ALSO BY PIERS BRENDON

Hurrell Froude and the Oxford Movement
Hawker of Morwenstow
Head of Guinness
Eminent Edwardians
The Life and Death of the Press Barons
Winston Churchill: A Brief Life
Our Own Dear Queen
Ike: The Life and Times of Dwight D. Eisenhower
Thomas Cook: 150 Years of Popular Tourism
The Windsors (with Phillip Whitehead)
The Motoring Century: The Story of the Royal Automobile Club

THE DARK VALLEY

THE DARK VALLEY

A PANORAMA OF THE 1930S

PIERS BRENDON

ALFRED A. KNOPF   NEW YORK   2000

THIS IS A BORZOI BOOK
PUBLISHED BY ALFRED A. KNOPF

Library of Congress Cataloging-in-Publication Data
Brendon, Piers.
The dark valley: a panorama of the 1930s / Piers Brendon.—1st ed.
          p.   cm.
"Originally published in Great Britain by Jonathan Cape, London, in 2000"—t.p. verso.
Includes bibliographical references and index.
ISBN 0-375-40881-9 (alk. paper)
1. Europe—History—1918–1945.   2. World politics, 1933–1945.   3. National socialism.
4. Japan—History—1926–1945.   5. Soviet Union—History—1925–1953.   I. Title.

D727 .B654 2000
940.5'2—dc21   00-034918

Manufactured in the United States of America
First American Edition

For Tom Rosenthal

with gratitude and affection

Contents

PART THREE: **CANYON**

PART FOUR: **DEEPENING GLOOM**

PART FIVE: **CHASM**

List of Illustrations

Acknowledgements

THIS book took many years to write and the debts of gratitude which I have incurred are correspondingly heavy.

I must first thank colleagues at Churchill College, Cambridge, who have helped me in many and various ways, notably Natalie Adams, Alan Kucia, Carolyn Lye, Gavin McGuffie, Sharon Maurice, Allen Packwood and Katharine Thomson.

Old friends have been unstinting with aid and advice. Professor P. N. Furbank read several chapters and made characteristically penetrating comments. I owe a lot to Professor Richard Overy. Tom Sharpe cheered me when I flagged. So did John and Maria Tyler, who also read the Spanish chapters. Sydney Bolt recalled the 1930s with wit and wisdom, conjuring up the dramas of the Cambridge Gramophone Society (a Communist Party alias) and singing the old songs with undiminished zest:

> The bourgeois keep their women
> in beautiful apartments and palaces,
> But the tendency of the rate of profit to fall
> exposes their worn-out fallacies.

("Or was it phalluses?" Sydney wonders.)

Peter Pagnamenta not only read the Japanese chapters, he also masterminded the transformation of some of the British material into two television documentaries on "1939," made by Blakeway Productions. Entitled *The World We Lost* (produced by Peter Jamieson) and *Did We Have to Fight?* (produced by Rachel Allen), they were shown on Channel Four to mark the sixtieth anniversary of the outbreak of the Second World War. Peter Pagnamenta was Executive Producer for both programmes and although I was credited with writing the script many of the best lines were his.

I must also thank Dr. Melveena McKendrick and Carolyn Cooksey for help, respectively, with Spanish and Italian matters. My sister-in-law, Junko

Brendon, assisted over a number of Japanese points. My wife Vyvyen, although preoccupied with her own books, never ceased to believe in mine and to sustain my efforts.

I must acknowledge permission to quote from the following copyright material: to the executors of the late Mr. M. Christie for the Christie Papers; Winston S. Churchill for the Churchill Papers; to Lieutenant-Commander Drax for the Drax Papers; to the Earl of Halifax for the Halifax Papers; to Mrs. E. Le Mesurier for the A. L. Kennedy Papers; to the Hon F. Noel-Baker for the Noel-Baker Papers; and to the Master and Fellows of Churchill College for the Phipps and Strang Papers.

Historians are born to make mistakes and, covering such a lot of ground in this book, I am especially vulnerable to error. However, I have been lucky enough to receive help from a number of distinguished authorities. They have examined the sections of the book in which they are particularly expert and have corrected me in countless ways. Moreover, they undertook this arduous task out of the kindness of their hearts. So I am enormously grateful to Professor Christopher Andrew, who read the French chapters; to Harry Browne, who read the Spanish ones; to Professor Martin Daunton, who read the British ones; to Dr. Jonathan Haslam and Dr. Peter Squire, who read the Russian ones; to Professor Warren Kimball, who read the American ones; to Dr. Stephen Large, who read the Japanese ones; to Dr. Detlef Mühlberger, who read the German ones; and to Professor John Pollard, who read the Italian ones.

One other outstanding and exceedingly busy scholar, Dr. Zara Steiner, who probably knows the 1930s as a whole better than anyone, took on the immense labour of scrutinising the entire book. Her contribution, well above the call of academic duty or personal generosity, is beyond praise and thanks. Needless to say, those who helped me do not always agree with my judgements and I bear the responsibility for any mistakes that remain.

My friend and literary agent, Andrew Best, helped to engender this book. Despite the unconscionable time I took to write it, my publisher Dan Franklin has always been enthusiastic about the book. He has, moreover, provided me with a model editor in the person of Tristan Jones—no one has done more to improve the text. My thanks, too, to Lily Richards, who has done a wonderful job on compiling and selecting the pictures.

Tom Rosenthal originally commissioned the book and he has followed its progress with occasional impatience but with unceasing benevolence. I shall always be grateful for the chance he gave me to write what I wanted to write.

Introduction

I WAS conceived just before Britain's finest hour and born soon after it, in December 1940. But, like many war babies, I was nurtured by the 1930s. My father was a typical bourgeois intellectual of that decade: he smoked Gitanes, wore scuffed suede shoes, read the *New Statesman* as though it were Holy Writ and hankered to fight in Spain (but learned Spanish instead). My mother, who had attended a school which taught girls that they were the "future mothers of the sons of the British Empire," was by no means a radical or a Bohemian. But she too was a creature of her time: she smoked Craven A, attached importance to keeping the seams of her stockings straight, thought Evelyn Waugh the acme of sophistication and was shocked by hearing "common" accents on the wireless. Such thumbnail sketches do scant justice to my parents, who were as multifaceted as the age in which they grew up. But this background does suggest the personal source of my fascination with that age, which was as fateful as it was complex. It was an age scarred by an economic crisis which, in the view of Léon Blum and others, was as traumatic as the First World War. It was also, of course, the gestation period of the Second World War, which killed some 50 million people, destroyed old empires and produced a global order that survived for half a century and will cast its shadow well into the new millennium.

The aim of this book is to depict the 1930s generally and to portray in particular the great powers in the throes of the Great Depression. During the ten years after 1929 the seven countries treated here—America, Germany, Italy, France, Britain, Japan and Russia—traversed a dark valley inhabited by the giants of unemployment, hardship, strife and fear. Gradually the darkness deepened as the diffuse economic crisis condensed into one great political thunder-cloud. The book is therefore a case study of the global perils lurking at the heart of a major recession. It offers a wealth of past experience on which to base future judgement. And it suggests questions which still demand answers. How can social and political stability be preserved in the face of an economic blizzard? What can be done to lift the scourge of joblessness and to promote growth? Can leaders be stopped from provoking external conflict in order to divert the attention of citizens from internal ills? What threat do the frustrations and fanaticisms of contemporary "proletarian nations," in the developing world, pose to international peace? Should democracies appease or oppose alien dictatorships? As the powers that be devise new ways to poison and pollute the wells of knowledge, how do ordinary people learn the truth? The historian, as Friedrich Schlegel said, is "the prophet looking backwards." Glimpses of what could be in store for the world, dangers to avoid or opportunities to grasp, may be discerned in *The Dark Valley*.

The story of how the leading industrial nations passed from the Slump to a war in which they were all belligerents is told chronologically. Unlike painters, who can present a vast composition on a single canvas, writers must proceed in linear fashion. But in so doing writers of large histories, especially, risk losing the narrative thread in the warp of simultaneous incident and the weft of related interpretation. I try to avoid this hazard by taking the action forward country by country, in a series of long strides. Sometimes the same events are seen from different angles. But usually the spotlight focuses on the peculiar circumstances of each country, illuminating the diverse national experiences as they coalesced into a single destiny. The march of events is swift and there are only two significant detours. Part One of the book sets the scene for the whole at some length: it begins with the Great War (at Verdun) and ends with the Great Crash (on Wall Street), including such crucial events as the Russian Revolution, the Peace of Versailles, the "March on Rome," the German hyper-inflation and Hitler's Beer Hall Putsch, earthquake and imperial enthronement in Japan, and Britain's General Strike. Part Three, which literally and figuratively forms the hinge of this volume, consists of two successive chapters devoted to Spain, whose civil war was widely regarded as both the defining episode of the period and the dress rehearsal for the Second World War. The book concludes sharply with the nations plunging into the chasm of that great conflict, the terminal point of the dark valley of Depression.

The political and economic bones of the story give it shape, forming the framework of a synthesis based on a mass of published sources and a selection of original material. But I endeavour to make the dry bones live, to clothe them with flesh and blood. Mine is a landscape with figures, a peopled panorama limned in microscopic particulars. At its most obvious this means that the following pages contain a series of brief lives. There are cameos of leaders such as Woodrow Wilson, Hoover, Roosevelt, Hindenburg, Brüning, Hitler, Mussolini, Pius XI, Lenin, Stalin, Clemenceau, Tardieu, Laval, Blum, Daladier, MacDonald, Baldwin, Chamberlain, Churchill, Hirohito, Konoe, Tojo, Franco, Schuschnigg, Chiang Kai-shek, Mao Tse-tung and Haile Selassie. But this does not exhaust the cast list. Playing a supporting role are figures as diverse as George Orwell, Leni Riefenstahl, Prince Saionji, Vyacheslav Molotov, Italo Balbo, Philippe Pétain, Anthony Eden, Manuel Azaña, Hermann Göring, André Malraux, Harry Hopkins, Nikolai Bukharin, Elsa Schiaparelli, Ishiwara Kanji, Sir Oswald Mosley, Jesse Owens, Galeazzo Ciano, Lavrenti Beria, Ernest Hemingway, Lord Halifax, La Pasionaria, Heinrich Himmler, King Edward VIII and Mrs. Simpson. My main *dramatis personae* did so much to shape the twentieth century that their names fill the mind like proverbs. Yet, although recognisably modern, they are already fading into the mists of time and from the vantage-point of a new millennium they seem remote historical personages. They deserve to be resurrected *en galère* in the context of their age.

So this book accords with Carlyle's maxim that history is the sum of innumerable biographies. But it also explores the human dimension in other ways. I cannot claim, with the *News of the World,* that all human life is here: fat though it is, this volume does not aspire to be comprehensive, let alone encyclopaedic. There are obvious gaps, many of them the result of ignorance. The book contains little or nothing about science, religion, philosophy, music and high culture. I am most acutely aware of the poverty of the female dimension. However, I do attempt to put the reader in touch with the prevailing texture, colour and tone of 1930s life. And in the spirit of Richard Cobb, who deplored the "artificial collectivities" which historians impose upon the past, I accumulate personal minutiae. This tome is a parcel of epitomes.

The contemporary experience is conveyed via details of the clothes people wore, the food they ate, the cigarettes they smoked, the work they did or lacked, the beliefs they held, the jokes that made them laugh, the books and newspapers they read, the films they saw, the pleasures they enjoyed, the sufferings they endured, and the rooms, buildings, villages, towns and cities in which they lived. I try to conjure up the ambience of places as far apart as Paris and Kyoto, Jarrow and Geneva, Vienna and Shanghai, Toledo and Tripoli, Barcelona and Chungking, Magnitogorsk in the Ural Mountains and Norris in the Tennessee Valley. I describe conditions in the concentration camps of Dachau and Kolyma, the circumstances of the Ukraine famine and the American Dust Bowl, the making of Renault cars and the breaking of Zeppelin airships. I visit the Kremlin, the White House, Hitler's Berghof, the British Foreign Office and the Quai d'Orsay. I open the doors of palaces in Versailles, London, Rome, Prague, Tokyo and Addis Ababa. I examine constructions or monuments of the time, many of which are rich in symbolism: the Empire State Building, half empty because of the Depression; Lenin's tomb, which served as a platform for Stalin; the Maginot Line, France's defensive mentality set in concrete; the Eternal City, remoulded in the image of the Duce; the Moscow metro, a Communist showpiece built by latter-day serfs; the Berlin Olympic stadium, where nationalism outstripped internationalism; the Paris Exposition of 1937, designed to promote peace but dominated by the martial pavilions of totalitarianism; the Telefónica skyscraper in Madrid, a beacon of electronic communication devoted to censorship and misinformation.

I deal in anecdote as well as character, for often an epiphany is worth a thousand words of exposition. So these pages brim with vignettes. There are circumstantial accounts of momentous events such as the Invergordon Mutiny, the Bonus March on Washington, the Nazi book-burning, the Night of the Long Knives, the Concorde riot, the conquest of Ethiopia, the Tokyo military revolt, the bombing of Guernica, the rape of Nanking, the *Anschluss,* the great Soviet purges. Such episodes are included for their intrinsic importance. But they also enable me to develop the main theme of the book, which concerns the manipulation of perception and the distortion of reality. Propaganda became part of the air people breathed during the 1930s. All the major occurrences of the day were the subject of organised deception which ranged from the big, amplified lie to a delicate economy with the truth. Moreover, many public spectacles were specifically mounted and choreographed with propagandist intent. King George V's Silver Jubilee celebrations and his son's coronation were a democratic riposte to Hitler's barbaric pageants at Nuremberg. Stalin's purge trials dramatised a new kind of tyranny. Mussolini's aerial circuses advertised the virility of Fascism. The unveiling of countless war memorials in France not only marked the nation's immense sacrifice but stressed its incapacity to face another blood-letting. Hollywood created celluloid myths to banish the Depression and affirm the New Deal. The machinations behind the scenes were at least as important as the performances acted out on the stage.

Of course, to lie is human and deceit has always been the element in which politicians, more than most people, live—their salamander's fire. "Lord, lord," said Falstaff, "how this world is given to lying!" Similarly the manufacture of illusion has invariably been part of the business of government. Rulers as remote as Rameses II, Augustus Caesar and Louis XIV have exemplified Montesquieu's dictum that the splendour surrounding monarchs forms part of their might. Yet the Depression years witnessed the dissemination of falsehood on a hitherto unprecedented scale. Never had science and art so combined to promote earthly powers. Goebbels and others developed novel techniques of thought control. New media such as radio and talking pictures were mobilised to sway the masses. Leaders used aircraft to grab the limelight and they emblazoned their messages on the sky. Dictators imposed their version of the truth by means of dogma and terror. They created new cults and persecuted unbelievers. Russia and Germany, and to a lesser extent Italy and Japan, had their own reality. Facts were moulded like plasticine into the approved shape, whether Communist, Aryan, Fascist or imperial.

Totalitarianism won adherents across frontiers, for the failures of capitalism were palpable during the Depression and the democracies suffered a sharp crisis of confidence. Hearing that Stalin had achieved planned progress and social equality, that Hitler had abolished unemployment and built autobahns, that Mussolini had revived Italy and made the trains run on time, people in Britain, France and the United States were inclined to believe that Utopia was another country. Many converts suppressed their critical faculties in all sincerity and naïveté: on the basis of a visit to Moscow in 1939, for example, Sir Charles Trevelyan told the *Daily Telegraph* that Russian public opinion was the best informed in the world. Many others thought it a small matter, at such a fraught time, to sacrifice veracity on the altar of ideology. In fact the Great Depression may best be understood as the moral equivalent of war, whose first casualty is truth.

Naturally people did not lose the ability to make up their own minds during the 1930s. All sorts of disparate creeds flourished in the West, where many were quite untouched by the political fundamentalism of the day. Even Germans under Hitler and Russians under Stalin remained free in their heads. But how free? Mass brainwashing did not work in the dictator states, but it had some effect in clouding apprehension. Confusion also reigned in the democracies, where citizens were sceptical about official information, especially after revelations that atrocity stories accepted as gospel during the Great War had been lies. Moreover, the general climate of opinion militated against certainty. The old Victorian orthodoxies were crumbling under the assaults of subversives from Samuel Butler and Edward Carpenter to H. G. Wells and Lytton Strachey—to say nothing of world-shakers such as Darwin, Freud and Einstein, let alone Heisenberg. Thus many became a prey to half-belief and double-think—*1984* began in 1931. This is not to deny that dialectical vacillation and dual consciousness are perennial conditions. As Montaigne argued in his essay on inconstancy, paradox is integral to personality. "The daemon of Socrates affords a memorable instance," declared Gibbon, "how conscience may slumber in a mixed and middle state between self-illusion and voluntary fraud." Yet never was conviction more fractured or doubt more pervasive than during the 1930s. Then, to a greater degree than ever before or since, humanity saw through a glass darkly. It is always hard to unearth what Victor Hugo called "that huge blind mole, the Past," but never more so than from the Kafkaesque burrow dug in the Depression.

This work therefore includes a pronounced epistemological dimension. It investigates how, and how far, contemporaries knew what they knew and the extent to which our own view of the time is fogged by their uncertainty. It surveys the strategies of delusion and self-delusion, the techniques of obfuscation, euphemism and selective amnesia, the mechanisms of willingly suspending disbelief and accepting the evidence of things not seen. Above all it elucidates the way in which political power obscured knowledge and economic catastrophe darkened understanding. This theme is reflected in the metaphor which recurs again and again in one form or another and which gives the book its title.

Many people during the 1930s remarked that they were passing through a dark valley, the valley of the shadow of death, a vale of tears in which the forces of darkness threatened to overwhelm the angels of light. The imagery was biblical (rather than Freudian) but darkness was no mere image: it literally covered the earth during the Depression. If the lamps went out in 1914, if the blinds came down in 1939, the lights were progressively dimmed after 1929. As H. G. Wells observed (in *The Shape of Things to Come* [1933]), the "polychromatic visual clamour" of Broadway, Piccadilly Circus, the Champs-Elysées, the Kurfürstendamm and the Ginza died away. Opacity "recaptured the nocturnal town. 'Night-life' became stealthy and obscure, with an increasing taint of criminality." The neon brightened later and by 1934 the photographer Man Ray, poet of the darkroom, could speak of an "age of light." The glare was increased by dictators keen to appear in a good light. As that phrase suggests, the central metaphor of this book is a mixed metaphor. Darkness invariably presented itself as light and was occasionally mistaken for it. Light, which Sir Thomas Browne called "the shadow of God," was equally ambiguous. It was often refracted through a prism of incomprehension and at times partially or wholly eclipsed. So my purpose is clear, if ambitious. It is to shed new light on a dark, dishonest decade. It is to cast a broad beam of illumination into a gloomy period, a period when the world was struggling with one crisis and hurtling towards another, the greatest in its history.

PART ONE

APPROACH

I

THE HARVEST OF ARMAGEDDON

WELL before dawn on 21 February 1916, when powdery snow lightened the darkness shrouding the lines of trenches gashed across the face of northern France, a 15-inch Krupp naval gun fired the first shot in the battle of Verdun. Its long barrel rising through the camouflage netting of its hiding-place in a wood near Loisin, it gave a full-throated roar and vomited a huge projectile 15 miles into the fortified city. The shell burst in the courtyard of the Bishop's Palace, "knocking a corner off the cathedral."[1] Others followed but not until sunrise did the main German bombardment begin. In the dead silence moments before the onslaught, French soldiers of the 56th and 59th Light Infantry Battalions, dug into a bosky hillside north of Verdun known as the Bois des Caures, saw snow fall from trembling branches. Then they were engulfed by a tornado of fire and steel. The barrage could be heard a hundred miles away in the Vosges Mountains, "an incessant rumble of drums, punctuated by the pounding of big basses."[2] Close at hand its impact was tremendous. One of the earliest victims was a water carrier who, with his horse and cart, was blown to smithereens by a direct hit from one of the 1,200 German guns. His comrades expected the same fate as they clung to the earth and, Jules Romains wrote, breathed "the smell of a tormented world, a smell like that of a planet in the process of being reduced to ashes."[3] The trenches of the First World War have been compared to the concentration camps of the Second. So they were, in the sense that they witnessed bestial suffering. By that analogy Verdun was Auschwitz.[4]

Actually Verdun was not the bloodiest battle of the war—that grisly distinction belongs to the Somme. Moreover, the carnage was so unspeakable elsewhere, notably on the Eastern Front, that governments sought refuge in censorship and lies, reporters dealt in euphemisms like "baptism of fire" and even poets felt lost for words. In every sector the combatants saw a new vision of hell, experienced an "iron nightmare."[5] They occupied killing fields in which the quick and the dead were buried in the same stretch of tortured soil, men gouging holes in the ground like the rats which fed on corpses regularly exhumed by scorching metal. Amid the stench and squalor of a gigantic shambles, legions of doomed youth emerged to be scythed down by machine-guns and crucified on barbed wire. They endured an inferno of shells: shrapnel which tore flesh to pieces and high explosive which pulverised bone and stone alike. They encountered the hideous inventions of perverted technology: flame-throwers and poison gas. Even in so-called "quiet sectors" of the line, those in which (one French officer complained) generals "plague us with their visits,"[6] a 2nd lieutenant's commission was, as Wyndham Lewis said, tantamount to a death warrant.

Yet, even taking Passchendaele into account, Verdun was the most terrible battle of the war. This was because of time and space: it lasted longest and was most concentrated. It continued at maximum intensity for much of 1916 and erupted sporadically until the armistice. And the kind of fighting which no one chronicled with more Zolaesque vehemence than Henri Barbusse was aimed at a single target on the narrowest of fronts:

> the woods are sliced down like cornfields, the dug-outs marked and burst in even when they've three thicknesses of beams . . . all the roads blown into the air and changed into long heaps of smashed convoys and wrecked guns, corpses twisted together as though shovelled up. You could see thirty chaps laid out by one shot at the crossroads; you could see fellows whirling around as they went up, always about fifteen yards, and bits of trousers caught and stuck on the tops of the trees that were left . . . And that went on for months on end, months on end![7]

Probably more soldiers were killed per square yard in defence of Verdun, symbol of French honour, than in any other conflict before or since. The figures are difficult to compute, but nearly 300,000 Frenchmen and Germans died and another 450,000 were wounded. The German commander, General Erich von Falkenhayn, thus fulfilled his ambition to bleed the enemy white. Admittedly, his own forces paid an almost equally horrifying price. But the French armies, most of which were sooner or later dragged into the charnel-house of Verdun, suffered more. They were crushed by a weight of artillery "against which courage had no resource."[8] Soon hopes of glory gave way to talk of butchery. French soldiers had entered the war with sublime faith in the offensive, symbolised by their red *képis* and pantaloons (where the British wore khaki and the Germans grey). Now some began to think in terms of a defensive strategy whereby casualties would be kept to a minimum. The embodiment of this philosophy was General Philippe Pétain.

Pétain was given command at Verdun when a German breakthrough seemed imminent. A peasant's son with a patrician's air, he looked every inch a general—always an important consideration with the military. He was a large, impassive man with icy blue eyes, a sweeping white moustache and pale, marmoreal features. As Pétain himself acknowledged, "I have a chilling mask."⁹ Coldness, indeed, was the characteristic which this stoical soldier presented to the world: he treated politicians with glacial disdain and adopted a frigid formality with his staff. But passions seethed beneath Pétain's arctic exterior. He had many love affairs, often with other men's wives and once with a woman apparently procured for him by the Germans. When summoned to Verdun he was nowhere to be found; his ADC finally tracked him down in the Hotel Terminus at the Gare du Nord in Paris. Outside a bedroom door he was able to identify "the great commander's yellowish boots with the long leggings, which, however, on that evening were agreeably accompanied by some charming little *molière* slippers, utterly feminine."¹⁰ Being, as a friend once said, more of a slave to his flesh than to his duty, Pétain insisted on finishing the business of the night. But once at Verdun he showed a stern regard for the flesh of the French *poilu*. He limited losses, relying on *matériel* rather than men. He acted defensively, reorganising the artillery and keeping it well supplied with ammunition. He constantly sent fresh troops to relieve those exhausted by the attrition of the firing line. He visited casualty clearing stations—unlike the British Commander-in-Chief, Douglas Haig, who felt it his duty not to sicken himself by such experiences. Eventually Pétain became the "saviour of Verdun." He thus earned himself lasting fame and popularity. In 1935 he came top of a newspaper poll conducted to find a dictator for France.

However, Pétain's methods were anathema to the offensive-minded high command. So, in April 1917, General Robert Nivelle was permitted to launch another frontal attack, this time against well-protected German lines on the Aisne. It was a disaster. Though incurring a modest loss compared to the hecatombs of Verdun, it broke the fighting spirit of the French armies. Two-thirds of their units were now affected by mutinies. These ranged from minor acts of indiscipline to violent disturbances. Some troops sang the "Internationale" and proposed to march on Paris. But most were protesting against the slaughter caused by futile assaults on heavily fortified positions. The authorities effectively hushed up the mutinies, punishing the ring-leaders (50 of whom were executed) and making concessions (more leave, better food) to the rest. But this spontaneous insurrection terrified the leaders of France, because it raised the twin ghouls of defeat and revolution. Pétain himself, infected by a pessimism that amounted to defeatism, muttered that France should begin peace negotiations. As it happened, all belligerent nations experienced mutinies or considered peace proposals in 1917. But it was in France, whose poignant war memorials would record the loss of 1.3 million soldiers (over a quarter of all men aged between 18 and 27), that the mood of war-weariness was overwhelming.

That mood was prophetically expressed by a character in Barbusse's *Under Fire* who exclaimed:

> The future, the future! The work of the future will be to wipe out the present, to wipe it out more than we can imagine, to wipe it out like something abominable and shameful ... Shame on military glory, shame on armies, shame on the soldier's calling that changes men by turns into stupid victims and ignoble brutes.[11]

Looking forward to the arrival of the Americans, French *poilus* were for the present prepared at least to defend the motherland. And defence was later to be elevated to the status of a cult, its fetish being the Maginot Line, modelled on the fortresses which had protected Verdun. But hostility to war and, by extension, to the military, became so widespread during the 1920s and '30s that cadets at St. Cyr were advised to doff their uniforms and go out wearing civilian clothes. Verdun spawned a feeling in France, so passionate as to be palpable, that this must be the war to end war. As a young lieutenant wrote in his diary just before his death in that battle, "They will not be able to make us do it again."[12]

The Great War invaded the mind of mankind, becoming "the essential condition of consciousness in the twentieth century."[13] The pain and grief of Verdun, in particular, seared the French psyche like phosgene gas in a soldier's lungs. People had their own recurring nightmares: of men drowning in shell-holes; or walking on corpses during an attack; or going mad in the underground fighting in Forts Vaux and Douaumont; or being more anguished by their horses' suffering than by their own; or collapsing from hunger, thirst and exhaustion when supplies failed to reach the front line; or weeping just because they could no longer bear the mud, the lice and the squalor. Despite horrors best captured in Otto Dix's grotesque paintings of mutilated war victims, or perhaps because of those horrors, Verdun exercised such a fascination that during the 1930s survivors constantly returned to it. They visited the grim ossuary of Douaumont, formally inaugurated in 1932. It was said to contain the bones of 130,000 soldiers, but they were not arranged in ornamental patterns like the frieze of skulls and the tracery of tibias that imposed a macabre retrospective order on battle in the ossuary at Solferino; instead they were heaped together higgledy-piggledy to represent the chaos of conflict. The Verdun ossuary remains the most extraordinary monument commemorating the First World War: a long, rounded chamber resembling the casemate of a fort, surmounted by a "funerary stela"[14] less like an obelisk than an enormous high-explosive shell. This and the other war memorials, notably the one to the Unknown Soldier (carefully exhumed from an area of Verdun deemed free of Jewish and Negro corpses) at the Arc de Triomphe, reinforced French feelings that such an immense sacrifice "must never be allowed to happen again."[15] So did the still-shattered landscape of Verdun, to which the ancient combatants were drawn. There they would reminisce and explore, trying to find the location of this dugout or that battery. "I was in Death Ravine . . ." "Which one?" Some of these pilgrims camped amid the mounds and craters, occasionally "getting their heads blown off when their fire heated up an explosive shell."[16] At Verdun the iron entered into the Gallic soul.

According to a myth much propagated by writers, a kind of camaraderie had existed between soldiers facing each other across No Man's Land. They were supposed to be united in mutual respect, and in common contempt for staff officers safely behind the lines who could blithely order them to fight to the last man. The myth was not without foundation, but anyone who reads the unpublished diaries and letters of *poilus* or tommies will be more impressed by their violent hatred of the foe. The hatred was compounded by an abiding fear, which was particularly pervasive in France, where the war produced a disastrous fall in the number of births. In 1928 Charles Lambert warned that "the demographic peril" was "as formidable as the German army."[17] Population stasis, which occurred in the 1930s, weakened the nation's capacity in every way, helping to make the Depression France's "economic Sedan."[18] France won in 1918. But Falkenhayn, whose own hair turned white during the months of Verdun, had succeeded in bleeding it white. As the politician Georges Mandel said in 1940, France's people believed that it "could not stand another bleeding like that."[19]

Another such bloodbath was a frightful prospect. But as France tasted the sweets of victory, there were many in Germany who were consumed by the bitterness of defeat. They vowed to reverse the verdict and to exact vengeance at whatever cost. And they believed that Verdun had forged a new Teutonic cadre: ruthless, mechanised, steel-helmeted "proletarians of destruction" for whom, Arnold Zweig wrote, there "is no truth, and everything is permitted."[20] The most fanatical of these nationalists was, of course, a young Austrian corporal named Adolf Hitler. As a down-and-out artist in Munich he had welcomed the war with rapture, thanking God for having matched him with this hour. Though said to be lacking in leadership qualities, he had conducted himself bravely. He had been wounded and had won the Iron Cross, first class, allegedly for capturing single-handed more than a dozen French soldiers—cynics later suggested that he had surrounded them. Writing from the trenches he had expressed a fervent hope that a new, purer Germany would emerge from the crucible of war,

> so that by the sacrifice and agony which so many hundreds of thousands of us endure every day, that by the river of blood which flows here daily . . . not only will Germany's enemies from the outside be smashed, but also our domestic internationalism [a euphemism for Jewry] will be broken up.[21]

Pale-faced, with intense, staring eyes and a much fuller moustache than he later wore, Hitler oscillated between moods of lethargic day-dreaming and daemonic enthusiasm. His fellows regarded him as a Bohemian and an eccentric. But Hitler was far from alone in finding a kind of fulfilment in the war. It gave him comradeship, discipline, the excitement of taking part in an heroic adventure and the sense of purpose which stemmed from proving that he and his race were fittest to survive. This social-Darwinist destiny was abruptly denied him in 1918. On 13 October Hitler was temporarily blinded in a British gas attack south of Ypres. He was sent to Pasewalk hospital in Pomerania. It was here, a month later, that the chaplain gave him the news of the armistice.

As he described the moment in *Mein Kampf*:

> Everything went black before my eyes; I tottered and groped my way back to the dormitory, threw myself on my bunk and dug my burning head into my blanket and pillow . . . And so it had all been in vain. In vain all the sacrifices and privations; in vain the hunger and thirst of months which were often endless; in vain the hours in which, with mortal fear clutching at our hearts, we nevertheless did our duty; and in vain the death of two millions . . . Would [their graves] not open and send the silent mud- and blood-covered heroes back as spirits of vengeance to the homeland which had cheated them with such mockery of the highest sacrifice which a man can make to his people in this world?

The language was melodramatic, as befitted a propagandist tract dictated by a demagogue of genius. The history was tendentious: here was the unvarnished myth that the new provisional government—in reality forced to act as a result of military, political and social collapse—had stabbed an undefeated Germany in the back. The autobiography was misleading: this was not quite the turning-point in his career that Hitler claimed. But all too real was the molten passion, from which Hitler would forge his brutal weapon of Nazism. As he wrote, "The more I tried to achieve clarity on the monstrous event in this hour, the more the shame of indignation and disgrace burned my brow . . . I, for my part, decided to go into politics."[22]

Nazism was not the only revolutionary growth to spring from Great War battlefields so prodigally fertilised with blood. During and after what was a cultural caesura as well as a political watershed, rebels and insurrectionaries mounted attacks on every aspect of an old order that had so patently failed. Its famed *douceur de vivre* had culminated in a stupendous conflict. Its religion had bestowed divine sanction on the carnage. Its industrial achievements had made possible assembly-line massacres. Its mass media of communication had manufactured propaganda on an unprecedented scale. A botched civilisation, as Ezra Pound called it, had begotten scientific barbarism. Barbarism bred more barbarism, which in Russia took the form of Bolshevism. The point was well made by Boris Pasternak, who (in *Doctor Zhivago*) blamed the war for shifting the world from a "calm, innocent, measured way of living to blood and tears, to mass insanity and to the savagery of daily, hourly, legalised, rewarded slaughter." Moral disintegration followed, in which individuals lost the power to speak, and even to know, the truth. "It was then that falsehood came into our Russia."[23]

PALE winter sunshine filtered through bare branches along the fashionable avenues of St. Petersburg[24] near the Tauride Palace, seat of the Russian parliament; but in the distance storm-clouds gathered as, almost exactly a year after the start of the battle of Verdun, the Romanov empire began to collapse under the hammer blows of war. From a long way off the sounds of a disturbance could be heard. Men were shouting. Horses' hooves clanged over cobbles. Lorries full of soldiers brandishing rifles screeched round corners. Then came the faint strains of a memorable tune. Monsieur Darier, French tutor to Count Paul Ignatieff's children, stopped his dictation and with his pupils ran to the windows of the yellow baroque mansion on tree-lined Fourstatskaya Street. "The Marseillaise!" he cried. "The Marseillaise. Hurrah!"[25] They thought that the Russian armies must have won a victory on the Eastern Front. In fact, that day in late February 1917 marked the beginning of the greatest political convulsion since the French Revolution.

Soon there were outbreaks of violence. Police and troops clashed with strikers, who had been driven to desperation by the bread shortage. To isolate the poorer districts of the city sentries guarded the bridges over the Neva, but rioters swarmed across the frozen river. In their shabby clothes and broken boots they were at first an unfamiliar whiff of the slums, later a terrifying reminder of the *sans-culottes*. Some waved red flags or banners saying "Down with the Tsar." Others clutched rocks or lumps of ice. A few had revolvers or hand grenades. They cried "Give us Bread" and "Down with the War." And they surged towards Znamenskaya Square. Here a revolutionary orator was addressing a crowd surrounding the huge equestrian statue of Alexander III, known locally as "the Hippopotamus." Attempting to break up the demonstration, Lieutenant Krylov, commander of the mounted police, aimed his pistol at the speaker. An appalled hush fell over the gathering. But before he could pull the trigger a Cossack "spurred his horse forward and cut Krylov down with his sabre."[26]

This was a fateful act, the first assault by a soldier on the forces of law. It foreshadowed not just the subversion of established political authority but the inversion of an entire social order. In the skirmishes that ensued more troops joined the demonstrators. The Volynsky regiment mutinied and others followed suit. The whole edifice of the old regime, undermined by war, weakened by ramshackle organisation, sapped by rampant inflation and riddled with injustice, fell to the ground. On 2 March, after inept attempts to quell the uprising, Tsar Nicholas II abdicated. So the 300-year-old Romanov dynasty came to an end.

A weak left-wing provisional government took its place, though real power lay with the spontaneously formed workers' and soldiers' councils, or soviets. But they were split into revolutionary factions and confused by contradictory aims—they wanted both to achieve peace and to avoid defeat. The Allies therefore felt safe in hailing the overthrow of tsardom as a triumph of liberty. Americans were also pleased, for now they could enter, with a clear conscience, what was plainly "a war between Democracy and Absolutism."[27] In fact absolutism, with its detested system of social inequality, was so deeply engrained in Russia, while democracy was so weak, that a second revolution was well-nigh inevitable. But hardly anyone, including the most committed revolutionaries, could see it at the time.

Indeed, the first leader of the Bolsheviks to return from exile, Joseph Stalin, initially called for "order"[28] and wanted to cooperate with the government. (He later cut this fact from his official biography, one of so many Soviet re-shapings of the past in the interest of the present that a student of history complained, "You never know what's going to happen yesterday.")[29] Stalin's moderation put him at odds with more radical party members, who excluded him from their Central Committee "in view of certain personal traits"[30]—presumably his manners, which were as foul as the black *makhorka* tobacco he smoked in his pipe. This ostracism, together with the radical N. N. Sukhanov's celebrated remark that Stalin was at this time nothing more than "a grey blur," has disposed historians to counter Stalin's own myth-making by minimising his role in the events of 1917.[31] Recently it has even been suggested that he was so "dogged by a sense of having somehow missed the revolution" that he was impelled to remove the witnesses and conduct a terrifying revolution of his own during the 1930s.[32] But Stalin was always there and not always in the background.[33] He seldom spoke. He was inconspicuous in his dark suit, Russian blouse and felt boots, though several witnesses noticed the cynical expression that sometimes played over his swarthy, pock-marked features. Cautious and calculating, he lacked the charisma and dynamism of Leon Trotsky. But he was a sinister, brooding presence in the eye of the revolutionary storm.

No one did more to cause that storm than the Bolshevik leader, Vladimir Ilyich Lenin. On 16 April, after his famous journey through Germany in the "sealed train," he was given a rapturous, and carefully stage-managed, welcome at Petrograd's Finland Station. Crowds waved red flags, bands again played the "Marseillaise" and the returning revolutionary was presented with a bouquet of flowers. Squat, bearded, snub-nosed, stoop-shouldered, wearing a Swiss wool coat and a Homburg hat (soon swapped for a worker's cap) on his bald, high-domed head, Lenin looked like a clerk on an outing. But above high Asiatic cheek-bones his eyes blazed with the fervour of a messiah whose hour had come. At once he proclaimed the socialist millennium:

> Dear Comrades, soldiers, sailors, and workers! I am happy to greet in your persons the victorious Russian revolution, and greet you as the vanguard of the world-wide proletarian army.

Theirs was no local victory, he continued, but the first stage of the international socialist revolution. Soon working-class combatants on all fronts would turn on their bourgeois exploiters. The imperialist war between countries, which marked the final crisis of capitalism, would become a civil war between classes. From this the masses would emerge triumphant and establish the dictatorship of the proletariat.

Such was the thaumaturgic power of Lenin's oratory that he brought the dry bones of Marxism to life. As the weary insurrectionist Sukhanov wrote, "Suddenly, before the eyes of all of us . . . there was presented a bright, blinding, exotic beacon, obliterating everything we 'lived by.' "[34] Addressing—and dressing down—his Bolshevik supporters, Lenin soon formulated his immediate policy. There would be no accommodation with the government. Abroad, hostilities must cease. At home, he came not to bring peace but the sword. The class war must be ruthlessly prosecuted. There could be no compromise with other parties. Land to the peasants. All power to the soviets. For Sukhanov this "thunderous speech" was another revelation: "It seemed as if all the elements of universal destruction had arisen from their lairs, knowing neither barriers nor doubts, personal difficulties nor personal considerations, to hover over . . . the heads of the bewitched disciples."[35]

The world gasped when, in October 1917, Lenin realised his revolutionary vision. It was, he claimed, the government's threat to purge the Bolsheviks which precipitated their coup. But its success resulted not so much from Bolshevik strength as from national weakness. Under the intolerable pressures of war, the whole fabric of Russian society was disintegrating— the countryside chaotic, the cities starving, the troops voting against war with their feet. Most Russians had nothing to lose but their chains. So when the armed uprising took place there was only token resistance. The storming of the Winter Palace, seat of the provisional government, had less military than symbolic significance: the cruiser *Aurora* fired nothing but blanks; trams continued to trundle across the Neva bridges. Naturally the heroic legend grew with the telling, but more people were killed during Eisenstein's filmed reenactment of the drama than during the event itself. Nevertheless, the revolution was terrifying. Maxim Gorky maintained that it was not so much a revolution as a "pogrom of greed, hatred and vengeance";[36] but there was no denying the absolute fanaticism of the revolutionaries. Trotsky consigned the Bolsheviks' allies as well as their enemies to "the dustbin of history."[37] Lenin announced that "We shall now proceed to construct the Socialist order."[38]

Lenin was an unscrupulous pragmatist. But at first the new order looked like the doctrinaire fulfilment of the Communist Manifesto. The State took control of everything. Banks and factories were nationalised. Private shops were shut. Landlords were dispossessed. Against the kulaks, the supposedly richer peasants, Lenin preached and practised "a ruthless mass terror."[39] He further said that, "We are exterminating the bourgeoisie as a class."[40] Those who survived became squatters in corners of their own houses; Boris Pasternak, for example, found himself sharing his father's old flat, now narrowly partitioned, with six other families. Vestigial liberalism and incipient democracy were crushed, along with all types of resistance.

To assist what they believed to be the inevitable and ultimately benign process of history, Communists spurned bourgeois morality. An autocracy came into being more totalitarian than anything dreamed of by Ivan the Terrible or Peter the Great. The imperial secret police, the 15,000-strong Okhrana, acting under relative legal restraint, had been responsible for the deaths of some 14,000 people in the half century before 1917. By 1921 its successor, Lenin's Cheka, consisted of 250,000 officers (including 100,000 border guards), a remarkable adjunct to a State which was supposed to be withering away. In the first six years of Bolshevik rule it had executed at least 200,000. Moreover, the Cheka was empowered to act as "policeman, gaoler, investigator, prosecutor, judge and executioner."[41] It also employed barbaric forms of torture. New Communist was not just old tsarist writ large. He was the zealot of a secular faith whose mission was to revolutionise the world.

Some outside Russia welcomed the prospect, which combined the afflatus of chiliastic religion with the sobriety of scientific materialism. Here was the promise of an end to the capitalist system, which institutionalised greed and exploitation, whose by-products were unjust empires and cruel wars. Instead each would give according to his ability and receive according to his need. The Communist creed tapped the idealism of the generation which mourned the lost generation. Old socialists like George Lansbury said that the Bolsheviks were "doing what Christians call the Lord's work" and that Lenin's devotion to the cause of humanity made his whole life like "that of one of the saints of old."[42] Communism also appealed to those who craved power. Soon Communist parties were springing up everywhere, encouraged by money and propaganda from Russia (in Britain, for example, the Soviet trade delegation sold tsarist diamonds to subsidise the *Daily Herald*).[43] In 1919 Red revolution broke out in Germany and Hungary. In 1920 some 35 countries sent delegates to the second Congress of the Communist International (Comintern) at Petrograd. It predictably resolved that "The international proletariat will not sheathe its sword until Soviet Russia becomes a link in the federation of Soviet republics of the whole world."[44]

The world rejected the revolutionary gospel of the Bolsheviks just as it had rejected that of the Jacobins, and for much the same reasons. The Red gospel was the herald of civil war between the classes, followed by a novel kind of tyranny. What Winston Churchill called "the plague bacillus of Bolshevism" was capable of destroying civilisation. Like many others, he became obsessed by the danger, denouncing the Bolsheviks "who hop and caper like troops of ferocious baboons amid the ruins of cities and the corpses of their victims."[45] Churchill did more than anyone to try to eradicate Bolshevism by sustaining "White" tsarist forces on the periphery of Red Russia. But though the Communist regime survived this onslaught, its hopes of exporting revolution were dashed. The German and Hungarian uprisings were suppressed. In America, where Secretary of State Lansing warned that Bolshevik forces "are menacing the present social order in nearly every European country and . . . may have to be reckoned with even in this country,"[46] there was a Red Scare. In England the Labour party repudiated Communism, which was not surprising in view of Lenin's offer to support their leaders as a rope supports a hanged man. In Japan the authorities passed a law against "thought crime," and the "thought police" (by no means a figment of George Orwell's imagination) devised new methods of reminding offenders of their loyalty to the Emperor.[47] In France the Right branded Communism as a German aberration and the Left split over whether to embrace it. In Italy fear of Communism helped to bring Mussolini's Fascists to power.

After 1917 the spectre of Communism haunted not only Europe but the world. To some it was a genial ghost of hope, to others a monstrous apparition of despair. For the time being, it had been kept at bay because, despite trials and tribulations, the capitalist system remained strong. But when it began to falter, during the stock market Crash of 1929 and the subsequent Depression, a fearsome alternative was at hand.

THE Bolsheviks, who had exposed the secret imperialistic war aims of the Allies and accepted humiliating German terms at the Treaty of Brest-Litovsk (1918), were excluded from the peace conference at Paris. Indeed, those who did attend spent much of their time trying to devise means of destroying Bolshevism. These included direct intervention, creating a *cordon sanitaire* of small states on Russia's western border, issuing propaganda about the Red Menace and setting up an International Labour Organisation to fix fair conditions for workers. Herbert Hoover, head of the American Relief Administration, also deployed his food supplies judiciously, convinced that Bolshevism was "the pit into which all governments were in danger of falling when their frantic peoples were driven by the Horsemen of Famine and Pestilence."[48] Containment of Bolshevism was, as Thorstein Veblen said, "the parchment on which [the Treaty of Versailles] was written."[49]

Although Russia could be isolated, however, Bolshevism could not be contained. In the view of Hoover and many others it was the wolf at the door of the world. And the large Communist movements that formed in France, Germany and Italy, to say nothing of the smaller parties in Britain, the United States and Japan, gave Moscow a sinister and pervasive influence abroad. Communists were a revolutionary fifth column in the citadels of capitalism. There they polarised opinion, provoked right-wing reactions and so eroded the liberal centre ground that it sometimes gave way under pressure. The statesmen of Versailles would have done better to treat with the new Russia instead of making an ogre of Communism.

Much more serious, though, was their alienation of Germany, which provided Hitler with a burning grievance and a plausible pretext for aggression. This was a tragedy. It was also a bitter irony, for everyone engaged in making the peace settlement of 1919 was resolved to prevent a repetition of the Great War. That was the war to end war; this must not be the peace to end peace. Harold Nicolson, then a young diplomat, wrote: "We were preparing not Peace only, but Eternal Peace. There was about us the halo of some divine mission."[50] Chiefly responsible for these lofty aspirations was President Woodrow Wilson. He was inspired by a moral vision of sublime grandeur. This was nothing less than the regeneration of the Old World by the principles of the New. These would be embodied in a League of Nations (whose Covenant, or constitution, would be enshrined in the Treaty) which would ensure that war should be no more. Arriving aboard the *George Washington,* named after the president who had warned against foreign entanglements, Wilson was hailed as the saviour of Europe. In France peasant families knelt to pray as his train passed; in Italy wounded soldiers tried to kiss the hem of his garments. But "Wilson the Just"[51] quickly disappointed expectations. Everything about him served to disillusion those he dealt with: his prim pince-nez and his pontifical manner, his woolly naïveté and his stubborn arrogance, his long twitching face and his regrettably short legs, his insensitive hands and the nervous little laugh with which he sought to disguise his failures in comprehension. No doubt Wilson was something of a Presbyterian minister manqué, as J. M. Keynes charged.[52] Georges Clemenceau, indeed, said that talking to Wilson was "something like talking to Jesus Christ."[53]

However, though Wilson was suspicious of the motives of everyone except himself, his idealism was far from being naïve. Nor was it adamantine. He was not bamboozled by the sharp wits of David Lloyd George and Clemenceau, as Keynes argued in his brilliant polemic *The Economic Consequences of the Peace.* However Keynes was right in detecting that the President possessed a Gladstonian elasticity of conscience where his own actions were concerned. As Lloyd George remarked, Wilson talked "a lot of sentimental platitudes" and believed them with the utmost sincerity. But, like every politician, the British Prime Minister continued with the indulgence of one who knew what he was talking about, "occasionally he has to deviate."[54] Podsnap rather than Pecksniff, Wilson behaved like some latter-day Moses. He worshipped before the Ark of the Covenant and issued his Fourteen Points—prompting Clemenceau's immortal riposte,

"God only had ten." But all too soon the President was qualifying the Fourteen Points with "Four Principles" and modifying them with "Five Particulars." Finding that one principle conflicted with another particular, he made compromising declarations about both. He insisted on a just peace, yet spoke of "the very great offense against civilization which the German State committed, and the necessity for making it evident once for all that such things can lead only to the most severe punishment."[55]

This view, needless to say, was shared by Clemenceau, though otherwise the two statesmen had precious little in common. The aged French Premier was a hard-headed realist, impatient with political abstractions and utopian ideals. Shrewd, witty, cynical and capable of a sabre-toothed ferocity which had earned him the nickname "the Tiger," Clemenceau was a man of the past. With his great walrus moustache, with the beetle brows that almost hid his tired brown eyes, with the yellow parchment skin that seemed to belong to some Asiatic Nestor, he looked like an anachronism. His old-fashioned clothes added to the impression: the square-tailed coats; the shapeless hats; the thick, black, buckled boots; the lavender suede gloves which he wore because of the eczema on his hands—though some said it was to hide his claws. Even his diet was archaic: his breakfast, for example, consisted of a Vendéen peasant dish, half porridge, half stew. Clemenceau's memories also went back a long way. As he told Wilson, "I have known men who saw Napoleon with their own eyes."[56] Clemenceau recalled witnessing from the heights of Montmartre the Germans burning the Castle of St. Cloud during the Franco-Prussian War. More recently, he had seen men marching up the line to death at Verdun carrying bunches of violets which they threw at him with shouts of "Vive la France."

After the armistice Clemenceau faced the most challenging task of a career which had involved him in such bitter struggles as the defence of Dreyfus. He wrote, "We have won the war; now we have to win the peace, and it may be more difficult."[57] His difficulties stemmed not just from Woodrow Wilson, whose high-minded formulae would simply, in the Tiger's view, leave Germany capable of taking its revenge a generation hence. They stemmed also from implacably revanchist opinion in France, typified not only by President Poincaré and Marshal Foch, but by the crowds who stoned the German delegation at Versailles. Most Frenchmen demanded a Carthaginian peace. Germany must be destroyed as a military nation, stripped of the sinews of war—arms, cash, territory, industrial capacity. Although Clemenceau wanted the fruits of victory, he would not go that far. He rejected Foch's proposals to extend the French frontier to the Rhine or to create a "buffer state" between France and Germany.[58] Instead he was prepared to accept British and American pledges of an alliance guaranteeing French security—these were broken, though at the time Lloyd George even offered to build a Channel tunnel to ensure the speedy arrival of an expeditionary force. No one but Clemenceau could have countenanced such an agreement. No one else had the prestige, or the physical courage. When a would-be assassin managed to wound him during the peace conference, lodging a bullet in his ribs, he merely deplored the state of French marksmanship.

As Lloyd George came to realise, Clemenceau would concede far too little to break the vicious cycle of aggression. At the same time the British Prime Minister had to look over his shoulder at democracy. For the spirit of vengeance was not confined to France. Lloyd George's difficulties were compounded by the vitriol of Lord Northcliffe's populist press—and by remarks made during the recent British general election about hanging the Kaiser and squeezing Germany until the pips squeaked. Yet the Welsh Wizard thrived on difficulties. He had, for example, gratuitously complicated his life by bringing Frances Stevenson, his mistress and secretary, to Paris, where she behaved like an unofficial wife, indulging him with chocolate *langues de chat* biscuits in his flat on the Rue Nitot. No one could match Lloyd George's mesmeric persuasiveness as an orator and his uncanny ingenuity as a negotiator. Observing him change his ground when he discovered that the areas shaded green on a Foreign Office map signified trees not Greeks, Harold Nicolson marvelled at his "kingfisher" quickness.[59] Keynes said that the Prime Minister possessed "six or seven senses not available to ordinary men," which gave him an "almost medium-like sensibility to everyone around him."[60] Winston Churchill paid tribute to his supreme mastery of "the art of getting things done."[61]

In Paris Lloyd George clearly perceived what must be done. The peace settlement should be harsh enough to satisfy the Allies, in particular to assuage the inherited and acquired fears of the French, and moderate enough to conciliate the Germans, who might otherwise succumb to Bolshevism. Lloyd George warned the other delegations:

> You may strip Germany of her colonies, reduce her armaments to a mere police force and her navy to that of a fifth-rate power; all the same, in the end if she feels that she has been unjustly treated in the peace of 1919 she will find means of exacting retribution from her conquerors.[62]

In view of such prescient caveats, why did the plenipotentiaries at Paris go on to make "peace with a vengeance"?[63]

The answer, in short, is that past wounds went too deep. The nations were, in a phrase of Auguste Comte which Clemenceau liked to repeat, "living the dead."[64] As Herbert Hoover graphically recorded:

Destructive forces sat at the Peace Table. The future of twenty-six jealous European races was there. The genes of a thousand years of inbred hate and fear of every generation were in their blood. Revenge for past wrongs rose every hour of the day. It was not alone the delegates that were thus inspired. These emotions of hate, revenge, desire for reparations, and a righteous sense of wrong were at fever heat in their peoples at home.[65]

Irreconcilable differences were apparent from the first, when the Council of Ten, two delegates from each of the great powers (the United States, Britain, France, Italy and Japan), gathered at the French Foreign Ministry on the Quai d'Orsay in January 1919.

They were conducted through high corridors, smelling of beeswax and coffee, to the minister's office. This was a magnificent Second Empire room with great double doors, a huge bronze chandelier, carved oak wainscoting and a series of Gobelin tapestries depicting those scenes of Henri IV's life which were fit to be represented. On the white mantelpiece stood a gold clock and a marble statue of Liberty holding a torch. Three long windows looked south over a formal courtyard with lawns, lilacs and splashing fountains. The delegates sat around a large U-shaped table. Clemenceau presided, his back to the blazing log fire, the iron hands in the velvet gloves toying with an ivory paper-knife which once, in a fit of irritation, he snapped. Sometimes abrupt and rude, more often patient and suave, he found it impossible to reconcile the many divergent national aspirations. So while much of Europe continued a prey to hunger, disease and strife, the conference ran into the sand. During interminable translations Wilson often read a newspaper. Lansing sketched hobgoblins. Lloyd George talked. Arthur Balfour, the feline British Foreign Secretary, catnapped, as did the Tiger himself. Count Makino of Japan silently, impassively observed.

So the Big Three adjourned to meet at Wilson's house in the Place des Etats-Unis or in Lloyd George's nearby flat or in Clemenceau's room at the Ministry of War. There they abandoned Wilson's principle of open covenants openly arrived at, consulting others only when they needed expert advice. Engaged in their immense haggle, they were occasionally to be seen crawling round their maps on the hearth rug. Sometimes they agreed and, according to Balfour, "were so pleased with themselves for doing so that they quite forgot to tell anyone what the agreement was."[66] Sometimes they almost came to blows. André Tardieu observed their different styles of argument. "Sitting bolt upright in his chair," Wilson debated like a college professor. Lloyd George "argued like a sharpshooter, with sudden bursts of cordial approval and equally frequent gusts of anger, with a wealth of brilliant imagination and copious historical reminiscences." Clemenceau "proceeded by assertions, weighty, rough-hewn and insistent."[67] Against such granite obstinacy the darting manoeuvres of the British Prime Minister made only limited headway, as Clemenceau's dismissive comment suggests: attending an opera he murmured, "Figaro here . . . Figaro there . . . he's a kind of Lloyd George."[68] Even the Puritan tenacity of the American President was gradually eroded, a process which incensed his fellow negotiators. Finding the ubiquitous Colonel Edward M. House, Wilson's familiar, easier to deal with, Clemenceau was delighted when the American President fell ill. He suggested that Lloyd George should bribe Wilson's doctor to make the malady last.

Still, despite anguished last-minute protests from Lloyd George himself, they finally arrived at an agreement, though the effort to represent it as the outcome of his principles strained even Wilson's powers of sophistry. Germany's colonies were to be confiscated, Britain and France getting the lion's share, Japan receiving some Pacific leftovers. Annexation was disguised by making the colonies "mandated territories"; in theory they were to be held in trust, a shadow of Wilson's hope that their control would be vested in the League of Nations. Germany was forced to admit war guilt, symbolised by the black crosses (for shame) which had to be erected over German war graves, as opposed to the white crosses (for purity) in French cemeteries. Heavy reparations were imposed, despite Wilson's earlier determination to eschew punitive damages. Germany was also to be surrounded by small states fashioned from the ruins of the Habsburg and Romanov empires, despite Lloyd George's warning that he could not "conceive any greater cause of future war."[69] On paper Poland, Czechoslovakia and Yugoslavia were unified self-determining nations, but their frontiers had been the subject of much controversy and all contained ethnic minorities, including Germans. Poland was to be given access to the sea via a contentious corridor which divided East from West Prussia and contained the newly created "free city" of Danzig. Another violation of the principles of democracy and nationality was the ban on Germany's uniting with Austria unless permitted to do so by the League of Nations, from which she was excluded. Finally, Germany was to be almost totally disarmed. It was stripped not only of its fleet but of its merchant marine. The Rhineland was to be neutralised and occupied for 15 years. The Saar coal-mining region also temporarily went to France, while Alsace and Lorraine were restored for good. When Clemenceau was asked whether the victorious Allies had forgotten anything he replied: "Yes! We have forgotten something very important. We have forgotten to ask for the Kaiser's breeches."[70]

Many Frenchmen might have taken that remark seriously, including

Foch, who insisted that such mild provisions made war inevitable within a generation. Others reached the same conclusion for the opposite reason—that the terms were wickedly vindictive. William C. Bullitt, for example, resigned from the American delegation in disgust, telling Wilson that he had delivered "the suffering people of the world to new oppressions, subjections and dismemberments—a new century of war."[71] The eminent French diplomat Paul Cambon agreed: Versailles had laid the foundations for "a just and durable war."[72] Herbert Hoover was so agitated by terms that "contained the seeds of another war"[73] that he went for an early morning walk in the deserted streets of Paris, where he encountered General Smuts and Maynard Keynes, each man instantly divining that the others were moved to be out at that hour by similar anxieties. Lloyd George himself believed that Versailles was more of a "hell-peace" than a "heaven-peace" and forecast that "we shall have to do the whole thing over again in twenty-five years at three times the cost."[74]

This sort of response was tepid beside the fiery resentment which erupted in Germany. The armistice had been bad enough but at least its "outrageously cruel conditions"[75] were tempered by Wilson's magnanimous Fourteen Points. Now the Allies threatened to renew the war unless Germany signed a treaty which would destroy the Reich that Bismarck had forged with iron and blood. Hitler would later sum up German feelings of outrage for the benefit of a British ambassador: "Freely negotiated agreements, yes! But blackmail, no! Everything that comes under the heading of the *Treaty of Versailles* I regard as extortion."[76] Despite Germany's hopeless position, the government considered resistance and President Ebert telephoned to consult Hindenburg. The Field Marshal could not bring himself to admit Germany's military impotence, let alone take responsibility for it. He told General Groener, "You know what the answer must be. I am going for a walk."[77]

So, on 28 June 1919, the treaty was signed in the Hall of Mirrors at the Palace of Versailles, where the German Empire had been proclaimed after the defeat of France in 1871. Outside, sunshine glittered on the spearheads of the blue-clad lancers flanking the square. The great staircase was lined by troopers of the Republican Guard, each standing immobile with drawn sword. Their uniforms were identical to those which the Guard had worn at Waterloo: silver helmets crested with horsehair plumes, shining cuirasses over blue tunics with red facings, white buckskin breeches and huge spurred riding boots. On the walls hung the flags of the Great War's victors, dominated by the tricolor. The audience, including many journalists, settled down on scarlet benches. The plenipotentiaries arranged themselves on a dais, the French Premier directly under a motto saying:

"Le Roi règne par lui-même." When Lloyd George chaffingly said that Clemenceau might have written it himself, the Tiger growled: "If I had, it would have been 'Moi' not 'Roi'. . . ."[78]

Finally, as silence fell, Clemenceau's voice rang out in rich, melodic tones: "Faites entrer les Allemands."[79] The frock-coated German emissaries appeared. They behaved with dignity but looked, as everyone noticed, more like prisoners in the dock than the representatives of a great power. No words were uttered. They signed the treaty, its hundreds of articles printed on Japanese vellum. Then they bowed stiffly and withdrew. Simultaneously the guns of St. Cyr began to boom and the fountains in the gardens below started to play. With an air of relief the other leaders swiftly appended their signatures and departed. The ceremony had been a disaster. As one diplomat recorded in his diary, it was a tableau of revenge. Every detail was designed to give "the utmost insult to Germany . . . Just the necessary note of reconciliation, of hope, of change of view, was absent."[80] Contrary to what had been intended, many people had actually felt sorry for the humiliated Germans. It was a contagious sympathy, on which Hitler would play with diabolical skill.

However, it was not just the vanquished who resented the treaty. Japan was far from satisfied. Admittedly the leader of the Japanese delegation, Prince Saionji Kinmochi, cherished the spirit of cooperation that he thought had "emerged as a new principle from the . . . peace conference."[81] An elder statesman so venerable that one of his first official acts had been to promote the training of Japanese troops with guns rather than bows and arrows, Saionji nevertheless loathed militarism. He venerated many of Wilson's liberal ideals—some of them, indeed, more than Wilson did. The Prince had imbibed Rousseau during a voluntary exile so protracted that he spoke perfect French, with a Marseilles accent. In fact, though he still thought about natural objects and emotions in Japanese, he thought about technical subjects in French. During the conference he indulged his passions for Vichy water, for well-tailored suits and for his geisha mistress (who was named Flower Child), keeping in the background and seldom taking advantage of his long friendship with Clemenceau. But when Wilson, for domestic reasons, refused to accept a Japanese clause enshrining racial equality in the Covenant of the League of Nations, Saionji took advantage of his confusion to secure Shantung, Germany's former sphere of influence, for Japan. This so incensed the heterogeneous Chinese delegation (one of whose members, T. C. Wang, was technically in rebellion against the Peking government) that they alone refused to sign the treaty. But, despite this concession, elements of the Japanese delegation were also in revolt.

Its most junior member in diplomatic status, though its most senior in social distinction, was Prince Konoe Fumimaro. If Saionji was "Japan's Lord Rosebery,"[82] Konoe was its Balfour—detached, lackadaisical, charming, sophisticated, fastidious. Konoe was interested in abstract ideas: before the war he had translated Oscar Wilde's *The Soul of Man Under Socialism* into Japanese. He could sit at a dinner table between two men of diametrically opposed views and convince each that he agreed with him. But Konoe was also a nationalist. Where Saionji was content with the status quo, Konoe argued that it only suited the interests of the "have" powers. Japan, like defeated Germany, was a "have-not." Konoe opposed the treaty because it institutionalised economic imperialism and racial discrimination. As he wrote in 1933, "It is not only futile, but unreasonable and unjust to eliminate war, while the real cause of conflict, the unfair conditions in the world, remains intact."[83]

That Versailles had reasserted the unjust old order, despite Wilson's quixotic window-dressing, was a view widely held in the United States. The British and French empires had grown as a result of its provisions. Freedom of the seas, one of Wilson's Fourteen Points, had not been established. Germany had been abased and antagonised. The League of Nations seemed to be a mechanism for entangling the New World in the dangerous and dishonest affairs of the Old, to say nothing of involving it (as Senator James A. Reed of Missouri warned) with "black, brown, yellow and red races, low in civilisation and steeped in barbarism."[84] Despite all Wilson's efforts, efforts which ruined his health, the Senate refused to ratify the treaty. This was a momentous decision for it meant that the people of the United States were washing their hands of Europe and returning to isolationism.

However, while America abandoned its vital political role on the international stage, there was no escaping the fact that it was now the greatest creditor nation in the world. Thus it would inevitably take a major part in the international economic drama played out during the next decades. Many, indeed, believed that this was fated to be a tragedy, that the fragile edifice of global industry and transport, commerce and finance, had been irretrievably smashed by the war. As Sir Arthur Salter recorded: "Prophecies of universal bankruptcy, of a return to the conditions of barter, of a rapid or gradual sagging of standards and modes of life to the levels of the days before the Industrial Revolution, were frequent and sometimes, apparently, authoritative."[85] But recovery, if it could occur despite the war's staggering legacy of debts and reparations, had to be generated in the United States. And prosperity would depend, as never before, on a stable American economy. Its collapse, following the stock market Crash of 1929, precipitated the world Depression—an effect of one war, a cause of a second.

Particularly sensitive to global economic conditions, Italy was another dissatisfied victor nation. Hers had been, in the words of the flamboyant poet Gabriele D'Annunzio, a "mutilated victory."[86] Though receiving new territory in the Tyrol and Dalmatia, Italians felt that they had been cheated of their full share of the spoils. Italy's ambitions focussed particularly on the Adriatic port of Fiume, which had a large Slav population. Wilson flatly refused to hand it over, so angering the Italians—they were said to be "fiuming"—that the Prime Minister, Vittorio Emanuele Orlando, withdrew from the conference. Then, in September 1919, D'Annunzio occupied Fiume at the head of a nationalist legion. According to the poet, he and his heroic force were inspired by the chance to recapture the mystical exaltation and the redemptive splendour of bloodshed, as experienced during the Great War: "Where masses of slaughtered flesh decompose, here sublime fermentations are born."[87] So, until evicted by an embarrassed and increasingly discredited Italian government in 1921, D'Annunzio set up what was, at least from the histrionic point of view, a fascist dictatorship. This bizarre adventure not only anticipated Mussolini's "March on Rome," it foreshadowed other violent revolts against the international order established at Versailles. It was one more portentous failure of a peace conference which had opened with hopes too high and too varied, hopes which could perhaps never have been realised, especially in the poisoned aftermath of Armageddon.

II

THE ROOTS OF FASCISM

ONE of the most raucous voices calling for Italy's entry into the First World War had been that of the Bohemian journalist, political agitator and self-styled man of destiny, Benito Mussolini. Ever an opportunist, he had advocated pacifism until the popularity of chauvinism became evident. Italians could not remain "inert spectators of this tremendous drama," he declared.[1] Intervention was a matter of national honour. It was also, for Mussolini, a means to an end. Full of the half-digested catchphrases of radical philosophers such as Sorel and Nietzsche, he glorified violence and saw himself as the embodiment of the will to power. Blood was the essential fuel and lubricant to turn the wheels of history. War would act on modern Italy as the barbarian invasions had once done on the Roman empire, sweeping away decadent institutions so that virile new structures could rise on their ruins. Mussolini, Superman in the making, would be architect of a revived Italy. In 1915 he fostered Revolutionary Action Groups (Fasci) to agitate for intervention. "Today it is War," he cried, "it will be Revolution tomorrow!"[2]

Mussolini was bombastic, inconsistent, shallow and vainglorious. But he was also, in some respects, a true prophet. The war proved a catastrophe for Italy simply because it lacked the resources to sustain it. Despite its pretensions to being a great power, Italy was a new, poor, fragmented and undeveloped nation. It suffered acutely from the disruption that followed the war. In 1920 the lira lost more than half its value and inflation raised the cost of living, afflicted the middle classes and led to serious civil disorder. The chaos was compounded by the hordes of demobilised soldiers who, having been fed on pledges that their sacrifice would not be in vain, now found themselves jobless and landless while war profiteers lived in ostentatious luxury. Italy's parliamentary institutions, already stunted and shaky, were further undermined by Orlando's failure at Versailles and by D'Annunzio's success at Fiume. Between 1919 and 1922 one weak government followed another as Italy rapidly became ungovernable. Mussolini was not far wrong in declaring that democracy itself had been killed during the war.

Mussolini's own strategy—to obtain power for himself—was as steady as his tactics were mercurial. At first, as a professed socialist, he behaved like a Latin Lenin. In March 1919 he revived his *Fasci,* making a fruitless attempt to form revolutionary cadres from embittered and ambitious ex-servicemen, with promises of profit-sharing for industrial workers and smallholdings for peasants. But in 1920 the strikes, riots, factory occupations and agrarian disturbances increased to such an extent that Red revolution seemed imminent. Mussolini realised that there was more to be won from attacking Bolshevism. During the winter of 1920–21 his Fascist movement gained enormous support as a result of the successful deployment of counter-revolutionary terror. With the connivance of the government and the active backing of industrialists and landowners, Mussolini's black-shirted squads raided the political headquarters of their opponents, destroyed trade union offices, burnt down cooperative institutions, smashed left-wing presses, assaulted Socialists with knuckledusters and coshes, and forcibly fed Communists on castor oil. Hundreds were killed and thousands injured. By July 1921 Mussolini could proclaim, "Bolshevism is vanquished."[3] It was now time to deny his more radical pronouncements against the monarchy and the Church, and to temper street violence with political intrigue.

How could Mussolini justify the chameleon changes, the abrupt *volte-faces,* the flagrant internal contradictions of Fascism? The answer is that Fascism was not "being" but "becoming," not a creed but a dynamic. Mussolini made up his own reality as he went along, like his admirer Luigi Pirandello. The playwright had anticipated Fascism, as one critic wrote, "in so far as it denies the concepts of the absolute and affirms the vital necessity of the continuous creation of *illusion,* of relative realities."[4] Mussolini was an animator of fantasy, the chief character as well as the author in his own theatre of the absurd. Fascism was form rather than content, style rather than substance. It was, as Mussolini said, "a doctrine of action."[5] It was a revolt against the crippling alienation and the stultifying conformity of bourgeois society. More than that, it was a kind of political mysticism. Mussolini himself, as a French observer wrote, was "a mystic of risk, with a quasi-religious faith in the absolute value of dynamism, considered as having an efficaciousness superior to all the calculations of reason."[6]

Fascism was a belief in the common bond of nationhood enshrined in the personality of a charismatic leader. The gospel that the leader preached was less important than his magical capacity to evoke the latent genius of his people. Fascism relied on propaganda before policy, mythology before history. It conjured with rhetoric, ritual, incantation and pageantry. It exploited symbolism: *fasci* meant "groups" and *fasces,* ubiquitous in Mussolini's iconography, were the bundles of rods with an axe which had been carried before Roman magistrates as an emblem of authority. Much of the liturgical side of Fascism was borrowed from D'Annunzio—the Roman salute (which Mussolini considered more "hygienic" than shaking hands), the demagogic techniques, the chanted responses of the crowd, the names of the squads, the Giovinezza hymn, the black shirts and fezzes, the badges, banners, slogans and war cries. Regarding the masses as a herd of beings to be governed (in Tom Paine's famous phrase) by fraud, effigy and show, Mussolini changed his policies as he changed his mistresses. The changes, indeed, brought him valuable publicity and helped to capture the popular imagination. With his spontaneous intuitions and his brutal inclinations, Mussolini alone appeared capable of breathing new spirit into Italy. Fascism was all things to all men.

Its adherents, too, were heterogeneous and their proceedings were various. In general, urban Fascists wanted to turn the movement into a victorious political party, whereas those from the countryside sought to achieve their ends by means of violence. Mussolini skilfully exploited both tactics. He gained 35 parliamentary seats (out of 510) in the election of 1921 and began to treat with rival political leaders, whose parties were divided and unnerved, like a seasoned power-broker. At the same time he took advantage of the guerrilla warfare being waged by his more aggressive followers. While Blackshirt detachments attacked socialists, occupied cities and extorted concessions from weak governments, Mussolini posed as the champion of order. Most of the middle classes supported him. So did many soldiers and policemen, who were given to sending wreaths to the funerals of Fascists killed in street fighting. Instead of taking strong measures, the ineffective Prime Minister, Luigi Facta, issued appeals. There was "nothing at all patriotic," he bleated, "in one Italian assassinating another."[7] Mussolini responded by organising a coup while still trying to talk his way into power. At a great rally in Naples towards the end of October 1922 he took "a solemn oath that either the Government of the country must be given peaceably to the Fascisti or we will take it by force."[8]

Bullying, bluster and bluff did their malign work on a government that was at once complacent and infirm. On 27 October squads of Blackshirts occupied post offices, telephone exchanges, railway stations and the like. Other *Fasci,* having seized power in many rural areas of northern and central Italy, prepared to march on Rome. Mussolini himself led from behind. In Milan that evening he took his long-suffering wife, Rachele, to the theatre, which he loathed. "The news has got around that the Fascists have mobilized," he whispered to her during the performance, "we must pretend to know nothing about anything."⁹ The mobilisation was more of a demonstration than an insurrection. The Fascist forces were so ill-equipped and badly organised that they could easily have been routed. But, convinced that he was facing civil war, King Victor Emmanuel III refused to sign a proclamation of martial law. Facta resigned and, after fevered negotiations, Mussolini was invited to become Prime Minister. He arrived in Rome via Wagons-Lits train on the morning of 30 October and was welcomed at the station by cheering crowds. Dressed in a curious costume, including a crumpled black shirt, white spats and a bowler hat, he drove through pouring rain to the Quirinal Palace. There he supposedly greeted the diminutive King with these words: "Majesty, I come from the battlefield—fortunately bloodless."¹⁰

No one propagated the myth of a bloody and heroic seizure of power more brazenly than Mussolini. Shortly before 30 October he declared that, "Only the myth can give strength and energy to a people about to hammer out its own destiny." Later he was even more explicit: "And why do I insist on proclaiming that that October was historically a revolution? Because words have their own tremendous magic power."¹¹ Mussolini was no mere myth-maker: after all, he had so demoralised the Italian State that it gave up without a struggle. But the "March on Rome" was far from being the Garibaldi-like adventure into which it was transformed by Fascist rhetoric. As Mussolini took up the reins of government his bedraggled Blackshirts limped into the capital. They had less in common with Caesar's legions than with Falstaff's followers. Their uniforms were an extraordinary motley, including nondescript trousers and multicoloured socks, headgear which was anything from felt hats to skull caps, footwear that ranged from top boots to dancing pumps. Some had rifles and bayonets, others riding crops or bludgeons. A man from Ancona carried only a baseball bat. At one stage of the proceedings, when Mussolini was supposed to be reviewing his troops, he closeted himself in his office with a woman.¹²

Thus although the "March on Rome" was a combination of parade and field day, it was also a triumph. The Fascists, wearing "rapt expressions, as if in a dream," were welcomed with immense enthusiasm. The Roman populace hailed them as liberators, showered them with flowers and laurel wreaths, and carried members of Perugia's daredevil "disperatissima squadron," Mussolini's bodyguard, on their shoulders. Everywhere flags hung from windows and placards announced "Victory is ours. Any conflict is useless."¹³ Actually the Blackshirts showed that they were not averse to beating and killing socialists in poorer parts of the city. Shouting anticlerical slogans and singing obscene songs, they also harassed the conservative editor of *Civiltà Cattolica,* Father Enrico Rosa, though, as if to illustrate Fascist ambivalence towards the Church, some doffed their fezzes and went to pray in St. Peter's. Mussolini, keen to maintain discipline, instructed them to demobilise after one final procession. This lasted six hours and Mussolini himself took a leading part, strutting in the sunshine and proudly displaying on his black shirt his Fascist badge and war wound stripes. Through the crowded streets of the capital they trooped, singing Fascist songs, placing wreaths on the tomb of the unknown soldier and cheering the King when he came out to wave from the balcony of the Quirinal Palace. Then they dispersed, entrained and returned home. For all its swagger and braggadocio, the "March on Rome" did signify the victory of despotism over democracy. Hitler grasped its significance at once, and Nazism gained immediate impetus and prestige. Referring to his own Stormtroopers, Hitler remarked: "The brown shirt would probably not have existed without the black shirt. The march on Rome, in 1922, was one of the turning-points of history."[14]

Few at the time could see this. The *New York Times* commented patronisingly that the Fascists had achieved a "revolution of the peculiar and relatively harmless Italian type."[15] Mussolini formed a coalition government, preserved an impression of continuity and never became a totalitarian ruler to compare with Hitler or Stalin. He donned a frock coat and a butterfly collar when visiting the King and had himself schooled in bourgeois etiquette (though he never became a Beau Brummell and could still sometimes be seen eating his food with a knife). He tried to project an image of dignity and respectability, controlling his own press, bribing or intimidating foreign correspondents—subjecting them, as he cynically put it, to "the olive or the club."[16] Privileged journalists were allowed to interview him, first in the Chigi Palace and later in the gold-coloured Palazzo Venezia. This was a great fortress in the centre of Rome, built by medieval popes with stones taken from the Colosseum and now staffed by Fascist lackeys in silver-laced uniforms.

Here, in the grand echoing Hall of the Mappa Mundi, home of the first terrestrial globe, Mussolini was to establish his office. It had three huge windows, painted columns, gilded torches (fitted with electric lights) in the corners, a decorated ceiling featuring the Lion of St. Mark and the she-wolf of Rome, and mosaic tiles on the floor depicting nude women and children bearing fruit. The hall was so large that Mussolini communicated with entering flunkeys by hand signals and it was empty apart from Mussolini's massive rosewood desk, itself unadorned except by a bronze lion. Approaching the dictator was an ordeal, for he seldom greeted guests at the door and later decreed that his ministers should run the last 20 yards into his presence. Enthroned on high, Mussolini exuded animal magnetism. But he could be modest, courteous, charming and sardonic. Many visitors were impressed, not least Winston Churchill, who was suspected of wishing to become an English Mussolini. Churchill did not altogether discourage this notion before 1935, saying that in Italy he would be a Fascist and stressing the need for leaders who "feel themselves to be uplifted above the general mass." There were no giant peaks on the "democratic plateau," there was no "venerated 'El Capitan' or 'Il Duce,' casting its majestic shadow in the evening light."[17]

Witnesses less susceptible to the allurements of power were inclined to dismiss Mussolini as a comic-opera Caesar, "a Napoleon turned pugilist."[18] One woman journalist (whom he tried to seduce) was put off by Mussolini's "absurd attitudinising"—the scowling forehead, the rolling eyes, the pouting mouth, the snapping jaw, the shaven head thrown back, the huge chin thrust out.[19] Mussolini's compulsive exhibitionism was part of his cult of machismo. Whenever possible he bared his chest for the benefit of the cameras and he made much of his furious bouts of exercise—riding, fencing, swimming, bicycling, boxing, playing tennis, doing gymnastics. More private manifestations of virility were visited on the many females who succumbed to his crude advances. Indifferent to the looks of his conquests (though he liked them to smell strongly of scent or sweat—he himself seldom washed, preferring to dab his body with eau-de-Cologne), Mussolini thrust himself forward with sadistic vigour, dragging them to the floor while removing neither his trousers nor his shoes. Apparently "his brutality and savage curses in moments of climax were followed by words of tenderness, however brief and however commonplace, when he was satisfied." And at least one woman was favoured, after he had lifted himself from her person, with an air on his violin.[20] Equally theatrical were Mussolini's public performances, his harangues to crowds from his balcony, which he called his "stage." He spoke in short, strident sentences, making chopping gestures with his right hand. Often he paused and posed for dramatic effect—head up, torso erect, arms akimbo—looking like nothing so much as a music hall villain.

Yet Mussolini was no more the comic figure he seems in flickering newsreels than he was the old-fashioned accommodationist visualised by other politicians at home and abroad. He was a peculiarly twentieth-century species of political gangster. Fascism was not just the negation of democracy, it was government by terror. Mussolini certainly snuffed out parliamentary power. But he also encouraged acts of violence against his opponents, of which the murder of the Socialist deputy Giacomo Matteotti in 1924 is the best-known example. Mussolini relished thuggery as a form of manliness and declared that his regime "could not be prosecuted except at the bar of history."[21] This conveniently remote tribunal enabled him to rule by means of crime. He employed ruffians such as Roberto Farinacci, the viciously anti-Semitic boss of Cremona who was sometimes known as "Mussolini's left hand." He suppressed civil liberties, expropriated property, imposed censorship, tapped telephones, destroyed independent trade unions, imprisoned people without trial. He appointed himself "head" of government and built up a mystique of the Duce, the infallible, omnipotent Leader, who was capable of performing miracles. (It was said that he stopped Mount Etna's lava from destroying a village.) Nothing less than playing the role of quasi-divine dictator could satisfy Mussolini's extravagant longings. As he said soon after coming to power, "I am possessed by a frenzied ambition which torments and devours me from within like a physical illness. It is, through my own will-power, to carve a mark on the age—like a lion with his claws, like this." Then with outspread fingers he made a savage, slashing motion.[22]

It was a symbolic gesture hardly impaired by the fact that he bit his finger nails "not merely to the quick but almost to the moons."[23] Whether they regarded him as saviour, buffoon or barbarian, contemporaries were bound to acknowledge that Mussolini had made his mark. Out of the blazing passions of war and the blighted hopes of peace he had distilled a new political force. It drew strength both from national exaltation and from national humiliation; for despite victory won at such terrible cost Italy remained, as Mussolini insisted, in comparison to more exalted powers a "proletarian nation."[24] It also drew strength from fears of Bolshevism, which was widely seen not as an alternative form of tyranny but as the stark antithesis of Fascism. Communists themselves identified Fascism as the final crisis of capitalism, in which the workers were terrorised into submission. Capitalists, or some of them, believed that the political dynamism and discipline of Fascism complemented their own economic efforts, especially after the Crash. "In 1929 the pillars of the temple that seemed to defy the centuries crumbled in a vast uproar," Mussolini declared. "The crisis through which we are passing is not a crisis *in* the system; it is a crisis *of* the system."[25] During this crisis the global battle-lines between Left and Right hardened, leaving little room for compromise. Many non-Fascists admired Mussolini for having created a state which seemed strong enough to withstand the economic holocaust. Many others feared that Mussolini's Roman Empire would plunge Europe into a new dark age. After the Great War T. S. Eliot had described the Waste Land as "a heap of broken images." With equal pessimism the Auden generation witnessed the consecration of the new icons of Fascism—black shirts, loud-speakers, rubber truncheons, barbed wire, jackboots.

A DRESS rehearsal for the world crisis of 1929 seemed to be taking place in the Germany of 1923. The lost war and the cruel peace had reduced the new Weimar Republic to a condition bordering on anarchy. Short-lived governments were challenged by separatist organisations and putsches from the Left and Right. There was a rash of political assassinations. Riots and strikes proliferated. Poverty and hunger stalked the land. France's intransigent President Poincaré demanded prompt payment of reparations, fixed at the enormous sum of 132 billion gold marks; and when the Germans defaulted in January 1923 French troops marched into the Rhineland, proposing to dig out the Ruhr's coal, as Lloyd George said, with bayonets. More insidious still, inflation was destroying the value of money like some financial cancer.

In this poisoned atmosphere extremist political groups flourished, among them the small but well-disciplined National Socialist party in Bavaria. Its spell-binding leader Adolf Hitler intuitively grasped the fact that the social chaos caused by the mark's precipitous fall was the humus of Nazism. In one speech the "German Mussolini," as Hitler was sometimes called,[26] told a story which epitomised the cataclysm. It concerned an old woman who had rejoiced when her small postcard shop did well during the Munich gymnastic festival.

> But now the old woman is sitting in front of an empty shop, crying her eyes out. For with the miserable paper money she took in for her cards, she can't buy a hundredth of her old stock. Her business is ruined, her livelihood absolutely destroyed. She can go begging. And the same despair is seizing a whole people. We are facing a revolution . . .

It would occur, Hitler said, when the farmer stopped selling food for currency good only for papering "his outhouse on the manure heap." Hitler pinned his faith in the "revolt of the starving billionaires."[27]

It now seems clear that German governments were themselves, at least in part, responsible for the "flight from the mark." As the entrepreneur Hugo Stinnes said, they had to spend beyond their means in the terrible aftermath of the war in order to sustain life and to find work for returning soldiers. Otherwise "Bolshevism would have seized Germany."[28] But the German authorities also aimed to avoid paying reparations. They deliberately engineered[29] currency depreciation in order to promote cheap exports and to exert "economic pressure on the Allies."[30] However, reparations, though in practice much less onerous than the Germans claimed and in any case paid for by foreign loans, also contributed to inflation. Added to the crippling burden of debt caused by the war itself, they adversely affected the balance of trade and undermined confidence in German stability. The massive toll in cash and kind led to a severe budget deficit which governments found themselves unwilling and unable to make up through taxation. So they printed money, in ever increasing quantities. In January 1919 there were 9 marks to the dollar; three years later there were 192. Stimulated by the assassination of the Jewish foreign minister Walter Rathenau in 1922, the "currency debauch" worsened. The British ambassador quipped that "German finance is dying beyond its means."[31]

In January 1923 it seemed that France was determined to finish the work of war and peace, for Poincaré insisted that Germany pay while making it impossible for it to do so. As Britain dithered and the United States withdrew, France began to exploit the Ruhr, Germany's industrial powerhouse, for its own ends. Berlin retaliated with a doomed strategy of passive resistance which cost 40 million marks a day. Forgetting their own punitive treatment of defeated Russia, the Germans found a new unity in common mortification. The Reichsbank made valiant efforts to hold the mark at a rate of about 2,000 to the dollar. But when these efforts failed it rose to astronomical heights. In July 1923 there were 353,412 marks to the dollar; in August, 4,620,455; in September, 98,860,000; in October, 25,260,208,000; in November, 4,200,000,000,000. It was the most colossal inflation in history, making the assignats of the French Revolution look almost as good as gold. To produce this currency 300 paper mills and 2,000 printing plants worked round the clock; eventually it cost more to print the notes than they were worth. Banks had to take on more clerks to count the noughts. They used the blank side of the notes as scrap paper because it was cheaper than buying pads. Eventually stacks of cash were not counted at all but weighed or measured with a ruler.

Life was transformed into a bizarre paperchase. Patrons of restaurants found their meals becoming more expensive as they ate. Factory workers saw their wages shrinking in value as they queued to collect them. However fast they ran to the shops, prices outstripped them. Shopkeepers, indeed, looked on their customers almost as thieves for taking goods which could only be replaced at prohibitive expense. Peasants refused to sell their produce for paper money, saying: "We don't want any Jew-confetti from Berlin."[32] Beggars rejected anything less than a million marks. New notes appeared, issued by municipalities and acceptable locally. Forgeries added to the confusion. Some people paid in kind:

theatre seats were sold for a couple of eggs; prostitutes offered their services for cigarettes. Interest rates rose to 20 per cent a day and loans were made in terms of rye or coal or even electric kilowatts. Bureaucrats in the Finance Ministry took part of their salaries in potatoes.

Those who possessed foreign currency were impossibly rich, for no one had enough marks to change anything but the smallest denominations. Ten dollars would purchase a large modern house. Foreign profiteers took advantage of the situation to make a killing, while American tourists lit their cigarettes with million-mark notes and pasted larger denominations on their suitcases, further exacerbating German chauvinism. In the words of one contemporary, "Germany was a rapidly decomposing corpse, on which the birds of prey were swooping down from all directions."[33] At the height of the inflation, according to a familiar story, a woman who left a basket of marks on the pavement came back to find the basket stolen and the marks in the gutter. Currency notes were used as lavatory paper. Germans talked of the death of money. Stephan Zweig minted a compelling metaphor for that awesome demise in his story of a blind man whose family had secretly sold his cherished collection of drawings in order to keep alive, replacing them in his portfolio with blank sheets of paper.[34] In the same vein, Hitler dismissed the Treaty of Versailles as a scrap of paper.

Not everyone suffered. Landowners actually benefited, often paying off their mortgages in depreciated marks. So did industrialists, especially if they sold abroad. Trade-unionists had a measure of protection. But at a time when a pound of ersatz butter could cost a labourer's daily wage and it might take five months' earnings to buy a suit of clothes, the working class was sucked into a maelstrom of misery. Even worse off were pensioners and those living on fixed incomes. Their savings vanished and they faced not only indigence but starvation. Here was a revolution as sweeping as that of the Bolsheviks. At a stroke property was destroyed and "the bourgeoisie was proletarianised."[35] Middle-class values were turned upside down: debtors were virtuous while thrift was a vice; wealth was no longer the index of worth. As one contemporary said, "Inflation finished the process of moral decay which the war had started."

Crime spread: so many potato fields were raided that police had to guard them in order to preserve the seed crop. There was an increase in suicide, malnutrition, illness and emigration. Infant mortality rates rose. Economic paralysis set in, unemployment grew, strikes and disturbances spread, shops were ransacked and towns looted. Corruption and anti-Semitism flourished—the Jews were accused of exploiting the tragedy. Germany's physical and psychic health decayed together. Life became "madness, nightmare, desperation, chaos."[36] Observing that the inflation had revived Germany's "old, bristling, savage spirit," D. H. Lawrence said: "Money becomes insane, and people with it."[37] Sexual decadence seemed to be a by-product of the bankruptcy of traditional values. A foreigner exclaimed, "Nothing brought you so much face to face with the pathological distortion of Germany's postwar mentality as the weird night life of Berlin."[38] Describing the way in which inflation infected everything, one historian has written that it was a "revolutionary influence much more powerful than the war itself."[39]

Inevitably this crisis threatened Germany's fragile democracy. Since the State was unable to protect its citizens they were bound to look elsewhere, especially when, in September 1923, the impotent government surrendered to French coercion in the Ruhr. Many workers turned to the Communists; Saxony and Thuringia were menaced by Red revolution. Many of the dispossessed middle class were seduced by right-wing movements. None was more rabid than the National Socialist party, which promised to restore a strong, unified Reich that was both anti-capitalist and anti-Bolshevist. And no one articulated petty-bourgeois bitterness more vehemently than its leader, Adolf Hitler, who larded his speeches with hideous invective against money-grubbing Jews. As Otto Strasser said, "His words go like an arrow to their target, he touches each private wound on the raw, liberating the unconscious, exposing its innermost aspirations, telling it what it most wants to hear."[40] Damning Weimar as a "robber's state," Hitler declared that people starving on billions must withdraw allegiance from a Republic "built on the swindling idea of the majority." They must embrace instead dictatorship.[41] To financial problems Hitler had only political solutions. He aimed to smash the State which had encompassed Germany's defeat and ruin, and build one which enshrined racial purity and national greatness—with himself at its head. The shackles of the past could only be broken by his indomitable will. "For liberation something more is necessary than an economic policy," he declared, "something more than industry: if a people is to become free, it needs pride and will-power, defiance, hate, hate and once again hate."[42] Noting that Germans needed to humiliate others in order to compensate for their own sense of mass worthlessness during the "witches' sabbath of devaluation,"[43] Elias Canetti thought that without it the Führer could not have induced them to participate in the destruction of the Jews.

Hitler was a small, nondescript figure. His complexion was pallid, his limbs were ill-coordinated, his lank hair flopped over a receding forehead, his toothbrush moustache was the image of Charlie Chaplin's. Only expressive, sensitive hands and luminous blue eyes saved him from being totally unprepossessing. In his heavy boots, blue serge suit, broad-brimmed black hat and dirty mackintosh, he resembled, in the words of his affluent acolyte "Putzi" Hanfstaengl, "a suburban hairdresser on his day off" or "a waiter in a railway station restaurant."[44] Hitler's style of life was shabbier still. He rented a small, dingy room in a poor district of Munich. It contained a single bed, a few sticks of furniture and a couple of threadbare rugs to cover the worn linoleum. Hitler's habits were Bohemian: he was erratic and unpunctual. So were his tastes: he had an insatiable appetite for sweet things, cream cakes, coffee flavoured with squares of chocolate, white wine enriched with spoonfuls of castor sugar. In the presence of upper-class people his manners were gauche. Yet even at this stage Hitler had developed "unmistakably Napoleonic and Messianic airs."[45] Accompanied by a savage Alsatian dog, he swaggered about packing a pistol and cracking a rhinoceros-hide whip. His pretensions knew no bounds. He once exclaimed, "I must enter Berlin like Christ in the Temple of Jerusalem and scourge out the money-lenders."[46] Absurd as his rhetoric sounds, when Hitler spoke he convinced audiences that he really was the saviour of Germany. He was transfigured by oratory.

No prophet ever had a more vivid appreciation of the "magic power of the spoken word." As he wrote in *Mein Kampf*:

> The broad masses of the people can be moved only by the power of speech. And all great movements are popular movements, volcanic eruptions of human passions and emotional sentiments, stirred either by the cruel Goddess of Distress or by the firebrand of the word hurled among the masses.

Hitler despised the kind of middle-class political meetings where professorial figures in frock coats and monocles *read* their speeches in hushed tones to a somnolent audience. "Only a storm of hot passion can turn the destinies of peoples," he believed, "and he alone can arouse passion who bears it within himself."[47] Hitler himself was so passionate that Hanfstaengl described his perorations as "an orgasm of words."[48] They induced ecstasy in his audiences and it later became his practice, at the climax, to crush his spectacles in his clenched fist. To quote another witness, who had never experienced such "hypnotic mass-excitement," he displayed the "fanatically hysteric romanticism of a brutal will."[49] But if Hitler played the demiurge he also learned the tricks of the demagogue. Apparently he studied the techniques of Ferdl Weiss, a popular Munich comedian. He rehearsed in front of a looking-glass, timed his entry to perfection, used every aid—bands, banners, spotlights, salutes. Emblazoned all around was the swastika, described by Barbusse as "two interlaced gibbets."[50] Hitler varied his rhythm and orchestrated the crowd's responses like an inspired musician. He began quietly. Often he reviewed the past and, like some black alchemist, transmuted the gold of history into the dross of propaganda. Then would come fiery denunciations of Versailles, the "November criminals"[51] of the Weimar Republic and the Jews. Rant would be followed by rapturous invocations to *Deutschland Über Alles*. Hitler lost about five pounds in weight during every speech, though he drank small bottles of mineral water throughout. He sometimes took a block of ice to the rostrum to cool his hands. But he sweated so profusely that the dye running from his suit stained his shirt and underwear blue.

If Hitler was Savonarola on the platform, he was Machiavelli behind the scenes. He manoeuvred adroitly through the turbulent shoal-waters of German politics, ever seeking a passage to power. Exploiting the deep divisions between the central government and the right-wing authorities in Bavaria, where the Nazis were tolerated because of their violent attacks on the Communists, Hitler tried to create conditions for a coup. Modelling himself on Mussolini, he dreamed of a march on Berlin. He also kept his followers, especially the party's paramilitary arm, the Stormtroopers, in a state of frenzied expectation. Unpaid, undernourished and badly clothed, the brown-shirted SA yearned to beat out their frustrations in an act of violence such as Hitler had long promised. It was partly in response to this pressure, partly because he judged the political situation ripe for revolt, that he staged his putsch.

On the evening of 8 November 1923 the three leading figures in Bavaria—State Commissioner Kahr, army commander Lossow and police chief Seisser—were attending a political meeting at the Bürgerbräukeller, one of the biggest beer halls in Munich. It attracted a large, fashionable crowd who filled the cloakroom with their top hats, swords and uniform coats. Shortly after 8:00 P.M. Hitler, wearing a trench coat over ill-fitting evening dress, arrived in his new red Benz car. Followed by his entourage he pushed his way through the police cordon and sat by one of the pillars in the vestibule, gnawing his finger-ends and sipping a litre of beer which had cost a billion marks. Half an hour later, in the middle of a dull speech by Kahr (who disappointed hopes that he would declare Bavaria's secession from Weimar and the restoration of the Wittelsbach monarchy), lorry-loads of Nazi Stormtroopers surrounded the beer hall. As their leaders burst through the doors Hitler cast aside his beer mug and fought his way through the throng, firing a shot into the ceiling from his Browning automatic. From the rostrum he bellowed, "The National Revolution has begun."[52]

In a state of savage euphoria, Hitler herded the triumvirate into a side-chamber at pistol-point. Here, after protracted argument, he obtained their reluctant cooperation in setting up a separate state, the first stage, he hoped, in the overthrow of the Weimar Republic. He was assisted by Erich Ludendorff, who appeared in the full-dress uniform of the Imperial Army. The former Quartermaster General always maintained that the putsch came as a complete surprise to him, but he had emptied his bank account a couple of days beforehand and he now lent his immense prestige to the Nazi cause. Hitler also won over the beer hall crowd which had earlier heckled his "South American" melodrama. His speech was a rhetorical performance worthy of Shakespeare's Mark Antony. As a witness recorded, Hitler "turned them inside out, as one turns a glove inside out, with a few sentences. It almost had something of hocus-pocus or magic about it." But after an uneasy show of unity Hitler made the mistake of allowing Kahr, Lossow and Seisser to slip away with the departing crowd. They at once repudiated promises extorted by force and began to organise resistance to Hitler. Sipping a glass of red wine, Ludendorff vaingloriously asserted that "The heavens will fall before the Bavarian Reichswehr turns against me."[53] But as the night passed it became clear that the tide was running against the putsch.

The next morning Hitler resolved on a final desperate gamble—death or glory. At the head of a ragged column of some 2,000 Stormtroopers— all singing, many carrying rifles, some with fixed bayonets—the Nazi leaders marched under an overcast sky towards the centre of Munich. On the Ludwig Bridge they blustered and beat their way through the first police road-block. But as they approached the Odeonsplatz through the narrow Residenzstrasse, they encountered another detachment of police. Who fired the first shot has never been established, but within moments the street was raked with gunfire. Hitler fell to the ground—either from an old soldier's reflex or pulled down by his dying comrade, Erwin von Scheubner-Richter, with whom he had linked arms. Fifteen other Nazis and four policemen were killed. Others, including Göring, were wounded. Only Ludendorff, immaculate in mufti, unbending in pride, marched straight on into the ranks of the police—who promptly arrested him. The Nazi forces scattered. Two days later Hitler himself was picked up by the police, who found him hiding in "Putzi" Hanfstaengl's attic.

The Beer Hall Putsch has often been dismissed as a fiasco worthy of its name, a storm in a stein. It is true that the Nazis were dispersed by a whiff of carbine shot. But at the time the British Ambassador thought the coup "looked very much like the beginning of civil war."[54] Moreover, the putsch brought Hitler to national prominence, so much so that he regarded it as "perhaps the greatest stroke of luck in my life."[55] The subsequent trial allowed Hitler to present himself as much more than a local rabble-

rouser—now he was the leader of a serious political party. He and his
co-defendants were treated with the utmost indulgence and Hitler was
permitted to speechify from the dock. He claimed sole responsibility for
the putsch, upstaged Ludendorff and turned the court into a theatre of
propaganda. "The man who is born to be a dictator is not compelled,
he wills," Hitler said, "he is not driven forward, he drives himself forward."[56] His sentence for high treason—five years' imprisonment—was so
lenient as to imply that the authorities themselves had been found guilty.
Hitler was now frequently acclaimed as *"Der Führer"* and even his gaolers
adopted the *"Heil Hitler"* greeting.

By then the mark had been stabilised. The new Currency Commissioner, Hjalmar Schacht, had introduced the Rentenmark, soon to become the Reichsmark. This was valued at a trillion old marks (of which
the Reichsbank now had supplies enough to fill 300 ten-ton railway
trucks) and was nominally secured on all land in Germany. The economy
remained exceedingly fragile, in part because inflation had reduced funds
available for investment. But high interest rates attracted foreign capital
and under the Dawes Plan American subventions helped to achieve a
patchy revival in Weimar fortunes. Indeed, between 1924 and 1930 Germany received more in loans from abroad than it paid in reparations.
However, the country's dependence on alien investment was a sign of
domestic weakness: when American credit was to be withdrawn as a result
of boom and bust on Wall Street, Germany would suffer accordingly. In
the meantime recovery boded ill for the Nazis and, as a British diplomat
noted, "Hitler's greatest enemy is the Rentenmark."[57] The Führer would
have to change his tactics and hope that he could climb to power over the
ruins of a new economic catastrophe. That catastrophe, when it came, was
made worse because the hyper-inflation of 1923 had traumatised not just
Germany but the world. In 1929 governments were so determined to protect their currencies and balance their budgets that they resisted the temptation to spend their way out of the crisis. So the Slump turned into the
Depression.

AS THE inflationary crisis was reaching its climax in Germany, a cataclysm
of an entirely different kind occurred on the other side of the globe.
Moments before noon on Saturday 1 September 1923, Japan was struck
by a massive earthquake. The inhabitants were accustomed to seismic
upheavals, superstition attributing them to the movements of the giant
catfish Namazu which lived under their volcanic isles. Indeed, when the
architect Frank Lloyd Wright visited Japan he was amazed to discover that

the needle on the seismometer was never still. But this was different. It measured 8.3 on the Richter Scale, which made it significantly stronger than the force that had razed San Francisco in 1906, and its epicentre was only 30 miles south of Yokohama.

According to witnesses, the first shock felt like "a grinding blow beneath our feet."[58] It rose to a sickening "crescendo of turmoil."[59] This lasted only about fifteen seconds but its effect was stupendous. As the captain of a vessel in the port of Yokohama observed, the whole city undulated "like the surface of the ocean under a great storm."[60] With a deafening roar nearly all the buildings in Yokohama and most of those in Tokyo toppled to the ground. Acres were flattened and many thousands were killed at once. Rows of new houses vanished under landslides while medieval ruins, buried for hundreds of years, suddenly came to light. Roads were gashed with crevasses large enough to swallow an automobile; trains crashed as railway lines buckled and bridges collapsed; tram and telegraph wires festooned the streets like monstrous spiders' webs. What one witness called the "insanely malicious forces of nature" appeared to have battered nearby villages into the ground with "a gigantic flail."[61] While the earth continued to tremble and choking yellow dust filled the air, the survivors, many crazed with fear, fled into parks and open spaces.

Almost at once fires began, as charcoal cooking braziers *(hibachi)* kindled the remains of wood and paper dwellings. Gas flaring from broken pipes added to the conflagration. It was fanned by a wind known as *tatsumaki*—the dragon's twist. This spread sparks to the futons, or padded quilts, carried by many refugees, turning them into involuntary pyromaniacs. It also drove flames over the wide Sumida River, where thousands of people sheltering at a clothing depot in the working-class suburb of Honjo were incinerated. In Yokohama huge oil storage tanks on the hillside burst, releasing an avalanche of fuel which quickly ignited. Many sought refuge in canals or at sea, only to be burned alive as streams of blazing oil covered the water. Boats in the harbour were set alight or sunk by tidal waves. On land incandescent tempests erupted. They were nothing like the familiar city blazes known as the "flowers of Edo," but rather a terrifying adumbration of the fire-storms caused by saturation bombing during the Second World War. Many suffocated, like those in the crush at Hongo Station. Others were whirled into the air, human brands plucked from the burning. Thousands died in "ghastly, grotesque attitudes,"[62] their arms upraised in a hopeless attempt to ward off the furnace heat. After dark, people ten miles away could read by its light. Immersed in billows of flame which roared like heavy guns, Yokohama presented "an amazing, grand and terrifying spectacle."[63] Amid the glare and stench of death, the

impression of war was compounded: soldiers started to dynamite buildings in order to make fire-breaks and to shoot the wild animals which were
roaming the streets after escaping from their shattered cages in the zoo.

Despite all efforts the holocaust lasted for several days. The Japanese
responded variously. In the frenzied exodus from the cities some fugitives
were trampled underfoot. Martial law was declared, but there were cases
of hysteria, cowardice, looting and "foul work by ghouls."[64] Large stocks
of rice had been destroyed and food riots occurred. More horrible was the
wave of paranoia which soon engulfed the nation. Searching for scapegoats, people blamed the inferno on immigrant Korean workers—for
whom they felt an atavistic racial antagonism. The authorities claimed to
have uncovered a gigantic Korean plot involving arson, looting, bombing
and murder. Fifteen thousand Koreans were interned and many others
were tortured and massacred. Some were literally crucified. Japanese
youths armed with spears and swords acted as vigilantes and "appeared to
have lost their reason."[65] The police behaved no better, rounding up a
number of left-wing radicals, some of whom were beaten and killed. An
army officer took the opportunity to assassinate the imprisoned anarchist
leader Osugi, breaking his back with a ju-jitsu hold and then strangling
his common-law wife and child. He was never brought to justice.

Fears of subversion were not entirely groundless. Among the crowd
seeking sanctuary inside the walled and moated gardens of the Imperial
Palace, one man cried ominously: "Remember Russia!"[66] Later these 247-
acre grounds, with their exquisite pavilions and pools, terraces and courtyards, streams, bridges and flowers, were thrown open to refugees. The
Prince Regent Hirohito, who had become head of state in 1921 as a result
of his father's madness, was absent from Tokyo but several members of his
family were killed. Although he soon returned, there was some resentment
at his failure adequately to reassure and commiserate with his subjects.
Doubtless Hirohito was inhibited by protocol, which ruled out spontaneous demonstrations of emotion. But three months after the earthquake
a young socialist attempted to assassinate him because he had not raised
an ideal state on the ruins.

It was one of the many paradoxes of Japan that violent social indiscipline could coexist with adamantine social order. Zen Buddhism, with its
doctrine that salvation lies in following the dictates of one's heart whatever
the earthly consequences, encouraged a sublime nonconformity. At the
same time the Japanese were so devoted to the ideal of national polity
(kokutai) that they sometimes burst the bounds of orthodoxy and became
more imperial than the Emperor. Yet their commitment to fulfilling obli-

gations at any cost, not excepting hara-kiri, resulted in a community spirit almost inconceivable to individualistic foreigners, who were inclined to disparage it as an archaic hangover from feudalism or a sinister portent of the "hive mentality." However, many Westerners caught up in the earthquake benefited from the self-denying code of their Oriental servants, who often sacrificed their own interests in order to save their employers' lives or to rescue their possessions. Most Japanese, indeed, behaved with exemplary courage and restraint, and some were heroic.

So bad had the destruction been in Tokyo that it was initially feared that the capital would have to be moved to another site. But citizens took heart from Premier Yamamoto's exhortation to "unite and rebuild."[67] Salvage work began almost immediately and some construction started before the ashes were cool. People waited stoically in food queues two miles long. There were many patriotic demonstrations. None was more moving than that prompted by a schoolmaster who, after fire had swept through a host of his companions, cried: "All present shout three banzais with me." Two hundred voices were raised in the most pitiful cheer ever heard.[68]

Because communications were cut, the outside world was slow to grasp the scale of the Japanese tragedy: perhaps 140,000 dead, tens of thousands injured and devastation which was likened to that of Armageddon. As one witness wrote, "Imagine the Somme battle-fields and the ruins of Ypres on a gigantic but concentrated scale and you have a picture, though not even realistic enough, of Tokyo and the country around."[69] At two billion dollars, the cost of renovation amounted to 40 per cent of the country's gross national product. It not only wiped out the 400-million-dollar profit which Japan had made out of the First World War, it crippled the entire economy. In the words of an American authority, this was "the greatest financial catastrophe of the age."[70]

Foreign countries, particularly the United States, responded generously to the disaster, donating millions of dollars and enabling relief agencies like the Red Cross to deliver food, clothing, tents, medical supplies and other aid to the stricken cities. But this largesse did little more than point up the contrast between America's wealth and Japan's poverty. It was poverty so acute that the masses could seldom afford to eat much more than rice and salt—Prince Saionji hailed it as a notable improvement when they were later able to augment this diet with bean paste (*miso*) and soy sauce. During the various economic crises of the 1920s, farmers—and agriculture employed half of Japan's 60 million people—had no recourse but to sell their daughters into prostitution. Sometimes it seemed as though this were Japan's most prosperous business: after the earthquake the brothel-keepers of Tokyo's Yoshiwara district rebuilt their premises more quickly than anyone else because they could afford to pay the highest wages.

Admittedly, Japan's advance since the nominal restoration of power to the emperors in 1868—the beginning of the Meiji ("Enlightened Rule") era—had been one of the most astonishing achievements of modern times. Within the lifespan of Prince Saionji, Japan had turned itself from a backward, isolated state into the greatest power in the Orient. It had defeated Russia, annexed Korea, Taiwan and other islands, and was casting avaricious glances towards China. Before 1853 any Japanese who built an ocean-going vessel was liable to the death penalty; by the 1920s Japan possessed the third largest shipping industry and navy, and the largest fishing fleet, in the world. Other manufacturing enterprises had also sprung from nothing, such as textiles. When the ailing Lord Northcliffe visited Tokyo in 1921, he noticed that all the weaving machinery had been made in Britain and that "it takes at least three Japs to do the work of one European."[71] Within a decade the "rising giant of the East" was poised to overtake John Bull's massive production of cotton textiles and one Japanese did the work of ten Britons thanks to the Toyoda automatic loom—when Platt Bros of Oldham bought the right to manufacture it in England they had to be taught how to do so by Toyoda engineers.[72] The Japanese themselves were always willing to imitate and improve on Western technology. Their success also resulted from an ability to translate patriarchal fealty into commercial loyalty, something the big business combines (zaibatsu) exploited to keep their wages and prices low. Routed by the trade mark "Made in Japan," foreigners increasingly took refuge behind tariff barriers. When the global Depression led to even fiercer competition, the Japanese felt a strong temptation "to cast the samurai sword into the mercantile scales" that seemed so unfairly weighted against them.[73]

This aggressive proclivity was encouraged by further Japanese resentments towards the West. Like those other victors, France and Italy, Japan emerged from the First World War with the neuroses of a defeated nation. Denied its demands at Versailles, it was humiliated at the Washington Naval Conference in 1922. By the terms of the agreement Japan was allowed fewer warships than America and Britain, who, as a subsequent Prime Minister Baron Hiranuma said, discarded their old alliance "just as she would a worn-out sandal."[74] Two years later the United States prohibited Japanese immigration, at a stroke turning gratitude for American aid after the earthquake into bitterness. Nippon declared a national day of mourning, and one man protested by committing suicide in front of the American embassy. Militarism, so unpopular after the war that (as in

France) soldiers preferred to wear mufti, revived. Liberal internationalists like Saionji found it increasingly difficult to maintain their predominance. Nationalist secret societies and blood brotherhoods proliferated, some of them engaging in political assassination. The outstanding proponent of the nationalist cause, Kita Ikki, declared that his country was entitled to seek equality with millionaire empires like Britain and huge landowners like Russia: "Japan with her scattered fringe of islands is one of the proletariat, and she has the right to declare war on the big monopoly powers."[75]

Kita's radical rhetoric, which influenced men such as Prince Konoe, reinforced the traditional idea that it was Japan's manifest destiny to bring "the eight corners of the world under one roof" *(hakko-ichiu)*.[76] At its most mistily magnanimous this was the aspiration to achieve universal brotherhood. Japanese were taught to regard themselves as the chosen people, the uniquely virtuous *Yamato,* the children of the sun. As "a messianic nation" they were, to quote a Western observer, "charged with a divine mission to subjugate, pacify and civilize the world."[77] Or as a Japanese professor explained, "Nippon's national flag is an ensign of 'red heart' or fiery sincerity. It alludes to the heavenly mission of Japan to tranquillize the whole world."[78] So high-minded notions of fraternity were imperceptibly transformed into self-serving ones of hegemony. Patriotic devotion tended to become imperialistic fanaticism. Major-General Nonaka expressed his country's burgeoning ambitions graphically: "The ultimate conclusion of politics is the conquest of the world by one imperial power . . . The Japanese nation, in view of her glorious history and position, should brace herself to fill her destined role."[79] The inspiration and the focus of the national cult was, of course, the emperor himself, who was worshipped as a living god.

Actually Hirohito, ruling in his father's stead, expressed some doubts about his divine ancestry. But Saionji assured him that it was a useful myth. In particular, the belief that the 2,600-year-old dynasty had descended in direct line of succession from the sun goddess acted as a social cement for a people still torn by ancient clan rivalries. The imperial indoctrination began at school, where children bowed towards the Son of Heaven's picture and repeated that their dearest ambition was "To die for the Emperor."[80] (One lot of pupils nearly did when, during a fire, their headmaster neglected them and injured himself in order to rescue the Emperor's photograph.) Hirohito, a small, delicate, sensitive young man, intelligent but lacking in self-confidence, had been brought up to pay an even stricter regard to duty. Though short-sighted, he had been for a time denied spectacles lest they cast doubt on his divinity. He was so governed by protocol that almost any impromptu action was rebuked; later he was not even permitted to travel in the same railway carriage as his own children because there was no precedent for it.

From his youth Hirohito had been drilled in the samurai's chivalric code of *bushido,* itself largely a Meiji fabrication designed to provide (along with Shinto) a "new Japanese religion of loyalty and patriotism."[81] In this it was similar to the "invented tradition" of ritual with which the British monarchy attempted to secure the allegiance of the masses in a democratic age.[82] And it is significant that Hirohito regarded his experiences at the court of Windsor, itself a monument to clotted formality, as a singular taste of freedom. During his European tour, which took place in 1921, he danced, hunted, wore plus-fours, ate bacon and eggs for breakfast (a custom he continued in Japan) and so enjoyed playing golf with the Prince of Wales that he built a nine-hole course in the grounds of the Imperial Palace. In France, Hirohito bought a bust of Napoleon, which he placed in his study. It was joined in the later 1920s by one of Darwin and after 1945 by one of Lincoln.

Doubtless the last two sculptures reflected his interest in marine biology and his accommodation with the United States. But the bust of Napoleon was not the purchase of a man impatient for martial glory. Hirohito was horrified by the sight of Verdun. As one court official later remarked, he was not only a scientist and "an extremely liberal person," he was also "a pacifist."[83] After his father's death (in 1926) Hirohito chose *Showa,* or "Radiant Peace," as the name for his new reign. Moreover, no one knew better than Hirohito that the emperor's powers, though theoretically as absolute as a theocracy could make them, were in practice negligible. In fact the only way to preserve his power was not to exercise it. As Saionji said, the emperor could not command the armed forces in case he was disobeyed, thus casting an "inexcusable blemish on sovereign authority."[84] Nor was the emperor always even kept informed of what was done in his name. When the army, pursuing its aggressive designs against China, assassinated the Chinese warlord Chang Tso-lin (known as the Old Marshal) in 1928, the new Prime Minister, Baron Tanaka, told Hirohito that no Japanese officers were involved. Later Tanaka admitted the truth to the Emperor, who was so angry that he did not "care to listen to him again"— whereupon the premier resigned in tears.[85]

The fact was that Japan had always been a country of subtlety and circumspection, of Shoguns, mayors of the palace, *rois fainéants. Gekokujo,* insubordination by which juniors were in some ways able to dictate to seniors, was a potent factor in Japanese life. Where sovereignty lay during the 1920s (and afterwards) remained a mystery, one not to be resolved by a press which the Emperor thought should be censored even more strictly than it was. Few realised that behind the scenes raged a perpetual struggle for power—between the deeply entrenched bureaucracy, the increasingly assertive military (though the army and navy sometimes looked set to fight each other and both services were riven by factions) and the Japanese parliament, the Diet (nominally elected by universal male suffrage after 1925, actually elected by well-nigh universal corruption). Also taking part in the power struggle were the rich *zaibatsu,* the nationalist societies and the imperial court. The Japanese people and foreign observers saw only what was acted out on the public stage. No performance was more moving than the complex rituals marking the imperial succession, some of which went back to the mythical origins of Japan when the sun goddess, angered by her brother the god of thunder, shut herself up in a cave and plunged the world into darkness.

Hirohito's ceremonial accession to the throne in November 1928 provided the most brilliant spectacle. It took place in the ancient capital of Japan, Kyoto. Set amid green mountains, the city was a jewel casket of shrines, pagodas, giant bells, stone lanterns, huge Buddhas and miniature landscape gardens. To welcome the Emperor it was decorated with bunting, flags and ideograph banzais. Along the route from the railway station crowds squatted on straw mats 10 to 20 deep, though the upper storeys of buildings were deserted as no one was permitted to look down on the Son of Heaven. As bugles sounded and the glittering procession passed smoothly over a carpet of clean sand on Karusama Avenue, people bared their heads (or lowered their paper umbrellas) and made deep obeisance. The most splendid of all the many rites that followed took place in the Enthronement Hall at the Sento Imperial Palace. With its austere lines and curved roof of white cypress bark, the vast open pavilion, known as the *shishenden,* was a gem of Japanese temple art. At its centre, scarcely visible from the large courtyard 18 steps below, stood the August High Seat, or *Takamikura.* This was a red and black lacquer throne in the form of an eight-pillared palanquin, carpeted with scarlet silk, curtained with brocades of scarlet, green and purple, decorated with mirrors, golden arabesques and fabulous beasts, and surmounted by a great gold phoenix with outstretched wings. Nearby was a smaller throne for the Empress Nagako, the first consort to attend the ceremony.

At a signal from drums and gongs 2,000 guests were ushered through the vermilion gates into the courtyard, its pebbles individually polished to reflect the sun. They made a "human frame" for the imperial picture, taking their places each side of a central avenue flanked by banners and standards featuring the sun and the moon, heraldic animals and royal chrysanthemums, and raised in colourful array on black lacquer spears whose silver and gold points glinted in the sunshine.[86] Most picturesque of all was the guard of archers, dressed in crimson surcoats and medieval armour and carrying samurai swords with white sharkskin hilts and gold mounts—gifts of the Emperor. Close to the throne gathered the imperial princes and other dignitaries, including the Prime Minister, all in ceremonial costume. The Emperor and Empress mounted their thrones and the curtains were drawn back. Hirohito wore robes designed when Europe was in the Dark Ages. They were dull orange, to represent the rising sun, and decorated with emblematic plants and beasts: bamboo and paulownia, phoenix and kirin. The Empress was dressed in a flowing violet gown over a red skirt with a long white train embroidered with birds and flowers. The Emperor was invested with the legendary symbols of majesty: the sacred mirror which brought life to earth, the sword of the clouds of heaven and the jewel necklace given to the first emperor, Jimmu Tenno, by the sun goddess to typify the ruler's virtues. Then he read the imperial rescript, adumbrating a reign of radiant peace and stressing his paternalistic role: "Our Ancestors looked upon the state as their own household and the people as their very children."[87] Baron Tanaka congratulated the 124th Emperor on his accession and the Premier's thrice-repeated cry, wishing the Son of Heaven life for 10,000 years, was echoed in the courtyard and broadcast throughout Japan and around the world: "Tenno Heika Banzai."[88]

This was the first time that the accession ceremony had been witnessed by journalists. Hundreds of newspapermen, radio commentators, photographers and film crews recorded the event for a mass audience. Even the infant medium of television was present—whereas TV cameras were excluded from the British coronation service in 1937, largely because, as the Archbishop of Canterbury noted, there was "no possibility of censoring."[89] Of course no one witnessed the most solemn rites, as Hirohito, almost immobilised by the impedimenta of office, conjured with the imperial mysteries. But nothing better epitomised Japan than the broadcasting of the public aspects of this ancient Oriental ceremony by means of modern Occidental technology. It typified a contrast which was apparent in myriad less spectacular ways, from the peasant riding in an electric tram and lighting his pipe with a tinder and flint to the high-fronted modern cinemas advertising their programmes with brilliantly coloured banners fastened on bamboo poles and employing orators *(benshi)* to explain the action.

As one newspaper wrote, the earthquake had "revolutionized" Tokyo's life.[90] It was a titanic clearing operation which opened the way to novelty in every sphere. After the earthquake (which Frank Lloyd Wright's sprawling, modernistic red and yellow brick Imperial Hotel had triumphantly survived, though the floor of its banqueting hall dropped two feet) a forest of steel and concrete buildings sprang up and Tokyo developed one of the most architecturally avant-garde city centres in the world. Its offices, staffed with employees dressed in Western fashions, were full of lifts, swivel-chairs and telephones. Its gleaming new department stores modelled themselves on Harrods and Bloomingdale's, and customers no longer removed their shoes at the entrances. If the Marunouchi district was Tokyo's Wall Street, the Ginza (Silver Way) was its Piccadilly—complete with "stick girls,"[91] female gigolos who attached themselves to men like walking-sticks. Moreover, its streetcar and subway systems were an improvement on those of London and New York. Narrow, muddy alleys gave way to broad asphalt boulevards with stone-flagged pavements. Canals were filled in to make roads and by 1941 six new bridges spanned the river. Whereas before the earthquake there had been only 12,000 automobiles in Japan, there were 100,000 by the end of the decade. The taxi superseded the rickshaw just as the motorboat overtook the sampan. The armed forces were equipped with some of the most sophisticated weapons in the world. Japan made more films than Hollywood. Education and literacy were almost universal. The nation's modern boys and girls, known as "mobos" and "mogas," enjoyed ballroom dancing, cafés, Western food, Charlie Chaplin, jazz and abstract art. Many "mobos" regarded baseball as Japan's national game. Some "mogas" went to beauty parlours, wore lipstick, cut off their long hair and sported the Eton crop. At the end of the 1920s one Tokyo magazine remarked on the "intense desire of the Japanese to keep pace with the Western peoples in their onward march towards higher culture and refinement."[92]

Yet at the same time Japan was the land of tea ceremonies and flower arrangement, kites and kabuki theatre, bonsai trees and haiku poems, sake and sukiyaki, sumo wrestlers and geisha girls, soothsayers and spirit shrines. Despite the massive rebuilding programme, Tokyo and Yokohama, joined in one great urban sprawl during the 1930s, gave the impression of being little more than a huddle of "dirty, dilapidated, ramshackle wooden shops and shacks."[93] The air smelled faintly of soya beans. The roads were thronged with people wearing kimonos and clogs, and carrying their packages in *furoshiki,* square pieces of ornamented silk or cotton. Half-naked urchins abounded, as did ox-carts driven by farmers dressed in rags or wearing raincoats and sandals of straw. There was no regular street lighting and the night markets were illuminated by lanterns. There was no modern sewage system and the night-soil was taken away in handcarts. Japanese houses, low structures of grey tile, stone, wood and paper, were made of standardised parts. But they were packed together higgledy-piggledy, especially in the poor, low-lying east end of Tokyo. Outside they were guarded by lucky charms and emblems (plum blossoms, oranges, even a lobster) to ward off evil spirits. Inside they offered no privacy, a concept difficult to express in Japanese. Certainly they afforded no protection against the nightly din of barking dogs. They contained no furniture and were decorated with little more than a painted scroll and a vase of flowers on the domestic altar or "god shelf" *(kamidana)*. Families sat on lemon-yellow, fragrant-smelling mats *(tatami)*, eating their food with chopsticks. Rigid etiquette prevailed: wives deferred slavishly to husbands, children humbly honoured parents. Marriages were arranged. Sons who entered the armed services were respected for adopting the samurai code of chivalry, which dated back to the time of the Crusades. The police played a quasi-feudal role: they even told householders when to do their spring-cleaning. In smart offices the abacus was more in evidence than the calculating machine and Tokyo (a city of 2.5 million inhabitants in 1928) had only 60,000 telephones.

Propagandists maintained that "the Old and the New stand shoulder to shoulder in Japan today."[94] Actually the tug of war between them was as longstanding as the rival slogans: "revere the emperor and expel the foreigners" and "join Europe and leave Asia behind."[95] The struggle between conservatives and innovators permeated all levels of life. It was most evident in the matter of foreign fashions such as kissing in films and doing the foxtrot. The former was invariably "tabooed by censors." The latter was often banned by police, who closed dance halls on the ground that "they tend to arouse the voluptuous instincts of patrons, which in turn are bound to have an undesirable effect on public morals."[96] That may sound odd coming from a people with the most elaborate system of licensed brothels in the world, but it was less an expression of puritanism than of nationalism. Japanese traditionalists, who saw nothing wrong with nudity in mixed bath-houses, just as easily denounced swimming costumes as a corrupting import. Indeed, ardent patriots repudiated everything from abroad, even technology. The writer Kobayashi Hideo said that if Western modernisation was a "tragedy" its second manifestation in a Japan wedded to the past was a "comedy."[97] Traditionalists scornfully rejected plans to adopt Roman script in place of the thousands of ideograms which made the written language hard for them but almost impenetrable to outsiders. To imitate the culture of the West in any way would be to impair the purity of the Japanese spirit.

The sacred source of that spirit, many believed, lay in the countryside;

and here the earthquake, which had ravaged Japan's most modern cities, taught a powerful lesson to those with ears to hear. One farmer wrote:

> Of late the vainglorious striving of [those] city people had reached extremes that caused poor, simple farmers no end of anxiety. With their elegant clothes and their gold teeth, gold rings and gold watch chains, they flitted from one lavish social affair to another. They would go off on trips to the seashore or the mountains to escape the heat . . . and tour the famous sites. But now all that has vanished as if in a dream, consumed by fire, and suddenly they find themselves reduced to misery. It seems that Heaven found it necessary to chastise them with a natural disaster in order to protect the nation.[98]

Rural conservation became such a fetish that poachers who tried to steal a twig could be shot on sight among the Kiso mountains, where forests of cedars and cypresses, red pines and oaks, grew with primeval density in *himitsu-no-tani*—ravines that never see the sun.

The preservation of the Japanese spirit was deemed so vital that chauvinists, especially among the military, became as paranoid about alien infiltration as Westerners had once been about the Yellow Peril. There were real fears that the Americans might build a tunnel under the Bering Strait which could pose a threat to Japan. Emperor-worship took extreme sectarian forms. Japanese resentment against rich but idle foreign nations grew more acute when times were hard. They were hard in 1927, when banks became so desperate to restore confidence after a financial panic that they piled notes by tellers' windows even though there had been time to print them on one side only. At the end of that year a writer in the *Japan Advertiser* predicted that a further financial crisis could not be long delayed:

> Such a panic will mean a general collapse and will be a revolution. The immensity of the task facing it will put to flight not only political parties but most of the present ruling interests in the country. Then the field will be cleared for the appearance of a Mussolini, and it is almost certain that the Army will rally to his support.[99]

This forecast was impressively close to the mark. The slump of 1929 plunged the nation into the years of economic depression, political turmoil and military strife known to Japanese as the "dark valley."[100]

III

THE BANE OF CAPITALISM

PARADOXICALLY, Japanese of all persuasions found much to admire in another offshore island race with exalted notions about its destiny. As the "world's greatest capitalist country"[1] and the world's strongest imperialist power, Britain offered Japanese nationalists an alluring model. Of course, they recognised that Britannia no longer ruled the waves. Nor did she dominate the globe as she had done before the Great War. But she remained so formidable, even in the Far East, that Japanese naval leaders were anxious to avoid unnecessary friction. As Vice-Admiral Oikawa remarked in 1936, "I saw that Britain's might, which is centred around Hong Kong, is tremendous."[2] Britain also compelled the admiration of Japanese progressives, who respected its constitutional monarchy, liberal traditions and parliamentary processes. Even a Francophile such as Prince Saionji extolled the virtues of a civilisation which seemed to be the most advanced that the earth had ever known.

Yet much of what the Japanese saw in Britain was an illusion. Although still imposing, the workshop of the world was in danger of becoming a museum of industrial archaeology. The British economy had been severely disrupted by the war and largely depended on heavy industries—coal, iron, steel, textiles and ship-building—which were in decline. Throughout the 1920s exports fell below the levels of 1913 while imports rose above them. And there were always more than one million people out of work. With a quarter of the world painted red on the map, Britain's imperial façade was also impressive. But the struggle to preserve and defend this huge miscellany of territories between the wars stretched the mother country's resources to breaking-point. And some observers perceived that the unprecedented extent of these dominions presaged imminent imperial collapse. As the Fabian Beatrice Webb wrote in 1929, "The British Empire is suffering from a sort of senile hypertrophy, which has been quickened by the exhaustion of the Great War, and the increased responsibility of the

Mandates for Palestine, Iraq and African territories."[3] As for the urbane conventions of Britain's political life, they disguised the instinctive authoritarianism of governments which had hardly come to terms with democracy. They also masked the social divisions which were made more bitter by labour troubles and economic depression.

This is not to suggest that there was any significant revolutionary tradition among the British working class. Indeed, hearing that strikers and policemen had played a friendly game of football, Lenin declared that all British classes, from the proletariat to the aristocracy, were incurably bourgeois. In the same vein Harry Pollitt, a leader of the Communist Party of Great Britain (founded in 1920), complained that the workers "cared only for beer, tobacco and horse-racing, and it will take twenty years to educate them."[4] Later, when Pollitt was imprisoned in Wandsworth for his opinions, a professional burglar said: "Serve you bloody well right, you've no respect for private property."[5] British society, described by George Orwell as the most class-ridden in the world, was fundamentally deferential. And trade-unionists such as the bibulous railwaymen's leader Jimmy Thomas, who told the House of Commons that less than "2 per cent of the people would vote for a revolution,"[6] aimed not to beat the system but to join it. They "piss[ed] in the same pot"[7] as the bosses, ordinary workers complained. They wore evening dress, hobnobbed with the rich, hankered after knighthoods and kowtowed to royalty. To quote Beatrice Webb again:

> Owing to its social prestige and its envelopment in London society, the Court is a shocking—I use the term deliberately in its double meaning—atmosphere for Labour politicians. It stimulates the unutterable snobbishness of the lower type of Labour representatives like Jimmy [Thomas], it wiles away the integrity of aesthetes like J. R[amsay] M[acDonald], while it gobbles up *arrivistes* like Ethel Snowden and it even deteriorates decent folk like the Alexanders and the Clynes.[8]

Ramsay MacDonald, the Labour party leader, was notoriously susceptible to the charm of duchesses and eagerly submitted to the aristocratic embrace. In socialist company he sang "The Red Flag"; but privately he deplored the sentiments as much as the tune, regarding it as "the funeral dirge of our movement."[9]

All the same, there was much working-class sympathy for the Bolsheviks and corresponding resistance to the British government's intervention on the side of the White Russians. In some of the post-war labour disputes trade-unionists employed Communist rhetoric to plead their cause. In 1920, using the soviets as their model, militants formed Councils of

Action, and places like "Red Clydeside" seemed bent on actually waging class war. Their aspirations were summed up by a transport workers' leader who told a meeting at the Albert Hall, "I hope to see the Red Flag flying over Buckingham Palace."[10] King George V was not the only one "in a funk" about the "danger of revolution."[11] Lloyd George's coalition government responded by rushing through an Emergency Powers Act (1920) awarding itself the draconian controls conferred by the wartime Defence of the Realm Acts (DORA). It also took secret measures to counter the Red Menace. These included spying on suspected subversives and mobilising the middle classes, themselves resentful at having been financially squeezed during and after the war. Plans were made to arm loyal citizens and to form "battalions of stockbrokers."[12] At one cabinet meeting the First Lord of the Admiralty regretted that he personally possessed no pistols less than 200 years old.

When the post-war boom collapsed in 1921, organised labour was at a disadvantage. Falling wages provoked strikes but rising unemployment made them less likely to succeed. Of all Britain's industries, coal mining, at one million strong the country's largest, was worst affected. Britain's civilisation, as Orwell would insist, was "founded on coal";[13] but the world was moving to oil. In any case, British pits were mostly antique, inadequately mechanised and increasingly uncompetitive. Conditions of work were correspondingly bad, a fact best illustrated by the appalling accident rate. Between 1922 and 1924 (inclusive) 3,603 miners were killed and 597,198 were injured. In 1923, on average, 5 miners were killed every working day; 32 were injured every hour. Even those miners who escaped death or disablement were liable to be worn out at the age of 40, their broad backs scarred by overhead beams, their pallid faces veined with subcutaneous coal-dust, their eyes rolling with nystagmus, their lungs choked with silicosis.

Yet in many tightly-knit communities in depressed areas like South Wales and Scotland the pit provided the only work. Indeed the vista from rows of jerry-built houses was bounded by coal—slag-heaps, ash-pits, colliery workings. Above ground, miners in cloth caps, mufflers, threadbare suits and patched boots eked out "days of semi-starvation" on wages of under £2 10s. a week (the average in 1925). Below ground, nearly naked and often on their knees, amid heat and dust, fumes and water, as well as their own sweat and sewage, men hewed coal for seven hours at a stretch—journeys from shaft to face, sometimes several miles long, did not count as part of the shift. One visitor to a pit commented, "It is like going down into the depths of Hell."[14]

From the abyss miners rose in 1925 to resist a further attack on their living standards. Lower wages and longer hours were essential, the owners insisted, if Britain was to compete with foreign pits. Those of a revived Ruhr were thought to be particularly damaging to their British rivals at a time when the pound had been pegged at a high rate by Britain's return to the gold standard. The miners, who regarded their employers as the "most heartless, soulless lot" of parasites that ever lived,[15] sought salvation in nationalisation. This the Conservative government, led by Stanley Baldwin, rejected. But the Prime Minister was unprepared for the aggressive obstinacy of the Miners' Federation. Its secretary, A. J. Cook, a lanky, blond Leninist with (as Beatrice Webb noted) glittering, china-blue eyes set close together, encouraged the pitmen with his revivalist rhetoric. Its president, Herbert Smith, a stout, cloth-capped Yorkshireman, formerly a prize-fighter and famous for responding to compromise calls with a blunt "Nowt doin'," epitomised the intransigence of his followers. The miners were supported by railwaymen and transport workers. And though this Triple Alliance had proved feeble enough in the past to be nicknamed the "Cripple Alliance," it persuaded the government to buy off a strike with a subsidy. This was to last until 1 May 1926, by which time a Royal Commission under the chairmanship of Sir Herbert Samuel would have reported on the coal industry. Meanwhile the government got ready for a trial of strength. It set up a nominally independent Organisation for the Maintenance of Supplies (OMS), known derisively by workers as the "Organisation of Mugs and Scabs."[16] The less systematic nature of the trade unions' preparations was summed up by Cook's promise to collect "grub" for the miners starting, apparently, with the extra tin of salmon which his mother-in-law bought every week. As Jimmy Thomas classically remarked, "By God! A British revolution based on a tin of salmon."[17]

Thomas might scoff but by May 1926 the *Manchester Guardian* feared that Britain was facing the "most devastating civil conflict of which this generation has had experience," a trial comparable to the Great War.[18] The recommendations of the Samuel Commission (present pay cuts for miners in return for the future reorganisation of their industry) had proved acceptable only to the government. When the subsidy ran out, the pit owners insisted on immediate wage reductions. The miners, intoning "Not a penny off the pay; not a minute on the day,"[19] were locked out of the collieries. The Trades Union Congress (TUC) thereupon called out four million workers on a "national strike," avowing that this was nothing more than an industrial action aimed at defeating the attempt to starve the miners into submission. Moderate Tory that he was, Baldwin instinctively sought a compromise. But late on Sunday 2 May printers on the *Daily Mail* refused to set up in type an editorial asserting that the "general strike is not an industrial dispute; it is a revolutionary movement, intended to inflict suffering upon the great mass of innocent persons in the community and thereby put forcible constraint upon the Government." This allowed diehards in the cabinet—notably the Chancellor of the Exchequer, Winston Churchill, a flamboyant *condottiere* who never ducked a fight, and the Home Secretary, Sir William Joynson-Hicks, a puritanical reactionary known as Jix or "Mussolini Minor"—to stiffen the Prime Minister's resistance. So the government broke off negotiations and when TUC representatives tried to resume them they found that Baldwin had gone to bed. The *Mail* stoppage had been, as one journalist remarked, "a mere frontier incident, and when a frontier incident starts a war everyone knows that it is an excuse."[20]

There was incessant talk of war, but the most remarkable feature of the General Strike was its peacefulness. It was, as one participant said, "the greatest industrial struggle that the country, or indeed, the world has ever known."[21] Yet it was generally conducted with the kind of sporting spirit on which the British prided themselves. As the fog lifted on the fine sunny morning of 4 May it became clear that the strike was rock solid: no buses or trains ran, the mines were deserted, the blast furnaces were silent, newspapers were rare and thin, pickets guarded the docks, factories depending on electricity shut their doors. However, as Churchill's propaganda sheet the *British Gazette* put it, "On foot, squeezed into cars, standing in vans, riding pillion, pedalling on cycles, swarming Citywards by every road and route, London came . . . doggedly and cheerfully to work."[22] Actually the capital was almost paralysed by traffic jams. But this account captured the air of chirpy improvisation that marked the strike. It was literally a nine-day wonder, an interlude in which dissidence was strangely blended with innocence. Pickets on *The Times* touched their caps to its proprietor, Lord Astor. In some places strikers themselves assisted with the distribution of food and milk, or enrolled as special constables. Even the undergraduates from Oxford and Cambridge, half of whom joined the mass of volunteers who tried to keep services running, scarcely seemed to realise that they were strike-breaking. Afterwards, when recalling their role, former scabs in Oxford bags and blacklegs in blue stockings felt ashamed. But at the time it just seemed rather a lark. Amabel Williams-Ellis spent the days "helping those organizing the strike" and the evenings helping her architect husband to entertain strike-breaking bus drivers.[23]

Yet there were real fears that a struggle which, according to Baldwin, placed Britain nearer to civil war than it had been for centuries, would end in carnage. On 5 May, Lady Diana Cooper asked her husband Duff, a

Conservative MP, "how soon we could with honour leave the country." He replied, "Not till the massacres begin."[24] Such fears were exacerbated by Churchill, who opined that "a little blood-letting" would do no harm[25] and at times seemed bent on provoking it. The *British Gazette,* of which Baldwin had appointed him editor in an effort to confine his aggression to words, pilloried strikers as "the enemy" and demanded their "unconditional surrender."[26] Churchill was also responsible for sending armed convoys to bring food from the docks. Some of the trade-unionists were equally belli-cose: Cook preached class war and foretold the downfall of capitalism. And many clashes occurred between strikers and strike-breakers. Pickets overturned trams and set them on fire. Baton-wielding police charged stone-throwing crowds. One letter reached Baldwin from a blackleg bus conductor who had to tell his passengers to put up their umbrellas to pro-tect themselves from flying glass and concluded, "facing some of these rough mobs is not exactly a pleasant job. I find the women very bad in parts (I mean in parts of London), the language simply awful and my rain-coat is well stained with spittle."[27] But the conflict was sporadic and mainly confined to poor districts (where special constables were some-times horrified by squalor which they had never before encountered). Only about 5,000 arrests were made and most people in the country were scarcely inconvenienced by the strike.

Throughout the TUC showed extraordinary restraint. Although confi-dent that they had moral right on their side, trade union leaders feared that their challenge to an elected government was constitutionally dubious if not downright illegal—as Sir John Simon, a former Attorney-General, pronounced it to be in the House of Commons. Simon's judgement was questionable as regards statute law, though the British constitution, being unwritten, invariably means what the government of the day wants it to mean. In any case, Churchill's proposal to outlaw the strike, arrest its lead-ers and seize union funds could easily have been put into effect. The TUC countered this threat by vehemently denying revolutionary intentions. It avoided Bolshevik terminology and sent back a cheque for £26,000 donated by the Russian Central Council of Trade Unions. It permitted all essential and many inessential services to continue. And it produced such a drably neutral newspaper, the *British Worker,* that even the police who raided it could find nothing to prosecute. Strikers themselves often pre-ferred to read Churchill's colourful effusions.

The TUC's studious moderation was matched by that of Stanley Bald-win. The Prime Minister was a religious man who, together with his wife, prayed every day on his knees and shared the puritanism (as well as some

of the literary skill) of his cousin Rudyard Kipling. Baldwin had a romantic vision of Britain as one nation and he cherished nostalgic memories of
the happy paternalistic relationship that had prevailed between master
and man in his family's ironworks. Baldwin's genuine patriotism was
expressed in 1919 by his anonymous gift of £150,000 (20 per cent of his
fortune) to help pay off the war debt. His political career was based on
rejecting the cynical and corrupt practices of Lloyd George, whose cabinet
Baldwin described as a "thieves' kitchen."[28] Baldwin felt a real sympathy
for the plight of the poor. In 1920 he visited Dundee, where slum children
still went about in bare feet, and, as he wrote, "I as near as two pins sat
down and howled . . . They seemed to know one would give one's life to
help: they can't know how impotent one is."[29] With his modest country
tastes, his preference for character over intellect, his sterling aversion to
foreigners, his phlegmatic mien and his unfashionable clothes—wing collars, baggy coats and shapeless hats—Baldwin looked the picture of John
Bull. He radiated sincerity as much as authenticity. As his biographer
G. M. Young wrote, he had a "marvellous power of sending a wave of
emotion in circles from the Chamber [of the House of Commons]. At
times I think he is the greatest orator in English history."[30]

Baldwin stated categorically that, "The General Strike is a challenge to
Parliament and is the road to anarchy and ruin."[31] And he demanded that
it should be called off "absolutely and without reserve." But he also made
conciliatory overtures which were extremely effective. Audibly striking a
match to light his pipe before speaking, he concluded a fireside chat,
transmitted to the nation by the British Broadcasting Company, by asking: "Cannot you trust me to ensure a square deal for the parties, to secure
even justice between man and man?"[32] Many working men believed that
they could trust him. When a Labour MP told the Durham miners that
"Mr. Baldwin had let them down and was as crooked as Mr. Lloyd
George," the President of the Northumberland Federation contradicted
him, declaring that the Prime Minister was "an honest and kindly man
who had done all he could for them."[33]

Yet Baldwin's air of benign impartiality was as misleading as his imper-
sonation of a rustic squire. As a friend wrote, "The most elusive factor in
S. B.'s make-up was his infinite capacity for closing up like an oyster and
playing the part of the simple, rather stupid Englishman."[34] Beneath the
Premier's taciturn exterior there was an astute intelligence which some-
times revealed itself in sharp remarks—such as his accusation that Lloyd
George had been caught telling the truth, or his observation that
Churchill when up to mischief looked like a cat stealing out of a dairy.

Belying his stolid manner, Baldwin was a prey to sudden impulses, moods of "appalling frankness" and extraordinary gaffes—he once told a charity meeting, "I want every one of you in this audience to be responsible for one unmarried mother."[35] Baldwin's buried emotions sometimes betrayed their presence by his curious parliamentary habit of "making an excruciating grimace and then planting a smacking kiss on the Order paper."[36]

He felt strongly about the miners, privately believing that they were led by "latent atheist bolshevists." He also felt strongly about the pit owners, being exasperated by their bone-headed stubbornness. But Baldwin treated the latter as "friends" with whom ministers should collaborate.[37] The Premier was not unduly snobbish, but such was the prevailing social apartheid in Britain that he looked on employees as a separate order of beings from employers. Everything about the miners proclaimed the great divide— accent, education, appearance, manners. At one meeting Herbert Smith took out his false teeth, cleaned them with a handkerchief and put them back into his mouth. Class-consciousness was second nature to Baldwin as to all Englishmen, and he revealed it incidentally in such remarks as: "The intelligent are to the intelligentsia what a gentleman is to a gent."[38]

Baldwin was, to paraphrase one commentator, a closed mind disguised as an open book. His apparent even-handedness and his repeated pleas for "peace in our time" concealed a ruthless determination to maintain the social order and to beat the strikers. So his government used the police and the courts to harass them. It tapped the TUC's telephones and intercepted their telegrams—some union joker devised a code in which the police were known as "Beauty." It discouraged the generous provision of Poor Law relief in order to wage a gradual but "remorseless war of attrition against the miners." (The Minister of Health, Neville Chamberlain, was lampooned as "the Minister of Death," but he remained convinced that the miners were never "within sight of starvation, hardly of under-nutrition.")[39] Above all, realising that it must win the hearts and minds of a people inclined to sympathise with the strikers, Baldwin's government skilfully deployed the weapon of propaganda.

In this endeavour Churchill's *British Gazette* was more of a hindrance than a help. It was blatantly partisan, suppressing some items (like the Archbishop of Canterbury's appeal for peace), inventing others (such as the return to work of 400 miners at Gallis Green colliery, which had not been in use for years) and trumpeting the government's cause so wildly as to bring it into disrepute, if not derision. Churchill behaved like Napoleon, his colleagues complained. He himself confessed to finding the *Gazette* a "combination of a first-class battleship and a first-class general election." And he utterly declined, in his celebrated phrase, to be impartial as between the fire engine and the fire.[40] But Churchill was conducting propaganda in the lurid fashion of the Great War only a few months after the government had been obliged to admit that the most appalling atrocity story from that war was a lie. This tale told of German factories turning corpses into soap and margarine; at the time it inspired Kipling to write a poem about Charlotte spreading her dead lover "lightly on her bread," but it later boomeranged viciously, casting doubt on the trustworthiness of all official information.[41]

To make its case in a more sophisticated fashion, the government employed the new, nominally independent BBC. Baldwin put his friend J. C. C. Davidson in charge of publicity. Davidson resisted Churchill's efforts to turn the BBC into "a Governmental propaganda agency . . . for the simple reason that the people you want to influence are those who would have at once ceased to listen had we announced that all the news was dope." But the BBC's news *was* "dope": it gave the illusion of objectivity while being carefully selected and slanted to suit the authorities. Davidson's liaison officer took part in drafting the bulletins and Davidson himself approved them before they were broadcast. He also managed to deny the Archbishop of Canterbury, the Leader of the Opposition and all trade-unionists access to the air waves. And he boasted that "my unofficial control was complete."[42]

Some strikers realised that the BBC was the "chief engine" in the government's "propaganda combat."[43] They nicknamed it the BFC, "British Falsehood Corporation."[44] But many thought that the BBC's "pontifical anonymous mugwumpery"[45] (Churchill's expression) must be unbiased. At the very least its director, John Reith, a towering figure with bushy eyebrows and a bullet scar across one cheek, seemed a model of Calvinistic rectitude. In fact Reith had a convenient capacity to appear fiercely independent while being tamely compliant. He told Davidson, "Assuming that the B.B.C. is for the people, and the Government is for the people, it follows that the B.B.C. must be for the Government."[46] The pattern for the inter-war years (and beyond) was set: the BBC, which became a public corporation in 1927, pretended to autonomy and impartiality while censoring itself at the government's clandestine behest. Official secrecy, the political analogue of hypocrisy, was so deeply engrained in British life that Baldwin considered this system to be perfectly proper. Thus truth became the first casualty of the class war that never was in 1926. But it had been so mutilated during the First World War that it was never the same again, as Ezra Pound memorably wrote in *Hugh Selwyn Mauberley* (1920). Those who had

walked eye-deep in hell
believing in old men's lies, then unbelieving
came home to a lie
home to many deceits
home to old lies and new infamy.

Baldwin, for all his high-mindedness, helped to make the 1930s a low, dishonest decade.

So the BBC became an institution, somewhat akin to the monarchy which it did so much to promote—during the age of hunger marches, as one historian has written, the Corporation regarded its coverage of royal occasions as "the triumph of outside broadcasting."[47] The Sovereign, too, affected to be above the political battle while surreptitiously supporting the status quo. He was "gravely disturbed" by the General Strike, though when Jimmy Thomas visited Buckingham Palace the King spoke more in sorrow than in anger: " 'Well, Thomas, if the worst happens, I suppose all this—' (with a gesture indicating his surroundings) '—will vanish?' "[48] While professing "paternal benevolence" towards his subjects George V urged the government to arrest trade union leaders and declare martial law. Still, there is no denying that the King, who modestly but accurately described himself as an ordinary little man, was often uncannily in tune with public opinion, or at any rate with middle-class opinion. When, on 12 May, the TUC General Council responded to Baldwin's conciliatory stance by adopting a face-saving compromise and calling off the strike unconditionally, George wrote in his diary:

> Our old country can well be proud of itself, as during the last nine days there has been a strike in which 4 million people have been affected, not a shot has been fired and no one killed. It shows what a wonderful people we are.[49]

Foreigners agreed. American visitors were amazed that the police remained unarmed. French journalists noted that more casualties occurred at the Joan of Arc celebration riots in Paris on 10 May than during the entire strike—which in their country might have precipitated a revolution. The general mood of self-congratulation fostered rose-tinted memories of the strike.

Yet, though satisfactory as far as Britain's constitutional democracy was concerned, the General Strike was a catastrophe for organised labour. Its leaders had been so anxious to refute the charge that they were insurrectionists that they betrayed their rank and file, who were astonishingly loyal to the last. At the very time when union chiefs were calling out more men and exhorting all strikers to stand firm and trust them, they were also conducting secret negotiations with Sir Herbert Samuel. Baldwin would not see them until they had formally called off the strike. And, in the words of Lord Birkenhead (who felt "great personal contempt both for Cook and Smith"),[50] their surrender was "so humiliating that some instinctive breeding made one unwilling even to look at them. I thought of the Burghers of Calais approaching their interview with Edward III, haltered on the neck."[51] They obtained no guarantees from the government, having to content themselves with Baldwin's vague assurances of goodwill. The formidable transport workers' leader Ernest Bevin was appalled by what they had done, telling his colleagues: "the best way to describe today, if we are not quick, is that we have committed suicide. Thousands of members will be victimised as a result of this day's work."[52] He was right. It was only the menace of further stoppages from local trade union branches that got men back to work on their previous terms. Baldwin pleaded that there should be no malice, recrimination or triumph; but in some industries, notably the railways, activists were punished. Moreover, after the crisis, Baldwin gave way to one of those fits of lethargy which made him the despair of his friends: he himself confessed privately that he was "not one of the world's workers"[53] and Neville Chamberlain compared him to a spinning top— "You must keep whipping him or he falls over."[54] Giving the lie to his façade of moderation, the Prime Minister permitted his right-wing cabinet colleagues to pass a Trades Disputes Act (1927), which banned sympathetic strikes and otherwise discriminated against organised labour. One union leader, J. R. Clynes, called it "the worst piece of vindictive and spiteful class legislation which our country has ever known."[55]

As for the miners, they refused to capitulate, engaging in a bitter struggle which had uncanny similarities to the coal strike directed by Arthur Scargill during the mid-1980s. Cook exhorted his men with the inspiration of an evangelist. Smith led them with the skill of a Great War general. "What we want is human signposts pointing the way to the New Jerusalem," cried Cook.[56] Refusing all compromise, Smith conducted his legions into the Slough of Despond. Churchill himself, as magnanimous in victory as he had been implacable in conflict, could not achieve a settlement despite his efforts to coerce the "recalcitrant owners,"[57] efforts which, as one said, they might have "expected from the extreme Socialist party if in power."[58] So when, after seven months, starvation forced the miners back to work they had to accept longer hours and lower pay. The owners encouraged the formation of a breakaway union. They also ensured that enough pitmen remained unemployed to keep the rest docile: places such as the Rhondda seemed like "occupied territory," with groups of defeated miners squatting on their haunches in the streets playing pitch-and-toss for buttons because "they had no half-pennies to venture."[59]

The Miners' Federation was in no state to renew hostilities, in spite of large subventions from Russian miners, who donated twice as much as had English trade-unionists when their own earnings were less than British strike pay. Doubtless these contributions were involuntary, made in the name of a revolution which more starry-eyed Soviet leaders thought imminent—though realists like Radek were sure that the General Strike was nothing more than a wage dispute. However, British ministers became so obsessed with Bolshevik subversion that in 1927 they tried to nail it by quoting from deciphered telegrams, thus causing the Russians to change their codes. Britain then broke off diplomatic relations with the Soviet Union.

The General Strike and its aftermath made an interesting if paradoxical prelude to the years of Depression. Awareness of the great gulf fixed between Britain's two nations increased. Outraged by injustice, many workers, especially miners, were imbued with a spirit of radicalism which expressed itself in everything from hunger marches to fights against fascism. The prevailing aestheticism of the 1920s began its transformation into the political culture of the 1930s. The Communist Party of Great Britain doubled in size and the bogey of Bolshevism loomed ever larger in the imagination of the middle and upper classes. On the other hand, the Party had only 10,000 members. Its influence was minimal, especially as the extreme hardship which nourished it was largely confined to depressed areas of the north and west while elsewhere living standards rose. The spectre of workers' control was exorcised by the failure of the General Strike. Trade unions afterwards restricted themselves to purely industrial disputes and the "political left was disabled for a generation."[60] To Ramsay MacDonald's delight the strike taught socialists what the Nazis had learned at the Beer Hall Putsch—that they must seek power through the ballot box. The lesson for the Tories was that Baldwin's emollient approach disarmed dissent. Cooperation was preferable to confrontation and at times of crisis Britons must all pull together. Appeasement had its place at home as well as abroad. So it was that Baldwin's Britain muddled through "the Devil's decade."[61]

CUTTING up the past and labelling the snippets is one way of trying to impose order on the flux of history. Doubtless it is always unsatisfactory—ages merge, epithets mislead. But whereas the horrors of depression and war made the 1930s a relatively uniform period—low, dishonest, dark, as contemporaries repeatedly observed—the 1920s, which spawned a multi-tude of tags, can best be seen as an amalgam of opposites. Nowhere was this more true than in America. During the New Era, the United States, freed from European entanglements, was struggling to return to what President Harding (speaking a language of his own) called "normalcy." The "time of wonderful nonsense," also known as the gay twenties, was the dry decade. During an epoch of isolationism good Americans, when they died, went to Paris. The roaring twenties, the jazz age, the age of the lost generation: these are evocative titles but they reveal nothing about an America whose business (in the words of Harding's successor, President Coolidge) was business and whose businessmen were (often) standardised citizens like Sinclair Lewis's George F. Babbitt. Nor do they suggest a reign of uninspired conservatism under the auspices of the bungalow-minded Warren Harding (satirised in Scott Fitzgerald's play *The Vegetable*) and the intellectually anaemic Calvin Coolidge, whose presidency (according to Harold Ickes) indicated that the country had returned to "subnormalcy."[62]

The most striking feature of this contrary decade was the collapse of the Harding-Coolidge prosperity in the greatest crisis ever to afflict American capitalism. Mark Sullivan, who scrutinised his times more closely than most journalists, said that the process could be summed up in three con-temporary song hits: the "serene and confident" overture "Smiles"; fol-lowed in the mid-1920s by that "paean of exuberant affluence" "My God, How the Money Rolls In"; and ending with a "crashing finale," the "uni-versally familiar and uniquely appropriate song of indigence," "Buddy, Can You Spare a Dime?"[63] It was not quite that simple. Great swathes of the country, notably the rural areas where nearly half the population still lived, were not only untouched by the decade's economic boom but worse off than before. In America's house there were many mansions. But noth-ing better explains the contradictions of the age than the antithesis between log cabin and skyscraper, between the old values of the land and the new civilisation taking shape on the sidewalks of New York.

Gleaming skyscrapers were the most potent symbols of the wealth of urban America. They were not simply the architecture of a mass society. They were, in the words of an admiring French visitor, "the dwellings of the supertrusts; they were the Eiffel Tower cathedrals which shelter Mr. Rockefeller, the Emperor of Petroleum, or Mr. Morgan, the Czar of Gold."[64] The tallest of them, the Empire State Building, was built by the financier John J. Raskob shortly after the Crash as a monument to "the American way of life that allowed a poor boy to make his fortune in Wall Street."[65] Even those in the city or the suburbs who did not make a fortune benefited from rising standards of living. They read the sophisticated advertisements, visited the expanding chain stores, admired a cornucopia of goods (many wrapped in the glistening new substance of cellophane), succumbed to salesmanship as slickly synthetic as rayon or plastic, and bought exciting "durables" like vacuum cleaners, refrigerators, washing machines, coffee percolators, phonographs, telephones and radios. Automobiles, naturally, were the prime icons in this consumer revolution. And by 1925 Henry Ford's assembly line was turning out a Model T every ten seconds. Buying on the instalment plan, factory workers themselves could acquire a Tin Lizzie, which sold for as little as 300 dollars. But few of those who built the cars relished the dictatorial brand of welfare capitalism which caused Ford to be described as "an industrial Fascist—the Mussolini of Detroit."[66]

Automobiles were vehicles of emancipation. They took city folks with leisure to the baseball game, the speakeasy or the cinema (a secular shrine now more patronised than the church). Holiday-makers drove to the seaside where they wore skin-tight swimsuits and acquired a tan; before the war genteel people had protected their pallor from the glare—but this was the era of the "solar revolution" and heliotherapy was all the rage.[67] Cars fostered a more mobile frame of mind (as well as ribbon developments of gas stations and hot dog stands). Flappers in flivvers set new fashions. They abandoned their chaperones, discarded their corsets, bobbed their hair, rouged their cheeks, painted their fingernails, wore flesh-coloured stockings, drank cocktails and smoked in public—the sale of cigarettes increased from 47 billion in 1920 to 125 billion in 1930. What they did in private was a subject of much prurient speculation. The practice of vamping seemed suggestive. So did the vogue for "It," defined by Elinor Glyn as "that strange magnetism which attracts both sexes."[68] There were grounds for regarding dances like the Charleston and the Black Bottom as syncopated sensuality, and cheek-to-cheek foxtrots were thought to be vertical indications of horizontal inclinations. Freud was almost as popular as Ford. It was commonly supposed that as hemlines went up morals went down. And moralists denounced automobiles as mobile houses of prostitution.

Probably there was an increase in promiscuity. It was stimulated by the new tabloid press (*The Graphic* was known as "The Pornographic") and by Prohibition, introduced in 1919, which led to a widespread flouting of traditional standards. In the view of Colonel Robert McCormick, boss of the Chicago *Tribune,* even the Teapot Dome oil affair (a notorious government corruption scandal) was the fault of Prohibition, which had turned the United States into a nation of lawbreakers. There was certainly a growing acceptance of divorce. But sex was by no means the only American preoccupation in an age which witnessed crazes for mah-jongg, Couéism (an early form of psychotherapy), marathon dances, crossword puzzles and miniature golf; or which hero-worshipped Babe Ruth, Bobby Jones, Jack Dempsey, Rudy Vallee and Charles Lindbergh, to say nothing of a host of movie stars. The car itself could be as much of a distraction from sex as an encouragement to it. John Steinbeck was doubtless exaggerating in *Cannery Row* when he said that most babies were conceived in Model Ts; but he may well have been right to say that two generations of Americans knew more about the Ford coil than the clitoris.

Meanwhile, down on farms lit by kerosene lamps and approached over dirt roads, rural America endured dearth amid plenty thanks to chronic over-production together with low prices, and revolted against the spree of the cities. Old Puritanism condemned new hedonism, especially where the illegal liquor business was concerned. But Prohibitionists were also protesting against an urban culture, a culture spawned by immigrants and deemed to be radical, degenerate and vicious. The revival of the Ku Klux Klan, which at its peak during the mid-1920s attracted five million members, was also a form of rustic rebellion. True, the white-hooded Hydras, Kleagles, Terrors, Furies and Exalted Cyclopses of the "Invisible Empire" had legions of enemies, not just their traditional black targets in the countryside but a burgeoning city population of Catholics, Jews, aliens and assorted moral "deviants." Still here was bucolic bigotry combined with small-town fascism.

Equally obscurantist were legislators who banned the teaching of evolution in several southern states, which led to the celebrated "Monkey Trial" in 1925. When John Thomas Scopes, a biology instructor, was fined 100 dollars for disseminating Darwinism at the Central High School in Dayton, Tennessee, that flail of the "booboisie," H. L. Mencken, characteristically concluded that "the mob has made its superstitions official."[69] In fact it was a reassertion of that old-time fundamentalism so deeply rooted in the soil of the countryside. Of course, the divide between metropolitan and rural life was never hard and fast. Progressive ideas, for example, flourished in the forests of Wisconsin and the cornfields of Nebraska. And even the most hardened urbanites cherished a nostalgia for a pastoral past. In his celebrated model village filled with antiques (including fiddlers playing square dances), Henry Ford tried to recreate it, as John Dos Passos said,

> so that everything might be
> the way it used to be,
> in the days of horses and buggies.[70]

Bound up with God, motherhood and apple pie, such Arcadian simplicities were so much a part of ideal America that even silent Calvin

Coolidge waxed lyrical about them. In his *Autobiography*, a deadly reflection of a desiccated personality, Coolidge eulogised the pristine, natural quality of New England life as he had experienced it in boyhood. Despite the drudgery and inconvenience, the rough overalls and cowhide boots, he enthused about picnics, parties, fairs and husking bees. "Even when I try to divest it of the halo which I know always surrounds the past," he wrote, "I am unable to create any other impression than that it was fresh and clean."[71] Honest, frugal, backward-looking and (in public at least) "as expansive as a letter-box,"[72] Coolidge seemed to embody immemorial American verities and values. Though not without sly and sometimes cruel wit, he spoke (when he spoke) in strings of clichés agreeable both to Main Street and to Park Row—when given their theme, a journalist such as James Thurber could report his speeches without the inconvenience of having to listen to them. After Harding's death in 1923, Coolidge was sworn in as President by his father, who was a notary public, at a simple ceremony in the lamp-lit living-room-cum-office of his white Plymouth house. Undemonstrative though he was, Coolidge permitted himself to be photographed hay-making during the 1924 election—his spotless smock was much mocked.

Yet the small-town President was indulgent towards capitalists of great wealth. As that spokesman for Middle America William Allen White said, President Coolidge

> pitchforked the muck of oil and petty graft from the Augean stables of the White House, but he let in, all smartly frock-coated, plug-hatted, high-collared, bespatted and smugly proud, another crew which was to devastate his country more terribly than Harding's greasy playfellows. All the day the friends and emissaries of Kreuger, the match king, Insull, the utilities king, Wiggin, the wizard, Mitchell, the manipulator, Doherty, the monarch of gas, the Morgans, the Rockefellers, and Mellon in person, the bad and the good, unchecked and unidentified, sat at his council table.[73]

Coolidge believed that government was the handmaiden of commerce. He also believed, more fervently than Jefferson himself, that less government was better government. So while big business grabbed "the country by the throat,"[74] as the Progressive senator George Norris remarked, Coolidge displayed a "genius" for "alert inactivity."[75] This carrot-topped, blue-eyed, sharp-featured, freckle-faced, twangy-voiced chief executive was a political minimalist. When, in 1928, Treasury Department officials showed him how vital it was to control the runaway investment market, the President froze them off with a blast of silence. Then, like the good husbandman he was, Coolidge spent the afternoon in the basement of the

White House counting the apples in a barrel sent to him by a friend from Vermont.

Coolidge's successor, Herbert Hoover, was also a countryman, the first president to be born west of the Mississippi. Hoover made much of his idyllic youth amid the Iowan corn, where his father had been a Quaker blacksmith. He extolled the delights of Aunt Millie's cooking, the joys of the swimming hole, the thrill of Indian-taught hunting, the happiness of fishing with a willow pole and "butcher-string line, fixed with hooks, ten for a dime, whose compelling lure is one segment of an angleworm and whose incantation is spitting on the bait."[76] Of course, Hoover was no hick. Orphaned at a tender age, he had become a successful mining engineer, travelled all over the world and amassed at least a million dollars by the time he was 40—he reckoned that anyone who could not make a fortune by that age was "not worth much."[77] Turning to public service, he had fulfilled his ambition to be a "food dictator"[78] at home and abroad during and after the war. Hoover paid lip-service to cooperation, which meant that everyone should get together and do exactly as he told them. According to a member of his staff, he expressed himself in few words: "One was 'yes' and the other was 'no.'"[79] But his "herculean efforts" saved "perhaps one-third of the population of postwar Europe" from starvation.[80] Moreover, tough and curt, pragmatic and idealistic, he refused to allow Western hostility towards Bolshevism to stop him from feeding millions of Russians during the disastrous famine of 1921–2.

As Secretary of Commerce under Harding and Coolidge, Hoover proved equally abrupt and adept. Laissez-faire was all very well but Hoover took action where necessary. Thus, for example, he controlled the distribution of radio frequencies. (This infuriated the evangelist Aimee Semple McPherson, who told him to keep his "minions of Satan" away from her stations because when she offered prayers to the Almighty "I must fit into His wave reception."[81] Then she eloped on a motorcycle with Hoover's inspector.) Hoover was an early believer that radio was "the most important new instrument for intellectual communication since Gutenberg began to cast in movable type."[82] And he was the first American president to appear on television. He was also, in the words of Walter Lippmann, "the first American President whose whole public career has been presented through the machinery of modern publicity . . . [which portrays] him as the master organizer, the irresistible engineer, the supreme economist."[83] As Secretary of Commerce Hoover issued a plethora of publicity material and as Republican candidate for the presidency he employed the most sophisticated propaganda techniques. One of his advisers was the New York advertising man Bruce Barton, who had done such a remarkable job of promoting Jesus Christ in *The Man Nobody Knows* (1925)—the Son of God was famously billed as a dynamic entrepreneur who had taken twelve men from the lowest rungs of business life and created an organisation which changed the world. Barton's talents were deployed to point out that Hoover was not, as H. L. Mencken charged, "a fat Coolidge." Rather he was a progressive conservative, a forward-looking political engineer who was at the same time wedded to the homespun values of American individualism. Hoover had seen American farmers, whom he had encouraged to over-produce during the war, reduced almost to the status of peasants during the 1920s. Mencken went so far as to say that farmers were not members of the human race. But Hoover lost no opportunity to praise them. They were a breed set apart from "the insidious forces of moral degeneration which are such corroding influences in the life of our great cities."[84]

The quintessential representative of those cities was Hoover's Democratic opponent in the presidential race of 1928. Alfred E. Smith was born in 1873 in a tenement on New York's Lower East Side, under the shadow of the Brooklyn Bridge (whose construction he subsequently claimed to have superintended). The child of respectable, second-generation Irish-Italian immigrants, he was brought up on the waterfront. The East River was Al's swimming-pool. His gymnasium was the rigging of sailing ships unloading their cargoes from all over the world. He learned music from itinerant German bands. Much of his schooling was picked up in streets lined with warehouses, dives and ships' stores, and thronged with sailors, longshoremen and teamsters—the sound of his father's wagon clattering over the cobble-stones was among his earliest memories. Smith's alma mater, he later said, was the Fulton Fish Market.

Here he began his working life. But Al Smith was ambitious and he soon got his feet on the Tammany ladder which had enabled many a likely lad to climb out of the slums. He made himself useful to the corrupt Democratic machine and proved to have outstanding political gifts. Though "unspoiled by formal education," his mind was "first-class." He was shrewd, quick and full of common sense. He possessed a phenomenal memory and was never at a loss for racy repartee. When someone from Ossining, site of a state prison, proposed a literacy test to exclude immigrants from the ballot, Smith replied that not all Americans who could read and write were qualified to cast an honest vote and that Ossining contained "people who could not only sign their own name but that of others as well."[85] With his resonant voice and flamboyant manner Smith was an actor manqué. He had a flair for the dramatic utterance, once denouncing the press magnate William Randolph Hearst as "the pestilence that walks in darkness."[86] He dressed like a dude in natty striped suits and pink and crimson neck-ties, topped by the rakishly slanted brown derby hat which became his political trade mark. Smith was also as honest as a Tammany man could be and in the state assembly he promoted social welfare legislation which, to Boss Charles Murphy's surprise, actually won votes. By 1919 Smith was Governor of New York. In 1924 he was defeated at the Democratic presidential convention, where Franklin D. Roosevelt hailed him as "the happy warrior." Gaining the nomination in 1928, he swore to beat the pants off Hoover.

In this endeavour Smith had several crippling disadvantages. It was not that he was too progressive; he accepted large campaign funds from big businessmen such as John J. Raskob and vied with Hoover in conservatism. But the very fact that there were few serious differences between the candidates highlighted the issues of Smith's Roman Catholicism and his hostility to Prohibition, about which Hoover temporised. Smith's opponents made much play with the evils of rum and Romanism, jug and Jesuit. As his train approached Oklahoma City he saw a line of burning crosses in the fields, symbols of the Ku Klux Klan. They were portents of further bigotry, including a campaign of slander to the effect that if Smith were elected "bootleggers and harlots would dance on the White House lawn."[87] But Smith had a greater handicap: he was so metropolitan that he was provincial. He gloried in his native city, declaring that he would rather be a lamp-post in New York than Governor of California. He was vague about the whereabouts of Wisconsin and asked, only half-jokingly, "What are the states west of the Mississippi?"[88] Worse still, in the opinion of many voters, every time Smith opened his cigar-chomping mouth he betrayed his origins, saying "woik," "foist," "ain't," "raddio" and "horsepital." H. L. Mencken reckoned that "The essential issue in America during the next fifty years will be between city men and yokels."[89] But in 1928 it was still vital to satisfy "the moral yearnings of the rural communities."[90]

Hoover did satisfy them. He espoused the old-fashioned virtues of rural self-sufficiency—plus the rather newer policy of increased farm relief. He also favoured peace, protection and progress through technology and education. He forecast more broadly-based prosperity and declared that the country was "nearer to the final triumph over poverty than ever before."[91] He promised two chickens in every pot and two cars in every garage. Harry Truman later said that he meant "two families in every garage,"[92] but at the time Hoover's vision of the vanishing poorhouse was impressive. So was the man himself. He lacked Smith's wit and charm; he had no small talk; and such was his scowling concentration on the job in hand that he was often rude and inconsiderate. But beside the dapper contender from New York he looked, in every sense, a heavyweight. Hoover had a high forehead, a pugnacious jaw and a habit of looking people straight in the eye. He was unconcerned with trifles. No dandy, he flung on scruffy blue serge suits and thought nothing of wearing broken shoe laces or collars without studs. He bolted his meals and let his dogs lick his plate while it was still on the table. Instead of keeping a notebook he scribbled down ideas on odd scraps of paper which his secretary rescued from his pockets every morning. Hoover worked with ferocious energy, exercising only briefly with an eight-pound medicine ball and occasionally relaxing with a detective novel. Despite his aloofness he attracted loyalty, even devotion. On first meeting him William Allen White was "mesmerised by the strange low voltage of his magnetism."[93] The American people felt that attraction. At the election Smith did relatively well in the cities. But he lost heavily in the countryside, splitting the Solid South and gaining only 15 million votes to Hoover's 21 million.

By dint of character and experience the new President could hardly have been better qualified for his job. Confidence in him was at once demonstrated by a "Hoover boom" on the stock exchange. "We were in the mood for magic," wrote Anne O'Hare McCormick. "We had summoned a great engineer to solve our problems for us; now we sat back comfortably and confidently to watch the problems being solved."[94] Tragically, Hoover proved unable to cope with the "economic hurricane"[95] that struck the United States only a few months after he entered the White House. Despite his record of humanitarian work, it is clear that Hoover was almost as keen as Coolidge to keep the State out of the nation's business. True, he preached and practised modest measures of reform and hoped to stimulate individual initiative. But recent attempts to depict him as a "progressive," prepared to take federal responsibility for engineering the common weal, are unconvincing.[96] Hoover resolutely opposed government intervention because he feared that it might sap self-sufficiency or crush freedom. The term "planned economy" was anathema to him. It was, he later wrote, "an emanation from the cauldrons of all three European collective forms," Communism, Socialism and Fascism. Moreover, "Every collectivist revolution rides in on a Trojan horse of 'Emergency.'"[97] Sound though this observation was, it scarcely applied to the United States, where the roots of democracy ran deep. But even during the darkest days of the American emergency Hoover would doggedly defend those shibboleths of the private enterprise system—voluntary action, business self-regulation, balanced budgets, market forces. He refused to recognise the unacceptable face of capitalism. Yet a couple of weeks before he took office in 1929 its existence was amply demonstrated: on St. Valentine's Day seven free en-

terprise bootleggers were massacred in Chicago, victims of market forces
to a man.

Despite his convictions Hoover had watched the stock market boom
with alarm throughout the 1920s. He predicted "inevitable collapse"[98] and
later he was to describe massive speculation as a crime far worse than murder. In May 1929 he turned many of his own securities into gilt-edged
bonds and he called for restricted credit to damp down share buying.
Although interest rates rose slightly they did little to discourage investors.
This was partly because Hoover had retained Andrew Mellon as his Treasury Secretary, a man whom he later described as a dyed-in-the-wool reactionary. Mellon's policy of reducing taxation had not only made him and
his millionaire friends a fortune (some of it returning to the Republican
coffers in the shape of campaign contributions) but had helped to promote the great bull market.

Just when this began is debatable. But the original rise in stocks was
based soundly on America's prodigious economic performance during and
after the Great War. Output almost doubled during the 1920s, when
America produced more than the other six great powers put together.
Exports grew by over 25 per cent during the decade—much faster than
imports—and American merchandise replaced British goods in many foreign markets. New York also succeeded London as the banking capital of
the world, lending and investing billions of dollars abroad. A golden era
seemed at hand. But during the mid-1920s the growth of stock prices
began to outstrip that of profits; share values soon ceased to bear much
relation to the earning powers of business. By no means all shares made
spectacular climbs; there were more or less serious dips in the market.
Bank failures and the collapse of the Florida land boom in 1926 discouraged euphoria. But between 1925 and 1929 production accelerated faster
than at any time in history. In 1929 the United States generated more electric power than all other countries in the world combined. And like soap
bubbles blown by a child, the worth of key industrial shares ballooned
ever more brilliantly. Wall Street inspired visions of boundless wealth.
Confidence blossomed. Buying stocks on margin (i.e., on credit) became
at first a fashion, then a frenzy. Brokers' loans increased from one billion
dollars in 1920 to seven billion in 1929. A boom psychology developed,
fostered by a variety of considerations, not all of them spurious. There was
no danger that Republican governments would use anti-trust legislation
to hamper business. Real wages were advancing modestly but significantly.
Trade union membership was declining. Interest rates remained low. After
1925 the prospects for international peace looked bright.

On the other hand speculators were also buoyed up by cheerful irrelevancies such as Lindbergh's flight, or Babe Ruth's record number of home runs, or the conspicuous consumption in Hollywood films, or the birth of Mickey Mouse. They were led on by unscrupulous advertising, including patriotic slogans like "Be a Bull on America" and "Never Sell the United States Short."[99] They succumbed to the blandishments of men such as John J. Raskob, who memorably declared in the *Ladies' Home Journal* that "Everybody Ought to be Rich." They followed the tips of venal broadcasters and newspapermen, who took bribes to promote shares—even Hearst and his star columnist Arthur Brisbane were not above conspiring to puff their own "interests."[100] In the market, self-regulation permitted a multitude of sins: pushing up the value of shares through syndicates or "pools," insider dealing and the issuing of fraudulent stock. As Professor William Z. Ripley told Calvin Coolidge, here was a scene of "prestidigitation, double-shuffling, honey-fugling, hornswoggling and skulduggery."[101] But by 1929 such malpractices seemed to excite investors just as, during the South Sea Bubble of 1720, Englishmen had rushed to buy stock in companies formed to produce a wheel for perpetual motion, or to traffic in the truly national commodity of woad, or to exploit a machine-gun ingeniously designed by its inventor, James Puckle, to fire round bullets at Christians and square ones at Turks, or even to support an undertaking which would in due time be revealed.

Greed and gullibility were scarcely less marked during the long hot summer of 1929. Seaboard Airline attracted thousands of investors so intoxicated with the possibilities of aviation that they did not discover that it was actually a railroad company. Some speculators traded not so much in futures as in eternity, purchasing gold-plated funeral caskets and ornate mausoleums equipped with sealed boxes for their share certificates. Those intent on speedier returns favoured the new investment trusts which were being floated almost every day. These were companies which sold shares and placed the money in a wide range of securities, thus in theory spreading the risk for investors and giving them the benefit of expert fund management. In fact the trusts themselves bought on margin and when honestly run they found that their most profitable investment was lending money to brokers—who in turn extended more credit to speculators, who then bought more shares. "It resembled nothing more than a dog chasing his own tail," wrote one economist. "Paper values rose without substance, and few thought to question the boom in which all made money and there were few losers."[102]

Share prices spiralled dizzily as the weather grew warmer. The *New York Times* average of leading industrial shares (the focus of most speculation), which had stood at 106 in May 1924, 245 at the end of 1927 and 331 at the beginning of 1929, rose 52 points in June, 25 in July and 33 in August, reaching 449 on the last day of that month. The volume of business grew correspondingly and on 12 June, for the first time, more than five million shares were traded on the New York Stock Exchange. Neither the World Series nor the talking pictures could compete in fascination with the stock exchange ticker as it tapped out dreams—and realisations—of avarice. To hear its staccato symphony investors throughout the country thronged smoky brokers' offices which, with their swing doors, half-darkened windows and mahogany chairs, resembled financial saloons. Like addicts deprived of a drug, they became frantic when separated from the ticker, which was installed in hotel lobbies and on ocean liners—one broker even contemplated putting a ticker on the moon. Terrestrial chauffeurs, barbers, beauticians and valets dabbled in Wall Street. Bishops and actresses chanced their luck. Bootblacks purveyed stock exchange gossip and a beggar gave the multi-millionaire Bernard Baruch advice on how to make a mint. So great was the excitement that one dealer thought the Stock Exchange should be moved to Yankee Stadium. The prevailing atmosphere was conveyed by a verse in the *Saturday Evening Post*:

> Oh, hush thee, my babe, Granny's bought some more shares,
> Daddy's gone out to play with the bulls and the bears,
> Mother's buying on tips, and she simply can't lose,
> And baby shall have some expensive new shoes![103]

In fact probably no more than 1.5 million people out of the United States' population of 120 million were actively engaged in speculation. And there were only 600,000 margin accounts. But few disagreed with New York's playboy mayor, Jimmy Walker, who described the continuing bull market as "the eighth wonder of the world." Everyone followed the drama on Wall Street, if only in the headlines. Foreigners were also impressed by the spectacle for, as the great bear gambler Jesse Livermore said, the New York Stock Exchange was now "a colossal suction pump" steadily draining the world of capital and "fast producing a vacuum in Europe": the Gulf Stream went one way, the Gold Stream went the other. The still fragile German economy, which relied on huge loans from the United States, was particularly hard hit. An Italian newspaper gave the view from Europe: "With more authority than the League of Nations, and with more subtlety than Bolshevism, another world power is making a direct appeal to the strongest instinct of human nature. The new power is Wall Street."[104]

Lone voices did warn about an impending collapse. Alexander Dana Noyes, veteran financial editor of the *New York Times,* issued pessimistic forecasts. Paul M. Warburg of Kuhn, Loeb & Co. said that if the "orgy of unrestrained speculation" were not stopped it would "bring about a general depression involving the entire country." The economist Roger W. Babson disseminated such gloom that he was nicknamed the "Prophet of Loss." But the Cassandras were accused of "sandbagging American prosperity."[105] The urge to talk up the market in 1929 was as powerful as the impulse to speak peace in 1939. Even the likes of Bernard Baruch, who was sufficiently jumpy to sell some of his holdings for gold, made bullish prognostications. Baruch stated in June that the "economic condition of the world seems on the verge of a great forward movement." Others were even more starry-eyed. The optimistic incantations of bankers and brokers were understandable. But most commentators and academics echoed them, none more famously than Professor Irving Fisher of Yale, who estimated that "stock prices have reached what looks like a permanently high plateau."[106] Astrologers might have been better guides, but they were not. On 2 September 1929 Evangeline Adams, the most fashionable crystal-ball gazer of the age, declared that "the Dow-Jones could climb to heaven." The following day the great bull market reached 452 on the *New York Times* share index, which is generally regarded as its historic peak.

Thereafter, for about six weeks stocks traded nervously: there were several sharp falls and partial recoveries. Fluctuations had occurred before. But never had there been such a large and unstable edifice of credit. Furthermore, industrial output had begun to decline and all over an increasingly fruitful earth the price of agricultural commodities was falling. Business failures in Germany and the collapse of Clarence Hatry's crooked financial empire in London added to anxiety in New York. Perturbed by such developments, one or two pundits wrote about the dangers of overstaying the bull market. But the crowds drawn to Wall Street as to some new El Dorado still hoped, and half-believed, that share prices would surge upwards once again. So did many of the professionals. On Tuesday 22 October the sleek and sophisticated Thomas J. Lamont, senior partner at J. P. Morgan, sent Herbert Hoover a memorandum saying, "The future appears brilliant . . . we have the greatest and soundest prosperity, and the best material prospects of any country in the world." The following day shares fell sharply amid hectic trading. The day after that—Black Thursday—the stock market succumbed to blind panic. A tidal wave of selling overwhelmed Wall Street. Chaotic scenes took place on the floor of the New York Stock Exchange. Hysterical traders ran, bellowed, cursed and gesticulated. With sweat pouring down their faces and their collars and shirts in tatters, they resembled battle-scarred "soldiers, crazily flinging

handfuls of torn ticker tape and order pads into the air."[107] Terrified speculators converged on the great white Exchange and police were drafted into
the area to keep control. All over the country people packed into brokers'
offices, but since the ticker could not keep up with the volume of business, they had no way of knowing the state of their fortunes. At midday
Lamont and other financiers organised multi-million-dollar support for
the market. Acting on their behalf, Richard Whitney, vice-president of the
Stock Exchange, strode onto the floor and ostentatiously bought important shares at above the asking price. Stocks rallied strongly. And Lamont
insouciantly told reporters that there had been "a little distress selling" for
technical reasons but that the market was fundamentally sound. This
refrain was taken up by others, notably President Hoover, who said that
American business itself was fundamentally sound. Yet nearly 13 million
shares had been traded, a record, and 3 billion dollars had been wiped off
the value of shares. The *New York Times* share index had fallen from its 452
peak to 372 and tourists were paying 50 cents for pieces of the black day's
historic ticker tape.

The significance of all this evidently sank in over the weekend. On
Monday 28 October there was a "nation-wide stampede to unload."[108]
Nearly 10 million shares were traded and the *Times* index fell by 49 points,
the steepest decline in its history. This time no one mounted a rescue
attempt. And the next day, Black Tuesday, proved even more catastrophic.
The New York Stock Exchange opened amid a deluge of selling orders.
Prices dropped precipitously. The floor became a pandemonium. Dealers
besieged the 17 horseshoe-shaped trading posts, waving, swearing, scrambling, clawing and screaming. Shrill cries of "Sell at the market!" could be
heard above a swelling diapason of rage, bewilderment and despair. The
roar conveyed a palpable sense of horror, as if in response to some monstrous natural calamity. It was the voice of wounded Wall Street and it had
"an eerie quality," wrote one reporter, "like chords from a primitive
requiem."[109] Men tore their hair and wept unashamedly. Some shrieked
that they were ruined. The ticker lagged so far behind that others, denied
that certainty, were tormented by doubt and fear. The air was blue with
smoke as frantic traders kept lighting and stubbing out cigarettes. Dr.
Francis Glazebrook of the Stock Exchange Medical Department, who had
treated shell-shock cases during the war, recognised similar symptoms in
the patients who crowded into his clinic that day. By its end 16,383,700
shares had been traded. Many of the investment trusts were wiped out, the
Times index had fallen 43 points and paper losses amounted to 10 billion
dollars. This figure was almost as much as America had spent on the Great
War, substantially more than the entire national debt and twice the

amount of all money in circulation throughout the United States at the time.

At least a million Americans were directly and immediately affected by the Crash. As J. K. Galbraith wrote, even the wealthy were "subjected to a levelling process comparable in magnitude and suddenness to that presided over a decade before by Lenin."[110] Cornelius Vanderbilt III, for example, apparently lost eight million dollars in an hour on Black Tuesday. Few rich investors were unscathed and many dismissed their servants and cut down on their luxuries. Those with fewer resources suffered worse. Some had to give up possessions bought on credit but managed to salvage something from the wreckage. Others failed to keep up the mortgage payments on their houses and found themselves without a roof over their heads. Still others lost everything. Many fell back on charity. A few committed suicide, though rumour exaggerated their numbers and jokes circulated about speculators booking hotel rooms not for sleeping but for jumping, or jumping arm in arm because they had a joint account. Determined speculators merely postponed the evil day, going back into the market when it improved the following week. Perhaps this was in response to encouragements like that of John D. Rockefeller Sr., who announced that he and his son were purchasing "good common stock."[111] Only they had the money, riposted the ruined singer Eddie Cantor. (It was a fair comment in view of Rockefeller's own remark on hearing that old J. P. Morgan's estate had been valued at 77.5 million dollars: "And to think that he wasn't even a rich man.")[112] However, gamblers bent on recouping their losses were caught when the market started to slide again in November, reaching a low of 224 points on the *Times* index. And, to anticipate, those who plunged once more during the rally of 1930 were punished in the course of a long, remorseless decline which began in May and reached its nadir (at 58 points) in July 1932. This was a fall of nearly 400 points from the autumn of 1929—when, as Scott Fitzgerald said, the Jazz Age leaped to its "spectacular death."[113]

Few things are more incalculable than the ebb and flow of confidence. Just what prompted speculators to behave like lemmings in October 1929 remains a matter of . . . speculation. Whatever claims there were to wisdom after the event, hardly anyone anticipated the Crash—Bernard Baruch's fortune decreased from 20 million dollars to 16 million. Franklin D. Roosevelt, Governor of New York, made no effort to regulate the Stock Exchange and went out of his way to avoid banking reforms. President Hoover called for credit controls but did virtually nothing to hold back the bull market. Nor did he attempt to reduce financial inequalities, perhaps the most fundamental cause of the Crash. In 1929 the wealthiest 24,000 families earned as much as the poorest 11.5 million families. These 24,000 families (who benefited from Mellon's tax reductions) also possessed over a third of American savings, whereas 80 per cent of the population had no savings at all. High profits and low wages accentuated this imbalance. So while the rich had pots of money to invest in stocks the poor could hardly afford to buy necessities, let alone manufactured goods. Ultimately the mass production economy was undermined by the fact that consumers, particularly those in the depressed countryside, lacked purchasing power. The resultant business shakiness plainly sapped faith in the stock market, though to what extent the decline in industrial output during the summer of 1929 prompted the autumn Crash it is impossible to say. But the Crash itself played a major part in causing the Great Depression.

As people tightened their belts, there was a sharp drop in the sale of automobiles, radios and other consumer goods. Industrial output fell and unemployment rose. Even worse hit were the producers of raw materials, who were competing fiercely in a shrinking market-place at a time when banks were reducing the credit of bulk buyers. The price of imports such as coffee, rubber and tin declined even more steeply than that of exports like wheat, corn and cotton. As foreigners found themselves unable to pay for American merchandise, international trade imploded. The Crash reverberated all around the globe, notably in Germany where the economic crisis gave Hitler his chance to seize power. In the United States the most important commodity to be damaged was confidence. Not only was there disillusionment with Wall Street but the prestige of business was shattered. Bank failures increased—American banks were anyway grossly under-capitalised because (until the 1960s) they were only allowed to operate in their home states. Bankers were discredited: *Time* magazine coined the term "bankster" and Depression jokesters quipped, "Don't tell my mother I'm a banker, she thinks I play the piano in a brothel."[114] Capitalism itself was called into question. For a time, admittedly, most people did not realise what had hit them; assuming that the Crash resembled financial panics of the past, they anticipated a recovery. As late as 1932 Edmund Wilson wrote a book about the aftermath of the Crash called *The American Jitters;* in the light of history he changed its title to *The American Earthquake,* for the collapse of the stock market seemed "like a rending of the earth in preparation for the Day of Judgement."[115] Depression psychology, with its burden of hopelessness, stemmed directly from this financial upheaval, which helped to "make the thirties a decade of fear."[116] As the world plunged into an abyss, individuals were blown about like snow-flakes. No one could guess what lurked in the shadows.

PART TWO

INTO THE ABYSS

IV

DEPRESSION IN AMERICA

ON Monday 21 October 1929, three days before Black Thursday, Herbert Hoover was in Michigan to preside over a jubilee celebrating the Golden Anniversary of the Festival of Light. Organised by Henry Ford, it marked his hero Thomas Edison's invention of the incandescent lamp at Menlo Park 50 years previously. Ford opened the Edison Institute and Greenfield model village, including a reconstruction of Menlo Park so faithful that even the dirt on the ground was authentic—to Edison's amazement, Ford had imported seven truckloads of clay from New Jersey. All over the world Edison's achievement was saluted: in New York, Broadway and Fifth Avenue blazed with golden lights, and as far away as Tokyo the thoroughfares were specially illuminated. Hoover's address was a hymn to progress. In particular he congratulated the scientists and industrialists from whose efforts "we gain constantly in better standards of living, more stability of employment, lengthened human life and decreased suffering." He concluded brightly, "Our civilization is much like a garden. It is to be appraised by the quality of its blooms."[1] Even Hoover's pachydermal self-confidence must have been shaken by the speed with which the sun set on the New Era and the blooms in the American garden withered.

If so, the President did not show it. He saw it as his duty to put a brave face on the Crash, so brave, in fact, that he had hardly ceased to deny its seriousness before he started to declare that the worst was over. At first most people supported the presidential line. It was well expressed by the New York *Daily News:*

> The sagging of stocks has not destroyed a single factory, wiped out a single farm or city lot or real estate development, decreased the productive powers of a single workman or machine in the United States. All these things are still there, and when they are essentially sound, as this country is, the more magnificently they recover.[2]

The President's commitment to ensure recovery was never in doubt. As his leisure-loving Secretary of State, Henry Stimson, remarked, Hoover's "cure for all his troubles . . . was more and harder work."[3] The first president to have a telephone on his desk, Hoover attempted to make government a model of industrial efficiency. He held incessant meetings with business leaders and tried to persuade them to maintain investment and wages. Henry Ford achieved a publicity coup by actually raising daily pay from six to seven dollars, but he kept it at this level only while it remained profitable to do so and to earn this sum his workers had to increase their productivity, via a speeded-up assembly line, by almost 50 per cent. In an effort to stimulate growth Hoover also cut taxes. But this was at once dubbed "rich relief"[4] since it affected only high earners, the focus of Andrew Mellon's most anxious solicitude. For the less well-off, Mellon believed that the Slump was not altogether a bad thing: it would "purge the rottenness out of the system" and encourage moral virtues like thrift and hard work as well as ensuring the survival of the fittest.[5] Hoover did not go quite that far. Indeed, his main endeavour was to boost confidence by his own optimistic pronouncements. He seemed to be whistling ever more loudly in the dark.

Yet the public wanted encouragement and on 1 January 1930 6,000 citizens lined up at the White House and shook hands with the President, a New Year's Day ceremony he was to abandon as the Depression got worse. Hoover himself talked about "Depression" in order to avoid using the term "Panic" and he announced "that business could look forward to the coming year with greater assurance."[6] He even went so far as to declare that unemployment was falling. No one was more outraged by this assertion than Governor Roosevelt's State Industrial Commissioner, Frances Perkins. Aged 50, this former social worker had long concluded that women in politics reminded men of their mothers and had resolved to "comport" herself accordingly, wearing a simple black dress with a white bow at the front and a small, dark tricorn hat.[7] But beneath her modest exterior Frances Perkins possessed an incisive intellect and a steely will. Eager not only to contradict Hoover but to educate Roosevelt, who was slow to appreciate the seriousness of the crisis, she provided figures which refuted the President's claim. Right across the country headlines carried her correction and over the telephone Roosevelt's "cheerful voice" boomed, "Bully for you!"[8] He learned the lesson she taught. Unemployment climbed from under two million in 1929 to five million during the course of 1930. In the cities bread lines appeared, evictions multiplied, municipal lodging houses filled, charity organisations doubled their expenditure, distress grew. When Manhattan's Little Church Around the Corner opened a soup kitchen in March, the line of hungry men stretched so far up Fifth Avenue, the city's smartest street, that it was reckoned unseemly. The police crowded them three abreast into 29th Street where, because supplies ran out, 2,000 went away hungry. About the same time unemployed men took part in Communist-inspired demonstrations in New York, Los Angeles, Seattle and Chicago. They demanded "Work or Wages" and received doses of tear gas and police violence.[9] America's system of relief was so primitive that once they had spent their pitiful savings and pawned the last of their possessions, the mass of job seekers seemed to have little prospect other than slow starvation.

"We didn't know the Depression was going on," recalled William Benton, who founded Benton & Bowles advertising agency in 1929, made a quick hit with commercials on the *Amos 'n' Andy* radio show, devised programmes such as the *Maxwell House Show Boat* that were almost as popular, and retired a millionaire in 1935. "There was plenty of money around," said another who prospered during the same period.[10] Indeed, affluence was, as yet, more conspicuous than poverty and it could even be said that the Depression was "nearly invisible to the casual eye."[11] Admittedly, shoeblacks and panhandlers haunted the sidewalks. Stores were less crowded, taxis less busy, trains shorter (Pullman cars often deserted), trucks fewer, restaurants and speakeasies emptier, "To Let" signs more numerous and building work almost at a standstill. But despite all this, despite the more acute hardship in the countryside, despite even the growing number of commercial collapses, mortgage foreclosures and bank failures (1,352 in 1930, compared to 659 the previous year), it was possible to ignore the Depression—and to swim against the tide.

Politicians and journalists could afford to be more preoccupied with issues such as naval limitation, tariff barriers, judicial appointments, Prohibition and the public ownership of electric power and other utilities. Hoover himself hid any worries he might have had and eschewed drastic remedies for distress. Putting his faith in self-help, local responsibility and voluntary agencies like the Red Cross, the President set his face against significant government action. He appointed committees and held conferences, but he permitted only a tiny increase in federal public works such as building interstate highways or veterans' hospitals. He even refused to support Senator Robert Wagner's proposal to establish a federal employment service. Yet during the disastrous drought of 1930 he did provide money for feeding livestock. An Arkansas congressman accused the President of being willing to feed "jackasses but . . . not starving babies."[12]

Referring to Hoover's relief of hunger abroad, Senator Alben Barkley suggested that the "best way to feed the unemployed would be to move them to China or Russia."

The President became more and more sensitive to such criticisms and hit back angrily. He accused his enemies of playing politics with human misery and endorsed Woodrow Wilson's view that senators' heads were knots which kept their bodies from unravelling. He described Congress as "that bear garden up there on the Hill" and said that one of its inmates was "the only verified case of a negative IQ."[13] Hoover was equally ill-tempered with those members of the press who were less than deferential. He resented invasions of his privacy even more than attacks on his policy. He hated stories about his penchant for driving the presidential limousine at high speed or about the system of signals by which his wife gave orders to the White House staff. (Hoover himself, whom the servants nicknamed "His Majesty," hardly ever addressed them and the First Lady would, for example, touch her spectacles to indicate that they should clear the table.)[14] The President instructed the Secret Service to keep reporters at bay and they countered by exaggerating his hard-heartedness. In fact he did not lack compassion: he donated much of his salary to charity, and his wife wore cotton dresses to promote the textile industry. But though exuding "lofty purpose,"[15] Hoover seemed cold, aloof and unsympathetic. Instead of seeking radical solutions to a human tragedy, he tinkered with the economy. However, he also allowed himself to be sucked into the fatal policy of protectionism, which would damage the United States more than any other country. In June 1930 he reluctantly signed the Smoot-Hawley tariff bill, the effect of which (predicted by a thousand economists) was to provoke massive retaliation abroad and to tighten the garotte on world trade. In the mid-term elections Hoover received a resounding vote of no confidence, especially from farming districts, and the Republican party effectively lost control of Congress.

During the clear, bitterly cold winter of 1930–31 the Depression became more difficult to disregard or deny, though Hoover kept saying that "the tide had turned." All over the country factories and businesses were closing. Wages, shares, prices and industrial production were falling, while crops fetched so little that they were barely worth harvesting. Banks and finance houses were crashing. Personal and public indebtedness was rising. So was unemployment. Hoover said that it was "shamefully exaggerated,"[16] but there were unemployment riots in Boston and other cities. And now white-collar workers joined the ranks of the jobless, many of them scraping a pittance by selling five-cent apples on the sidewalks. In their washed, frayed shirts, their shiny, threadbare suits, their polished, mended shoes, these shabby-genteel wraiths were a terrible reminder of middle-class vulnerability to the catastrophe. The President now blamed it on external factors. In due course Hoover would also assert that, "Many persons left their jobs for the more profitable one of selling apples."

It was more difficult to be insouciant about those now being destroyed by the Depression, about nameless families squatting in doorways or bivouacking over hot-air gratings or building tar-paper shacks on waste ground or dredging through trash cans and refuse dumps for food. The plight of the rural poor was quite as alarming, particularly in drought-stricken areas where ragged families huddled in district schools for lack of fuel to heat their homes and starving farmers had no recourse but to raid grocery stores. But whereas in Chicago even Al Capone founded a soup kitchen (costing him 300 dollars a day), Hoover refused to seek effective national shelter from the gathering economic storm. Instead the President looked for silver linings. He asked the crooner Rudy Vallee for a cheerful song. In February 1931 he told Senator Clapper, "What the country needs is a good big laugh . . . If someone could get off a good joke every ten days, I think our troubles would be over."[17] In fact, as Henry Stimson noted in his diary, Hoover's cabinet was singularly bereft of humour. Outside there were jokes, many of them bitter plays on the President's name: shantytowns were dubbed "Hoovervilles"; newspapers were "Hoover blankets"; jackrabbits were "Hoover hogs"; cardboard for mending shoes was "Hoover leather"; and so on. He was not amused. And his relationship with more serious commentators deteriorated still further after the appointment of a rebarbative new press secretary, Theodore Joslin; it was, quipped one reporter, "the first known case of a rat joining a sinking ship."[18] Hoover soldiered on doggedly. He was quoted as saying that the "slump" was "mental"—all in the mind.[19] In a speech at Valley Forge, he declared that "the trial of human character through privation and suffering" was a "triumph of the American soul."[20]

At 11:30 on the morning of 1 May 1931 Hoover pressed a button in Washington and switched on the lights of a more obvious American triumph, the Empire State Building in New York. Topped by a steel tower designed for mooring dirigibles (which were barred from the city), it was the loftiest structure on earth. New Yorkers delighted in its vital statistics: 1,250 feet high, weighing 600 million pounds, constructed with 10 million bricks, containing 67 elevators and 6,400 windows, and capable of accommodating 25,000 office workers. It had been put up in a single year at a cost of 52 million dollars (much cheaper than the original estimate because of the fall in price of materials and labour). It had also cost the lives of

48 construction workers, including one who was fired and jumped off the building. Dressed in a dark coat and a black derby, Al Smith, president of the Empire State Company at a reported annual salary of 50,000 dollars, conducted the opening ceremonies after his granddaughters had cut the ribbon across the Fifth Avenue entrance. Inside the four-storey hall visitors admired the grey and crushed strawberry marble, the galaxy of gold and silver stars on the cream ceiling, and elevator doors, picked out in silver and black, which reminded Edmund Wilson of the entrances to Egyptian tombs. On the 86th floor guests marvelled at the views, one exclaiming: "There's Central Park, no bigger than a football gridiron."[21] The beleaguered Mayor Jimmy Walker praised the building as a place "further removed than any in the world, where some public official might like to come and hide."

Governor Roosevelt congratulated its owners on their "grasp of the needs of the future."[22] But it became apparent almost at once that the skyscraper was a monument to the past, to the era of prosperity in which its builder, John J. Raskob, had made his fortune. It was now a monstrous white elephant. Only 20 per cent of its space was rented and by 1934 the building was losing a million dollars a year. Unkindly known as "Al Smith's last erection,"[23] it struggled to avert financial detumescence. Many of its floors were closed off and one Dartmouth honours graduate was delighted to secure the job of flushing all its unused lavatories every day to prevent chemicals in the water from marring the porcelain finish. During the Depression nothing was more poignant than the existence of poverty in the midst of plenty. And nothing more vividly symbolised that condition than the glittering vacancy of the Empire State Building.

Confronted by growing misery, Hoover himself sounded increasingly vacuous; the socialist Norman Thomas justifiably attacked him for leaving the unemployed to "subsist on patriotic oratory."[24] At Indianapolis in June the President ridiculed the notion that America could legislate itself out of a "world-wide depression"—it was about as "accurate as the belief [that] we can exorcise a Caribbean hurricane by statutory law." The only way to alleviate the effects of the Depression and to avoid dictatorship was by "organizing cooperation" and "stimulating every element of initiative and self-reliance." He therefore denounced uneconomic public works as "sheer waste." And he condemned "a dole,"[25] the demoralising effects of which have so often troubled the affluent.

Roosevelt himself abhorred a dole. But with one eye on the White House and the other on the huddled masses, he announced in August 1931 that government was the servant of the people and that when they could not help themselves state aid was imperative, "not as a matter of charity, but as a matter of *social duty*."²⁶ Roosevelt thereupon raised state income taxes to fund a Temporary Emergency Relief agency. Almost by chance he appointed as its executive director an outstanding professional social worker, Harry Hopkins. Tall, gaunt, rumpled, Hopkins was "an ulcerous type" according to one colleague, "intense, seeming to be in a perpetual nervous ferment—a chain smoker and black coffee drinker."²⁷ Within three months Hopkins was getting relief to nearly ten per cent of the state's population, a portent of things to come. But this still left 1.5 million people fending for themselves. And when Hopkins's 20-million-dollar allocation ran out Roosevelt was cautious about borrowing more, doing so only because his state was faced by circumstances so grave that they were "akin to war conditions."²⁸

Everywhere the Depression was likened to war. Professor Arnold Toynbee felt as though "Fate and Folly were making a concentrated attack upon the citadels of Civilization" and said that if "the world crisis of 1931 may be regarded as comparable to the World War of 1914, then the failure of [Austria's largest bank] the *Credit-Anstalt* at Vienna . . . may be taken as the analogue to the murder of Archduke Franz Ferdinand at Sarajevo."²⁹ The entire European financial structure was threatened by this failure and the repercussions were bound to affect America. "We have all been saying to each other that the situation is quite like war," wrote Henry Stimson.³⁰ And he lavished praise on Hoover for his bold assault on the problem—offering a year's moratorium on the payment of war debts. As it happened this restored European confidence for only a short time and, to let Toynbee complete his military metaphor, "the salvos rapidly increased in frequency and intensity until they became a continuous stupefying drum-fire, which confounded the ordinary multiplicity of human sensations in the single sense of a 'totalitarian' ordeal."³¹

Hoover's domestic tactics were equally ineffective. The President's Organization for Unemployment Relief (POUR was its apt acronym), set up in August 1931, proved even more inept than its predecessor, an Emergency Committee which had at least recommended public works. POUR offered no direct federal aid and was little more than a propaganda agency. Even in this sphere it was singularly maladroit. Under the slogan "Dollar, go forth like David!" one of POUR's advertisements exhorted readers to spend in order to defeat Goliath "who wants to spread hunger and illness and despair among you." An unemployed man wrote bitterly to POUR's head, Walter S. Gifford,

You and Pres. Hoover show at times about the same degree of intelligence as Andy [of the *Amos 'n' Andy* radio show] does. The other night Andy was going to send a fellow a letter to find out his address. You have told us to spend to end the slump, but you did not tell us what to use for money.[32]

Actually the President did try to expand credit during the nightmarish autumn of 1931—a time when more big banks crashed, Britain went off the gold standard, the precious metal flooded from the United States to Europe as overseas speculators cashed in their paper dollars, and so many Americans took to hoarding that perhaps a quarter of the nation's currency was hidden in mattresses or buried in gardens. But, by the inexorable logic of the market-place, the more someone needed money the less likely he was to receive it. Strong banks would not lend to weak ones, or to impecunious concerns, let alone to customers without collateral. So Hoover established the Reconstruction Finance Corporation with a federal appropriation of two billion dollars to give credit to banks and other big institutions. But this only increased their indebtedness while doing nothing to augment the purchasing power of the people or to help those in acute distress: the economist Rexford Tugwell compared it to trying to fertilise the soil by putting manure in trees. Hoover was eloquent about the absurdity of trying to squander one's self into prosperity. But he had hesitantly conceded the principle of deficit financing, declaring that in time of war no one dreamed of balancing the budget. However, said Roosevelt, who agreed that "the Nation faces today a more grave emergency than in 1917," the President had forgotten "the infantry of our economic army."[33]

BETWEEN the autumn of 1931 and the following spring the casualty lists of the Depression lengthened like those of the Great War. More than ten million people were unemployed but only a quarter of them were receiving relief. Indeed, about a quarter of the entire population, some 30 million Americans, were without any income at all. Two million vagrants, many of them youths, roamed the country looking for work. Twenty per cent of the nation's school children were underweight; in the poorest communities—among the share-croppers of Alabama or the coal miners of Pennsylvania, Kentucky and West Virginia—over 90 per cent were affected. For those in work average wages fell from 1929 levels by a fifth, to $22.64, though in Tennessee mills and New York sweatshops women were paid anything from $2.39 to $0.50 a week. Half a million Americans moved from city to country in search of subsistence. During the early

1930s, for the first time in the Republic's history, more people left the United States than arrived (though this was partly a result of Hoover's bar on immigration). Between 1929 and 1932 the birth rate fell from 18.8 to 17.4 per 1,000 and the suicide rate rose from 14 to 17.4 per 100,000.

In Montana thousands of acres of wheat went uncut because they would not pay for the price of harvesting—sixteen bushels would earn enough to buy a four-dollar pair of shoes. In Iowa a bushel of corn was worth less than a packet of chewing gum. Apples and peaches rotted in the orchards of Oregon and California, just as cotton did in the fields of Texas and Oklahoma. Western ranchers killed their cattle and sheep because they could not pay to feed them. Yet there was hunger amid abundance. Bread lines stretched under choking grain elevators. Malnutrition and associated diseases like rickets and pellagra were commonplace. President Hoover insisted that "Nobody is actually starving,"[34] a cry that others frequently echoed.[35] But there *were* cases of starvation. Congressman George Huddleston was probably not far wrong when he claimed that they ran into thousands:

> I do not mean to say that they are sitting down and not getting a bite of food until they actually die, but they are living such a scrambling, precarious existence, with suffering from lack of clothing, fuel, and nourishment, until they are subject to be swept away at any time, and many are now being swept away.[36]

Those charged with relieving destitution, both private agencies and public figures, failed dismally. Mayor Anton Cermak of Chicago acknowledged that, "We have no cash" and he personally telephoned people who owed over 20,000 dollars in taxes, begging them to pay what they considered a fair share of their debt.[37] Such expedients were hopeless. Half Chicago's working population of 1.6 million were idle and many city employees went unpaid for long periods, including the teachers (who nevertheless helped to feed thousands of hungry school children out of their own resources). With its wasteland of derelict factories and lifeless rail yards, its wilderness of unkempt parks and uncleaned streets, its jungle of slum tenements and teeming flophouses, Chicago was "Skid Row, U.S.A."[38] In Detroit, where two-thirds of the population were either out of work or on short time and 4,000 children daily stood in bread lines, the liberal Mayor Frank Murphy paid out 2 million dollars a month to ease distress. But he had to reduce this figure drastically when the city was faced with bankruptcy. Mayor Curley of Boston, who warned Hoover that his policies threatened to make the United States "a nation of beggars," had the same experience.[39] So did scores of other local authorities.

Governor Gifford Pinchot of Pennsylvania, who donated a quarter of his 52,000-dollar income to poor relief, was thwarted in his efforts to raise loans and taxes. Furious at the "Pollyanna view" of the Depression still being taken by some, including those controlling the mass media, he released a story about ten paroled prisoners who were so appalled by life outside the penitentiary that they voluntarily returned to it.[40] In Oklahoma, where no relief was left for the able-bodied once the aged and infirm had been assisted, the eccentric Governor "Alfalfa" Bill Murray failed in his attempt to levy income tax despite a willingness to use radical methods and to declare martial law. Few others went so far. But one man was quite impervious to the constraints of economic orthodoxy. He was Huey Long, the dictatorial Governor of Louisiana, who became a Keynesian without knowing it. By the simple process of increasing Louisiana's debt from 11 million to at least 125 million dollars, he financed huge public works, employing more men on building highways than any other state in the Union. He also ensured that fewer banks failed than anywhere else, blackmailing the strong ones into subsidising the weak.

In lieu of assistance, though, Americans resorted to extraordinary shifts. In Kentucky miners ate wild greens, violet tops, forget-me-nots and "such weeds as cows eat."[41] In Pennsylvania they devoured roots and dandelions. Some of the unemployed availed themselves of scraps kindly donated by Princeton dining clubs. Others consumed leftovers from restaurants, as recommended by Secretary of War Patrick Hurley. In Kansas farmers burned wheat to keep warm—a bushel now fetched only around $0.30, as compared to $3 in 1920. Corn, too, was cheaper than coal; as it blazed in stoves all over the prairies the air turned thick with blue smoke and a smell rather like that of coffee roasting. In Washington State lumberjacks started forest fires to earn money fighting them. In Arkansas families lived in caves. When the Russians advertised for 6,000 skilled workers more than 100,000 applied to go to the Soviet Union. Nearly 30 states established systems of barter and in Washington State stores issued and accepted wooden currency. To prevent the school system from collapsing entirely, teachers were often boarded out with families on a rota basis. Students found ever more ingenious methods to work their way through college— at Ohio State University two young men started a "dog laundry," washing and coiffing the pets of the opulent.

More radical solutions to domestic ills were much canvassed but had little effect. "People were talkin' revolution all over the place," recalled one contemporary.[42] President Hoover himself worried that "timid people, black with despair, have lost faith in the American system" and were now advocating foreign "economic patent medicines." He warned of the "armed revolutions" that had occurred "in a score of countries" during the previous two years and declared that in the United States there was no need for "revolutionary change."[43] Many Americans disagreed. Some wanted revolution from above and the establishment of a "corporate state" along Fascist lines. The explosive General Hugh Johnson, who was to be a pioneer of Roosevelt's New Deal, called for "Musellinny, Dictator, pro tem."[44] When a young man solicited Newton D. Baker's support for the Chicago Student Congress Against War and Fascism, the pacifist former Secretary of War responded: "Maybe it would be a good thing if we had a war. Kill off some of our unemployed."[45]

Others went to different extremes. Edmund Wilson was one of a number of middle-class intellectuals who concluded that "Karl Marx's predictions are in the process of coming true." Capitalism was in crisis because of its inherent contradictions: economic competition resulted in greater industrial efficiency at the expense of the workers, so "the more cheaply and easily goods can be produced, the fewer people are able to consume them."[46] By contrast, Wilson was impressed by the apparent success of Stalin's Five Year Plan, which the *New York Times*'s Moscow correspondent in Russia, Walter Duranty, described as "a stroke of genius."[47] But though some Americans agreed with the journalist Lincoln Steffens that all roads led to Moscow, few travelled that far. The Communist party numbered only 12,000 by 1932, though Representative Hamilton Fish's Congressional investigation conjured with figures as large as 500,000, adding that the leaders were mostly "of Jewish origin" and that their followers "speak English with an accent, if at all."[48] The bourgeoisie were certainly alarmed by the Red Menace, by the prospect of barricades in the streets, the massacre of property owners, the communalisation of American women and associated horrors. In Kansas the Daughters of the American Revolution made children's street-crossing guides use green flags instead of red ones in case the young should learn to accept the red flag as an emblem of authority. But there was no revolutionary rift between bourgeoisie and proletariat. Indeed, guilt-ridden middle-class liberals seeking a new faith were probably more inclined to embrace Communism than were embittered members of the working class, whose main concern was survival.

However, while political apathy was widespread among victims of the Depression, some were driven to protest. During 1931 there were strikes and disturbances amounting almost to guerrilla warfare in the coalfields of Pennsylvania. Sporadic outbreaks of violence and looting occurred elsewhere. Disorders shook Chicago and other cities. Even blacks, inured to economic depression at the best of times, rebelled. In December 1,600 hunger marchers arrived in Washington, D.C., led by the Communist

Herbert Benjamin, whom the Secret Service dubbed "an agitator of the worst type."[49] To his great credit, Hoover was contemptuous of Red Scares and he ensured that the demonstrators were provided with army tents, cots, blankets and rations. Riding his large blue motorcycle, the capital's enlightened police chief, Brigadier General Pelham D. Glassford, even headed their parade down Pennsylvania Avenue. They speechified, sang the "Internationale" and waved banners threatening to fight for the workers in the next war. But they were carefully hemmed in by the forces of law and order, who kept clubs, tear gas and machine-guns at the ready, and ensured that no personal appeals were made to their elected representatives.

Peaceful protest was difficult. For in America's liberal democracy, by a sad paradox, the standard methods of maintaining social control were viciously authoritarian. Throughout the country the police frequently employed terror and torture. The latter was euphemistically known as "the third degree" (of pressure—after arrest and incarceration) and it approached, as one critic said, "the ingenious cruelties of the Spanish Inquisition."[50] Policemen were apt to treat the unemployed as hobos, pickets as criminals, demonstrators as insurrectionaries. But the various private armies which industrialists recruited to protect their interests, such as that created by Henry Ford after the fatal Dearborn riot in March 1932, or Pennsylvania's murderous Coal and Iron Police, were little more than gangs of hoodlums. They were a brutal by-product of the approach towards industrial relations memorably summed up by R. B. Mellon, Andrew's brother: "You couldn't run a coal mine without machine guns."[51] At times Americans even anticipated techniques later refined by the Russians: in Oregon, for example, political agitators were sent to lunatic asylums. The prison authorities, too, meted out savage punishments to offenders, while the chain gang was a reversion to medieval barbarism. So was lynch law, which was by no means confined to the South.

His humanitarianism notwithstanding, in the summer of 1932 Hoover involuntarily presided over one of the most shocking instances of state coercion in American history. By then over a quarter of the labour force was out of work and the unemployment figures were still rising. The downfall of the fraudulent commercial empires of Ivar Kreuger and Samuel Insull had caused further distress. Bitterness was exacerbated when a Senate investigating committee uncovered sensational evidence of Wall Street's sleazy practices, notably finance houses' "preferred lists" of important people who got the chance to buy shares at advantageous prices before a flotation. Cornbelt farmers were taking violent action in an effort to stave off "degradation, bankruptcy, dissolution, and despair."[52] And for much the same reason 20,000 unemployed Great War veterans converged on Washington, D.C. Their leader was Walter W. Waters, a fair-haired, blue-eyed ex-sergeant who had once worked as superintendent in an Oregon canning factory. Their purpose was to demand immediate payment of the "bonus," the veterans' endowment policy which was due to mature in 1945. This was worth, on average, 1,000 dollars per man and Waters' proud but tatterdemalion army became known as the BEF, the Bonus Expeditionary Force.

Arriving in the capital from all over the country, their numbers swollen by the attendant publicity, their progress hastened by states keen to pass on the problem to the federal authorities, the veterans put up huts in open spaces or squatted in empty buildings near the seat of government. Most camped on the mosquito-ridden Anacostia mud flats, nicknamed "Hard-Luck-on-the-River." Scavenging for canvas, sacking, lumber, bricks, corrugated iron, packing cases, oil drums, old mattresses—anything for building or furnishing their shacks—the men raised a pathetic Hooverville within sight of the Capitol. It became a quagmire during the frequent rain storms, a dust bowl in hot weather. But they kept it as clean and sanitary as possible, digging latrines ("Hoover villas") and even cultivating small gardens. Some brought their families. The men were dignified and well disciplined. Their parades and rallies, held daily throughout June and July 1932, were restrained affairs. Even the provocative "Death March," a single file shuffling round the Capitol for three days and four nights, was non-violent. This was the brain-child of the leader of the Californian contingent, Roy Robertson, a man with a charismatic personality and a spinal injury for which he had a brace protruding over his head, giving the sinister impression that he was wearing a hangman's noose.

Despite competition from Robertson and others, Waters kept command. He even considered founding a Mussolini-style militia, the Khaki Shirts, though there was nothing in the charge that the BEF had engaged in a Fascist "March on Washington." For most of the time most veterans obeyed his orders, including stern prohibitions such as, "No panhandling, no liquor, no radical talk."[53] By and large the veterans were middle-aged, middle-class and politically middle-of-the-road. They saluted the Stars and Stripes, not the Red Flag. They sang "America," not the "Internationale." They took as their watchword, "Eyes front, not left."[54] The few Communists in their ranks (so abused by the militantly patriotic bonus marchers that they sought police protection) were naturally as eager to claim responsibility for the BEF as conservative Americans were to denounce it as a legion of Reds. Military intelligence (to use the oxymoronic term in its technical sense) sustained such myths: one report declared that Bolshevik elements in the BEF were controlled by the Jewish motion picture company Metro-Goldwyn-Mayer, itself supported by the USSR.

Depression bred suspicion. Indeed, it created a climate of paranoia. Robbed of self-confidence and self-respect, the veterans believed that they were the victims of financial conspiracy and political oppression. As it happened, Hoover did discriminate against them, but only because he regarded veterans as a relatively privileged group. In 1932 their benefits were the largest item on the federal budget and few politicians or newspapers approved of giving them further subventions. Hoover had already done much for the veterans and he did more for the BEF in Washington, quietly authorising the provision of tents, cots, blankets, cheap food and medical assistance. Unfortunately for his reputation, the President barricaded himself inside the White House, refused to meet Waters and kept his benevolence dark, fearing that news of it would encourage more veterans to come to Washington. So the police chief, Brigadier General Glassford, got the credit, adding to the plaudits he had already earned as a sympathetic mediator and a skilled publicist. Hoover was again indulgent when a large majority in the Senate turned down the bonus; he secured a grant of 100,000 dollars to pay for the BEF's return home. Most departed, but many had nowhere to go and clung to their toehold in Washington.

Despite Glassford's diplomacy, frustration led to confrontation. Trouble broke out over the veterans' occupation of several buildings near the Capitol which were due for demolition. On the morning of 28 July 1932 a near-riot occurred when Glassford tried to evict them. In the ensuing mêlée police shot two veterans dead and wounded others while suffering a number of injuries themselves. Amid much confusion federal intervention was called for. The flame-haired Secretary of War Patrick Hurley wanted to declare martial law but Hoover refused, giving strict instructions that the army should simply clear the disputed buildings. Tragically, the army's flamboyant Chief of Staff, General Douglas MacArthur, had no compunction about disobeying orders he disliked. In deference to the anti-military prejudices of the time officers at the War Department wore mufti, but MacArthur now donned his individually designed uniform with its English whipcord jodhpurs and its six rows of ribbons. He also sent his aide, Major Dwight D. Eisenhower, home to change. Ike protested, partly because he thought the Chief of Staff had no business conducting operations personally and partly because it was such hell getting on his boots. MacArthur, like other self-appointed men of destiny, was unmoved by such objections. He told Glassford, "We're going to break the back of the BEF."[55]

So, in the late afternoon of 28 July, four troops of cavalry, six whippet tanks and four companies of steel-helmeted infantry with fixed bayonets and machine-guns advanced down Pennsylvania Avenue. They were accompanied by 300 city police and squads of Secret Service and Treasury agents. Not realising the advancing troops' purpose, the old soldiers of the BEF initially cheered MacArthur's young ones. But the latter deployed and waded into veterans and bystanders alike. The infantry fired tear-gas bombs and set fire to small squatters' camps en route. The cavalry charged down the sidewalks as well as the street, beating terrified people with the flats of their sabres (though George S. Patton Jr. afterwards claimed to have cut off a veteran's ear). The crowd of onlookers, mostly shoppers and office workers on their way home, booed, hissed and harassed MacArthur's men. The BEF—astonished, furious, and demoralised—put up little resistance and retreated to Anacostia Flats. Scores of people were injured. Hoover sent MacArthur two specific orders not to follow the veterans over the river. But the General was "very much annoyed [at] having his plans interfered with in any way until they were executed completely."[56] Late that evening they were carried out when, after a pause for food and rest, troops crossed the bridges. Overawed by the show of force, the veterans snatched up what tattered possessions they could carry and fled. Amid the glare of the burning shantytown they melted away, to become refugees in their own land.

It was later said that the veterans set fire to their own huts as a last gesture of defiance. In fact MacArthur ordered the holocaust and by morning the Hooverville was gutted. The Chief of Staff himself gave a press conference (against Eisenhower's advice) at which he insisted that stern measures had been necessary because the BEF was "animated by the essence of revolution."[57] He went so far as to say that if it had remained in Washington for another week the government might have been imperilled. Journalists ridiculed the notion that a successful uprising could have been achieved by "10,000 homeless, half-starved, unarmed victims of our social disorder!" And they accused Hoover of staging the entire episode for electoral purposes, so that he could claim to have averted revolution.[58] Actually Hoover was furious and in private he rebuked MacArthur. But with a political clumsiness that seemed to have become second nature to him, the President publicly supported the General. Eventually he even convinced himself that Red plotters had been at work. Amid growing bitterness, the government further declared that the BEF was full of criminals. But the Veterans' Bureau proved that at least 94 per cent of the bonus marchers had genuine war records and Glassford showed that Washington's crime rate was actually below average in June and July 1932, adding piquantly that the BEF's criminal record was relatively better than that of the three post-war cabinets.

Despite a barrage of criticism, the President stuck to his guns. And at the end of an exhausting campaign he blurted out, "Thank God you still have a government in Washington that knows how to deal with a mob."[59] With its echoes of Communist and Fascist tyranny, this remark was the final nail in Hoover's political coffin. Of course, his failure to defeat the Depression made it virtually impossible for him to win the forthcoming presidential election. But by taking responsibility for the bonus rout and by justifying it so unconvincingly, Hoover destroyed at a stroke his long-established reputation as an honest humanitarian. Instead he had become, it was commonly said, the first American president to make war on citizens in the streets of their own capital. Certainly Franklin D. Roosevelt, who was to run against Hoover, had every reason to be grateful to General MacArthur: Roosevelt regarded him as an embryonic Mussolini and one of the two most dangerous men in the country (the other being Huey Long). While sitting on the porch at his Hyde Park home listening to a radio report of MacArthur's famous victory over the BEF, Roosevelt allegedly turned to his friend Felix Frankfurter and said, "Well, Felix, this will elect me."[60]

By then, indeed, Herbert Hoover was the most unpopular president since Rutherford B. Hayes had occupied the White House 50 years previously. He had fostered so many illusions about the imminent return of prosperity that, amid the wreckage of millions of lives, nothing was left but disillusionment. Hoover had failed to meet the greatest peacetime crisis in the Republic's history. He had, critics plausibly argued, secured "bigger and better opportunities for the rich men to inherit the earth" but afforded poor men only "the right to starve while standing on [their] own feet." Whatever he felt, he had expressed no real emotion about the country's plight. The writer Sherwood Anderson suggested that Hoover's long stay in China had inclined him to think of poor Americans as coolies. *The Nation* went so far as to accuse Hoover of "cold-blooded . . . murder."[61]

Yet by the end of his presidency Hoover was spending unprecedented sums on public works. They were too little and too late but the President got no credit anyway. He had ceased to carry conviction. He seemed an increasingly tragic figure, eclipsed by a catastrophe the scope of which he scarcely grasped. He talked confidently but looked grim and anxious. He lacked not only bonhomie but histrionic talents. He was a leader who shunned the limelight and scorned dramatic gestures. During the election campaign he alienated voters by his lacklustre mien and his obvious dislike of crowds. A British journalist was struck by the dispiriting influence of Mr. Hoover's personality, his unprepossessing exterior, his sour, puckered face of a bilious baby, his dreary, nasal monotone reading interminably, and for the most part inaudibly, from a typescript without a single inflection of a voice or gesture to relieve the tedium.[62]

Hoover seemed an engineer first and a human being second. His most loyal press supporter, William Allen White, said: "Politics after all is one of the minor branches of harlotry, and Hoover's frigid desire to live a virtuous life and not follow the Pauline maxim and be all things to all men, is one of the things that has reduced the oil in his machinery."[63]

BY a strange congruence Hoover's Democratic opponent, Franklin Delano Roosevelt, was criticised precisely because he did attempt "to be all things to all men."[64] Roosevelt seemed both weak and devious, prone to compromise, intent on popularity, a politician in every sense of the word. Walter Lippmann, doyen of American commentators, stamped his authority on this view. He lambasted Roosevelt for his "two-faced platitudes" and declared that the candidate was "an amiable man with many philanthropic impulses, but he is . . . too eager to please."[65] Exposing "Furtive Frank's" ingratiating inconsistencies and complaisant superficialities, other journalists called him "the corkscrew candidate" and the "Feather Duster."[66] Huey Long, who scandalised Hyde Park with his loud suit, orchid shirt and pink necktie, agreed. Hardly a model of political integrity himself, he thought charm an inadequate substitute for conviction. "When I talk to [Roosevelt] he says 'Fine! Fine! Fine!' But [Senator] Joe Robinson goes to see him the next day, and again he says 'Fine! Fine! Fine!' Maybe he says 'Fine!' to everybody."[67] Much in Roosevelt's career suggested that this was exactly what he did.

From the first he was preternaturally dutiful towards his possessive mother, Sara, an iron matriarch who regarded the Roosevelts as too grand to dine with the Vanderbilts. Franklin, born in 1882, was an only child and a distant cousin of the future President, Theodore Roosevelt—a relationship he never hesitated to exploit. His childhood was privileged, protected and peripatetic. At Hyde Park, where his father played the squire on his estate beside the Hudson River, Franklin enjoyed country pursuits and outdoor sports such as horseback riding and sailing. Aged 14 he was sent to Groton, where he came under another dominating influence, that of its Arnold-like headmaster the Rev. Endicott Peabody (who would vote for Hoover). At Harvard Roosevelt shone socially if not academically. But he was to describe his failure to become a member of the exclusive Porcellian Club as the greatest disappointment of his life, a curious revelation of spiritual dilettantism. Roosevelt conformed to the point of priggishness, even to the point of mendacity—he was a fluent and plausible liar. He sought easy accommodation, avoided bruising confrontation. He seemed lazy, shallow, affable, arrogant and patrician. Perhaps it was pride of caste when, in 1905, he married his awkward, unattractive cousin Eleanor, President Teddy's favourite niece. Or perhaps he was taking the line of least resistance. It is impossible to tell because, for all his self-confident bonhomie, Franklin was ultimately inscrutable. From his youth up he had protected his psychological privacy. He never exposed the core of his being, though he did occasionally reveal his ambitions. In 1907 he informed his fellow clerks in the Wall Street law office he had joined that his goal was the White House. He would win a seat in the state assembly, secure appointment as Assistant Secretary of the Navy and then become governor of the Empire State. "Anyone who is governor of New York has a good chance to be President with any luck."[68]

Roosevelt carried out this programme with remarkable fidelity. It is true that in 1910 he became a Democratic state senator, but otherwise he followed in his Republican cousin Teddy's footsteps. In particular he aspired to be both conservative and progressive, finding the golden political mean and drawing support from the widest possible constituency. So although he made his reputation by challenging the crooked Tammany machine, he afterwards took care to mend his fences with the New York powerbrokers. In 1932 Walter Lippmann could remark that it was only through the magic of his name that Roosevelt had managed, "in spite of a working alliance with Tammany, to dissociate himself from it."[69] By the same token Roosevelt maintained cordial relations with Josephus Daniels, Secretary of the Navy, while secretly undermining his boss in order to promote his own career. However, it was not in government offices where decisions were made or in smoke-filled rooms where influence was peddled that Roosevelt really shone. His genius was that of the communicator. Having overcome initial difficulties—the habitual tilt of his chin was taken for haughtiness—he established an uncanny rapport with voters. He was interested in people and sensitive to their concerns. Tall and handsome, he conveyed human warmth. "My friends . . . ," he said, but unlike Ramsay MacDonald, who used the same formula, Roosevelt sounded as if he meant it. His speeches were little better than clichés. But he charged them with his own dynamism. His optimism was infectious. He radiated good cheer.

Roosevelt needed all the good cheer he could muster to cope with the setbacks of middle age—the souring of his marriage as a result of his love affair with Eleanor's social secretary, Lucy Mercer; his defeat as Democratic candidate for the vice-presidency in 1920; and, worst of all, the attack of poliomyelitis which left him partially crippled the following year. Actually, in the view of Frances Perkins and others who knew Roosevelt well, this affliction transformed him from playboy politician into mature statesman. It supposedly purged him of frivolity, giving him a new humility, a sense of compassion and understanding, a spiritual serenity. Doubtless there is something in this. But the old Roosevelt was anything but defunct. The inveterate campaigner survived. He was still inclined to vanity, insincerity and occasional cruelty. His memory was as retentive as ever but his concentration span was just as short—he continued to skim rather than read. Immensely buoyant, jovial and energetic as always, he remained foxy, evasive and impenetrable. Most important of all, Roosevelt's charisma persisted. It was, if anything, enhanced. He proved that with his famous "Happy Warrior" speech nominating Al Smith at the Democratic convention in 1924. Boss Pendergast of Kansas City, who was powerful and cynical enough to boast that he had sent his "office boy" Harry Truman to the Senate, exclaimed after this speech that Roosevelt had "the most magnetic personality of any individual I have ever met." And one of Roosevelt's own correspondents said that, "His very crutches have helped him to the stature of the Gods."[70]

Four years later he again demonstrated his hold over the electorate. Although making every effort to regain the use of his legs, Roosevelt had kept himself in the forefront of national politics—he even claimed to be an honorary Southerner on the strength of his stays at the curative centre which he had built up at Warm Springs, Georgia. Thanks to his disability he had been able to distance himself from his party's failures and associate himself with its successes. Assisted by his political familiar, Louis Howe, an asthmatic, chain-smoking ex-journalist who looked like a "mediaeval gnome"[71] and behaved like a modern Machiavelli, Roosevelt had maintained contact with leading Democrats throughout the country. And, though reluctant to accept what he thought was an ill-timed draft from Al Smith, he finally agreed to run for the governorship of New York State in 1928. In his graphic way Smith dismissed doubts about the candidate's health—"A Governor does not have to be an acrobat"[72]—and Roosevelt won by a whisker. To Al Smith's surprise he then proceeded to govern.

This meant that he refused to be Smith's puppet at Albany, where he treated the governor's dingily baroque mansion as an antechamber to the White House. Roosevelt took initiatives that marked him down as a strong, progressive leader: he promoted state regulation of electric power, unemployment insurance and public works. On the other hand he con-

ciliated bankers, businessmen and conservatives. He even invited Tammany to investigate itself, which was rather like asking Al Capone to assess
his own taxes. Roosevelt's balancing act stemmed as much from intellectual as from moral flexibility. One of the most pleasing traits of his character was an extraordinary openness to new ideas. By 1932 he had recruited a
"Brain Trust" of academic advisers to supply them. Its leader, Professor
Raymond Moley, was actually perturbed by Roosevelt's "autointoxication
of the intelligence." But he and other Brain Trusters, notably Rexford Tugwell and Adolf Berle, took full advantage of Roosevelt's ideological eclecti-
cism. His speeches rang with their thoughts and phrases—Moley, for
example, suggested his appeal on behalf of the "forgotten man" at the bottom of the economic pyramid[73]—and they encouraged him to tackle the
Depression by means of "bold, persistent experimentation."[74]

Still, ever the pragmatist, Roosevelt regarded principles as good servants
but bad masters. His most crucial act of political trimming, even more
important than his damp compromise on the Prohibition issue, was to
abandon his long commitment to the League of Nations in order to
appease isolationists such as William Randolph Hearst. When the Democratic Convention seemed set on deadlock at the end of June 1932, Hearst
used his influence to swing the Californian delegation (pledged to "Cactus
Jack" Garner) to Roosevelt. Inside the barn-like Chicago Stadium the
band played what was to become Roosevelt's campaign tune, "Happy
Days Are Here Again." The candidate himself, breaking with tradition,
flew to Chicago—a dramatic political move perhaps copied from Hitler's
aeroplane electioneering over Germany. In his acceptance speech Roosevelt pledged himself to "a new deal for the American people."

Nicknamed "Red, White and Blue"—the colours, respectively, of his
complexion, hair and eyes—Jack Garner was Roosevelt's choice as candidate for the vice-presidency. It was an office which the plump, stetsoned
Texan reckoned "not worth a pitcher of warm piss"[75] and he contributed
little to the campaign except confidence. He said that to be elected Roosevelt only had to "stay alive 'til November."[76] Roosevelt was equally confident, though he was also superstitious enough (Moley claimed) to wear
the same hat throughout the campaign. This he conducted with his usual
exuberance, blithely holding together a Democratic coalition stretching
from Al Smith to Huey Long. During it he paid even less heed to the hob-
goblin of consistency. As Hoover said, Roosevelt's tariff policy, woven
together from contradictory strands, put him "in the dreadful position of
the chameleon on the Scotch plaid."[77] Roosevelt always posed as a farmer
himself but his farm programme was a bundle of incongruities cleverly
designed, as Moley said, to win "the Midwest without waking up the dogs

in the East."[78] Roosevelt criticised Hoover for having unbalanced the budget and he promised to cut government spending (though not at the expense of the starving), while also pledging federal relief and public works. But he won hearts if not minds. Hoover's policies were more coherent but less attractively presented, and anyway the President was now hated. Crowds booed him and waved hostile placards. One telegram urged him to "Vote for Roosevelt and make it unanimous."[79] Hoover himself said that his campaign train reminded him of Warren Harding's funeral cortège. Roosevelt, by contrast, beaming and waving his cigarette-holder, brimmed with vitality. Having triumphed over his own affliction, he alone seemed capable of defeating the economic paralysis crippling the country.

Victory in the election was duly achieved: Roosevelt got 22.8 million votes to Hoover's 15.75 million. Victory over the Depression was quite another matter. By the winter of 1932–33 perhaps as many as 15 million people were unemployed, a third of the labour force. Industrial production had halved since 1929. The value of exports had decreased by 69 per cent and the American share of world trade had shrunk. Investment had virtually ceased. In three years agrarian incomes had fallen from 12 billion dollars to 5 billion and violent resistance to the forced sale of farms was growing by the day. The nation seemed to be sliding inexorably into the abyss of starvation, bankruptcy and despair. Contemporaries coined new superlatives to comprehend the scale of the crisis. The State Department's economic adviser Herbert Feis suggested that bonds and currency should no longer be engraved with traditional scenes of "fertile prairies, powerful machines, speeding locomotives and busy factories" but with

> pictures of lines of men before factory gates or in relief lines under dark skies, and of distraught farmers in fear of losing their houses and lands, and burning their wheat and dumping their milk in gutters rather than accept the miserable prices which they could get.[80]

Felix Frankfurter considered that the "historian of the future will find new words behind the initials B.C. and A.D. I think they will connote, in addition to the great sacred weight those initials now carry, Before Crash and After Depression."[81]

Refusing to accept responsibility without power, Roosevelt resisted Hoover's clumsy attempts to involve him in various ameliorative efforts. The President-elect remained non-committal while striving to seem cooperative. This was an unpopular stance but it was offset by his spectacular courage under fire during an assassination attempt at Miami in February 1933—Chicago's Mayor Cermak, with whom he was talking at the time, later died of gunshot wounds. But though Roosevelt coolly proceeded with the business of planning and cabinet-making, he was constantly reminded that the Depression was pregnant with social dangers. There was more talk of revolution and all sorts of voices called for an authoritarian style or form of government. Major Dwight D. Eisenhower was nicknamed "Dictator Ike" because he believed that "virtual dictatorship must be exercised by our President."[82] Walter Lippmann, who in 1931 had dismissed as "a counsel of despair" pleas that the President should take war powers to overcome the Depression,[83] now told Roosevelt: "You may have no alternative but to assume dictatorial powers."[84] At a time when Hitler was taking advantage of the Reichstag fire to establish totalitarian rule, German newspapers said that "America is ripe for a dictator."[85] Even Eleanor Roosevelt wished that the United States had a benevolent dictator who could force through reforms. Her husband regarded her quizzically and replied that one "could not count upon a dictator staying benevolent."[86]

Strong measures were certainly essential. During the first two months of 1933 nearly 400 banks failed as depositors withdrew their funds and succumbed to "hoarding mania." They held on to what cash remained after buying "a great deal of canned food" for storage "against a possible siege."[87] To prevent the complete disappearance of the dollar, state governors increasingly declared "bank holidays." Finally, at the beginning of March, the malaise spread to the financial centres of Chicago and New York. Even the affluent ran short of cash. Film stars had to borrow money. Groucho Marx, with 50 dollars, was a plutocrat. Fay Wray, heroine of the newly-opened *King Kong*, found herself with only $2.80—and the citadels of civilisation under assault from the monster Depression seemed as vulnerable as the Empire State Building in the grip of the giant ape. Economic life was at a standstill. The lamps seemed to be going out all over the United States. A current hit expressed the mood: "Dancing in the Dark." America, as J. M. Keynes had suggested, appeared to be entering a new Dark Age which would last for a thousand years.

Inauguration Day, 4 March 1933, dawned grey and overcast, though pale shafts of sunlight occasionally glinted through the clouds. In Washington a chill wind whipped up the bunting and the flags (flying at half-mast to mark the death of Nebraska's Senator Tom Walsh). Large crowds waited anxiously and expectantly, making wry jokes about how they would find the money to pay their hotel bills. The change of government was conducted in an atmosphere "comparable to that which might be found in a beleaguered capital in war time." During the open-car journey from White House to Capitol, Hoover was taciturn and Roosevelt tense.

As he took the oath on his seventeenth-century Dutch Bible the new President was unwontedly grim. His face was stern as he delivered the inaugural address. But his carefully crafted sentences were luminous with hope. There was "nothing to fear but fear itself." "Plenty is at our doorstep." The "unscrupulous money-changers" had fled from the temple, which must be returned to its "ancient truths." But if morality was needful, so was action now. "Our greatest primary task is to put people to work." The government must help directly with "relief activities." The constitution was adequate but if necessary "I shall ask Congress for . . . broad executive power to wage a war against the emergency as great as if we were . . . invaded by a foreign foe."[88] This pledge received the loudest cheer. But would Roosevelt really sacrifice democracy on the altar of recovery? Nothing in his manner suggested such fell purpose. Indeed, when he had finished speaking his countenance once more lit up with the old, infectious smile. Amid the encircling gloom he glowed with confidence. As Lillian Gish said, he seemed "to have been dipped in phosphorus."[89]

V

THE TRIUMPH OF HITLER

FRANZ Kafka's novel *America,* published in 1927, begins with its hero sailing into New York harbour as "a sudden burst of sunshine illumines the Statue of Liberty."[1] Many Europeans were equally dazzled by the brave New World during the 1920s, and Germans in particular regarded the United States as the land of the future. Bertolt Brecht, for example, was fascinated by its skyscrapers, six-day bicycle races, industrial efficiency, jazz. "Hello!" he wrote in the "Song of the Machines,"

> We want to speak to America,
> Across the Atlantic waters to the great cities
> Of America, hello![2]

Brecht drew political inspiration from the Soviet Union, but it was in the United States that he found imaginative stimulus. According to the artist George Grosz, he even modified his Russian commissar's look—leather coat, cap and tie, convict haircut, stubbly chin and steel-rimmed glasses— to accord with what he supposed was American fashion, tapering his trousers and padding his shoulders. So when America succumbed to the Depression, Brecht was powerfully affected. "What men they were," he exclaimed, "their boxers the strongest, their inventors the most adept, their trains the fastest, and it all looked like lasting for a hundred years. And now the sudden crash—what a bankruptcy, how great a glory that has vanished!"[3]

The transatlantic débâcle seemed to herald the collapse of capitalism everywhere, something Brecht had foreshadowed in his opera *The Rise and Fall of the City of Mahagonny.* Completed by the spring of 1929, this is a bitter exposé of bourgeois society as a gehenna of crime and vice which eventually goes up in flames. After the Wall Street Crash Brecht wrote another drama, *St. Joan of the Stockyards,* a satirical fable about the martyrdom of a Salvation Army lass, Joan Dark, amid the moral and physical squalor of the Chicago meat business. Despite their American settings it is clear that in these works Brecht was chiefly excoriating Germany. The Nazis thus protested about *Mahagonny*, disrupting its performances with rioting in Leipzig and surrounding the theatre at which it opened in Berlin with brown-shirted Stormtroopers (*Sturmabteilung,* or SA) shouting *"Deutsche erwache!"*[4] Yet curiously enough Hitler did not altogether disagree with Brecht. He saw the Depression in America as "the last disgusting death-rattle of a corrupt and outworn system."[5] And he reviled the Weimar Republic as a monster of degeneracy.

Sired by defeat and spawned by the "syphilitic peace"[6] of Versailles, Weimar was impotent as well as decadent. That, at any rate, was Hitler's explanation of the uneasy accord which Germany reached with its former enemies under the direction of Gustav Stresemann, Foreign Minister between the great inflation of 1923 and the great Depression of 1929. Hitler might rage about national humiliation, but Stresemann gained Germany a voice in the councils of the nations. With his podgy fingers (invariably clutching a cigar), his broad jowls and his hair *en brosse,* Stresemann was said to look like a brewer. But he had a delicate diplomatic touch and he aimed to strengthen his country by achieving *détente* with its neighbours. At Locarno in 1925 he accepted Germany's western frontiers (though he still hankered to move eastwards) and fostered a spirit of international goodwill. The same year the aged Field Marshal Paul von Hindenburg was elected President, which seemed to portend some sort of return to militarism and monarchism. Yet Stresemann took Germany into the League of Nations (without alienating Russia). And in 1928 he signed the Kellogg-Briand Pact renouncing war as an instrument of policy. Here was the apogee of inter-war idealism whereby nation would speak peace unto nation. But, cried Hitler, this did nothing to change the lot of the betrayed and enslaved Fatherland. As for the Young Plan of 1929, which reduced and re-scheduled Germany's reparations payments, it merely confirmed the status quo. In the view of passionate nationalists such accommodations were a demeaning acknowledgement of war guilt. Stresemann, said Joseph Goebbels, Nazi *Gauleiter* of Berlin, was "the incarnation of everything rotten in Germany."[7]

That Weimar's successes could so easily be represented as failures pointed to grave political weakness. But the Republic was also morally vulnerable. Germany was in many respects a profoundly conservative society. Manners and dress were formal. The hand-shaking ceremony was, if possible, even more elaborate here than in France. When carrying out their duties official executioners wore top hats, white gloves and frock coats. Officers and gentlemen clung rigidly to their code and duelling, though illegal, was still common. Few complained when the police im-

posed social discipline. They licensed, inspected and even graded prostitutes of both sexes, who could be sued if they infected their clients. There
were countless societies for the organisation of culture, leisure and sport.
Even hiking was regimented, as the bands of Wandervögel with their
swastika emblems and *"Heil "* salutes (both borrowed by Hitler) amply testified. The German bourgeoisie prized order and respected authority. Yet,
as though desperate to escape from a demoralising past, many of the new
republicans cast off the shackles of orthodoxy. Weimar became a byword
for liberalism, modernism and hedonism, for avant-garde art and architecture, for social deviance and sexual decadence.

Nothing excited critics to greater flights of hyperbole than Berlin's reputation as a modern Sodom:

> In the whole of *The Thousand and One Nights,* in the most shameless
> rituals of the Tantras, in the carvings on the Black Pagoda, in the Japa-
> nese brothel pictures, in the vilest perversions of the Oriental mind, you
> couldn't find anything more nauseating than what goes on there, quite
> openly, every day.[8]

Thus warned, Christopher Isherwood naturally determined to visit the
German capital as soon as possible and stay for a very long time. Others
did the same: 150,000 of Berlin's 4.3 million inhabitants were foreigners.
But no city could live up to such alluring advertisements. And Berlin,
with its muster of straight grey streets named after national heroes and its
drab uniform squares filled with the statues of forgotten generals, seemed
more a monument to the Prussian spirit than the site of a new Babylon. To
the satirist Kurt Tucholsky the very idea that the Kurfürstendamm could
compete with Montmartre, that Berlin could rival Paris as a metropolis,
seemed ridiculous: "Children," he admonished, "the chickens cackle in
Potsdam Square."[9] Still, on the candelabra-lit Kurfürstendamm the prostitutes did parade in their red boots, ogled from fashionable cafés by gross
profiteers who might have stepped straight out of Grosz cartoons. The
neon-illuminated Friedrichstrasse was described by one indignant visitor
as "the pornographic shop-window of Germany's shame."[10] Sleazy clubs
offered anything from cocaine to fetishism and perversions abounded: one
coven of coprophagists gorged a prostitute on chocolate, gave her a laxa-
tive and settled down to a feast. There were so many homosexual bars,
transvestite dance halls and nude cabarets that an enterprising publisher
issued a *Guide to Vicious Berlin.* Outside the palace at the bottom of Unter
den Linden were two stone lions, one of which was said to roar whenever a
virgin walked by.[11]

Berliners were noted for their sardonic wit and coarse speech. And if their city was less sophisticated than they thought, it was in many ways more permissive than Paris, where both *The Threepenny Opera* and *The Blue Angel* (Joseph Von Sternberg's film starring Marlene Dietrich) were banned. Berlin, which had what Hitler damned as a mongrel Marxist population, was the capital of "cultural Bolshevism." And Hitler, who loved virile lederhosen and regarded even Viennese waltzes as effete, inveighed against its various manifestations. They included Bauhaus architecture, Dadaist art, Jewish psychoanalysis, experimental theatre, short skirts, suede shoes, foxtrots, lipstick, bobbed hair, jazz. Such debauchery subverted the national spirit, he maintained, and he accused Weimar of fostering cultural treason. But playing on the fears of conservative, provincial Germany, though effective, was not enough. Hitler, who was himself paradoxically a manifestation of the revolutionary Weimar spirit, believed that the best propaganda was blood running in the gutters. He determined to challenge the Communist enemy in its stronghold—on the streets of "the reddest city outside Russia."[12]

Hitler's instrument for this task was a well-educated young acolyte and agitator named Joseph Goebbels. Unlike some other Nazis in the north, Goebbels was prepared to serve the Führer with the loyalty of a zealot. Indeed, once converted, he literally worshipped Hitler, filling his diary with paeans of devotion. Hitler was a political prodigy who could conquer the world. He was an artist-statesman, a kind master, a beloved friend. Staying with him in Bavaria, Goebbels had what amounted to a mystical experience. The Führer, he wrote,

> is a genius. The natural creative instrument of divine destiny. I stand by him profoundly moved. He is like a child, dear, good, compassionate. He is as nimble and clever as a cat. Like a roaring lion, he is great and gigantic. What a fellow, what a man . . . After supper we sit in the garden . . . for a long time and he preaches about the new state and how we are to fight for it. In the sky a white cloud takes the form of a swastika. A glittering light shines in the heavens. It cannot be a star. Is it a sign of Fate?[13]

For all his adoration, Goebbels was an unlikely Nazi. Dwarf-like and club-footed, he was by no means a model member of the master-race, something his enemies harped on with glee. Ribbentrop would call him Mickey Mouse. Yet with his penetrating brown eyes, wide expressive mouth, and slender sensitive hands, Goebbels was an oddly fascinating character. He had the cadaverous features of an ascetic and the hot passions of a libertine, charming women and doing much to earn his subsequent nickname, "the he-goat of Babelsberg."[14] He was a facile liar, claiming that his foot was the result of a war wound instead of (probably) infantile paralysis. Perhaps it was bitterness about his deformity, which must have been psychologically crippling in the context of National Socialist eugenics, that made Goebbels a monster of malevolence—one senior Nazi, Gregor Strasser, said he was "Satan in human form."[15] Like Hitler, Goebbels was a revolutionary who lived in a world of moral entropy. He also proved to be a demagogue second only in potency to Hitler.

His voice, a powerful and skilfully modulated baritone, could be anything from a scream to a caress. It was an extraordinary thing to emerge from so puny a frame, "as if Niagara came pouring from an eye-dropper."[16] Goebbels' gestures were equally dynamic, the erect right arm which added to his stature, the eyebrows raised in sublime anger, the eyeballs rolling with mockery and scorn. Glib, resourceful, sarcastic, mordant, he deployed both sophisticated argument and crude invective. From his great gash of a mouth flowed warped and tainted versions of the truth as well as venomous exhalations of pure fanaticism. A virulent anti-Semite and a consummate actor, Goebbels practised his speeches in front of a mirror and played on the emotions of his audiences with cynical ease. His technique was different from that of Hitler, who seemed to reach out for the souls of his hearers: Goebbels whipped their bodies into what Albert Speer called "wilder and wilder frenzies of enthusiasm and hatred, a witch's cauldron of excitement."[17] Son of a poor white-collar worker himself, Goebbels was particularly adept at exploiting the atavistic prejudices of the lower middle class. But he was not satisfied with subtle oratorical effects or even with the barbaric pageants in which he set them. Insurrection spoke louder than words. Goebbels propounded the maxim that, "He who conquers the streets conquers the masses; and he who conquers the masses conquers the state."[18] The streets of Berlin were obviously the prime target. For, to quote another of Goebbels' maxims, "Whoever has Prussia has the Reich. And the road to power in Prussia is via the conquest of Berlin."[19]

Actually Goebbels was not pleased by the prospect of being sent to the capital, even as a "saviour"[20] of the National Socialist cause. Berlin, he primly remarked, was a sink of iniquity amid a wilderness of masonry. "The breathtaking tempo of this monster of cement has made men hard and soulless and devoid of compassion." Moreover in 1926 the Berlin Nazi party was in a hopeless situation. It was plagued by division and debt. Its headquarters was a basement in the Potsdamerstrasse known as the "Opium Den," filled with tobacco smoke and so dark that the electric light was kept burning all day. The party had only about 1,000 members and Goebbels quickly expelled a faint-hearted 400. Arrogant and ambitious, the new *Gauleiter* wanted a hard core of dependables. On 1 January 1927 he moved from the Opium Den to new offices in Lützowstrasse and addressed his faithful followers thus: "Berliners may insult us, slander us, fight us, beat us up, but they must *talk* about us. To-day we are six hundred. In six years we must be six hundred thousand!"[21]

Goebbels set about fulfilling this prophecy with frenetic vigour and in the process he developed techniques that helped to make him one of the most influential propagandists in history. To his enemies he became the Lucifer of lies. And Goebbels himself acknowledged that propaganda had absolutely nothing to do with truth. All that mattered was its success. On the other hand, he liked to say that Jesus Christ had been a master of propaganda and that "the propagandist must be the man with the greatest knowledge of souls."[22] Propaganda was, indeed, the gospel of Nazism, the light to lighten the Gentiles. And as the "Mahatma Propagandhi"[23] during the Third Reich Goebbels proclaimed that his mission was to conduct the spiritual mobilisation of the German people. By the same token his present task was to sap the moral foundations of the Weimar "system." He did so, as Hitler had proposed in *Mein Kampf* (a book which Goebbels read with fascinated attention), by encouraging "a fanatical outburst of [*völkisch,* i.e. racist] and national passion."[24] He plastered Berlin with flaming red posters. He held Nazi meetings in predominantly Communist areas. When fights broke out he mustered wounded Stormtroopers on the speaker's platform. He founded a guard of honour consisting of tall, uniformed Aryans and invented ceremonies such as the solemn entrance of flag-bearers. He organised marches through poor districts like "Red" Wedding, with its interminable rows of sombre tenements. He provoked attacks on Jews in smart boulevards like the Kurfürstendamm, with its glittering shops, restaurants and entertainment palaces. "Berlin needs its sensations as a fish needs its water," Goebbels declared.[25] Nothing was more sensational than terror in the streets.

The police responded, in May 1927, by banning the Berlin Nazi party. However, Goebbels proved adept at running an underground organisation. He founded apparently innocuous sporting clubs to keep his men together and, to circumvent the prohibition of brown uniforms and Nazi insignia, he made them wear white and use bottle tops as badges. He also started a weekly newspaper, *Der Angriff* (The Attack). Although, by his own admission, its early editions were piffle, it became the authentic voice of Goebbels in print. One of his nastiest campaigns was the persistent vilification of the Jewish Deputy Chief of Police, Bernhard Weiss, whom he lampooned as "Isidor." But for all this sound and fury the Nazis made little headway. By 1928 Hitler seemed to have faded into "oblivion."[26] Never having met a Nazi, the writer Robert Neumann declared: "Hitler doesn't exist."[27] And in the May elections the National Socialist party won only 2.6 per cent of the vote, entitling it, under Weimar's system of proportional representation, to 12 seats in the Reichstag. Among the Nazi deputies chosen were Hermann Göring, who immediately began to feather his own nest, and Joseph Goebbels, who announced that National Socialists would become parliamentarians in order to destroy parliament. "We will move into the Reichstag to supply ourselves at the arsenal of Democracy with its own weapons."[28] The principal benefit membership conferred, Goebbels added, was that he now had the freedom to call Weimar "a dung heap" rather than a " 'state.' "[29]

This was a scatological version of Oswald Spengler's view that Weimar was not a state but a business enterprise, "a dictatorship of the party bosses . . . erected in smiling comfort over the corpses of two million heroes who died in vain, over a nation which withered away in misery and torture of the soul."[30] Spengler was no Nazi and Goebbels merely gave a vulgar gloss to opinions which could be heard on the Left as well as the Right. But was Weimar really riddled by decay and doomed to destruction? Despite crippling handicaps, the Republic displayed remarkable resilience and its collapse was by no means inevitable. By 1929 it was enjoying prosperity, admittedly patchy and precarious, such as most of its citizens had never before experienced. Industry was doing relatively well. Germany had a favourable trade balance of 387 million marks in 1930 and overtook Britain as the second largest exporting nation. Trade unions were strong. Taxation was heavy but wages were high. The foundations of a modern welfare state had been laid. The parliamentary constitution was working, albeit uneasily. The army was reluctantly cooperating with the State. President Hindenburg tolerated leftists in Weimar's coalition governments, though he was credited with insisting that the imperial black-white-and-red flag should fly beside the banner of the Republic—whose colours, according to its adversaries, represented the Black International of Roman Catholics, the Red International of Socialists and the Yellow International of Jews. The only serious controversy in foreign affairs concerned the Young Plan.

The Plan eased the economic burden of reparations but reminded Germany of the psychological burden of war guilt. Even so, the payments were quite heavy and set to continue until 1988: Goebbels denounced the Young Plan as a "death penalty passed on the unborn."[31] Hitler ignored the fact that it also secured the early evacuation of the Rhineland and, rousing himself from a sentimental romance with his buxom niece Geli Raubal, declared that it would enslave the German people. In an attempt to defeat

The Crash: Wall Street on "Black Tuesday," 29 October 1929

The Inauguration of President Franklin D. Roosevelt, 4 March 1933

Public Power: Roosevelt visiting the Tennessee Valley Authority, 1934

FDR stands up for
the "forgotten man"

Miss Prosperity, 1935:
her dress is made of
bonds sold to promote
the New Deal

Germany's new
Chancellor, Adolf Hitler,
humbly greets President
Hindenburg

Hitler stars in his
own theatre of power,
Thanksgiving Day, 30
September 1934

Heroic images were projected throughout Italy to foster
the cult of the Duce

Mussolini in Tripoli, where he posed as the successor of the
Roman emperors and as the "Protector of Islam"

Soviet collective farmers on the Gigant Estate hail the brave new era

Stalin, Molotov (*left*) and Voroshilov (*right*) wear Uzbek national
dress at a collective farm meeting, 1935

"The Driver of the Locomotive of History" points the way ahead

Refugees from the Depression:
"Okies" in a makeshift shelter at Blythe, California, August 1936

it, he even entered into an alliance with the dour Nationalist leader Alfred Hugenberg. The Nazi-Nationalist coalition lost when the Young Plan was endorsed by a plebiscite in 1930. But by this time Hitler had demonstrated that he was the embodiment of a dynamic future, while the short, paunchy Hugenberg, with his bushy white moustache, his stand-up collar, gold watch-chain and cut-away coat, was just what he seemed—the personification of the past. Hitler had used Hugenberg's funds and his press to appeal to a wider and more respectable constituency, transforming Nazism from a splinter group into a national party. And Goebbels had taken the opportunity to make some flaming propaganda—when the President ratified the Young Plan, *Der Angriff* asked, "Is Hindenburg still alive?"[32]

THE Nazi advance would hardly have been significant but for the Depression. This did not come entirely out of the blue, though before its arrival the usual academic soothsayers (such as the Bonn sociologist Joseph A. Schumpeter) were to be found pronouncing that no disasters of any kind were likely. Even when Wall Street crashed alarm bells did not ring in Germany, where most people felt a sense of *Schadenfreude,* swapping jokes about hitherto rich relations in America who now wrote begging letters home. Nevertheless, the Depression struck Germany harder than anywhere else except the United States. In part this was because the German economy relied so heavily on short-term foreign loans, which soon dried up after the stock market collapse. Furthermore, poverty was already widespread. In particular, there was considerable distress among peasantry and small farmers (nearly a third of the population) who were hit by debt, high interest rates and foreign competition. Before October 1929 some two million people were out of work; by January 1930, as exports dwindled and factories closed, the figure had risen to more than three million.

With demoralising speed the Depression took its familiar toll. In Berlin and other cities queues formed outside government employment offices. Buskers, beggars, bootlace salesmen and match sellers haunted the streets, though before the Crash Berlin had probably been the most mendicant-free capital in Europe. Men played draughts in labour exchanges or scavenged the pavements for cigarette butts. Wearing coarse brown breeches and dirty yellow shirts, the workless gathered at Nazi centres where Stormtroopers fed them for a few pfennigs. In Berlin alone there were between 20,000 and 30,000 young waifs living in gangs and surviving on crime, some of them syphilitics and drug addicts. Erich Kästner described the capital, in his Depression novel *Fabian* (1931), as a vast city of stone which was rotten to the core. Around Berlin, in forests, parks and suburban allotments, villages of packing-case shacks sprang up. Peasants guarded their potatoes with guns. Share prices tumbled and small businesses failed. Pawnbrokers flourished. So did astrologers, numerologists, seers and other charlatans. One popular Berlin revivalist had a recipe for salvation consisting of "prayer and cream cheese."[33] Suicides increased, particularly among middle-class people for whom the shame of poverty was too much to bear.

The State itself could not bear the shock. For other countries the Depression was primarily an economic crisis; for Germany the crisis was primarily political. Reeling from the blows of war and peace, Weimar was psychologically incapable of withstanding a fresh onslaught. The advocates of democracy were discredited and the Republic was peculiarly vulnerable to critics who blamed it for the catastrophe. Hitler's bastard philosophy was especially compelling: the State was a racial organism, not a business organisation; there were no economic problems, only political ones; the force of the Leader's will must be unleashed and German blood must be "freed"; "no resurrection of the German people can occur except through the recovery of outward power."[34] Communist prophecies about the imminent collapse of capitalism were also persuasive and many of those alienated from Weimar enlisted under the Red banner. But most Germans hated and feared this radical, atheistic, foreign creed. Hitler appealed more to the disillusioned middle classes thrown on to the dole, to farmers unable to meet their mortgage repayments, to unemployed young workers who found comradeship, purpose and all the excitements of licensed vandalism in the ranks of the Nazi SA. As early as February 1930 Hitler predicted "with almost clairvoyant certainty" (and chilling accuracy) that "the victory of our movement will take place . . . at the most in two and a half to three years."[35]

Hitler's certainty was prompted in part by the Depression itself. One such upheaval, he said, would provoke another: "The impossible will become possible, miracles will happen!"[36] He was also convinced that he was the predestined saviour of Germany. Providence had chosen him to make the nation great and he once told Joachim von Ribbentrop, his future Foreign Minister, that "before big decisions he always had a feeling of absolute certainty."[37] After surviving a car accident Hitler remarked that in fact nothing could have happened since he had not completed his task. The Führer was able to transmit this faith not only to his immediate followers, most of whom, like Goebbels, allowed themselves to be mesmerised by him (though they were also inspired by baser motives). For the first time he could also project his charismatic presence on to a wider screen. At such an apocalyptic moment the power of his personality cult was overwhelming. Witness the confession of a typical convert: "there was only one thing for me, either to win with Adolf Hitler or to die for him. The personality of the Führer had me in its spell."[38]

Nazi devotion took many forms. Some tried to touch Hitler, as though he were endowed with thaumaturgic powers. Others built little domestic shrines to him. Widows sent him small gifts. A tubercular party member gazed at the Führer's portrait for hours "to gain strength."[39] School girls painted swastikas on their fingernails, and one group of blonde maidens vowed to "Heil Hitler" and give the Nazi salute at the point of orgasm. Many Germans were, of course, immune to Hitler's animal magnetism. At one tumultuous rally organised by Goebbels in the Berlin Sportpalast, a stadium seating 15,000 people, all the trappings of demagoguery were deployed—ranks of Stormtroopers, massed banners surmounted by Roman eagles, a brass band playing military music, the scowling protagonist's portentous entry, the heel-clickings and salutes, the impassioned speech and the ecstatic responses. But though Hitler worked his enchantment on the crowd, sending them into "a kind of hypnotic trance" with his "repetitive rhythm" so that they emerged with "shining faces and dreamy eyes," the German journalist Egon Larsen found the entire performance phoney, primitive and ludicrous.[40] Sefton Delmer, a British newspaperman who attended the meeting, concluded quite simply that the Führer was a "crackpot."[41]

Sophisticated minds found it fatally easy to underrate Hitler. Thomas Mann said that he offered merely "politics in the grotesque style with salvation-army attractions, mass fits, showground-stall bell-ringing, hallelujahs, and dervish-like repetition of monotonous slogans till everyone is foaming at the mouth."[42] Yet such antics at least showed that the Nazis possessed dynamism, something singularly lacking in the Weimar authorities, who played into Hitler's hands. Faced with the problem of financing vastly increased welfare benefits—or cutting them—the government split. So at the end of March 1930 President Hindenburg, prompted by his "Field-Grey Eminence" General Kurt von Schleicher, appointed a Catholic conservative as Chancellor: Heinrich Brüning. Having served heroically as commander of a machine-gun unit during the war, Brüning was used to taking orders and he revered the old soldier who now demanded his allegiance. They made a "strange contrast,"[43] the Junker Field Marshal and the son of a wine and vinegar merchant sitting together in the great office of the Presidential Palace which overlooked the garden bathed in pale sunshine.

Hindenburg, aged 83, a vast, immobile hulk with curling moustache and bristling hair, seemed to be the incarnation of Prussian military might. Brüning, aged 44, slight, balding, bespectacled, thin-lipped and slope-shouldered, with a habit of speaking quietly as though he were afraid of being overheard, looked like a priest manqué. Hindenburg, with his gargantuan appetite, ruddy skin and blue, tear-prone eyes, resembled an enormous baby; but he was increasingly given to bouts of senility and it was said that he would sign anything put in front of him, even sandwich papers. Brüning was tough and resolute but so modest that he arrived at the Reich Chancellery with one suitcase and so shy that when greeted by crowds in Munich he pulled down the blinds of his railway carriage. Hindenburg liked to distance himself from responsibility and boasted that the only books he had ever read were the army manual and the Bible. Brüning was hard-working and well informed. He was also narrow-minded and high-minded, inclining to interpret patriotism as loyalty to the President. Hindenburg took the same view.

Both men were authoritarians. Neither possessed much political finesse. Brüning thus determined on a stubbornly orthodox policy. He would raise taxes, lower the dole, balance the budget, avoid inflation and honour Germany's obligations under the Young Plan. And when he could not get parliamentary support for this programme Hindenburg agreed to allow him to rule by emergency decree according to the notorious Article 48 of the 1919 Weimar constitution. So the democratic pass was sold before the advent of the Nazis.

With the Reichstag neutralised, public attention focussed on the struggle in the streets. In Berlin Goebbels redoubled his efforts, achieving a notable propaganda coup by making a martyr out of a pimp. Perhaps Horst Wessel, a young Stormtroop commander, did not actually live off immoral earnings, but he was certainly a womaniser and a brawler and he was murdered in a sordid crime of passion. Representing him as a hero slain for the cause by diabolical Communists, Goebbels elevated Horst Wessel to the Nazi pantheon. His funeral, like that of other SA members who fell in the "struggle," was the occasion for a provocative demonstration; his grave became a shrine; a clichéd song he had written (set, ironically, to an old Communist tune) became the movement's anthem; and his name was chanted as a battle cry. It was often heard in the capital as party feuds grew more violent in the noxious atmosphere of Depression. The British writer Stephen Spender was struck by "the sensation of doom" to be felt in the streets during this period of what he called *"Weimardämmerung."*

The feeling of unrest in Berlin went deeper than any crisis . . . In this Berlin, the poverty, the agitation, the propaganda, witnessed by us in the streets and cafés, seemed more and more to represent the whole life of the town, as though there were almost no privacy behind doors. Berlin was the tension, the poverty, the anger, the prostitution, the hope and despair thrown out on to the streets. It was the blatant rich at the smart restaurants, the prostitutes in army top boots at corners, the grim, submerged-looking Communists in processions, and the violent youths who suddenly emerged from nowhere into the Wittenbergplatz and shouted: *"Deutschland erwache!"*[44]

Towards the middle of 1930 another British observer, the Military Attaché in Berlin, expressed fears that the brown-shirted Stormtroopers would destroy Brüning's government and replace it with a "mad-dog dictatorship." They got their chance to try in the September general election. Goebbels, by now in charge of all Nazi propaganda, ran a campaign which quite eclipsed the efforts of the other 23 parties competing for votes. As well as loudspeakers, he used jackboots, rubber truncheons and knuckledusters to make the Nazi point. He distributed millions of brochures. He stuck posters everywhere. He organised thousands of mass meetings, many of them in the open, where they were lit by phalanxes of blazing torches. Hitler spoke until he was hoarse, using to the full his "extraordinary gift for hypnotising his audience and gaining adherents," many of them, the British Attaché averred, "quite reasonable people."[45] Brüning's analytical orations were bloodless by comparison; and in a futile effort to counteract Hitler the Social Democrats opened a school of oratory. The Führer gave few clear indications of policy: indeed, it has been said that Hitler never made political speeches, only philosophical ones. His epigones were equally vague, one speaker telling an enthusiastic small-town audience: "We don't want lower bread prices, we don't want higher bread prices, we don't want unchanged bread prices—we want National Socialist bread prices!"[46] Hitler did make specific appeals to certain groups, such as farmers and soldiers, but he concentrated on the nation's wrongs and his determination to right them. He promised leadership, rebirth, redemption, unity, empire. While vowing to purge the poisons from the German body politic he sent them coursing hotly through its veins. Against a background of grievance and misery, propaganda and organisation triumphed. On polling day the Nazis won nearly 6.5 million votes; this gave them 107 seats in the Reichstag, where they were now the second largest party (after the Socialists). As Fritz Stern remarks, Hitler had proved himself "the greatest magician-manipulator of the violent instincts of an outraged, perplexed people that the modern world has seen."[47]

The amazing election result, widely interpreted as a flight into unreason, horrified civilised people in Germany and abroad. Hindenburg resolved that Brüning's government should continue. But its task was made much more difficult by a grave loss of confidence in German financial stability, large capital withdrawals and an abrupt twist in the spiral of Depression. Politically, too, Hitler kept up the pressure. When the Reichstag met in October, Nazi deputies defied the ban and appeared in their brown uniforms. Maintaining that the Reichstag was an Augean stable, they proceeded to treat it as such, in the spirit of National Socialist students who chanted, "We shit on freedom."[48] Meanwhile Stormtroopers demonstrated illegally in front of the building and then went on the rampage. Frustrating police efforts to disperse them, they broke the windows of Jewish shops and beat up Jewish-looking people in the streets. Goebbels arranged this display knowing exactly what it involved. For, ironically, a dissident group of the SA had recently smashed up his smart new office in the Hedemannstrasse and he had been obliged to call the police. Discipline had now been restored after a purge of opposition factions—the Horst Wessel detachment had to be disbanded altogether on account of infiltration by Communists. And Goebbels continued his efforts to sabotage the State by means of organised hooliganism.

He brought off a characteristic coup in December 1930 when the American film of Erich Maria Remarque's novel *All Quiet on the Western Front* was first shown in Berlin. This best-selling book was one of a number published on the same theme at the end of the 1920s, when writers had had time to digest the experience of the First World War and were, perhaps, becoming apprehensive about the possibility of a second. Remarque had evoked the conflict in all its stark horror and tragedy. He had also made it clear that by the summer of 1918 German soldiers in the trenches knew that the war was lost and desperately wanted their leaders to make peace: "Breath of hope that seeps over the scorched fields, raging fever of impatience, of disappointment, of the most agonizing terror of death, insensate question: why? Why do they not make an end?"[49] The Nazis were naturally incensed by Remarque, who not only exposed the fatuity of their martial rhetoric but also shattered their most cherished myth— that the "November criminals" had stabbed the undefeated German army in the back.

Goebbels retaliated by sending dozens of Stormtroopers to the Mozartsaal cinema in Nollendorfplatz. There in the darkness they bawled insults: "filthy film," "pigsty" and "throw the Jews out." Goebbels himself cried, "Hitler is at the gates of Berlin."[50] His henchmen let off stink bombs, hurled paper bags of sneezing powder from the balcony and released white mice among the seats. Goebbels afterwards chortled that within ten minutes of the start of the film the cinema had become a madhouse. But this was no schoolboy jape. Once police had cleared the auditorium Storm-troopers proceeded to attack "'dirty Jews'" outside.[51] For several more days the cinema became a focus for riotous demonstrations. Then the censor banned the film as being injurious to German prestige. Though approved by Hindenburg himself, this was a cowardly retreat in the face of vicious intimidation. It boded ill for the Weimar Republic.

Actually in this episode Goebbels did not have the last laugh. An anonymous contributor sent a short story about trench warfare to *Der Angriff* (now a daily paper) and after publication it was revealed to be a section of *All Quiet.* There was much ribaldry about the deception and Goebbels, for a wonder, was left speechless. But the Nazis kept up the attack. Hitler's old captain, Ernst Röhm, reorganised the brown-shirted Stormtroopers. In 1931, recruiting largely from the ranks of the unemployed, he increased the size of this force from 100,000 to 300,000. It became less of a "robber band" such as Goebbels had fostered and more of a paramilitary cadre, dealing out brutality in a more systematic fashion while retaining a degree of respect from the regular army. Hindenburg and Schleicher, for example, discouraged Brüning from suppressing the SA, fearing a civil war. Brüning attempted to regain his freedom of action abroad, not least by mooting a customs union with Austria. But the French, suspecting that this presaged a political confederation, made Austria's withdrawal a condition of providing funds in the wake of the Creditanstalt Bank's failure in May 1931. This financial arm-twisting was a serious humiliation for Brüning, and Hoover's moratorium on war debts was no compensation. For almost immediately after its announcement, undermined by the collapse of one of Germany's largest textile manufacturers, the great Darmstadt and National Bank closed its doors. This provoked a general run on the banks and a massive capital outflow from Germany. Business was virtually paralysed and the country teetered on the edge of bankruptcy. The Chancellor did his best to stem the panic, arranging bank holidays, closing the stock exchange and tightening Germany's belt. But the new financial crisis magnified old terrors. The spectre of 1923 had risen. Returning to Berlin in mid-July 1931 the British Ambassador was struck by the "unnatural silence hanging over the city, and particularly by an atmosphere of extreme tension similar in many respects to that which I observed in Berlin in the critical days immediately preceding the war." The difference was that Germans were now overcome by "an almost oriental lethargy and fatalism." It was attributable to renewed "fear of inflation."[52]

Introspection was a key feature of the Depression in its first phase: each country concentrated on its own woes and thought itself worst affected. So Brüning received no help from the foreign governments he assiduously

courted, with the temporary exception of America. He failed to get reparations cancelled permanently or to obtain equality of armaments as
stipulated at Versailles. Moreover, like Herbert Hoover, he became the
scapegoat for the disaster at home. Booed and vituperated as "the Hunger
Chancellor," he seemed to be administering hardship rather than alleviat-
ing it. His only solution was further austerity, which was like recommending thrift to the destitute. He freely admitted that the coming winter, with
over five million people out of work, would be the worst in a hundred
years. The Nazis took full advantage of such candour. Goebbels trumpeted that the workless, given stones instead of bread, had "fallen prey
to the blackest despair."⁵³ Röhm stepped up violence in the streets, often
with fatal consequences. Hitler rallied the faithful and contemptuously
exploited his allies on the Right. Using Mussolini's tactics, he strove to
bluff, bully and bluster his way into power. He threatened a coup but
promised to act legally. At his first meeting with Hindenburg in October
1931 Hitler made a deplorable impression. He was in an overwrought state
anyway because his niece Geli Raubal had recently committed suicide, an
event which perhaps caused him to become a complete vegetarian (apart
from occasional liver dumplings) because he felt that eating meat was "like
eating a corpse."⁵⁴ Furthermore Hindenburg, whom he despised as a cautious, orthodox bourgeois, bore a striking resemblance to Hitler's father,
who had beaten the young Adolf. So, nervous but emphatic, Hitler apparently subjected the Old Gentleman to a characteristic harangue. The victor of Tannenberg declared that he did not want to see the "Bohemian
corporal" again.

The President was increasingly given to "mental blackouts."⁵⁵ Even his
memories of Tannenberg itself had grown dim, though he could still recall
the happy days of the Franco-Prussian war. Yet this monstrous shell of a
man stood between Hitler and supreme power. Thus Hindenburg became
the focus for private intrigue and public challenge. Hitler finally seized
the prize through backstairs manoeuvring, but only after fighting no fewer
than five elections in the course of 1932: two for the presidency, against
Hindenburg himself, in March and April; another in April for state parlia-
ments; and two for the Reichstag, in July and November. They were
bitterly contested against a background of acute Depression. Industrial
production had fallen to about 60 per cent of 1929 levels and profits had
almost halved. Food prices were high, thanks largely to Hindenburg's
efforts to protect other large landowners. Yet peasants, burdened by debts
and taxes, got low prices for their produce. Real wages had fallen, often to
below the legal minimum. According to official statistics, just over six million people were unemployed at peak periods; but by the end of 1932 the

true figure was closer to nine million, about a third of the workforce. The dole of around 16 marks a week was barely enough to keep body and soul together, yet some 20 million Germans relied on it and more than a million had no support at all. The nation was scourged by hunger, fear, hopelessness, misery and violence. Once again Christopher Isherwood conjures up the prevailing atmosphere most vividly. Berlin was in a "state of civil war."

> Hate exploded suddenly, without warning, out of nowhere; at street corners, in restaurants, cinemas, dance halls, swimming-baths; at midnight, after breakfast, in the middle of the afternoon. Knives were whipped out, blows dealt with spiked rings, beer-mugs, chair legs or leaded clubs; bullets slashed the advertisements on the poster-columns, rebounded off the iron roofs of latrines. In the middle of a crowded street a young man would be attacked, stripped, thrashed and left bleeding on the pavement; in fifteen seconds it was all over and the assailants had disappeared.[56]

After his dramatic announcement at the Berlin Sportpalast in February 1932 that Hitler would be a candidate for the presidency, Goebbels did his best to import the tactics of the street brawl into the Reichstag. The malign little revolutionary infuriated the assembly by associating Hindenburg with the betrayal at the end of the war and with the "party of deserters." White with rage, a Social Democrat who had lost an arm in the trenches told Goebbels that he had achieved the total mobilisation of human stupidity and "appealed to the brute beast in man."[57] Scenes of bedlam followed, culminating in a Nazi attempt to howl down Brüning. The British Ambassador, an eyewitness, said that when Goebbels and his henchmen advanced to the rostrum shaking their fists at the Chancellor he was reminded of an episode at the Chinese parliament in Peking before the war when the Speaker had had to escape through the back door. But this was just the prelude to a campaign organised by Goebbels which was, as he had hoped, "a masterpiece . . . of propaganda."[58]

On a scale never before seen, he deployed the arts of mass suggestion—posters, gramophone records, films, leaflets (some flung from aeroplanes), and advertisements revealing that Hindenburg was the candidate of the Jews. The very fact that the Nazis were denied access to the wireless gave their electoral activities an energy lacking in those of Hindenburg. Every city, town, village and hamlet was canvassed in a political campaign so violent that it seemed a continuation of war by other means. Brüning resisted, speaking energetically on Hindenburg's behalf, but the President himself did little except allow himself to be filmed taking the salute at a march-past of goose-stepping troops. He was, an American journalist reported, "a veritable mountain of a man in General's pink and gray, whose black and gold spiked helmet towered a full head above the tall and slimmer figures of his gray green-clad staff." [59] In his old trench coat Hitler looked less impressive. But he was a whirlwind, fanning the basest passions and the highest hopes of audiences in a *tour de force* of mob oratory. Goebbels, ever playing the prophet to his god, extolled the flaming new faith which had been born out of Stygian despair: "Millions and millions of National Socialists have discovered in the movement a new point and purpose to their lives . . . This is the work of Adolf Hitler. The masses see in him their last hope, and his name has become for millions the shining symbol of Germany's will to freedom." [60]

At the poll 11.3 million votes were cast for Hitler, compared to 18.6 million for Hindenburg (and nearly 5 million for Ernst Thälmann, the Communist candidate). The President just failed to win an outright majority so there had to be a second ballot the following month, in April 1932. Knowing that his party could not afford to stand still, Hitler renewed the contest with none of his initial hesitation. And Goebbels developed a novel electioneering technique—flying the Führer around the country from one rally to another. "Hitler over Germany" he called it, relishing the slogan's ambiguity. Goebbels also delighted in the aerial experience, though the plane was little more than a winged margarine box. He noted that the Führer alone needed no oxygen to sustain himself at 6,000 metres and found that, when shared with Hitler, the heights were "serene and luminous." [61] According to Sefton Delmer, the *Daily Express* reporter who managed to insinuate himself into Hitler's entourage, the Führer was dull and morose during these flights. But then a transfiguration would occur. Arriving late and at night to enhance the dramatic effect, the noisy, flimsy aircraft would descend in darkness and sometimes storm, its lights blinking, as though Hitler were "the incarnation of Siegfried the Light-God." Hitler was galvanised by the ardour of his followers and a new glitter came into his eyes. It was, Delmer reckoned, the *"leutseliges Leuchten,"* the "gracious shining" attributed to the Hohenzollern kings, or "the light in the eyes of a Messiah predestined to lead Germany to its place in the sun." [62] Goebbels called Hitler's rallies "the divine services of our political movement." [63]

Despite these religious exercises Hindenburg won the year's second presidential election easily, with 19.4 million votes to Hitler's 13.4 million. And when, amid rumours of imminent civil war, Brüning banned the SA, confiscating their weapons and expelling them from their premises (often beer halls, which could be hired cheaply during the Depression), it looked as though National Socialism had suffered a serious check. But in various state elections the Nazis fought back bitterly, gaining 36 per cent of the total vote and increasing their representation in the important Prussian Diet from 6 seats to 162. After this victory, Brüning's government began to crumble.

GENERAL von Schleicher, head of the army's political bureau, confidant of the President and close friend of Hindenburg's boorish son Oskar, had become convinced that some accommodation would have to be reached with a party attracting so much popular support. Tall, fleshy, pallid, sharp-eyed and shaven-headed, Schleicher regarded himself as a soldier-statesman without equal. He had, indeed, many qualifications for the role—charm, wit, intelligence and self-confidence. Cynical of mind and caustic of tongue, he convinced himself and others that he was a strong man. Schleicher—the name means "crawler" in German—also possessed a serpentine capacity for intrigue. Employing it unscrupulously, he discredited Brüning, who, in a last desperate effort to combat the Depression, had proposed settling ten per cent of the unemployed on bankrupt estates in east Germany. Hindenburg was still smarting from the indignities he had suffered during the elections, for which he blamed Brüning as much as Hitler, and he lent an ear to fellow Junkers who damned this project as agrarian Bolshevism. He also heeded Schleicher, who stated that the army had lost confidence in the Chancellor. So, at the end of May 1932, Brüning resigned. Schleicher then showed his lack of that indispensable political attribute—judgement. And the Weimar Republic began to move quickly down the slippery slope to self-destruction.

Schleicher chose as Brüning's successor a man hopelessly unqualified for the post. Franz von Papen was an aristocrat at a time of populist excess, a rich man in the midst of economic travail and a dilettante confronted by the might of nascent Nazism. Not that Schleicher selected him for his brains: when someone remarked that Papen had no head for administration the General replied, "He doesn't need a head, his job is to be a hat."[64] However, being so obviously ineffectual as Chancellor, Papen discredited both his patron and the State. He was vain, shallow, amusing, ambitious and incompetent. As the French Ambassador memorably remarked, "Papen enjoyed the peculiarity of being taken seriously by neither his friends nor his enemies."[65] With his uhlan's dash, his polished manner and his equine face, which was bisected by a thin pencil moustache, Papen had distinguished himself more on the hunting field, in the salon and the boudoir than in the political sphere. He had been expelled from the United States in 1916 for using his position as Military Attaché to organise acts of sabotage and had carelessly revealed the names of his accomplices.

Although he later managed to ingratiate himself with Hindenburg, who regarded him as in every sense a nobleman, Papen had not otherwise excelled; and as a speaker in the Prussian Diet he gave "the impression of a little man standing on tiptoe."[66] Reactions to his appointment ranged from angry incredulity to raucous hilarity. Papen was, in Count Kessler's words, "A character from Alice in Wonderland."[67]

This impression was compounded by Papen's nonchalantly-chosen, right-wing "Barons' Cabinet" and by an initial pronouncement which attributed the Depression to the socialisation of German industry and blamed the welfare state for rotting the moral fibre of the nation. With such a studied insult to Germany's millions of unemployed it seemed almost as though Papen were trying to fulfil a prophecy he had earlier made to a French friend: "Aprés Brüning le chaos."[68] Chaos was made more certain by a deal that had been struck with Hitler, who gave vague assurances that he would tolerate Papen's government in return for definite promises that it would lift the ban on the SA and dissolve the Reichstag. So the summer of 1932 was dominated by a general election campaign which reached a new pitch of violence. There were constant provocations, skirmishes and assaults. Murder and arson became commonplace. The streets were torn by bombings and shootings. One witness described the organised terror of the Nazis as "a continuous St. Bartholomew's Massacre, day after day."[69] Even at peace the capital was filled with an air of menace:

> the party flag was everywhere in evidence. Huge posters, pictorial homilies, and Nazi slogans screamed from windows and kiosks, blazoning forth messages about honour and duty, national solidarity and social justice, bread, liberty and the beauty of sacrifice—all proclaiming the consummate skill with which Hitler had been leavening the masses. Passers-by wore tiny lapel emblems; uniformed men elbowed their way through the crowds, the swastika circling their brawny arms. On every news-stand the *Beobachter* and *Angriff* were piled high.[70]

With dandified vigour Papen strove to assert himself. At the International Conference on Reparations at Lausanne he reaped what Brüning had sown and got German war debts reduced to a final payment (never made) of three billion marks. In the eyes of his fellow statesmen Papen had the inestimable advantage of not being Hitler, and they were anxious to sustain him. But looking across the conference table at Papen, Edouard Herriot whispered to Lord Simon: "The more I study the face of a German cavalry officer, the more I admire—his horse."[71] The Nazis decried Papen's success at Lausanne as a further shameful acknowledgement of war guilt. Nor were they outwardly grateful for his suppression of their most steadfast enemy, the left-wing government of Prussia, though privately Hitler acknowledged that the Chancellor had established a dictatorship there—which got people used to the idea. But this was a convenient accident. Hitler despised Papen to the depths of his soul, ranking him with Brüning as a coward and a poltroon: "They underestimate me because I have risen from below, from the 'lower depths,' because I haven't had an education, because I haven't the 'manners' that their sparrow brains think right."[72]

In addition to hammering away at familiar themes like national revival and the Red Menace, Hitler exploited voters' fears that the Depression was becoming ever bleaker. Despising professional economists—"Where are your storm troops?"[73] he once asked, anticipating Stalin's question about the Pope's divisions—Hitler made claims that only he could put Germany back to work. They were easy enough to ridicule, especially as they were combined with promises that in the Third Reich every German girl would find a husband. Scoffers said that "Hitler was planning to give employment in straightening the Crooked Lake, painting the Black Forest white, and putting down linoleum in the Polish corridor."[74] Yet partly because Goebbels was raising propaganda to the level of a "political art"[75] and partly because Hitler struck a real chord in the traumatised psyche of the German people, the Nazis more than doubled their Reichstag representation. When the votes were counted at the end of July 1932 they had won 230 seats out of a total of 608.

Hitler thought that his hour had come. But when the SA once again seemed to threaten a coup, the government decreed that political terrorism would be punishable by death. What is more, Papen and Schleicher would only offer Hitler the vice-chancellorship, even when he subjected them to one of his famous rages "whereby the vein on his forehead from the top of his nose to his hairline swelled and grew blue in the most terrifying way."[76] At a subsequent meeting with Hindenburg this exclusion was confirmed. Standing with the aid of his cane and not offering Hitler a seat, the President brusquely dismissed the Führer's pretensions. He angrily protested about the excesses of the SA and refused to let Hitler attain the position that Mussolini had held after the "March on Rome." The Field Marshal reprimanded the Corporal to his face and expressed contempt for him afterwards, remarking to his secretary: "That man for Chancellor? I'll make him a postmaster and he can lick the stamps with my head on them."[77] Hindenburg also moved with unaccustomed speed to make public his version of the interview, for once catching Goebbels off guard. Despite this humiliation Hitler, who had spent hours pacing up and down at Goebbels' home outside Berlin and had finally been obliged to calm his nerves with music, resisted the temptation to try to take power by force. He did spurn legality, it is true, in an effort to maintain the Nazis' revolutionary afflatus. He publicly declared that five Stormtroopers, who had been condemned to death for brutally murdering a Communist labourer in his own home, were national heroes. And when the Reichstag met in September 1932 Göring, its president, ostentatiously averted his gaze from the frantic Papen, who was brandishing a dissolution order in its familiar red portfolio, in order to pass a huge vote of no confidence in the government.

However, this farcical episode merely made another election inevitable. Papen hoped to wear the Nazis down and he was not altogether disappointed. This was due partly to their depleted treasury and partly to exhaustion. So desperate was the financial situation that Stormtroopers were sent on to the streets with collecting boxes and at one moment the party's whole future seemed to depend on raising a loan of 2,000 marks from its own Press Officer, Otto Dietrich. Hitler and Goebbels campaigned until they dropped. And to keep up the party's momentum the Führer ordered its members to vie with the Communists in supporting a transport strike in Berlin. The strike was the culmination of many bloody industrial disorders resulting from the government's strict policy of holding down wages and benefits. Now strikers let loose new terror against strike-breakers. Stormtroopers dug up tram rails and smashed streetcars. The capital came to a standstill and Goebbels described Berlin as a city of the dead. Yet, he continued, the streets were "crowded with people. They move in grey masses through the thoroughfares. An indescribable state of apprehension is everywhere apparent. The wildest rumours are spreading." In fact, the whole country was in such a state of "mental anarchy" that unless a strong hand intervened the result would be "absolute chaos."[78] The wish was naturally father to the thought. But when Germany went to the polls for the general election of 6 November 1932 the Nazis lost over two million votes, which reduced their representation in the Reichstag from 230 seats to 196.

Nevertheless, despite Communist gains, the Nazis were still the largest party. And when it became clear that Papen could not obtain their cooperation to form a parliamentary majority he was obliged to resign. Complex negotiations followed in which Hitler insisted on receiving full powers as Chancellor. His way was blocked by Hindenburg, privately pilloried by Hitler as "that feeble-minded old bull, that senile dodo, that . . . old cab-horse."[79] The resolution to this impasse was achieved by the "Field-Grey Eminence," General von Schleicher, who slid furtively from the shadows. Fearing civil strife from the Communists and hoping to split the Nazis, he manoeuvred himself into the chancellorship. Hindenburg, though bitter at losing the congenial Papen, bowed to what seemed military necessity. But Schleicher proved too clever by half. His attempt to drive a wedge between Hitler and Gregor Strasser, who represented the stunted "socialist" element in National Socialism, backfired disastrously. Strasser not only refused Papen's offer of the vice-chancellorship but, when Hitler accused him of treachery, resigned his position in the Nazi party.

For a moment the Nazis, impoverished, demoralised and divided, appeared to be on the point of disintegration. Hitler's nerves were stretched taut: for hours he paced up and down his room at the Kaiserhof Hotel (strategically situated opposite the Chancellery) pausing only to exclaim, "If the Party once falls to pieces, I shall shoot myself without more ado."[80] But intimations of its demise were premature. Strasser's departure made it more respectable in the eyes of conservative industrialists, who had previously discerned frightful similarities between Nazism and Bolshevism. They now saved the party from bankruptcy, their mood involuntarily encouraged by Schleicher. He alienated the business community by controlling prices and maintaining wages in a despairing effort to mitigate the effects of the Depression. He also revived Brüning's plan of land settlement in the east, further offending Hindenburg and the Junkers, who wondered whether they had a "Red General" in their midst. But it was the hapless Papen who finally brought down Schleicher. On 4 January 1933 he secretly met Hitler in Cologne, initiating an intrigue which was to bear the most bitter fruit in history.

While the Nazis concentrated all their resources on propaganda, winning a massive electoral victory in the tiny state of Lippe and staging a huge demonstration in front of the Communist headquarters in Berlin, Papen poured poison into the ears of Hindenburg. So when Schleicher asked for a dissolution of the Reichstag—he, like Papen, had failed to obtain a parliamentary majority—the President refused. Schleicher had no option but to resign. More negotiations followed. Hitler still insisted on the chancellorship but agreed that Papen should be his deputy and that only three of the eleven cabinet posts should go to Nazis. Eventually Hindenburg capitulated. Papen, like so many others, was confident that he could civilise Hitler, whose barbaric utterances seemed a mark of his political gaucherie. Hindenburg was tired of responsibility and perhaps moved by Nazi threats to reveal details of tax evasion on his Neudeck estate. So Hitler came to power thanks to the chicanery of a political fop and the weakness of an old soldier, human frailties which proved fatal to a sick republic mortally wounded by the Depression.

After hours of tortured waiting, Nazi leaders at the Kaiserhof Hotel spied Hitler emerging from the Reich Chancellery. He had been sworn in at about noon on 30 January 1933 and Goebbels, greeting his exultant leader, was for once "dumb with emotion." "The day passes like a dream," he wrote. "Everything is like a fairy tale."[81] That evening tens of thousands of brown-shirted Stormtroopers massed in the Tiergarten, tramped under the Brandenburg Gate and turned into "the promised land of Unter den Linden and the Wilhelmstrasse, marching with the triumphant, ecstatic air of soldiers taking possession of a long-beleaguered city."[82] They surged onwards in a flood of fire, torches held aloft, boots crashing on asphalt, voices raised as brass bands blared out the Horst Wessel song, "Fridericus Rex" and "Deutschland Über Alles." Onlookers added to the din, cheering wildly and shouting *"Heil Hitler"* and *"Heil, Heil, Sieg Heil!"* while boys who had climbed trees in the Wilhelmplatz yelled and whistled with ear-splitting shrillness. As the column goose-stepped past the old, grey Chancellor's Palace there was a subdued ovation for the President, dimly visible at a lighted window closed against the chill, clear night air. A towering figure, he kept nodding his head to the music and beating time with his cane. Many wondered what thoughts were running through that massive head and the story later went round Berlin that he had turned to his secretary with the words: "Ludendorff . . . how well your men are marching, and what a lot of prisoners they've taken!"[83]

When the procession reached the Chancellery balcony on which Hitler was standing, illuminated by a blaze of searchlights, there were frenzied outbursts of applause. Even Papen found this ominous:

> When I compared how these masses which viewed themselves as the representatives of a new era marched with restrained joy by Hindenburg, the symbol of the past, and how they saluted the Messiah of their hopes with the fervour of revolutionaries, I had the feeling of listening to a fanfare announcing a period of radical changes.[84]

Hitler had, indeed, promised such changes: a dictatorship would be established, heads would roll, Jews would be eliminated. The worst of these threats might be dismissed as the rhetoric of the hustings, but many observers were baffled by German enthusiasm for "a leader who tells them they are not fit to govern themselves."[85] However, the people were not cheering the eclipse of democracy so much as the re-kindled glow of national pride. In the words of Fritz Stern, "The eerie show of light and darkness was a signal of invincibility and a threat of intimidation . . . [marking] a rebirth of the German nation."[86] As capitalism faltered and Communism loured, the crowd was expressing its faith in fascism. Mussolini had shown the way and now Hitler would take up the torch. Millions of Germans believed that only this man, framed against the Chancellery window in a dazzling nimbus of light, could lead them out of the Depression. So he did. But Hitler's path of glory led to the grave, to the final catastrophe which had long haunted his mind, to the twilight of the gods. Soaked in the romance of Wagner, whose great opera cycle *Der Ring des Niebelungen* culminates in Wotan's burning Valhalla, Hitler seemed to relish the prospect of ending his days in an inferno of fire and blood. Shortly before becoming Chancellor he adumbrated that terrible conclusion: in defeat "we shall never capitulate—no, never . . . We may be destroyed, but if we are, we shall drag a world with us—a world in flames."[87] And he hummed a motif from *Götterdämmerung*.

VI

THE DUCE AND THE POPE

BEFORE Hitler became Chancellor he paid tribute to the ruthlessness of Mussolini's dictatorship by calling him a Prussian. The Duce would have appreciated the compliment, though in his earlier years he had reviled all things Germanic and nursed the ambition "to make Romans out of Italians."[1] But by the end of the 1920s, with his hold on power secure, Mussolini became intent on Prussianising Italy, changing its people from merry mandolin players into aggressive warriors. Discipline would be instilled, if necessary with a stick, though the Duce also toyed with more grandiose schemes. One such plan was to reafforest the Apennines in order to create a harsher climate which would transform "our good-for-nothing Italians, this mediocre race,"[2] into hardy Nordic Aryans. Like most of Mussolini's projects, this came to nothing. For Fascism was mainly a matter of fantasy. Dreaming up sensations and inventing headlines to dramatise them, Mussolini was as much the editor as the dictator of Italy. His totalitarianism was never total, though from the first many people, including Pope Pius XI, believed that his domineering spirit alone might "be able to regenerate Italy." The Supreme Pontiff, who had received the keys of St. Peter eight months before Mussolini's "March on Rome," prayed that such a shining luminary might "guide and enlighten humanity."[3]

His orisons must be seen in the light of papal history. Ever since 1870, when the Papal States had been unwillingly incorporated into a united kingdom of Italy, Popes had remained voluntary prisoners in the Vatican, immured behind its massive bronze gate and refusing to set foot on ground desecrated by the forces of Savoy. The loss of temporal dominion had been accompanied by an assertion of spiritual power: the successors of St. Peter declared themselves infallible when speaking *ex cathedra* on matters of faith and morals. They refused to reconcile themselves with the new state or to harmonise themselves "with progress, with liberalism and with modern civilization."[4] That diabolical trinity, anathematised in Pope Pius IX's *Syllabus of Errors,* clearly held little attraction for Mussolini. Here

was an important ground for sympathy between Fascism and Roman
Catholicism, but their similarities were already legion. Both were autoc-
racies ranged against Freemasonry, Communism and democracy. Both
relied on ceremonial and censorship, dogma and propaganda. Both opposed birth control and other modern fashions. Both exalted their own
martyrs and favoured the subordination of women. Like the Pope, the
Duce claimed infallibility. Many wearing black shirts and black soutanes
believed that a *rapprochement* between the two faiths might be as advantageous as the alliance familiar elsewhere between throne and altar. The Fascist State would receive a pontifical blessing in return for lending the
Church its secular arm. The Pope would re-enter the life of the nation and
reinvigorate its spirit. But though both sides felt the attraction of the
alliance, both knew that the claims of God and the claims of Caesar were
proverbially hard to reconcile. Now that the champions of Church and
State were competing tyrants the difficulties were compounded. Thus
the stage was set, against a backcloth of acute Depression, for a clash of
characters as well as creeds. Commenting on the conflict between Pope
and Duce, the German Ambassador wrote: "the real danger of a sudden
eruption lies not so much in the inflammable material, as in their ever-
increasing totalitarian and absolutist pretensions."[5]

Thanks to Vatican secrecy and Catholic hagiography, the personality
of Achille Ratti, Pope Pius XI, remains shrouded in obscurity. Short, stout
and sleek, with myopic eyes peering through gold-rimmed glasses, he
looked soft. Most of his career had been spent amid the dusty incunabula
of the Ambrosian Library in Milan, and in its prim precision his thin
nasal voice seemed that of a scholar. But like many middle-class Lom-
bards, he was a hard-headed man of business. His lonely hobby was
mountaineering, and at the age of 65 this obstinate Alpinist scaled the
throne of St. Peter. He had been a surprise choice and on his accession the
College of Cardinals was shocked by immediate revelations of his "dictatorial nature."[6] "After he became Pope there was only one word on every
tongue, *obbedire,* obey."[7] Pius rebuked one prince of the Church for giving
him unsolicited advice. His early encyclicals proclaimed the theocratic
authority of his office with a boldness which would have done credit to
Gregory VII or Innocent III. But his terminology was sometimes shock-
ingly modern: "if a totalitarian regime exists—totalitarian in fact and by
right—it is the regime of the church."[8] Austere yet emotional, daring yet
conservative, devious yet intransigent, charitable yet caustic, he asserted
his prerogatives with uncompromising vigour. Visitors were impressed by
his "tremendous force of character," and they noted the Pontiff's trick of
pulling his skullcap over his ear before some explosion of wrath.[9] When

the cardinals in a body endorsed his policy of reaching an accord with Mussolini, the Pope remarked: "Had they all been opposed I would have acted just the same."[10]

Meanwhile, to the disgust of many Fascists, Mussolini himself had ostentatiously sloughed off his earlier hostility to the Church. There seems little doubt that he was a heathen at heart. The son of a fiercely anticlerical blacksmith who named him after the Mexican foe of ecclesiastical privilege Benito Juarez, Mussolini was brought up in the Romagna, most seditious of the papal provinces. He had savagely rebelled against seminarian education. His first pamphlet was entitled "God does not exist" and he wrote a juvenile novel which had a lecherous cardinal as its hero. Priests he had described as "black microbes who are as fatal to mankind as tuberculosis germs."[11] He had scorned the Holy See and mocked God. Energetic blasphemy doubtless betrayed elemental superstition, something Mussolini seldom bothered to hide. In delinquent, vagabond youth he had worked for a time as a fortune teller and he was always quick to make signs against the evil eye. Hearing the news of Lord Carnarvon's sudden death in 1923, Mussolini ordered that his gift, an Egyptian mummy found in Tutankhamun's tomb, should at once be banished from the Chigi Palace. But if he set great store by luck, the Duce's approach to the Vatican was based on *Realpolitik*. The Catholic Church was not only a universal organisation, it was the most powerful force in Italian society—over 2 per cent of the 44 million population were in holy orders. Claiming a divine commission, the papacy was also a link with a glorious temporal past. It was, as Hobbes had said, the ghost of the Roman Empire sitting crowned upon its grave. To have the support of this venerable institution would be of inestimable benefit to the new order. It would make Fascism respectable. It would augment Italy's standing in the world. It would garb the nation in the seamless robe of totalitarianism. Mussolini would become Caesar.

So the Duce strove to ingratiate himself with the Holy See. Unlike Bolshevism, he declared, Fascism did not vainly endeavour to efface God from the soul of man. To prove it, he granted a series of boons to the church, making religious teaching compulsory in schools, restoring the crucifix to public buildings, raising clerical stipends, strengthening the laws against blasphemy, sustaining Vatican finances and suppressing freemasonry. There were smaller gestures too. The Duce donated the Chigi Palace library to the Vatican (he needed the space, it was said, for his big ideas); he gave free railway passes to cardinals; at Easter he sanctioned the ringing of the great bell on the Capitol, which had belonged to ancient Rome and had been silent since 1870. Cautiously the Pope reciprocated. In particular he grasped at the chance of saving Italy's soul even though it involved the sacrifice of his own parliamentary allies. Putting his trust in Catholic Action, a non-political organisation for reforming society, he fatally undermined the Catholic Popular Party. Thus he helped Mussolini to establish his dictatorship. When Fascist thugs murdered the Socialist deputy Matteotti, Pius XI refused to see his wife or mother and the Vatican's organ *L'Osservatore Romano* continued to sustain Fascism. So did Father Rosa's Jesuit journal, *Civiltà Cattolica*. When Mussolini himself was nearly assassinated in 1926 the Pope said that the Duce's peril was also the country's, attributed his delivery to "the almost visible intervention of Divine Providence" and joined in "the veritable hurricane of jubilation, rejoicing and thanksgiving" which greeted his "miraculous preservation."[12]

Tension still existed between Church and State, both of which, despite their hierarchical structure, were riven by internal factions. Sometimes Fascists violently attacked bodies like Catholic Action, and there was constant rivalry over who would control the citizens of the future. Often bitterness overflowed into minor issues, such as the new method of dating which replaced BC and AD with EF *(Era Fascista)*. In one dispute the Vatican objected to an indecorous public display by girls of the Fascist youth organisation *Balilla,* who paraded through Rome clad in gym slips and armed with rifles; eventually a compromise was reached whereby the girls carried bows and arrows. On larger matters the antagonists also sought grounds for compromise and for three years negotiations proceeded to find a comprehensive settlement to the "Roman Question," the problem of reconciling the papacy and Italy. By the beginning of 1929 all obstacles had been overcome. But the Pope almost baulked at the last moment, complaining hysterically that he was being rushed into an agreement which should be signed by his successor. "No, no, Your Holiness!" insisted his wily negotiator, Francesco Pacelli (brother of the future Pius XII): "Now or never!"[13]

So, shortly before noon on 11 February 1929, Mussolini, smart in top hat and morning suit, met Pius XI's Secretary of State Pietro Gasparri, a study in scarlet cape and gloves with gold tassels dangling from his red Cardinal's hat. The historic venue, from which the Concordat they signed took its name, was the Lateran Palace. Home of the Popes for a thousand years, it stood on land supposedly given to the Bishop of Rome by the Emperor Constantine. The current representatives of Church and State repaired to the Hall of Missions, a colossal, echoing chamber with gilded ceiling, marble floor, elaborately frescoed walls and five great windows overlooking the Piazza San Giovanni. Close to the spot where Leo III had greeted Charlemagne, they sat on ornate Chinese chairs at a vast, oblong Philippine table, gifts to the Holy See from Catholics abroad. Gasparri, who had been involved with the Lateran Pacts from their inception, acted as host. Sprung from Tuscan peasant stock, he was a cunning conservative. The Vatican did not like revolutions, he once remarked; it had too many windows on the street. Squat and ugly, Gasparri imperfectly concealed his cynicism behind a veneer of geniality and untidiness—his scarlet skullcap was invariably askew and traces of food and snuff marred his purple robe. On one occasion, charged with lying, he said that he was only following hallowed diplomatic practice, and in any case the Pope would forgive him. The Cardinal signed first and handed over the heavy gold pen to the Duce. It was a papal present to Mussolini, who appended his own signature. After photographs and handshakes, the delegates drove off through an expectant crowd in the pouring rain to the competing strains of the Te Deum and the Fascist cry, invented by D'Annunzio, *"Eia, Eia, Alalà!"* According to one story, presumably *ben trovato,* on his way back to the Vatican Gasparri saw two men fighting in the street and commented, "Oh, no doubt they have signed a concordat."[14]

Meanwhile, in the Vatican the Pope himself was addressing priests who would soon be conducting Lenten services. After suggesting the kind of topics on which they might preach, including the indecency of contemporary fashions and the excesses of "that movement which is called by the non-Italian name of 'sport,'" he announced that the Pacts were at that very moment being signed "over in Our palace of the Lateran." Perhaps the agreement would not satisfy everyone, Pius continued, "a thing which even God Almighty does not often succeed in doing."[15] But His Vicegerent on earth would be unmoved by criticism. The Pope was moved, however, by the access of enthusiasm which greeted the Concordat. In a trice the streets of Rome were decorated with yellow and white papal flags, often flying from windows beside the green, white and red tricolor of Italy.

The following day a huge congregation filled St. Peter's, and the square outside was a sea of black umbrellas as 200,000 people gathered in the rain. A fanfare of silver trumpets heralded the Pope's arrival in the basilica, which provoked "extraordinary scenes of popular devotion." He was preceded down the nave by white-haired cardinals in scarlet robes and ermine capes. Then followed Swiss Guards carrying enormous serpentine swords and wearing the red, black and yellow uniforms designed by Michelangelo, and Noble Guards in Elizabethan ruffs with rapiers in their belts. Two *flabelli* (semi-circular white ostrich feather fans) cleared the air in front of the Pope's *sedia gestatoria*. Borne aloft, he wore the triple crown and a full white silk cloak beautifully embroidered in gold. He raised his hand, its green fisherman's ring glinting in the light from thousands of candles, to bless the dark-garbed worshippers. Some fell to their knees, others waved handkerchiefs, many shouted *"Evviva il Pappa Ré"* (Long live the Pope of Conciliation). Amid "wild applause and frantic cheering" the procession traversed the length of the church. The Pope took his seat on a canopied throne of white and red damask to the left of the altar. The cardinals filed by and kissed his ring in fealty. During the Mass "hidden electric lights played upon him, throwing him into bold relief—the cynosure of all eyes."[16] After the service similar scenes took place in St. Peter's Square. In response to the chanting of the crowd the Pope appeared at the balcony over the main entrance to the basilica. As he gave his silent benediction the people moved in unison like some vast, primeval beast: umbrellas came down, hats were doffed and all knelt together on the wet pavé. Pius wept.

Jubilation was also manifested outside the royal palace and the little King Victor Emmanuel III, adamantine anticlerical though he was, emerged to greet the throng. Only Mussolini refused to show himself. Eventually the crowds dispersed, many people strolling through the illuminated streets now that the rain had ceased, or admiring the façade of St. Peter's which was lit up with torches. Abroad there was almost universal praise for a settlement reached by the "genius and statesmanship of the Vatican and of the Palazzo Chigi."[17] At home *L'Osservatore Romano* spoke for the rejoicing citizens when it hailed Mussolini as the "man whom Providence has sent Us." He was a man who, like Pius himself, did not believe in the "villainous fetishes of liberalism." Thanks to the Duce, concluded the papal paper, "Italy has been given back to God and God to Italy."[18]

Mussolini had certainly made large concessions. The Vatican, all 109 acres of palaces, churches, treasure houses, courts and gardens, became a sovereign state. The Pope received an indemnity of 1,750 million lire to compensate for the loss of his former territories. Roman Catholicism was declared the official religion, with a major part to play in educational and matrimonial affairs. Catholic Action, which Pius XI called "the apple of Our eye," was allowed to continue in a restricted form.[19] The Pope also gained many less important advantages, such as control of the Catacombs, assistance with radio transmissions, a state-built railway station inside the Vatican City and the outlawing of improper behaviour like dancing during Lent. Nevertheless, shrewd observers considered that Mussolini had got the better of the bargain and that the Church had seriously compromised itself by treating with him. The sometime French Premier Edouard Herriot said that the papacy had united itself to "a regime which has destroyed the constitutional liberties of a great nation."[20] Now wedded to a policy of coming to terms with earthly powers, the Pope professed himself willing to make a pact with the devil if he could thereby advance the cause of religion. But some Catholics feared that he really was endorsing, in the Fascists, the powers of darkness. A member of the "black" Roman nobility, diehards who had always refused reconciliation with the house of Savoy, whispered: "It is a pity that we are no longer in the Middle Ages, when we could have administered a little poison to this Pope."[21] One punster had the Pope introducing himself to Mussolini with the words, *"Pio Undecisimo,"* to which the Duce replied, *"Pio tutti"* (I take everything).[22]

Mussolini took what mattered to him—prestige and power. He had succeeded where Cavour had failed and he revelled in the international acclaim, savouring this triumph above all others until his dying day. It added to his pleasure when anti-Fascist Catholics likened him to Napoleon, who had also arranged a concordat with the Holy See to cement his despotism. Mussolini's dictatorship was set in concrete by the election held in March 1929, the month after he had signed the Lateran Pacts. The Church endorsed him and for the first time many Catholics voted for Fascists with a clear conscience. Catholic Action, intent on having the Concordat ratified by parliament, instructed its members to support Mussolini. Priests often led their flocks to the polling booths. Admittedly the election was little more than a cynical charade—on a par with the Duce's becoming President of the National Anti-Blasphemy League. Mussolini selected the candidates and voters could merely signify "yes" or "no" to the entire list on ballot papers of different colours which had to be placed in transparent urns. Coercion, under these circumstances, was almost superfluous and it was scarcely surprising that over 98 per cent of the nearly nine million voters endorsed Mussolini's slate. The Duce had memorably described liberty as a putrefying corpse and opponents of his regime now lamented that in Italy the Pope had nailed down the lid on its coffin. Mussolini liked the metaphor and in May 1929 he essayed a bold variation on it. Appeasing anticlericals among his own followers, he brusquely asserted the sovereignty of the Fascist State as against a Catholicism which, had it not grown up in Rome, might have remained an obscure Middle Eastern sect like the Essenes. "We have not revived the temporal power of the Popes," he told parliament. "We have left them with as much territory as would suffice for them to bury its corpse."[23]

Shocked and outraged, the Pontiff declared that Mussolini had betrayed him. He issued a stern public rebuke, condemning the Duce's religious observations as heretical and setting forth the Church's claims to superiority over the State. The quarrel, ominous for the future, was patched up so that the Concordat could be ratified. But during debates on it in the

Senate both parties were subjected to a devastating attack by Italy's most famous philosopher, Benedetto Croce. Once a defender of Fascism, he now dismissed the Duce as an adventurer who "nourishes himself on the applause of the crowd," a petty tyrant with a diseased brain and feet of clay. By making a pact with such a leader the Pope proved himself to be "narrowly reactionary and definitely anti-proletarian." Democracy, Croce continued, was for Pius XI "a diabolic masonic creation." The Pope had "discovered in Mussolini a pillar of the hierarchic principle in the state, a divine instrument called upon to impose the dogmatic doctrine of absolute sovereignty on a people led astray by the nefarious liberal revolution."[24]

Croce's criticisms hit the mark. Of course the Church is always mired in the world, and despite everything Pius XI did his best to keep it clean. For example, he repudiated Cardinal Schuster's statement that, "From the very beginning, Catholic Italy and even the Pope himself have blessed Fascism."[25] Moreover, he continued to assert, always forcefully and sometimes successfully, the prerogatives of the Church against the State. But by negotiating something that looked like an unholy alliance with a dictator on his doorstep the Pontiff undermined the moral authority of his office. Like some Borgia of yore he seemed to endorse a *condottiere* who openly proclaimed violence to be a virtue and practised what he preached. The Pope gave the impression that the Catholic Church in Italy was the Fascist party at prayer; and he implied that the citizen, like the worshipper, might best do his duty on his knees. Catholicism was the State religion and Fascism was the ordained polity; certainly many Italians, with the fervent encouragement of the priesthood, regarded them as two sides of the same coin. To paraphrase the young John Henry Newman: if the Pope himself was not a Fascist he had the misfortune to resemble one.

In the context of his time, it may be argued, Pius was bound to side with Fascism against Bolshevism. Zealots of the Red faith not only persecuted Christians and turned churches into anti-God museums, they threatened to subvert the world. But it became increasingly plain, especially when cardinals hailed Mussolini's war in Ethiopia as a "Catholic Crusade,"[26] that the Vatican was merely associating with one form of murderous totalitarianism rather than another. This had grievous consequences, as Pius eventually came to realise. In Italy the Church seemed to lose its independence. It appeared to be little more than a colourful adjunct to the circuses—military parades, free football matches, firework displays and so on—which were supposed to compensate for a dearth of bread. In the eyes of many foreigners the earthly mirror of the heavenly light grew dim. As the economic crisis struck, more and more people sought secular salvation in the gospel according to Karl Marx. They converted to Communism, feeling that nothing less than a revolutionary creed could cope with a problem that threatened to engulf the globe. After all, the Pope himself declared the Depression to be "the worst calamity that has befallen man since the Flood."[27]

MUSSOLINI's antediluvian economic policies made matters worse for Italy. Like Winston Churchill, the Duce tended to see economics as another form of national strife. But despite fanfaronades of propaganda and a plethora of "faked statistics,"[28] those with eyes could see that his belligerence sapped the nation's strength. In 1925, insisting that Italy should be self-sufficient in food, Mussolini had announced "the Battle for Grain." But by erecting tariff barriers against cheaper foreign cereals he subsidised inefficient Italian agriculture, which entered a decade of decline. Because fodder became so costly he also diminished the number of livestock and debased the diet of the people. In 1926 the Duce had fought "the Battle of the Lira," swearing that he would defend it against inflation to his dying breath, to the last drop of blood in his body. Again like Churchill, who had just returned Britain to the gold standard, Mussolini over-valued the currency (at 90 lire to the pound) for reasons of national prestige. This made Italian exports more expensive, damaged industry, forced down wages and increased unemployment. Yet the dictator managed to prevent inflation, as Keynes thought he could not, thanks to the economic efficacy of "a good dose of castor oil."[29]

In the same year as "the Battle of the Lira" Mussolini had established his "Corporate State." It aspired to fuse capital and labour into a single body whose head was the Duce. Combining private enterprise with public duty, this organism would regulate the economy and society in a way that was neither capitalist nor Communist but Fascist. But although the corporate state neutralised trade unions, diminished strikes and fostered large cartels, it increased bureaucracy at the expense of efficiency. Trivial regulations proliferated: for example, parents were forbidden to have their children christened with names such as Cavour, "which sound as an offence to the present institutions."[30] Little was achieved by the corporate state. It was always rhetoric rather than reality, a largely successful attempt to convince the public that the naked dictator had donned a new suit of clothes. In fact Italy had failed to share significantly in the prosperity of the 1920s and its economy was depressed even before the advent of the Great Depression.

By 1929 Italy's annual income, at 400 billion lire, was less than a quarter of Britain's. Its wages were among the lowest in Europe—if, on a relative index of average income per head, Britain was 100, Germany was 73 and Italy only 39. (The United States, by contrast, was 190.) Industrial workers, earning around 25 lire a day, barely got by, while agricultural labourers (about half the population) sometimes lived at subsistence levels. In Sardinia and Calabria, as Mussolini himself acknowledged, there were towns where the inhabitants survived for months by eating wild plants. Intent on increasing the population ("the Battle for Babies"), Mussolini forbade emigration; but a tide of internal migrants swelled the slums around cities such as Naples, Rome and Turin. Later Mussolini tried to blame the state of the Italian economy on the Wall Street Crash, which "exploded unexpectedly like a bomb" leaving the world as much aghast as it had been "at the announcement of the death of Napoleon." American prosperity had been the subject of envy and amazement in Europe, he said. And in the days that followed Black Thursday Italy was driven back on to the "high seas."[31]

However, this piece of special pleading could not hide the fact that Italy was already low in the water and peculiarly vulnerable to the rising waves. Between 1929 and 1933 industrial production fell by more than a quarter and throughout the 1930s Italy's rate of growth was lower than that of almost all other European countries. Industrial wages also declined by 25 per cent. And some farm workers lost about half their incomes as the price of raw materials tumbled—wheat by a third, wine by almost two-thirds. The number of unemployed rose from about 300,000 to well over a million. There were some rickety social welfare provisions but a daily dole of 3.75 lire scarcely kept starvation at bay. In Trieste women kept alive by eating pigeons which their children killed with stones. Peasants in Lucania lived almost exclusively on bread, sometimes spiced with raw tomato, red pepper, garlic or olive oil. When it was shown that even the average adult diet delivered 200 calories fewer than the nutritionists' recommended daily intake, Fascist economists took to harping on the nourishing qualities of polenta. "Fortunately," Mussolini blustered, "the Italian people are not yet accustomed to eat several times per day and, having a modest standard of living, feel want and suffering less."[32] Between 1927 and 1934 the birth rate fell from 27.5 per thousand to 23.4, despite the Duce's propaganda, despite a tax on bachelors, despite even the efforts of a prefect who promised to make a personal contribution to solving the problem.

The value of stocks and shares declined by about 40 per cent. The Bank of Italy's reserves shrank by a third and many other banks, weakened by Mussolini's deflationary policies, had to be "salvaged."[33] Business bankruptcies increased: well over a third of all industrial concerns with capital under a million lire were losing money by 1932. Mussolini was slow to respond. At first he was inclined to dismiss the Depression as a "rich man's panic."[34] He was attracted by the notion that it gave Italians the chance to be Stoics again: "Perhaps we are moving towards a period of mankind levelled to a lower plane. We need not get alarmed about this. It may be a very strong humanity, capable of asceticism and heroism the like of which we cannot at present imagine."[35] This was not a position he could sustain for long, particularly when people started to remark that the Fascist salute was a way of showing "how high the grass would soon grow in the streets of Rome."[36]

Thronged with trams, cabs, carts and motor buses, the streets of Rome were, in the words of one supercilious visitor, "gutters rather than thoroughfares."[37] They did not at all conform to Mussolini's notion of the grandeur that was, and should again be, Rome. *Folie de grandeur* might best explain his plans for the city, put forward in a speech from which he promised "vigorously to exclude all rhetorical divagations":

> In five years Rome must appear wonderful to the entire world, vast, orderly and potent, as she was in the days of the first empire of Augustus. The trunk of the mighty oak must be freed from everything that still overshadows it. Space must be cleared around the Forum, the Theatre of Marcellus, the Capitol and the Pantheon. All that grew up during the centuries of decadence must disappear. Within five years the hill of the Pantheon must be made visible through a broad avenue leading from the Piazza Colonna. Parasitic and profane excrescences must be torn from the majestic temples of Christian Rome. The immemorial monuments of our history must loom gigantic in their necessary solitude. Then the third Rome will extend over other hills, along the banks of the sacred river to the shores of the Tyrrhenian Sea . . . Not least of the merits of Fascism is that it has given once more a moral and political capital to the nation. Rome now takes pride of place in the new consciousness of the victorious fatherland.[38]

Fortunately little of this scheme was implemented. It was too expensive, whereas it cost the dictator little to drop the plan—merely the expenditure of words which were certain to be greeted with "a chorus of ecstatic approval."[39]

However, in opening up the area round the Colosseum, excavating Trajan's forum and beginning the Via del Mare, Mussolini did destroy priceless relics of medieval and Renaissance Rome, substituting crude memorials to his own regime. Furthermore, by creating vast open spaces he paved the way for Roman monuments to become traffic islands. This was the fate of the Mausoleum of Augustus, which Mussolini extracted, in the words of an inscription still visible, "from the shadows of centuries."

The whole scheme was a brutal piece of architectural propaganda. The tomb was gutted of subsequent accretions and restored to a solemn state of ruination. The Ars Pacis Augustae (the magnificent altar of peace celebrating the Emperor's military triumphs and, in Fascist eyes, Roman dominion over "all the decrepit civilisations of the old world") was resurrected. The square was opened to the Tiber, conjuring up a contemporary image "of the flow of centuries before the solid reference point of one name and one immortal idea." The murals and sculptures on the new buildings set around the square were decorated with imperial and Fascist symbols suggesting that Mussolini was the heir of Augustus. Yet the effect was diffuse and the whole has rightly been described as a "colossal mistake."[40]

This could not be said of all Fascist architecture. Some, such as that of Giuseppe Pagano, was genuinely original. Giovanni Greppi's gigantic war memorial, a funereal fortress at the summit of Monte Grappa, added an awesome dimension to the sublime spirit of the place (and amply fulfilled the Duce's wish that such monuments should be pantheons rather than cemeteries). The new town of Sabaudia, designed by Luigi Piccinato and others, was beautifully integrated into its reclaimed landscape. But, like Hitler and Stalin, Mussolini had a penchant for grandiloquent chauvinism. He liked to set his bombast in concrete. This was reflected in many of the sports stadiums, railway stations and official buildings erected during the 1930s, which were models of neo-classical hubris.

Such edifices did not merely express vain imperial aspirations. In his early days in power Mussolini had flirted with laissez-faire, but by the mid-1920s he had come to believe that Fascism involved State intervention in the economy. Hence not only the epic monuments but also the public works—low-cost housing, irrigation projects, land-reclamation schemes (among which was the draining of the Pontine marshes, originally attempted by Julius Caesar) and road improvement programmes (including the construction of the first *autostrada*). Big business, too, received assistance. Mussolini set up organisations such as the Institute for Industrial Reconstruction which bought stock in needy banks and corporations. This gave the State a major stake in important enterprises, notably steelworks and ship-building. It also seemed a step towards realising the Duce's dream of autarky, without which Italy could not fulfil its destiny as a great warrior nation.

Mussolini dramatised his concern for Italian victims of the Depression, asking rhetorically: "Can the state repeat the gesture of Pontius Pilate?"[41] His own gestures were more generous but equally ineffective. He visited the Mezzogiorno and promised to clear the slums. But nothing was done and the Duce contented himself with announcing periodically that the southern problem was solved. After the Wall Street Crash Fascist agents in America encouraged Italian emigrants to return home where they would find work and wages. In fact they found bad conditions made even worse by the drying-up of funds sent back from the New World. "Damn 1929 and the bastards who got me back here," exclaims a returned "American" in Carlo Levi's novel *Christ Stopped at Eboli*. As this marvellous evocation of Lucanian village life reveals, the former emigrants soon became peasants again, inhabitants of "a dark, mysterious world of their own where there was no hope." Short swarthy men in rough black suits, they cultivated meagre patches of soil and shared windowless hovels with their families and beasts. Their way of life had changed little since the Middle Ages and the only poetry in their "dark, desperate epic" was the romance of brigandage. Occasionally, when provoked by some particularly flagrant injustice, they might set fire to a tax office or slit the throat of their overlord.[42] In the north, where over 80 per cent of Italy's industry was concentrated, there were also sporadic riots and demonstrations. Sometimes Mussolini made concessions to violence, doling out money or setting up soup kitchens. But in general the unemployed were controlled by brutal repression just as those in work were disciplined by fierce paternalism. One Turin worker recalled: "The bosses were bosses and we were like, I don't know, like slaves."[43]

As these conflicts suggest, with a species of totalitarianism haphazardly tacked on to existing institutions, Mussolini aspired to regiment a society profoundly fissured and fragmented. There were divisions between and within classes, regions, districts and villages. The rich despised the poor and lorded it over them, often using the familiar form of address in the most arrogant fashion. Men and women thought of themselves as Florentines, Venetians, Genoese or Neapolitans first and Italians second. When making a journey outside their own province Piedmontese commonly said, "I'm going to Italy."[44] Local pride, *campanalismo*, eclipsed national patriotism. Local dialects emphasised and compounded the differences: to the inhabitants of Ignazio Silone's Fontamara "Italian is a language learnt at school, like Latin, French or Esperanto."[45] Village vendettas were regular events and even in the most tightly-knit communities feuds were commonplace. In the south, for example, it was a matter of life or death for impoverished gentry to obtain minor posts such as druggist, priest or marshal of carabinieri in order to preserve their status and dominate the peasants. So, to quote Carlo Levi again, their lives were a struggle for petty power, a "struggle which the narrowness of their surroundings, enforced idleness, and a mixture of personal and political motives render continuous and savage."[46] Under the impact of the Depression the rifts in Italian society grew deeper. The Duce did not have to divide in order to rule. Rather his task was to promote a mystical unity with himself as its incarnation. To deal with the Depression Mussolini had no planned economy, no proper investment programme, no new deal. His remedial measures were the usual mixture of opportunism, improvisation and self-advertisement. As a foreign observer remarked, it was impossible to

> over-emphasise the depth of Italian ignorance, especially rural ignorance, of political affairs. These people are provincial, even parochial, in a dark, primitive sense. Any bluff will impose upon them, if it is outside their tiny, limited, blinkered experience.

Central to the task of welding the nation into a homogeneous whole was the cult of the Duce. Mussolini promoted himself with vainglorious abandon. His picture was everywhere and when he so forgot himself as to shake hands, the newspapers faked the photograph and showed him giving the Roman salute. Sculptures of the Leader also multiplied, among them equestrian statues whose eyes lit up at night, flashing green, white and red. Streets and squares were named after him and the Fascists even christened Mont Blanc "Monte Mussolini." Slogans proliferated: "Mussolini is always right" and "We shall go straight ahead" (famously displayed outside Naples on a hairpin bend). Cinema audiences had to stand when the Duce appeared on film. Like the carefully censored newsreels, radio always exhibited him in a starring role, wooing and winning the Italian people with bravura displays of political charisma and personal machismo. Despite, and perhaps because of, the posturing and pouting which seem so ludicrous in retrospect, Mussolini projected pure animal magnetism. To many he seemed the embodiment of the Italian spirit. As one Fascist wrote:

> Mussolini is not only like the hero envisaged by Carlyle, a "missionary of order," but, above all, an exciter of life, a leader to glory, a man who knows how to take the Nation, make it confront itself, make it participate in a passionate faith, interpreter of the aspirations and the anxieties of the multitude. There is in him the sense of the real marvellously fused with the spiritual and historical necessities. He has fixed the directions of our destiny, has established the necessary tables of our law . . . This man, whom divine Providence has called to the leadership of the Italian people, has passed through the torment of terrible experiences, through the fire of formidable passions. Thus, rich with a prodigious human sensibility, he has understood that not merely the forces of economic brutality, not physical laws alone, regulate the destiny of peoples.[47]

Such adulation, whether genuine hero-worship or calculating sycophancy, magnified Mussolini's delusions of grandeur. DUCE, his obligatory title, was capitalised in the newspapers and the initial letter of His personal pronoun, like God's, was printed in upper case. Mussolini believed that the press should be like an orchestra, with many different instruments all playing the same tune—his tune.

He also liked to tell foreign diplomats that "press censorship took place after not before publication."[48] In fact detailed instructions went out to editors in advance saying what they should and should not print. A typical order forbade articles on the Depression: "The papers should rather concern themselves with the signs of recovery."[49] Controlled by Mussolini's acolyte Manlio Morgagni, the wire service Agenzia Stefani systematically distorted the news. Italian newspapermen were anyway thoroughly "Fascistized" and those who proved obdurate could be confined, along with other political prisoners, to the barren islands of Lipari and Lampedusa, Mussolini's fiery Siberia. Foreign reporters were flattered, bribed, intimidated or expelled. Mussolini wove a "highly paid and widespread network of propaganda . . . round journals published in New York, Paris, London and Berlin."[50] He took endless trouble to win over prominent journalists. He received Anne O'Hare McCormick, it was said, like the Queen of Sheba, and she returned the compliment by representing him in the *New York Times* as the last and greatest of the Roman emperors. The Chicago *Tribune*'s George Seldes, by contrast, was ignominiously deported, and not until after the invasion of Abyssinia would anyone in America publish his fine study *Sawdust Caesar*. This was partly, a New York publisher explained, because of "the threat of bombings and stilettos" and partly because an attack on Mussolini would not sell well in the United States.[51]

Italy lacked a Goebbels to make propaganda a black art (though the little Nazi plagiarised Mussolini's musical analogy, saying that "We don't want everyone to blow the same horn at all, but only want them to blow according to *one* plan").[52] But over most aspects of Italian life the skull-and-crossbones of Fascism fluttered, however raggedly. Culture served Mussolini, since dissenters—among them Arturo Toscanini—were beaten up and driven out. Anyway, some artists genuinely supported Fascism. The Futurist Filippo Tommaso Marinetti, whose famous 1909 manifesto had been a revolt against the liberal creed of the nineteenth century and who extolled "the beauty and necessity of violence,"[53] could even claim to have shaped its ideology. Indeed, like Mussolini, Marinetti wished to effect a fundamental redefinition of the Italian character. Not content with trying to abolish the past, he wanted to abolish pasta. This was because it made people "heavy, brutish . . . sceptical, slow and pessimistic."[54]

Spaghetti sapped Italian virility and strands of vermicelli tied Italian thought into knots. How could Italians be re-made as warriors, Marinetti asked, while weighed down by their "biquotidian pyramid of pasta"? What was the point of a man's raising "his arm in the Roman salute if he can rest it without effort on his bulging stomach"?

To revive the national spirit, to be an optimistic antidote to the global economic crisis and to boost the sale of homegrown food (cheap rice instead of expensive imported grain), Marinetti called for a "culinary revolution." It would transform eating into an aesthetic and patriotic experience. It would replace macaroni, tagliatelli and other elements of the "absurd Italian gastronomic religion," with dishes such as *Ultravirile* (a lobster concoction), *Elasticake* (a zabaglione and liquorice pudding) and *Aerofood.* The last was described thus:

> The diner is served from the right with a plate containing some black olives, fennel hearts and kumquats. From the left he is served with a rectangle made of sandpaper, silk and velvet. The foods must be carried directly to the mouth with the right hand while the left hand lightly and repeatedly strokes the tactile rectangle. In the meantime the waiters spray the napes of the diners' necks with a *conprofumo* [complementary scent] of carnations while from the kitchen comes contemporaneously a violent *conrumore* [noise having affinity to flavour] of an aeroplane motor and some *dismusica* [associated music] by Bach.

This campaign created a stir. And Marinetti certainly expressed the Fascist passion to trumpet the cause of "our . . . dynamic and dramatic peninsula, envied and threatened on all sides, poised to realise its immense destiny, [which] must consider national pride as its first law of life." But feasts of *Aerofood* were little more than Futurist fantasies, on a par with Marinetti's "really miraculous idea, which may even have escaped Marconi," to broadcast "nutritious radio waves."[55]

Less avant-garde and more practical ways were sought to sell Fascism to the masses. Sport was used to promote the regime. So was education. School and university teachers were obliged to take loyalty oaths and during the 1930s attempts were made to give the curriculum a Fascist bias. The youth organisation Balilla had children marching from the age of six. Achille Starace, the Party Secretary, tried to impose a Fascist style of behaviour on leisure. Described as Mussolini's choreographer, Starace so adored uniforms that he was said to dress up as an Eskimo before going out to buy an ice-cream. Mocked for his vanity, he was also ridiculed for his love of arbitrary regulations. Moreover, his efforts to regiment Italian society met with limited success except on a superficial level.

Somewhat more effective were grand shows such as the Fascist Exhibition to mark the tenth anniversary of the "March on Rome." This must be "ultra-modern," Mussolini insisted, bereft of "melancholy souvenirs in the style of the past." So the *palazzo* on Rome's Via Nazionale which housed the exhibition was turned into something between a futuristic fortress and a secular cathedral, enhanced by night-time floodlights which illuminated an enormous red and white metallic "X." Inside was a series of rooms full of lights, colours, sounds, displays and images illustrating the history of Fascism, including such sacred emblems as the cudgel and the bottle of castor oil, together with bloody shreds of Mussolini's clothing. The rise of Fascism was dramatised by a blown-up picture of a rally before which a mass of gleaming mechanical hands rose in the Roman salute, powered by three turbines symbolising "the strength and will of the people—disciplined by its faith." The "March on Rome" was represented by a gigantic bas-relief featuring a Roman sword slashing through chains, a soaring eagle and marble fasces rising inside the red-tiled triumphal arch of Vittorio Veneto "like a huge, living flame."[56] Mussolini himself, to whom Italian heroes from Garibaldi to D'Annunzio were shown as mere prophets, was deified in an antechamber to the *Sacrarium*. This was the shrine to Fascist martyrs and the climax of the exhibition. Bathed in deep blue light, it inspired devotees to an ecstasy of mixed metaphors.

> In the Sacrarium is the mystery of the Revolution. In the Sacrarium is the heart of the nation. In the Sacrarium is the inextinguishable flame. From the Sacrarium issue the roots which will sink, in the intangible solidity of time and space, the Fascism of Mussolini in the world. From the Sacrarium is diffused the light of the path and the immortality of the Idea to all Italians transformed by the Revolution.[57]

Italians were not transformed by the revolution, though nearly four million attended the exhibition and many were genuinely moved. However, as the Depression deepened, Mussolini needed ever more spectacular propaganda coups to make his compatriots a homogeneous, obedient people. One method was to provide flying circuses, to write the marvels of Fascism in the sky.

THE impresario and star of these aerial stunts was Italo Balbo, Fascist boss of Ferrara and Minister of Aviation from 1929 to 1933. Fancying himself a poet of action, Balbo had fought courageously during the Great War; he afterwards attacked socialists at home with equal belligerence. He was often credited with inventing the castor oil treatment for political opponents. If so, this was not the worst of his crimes, which he boldly justified by asserting that patriots should not shrink from spilling blood. Ruthless, restless, exuberant and gregarious, Balbo swaggered about in a uniform consisting of black shirt, grey-green jodhpurs, *ardito*-style jacket with black flame insignia and Alpine hat, later changed for a fez. He wore a goatee beard and was as ardent a womaniser as the Duce himself, with whom, he said, "my soul vibrate[s] in harmony."[58] Also like Mussolini, who first travelled by plane in 1918 and felt in his veins "the truly Dionysiac intoxication of the conquest of the azure,"[59] Balbo became intoxicated with flying. He regarded it as the apotheosis of the Fascist qualities of power, speed, virility and heroism. Already public interest in aviation was kept at fever pitch by the record-breaking exploits of pilots male and female. Marinetti even predicted that, "The day will arrive when the sky, hitherto considered man's roof, will become his pavement."[60] Thus Balbo saw flying as the ideal contemporary medium for both advertising the achievements of the regime and promoting his own career. He subscribed to the theories of General Giulio Douhet, who argued that fleets of bombers would make a decisive impact on the next war. So rather than sponsoring individual pioneering flights, Balbo initiated a series of mass aerial cruises. At the end of the 1920s his squadrons of seaplanes, with their specially trained crews, made two dramatic Mediterranean expeditions. At the beginning of 1931, 9 out of his flight of 12 aircraft crossed the South Atlantic to world-wide acclaim. No feat of showmanship so boosted Fascist prestige.

"Propaganda is the instinctive need of the convinced," Balbo declared. "It appears absurd that others do not think like me."[61] Despite recent claims that these were years of "consensus,"[62] and evidence that acceptance of Fascism (though perhaps based on "wishful thinking") was widespread, "genuine and passionate,"[63] many Italians did think differently. And a handful actually turned Balbo's chosen method of propaganda against Fascism. Several exiles flew lonely missions from France and Switzerland to drop leaflets denouncing Mussolini over Milan and Rome. The most famous of these flights was made by Lauro de Bosis in October 1931, not long after Balbo's spectacular South Atlantic adventure.

Aged 30, de Bosis was a scholar, a poet and an idealistic conservative whose opposition to Mussolini had so far been somewhat equivocal. To purge his guilt and to awaken the liberty-loving spirit of Italy, he hit on the idea of a sacrificial flight. As he wrote in a poem about Icarus, he would aim at "a noble goal" and if he fell into the sea his mother would be able to say: "Son, child of mine, thou art not dead. Mine eyes have seen thee like a god illuminated by the sun."[64] Before setting off de Bosis also penned a moving and prophetic manifesto entitled "The Story of my Death," which was later published by newspapers in Europe and the

United States. It was full of intimations of mortality and concluded that if
"my friend Balbo has done his duty" the Italian air force would be waiting
to destroy him.[65] This did not matter.

> I shall undoubtedly reach Rome, and once my business there is done, I
> can close the balance of my life . . . Above all one must show the young
> that the liberal cause has still got enough appeal to make a man happy to
> give up his life for it . . . What I most condemn in fascism [is] that it has
> brought out all that is cruel and medieval in human nature, to catch
> men's souls. [It is a] romantic corruption of the spirit, [a] reversal of all
> essential values . . . Mussolini has isolated Italy: no news arrives there
> from abroad; she stews in the barbaric and hypnotic sauce that her chef
> prepares for her every morning. The earth and the sea are his, but the sky
> still belongs to free men.[66]

In the absence of radar de Bosis proved right. With only seven and a half
hours of solo flying experience to his credit he set off from Corsica in his
russet-coloured, white-winged *Pegasus* and glided like a phantom over the
Eternal City. He flung out a shower of leaflets denouncing Mussolini's
corrupt and tyrannical government, appealing to the King and urging a
boycott of every Fascist enterprise and ceremony. They floated on to the
green lawns of the Quirinal Gardens and the outdoor cafés in the Villa
Borghese. They landed like snowflakes on the Piazza di Spagna and the
Piazza Venezia. De Bosis was not shot down but on his return journey he
apparently ran out of fuel and crashed into the Mediterranean. No trace of
him or of the *Pegasus* was ever found. Commenting on this act of self-
immolation, *The Times* said: "So long as there are men like Lauro de Bosis,
the safeguarding of freedom is assured."[67]

Actually the gesture had little real effect. But Fascism, ever preoccupied
with symbol and mime, was sensitive to such pin-pricks. Balbo was particularly humiliated and correspondingly keen to wipe out the stigma with
an unprecedented propaganda coup. His Wing Days, modelled on the
RAF flying displays at Hendon, were not enough. Nor were the gigantic
12-engined DO X flying-boats which were designed to carry 150 passengers, to supersede dirigibles and to be the jumbos of their age (in fact they
became flying white elephants which were soon firmly grounded). Balbo
needed a global triumph. So, in July 1933, after a tense wait for favourable
weather, he led a sky-borne armada of 24 Savoia Marchetti flying-boats
across the North Atlantic. They travelled in a series of hops at an average
speed of 130 miles per hour. On the last lap of their journey, from Montreal to Chicago, Balbo's fliers were escorted by 43 American fighters
which spelled out the word ITALIA as the Savoias, their silver wings and
tri-coloured tails glinting in sunshine against a thundery sky, made perfect

formation landings near the Navy Pier on Lake Michigan. Exhausted and still shuddering from their aeroplanes' vibrations, their crews were greeted with unbridled enthusiasm.

There were processions, receptions, speeches, ceremonies, telegrams and flowers. Mayor Ed Kelly (with his eye on Chicago's 300,000 Italian-Americans) gave Balbo, immaculate in his white uniform, a golden key to the city. Balbo became a fully-fledged member of the Sioux, christened Chief Flying Eagle, having first ascertained that other distinguished white men had accepted the honour. A million citizens, many of them giving the Fascist salute, hailed the gallant airmen as they paraded on Michigan Avenue. July the fifteenth was designated Italo Balbo Day and Seventh Street was named Balbo Avenue. When he visited the World's Fair its Federal Commissioner Harry S. New said that if Balbo remained in the United States he might be elected President. After meeting the current occupant of the White House, who seemed to share many of Mussolini's views, Balbo complimented him on being "a dictator."[68] Not all was sweetness and light. Organisations such as the Italian League for the Rights of Man distributed "thousands of flaming circulars attacking General Balbo." But most people were thrilled by his achievement, which the *New York Times* regarded as the "greatest mass flight in aviation history."[69] Major Dwight D. Eisenhower, who acted as one of Balbo's military hosts, said that the General's grand manner and sense of publicity made him almost more American than Italian. After the war, to the embarrassment of Italian officials, Ike reiterated his approval of Balbo.

In the United States Balbo was delighted to beat the patriotic drum, to laud the flourishing state of Italy under Fascist leadership at a time when the New World was in the trough of Depression. But he was conscious that Mussolini was increasingly resentful of being eclipsed. Plaintive requests crossed the Atlantic that something, perhaps a skyscraper, should be named after the Duce—but the Americans would not oblige. Balbo's return home was all the more perilous for being so triumphant. It was ecstatically evoked in Marinetti's broadcast commentary, which gave the poet ample scope to indulge in favoured Futurist devices such as "integral onomatopoeia" and "telegraphic lyricism"—to say nothing of the "death of syntax."

> Listen to the music of the sky, with its mellowed tubes of pride, the buzzing drills of miners of the clouds, enthusiastic roars of gas, hammerings ever more intoxicated with speed and the applause of bright propellers. The rich music of Balbo and his transatlantic flyers hums, explodes and laughs among the blue flashes of the horizon . . . The cruiser *Diaz* fires salvos. The crowd shouts with joy. The sun mirrors the

Italian creative genius . . . The delirious crowd yells: "Here he is, here he is, here he is! Duce! Duce! Duce! Italy! Italy!" The rumble, rumble, rumble of the motors that pass a few yards from my head. . .[70]

Mussolini and the royal family welcomed Balbo at Ostia airport, now decorated with Gherardo Dottori's mélange of propellers, wings, cockpits and engines—a dramatic vision of the new school of aero-painters as well as a celebration of the success of the heroes of the ether. Amid a rapturous throng the fliers drove to the Piazza Colonna, which was brilliantly illuminated by searchlights. The next day they marched under the Arch of Constantine and Mussolini made Balbo an air marshal. All the time, however, the glowering Duce was doing his best to steal his subordinate's thunder and to edge him out of the limelight. Telegrams were published between the two men to show that Mussolini had virtually directed the epic flight himself. The newspapers talked of "*The Wings of Mussolini* under the guidance of Balbo."[71] Huge posters showed the Duce dressed in flying kit beside a squadron of aircraft. And as soon as the sensation had died down, Mussolini deprived Balbo of the aviation portfolio and sent him off to govern Libya. Balbo thus became a victim of his own propaganda. So indeed did the Italian air force, whose general development was neglected for the sake of eye-catching stunts. When Mussolini entered the Second World War only two fighter groups possessed modern monoplanes and one of the earliest achievements of the ill-trained anti-aircraft gunners was to shoot down Air Marshal Balbo himself. Fascism, with its mania for showmanship, was always apt to sacrifice substance for accident.

In the arena of showmanship, as Mussolini ruefully discovered during the years when Balbo tried to inscribe the Fascist message in the heavens, the Roman Catholic Church had nearly 2,000 years' experience. Indeed, devout Catholics were apt to see Fascism, like Marxism, as a diabolical parody of their religion. Mussolini's hymns and creeds, rituals and exhortations, banners and badges, seemed to mock the solemn appurtenances of the true faith. The Duce himself feared that the Church was becoming a focus of opposition to his own dictatorship. He disliked the Pope's narrow greed for power, shrewdly recognising that it aped his own: "The fact is that we both have the mentality of the peasant."[72] And since the Lateran Pacts he had become suspicious that Pius was turning the tables on him. "We intended that the Church should become a pillar of the Regime," he said in 1931. "We never thought for a moment that the Regime would become the servant of the Church!"[73] Roused by the agitation of his anti-clerical followers, the Duce was particularly worried by the revival of Catholic Action, the Pope's lay organisation for promoting Catholicism among youth, women, trade unions and other sections of society. It threatened to undermine, if not to challenge, Fascist authority at a time when that authority was weakened by the Depression. So in May 1931, after various preliminary skirmishes (including an attack by young Fascists on the Jesuit headquarters in Rome which housed Father Rosa's *Civiltà Cattolica*), Mussolini suppressed important centres of Catholic Action.

This precipitated the sharpest crisis between Church and State of the entire Fascist period. Pope Pius issued a furious encyclical *Non Abbiamo Bisogno,* denouncing Mussolini's totalitarian state in general and its attempts to control education in particular. The Supreme Pontiff, who had himself been vilified in Rome by Fascist crowds crying "Death to the traitor Ratti,"[74] condemned the violence with which Catholic Action had been disbanded and the falsehoods uttered by the captive press. He suggested that Mussolini had signed the Concordat in the hope of dominating the Church and not from any love of religion. He proposed that Catholics swearing loyalty oaths to the Duce should make a mental reservation that these took second place to the laws of God. Finally, he damned the regime's efforts to convert the young to "Statolatry"—"a real pagan worship of the state."[75] The Vatican employed Monsignor F. J. Spellman, the future cardinal, to smuggle the encyclical out of the country. *L'Osservatore Romano* published it inside Italy, appearing five hours early in order to elude the vigilance of the censor. Mussolini was livid and stepped up his persecution of Catholic Action. The Pope privately let it be known that he might excommunicate the Duce. When someone suggested that the Holy See should seek arbitration Pius exploded with righteous indignation. Banging both hands on the table, he shouted breathlessly:

> The rights and prerogatives of which I am the repository are of a divine nature. They have been entrusted to me, as Pope, and I cannot depart from them in any way . . . On such questions no compromise is possible . . . I would even withdraw into a monastery if I was forced, but I will never abandon what I believe to be my mission, never, never, never![76]

Yet it turned out that a compromise was possible after all. Neither Pope nor Duce wished to jeopardise the Lateran Pacts. So peace overtures were made by both sides and in September 1931 a second accord was reached. Catholic Action would continue its religious work under the direction of the bishops but would keep out of politics. It would not display its own flags or insignia, and all pupils in Catholic schools would join the Balilla. The Vatican also made other concessions, such as dismissing Father Rosa from his job as director of *Civiltà Cattolica.* Though still "filled with animus against the Pope,"[77] Mussolini probably gained more than he lost from this agreement, which put the Church firmly in its place. At any rate, when he visited the Vatican on 11 February 1932, the third anniversary of the signing of the Lateran accord, the Duce apparently made no humiliating genuflections; though there was a slight awkwardness about his initial exchanges with the Pope and he was reported (by newspapers anxious to conjure up visions of Canossa) to have kissed the Holy Father's slipper. Actually, according to Mussolini's minute of the meeting, Pius was the more conciliatory. He expressed happiness that the difficulties between Catholic Action and the Fascist party had been resolved. He also said that, "I do not see, in the whole of Fascist doctrine—with its affirmation of the principles of order, authority and discipline—anything contrary to Catholic conceptions." Quite the reverse: "Fascist totalitarianism" in material matters should collaborate with "Catholic totalitarianism" in the spiritual sphere, especially during "these times of crisis and great misery." The Pope sealed their alliance with a gift: "I wish to give you in remembrance of this day, three medals, two of which recall the Crucifixion and the third, the radio. Sometimes I think how the message of Peter and Paul could have been facilitated had they had this means at their disposal."[78]

It was fitting that these two autocrats should conclude their interview on the subject of propaganda—hollow pillar of the Church, lying buttress of the State. Their very meeting was itself a form of propaganda, a show of harmony from which each hoped to gain. The Pope's moral authority could hardly have been enhanced by associating with Mussolini. But the Duce afterwards behaved as though he had achieved the consecration of absolutism, larding his speeches with references to the saving grace of the Fascist faith. "In this dark, tormented and already tottering world," he told his parliament at the end of 1932, "salvation can only come from truth in Rome and from Rome it will come."[79] However, in a world darkened by Depression mystical unity was not enough to guarantee the survival of the nation. The global convulsion was releasing new forces, notably National Socialism in Germany. Mussolini, who maintained both that Fascism was not for export and that it was the universal movement of the age, was at once flattered and vexed by the triumph of Nazism. In public he welcomed it, but he was privately apprehensive about the danger to his northern flank. Yet he was attracted by this barbaric new expression of power and sought to assert his own political virility. Fascism would become more warlike as the 1930s progressed. For the alternative to belligerence was decadence, the Duce believed, and anything was better than that. Italy must never become like France, which had been ruined, Mussolini declared, by "alcohol, syphilis and journalism."[80]

VII

THE DECADENCE OF FRANCE

MUSSOLINI'S strictures on France were not absurdly wide of the mark. Between the wars Frenchmen drank about three times as much alcohol annually as Italians, most of it in the form of wine—200 litres per head, helped down by assurances from the Minister of Agriculture that French wine was the best antidote to alcoholism and, maybe, by the amiable linguistic convention that it *se boit* (drinks itself). There was also one bar for every 81 inhabitants of France as compared to one for 225 in Italy (and 425 in Britain). At the same time perhaps four million people, ten per cent of the French population, were infected with syphilis,[1] though matters improved a little after 1929 with the surreptitious import for the mass market of American "Dreadnought" contraceptive sheaths. It may seem perverse, finally, that someone who prided himself on having been a newspaperman should also blame journalism for wrecking France. However, Mussolini was referring to the government's failure to control the French press, which was arguably the most vicious and corrupt anywhere. Newspapers had hardly changed since Balzac depicted them as garish "intellectual brothels" in *Illusions Perdues*. Their clients were individuals, commercial concerns and governments, either French or foreign. During the Great War some papers had taken bribes from Germany and the practice continued when the Nazis came to power, prompting *Time* magazine to describe the French press, in May 1939, as the "sewer of world journalism." Still, even if there was some truth in the Duce's criticisms they doubtless also reflected his anger at Gallic contempt for both his regime and his country. Frenchmen were apt to call Fascists *"fessistes"* (arse-ists) and to say that black shirts were an Italian invention for saving on laundry bills.[2] "In France we have no friends," Mussolini declared. "All of them are against us. In the eyes of every Frenchman we are only 'sales macaroni.'"[3]

That a racial hierarchy existed in which those above were entitled to despise those below was generally accepted at the time. The British, even more than the French, were masters of the art of chauvinism, treating lesser breeds with a lofty disdain which was the mark of effortless superiority. That ubiquitous royal flunkey Sir Alan Lascelles, for example, described the Italian-American anarchists Sacco and Vanzetti, victims of one of the most celebrated causes of the 1920s, as "those two ice-cream merchants who are due to be electrocuted tomorrow and whose names escape me."[4] Much of Mussolini's braggadocio was designed to raise Italian standing in the world, even if this meant treading on supposed inferiors. Moreover, despite a gut feeling that France was rotten to the core, the Duce could not but be struck by its prestige and power in 1929.

The French army was the strongest on earth. Paris could claim to be the cultural centre of the world. The French empire, with 80 million inhabitants and 4 million square miles of territory on which the sun never set, was second only to that of the British. National pride in Greater France was augmented rather than diminished by the brutal suppression of colonial people, as happened in Tonkin in 1930, and French schoolchildren were taught to believe that their country, not Mussolini's, was the "heir to Rome."[5] French industry was growing faster than the industries of its European and American rivals. Indeed France was almost keeping pace with Japan and its car industry was the second largest in the world. French banks held much of the globe's gold, amounting to one quarter by 1932. After the serious inflation of the 1920s Prime Minister Poincaré had stabilised the franc, thus helping to secure favourable terms of trade and a healthy balance of payments. In November 1929 the new Premier, André Tardieu, proposed to spend the surplus on the creation of a modern welfare state, so introducing France to "the politics of prosperity."

Tardieu, who dominated the political life of the nation for the next three years, was an intellectual Napoleon. A Parisian *haut bourgeois* whose self-confidence was as overweening as his brilliance, he had passed out top of the Ecole Normale, piling up "prizes and diplomas as a juggler piles up eggs." His head seemed literally to bulge with ideas—as a young infantryman Tardieu had at first been obliged to drill in a bowler hat while an outsize military cap was made to order. He wrote with astonishing clarity and ease, seldom correcting a word, and by the age of 24 (in 1900) he was the highest-paid journalist in France. Skipping nimbly between the professions of commerce, literature, academe, politics and diplomacy, he earned golden opinions. "There are six Great Powers," said the German Chancellor von Bülow, "and then there is André Tardieu."[6] Tardieu also earned gold *tout court,* becoming involved in a couple of pre-war business scandals which tarnished his reputation—during the 1930s cartoonists often portrayed him as a shark. But he served gallantly in the trenches, adding the Croix de Guerre to the Légion d'honneur, and afterwards did sterling service as Commissioner for Franco-American War Cooperation. In the heat of a Washington summer he may have "dozed off from time to time" but, it was said, "his hand kept on writing."[7] This was no happy anticipation of Surrealist automatism: Tardieu believed in hard work and, when acting as Clemenceau's lieutenant during the peace conference, in hard bargaining. He had no patience with the pacific policy of Aristide Briand, dismissing it as "a dead dog floating with the stream."[8] Instead, he admired the aggressive achievements of American technocracy and sought to emulate them in France. Having climbed by way of several ministerial offices to the top of the political ladder, he now aimed to re-equip industry and improve agriculture along modern scientific lines. At the same time, conservative though he was, he intended to mitigate the rigours of capitalism through a radical programme of public works, social insurance, free secondary schooling, family allowances and better health care. Setting out his policy for prosperity on 25 November 1929, Tardieu proclaimed that youth had come to power.

This was something of an exaggeration. According to the old German jest, France was ruled by men of 75 "because the men of 80 are dead."[9] However, as it happened, the very day before Tardieu made his pronouncement an age had ended. Tardieu's own mentor Georges Clemenceau, the nation's most venerable and venerated elder statesman, had breathed his last. Sustained through the 1920s by an *amitié amoureuse* with a married woman over 40 years his junior—perhaps his happiest relationship in a life of domestic as well as political strife—Clemenceau had made no concessions to age or to anything else. Within a few months of his eightieth birthday, the Tiger had killed two real tigers in the Indian jungle. To the last he had continued to espouse the principles of Versailles, fiercely condemning compromisers such as Briand, who sought general disarmament and the conciliation of Germany. "Even with one foot in the grave," he said, "I have another to kick the backside of that blackguard."[10] When Tardieu himself came to terms with Briand, Clemenceau declared that France was unsafe in the hands of such men and that "I will die unhappy."[11] The prospect of extinction itself he faced with characteristic sang-froid, remaining true to his anticlerical principles and asserting that death was no more than "a dreamless sleep." Even great achievements were nothing but "wisps of smoke which [men] call glory" and prize because "they find in them something that smacks of survival after death."[12] For as long as possible Clemenceau refused to lie down and he reportedly left instructions that he should be buried in a vertical position. Finally, aged 88, he died.

France mourned as Clemenceau lay in the small blue and grey bedroom of his fashionable Passy apartment, with its clutter of mementoes and its Maples furniture. He was dressed in blue clothes and wore the double-pointed field cap which had been his only helmet on visits to the front line. Braving the rain squalls, crowds stood outside in the Rue Franklin as public men came to bid their adieux to the Father of Victory. Tardieu reported that "he lies magnificent and calm." The Prime Minister also reflected on the invincible courage of one who had been both "an aristo-crat and an autocrat. His father used to sit at the family table on a kind of throne, and it was in that way that M. Clemenceau lived among us." But unlike that other saviour of France, Ferdinand Foch, who had died earlier in the year and whose obsequies had been conducted with elaborate pageantry, Clemenceau had decreed that his funeral was to be unadorned. There were to be no eulogies, no oblations, no ceremonies. There was to be no inscription, only a plain white stela featuring Athene, goddess of wisdom, whose lance pointed to his resting-place. In his coffin were to be laid the iron-knobbed stick which he had taken on his tours of the trenches and a bunch of flowers picked for him in No Man's Land, his most treasured souvenirs of the war.

So Clemenceau's faithful chauffeur drove his master on a final journey to La Vendée (over roads so mired that several times the vehicle had to be pulled by oxen), to the family's land at Le Colombier near the village of Mouchamps. Here in the valley of Le Petit Lay, where green and brown fields were divided by ragged hedges and scrawny woods, Clemenceau was buried beside his Jacobin father. The interment, attended by a few close friends and relations and watched by neighbouring peasants (some of whom furtively made the sign of the cross), took place in mud and rain and lasted only ten minutes. It was a retrospective *memento mori,* a stark reminder of the grim circumstances in which a whole generation of fight-ing Frenchmen had gone to their graves. Even the position in which Clemenceau was buried had its poignant symbolism—so, at least, com-mentators said. Upright in death as in life, he stood for the indomitable spirit of France. His was an inextinguishable "soul of fire."[13] His sepulchre evoked spectral memories of the bloody killing fields of Verdun, where a sergeant had pronounced the phrase that echoed round the world: "Arise ye dead!"[14] Unhappily the symbolism was not quite sustained by the reality. If reporters had taken the trouble to visit Clemenceau's grave, remote and dark under the shade of a large cedar tree, they would have discovered that he was buried horizontally like everyone else. Never-theless, he remained one of the nation's most potent icons. General de Gaulle memorably invoked him, after the defeat of 1940, to sustain his compatriots' faith in the resurrection of France: "From the depth of your Vendéen tomb, Clemenceau, you do not sleep."[15]

Despite Clemenceau's wishes, his passing was marked by certain last rites. Eager to bask in the Tiger's reflected brightness, members of the National Assembly could not resist making lapidary orations. "The voice of the whole people spoke through the lips of that old man," Tardieu told the Senate, "opening up the paths of hope to the generations of tomorrow."[16] Throughout France flags flew at half-mast. War veterans marched past the Tomb of the Unknown Soldier beneath the Arc de Triomphe. A salute of 101 guns was fired. As the shots rang out the streets of Paris fell silent, as on Remembrance Sunday. There was even a pause in the *haute couture* district around the Rue de la Paix, where apprentice dress-makers were parading in fantastic carnival garments to celebrate the festival of Saint Catherine. Then the revel went on in its usual style.

The same, despite shades of past war and adumbrations of conflicts to come, might be said of France. One month before Tardieu's proclamation about prosperity Wall Street had crashed. Yet Frenchmen hardly noticed or, if they did, expressed confidence that Europe would benefit from the bursting of the American "abscess."[17] True, behind the old-fashioned railings and the Corinthian columns of the Paris Bourse, where share prices were still chalked on a blackboard, some did feel apprehension. The "gold-skinned men" who, as James Joyce said, quoted "prices on their gemmed fingers," sensed the seismic tremor. A few rich speculators who had invested abroad were hard hit; one, Maurice Sachs, wrote in his diary on 24 October, "We have nothing left."[18] Jewellers and art dealers lost fortunes as overseas orders were suddenly cancelled. The cafés and hotels of Montparnasse emptied. So did tourist haunts where young women kept out the cold with feathers, sequins and spangles—the *Folies Bergère,* the Lido, the Moulin Rouge. At the Ritz, journalist Janet Flanner observed, pretty ladies had to pay for their own cocktails. Yet fancy-dress balls had never been more extravagant and Parisian parties were "unusually frequent" and fantastic. The fashion designer Jean Patou, for example, roofed over her garden, covered walls, ceilings and trees with silver foil and gave lion cubs to her guests as prizes.[19]

Looking back on the global crisis which began in 1929, the far-sighted politician Paul Reynaud wrote:

> The oceans were deserted, the ships laid up in the silent ports, the factory smoke-stacks dead, long files of workless in the towns, poverty throughout the countryside. Argentina saw the wheat and livestock prices collapse; Brazil the price of coffee; America, that of corn and cotton;

Malaya, of rubber; Cuba, of sugar, and Burma, of rice. Then came the stage when wealth was destroyed. The Brazilians threw their sacks of coffee into the sea, and the Canadians burned their corn in railway engines. Just as a man leaving a house at a moment's notice, burns his papers, civilization seemed to destroy, before disappearing, the wealth it had created. Men questioned the value of what they had learned to admire and respect. Women became less fertile . . . The crisis was even more prolonged than the war. Nations were economically cut off from one another, but they shared the common lot of poverty.[20]

Yet for a couple of years France seemed so insulated from the Depression that it was known as "the happy isle."[21]

Tardieu's measures—spending government surpluses, introducing welfare measures, encouraging the rationalisation of industry—had some effect. There was even a reaction against the yoking of human beings to machines: René Clair's film *A Nous la Liberté* (1931) anticipated Charlie Chaplin's *Modern Times* by five years. But Clair himself seemed to visualise that mechanisation could bring emancipation. Moreover, with virtually no unemployment, national self-confidence was high. When General Motors closed its French sales organisation towards the end of 1929 Renault hired most of its workforce. And a huge advertisement for Citroën blazed among the "zigzag skysigns" which wriggled on the Eiffel Tower, George Orwell noted, "like enormous snakes of fire."[22] "The great name shines," wrote Ilya Ehrenburg, and all around it "tongues of mystical flame dart from earth to heaven." These were not merely 200,000 electric bulbs fed by 90 kilometres of wiring. They were "a new revelation, the tablets of Mount Zion: Come to your senses! Join us! You must buy immediately—ten horsepower, a new model!"[23]

André Tardieu himself was the glittering new embodiment of Gallic self-confidence. With his bejewelled pince-nez and his gold cigarette-holder (a present from Czar Ferdinand of Bulgaria), with his immaculate silk hats and his fashionable waistcoats, he was a peacock among politicians. In the mornings he could be seen walking his pair of dachshunds along the Avenue de Messine. Before the National Assembly he flaunted his paunch like a promotion for prosperity politics and his "forehead—vast, arched, powerful—tower[ed] like a bastion against the assaults of mediocrity."[24] In the evenings he would go to the Opéra, flit in and out of aristocratic salons, dine twice off the best food and wine, and carouse half the night in raffish company. With his jaunty manner, his racy conversation and his dictatorial pretensions, Tardieu provoked his colleagues. Discriminating opponents such as Joseph Paul-Boncour admired him in spite of themselves—"ardent, combative, peremptory, [he had] one of the best organised minds I have ever known."[25] But Tardieu was a standing affront to the average provincial deputy, the average deputy himself being, according to Richard Cobb, a bearded figure "of considerable girth, as if representing agricultural interests in his sheer size."[26] Such parliamentarians attacked Tardieu as a *condottiere,* a *boulangiste,* a latter-day Napoleon, an incipient Mussolini. "If it's war you want, gentlemen," the Prime Minister retorted brusquely, "I'm willing."[27]

Tardieu probably had more comprehension of the impending storm than his parliamentary colleagues, most of whom were economically illiterate, and he was certainly willing to fight for more power to meet it. The constitution of the Third Republic, designed precisely to prevent the emergence of another Napoleon, had strengthened parliament at the expense of government. Referring to the National Assembly, in which the directly elected Chamber of Deputies was more powerful than the Senate, President Gaston Doumergue said: "France has 600 dictators."[28] Consequently the executive was always in a difficult position and often in an impossible one. Between 1870 and 1940 there were no fewer than 108 ministries. During the inter-war years they lasted, on average, six months. (Deputies could bring down governments without causing general elections, which were held every four years.) Ministries consisted of coalitions formed from members of the many groups—there was even a "group of deputies not members of any other group."[29] Deputies sat in a Left-to-Right semi-circle in the great red, white and gold Chamber of the Palais Bourbon and party labels were virtually meaningless. As one member of parliament said, "I am a Deputy of the Left, I sit in the Centre and I vote Right."[30] The large Radical party was conservative on almost every issue except that of anticlericalism and united only in the sense of wanting to milk the State. Radicals were likened to radishes, "red outside, white inside, and sitting in the middle of the butter-dish."[31] This was mild compared to the insults swapped in the Chamber, which sometimes did not stop at words. Fist-fights were common and during the early 1930s the National Assembly voted that members should not bring in their canes in case they should be used as weapons. Even respectable members of the Senate, elected by local councils, came to blows. What hurt most was the truth—that most politicians did get into the butter-dish, if not the pork barrel. Constituents were cynical about corruption. Indeed, many were equally venal, eager to obtain favours from their elected representatives in Paris. As a ministry became more precarious it was more inclined to generosity; so, as André Malraux wrote, "the personal interests of the Deputy lie on the side of instability."[32] Far from being able to set himself up as a dictator, Tardieu had to appease the grasping factions. His own cabinet contained 33 ministers. "It's not a cabinet," exclaimed the Radical leader Edouard Daladier, "it's a tribe."[33]

Thus Tardieu could do little. Indeed, so impotent were all its governments that historians have described France between the wars as a "stalemate society."[34] Yet the impression of stasis is not altogether accurate. Nor is the complementary suggestion that France was hopelessly unstable because governments kept changing, as though the game of ministerial musical chairs was central to the life of the nation. The truth is that whoever was in office, the Civil Service was in power. France had a long tradition of directorial administration. Officials of all sorts had wide-ranging authority which they exercised with vigour and (often) with discretion. Take the energetic Prefect of Police in Paris, Jean Chiappe, for example. He established pedestrian crossings between rows of metal studs, banished several herds of goats from the inner city and prevented Paris's 25,000 prostitutes from soliciting too blatantly in the streets, though his plan to improve still further the "moral tone" of the capital by abolishing *vespasiennes,* the stinking iron pavement pissoirs, met with insurmountable male opposition.[35] There was much less opposition to the system of preventive detention (similar to the arbitrary arrest achieved by *lettres de cachet* under the Ancien Régime) which Chiappe employed chiefly to suppress the Communists. This was because most people, however much they cherished their revolutionary tradition, accepted the status quo. Before the Depression and the rise of Hitler they were unmoved by challenges from political extremists of Left and Right. Bourgeois and peasant gave their allegiance to the secular republic. In this land of 40 million individualists, the conservative consensus ruled. Less government was better government and if it did not work well . . . it worked after a fashion. In this it was like the plumbing in a country where most lavatories were "Turkish" holes in the ground. It was like the telephone service, where making a call from a post office could involve a wait of up to three hours. It was like the dirty, antiquated railways, where trains that attempted to run on time seemed liable to crash. It was like the safety matches which, after myriad splintering strikes, failed to ignite or glowed without flame, only to explode into sulphurous life, hop from their sticks and burn a hole in the carpet.

Gallic logic notwithstanding, Frenchmen prided themselves on their mastery of the art of muddling through—*débrouillage*. Nowhere was this art practised with more aplomb than in Emile Zola's bursting "belly of Paris," Les Halles. Situated in a tangle of mean streets just behind the Bourse, this monstrous food market was of far more interest to the average sensual man than the temple of stocks and bonds. In fact the 50-square-yard area closest to the Bourse which was devoted to the sale of mushrooms gave rise to flights of lyricism that could never have been prompted by mere money. There, heaped in a massive array of boxes and baskets, were not just common or garden *boules de neige*

> but pungent little *cèpes* from the south that incite to abandon and the wholesomeness of sin, large pine needle mushrooms from up near Lille, the special medium mushrooms from outside Rouen with the flesh tones of Jeanne d'Arc to be ravished by irreverent teeth and swallowed as a substitute for magic.[36]

But mushrooms were only drops in the ocean of produce which nightly flooded into Les Halles, threatening to overwhelm the ten huge pavilions built by Napoleon III—his "umbrellas of glass and iron."[37] For miles around the city centre roads were clogged as wave upon wave of wagons struggled to deliver their tide of merchandise—chicory from Roussillon, tomatoes from Cavaillon, cabbages from Anjou, apples from Normandy, carrots from Nanterre. They brought in shoals of mackerel from the Channel ports, trout from the Vosges, eels from Brittany, squid from the Mediterranean, crayfish (Zola's "liquid fire") from the Atlantic. Gory tumbrils carried freshly butchered carcasses from the abattoirs of Vaugirard and La Villette, beef from Savoy and Charente, mutton from the Pyrenees and the Auvergne, poultry from Périgord and pork from Corréze.

Little had changed in the life of Les Halles since Zola's classic evocation 60 years before. Still the giant hangars magnified a deafening cacophony: the crack of whips and neighing of horses, the crash of iron hooves and wooden clogs on the pavé, the curses of blue-bloused porters (some wearing the red stocking caps of liberty like their Jacobin forefathers), the jostle of crammed barrows and overflowing trolleys amid towers of crates and pyramids of boxes, the hoarse cries of sellers and the answering clamour of buyers, the tumult of tormented souls in a mercantile pandemonium. Still each dawn transfigured this infernal world, glancing through the shutters, chasing the shadows from the hollows in the roofs, illuminating the forest of pillars and bathing even the dimmest provender in a lambent glow. Still the senses were ravished by the sight and smell of mountains of tangerines, plateaux of raspberries, jungles of thyme, morasses of pâté, prairies of dahlias, seas of shrimps. Still, as Zola had noted, much of the produce rotted before it could be sold, so that the market was "a vast ossuary, a graveyard of corpses, a charnel-house of stench and putrefaction."[38] Zola made it all so romantic that when their nightclubs closed elegant *flâneurs* flocked to this cornucopia of squalor, to drink onion soup and ogle the prostitutes. But even before the Great War an official commission had recommended moving Les Halles, "of which the filth and smell are so annoying just a few steps away from the Louvre, the Hôtel de Ville, and the stock exchange, and which blocks, for long hours, all the movement in the most important streets."[39] In 1925 Le Corbusier favoured a plan to raze the whole area and erect 18 identical giant towers. During the 1930s conditions in Les Halles got worse. Two more pavilions were built and lorries in ever-increasing numbers added to the congestion, impregnating the ripe atmosphere with petrol fumes.

Les Halles did work, but in a grotesquely archaic fashion. The market was almost a lampoon on the predominance of Paris, which affected every aspect of national life. Some 40 per cent of the produce brought to the capital was then sent back to the provinces, often to cities quite close to its place of origin. Thus lettuces from Perpignan might go to Lyon via Les Halles. Of course this itinerary, with its incessant loading and unloading, immensely inflated prices—in the case of fruit and vegetables by something like 500 per cent. Indeed, it cost less to transport the lettuces from Perpignan to Paris than from the Gare d'Austerlitz to Les Halles, where agents, concessionaires, dealers and middlemen added to the toll. It was this colossal vested interest, as the historian Herbert Lüthy said, that caused "the incredible gap between the excessively low prices paid to the French producer and the excessively high prices paid by the French consumer. But the impregnable fortress of the Halles has rebuffed every effort at rationalisation."[40] In many respects, then, the Parisian market was a paradigm of the national condition. It was old-fashioned, over-centralised, protectionist, inefficient, corrupt and impervious to change. Its veneer of vitality concealed a core of decay. Though propelled by the momentum of the ages and sustained by a nexus of private interests, Les Halles threatened to grind to a halt. The nation's alimentary canal faced terminal constipation. Les Halles typified what historians have called the "blocked society."[41]

INNER stagnation was indeed, despite the early appearance of vigour, the essential condition of France during the 1930s. And paradoxically it was not her ostensible strength but her fundamental weakness that protected Marianne from the initial onslaught of the Depression. French exports were competitive, but only because the franc had lost four-fifths of its pre-war value during the 1920s. Relying on a buoyant home market, France anyway sold fewer goods abroad than great capitalist powers such as England and Germany; so it was less affected by the decline of global trade. French industrialists were cushioned against the slump because they had made large savings—by failing to invest in expansion and modern equipment. The short-term foreign money which flowed into France between 1929 and 1932 only did so because of the determination of successive governments to defend the franc against further inflation—a policy which would soon leave French exports disastrously over-priced. Unemployment was low because France had been shorn of manpower during the war—1.3 million dead and 1.1 million made permanent invalids. Of course, the population problem was obvious, but this did not stop busy *faiseuses d'anges*—"angel-makers"—from performing perhaps as many as a million abortions a year, an illegal practice at least partly explained by peasants' reluctance to divide land equally among their children as stipulated by Napoleonic inheritance laws. Anyway, the consequences of all these ills was that the Depression took longer to harm France than any other country, and that it also lasted longer. Furthermore, when early hopes that France might escape the economic crisis were dashed the result was bitter disappointment, social stress and political ferment.

French demoralisation was exacerbated by a pervasive sense of military insecurity. Men, women and children feared that Germany, with its 60 million people, would seek revenge on France, with its 40 million. Tardieu, whose interventionist policies aimed both to modernise and to protect the French economy, evolved a dual strategy to meet the German threat—conciliation and defence. In pursuit of the first goal he had achieved an accord with his old enemy Briand, France's "pilgrim of peace," placing him in the Quai d'Orsay in 1929 to follow a foreign policy of *détente*. This meant a gradual loosening of the bonds of Versailles, much to the horror of Clemenceau, who, shortly before his death, compared Tardieu's attitude to the treaty with that of "a father who kills his child."[42] But Tardieu was, above all things, a pragmatist. He recognised that France would be no match for a revanchist Germany. He saw that little alliances with states like Poland and Czechoslovakia would not give France security, and he mistrusted Communist Russia to the core of his *soigné* being. Much to the fury of his country's allies and enemies, Tardieu tried to transmute French gold into French might; but he also knew that there was no alternative to the popular policy of peace espoused by Briand. So began one of those dangerous liaisons that add piquancy to politics.

Briand was oil to Tardieu's vinegar. Whereas Tardieu had always moved in grand circles—his uncle had been Napoleon III's physician—Briand had been born (in 1862) over the Café de la Croix Verte in Nantes. The Premier knew everything whereas the Foreign Minister was famed for what Jean Jaurès once called his "encyclopaedic ignorance." Tardieu was incessantly active while, to his indignant amazement, Briand did absolutely nothing for hours on end. Tardieu was a dandy; Briand was small, unprepossessing, ill-kempt and badly dressed. Everything about him drooped: his uncombed locks, his huge gendarme's moustache, the eternal *mégot* (cigarette end) in the corner of his mouth. He seemed soft and flabby, though women did not find him so. Indeed, Briand was notorious for his amours. As a radical young politician he had been caught naked in a field with the beautiful wife of a banker, which prompted an opponent to describe him as "a sans-culotte in search of his trousers." Later Briand had a fling with La Belle Otero, most flamboyant of the *Grandes Horizontales,* once travelling all the way to Cannes to wish her a happy birthday. There was much speculation over the source of Briand's sex appeal. One of his mistresses explained that though he had a plebeian mouth his hands were the hands of an aristocrat. Some people extolled his "violoncello voice." Others pointed to Briand's manner, his expressive gestures, his feline charm.[43] "Briand's charm worked on Tardieu," it has been said, just as "Tardieu's intelligence won over Briand."[44]

Perhaps the Foreign Minister's essential secret lay in his sympathetic understanding of human nature. Wily, witty and ingratiating, he both recognised and shared the general desire for peace. He also seemed capable of realising it. At the time this naturally incurred the wrath of the Right. In 1930 the cartoonist Sennep represented Briand as offering Germany the Hexagon—France—on a plate with the words, "A little morsel."[45] When Briand died two years later, Charles Maurras' flaming royalist rag *L'Action française* printed a bitter obituary, reflecting on his "unjust natural death" and suggesting that he should have been killed for his treachery.[46] Later still, of course, the winner of the Nobel Peace Prize was to be stigmatised as the apostle of appeasement. In fact, as Tardieu's Foreign Minister, Briand was a pertinacious defender of France's interests and a vital asset to the government. And although his proposal for a United States of Europe might have been visionary, prior to the rise of Hitler it was by no means unrealistic to hope that some *modus vivendi* could be arranged with Germany. When France finally quitted the Rhineland in June 1930 Tardieu expected Germany to appreciate that it was "the most generous gesture in French history."[47]

However, though Tardieu's primary concern was to seek peace with his country's great rival, he was also determined to embed French security in concrete. The second arm of his foreign policy, a plan he had contemplated during the war years, was to build a chain of fixed defences along France's north-eastern frontier. Others supported this project but it was named after Tardieu's formidable War Minister, André Maginot, a giant who had been crippled while serving as a sergeant at Verdun. "I'm like my leg," he used to say, "I won't bend."[48] The fortifications were approved by parliament in 1930 and were operational six years later. One hundred and fifty miles long and seven miles deep, they formed the mightiest bastion in history. The first line of defence was a lightly-held screen, designed to trip up a surprise attack. Then came a bristle of obstacles whose purpose was to pin down infantry and tanks: barbed wire, pill-boxes, ditches, land-mines, and dragon-toothed iron rails projecting five feet out of their concrete beds. Behind them, three miles apart and supported by armoured domes with overlapping fields of fire, were the main forts. Though built to no standard pattern, all had massive double carapaces of concrete and steel to absorb bomb blasts.

Sixty feet below their camouflaged turrets was a labyrinth of tunnels, bunkers, barracks, vaulted galleries, command posts, electric lifts, diesel generating chambers and mechanical ventilating systems (to expel smoke and poison gas). There were even infirmaries and cinemas, as well as a modern drainage system—which had to be improved once it was found that soldiers blocked the lavatories with old socks, razor blades and empty bottles. Rumour had it that in an attack the dead would be dissolved in acid and flushed down these drains, but in fact each fort was supplied with its quota of galvanised iron coffins. Communications were secured by telephone lines implanted in concrete. Subterranean electric railways transported ammunition to magazines protected by 17-ton metal doors which closed automatically in the event of an explosion. As well as being equipped with mitrailleuses and anti-tank guns, the forts had a range of artillery—75s, howitzers and mortars—and they were capable of firing four tons of shells a minute. The garrisons (which ranged from 200 men to 1,200) stayed underground for long periods at a time, despite the sewage smell, the artificial light and damp so bad that the soldiers were forced to write letters in pencil since ink would not stick to the page. These pallid troglodytes, many of them technical specialists, were an élite and were treated as such. These "crustaceans of the ramparts," convinced of their invincibility, possessed the highest morale in the French army.[49]

Their confidence was understandable, despite retrospective judgements which dismiss the Maginot Line as a titanic instance of hubris and folly, the ultimate military mare's nest. In fact, it protected France's heaviest concentration of natural and industrial resources, not least in the disputed provinces of Alsace and Lorraine (Maginot's own home). The Line's construction provided work during the Depression and investment in defence at a time when no other major military expenditure would have been sanctioned. It gave promise of vengeance for Verdun, in that only the aggressors would suffer a bloodbath. What Pétain called these "battlefields prepared in peacetime"[50] did not entirely rule out a war of mobility. This was because the Maginot Line ceased at the border of France's ally Belgium, on whose soil the German invader could best be opposed. But, above all, this "subterranean fleet"[51] (Maginot's expression) would compensate for France's depleted manpower during the "hollow years" of the later 1930s when, as a result of fewer births between 1914 and 1918, the number of young men available for military service halved. The "foundations of the Maginot Line," it has been aptly said, "were the war cemeteries of France."[52] Even the Chief of Staff, General Maxime Weygand, who told Maginot that the existence of a powerful army was "a question of to be or not to be,"[53] concluded that the Line created a "safe [position] for a considerable time without any great effort by France."[54]

Not all shared this optimism. The more the Maginot Line was said to be "impregnable," the more some civilians were disposed to conclude with Aldous Huxley that its existence "[was] the guarantee that in any future war Paris [would] be bombed" from the air.[55] Likewise some military men dismissed it as the "Imaginot Line."[56] Army officers reflected on Napoleon's "axiom of war that the side which stays within its fortifications is beaten."[57] Colonel Charles de Gaulle was neither the first nor the only senior figure to inveigh against "an army of concrete," or to assert that "static security . . . can never be complete."[58] Despite plans to grapple with the enemy in Belgium, it was clear that the Great Wall of France was the supreme monument to defensive dogma, which was as rampant before the Second World War as offensive spirit had been before the First. "How could anyone believe that we should contemplate the offensive when we have spent billions to establish a fortified barrier?" exclaimed one War Minister, dismissing de Gaulle's proposals and ignoring France's commitments to eastern Europe. "Are we stupid enough to go in front of this barricade in pursuit of all kinds of adventure?"[59]

The barricade unquestionably engendered a "Maginot mentality," a demoralising apathy, a grand illusion that the nation could resist invasion without really fighting. It acted as a "brake on . . . operations"[60] in an army led by an "assortment of Methuselahs."[61] It sapped the initiative of soldiers more than usually intent on preparing to fight the previous war. "Obsessed by their defensive dream," wrote a biographer of Pétain, "the French authorities saw tanks and aeroplanes as being mere appendages to the infantry."[62] Even if the generals had been more far-sighted there was no avoiding the fact that this monstrous bulwark, which cost seven billion francs, devoured a disproportionate amount of the army's budget. In 1940, when the fallacies, inadequacies and flagrant incompleteness of the Maginot Line were so amply demonstrated, most *poilus* found themselves fighting with 1886 Lebel rifles and some had the even older Gras.

This is to anticipate. In 1930 Tardieu's dual strategy of conciliation and defence seemed plausible. His confidence that the nation was entering an unprecedented era of prosperity appeared justified, particularly when Frenchmen considered the disastrous effects of the Depression elsewhere. France, indeed, was the envy of the world. The Gallic cock, perched on a pile of gold, crowed in many foreign cartoons. With his head thrown back and his dazzling, menacing smile, Tardieu himself was a gift for cartoonists. But though mocked for his social arrogance, he was admired for his intellectual fecundity. Sparking off ideas like a catherine wheel, he seemed eminently to merit his nickname "the Marvel." However, not even André Tardieu was immune from the factionalism and corruption which vitiated French public life. Many of his welfare policies were opposed by the Radicals simply because they had proposed them first. "So you are going to shoot me," Tardieu exclaimed, "at the very time when I come before you bearing your children in my arms?"[63] Frustrated by the Left, Tardieu moved further to the Right. He attacked the Communists and bribed the bully boys of organisations such as Action Française (the political avatar of Maurras' newspaper, which was not just royalist but virulently nationalist) to cheer his speeches. When a scandal involving the collapse of the Oustric Bank brought down his government at the end of 1930, Tardieu (and Briand) teamed up with the renegade Socialist Pierre Laval, whose conservative ministry lasted until 1932.

Premier Laval, who had been Tardieu's Minister of Labour, was (as much as Briand) his political antithesis. He was cunning rather than clever, emollient rather than brusque, populist rather than authoritarian, peasant rather than bourgeois. Laval came from the high Auvergne, where his grandfather had been an illiterate shepherd and his father ran the Hotel du Centre at Châteldon. Here amid the gossip and the smoke of tobacco, among the cards, drinks and dominoes, Laval had early learned to "practise camaraderie like a science."[64] With his slippery charm and his unpretentious amiability, he found it easy to be all things to all men. After qualifying as an advocate, he took his first step towards political advancement by defending left-wing agitators, assuring them: "Comrades, I am a manual lawyer."[65] In 1914, aged only 29, Laval was elected deputy for Aubervilliers, on the outskirts of Paris, where he appealed both to city snobs in their semi-rural retreat and to slaughter-house workers who supplied Les Halles. Laval dressed respectably. He wore dark suits and hats, white ties and spats, and he carried a cane. But he was said to look like a rich Gypsy or a wily Oriental. His skin resembled tanned leather stained with prune juice. His cheekbones were high. His heavy-lidded eyes were almond-shaped and chestnut-coloured, except during rare flashes of anger when they turned black. Imaginative opponents accused Laval of being an Arab Freemason or an Algerian Jew. Softly he denied the impeachment, while admitting ironically: "I do have a fault. I am an Auvergnat."

At first opposing and then supporting the war, Laval kept well away from it, earning himself the nickname "Pierre Far-From-Front." Instead he slowly mastered the art of political patronage, doing favours, arranging deals, bartering influence. He climbed the ministerial greasy pole and quitted the Socialists without antagonising them, though some joked that he had arranged to be born with a palindromic name that looked the same whether he was moving from Left to Right or vice versa. He enrolled as a disciple of Briand and made friends with Tardieu. He flattered the Senate and came, by means of lucid oratory, to "dominate the Assembly like a lighthouse." At the same time he acquired a network of business interests, including newspapers and a radio station, and set himself up as a country gentleman. But this "peasant peer" and "suburban Louis XI"[66] never lost the common touch. Indeed he disliked the grand life, and if his manners became refined he retained the rural habit of taking out his pocket-knife at table to cut the rind off cheese. Laval preferred to enjoy happy domesticity among his cows or to hobnob in cafés with cronies and constituents, smoking—Gitanes, Gauloises, Camels, anything—until his fingernails were saffron. But it was noticed that he never offered his cigarettes to others. Even as Prime Minister he sought congenial informality. On an official visit to Berlin in 1931 he sneaked out after a banquet to sample frankfurters and sauerkraut. The dish played such havoc with his duodenal ulcer that he turned "yellow as a quince" and tried to ease the pain by walking up and down Unter den Linden, to the discomfiture of the guard of honour which had to present arms each time he passed.[67]

Like the political fixer he was, Laval sought to make friends and influence people, notably by employing France's golden treasury. As willing to drive a hard bargain from a position of strength as he was later to accept a humiliating settlement in a state of weakness, he prevented the proposed Austrian-German customs union in 1931 by threatening to withhold credit from Austrian banks. He also took a hard line over the question of war debts and reparations. So hard, in fact, that he provoked President Hoover to declare that a revived France always "gets rich, militaristic and cocky; and nobody can get on with her until she has to be thrashed again." Still, on his visit to the United States in the autumn of 1931 Laval did make a good impression. He declared himself vastly impressed by the skyscrapers (seen through a blizzard of ticker tape), signed autographs tirelessly and won over the Americans with his unforced charm. *Time* magazine made him its "Man of the Year"—he was the first Frenchman to receive that accolade—and on his return Parisian papers dubbed their Auvergnat Premier "the Hoovergnat." Brüning also warmed to Laval, who sought *détente* in the spirit of Briand and argued that "we will be neighbours of Germany for ever."[68] But with Hitler breathing down his neck Brüning could not accept Laval's scheme to renounce rearmament in return for a French loan of 150 million dollars. And at this stage Laval himself was concerned to appease French nationalists, who in November 1931 smashed up the International Disarmament Conference at the Trocadéro, to the bewilderment of an audience of radio listeners who could not understand the unexplained noises. Even the British found Laval congenial, especially when he advanced funds in an unsuccessful effort to relieve their financial plight. But when, in September 1931, Britain abandoned the gold standard, a move swiftly followed by other countries, the franc was overvalued and French exports were over-priced. Suddenly the storm-clouds of the Depression, which had been gathering throughout the year, burst over France.

DURING 1931 industrial production declined by nearly a fifth. Unemployment rose from 12,000 to 190,000. Over 100 banks closed their doors and business bankruptcies increased by 60 per cent. Farm prices collapsed. Since a third of France's population was engaged in agriculture and rural constituencies were over-represented in parliament, the government helped in various ways, stockpiling wheat, buying alcohol to mix with petrol, discouraging over-production. Above all, it imposed strict controls, quotas and duties on imports. But protectionism had the unfortunate effect of sustaining old-fashioned farming methods, and from 1928 to 1934 peasant earnings fell by more than half. Laval and his successors were no more successful when dealing with budget deficits, which first appeared in 1931. After the inflationary traumas of the 1920s the only practical policy was rigid economy and a general tightening of belts. Although more vagrants did seem to be sleeping under the bridges of Paris, there was at first little overt distress. This was because falling prices cushioned consumers against the effects of falling wages, farmers and shopkeepers had recourse to their savings, and peasants reverted to subsistence cultivation. Nevertheless, as Roger Martin du Gard wrote in 1931: "The future appears laden with catastrophic events."[69] The Depression imposed increasing strains on French society and, eventually, intolerable stress on the Third Republic. It undermined faith in capitalism, stimulated extremist movements and ushered in a "time of hate."[70]

The first political victims of this cumulative crisis were Laval and Tardieu, whose conservative coalition was defeated by a left-wing alliance at the general election of May 1932—two months after the death of Briand. Tardieu, who had attacked the Communists very effectively in radio broadcasts (though there were only two million listeners), became more than ever convinced that the constitution must be reformed. By now almost an extinct volcano, he was embittered by the failure of his bright hopes for prosperity and cherished dark thoughts about an authoritarian future. Meanwhile Laval bided his time, calculating that the Left would come to grief on the jagged rocks of the Depression. He was right. Over the next two years there were six different ministries, all equally impotent. Five were led by Radicals, including the warring Edouards, Herriot and Daladier, and one by Joseph Paul-Boncour, the ambitious, flamboyant former Socialist who was "endowed by nature with an opulent shock of white hair" and nicknamed "Robespierrot."[71] The Radicals, the largest party, were unable to cooperate with one another or with anyone else. They felt an ideological sympathy for the Socialists but a practical repugnance. Now that Providence had given them power they meant to enjoy it, in the spirit of Marcel Pagnol's Monsieur Topaze; but they were inhibited by Republican rhetoric from doing so through obvious collaboration with reactionaries. In fact, nothing better summed up the Radicals' situation than the hoary joke that Frenchmen have their hearts on the left and their wallets on the right. Radical ministers were decisive only in negation and Radical deputies dithered over every issue except elevating "fraud into a system of government."[72] Apart from a gut feeling that they must "balance the budget or die" they had no understanding of the Depression, and no policy for dealing with it, other than by vague calls for an "Economic 1789."[73] When ministers raised economic questions Edouard Herriot would "hold his head in his hands in despair and tell them to do what they thought right." Edouard Daladier, Herriot's rival and former pupil, actually went to "night school" in an effort to penetrate the mysteries of the dismal science. This proved an unhappy experience. Daladier learned about a scheme invented by an Austrian named Woorgl for "melting money"—issuing notes designed to stimulate growth by losing 12 per cent of their value each year—which raised the spectre of the revolutionary assignat and horrified his colleagues.[74]

The Radical leaders typified their party's self-indulgence and irresolution. Herriot, who had progressed from humble military origins to out-standing academic achievements, was a monstrous gourmand who liked to order the entire menu in restaurants. He was fond of describing himself as an "average Frenchman,"[75] though his appetite, erudition and oratorical powers were anything but ordinary. Even Herriot's vanity was larger than life: when meeting people he disliked, he would stare pointedly into space and offer them a single finger of his hand to shake, in the manner of a Bourbon king. Yet this rumpled pipe-smoker was essentially a man of moderation. Sensual, genial and deliberate, he remained a good Mayor of Lyon in spirit and in fact, sometimes quitting the counsels of the nation to preside over the municipal council. Daladier, stubborn, stolid, taciturn and abrupt, seemed a much stronger character. The son of a Provençal baker, he had a hard head, a thick neck and a bad temper. These attributes, together with the fact that (according to his enemies) the rustic Daladier still smelled of the stable, earned him the nickname "the Bull of the Vaucluse." The impression was misleading, as colleagues soon saw: some said that he was more like "a hesitant cow," others that he had the horns of a snail.[76] When Daladier banged his fist on the table, one observer noted, "it is a sign that he is preparing to give in."[77]

Neither Herriot nor Daladier was willing or able to take vigorous measures. They clung to financial orthodoxy, reducing official salaries, trying catchpenny expedients such as State lotteries, raising short-term loans to stave off catastrophe, conducting the economy on the principles of a worried housewife. For all their progressive protestations, they failed to tackle crying social evils. Women remained in the subordinate, voteless state to which Napoleon had consigned them, unable even to obtain a passport without male consent. The police went on torturing those not in a position to make a fuss. Nothing was done about slums which were among the worst in Europe. In factories the systematic use of spies continued. The guillotine still did its bloody work, despite pleas for its abolition made before the execution of the mad White Russian Gorgulov who assassinated President Doumer in 1932. The protesters' purpose was not to secure the abolition of the death penalty on humanitarian grounds; it was to have modern technology applied to a process which still relied on horse-drawn, lantern-lit tumbrils as used during the Terror.

Abuses endured in prosperity provoked trouble during time of trial. By the freezing winter of 1932–3 French production had fallen to two-thirds of its 1929 level and over 250,000 people were unemployed. Distress was now visible on the streets of Paris as queues formed outside barracks to snatch scraps of food left by soldiers. Returning from three years of relative affluence in the United States, Maurice Sachs was appalled by the change in Paris, which had become an "abyss of misery, suffering and disorder":

> the theatres nearly empty, Montmartre almost abandoned . . . every sign of penury lying on the luxurious surface of life like leprosy; factories shut, businesses bankrupt, intellectuals everywhere unemployed; too many lawyers, doctors, littérateurs, too many unskilled workers; grey faces and bad news everywhere.[78]

For years extremist groups such as Action Française had used any available excuse to attack the Third Republic: the alleged pro-Semitic bias in the film *Ben-Hur;* the sexual peccadilloes of ministers like Briand; a play about the Dreyfus affair, withdrawn in 1931 after street riots and stink-bombs in the theatre; Herriot's non-aggression treaty with the Soviet Union; and his attempt to continue paying war debts to the United States after German reparations had ceased, which was frustrated with fatal results to his government in December 1932. But now disturbances of all sorts spread through France.

Tax payers revolted in Burgundy, Normandy and Languedoc. In Nîmes veterans howled down proposed cuts in pensions. Students clashed with gendarmes on the Left Bank. In Chartres farmers and peasants, some carrying pitchforks, attacked the Prefect and engaged in running battles with the police. In fact the peasant, described by Herriot as "our silent master,"[79] found his voice on the rack of the Depression. Bodies like the Agrarian Party sprang up to promote the interests of this five-million-strong constituency, which became a politically conscious force for the first time. That dung-heap demagogue Henri Dorgères gathered a following which he transformed into the Peasant Front, complete with green shirts, the motto "Believe, Obey, Serve" and the symbol of a crossed pitchfork and sickle.

Other suffering groups also began to organise, particularly members of the petty bourgeoisie disillusioned with democracy. Many leagues and associations, more or less fascist, formed or developed. Admirers of Hitler, who had just come to power, started the Social-National Party. The veterans' Croix de Feu, whose emblem was a fiery cross surmounted by a skull, blazed into hectic life under the inspirational leadership of Colonel Count François de la Rocque. This sternly enigmatic authoritarian declared that the country was in danger and proposed to restore virtue by means of marching men. Others were also on the move. State officials took to the streets to protest against pay reductions. Lorry drivers rioted. Textile workers and miners went on strike. Shopkeepers and small businessmen demonstrated. Towards the end of 1933 the Communist Party (which because of its slavishness to Moscow had only 35,000 members, a tenth of the combined fascist strength) organised a "Hunger March" from Lille to Paris.

By then the financial crisis was reducing France to chaos. The trade deficit was crippling. The jobless numbered well over 300,000. Ministries fell like skittles and the middle ground of politics was exposed to fire from all sides. Having suffered what General Weygand called "a veritable Calvary" of cuts,[80] the army was thought to be preparing to mount a coup, so much so that Daladier refused to renew Weygand's annual authorisation of command which fell due on 1 January 1934. The nation succumbed to "intellectual turmoil"[81] and political angst. Fear of rising unemployment eclipsed anxiety about falling population and there were calls for eugenic measures on a par with those of the Nazis, including the sterilisation of people suffering from "physiological and mental defects, [and] impulses of a criminal or sexual order."[82] Racist invective plumbed revolting new depths: the novelist Georges Bernanos likened Jews to embalmers patiently pumping out through the nostrils the grey matter of France itself. The State seemed rotten. Parliament was discredited. All the established political parties were in ferment, notably the Socialists, who split from those of their number who appeared bent on becoming National Socialists. One of these militants, Barthélemy Montagnon, expressed a general view: "we are in the midst of a Revolutionary age!"[83] Or as Léon Daudet, that gadfly of *L'Action française,* put it: the country was being swept by a "Wind of Panic."[84]

Sensing that this wind would freshen into a hurricane which might smash the Third Republic, *L'Action française* became more violent than ever. The plump, malicious Daudet stabbed and slashed with his poisoned stiletto, fearful that France would fall victim to the Scylla of Communism or the Charybdis of Nazism. The white-bearded, misanthropic Maurras wielded his anti-Semitic bludgeon as though determined to clear the way single-handed for a royalist revival. Several events assisted *L'Action française* to become the megaphone of middle-class disaffection. In December 1933 the Comédie Française caused an uproar by staging Shakespeare's *Coriolanus,* which, with its talk of "ignoble tribunes," "reckless senators" and the "mutable, rank-scented many," seemed intended to encourage the establishment of a dictatorship. Just before Christmas 1933 a terrible railway accident occurred at Lagny near Paris when the Strasbourg express crashed into a crowded local train, killing or injuring over 500 people. There followed a bitter public row over the inadequacy of the safety precautions and the slowness of the emergency services. Finally, another financial scandal broke, whose ramifications reached right into the cabinet. Such affairs were usually passed off with sallies such as *Rire's* cartoon captioned: "Tonight we shall be entertaining a minister and two deputies. Count the silver."[85] But the Depression had so upset French equilibrium that the Stavisky scandal shook the State to its foundations.

The son of a Jewish dentist who had emigrated from Kiev to Paris before the turn of the century, Serge Alexandre Stavisky was a well-known underworld figure by the 1930s. Melodramatic papers even dubbed him the "king of crooks." Flashy, charming, with a "velvet look" and the "eyes of a gazelle," he had been involved in a series of shady dealings as gigolo, drug-dealer, impresario, police informer and fraudster. Gradually his swindles had grown larger and with them his ability to buy Hispano-Suizas, race-horses, newspapers and politicians. His influence with the authorities was such that he managed to have the trial of a case pending against him postponed no fewer than 19 times. Stavisky's final coup was to sell bonds worth 200 million francs based on the assets of Bayonne's municipal pawnshop. In this unlikely but ingenious enterprise he was aided by a number of corrupt officials, including the Mayor and Deputy of Bayonne, Joseph Garat. Moreover, shortly after news of the crime broke, at the end of December 1933, it emerged that Stavisky had obtained two letters recommending investment in Bayonne bonds from a Radical cabinet minister, Albert Dalimier. Press and public bayed for blood, but Stavisky had disappeared. So on 7 January 1934 *L'Action française* urged its readers to besiege the Chamber of Deputies, cry "Down with the Thieves" and "clamour for honesty and justice."

The following day a new bombshell burst: Stavisky was dead. The official news agency Havas announced that police had traced him to a villa in Chamonix and that as they were forcing the door the king of crooks had fired a bullet through his own head. French faith in their guardians of law and order being what it was, almost everyone concluded that the police had murdered Stavisky to protect his highly-placed political accomplices. There was a howl of derision and anger. Even the respectable papers, finding the official story full of holes, printed the word "suicide" in inverted commas; the *Populaire* said that Stavisky had been "suicided."[86] One cartoon showing a smiling police chief with his arm round Stavisky's shoulder in a fond embrace was captioned, "M. Jean Chiappe collars Stavisky."[87] In parliament, as in the press, charge and counter-charge flashed like lightning through an atmosphere laden with rancour, suspicion and hatred. A right-wing deputy named Philippe Henriot accused two cabinet ministers, Joseph Paul-Boncour and Anatole de Monzie, of having visited Stavisky's pregnant girlfriend (later wife) when she was in hospital under police supervision for a purpose other than that of giving her legal advice. Bearding the author of this calumny in the lobby and employing a phrase which, as one paper noted, does "not figure in the Dictionary of the French Academy," de Monzie roared: "I do not — women in hospital!"[88] A duel between the antagonists was only just averted.

Meanwhile violence had broken out in the streets. Nearly every night the young frondeurs of Action Française and their nationalist allies held riotous demonstrations in the vicinity of the Palais Bourbon, the seat of parliament. Shouting "Down with the Thieves," "Down with the Murderers," they caused huge traffic jams and widespread damage. But it was noted that Chiappe's police treated them more gently than they did the Communists, who were easily identified by their caps, mufflers and overalls. Finally, at the end of January, the two-month-old government of the Radical Camille Chautemps resigned. Though he had proved oddly insouciant over the Stavisky scandal, preferring to stiffen the libel laws than to hold an inquiry, Chautemps still commanded a majority in the Chamber. For the first time in the history of the Third Republic parliament capitulated to the mob.

In an attempt to restore order President Lebrun, who had succeeded the assassinated Doumer, brought back Daladier. The Prime Minister tried to form a government of national unity but had to be content with many of the old familiar faces. So, to stamp his authority on the State and to win Socialist support, the Bull of the Vaucluse dismissed the director of the Comédie Française responsible for the staging of *Coriolanus* and replaced him with the head of the detective service, the Sûreté—an appointment which, in the face of widespread ridicule, he was quickly obliged to rescind. More controversial still, Daladier removed the dapper little Corsican police chief Chiappe, who was popular with the Right and departed with an ill grace. Further small disturbances followed and rumours were rife—of insurrections, bomb plots, the deployment of Senegalese troops armed with machine-guns. Before the meeting of parliament and the demonstrations which were planned to coincide with it, there was an ominous pause. Taxi-drivers were on strike, but this did not explain the uncanny silence in the streets. It was as though Paris were holding its breath.

Then, on the warm, overcast afternoon of 6 February 1934, as Daladier began to make his opening declaration to the Chamber, pandemonium erupted. The Prime Minister was assailed by howls, taunts and catcalls. "Dictator!" cried the Right. "Provocateur!" retorted the Left, when Tardieu tried to intervene. Communists sang the "Internationale." Deputies came to blows and several times the sitting had to be suspended. That evening Daladier got his vote of confidence, but by then all eyes were fixed on a bloodier battle which had broken out just across the Seine, in the Place de la Concorde. Into this enormous amphitheatre, which had witnessed the guillotining of Louis XVI and Marie-Antoinette, a vast throng had converged from meeting-points all over Paris. Many were royalists, nationalists and fascists of different persuasions: Camelots du Roi, Jeunesses Patriotes, members of Solidarité Française and so on. They were joined by disciplined cohorts of ex-servicemen with their medals, armbands and tricolors, by a phalanx of Communists, and by a ragged legion of the unemployed—to say nothing of the army of onlookers. The mass was moved, as one reporter noted, by an "odd mixture of aggressive reaction, of real indignation at the scandals of public life, of economic discontent, of disillusionment with democracy as practised."[89] Such motives might have produced a putsch, as a small minority of the rioters, who came armed with pistols, seem to have planned. But there was no Danton or Mussolini among their leaders: Colonel de la Rocque did little more than march up and down, and Maurras spent most of the night writing poetry. What is more, most of the demonstrators were united only in a frenzy of negation. They wanted to beat out their anger at corruption and Depression on the heads of police and deputies. Their violence was certainly designed to inflict grievous bodily harm but they were not guilty, as the Socialist leader Léon Blum charged, of the "attempted murder of the Republic."[90]

The riot began towards dusk when demonstrators started hurling stones and lumps of asphalt at the police, who were sheltering behind vans barring the way across the Concorde Bridge to the Palais Bourbon. Gardes Mobiles tried to break up the crowd with periodic cavalry charges into the square. Their helmets shone and their sabres flashed in the glare of a burning bus and the glow of the floodlit Luxor obelisk, but they were repeatedly driven back. The rioters threw marbles under the horses' hooves, slashed open their bellies with razors attached to walking sticks and tore up iron railings from the Tuileries Gardens to use as javelins. Turning over cars and uprooting trees, tearing up lamp-posts, benches and paving-stones, they raised barricades. Flying columns of truncheon-wielding gendarmes who tried to destroy them were met with a hail of missiles. As each side received reinforcements and carried off its casualties, some of whom had received terrible wounds, the opposing forces surged back and forth amid the flicker of flames, the stench of burning rubber and the tumult of conflict. Who began the shooting is not clear. Many witnesses blamed the rioters, some the police. People in the crowd pushed forwards to see who was letting off what they thought were Chinese crackers, only to be hurled back in "mass panic" by a fusillade from the bridge. Women cried, "Assassins, assassins" and a "thrill of horror" spread "like wildfire over the city."[91]

So did the rioting. The Ministry of Marine, opposite the Crillon Hotel on the north side of the Place de la Concorde, was set ablaze and the firemen were stoned. Communists rampaged up the Rue Royale, fighting mounted police, wrecking newspaper kiosks and smashing the illuminated traffic beacons—one young man was heard to say that this "would make work for the unemployed."[92] Driven down the Rue de Rivoli by another contingent of Gardes Mobiles, more rioters shattered shop windows and set fire to cars. In the Place Saint-Michel students of the newly-formed University Front were dispersed by baton charge.

The deputies, smuggling themselves through the police cordon, went in fear of their lives. Herriot, easily recognised by his bulk, was set upon and coolly remarked on having "the honour of not being brutalised by the canaille . . . but by more distinguished persons who were there to defend the cause of order." A courageous Communist saved him from being thrown into the Seine: "I felt humiliated," Herriot wrote in his memoirs, "by the thought that a Mayor of Lyon could finish his days in a river other than the Rhône."[93] Meanwhile, in the Place de la Concorde the fight went on with renewed fury, rioters advancing on the bridge, police and guards mounting savage counter-attacks, vicious skirmishes breaking out on the periphery, volleys of shots being fired at intervals. By midnight both sides were exhausted and, like the flames of the burning vehicles, hostilities gradually died down. Fifteen people had been killed and 2,000 seriously injured.

This had been the worst internal disorder to afflict France since the 1871 Commune. The next morning Parisian papers blazed with headlines such as "A Day of Civil War."[94] In the heat of the moment it was an understandable exaggeration. The fact was, however, that Daladier (whose first impulse had been to censor the dispatches of foreign correspondents) resigned with such ignominious haste that he did not even consult his cabinet. Once again power had stemmed from the barricades. The new national government of the aged ex-President Gaston Doumergue reflected the hopes of the reactionary in the street and the fears of the Radical in the Chamber. Among those given office were Pétain and Laval. Tardieu entered the government though, like Herriot, he was appointed joint Deputy Prime Minister without Portfolio. "Herriot and I," he quipped, "are going to shut ourselves up in a café and play cards."[95]

In the bloody wake of 6 February few Frenchmen looked so cheerfully to the future. Since 1929 they had seen their country sink from its gleam-

ing peak of prosperity into a dark valley of Depression. The economic crisis appeared to have sapped France's will to defend itself, menaced though
it was by rampant Nazism without and creeping fascism within. The riots
were, in Mussolini's view, a convincing argument for fascist discipline; and
politicians such as Laval were not ashamed to declare that "the parliamentary system is decidedly incapable of functioning except in times of prosperity and ease."[96] France's democratic friends were scarcely a support.
The United States was isolated and resentful over the cancellation of war
debts. A cover of *Life* magazine lampooned the emblem of the French
Republic, picturing a blonde Marianne dancing on a heap of gold and
singing, "I can't give you anything but love." Depressed Britain was preoccupied with the safety of its global empire, strangely detached from
Europe and affected by a Francophobia "pervasive even at the highest
levels."[97] Perfidious Albion was less than cordial about the entente. So, it
seemed, France on its own might easily abandon democracy for dictatorship. In the lurid light of boulevard bonfires the Third Republic looked
hopelessly decadent, if not ultimately doomed.

VIII

THE SLUMP IN BRITAIN

FROM time immemorial Britain had regarded France as its natural enemy, but it took the Great War alliance between the two powers to expose the full depths of their hostility. "Anti-French feeling among most ex-soldiers amounted almost to an obsession," according to Robert Graves, who recorded the opinion of his shell-shocked fellow-poet Edmund Blunden: "No more wars for me at any price! Except against the French. If there's ever a war with them, I'll go like a shot."[1] Tales proliferated about French peasants charging English Tommies rent for the trenches they were defending, and Gallic pusillanimity was contrasted with Teutonic gallantry. Many believed that Britain had been fighting on the wrong side and Lord Mount Temple was not alone in saying that if "another war comes . . . I hope the partners will be changed."[2]

This mood weakened the democratic entente. Even the normally Francophile Churchill was disgusted with French greed and intransigence during the Versailles negotiations. The manic-depressive Governor of the Bank of England, Montagu Norman, for years refused to visit French health resorts on the grounds that he might there encounter French bankers—though he was prepared to consult the celebrated Doctor Coué in order to convince himself that "every day, in every way, I feel better and better."[3] Stanley Baldwin so disliked foreigners, particularly Frenchmen, that he went to elaborate lengths to avoid sitting next to them at table. Ramsay MacDonald, who had succeeded him as Prime Minister at the head of a minority Labour government in June 1929, inveighed not only against the "crooked diplomacy"[4] of André Tardieu but against "the whole crew of French politicians—underhand, grasping, dishonourable."[5] Meeting them once *en masse*, MacDonald asked Madame Herriot if her husband was the only honest man present; she replied tactfully that there were two.

Despite his high-minded internationalism, MacDonald was doubtless influenced by a national antipathy so pronounced that it might have

sparked off "an explosion of public opinion against France."[6] Gallic corruption apart, he was perturbed by France's implacable hostility towards
Germany, by its ruthless use of economic diplomacy and by its "purely
militarist" mentality. "France," he said at the beginning of his second premiership, "becomes the peace problem of Europe."[7] Like Briand, Mac-
Donald saw it as his prime duty to avert a new conflict. Though never a
pacifist, he had opposed the Great War. Then he condemned the punitive
peace, favouring disarmament instead. Nor would MacDonald have any
truck with class warfare. After an early flirtation with the Russian revolutionaries he concluded that Bolshevism was tantamount to barbarism. His
own socialism was not entirely bogus, though Harold Nicolson suggested
that it was as much the genuine article as Harris tweed made in Bavaria.
But it was principle rather than practice. It was a utopia to be glimpsed
through the mists of romantic rhetoric and to be realised gradually—if at
all. MacDonald's socialism, as one critic wrote,

> is that far-off Never-Never-Land born of vague aspirations and described
> by him in picturesque generalities. It is a Turner landscape of beautiful
> colours and glorious indefiniteness. He saw it, not with a telescope, but
> with a kaleidoscope.[8]

An idealist rather than an ideologue, a champion of "vehement moderation," MacDonald instilled confidence—even in his political opponents.
He was the Labour party's answer to Stanley Baldwin, and in 1929 he
might just as easily have campaigned on the Conservative slogan, "Safety
First."

But was MacDonald the man to lead Britain out of difficulties which,
even before the economic blizzard, were more acute than those of France?
Certainly he looked the part. He was tall and handsome, with piercing
brown eyes and wavy grey hair, a broad moustache and a voice which convinced acolytes that he was "a second Messiah coming amongst them."
Nicknamed "Gentleman Mac," he had the bearing of an aristocrat and he
did nothing to dispel the rumour that his father had been a marquis.
Actually his father was a ploughman and he had sired MacDonald on a
Scottish servant girl whom he had never married. Bastardy was a deep,
unacknowledged wound in the son's psyche as well as a serious social
stigma. MacDonald had been toughened by hardship: during his early
days in London he had lived on nothing but water and oatmeal sent from
his mother's home at Lossiemouth, for which he duly paid. He had also
been inspired by high hopes of social reform: he had taken his first political steps at the East London Ethical Society, where, wearing his red tie, he
had sung hymns to progress with his fellow idealists. With his political

flair, his intellectual power and his "nervous electric energy,"[9] he had done much to create the Labour party.

Moreover, he had emerged with glamour enhanced from the personal tragedy of his beloved wife's death. And he had survived, with prestige augmented, the political setback of his courageous wartime isolation. Both events had seared MacDonald to the core. Asked in 1936 why he had never remarried, he replied: "My heart has been in the grave for a quarter of a century."[10] Viciously abused as a traitor during the war, he had at one time "talked of suicide."[11] His 1924 ministry had been little more than a fiasco. Furthermore MacDonald had suffered personal indignities as Prime Minister. He had been so poor that he was obliged to dine in the officially-heated banqueting rooms at 10 Downing Street to save on coal in his private apartment. He had had to travel by bus and tube until given the money to purchase a motor car by a biscuit manufacturer, whose subsequent ennoblement tarnished the Prime Minister's reputation. Nevertheless MacDonald's long suffering seemed somehow to have sanctified him. To his charismatic presence and his melodious eloquence—those rolling Scottish "r"s—the Labour leader added a visionary gleam, a distillation of Celtic twilight. He fascinated devotees with his air of martyred melancholy, brooding mystery, "unfathomable depth."[12] He was, as one admirer wrote, "the Hamlet of the Labour Party . . . the soul of the movement."[13] Even outsiders were impressed by his spiritual strength (though few knew that he dabbled in spiritualism). Shortly after MacDonald became Prime Minister in 1929 the journalist A. G. Gardiner wrote that he "is made of a metal that has been tried in the fiercest fires of adversity and has only hardened and strengthened in the process."[14]

In fact MacDonald's strength was strangely alloyed with weakness. Perhaps because of his illegitimacy, he was constitutionally insecure and hyper-sensitive to criticism. As proud of his intellect as of his appearance, he could never "allow that there was anything he did not know. He would talk science with scientists, music with musicians, medicine with doctors, Buddhism with Indians."[15] (The Indians delighted him by saying that he was a reincarnated Brahmin.) Intolerant of all who questioned his omniscience, MacDonald was alternately aloof and condescending towards his colleagues. Malcolm Muggeridge remembered him as a picturesque figure in a tweed knickerbocker suit and a flamboyant tie "who shook hands by extending two fingers, made conversation by asking fatuous questions, and engaged in little playfulnesses almost like royalty."[16] To royalty itself and to his other social superiors MacDonald was infinitely more ingratiating. He formed an "intimate social relationship" with Sir Oswald Mosley such as never existed between himself and "plebeian members of the Labour Party."[17] He revelled in his friendship with the Marchioness of Londonderry, sending her fey poems and addressing her mock-medievally as "My Dear Ladye." He engaged in sentimental affairs with other Society ladies, writing letters not so much romantic as necromantic: "What a day yesterday was in the air. I sang songs to the winds & the clouds & the mists, admired the handsome fur boots I was wearing & was as vain as a peacock."[18] While they acknowledged MacDonald's indispensable political gifts, Labour politicians were increasingly impatient with their leader. One Scottish MP likened him to that other Highland product, the collie: "Brilliant, vain, jealous, loyal and untrustworthy."[19] Beatrice Webb declared that MacDonald was "an egotist, a poseur and a snob, and worst of all he does not believe in the creed we have always preached—he is not a socialist and has not been one for twenty years; he is a mild radical with individualist leanings and aristocratic tastes."[20]

   This was a characteristically acute assessment. MacDonald was essentially a decorative figure: having urgently radioed the Foreign Office for sartorial advice from his transatlantic liner, he eschewed cloth cap for top hat and morning coat on his visit to the United States in the autumn of 1929 and made an excellent impression. But he had no comprehension of the impending economic crisis and no remedy, socialist or otherwise, for Britain's longer-term economic ills. The worst of these was unemployment, which Labour had pledged itself to tackle via schemes of national reconstruction. In practice MacDonald did little more than set up committees and launch inquiries. As Baldwin remarked with unwonted sharpness, the King's speech setting out Labour's programme could be summed up as, "My Ministers are going to think"—which prompted the obvious retort that this was more than the Conservatives had ever done.[21] In the event, unemployment almost doubled during the first year of MacDonald's administration, rising to a figure of two million, and he did not so much bend his brain as wring his hands. In December 1929 he wrote in his journal: "Unemployment is baffling us. The simple fact is that our population is too great for our trade . . . I sit in my room in Downing Street alone & in silence. The cup has been put to my lips—& it is empty." There was much more in this vein, as MacDonald wondered if the sun was setting on the empire, worried about the rise of tariffs and the decline of trade, brooded on the backwardness of British industry, dreamed about the dearth of work, complained that the harvest of Depression which he was now reaping had been sown by warmongers like Lloyd George. Never lucid, MacDonald was showing signs by 1930 of his sad lapse into final incoherence. "I cannot see any daylight through the forest of unemployment," he wrote. "All kinds of evil possibilities are as real to me as though I was in them, & my head won't work."[22]

Nor would the round, bald head of Jimmy Thomas, once the railwaymen's leader, now Lord Privy Seal and the minister charged with the task of curing unemployment, who preferred drinking to thinking at the best of times (a colleague once twitted him with having consumed 9 gallons of champagne in 150 days). Thomas would often complain of having "an 'ell of an 'eadache," prompting Lord Birkenhead's famous reply: "Try a couple of aspirates."[23] In fact Thomas acted the proletarian for all he was worth: Beatrice Webb said that he dropped his aitches as carefully as a beautiful woman puts on her make-up. He enjoyed hobnobbing with smart new cronies from turf and 'Change, where he used inside knowledge to speculate in stocks, and he played shamelessly to the gallery. When a railwayman shouted, "You have sold us, Jimmy," Thomas retorted: "Well, I've been trying bloody 'ard, but I'm darned if I can find a buyer."[24] George V liked his bluntness (Thomas told him that Balmoral was a "bloody dull 'ouse")[25] and laughed at his earthy jokes, though not so heartily (as myth has it) that he burst an abscess in his back.

Although Thomas was regarded as having "the adaptability of a Jack-of-all-Trades and the versatility of a one-man band,"[26] he proved quite incapable of grasping the scope of the unemployment problem, let alone of finding solutions to it. He was by no means torpid, though there was a grain of truth in the *Pravda* cartoon which showed Thomas reclining in an armchair surrounded by flunkeys and saying, "At last I can do something for the unemployed."[27] He chased any number of red herrings, here proposing the erection of concrete telephone poles, there planning a traffic circus at the Elephant and Castle. He made futile efforts to drum up trade in Canada, claiming to have secured orders for British ships—they proved evanescent, "ships that pass in the night."[28] But by the time of the Wall Street Crash, preceded in England by the collapse of Clarence Hatry's fraudulent financial empire in September 1929, Thomas had done virtually nothing except promote a few road-building schemes. Very soon, according to "Uncle" Arthur Henderson, Labour's stolid Foreign Secretary, Thomas was "completely rattled and in such a state of panic that he is bordering on lunacy . . . the p.m. fears suicidal mania."[29]

Even if Thomas had been more imaginative, however, he could not have achieved anything, owing to the adamantine financial orthodoxy of Philip Snowden, Chancellor of the Exchequer. A tough, blunt Yorkshireman who had been crippled (probably as a result of spinal tuberculosis) in 1891, Snowden burned with the gem-like flame of radical Nonconformity.

Fiercely wedded to the narrow canons of thrift and sobriety, Snowden was blind to other considerations. He permitted himself few pleasures apart from Turkish cigarettes at 3d. for 20, which he chain-smoked in an ivory holder. He had no aesthetic interests, though he could sing two songs— "On Ilkla Moor baht 'at" and "The Red Flag." (The latter he taught to the newspaper magnate Lord Beaverbrook, an unlikely convert despite his weakness for revivalist hymns.) In contrast to MacDonald, however, Snowden was blessed with a luminous clarity of mind. He expressed his views with the conviction of a fanatic and jokes abounded about his eagerness to set up a guillotine in Trafalgar Square for "the idle rich" (a phrase he apparently invented). Possessing ash-blond hair, steel-blue eyes and a paper-white face, he seemed a sea-green incorruptible. When speaking he would jut his hatchet chin forward and "his long tongue would come out from between his thin lips like a serpent to hiss and sting."[30]

Almost at once foreigners felt the lash of that tongue, when at an international conference at The Hague in 1929 Snowden refused to accept a reduction of Britain's share of German reparations under the Young Plan. He made no bones about his hostility to the French, who protested about his "terrible accountancy"[31] and booed him in Parisian cinemas. Snowden almost provoked a duel with the French delegate, Henri Chéron, who later expressed the hope that Britain's next negotiator would hail from as far away from Yorkshire as possible, preferably Land's End. "Cripple psychology," commented Hugh Dalton, a junior member of MacDonald's government, "waving his crutches round and round his head and yelling insults at foreigners, amid rapturous applause from all the worst elements in England."[32] Among them was King George V, who was so pleased with the performance of the "Iron Chancellor" that he invited him and his handsome wife Ethel to Sandringham. Snowden was much gratified, though the King's country house was one of the ugliest in England and it was home to 75 dogs. Ethel later said that she needed no friends in the Labour party because she was on such intimate terms with the royal family.

Whatever Snowden's psychology, his tactics were equally effective in the House of Commons. He believed passionately in balanced budgets, free trade, the gold standard, redistributive taxation and reducing the national debt. He had no faith at all that government spending on public works could lessen unemployment, reckoning that the money obtained by loans or taxes would correspondingly diminish private investment. Thus, to Winston Churchill's huge delight, Snowden's budgets hardly differed in principle from his own during Baldwin's administration—which did not stop Churchill from attacking them with his usual ebullience. He compared Snowden to Jekyll and Hyde:

> On the one hand we have the severe Treasury pedant, accepting with double joy the narrowest doctrines and dogmas of departmental officials, and on the other hand we have the Socialist agitator endeavouring to excite the masses to the pillage of the wealth of this country.[33]

In presentation, of course, the contrast between the two Chancellors was marked, for Snowden "eschew[ed] all rhetoric."[34] As the Conservative MP Leo Amery noted, he offered the Commons "a glass of very dry ginger ale as compared to the magnum of sweet champagne Winston used to give us."[35]

To combat the malign effects of the Depression Snowden raised taxes and curbed government expenditure. During the London Naval Conference early in 1930 he obliged MacDonald to reverse his (and the Admiralty's) expensive ship-building programme, which enabled Britain to reach agreement on a "naval holiday" with the Americans and the reluctant Japanese. Like some fiscal Canute, Snowden resisted the rising tide of protectionism. Although he permitted some ameliorative measures such as small increases in unemployment benefit and a relaxation of the harsh terms on which it was given, he refused to countenance schemes of job creation which did not pay for themselves. The most potent and practical of these schemes was proposed by Jimmy Thomas's ambitious junior minister Sir Oswald Mosley. Helped by the Cambridge economist Maynard Keynes and drawing on other ideas, notably those set out in Lloyd George's Liberal manifesto *We Can Conquer Unemployment,* Mosley put forward a revolutionary programme of State intervention, economic reconstruction and public works to be financed by government loans. He also wanted the regulation of trade by tariffs so that Britain could be "insulated" against the "electric shocks of present world conditions."[36]

Despising Thomas and desiring action, Mosley submitted his proleptic New Deal directly to MacDonald. Having dismissed Lloyd George's manifesto as a religious tract sub-edited by Satan, the Prime Minister was unlikely to embrace Mosley's scheme. So he and his cabinet colleagues were only too pleased when it was condemned by the Treasury and its inflexible chief. Precisely because Snowden had always been at heart a liberal rather than a Socialist, he anathematised the kind of central direction which Mosley advocated. It smacked of dictatorship, as Mosley himself implied when he said that Napoleon could carry out his proposals. At one meeting Snowden chided Mosley: "You are a young man who cannot remember previous depressions; they have often recurred in my lifetime and have passed away." The Chancellor extolled the self-correcting equilibrium of the free market, which would gradually expand to absorb British production. "For instance, when I was a boy, negroes did not ride bicycles; now they do ride bicycles and workers in Coventry are employed to make those bicycles."[37]

When his memorandum was rejected Mosley resigned, declaring that Snowden's policies, not his own departure, would wreck the government. Mosley then appealed to the parliamentary Labour party, which sympathised but followed its leaders. Most Labour MPs anyway mistrusted this wealthy deserter from the Tory ranks who, with his well-groomed moustache and his toothy smile, looked like a bold, bad music hall baronet and spoke to them (as Clement Attlee complained) "as though he were a feudal landlord abusing his tenants who are in arrears with their rent."[38] In a rash, fierce blaze of impatience, Mosley took his case to the House of Commons on 28 May 1930. Tall, aquiline and immaculate in black coat and striped trousers, he made an eloquent speech, justifying his resignation and forecasting "a real crisis" or "a gradual paralysis" during which Britain would sink to the level of Spain.

> What a fantastic assumption it is that a nation which within the lifetime of every one has put forth efforts of energy and vigour unequalled in the history of the world, should succumb before an economic situation such as the present. If the situation is to be overcome, if the great powers of this country are to be rallied and mobilised for a great national effort, then the Government and Parliament must give a lead.[39]

With MacDonald in command there was no chance of that, even though plans such as Mosley's offered the government "a real historical option"[40] to laissez-faire orthodoxy. The Prime Minister did, it is true, remove Thomas, making him Dominions Secretary, an easy wicket thanks to Tory divisions over imperial preference and Indian independence. Moreover, MacDonald himself took charge of unemployment policy, prompting a flurry of activity. He received deputations, formed committees, set up inquiries, consulted experts. He even consulted the Opposition. But the number of jobless mounted remorselessly, as did the Prime Minister's excuses. He blamed Lloyd George. He blamed the French. He blamed the capitalist system. He blamed the unemployed themselves, invoking those familiar figures of Conservative demonology—work-shy men and fur-coated women arriving by motor car to collect their dole. MacDonald had a Victorian feeling that the State should not act as Lady Bountiful any more than it should lord it over the free market. He was not dogmatic; indeed, he deplored Snowden's "hard dogmatism expressed in words & tones as hard as his ideas."[41] MacDonald was prepared to discuss anything, though his talk tended to ramble off into the gorse-clad hills of Lossiemouth, or to wander through the byways of culture and the highways of Society. But at heart he believed that nothing could be done. The Depression was a natural cataclysm. MacDonald doubtless lacked the will to act but, more important, he lacked the conviction. Lord Beaverbrook compared him to a Baptist preacher who had lost his faith but still had to go on preaching.

As the number of unemployed rose to 2.5 million by the end of 1930 there were real concerns about Britain's political stability. Both government and party system lost credit. MacDonald was kept in office only by a cynical Lloyd George fearful of an election. Socialists, Conservatives and Liberals squabbled ferociously among, as well as between, themselves. The rotten structure of Westminster could surely not withstand another "hungry thirties" like that of the previous century. In the face of Depression Fabian faith in "the inevitability of gradualness" looked naïve. Beatrice Webb was not alone in anticipating that Britain would become embroiled in a global revolution which would sweep away both parliamentary democracy and capitalism itself:

> The U.S.A., with its cancerous growth of crime and uncounted but destitute unemployed; Germany hanging over the precipice of a nationalist dictatorship; Italy boasting of its military preparedness; France, in dread of a new combination of Italy, Germany and Austria against her; Spain on the brink of revolution; the Balkan states snarling at each other; the Far East in a state of anarchic ferment; the African continent uncertain whether its paramount interest and cultural power will be black or white; South American states forcibly replacing pseudo-democracies by military dictatorships; and finally—acutely hostile to the rest of the world, engulfed in a fabulous effort, the success of which would shake capitalist civilization to its very foundations—Soviet Russia.[42]

Nothing was more calculated to precipitate revolution than inflation. As Lenin himself had remarked, the best way to undermine the capitalist system was to debauch its currency. Debauchery approached as tax yields fell by nearly a third and the cost of unemployment benefit rose from 12 million pounds in 1928 to 125 million in 1931. Fearing national bankruptcy, Snowden inveighed against the microbe of inflation, while MacDonald dwelt darkly on the prospect of working men having their wages delivered by pantechnicon. It was evident that the government was losing its nerve. Snowden, whom Lloyd George described as a "poor limp creature who is on the point of a serious attack of syncope which may involve us all in disaster," warned that drastic measures would be necessary to alleviate the situation. As for the Prime Minister, Lloyd George said that he was "as near a broken man as I have seen in a big job." Conjuring with Churchill's recent description of MacDonald as "the boneless wonder," the Welsh Wizard continued:

> He looked tired, faded & spiritless. The fizz is out of him. He is no longer riding the clouds. He is like a man who has fallen from the top of the Taj Mahal where he has been posing & gesticulating for weeks. He hasn't a bone in his body. It is all pulp. His difficulties are almost overwhelming. He has to face a realised deficit *this* year of £40,000,079 & an anticipated deficit of £70,000,000 next year! I had no idea that it was as bad . . . it was like talking to a white rabbit. This ranting hero of the Socialist halls squealed with terror when he was invited to face the wrath of the financial weasels of the City.[43]

What most concerned the City's rich was naturally the amount of money being paid to the country's poor. Wages were too high, they believed, which made Britain uncompetitive—exports had halved in value since 1929. Also too high were pensions, the mania for which, in the opinion of Sir Ernest Benn, was "unEnglish, immoral, degrading and disastrous."[44] There had been "an orgy of extravagance on social reform"[45] which had given Britain the most expensive and comprehensive system of unemployment relief in the world. Admittedly it operated in a piecemeal fashion and MacDonald himself acknowledged that 26 shillings a week for a married couple was "not a living wage."[46] Nevertheless, the nation seemed to be living beyond its means. This conclusion was sustained by the reports of two committees of inquiry in the summer of 1931. The second, that of Sir George May, was particularly alarmist. It shook people abroad as well as at home by predicting a budget deficit of 170 million pounds in a full year and recommending draconian economies, including a 20 per cent cut in unemployment benefit.

Meanwhile the European financial storm which followed the collapse of the Creditanstalt bank began to approach British shores. Initially the Bank of England had tried to prop up Austrian and German credit with further loans, in the spirit of Hoover's moratorium on reparations. But as the French sought to wring political concessions from their old enemy— MacDonald found their behaviour "inconceivably atrocious"[47]—foreign funds flooded from German banks, until many closed their doors. So the City, with its huge long-term loans to Germany frozen, came under pressure in its turn. Foreign creditors, many of them French, sold sterling. London's financial life-blood began to drain away in a golden haemorrhage. In less than 4 weeks the Bank of England lost 60 million pounds' worth of bullion and foreign exchange. In a state of nervous prostration its Governor, Montagu Norman, fled to North America for a long holiday, having insisted that "ration books should be printed in case the currency collapsed and the country had to revert to barter."[48]

Neither higher interest rates nor American and French loans could stop the run on the pound. By the beginning of August London bankers told Snowden that the picture could not be blacker and warned MacDonald that Britain would go over the precipice unless foreign confidence was restored by a balanced budget. The Chancellor proposed to achieve it not only by raising taxes but also by a ten per cent cut in unemployment benefit. Without this, he warned bleakly, "The deluge."[49] Others talked of an "economic 1914."[50] So, after bankers and trade-unionists had applied conflicting pressures, after much external consultation and internal wrangling, the cabinet split. Nine members opposed penalising the indigent for the failures of the opulent. Eleven ministers took the view that everyone must make sacrifices to preserve the currency and that, in any case, the unemployed were cushioned by lower prices. Emerging from this stormy meeting, to which he had contributed nothing except a few doodles on a blotter and a final request for his colleagues' resignations, MacDonald exclaimed: "I'm going off to the Palace to throw in my hand."[51]

ON the short journey up Whitehall, through Admiralty Arch, along the Mall and past the Victoria Memorial—a processional way quite recently established for displays of pageantry designed to mobilise imperial loyalty behind the sovereign—MacDonald might have had time to reflect on the oddity of his position. Here he was, the socialist leader of a parliamentary democracy, going to decide the fate of the nation in secret conclave with the crowned head of a hereditary monarchy. The contrast between the purposes of the modern State and the trammels of feudal tradition became even more apparent once he reached Buckingham Palace.

The Palace was a vast museum full of the treasures of the ages. Its 600 rooms were crammed with Aubusson carpets and Axminster rugs, Meissen porcelain and Sèvres china, Japanese perfume burners and Chinese cabinets. They contained Gobelin tapestries, gilt thrones, ebony commodes, malachite candelabra, marble vases, boulle tables, walnut grand pianos, silk panels and damask walls, as well as bric-à-brac so antique that it was liable to disintegrate at the touch. There was a picture gallery full of old masters. There were innumerable barometers and 300 clocks which provided two men with full-time employment. King George himself collected rich snuff boxes and Queen Mary, who liked to surround herself with plaques, miniatures, statuettes, intaglios, wax profiles, baubles and bibelots of all sorts, had "assembled an immense collection of *objets d'art*."[52] (Many were acquired by Sovereign scrounging that amounted to kleptomania—when she visited Asprey's, the Bond Street jewellers, staff were instructed to lock away valuable trinkets because of her habit of pocketing them.)[53] The State Apartments were models of magnificence: the Grand Hall with its crimson carpets and marble columns; the Throne Room with its seven cut-glass chandeliers and Louis XVI wood-carvings; the Blue Drawing Room with its gold-framed mirrors, brocaded walls and decorated ceiling; the domed Music Room with its five huge windows overlooking the Palace gardens and lake; the Ball Room with its great organ and canopied thrones . . . and many others.

Here was the setting for a monstrous tableau vivant of archaic custom. On State occasions the King and Queen were attended by a host of functionaries including the Lord Chamberlain and the Lord Steward, who preceded them into banquets walking backwards. There was the Honourable Corps of Gentlemen-at-Arms, bearing swords and wearing scarlet jackets heavily ornamented with gold lace and tall burnished helmets with white horse-hair plumes. There were the square-bearded Yeomen of the Guard with their halberds and maces, dressed in black velvet hats, white ruffs and scarlet doublets and tunics embroidered with royal emblems. Also performing arcane rituals were ladies of the household, equerries, gentlemen ushers, pages and footmen matched in pairs by size and dressed in scarlet coats with gold trimmings, red velvet breeches, white stockings and buckled shoes. These gorgeous flunkeys were the standard-bearers of an army of servants who dwelt hugger-mugger in "beetle-ridden basements."[54] Beneath even them, as King Edward VIII later discovered, came a "troglodytish individual" who apparently slept in an enormous, tallow-filled room in the bowels of the Palace and "help[ed] with the candles."[55]

Above stairs, the focus of the hive's constant solicitude, King George and Queen Mary proceeded according to the unvarying rhythms of time-worn protocol. The Queen, a stiff, bloodless figure, was anyway something of a regal marionette; Beatrice Webb described her as "an exquisitely executed automaton."[56] She was not stupid but, like her husband, she was awesomely remote from the everyday life of the nation. Visiting the East End of London she eventually exclaimed to a group of its people, "Why, why do you live here?"[57] The King, a dull, voluble man with no interests except shooting, stamp-collecting and clothes, was conservative to the point of ossification. He hated novelty almost as much as he hated abroad: "Amsterdam, Rotterdam, and all the other dams! Damned if I'll go."[58] He maintained pre-war standards in everything, had his trousers creased at the side and put on the same collar stud he had used for 50 years. He carried on with the presentation of débutantes, insisted on traditional Court dress (spectacles must not be worn without permission) and could think of nothing when meeting Gandhi except the impropriety of his entering Buckingham Palace with "bare knees."[59] Political novelty the King found particularly offensive and, as Lloyd George once complained, the "whole atmosphere" of the Court "reeks of Toryism."[60] Yet as a constitutional monarch the Sovereign had to remain above the battle. In the words of J. C. C. Davidson, King George

> was very right-wing and he knew where his friends really lay, and that the Conservative Party was the King's Party and a radical party was not. But he managed to persuade the Labour Party that he was entirely neutral. That must have required a good deal of self-discipline.[61]

Only thus, in an age when crowns and thrones were showing a distressing tendency to perish, could George hope to survive as head of a united nation. So, on the fateful Sunday evening of 23 August 1931, when Ramsay MacDonald arrived looking "scared and unbalanced,"[62] the advice which the King gave him was to remain at his post. However, he should not stay as a Labour Prime Minister but as the head of a coalition government of national salvation.

The royal prerogative was therefore used, as it invariably is in Britain, not so much to prevent change as to ensure that the more things change the more they stay the same. The ideal situation from the King's point of view was a National Government nominally led by a sentimental Socialist (one happy to wear the regulation knee breeches at Court) but dominated by staunch Tories. MacDonald's feelings, as he emerged from the Palace, were mixed. He recognised that he might be committing political suicide. He guessed that he would incur the odium of the Labour party without gaining the respect of the Conservatives. Yet in many ways the latter promised to be more congenial colleagues. He had long hankered for some sort of *rapprochement* with them, though the strain of bringing the National Government to birth induced a kind of morning sickness—the vomiting left him as weak as a kitten. Evidently MacDonald succumbed to the continuing allure of high society and high office. Having led the country into the crisis the Prime Minister was buoyed up by his Sovereign's assurances that he was the only man to lead it out. He allowed the King to persuade him that it was his patriotic duty to stay, at least temporarily, and to put country before party at a time when the Socialists were behaving like deserters.

MacDonald himself was accused of desertion when he formed a cabinet

consisting of four Labour men (including Snowden and Thomas), four
Tories (including Baldwin and Neville Chamberlain, but not Churchill)
and two Liberals (excluding Lloyd George, who was ill). Most of the
Labour party opposed the National Government and some of its members
were so bitter that they nurtured dark suspicions of conspiracy as well
as betrayal. Victims of a bankers' ramp, they had surely been jockeyed out
of power by a palace revolution. The Crown, they believed, had acted in
an unconstitutional fashion, when its proper role, according to Professor
Harold Laski, was "that of dignified emollient rather than of an active
umpire between conflicted interests." There was something in this charge,
though since Britain's constitution was unwritten and since the sacrosanct
monarchy was surrounded by an "organized silence,"[63] it could not easily
be proved. Few realised at the time what has subsequently become clear,
that "the King's anti-Socialist bias played a large part in his motivation."[64]
Anyway, since the Labour party's republicanism was even more theoretical
than its socialism, it was not inclined to launch a concerted attack on the
throne.

Instead its members vented their spleen on MacDonald, who was well
compensated by aristocratic adulation—as he had memorably and gleefully told Snowden when the National Government was formed, "tomorrow every Duchess in London will be wanting to kiss me."[65] Snowden
himself became a target when he stood up in front of massed ranks of
Conservatives and Liberals on 10 September to present his emergency
budget to the House of Commons. This he balanced mainly by tax
increases (which the Tories were now prepared to swallow) and cuts in
public service pay and unemployment benefits—a single man's dole fell
from 17s. a week to 15s. 3d. The furious Labour party, now led by Henderson, conveniently forgetting that it had already accepted most of
Snowden's measures, assaulted him root and branch. Snowden retaliated
with stunning invective, damning his erstwhile friends as Bolsheviks. But
though he could quell domestic opposition he could not, in the face of
continuing European financial instability, stem the flow of gold from London. Foreign confidence was further shaken when Snowden's economies
apparently jeopardised the security of Britain's most powerful institution,
the Royal Navy. The Admiralty had been exceedingly cavalier in its announcement of the pay reductions to ratings and on 14 September some
sailors of the Atlantic Fleet disobeyed orders, thus sparking off an event
which became known as the Invergordon Mutiny.

Harbouring close to the small town of Invergordon in Scotland's Moray
Firth were the most powerful vessels in the world, among them the battleships *Nelson* and *Rodney*, grey leviathans an eighth of a mile long and

equipped with 16-inch guns capable of firing 1-ton shells a distance of 20 miles. Although the men endured harsh discipline, slaved at endless spit-and-polish tasks and slung their hammocks where they could on cramped mess-decks, conditions here were probably better than in any other navy in the world—better, certainly, than those in the Chilean navy, where a major mutiny over pay cuts (which brought down the government) had just been brutally suppressed. The lash had gone, while indulgence in those other celebrated British naval traditions, rum and buggery, was now largely optional. Hard tack had vanished and the food was fairly good. Young leaders of the mutiny such as Len Wincott, brought up in the Leicester slums, and Fred Copeman, a workhouse boy, found their lot vastly improved in the navy. But there were grievances, particularly over class discrimination, which life in the services seemed to accentuate. If an ordinary seaman caught venereal disease a black mark (in red ink) was entered in his record; whereas an officer who was similarly afflicted incurred no penalty, his indisposition being jocularly dismissed as a case of "wardroom lumbago."[66] Promotion within the ranks was slow. From the ranks it was rare, despite Labour's endeavour to introduce naval "democratisation."[67] (The problem was not only that officers resented promotions from the lower deck; matelots also liked their officers to be gentlemen.) The men's main source of discontent, though, was over pay. On three or four shillings a day they could hardly support their families. As an Admiralty committee reported, "When a pair of boots has to be mended some other thing has to be done without."[68] To make extra money men set up little businesses on board ship—as barbers, launderers, cigarette-makers and the like. But, as one witness recalled, "You could see the poverty . . . I'd read a lot of Dickens and I'd seen the Cruikshanks: these people, a lot of them, were caricatures. It showed in their faces that they'd suffered." So when news spread of cuts which docked the pay of some able seamen by as much as 25 per cent (whereas some officers were losing less than 4 per cent), the result was a spontaneous outburst of rage.

Shocked watches on shore leave gathered at the big canteen by the football fields at Invergordon. There were noisy discussions and inflammatory speeches. Men feared that their wives would be evicted or would turn to prostitution. In an atmosphere of rowdiness, drunkenness and indiscipline some planned to strike—they were careful not to talk of mutiny—by refusing to put to sea for exercises. This they duly did at 6:00 in the morning of Tuesday 15 September, to the amazement of the boy sailors who called hands to duty. As one later said, "To me, that was like the sea drying up."[69] The crews of the half-dozen capital ships involved were not hostile towards their officers. They simply ignored orders, disregarded appeals and milled around aimlessly. There was little or no organisation, though the men encouraged one another by cheering from ship to ship. Some talked of training their guns on Ramsay MacDonald's house at nearby Lossiemouth. Others sang "The Red Flag." But they also stood up when Marine bands played "God Save the King"; and despite sedulous efforts the Admiralty was never able to find evidence of a Communist conspiracy. The only coherent demands were formulated in a "loyal" manifesto dictated by Len Wincott on board the *Norfolk*. This implored the Admiralty "to amend the drastic cuts in pay" which "threaten tragedy, misery and immorality amongst the families of the lower deck." Otherwise the stoppage would continue.[70]

Hotheads at the Admiralty apparently considered suppressing the mutiny by force. And Jimmy Thomas said that if he had been in charge the mutineers would have been "disciplined for an example" instead of being allowed to "sovietize the British Navy."[71] The First Lord, Austen Chamberlain, painfully conscious of his department's bungling, took a conciliatory line. He ordered ships of the Atlantic Fleet to disperse to their home ports and promised to give sympathetic consideration to the men's grievances. This policy was successful: two days after it started the mutiny petered out and the cuts were reduced to a flat rate of ten per cent. Less honourably, the navy inflicted what Fred Copeman called the "maximum amount of punishment without technically breaking the Admiralty's promise" that there would be no reprisals. Some of the arbitrarily chosen "ring-leaders" were made to do exhausting special gunnery drill dressed in oilskins, and others were discharged from the service. Copeman and Wincott went on to join the Communist Party, the former fighting for the International Brigades in Spain and subsequently becoming a Moral Rearmer, the latter emigrating to Russia, where he finished up in one of Stalin's gulags. Later a few of the more inept senior officers were also quietly removed.

Meanwhile the silent service buttoned its lip and the government, its addiction to secrecy reinforced by fears of a renewed financial panic, tried to hush up news of the mutiny. Chamberlain talked in euphemisms and told parliament that "the movement had never been general."[72] He was ably assisted by newspapers like *The Times,* which had long since abandoned its prickly duty of disclosing inconvenient truths for the more comfortable role of Establishment pander. It concentrated on reporting such items as the winning of the Schneider Trophy by G. H. Stainforth in the Supermarine seaplane (ancestor of the Spitfire) which beat the world record and flew at just over 400 miles per hour, the visit of Gandhi to the East End poor (who were better off, he said, than the starving and enslaved people of India), and the Japanese attack on the Chinese at Mukden. If anything, such reticence actually encouraged sensational stories in the foreign press. As the diplomat Sir Robert Vansittart remarked, "Europe thought that revolution had started, that troops were unpaid, and mobs starving."[73] Many Continental journalists, particularly in France, saw the hand of Moscow behind the mutiny. But Communists in Russia were bewildered by the whole affair. They remembered the battleship *Potemkin* (Eisenstein's film was banned in Britain) and assumed that the British proletariat, forced by the bourgeoisie to bear the burden of the capitalist crisis, would respond with revolution. They could not understand why there were "no acts of violence, arrests or executions."[74]

DURING September, it is true, riotous demonstrations against the cuts took place in London and elsewhere. But the main impact of Invergordon was further to shake foreign confidence in the pound and to increase withdrawals of gold from London: 43 million pounds fled abroad in three and a half days. What could be done to meet the crisis? It seemed inconceivable that Britain, financial pivot of the world, should abandon the gold standard. Indeed, when a journalist raised the idea just before the mutiny, Sir Warren Fisher, head of the Civil Service and Permanent Secretary to the Treasury, "got to his feet, his eyes flashing, his face flushed with passion," and said that "any such suggestion is an affront to national honour" and "quite unthinkable."[75] A week later, with Britain's credits nearly exhausted, a bill was rushed through parliament suspending the Bank of England's legal obligation to sell gold for sterling at a fixed price. Returning home from America, Montagu Norman, Governor of the Bank (which was nicknamed the Old Lady of Threadneedle Street), received the news by cable couched in the best code his subordinates could devise. It said, "Old Lady goes off on Monday." Utterly mystified, he concluded that his mother must be taking a holiday.

The violation of financial orthodoxy, when he finally discovered that it had taken place, came as a terrible blow to Norman. As Baldwin remarked, "Going off the gold standard was for him as though a daughter should lose her virginity."[76] Doing its best to exploit the trauma, Labour issued posters proclaiming: "Three cheers for the British Navy! They beat the Kaiser at Jutland and Montagu Norman at Invergordon."[77] Certainly Britain's position as the banker of the world was damaged. Sterling sank to around two-thirds of its former value, though this actually gave Britain an advantage over its European neighbours which resisted depreciation through fear or for misguided reasons of prestige. Other states moved towards managed currencies, some 25 going off gold at once and others following suit later—Japan abandoned it in December 1931, for example, when the yen came under pressure. The collapse of the international standard of valuation bred greater disillusionment with capitalism. It also fostered economic nationalism, whether expressed through protective tariffs or efforts to achieve autarky, which easily translated into political aggression. Yet in Britain the practical repercussions of the financial upheaval were slight. Wages remained stable, prices actually fell (due to the downward pressure on sterling from international markets) and steadily declining interest rates helped British recovery. As Baldwin told Lady Grigg, "We have fallen over the precipice, missus, but we are alive at the bottom."[78]

With this achievement to its credit the National Government felt confident of winning a general election. The October campaign, conducted in an atmosphere of crisis and punctuated with accusations of treachery, was unusually fierce. Snowden described the policies of the Labour party as "Bolshevism run mad" and warned that his former friends would endanger Post Office savings accounts.[79] MacDonald waved devalued German 50-million-mark notes in the air to illustrate the financial havoc which a Labour government would wreak. The King privately canvassed for the National coalition and the Archbishop of Canterbury publicly endorsed the patriotic endeavours of its trustworthy leaders. Clouds of rhetoric hid the fact that they could not agree on a policy. Instead they asked the electorate for "a doctor's mandate" to cure Britain's ills as best they might. And when this was granted—the National Government winning a huge majority of 556 seats, most of them going to the Tories, and Labour being reduced to a rump of 52—they "agreed to differ" over what healing nostrums to prescribe. The result was a characteristic British compromise, the bland leading the bland. Where other nations responded to the Depression with radical initiatives—the New Deal, the Popular Front, the Corporate State, the Five Year Plan, militarism or dictatorship—Britain plumped for a conservative consensus. Lloyd George, Churchill and Mosley remained in the wilderness while safe, mediocre, hollow men— MacDonald, Baldwin and Neville Chamberlain—occupied the seats of power.

This meant, of course, that there would be no rash adventures or extremist panaceas, which would anyway have been inappropriate to the more benign conditions prevailing in Britain. But it also ensured that the policies of the National Government were unimaginative and ineffectual. Tariffs, which soon caused the resignation of laissez-faire champions such as Snowden, did more to harm than to help the British (and the world) economy. Equally unsuccessful were the efforts of Neville Chamberlain, the stern new Chancellor, to promote a system of imperial free trade. (By raising trade barriers against the rest of the world the inaptly named British Commonwealth did permit a modest increase in the mother country's exports to her dominions and colonies, which encouraged nations like Italy and Japan to lust for imperial possessions of their own. Actually, despite the prestige they conferred, empires were more trouble than they were worth.) Chamberlain's efforts to cut public spending, where they were effective, hampered growth and did nothing to alleviate unemployment. They also damaged the social fabric (school-building, for example, almost ceased) and weakened the nation's defences—when struck by the Depression, Britain, like France, undertook virtual disarmament.

The government paid lip service to planning, one of the shibboleths of the age, lending a tentative hand to agriculture. But it did little to help depressed areas in the north and west. Still less did it assist declining industries such as ship-building and coal, even though Chamberlain himself had acknowledged, shortly after the General Strike, that the "devastation in the coal-fields can only be compared with the war devastation of France."[80] Involuntarily, by failing to balance his budgets and by making money cheap, Chamberlain did somewhat assist in the recovery which began within 18 months of the National Government's triumph at the polls. And naturally he claimed the credit for it. In fact it largely resulted from the favourable terms of trade, which lowered the price of imports by as much as a third. Thus the cost of living fell and those in work benefited accordingly. By a strange paradox, therefore, the devil's decade spawned the affluent society. Indeed, so marked was the growth of prosperity among wage and salary earners that one eminent authority has described the "hungry thirties" as a "myth."[81] Another has declared that "the outstanding fact about the English depression is its mildness, which makes it doubtful whether that term is applicable at all."[82]

There is much to support this view. Economic growth was strong and the standard of living in whole areas of the country, notably the south and east, was buoyant. The 1930s witnessed the birth of the middle-class house-and-car culture which prevails today. During the decade nearly three million houses were built, many of them in pebble-dash suburbs or along ribbon developments, and the number of cars doubled, to reach two million. This boom stimulated the manufacture of other goods—furniture, telephones, radios, cookers, vacuum cleaners, anglepoise lamps, even sets of Monopoly (which eclipsed mah-jongg). Despite the poor performance of its heavy industry, Britain "did not lag behind Germany in manufacturing productivity as a whole before the Second World War"[83] thanks to such items as food, drink, clothing and cigarettes. New lines were developed and brand names were advertised prodigiously—Kensitas, Elastoplast, Brylcreem, Nescafé, Yeastvite, Kraft Cheddar, Mars Bars. Where previously pets had been fed kitchen scraps their fond owners now bought them Chappie. To meet consumer demand chain stores such as Woolworth's and Marks & Spencer expanded. Garages and factories proliferated along new bypasses. Other signs of affluence were equally apparent: dance halls, dog-tracks, municipal swimming-pools and gaudy picture palaces, which were attracting over 20 million people a week by 1939. The same number made annual visits to the seaside. More holidays with pay encouraged experiments with leisure and many took to outdoor sport, including biking, hiking and camping. Some became nudists, joining that rogues' gallery of sandal-wearers, moral rearmers, fruit-juice drinkers, vegetarians, pacifists, Esperantists, beavered woodcraft folk and assorted faddists who were prominent enough during the 1930s to be satirised by Aldous Huxley and George Orwell. The point was that unorthodoxy was affordable. Between the wars average incomes rose by a third. Moreover—thanks to better social services, diet and health (though more people, an estimated 80 per cent of men and 40 per cent of women, smoked)—the quality of life improved.

Yet the Depression cast its pall even over those in work and over regions where new industries thrived. In the words of the playwright Ted Willis, who was brought up in a respectable working-class suburb of north London, "it was impossible not to sense and to share the atmosphere of fear and foreboding which lay on the district like a frost." Periodically Willis's mother would snatch her family's own food off the table and take it round to neighbours, replying to her son's protests: "Stop whining! You're hungry. They're starving!"[84] In the Midlands, the west and the north, the Depression was palpable and universal. Regions whose vitality had made Britain the world's workshop were now industrial graveyards. Coal production had shrunk by a fifth since 1929 and many mining villages in South Wales, Yorkshire and Scotland had no work at all. Ship-building in 1933 amounted to an astonishing seven per cent of its 1914 level. The Tyne and the Clyde presented a picture of dereliction—mouldering warehouses, rusting cranes, rotting ships.

Jarrow, light of the world during the Dark Ages, now epitomised "some of the worst darkness known to the human spirit."[85] Eighty per cent of the population was unemployed and the town was "utterly stagnant."[86] Many of its shops had closed, though not pawnbrokers or undertakers. Funerals were "the remaining bit of pageantry available to the poor"; death was the only spree they had left. J. B. Priestley, who made these observations, added that Jarrow and similar places in Northumberland and Durham "looked much worse to me than some French towns I saw at the end of the war, towns that had been occupied by the enemy for four years."[87] In Lancashire bitter industrial strife broke out as textile workers were caught between the Scylla of unemployment and the Charybdis of sweated labour. Textile production, which still accounted for 40 per cent of Britain's exports, had fallen by two-thirds between 1929 and 1933. So many mills went out of business that the smut wore off buildings: to the amazement of its inhabitants, Blackburn began to look clean. Former mill-owners were reduced to picking up cigarette ends in the street. The government euphemistically designated some of the distressed parts of Britain (though not Lancashire) "special areas." Each one was, as the novelist James Hanley wrote, "a new kind of social hell with nothing special about it except the demoralization of a whole people, physical and moral."[88]

Even skilled workers who managed to hold on to their jobs were hard pressed. An engineer, for example, might earn 45 shillings a week: of this 25 shillings went on food, 10 on rent, 5 on coal, gas and insurance, leaving 5 shillings over for clothes, Woodbines and recreation. On this kind of income, a man could barely afford to marry. And, as Walter Greenwood showed in his celebrated novel, love on the dole was a vale of tears. When its hero realises that he has received a life sentence of pauperdom he exclaims, "Ah may as well be in bloody prison";[89] he is only rescued by his sister's selling herself to a libidinous bookmaker. Such transactions really did take place: Ted Willis recalls a mother trading her daughter for a hundredweight of coal.

The tragedy of unemployment was enacted against a background of sordid streets, foetid alleys, mephitic courts, decaying houses and suffocating rooms. Here were be-shawled women shuffling over the cobbles in clogs, gaunt children in ragged hand-me-downs who even at play on scrubbed pavements looked like "little old people,"[90] and an army of mufflered men in shabby suits and patched boots. They hung around in groups, fighting aimlessness and apathy. They tramped from decrepit workshop to moribund factory. They haunted the labour exchange, its bare bricks painted in regulation chocolate and green, its atmosphere stinking of poverty and misery, its heedless clerks imposing the discipline of bureaucracy on furtive "idleness." In November 1931 the National Government stiffened up that discipline. The Means Test was imposed, whereby the household resources of about a million long-term unemployed were taken into account. Thus a man would have his benefit cut if investigators found that he had savings or if his children were earning small sums—a circumstance which often led to the breakup of families. The psyche of the working class was indelibly scarred by this degrading inquisition.

But hardship hurt more than humiliation. Unemployment and the Means Test were rightly described as "a steadily growing disease eating deeper each week into the family resources."[91] As even *The Times* admitted, half the population was "living on a diet insufficient or ill-designed to maintain health,"[92] and the proportion reached three-quarters in areas of high unemployment. In 1938 Professor Richard Titmuss estimated that malnutrition had been responsible for the deaths of 150 people for every day of the previous decade. There was, he wrote, "intense poverty, so considerable and so widespread, but at the same time so veiled and hidden by British stoicism and complacency, that public opinion has hitherto refused to recognise it."[93] This was partly because, as Sir John Boyd Orr discovered during his famous investigation entitled *Food, Health and Income* (1936), "The Establishment put up the strongest possible resistance to informing the public of what the true position was regarding undernourishment among their fellow citizens."[94] Orr made a small contribution to a vast amount of social research carried out during the 1930s, which encompassed everything from the detailed studies of Seebohm Rowntree to the wide-ranging surveys of Mass Observation. Even the travel firm Thomas Cook added to this body of knowledge, by taking sightseers on tours of the East End.

Yet that region, like many others, was still as much the subject of myth and speculation as it had been when Charles Booth had conducted his celebrated metropolitan inquiry at the turn of the century. Then he had written, "East London lay hidden from view behind a curtain on which were painted terrible pictures: Starving children, suffering women, overworked men; horrors of drunkenness and vice; monsters and demons of inhumanity, giants of disease and despair."[95] Booth had attempted to twitch back the curtain, with some success. But it had closed again by the 1930s. Then another social investigator could remark: "the East End is as unknown to us as the Trobriand Islands."[96] Each generation apparently had to acquaint itself anew with the people of the abyss, to discover for itself areas such as outcast London, which were cut off socially, physically and psychologically from the rest of the country. Here was a familiar *terra incognita,* much like the Third World today. In her grand way the Marchioness of Londonderry typified the common attitude as she talked "about starving and dying children, ordered cocktails, 'phoned to a servant to take the dogs out for their exercise" . . . and so on.[97]

The unemployed did what they could to express their grievances. They took part in protests, rallies and hunger marches, many organised by Wal Hannington and the Communist-dominated National Unemployed

Workers' Movement. Often the agitation culminated in violence and during the autumn of 1932 there were pitched battles between demonstrators and police on the streets of London. Despite the fact that in Britain, paradoxically, social cohesion was as marked as class stratification, revolution seemed imminent. A sinister portent was that many of the unemployed had abandoned traditional working-class reverence for the royal family. "Up the Reds," they cried, "Down with Royalty."[98] When visiting London's East End the Duke of York (the future King George VI) was assailed by Cockneys shaking their fists and shouting, "Food! Give us food! We don't want royal parasites!"[99] Such outbursts were an understandable response to the scandal of destitution amid abundance. Supporters of the established order were at their wits' end to defend a system productive of such injustice, particularly as it had also caused what Beatrice Webb called "the worst collapse of profit-making enterprise the world has ever seen."[100]

Now many faithful conservatives began to fear that capitalism was in a state of terminal decline. T. S. Eliot wrote, "The present system does not work properly, and more and more people are inclined to believe that it never did and never will."[101] Evelyn Waugh worried that the "seeming-solid, patiently-built, gorgeously-ornamented structure of western life was to melt overnight like an ice-castle, leaving only a puddle of mud."[102] Those on the Left were still more apocalyptic. H. G. Wells believed that global revolution was inevitable, a prelude to the emergence of a "socialist world-state."[103] In his influential book *The Coming Struggle for Power* John Strachey, once an acolyte of Sir Oswald Mosley and now a propagandist for Communism, argued that the proletariat would revolt against their exploiters and establish a new civilisation based on the common ownership of the means of production. But having forecast utopia Strachey conjured up phantasmagoria. He declared that capitalism could survive the Depression only if Britain became a brutal autocracy. "Direct, open terror against the workers, violent aggression against its rivals, can alone enable a modern empire to maintain itself. A name for such a policy has been found: it is fascism."[104]

Fascism became Sir Oswald Mosley's solution to the Depression. After the Labour party had rejected his proposals and the electorate had rejected the short-lived New Party he formed in 1931, Mosley went to Rome. Here he confirmed his view that the crisis would spawn a British movement like the Duce's. As Harold Nicolson recorded, "Tom cannot keep his mind off shock troops, the arrest of MacDonald and J. H. Thomas, their internment in the Isle of Wight and the roll of drums around Westminster."[105] However, Mussolini advised Mosley not to aim for a military coup but to form a party calling itself fascist. This Mosley did in October 1932. Though maintaining its Britishness with nationalistic fervour, the British Union of Fascists was slavishly imitative. It adopted the fasces symbol, the Roman salute, the black shirt and the characteristic pageantry. Mosley acted as his own impresario and stage manager, marching into meetings with a uniformed bodyguard, illuminated by spotlights and greeted by fanfares. He adopted Mussolini's trick of rolling his exophthalmic eyes so as to show the whites all round the pupils. Melodrama was provided by the Leader's practised demagogy and by ritual outbreaks of violence as Blackshirt stewards ejected hecklers. Thanks to all this, to large sums of money secretly sent from Italy and to the support of Lord Rothermere's newspapers, the BUF attracted some 50,000 members by its high point, in 1934.

Fascism was fashionable and it would be easy to dismiss Mosley's movement as a form of political chic. Many thought that he himself was a dilettante. Churchill dismissed him as a "gilded butterfly."[106] Trotsky regarded him as an "aristocratic coxcomb."[107] F. E. Smith called him a "perfumed popinjay of scented boudoirs."[108] Flâneur, partygoer, habitué of nightclubs, Mosley seemed incurably frivolous. *Action,* for example, the paper of the New Party, had juxtaposed its leader's diatribes with gardening notes by Vita Sackville-West and articles by the scientific guru Gerald Heard on subjects such as "Will Eels Show Us Where Lost Continents Lay?" Some of Mosley's schemes to reduce unemployment were equally bizarre: he once suggested making a mid-city airport on the roof of Victoria Station. He hardly even seemed serious in his energetic pursuit of women. As his son Nicholas records, after some unsatisfactory sexual slumming with the wife of a colleague during his socialist days Mosley coined the amusing slogan, "Vote Labour: Sleep Tory."[109] Beatrice Webb reckoned that Mosley was fundamentally decadent, lacking in the fanaticism of a Hitler. It was a view shared by James Lees-Milne, who witnessed Mosley at a meeting:

> His eyes flashed fire, dilated and contracted like a mesmerist's. His voice rose and fell in hypnotic cadences. He was madly in love with his own words . . . The posturing, the grimacing, the switching on and off of those gleaming teeth, and the overall swashbuckling so purposeful and calculated, were more likely to appeal to Mayfair flappers than to sway indigent workers in the Potteries. I did not then, and do not now, think that the art of coquetry, ought to be introduced into politics.[110]

When Mosley himself discarded his double-breasted waistcoats and amber ties in favour of the Blackshirt uniform, dressing up "like a fencing instructor with a waist fondly exaggerated by a cummerbund and chest and buttocks thrust out,"[111] it was easy to believe that he merely represented an effete "Savile Row Fascism."[112]

Actually Mosley had a vicious streak and he sought to promote the BUF by violent means. He professed respect for the law and reliance on "the good old English fist."[113] But his followers often resorted to knuckledusters and rubber truncheons. Contingents of them were kept under military discipline at a barracks in Chelsea equipped with cellars which were said to be ready for use as punishment cells. Mosley fostered Fascist aggression because he believed that "when the crash came the man who could control the streets would win."[114] His tactic was to provoke retaliation, especially from the Communists, in the hope of further destabilising society and precipitating the ultimate crisis which would thrust him into power. Mosley had a curious ability to transmute thuggery into a kind of idealism. Writing quite recently, one of his most turbulent followers confessed: "I was completely bowled over, fascinated and imbued with an inner feeling of spiritual uplift."[115] According to one concerned contemporary, he appealed particularly to the "lower middle classes" and to the "adolescent unemployed," who were vulnerable to the attraction of "semi-militarised forces" during a "period of heavy depression."[116]

They were also vulnerable to the appeal of Mosley's rhetoric, especially in the revivalist atmosphere of the BUF's cut-price Nuremberg rallies. Intellectuals might dismiss his speeches as booming banalities "without a flicker of wit or wisdom."[117] But when, at a well-attended Albert Hall meeting in the spring of 1934, Mosley proclaimed that fascism was "in accord with the new economic forces of the modern age and with the spiritual urge of the post-war world,"[118] he was cheered to the echo. Ward Price of the *Daily Mail,* admittedly an odious toady to fascist dictators of all sorts, described Mosley as "the paramount political personality in Britain" and declared that "the Blackshirt Movement was caught up on such a wave of deep-seated popular enthusiasm as must sweep it to victory."[119]

Eager to fulfil this prophecy, Mosley organised a further show of strength at Olympia, the huge exhibition centre in Kensington, on 7 June 1934. This was one of the largest indoor meetings ever held in Britain. Over 12,000 people attended, including peers, MPs and affluent fellow-travellers of the Right who arrived in Rolls-Royces and evening dress. Outside the hall they encountered a crowd of hostile demonstrators from the East End. Many had marched at the behest of the Communists, who were (according to a police report) "making every effort to bring off a spectacular coup against the fascists in order to counteract the loss of prestige the Party has suffered in recent by-elections." Waving banners and uttering "offensive and sometimes obscene expressions," they manifested "intense bitterness" towards the Blackshirts. Despite a strong police presence there was some disorder. But at first hostilities were mainly confined to raucous chant and hoarse slogan. Fascists bawled "Britain Awake":

> We bring a saving revolution,
> We will avenge the long betrayed.[120]

Communists countered with

> Hitler and Mosley, what are they for?
> Thuggery, buggery, hunger and war![121]

Taking their cue from America (where Bonnie Parker and Clyde Barrow had just been shot and John Dillinger was still being hunted), they also shouted: "Mosley, public enemy No. 1."[122]

After much delay Mosley finally made his entry. Preceded by a phalanx of Blackshirts bearing Union Jacks and Fascist standards, illuminated by four searchlights, hailed with roars of "Mosley" and saluted by a mass of upraised arms, he strutted the whole length of the arena and mounted the rostrum. He began by warning that this was to be an orderly meeting but, as if to answer that challenge, interruptions began almost at once. They broke out at intervals in different places around the hall, "obviously according to a prearranged plan." What is more, some of the hecklers had equipped themselves with razors and knuckledusters. But the Blackshirts were also prepared for violence. Mosley was intent on showing that he could match Hitler's Stormtroopers for ruthlessness, though he argued that in throwing out hecklers his men were fighting for free speech—an odd claim considering that his lieutenant William Joyce (the future Lord Haw-Haw) declared that "under Fascism freedom of speech would not be allowed."[123] So every time dissentient voices were raised Mosley stopped orating, the spotlights switched to the heckler and a gang of jackbooted Blackshirts threw him out with unconstrained ferocity. The police were horrified to see stewards coshing and kicking members of the audience, but they had been ordered not to intervene inside the hall. No lives were lost, but many hecklers emerged with more or less serious injuries and a couple landed on the pavement without their trousers—debagging then being regarded as a mark of shame to the victim rather than a sign of retardation in the perpetrator. Women, too, were subjected to violence and so were "people who got up in the hall merely to protest against what they regarded as brutality."[124]

News and comment about the "Blackshirt brutality that shocked England"[125] filled the newspapers for weeks after the Olympia rally. Many witnesses expressed outrage at what they had seen. The Conservative MP W. J. Anstruther-Gray wrote in the conservative *Daily Telegraph:*

> If anyone could have told me before I went to that meeting last night that I would ever be in sympathy with Communist interrupters, I would have called him a liar. But I had not been at that meeting for more than a few minutes before all my sympathies were with the men that were being handled with such gross brutality . . . Something must be done to prevent a recurrence of last night's disgusting behaviour.[126]

The Home Secretary was inundated with similar protests, many critical of the passivity of the police. This was difficult to defend since it was obvious that breaches of the peace had taken place at Olympia which called for official intervention. Moreover, as one constable who had witnessed the entire disturbance noted, the "enthusiastic zeal" with which his superiors prosecuted Communists was in stark contrast to their attitude towards Fascists, which "ranged from indifference to approval."[127] It was said then and later that the forces of law were equally hostile to anyone committing an offence. But it is clear that magistrates as well as police had been indulgent towards Blackshirts. And even the Home Office had not treated them as a serious challenge. Learning of Mosley's scheme to manufacture "Black Shirt" cigarettes which his followers would be instructed to smoke (just as Hitler's Stormtroopers did their specially-made "Sturm" brand), one official chortled: "Truly the way of Fascists will be hard if their taste in cigarettes is to be made to conform with their political convictions." After hearing eloquent indictments of the "menace of Fascist militarism,"[128] the Home Secretary himself was still inclined to equate Blackshirts and hunger marchers.

The public, however, was quite clear about the difference. There was a powerful reaction against Mosley. This turned into a positive revulsion three weeks later when Hitler dealt out murder to dissident Stormtroopers during the "Night of the Long Knives," an event which turned British opinion against the Nazis as surely as the September Massacres had once turned it against the Jacobins. The BUF applauded the purge on the grounds that Röhm and his friends were degenerates. They thereby incurred odium for serving Hitler, just as the British Communist Party did for worshipping Stalin. Rothermere, whose *Daily Mail* had initially justified Blackshirt excesses at Olympia, withdrew his support, as did Mussolini once he became convinced that Fascism could not succeed in Britain. Membership of the BUF fell by four-fifths within a year. Seeking to prevent the slide, Mosley adopted the Nazi view that a dynamic creed "cannot flourish unless it has a scapegoat to hit out at, such as Jewry."[129] Although a more or less mild anti-Semitism was almost universal in Britain, Mosley's vicious rhetoric, which attracted the approval of Julius Streicher among others, put him even further beyond the pale. In East London, where there was a large Jewish community, the BUF did make progress. But it could so little aspire to being a national movement by 1935 that Mosley had to urge his followers to boycott the general election, employing the feeble slogan, "Fascism next time."[130]

So when other countries were bobbing like corks in the wake of the Depression, Britain preserved a relative equilibrium without benefit of a New Deal, let alone a Five Year Plan. Riots shook France, a socialist uprising convulsed Austria, bitter strife racked Spain, State terrorism did its bloody work in Germany and Italy, "government by assassination" prevailed in Japan. Having crushed internal opposition, the authoritarian states increasingly sought external outlets for their energies and for the social tensions engendered by the Depression. Not content with scapegoats at home they wanted sacrificial lambs abroad. It is significant that, in addition to attacking Jews in Britain, Mosley himself tried to stir up national hostility against the Japanese. His *Fascist Week* was full of headlines such as "THE REALITY OF THE YELLOW PERIL." It insisted that Nippon's commercial rivalry was Britain's gravest economic problem and called for an "embargo on Japanese goods." "Japan is the cuckoo among nations," it shrilled, "Japan is the modern pirate."[131] Certainly Japan, the newest industrial nation, was catching up with Britain, the oldest, at an extraordinary rate between the wars. The Land of the Rising Sun actually seemed capable of eclipsing the empire on which the sun never set. But the Far Eastern colossus was to be seriously hurt by the Depression. Accordingly Japan became the first major power during the 1930s to export its aggression.

IX

JAPAN'S IMPERIAL DESTINY

ACCORDING to the Japanese maxim, which might stand as an epigraph for the nation's history in the aftermath of the 1929 Slump, "internal disorder leads to external troubles."[1] Despite amazing economic progress, which had enabled Japan to survive hard times following the Yokohama earthquake, the country still had a much lower standard of living than industrial pioneers such as Britain. The salary of a senior army general was less than 500 pounds a year, while a tenth of greater Tokyo's 5 million inhabitants existed on as little as 7 yen a month (14 shillings or 3.50 dollars). In the villages, where nearly half of Japan's 64 million people lived, peasants barely managed to subsist on the tiny plots which they tended, as Kipling had observed, with "comb and toothpick."[2] Actually, though it possessed the smallest arable acreage per head of any country in the world, Japan had the most productive agriculture. And from 1927 to 1930 rice harvests were unusually abundant. But this bounty of nature caused a disastrous drop in the price of "the king of grains."[3] Thus the Japanese, possessing few raw materials and reliant on international trade, were shattered by the Depression. Nowhere else did the economic crisis implode more viciously or explode more rapidly. It pervaded the life of the country and warped the psyche of its inhabitants. It emphasised the poverty and fragility of their existence in a land so bereft of raw materials, so reliant on foreign trade. As the contemporary journalist K. K. Kawakami wrote, the Depression dealt Japan "a staggering blow and has profoundly affected the mental outlook of the entire nation . . . a pall of gloom has been cast about the people."[4]

The slump in agricultural prices was catastrophic. Farming families, whose average annual income was only 300 yen, found that their rice fetched a third less in 1930 than it had in 1929. They could not even cover their costs, let alone reward themselves adequately for back-breaking toil knee-deep in the paddy-fields. Worse still, owing to the increasing popularity of rayon as well as to the collapse of the American market, the price of their other main cash crop, the "God-sent merchandise"[5] of raw silk, fell by more than half. This devastated the rural economy, making it hardly worthwhile for farmers to remain in the arduous service of "the honourable little gentleman," as the silkworm was styled. Not since the turn of the century had they received so little for their harvests. Now, with higher rents and debts to usurious money-lenders of some 600 yen per rural household, they could barely support their families. In some areas money virtually disappeared and farmers lived by barter—two quarts of rice for a packet of Shikishima cigarettes.

The situation was made worse by a population explosion resulting in four births a minute—nearly a million new mouths to feed each year. As the contemporary cliché ran, Japan combined "an Oriental birth rate with an Occidental death rate."[6] For nationalistic rather than moral reasons, the authorities opposed birth control. When the American campaigner Margaret Sanger visited Japan in 1922, her literature was confiscated and she was forbidden to lecture. Later one of her Japanese followers was stabbed. But when the Depression struck, "the masses were driven into becoming a huge laboratory for contraception by necessity." As one magazine charmingly put it, "Groping in the dark, sometimes in violation of official regulations, they learned various devices."[7] The device which Japanese men liked least was the condom, which one later compared to putting on Wellington boots in order to take a bath.

Prince Saionji said that conditions in the 1929 Depression were not as severe as they had been in a similar slump three-quarters of a century before when people had "gone around crying loudly, 'I'm hungry, I'm hungry,' and . . . actually collapsed from hunger."[8] But in some districts there was malnutrition amounting to starvation. In the Tohoku region (where harvests failed) peasants were reduced to eating millet, roots, bracken, barnyard grass, rice husks mixed with chestnuts and acorns, the stems of water lilies and bark stripped from trees. They devoured cats, dogs and other animals. There were reports of cannibalism and cases of suicide. As one newspaper recorded, school children too frail to beg could "only gaze with their sad eyes. The skin on their faces hangs down flabbily and the joints of their hands and feet are swollen with the flesh dried up. They look like weak little old men."[9] Young men were sometimes told not to return from military service alive so that their families could benefit from State money. So many farmers sold their daughters into prostitution (for an average of 150 yen each) that the countryside was emptied of pretty girls. Some farmers also sold their tiny holdings or tried to extort better terms from landlords—two-thirds of farmers rented some or all of their land. They postponed marriages, wore their clothes into rags, left roofs unthatched, gave up luxuries such as soap and sugar, used mulberry leaves as fertilizer and worked harder at an occupation which already, as the old saw had it, forced them to "leave in the morning, the stars still shining, return at night walking on moonlight shadows."[10] Toil, though, could be self-defeating. Destitute farmers sometimes concluded, "Better to remain idle and eat less than work hard and eat more than can be earned."[11] Conditions were only marginally improved by voluntary self-help organisations—which everyone, in the Japanese manner, joined. Measures of government assistance were also ineffective, at least at first. Farmers, *hyakusho,* lived up to their customary name—unfortunates.

Yet the agricultural community regarded itself, and was generally regarded, as "the backbone of the nation, the source of its military strength, and the guardian of its traditional virtues against alien influences."[12] So the plight of the farmers became a source of increasing rancour and strife inside Japan. The failure to improve conditions discredited not just the politicians but the democratic system which produced them and the capitalist system which sustained them. It exacerbated jealousies between rich and poor. It widened the rift between town and country. Above all it alienated the army, which took most of its recruits from the countryside. Many officers came from the small land-owning class, while the best troops were drawn from the hardy northern peasantry worst affected by the Depression. Commanders such as Tojo Hideki, who tried to act as a father to his men, heard their pitiful tales of hunger and despair. "Soldiers can't concentrate on their duty," he said ominously, "if they have personal worries."[13] Thus peasant pauperism fostered military extremism. Fanatical young officers, inspired by "romantic agrarian nationalists" such as Gondo Seikyo,[14] sought to purge the nation through terror at home and aggression abroad. They aimed, somewhat vaguely, to purify the Japanese national essence or way of life *(kokutai)* in their own islands, establishing social justice through a restoration of direct imperial rule. And, rather more precisely, they proposed to fulfil Japan's manifest destiny overseas by conquests which would provide raw materials, markets for its manufactured goods and living-space for its surplus population.

The impact of the Depression on Japanese industry, though more short-lived, was also profound. Not since the nation began to modernise during the Meiji era had it suffered such a severe setback. The textile industry, which employed a quarter of the manufacturing workforce and produced two-thirds of Japanese exports, was hit particularly hard. Prices dropped by a third, wages fell by a quarter and thousands of workers lost their jobs. Heavy industry, supported by government subsidy, was not so badly affected. But production declined sharply and the value of all Japanese exports halved between 1929 and 1931. Foreign protectionism made matters worse. America's Smoot-Hawley Tariff Act, described by one historian as "a virtual declaration of economic war on the rest of the world,"[15] raised duties on Japanese goods by an average of 23 per cent. In Japan hundreds of small-scale enterprises went out of business. By October 1930 the official unemployment figure had risen to 322,527, though independent surveys put it at well over 2 million. Most of these were unskilled workers. There was little unemployment relief, with the result that some returned to their villages, placing additional strain on the rural economy. Others took to rag-picking, rubber collecting, scavenging for waste paper, begging and petty crime. Thousands of unemployed workers in their baggy trousers *(mompei)* hung around in parks and on street corners. They pockmarked whole neighbourhoods, wrote the novelist Mishima Yukio, as though with some "secret plague."[16] They queued for soup dispensed by the Salvation Army. Many slept in the open and some died of exposure.

Industrial paternalism was the rule in Japan: less than eight per cent of the labour force belonged to trade unions and the employees of large companies were aptly described as "captive children reared into workers."[17] Yet there were hundreds of industrial disputes. Some strikes were spontaneous and unorganised. Some were eccentric: workers sat for long periods on the tops of factory chimneys, which was quite an effective tactic (though the first man to protest in this way was imprisoned for "infringing domiciliary rights").[18] Other strikes were violent. At the Mitsubishi and Kawasaki dockyards in Kobe there was bloody fighting between thousands of demonstrators and police supported by troops with drawn swords. In 1930 tear gas was used for the first time, to disperse trade-unionists surrounding the Tokyo city electricity bureau. Masses of workers besieged the Tokyo Muslin Company, surging with linked arms towards its gates to the beat of a big bass drum and being repeatedly driven back by hired strike-breakers armed with high-pressure hoses. Employers also retaliated by locking girl strikers into their company dormitories, whereupon their male colleagues would gather outside to shout encouragement. Massive labour rallies took place, one of the largest being held on May Day 1930 in Tokyo's Hibiya Park. Economic distress and civil disturbance bred what has been called the "politics of despair."[19]

The Depression smashed the liberal, parliamentary, internationalist consensus which had, broadly speaking, prevailed in Japan during the 1920s. Many people concluded that if democracy led to dissension, patriots should follow *Kodo,* the Imperial Way. If laissez-faire caused chaos, authoritarianism would impose order. If free trade and cooperation with the West produced crises like that of 1929, the Japanese should embrace economic nationalism and political chauvinism. Moreover, if orthodox deflationary policies resulted in massive social hardship, the State should intervene, financing its ameliorative efforts with loans. Thus the scene was set for a revolution in the affairs of Nippon.

No one opposed this more vigorously than Hamaguchi Yuko, who had succeeded Tanaka as Prime Minister in 1929. A tiny man who had almost been left to die of exposure as an infant because his father, a forestry official on the island of Shikoku, could not afford a large family, Hamaguchi had married money, attended Tokyo Imperial University and gone into politics. His devotion to duty was well illustrated by the fact that, to promote the government's Tobacco Monopoly Bureau of which he was chief, he had taken up smoking against doctors' orders. Eventually he had become the president of the Minseito party. Nicknamed "the Lion," he was a byword for courage and he fiercely resisted the moves of the militarists. Also known as "the Lord High Executioner,"[20] he cut government expenditure to the bone, combining thrift with honesty in a fashion rare among Japanese politicians. However, Hamaguchi's economic judgement was flawed and the obstinacy with which he pursued his political ends provoked bitter opposition. Convinced that Japan would benefit from exchange stability, he returned to the gold standard in January 1930. It was about the worst time he could have chosen, particularly as, for reasons of prestige, the yen was set at too high a rate—like Churchill's pound and Mussolini's lira. Japanese goods were grossly over-priced and, in the atrocious trading conditions, "the bottom dropped out of the export market."[21] Hamaguchi urged his compatriots to tighten their belts. He staunchly supported his Finance Minister, Inoue Junnosuke, who was as committed as Philip Snowden to the ideal of balanced budgets. But the government's retrenchment schemes had little effect and the Industrial Rationalisation Bureau, set up in June 1930, failed in its ambitious aim to revolutionise the entire economic system of the country.

Hamaguchi also backed the pacific policies of his sage Anglophile Foreign Minister, Baron Shidehara Kijuro. Although Shidehara was more imperialistic than he has sometimes been painted, his prime concern was to maintain international cooperation in the spirit of Briand and Kellogg. The major challenge to this policy came from naval nationalists led by Admiral Kato Kanji. He insisted that Japan should improve its position in relation to rival fleets at the London Naval Conference in 1930. Eight years earlier the powers had agreed in Washington that Japan's naval strength should be limited to 60 per cent of the capital ships allowed to Britain and America. Now, Kato told Hamaguchi, 70 per cent "is the absolutely lowest ratio and is a matter of life and death for our navy. If an agreement for that ratio is not secured, we must resolutely break off negotiations."[22] The Prime Minister disagreed, arguing that arms limitation would promote prosperity as well as peace. Kato rejoined that national security must come before affluence and that it was his duty to fight wars, not to prevent them. But, despite the threats and intrigues of Kato's aggressive "fleet faction," supported by the opposition Seiyukai party and reactionary members of the Privy Council such as Baron Hiranuma Kiichiro, the Japanese negotiators in London eventually agreed to a ratio of 65 per cent. This was a brave compromise; Secretary of State Stimson said publicly, "I take my hat off to the Japanese Government."[23] The Japanese public also seemed to be pleased with the outcome, at least initially, for at Tokyo station crowds greeted returning delegates with uninhibited enthusiasm, waving banners, tossing bouquets and shouting banzais.

However, opponents of the Treaty were irreconcilable. "It's as if we had been roped up and cast into prison by Britain and America," Admiral Kato declared.[24] After making public protests and hinting at insubordination to the Emperor, Kato resigned. But his military and political friends would not let the matter rest. They drummed up opposition to the "traitorous treaty" and claimed that Hamaguchi, by ignoring the "right of military command" to decide on questions affecting the safety of the State, had acted unconstitutionally.[25] Articles 11 and 12 of the Meiji constitution did indeed give the military some independent authority, but this was generally thought to relate to operational matters. By asserting that the Supreme Command had powers to intervene in almost every sphere of government, Kato and his allies opened a Pandora's Box of troubles which, over the next 15 years, wrecked their country. Heedless of impending evils, they stoked the fires of Japanese jingoism. A member of the Black Dragon society, one of many ultra-patriotic organisations proliferating at this time, presented the returning leader of the Japanese delegation to London, Wakatsuki Reijiro, with a ceremonial dagger wrapped in a silk cloth—an invitation to commit hara-kiri. An attempt was made to assassinate another delegate, Admiral Takarabe Takeshi. Adopting the traditional form of protest, a middle-ranking naval officer committed suicide, shooting himself on board the sleeping-car of a Tokyo train. Takarabe commented: "At last, a human sacrifice has been offered in opposition to military reduction."[26]

Other human sacrifices were to follow. The Naval Treaty was the last achievement of the Japanese liberals between the wars. Henceforth the influence of such men as Prince Saionji and Baron Shidehara would wane as that of the militarists and nationalists waxed. Admiral Kato, Baron

Hiranuma and their supporters used the Treaty as a focus for all the ills and frustrations that plagued Japan—fear of being crushed between capitalist Anglo-American forces and Communist Sino-Soviet hordes, resentment at the lowly position Nippon occupied in the councils of the nations, anguish at the sufferings it endured as a result of the Depression. The treaty dispute acted as a crucial catalyst. As Marquis Kido Kiochi, chief secretary to Lord Privy Seal Makino, later said: "Excitement ran high through the length and breadth of the country. It is no exaggeration to say that a big transformation, which later overtook Japan, eventually making her what she is now, was started at that time."[27]

IN these circumstances zealots increasingly turned to violence. One such was a young man called Sagoya Tomeo, who belonged to the Nation-loving Society *(Aikoku-Sha)*. In November 1930, fortified by a night of "wild orgy" financed by some mysterious paymaster,[28] he waylaid Premier Hamaguchi at Tokyo's great red-brick railway station (modelled on that of Amsterdam) and shot him in the stomach with a Mauser pistol. Apparently Sagoya was protesting not only about the Naval Treaty but about Hamaguchi's response to the Depression. But the public was so shocked by his action that it did not at first consider his motives, though as the decade progressed the "sincerity" of an assassin sometimes tilted the scales of justice in his favour, especially as Japanese tended to believe that the victim was in some way culpable. As it was, Sagoya served only three years in prison before receiving an amnesty. Hamaguchi himself survived the attack for a few months, lingering in office until the following spring. But "the Lion" had been mortally wounded. Feeling himself near death he rose from his bed, donned a ceremonial kimono and bowed towards the imperial palace.

After the elimination of this "peace warrior"[29] individual assassination and mass murder became instruments of policy. Nationalist organisations abounded, none more rabid than the Cherry Blossom Society. Its name symbolised the loyal samurai dying in his prime with beauty unsullied and it appealed to middle-ranking army officers. Its founder, Lieutenant-Colonel Hashimoto Kingoro, a short, tough, sour successor of the samurai, had just returned from a three-year tour of duty in Europe. Detesting liberalism, capitalism and Communism in almost equal measure, he was a fierce proponent of militarism, anti-white racism and "fascism-in-the-name-of-the-emperor."[30] This creed was spelled out in the Cherry Blossom Society's manifesto. It declared that, having defeated the navy, the "poisonous sword" of the party politicians was about to be turned on the army, guardian of the true interests of the nation. These politicians were indifferent to the fact that "farming villages are devastated, unemployment and depression are serious" and that grave "population and food problems are minute by minute threatening the people."[31] They practised soft diplomacy instead of extending Japanese power. They were also poor representatives of democracy, "indulging in drinking and amusements, taking graft" from the *zaibatsu,* howling and fist-fighting during sessions of the Diet in a way which the soldiers found "unbearably disgraceful."[32] Unfortunately the Supreme Command lacked the courage to "wash out the bowels" of the politicians, so the Cherry Blossom Society would have to do it for them.[33] Hashimoto wanted to purge Japan by means of a "grand coup d'état,"[34] prior to establishing "national socialism under the aegis of the Emperor."[35] Secretly encouraged by senior officers such as General Tatekawa Yoshitsugu and civilian extremists such as Okawa Shumei, Hashimoto plotted to storm the Imperial Diet in March 1931. But at the last moment his superiors thought better of it. And his chosen dictator, War Minister Ugaki Kazushigo, withdrew his equivocal support—which later, still more equivocally, he denied ever having given. Cliques, which grew like cancer inside Japan's highly-disciplined army, would make many such false starts over the next few years. But one reason why the March putsch proved abortive was that officers even more influential than Hashimoto were at that very moment conspiring to launch a massive act of aggression abroad.

Chief among them was another lieutenant-colonel, Ishiwara Kanji. Born in 1889, the second son of a policeman from Tsuruoka, he was one of the most brilliant students ever to graduate from the Army Staff College, where he had received the imperial sword of honour and later became an instructor. Ishiwara had also served in Korea, done a spell in Germany (where he became convinced of the importance of air power), and explored China on horseback. He was an insubordinate subordinate, disregarding military convention and coining rude nicknames for his superiors (he called Tojo "Dear Dunderhead").[36] But Ishiwara's juniors admired his quixotic temper. Vigorous, outspoken, uncompromising and supremely self-confident, he was rash in both thought and deed. In fact he combined to an extraordinary degree the attributes of the mystical visionary and the ruthless pragmatist.

He held the nationalist view that the army was a divinely-ordained instrument of global salvation, destined to bring civilisation under one enlightened, Japanese roof. But he also believed that there would first have to be a "Final War"[37] for control of the world. Japan's chief enemy would be the United States. Hostilities would break out when technology had advanced far enough to enable aeroplanes to fly around the earth and, coincidentally, 50 years after the outbreak of the Great War and 2,500 years after the death of Buddha. To prepare for this apocalyptic conflict, Ishiwara said, Japan should seize control of Manchuria. China's province was the "granary of Asia."[38] It was the source of raw materials without which the forces of Nippon could not hope to sustain the titanic struggle which Ishiwara foresaw. It was the repository of mines and factories which would relieve unemployment in Japan and assist its people to climb out of the dark valley of Depression. As Ishiwara stated,

> It is a publicly acknowledged fact that our national situation has reached an impasse, that there is no way of solving the food, population, and other important problems, and that the only path left open to us is the development of Manchuria and Mongolia.[39]

This would be no mere colonial conquest: it would provide the model for an imperial-fascist state such as the army should impose on the mother country. That would be an easy task, Ishiwara thought, for Japan would become unified and transfigured by war.

The most remarkable thing about these fearsome fantasies was that Ishiwara had the power to turn them, or some of them, into reality. Of course, other empire-building men-on-the-spot have pitched their unwilling countries into war. But this obscure lieutenant-colonel on the staff of the Kwantung Army not only transmuted the martial ardour of his seniors into active aggression, he also dragged the Tokyo government, step by reluctant step for months on end, in the train of his fiery chariot. How did he do it? Acting in the aftermath of Hashimoto's "potent manifestation of defiance of the superior by the subordinate,"[40] Ishiwara was in fact ideally placed for the task. He held the prime planning post on the garrison of Kwantung, the leased region of China which Japan had gained after the Russian War in 1905. This force was itself strategically situated to exploit the other fruits of that victory—the extensive rights and privileges which Japan enjoyed in China, notably control of the South Manchurian Railway. Other powers also had a stake in China, which was too vast to be assimilated into a single empire but had been virtually destroyed as a nation state by over a century of strife—more people had been killed during the Taiping rebellion than in the Great War. But many Japanese, particularly those in Kwantung, regarded China as their country's natural sphere of influence. The first stage of Japan's divine mission was to secure the Orient for Orientals, to enforce (as Kita Ikki recommended) "an Asian Monroe doctrine."[41] China was a woman while Japan was a man, nationalists intoned; the Japanese were people of clay while the Chinese were people of sand. As a preliminary, however, to securing China's kowtow, Japan would have to overwhelm Manchuria, itself a holy land "consecrated by the sacrifice of one hundred thousand brothers who shed their blood in the war led by the great Meiji emperor."[42] So, in spreading the gospel of the sword among the 10,000-strong Kwantung Army, Ishiwara was preaching to the converted.

Among his disciples the most important by far was Colonel Itagaki Seishiro, the senior staff officer. A striking contrast to the abstemious Ishiwara, he was famed for sensual excesses in an army notably devoted to bed and bottle. An habitué of geisha houses, Itagaki indulged in sake-drinking contests lasting for three days at a time. But he never missed a drill, for there was a roughness and toughness about this squat, broad-mouthed soldier which doubtless stemmed from his peasant upbringing. Bitter about the impoverishment of his class and convinced that Japan was a divine nation with a global mission, Itagaki warmed to the radicalism of his ardent junior. Complementing Ishiwara, he was also more responsible than anyone for implementing his ideas. As the charismatic General Araki Sadao wrote, "Itagaki was a straightforward, uncomplicated fellow; Ishiwara was a man of lightning intellect, but [they] got on well together."[43] Together they spied out the land, laid plans, raised money and manufactured provocations. They also tried, with the elliptical subtlety for which the Japanese language is perfectly suited, to draw the Tokyo Supreme Command into their plot. In this they largely succeeded, for the army's leaders were eager to find some excuse to resist the government's impending defence cuts. But Ishiwara and Itagaki kept the Emperor's senior military advisers, and thus the government, in the dark. They did not even confide in the commander of the Kwantung Army. He was General Honjo Shigeru, a dapper, urbane figure with grizzled hair and a medieval military mind who would, Ishiwara surmised, act as his puppet. When, after hostilities had broken out, the General showed an anguished inclination to heed pacific instructions from Tokyo, Itagaki simply said: "Never mind Honjo, it's Ishiwara's war."[44]

During the summer of 1931 the Japanese public was carefully prepared for Ishiwara's war. Seiyukai politicians made aggressive speeches about Japan's being a potted plant and needing living-space. Soldiers rattled their sabres in the direction of China, where violations of Japan's treaty rights, boycotts of its goods and other incidents created friction. One regimental commander intimated to his reservists that "war would break out in the near future," shouting so agitatedly that one of them, a fish dealer, whispered: "The Commander must have become demented."[45] Japanese settlers and Korean colonists under the protection of their flag in south Manchuria complained about being victimised by the Chinese and said that Tokyo's indifference to their fate was akin to "dancing on a volcano." Planes of the 3rd Air Regiment scattered leaflets over Japanese cities setting out their country's rights in Manchuria under the headline, "Wake up to National Defence!"[46] Amplified by loudspeakers in the streets, Tokyo radio broadcast inflammatory statements. Newspapers printed rumours of war. Eventually they grew so insistent that the Emperor instructed Hamaguchi's weak successor, Wakatsuki Reijiro, to ensure the continuation of "friendly relations with China." The Prime Minister in turn told the burly, bull-necked War Minister, General Minami Jiro, that the indiscriminate use of force in Manchuria "may prove to be the basis of a blunder." Convinced by hearing more definite evidence of the plot, Minami finally dispatched General Tatekawa, who had supported Hashimoto's March plot, to warn the Kwantung Army against rash actions. This dashing cavalryman was chosen for the odd reason that, as an acknowledged extremist himself, he would be able "to restrain the young reactionary elements in Manchuria."[47] It was, as one historian has remarked, rather "like telling a pyromaniac to forestall an attempt at arson."[48] When Tatekawa arrived at the Manchurian capital, Mukden, on 18 September, he allowed Itagaki to take him to the Kikubun restaurant where he drank sake all the evening and failed to pass on his official message. Shortly after 10:00 P.M. an explosion occurred on the South Manchurian Railway. It was the first blast in a war that would go on for nearly 15 years and culminate in the atomic holocausts of Hiroshima and Nagasaki.

Ishiwara and Itagaki had laid their plans well. A specially trained Japanese unit placed 42 yellow packages of blasting powder on the line. Their detonation enabled other units, who were officially there to guard the railway zone but had been practising night assaults, to provoke hostilities with the Chinese forces stationed in Mukden. Heavy siege guns, which the Kwantung Army had smuggled into the city, opened fire on the Chinese barracks. By dawn the Japanese had occupied the huge arsenal, the airport, the international area and the Walled City. The streets teemed with Japanese "armed reservists" imported by the army, many of whom were, according to Prince Saionji, "fascist gangsters."[49] Reinforcements were brought in and other key points on the South Manchurian Railway to Changchun were secured. General Honjo received news of the

Manchurian Incident ("incident" being the Japanese euphemism for all manner of outrages) in his bath in Port Arthur. Ishiwara then morally coerced him into leading his followers.

So Honjo travelled across the windswept Manchurian plain to the city of Mukden, by day an ugly sprawl of nondescript buildings, by night "a dark plaque on which the lighted streets cut cubist hieroglyphics."[50] He established his headquarters in the large South Manchurian Railway office. This was situated opposite the new Yamato Hotel and overlooked the parkland monolith commemorating Japanese soldiers who had fallen in the war against Russia. Here, in his stuffy second-floor office papered with maps and filled with bonsai trees and chrysanthemums, the stout little commander told journalists over lidded, egg-shell cups of fragrant tea that Japan had simply retaliated against Chinese aggression. His intention was to restore freedom and prosperity to 30 million Manchurians tyrannised over by warlords. He proposed "to bring genuine spring back to this frozen land."[51] Such explanations cut no ice with foreigners or with the Japanese civilian authorities. Premier Wakatsuki suspected and regretted "a conspiracy of the Japanese Army."[52] Foreign Minister Shidehara turned "deathly pale" on hearing the news,[53] rightly assuming that it meant the military were out of control. Soon after the explosion on the night of 18 September, a Japanese diplomat in Mukden had rushed to Itagaki's residence insisting that, "This problem must be settled by diplomatic negotiation." Itagaki shouted angrily, "The army is on the march. This is an act of the Supreme Command. Does the consul intend to obstruct it?" There was no reply and Itagaki's co-conspirator, Major Hanaya, drew his sword with the threat: "There'll be no mercy for those who stand in the way of the Supreme Command!"[54]

THIS episode is a paradigm of the Japanese condition over the next few years, as militarists and nationalists engaged in their murderous struggle to dominate successive governments. Initially the struggle centred on the efforts of Ishiwara and Itagaki to extend their war until they had conquered all Manchuria. Supported by the Emperor himself as well as by Saionji and other influential figures, Wakatsuki and Shidehara tried to contain the aggression. But the Kwantung Army pressed on regardless. Its leaders created spurious provocations. They claimed to be acting in self-defence. They inflated the menace of a revived Russia under Stalin and a unified China under Chiang Kai-shek, leader of the Kuomintang (Nationalist) party. They applied to the full the "time-honoured principle of command authority . . . in the area of operational planning."[55] They presented their government with a series of *faits accomplis,* such as the bombing of Chinchow in early October. They exploited divisions within the War Ministry and the Cabinet, where General Minami said: "Should Japan be determined to wage war on the whole world this can readily be done."[56] They spurned military messengers from Tokyo such as Colonel Imamura Hitoshi, who urged that "the arbitrary decisions of field elements" were threatening the unity of the nation. "What's the matter?" retorted Ishiwara, "Doesn't central headquarters have any backbone?" And when Imamura tried to continue the argument Ishiwara rudely rolled over on his tatami mat and went to sleep.[57] The Kwantung officers even denounced Hirohito's order to withdraw as an "outrageous act," declaring that "regardless of what the Emperor may say, the troops can't be withdrawn"[58]—with the result that imperial advisers decided that he should not endanger his prestige (perhaps also his person) by issuing further statements. Ishiwara and Itagaki even threatened to sever relations with the mother country and to mount a coup in Tokyo. And when, in mid-October 1931, Hashimoto tried to overthrow the government again (this time attempting to promote General Araki Sadao as his fascist figurehead), the Kwantung Army said that the arrested plotters should be treated leniently "in appreciation of their spirit, as from another viewpoint, they are rare treasures to the nation."[59]

Faced with this sustained pressure, Wakatsuki was reduced to despair and in December his government collapsed. With it went the conciliatory diplomacy of Shidehara. In his efforts to explain the actions of the military while upholding the prestige of the country, he had exhausted even the Japanese capacity for obfuscation. But the League of Nations could do little more than huff and puff about Japan's breach of the Covenant, the Kellogg-Briand Pact and the Nine Power Treaty (signed in 1922) which guaranteed them an "open door" into China. This impotence reflected the fact that the nations of the world, even if they had been inclined to take action over the Manchurian Incident, could think of nothing but their own parlous state. Britain went off the gold standard a couple of days after the explosion at Mukden. Anyway Britain wanted to protect its valuable Far Eastern trade and was not entirely averse to seeing imperialist Japan facing Communist Russia. Nor was France, vulnerable at home and concerned about the safety of Indo-China. Moreover the European press was inclined to praise Japan for having created in Manchuria "a flourishing oasis in a howling desert of Chinese misrule."[60] China itself was tormented by flood, famine, poverty, banditry, warlordism and civil strife. The Soviet Union was preoccupied with collectivisation and the Five Year Plan. America was paralysed by the economic crisis and Hoover concluded that he must talk softly because he did not have a big stick. Even the more militant Stimson made calming gestures towards Japan in response to his ambassador's advice that criticism "only further inflamed the situation and played into the hands of the chauvinistic elements."[61]

Prince Saionji did his best to prevent these elements from dominating the next government by choosing as Prime Minister the Seiyukai leader Inukai Tsuyoshi. A cunning operator, Inukai was known as "the old fox."[62] But this goatee-bearded septuagenarian was also notoriously goatish, as agile at womanising as at hiking, which he liked to do from his villa on the sacred slopes of Fujiyama. Short, thin, grey, with sharp eyes and a sly expression, he was unusual in larding his speeches with jokes. But no one was more passionately the politician. From the liberal viewpoint Inukai was the ideal compromise candidate for Premier: he advocated a forceful foreign policy but he opposed the pretensions of the army. In this he was supported by the powerful new Finance Minister, Takahashi Korekiyo, who dismissed talk about "the prestige of military command" as "nonsensical."[63]

Takahashi was aged 78 and in poor health. But he was fearlessly outspoken and he enjoyed immense prestige. Jovial and rotund, he was nicknamed "Dharma" after the pot-bellied god of good fortune represented by armless and legless dolls which, when pushed over, automatically right themselves. He also had vast experience, which was to stand him in good stead over the next four years. Takahashi's origins were humble: he was the son of a court artist and a parlour maid, and he said that he would rather join his ancestors than talk about them. But after working as an indentured labourer in the United States, and as a manservant to a geisha and a teacher of English in Japan, he had carved out a distinguished career in banking. He had helped to pay for the war with Russia and in 1913 he had become Finance Minister, an office he was to hold no fewer than six times.

His first task in 1931, when the world still languished "in the valley of depression,"[64] was to take Japan off the gold standard. At a stroke this stopped the catastrophic outflow of specie and, with a 40 per cent devaluation of the yen, restored Japan's competitiveness. Rejecting orthodox advice to balance his budgets, Takahashi proceeded to raise loans by issuing government bonds. He subsidised heavy industry and pumped huge sums into village relief. He lowered interest rates and stimulated demand. He encouraged mergers and cartels. He promoted exports and reduced unemployment. He introduced trade protection and exchange controls. In the midst of the world depression this "pioneer of international economic policy"[65] presided over a Japanese "industrial boom."[66] It naturally provoked hostility from competitors. By the mid-1930s Lancashire cotton manufacturers were issuing statements such as:

> The present advance of Japanese commodities in the markets of the world constitutes a dire menace to the industrial organisation of all countries. Should this situation continue, Japan will eventually prove a common enemy of the world.[67]

Furthermore, as Takahashi recognised, the boom was partly caused "by orders for war supplies,"[68] paid for with borrowed money. So he was in the paradoxical position of financing military expansion which he profoundly deplored. In the short term, contemporary economists noted, the increased expenditure of the armed services "played in the Japanese recovery the stimulating role assigned by the Keynes school to programmes of public works."[69] In the longer term the demands of the military became so excessive that they proved "fatal"[70] to Takahashi and disastrous to his country.

However, by the beginning of 1932 the tide of public opinion had turned. Liberalism was seen as a sign of weakness, whereas the heroic militarists appeared to be fighting for the nation's vital interests. The rampant spirit of chauvinism was embodied in Inukai's War Minister, General Araki Sadao, the army's choice. He was a flamboyant figure who had personally revived the ancient art of sword-making. He himself liked to wear a samurai sword, encouraged young officers to do the same and practised fencing with a dummy. A mystic worshipper at the shrine of Japan's glorious past, he recommended hara-kiri rather than surrender. He also wrote an article entitled "The Horse and National Defense," though he was by no means the sort of military primitive who preferred spears to guns. In fact, one Western observer visualised him as Japan's Moses, "shooting his way out of Egypt in an armoured car, insisting the while upon the literal observance of the ten commandments and the feast of the Passover."[71] Admired by his juniors as "a fire-spitting, sabre-rattling disciple of Mars,"[72] Araki had resisted their attempts to make him a dictator in October. Instead he warned them that "the Kusanagi sword [the legendary weapon by which an ancient royal prince had conquered the rebellious people of Japan] should always be polished: but it should not be indiscriminately drawn from its scabbard." Nevertheless the genial Araki remained their idol. They hailed him as "a god-like man of high character."[73]

Born in 1877, the son of a poor soya sauce manufacturer, Araki had begun his career as an apprentice in a pickle factory. But he proved an inspired soldier, realising as early as 1914 that Germany would lose the

First World War and developing an inveterate hatred of Communism when he saw it at close range during the Bolshevik revolution. His hostility to the USSR was reflected in an oil painting of the Russian surrender at Port Arthur in 1905 which was almost the only decoration in his Spartan quarters. An ascetic who drank no sake, the hollow-cheeked, handlebar-moustached, colourfully be-ribboned General also condemned the evils of capitalism and its parasitic beneficiaries. He spoke with vatic fervour about the need for spiritual strength. He even believed that earthquakes were good for Japan, bolstering the character of its people, encouraging self-denial and teaching indifference to material possessions. Attaching significance to the fact that he had been born under the sign of the Tiger, Araki drew little sketches of tigers and presented them to visitors as souvenirs. They were impressed. No one articulated faith in Japan's "holy mission in the world"[74] with greater "religious intensity."[75] No one preached Japanese imperialism more volubly—or more bombastically. It was his ultimate aim, Araki declared, to instill into the nation the soul of a soldier. Even the thin blood of the aged Saionji, who regarded such hopes as Utopian, was stirred by Araki's tumultuous eloquence. The General kept young officers in a state of "constant ferment."[76] By giving them their heads he sabotaged Inukai's efforts to enforce civilian rule. Declaring that "the true spirit of our nation has been quickened to life through the Manchurian crisis,"[77] Araki also permitted an almost uncontrollable expansion of the Japanese war in China, which subsequently brought on a nervous breakdown and retrospective regrets. "I didn't want to do the things that are being done in North China," he said in 1936, but "the situation . . . was already there . . . it is like telling someone not to get involved with a certain woman. There is nothing you can do about it . . . if the woman is pregnant."[78]

Fatalism combined with activism is one of the most bewildering Japanese characteristics. Like many of his countrymen, Araki saw himself as a pawn of fate. As much as any Surrealist he believed in the certainty of chance. He willingly swayed with the "tide of events" *(taisei)*, displaying a "voluptuous contentment in being buffeted by the great forces beyond his control."[79] Yet in prophetic vein he himself juggled with cosmic forces. He declared that:

> We cannot let things drift any longer. We are the leading Asiatic power and we should now take matters into our own hands. We must be active, ever expending the last portion of our national strength. We must be prepared to wage a desperate struggle. The Whites have made the countries of Asia mere objects of oppression and imperial Japan should no longer let their impudence go unpunished.[80]

Like Ishiwara, Araki saw the Manchurian Incident as a prelude to global war (though his prime target was Russia) and he approved the army's northward push: Chinchow was taken early in January 1932 and Harbin a month later. Araki also endorsed the Kwantung Army's plans for the conquered territory as adumbrated by Itagaki in a lecture to Hirohito's advisers at the Imperial Palace on 11 January. As Marquis Kido recorded, "Col. Itagaki gave hints that Manchuria would be placed under a new ruler, and that the Japanese army would take charge of a national defense of the new Manchurian state."[81] To disguise these intentions and to retaliate against damaging Chinese boycotts of Japanese goods, the armed services, again with Araki's blessing, took the momentous step of extending the war southwards. They used as a base their enclave in the great international entrepôt of Shanghai, where even the clanging tramcars were plastered with slogans like "Overthrow Japanese Imperialism" and "Sever Economic Relations with Japan."

CHINA'S commercial gateway, its largest manufacturing centre and its most populous urban area, Shanghai was the most cosmopolitan city in the world. A magnet for emigrés of every race and "a thicket of spy agencies,"[82] its International Settlement (plus the separate French Concession) profited enormously from extra-territorial administration, favourable tax rates and peace—nationals whose countries were at war suspended hostilities in Shanghai. Here, close to the vast mouth of the yellow Yangtse and guarded by the guns of grey warships flying the flags of many nations, flourished a strange, polyglot, quasi-colonial community. The highest buildings in Asia, monuments to the dominion of the *taipan,* were secured on their concrete rafts embedded in the silty Bund. Surveyors regularly checked the foundations of the Hong Kong & Shanghai Bank's skyscraper in case it sank under the weight of silver in its vaults. Palatial cinemas proliferated, showing films in English, French, Italian and Japanese. So did garish nightclubs, frothy soda fountains, drab mission halls, gay amusement parks with miniature golf courses, neon-lit department stores like Sun Sun's and more automobiles than in all the other Chinese cities combined.

Like a phosphorescent tide, the native world lapped against this foreign bastion, though Chinese were banned from its parks. The Chinese city was a warren of wooden sweatshops, teeming bazaars, dilapidated godowns and smoke-belching factories. Its sordid slums pullulated with traders, mendicants, gamblers, gangsters, drug addicts, slave children and coolies. According to a contemporary estimate Shanghai contained more prostitutes per head of population than any other city on earth: one in 130, compared to one in 250 for Tokyo, one in 481 for Paris, one in 580 for Berlin and one in 960 for London. There were 1,500 opium dens and the crime rate was twelve times higher than that of Chicago: visiting policemen from the Windy City begged to be allowed to "go home."[83] Shanghai even possessed a leper colony. In the sultry air (and near land fertilised by human manure distributed by the municipal "honey carts") disease was as rife as famine. Each year nearly 30,000 corpses were picked up from the streets and one "Shanghailander" newspaper urged that the police should sweep them clean of deformed beggars, whom it called "this refuse."[84] Such a simmering cauldron was easily brought to the boil. In January 1932 the Japanese had no difficulty in provoking a murderous affray as a pretext for military aggression, especially after a Chinese paper had deplored the recent failure of an assassination attempt (by a Korean nationalist) on Hirohito—which the Japanese themselves described, in a classic periphrasis, as "the Emperor Disrespect Incident."[85]

Eager for the navy to steal some of the army's thunder, Admiral Shiozawa Koichi deployed 2,000 blue-jacketed, white-putteed marines equipped with rifles, machine-guns, light artillery and armoured cars. Late on the moonless night of 28 January 1932, under the lurid glow of flares, they attacked the heavily-populated Chapei district, just north of the International Settlement. They were backed by detachments of "reservists" who subjected civilians to appalling atrocities, looting, raping, burning and murdering at will. The next day carrier-borne aircraft bombed the area, smashing the flimsy structures to atoms and causing fierce conflagrations, with flames leaping 100 feet into the air. Seaplanes flew so low to strafe the inhabitants that it was possible to see the faces of the pilots who, in martial Japanese fashion, were supplied with swords and pistols but not parachutes. From the safety of the International Settlement Westerners drove their Buicks to photograph the charred ruins and to view dead bodies being torn apart by snarling dogs. Meanwhile a "brown wave" of refugees fled with their possessions piled into trams, cars, carts, rickshaws and wheelbarrows.[86] Old men shuffled by, clutching bamboo birdcages. Young women hobbled on tightly-bound feet tugging children quilted against the cold. By contrast the Communist-trained Chinese 19th Route Army, thought to be a rabble in pagoda-shaped straw hats, rubber-soled canvas shoes and grey cotton uniforms (the insignia fastened to their shoulders with safety pins), stood firm. After prolonged combat they even managed to counter-attack. So, having grievously lost face, the Japanese navy had to call in the army. But even when attacked by thousands of steel-helmeted troops equipped with tanks and howitzers and protected against the snow by olive-drab woollen overcoats, the Chinese fought on tenaciously. Their snipers, hiding in buildings and bamboo thickets behind the Japanese lines, were particularly effective. One nearly managed to kill General Ueda Kenkichi in his field headquarters, shooting a hole just above the red band in his hat. He was most upset, complaining to the American journalist Edgar Snow: "The Chinese have no sense of honour or what is proper in warfare. Sniping is outlawed by most civilized countries."[87] When the pressure got too much for them the Chinese managed to retreat in good order, whereupon the Japanese claimed victory. So, in May, after protests from the League of Nations and the United States and complex negotiations, an armistice was signed and peace came once more to Shanghai.

However, as a result of the fighting (particularly the bombing of civilians—the first major instance in history), public opinion in Europe and America moved decisively against Japan. But governments, hag-ridden by the Depression, which Henry Stimson described as "an emergency like war," were still cautious about reacting in a way that might lead to real conflict. Thus the economic crisis not only prompted Japanese aggression, but also inhibited the great powers from doing anything about it. Britain's position was particularly weak, considering its vast interests in the East. As Neville Chamberlain wrote, "If we got into a real quarrel with Japan she could blow our ships out of the water one by one as they tried to get out of the Whangpoo."[88] Such considerations did cause the London government to abandon the Ten Year Rule, by which it had been decided that Britain need prepare for no major war within a decade, though the Treasury warned that financial risks were still greater than military ones. In the meantime, Britain continued with its policy of appeasement, refusing even to support Stimson's expostulations about Japan's "utterly unwarranted" actions in Shanghai.[89] However, at the League Britain did endorse the American doctrine of "non-recognition"—the refusal to acknowledge political changes brought about in violation of peace treaties. This included the state of Manchukuo, which the Kwantung Army established in place of the Chinese province of Manchuria early in 1932. It was a nominally independent and supposedly egalitarian cooperative of five races under a five-coloured flag. But its puppet status was obvious from the first. The proclamations and blood-red posters announcing the creation of this "ideal Paradise Land" were issued in Japanese.[90] And if its "Chief Executive," the lanky, bespectacled, forlorn Henry Pu Yi, last Manchu Emperor of China (who now dressed in frock coat and spats), had any ideas of living up to his new title he had only to observe that his Mukden palace was situated just across the road from the state prison. As Pu Yi later attested, whatever statements he made were "dictated by Itagaki."[91] An American said that the new country should be called "Japanchukuo,"[92] while a French writer christened it "Manikinchuria."[93]

The Kwantung Army's ideal for its private fief, quite genuine when enunciated by zealots such as Ishiwara who believed in Japan's civilising mission, foundered on the rock of colonial self-interest. This is not to say that its masters failed to develop the country: the new capital Hsingking (formerly Changchun) was a good, if drab, advertisement for their regime, with spacious parks, broad avenues and an imposing business district. But the Japanese could not disguise their intention to exploit Manchukuo. In the words of the Great East Asian Propaganda Society (which was controlled by Honjo and Itagaki), the ultimate purpose of Manchukuo was to "serve the allied and friendly Nippon in her struggle against the Anglo-Saxon world as well as against Comintern aggression."[94] Industry, commerce and agriculture were fostered for the benefit of the colonists and the mother country. Thus, for example, the Japanese monopolised the trade in soya beans—"meat, bread and business" to millions in the East and a commodity of which Manchuria produced half the world's supply.[95] Also extremely lucrative was the State opium monopoly which Honjo established: it was estimated that about 20 per cent of Japanese immigrants were engaged in drug dealing. Many others were profiteers, adventurers, brothel-keepers and assorted hoodlums (ronin), who descended on the new state like a flock of harpies.

Kidnapping, extortion, rape, robbery and murder made a hell of Harbin and other cities. The Japanese blamed these evils on Chinese bandits and guerrillas, who were indeed active. But they turned a blind eye to what one of their countrymen called the "mad carnival of debauchery carried out by gangs of ignorant bullies."[96] When Japanese were accused of crimes the newspapers had to refer to them as "foreigners." And the seven different Japanese police forces (one of them headed for a time by the officer who had murdered the radical Osugi after the 1923 earthquake) were chiefly engaged in repression. To this task they brought a brutality that self-proclaimed master races invariably reserve for lesser breeds. At its worst this took the form of the hideous bacteriological experiments which the army's infamous Unit 731 carried out on Chinese peasants and condemned prisoners, some sent by Ishiwara himself. Such perversion of science had become a "routine procedure"[97] by 1938, most of the so-called *marutas* ("logs of wood") infected with anthrax, typhoid, plague and other germs being Chinese POWs, but it remained a deadly secret. Still, the head of Japanese Intelligence in Manchuria (admittedly an extremist) made no bones about the nature of his country's imperialism:

> we have no intention of imparting our civilization to the people whom we have conquered or shall conquer. They will simply disappear. The Koreans will be eaten by vices; the Chinese will be victims of opium and other narcotics; the Russians will be ruined by vodka. They will be annihilated. Alone the descendants of Amaterasu-O-Mi-Kani, the Sun Goddess, will people our Empire. And this is but the first part of our programme of the tasks which the Gods have given to our people . . . Nothing can stop Japan from becoming the greatest Empire on earth![98]

Such forthrightness was uncommon among a people who cherished the proverb: "Behold the frog, who when he opens his mouth displays his whole inside."

But one leading figure who scorned to "pile circumspection on circumspection"[99] was General Araki. He frankly told the Lytton Commission, sent by the League in 1932 to investigate the situation in Manchuria, that the region would "never be allowed to return to Chinese hands."[100] Japan needed Manchukuo not only because it represented a way out of the Depression but, in the last resort, for reasons of national prestige. This was the kind of tub-thumping talk that infuriated cabinet ministers, particularly Takahashi, who aspired to "train [Araki] gradually into a statesman" and maintained that the army had been sent to Shanghai "to recover its prestige even at the expense of the nation." Other liberals agreed. The Emperor himself urged restraint and worried so much about the "rampancy" of the army that he could not sleep.[101] And the Japanese Ambassador to Italy, Yoshida Shigeru, declared that the insane Shanghai incursion "reflected a fascist tendency within the country."[102] That tendency was also reflected in the "violence and terror" employed in Japan as in Manchuria during the early months of 1932.[103]

Holding corrupt politicians and greedy capitalists responsible for "injustice at a time of severe economic pressure,"[104] members of ultranationalist groups first murdered the former Finance Minister, Inoue, and then Baron Dan Takuma, head of the Mitsui *zaibatsu,* which henceforth paid them protection money. At the same time Araki was involved in a "deep plot" to achieve an "internal political revolution."[105] Its aim was to replace party cabinets such as that of Inukai, who was trying to use the Emperor to check the military, with national governments which would serve the entire people by following the Imperial Way. It was the burning sense that Inukai was neglecting certain sections of the community, particularly the desperate farmers, which inspired his own assassination.

On the late afternoon of 15 May 1932, when the magnolias were in bloom, two taxis containing nine young officers in the army and navy drew up in front of the Yasukuni Shrine. Situated in a small hilltop park amid the cheap cafés and second-hand book shops of Tokyo's university district, it was sacred to the memory of the nation's war dead. The officers entered through the huge metal torii cast from captured cannon, passing the rows of stone lanterns and the bronze statue of the first Meiji War Minister, who had been assassinated in 1869. They worshipped, doffing their caps and bowing to the unseen mirror of the sun goddess. Then they re-embarked in the taxis and drove down cherry-lined Green Leaf Avenue to the Prime Minister's official residence, a building resembling a large hotel, which had been put up after the earthquake. After splitting up to search its lobbies and corridors, one contingent broke into Inukai's private apartment. Calmly he lit a cigarette, invited them to take off their shoes and said, "Let us talk it over before you shoot."[106] But at that moment another group of officers burst in, led by Lieutenant Yamagishi clutching a dagger and shouting: "No use talking . . . Fire!"[107] Revolver shots rang out and the Prime Minister slumped to the matted floor with bullets in his neck and stomach. The "old fox" was a long time dying: tended by his daughter-in-law, he murmured in his delirium, "If only we could have talked."[108]

Meanwhile his killers made their way to the metropolitan police headquarters, where they surrendered. Other members of their so-called "Young Officers of the Army and Navy and Farmers' Deathband" also capitulated, after having mounted violent but largely ineffectual attacks against a variety of additional targets. These included Lord Privy Seal Makino's house, the Bank of Japan and the Hatatogo power station—one of the conspirators said afterwards that he had wanted to make those living in luxury sit in darkness for a while. Happily they had stifled still wilder caprices, having abandoned plans to provoke a war with the United States by killing Charlie Chaplin, who was then on a visit to Japan. But for the first time uniformed officers had staged a serious coup d'état: some of them had tried to make Araki the leader of a purified Japan. He had resisted. Indeed, fearing a popular reaction against the military, he resigned. There was widespread condemnation of the young officers immediately after Inukai's murder and, as Marquis Kido recorded, the "cry against the military's tyranny is heard everywhere."[109] So, paradoxically, Araki was brought back as War Minister because he seemed to be the only general who could control "the explosive temper of the army."[110] He did so by a public display of sympathy for the assassins:

> When I consider why these naive youths acted as they did I cannot hold back my tears. They did not seek fame or advantage. What they did, they did in the genuine belief that it would be for the good of the empire.[111]

Others were so impressed by the plotters' sincerity that they sought to match it. During the trial (which resulted in light prison sentences, later commuted) thousands of petitions for clemency were signed, often in blood. Araki also received a grisly package of nine amputated little fingers from men wishing to take the place of the accused who, they feared, might be executed.

THUS the country's mood changed as chauvinist propaganda became more insistent and the military tightened its political grip. As the army had hoped, party government died with Inukai. His successor, Admiral Saito Makoto, headed a coalition cabinet of "national unity," aptly described as "a compromise between dictatorship and parliamentarism."[112] Saito himself did not favour fascism—neither Saionji nor the Emperor would have countenanced a leader with such tendencies at that time—but the new Premier did have a "natural gift for inaction"[113] and a perplexing ability to make himself misunderstood. Araki therefore dominated the government. Advocating a re-kindling of the samurai spirit, he was responsible for what a British diplomat called "a devil's brew of ultra-nationalistic incitement."[114] As the American Ambassador added, Araki fostered "war fever": he demanded more military training in schools where children were already being induced to give their pocket money to buy "patriotism" tanks and planes.[115] He also favoured more indoctrination among university students who, despite wearing uniforms and being forbidden to meet in groups of more than five, seemed given to dangerous thoughts. In the cabinet only Takahashi spoke out against the intellectual discipline which the War Minister was attempting to impose on society as a whole. When Araki argued that public opinion would not have tolerated the Foreign Ministry's proposed non-aggression pact with the Soviet Union, which he had just quashed, Takahashi retorted:

> There is no such thing as public opinion at present. If you say anything unfavourable [about] the Army, then the Kempei [military police] rattle their swords or point a gun or threaten you. There is nothing so severe as the present suppression of free speech. It is a fact that when a cer-

tain newspaper publisher in Kyushu wrote something unfavourable [about] the Army, they threatened him by having an airplane circle around the paper plant and said that they would bomb the plant. The situation of the Kempei following statesmen around as if they were spies is very disgusting.

Flushing with anger, Araki insisted that there was free speech in Japan.

The two ministers clashed again over the army's determination to extend its Manchurian empire to the Great Wall by annexing the mountainous province of Jehol. Takahashi warned that this would ensure the hostility of the League of Nations and provoke a disastrous "fight against the entire world."[116] But, drunk with national spirit, Araki was happy to declare that *Kodo,* the Imperial Way, "should be spread and expanded all over the world, and every impediment to it brushed aside—even with the sword."[117] Anyway, in the wake of the critical Lytton Report, which was extremely well informed (despite elaborate Japanese attempts to conceal the truth) and called for the withdrawal of Nippon's forces from Manchuria, Araki was determined to break with the League. He was also opposed by Saito, who thought Japan would lose its position in the world, and by the Emperor, who was so worried by the prospect that he shed several pounds in weight. But, supported by the army, the fiery little General was adamant. "We are being restrained on all matters by our membership of the League," he told the cabinet, "only by leaving . . . can we attain our independence."[118] With equal assurance he ridiculed the notion that Western nations, all of whom were "suffering from the depression," would impose economic sanctions on Japan, let alone "wage war for the sake of the League."[119] So the attack on Jehol was launched, which quickly led to its capture (some of the opposing troops having never before seen tanks or even aeroplanes) and an armistice with China. The League of Nations responded with a historic ten-hour message broadcast to the world from Geneva in Morse Code announcing its substantial confirmation of the Lytton Report and its virtual condemnation of Japan.

The Japanese representative to the League, Matsuoka Yosuke, had expended much energy, ingenuity and cash in an effort to prevent the League from censuring Japan. But his qualifications for this task were doubtful. He had, it is true, spent several of his formative years in the United States, graduating from Oregon Law School in 1900, and his English, if not always coherent, was amazingly voluble. In private conversations he effervesced with boyish charm. He had also gained much diplomatic and political experience abroad, notably in Manchuria, where he had held important positions on the railway and had come to the conclusion, about which he lectured the Emperor in 1932, that "according to the principle of biology" such near neighbours as China and Japan were natural enemies.[120] However, Matsuoka was frankly contemptuous of the West, reckoning that democracy must yield to more virile systems of government and telling Mussolini that, although Fascism might work in Italy, Japan would create a form of imperial totalitarianism. What is more, Matsuoka, a slight, bespectacled figure whose closely cropped hair stood "straight up like a pen-wiper,"[121] was volatile to the point of dementia. Before he set off for Geneva, Yoshida Shigeru told him, "You should go to an insane asylum, douse your head in water, and then leave after you've cooled down a bit."[122]

Matsuoka showed no signs of having undergone this treatment when he arrived there via the Trans-Siberian Railway. Establishing his large delegation (which included Ishiwara) at the Hotel Métropole, he bubbled with ideas for converting League members to his viewpoint, sometimes emerging from his room late at night wearing a brown kimono and clutching a bottle of aqua vitae. Matsuoka hectored the Assembly unmercifully. He asserted that every single Japanese backed the army's policy in Manchuria and demanded, "Do you suppose that they were all insane?"[123] At least once he shocked his fellow delegates by abandoning his prepared speech and comparing them to the killers of Christ. "Japan stands ready to be crucified," he orated. "But we do believe that, in a very few years world opinion will be changed and that we also shall be understood by the world as Jesus of Nazareth was!"[124]

The Assembly was merely the formal face of the League and a surprisingly drab one. For while its palatial new home rose beside Lake Geneva the Assembly met at what one disappointed visitor described as "a second-rate hotel in a back-street, with a garden containing only a few old Brussels sprouts." To accommodate the Disarmament Conference this greenish-yellow, four-storey building had a khaki-coloured, iron-and-glass extension which "looked like a mixture of a garage and a greenhouse."[125] Statesmen in silk hats and frock coats processed through the hotel's lobby with its potted palms and its red cord carpet, past the lounges with their creaking parquet floors and faded Victorian furniture, to deliberate in a large, stuffy white hall filled with desks and hazy with the tobacco smoke of all nations. But the League's real business was conducted elsewhere in the mist-ridden city of Calvin, itself once described by Ramsay MacDonald as "a perfect hot-bed of intrigue and a forcing-house of rumour."[126] Accordingly Matsuoka spent much of his time trying to negotiate and exert influence behind the scenes. Encouraged by the conciliatory British, he did not take quite the "uncompromising stand" he later pretended.[127] He also did his best to suborn the press, bribing some journalists and entertaining others at parties "conceived on Lucullan and Bacchanalian lines."[128]

On 24 February 1933 people queued for hours to get into the session of the Assembly, held in one of the halls of the Disarmament Conference building, at which the Japanese plenipotentiary would make his final appeal for the League's rejection of the (revised) Lytton Report. Back in Biblical vein Matsuoka first challenged the nation that was without sin to "cast the first stone" at Japan.[129] Then, swaying slightly at the rostrum and speaking in a low, emotional voice, he reiterated his case. China was not a state but a chaotic region "larger than Europe" with as many governments and almost as many languages. The League's proposal for an independent Manchuria to be established under Chinese sovereignty was therefore unworkable and unacceptable. Only Manchukuo under Japanese protection could achieve peace in the Far East.[130] The Assembly, presided over by the pale-faced Belgian Foreign Minister Paul Hymans, was not convinced. Watched by the packed, hushed audience in an atmosphere of electric tension, 42 delegates voted to adopt the Report, to condemn Japan's actions and to deny their puppet state international recognition. Siam abstained and Matsuoka, his voice on a "rising inflexion," uttered a solitary "No."[131] Slowly and sadly, Matsuoka returned to the rostrum to express his regrets in a dignified "Sayonara speech." His country had, "for the sake of peace, borne the unbearable but the resolution was something that Japan could in no way accept."[132] Then he returned to his seat at the end of one of the long green benches, gathered up his papers, motioned to the other members of his 30-strong delegation and, in utter silence, marched out of the hall. Japan's participation in the League of Nations was at an end. According to one witness Matsuoka burst into tears as he passed through the door, saying: "Japan has left the League with a heavy heart."[133] According to another he kept his composure and betrayed only one sign of strain—puffing vigorously at an unlighted cigar.

After this dramatic exit, Hymans' words about the League's continuing to work to "ensure the peace of the world" rang hollow.[134] Coming on top of its unsuccessful attempts to secure disarmament and alleviate the Depression, the League's failure to restrain Japan was disastrous. It fatally undermined the principle of collective security and gave international sanction to the policy of appeasement. At a time when all members of the League were punch-drunk from the economic crisis, when Roosevelt was about to launch the New Deal, when Hitler was poised to create a totalitarian state, when Stalin was striding through blood to make a brave new world, it was understandable that the great powers should avert their gaze from Japan's aggression. But by resorting to non-recognition and relying on moral condemnation the League demonstrated that it was not prepared to enforce its will. The tragedy of the 1930s was that supporters of the League's ideals took so long to realise that peace could only be defended by war.

For Japan quitting the League was a fateful step into the valley of shadows. Matsuoka himself seemed to have some inkling of this. For he had warned the Assembly not to adopt the report, which would lead inevitably to Japan's exit, because a disintegrating China and a menacing Russia already threatened the peace of the world; so "we look into the gloom of the future and can see no certain gleam of light before us."[135] Now Matsuoka's country had been solemnly arraigned before the bar of the world as an international criminal. Nippon was bitterly scornful that the League had been unable to exact punishment and supremely confident that, after pausing to digest Manchuria, it could pursue its expansionist course unscathed. But pariahdom also provoked paranoia. Japan felt persecuted and indulged in messianic passions. Militarists took stricter control of the country's destiny despite their gross ignorance of the outside world, their internecine factionalism and their hysterical bellicosity—in 1933 the Deputy Foreign Minister lamented, "The Army seems determined to attack Russia in 1935, and the Navy the United States in 1936."[136] Nationalists brandished ever more fiercely "the Sun Flag of the Land of the Rising Sun" which would, according to Kita Ikki, "light the darkness of the entire world."[137]

Isolation bred intransigence. Matsuoka insisted on coming home from Geneva via Britain and America to avoid showing "even a slight indication of compromise" and to demonstrate "Japan's solitary dignity."[138] Ishiwara, too, returned via Britain. In Geneva he had shunned the League, preferring to shop for books and prints of his heroes, Napoleon and Frederick the Great. In London, wearing traditional Japanese costume at an embassy reception given in his honour, he coolly defended his Manchurian activities. But he then crossed the Soviet Union, where he was more discreet. Ishiwara did not complain that among the other passengers on the Trans-Siberian Railway were lice. Rather, he complimented the Communists on their "remarkable feats" in building a new state. But, as he later drily commented, "I didn't say whether I thought executing several hundred thousand people good or bad."[139]

X

STALIN'S REVOLUTION

ISHIWARA'S estimate that building the new Soviet State had involved the execution of a few hundred thousand people was a shot in the dark. It was hopelessly wide of the mark. For while the rest of the world grappled with the Great Depression the USSR suffered a self-inflicted catastrophe that cost countless millions of lives. Indeed, at the very time when the citadels of capitalism were crumbling the Communist Colossus seemed to be engineering its own downfall. Claiming to be protected from external conditions by the socialist system yet feeling profoundly vulnerable because of its economic backwardness, the USSR forged new armour at awesome cost in blood and treasure. In the name of survival it gashed terrible wounds in its own flesh. To catch up with the industrialised world it reverted to methods which made the tsars seem civilised. The "Red Tsar" responsible for these acts of barbarism was, of course, Joseph Stalin.

His colleagues had long been aware of his brutal propensities. The first head of the Cheka secret police, Felix Dzerzhinsky, took the job because otherwise it would have fallen to Stalin and "He would nurse the baby with blood alone."[1] But throughout the 1920s Stalin had risen by guile more than force. He was secretive and self-sufficient and he had a memory like a machine. A supreme bureaucrat, nicknamed "Comrade Card-index," he had climbed to power through committees. As General Secretary of the Central Committee of the Communist Party he had outmanoeuvred his rivals one by one. He had defeated Lev Kamenev, who called him a "ferocious savage," and Grigori Zinoviev, who described him as a "bloodthirsty Ossetian" with "no idea of the meaning of conscience."[2] He had exiled the inspiring Trotsky, who denounced him as "the grave-digger of the proletarian revolution."[3] He had isolated the intellectual Bukharin, who regarded him as a "debased Genghis Khan."[4] By 1929 Stalin had established what Trotsky called "the dictatorship of the secretariat."[5] He was thus able to initiate a revolution more far-reaching than Lenin's. At the time its full horror was hidden by a fog of propaganda. But during the

Second World War Stalin told Churchill that his "revolution from above" had surpassed, in the severity of its impact on the Russian people, the German invasion itself. It was no wonder that at night the floodlit Red Flag, which a concealed wind-machine kept flying above the crenellated walls, tented towers and gold domes of the Kremlin, reminded contemporaries of a "pool of blood suspended in the darkness."[6]

Also gleaming from the Kremlin's battlements were the gilt double-headed eagles of the Romanovs, not replaced until 1937 by Stalin's huge illuminated red glass stars. Other royal relics littered the palaces, cathedrals and barbicans of this 65-acre museum, not just State treasures such as the crown jewels but priceless bric-à-brac: the red velvet, gold-embroidered saddle of Ivan the Terrible, the engraved armour of Boris Godunov, the huge boots which Peter the Great made for himself, Catherine the Great's silver wedding dress. But time had moved on in the Kremlin: the clock on the Saviour Tower no longer chimed the "Preobrazhensky March" but the "Internationale" (so tuneless that it was hardly recognisable). In 1929 Stalin demolished various imperial and ecclesiastical edifices to clear the ground for Communist monuments such as the military academy. Moreover, the kite-shaped fortress overlooking the Moscow River became more impregnable than ever. It was Stalin's Castle, a nightmarish labyrinth shrouded in "cloud[s] of secrecy"[7] and enclosed by walls of terror. Elaborate measures were taken to preserve the safety of Russia's man of steel. There were sentries at every corner. Crack secret police patrolled the corridors and grounds. Guards checked the identity of all visitors against their photographs. Passwords were constantly changed. The air was tested for traces of poison gas. At the centre of this stronghold Stalin himself dwelt with becoming simplicity—in the imperial servants' quarters of the Poteshny Palace. His small study was plainly furnished with a bookshelf, a battered leather ottoman and a writing table. On it stood two photographs: one of his daughter Svetlana, the other of Lenin reading *Pravda*. No pictures hung on the walls. Instead there was a plaque inscribed with Dante's line, "Go your way and let people talk"; and an intaglio profile of the wife of Zeus above Pushkin's sonnet, "Hera, the far-famed goddess of power."[8]

The adjoining bedroom was similarly modest: the windows were narrow, a couple of rugs covered the worn floor and Stalin slept under an old army blanket. Nothing in his personal appearance suggested that he was the embodiment of power. He invariably wore a plain khaki tunic buttoned up to the chin and uniform trousers stuffed into long black boots. He was short and swarthy with thick, greying hair, deep, dark, slightly squinting eyes, a nicotine-stained moustache and bad teeth—having a penchant for medical murder himself, Stalin did not trust dentists. Some people, to be sure, perceived a monster. Boris Pasternak said that Stalin was "the most terrible creature he had ever seen, a crab-like dwarf with a yellow, pock-marked face and a bristling moustache."[9] Another poet, Osip Mandelstam, was repelled by "the huge laughing cockroaches on his top lip."[10] When Stalin laughed, the critic Kornelii Zelinsky noted, "His eyebrows and moustache move apart and something cunning appears. Tigerish, in fact."[11] Other outsiders discerned Stalin's "brutal lack of scruple" and even the sycophantic *New York Times* correspondent Walter Duranty found him "crude," "hard and cruel."[12] Insiders were exposed to the autocrat's feral rages, drunken buffoonery, paranoid suspicions, caustic cynicism and obscene invective. Women were by no means immune, not even the highest in the land. Stalin once told Nadezhda Krupskaya that she was a syphilitic whore and later said that if she misbehaved he would make someone else Lenin's widow.

Yet for the most part visitors were overwhelmed by Stalin's simplicity and sincerity, by his unaffected friendliness and his unassuming demeanour. H. G. Wells thought him kindly, "candid, fair and honest"[13]— and tried to get him to join the P.E.N. Club. The American journalist Eugene Lyons emerged from a rare interview saying, "I like that man."[14] After his first meeting with Stalin the British Ambassador Lord Chilston told his staff, "Do you know, I think the chap's a gentleman."[15] It was hard to reconcile the shy Kremlin recluse with the dictator around whom a personality cult was forming so extravagant as even, apparently, to surprise its subject. "If this goes on," Stalin remarked to one of his bodyguards, "some night I'll find my own statue in my bed."[16]

Stalin always claimed that he discouraged personal adulation. In fact he craved it, once growling over a portrait showing his pock marks that artists see too much. The semi-cripple with the withered left arm and two toes joined on his left foot was inordinately vain. The shoemaker's son from Georgia responded with whiplash ferocity to any slight. The sometime seminarian from Tiflis built power on the foundation of awe. The Red revolutionary established his legitimacy by becoming the heir of Lenin. But it was not enough to be the guardian of Leninist orthodoxy, even though, as Zinoviev complained, Stalin could thereby claim to be infallible. Stalin must also be the high priest of Lenin's own cult. For Lenin had been genuinely revered, not because he inspired terror but because he embodied hope. On his death huge queues had formed outside the Hall of Columns in what had formerly been the Nobles' Club, where his body lay. Bonfires were lit in the streets to ward off the intense cold. Amid the crowd were Pasternak and Mandelstam, the latter joking that people had come to complain to Lenin about the Bolsheviks but "it won't do any good." In fact Mandelstam marvelled at the spectacle of the "Moscow of ancient days burying one of her tsars," and his wife Nadezhda concluded that Lenin's funeral was "the last flicker of the Revolution as a genuine popular movement."[17] Stalin wanted to be the keeper of that flame. He needed to preserve Lenin for his own purposes. Perhaps inspired by Howard Carter's discovery of the mummified Tutankhamun, Stalin advocated the embalming of Lenin's body. And in 1929 he approved the construction of a permanent shrine, beside the rose-coloured Kremlin Wall in Red Square, for the supreme effigy of Communism. It was a marvellous fulfilment of Lenin's own (frustrated) ambition to create "monumental propaganda"[18] and an extraordinary realisation of his remark that great liberators are often fated after their deaths to serve as the icons for some new tyranny.

Lenin's mausoleum was a stepped pyramid of russet and dark grey granite (grey being a "worker's colour"),[19] and it became the focus of intense devotion. Just what superstitions this pharaonic monument inspired in a godless theocracy it is impossible to say, though the poet Vladimir Mayakovsky did suggest that Lenin's preserved body symbolised the everlasting life of Communism. Anyway, a perpetual procession of votaries shuffled towards the immobile guard of honour, under the porphyry inscription of Lenin's name, through the bronze portals, down the dimly lit steps, into the labradorite-tiled Funeral Hall and past the immortal corpse. It lay in a scarlet-lined, glass-topped sarcophagus based on a sable plinth surrounded by magnificent blooms, which were changed daily. The head rested on a red silk cushion. A cloth of purple and black satin shrouded the loins and legs. The torso was dressed in a khaki gabardine tunic with the Order of the Red Banner pinned over the heart. The little hands, nails carefully manicured, were crossed. The auburn beard was trimmed. The eyes were closed as though in sleep. The lips were fixed in the ghost of a smile. The yellow-white skin was drawn smoothly over the high cheek-bones and domed forehead. The flesh was in the pink.

It was kept so in a marinade of chemicals. Lenin's embalmers regularly swabbed his exposed surfaces with a secret "balsam," impregnating the tissue, which did not become waxy but remained firm and resilient. They paid particular attention to the face, its lips stitched together, its eyelids sewn over false eyes, its skull void of grey matter—the brain had been sent to the Lenin Institute, where it was sliced into 30,000 pieces for scientific study. Every 18 months the whole body experienced a little resurrection—it was given a "general overhaul."[20] The inner cocoon of rubber bandages was unwrapped and the stick-like limbs and eviscerated trunk were bathed in a solution of glycerine and potassium acetate (while the embalmers sometimes got drunk on the 96 per cent proof spirit used in the preservation process). The survival of these cosmetic taxidermists depended on Lenin's own survival. To foreign journalists they nervously demonstrated the continuing elasticity of his flesh, pinching the cheeks and tweaking the nose. Plainly Lenin possessed enough *élan vital* to defy rigor mortis.

Only the occasional Doubting Thomas needed such reassurance. One determined sceptic was the poet E. E. Cummings, who regarded the "trivial idol throned in stink" as another Soviet "fake 'reality'" and claimed to have seen "better gods" and "mightier deeper puppets" on Coney Island. But most pilgrims, particularly those from abroad, saw Lenin with the eyes of faith. Edmund Wilson was enraptured by "a beautiful face, of exquisite fineness; and—what proves sufficiently its authenticity—it is profoundly aristocratic."[21] Visitors literally viewed the saviour of the proletariat in rose-tinted light. Bathed in a damask glow he lay, the form conserved, the contents transformed. Lenin had become, in his final state, a weird embodiment of dialectical materialism: the corporeal phantom of revolution, the hollow incarnation of Bolshevism.

But the ox-blood ziggurat was important less as a tomb for Lenin than as a platform for Stalin. From its polished eminence he presided over interminable parades in the vast asphalt amphitheatre of Red Square—the old cobblestones had been replaced and the onion-domed St. Basil's Cathedral was now an anti-God museum, but so far little else had changed and plans to erect a 50-storey monumental building in the shape of a factory chimney came to nothing. Nothing, indeed, could be permitted to overshadow Stalin as he stood for hours on the little wooden pedestal that added inches to his stature. Here he smoked and spat. He eased his creaking shoulders inside a German-made bullet-proof waistcoat and stamped his aching feet above the sacred husk of Lenin. He raised his hand, palm outstretched, in "a little gesture that was at once a friendly wave, a benediction and a salute."[22] He became the sinister cynosure of frightened eyes.

The "opening episode" of Stalin's personality cult was the celebration of his fiftieth birthday on 21 December 1929.[23] Russian newspapers filled their first four pages with column after column of fawning tributes to "the peerless warrior of Communism," "the iron Leninist," "Socialism's victorious chief."[24] Clouds of incense wafted towards Moscow from every town, village, factory and barracks in the land—a land occupying a sixth of the world's surface and embracing 160 million people of 100 races speaking 200 languages or dialects. In birthday greetings and speeches Stalin was exalted as Lenin's most faithful disciple. In his reply Stalin identified himself with the Communist cause and (reaching instinctively for the imagery of the abattoir) he vowed to shed for it "if necessary all my blood, drop by drop."[25] A drive began to recruit new members of the Party in his name. Icons of the leader proliferated—by 1933 there were 103 busts or portraits of Stalin in Gorky Street alone, compared to 58 of Lenin. He was hailed as the *Vozhd,* equivalent to Führer, Duce or Caudillo. Soon, indeed, Stalin was being elevated from Superman—"Driver of the Locomotive of History"—to Almighty God: "O Great Stalin, O Leader of the Peoples, Thou who didst give birth to man, Thou who didst make fertile the earth."[26] Many Western observers, even those favourably disposed towards the regime, were repelled by the idolatry. But Walter Duranty observed that Stalin had merely revived "the semi-divine, supreme autocracy" of the tsars. He had established himself on the Kremlin throne "as a ruler whose lightest word is all in all and whose frown spells death."[27] This conformed to an Oriental tradition going back to Tamerlaine, who had marked his victories with "pyramids of skulls."[28] Though ingratiating and patronising, Duranty could also be discerning. Later Osip Mandelstam would pose the question: "Why is it that when I think of *him* [Stalin], I see heads, mounds of heads?"[29]

PART of the answer lies in the campaign which Stalin launched six days after his fiftieth birthday, a campaign resisted so violently that only his inflated prestige enabled him to carry it through—and to survive. Having found that his plans to revolutionise industry were being jeopardised by a shortage of grain, Stalin determined to speed up his programme of forcing peasants *(muzhiks)* into collective farms and he announced a new policy of "liquidating the kulaks as a class."[30] The kulaks (literally, grasping "fists"; metaphorically, rich peasants) were portrayed as a reactionary agricultural bourgeoisie intent on choking Communism with "the bony hand of famine."[31] It is true that these more enterprising farmers had taken advantage of Lenin's New Economic Policy, introduced after his own attempt to squeeze grain out of the peasantry had led to widespread revolt and famine in 1921, to sell their surplus produce on the open market and acquire a few implements and animals. Moreover they preferred to hoard their grain or feed it to their livestock (meat and dairy products fetched higher prices than cereals) rather than dispose of it to the State. But these better-off peasants were anything but the greedy capitalists of Stalin's fantasies. As Zinoviev said, "We are fond of describing any peasant who has enough to eat as a kulak."[32] Nevertheless Stalin decreed that the kulaks were class enemies. Their persecution would terrify the lesser peasants into joining collectives, which would in turn reap huge benefits from exploiting the kulaks' property. Thus socialism would come to the countryside and peasants would be transformed into proletarians. Huge agricultural factories would produce the food without which Russia must remain a backward nation; food itself became a State monopoly. In the Communist historical process the eradication of the kulaks was incidental to the elimination of private farming. Stalin quoted the Russian proverb: "When the head is cut off, one does not mourn for the hair."[33]

So Stalin declared war on his own people—a class war to end class. In the first two months of 1930 perhaps a million kulaks, weakened by previous victimisation, were stripped of their possessions and uprooted from their farmsteads. They were among the earliest of "over five million"[34] souls deported during the next three years, most of whom perished. Brigades of workers conscripted from the towns, backed by contingents of the Red Army and the OGPU (which had replaced the Cheka), swept through the countryside "like raging beasts."[35] They rounded up the best farmers and their families, banished them to the barren outskirts of their villages or drove them into the northern wastes. Often they shot the heads of households, cramming their dependents into "death trains"—a prolonged process owing to a shortage of the blood-coloured cattle trucks known as "red cows." While they waited, women and children expired of cold, hunger and disease. Muscovites, at first shocked by glimpses of the terror being inflicted on the countryside, became inured to the sight of peasants being herded from one station to another at gunpoint. A witness wrote:

> Trainloads of deported peasants left for the icy North, the forests, the steppes, the deserts. There were whole populations, denuded of everything; the old folk starved to death in mid-journey, new-born babies were buried on the banks of the roadside, and each wilderness had its crop of little crosses of boughs or white wood.[36]

The survivors of these ghastly odysseys were concentrated in primitive camps which they often had to scratch with their bare hands from taiga or tundra. They were then set to work at digging canals, lumbering and other projects, Stalin having recently been dazzled by the prospect of "constructing socialism through the use of prison labour."[37]

Whatever Stalin may have envisaged, the assault on the kulaks was less like a considered piece of social engineering than "a nation-wide *pogrom*."[38] Often the urban cadres simply pillaged for private gain, eating the kulaks' food and drinking their vodka on the spot, donning their felt boots and clothes, right down to their woollen underwear. Moreover, the spoliation was marked by caprice and chaos since it was virtually impossible to decide which peasants were kulaks. Peasants of all sorts (including women) resisted, fighting back with anything from sporadic terror to full-scale revolt. There were major uprisings in Moldavia, the Ukraine, the Caucasus, Crimea, Azerbaijan, Soviet Central Asia and elsewhere. To quell them Stalin employed tanks and even military aircraft, unusual adjuncts to agrarian reform (though Lenin had also used poison gas). Some units refused to kill their countrymen and these he punished. Where troops did not mutiny, their morale was shattered. "I am an old Bolshevik," sobbed one OGPU colonel to a foreign writer. "I worked in the underground against the Tsar and then I fought in the civil war. Did I do all that in order that I should now surround villages with machine-guns and order my men to fire indiscriminately into crowds of peasants? Oh, no, no!"[39]

Some kulaks fled from the holocaust, seeking refuge in the towns or the woods and selling as many of their possessions as they could. Braving the machine-guns of the blue-capped border guards, others crossed into Poland, Romania, China or Alaska, taking portable property with them, occasionally even driving their flocks and herds. Some tried to bribe their persecutors. Some committed suicide. Some appealed for mercy, of all Communist commodities the one in shortest supply. Like the troops, some Party members were indeed horrified at the vicious acts which they were called upon to perform. One exclaimed, "We are no longer people, we are animals."[40] Many were brutes, official gangsters who revelled in licensed thuggery. Others carried out the persecutions for fear of joining the victims. Others belonged to the semi-Christian "tradition of social levelling stretching back to the peasant commune."[41] Still others were idealists of a different stamp, convinced that they were doing their "revolutionary duty."[42] They had no time for what Trotsky had once called the "papist-Quaker babble about the sanctity of human life."[43] According to Marx's iron laws of history, they shed the blood of the kulaks to achieve the dictatorship of the proletariat. Without this sacrifice the Soviet Union could not modernise and socialism could not survive. As one apparatchik expressed it: "When you are attacking there is no place for mercy; don't think of the kulak's hungry children; in the class struggle philanthropy is evil."[44] This view, incidentally, was often shared by Western fellow-travellers. Upton Sinclair and A. J. P. Taylor both argued that to preserve the Workers' State the kulaks "had to be destroyed."[45]

Whether facing expropriation and exile or collectivisation and servitude, masses of peasants retaliated by smashing their implements and killing their animals—live beasts would have to be handed over to the collectives whereas meat and hides could be respectively consumed and concealed. In the first two months of 1930 millions of cattle, horses, pigs, sheep and goats were slaughtered. Many others starved to death because grain was lacking or the collective farmers neglected them. A quarter of the nation's livestock perished, a greater loss than that sustained during the Civil War and one not made up until the 1960s. It was ironic, therefore, that on 2 March 1930 Stalin should call a halt in an article in *Pravda* entitled "Dizzy with Success." This declared that over-zealous local officials had made mistakes and that peasants should not be forced to join collectives. Under the spur of coercion no fewer than 15 million households (numbering over 70 million souls, or 60 per cent of all peasants) had already done so. But now, within a few weeks, nine million households withdrew from what they regarded as a new form of serfdom. Processions of peasants marched round villages with copies of Stalin's article blazoned aloft on banners. As a foreign journalist recorded, Russia's *muzhiks* had lived under "lowering clouds of gloom, fear and evil foreboding . . . until the colour of them seemed to have entered their very souls."[46] Now, thanks to Stalin, the pall had lifted and the reign of terror had ceased.

It was a false dawn. Stalin was retreating the better to advance. The only Bolshevik leader whose parents had been serfs, he knew the peasants and regarded them as the scum of the earth. Not for him the romanticism of a Tolstoy, who saw the *muzhik* as a spontaneous child of nature. Rather, Stalin agreed with Maxim Gorky who wrote that "the fundamental obstacle on the path of Russia's progress towards Europeanisation and culture" was "the overwhelming predominance of the illiterate countryside over the town, the zoological individualism of the peasantry and its almost total lack of social feelings."[47] Known as *chorny narod,* "the dark people," the peasants were indeed brutal and obscurantist. Scattered in 600,000 villages and other small settlements over the interminable steppe, they dwelt in fly-ridden, cockroach-infested hovels with thatched roofs and mud floors, sharing the space, as often as not, with their animals. Thrashing their lean oxen or their gaunt women, millions tilled the soil with wooden ploughs "at least as old as the Pharaohs."[48]

More like the coolies of Asia than the farmers of Europe, the *muzhiks* knew nothing but poverty. Indeed, they had kept hunger at bay only since the mid-1920s. Bundled into putrid layers of ragged homespun (though some factory-made garments were appearing), they huddled around their stoves during the long dark winters, gossiping and brawling just as Chekhov had described in his classic story "Peasants." They saw their children and animals die and their huts go up in flames—"the red cockerel" devoured 400,000 homes a year. They resisted outside authority and visited barbarous punishments of their own on wrongdoers within the community. They smoked home-cured tobacco rolled up in newspaper. Otherwise their anodynes were religion, sex and drink. Smoke-blackened icons filled their houses, portents of heavenly recompense for lives nasty, brutish and short. Promiscuity was almost universal and the "most daring familiarities" took place in public, while the "usual talk was a running fire of obscenities and the gestures were as bad as the language."[49] Drunkenness was such a "normal phenomenon" that Party members themselves defended it as "necessary for the worker in view of the hard conditions of his life";[50] so they could scarcely blame the peasant for drowning his sorrows in vodka.

Stalin, however, though not averse to binges of his own, was determined to subject the *muzhik* to socialist discipline, to change his character by continuing the revolutionary change in his circumstances. In the autumn of 1930 he resumed the policy of forcible collectivisation. Peasant anguish was fed by rumours that women would be socialised, that unproductive old people would be prematurely cremated and that children were to be sent to crèches in China. Such fears did not seem extravagant, for the authorities were themselves offering peasants apocalyptic inducements to join the collectives: "They promised golden mountains . . . They said that women would be freed from doing the washing, from milking and cleaning the animals, weeding the garden, etc. Electricity can do that, they said." Under the hammer and sickle all things would be made new.

In 1930, Year XIII of the Communist era, a new calendar was introduced. It began the year on 1 November and established a five-day week: Sundays were abolished and rest days rotated so that work could be continuous. The anti-God crusade became more vicious and the church was portrayed as the "kulaks' *agitprop* [agitation and propaganda agency]."[51] Priests were persecuted. Icons were burned and replaced with portraits of Stalin. The bells of basilicas were silenced, many being melted down for the metal. Monasteries were demolished or turned into prison camps. Abbeys and convents were smashed to pieces and factories rose on their ruins. Churches were destroyed, scores in Moscow itself. Chief among them was the gold-domed Cathedral of Christ the Redeemer, Russia's largest place of worship and (according to the League of Militant Atheists) "the ideological fortress of the accursed old world,"[52] which was dynamited to make way for the Palace of Soviets on 5 December 1931. Stalin was unprepared for the explosion and asked tremulously, "Where's the bombardment?"[53]

The new Russian orthodoxy was instilled through everything from schools in which pupils learned to chant thanks to Comrade Stalin for their happy childhood to libraries purged of "harmful literature," from atheistic playing-cards to ideologically sound performances by circus clowns. An early signal that the Party was becoming the arbiter of all intellectual life was the suicide of Vladimir Mayakovsky: he was tormented by having turned himself into a poetry factory; he had stepped "on the throat of my own song."[54] (Even so he became a posthumous propagandist: as Pasternak wrote, "Mayakovsky began to be introduced forcibly, like potatoes under Catherine the Great. This was his second death. He had no hand in it.")[55] Of more concern to the average Soviet citizen was the socialist transformation of everyday life: the final elimination of small traders and private businessmen, the establishment of communal kitchens and lavatories, the direction of labour, the proliferation of informers (a marble monument was raised to Pavel Morozov, who supposedly denounced his father as a kulak), the purging of "wreckers" and the attempt to impose "iron discipline"[56] at every level. Stalin called for an increase in the power of the State to assist in its withering away. Like Peter the Great, he would bend Russia to his will even if he had to decimate the inhabitants—as he had once presciently observed, "full conformity of views can be achieved only at a cemetery."[57]

Destroying the nation's best farmers, disrupting the agricultural system and extracting grain from a famished countryside to export in return for Western technology—all this had a fatal impact on the Soviet standard of living. By 1930 bread and other foodstuffs were rationed, as were staple goods such as soap. But even rations were hard to get: sugar, for example, had "ceased to exist as a commodity."[58] The cooperative shops were generally empty, though gathering dust on their shelves were items that no one wanted, among them French horns and hockey sticks. There were also "tantalisingly realistic and mouth-watering"[59] wooden cheeses, dummy hams, enamelled cakes and other fake promises of future abundance. On the black market bread cost 45 roubles a kilo while the average collective farmer earned 3 roubles a day.[60] Some Muscovite workers shortened the slogan *"pobeda"* (victory) to *"obeda"* (food), or even to *"beda"* (misfortune).[61]

In response to such scarcity the Communist urge to acquire private property was rampant. Rubbish was not thrown away but traded. Queueing was universal and people often joined lines without knowing what commodity they were waiting for. They began to gather outside butchers' shops in the capital at 2:00 A.M. But they were philosophical about it, joking that in Russia freedom consisted of being able to join another queue. (It was possible to get a permit to buy railway tickets without queueing, but when a foreign journalist tried to use one he found himself joining a queue of other such permit holders.) Muscovites lived mainly on sour black bread; grey, cardboard-like macaroni; vegetables such as beetroot and cabbage; salted smoked Arctic fish which made their gums bleed and a sausage known as "Budenny's First Cavalry."[62] All the restaurants were now under socialist control and their offerings were revolting. Works canteens dispensed dishwater soup or (like the one at the Dnepostroi hydroelectric plant) a "bluish swill that stinks like a corpse and a cesspool."[63] It was possible to acquire better food from semi-legal bazaars (often by barter) and from some government shops. These were known, because of their displays of rare luxury goods, as "Stalin museums." Buyers could obtain delicacies such as radishes ("Stalin lard") and rabbits ("Stalin cows")—in fact Stalin did support rabbit farms and an institute to promote the "Rabbitization of Russia" was set up outside Moscow in 1932, followed shortly by the first trial of "rabbit-wreckers."[64] Best stocked of all were the hard-currency Torgsin shops (opened in 1931) where some customers literally paid with the gold fillings from their teeth.

Russian life was everywhere crumbling under the iron heel of Stalin's socialism. Moscow, an Asiatic sprawl of zigzag streets, squat wooden houses and multicoloured cupolas, seemed like a city at war. Gone were the garish signs of the bearded, long-mantled free traders who had loved to drink vodka and eat cucumbers in Slovanski Bazaar. Gone were fur-coated women on the pavements. Going were horse-cabs in the streets, along with their blue-robed peasant drivers. Instead, wrote Eugene Lyons, "Viscous ooze of swarming dung-coloured people, not ugly but incredibly soiled, patched, drab; the odour and colour of ingrained poverty, fetid bundles, stale clothes."[65] Visitors were especially struck by the unmistakable smell of Moscow. It was a compound of sheepskin, sawdust, vodka, black bread, drains, disinfectant, cheap perfume and unwashed humanity which stank (according to Henry Luce) of "rotten eggs in a damp cellar."[66]

With accommodation for one million people, Moscow housed over three million. The overcrowding was so oppressive that those who had permanent titles to apartments stayed put even if they were in danger of being arrested—a danger increased by jealous neighbours who sometimes denounced them in the hope of succeeding to their homes. Such was the medieval squalor of the capital that Frank Lloyd Wright proposed razing it to the ground and building a new garden city on its foundations. Le Corbusier, who scoffed that Moscow's layout was based on donkey tracks, put forward an equally devastating plan. Utopian socialists, too, visualised the withering away of the metropolis. It should be assisted, according to architect Konstantia Melnikov, by a "Laboratory of Sleep" which would nightly submerge citizens in sounds and smells scientifically chosen to induce a rural, collectivist mentality.[67] As it happened, Stalin's vicious underling Lazar Kaganovich insisted that Moscow should be transformed into a modern world capital. So streets were torn up, clouds of dust rose from demolished buildings and piles of masonry cluttered the highways. But the population increased faster than new apartments could be built and housing conditions did not improve. The general dilapidation gave visitors the impression that Moscow had been bombed.

Yet there were havens of luxury such as the gilded Opera House with its classical façade and the Metropole Hotel, where sexual Stakhanovites known as "Lubyanka Ladies" seduced foreigners at the behest of the OGPU.[68] But though Moscow had a bourgeois, as well as a proletarian, face it offered little in the way of night life. There were a few theatres and restaurants, but no clubs, cabarets, cafés, dance halls. Even Gypsy music was now banned. The newspapers failed to provide information, let alone entertainment—no fashion notes, cookery columns, crossword puzzles or comic strips, only official pronouncements in deadly jargon and an interminable litany of mendacious statistics about the Five Year Plan. Everywhere production quotas were exceeded while the quality of life deteriorated. Moscow was much better off than the provinces (while the primitive hinterland beyond the Volga was another world) but from its lower depths the tide of penury overflowed into the smarter avenues. It was a tide of haggard men in calico shirts, padded linen jackets and stiff-visored caps; scrawny, red-scarfed women with straw baskets; starveling beggars dressed in tatters (their numbers diminished by the demands of the Plan); and hollow-cheeked, tangle-haired waifs called *bezprizorniki,* thugs in the making, who sold vile "Sport" cigarettes outside factory gates for ten kopecks each and otherwise scavenged on the margins of life. Some slept in empty asphalt barrels on Red Square. "Give me a kopeck, little uncle," they would cry, "you may be my father. . ."[69] All these were the displaced persons in Stalin's socialist offensive, the walking wounded in the "battles" for grain and tractors fought by "shock brigades" on the agricultural and industrial "fronts." They were the casualties in the Soviet transformation of work into war.

THAT the USSR was engaged in a struggle for survival was an axiom of Communist life. Red banners slung across the streets of Moscow proclaimed, "We are all of us working as in time of war. For any failure to achieve what is planned a Communist bears a double responsibility."[70] Stalin had not foreseen the Depression. Indeed, like many Russians, he had been infected with *amerikanomaniya* and profoundly admired the methods and products of the world's most advanced capitalist country. Advocating "socialism in one country," he had virtually given up hope of a global revolution. In fact, he needed the bourgeois nations. They had to supply the technology without which socialism would fail. So their crisis was Russia's crisis. Stalin claimed that the Depression stopped at the Soviet frontier and he contrasted capitalist "economic *decline*" with Communist "economic *upsurge*."[71] But he knew perfectly well that the USSR now had to sell twice as much grain abroad to obtain the same amount of machinery. He appreciated the hostility his policy of dumping, or selling below cost price, aroused in the West. He believed that the capitalist powers would once again gang up on the Soviet Union. They would thus divert attention from their internal problems and export the aggression of their downtrodden masses. Early in 1931 Stalin's henchman Vyacheslav Molotov declared that the "world economic crisis" was "pregnant with great danger to the cause of peace."[72] Stalin himself uttered a memorable warning:

> One feature of the history of old Russia was the continual beatings she suffered because of her backwardness. She was beaten by the Turkish beys. She was beaten by the Swedish feudal lords. She was beaten by the Polish and Lithuanian gentry. She was beaten by the British and French capitalists. She was beaten by the Japanese barons. All beat her, because of her backwardness . . . It is the jungle law of capitalism. You are backward, you are weak—therefore you are wrong; hence you can be beaten and enslaved. You are mighty—therefore you are right; hence we must be wary of you.[73]

Stalin concluded this pungent speech by saying that the advanced countries were between 50 and 100 years ahead of Russia and that unless she caught up within a decade she would be crushed.

So there could be no compromise. While Stalin continued to complain that the country was "devilishly backward" the Party, as he said, whipped it forward.[74] Egalitarian ideals were scrapped to increase productivity. For example, skilled workers received extra incentives in the shape of higher pay, better food and improved accommodation—at the massive steel plant of Magnitogorsk in the Urals there was a whole hierarchy of canteens. But Stalin favoured the stick rather than the carrot and those infringing industrial discipline were harshly punished. Men were tied to their machines like helots. Those arriving late could be imprisoned. Dismissal might mean starvation—the loss of a work card resulted in the denial of a food card. Diligence was kept at fever pitch by the arrest and execution of large numbers of economic "wreckers," plus well-publicised show trials of "spies" and "saboteurs." Morbidly suspicious, Stalin seems to have persuaded himself of their guilt; but even if they were innocent their punishment would encourage the others. His solution to the shortage of small coins, hoarded for their tiny silver content because the gov-

ernment had printed so much paper money to pay for its own incompetence, was to shoot "wreckers" in the banking system, "including several
dozen common cashiers."[75]

In 1931 Stalin also tried to squeeze the last valuables, particularly gold,
from Russian citizens in order to purchase more foreign equipment.
Among the methods of torture used were the "conveyor," whereby relays
of interrogators deprived prisoners of sleep; the sweat- and ice-rooms, to
which victims were confined in conditions of intolerable heat or cold;
the tormenting of children in front of their parents. Alternatively the
OGPU might just beat their prey to death with a felt boot full of bricks.
These bestial practices were theoretically illegal but their employment
was an open secret. When a defendant at one show trial protested over-
indignantly that he had suffered no maltreatment in the Lubyanka, it was
too much even for a court which had solemnly swallowed stories of a conspiracy masterminded by the likes of President Poincaré and Lawrence of
Arabia: everyone simply roared with laughter. The Lubyanka, the tall grey
OGPU headquarters (formerly the office of the Rossiya Insurance Company) in Dzerzhinsky Square, was a place "fraught with horror."[76] Appropriately it was embellished with a sculpture representing the Greek Fates
cutting short the threads of human life. Stalin saw himself as the avatar of
destiny, the embodiment of the will of history, the personification of
progress. He explained to Gorky in 1931:

> Not everyone has the nerves, strength, character and understanding to
> appreciate the scenario of a tremendous break-up of the old and a fever-
> ish construction of the new, as a scenario of what is *necessary* and there-
> fore *desirable*. This scenario does not in the least resemble the heavenly
> idyll of a "general well-being" which provides the possibility of "taking it
> easy" and "relaxing pleasurably." Naturally with such a "baffling turmoil"
> we are bound to have those who are exhausted, distraught, worn-out,
> despondent and lagging behind—and those who go over to the enemy
> camp. These are the inevitable "costs" of revolution.[77]

The achievements of Stalin's revolution were almost as staggering as the
costs, even when propagandist fictions are discounted. Although its targets kept growing in the making, the first Five Year Plan was anything but
"Utopian." Initiated in 1928, its purpose was to transform the Russian
economy at unprecedented speed. As the British Ambassador reported, it
was "one of the most important and far reaching [experiments] that has
ever been undertaken."[78] Between 1928 and 1932 investment in industry
increased from two billion to nine billion roubles and the labour force
doubled to six million workers. Productivity too nearly doubled and huge
new enterprises were established—factories making machine tools, auto-

mobiles, chemicals, turbines, synthetic rubber and so on. The number of tractors produced rose from just over 3,000 to almost 50,000. Special emphasis was placed on armaments and factories were established out of the reach of invaders—by 1936 a plant at Sverdlovsk in the Urals was actually turning out submarines, which were transported in sections to the Pacific, the Baltic and the Black Sea. In just four years, by a mixture of heroic effort, "economic patriotism"[79] and implacable coercion, the foundations of Soviet industrial greatness were laid. Cities had grown by 44 percent. Literacy was advancing dramatically. By the mid-1930s Russia was spending nearly twice as much as the United States on research and development; by the end of the decade its output was rivalling that of Germany.

In this initial stage, of course, progress was patchy and the quality of manufactured goods was poor. There were many reasons for this, such as the unremitting pressure to increase quantity and the fact that (as Sukhanov had said) "one only had to scratch a worker to find a peasant."[80] The novelist Ilya Ehrenburg described new factory hands as looking "mistrustfully at the machines; when a lever would not work they grew angry and treated it like a baulking horse, often damaging the machine."[81] After visiting Russia David Low drew a cartoon of a dairymaid-turned-engineer absent-mindedly trying to milk a steam-hammer. Managers were little help. They were terrorised from above: an American specialist sharing a hotel bedroom with his mill boss was woken by "the most ghastly sounds imaginable" as the man ground his teeth in his sleep, tormented by stark, primitive "fears that none but his subconscious mind could know."[82] Managers in their turn were encouraged to behave like "little Stalins": as the Moscow Party chief Lazar Kaganovich said, "The earth should tremble when the director is entering the factory."[83]

The atmosphere of intimidation was hardly conducive to enterprise even if management had been competent, which it generally was not. At the Gorky automobile plant, which had been designed by engineers from Detroit, several different types of vehicle were made simultaneously on one assembly line, thus making nonsense of Ford's plan to standardise parts and performance. In the Urals asbestos ore was mined underground when it could have been dug from the surface by mechanical shovel far more safely and at a tenth of the cost. Everywhere so many older managers were purged that inexperienced young men had to be promoted—one found himself head of the State Institute of Metal Work Projects two days after he had graduated from Moscow's Mining Academy. Vigour could compensate for callowness. Foreign experts, often Communists and others fleeing from unemployment in the West, were impressed by the frenetic enthusiasm and hysterical tempo with which their Russian colleagues tried to complete the Five Year plan in four years, a task expressed in Stalinist arithmetic as 2 + 2 = 5. They were even more impressed by the suffering involved. In the words of an American technician who worked at Magnitogorsk, "I would wager that Russia's battle of ferrous metallurgy alone involved more casualties than the battle of the Marne."[84]

Magnitogorsk, situated on the mineral-rich boundary between Europe and Asia, was a monument to Stalin's gigantomania. Built to American designs, it was to be a showpiece of "socialist construction" and the largest steelworks in the world.[85] It was also the most important project in the Five Year Plan. So between 1928 and 1932 250,000 people were drawn willy-nilly to the remote "magnetic mountain" of ore, discovered in the eighteenth century, which was the "iron heart" of this new complex.[86] There were horny-handed peasants from the Ukraine, sparsely-bearded nomads from Mongolia, sheepskin-clad Tartars who had never before seen a locomotive, an electric light, even a staircase. There were Jews, Finns, Georgians and Russians, some of them products of three-month crash courses in engineering and disparaged by the American and German experts as "90-day wonders." There were 50,000 prisoners under OGPU supervision, including scientists, kulaks, criminals, prostitutes and child slave-labourers swept up from the gutters of Moscow. There was even a brigade of long-haired, bushy-bearded bishops and priests wearing ragged black robes and mitre-like hats.

To accommodate this labour force a rash of tents, earthen huts and wooden barracks sprang up on the rolling steppe. These grossly overcrowded refuges were verminous and insanitary, especially during the spring thaw when Magnitogorsk became a sea of mud and there were outbreaks of bubonic plague. Moreover, they afforded scant protection against the scorching summers and freezing winters. The same was true of the rows of porous, box-like structures for the privileged, set up with such haste that for years the streets lacked names and the buildings lacked numbers. These were the first houses of the socialist city which was to rise out of chaos during the 1930s, a city which would boast 50 schools, 17 libraries and 8 theatres but not a single church. There was, however, a Communist cathedral—the steel plant itself. No place of worship was built with more fervour or more labour. Its construction involved the excavation of 500 million cubic feet of earth, the pouring of 42 million cubic feet of reinforced concrete, the laying of 5 million cubic feet of fire bricks and the erection of 250,000 tons of structural steel.

Ill-clad, half-starved and inadequately equipped, the workers were pitilessly sacrificed to the work. Driven by terror and zeal, they were also the victims of incompetence. They lacked the tools and the skill to weld metal on rickety scaffolding 100 feet high in temperatures of –50 degrees Fahrenheit. Countless accidents occurred, many of which damaged the plant. Confusion was worse confounded by gross management failures. American experts were horrified to find that Party propagandists rather than engineers were determining priorities—tall, open-hearth stacks were erected earlier than they should have been because they "made a nice picture."[87] But despite every setback the stately blast furnaces rose from their concrete beds, to the tune of "incessant hammering, resembling machine-gun fire."[88] By 1 February 1932 the first pig-iron was produced. Although less than half built by 1937 (its target date for completion), Magnitogorsk was already one of the biggest metallurgical works on earth.

To the faithful it was a huge crucible for the Promethean energies unleashed by Russia's man of steel. Enterprises such as Magnitogorsk symbolised Stalin's successful "break" with the past *(perelom)* and Russia's great leap forward. It was a leap in the dark. But the shape of future terrors could be discerned and even committed Communists feared that too much was being sacrificed to the industrial Moloch. In the final speech at his show trial Nikolai Bukharin likened "our huge, gigantically growing factories" to "monstrous gluttons which consumed everything."[89] What they certainly consumed was vast quantities of grain, both directly to feed the workers and indirectly to exchange for the sinews of technology. In the two years after 1928 government grain requisitions had doubled and only a good harvest in 1930 enabled Stalin to commandeer 22 million tons (over a quarter of the total yield) from a countryside devastated by collectivisation and "dekulakisation." Yet in 1931 he took slightly more grain even though the harvest was poor. The result was massive rural famine. It was the largest organised famine in history until that of Mao Tse-tung in 1959–60, when "some twenty million Chinese starved to death."[90]

THE fertile Ukraine, where Stalin was already persecuting anyone suspected of local nationalism, suffered worst. But other regions were also affected, notably Kazakhstan, where about 40 per cent of the 4 million inhabitants died as a result of the attempt to turn them from nomadic herders into collective farmers. As early as December 1931 hordes of Ukrainian peasants were surging into towns and besieging railway stations with cries of "Bread, bread, bread!"[91] By the spring of 1932, when Stalin demanded nearly half the Ukrainian harvest, the granary of Russia was in the grip of starvation. While peasants collapsed from hunger Communist shock brigades, supported by units of the OGPU in their brown tunics and red and blue caps, invaded their cabins and took their last ounces of food, including seed for the spring sowing. They used long steel rods to probe for buried grain, stationed armed guards in the fields and sent up spotter planes to prevent the pilfering of State property. This was now an offence punishable by death or, to use the jargon of the time, "the highest measure of social defence."[92] The OGPU suspected anyone who was not starving of hoarding. It also attempted to stop peasants from migrating in search of food; but by the summer of 1932 three million were on the move. Some Communist cadres tried to avoid carrying out their task. One rebellious Party man reported that he could fulfil his meat quota, but only with human corpses. He fled, while others like him were driven to madness and suicide. But most activists were so frightened for their own skins that they enforced Stalin's ukase.

So the Ukraine came to resemble "one vast Belsen."[93] A population of "walking corpses" struggled to survive on a diet of roots, weeds, grass, bark and furry catkins.[94] They devoured dogs, cats, snails, mice, ants, earthworms. They boiled up old skins and ground down dry bones. They even ate horse-manure for the whole grains of seed it contained. Cannibalism became so commonplace that the OGPU received a special directive on the subject from Moscow and local authorities issued hundreds of posters announcing that "EATING DEAD CHILDREN IS BARBARISM."[95] Some peasants braved machine-guns in desperate assaults on grain stockpiles. Others robbed graves for gold to sell in Torgsin shops. Parents unable to feed their offspring sent them away from home to beg. Cities such as Kiev, Kharkov, Dnepropetrovsk, Poltava, Odessa and Belgorod were overrun by pathetic waifs with huge heads, stunted limbs and swollen bellies. Arthur Koestler said that they "looked like embryos out of alcohol bottles."[96] Periodically the OGPU rounded them up, sending some to brutal orphanages or juvenile labour colonies, training others to be informers or secret policemen. Still others became the victims of "mass shootings."[97]

Meanwhile adults, frantic to follow the slightest rumour of sustenance, continued to desert their villages. They staggered into towns and collapsed in the squares, at first objects of pity, later of indifference. Haunting the railway stations these "swollen human shadows, full of rubbish, alive with lice,"[98] followed passengers with mute appeals and "hungry eyes."[99] A few managed to get out of the region despite the guards (who confiscated the food of Ukrainians returning to help), but for the most part these "miserable hulks of humanity dragged themselves along, begging for bread or searching for scraps in garbage heaps, frozen and filthy. Each morning wagons rolled along the streets picking up the remains of the dead."[100]

Some were picked up before they died and buried in pits so extensive that they resembled sand dunes and so shallow that bodies were dug up and devoured by wolves. In the autumn of 1932 Stalin increased his squeeze on the villages, ordering blockades of those which did not supply their grain quotas and blaming kulak sabotage for the shortfall. It may well have been over the famine that on 5 November 1932 his wife Nadezhda Alliluyeva committed suicide. Certainly she had lost any illusions she might have possessed about her husband. Some time before her death Nadezhda yelled at him: "You are a tormentor, that's what you are! You torment your own son . . . you torment your wife . . . you torment the whole Russian people."[101]

The better to control his victims Stalin reintroduced the internal passport. Communists had always denounced this as a prime instance of tsarist tyranny. Now it enabled them to hide the famine, or at any rate to render it less visible, by ensuring that most deaths occurred outside urban areas. This is not to suggest that Stalin was prepared to acknowledge the existence of the tragedy. When a courageous Ukrainian Communist gave details of what was happening Stalin replied that he had made up "a fable about famine, thinking to frighten us, but it won't work."[102] It is clear, though, that Stalin was deliberately employing starvation as an instrument of policy. Early in 1933 he sent Pavel Postyshev to the Ukraine with orders to extract further deliveries from the barren countryside. Postyshev announced that the region had failed to provide the requisite grain because of the Party's "leniency."[103] The consequence of his strictness was that, over the next few months, the famine reached its terrible climax. Entire families died in agony. Buildings decayed, schools closed, fields were choked with weeds, livestock perished and the countryside became a gigantic charnel-house. About a quarter of the rural population was wiped out and the mortality rate only began to decline in the summer of 1933, after it had become clear that no more grain could be procured and the State's demands were relaxed. Altogether the famine claimed some five million lives and Stalin followed it with a more prolonged purge, arresting anyone he could blame for the grain shortage (Party men, vets, meteorologists) as well as suspected nationalists, including intellectuals, philologists and wandering blind bards. Whether Stalin was guilty of genocide in the Ukraine depends on how the word is defined. But in so far as his motives are penetrable it seems that he determined to yoke the peasant to the iron service of industry. As one OGPU boss explained it:

A ruthless struggle is going on between the peasantry and our regime. It's a struggle to the death. This year was a test of our strength and their endurance. It took a famine to show them who was master here. It took millions of lives but the collective farm system is here to stay. We've won the war.[104]

"Food is a weapon,"[105] as the Foreign Commissar Maxim Litvinov had once said, and Stalin deployed it with revolutionary cruelty and effect. The surviving peasants became not proletarians so much as serfs. One Party official explained their position to them thus: "Karl Marx, our dear dead leader, wrote that peasants are potatoes in a sack. We have got you in our sack."[106]

Despite the blanket of silence enveloping the Soviet Union, many of its citizens knew about the famine and recognised that collectivisation had been a catastrophe. They repeated the joke attributed to Party journalist Karl Radek about how to rid the Kremlin of lice: "Collectivise them, then half of them will die and the other half will run away."[107] By an extraordinary circumstance, however, many Westerners failed both to appreciate the deficiencies of the Soviet economy and to understand the nature of Stalin's State. This was partly because disillusionment with capitalism fostered illusions about Communism—doubtless a result of the perennial human need to believe that Utopia is a province of reality. It somehow seemed logical to assume that darkness in the west meant light in the east, a view sustained by the radiant confidence of committed Communists who, as Stephan Zweig found, believed *"Ex oriente lux."*[108] It was easy to see Depression, unemployment and chaos as the bitter fruit of free enterprise while regarding progress, full employment and the Five Year Plan as the bounty of State Socialism. As Arthur Koestler wrote,

> If History herself were a fellow-traveller she could not have arranged a more clever timing of events than this coincidence of the gravest crisis of the Western world with the initial phase of Russia's industrial revolution. The contrast . . . was so striking that it led to the equally obvious conclusion: They are the future—we, the past.[109]

Stalin himself tellingly ridiculed one of the most glaring contradictions of capitalism—the destruction of "surplus" commodities at a time of dearth in order to keep up prices and profits. He added that "in the U.S.S.R., those guilty of such crimes would be sent to a lunatic asylum."[110] In the face of such evident absurdities, it seemed only right and proper for Communists to commend an economy of shortages and corresponding "consumer asceticism."[111]

Thus unbiased visitors were not looking for famine but for the germs of a new civilisation; and those on the Left, especially intellectuals, anticipated a "worker's paradise."[112] Before setting off for Moscow in 1932 to experience "the veritable future of mankind,"[113] Malcolm Muggeridge made a bonfire of bourgeois trappings, including his dinner jacket. Arthur Koestler endorsed the slogan at the frontier—"Change trains for the twenty-first century"—and visualised Russia as

> a kind of gigantic Manhattan with enormous buildings sprouting from the earth like mushrooms after rain, with rivers queueing up before power stations, mountains being tossed into the air by faith, and people breathlessly racing, as in an accelerated film, to fulfil the Plan.

Koestler actually witnessed some of the worst effects of the Ukraine famine—a typhus epidemic, incessant funerals in Kharkov, whole districts depopulated—but for the time being he "remained a convinced Communist." By a feat of intellectual prestidigitation he persuaded himself that everything horrifying was the "heritage of the past" and any promising developments were the "seeds of the future."[114]

Muggeridge, on the other hand, soon perceived the truth and mocked the gullibility of other visitors. Lord Marley denied that official lies could have been told about the Five Year Plan—"Think how ashamed the Soviet Government would be if it were discovered that their statistics had been falsified"[115]—and believed that the authorities permitted food queues in Moscow because they "provided a means of inducing the workers to take a rest." Edouard Herriot was convinced that the milk shortage was due to the large amount allocated to nursing mothers.[116] George Bernard Shaw expressed his confidence that the Soviet Union was free from hunger by declaring that he had thrown his supplies of Western tinned food out of the train window, a boast which visibly shocked his hosts. Muggeridge himself, however, evaded the government's ban on journalists visiting the Ukraine (it said they might obstruct harvesting) and sent back some of the earliest reports of the famine to reach the West.

Many other eyewitness accounts followed. Yet the Kremlin simply denied the famine's existence. Like Hitler, Stalin believed in the efficacy of the big lie. In this case he backed it up by continuing to sell grain on the international market, a policy which made it seem inconceivable that Russians were starving. Lenin had done the same in 1921 but, unlike him, Stalin now rejected help from outside relief agencies such as the Red Cross. When Austria's Cardinal Innitzer appealed for aid to the Ukraine, citing cases of cannibalism, the Soviet government declared that reports of the catastrophe were "absolute inventions," adding that Russia had neither cannibals nor cardinals.[117] What Russia did have was an inglorious history of official deception going back at least to the seventeenth century, when

Boris Godunov himself had tried to conceal a famine, ordering Russians to turn out in their best clothes to impress foreigners with their prosperity. Potemkin, of course, gave his name to such chicanery. Hergé's famous strip-cartoon character Tintin mocked it during a Russian adventure in 1929. He discovered an empty Soviet factory where workers were burning straw and beating sheet metal to "fool poor idiots who still believe in a 'red paradise.'" [118] Stalin elaborated the ploy in an effort to dupe distinguished visitors.

Before Herriot's visit to Kiev in the summer of 1933, for example, the authorities created an alluring mirage of plenty. They mobilised the entire population to clean and decorate the streets, banished beggars and *bez-prizorniki,* and tied up the manes of militiamen's horses with white ribbons—something never seen before. To ensure Herriot's comfort at a Rostov hotel the local OGPU boss put his own bed at the Frenchman's disposal—a fact of which he probably never became aware. Wooed with meals gargantuan enough to satisfy even his appetite, Herriot was completely hoodwinked. On his return to France he declared that the Russian famine was nothing more than a product of Nazi propaganda. Most foreign correspondents, anxious to keep their snug berths in Moscow, took the same line. They made few efforts to evade the censor, who once told Muggeridge, in what he took to be a text for the age: "You can't say that because it's true." [119] Walter Duranty was the most cynical: privately he acknowledged that the famine had killed millions; in the *New York Times* he denied its existence, employing the Soviet euphemisms about "supply difficulties" and "food shortages." In a classic piece of obfuscation he declared: "There is no actual starvation but there is widespread mortality from diseases due to malnutrition." He concluded with that callous cliché so often applied to Communist Russia: "You can't make an omelette without breaking eggs." [120]

CONFUSED by the conflicting evidence, many Westerners reckoned that the reality lay somewhere between the extremes. The best accounts of Russia seemed too good to be true while the worst were surely incredible. In the words of the American exile Fred Beal, who had inspired strikers back home with glowing intimations of the Red Mecca only to become so disenchanted that he preferred to face a 20-year prison sentence in the United States rather than to remain there, "The horrors of Soviet life are such that few people in the Western world could be brought to believe them." [121] Many others regarded the clash of testimony as licence to suspend their critical faculties altogether. In an age dominated by what Pasternak called "the inhuman power of the lie,"[122] it seemed impossible to know the truth. So people could believe what they wanted to believe. Often this was nothing at all: preoccupied by their own concerns, many in the West simply averted their gaze, like a cat baffled by a mirror. Others created the Soviet Union in their own image. As a British poet wrote in 1932, the left-wing visitor found:

> Great factories rising
> An enthusiasm surprising
> For welfare and education;
> A New World in formation
> Much better than the Old–
> Just as he had foretold.

The right-wing visitor discovered:

> Breakdowns in transportation;
> Growing indignation
> With Communist oppression;
> A steady retrogression
> To chaos, bloody and red–
> Just as he had always said.[123]

Thus in the 1930s, to invert C. P. Scott's aphorism, facts were free but comment was sacred. Amid the welter of claim and counter-claim evidence became evanescent, like the shadows in Plato's cave. Reality kept changing its shape.

The Russians themselves were used to this protean flux: in the words of Stalin's reptilian State Prosecutor Andrei Vyshinsky, "We have our own reality."[124] The maxim applied particularly to Stalin, who was insulated more securely than most dictators inside a fantasy world, there to coin the paranoid paradox that the greatest saboteurs are those who never commit sabotage. But Stalin also made his own reality. He not only refused to acknowledge present truths such as the Ukraine famine, he systematically falsified the past. Where evidence was lacking, force could secure a simulacrum of belief. Just as innocent prisoners tortured in the Lubyanka became convinced of their guilt, so famished citizens half assented to official insistence that they lived in a land of plenty. To quote one authority:

Truth, they knew, was a Party matter, and therefore lies became true even if they contradicted the plain facts of experience. The condition of living in two separate worlds at once was one of the most remarkable achievements of the Soviet system.[125]

Despite his materialistic creed Stalin regarded even "objective circumstances" as malleable. Mathematics had to reflect the class struggle—N. N. Luzin was denounced as a counter-revolutionary "wrecker on the mathematical front."[126] Science must be properly proletarian. Only Soviet accounting was acceptable. The Party condemned "hooliganism in language" and urged its members to employ "Bolshevik-Leninist vocabulary" (and the Moscow dialect), addressing the masses "in one voice so as to raise them up to the proper class consciousness in the correct idiom."[127] (Foreign Communists sometimes gave themselves away—fatally in Germany—by using Newspeak terms such as "herostratic.") The Party also called for "Purity of Marxist-Leninist Theory in Surgery."[128] There could be no neutrality in chess. Logic itself had to take the "general line." As a belief in the dialectic tended to induce philosophical confusion, not to say schizophrenia, Marxists found it easier than most to decide that black was white. But such outrages against common sense were by no means unique to Stalin's Russia. As George Orwell noted, "Totalitarianism . . . probably demands a disbelief in the very existence of objective truth."[129]

Truth was certainly a will-o'-the-wisp at the 17th Party Congress, held early in 1934. Its very title, the "Congress of Victors," mocked the fate of a people who had become lean while the State had grown gross. The fact that real wages had fallen by almost half since 1928 did not stop Stalin saying that living standards had risen. Moreover, despite Party rumblings to the effect that he was "the evil genius of the Russian Revolution"[130] and moves to replace him with the independent-minded boss of Leningrad, Sergei Kirov, Stalin was lauded more extravagantly than ever. Karl Radek flew in the face of reality still more audaciously:

> All that we have gone through in the last years has shown how, having destroyed the freedom of the press and all other bourgeois freedoms, the working class under the Party's leadership has erected such freedoms for the creative activity of the masses of workers and peasants that the world has not seen before.[131]

Such assertions could appear plausible only to a world darkened by Depression. Where capitalism bestowed the kind of liberty which permitted those without jobs to remain unemployed, Stalin's service could seem perfect freedom.

The hoary Christian paradox raised its head again over the role of writers in a Communist society. They could only write freely, Stalin maintained, so long as they reflected reality as defined by the Party: "Literature comes from the heart of the people and can be created only in freedom.

Free creation, however, is conceivable solely in terms of socialist realism; national in form, socialist in character."[132] A competent versifier in his youth, Stalin liked to lay down the law on such matters for, as a student of his *feuilletons* has piquantly suggested, "Unacknowledged poets are the legislators of the world."[133] But Stalin's cultural repression, disguised though it was by Communist casuistry, smothered Soviet writers and artists for a generation. Some remained silent, feeling with Alexander Bogdanov that they could only work in a society which did not insist on the promulgation of its faith in fetishes, myths and clichés. Some left, like Yevgeny Zamyatin, who said that he could not write "behind bars."[134] Remaining "engineers of human souls" (to quote the famous phrase which Stalin later denied uttering)[135] manufactured their work on a socialist assembly line. They engaged in "Fordizing and Taylorizing art."[136] Boris Pasternak went so far as to say that "Literature ceased to exist."[137] Actually creative fires continued to burn underground. Literature did exist: but in hermetic form (such as the poems of Anna Akhmatova) or in a pre-Gutenberg state, either in samizdat or in the memories of its authors and devotees. Occasionally, as in the case of some of Mikhail Bulgakov's writing, it even survived in OGPU files, to emerge 60 years later when the system which had suppressed it collapsed.

Foreigners like André Gide, who believed that without a vision the people perish, were alienated from the regime by its stifling cultural conformity. The Soviet authorities tried their best to woo him. They arranged welcomes at each station (with banners thoughtfully carried on his train) and even filled a swimming-pool with handsome young Red Army soldiers (though after his defection they revealed that, while their guest, he had engaged in a homosexual act). Yet the writer was repelled by Communist attempts to secure "total unanimity of thought" through terror.[138] Visiting an exhibition of official "artists" in Tiflis, Gide was reminded of the sun god "Apollo who, when he was set to serve Admetus, had to extinguish all his rays."[139]

However, at the 17th Party Congress a Soviet spring seemed to be in the air. While capitalist countries continued to suffer under the Depression, the second Five Year Plan was driving Russia forward at a steadier pace. Clearly external forces had played their part in Stalin's revolution from above, precipitating frightful domestic sacrifices for the sake of foreign technology and helping to shape the desperate policy whereby Russia attempted "to starve itself great."[140] Far from being, as Litvinov claimed, "the only country in the world unaffected by the economic crisis,"[141] the USSR had been profoundly affected. But by 1934 people could ignore the broken eggs because the omelette showed signs of materialising.

More food appeared in the shops. Consumer goods such as scented soap were available. The planned economy was bearing fruit. The social climate was easier. In Moscow dance halls opened, as did public lavatories on Stalin's orders. Jazz was permitted. People attended a musical called *Jolly Fellows* and listened to the popular song "Masha and I by the Samovar." Playing tennis was no longer a sign of bourgeois revisionism. Convulsions inside the Party, which had led to the bloodless purging of nearly a third of its two million members in 1933, subsided. Many old Bolsheviks were rehabilitated. Now that 25 million individual holdings had been consolidated into 240,000 collective farms, peasants were permitted to have small plots and livestock. The victory of socialism in the countryside brought to an end the "saturnalia of arrests."[142] Stalin himself told the 17th Congress that there was nothing left to prove, "nobody to beat."[143] In fact the way in which the Congress acclaimed Kirov suggested that he was the man to beat. Kirov must have sensed something of Stalin's malice, for he told a friend, "Alyosha, my head is on the block. They're going to kill me."[144]

As it happened, Stalin would not be content with the death of Kirov. In the purges that followed it he was to eliminate 1,108 of the 1,996 delegates at the 17th Congress, as well as millions more. It was this holocaust which prompted the composer Dmitri Shostakovich to remark, in an echo of Mandelstam, that he could see in Stalin's time nothing but "corpses, mountains of corpses."[145] Yet in 1934 Stalin seemed benevolent and Russians looked on the bright side. At a demonstration in Red Square to honour the Party Congress Kirov himself gave "a fiery speech, a veritable ode to the new era that was dawning." Within a few months the OGPU had become the NKVD, a change of name which people hoped would herald a change of nature. Furthermore Stalin announced the framing of a new constitution for the Soviet Union and (though voters would find only one name on their ballot papers) it was billed as "the most democratic in the world."[146] This glowing prospect was the "Noon" in Koestler's novel *Darkness at Noon*. It was also the sunshine in one half of David Low's famous cartoon of the Soviet Union. The other half reflected the purges and consisted of sinister figures carrying out evil deeds in the dark.

XI

THE NEW DEAL

THE Soviet Union fascinated the United States; it shimmered "in many American minds with almost hypnotic intensity."[1] Even staunch Republicans, who could think of nothing but Red dictatorship, slave labour camps and the persecution of the Church, reluctantly came to admire the Five Year Plan. Main Street businessmen were also impressed, though they had been wont to joke that "Russia's word was as good as her bonds."[2] Communism, a system they had despised in years of prosperity, seemed capable of achieving economic miracles at a time when capitalism was on its knees. Herbert Hoover himself had proposed an American Plan and many of his conservative compatriots agreed that nothing less could save the nation. As for progressives, they tended to quell past uneasiness about Russian cultural tyranny and endorse Edmund Wilson's view that Communism was the moral top of the world where the sun never stopped shining. The need for planning was obvious to them, for it offered "the extreme of efficiency and economy combined with the ideal of a herculean programme."[3] In the opinion of journalist Ray Long, the Russian Five Year Plan was "the most important human step since the birth of Christianity."[4] Rexford Tugwell, perhaps the most radical of Franklin Roosevelt's Brain Trust, was less apocalyptic. But, noting the "popular interest in 'planning' as a possible refuge for persistent insecurity," he echoed Lincoln Steffens: "The future is becoming visible in Russia."[5]

Like most Americans Tugwell wanted democratic planning, though he acknowledged that by its very nature planning involved strong central direction. As will emerge, however, the New Deal was not Communist (or Fascist)—it was pragmatist. Roosevelt was interested in ideas but he was no ideologue. Unafraid of experiments, he would adopt whatever measures were necessary to counter the Depression. The President might pay lip-service to the notion of planning but he believed that the paralysis afflicting the nation could only be tackled by trial and error. It was symbolic not of Roosevelt's own physical helplessness (Tugwell surmised) but of America's plight that when he was wheeled for the first time behind the empty presidential desk and found himself alone with no visible means of communication—no buttons to press or buzzers to push—he let out a great shout. Before its echoes had died away several aides tumbled into the Oval Office. The New Deal, in its first hundred days, arrived no less precipitately.

Serene, smiling, confident, throwing out exuberant sallies, smoking two packets of Camels a day and handling his ivory cigarette holder "as a mandarin might have used his fan,"[6] Roosevelt began a dramatic whirl of activity. With the eager collaboration of Congress he initiated 15 major pieces of legislation in just over 3 months, signing (on average) a new bill every 3 days. There had never been such a flood of law-making, never such a swift, novel and radical presidential programme. The power of the White House was signally enhanced and excitable commentators concluded that Roosevelt had established "a benevolent and a necessary dictatorship."[7] Certainly a revolutionary new broom was sweeping through the offices of government. It was symbolised by the experience of Frances Perkins when she first sat down behind *her* desk, as head of the Department of Labor. Opening a drawer she shrieked for the caretaker: "Quick. There's a mouse in here. Get rid of it." It turned out to be not a mouse but the largest cockroach Frances Perkins had ever seen. The entire building was infested. Indeed, it was infested not only with cockroaches but with criminals: the new Secretary of Labor discovered that a number of officials had been involved in an illegal immigration racket. Roosevelt was characteristically relaxed about official rascality: "It's a great joke that it should be you who runs into crooks. Go ahead and clean them out."[8]

In carrying out the New Deal the President's first endeavour was to go to the financial heart of the matter—to save the banks and start money pumping once more through the nation's arteries. He did so by calling Congress into special session and proclaiming a national bank holiday: for a few days Americans had to live on scrip, wooden tokens, foreign coins, telephone slugs, stamps, cigarette coupons, barter and credit. Meanwhile, since there was no question of nationalising the banks, emergency legislation was prepared based largely on Hoover's plans. It authorised federal support for sound banks while empowering government auditors to check others and keep the insolvent ones shut. (A further measure, signed in June, guaranteed bank deposits.) To help restore confidence Roosevelt gave a press conference (the first of nearly 1,000 he held as President), so impressing reporters with his ebullience and openness that they applauded at its conclusion. He also gave the first of his radio talks to the nation. It was a *tour de force,* clear, easy, intimate and delivered in a mesmeric voice at just the right pace. With this "fireside chat," the precursor of 27 more, all carefully timed and formidably influential, Roosevelt proved himself "a master dramatist—a radio performer of 'star' quality."⁹ As the comedian Will Rogers said, FDR could take a complicated subject like banking and make everybody understand it, even the bankers. He could also inspire devotion and cast out fear. The President concluded his talk with the words: "Together we cannot fail."¹⁰ When the banks opened, deposits exceeded withdrawals. By April financial anaemia was averted: over a billion dollars had returned from hoards to vaults.

Roosevelt also earned the gratitude of wealthier members of society by his quick decision to cut government expenditure. The obvious target was the benefits paid to veterans, who were one per cent of the population but received over a quarter of the budget. Protests were inevitable. But when a new BEF marched on Washington Roosevelt avoided Hoover's mistakes. He accommodated the veterans in an old army camp, supplying them with tents, food, an infirmary, a band, latrines, showers and soft soap from his wife Eleanor, who took it upon herself to become the unofficial mother to the nation. Arguing that some must suffer for the good of all, Roosevelt also reduced the federal payroll, including the salaries of members of Congress. Moreover, he squeezed defence spending, which provoked a tirade from the army's Chief of Staff. According to General MacArthur's inflated account of the episode, he told his Commander-in-Chief that "when we lost the next war, and an American boy, lying in the mud with an enemy bayonet through his belly and an enemy foot on his dying throat, spat out his last curse, I wanted the name not to be MacArthur, but Roosevelt." Roosevelt seldom lost his temper but on this occasion he roared, "You must not talk that way to the President!"¹¹ The General naturally capitulated and the financial pinch became so tight that his bald-headed aide, Major Eisenhower, had to requisition his streetcar fare from the War Department building (opposite the White House) to the Capitol and back. Naturally big business was delighted: one tycoon opined that Roosevelt was the greatest leader since Jesus Christ.

The love-feast was to be short-lived. Having restored faith in government credit by these orthodox measures (and made it easier for the disadvantaged to swallow the pill by legalising low-alcohol beer and light wine), Roosevelt embarked on a more adventurous course. His aim was to bring relief to the unemployed and his first creation was the Civilian Conservation Corps. Known as the CCC, it was the forerunner of so many New Deal agencies designated by their initials that Roosevelt himself sometimes became confused and Al Smith accused the Brain Trust professors of playing "anagrams with 'alphabet soup.'"¹² Despite its name, the CCC was run by the army and it set 250,000 young men (as well as thousands of veterans) to work on projects such as reafforestation, flood control and soil conservation. They were paid a dollar a day plus their keep and they received basic education. Conservatives liked the thought of regimenting the nation's youth (a source of concern to liberals, who thought it smacked of Hitlerism or Stalinism, perhaps both) but they were perturbed by the cost. Roosevelt argued that the national budget was better than balanced and that emergency measures were necessary to meet the crisis. He provoked further anxiety with his next move. Eager to stem the flow of bullion abroad and to drive down the value of the dollar, thus making American exports more competitive while raising commodity prices at home, Roosevelt took the United States off the gold standard on 19 April 1933. Even members of the government were appalled. Secretary of State Cordell Hull feared runaway inflation and the demise of sound money. Budget Director Lewis Douglas declared that it was "the end of western civilization."¹³ Someone else suggested that the inscription on dollar bills should be changed from "In God We Trust" to "I Hope that My Redeemer Liveth."¹⁴

Roosevelt's Secretary of Agriculture, Henry A. Wallace, himself had a mystical faith which actually did find expression in the currency: in 1935 he persuaded the Treasury to put the Great Pyramid on the new dollar bill. But in 1933 he recognised that hope was just about all the farmer had to live on, a situation summed up by the nickname given to those who dwelt on the great plains: "America's Next Year People."¹⁵ With foreclosures, evictions and forced sales continuing and wheat prices lower than at any time since the reign of Queen Elizabeth I, the countryside was close to revolution. Wallace, with his red neck, his rustic shoes and his unkempt brown hair, looked like a farmer. In fact he was the scion of a distinguished agrarian-journalistic-political dynasty from Iowa and he was "illuminated with lofty purpose."¹⁶ He likened stock market capitalists to Chicago gangsters and regarded the Depression as a symptom of the collapse of the corrupt moral order of the past. The New Deal was the New Jerusalem. In his high piping voice Wallace spoke of creating new social machinery, but his language was that of an Old Testament prophet: "The millennium is not here yet, although the makings of it are in our hands."¹⁷ Wallace himself aimed to achieve the salvation of the husbandman. His method was to limit production, thus driving up prices and increasing rural purchasing power. This process, he remarked, was recommended by modern economists; by his illustrious uncle, Henry Wallace; and by Isaiah.

In May 1933 the Agricultural Adjustment Administration (AAA) was set up and it at once began a programme of paying farmers to reduce their output of staple crops such as cotton, corn, wheat, hogs and tobacco. This was by no means the limit of its work, an impression of which is well conveyed by one of the young lawyers recruited into its ranks. This was Adlai Stevenson, who wrote excitedly of having to negotiate

> with producers, processors or handlers of everything from Atlantic oysters to California oranges, and from Oregon apples to Florida strawberries. Walnut and asparagus growers from California, rice millers from Louisiana, lettuce shippers from Arizona, shadegrown tobacco handlers from Connecticut, potato merchants from Maine, candy manufacturers from Pennsylvania, chicken hatchers from everywhere, date and grape shippers and olive canners from California, pea canners from Wisconsin, peanut processors from Virginia, and the Carolinas.

To cap it all, Stevenson concluded, a couple of Congressmen from Georgia arrived and "calmly announced that the Packaged Bees Industry was going to hell!!"[18] Subsidies to farmers were paid by a tax levied on food processors, which ultimately came out of the consumer's pocket, and the policy was not without its critics. They became especially vociferous when ten million acres of cotton (a quarter of the nation's crop) were ploughed up and six million piglets were killed. Some echoed Stalin's charges about the absurdity of destroying wealth at a time of dearth. Others pointed out additional anomalies. For example, large farmers benefited most from the scheme, receiving handouts for abandoning their poorer land, spending it on machines which produced more from their better fields and dismissing their tenant sharecroppers, many of them Southern blacks already living at subsistence level. Nevertheless Wallace's programme was generally reckoned a success, especially when it was augmented, in June, with a measure to re-finance farm mortgages at low rates of interest. Farm incomes increased by a third between 1932 and 1935. The President of the Farm Bureau Federation described the AAA as the "Magna Carta of American Agriculture."[19]

On the same day that the AAA was established, Roosevelt signed the act setting up the Federal Emergency Relief Administration (FERA). This provided 500 million dollars to meet immediate needs. The FERA was actually little more than an expansion of Hoover's efforts, though it gave grants rather than loans. But it operated through local agencies and could only distribute half its appropriation directly; the other half depended on states spending three dollars for every one it contributed. Still, thanks to its director Harry Hopkins, the new organisation seldom allowed bureaucratic niceties to impede the flow of humanitarian aid. And by the autumn Hopkins, who had run a similar operation for Roosevelt in New York

State, had persuaded the President to give him more discretion in disbursing funds. Hopkins, indeed, became the chief architect of social policy during the 1930s, getting the government involved in relief work on an unprecedented scale.

This humane, hard-bitten professional social worker, who was said to combine the purity of St. Francis of Assisi with the shrewdness of a race-track tout, seemed living proof that the New Deal wedded realism to idealism. Outwardly cynical, addicted to poker, ponies and profanity, Hopkins was painfully sensitive to hardship and bubbled with schemes to alleviate it. Fond of the fleshpots, he conducted his public business with ostentatious austerity. He wore a frayed blue suit and inhabited a tiny office with peeling walls, pipes running from floor to ceiling and a pervasive smell of disinfectant. It was bare of anything but an unpolished desk and overflowing ashtrays. With his thinning hair, his scraggy neck and his gaunt face, Hopkins looked like an ascetic. He spent nine billion dollars on the relief of others, "carrying it off with a bright Hell's bells air," and died without a penny to his name.[20] He so impressed Congress with his sincerity that one Senator remarked: "If Roosevelt ever becomes Jesus Christ, he should have Harry Hopkins as his prophet."[21]

FEW enterprises caused the President to be so lauded and so cursed as his next major initiative: the establishment of the Tennessee Valley Authority (TVA) on 18 May 1933. Praised by supporters as "the greatest experiment in regional planning the world has seen outside Russia,"[22] the TVA was anathematised by detractors as "part of a vast Communist conspiracy to undermine the American way of life."[23] Actually, like Roosevelt's other ventures, it fitted no simple stereotype. When asked how he would explain the political philosophy behind the TVA Roosevelt replied jauntily, "I'll tell them it's neither fish nor fowl, but, whatever it is, it will taste awfully good to the people of the Tennessee Valley."[24] The TVA, in fact, was a series of improvisations, part practical and part visionary, designed to deal with a specific problem. The problem, which faced over 2 million people dwelling in the 40,000 square miles drained by the Tennessee River, was how to improve their wretched lot by harnessing its raging waters.

These, fed by 5 main tributaries, curved down from the Appalachians on a 650-mile journey into the cotton country of Alabama, through the corn belt of mid-Tennessee and across the grasslands of Kentucky towards the Mississippi. The river was tawny with vast quantities of topsoil from hillsides which had once been the forest hunting-grounds of the Cherokee but were now barren, eroded by over-intensive lumbering and farming. It was prone to disastrous flash-floods like that which had drowned Chattanooga in 1867. Moreover the calm waters of the lower Tennessee, bordered by cottonwoods and sycamores, were cut off from towns upstream by Muscle Shoals. These were 37 miles of rapids in the rugged foothills of the Cumberland Plateau with a fall of over 130 feet, almost that of Niagara. Here the torrent roared around rock barricades and foamed over flint ledges. The shoals were home to millions of mussels which had once fed the aboriginal inhabitants and were later a rich source of mother of pearl. During the First World War the government had begun to dam the river at Muscle Shoals. Its aim had been not so much to create a waterway as to lessen American dependence on Chile for nitrates, used for explosives as well as fertiliser, by building nitrogen-fixing plants powered by hydro-electricity. Many contemporaries grasped the enormous potential of this undertaking. One wrote: "The golden touch of Midas and the mines of Solomon represent but a widow's mite when compared with the penned-up productiveness of Muscle Shoals."[25] Henry Ford actually offered to buy the entire business, which on completion of the huge Wilson Dam in 1925 not only submerged Muscle Shoals under 40 feet of water but also generated an eighth of the nation's electricity. However, he was prevented by the Progressive Senator George Norris, who called Ford's proposal "the most wonderful real estate speculation since Adam and Eve lost the title to the Garden of Eden."[26]

For many years Norris had cherished notions of using the Tennessee River for the common weal—essentially to produce cheap electricity, incidentally to manufacture fertiliser, to control floods and to improve navigation. But both Coolidge and Hoover vetoed his bills. The political climate began to change with the advent of the Depression, especially when details emerged about the rapacity of private power utilities. Long their opponent and a champion of conservation, Roosevelt nurtured even more ambitious plans than Norris. He saw the TVA as a "laboratory in social and economic life,"[27] an "experiment in civilisation." It was a means of transforming the life of a region where many of the rural population wore homespun, lived in log cabins, drank moonshine whisky, slept on husk mattresses, suffered from diseases such as pellagra, hookworm and malaria, and won bare subsistence from land fit only for raising "hog and hominy."[28] Improving the veteran Senator's bill, the President told Congress that the Muscle Shoals project could encompass soil erosion control, reafforestation, improved land management and industrial diversification. "In short, this power development of war days leads logically to national planning for a complete river watershed involving many states and the future lives and welfare of millions."[29]

To head the TVA Roosevelt chose Arthur Morgan, an innovative engineer turned successful college president, whose vision of what the agency could perform was even more extravagant than the President's own. Morgan, the saintliest man Senator Norris had ever met, dreamed not only of transforming the environment but of accomplishing thereby the secular salvation of the people. He proposed that the TVA should create a "new social and economic order," one which had less in common with the likes of Magnitogorsk than with old-fashioned utopian communities such as Brook Farm. Morgan favoured the revival of handicrafts and folk-ways. He wanted the Valley inhabitant to be "the individualist of American industrial life. With artistic and scientific guidance, he can make the goods which America needs to take the curse off its mass-production civilization."[30] One of Morgan's first acts was to put forward a code which included such improving precepts as this: "Intemperance, lax sex morality, gambling, the use of habit-forming drugs are not in keeping with the spirit of the Tennessee Valley Authority."[31] In other respects, too, Morgan seemed more of a crank than a visionary. He dabbled in eugenics, the occult and food faddism. He once even suggested that the Tennessee Valley should adopt "a sort of local money"—one journalist suggested that it could be a currency of "coon skins." However, Morgan was not given his head at the TVA. Roosevelt, whose instinct was always to divide and rule, and to create consensus from conflict, appointed incompatible colleagues to its board. One of the other directors was David Lilienthal, an astute, ambitious lawyer who liked the "taste of blood," particularly if it was that of private utility companies. Morgan, a political innocent, was inclined to cooperate with the companies. So, from its inception, the TVA was riven by a feud and "run by a debating society."[32]

This helps to explain why the operational plans of the TVA were flawed. For example, when a lake was created by the Norris Dam, the removal of the living was managed with much less tact than the re-burial of the dead. But although the TVA was sometimes ruthless and sometimes inept, it did initiate a revolution in the life of the Tennessee Valley. When completed, a series of 9 dams controlled the 60 billion tons of water which annually flowed down the Tennessee River; and 11 more dams shackled its tributaries. In its entirety this engineering work dwarfed the Dnepostroi Dam and was larger than that of the Panama Canal. The dams helped to form the largest inland waterway system in the world and they transformed the Tennessee River into a series of lakes covering a total of 900 square miles, an area so huge that barges had to be specially constructed to withstand waves. Between these concrete colossi the water ran blue, a tribute to the TVA's massive programme of replanting and soil conservation. The TVA's dynamos produced more electricity than the entire output of Central and South America. During the inter-war period prices fell by more than a third and electricity came to an area where, in 1930, 95 per cent of the rural population were without it. (So that the inhabitants could take advantage of this new luxury the TVA arranged the sale of appliances—cookers, radios and refrigerators—at the cheapest rates.) However, the dams, locks, spillways, floodgates, gantries, turbines, generators, power houses and visitor centres of the TVA were not merely vast pieces of mechanical, or even social, engineering. They aimed to be utilitarian works of art, icons of the machine age. As Julian Huxley wrote, they were "the medieval cathedrals or renaissance palaces" of the New Deal.[33] They were an architectural as well as a literal endeavour to give more light.

Equally eye-catching was the construction of the new community of Norris, extolled by many as "the first all-electric town."[34] Built close to the Norris Dam, it consisted of 300 dwellings, set in green belt land, each one having a 4-acre plot for subsistence farming. The houses, built of cinder block, were somewhat drab. But boasting four or five rooms, indoor plumbing and electric lights, they looked like mansions to Tennessee farmers, a third of whom did not even have outdoor privies. With its electrically-heated school (the first in the world), its cooperative enterprises, its dormitories for unmarried workers, its enlightened further education programmes, its interdenominational church services, its low rents and high wages (in an area where so little cash was in circulation that barter was a way of life), Norris seemed to be a model of what planning could accomplish. It was not planning along Communist or Fascist lines, as Arthur Morgan pointed out: the New Deal "is not taking the road of Russia or of Germany, but the way of cooperation and good will."[35]

That these qualities were not always enough was illustrated by the fate of the town, which never reached its full potential and later became a garden suburb of Knoxville. That the TVA brought illumination to an obscurantist region is shown by the fact that many Tennesseans, among them such stubborn individualists as hill-billies and Holy Rollers, came to believe that government did have a certain responsibility for the welfare of citizens. The TVA was well-nigh universally popular in the Tennessee basin. Although its racial policies seemed dangerously liberal to the South (blacks were still segregrated but they were paid the same wages as whites), in Memphis and other cities "the agency's name became a shibboleth."[36]

When Lorena Hickok, journalist, social investigator and close friend of Eleanor Roosevelt, visited Tennessee in 1934 she reported excitedly that 10,000 men were working on TVA enterprises, "building with timber and steel and concrete the New Deal's most magnificent project, creating an empire with potentialities so tremendous and so dazzling that they make one gasp." In the midst of the Depression she had found a hope for the future: "A Promised Land bathed in golden sunlight, is rising out of the gray shadows of want and squalor and wretchedness down here in the Tennessee Valley."[37]

To improve prospects and to revive the economy on a country-wide scale Roosevelt next created the National Recovery Administration (NRA). The NRA, hastily spatchcocked together in mid-June 1933, aimed to substitute industrial cooperation for the "cannibalistic"[38] competition which had prevailed since the onset of the Depression. In place of an anarchic system of sweating in the factory and undercutting in the market-place it would establish a stable structure of wages and prices, thus increasing the purchasing power of workers and encouraging manufacturers to raise production. It would improve conditions of work and eliminate unfair trading practices. Furthermore it would permit labour to organise unions and engage in free collective bargaining. And it would dispense with anti-trust laws that prevented business from fixing prices. The mechanism designed to achieve all this, and thereby to reverse the vicious spiral of decline, was the NRA code of fair competition. Each industry was to have a code, either adopted voluntarily or imposed by the government. And the man given the task of putting these codes in place was Hugh S. Johnson. As head of the NRA, this red-faced, square-jawed, bull-necked former cavalry general was in charge of the largest peacetime effort ever made to mobilise American industry. In a characteristically colourful utterance Johnson forecast: "It will be red fire at first and dead cats afterwards. This is just like mounting the guillotine on the infinitesimal gamble that the axe won't work."[39]

Johnson's frontier childhood had been hard and as a soldier he was so gruff that even his commanding officer General "Black Jack" Pershing acknowledged, "He really seems ready to devour you, bones and all." But Johnson was also a sentimentalist who wept uncontrollably at the arias in *Madame Butterfly* and sympathised warmly with the victims of the Depression. A qualified lawyer and a businessman of some experience though little success, he had become associated with the Brain Trust. Yet he was impatient with their "poppycock discussions," during which he would squirm, sweat, pull his hair, stretch, scratch and crouch. Johnson wanted a "jazzed-up" version of Mussolini's Corporate State so much that he was prepared to ride roughshod over legal niceties. "You don't seem to realize that people in this country are starving," he told one critic, "that industry has gone to pot . . . unless we stimulate it . . . and that this law stuff doesn't matter."[40]

Roosevelt was much taken with Johnson despite, or perhaps because of, warnings that he was "dangerous and unstable,"[41] excitable and erratic, "dictatorial and absolutely beyond control."[42] This last caveat came from Secretary of the Interior Harold Ickes, and Roosevelt was concerned enough to give him, instead of Johnson, responsibility for spending the 3.3 billion dollars which the NRA bill had appropriated for public works. This money was designed to relieve unemployment and to stimulate consumer demand (though it was never enough to make a significant difference) and Johnson, assuming that he would be in charge, had already begun to set up a Public Works Administration. When Roosevelt called him into a cabinet meeting and said, lavishly sugaring the pill with praise, that supervising national recovery was so vital that he was being relieved of the pedestrian job of looking after public works, the General turned first red, then puce and finally purple. As the cabinet dispersed he remained slumped in his chair, murmuring in a broken voice, "I don't see why, I don't see why."[43] Frances Perkins had to take Johnson for a two-hour drive round Washington to calm him down and prevent his resignation.

His morale restored, the General took off his coat, rolled up his sleeves and toiled "like ten demons."[44] His first and most successful effort was to secure agreement on a code for the textile industry whereby minimum wages were set and child labour was abolished. Other codes followed. Johnson persuaded steel barons, automobile magnates, mine owners and other "Brahmins of Big Industry"[45] that it was their patriotic duty to display the Blue Eagle, emblem of the NRA. Inevitably there were mavericks: "Hell," growled Henry Ford, "that Roosevelt Buzzard! I wouldn't put it on the car." But even Ford complied with the code and Johnson's only sanction against him for refusing to sign it was to institute a government boycott of his products, which was ineffective. The truth was that Johnson feared to compel adherence because he suspected (with good cause) that the NRA codes were unconstitutional. So he resorted to moral pressure and extravagant publicity. Described as "the greatest master of ballyhoo since Barnum,"[46] the General mounted a huge campaign to promote the NRA. He organised flying displays, motorcades, torchlight processions, mass rallies, brass bands, billboards, films and demonstrations. He also held press conferences in which he amused and amazed journalists with his pungent language. Johnson used words like "hornswoggler" and "chiseller." He called Ogden Mills a "little son of the rich." Johnson said that his offices in the new Commerce Building, the apple of Herbert Hoover's eye, reminded him of the pay toilets in Union Station. He denied having any political ambitions, saying that he would rather "be down between Brownsville and Matamoros where the owls fucked the chickens"[47] (only to be rebuked by a minister from St. Louis as a "cussing man . . . more proficient in profanity than in prayer").[48] Asked what would happen to those who refused to go along with the NRA codes, Johnson replied: "They'll get a sock on the nose."[49]

However, observers soon noted that inside General Johnson's iron glove was a velvet hand. Even when the codes were accepted they were full of loopholes and he could not prevent employers from using them for their own purposes—to raise prices, limit production and restrain competition. Thus, in the precise opposite of their intended effect, the codes actually contributed to commercial stagnation. Johnson, in many ways a conservative, conciliated the captains of industry and conceded little to organised labour except where it was already strong, as in the mines. Moreover, despite his sabre-slashing assault on red tape, he became entangled in the minutiae of drafting codes for the production of corn-cob pipes, fly swatters, dog food and striptease acts. This provoked first ridicule and then reprobation, especially as by 1934 there seemed to be substance in William Randolph Hearst's gibe that NRA stood for No Recovery Allowed, perhaps even in his allegation that it was State Socialism. A "volcano of invective"[50] at the best of times, Johnson erupted against his attackers, calling them "social Neanderthalers," "Old Dealers," "witch doctors of the let-things-alone school."[51] He worked harder than ever, often for 15 hours a day. He charged about the country in a blaze of headlines and a haze of cigarette smoke—the General chain-smoked Old Gold, lighting one while he still had two burning in the ash-tray. As the pressure mounted he also drank more heavily, which led to violent rows in the office and sudden disappearances to an inn overlooking the Hudson near West Point. Eyes bloodshot, hair dishevelled, paunch sagging and clothes rumpled, Johnson thrashed around ever more recklessly and ineffectively. He also became increasingly paranoid about the press, engaging in a memorable spat over his assertive secretary and mistress Frances Robinson, known as "Robbie." He justified her high salary by saying that Robbie was much more than a secretary and, when reporters delightedly pounced on the remark, Johnson accused them of hitting below the belt. The General's lieutenant Donald Richberg, who had the appearance of "an amiable woodchuck" but the inclinations of an Arctic skua, stabbed him in the back. Making the most of Johnson's tumultuous indiscretions, Richberg told Roosevelt that "a team of horses can't be driven in harness with a wild bull."[52]

With much reluctance and more flattery the President eased the General out of office in September 1934. Disgruntled and eventually disillusioned with the New Deal, Johnson wrote a book justifying his stewardship entitled *The Blue Eagle from Egg to Earth,* which the new chief of a reorganised NRA, none other than Richberg himself, dubbed "The Blue Eagle from Egg to Egomania."[53] Yet for all Johnson's flamboyant narcissism the fact remained that he had starred in a drama such as had never before been performed on the national stage. It was no mere entertainment, for the NRA created two million jobs and established minimum scales of pay. Above all it inspired the hope that recovery could be achieved, as Johnson said, "by cooperation instead of by absolute dictatorship."[54] Unfortunately histrionics could not persuade business to cooperate and rhetoric was no substitute for regulation. Johnson's extravaganza raised expectations without raising wages sufficiently to stimulate demand for goods, the key to dispelling the Depression. So, even before the General relinquished command, and well before his agency was declared unconstitutional (in May 1935—for vesting unwarranted power in the presidency), the NRA had become "the light that failed."[55]

More successful was that part of the national recovery effort, the Public Works Administration (PWA), which Roosevelt had entrusted to Harold Ickes. Brought up by a Calvinistic mother in humble circumstances, Ickes was a Puritan so sure of his own righteousness that he thought nothing of tapping the telephones of his staff to ensure that they were free of graft. Through hard work and ability he had qualified as a lawyer, practising in Chicago, where he had hobnobbed with gangsters and prosecuted crooked business interests. An advanced Progressive, he had helped to manage Theodore Roosevelt's political campaign and he later transferred his allegiance to Franklin, who took an immediate fancy to him. Fair, beefy and bespectacled, Ickes waddled about with such purposeful energy that Roosevelt privately nicknamed him "Donald Duck." But as Secretary of the Interior he became the most belligerent champion of the New Deal. He was vividly outspoken: he said that Huey Long suffered from intellectual halitosis and that General Johnson was afflicted by mental saddle-sores. He delighted in his reputation as a curmudgeon. He flayed predatory "big dealers," who considered him a "bad egg" (Hearst's expression)[56] and compared him to Goebbels. In fact he was the first member of the government to denounce fascism and he embarrassed the State Department by calling Hitler, "Esau, the Hairy Man." Testy towards his colleagues, Ickes exercised "generally wholesome talents for terror" towards his subordinates.[57] He once caught out ten members of his department by including bits of *Alice in Wonderland* in a typed WPA application which they failed to notice despite indicating that they had read it. Ickes was, in short, an authoritarian liberal. He controlled the PWA with ferocious efficiency and meticulous honesty, employing sleuths to spy on his own inspectors. He thus fostered a series of splendid projects, clearing slums and building or reconstructing roads, canals, bridges, docks, airports, sewers, hospitals, schools, power plants, gaols and public offices. No American ever made more mark on his native landscape. Ickes also had an impact on the social topography, sustaining decent wage scales, improving conditions of work, supporting union membership, hiring blacks and Indians. But the Secretary of the Interior was so punctilious that he moved slowly and spent cautiously—at a time when a quarter of the population was still out of work.

IF Roosevelt had not lifted the Depression in his first hundred days as President, he had dissipated the pall of fear which hung over the United States. It was a task that had seemed impossible when he took office. At the beginning of March 1933 one supporter had written, "I really tremble for the new administration because the great rank and file of the people are expecting a miracle."[58] After Roosevelt's inaugural address many Americans felt that he was the man to perform it: "They were ready to believe that he could see in the dark."[59] By the middle of June they concluded that a miracle had indeed occurred. As the *New York Times* noted, Roosevelt had turned the emergency into a personal triumph:

> That was because he seemed to the American people to be riding the whirlwind and directing the storm. The country was ready and even anxious to accept any leadership. From President Roosevelt it got a rapid succession of courageous speeches and efforts and achievements which inclined millions of his fellow citizens to acclaim him as the heaven-sent man of the hour.[60]

Roosevelt's measures may have been largely unpremeditated, surprisingly incoherent and frequently ineffective. All too often his overlapping agencies engaged in feuds of their own and he never harnessed their energies to achieve real economic recovery. Yet in just over three months the President averted catastrophe, restored the nation to psychological equilibrium and incidentally buttered his own political parsnips for life. He imbued the United States with a sense of purpose, unity and dynamism. He epitomised compassion in government. He reinvigorated public service and, like John F. Kennedy after him, got the young involved. He gave promise that the resources of democracy were equal to the crisis and that capitalism could heal itself. He exuded optimism. As Harold Ickes said, "It's more than a New Deal. It's a New World."[61]

Roosevelt's achievement was indeed a personal one. He conveyed a sense that the New Deal was a great adventure, a heroic struggle which would culminate in victory over the Depression. His zest for this enterprise found expression in the obvious delight he took in the appurtenances of his office. The White House itself was transformed by his exhilarating presence. When H. G. Wells had visited Hoover there he had found "a sickly overworked and overwhelmed man" inhabiting "a queer ramshackle place like a nest of waiting-rooms with hat-stands everywhere, and unexpected doors . . . through which hurrying distraught officials appeared and vanished." Calling on Roosevelt he "found that this magic White House had changed back again to a large leisurely comfortable private home."[62] Where Hoover had addressed Wells like a public meeting, everything under Roosevelt was informal and relaxed.

The house was lived in to the point of shabbiness. The food was notoriously bad: gourmet visitors were particularly revolted by the salads, which sometimes concealed "bits of marshmallow in their dreadful depths."[63] The patrician President sent away for bargain mail-order shirts. His bedroom was almost Spartan: he slept on a thin mattress in a narrow iron bedstead covered with a white seersucker counterpane; there was little in the way of decoration except pictures, a collection of miniature pigs on the marble mantelpiece and the tail of his father's horse Gloucester over the door. The adjoining second-floor Oval Study was scarcely less modest. The walls were painted battleship grey and a large green rug covered the floor. The President's massive oak desk, made from the timbers of the *Resolute,* was crowded with curios, gadgets and souvenirs. Books, model ships, photographs, naval paintings and flags added to the clutter. The impression that 1600 Pennsylvania Avenue was a family home was strengthened by the First Lady, whose hospitality was as warm as it was frugal. Vulnerable and impulsive, radiating "spiritual energy"[64] but possessing the common touch, Eleanor Roosevelt not only acted as her husband's (frequently ignored) liberal conscience, she also acted as his hostess in a singularly unpretentious White House. Her efforts had more than domestic import since, as one of her staff said: "This goldfish bowl is made out of magnifying glass."[65] What people saw inside it was the smiling face of democracy.

Nevertheless critics, some of whom had earlier called for a dictatorship, increasingly damned Roosevelt for having established one. This charge, which reveals much about the power of ideas to transcend reality, soon became the common currency of polite conversation. It was repeated in the press, most rabidly by Colonel Robert R. McCormick's Chicago *Tribune*, which described Mussolini, Stalin, Hitler and Roosevelt as the four horsemen of the Apocalypse. It was first heard from the pulpit in the summer of 1933, when Roosevelt was denounced as a "dictator" by the President of the Church of Latter-day Saints.[66] Similarities can be adduced, it is true, between Roosevelt's remedies for the Depression and those of fascist and Communist leaders. FDR himself said that he was doing, in a more orderly way, "some of the things that were being done in Russia and even some of the things that were being done under Hitler in Germany."[67] The President built highways while the Führer built *autobahns*. Roosevelt regarded the CCC work camps as a means of getting young people "off the city street corners"; Hitler described similar projects as a way to keep the youth from "rotting helplessly in the streets."[68] When Roosevelt refused to cooperate at the World Economic Conference of June 1933—he feared its attempts to stabilise international currency would interfere with his price-raising efforts in the United States—Hjalmar Schacht, President of the Reichsbank, congratulated him for being an economic nationalist like the Führer. He may even have been influenced by writers such as Stuart Chase, populariser of the term "New Deal," who likened Communism to "the flaming sword of Allah" seen "over the plains of Mecca."[69]

However, Roosevelt's diplomatic recognition of the Soviet Union in November 1933 was not prompted by any ideological sympathy. On the contrary, religious Americans went so far as to hope that he had "restored God to Russia."[70] In fact the President wanted good relations with the USSR to counter Japan and to promote trade. At home he was clearly trying to preserve the American way of life. His version of the planned economy was not socialism but state capitalism. His purpose was to reinvigorate private enterprise with injections of public spirit—and public money. Roosevelt's New Deal was a world away from Stalin's *perelom,* his break with the past. Despite what Hearst might say, the TVA was by no means Soviet. The AAA could not be confused with Stalin's agrarian revolution: Wallace was trying to save American kulaks. The public works schemes of Hopkins and Ickes were designed to restore individual dignity, not to promote collectivism. Though often called a "Parlour Pink," Rexford Tugwell was, as General Johnson said, "about as Red as a blue hen."[71] Sinister enough in all conscience, J. Edgar Hoover's Federal Bureau of Investigation (FBI) was no "miniature American Cheka";[72] in fact, promoted with Hollywood hoop-la, it smacked less of the secret police than the Keystone Kops. Roosevelt's emergency measures aimed to increase national prosperity rather than to augment presidential power. Nothing could have induced him to emulate the brutal Caesarism of Stalin.

Equally, the President was repelled by Hitler's organised savagery, especially as expressed in war-mongering and anti-Semitism—though in practice FDR would do as little to succour German Jews as to assist American blacks. As chief of the world's greatest trading nation he did not, like Hitler and Mussolini, lust for autarky; though at a time when European states were refusing to pay their war debts Roosevelt was inclined to ignore the warning of his Secretary of State, Cordell Hull, that economic wars are the germs of real wars. While the President was influenced by isolationism—he wrecked the World Economic Conference with his bombshell message urging each nation to set its own house in order—he aspired (as his later policies showed) towards internationalism. Furthermore Roosevelt's New Deal hardly compares in essentials with Hitler's *Gleichschaltung* (coordination). The Blue Eagle could not be mistaken for the swastika. The fireside chat was the antithesis of the Nuremberg rally. Organised labour flourished under Roosevelt, whereas Hitler smashed the trade unions. Roosevelt's manipulation of the media bore no relation to the national brainwashing attempted by Goebbels. The President did not possess, as the *New York Times* sagely observed, "a private army of, say, 2,000,000 Blueshirts."[73] The American constitution remained intact. No senators were sent to concentration camps; no congressmen were forcibly fed on castor oil. True, there were Americans who believed that a little castor oil might have started the wheels of industry going, not least the red-necked, red-suspendered, Red-hating Governor Eugene Talmadge of Georgia. But Roosevelt organised no "Fascist movement"[74]—a vital necessity, in the opinion of Sir Oswald Mosley, if the President were to become a bona fide dictator.

The fact is that, more than most presidents, Roosevelt existed in a deliberate dimension of ambiguity. He was eclectic and evasive to the point of contradiction and obfuscation. He was prepared to try whatever expedient looked good at the time. When the small boom that coincided with the first hundred days of the New Deal began to falter, Roosevelt initiated another of his overlapping relief agencies, Harry Hopkins's short-lived Civil Works Administration, which found temporary employment for over four million people during the cold winter of 1933–4. On the false assumption that the Depression could be cured by fixing prices rather than by stimulating demand, over that winter he also juggled with the value of gold against the dollar, offering a few cents more than the European bullion market. To his admirers Roosevelt was a bold empiricist who was wonderfully accessible to new ideas. The "unblinkered mind," said H. G. Wells, was in possession of the White House.[75] To his enemies the President was an unscrupulous opportunist, prepared to embrace any creed to remain there. As H. L. Mencken wrote, if Roosevelt became convinced that coming out for cannibalism would get him votes "he would at once begin fattening a missionary in the White House backyard."[76] Roosevelt contented himself with rejecting all foreign "isms"—even cannibalism—though he remained studiously vague about his positive beliefs. A young reporter once pressed him to define his philosophy. " 'Philosophy?' asked the President, puzzled. 'Philosophy? I am a Christian and a Democrat—that's all.' "[77]

Such a philosophy was doubtless sounder than the views of rivals who claimed that they could resolve the crisis. It was more wholesome than the incipient fascism of Father Charles E. Coughlin, the radio priest whose mellifluous brogue seduced millions of Americans—he received more letters than the President himself and when he was broadcasting it was possible to walk down city streets, even in Protestant or Jewish neighbourhoods, and not miss a word of "The Golden Hour of the Little Flower" because it could be heard coming from every house. The New Deal was infinitely more civilised than the thuggish populism of Huey Long, whose wealth-sharing plan was a demagogic means to obtain total power—the pretensions of the "Kingfish" were symbolised by his Governor's mansion in Louisiana, which was designed to resemble the White House. Roosevelt's beliefs were less cranky than the panacea proposed by Dr. Francis E. Townsend, who wanted to give old people 200 dollars a month. And they were more practical than the Utopian Socialism of Upton Sinclair, whose EPIC struggle to End Poverty In California was defeated in 1934. Many other dissidents had sky-blue schemes designed to resolve (or to appear to resolve) the troubling inequities of privilege, wealth and power and to give individuals in the grip of implacable economic forces control (or the illusion of control) over their own destinies. Roosevelt had most sympathy for Sinclair. But the President would not endorse him, saying that he (Roosevelt) could only go as fast as the people would let him.

That speed he gauged almost to perfection, now tacking towards conservatism, now trimming his sails in the radical breeze. Thus he made frequent overtures to the business community, to laissez-faire capitalism and to the principle of self-reliance. On the other hand he attempted to regulate Wall Street, establishing the Securities & Exchange Commission (SEC) in 1934. Then again he shocked liberal opinion by appointing as its head the free-booting financier Joseph Kennedy, which was, as Louis Howe remarked, "like setting a cat to guard pigeons."[78] The following year his Social Security Act gave a modicum of protection (largely paid for by contributions) to some of the neediest members of society, the old, the young, the handicapped, the unemployed, the poor. But it fell far short of being the kind of "cradle to the grave" insurance that the President had envisaged, not least because he retreated before vested interests such as doctors and Southern landlords. Other progressive moves followed the Supreme Court's striking down of the NRA in 1935. Most notable was the Wagner-Connery Act, a charter for trade unions, whose membership increased from 2 million to 11 million during the 1930s. But although unemployment fell by a third and national income rose by a third during Roosevelt's first three years in office, the crisis showed no sign of abating for millions of Americans.

Many expressed their anguish in strikes, protests, disturbances and riots. Violent labour disputes in cities as far apart as San Francisco and Minneapolis fed fears of revolution from the Left or Right. Some warned of impending civil war. Roosevelt himself apparently said that if he failed he would not be the worst president in American history but the last. Other observers saw the Depression as the seedbed of wider conflict. Reporting on conditions in Rhode Island at the end of 1934 Martha Gellhorn wrote, "I don't want to howl doom, but it is really a horrible mess. I should think it would be a cinch to run a war these days, with a good many of the world's young men having nothing better to do anyhow than get shot; and at least fed a bit beforehand."

Which region of the United States suffered worst was a matter of opinion. The traveller Lowell Thomas found the soft-coal patches of West Virginia the "foulest cesspool of human misery this side of hell."[79] But other witnesses discovered conditions equally bad in nearby mining districts of Kentucky (which was riven by industrial strife) and Pennsylvania (where some families lived in abandoned coke ovens). Urban investigators could not believe that there was anything more terrible than the plight of the cities, Detroit with its silent factories, Philadelphia with its disgusting "bandbox" slums, Chicago and New York at the end of their tether. Depression was a perennial condition for blacks, but now everyone in the South was, as the contemporary historian W. J. Cash noted, "either ruined beyond his wildest previous fears or stood in peril of such ruin."[80] Among poor whites the most deprived were probably the share-croppers of Arkansas. In their squalor, wretchedness and despair they reminded one visitor of Chinese coolies. Lorena Hickok was so appalled by the human anguish she encountered in the Dakotas that she dubbed them America's Siberia.

PROBABLY there was no more distress under the big sky of middle America than elsewhere on the continent. But to compound the Depression the great plains were afflicted by an overwhelming natural catastrophe—drought. A dry cycle began in 1930 which not only ruined farmers but threatened to destroy the land itself. The worst damage occurred at the convergence of five states: Oklahoma, Texas, New Mexico, Colorado and Kansas. This vast swathe of territory (a swamp in the time of dinosaurs, whose bones were often exhumed) was America's "dust bowl."[81] It experienced the ecological equivalent of the financial crash. And, like the Wall Street disaster, the Dust Bowl was caused by the untrammelled operation of free market forces. Farmers had sown greed, exploiting the ground beyond what it could bear, and they reaped a whirlwind. In fact the topsoil of the plains had always been liable to blow away when fire or grasshoppers destroyed its sparse thatch of greenery. But what now threatened to turn prairie into desert was a novel combination of overgrazing and industrialised agriculture. With their tractors and disc ploughs sodbusters had literally busted the sod, pulverising the fragile earth and tearing the heart out of the humus. The impact of this mechanised rape did not become apparent until the 1930s drought. Then the wind sucked up the scarred and scorched earth. Swirling dust devils climbed high into the air and swept over the continent. The great blow of May 1934, for example, carried 350 million tons of dust thousands of miles, blanketing Chicago, darkening the doors of the White House, causing a haze in Savannah and begriming ships far out in the Atlantic. In winter red snow fell on Maine.

People joked about the "dirty thirties" but most storms were confined to the Southern plains. There they took the form of prolonged sand siroccos or sudden black blizzards which rolled over the countryside like biblical plagues. The fine grains blasted the paint off buildings. They wrecked engines. They blinded and suffocated animals. They scourged humans. To protect themselves people wore goggles, scarfs and masks, and coated their nostrils with vaseline. But any movement caused a miniature maelstrom and nothing could keep dirt out of ears, mouths, noses and lungs. Householders tried to seal their doors with oiled cloth and their windows with gummed paper, but every interior surface became covered with a powdery film, sometimes deep enough to ripple like the sand at low tide.

Outside, thick deposits of silt rose to smother the clapboard shacks, many of which were abandoned. The wind whipped prickly rolls of sage-brush and tumbleweed over the panhandle. Drifting dunes gave even the most familiar landscape an eerily lunar quality. Dust filled the furrows and clogged such tender shoots as had emerged from the parched earth. Livestock starved as their pasture disappeared. All around was desolation— barren fields, dead trees, crippled windmills, submerged fences, choked wells. It was as if the land itself were being buried in an immense Golgotha, with the copper empyrean as its pall. There were days of almost complete obscurity and weeks when midday was like twilight and "the sun's rays struggled through the gloom with a strange bluish luminescence."[82]

The Dust Bowl provided contemporaries with a potent symbol for the Depression decade. It spelled the bankruptcy of an economic order based on exploitation. It typified the industrial destruction of agrarian harmony, until then an idyll to which most people, including the President, paid homage. It was a metaphor of metamorphosis—the transformation of brave new world into wasteland, the turning of American dream into nightmare. The dust storms that raged over the plains seemed, as Woody Guthrie sang, "our judgement" and "our doom." They provoked apocalyptic terrors and wellnigh extinguished hope. When a cloud of dust obscured the sun at noon, one Oklahoman "feared that the Lord was returning to gather his flock."[83] A woman from Concordia noted in her journal, "This is the ultimate darkness. So must come the end of the world."[84]

Such sentiments were understandable. But dust should not obscure the truth, as it does to some extent in John Steinbeck's powerful documentary novel *The Grapes of Wrath*. The book begins with a graphic evocation of the dust-muffled landscape of Oklahoma, as if to suggest that a natural disaster was the root cause of the "Okie" migration to California. Actually the prime mover was poverty, itself the result of Depression and drought, of farm mechanisation and unemployment, of soil erosion and New Deal policies. The AAA's soil conservation and crop restriction measures fostered rural depopulation. Subsidised landlords were inclined to buy machines to do the work of men and Okies described themselves as being "tractored out" of their farms. Hence the pathetic odysseys of families such as Steinbeck's Joads, who went west to seek their fortune and found only further destitution. This was not because the fruit-filled countryside of their fantasies did not exist. The Joads were awestruck by their first sight of California, stopping their overloaded jalopy in the middle of the road and gazing hungrily at the sunlit "valley golden and green before them."[85] No, it was simply that (until the coming of war and the growth of defence industries) people like the Joads could not get a stake in the promised land. Unqualified for relief until they had been there a year, and paid starvation wages for casual work by fruit farmers, they squatted in "little Oklahomas," ditch-bank camps described as "filth-festering sores of miserable humanity."[86] Denied a harvest of happiness, they reaped the grapes of wrath.

Steinbeck's novel was one of the most moving and memorable accounts of the Depression years. But it also helped to foster the myth that the Dust Bowl was entirely impoverished and deserted. Certainly there was a spectacular exodus. During the 1930s Oklahoma lost a fifth of its population and the figure for Dust Bowl counties was much higher—at a time when mobility was diminished by the Depression. However, most people did not move far and the remaining majority survived surprisingly well. True, the cosmic scale of a tragedy which gave some nine million productive acres of high plains back to nature left some farmers distraught, demoralised, bewildered and apathetic. But many faced the crisis in the spirit of their pioneer ancestors. They disconnected the telephone, stopped the newspapers, put off charity, substituted cheap lye for washing powder, caught jackrabbits for the pot, made hand towels from cement sacks and dresses from chicken-feed bags. They took advantage of the life-giving transfusions of federal cash, selling livestock to the government under the Drought Cattle Purchase scheme and earning 20 cents an acre by ploughing along the contours of their land to reduce erosion. They sent their children to schools which never closed and in some cases they managed to find the money to buy new tractors. They even remained cheerful. Dust Bowl humour became the fashion. Will Rogers said that only advanced civilisations were covered in dirt—California couldn't manage it. The sign in a store window on the Great Plains read: "Great bargains in real estate. Bring your own container."[87]

The incoherence of the New Deal was well illustrated by the fact that one of its agencies (the AAA) helped drive the poor Okies to California while another, Rexford Tugwell's Resettlement Administration (RA), gave them loans to stay at home. The RA itself was riddled with anomalies. On the one hand it fostered a spirit of sturdy individualism by encouraging farmers to cultivate their own marginal land; on the other it offered to set them up in green belt settlements and agricultural collectives. Similarly, by establishing clean, well-organised camps in California the RA found itself inadvertently subsidising the large fruit growers. However, critics did not so much attack the muddles of the New Deal or even its failure to achieve national recovery. They condemned its frills, work projects such as those devised by Hopkins's dynamic organisation, the Works Progress Administration (WPA, created in 1935), for writers, actors, artists and musicians.

(They too had to eat, as Hopkins sagely remarked, and his assistance was actually one of the most imaginative aspects of the New Deal.) Critics also denounced Roosevelt's fiscal irresponsibility, his demoralising of the poor by means of handouts and his centralising tendencies, which were sustained by a vast new federal bureaucracy. The last was typified by interfering agencies such as the SEC and the Food and Drug Administration (FDA), and by the horde of New Dealers, often lawyers and professors, who descended on Washington and whose heads were turned by their proximity to power. Rexford Tugwell, for example, soon gave up saying "Roosevelt and I" and just said "I." Ray Moley behaved like "the greatest person on the planet"[88] and the newspapers intoned: "Moley, Moley, Moley, Lord God Almighty."[89] When he over-reached himself, the *New York Times* likened his fall to that of Lucifer.

The assaults on the New Deal took many forms, from conservative decisions by the Supreme Court, via vituperation from newspapers and businessmen, to Al Smith's teaching the tiger in Central Park Zoo to roar at the name of Roosevelt. The President responded to his critics in characteristically pragmatic fashion: what is sometimes known at the "Second New Deal" (launched in 1935) was no more homogeneous than the first. It was, indeed, a kind of creative anarchy, a form of improvised ingenuity. Thus when the AAA was declared unconstitutional in January 1936 the government continued to subsidise farmers under the guise of paying for soil conservation. Bobbing and weaving, Roosevelt declared his commitment to work not relief but allowed the budget deficit to grow to 3.5 billion dollars and then increased taxation on the rich. However, what mattered to the electorate was not Roosevelt's consistency but his concern. The President was plainly making a supreme effort to tackle the Depression.

This was the only issue that mattered, despite the international gloom precipitated by Japan's seizure of Manchuria, Italy's attack on Ethiopia and Germany's occupation of the Rhineland. These events, indeed, strengthened the traditional American determination to avoid foreign entanglements. Furthermore isolationism was reinforced by pacifism, by hostility to the military establishment so bitter that officers in the War Department worked in civilian clothes, and by revulsion against arms dealers, who were denounced as "high priests of war" and "death's recruiting agents."[90] Roosevelt himself hankered for collective security. But he could not ignore the isolationist spirit, pithily expressed by Senator Thomas D. Schall: "To Hell with Europe and with the rest of those nations."[91] And he signed the Neutrality Acts (1935–37), which were designed to keep the United States out of future wars—a move which the likes of Hitler and Mussolini welcomed as clearing the deck for their own aggression. The fact was that Roosevelt needed the support of the isolationists to carry through the New Deal. To defeat the Depression at home he stood aloof from the foreign fray. He sacrificed the alien scapegoat to the domestic underdog. And Americans applauded his compassion.

In the 1936 election Roosevelt shamelessly wore his warm heart on his sleeve: "Presidents do make mistakes, but the immortal Dante tells us that divine justice weighs the sins of the cold-blooded and the sins of the warm-hearted in different scales."[92] Alf Landon, the modest, liberal, Republican candidate could not match his opponent's rhetoric, let alone FDR's comment on his emblem, the Kansas sunflower—it was yellow, had a black heart and always died before November. Roosevelt did not pretend that he had solved all the nation's problems, for the unemployed still tramped the streets with the desperation of marathon dancers and six-day bicycle racers. But he insisted that things had improved over four years and he traded on the fact that the New Deal had been the salvation of millions of his countrymen. Many other people at home and abroad still reckoned Roosevelt an incipient dictator, and Nazi newspapers, always on the lookout for an American Führer, said that his second election victory would give him a free hand to reform a constitution that "belongs to the age of the oxcart."[93] With more justice Winston Churchill saw Roosevelt as the universal champion of democracy. The President's "impulse is one which makes toward the fuller life of the masses of the people in every land." As it "glowed brighter," Churchill said, it might well eclipse not only "the baleful unnatural lights which are diffused from Soviet Russia" but "the lurid flames of German Nordic self-assertion."[94]

XII

THE NAZIS IN POWER

LIKE Roosevelt, Hitler came to power in the darkest moment of the economic crisis and exploited the situation to dominate his nation. Each man played the hero in a drama of deliverance, a shining knight slaying the dragon Depression. And the first acts of both were designed to make an irresistible impact: in America through the euphoria generated during the Hundred Days; in Germany through the ecstasy of the Nazi "national awakening." However, the differences between President and Führer were fundamental. Roosevelt aimed to breathe new life into the American economy so that it could stand on its own feet, an independent entity generating peace and prosperity in a world of laissez-faire. Hitler intended to recreate the German economy as a kind of Frankenstein's monster, subordinate to his will and armoured for a war of racial supremacy. It was a war in which the Nazi conquest of America, now deemed by Hitler a "mongrel society"[1] because of the slump in its fortunes, would be the final stage in his march to world domination.

Hitler's economic approach gave him two advantages. First, recovery and job creation (both in train by January 1933) were signally assisted by military expenditure. This was always his priority, though initially it was to be camouflaged for fear of foreign reprisals. As he informed one of his first cabinet meetings,

> The next five years must be dedicated to the rearmament of the German people. Every publicly supported work-creation scheme must be judged from this standpoint: is it necessary for the restoration of the military strength of the German people?[2]

The Depression actually made rearmament easier: there was less civilian competition for labour and resources. Secondly, Hitler could impose financial discipline on his country which no democracy would tolerate. As he told Schacht, his guard against inflation was the concentration camp. So, at a time when the New Deal was floundering, Hitler quickly fulfilled his promise to give Germany "Bread and Work." He achieved this success through the power of the State and by it his own power was augmented. The Führer needed no reminding of the primacy of power.

To consolidate his position as Chancellor Hitler insisted on holding a democratic election to end democracy. He was confident that, having squared the army with promises of rearmament and seduced big business with talk of establishing a stable economic climate, he could obtain an overwhelming endorsement at the polls. For he now commanded the entire resources of the State, including the radio. As Minister of the Interior in Prussia Hermann Göring was especially active in employing the state apparatus. A gangster in charge of the police, he transformed the Prussian force into an auxiliary of the SA. Their particular task was to suppress the Communist opposition and Göring's instructions were to "Shoot first and ask questions afterwards."[3] The Communists, Stalin's victims as much as Hitler's, blindly insisted that there was nothing to choose between social fascists (i.e. Social Democrats) and actual fascists. The Führer, who told army chiefs that the Red "rot within the state must be expunged . . . through terror,"[4] intended to teach them differently. He got his chance on the night of 27 February 1933, when the Reichstag building was set on fire.

Most of the ugly sandstone structure on Königsplatz survived the blaze. But the debating chamber itself was gutted, "cut out of the building . . . as neatly as a stone from a peach."[5] This was because the oak-panelled amphitheatre filled with the tiered seats of the deputies was surmounted by a glass cupola, known to Berliners as "the biggest round cheese in Europe."[6] This dome cracked with the heat and acted as a chimney. Inside a pillar of fire rose vertically like a giant organ pipe, shooting out of the top and bathing the snow-clad trees of the Tiergarten in a lurid glow. So fiercely were the flames drawn upwards that when Göring arrived, eager to save the Gobelin tapestries, he was, despite his camel-hair-upholstered bulk, almost sucked into the inferno.

Shortly afterwards Hitler himself appeared in the Reichstag lobby, dressed in a flapping trench coat and a soft, broad-brimmed black hat. All his apocalyptic instincts were roused by the incendiary spectacle. But he at once began to seek ways of exploiting it politically. "God grant that this be the work of the Communists," he intoned. If the Reds got hold of Europe, he continued, warming to his theme, within two months "the whole continent would be aflame like this building." Papen then entered, immaculate in evening clothes amid the charred debris, smoking carpets and pools of water from the firemen's hoses. He had been giving a dinner at the exclusive Herrenklub in honour of Hindenburg, who, though apparently unmoved at seeing the Reichstag "looking as though it were illuminated by searchlights,"[7] had to be kept informed. Hitler grasped Papen's hand convulsively: "This is a God-given signal, Herr Vice-Chancellor! If this fire, as I believe, is the work of the Communists, then we must crush out this murder pest with an iron fist."[8] Some minutes more and Hitler had managed to work his furious suspicion into hysterical certainty. Leaning over the stone parapet of a balcony and "staring into the red sea of flame," his face scarlet with heat and excitement, he screamed at his entourage:

> Now there can be no mercy; whoever stands in our way will be mown down. The German people will not tolerate clemency. Every Communist functionary will be shot wherever he is found. The Communist deputies must be hanged this very night.[9]

Nor should their allies be spared, the Führer concluded, among whom he numbered the Social Democrats.

The rest of the night Hitler spent at the offices of the *Völkischer Beobachter* working with Goebbels on the Nazi version of the fire. They represented it as the "signal for bloody revolution and civil war,"[10] a St. Bartholomew's Day massacre to involve everything from political terror to the poisoning of reservoirs and communal soup kitchens. Though a Red insurrection was by no means impossible, few believed that the Communists would risk an open trial of strength with the Nazis. As *The Times* commented, "Clubs have been trumps and most of the trumps are in the hands of Göring."[11] Thus many people, including some of the top Nazis themselves, accepted the Communist account of the fire. This was speedily advanced by Willi Münzenberg's ubiquitous Red propaganda organisation. Citing a mass of circumstantial evidence, mostly spurious, its *Brown Book of the Hitler Terror and the Burning of the Reichstag* (1933) asserted that the Nazis themselves had secretly torched the building as a pretext for establishing a dictatorship. Thus what appears to be the truth—that an unbalanced Dutch Marxist named Marinus van der Lubbe had started the fire as a solitary protest against Nazism—was obscured for a generation. Hitler benefited most from the confusion. On 28 February he issued a decree for the protection of the State and its citizens, which was signed by Hindenburg. Annulling rights enshrined in the Weimar constitution and giving the government wide emergency powers, it was the death warrant of democracy. Among other things it sanctioned arbitrary arrest, the confiscation of property, the banning of free assembly and the suppression of free speech. No wonder Hitler regarded the Reichstag fire as a heaven-sent "beacon."[12] In its flames he forged the fetters of tyranny.

Yet despite detaining many of the Communist rank and file, despite employing all the arts of propaganda and demagogy, despite organising mass rallies, torchlight tattoos and violent demonstrations, Hitler managed to win only 43.9 per cent of the votes in the Reichstag election of 9 March. Still, after imprisoning Communist deputies and importuning Catholic deputies, he gained the necessary two-thirds majority in the Reichstag to pass an Enabling Act on 23 March 1933. Meeting at the Kroll Opera House, which was guarded inside and out by lines of Stormtroopers, the parliament transferred its legislative power to Hitler's government. With hardly a protest this elected body carried out the death sentence on democracy.

Hitler now moved quickly to crush the remaining obstacles in the way of his dictatorship, a process euphemistically described as *Gleichschaltung*—coordination. He began by subordinating the federal states to central control. He eliminated rival political bodies, making Germany a one-party state. He dissolved ex-servicemen's militias or incorporated them into the SA. He replaced key figures in the Civil Service with loyal Nazis. He set up a new secret police—the Gestapo. He initiated the systematic persecution of Jews. He adopted a carrot-and-stick policy towards the churches, intimidating refractory priests but negotiating a concordat with the Pope. Hitler smashed the independent trade unions, merging them into a government-controlled Labour Corps and sending many of their leaders to concentration camps. Camp guards were soon being warned against shooting prisoners because bullets cost three pfennigs each. Nazi brutality extended to the streets, where Stormtroopers took revenge on anyone thought to oppose the Führer. Christopher Isherwood described Berlin as a city which lay under an epidemic of fear, a city full of whispers telling of "illegal midnight arrests, of prisoners tortured in the SA barracks, made to spit on Lenin's picture, swallow castor-oil, eat old socks."[13]

Hitler also sought to impose ideological discipline on the Third Reich. This involved censorship and the inculcation of Nazi principles in every sphere, masterminded by the new Minister of Public Enlightenment and Propaganda—Goebbels. Goebbels' most notorious essay into cultural dictatorship occurred as early as 10 May 1933, with the burning of books said to contain "insidious poison which threatens the very roots of Germandom." Among them were works by Marx, Freud, Einstein, Proust, Gide, Zola, Wells, Heinrich Mann, Jack London, Ernest Hemingway, Upton Sinclair and about 150 other well-known writers. This literary *auto-da-fé* was carried out by Nazi students in most of Germany's 30 university towns. The Berlin bonfire, lit on sand-covered granite at the Opernplatz on Unter den Linden between the opera house and the university, was typical. The books, snatched by raiding parties from public and private libraries ("intellectual brothels"),[14] were brought in a cavalcade of cars and trucks escorted by squads of students bearing banners and singing Nazi songs. They were dressed in "red caps and green caps, purple and blue, with a chosen band of officers of the duelling corps in plush tam-o'-shanters, white breeches, blue tunics and high boots—with spurs." Reaching the square at midnight they flung the offending volumes on to the pyre, often bellowing an indictment of their authors: "Erich Maria Remarque . . . for degrading the German language and the highest patriotic ideal." Amid *"Heil Hitlers"* and general hullabaloo from the 40,000-strong crowd, Goebbels mounted the swastika-bedecked rostrum and declared:

> Jewish intellectualism is dead. National Socialism has shown the way. The German folk soul can again express itself. These flames do not only illuminate the final end of the old era, they also light up the new . . . The old goes up in flames, the new shall be fashioned from the flame in our hearts.[15]

There was much more in this vein. But the outside world was not only unconvinced, it was horrified by the immolation of German culture. Particularly shocking was the treason of the academic clerks, many of whom attended the book-burnings in full regalia of caps and gowns. The Rector of Göttingen University declared that he was "proud of the new appellation—barbarians."[16] Other scholars endorsed the purge and one distinguished scientist said that nature itself, in the form of molecular structure, corroborated Hitler's leadership principle. Protests against their intellectual abdication rang round the world. Helen Keller, whose own books had been burned, wrote: "History has taught you nothing if you think you can kill ideas." She added movingly that she had given all her royalties to German soldiers blinded in the Great War. In New York the American Jewish Congress held a vast rally at which speakers expressed their abhorrence for Hitler's assault on civilisation and condemned Nazi Germany for having "sinned against the light."

Such noble affirmations might have carried more weight if the principles of free expression had been fully applied in the democracies themselves. But some English libraries proscribed *All Quiet on the Western Front.* French censorship was arbitrary and pervasive. And on the very day of Hitler's book-burnings the Rockefeller family stopped the Mexican artist Diego Rivera from completing his mural depicting "human intelligence in control of the forces of nature"[17] in the great hall of the 70-storey Rockefeller Center because it included the figure of Lenin against a background of crowds of unemployed workers. Nevertheless, the Nazis' literary holocaust was recognised as a portentous reversion to savagery. As Heinrich Mann wrote, the Nazis burned "the books they were incapable of writing, the sum in fact of a whole spiritual culture from which they had been excluded by their own insufficiency."[18] John Heartfield linked the book burnings and the Reichstag fire in a brilliant photomontage entitled "Through Light into Night."[19] Milton's *Areopagitica* was quoted. Heine was invoked: "Wherever they burn books, sooner or later they will also burn human beings."[20]

Thus cultural totalitarianism was just as brutal in Nazi Germany as in Soviet Russia, and even more blatant. Addressing the Reichstag in the spring of 1933 Hitler made no bones about his intention to carry out

> a thorough moral purging of the body corporate of the nation. The entire educational system, the theatre, the cinema, literature, the Press, and the wireless—all these will be used as means to this end and valued accordingly . . . Blood and race will once more become the source of artistic intuition.[21]

Naturally Hitler claimed that there was an unbridgeable gulf between Nazism and Bolshevism. Indeed Goebbels employed some of his choicest calumnies against the Soviet Union. He asserted, for example, that moral dissolution had reached unprecedented depths at Magnitogorsk: the authorities banned the words "father," "mother," "son," "daughter," "brother," and "sister"; but they permitted incest.[22] However, in private Hitler acknowledged that "there is more that binds us to Bolshevism than separates us from it."[23] Fanaticism, so alien to bourgeois liberals, was what the two creeds had in common. Adherents abandoned their individual wills and shed their anomie. They found a collective identity and a common fulfilment in the Aryan race or the proletarian class—whose avatar was the quasi-divine leader. His word and his world-view became law.

Like Stalin, Hitler had his own reality to which everything had to conform, including supposedly objective circumstances. Thus the Third Reich insisted on "*völkisch* learning." This meant Gothic philology, and history as a Teutonic saga seen with "eyes of blood." But it also meant "Aryan biology," "Nordic physics" and "German mathematics." When scientists found that they could not do without the "Jewish" theory of relativity, they examined it "with a view to isolating the Aryan elements."[24] As the Rector of Freiburg University, philosopher Martin Heidegger, said in May 1933: "Not theses and ideas are the laws of your being. The Führer himself, and he alone, is Germany's reality and law today and in the future."[25] As in the Soviet Union, even chess came within the province of the State: one senior Nazi condemned Emanuel Lasker for having "by dint of low cunning, maintained himself as chess-champion of the world, thus, in true Liberalistic-Semitic fashion, depriving Nordic players of their legitimate rights."[26]

Hitler valued blood rather than brains. He despised the intelligentsia almost as much as the *"journaille"* (his term for journalistic *canaille*)[27] and even talked of eliminating them. So at every level education became indoctrination. Nazi day-nurseries used the prayer: "Führer, my Führer, my faith, my light."[28] Weimar school textbooks were pulped; teachers and pupils had to give the *"Heil Hitler"* salute at the beginning and end of each lesson; elaborate ceremonies were devised to fill juvenile minds with Nazi ardour; children were encouraged not to play "Cowboys and Indians" but "Aryans and Jews." By 1936 it was made compulsory for all adolescents, male and female, to join the Hitler Youth movement. About 15 per cent of the university professors and lecturers were dismissed and many others were victimised. Some wore Nazi uniforms and all were made to understand that their job was to teach official doctrine, not to determine truth. So, during the Third Reich, the great tradition of German scholarship was extinguished. The blinds were pulled down on the *Aufklärung*.

Art suffered a similar fate. Employing exactly the same arguments as Stalin, Goebbels declared that while artists should be free to create they must draw their inspiration from the people. This doctrine led to the proscription of "degenerate art" and the condemnation of those "poor unfortunates" who, as Hitler said, "feel meadows to be blue, the heavens green, clouds sulphur-yellow."[29] Hitler, the chocolate-box painter, yearned to sterilise the Cubists, Futurists and Dadaists of this world, none more odious than the "Propagandada"[30] George Grosz. Describing art as a public matter, with moral as well as aesthetic content, Goebbels arranged for it to be policed. In September 1933 he set up the Reich Chamber of Culture to superintend all artistic production. The Gestapo destroyed pictures by the likes of Oskar Kokoschka, who remained confident that his work would triumph over that of the Third Reich's "banal daubers."[31] Goebbels may have feared this too: at the exhibition of so-called "Junk Art" held in Munich in 1937 he employed actors to mingle with the crowds and pour scorn on the paintings.

In the same vein Musical Officers of Health tried to eradicate jazz and other "malignant growths of orgiastic dissonance."[32] Handel's *Judas Maccabaeus* was re-named *Wilhelm von Nassau*. The new arbiter of the theatre was failed playwright Hanns Johst, author of the famous boast that whenever he heard the word "culture" he wanted to reach for his gun. Like the theatre, literature was fatally impoverished by the exile of its greatest figures—Brecht, for example, left Germany the day after the Reichstag fire. The architecture of the Bauhaus was superseded by Ozymandian monuments in the style of bombastic neo-classicism dear to the Führer's heart. He was also fond of the cinema and on to its silver screen Goebbels was content to project fantasy. Propaganda had its place in selected films and newsreels. But most people regarded picture palaces (whose audiences quadrupled during the 1930s) as an escape from too much reality. Light entertainment was also the staple diet of radio, though loudspeakers in the streets made it hard not to hear Hitler's speeches. They set out the themes on which Nazi intellectual workers were forced to play a counterpoint after the crushing of an independent German culture. Like Stalin, Hitler aspired to national thought control. He aimed to put minds as well as bodies behind barbed wire.

YET for a totalitarian Hitler ruled Germany in a surprisingly anarchic manner. Ever the Bohemian, he avoided office routine—after Hindenburg's death he abandoned it altogether. He rose late, kept an erratic schedule and saw visitors according to whim. He spent several hours over a late lunch, talking inordinately but eating sparingly: he indulged himself only in the consumption of sweetmeats. Many were struck by the "extraordinary contrast" between Hitler's petty-bourgeois addiction to chocolate cake and "talk that revolved round death, revolt, gaol, murder, robbery."[33] The contrast was equally marked in Hitler's preference for sentimental cinema. Greta Garbo was his screen goddess and on most evenings he watched a romance, a comedy or a musical, often more than one, seeing his favourites (among them *King Kong*) over and over again. He also went to Bayreuth, where Wagner regularly reduced him to tears— behaviour which Hugh Walpole, when he had been obliged to share a box with this "curious tenth-rate fellow" in 1926, thought curable only by a few terms at an English public school.[34] These entertainments apart, Hitler's main recreation was architecture: he liked to sketch triumphal arches, concrete bunkers and monumental façades; he dreamed of constructing the largest hall in the world, 16 times the size of St. Peter's in Rome. (So jealous was he of its planned rival, the Congress Hall to honour Lenin in Moscow, that when the invasion of Russia began in 1941 Hitler remarked: "That puts paid once and for all to Stalin's building.")[35] He conducted evening business haphazardly, reading little but quizzing officials and filing away their answers in a prodigious memory. Mostly, though, he engaged in interminable monologues, reiterating familiar themes, reducing his coterie to a state of catatonic exhaustion and sometimes even droning himself to sleep. Talk, as Hitler's press chief Otto Dietrich said, "was the very element of his existence."[36]

The Führer was relatively austere in his domestic arrangements, living in a modest apartment on the first and second floors of the old Chancellery. But that austerity was tempered by his overweening architectural obsessions and a new Chancellery was designed by Albert Speer to reflect the might of the Third Reich. Similarly, Hitler's rustic retreat at Berchtesgaden, where he enjoyed relaxing at weekends in a light-blue Bavarian sports coat and a yellow tie, started as a simple, pine-panelled villa. The furniture, as Albert Speer recalled, was "bogus old-German peasant style and gave the house a comfortable petit-bourgeois look. A brass canary cage, a cactus, and a rubber plant intensified the impression." So did a clutter of knick-knacks and cushions embroidered with swastikas, sent to Hitler by admiring women. But Hitler soon transformed the Berghof, as it was called, into an uncomfortably elaborate chalet embellished with engraved silver, rich carpets, Gobelin tapestries, red Morocco leather chairs and mythopoeic paintings—he was fond of voluptuous female nudes. He installed large marble fireplaces for he loved staring into the flames. He also liked to gaze through the huge picture window in his 60-foot-long salon, across the awesome gulf to the Untersberg where, according to legend, Barbarossa slept, one day to rise and restore the glory of the German empire. From his lofty eminence Hitler soared to new heights of megalomania, proclaiming that here "my creative genius produces ideas which shake the world."[37] Yet, like any house-proud host, he came down to earth with a bump when the flower arrangements or the place-settings were not to his satisfaction.

Over more important matters Hitler was apt to procrastinate and change his mind. He operated by intuition, putting off decisions until the spirit moved him. A spasm of genius, he reckoned, was worth a lifetime of uninspired work. He despised orthodox functionaries, "dusty bureaucrats,"[38] "those [sleepy] Father Christmases at the Foreign Ministry,"[39] the military "saurians" in the Bendlerstrasse.[40] In theory Hitler insisted on centralisation according to the "Führer principle," yet in practice he added to officialdom. He set up and worked through competing authorities of his own, rather in the manner of Roosevelt. One historian has gone so far as to describe Hitler as in some respects a "weak dictator,"[41] not a view his victims would have shared. The Führer's technique was to let his subordinates fight among themselves and to act as "supreme arbiter,"[42] mesmerising them by his "hypnotic dilation of the eye."[43] Administrative chaos was inveterate because personal control was absolute.

Joachim von Ribbentrop, for example, was "spellbound" by the force of the Führer's personality; Hitler's "will was inflexible and the energy with which he pursued his aims unimaginable."[44] Field Marshal von Blomberg, the monocled Minister of Defence, said that a cordial handshake from the Führer could cure him of colds. Nazis less stupid than Ribbentrop (whom everyone except Hitler considered a nincompoop) and less compliant than Blomberg (who was nicknamed "the Rubber Lion") were equally overwhelmed. Göring, such a formidable character that he could dominate the war crimes tribunal at Nuremberg from the dock, was himself so dominated by Hitler that, as he said, the relationship "turned into downright mental prostitution for me."[45] Hjalmar Schacht never left Hitler's presence without feeling uplifted, even though he was independent-minded enough to criticise some Nazi policies towards the Jews and regarded himself as the "Economic Napoleon of the Twentieth Century."[46]

With his pince-nez, his stiff wing collars, starched shirts and striped trousers, Schacht was the model of the old-fashioned banker—which did not stop him denigrating Cordell Hull who, attired in his antique frock coat, "seemed to have stepped directly out of the era of Abraham Lincoln."[47] Another link with that era was Schacht's middle names, Horace Greeley, bestowed because his father, a clerk who briefly emigrated to America, so admired the famous editor. But Schacht shared none of Greeley's flamboyant idealism. He was a born opportunist, arrogant, clever and egotistical. First a publicist for bankers, then a banker himself, Schacht had emerged triumphantly from several financial scrapes to become the saviour of the mark after the great inflation. But in 1930, sensing the imminent collapse of the Weimar Republic, he had thrown in his lot with Hitler.

Although never a party member, Schacht raised large sums for the Nazis from his industrialist friends, as much as three million marks at a single meeting according to his own account. His reward was to be made (for the second time) President of the Reichsbank in 1933 and, the following year, Economics Minister. As it happened Hitler did not really trust this prim technician. Appearances were certainly against Schacht: "A tall, dry, spare, devil of a man, his features might have been hacked out by a billhook, and his long wrinkled neck was like the neck of a bird of prey."[48] But the Führer, who had no blueprint for saving Germany from the slump, hated anyone who tried to talk to him about economics, which should always, he insisted, be kept subservient to politics. Schacht took precisely the opposite line: "I am not a politician and I do not believe in politics," he once said. "Politics is what prevents progress."[49] Yet for the first three years of the supposed Nazi revolution Hitler gave almost complete control over German economic policy to this financial conservative.

It is true that Schacht's powers were carefully circumscribed. He had no say in matters of State like Germany's quitting the League of Nations and the Disarmament Conference in October 1933, a move which freed Hitler to rearm. He was not consulted about the signing of a non-aggression pact with Poland in January 1934, a tactic which, as the Polish dictator Marshal Pilsudski cynically but accurately observed, transformed his country "from Germany's *hors d'oeuvre* to her dessert."[50] Schacht was also made to understand that his overriding responsibility was "to *finance* rearmament in spite of the inherent dangers to the currency . . . out of nothing and furthermore under camouflage, [in order to make] a respect-commanding foreign policy possible."[51] Nevertheless Schacht was more responsible than anyone for pulling Germany out of the slough of Depression. Certainly he was helped by a fall in unemployment during the spring of 1933, which was due to a normal upswing in the business cycle—firms began to re-stock at a time when labour and raw materials were cheap. Also Germany had shed the burden of reparations and was embracing protectionism before the Nazis came to power in order to shield its economy from foreign competition. Furthermore Schacht was able to develop existing Weimar plans for creating work, especially through construction, electrification and road-building.

Schacht's real innovation, however, was the massive increase in State expenditure. Some of it went on subsidising agriculture and small business, though Schacht made no Keynesian attempt to stimulate demand for consumer goods—indeed, Germans were encouraged to save. Some of it financed a considerable growth in the Civil Service, which gave jobs to the Nazi boys at the cost of widespread bureaucratic confusion and corruption. But Schacht's main endeavour was to promote heavy industry, much of which was related to rearmament. Public investment doubled during Hitler's first year in power and it went on expanding at a dramatic rate. This was largely paid for with new credit notes called *Mefo* bills, accepted by government contractors and banks, earning four per cent interest and repayable after five years. Further "Schachtian devilries,"[52] as one economist dubbed them, were put forward in his New Plan of 1934. They included stringent import controls, disguised export subsidies, foreign exchange regulations and barter agreements with other countries—one of the more remarkable concerned the exchange of American copper plate for German water-lice, used to feed tropical fish. Additional trade manipulations, many of whose victims were vulnerable Balkan states, amounted to nothing short of fraud. Close supervision of the money markets ensured that private investment was directed towards big enterprises favoured by Hitler, such as engineering and synthetic oil and rubber production. In short, Schacht provided the tools to make the German military machine, the sinews of war.

As a result of all these efforts two million Germans found work within a year of Hitler's becoming Chancellor, and by 1936 the unemployment problem was virtually solved. This was the Führer's great achievement, one which magnified his popularity at home and his prestige abroad—the Governor of the Bank of England, Montagu Norman, for example, developed an "admiration and respect" for Hitler.[53] Although economic growth was uneven and levels of productivity were surprisingly low (facts obscured by rampant propaganda), under Hitler's aegis Germany recovered from the Depression more quickly and completely than any other country except Japan. Many concluded that the only cure for the Depression was totalitarianism, though of course many others considered that the remedy was worse than the disease. Most Germans, it must be said, were so grateful to Hitler for restoring a measure of national prosperity, not to mention national dignity, that they averted their gaze from the dark side of his rule.

That included not only the abominations of the concentration camps and anti-Semitism, which affected a minority—though they may, as Hitler thought, have given a thrill of excitement to the majority. It also involved the tightening of the State's grip on every individual. To avoid inflation Schacht needed high taxes, low wages and fixed prices, which the Führer was pleased to provide. So under the Third Reich living standards rose little, if at all, above the levels of 1929, though they were naturally an improvement on those of 1932. Admittedly alcohol consumption increased and signs proclaiming that "German Women do not Smoke"[54] were an inversion of the truth remarkable even by Nazi standards. But the quality of food eaten by the average citizen deteriorated. This was the era of *ersatz,* and Germans had their own wry jokes about it: margarine was known as "Hitler butter."[55] Following Stalin's example, the Führer further shackled workers. Dubbed "soldiers of labour,"[56] they were forbidden to change jobs without permission and severely punished for absenteeism. The employment of women was restricted and females were driven out of some professions in deference to the Nazi view that they should properly be concerned with children, church and kitchen. Just as procreation was officially encouraged, recreation was officially regimented. The "Strength through Joy" organisation supervised all sporting and leisure activities in the Nazi interest. Not only did the Depression enable Hitler to climb to power, it seemed to justify the establishment of a dictatorship which touched every sphere of German life.

THE most savage early assertion of Hitler's power, belying his claim that the Nazi revolution was bloodless, occurred on the "Night of the Long Knives." This purge was provoked by the SA, who felt cheated out of the spoils of the office which they had helped Hitler to win. Many of them wanted a second revolution; their aim was to establish a new order on the ruins of aristocratic privilege and bourgeois affluence. Many others wanted the three million Brownshirts to be incorporated into the German army as Mussolini's Blackshirts had been into that of Italy. In front of regular soldiers the SA sang: "The grey rock will be drowned in a sea of brown."[57] The Stormtroopers' leader, Ernst Röhm, was equally undiplomatic. Gross and coarse, his porcine face scarred by a war wound and his red nose bearing the marks of crude plastic surgery, Röhm looked like a hideous caricature of the *condottiere*. Famously homosexual, he picked his entourage for their looks and indulged in orgies which scandalised even Berlin. The shaven-headed Röhm was apparently bold enough to criticise the Führer himself, saying that Hitler was a ridiculous corporal, an " 'artist' . . . [who] wants to sit on a hilltop and pretend he's God."[58] Röhm liked his Stormtroopers to be radical—Berliners called them "beefsteaks" because so many were brown outside, Red inside. And he was "prepared to use force" to achieve the second revolution.[59] Yet he was a convinced Nazi as well as a brutal soldier of fortune and the height of his ambition was to become the head of Hitler's praetorian guard. Such pretensions were naturally anathema in the War Ministry, that monumental office on the Bendlerstrasse whose marbled halls and high-columned rooms were still the preserve of the Prussian Junker caste. The army's support would be vital to Hitler when the increasingly senile Hindenburg died, for the Führer planned to subsume the presidency into his own office. The price for that support was the scotching of Röhm's Stormtroopers.

The deal was not spelled out quite that blatantly; and the high command went to elaborate lengths to distance the army from this blood feud, which was after all a political matter. Moreover, Hitler himself vacillated; he had some sympathy for the radicalism of an old comrade like Röhm but remained suspicious that it represented a challenge to his authority. His suspicions were fanned by Röhm's rivals, notably Göring, who aspired to command the army himself, and Heinrich Himmler, who planned to expand his force of black-shirted Stormtroopers, the élite SS (*Schutzstaffeln*, or Protection Squad), which had started life as Hitler's bodyguard. This ambitious duo tried to convince Hitler that an SA uprising was imminent, and he may well have believed them. He may also have been influenced by Mussolini when they met for the first time at Venice in mid-June 1934.

On this occasion, it is usually said, the Duce, in his immaculate uniform complete with dagger and fez, upstaged the Führer, ill at ease in yellow mackintosh, grey felt hat and too-tight patent leather shoes. Actually, Hitler thought the Italian army ridiculous because, as the band played at too quick a pace, its troops did not so much march past as trot. The Italian navy astonished him, for where flags ought to have flown from the warship he inspected the sailors had hung out their washing. Still, as Mussolini moved the throng in St. Mark's Square to shrieking ecstasy, doctors and nurses standing by to succour those "overcome by emotion,"[60] there was no denying his charisma. The Führer's pilot had never seen "crowds so hypnotised by anyone, not even Hitler."[61] In private, Hitler said, the dictators "talked together like comrades,"[62] though the Duce complained that his guest had recited the whole of *Mein Kampf* from memory. But apparently Mussolini did urge Hitler to treat his internal opposition as he had treated Matteotti.

Still Hitler hesitated. On his return to Germany he kept out of Berlin. He posed wearing Tyrolean dress for photographers in Bavaria and inspected the Krupp steelworks in Essen, gazing with rapt intensity at torrents of molten metal cascading from fiery crucibles and flattened by gigantic power-hammers. But plans had been laid to eliminate the SA leadership and when, at the fashionable Hotel Dreesen in Bad Godesberg, Himmler presented Hitler with more "evidence" of Röhm's treachery the Führer screamed, "It's a putsch!"[63] Outside, over the Rhine, a thunderstorm raged. Inside, foaming and twitching, slapping the side of his boot with a rawhide whip and cursing Röhm, Hitler vowed to "settle that swine's hash" in person.[64] So, in the early hours of Saturday 30 June, he flew to Munich. Next to the pilot, Hitler stared into the darkness. As the dawn began to break Viktor Lutze, who sat among the Führer's entourage in the body of the Junkers 52 and would replace Röhm as head of the SA, hummed to himself:

> Red of the morning, red of the morning,
> Thou lightest us to early death.[65]

Meanwhile Röhm and his SA cronies had been enjoying a holiday at the attractive spa of Bad Wiessee on the Tegernsee. They had bathed naked in the beautiful lake, its limpid surface reflecting the wooden chalets, lush meadows and forested hillsides which made this Edwardian wateringplace so popular in the hot Bavarian summer. They had walked on the promenade and in the mountains, visited the *Schloss* and the rotunda, and drunk the sulphurous waters which were said to cure those afflicted with everything from heart disease to gout. At the Pension Hanselbauer leading Stormtroopers had also caroused late into the night, some disporting themselves with their catamites in a fashion which Goebbels, suddenly the puritan, would denounce as nauseating. All were fast asleep when Hitler, at the head of a convoy of SS men (some of them guards from Dachau) burst into the hotel at 6:30 A.M. and dragged the Brownshirts from their beds. Pistol in hand the Führer confronted Röhm, furiously accusing him of treason and (as one witness wrote) pacing up and down "with huge strides, fiery as some higher being, the very personification of justice."[66] The prisoners, Röhm wearing a blue suit and smoking a cigar, were bundled into a bus and taken to Stadelheim Prison in Munich. Then Hitler supervised the arrest of more SA functionaries arriving by train at the great grey municipal railway station. By 10:00 A.M. he was at the Brown House, where Goebbels sent a coded signal to Berlin—"Hummingbird."

On receipt of the signal Göring and Himmler widened the terror, sending out Gestapo and SS squads to settle scores not only with prominent Brownshirts but with older adversaries. In his palatial office on the Leipzigstrasse Göring strutted about "in a white military tunic and blue-grey military trousers, with high black boots that reached over his fat knees," his voice booming: "Shoot them . . . take a whole company . . . shoot them . . . shoot them at once!" So General von Schleicher and his wife were gunned down in their own house. Gregor Strasser, once Hitler's deputy and now his Trotsky, was shot in a cell at the Gestapo headquarters on Prinz Albrechtstrasse. Two of Papen's staff were murdered and he himself barely escaped with his life—which did not stop him from afterwards serving Hitler. Gustav von Kahr paid a hideous penalty for having opposed the Beer Hall Putsch in 1923: he was butchered with pickaxes. Several people were killed by mistake; a few intended victims escaped. Some SA men, loyal and uncomprehending to the last, were executed shouting *"Heil Hitler."* With a green pencil Hitler himself ticked names on his Munich death list, adding that of Röhm only later and with some reluctance. Then, having instructed the SA rank and file to take their orders from Lutze, he flew back to Berlin. His plane landed at Tempelhof airport in a livid sunset. The Führer disembarked, his white, puffy, unshaven face set off by the sombre tones of his clothes—brown shirt, black tie, brown leather coat, high black army boots. With "the gratuitously blood-red sky," it was, one official recalled, "like a scene out of Wagner."[67]

After a bath Hitler told a secretary, "Now I feel as clean as a newborn babe again."[68] The stains on his character were less easy to eradicate. All told, more than 100 people had been killed during the purge and, since Goebbels censored news of it, rumour vastly inflated the figure. Having concluded that he could not hush it up altogether, Hitler appeared before the Reichstag a fortnight later to broadcast his version of events. He lambasted the corruption of Röhm's circle and emphasised the threat which the Brownshirts had posed to the army, the Reich's sole arms-bearers. He asserted that an act of violence was the people's legitimate defence against revolution. And he declared in an extraordinary mixed metaphor: "I gave the order to shoot those who were the ringleaders in this treason, and I further gave the order to burn down to the raw flesh the ulcers of this poisoning of the wells in our domestic life."[69] Rising from their red plush seats in the brightly-lit Kroll Opera House, deputies greeted this admission of mass murder with wild acclaim.

Churchmen did not protest, and all over the country Germans were taken in by the "devil's masquerade."[70] Hitler seemed to have rescued them from the brown-shirted bullies and extortioners, preventing a vicious insurrection from below by a courageous *coup d'état* from above. He appeared to have dispensed "natural" justice, establishing a "pseudo-legal fiction of the Führer's charismatic authority."[71] He even gave the victims' families a State pension in a macabre effort to take the sting out of what some sardonically christened *"Reimowo"*[72]—short for *Reichmordwoche,* or "Reich murder week." At home, therefore, the Führer was not so much "admired" as "deified."[73] Abroad he was vilified. The world was shocked by the spectacle of a head of state "shooting down his former henchmen in the style of an American 'gangster.' " And Germany's neighbours trembled at this "foretaste of what they might have to expect if ever they were to fall under the domination of 'the Third Reich.' "[74]

They trembled still more a month later when Austrian Nazis shot their dictatorial Chancellor Engelbert Dollfuss during the course of an insurrection intended to achieve unification with Germany—*Anschluss.* This was one murder too many for Mussolini, with whom Dollfuss's family were staying at the time. He promised to support Austrian independence and moved troops to the border, forcing the Führer to disown his adherents in Vienna. The Duce, meanwhile, described Hitler as a "horrible sexual degenerate" and dilated on the superiority of Fascism over Nazism. Both were admittedly authoritarian, collectivist and anti-liberal. But his own creed was rooted in the great tradition of Italian culture, respecting religion, the family and the individual. By contrast National Socialism was "savage barbarism." Its chieftain was lord over the life and death of his people. "Murder and killing, loot and pillage and blackmail, are all it can produce."[75]

Such arguments, even if they had not been specious, would have made little impression on the German army, which supposed itself to be the main beneficiary of the Brownshirts' emasculation. In the Bendlerstrasse Röhm's demise had been celebrated with champagne. The soldiers, whose uniforms already bore the eagles and swastikas of National Socialism, had been accessories before the purge. Now they became "blood-brothers to the Nazis."[76] Hindenburg himself had congratulated Hitler for having nipped treason in the bud, apparently sending him a telegram which read: "He who wishes to make history must also be able to shed blood."[77] And when the aged President died in August 1934 Hitler exacted from the army a personal oath of loyalty and "unconditional obedience" to himself as Supreme Commander and "Führer of the German Reich and people."[78] This was a wholly new office, superseding the presidency. But the high command was unperturbed. It had connived at the breaking of law to assist in the making of order. The generals did not realise that they were inaugurating a tyranny without precedent, the supreme dictatorship of crime. This was too much even for the existentialist champion of crime, Jean Genet, who left Nazi Germany in disgust, concluding that to break the law in a state run by outlaws was to conform. To do evil in Hitler's realm "was to perform no singular action that might fulfil me," he complained; it was to "obey the customary order . . . The outrageous is impossible."[79] For the Third Reich and for the whole world, the Night of the Long Knives presaged a dark night of the soul.

THE defeat of the brown-shirted SA, which survived in weakened form, was a victory for the black-shirted SS, Hitler's supreme instrument of terror. As a reward for services rendered and as a deliberate counterweight to the Wehrmacht, Hitler made this crack corps independent, allowed it to form armed units, invested it with draconian police powers and gave it control over the entire network of concentration camps. So in place of the SA's heedless brutality came the systematic barbarism of the SS, barbarism planned with bureaucratic attention to detail and carried out on an industrial scale. The commander and virtual creator of this force, numbering 200,000 men by 1934 and destined to become almost a state within a state, was Heinrich Himmler. With his close-cropped hair, weak chin, sloping shoulders and podgy fingers, Himmler looked like a colourless functionary. Even in his all-black uniform, with its silver tabs, oak-leaf clusters and death's head insignia, he scarcely resembled a Nordic knight-errant. Indeed, the narrowed eyes behind a rimless pince-nez and the bowed lips ill-concealed by a Hitlerite moustache gave a faintly Mongolian slant to his appearance. But, like Stalin, this drear apparatchik was a personification of the banality of evil. Assisted by the reptilian Reinhard Heydrich, he created Hitler's OGPU. The SS, whose radiant symbol was the double lightning flash (a ⚡⚡ key was fitted to German typewriters), threatened to wreathe the entire world in night and fog.

Himmler's background was as prosaic as his personality. The son of a Bavarian schoolmaster, he appears from his "flat, virtually emotionless" adolescent diaries to have been an earnest, shy, conventional youth, unhealthy, inhibited about sex and pompous before his time.[80] Possessed to an extreme degree by the national passion for uniforms, he later claimed to have fought in the Great War, though in fact he was too young. But he did march with the anti-Bolshevik militias afterwards and, befriended by Röhm, he carried a Nazi banner during the Beer Hall Putsch. During the 1920s he contracted a marriage that proved unhappy and set up, unsuccessfully, as a poultry farmer. However, his hard work for the party was rewarded in 1929, when he was given command of the SS. During these years Himmler's devotion to Hitler was absolute: he clicked his heels when answering his master on the telephone and was sometimes seen in rapt communion with a picture of the Führer on his office wall. Himmler was both crank and clerk, visionary and pedant.

The SS, combining spurious mysticism with organised murder, reflected its author's character. Sometimes its members were known as the Nazi Jesuits. Certainly Himmler, who had been brought up a Roman Catholic though he was later to call for the Pope's public execution, admired the black-cassocked society's discipline. The Führer even went so far as to call him "our Ignatius de Loyola."[81] But Himmler also drew inspiration, in fashioning his élite, from the myths of King Arthur and the sagas of the Teutonic Knights. He developed an SS code of honour, including rules for duelling and committing suicide. As well as oath-taking ceremonies for initiates, he evolved a series of pseudo-chivalric, neo-pagan rituals to be performed in his medieval castle at Wewelsburg in the mountain forests of Westphalia. Here 12 senior SS paladins would sit round Himmler's massive oaken table in high-backed, pigskin-covered chairs inscribed with their occupants' names on silver plates and engage in something like a secular séance. Himmler apparently believed that he had the power to summon up the spirits of the dead and he seems at times to have regarded himself as the reincarnation of one of them, the Dark Age German King, Henry the Fowler.

Himmler also dabbled in astrology, mesmerism and homoeopathy. He favoured herbal remedies—every concentration camp perforce had its herbal garden. He also foisted his food fads on subordinates, urging the saving properties of porridge, mineral water and wild mare's milk. Above all Himmler insisted on the redemptive quality of blood, blood generated on German soil. This magic fluid he invoked with solemn incantation: "Only good blood, blood which history has proved to be leading and creative and the foundation of every state and of all military activities, only Nordic blood, can be considered." So Himmler recruited the "purest" possible specimens of the master-race, who were permitted to marry only their female counterparts. However, what these bogus notions of biological supremacy chiefly spawned was a sanguinary contempt for lesser breeds, "the offal of criminals and freaks . . . [with] slave-like souls."[82] These "sub-humans" were fit only for the concentration and extermination camps. It was in the organisation of these "mills of death"[83] that Himmler really fulfilled himself. Here was his proper memorial, for here the bloodless bureaucrat united with the bloodthirsty fantasist to produce an unprecedented apparatus of mass murder.

The first concentration camp proper, run by the SS, was established in March 1933 around a derelict explosives factory at Dachau near Munich. In fact Dachau, the largest of its kind, became the generic name and the model for all camps during the 1930s. At first the 2,000 or so prisoners were housed in bare concrete huts once occupied by the munitions workers. These were ringed by a wall, barbed wire, machine-guns on watchtowers and a high-voltage electric fence. But in 1937 the inmates, at this stage mostly political prisoners leavened with Jews, constructed an elaborate new camp as well as comfortable living quarters for the SS guards nearby. This camp contained bunk-filled barracks, showers, kitchens, stores, workshops, punishment cells, an infirmary and a smart red-brick crematorium. Its main gate bore the legend *"Arbeit Macht Frei"*—Labour Brings Liberty. Actually labour, all done at double time, brought torment, and the only motto fit for this hell on earth was "Abandon hope, all ye who enter here." For at Dachau men like Rudolf Hoess, who was to be Commandant of Auschwitz, and Adolf Eichmann, who later "boasted of five million murders,"[84] served their apprenticeship. Here the soul of Nazism was first made manifest.

The most diabolical cruelty was a psychological one. The SS tried to break the spirit of inmates by refusing to disclose the length of their "preventive detention," the euphemism for arbitrary imprisonment. This policy engendered what the Deputy Commandant happily called "a sort of prison psychosis."[85] The guards next sought to dehumanise their charges by a regime of unbridled savagery. Theodor Eicke, who became Commandant in June 1933 and went on (after shooting Röhm) to superintend all the camps for Himmler, was high priest of the "cult of severity." Himself the former inmate of a lunatic asylum as well as a prison, Eicke practised "hate indoctrination," telling the guards at Dachau: "Behind the wire lurks the enemy . . . show the enemy your teeth."[86] To toughen up his own men and to grind down the prisoners, he prescribed a formal programme of "floggings, solitary confinement and executions for infractions of the rules."[87] The programme became even more repressive inside the darkened punishment block, described by one inmate as "a veritable chamber of horrors run by sadistic maniacs."[88] But, penalised for pity and promoted for ferocity, members of the Death's Head units which ran the concentration camps found countless unofficial ways to terrorise the prisoners.

From the moment of their arrival, suffocatingly crammed into cattle trucks, detainees were "kept conscious that they were hunted beasts, without any rights whatever." All had to run the gauntlet of bawling SS guards who gave them an early taste of the jackboot, the rifle butt and the whip. Subsequent formalities included a filthy bath, the shaving of heads and the distribution of prison clothes, often grotesquely ill-fitting. In Dachau these were at first a motley, perhaps dungarees, or white linen garb, or even green frock coats, the old uniforms of the Prussian police. Later prisoners wore standard cotton jackets and trousers with vertical grey and blue stripes, aged leather boots or clogs and caps (though Jews, whose religion ordained head covering, were denied hats). In due course this dress was marked with a kaleidoscope of insignia to classify the prisoners—yellow stars for Jews, red triangles for political offenders, pink ones for homosexuals, brown for Gypsies, purple for Jehovah's Witnesses, green for criminals, black for "shiftless elements." Then followed roll-call, a terrible ordeal which sometimes lasted long into the night, when men collapsed and died under the blinding beams of the searchlights.

Life in Dachau, one inmate wrote, was "more brutal, more savage, more sadistically bloody than anything we had ever imagined."[89] Punctuated by blasts on the siren, it was a round of unbroken toil and ceaseless harassment. Some prisoners were literally worked to death. The weak in body or mind were especially victimised because they were regarded as "useless lives." The old might be deprived of blankets in winter so that they could die a "natural death."[90] Other prisoners were "shot while trying to escape," a phrase frequently used to disguise straightforward murder.[91] Still others were beaten, bullied or punished so viciously that they never recovered. Bespectacled intellectuals were a particular target of the guards, themselves mainly of working-class and peasant stock. Jews were ritually humiliated and made to sing anti-Semitic songs. When 20 Catholics attended a Mass in 1933 SS men forced them to spit in one another's faces and lick the spittle away. Even able-bodied inhabitants of this "gigantic torture chamber"[92] found it, on less than 1,000 calories a day, hard to stay alive. Most quickly lost a third of their body weight and their hair and nails almost ceased to grow. Potemkin meals were served to them when visitors appeared, but the prisoners' ashen faces, sunken cheeks and skeletal frames (a stark contrast to the sleek guard dogs) should have exposed the deception.

In fact the SS was able to obscure, if not entirely to conceal, the truth about camp conditions. These were shrouded in the "strictest secrecy." Inside Germany it was more than his life was worth for a released prisoner to expose the reality. Only a few foreign observers were admitted to the camps and then under close supervision. So in April 1933 one journalist reported that, "Life in Dachau seems to be halfway between that of a severely disciplined regiment and that of a hard-labour prison." A few months later another noted the inadequate diet and the "tortured looks on [prisoners'] faces, which ranged all the way from rage and bitterness to bewildered helplessness." Yet he remained convinced that Eicke "sincerely believed" his task to be "pedagogic rather than punitive."[93] The dread realities did begin to emerge over the next few years, as valiant efforts were made to smuggle out information, including "photographs taken illegally in Dachau."[94] At home rumours spawned the rhyme:

> Please, Lord, make me dumb
> So I won't to Dachau come.

Abroad witnesses reported terrible experiences.[95] Yet there was a common reluctance to face the reality.

In 1934 *The Times* commissioned its Munich "stringer" to write a "series of articles" on Dachau, a difficult and dangerous assignment, and then failed to print them.[96] As late as September 1936 the *New York Times* could suggest that "milder treatment" was now the rule inside Dachau, whereas at that very moment the new Commandant, Hans Loritz, was demonstrating what harshness really meant—the prisoners nicknamed him Nero. As with Russia, where the Gulag may have held as many as 2 million prisoners (in 1933) compared to 25,000 in Nazi camps, the waters were sufficiently muddied to enable people to interpret the evidence in the light of their prejudices. In view of previous atrocity propaganda it seemed reasonable to remain sceptical about lurid stories emerging from the civilisation of Schiller, Goethe and Beethoven. In fact, subjected to such incredible brutality, the prisoners themselves were apt to doubt the evidence of their senses and to conclude that it was all an "evil dream." Arriving "like cattle . . . at a slaughter house" and greeted with bestial violence, one of a group of detainees at Dachau wrote: "It was actually happening, yet it was impossible; such things simply could not happen."[97]

Hitler believed that terrorism was "absolutely indispensable . . . [to] the founding of a new power." The Bolsheviks understood that. But in his opinion they went too far. He himself preferred to use the old ruling class rather than to exterminate it. "Too much frightfulness," he said, "produces apathy."[98] Just enough compelled obedience. There were many signs that the climate of violence and murder engendered by the Nazis was changing German society. A piquant one was the new-found psychological health of the caste of official executioners, who sloughed off the disorders which had previously plagued them and felt a "new pride and confidence in their work."[99] Now, however, in the aftermath of Röhm's destruction and Hindenburg's death, the Führer aimed not only to coerce but to inspire.

THE Nuremberg Rally of September 1934 was the most spectacular hitherto mounted: the shrine of German romantics became the stage of Nazi fanatics. Nuremberg was transformed into a theatre of power, beside which the British coronation was a mere pantomime of pomp. The city's medieval alleys were filled with hosts of uniformed men. Forests of swastika banners obscured the carved gables. Baroque lamp-posts were festooned with loudspeakers. Gothic squares rang to the strains of martial music. At the Catholic hospice a picture of Hitler shared a candle with a portrait of the Virgin Mary. Nearby, in the enormous grassy (later granite) arenas where the faithful would parade, huge stands had been erected. Behind the speaker's rostrum at the Luitpold Stadium were flagpoles 130 feet high and flanking it were massive towers topped by stone eagles, each with a wing-span of 23 feet, built in sections at a film studio.

The whole extravaganza was, in fact, captured on celluloid by 18 cameramen working under the direction of Leni Riefenstahl. Her brilliant and repulsive documentary *Triumph of the Will* (a title selected by Hitler) elevated propaganda into an art form. Scenes were rehearsed and, on occasion, re-enacted in the studio. To heighten the drama the order of events was changed. And Leni Riefenstahl employed novel techniques—wide-angle shots, telescopic lenses, aerial photography. To film night parades, when spotlights would have spoiled the effect of the blazing torches, she distributed magnesium flares to bystanders—though the acrid smoke almost asphyxiated the guests of honour. Other devices were crude but powerful. As critics have often noted, the famous opening sequence—"a bold visual passage from darkness to light"[100] in which Hitler descends from the clouds, his plane casting the shadow of a cross over marching Stormtroopers—is heavy with messianic symbolism. Yet the atmosphere really was charged with religious fervour. The expression in the eyes of Hitler's disciples reminded the journalist William Shirer of Holy Rollers he had seen in Louisiana. The Führer's secret, Shirer reckoned, was that he had restored "pageantry and colour and mysticism to the drab lives of twentieth-century Germans."[101] At Nuremberg Hitler tried to inspire the devotion of the people by presenting himself as the incarnation of their destiny. The rally thus became a mixture of epiphany and mummery, the greatest sound and light show on earth.

Hitler was greeted with church bells and bugle fanfares. He was serenaded by massed bands and he made his entries and exits to the strains of the catchy "Badenweiler March." Nuremberg throbbed to the tramp of goose-stepping columns: Brownshirts, Blackshirts, soldiers, Hitler Youth, even the Labour Corps, with polished spades glinting in the sunshine. The city echoed to the delirious chant of *"Ein Volk, ein Reich, ein Führer."* Muffled drums rolled as Hitler, flanked by Himmler and Lutze, marched down the aisle between tens of thousands of silent Stormtroopers to lay a wreath at the war memorial in Luitpold Stadium. It was, as a witness to a later rally noted, "a superbly arranged gesture. Those men represented individualism as against the solid anonymity of the massed Brownshirts; they stood for leadership as against the blind obedience of the people."[102] At intervals between the parades, salutes, military manoeuvres, gymnastic performances, firework displays and other rituals, Hitler addressed the multitude. He announced the advent of the "Thousand-Year Reich."[103] He attacked Jewish intellectualism. He threatened to annihilate his enemies. But he said that with the passing of Röhm the black cloud over the movement had dispersed and that the party had never been more strongly united. He declared that Germany had a God-given mission and wanted peace.

The climax of the rally occurred at the Zeppelin Field on 7 September. Hitler's peroration came as darkness fell and the whole arena was then lit by 130 anti-aircraft searchlights shining vertically into the sky. Their beams formed what Albert Speer called the "first luminescent architecture," vast columns supporting the blue dome of a gigantic "cathedral of light."[104] The glow could be seen nearly 100 miles away, in Frankfurt. What remained hidden, as the party choreographers had planned, were the paunches of the 21,000 standard-bearers; for the klieg lights focussed on the swastika flags crowned with eagles as they were marched in ten columns through the ranks of nearly half a million Nazis to the floodlit grandstand. After an oath-taking ceremony Hitler drove slowly back through the thronged and cheering streets of Nuremberg at the head of a torchlight procession. Bonfires blazed on the hilltops and the parade "looked like a river of molten, bubbling lava which slowly finds its way through the valleys of the city."[105]

Goebbels later attributed Nazi triumphs to the "ritual of great party occasions" which had enabled him to foster the Führer cult and bestow on Hitler "the halo of infallibility."[106] In fact most Germans, though they gave Hitler credit for restoring national fortunes, probably did not succumb to the power of mass suggestion. There was strong subliminal resistance even to the most fundamental Nazi dogmas—jokers defined an Aryan as the "hind quarters of a prolet-aryan."[107] But some Germans were half-convinced, possessing genuine faith in Hitler while knowing it to be groundless: Ambassador André François-Poncet declared that "in no other race was sincerity so allied to mendacity."[108] Moreover, many people really did worship the Führer. Typically they confessed their creed in quite straightforward terms: "My belief is that our Leader, Adolf Hitler, was given by fate to the German nation as our Saviour, bringing light into darkness."[109] Attending the Passion Play at Oberammergau, the American Ambassador found that Hitler was identified with Jesus and Röhm with Judas—the only character played by a Jew.

At Nuremberg, too, doxology alternated with demonology: Hitler chose the next rally, in September 1935, to promulgate the infamous laws depriving Jews of citizenship and civil rights. To protect "German Blood and German Honour,"[110] the Nuremberg Decrees also prohibited them from marrying Aryans. Foreign opinion was outraged by this "cold pogrom." "There has never been anything quite like it in the history of the world," expostulated Lord Beaverbrook's *Sunday Express*.

> The physical excesses of 1933 continue. Jews are still murdered in the concentration camps; they are still beaten in the streets, and are still paraded through the towns with defamatory placards round their necks. But from this week-end the screw tightens ... There is nothing [German Jews] can do except run round helplessly in circles until they die.[111]

Hitler was indifferent to such sentiments. The announcement of the Nuremberg laws was a sign of sublime self-confidence, for the year between these two rallies had been one of almost unalloyed success for the Führer.

Admittedly there were still economic difficulties, but this did not worry

Hitler, who believed that it was enough to abolish *"the feeling of hardship"* by stimulating faith in the *Volk*.[112] That certainly seemed an effective strategy in January 1935, when the inhabitants of the Saar, the coal-rich region detached from Germany at Versailles, voted to return by an overwhelming majority. Hitler thereupon renounced German claims to Alsace and Lorraine, taking the sting out of French resentment and concealing a real advance by a rhetorical retreat. This was one of his prime diplomatic techniques and it frequently wrong-footed the other European powers. In March he responded to the announcement of British and French defence plans, themselves a reaction to his own rearmament, by instituting conscription, with the declared intention of creating an army of over 500,000 men. He also confirmed the existence of a German air force which, he mendaciously told Sir John Simon, was equal to that of Britain. Once again the Führer issued a verbal smokescreen. In a conciliatory speech he stressed Germany's wish for peace and exploited the guilt which nagged its former enemies over the Carthaginian peace. Faced with the repudiation of Versailles, Britain and France first dithered and then reached an accord with Italy at Stresa.

Hitler demolished it with ease. Playing on pacifist pressures in Britain and the desperate wish of its government to inveigle Germany into some sort of arms limitation framework, he negotiated an Anglo-German naval agreement. Its provisions, restricting German strength to 35 per cent of Britain's surface fleet (but allowing parity in submarines), hampered his programme of naval expansion not at all. Instead, the signing of this agreement ended the period of isolation which Germany had suffered following its withdrawal from the League, marked the "first triumph" of Nazi diplomacy,[113] and provided Hitler with the happiest day of his life. As it happened that day, 18 June 1935, was the anniversary of the battle of Waterloo—a piece of British tactlessness towards the French on a par with their giving General de Gaulle, when he fled to London in 1940, an office in Waterloo Place, off Trafalgar Square. The fact was that France had not been consulted about the naval agreement and felt betrayed by it. Admittedly France had just embraced its old ally, the Russian bear, now outrageously metamorphosed by what Winston Churchill called "the baboonery of Bolshevism."[114] But Britain had jeopardised the security of both democracies by permitting a challenge to its own Maginot Line—the fleet. Britain had sanctioned the violation of Versailles. It had split the "Stresa Front." And it had attempted to dignify weakness as a policy of appeasement. Mussolini for one was not deceived.

The Duce was already planning to star in the next act of the global drama, during which Italy would vanquish Ethiopia. As a preliminary he

studied the composition of Britain's population, discovering that it contained a preponderance of females and that 12 million Britons were more
than 50 years old, over "the age limit for bellicosity."[115] This confirmed his
view that Albion was inclined to passivity as well as perfidy. Any warnings
its decadent diplomats or effete politicians gave about African adventurism—and their silence at Stresa he interpreted as acquiescence—could be
ignored. France, too, could be discounted. It was preoccupied with Germany and in return for Italy's support at home Laval had secretly and
ambiguously given Mussolini a "free hand"[116] in Ethiopia. Germany did
not yet represent a military threat and Mussolini probably wanted to make
his grab for Africa before Hitler grew strong enough to make his for Austria. The Duce, who had not forgotten the murder of Dollfuss, was still
alienated from the Führer. Their encounter in Venice the previous year
had not been a meeting, he said, but a "collision." Hitler was a barbarian
and his racial theories were pernicious nonsense. By the canons of Nordic
purity, Mussolini pointed out, the Lapps would have to be honoured as
the highest type of humanity. But as the democracies hardened against
Italy's plans for colonial conquest Mussolini had cause to be grateful for
Germany's benevolent neutrality. Hitler, for his part, was intent on sustaining the authoritarian system of government. After all, Mussolini was
the "spiritual leader of the Nazi movement"[117] and an alliance between the
two systems was perfectly natural. So, as the clouds of war gathered over
Ethiopia, the Nazi-Fascist Axis was adumbrated in Europe. As one witness
to the formation of this brutal friendship observed, Hitler had cast Mussolini in the role of "partner in his own Satanic revolution."[118]

XIII

MUSSOLINI'S ABYSSINIAN ADVENTURE

MUSSOLINI had long dreamed of setting the "Dark Continent" alight. As a youth he had been shocked by the Ethiopian victory over the Italians at Adowa in 1896, when the Emperor Menelik administered the most devastating rebuff ever suffered by a European power in Africa. The figures—"ten thousand dead and seventy-two cannon lost"—hammered in Mussolini's head for years afterwards.[1] Like D'Annunzio, he regarded this disaster as a "shameful scar,"[2] a stigma on the Italian body politic that could only be washed away with blood. Revenge would be sweet, righting a cosmic wrong whereby black savages had defeated the forces of white civilisation. Revenge would also be compensation, in the shape of the last independent African country, for the meagre pickings Italy had obtained at Versailles. An empire would bring dignity to the State, virility to the regime and glory to the Duce. As it was, Italy had only a few tattered colonies, Eritrea and Italian Somaliland, Libya and the Dodecanese, which bore no comparison to the splendid possessions of Britain and France. Mussolini felt the hurt deeply. Only an imperial power could be great, Mussolini considered, and as early as 1932 he laid out four large relief maps in the Via del Impero showing how Rome had once embraced territory stretching from Hadrian's Wall to the first cataract of the Nile, from Parthia to the Pillars of Hercules. Aggression was the fulfilment of Fascism, in Mussolini's view, the proof that it had not become as decadent as the democracies, and Italian newspapers soon began to laud "the poetry of hatred and the beneficent hygiene of war."[3] Finally African conquest would be a Roman triumph worthy of Augustus, a dazzling monument to Mussolini's personal prestige.

These were the visceral motives inspiring him to embark on what King Victor Emmanuel was to call "the greatest colonial war in history."[4] But Mussolini was also prompted by more immediate considerations. In 1932, when he secretly commissioned General Emilio De Bono to prepare for the Abyssinian adventure, the Duce was preoccupied by the Depression.

Faced with the example of Libya, Italy's largest colony, which repaid only a tithe of what it cost to have and to hold, he could hardly hope that a conquered Ethiopia[5] would come to his rescue economically. Poor, remote and landlocked, Ethiopia could by no means fulfil the classic role of a colony—to be a source of raw materials and a market for manufactured goods. On the other hand, in an era of protectionism Italians could easily be persuaded of the advantages of having an exclusive economic domain in Ethiopia, just as the Japanese had been convinced about Manchuria. Mussolini, indeed, resented the flourishing Japanese trade with Ethiopia and scotched a royal dynastic marriage which would have strengthened this Afro-Asian axis.

Furthermore he had every incentive to divert the attention of Italians from the parlous state of their own country by reviving their long-felt fascination for the "lure of Africa."[6] He appreciated the possibilities of channelling internal frustration into external violence. He saw the chance of mobilising patriots behind the regime and he reckoned that militant nationalism could invigorate moribund Fascism. In 1932 he declared that Fascism carried "the anti-pacifist attitude into the life of the individual. 'I don't give a damn'—the proud motto of the fighting squads . . . sums up a doctrine which is not merely political: it is evidence of a fighting spirit which accepts all risks."[7] Mussolini visualised that Ethiopia would provide living-space for a population he was encouraging to expand and which could no longer find an outlet in the United States. He may also have hoped to relieve unemployment by his call to arms and men. At any rate many Italians saw an escape from the rigours of the Depression in the fertile cotton-growing regions of Gojjam and Jimma, among the rich coffee plantations of Kaffa and Sidamo, amid the gold and platinum of Yubdo and Birbir. Even well-informed outsiders believed Ethiopia to be "an Eldorado and Canaan combined."[8] Fascists sang:

> Hard-working warrior people who
> Follow your leader, Mussolini,
> He will open up the way for you,
> You shall have bread for your bambini.[9]

Mussolini did not put it quite like that, though he was clearly anxious that a people so beset by hardship might knock him off his pedestal. When he began to prepare them for their new imperial role, in 1934, he spoke of Italy's civilising mission. With transparently disingenuous emphasis he rejected the idea of "territorial conquests" while embracing that of "natural expansion," in the course of which Italy would help Africa to progress from its primitive state.[10] Yet in 1922, despite its frankly-expressed concerns about spreading the collective security blanket over part of Africa, which would therefore be taboo for colonial conquest, Italy had supported Ethiopia's admittance to the League of Nations. Indeed, it had done so in the face of Britain's protest that a nation tolerating slavery was unworthy of membership—a protest that lost some of its force when it emerged that His Majesty's Ambassador in Addis Ababa had several slaves on his domestic staff. Moreover, when the Crown Prince and future Emperor of Ethiopia, Ras Tafari Makonnen (otherwise known by his baptismal name, Haile Selassie, which means "Power of the Trinity"), visited Europe a couple of years later he had been greeted more cordially in Italy than anywhere else.

A tiny figure, only five feet four inches tall, Ras Tafari made up in dignity what he lacked in stature. As one of his American advisers put it, "he invariably looked out upon the world as from an inner eminence."[11] Aloof, arrogant, austere, he modelled his public behaviour on that of the Emperor Hirohito. Even abroad he acted like a deity receiving homage, preserving an Olympian calm not least in the face of racist slights. Most foreigners were struck, however, by the refinement of Ras Tafari's appearance: close-cropped curly hair, high brown forehead, trim crisp beard, long hawkish nose and large black eyes which alone betrayed his moods, sparkling with humour, glittering with disdain, suffused with melancholy. Though he spoke jerkily in a low, grating voice and his minute, exquisitely-shaped hands sometimes toyed with a jewelled ring or a gold fountain pen, Ras Tafari possessed the imperial gift of immobility. In the words of the journalist George Steer, he appeared "at all times, even in the middle of war, completely detached and poised above the mêlée, pursuing his quiet, rather delicate and well-dressed life without noting overmuch the noise which surrounded him."[12]

What went on behind this impassive exterior was a mystery. Ras Tafari had learned French from his tutor and imbibed more than a smattering of Western culture at mission school. But his most formative experiences had been in securing the succession to an empire where the norm was intrigue, murder and civil strife. He understood something of the modern world, favoured progressive schemes including the building of model prisons and was the first Ethiopian to fly. But he stemmed from the legendary world of Prester John, dispensed medieval punishments such as mutilation and identified himself with a people who believed that war-planes could be made to crash by spells. He encouraged the introduction of modern medicine but took precautions to protect his family from witchcraft. Dressed in a black, gold-embroidered silk cloak, white suit and solar topi, and carrying an elegant ebony walking-stick, he went to church in his red Rolls-

Royce like an English gentleman. Clad in a spangled toque, embroidered robes and ornate sandals, he also presided over feasts at which squatting warriors quaffed *tej* (mead) from drinking horns and gorged on raw meat, which they hacked with their daggers from the bleeding carcasses of oxen carried in on poles by slaves.

On his much-publicised European tour in 1924, Ras Tafari was evidently considered an exotic barbarian. Noting that his bowler hat and shiny, elastic-sided boots comported uneasily with a white *shamma* (toga) and jodhpur-like pantaloons, English newspapers asserted that the alien ruler took a particularly keen interest in the instruments of torture and execution at the Tower of London. After Matteotti's murder but before his corpse was found, a Roman periodical printed a cartoon of Ras Tafari whispering to the Chief of Police: "You can tell me in all confidence, did you eat him?"[13] However, in Britain the Crown Prince encountered marked official coolness, despite bringing gifts of lions for George V. The King disliked "nigger" rulers[14]—he scandalised the Foreign Office by maintaining that the social events of Ascot week had priority over his duties as a host and offered Ras Tafari the minimum of courtesy. By contrast Victor Emmanuel gave him a warm welcome and talked of strengthening the friendship between their two countries. Mussolini sought to impress the visitor with a theatrical performance and Ras Tafari was indeed struck by his "powerful face, his enormous eyes, his projecting jaw, his voice with its always changing inflections."[15] The Duce's monstrous geniality did not disguise his inveterate rapacity, and the Crown Prince was to reject his pressing offers of economic "help." Nevertheless, Mussolini reiterated Italian amity in the formal accord of 1928, which he confirmed as late as September 1934.

By that time, however, Mussolini feared that Ras Tafari was putting Ethiopia so firmly on the map that it might prove impossible to remove. In 1930 he had been crowned Emperor Haile Selassie I, Elect of God, Lion of Judah, King of Zion—he traced his ancestry back to King Solomon and the Queen of Sheba. The coronation, modelled on that of George V which had so impressed the Emperor's father, focussed the world's attention on this romantic corner of Africa. Twelve states sent representatives and the travel agent Thomas Cook advertised a tour to Addis Ababa. In practice Ethiopian pageantry left something to be desired: though the crown, royal vestments and regalia were newly made for the occasion, the Imperial Bodyguard wore khaki uniforms imported from Belgium as well as busbies made in England from the manes of African lions, and eight Austrian horses (the largest in the world) pulled a State coach once owned by the German Kaiser. The coronation, held in the candle-lit, incense-filled dimness of St. George's Cathedral, was a miasma of monotonous chanting and arcane ritual. Other ceremonies seemed to be a mixture of *The Arabian Nights* and *Alice in Wonderland*. The Emperor appeared and disappeared like a cross between Haroun al Raschid and the White Rabbit, protected by machine-guns and a crimson silk parasol decorated with sequins and gold tassels. The parades were a muddle of competing bands and conflicting gyrations. At one pantomime of valour native warriors boasted of their martial feats at Adowa—luckily the Italian representative, the Prince of Udine, did not understand Amharic. The firework display ended almost before it began in a single pyrotechnical explosion. All this gave scope for mockery from the likes of Evelyn Waugh. Blackly mischievous, he refused to see in Ethiopia anything more than a travesty of white civilisation mummed by outlandish natives, many of whom were "still primarily homicidal in their interests."[16]

Waugh's view that the Ethiopians were savages was sustained, curiously enough, by one of his bitterest critics, the explorer Wilfred Thesiger, who also witnessed the coronation. He was offended at the time by Waugh's grey suede shoes, floppy bow-tie and Oxford bags, and still more offended subsequently by his satire. For Thesiger regarded Ethiopians as noble savages, all the better for being relatively uncontaminated by the West. Ever since childhood, which he had spent at the British Legation—his father was ambassador—Thesiger had cherished nostalgic memories of Addis Ababa:

> The smell of rancid butter, of red peppers and burning cow dung that permeated the town; the packs of savage dogs that roamed the streets and whose howling rose and fell through the night; an occasional corpse hanging on the gallows-tree; beggars who had lost a hand or foot for theft; debtors and creditors wandering round chained together; strings of donkeys bringing in firewood; caravans of mules; the crowded market where men and women squatted on the ground, selling earthen pots, lengths of cloths, skins, cartridges, bars of salt, silver ornaments, heaps of grain, vegetables, beer—all this combined to create a scene and an atmosphere unlike any other in the world.[17]

Thesiger's romantic attachment to this part of Africa was unusual—he even characterised the Danakil tribesmen as cheerful, happy and hospitable, despite their penchant for killing and castrating unwary visitors, and wearing their victims' testicles on their wrists.

Nearly all outsiders judged Ethiopia by their own standards of technical achievement. So they were unimpressed by Addis Ababa, despite its sparkling upland atmosphere and its impressive position under the shadow of Mount Entoto. It was a sprawling shantytown of corrugated-iron-roofed bungalows and conical *tukuls* (thatched huts) with manure-coloured walls, all set about with grey-green eucalyptus trees—the Emperor Menelik had imported them from Australia because they grew fast and provided ample firewood, thus obviating the need for a nomadic village-capital. At Haile Selassie's coronation efforts had been made to smarten up the place: beggars and lepers were banished, the slums were hidden by whitewashed fences, a few roads were covered in asphalt and papier-mâché triumphal arches were erected. But nothing could conceal the fact that Addis Ababa, which means "New Flower," did not live up to its name. It had no sewage system—household refuse was thrown into the streets to be picked over by vultures, jackals and hyenas. Disease was rife, especially tuberculosis, leprosy and syphilis—the many prostitutes marked their dwellings with red crosses until the Emperor forbade it in response to protests from the International Red Cross. The best hotel, the red-roofed, grey-fronted Imperial, had no running water; its electricity supply was erratic and its bedroom walls were made of muslin. Even the paved roads were an obstacle course, full of loungers, priests, mendicants, wayfarers, camel trains, herds of bleating sheep, and chiefs who never moved without their tails of retainers. Whistling traffic police in pith helmets, blue tunics, white knee breeches and khaki puttees failed to keep order despite their hippopotamus-hide whips. Slowly the triumphal arches, which were surmounted with lions and crowns, crumbled. Yet for all its ramshackle squalor, Addis Ababa was 500 years ahead of the rest of the country, which was still a conglomeration of mountain fiefdoms in a desert wilderness. "Conditions here are appalling," wrote a European doctor. "The country is way back in the 15th century—ruled over by feudal lords."[18]

Nevertheless the Duce had reason to fear that the Emperor was transforming Ethiopia from a prospective colony into a modern nation. Haile Selassie set a personal example which impressed all visitors. He moved out of Menelik's old palace, known as the Great Gebbi. This was a jumble of pavilions which, with their lion mascots and wrought-iron balconies, looked as though they should be gracing the end of a pier. Apparently Haile Selassie felt uncomfortable in the home of his predecessors, though he did enjoy spying on the inhabitants of the city through a great naval telescope which he set up in one of the turrets. The vast blue banqueting hall, brightened only by the glitter of gold plate and the glorious embroidered silk fabric on which the Emperor reclined at meals, was too gloomy. The throne room, with its dark red walls, thick Persian carpets, gilded chairs and crystal candelabras, was too reminiscent of the court of an old-fashioned Oriental potentate.

Instead Haile Selassie built himself a new grey stone palace, called the

Little Gebbi, modelled on Lord Noel-Buxton's mansion in Norfolk which he had visited in 1924. It was lit by electricity and furnished by the Oxford Street firm of Waring & Gillow. It contained not lions but lapdogs: the royal beasts, whose roaring competed with the sound of drums at night, were kept in cages along the drive, while cocker spaniels, a gift from the Duke of Abruzzi, roamed the house. The rooms were airy and the dark wood was highly polished by imposing servants in red and green liveries, knee breeches and buckled, patent leather shoes—a European-style uniform designed for the Emperor by his Swedish military adviser General Virgin. The drawing-room mantelpiece was crammed with signed photographs of white royalty. In the dining-room there were chairs of blue leather for guests and red leather for the imperial couple. At the flick of a switch the throne room turned into a cinema. Like the Little Gebbi itself, the Emperor's hospitality was thoroughly sophisticated—gold-lettered menus, French cooking, fine wines and impeccable service. Standards were kept up to the mark by strict domestic discipline: a waiter who dropped a silver spoon was clapped in irons. Still, as one guest remarked, there was little to indicate that one was not in Mayfair but in "the heart of darkest Africa."

The same man observed that in all other spheres Haile Selassie had, since his European tour, "determined that his empire should emerge from the darkness of the centuries into the light of civilisation."[19] Progress, admittedly slow, was evident. In an effort to bind together a nation of 12 million people divided by countless tribal loyalties, 70 different languages and an archipelago of bare table-mountains slashed by deep, jungle-choked valleys, communications were improved. Already, a railway, used by the formidable "Rhinoceros Express," snaked up from the port of Djibouti in French Somaliland. Now more roads were built, including rough links from the capital to Dessye and Jimma. The postal service was improved, though in many places it still relied on men carrying letters in cleft sticks. The telegraph was extended, as was the primitive telephone system, though connections remained so bad that Ethiopians blew down the mouthpiece as though to clear the line. Wireless stations were established—radio was known as "the wind telephone."[20] Airfields were constructed and a few old planes were acquired. Schools and hospitals sprang up, though in pitifully small numbers. A Boy Scout movement was begun. More European advisers were imported, including Belgian officers who tried to turn warriors into soldiers.

The Emperor sold concessions to foreign companies that wanted to develop Ethiopia's resources, making himself a tidy fortune in the process, much of which he devoted to the common weal. In a land where the currency included bullets, bottles and ivory, he founded the Bank of Ethiopia (though he lodged his own balances abroad). He tried to abolish internal tariffs and because, as a primary producer, Ethiopia was so hurt by the Depression, he fostered trade with Japan, which could supply, say, cotton goods 80 per cent more cheaply than could the United States. He made sporadic efforts to eradicate slavery, though he was reluctant to attack a vested interest in which the Church and the aristocracy had such a large stake. Indeed, he was generally a conservative reformer, explaining to a visiting Frenchman:

> I believe European influence to be salutary and, in assimilating it thoroughly, my people can become strong, strong enough to follow the path of progress on their own. But you see, my country is like the Palace of the Sleeping Beauty, where time has stood still for 2,000 years. Minute precautions must therefore be taken when waking from this prolonged slumber . . . On the one hand I must resist the impatience of Western reformers and, on the other, the inertia of my people, who would shut their eyes if the light were too strong.[21]

There was, at any rate, no question about Ethiopians being ready for democracy. The new constitution, based on that of Japan, emphasised the sacred person of the Emperor, his inviolate dignity, his incontestable power. Haile Selassie resisted the slightest dilution of that power. Sometimes he personally supervised the repairing of roads and his permission was needed to buy firewood outside Addis Ababa market. As a close relation remarked, Haile Selassie was "one of the few rulers who can say with truth, 'L'Etat, c'est moi!'"[22] At the Emperor's parliament, whose members he appointed, the only person with the right to speak was . . . the Emperor.

Naturally Mussolini did not regard this arrangement as a sign of backwardness: rather it suggested that Ethiopia was becoming a cohesive, authoritarian state. As such it might in the long run threaten Eritrea and Italian Somaliland. Haile Selassie had already been nicknamed the "Black Napoleon."[23] Responding to Italian provocation, he announced that he was the emperor of all blacks, especially those enslaved by whites—which coloured official British attitudes towards him just as it delighted supporters of Marcus Garvey's campaign to win "Africa for the Africans."[24] In the short run a centralised, modernised Ethiopia might be able to resist an Italian assault. As the Emperor himself would observe: "Italy never ceased to look jealously at any act of civilization that was being carried out in Ethiopia."[25] Ethiopian progress combined with German rearmament to convince Mussolini that he should act swiftly. Time was working against him. The Duce had to enhance Italy's great-power status before the Führer grew strong enough to swallow Austria—it seemed probable that the *Anschluss,* on which Hitler was plainly bent, would lead to a direct confrontation between Italy and Germany in the Tyrol. Mussolini prepared his attack throughout 1934, making bellicose speeches, building up his forces, approving the construction of roads, railways, aerodromes, hospitals and water installations in Eritrea. The Emperor retaliated with protests and proverbs—he quoted King Solomon to the effect that "The wise man turns his tongue seven times in his mouth before speaking."[26] He imported what arms he could obtain and afford, concealing them in boxes marked "pianos" or "wire nails." He also appealed to Hitler, requesting chemical as well as conventional weapons: the Führer, anxious to keep Mussolini busy with a sideshow, secretly sent an encouraging reply as well as a quantity of rifles and machine-guns. Haile Selassie complained that he had to spend on munitions what he had saved for hospitals. But when asked whether he feared defeat by Mussolini he again conjured with his ancestors, recalling how David had defeated Goliath.

As the tension mounted, border incidents multiplied. On 5 December 1934 a serious clash occurred at Wal Wal in the Ogaden desert, on the disputed frontier between Ethiopia and Italian Somaliland. Actually, as the embarrassed Italians discovered, even their own maps showed that this group of wells was 60 miles inside Ethiopian territory. Nevertheless the Duce treated the skirmish as a *casus belli* and issued a virtual ultimatum. The Emperor appealed to the League of Nations, which he seemed to look on as a kind of fetish. On 30 December Mussolini drafted a secret directive calling for war, anticipating the use of an aerial armada which would deploy chemical weapons and ordering the "total conquest" of Ethiopia.[27] While the Emperor sought salvation from Geneva, the Duce pursued the more profitable course of ensuring the neutrality of the two powers which dominated the League.

In January 1935 the French Foreign Minister Pierre Laval came to Rome. He established a solid rapport with Mussolini, who later said that Laval was the only Frenchman for whom he had any regard. Both men were plebeian, crafty and unscrupulous, and Laval further endeared himself to the Duce by not caring a fig for Ethiopia. Indeed, until the Wal Wal incident he had apparently not known where that country was and he expressed astonishment that it was a member of the League of Nations. When a delegate mentioned its capital, the name seemed new to Laval: *"A-hé-ba. Que c'est chic, ça. A-bé-ba."*[28] At any rate, the French Minister was eager to follow the Quai d'Orsay's policy of giving Mussolini *carte blanche* in Ethiopia if there was something in it for him. There was: an agreement of mutual support directed against Germany in Europe and concessions to France in

Africa. As part of the deal, Mussolini would abandon his claims in Tunisia, where 100,000 of his countrymen had settled, while Laval was to hand over French territory adjoining the Italian colonies of Libya and Eritrea. This territory, Mussolini protested during the negotiations, was worthless. "I'm not a collector of deserts . . . I sent Marshal Balbo to take photographs of the areas you are prepared to cede to us. I have them here for you. They are lunar landscapes." "All the same," said Laval, alluding to a couple of oases, "there are two towns." "Two towns!" exclaimed Mussolini. "Of course," added Laval, "I'm not saying they are on a par with Rome or Aubervilliers." Mussolini was amused and the way was open for them, like two Mafia bosses carving up criminal territories, to reach an agreement over Ethiopia. What form it took and how it was signified— whether by nod or wink or Gallic shrug—is not known. But it was clear that France would not stand in the way of Italy's impending conquest. When a colleague asked if Mussolini had made any secret demands, Laval replied: "No . . . poor Abyssinia!"[29]

Neutralising Britain, where even the most flagrant practitioners of *Realpolitik* must always cling to the fig-leaf of morality, proved to be altogether more problematic. The Foreign Office understood Mussolini's plans for Ethiopia despite the reports of their ambassador in Rome, Sir Eric Drummond, who was peculiarly obtuse even by diplomatic standards. As late as February 1935, at the very time when Mussolini was telling his commander in Eritrea, General Emilio de Bono, that if the Emperor "should have no intention of attacking us we ourselves must take the initiative,"[30] Drummond assured his masters in Whitehall that the Italians had "no aggressive intentions" but were "genuinely afraid of overwhelming Abyssinian attack."[31] Even after he realised his mistake Drummond, who came to "love Fascism,"[32] according to the Duce's son-in-law Count Ciano, barely protested. Indeed, the Foreign Office rebuked him for feebleness. Yet the British government, though anxious to prevent an attack on Ethiopia which would outrage domestic public opinion and demolish the League of Nations, was itself eager to placate Mussolini. Like France, Britain aimed to use Italy as a counter against Germany. This was the object of Ramsay MacDonald and Laval when they met Mussolini at the Stresa Conference in April 1935. It was held at the Borromeo Palace on Isola Bella in Lake Maggiore. There, in the Music Room, a lofty chamber full of Renaissance paintings and Florentine mosaics, MacDonald and his Foreign Secretary, Sir John Simon, sitting on chairs covered with ancient Genoese velvet at a table draped in gold brocade, deliberately ignored the question of Ethiopia. Perhaps they hoped that it would go away. "These feeble creatures can't give us any serious trouble," Mussolini observed sardonically. "I expect the Abyssinians caught them young."³³ The impression that the British leaders were political eunuchs was confirmed when they quickly abandoned the spirit of Stresa for the chimera of the Anglo-German naval agreement.

Anyway, growing daily more bellicose, Mussolini was not long content that the Ethiopian matter should be passed over in silence. He pressed for positive acquiescence. The Foreign Office riposted drily that too much mental agility was required to blame Ethiopia for the current threat to peace. The Duce vented his wrath on the British Ambassador: the situation was intolerable; the Ethiopians were cannibals; his expensive preparations were nearly complete and could not be abandoned; going to war was his "will" and his "destiny."³⁴ Drummond, who failed to prevent his Italian servants from reading embassy documents, thus giving Mussolini (and Stalin, to whom the secrets were also sold) a priceless diplomatic advantage, advocated concession. The new Foreign Secretary, Sir Samuel Hoare, memorably dubbed by F. E. Smith "the last in a long line of maiden aunts," agreed. So did some made of sterner stuff: Churchill, for example, who was obsessed by the menace of a rearmed Germany and accepted the conclusion of a government report (later leaked by Mussolini) that no vital British interests were at stake in Ethiopia. Accordingly the suave, patrician Minister of League of Nations Affairs, Anthony Eden, was dispatched to Rome in an effort to buy off Mussolini with territory in the Ogaden—another desert. Haile Selassie, who would be compensated with a corridor to the port of Zeila in British Somaliland, was not consulted about his impending loss of territory. Mussolini was not satisfied with a settlement which gave him less than "everything, including the head of the Emperor."³⁵ Eden's mission was therefore abortive, though rumours that he quarrelled with the Duce seem ill-founded. Nevertheless, Mussolini did behave boorishly—"jaw thrust out, eyes rolling and popping, figure strutting and attitudinizing"³⁶—and Eden gave the impression that he thought "Wogs begin at Calais."³⁷ After their meeting the Duce remarked, "I never saw a better-dressed fool."³⁸

Relations between Britain and Italy now deteriorated sharply. In an impromptu speech, delivered to his black-shirted troops from the back of a truck at Eboli, Mussolini promised that they would conquer the whole of Abyssinia and that "we shall snap our fingers in the faces of the blond defenders of the black race."³⁹ What was particularly infuriating was British hypocrisy. Having swallowed the camel of Manchuria, they were straining at the gnat of Abyssinia. Holding incomparable colonial possessions themselves, they condemned Mussolini for wanting to occupy the last remaining place in the sun. "I think for Italy," he declared, "as the great Englishmen who have made the British Empire have thought for England."⁴⁰ This was fair comment. Yet already the tide of empire was turning. Colonies were becoming anachronisms, though Britons such as Winston Churchill, who even after the rape of Ethiopia called Mussolini "the Roman genius,"⁴¹ refused to admit it. Not until 1948 did Churchill acknowledge that "Mussolini's designs on Abyssinia were unsuited to the ethics of the twentieth century. They belonged to those dark ages when white men felt themselves entitled to conquer yellow, brown, black or red men, and subjugate them by superior strength and weapons."⁴²

Mussolini felt that, on the contrary, he was engaging in a heroic Darwinian struggle for the promotion of human progress. Speaking in anguished, strangled tones, the Duce warned Sir Eric Drummond that if there was any interference in what Fate had decreed he might in desperation make war on England. The British government, led once again by Stanley Baldwin (who was anxious to keep out of the Ethiopian business and did not want anything to interfere with his summer holiday), allowed itself to be intimidated by this absurd threat. The ill-prepared Admiralty in particular feared a "mad-dog act,"⁴³ perhaps to be undertaken by a group of young Italian aviators who styled themselves the "Suicide Club" and vowed to descend on British ships as living torches. Mussolini, by contrast, was not at all apprehensive when, in September 1935, Sir Samuel Hoare nailed his colours to the League of Nations' mast. In what was hailed as "the most impressive speech ever heard in Geneva"⁴⁴—even the white-gloved policeman on duty clapped—Hoare declared that his country was totally committed to the principle of collective resistance to acts of unprovoked aggression. Needless to say, collective resistance was a pipedream, which gave Britain every excuse not to take the lead. So, in a series of humiliating tugs, the Foreign Secretary tore down his brave banner. Knowing that Britain had ruled out any sanctions likely to be effective— such as closing the Suez Canal—Mussolini could ignore the European democracies just as he ignored isolationist America. (Cordell Hull uttered cautious admonitions in public but privately asked the Italian Ambassador why the Duce had not just bought Ethiopia.) The fact was that every British velleity, like every Papal equivocation, made Mussolini look more decisive. Brushing aside warnings from the army's Chief of Staff, General Pietro Badoglio, that he was leading the country to catastrophe, Mussolini hurled defiance at his enemies.

IN mid-afternoon on 2 October 1935 church bells and factory sirens summoned Italians to the squares of their towns and cities, where loudspeakers would broadcast the Duce's message to the nation. Millions gathered, many wearing uniforms, in one of the greatest manifestations of mass enthusiasm of the Fascist era. In Rome tens of thousands choked the streets leading to the Piazza Venezia, gathering beneath Mussolini's beflagged balcony and darkening the white marble steps of Victor Emmanuel II's monument. At dusk, under a leaden sky, the Duce made a dramatic appearance on his tiny spotlit stage. He stood there, a lonely, black-uniformed figure against the huge medieval wall, its crenellated battlements illuminated by flares. For 18 minutes he ranted, gestured and grimaced, his voice hoarse with emotion. Italy had been patient for too long, he cried; now she would take her place in the sun. The crowds responded predictably to this paean of devastation, stamping, cheering, waving banners and shouting, *"Duce! Duce! Duce!"*[45] But soon they began to disperse and it was apparent that Mussolini's inflammatory words had achieved only a temporary combustion. Through irresolution and ineptitude the British government had strengthened Mussolini's hand, uniting Italians behind him, alienating them from the League, reconciling them to closer relations with Germany and failing to prevent aggression against Ethiopia. Even so, Italy was at first less than enthusiastic about the war.

The next day, as the rainy season dribbled to its close in the horn of Africa, Mussolini's legions crossed the shallow, muddy Mareb River which marked the border between Eritrea and Ethiopia. Tongues of light pierced the dawn sky from searchlights behind their lines. Aircraft hovered overhead and artillery fired occasional warning shots into the bush. A hundred thousand troops, vanguard of nearly half a million, advanced in three columns on a broad front. They were preceded by native cavalry led by white officers, whose horses, according to a recent decree from Rome, all had to bear Italian names. Light Fiat-Ansaldo tanks also screened them and, supremely confident, the marching men sang "Little Black Face" and picked yellow flowers as the sun rose. They were a motley array, ranging from regular divisions to volunteer brigades, from fair, pith-helmeted north Italians to black, bare-footed Eritreans. Most flamboyant were the Blackshirts with their long beards and short carbines, their death's head and thunderbolt badges, their knives, war cries and mottoes—"The Life of Heroes Begins after Death."[46] Bringing up the dusty rear were big guns and immense convoys—American trucks, versatile Fiat cars known as "Mules," strings of four-legged mules—carrying everything from food and ammunition to a million freshly minted Maria Theresa silver dollars for bribing the Ethiopian chiefs. Almost entirely unopposed, this martial millipede crawled into the Tigrean foothills, inching its way towards the geographical fortress of Ethiopia, "a terrain of crag and precipice, where

Nature seems to have lost her temper with the landscape."[47] Keeping his troops supplied over such lines of communication was, as De Bono sagely informed Mussolini, "a task which would make even a bald-headed man's hair stand on end."[48]

This was partly because the Duce, determined that the mistakes of Adowa should not be repeated, had invested so much in the largest expeditionary force ever engaged in a colonial campaign. The port of Massawa could handle only 3,000 tons a day and ships queued, rusting offshore, for up to 6 months before unloading their cargoes, half of which comprised of timber to build barracks. De Bono soon worked out, perhaps by a proleptic process of lateral thinking, that it was cheaper and easier to use tents. As this suggests, the aged cavalryman was anything but a Napoleon. More Fascist than fighter, he had been mixed up in Matteotti's murder and had played the tyrant in Libya—though his yoke was easy compared to that of General Rodolfo "Butcher" Graziani, commander of Mussolini's southern forces, which were massing in Italian Somaliland. Although he posed as a champion of civilisation and proclaimed the abolition of slavery, De Bono showed within a few days of opening hostilities that he had no scruples about bombing Ethiopian women and children: "Do they expect that we'll drop confetti?"[49] But he was frugal with the lives of his own men. They nicknamed him "Little Beard," while he addressed officers as "dear ones" and men as "children." Mussolini, who believed that glory would only be won by bloodshed, kept urging him forward. The Duce now spent all his time in uniform poring over maps (though he never noticed when all the flags were inadvertently moved) and sometimes sent his commander more than 100 urgent telegrams a day. But it was as much as De Bono could do to take bombed and unresisting Adowa, site of Menelik's victory, and to occupy the sometime seat of the Queen of Sheba—the holy city of Axum, whose giant sandstone pillars were shipped back to Rome. Now the General was intimidated by a successful Ethiopian ambush. He was haunted by the chimera of a British attack from the Sudan—in fact all the Italians received from that quarter, despite sanctions, was monthly convoys of wheat. He became bogged down by transport difficulties. While De Bono stuck in Tigre the Duce fumed in Rome.

In Addis Ababa the Emperor coolly continued to direct a chaotic mobilisation. It had been signalled on 3 October with the beating of Menelik's war-drum in the courtyard of the Great Gebbi. The ceremonial crooked club struck the taut lion-skin in a series of loud single beats like the tolling of a bell. Silken flags in the national colours—green, yellow and red—were unfurled before an excited crowd of warriors, journalists and spectators. As the palace guards tried to control the throng, civil and military dignitaries appeared. Standing on a wooden chair, the Court Chamberlain proclaimed a holy struggle against the invaders and called Ethiopians to arms. There was wild applause, a flourishing of weapons and a dash to see the Emperor, who was on the balcony of the north tower. Silencing the shouts and the war cries, he urged them not to attack the Italians *en masse* but to strike ferociously in small numbers and melt back into the mountains. However, as the Emperor later acknowledged, his subjects were too wedded to their traditions of valour to fight like brigands. They preferred cold steel to bullets, pitched battles to guerrilla warfare. Unable to control his janissaries, Haile Selassie could only dispatch them to the front.

They swarmed like a feudal host, some with spears and swords, others with antique rifles and colourful bandoliers. They lacked almost everything a modern army needs. They had no supplies save what they and their camp followers could carry—mainly bags of millet. They had no medical services apart from a few Red Cross volunteers in tents which the Italians eventually bombed. They had no war-planes, hardly any artillery and little mechanised ground support. They had no proper communications and since their code was never changed the Italians could decipher the few wireless messages that were sent. The Ethiopians had no coherent strategy and no fixed chain of command. All they had was a common purpose and boundless courage.

Mussolini feared that this might be enough. In November 1935 he replaced the cautious De Bono with the now pugnacious Badoglio. Square-headed and thick-set, he was Italy's most famous military hero. Though involved in two colossal defeats, Adowa and Caporetto, Badoglio had masterminded victory over the Austrians at Vittorio Veneto. An ardent monarchist, he had begged for a battalion of Royal Carabinieri to sweep the Blackshirt rabble from the streets in 1922. However, he had made his peace with Mussolini and, despite earlier doubts, had resolved to back the war in Ethiopia. Dapper in dress and courteous in manner, Badoglio aped the style of the officer caste. But at heart he remained what he had always been, a Piedmontese peasant. He was fond of *boccia* (a game of bowls). He spoke little and smiled less. He was earthy, primitive, brutal, bent on mustering all the force at his command to crush the barbarous foe.

While Badoglio made dispositions Mussolini made threats. He himself was not seriously menaced by the League's initial sanctions. They included, as Lloyd George said, "elaborate arrangements to deprive Italy of those things she could do without."[50] The League banned the import of mules and camels, for example, but not cars and lorries. Indeed, the Duce benefited from such feeble opposition, posing as the dauntless national champion and glorying in his role as leader of *"Italia contra mundum."*[51] Although able to purchase strategic supplies from the Soviet Union and elsewhere, he conjured with notions of a siege economy. He ordered offices to shut early in order to save fuel, banned the sale of meat on two days a week and even (like Stalin) promoted the breeding of rabbits. However, Mussolini did fear the imposition of an oil embargo and warned that this would be an act of war to which he would retaliate even at the cost of his own destruction. Ostentatiously keeping a revolver on his desk, Mussolini convinced timid diplomats that he was "capable at any moment of an act of suicidal but disastrous folly."[52] So, in December 1935, Britain and France made another attempt to buy him off. Having assured his Chelsea constituents a month before that the government was not trying to "do a disreputable deal" behind the League's back,[53] Hoare hurried off to Paris after the general election and agreed on a peace plan with Laval. Its main stipulation was that about two-thirds of Ethiopia would be ceded to Italy and that in return Haile Selassie would receive an outlet to the sea. When this proposal was prematurely leaked to the press, there was a storm of indignation in France and a cyclone of public fury in Britain. Laval lost Herriot's support and his hold on power. Hoare was forced to resign, though his successor, Anthony Eden, had been almost as heavily implicated in the plan and had urged that Haile Selassie should give it "favourable consideration."[54]

In the event, both belligerents rejected it. But for Mussolini the abortive plan was a glittering triumph. Hoare and Laval had divided and discredited the European democracies. They had undermined the League and the policy of collective security. They had legitimised Fascist aggression by seeking to reward it. It was with more than usual plausibility that the Duce could declare, when inaugurating the new town of Pontinia on 18 December:

> The war which we have begun on African soil is a war of civilisation and liberation. It is a war of the people. The Italian people feels it as its own. It is the war of the poor, of the disinherited, of the proletariat. Against us are ranged the forces of conservatism, of selfishness, and of hypocrisy. We have taken on a hard fight against these forces. We shall continue this fight to the end.[55]

The rhetoric may have been catchpenny but Italians backed it with gold. On the same day they participated in one of the most successful ceremonies ever dreamed up by the Fascists—the donation of wedding rings to the war effort.

The statuesque Queen Elena, unkindly said to be twice the size of the pocket monarch she had married, initiated this "Day of Faith." Shortly before 9:00 A.M. she entered the crowded Piazza Venezia, where she was greeted by Party Secretary Starace, supreme architect of pageants. Huddled against the rain squalls in a trilby-style hat, fox-fur wrap and long black velvet coat, she mounted the broad white steps of the massive Victor Emmanuel monument, which was guarded by young Fascists. She threw her own ring and her husband's into one of three smoking bronze urns—the suggestion being that the metal was melted down for instant use. Then she was given two dark steel bands, each inscribed with the motto "Gold to the Fatherland," which were blessed by Monsignor Bartolomasi. The Queen next laid a wreath on the Tomb of the Unknown Soldier and, holding a lighted taper, delivered a short speech which was broadcast to the nation. In a low, clear voice, which at times trembled with emotion, she said:

> In ascending to the Sacrarium of the Altar of the Fatherland, together with the proud mothers and wives of our dear Italy, to lay on the Altar of the Unknown Warrior the wedding ring, symbol of our first joys, and of the greatest renunciations, as the purest offering of devotion to the Fatherland, bowing ourselves down to the earth as if to commune in spirit with our glorious sons who fell in the Great War [here she gave a Fascist salute which was imitated by all present], we invoke together with them before God, "Victory." Young sons of Italy, who are defending her sacred rights and are opening new paths for the brilliant march of the Fatherland, we wish that you may bring about the triumph of Roman civilization in the Africa which you have redeemed.

The crowd cheered ecstatically: "Long live the Queen," "Long live the House of Savoy."[56] Led by Rachele Mussolini, 250,000 Romans followed the royal example. Mostly women, all wearing black, some in fur coats but many in tattered clothes and hatless, they queued for hours to pay their solemn tribute. In Milan, in Naples, in Trieste, all over the country the same patriotic scene was acted out. Correctly interpreting the Pope's Delphic utterances as tacit support for the Catholic "colonisers of Africa,"[57] clergy gave their gold crosses and chains. Jews surrendered their own holy artifacts, including the gold key of the ark of the law from their synagogue in Rome. Pirandello handed over his Nobel Prize gold medal. Old opponents of Fascism were reconciled and even Benedetto Croce contributed his senatorial emblem. When Prince Doria's Scottish wife refused to give up her ring, she was assaulted; it became difficult to wear anything but a band of steel. Some of those were doubtless acquired in exchange for cheap rings bought for the occasion—jewellers' shops were stripped of their stock. But most donors made a heartfelt sacrifice and it was hard thereafter to convince them that it was vain.

Meanwhile Haile Selassie's horde had begun to grapple with the cohorts of Badoglio. Early piecemeal assaults proved damaging only to the Italian attackers and the Ethiopians perpetrated appalling atrocities on those who fell into their hands. Though generally ill-led, these warriors showed Spartan contempt for danger, braving bombs and shells, throwing themselves bodily at machine-guns, fighting tanks as though tanks were wild animals. "It was an incredible spectacle," said Haile Selassie, "men in flimsy cotton *shammas* attacking these steel monsters with their bare hands."[58] After suffering several setbacks Badoglio retaliated with poison gas—a weapon which other colonial powers such as Britain, France and Spain had used against "primitive" people during the 1920s.[59] He employed it on a large scale for the first time just before Christmas, initially in bombs, subsequently in spray pumped from aeroplanes. Falling in caustic yellow droplets, the lethal mist had a ghastly impact on barefoot, semi-naked Ethiopians. One Red Cross worker recorded:

> The patients were a shocking sight. The first I examined, an old man, sat moaning on the ground, rocking himself to and fro, completely wrapped in a cloth. When I approached he slowly rose and drew aside his cloak. He looked as if someone had tried to skin him, clumsily; he had been horribly burned by "mustard gas" all over the face, the back and the arms. There were many others like him: some more, some less severely affected; some newly burned, others older, their sores already caked with thick brown scabs, men and women alike, all horribly disfigured, and little children, too. And many blinded by the stuff, with blurred crimson apologies for eyes.[60]

The gas scorched earth and contaminated water. It ravaged villages, poisoned livestock and corroded Ethiopia's will to resist. One of the Emperor's best commanders, Ras Imru, later wrote: "I was completely stunned . . . I didn't know how to fight this terrible rain that burned and killed."[61] Probably its effect was more demoralising than devastating, though according to one contemporary estimate 250,000 Ethiopians were killed or wounded by this chemical scourge. Badoglio, who imposed such strict censorship that some correspondents simply packed up and went home, suppressed news of it. When victims of poison gas were produced, Italian newspapers declared that they were suffering from leprosy. So, like much in the 1930s, Mussolini's war crime was well known but unknown, clear as Ethiopia's blue sky but shrouded in a sulphurous haze. Even before hostilities began, Evelyn Waugh could confidently anticipate Italian policy towards the Abyssinians: "i hope the organmen gas them to buggery [*sic*]."[62] During the conflict the British government, for one, received "overwhelming" evidence that the Italians were using gas, including reports from its own envoys and even a sample of the poison.[63] Yet when the war was nearly over, Lord Halifax professed himself unable to confirm the many well-authenticated reports "so vitally affecting the honour of a great country."[64] Needless to say, Mussolini's resort to poison gas was not just dishonourable, it demolished all his claims to white superiority. The Emperor made this point trenchantly on 1 January 1936, when protesting against the use of the weapon: "Italy proceeds on her barbarous course with impunity and, according to her own profession, in the name of civilisation."

Aircraft were more responsible than gas for bringing Badoglio victory, though their employment involved similar moral obliquity. Rejoicing in their mastery of the skies, many pilots treated the war as a sport. Mussolini's sons, Vittorio and Bruno, were notorious in this respect. Vittorio boasted, "Over the radio we kept getting information, almost like hunting bulletins: 'There's a beautiful covey of fat doves at Castel Porciano.'" He waxed lyrical about the joy of killing his prey. "I still have in mind the spectacle of a little group [of Ethiopian cavalry] . . . blooming like a rose when some of my fragmentation bombs fell in their midst. It was great fun and you could hit them easily."[65] He was equally diverted by setting fire to Ethiopian villages, though his brother-in-law, Galeazzo Ciano, commander of the *Disperata* Squadron, was less easy to please. He complained that the *tukuls* were so flimsy that they gave no satisfaction to his bombardiers. Living, literally and metaphorically, on a heightened plane, some airmen manifested an apocalyptic fervour worthy of D'Annunzio. "When I saw the bombs fall," wrote Federico Valli, "I wanted to fling my heart after them." Others were shaken by the destruction they wrought, the agony inflicted by gas, the swathes of men mown down by strafing, the carnage caused when waves of Caproni bombers dropped high explosive on massed Ethiopians, "who bent double and clapped their hands over their ears as if they had been caught in a heavy hail storm." Occasionally the Italians experienced a frisson of danger aloft, when their foes retaliated with scattered machine-guns and Oerlikon anti-aircraft guns—the latter sometimes fired by the Emperor himself, though there is no record that he hit anything. Still, downed airmen could expect little mercy, which contributed to their sense of being engaged in "a heroic struggle, a sublime game with death."[66]

Aircraft could spot the foe, hamper his movements, damage his formations and impair his morale; but Badoglio knew that the war had to be

won on the ground. Luckily for him, the Emperor's orders about mass
assaults were disobeyed. During January 1936 large Ethiopian forces commanded by his cousin Ras Kassa attempted to overwhelm the Italian centre, at Tembien, by sheer weight of numbers. Badoglio recorded,

> Against the organized fire of our defending troops, their soldiers—many
> of them armed only with cold steel—attacked again and again, in com-
> pact phalanxes, pushing right up to our wire entanglements, which they
> tried to beat down with their curved scimitars.

Afterwards the Italian commander professed contempt for Ras Kassa: "no
gleam of an idea of manoeuvre flashed upon him."[67] But at the time
Badoglio was seriously worried by this pitiless assault, which nearly cut his
line in two. "In spite of our heavy fire," wrote a soldier to the mayor of his
native village in Lombardy, "the enemy came to within about six yards of
our machine guns."[68] Badoglio's Blackshirts fought poorly compared to
his blacks and he had to bring in regular reinforcements as well as airborne
supplies. In the event, valour was not enough to win the Ethiopians victory and the battlefield was strewn with their dead.

Having halted this advance, Badoglio himself went on to the offensive.
In order to move southwards he had to overwhelm the great stone sentinel
of Amba Aradam. This was a flat-topped mountain honeycombed with
caves, crevices and chasms, and rendered almost impregnable by its pre-
cipitousness and its natural zariba of brambles and thorny acacia. It was
garrisoned by the flower of Haile Selassie's army under the command
of his grizzled Minister of War, Ras Mulugueta. The hawk-eyed hero of
Adowa, who had killed more men with the sword than any living
Ethiopian, knew nothing of modern warfare. Mulugueta's certainties were
his rhino-hide shield and his silver-tipped spear. On his own men he
imposed a ferocious discipline, enforced by cruel punishments, and even
when sober he would sometimes speak harshly to the Emperor himself.
Mulugueta hated foreigners as much as he loved women; but his approach
to both was crude and, at 70, he was too old to adopt new techniques. In
February Badoglio subjected the Ethiopians' rugged fastness to the most
intensive aerial bombardment ever seen—a terrible prelude to Guernica,
Coventry, Dresden and Hiroshima. About 170 planes, supported by 280
guns, turned the six-mile by two-mile summit into an inferno. Blitzed
tukuls and bright green pepper bushes burst into flames and billowing yellow smoke blotted out the sun. Horses, mules and cattle, Mulugueta's
transport and his food on the hoof, were incinerated. Sheltering in caverns
and ravines, the Ethiopians could neither return fire nor stop the Italians
encircling their redoubt and, under cover of mist after torrential rain,

climbing its gentler southern slopes. Only a timely foray from warriors on the plain enabled Mulugueta to escape from this trap. But his host was reduced to a rabble and in the chaos of flight Ras Mulugueta himself was slain. On Amba Aradam the Italians cleared out the caves with hand grenades. They then burned some 8,000 Ethiopian corpses, turning the mountain into a gigantic crematorium and polluting the air all around for many weeks afterwards with the stench of charred flesh.

This crucial victory, the greatest colonial battle ever fought, almost put an end to organised resistance from the Ethiopians. However, harried from the air and assailed by dissident tribesmen on the ground, some lion-maned chiefs did continue the struggle. Ras Kassa led more bloody engagements on Badoglio's right flank. Scaling sheer cliffs before dawn, *Alpini* mountaineers helped to break his strong position at Tembien. Even when darkness fell again Italian aircraft inflicted appalling casualties on Kassa's fugitive forces. They dropped flares in the valley of the Gheva and turned night into day. Ras Imru gave a good account of himself, but he too was obliged to retreat. Moreover, in the southern deserts weak Ethiopian detachments were brushed aside when General Graziani recovered from his long military sleeping sickness. Finally the Emperor himself mustered fresh levies and rallied what remained of his old soldiery.

On 31 March 1936, at Mai Ceu in the central highlands, Haile Selassie launched a last-ditch attack on the advancing Italians. It was a measure of desperation, a doomed attempt to repeat the triumph of Adowa, and exactly what he had from the first advised his armies to avoid. From wireless intercepts Badoglio knew just what to expect. When waves of warriors charged his well-defended positions they encountered withering fire. Even so they mauled the Italian front line. But their losses were crippling and, in the dusk, as rain began to fall, the Emperor reluctantly ordered a withdrawal. In the confusion and bitterness of defeat his sang-froid for once deserted him. When Colonel Konovaloff, his White Russian adviser, asked what he intended to do, Haile Selassie replied: "I do not know . . . My chiefs will do nothing. My brain no longer works."[69]

Flight was the only option. Wearing a solar topi and riding a white horse, Haile Selassie led the remnant of his army down from the empire's mountain ramparts and on to the central plateau with its red pepper plantations, yellow cotton fields and hospitable people. But as it went his force disintegrated and it now became a matter of *sauve qui peut*. Having long torn at its flanks, jackal tribesmen in Italian pay moved in for the kill. They also raped and plundered in villages *en route*, while from above planes from an air force "at its peak"[70] caused havoc. The leader of a mobile Red Cross hospital commented: "This isn't war—it isn't even slaughter. It's the torture of tens of thousands of defenceless men, women and children with bombs and poison gas."[71] Despairing of mortal aid, the Emperor made a pilgrimage to the famous rock-hewn churches of Lalibela. There he fasted and prayed. But, apparently without benefit of divine assistance, he had to resume his retreat to Addis Ababa. He was hotly pursued by Badoglio's motorised "iron-will column," the first military detachment to be supplied from the air—three-engined Savoias dropped spaghetti, wine and even live cattle by parachute. The column also included horse transports so that the General could ride triumphantly into the city. Once in the capital himself, Haile Selassie again contemplated resistance. In a forlorn rhetorical flourish he appealed to the correspondent of *The Times,* "Do the peoples of the world not realize that by fighting on until the bitter end I am not only performing my sacred duty to my people, but standing guard in the last citadel of collective security?"[72] If they did realise it they were not prepared to help. Moreover the Italians had bombed the heart out of Ethiopia and shattered its fragile unity. So the Emperor chose exile.

Before going he apparently tore down the silk curtains around his throne and invited his soldiers to sack the palace and the city, leaving nothing for the Italians. He thus initiated an orgy of destruction and violence which allowed Badoglio to pose as Ethiopia's saviour. Moreover, it did not make for a dignified exit: on 2 May, a beautiful spring day, the Emperor drove to the station through a snow-storm of white feathers disembowelled by looters from hundreds of pillows and mattresses. With his family and a small suite of retainers, Haile Selassie boarded the "Rhinoceros Express" and steamed down to Djibouti. He arrived looking haggard and exhausted, with one arm bandaged on account of a poison gas burn. From there he sailed, first for Jerusalem and then to London, where an embarrassed British government, anxious to mend its fences with Mussolini, gave him reluctant asylum. It changed the route of his arrival so that he would not be cheered in the streets and when he was invited to tea in the House of Commons Prime Minister Baldwin skulked behind a table so that he would not have to be introduced.

Meanwhile, in the glorious May of 1936 Italian joy was unconfined. When Badoglio, shortly to be made Duke of Addis Ababa, telegraphed the news that he had occupied the Ethiopian capital and that the war was over, church bells rang and throughout Italy there were scenes of wild jubilation. The little King, shortly to be made little Emperor, burst into tears. "My legs were trembling," Victor Emmanuel later recorded. "That night, though I always sleep soundly, I got up, turned on the light, and went to look at a map of Africa."[73] The Pope, who had remained silent about the jingoistic excesses of the clergy and the use of poison gas, expressed satisfaction at the "triumphal felicity of a great and good people."[74] More messianic than ever, Mussolini appeared on his balcony to herald the annexation of the promised land, the founding of the third Rome, the triumph of civilisation. The multitude reached new heights of ecstasy and Italy echoed with the staccato chant of *"Duce! Duce! Duce!"* Savouring what one Italian paper called "a manifestation of devotion which acquired the aspect of an apotheosis,"[75] Mussolini seemed transfigured. "He is like a god," said one Fascist. "Like a god? No, no," said another, "He *is* a god."[76]

Certainly he was treated as one: peasants knelt in the fields as he passed, held their children up for him to bless, pasted his picture on their cottage walls beside that of the Virgin Mary. Victor Emmanuel, who now considered Mussolini a military, as well as a political, genius, made him a Knight of the Order of Savoy; the Duce in turn poured out lesser decorations, fostering his cult in the armed forces. "Never," reported the French Ambassador Charles Pineton, "has Italian support for Mussolini been more complete."[77] The Duce had turned a squalid colonial adventure into a great patriotic crusade. He had transcended the Depression and transformed domestic anguish into foreign aggression. He had become the embodiment of Italian passions and aspirations. He had completed his identification with Augustus, which was not only celebrated in art, architecture and books but in the great exhibition staged in 1937–8 to mark the bi-millennium of the Emperor's birth. One display was dedicated to "The Immortality of the Idea of Rome: The Renaissance of Empire in Fascist Italy."[78] It juxtaposed images of imperial and Fascist triumphal arches, equated Augustus's obelisk commemorating the conquest of Egypt with a pillar from Axum and set a painting of Roman matrons offering gold during the Punic Wars beside a picture of Queen Elena leading Italian women to sacrifice their wedding rings. All told, the Duce had restored the nation's pride. He had also, D'Annunzio said, created his own legend.

Increasingly self-intoxicated, Mussolini came to believe in it himself. His compatriots, too, so long force-fed on the pabulum of propaganda, swallowed it whole. Indeed, it survives to this day: in his multi-volume biography of the Duce, the distinguished historian Renzo de Felice declares that the "audacious, brilliant and happy action"[79] against Ethiopia was Mussolini's "political masterpiece."[80] In fact, the last major imperialist enterprise was not only a crime, it was a blunder. Bloodshed apart, it cost poor Italy 12 billion lire. It gave Mussolini delusions of power which led him into disastrous military operations against better-armed adversaries— for Badoglio's success in Ethiopia, like Kitchener's in the Sudan and

Schwarzkopf's in Iraq, was simply a matter of superior technology. In Europe the Duce found himself sliding inexorably into the arms of the Führer. Meanwhile Britain and France, vilified by Mussolini for support- ing the League's sanctions, began to master their economic fears and increase their defence spending. In Africa Mussolini became embroiled in a full-scale guerrilla war.

Ethiopians now started to fight as the Emperor had first wanted. They struck and vanished into the wilderness, confining the Italians to their for- tified positions; despite Mussolini's heavy investment in his new posses- sion (he even promised to learn Amharic) only 3,500 colonists settled there. The Duce instructed Graziani, who was appointed Viceroy, to employ the techniques of repression which in Libya had earned him the soubriquet "Breaker of Natives":[81]

> I authorise Your Excellency once again to begin conducting systematically the policy of terror and extermination against the rebels and the accom- plice population. Without the law of tenfold retaliation the wound will not heal quickly enough.[82]

Graziani, whom Evelyn Waugh famously described as an "amiable Chris- tian gentleman," used torture and gas freely, set up concentration camps and conducted mass executions. Like Stalin in the Ukraine, he tried to eliminate the natural leaders of the Ethiopian community: chiefs, priests, monks, school teachers, soothsayers. Even so he could not quell the revolt. The Ethiopian ulcer continued to torment Mussolini until the country's liberation in 1941.

Before that, Haile Selassie made one more appearance on the global stage. At the end of June 1936 he addressed the League of Nations at Geneva. With immense dignity the tiny cloaked figure mounted the ros- trum where a spotlight, falling full on him, emphasised his delicate fea- tures and dark complexion. As he began to speak a claque of Italian journalists at one end of the press gallery howled him down, blowing whistles and shrieking execrations. Delegates rose and faced the gallery in protest. In an effort to quell the disturbance someone briefly turned out the lights. Nicholas Titulescu, the Romanian Foreign Minister, shouted: "Throw out the savages." After a few minutes police dragged them from the chamber, arresting all but the most influential. Then the Emperor, who had been waiting with an expressionless countenance, made an elo- quent plea for morality in international affairs. He appealed to the con- science of the League and accused it of failing in its duty: "You abandoned us to Italy." Had not its connivance at the rape of Ethiopia set a "terrible precedent of bowing before force?"[83] What would happen next and what could he tell his people?

He was questioning a corpse. Damaged by its impotence over Manchuria, the League of Nations, as many had anticipated, was destroyed by its failure over Ethiopia. Like the preserved body of Lenin, it had the appearance of life but its veins were filled with embalming fluid. As Léon Blum noted bitterly,

> The League of Nations no longer condemns the Fascist acts of aggression; the League "notes," the League "does thus and thus," the League "deplores"—the League makes a hypocritical show of balancing between the criminal and his victim . . . Even more intolerable are the lies concealed in these formulae, and what can be read between the lines: the League's confession of impotence, its abject surrender, its acceptance of the fait accompli.[84]

The League could still serve as a totem but it had lost any power to taboo. Italian contempt for it was expressed not only by the newsmen who had demonstrated in front of Haile Selassie but by the fact that they were hailed as heroes at home. Like the sanctions, Mussolini gloated, "the League is a farce."[85] Perhaps collective security had always been a dream. But, as Arnold Toynbee wrote at the time, cowardly and mealy-mouthed politicians of Britain and France made no attempt to realise it in the face of naked aggression. As the dream dissolved into thin air the dictatorships became more belligerent and the democracies became more exposed to what Blum called "the contagion of war."[86] Prophesying war, indeed, was now the rule. Every skirmish on Europe's darkling plain foreshadowed the prospect of ignorant armies clashing by night. As he stalked proudly from the platform at Geneva, the Lion of Judah growled: "It is us today. It will be you tomorrow."[87]

XIV

LÉON BLUM AND THE
POPULAR FRONT

TORN by internal strife in the wake of the Concorde riot, France hardly liked to contemplate the black prospect of external conflict. The Left, in any case, favoured pacifism as much as it hated fascism. The Right not only sympathised with Mussolini but sought Italian friendship as a counter to German enmity. After the bloody clash of 6 February 1934, however, the French factions were more preoccupied with current mutual antagonism than with looming foreign hostilities. This was because the violence had dramatised political divisions inside France, polarised opinion more strongly than at any time since the Dreyfus affair and revived the ancient struggle between reactionaries and revolutionaries. It stimulated the growth of paramilitary leagues such as Jean Renaud's Solidarité Française, whose men wore blue berets and shirts, grey trousers and army boots, and Colonel de la Rocque's Croix de Feu, which within a couple of years would have nearly 500,000 members. It marked the birth of the fascist spirit in France: so at least thought the pro-Nazi writer Robert Brasillach, who each year on 6 February placed violets round the fountain in the Place de la Concorde. The riot also engendered solidarity between Socialists and Communists, hitherto implacable foes vying for working-class support.

Immediately after what they saw as the attempted "Fascist coup," the two main left-wing parties organised independent protests, which the police met with violence. But on 12 February 1934 they jointly backed a one-day general strike. Their members marched separately through the wintry mist to the Place de la Nation in eastern Paris, a traditional Jacobin centre and the site of Dalou's great bronze sculpture commemorating the "Triumph of the Republic." The demonstrators carried banners declaring that "Fascism Shall Not Pass" and that "The Republic Will Not Be Suicided"[1] (as Stavisky was supposed to have been). As the two columns approached one another, Léon Blum, leading the Socialists, feared that there would be a collision rather than a fusion with the Communists. But, as another witness recalled:

> After a silence, a brief moment of anguish, to the astonishment of the party and union leaders, this encounter triggered a delirious enthusiasm, an explosion of shouts of joy. Applause, chants, cries of "Unity, unity" . . . In fact the Popular Front had just been born before our eyes.[2]

Actually the birth of the anti-fascist "Popular Front"—a term not coined until 12 October 1934, by the Communist paper *L'Humanité*—was not so simple. As late as April 1934 Maurice Thorez, the slim, blue-eyed Communist leader, decried the Socialists as "social fascists" and refused to be associated with such "puke."[3] As always, he was abjectly toeing what he believed to be the Party line.

However, this changed later that spring as Stalin contemplated the defeat of Communism all over the world—in Germany, Japan, China, Spain, Britain and the United States. As a result of his uncompromising policy of setting class against class Communist parties outside the Soviet Union languished, that in France, with only 28,000 members, being the largest. In theory the global setbacks could be dismissed as a "temporarily successful" attempt by the "international bourgeoisie to divert the tide of revolution" which had been "set loose" by the Depression.[4] But in practice Stalin felt increasingly threatened by fascism in general and by Nazism in particular. Responding with Pavlovian predictability, he sought a *rapprochement* with France. Gaston Doumergue's national government viewed Communism with horror but Nazism with terror; so Louis Barthou, the cultured, aged Foreign Minister, was able to revive his country's traditional eastern alliance. Barthou was no Clemenceau. Indeed, he had occupied a lower circle in the Tiger's demonology than even Briand: "Barthou would murder his own mother. Briand would not murder his own mother, but he would murder someone else's mother!"[5] However, Barthou was the last master of the Quai d'Orsay to plan serious resistance to Hitler and he advanced negotiations so far towards a Franco-Soviet Pact that in May 1935 his successor, Pierre Laval, felt (reluctantly) bound to sign it.

Stalin worked in the dark and the details of his diplomacy remain obscure. In supporting a Popular Front he may well have been influenced by the French Communists themselves. The Party's ablest leader, Jacques Doriot—soon to become a fascist but then still the incarnation of the Red with "the dagger clenched between his teeth"[6]—had long advocated such a course. Plainly, though, Stalin was "the ultimate source of decision."[7] He wanted an end to the class-against-class policy everywhere; and he ordered

French Communists to switch their energies from fomenting revolution at home to resisting aggression abroad. He also approved the creation of an alliance with the Socialists and, indeed, with all the political forces inside France that were hostile to fascism.

Other factors also helped to form the French Popular Front, notably worsening economic conditions. By 1934 most countries were beginning to struggle out of the Depression: France, by contrast, was heading more deeply into it. Industrial production was down by a third compared to the levels of 1929 and exports were slipping even more rapidly. In a workforce of 12.5 million, unemployment was rising to a peak of more than 1 million—twice the mendacious official figure. The real incomes of peasants had fallen by 30 per cent; those of miners, shopkeepers and small businessmen by around 20 per cent. It is true that, because of the simultaneous collapse of prices, some workers (such as car makers) were actually better off in real terms. But their quality of life had deteriorated.

Exploiting trade union weakness, employers had "mechanised labour" according to the dehumanising dictates of the Taylor Plan. They broke down toil into component parts so that a worker might spend his whole time tightening a single bolt, becoming himself a mere cog in the production process. The bosses stiffened factory discipline, raised output quotas and accelerated assembly lines. This type of work was called in French *"travail à la chaîne"* and trade-unionists denounced it as "the organisation of exhaustion."[8] Liberal critics dubbed Taylorism the "American cancer."[9] Yoked to iron and steel, their movements orchestrated by the "huge drumbeat of machines,"[10] their days subject to the tyranny of the time-clock and the siren, workers left their benches grey, dazed hulks. Industrial accidents increased. Foremen behaved like gaolers. So strict was Louis Renault's regime that his vast Billancourt plant was known as the "penal colony."[11] New recruits to his 30,000-strong workforce were photographed and finger-printed. Smoking was prohibited. Time-keepers conducted a hated surveillance. Informers infested the cloakrooms and spies haunted the lavatories. The slightest infraction of the rules could result in instant dismissal.

So France suffered under the triple curse of joblessness, declining incomes and tightening bonds of economic servitude. Moreover, between 1934 and 1936 successive governments proved unable or unwilling to lift the curse. On the contrary, they became caught up in a series of financial crises caused by falling tax revenues and fixed obligations: half of public expenditure went for Great War pensions. Determined to defend France's prestige to the last centime, they would not countenance the only measure which could restore its global competitiveness—devaluation of the franc.

Instead they cut spending in a vain and painful attempt to balance the budget. Far from being a government of public safety, Gaston Doumergue's ministry was merely, as Colonel de la Rocque said, "a poultice on a gangrenous leg."[12] Known as "Gastounet," the Premier himself was antique, bumbling and so keen to present himself as a simple, unambitious man that he patronised a café near the Gare de Lyon to play *belote* with friends from the Auvergne. His government did undertake some initiatives: *Coriolanus* was stopped and modest public works were started. But apart from clinging to the fallacy that he was indispensable, the Prime Minister had only one political idea (gleaned from Tardieu). This was that the executive, having lost in authority, should gain in power. Deputies rejected the reform, not so much because it presaged dictatorship as because it threatened their own ascendancy.

Normally Gastounet's smile was as wide as Mistinguett's. But now the red-nosed, bowler-hatted Premier flounced out in a huff, to be replaced in October 1934 by another centre-right coalition led by Pierre-Etienne Flandin. Lanky, bland and Anglophile, Flandin aimed to revive France's economy by expanding credit. Simultaneously, at the Quai d'Orsay, Foreign Minister Laval sought to contrive its security through the Italian accord. There is no need to recapitulate the failures of French foreign policy—the collapse of the Stresa Front, the alienation of Mussolini over Ethiopia, the half-hearted agreement with Russia. But it must be said that France's timid performance on the international stage reflected its profound weakness at home. The French were willing to be dominated by "the English governess" not just because she was powerful but because they owed her money. Similarly France's eagerness to appease Germany— Laval refused to counter Nazi propaganda during the Saar plebiscite of January 1935—was prompted by "financial decline and the flight of capital."[13] For this Flandin's uncertain programme was partly to blame: the spindle-shanked Premier was depicted as a flamingo, not knowing which leg to stand on, the left or right. While proclaiming an end to State regulation of the economy he pursued a policy of industrial reorganisation, encouraging investment by expanding credit but failing to stimulate demand at a time when French goods were already the dearest in the world. Then, in the spring of 1935, growing budgetary deficits (assisted by Communist victories in local elections) provoked a "gold rush." Specie flooded from the vaults of the Bank of France, which was slow to raise interest rates. Its tardiness fostered the popular belief that the "200 families" in control of the bank were trying to force the government to embrace deflation rather than devaluation. Flandin himself declared that France was being chained to "the chariot of King Money." But he appeared an unlikely champion of freedom, especially as he had just broken his arm in a car crash, and his ministry collapsed.

On 6 June 1935, after a week of political turmoil, Laval became Prime Minister with plenary powers to defend the franc. He enjoyed issuing decrees, some of which had little to do with restoring confidence in the currency: one that singularly contributed to national security made it illegal for foreigners living in France to keep carrier pigeons. But Laval was unable to formulate a coherent economic strategy, even with the help of a "brains trust"—Communists called it a "brain of trusts."[14] Furthermore the Prime Minister handicapped himself by excluding from his counsels one of the brightest stars in the political firmament, Paul Reynaud, who favoured devaluation. "Over-valued currency," Reynaud urged, "is followed by a horde of speculators, as wounded game is tracked down by wolves."[15]

Dubbed the Mickey Mouse of the Chamber, Reynaud was not always taken seriously. His stature was small but his vanity was larger than life. He wore platform shoes, dyed his hair and practised what he hoped were rejuvenating exercises such as swimming, bicycling and gymnastics. His eyes were almond-shaped and his tiny, moustached head, set low on his shoulders, had an Oriental cast. It was said that "he had the countenance of a Samurai educated at Cambridge."[16] Reynaud was, indeed, an intellectual warrior, a paladin of new ideas—such as de Gaulle's notion of deploying squadrons of tanks in lightning warfare. He was also a master of the telling phrase and the devastating polemic. Speaking in a sharp, metallic voice and chopping the air with incisive gestures, he lambasted the "dictatorship of stupidity" that would be the ruin of France. Conservatives, who likened the battle of the franc to the defence of Verdun, reviled Reynaud: *L'Action française* declared that he had the "mug and morals of a termite."[17] But he won more and more converts, particularly when, in July 1935, Laval imposed economies on almost everything except social benefits and military expenditure. Ten per cent was cut from pensions, rents, dividends from government stock and the salaries of civil servants. These *fonctionnaires* had traditionally been protected and they now protested vigorously. Many supported the Popular Front, whose massive demonstration on 14 July was an important landmark on its march to power.

The date was chosen, of course, because it was the anniversary of the storming of the Bastille. By coincidence it was also the day on which Alfred Dreyfus was buried in Montmartre Cemetery. Around Dreyfus had crystallised opposition to all the chauvinist, ultramontane, anti-Semitic forces in France, whose resurgence, in the shape of quasi-fascist leagues, the Popular Front engaged to resist. As one newspaper said, "Dreyfus dies when France seems again divided against herself."[18] For this Laval was partly to blame, for not only did he seem to be the cornerstone of the "wall of money" (or "bankers' ramp," as the British called it), he openly sympathised with organisations such as the Croix de Feu. Thus encouraged, de la Rocque behaved ever more provocatively. Declaring that he did not give a fig for legality, the Colonel staged inflammatory rallies as far afield as Algiers. As it happened, he would take neither the insurrectionary road to power nor the parliamentary one. But at the time de la Rocque seemed as menacing as Mussolini, if not Hitler, and he threatened to "buzz" the "Red" suburbs of Paris with the Croix de Feu's aeroplanes on 14 July. Eventually he agreed to hold a parade after the official Bastille Day ceremonies. These included the greatest fly-past yet seen in France—600 aircraft (a quarter of its whole strength but mostly obsolescent) filling the blue sky with flashing wings and roaring engines. Below, Dreyfus's cortège had to cross the Champs-Elysées: male spectators doffed their hats and women made a sign of the cross while troops, not knowing whose bier it was, presented arms. Afterwards well-disciplined men of the Croix de Feu, each with a red, white and blue brassard and many wearing military medals, marched to the Arc de Triomphe and the Colonel re-kindled the flame at the tomb of the Unknown Soldier.

Meanwhile, as the sun broke through a morning mist thickened by clouds of tobacco smoke, supporters of the Popular Front assembled at the Buffalo sports stadium in Montrouge. They took a solemn oath to defend democracy and observed a minute's silence to honour Dreyfus. Later, Radicals marched beside Socialists and Communists (as well as fellow-travelling intellectuals such as André Malraux) from the Place de la Bastille to the Place de la Nation. For hour after hour the 400,000 demonstrators passed the July column where the great prison-fortress had once stood. There were representatives of every class—labourers, clerks, schoolmasters, lawyers, railwaymen, engineers, *fonctionnaires*. They policed themselves and fears of civil war dissolved in the sunshine. The hot tarmac was sticky under foot but idealism was in the air. Communists shouted "All Power to the Soviets" but they also cheered Daladier. They waved red flags and sang the "Internationale," but they also pledged allegiance to the tricolor and joined in the "Marseillaise." That evening accordions played and couples danced in the streets. A firework display blazed over the Seine. Throughout France similar demonstrations had taken place, with similar vows of left-wing unity. As the historian Marc Bloch put it, "something lived again of the spirit that had moved men's hearts on the Champs-de-Mars under the hot sun of 14 July 1790."[19] The Popular Front had come of age.

· · ·

IT was never the homogeneous body which hope painted that bright day. Indeed, it was only kept in being by hardship and by fascism. Hurt by Laval's cuts, the middle class suddenly began to sympathise with the working class. During the summer of 1935 the agricultural slump reached its nadir, which prompted further agitation by Dorgères' Peasant Front. In the autumn Colonel de la Rocque seemed to threaten a domestic putsch and Mussolini went to war with Ethiopia. While Laval temporised the Popular Front mobilised. But it was an insubstantial pageant of altruism and rhetoric. The Popular Front was not a political party but a "centre of liaison." What this meant was unclear. Thorez regarded the Popular Front as a mechanism of revolution at the service of the Comintern. Daladier saw it as an "alliance of the 3rd estate and the proletariat."[20] The common programme amounted to little more than opposition to fascism, but even over this opinion was divided. The Socialists, who had opposed Flandin's extension of conscription to two years, wanted to use only economic sanctions against Mussolini. The Communists, who at Stalin's behest had done a volte-face over the question of national defence, believed that, "Peace may require the eventual application of force."[21] There was much talk of planning and, under the goad of economic adversity which did not spare the bourgeoisie, even time-serving Radicals moved to the Left. Everyone thought that France needed some sort of New Deal. But there was little positive agreement after the ritual denunciations of the "200 families" and the "merchants of death"—arms manufacturers. Socialist and Communist trade unions merged. But no one knew how to raise the living standards of the masses without damaging France's grossly uncompetitive economy as a whole.

Nevertheless, during the dismal last days of Laval's administration many French people saw the Popular Front as a beacon of hope. Amid fresh political disturbances in the streets, further financial panic in the markets and new revelations of diplomatic chicanery in the shape of the Hoare-Laval plan, the Popular Front seemed to offer the prospect of good government. It would be government based on "the law of the League" not "the law of the jungle."[22] It would banish bribery and corruption: to augment his support Laval had had much recourse to the parliamentary "jam cupboard."[23] The Popular Front would not just brandish a clenched fist at fascism, it would extend an open hand to all men of goodwill. It would mobilise the masses, who were already galvanised, as Blum said, with "*élan*, confidence and enthusiasm."[24] It would recruit the intelligentsia—many of whom had signified their support at the International Writers' Congress for the Defence of Culture held in June 1935 at the Palais de la Mutualité. There, in an emotional fever as torrid as the weather, they aired much Stalinist propaganda along with what E. M. Forster imagined would be "the last utterances of the civilised."[25] In sum, the Popular Front promised to be a celebration of social communion, a consecration of human dignity, an apotheosis of fraternity. Its promise by no means excited everyone: Jean-Paul Sartre hoped for its victory but did not trouble to vote. Nevertheless it seemed certain to win at the general election due in the spring of 1936. Before that, however, during Albert Sarraut's caretaker ministry which followed the collapse of Laval's government in January, events occurred which were to make its victory doubly sure.

The first took place on 13 February 1936 when Léon Blum was attacked in the street by a gang of royalist hooligans belonging to the Camelots du Roi, the "fighting wing" of Action Française.[26] A fellow deputy, Georges Monnet, was driving Blum home for lunch from the Palais Bourbon when his Citroën B-12 was stopped on entering the Boulevard Saint-Germain by the funeral procession of the monarchist writer Jacques Bainville. Suddenly a voice cried, "There is Blum."[27] At once young thugs surged round the car, smashing the windows and tearing off the doors. Madame Monnet was injured by flying glass. Blum was dragged out, beaten and kicked. He was also hit over the head and badly cut by a stocky, leather-clad youth wielding the rear licence plate like a cleaver. Watching the scene with glowing eyes, women in fur coats cried, "Kill him!"[28] Blum probably would have been killed but for the intervention of building workers and civil servants from the nearby War Ministry, who rescued him and staunched his wounds. The Camelots du Roi melted away, one of them taking Blum's Bohemian-style, broad-brimmed black felt hat, his only sartorial concession to socialism—police later retrieved this trophy from the offices of *L'Action française*. Maurras' newspaper claimed that Blum himself had provoked the affray by driving into the crowd. But by chance an amateur cine-cameraman had filmed the whole incident. It caused outrage. Sarraut dissolved Action Française along with other royalist leagues. Maurras, who had called for Blum to be shot in the back, was prosecuted and imprisoned for several months. The Popular Front mounted a huge protest demonstration in defence of the democratic Republic. Convalescing in the country, the Socialist leader enjoyed enhanced power and conveniently diminished responsibility. Blum's blood was the seed of his cause. He had become the Popular Front's first martyr.

Blum also had personal qualities which made him a priceless asset to the Popular Front. In a land where intellectuals are actually admired he was the descendant of the *philosophes* of the Enlightenment. The personification of Republican virtue, he was the spiritual successor of the French revolutionaries who formulated the Declaration of the Rights of Man. A humanist as much as a politician, he inherited the mantle of the great Socialist leader Jean Jaurès.

It is true that, unlike the squat, soup-stained Jaurès, Blum by no means looked the part. Tall and willowy, with a creamy complexion, a silky moustache and rimless pince-nez, he seemed more of a *fin de siècle* aesthete than a new Jacobin. His hair was long and his gestures were languid. His voice was reedy and his manner was precious. His blue-grey eyes were "as tender and warm as a ray of sunshine refracted by a fanciful mirror" and he had slender, sensitive hands. They were the hands (according to an admirer) of "a miracle-working rabbi" and they compensated for his only inelegant feature—flat feet, which gave him a duck's waddle. Nevertheless, Blum danced and fenced exquisitely. He dressed like a dandy and he was liable to interview delegations of workers in his library at noon wearing slippers, mauve pyjamas and a silk dressing gown. Satirists made much of his effete fondness for spats, buttonholes, scented handkerchiefs, rattan canes, expensive cigars and velvet collars. Blum was called a "mandarin of decadence,"[29] "the revolution in pearl-grey gloves."[30]

Furthermore this model of Proustian refinement was the target of ever more vicious anti-Semitism. Daudet nicknamed him the "circumcised hermaphrodite"[31] and Maurras called him a "chameau"—a rotter—16 times in a 50-line article.[32] When he jokingly told Alfred Lebrun that a display of Louvre treasures at the International Exposition was the famous collection of silver which anti-Semitic papers accused him of possessing, the ponderous President returned later to find out if it were true. Most slurs Blum ignored. Some he met with steely dignity. When deputies in the Chamber shouted, "Go back to Jerusalem," Blum replied: "I am indeed a Jew . . . It is no insult to me to remind me of the race of which I was born a member, which I have never denied and towards which I feel nothing but gratitude and pride."[33]

Actually he had long adopted a secular, free-thinking creed instead of the more traditional beliefs of his father, who owned a prosperous haberdashery business in the Rue Saint Denis (a stone's throw from Les Halles), where Blum was born in 1872. But on matters of morality Blum was always willing to stand up and be counted, as he showed during the Dreyfus affair. In 1935 he criticised pusillanimous Jews who had lain low then and now vainly imagined that they could conceal themselves from the fascist onslaught. In short, Blum was a living exemplum of Winston Churchill's rule that courage is the most important political virtue because it guarantees all the rest.

Blum's bravery was matched by his precocity. At the age of five he was quoting La Bruyère. In 1889 he won a philosophy prize with an essay on which a teacher commented: "If a youngster of seventeen wrote that, he is a monster."[34] Averse to the discipline and to the cuisine of the élite Ecole Normale Supérieure, he left and qualified as a lawyer at the Sorbonne, afterwards practising successfully. Meanwhile he became a cultural critic and established a brilliant reputation as a man of letters. In one of his earliest works he eulogised the classical values of logical thought and lucid expression, his polestars. The antithesis of Ramsay MacDonald, Blum was an uninspiring orator but he spoke with luminous clarity. Sometimes his dedication to reason led to controversy. In 1907 he published a book condemning the double standard in sexual morality and advocating that young women as well as men should experiment with different partners before settling down to marriage. However, his critics were disarmed by Blum's transparent nobility of mind—his own family life was happy and quite free of scandal. More rashly still, four years later he fought a duel in the Parc de Princes with an enraged victim of his pen, wounding his adversary.

However, after the Great War (most of which, being too myopic to fight, he spent as a senior government official) Blum entered parliament and devoted his life to socialism. He quickly rose to prominence. This was partly because of his dialectical skill and his encyclopaedic memory—as Premier, despite having no interest in horse-racing, he could recite the names and pedigrees of all the winners of the Grand Prix since its inception in 1863. But mainly it was because Blum could best evoke "the glorious shadow of Jaurès."[35] In 1924, exactly ten years after the assassination of that so-called "peasant of genius," Blum gave a transfixing oration built round the symbol of night. The hall was darkened, women swathed Jaurès's statue in funereal crêpe, Mendelssohn's "Appel de la Nuit" was sung and Blum declared: "He is fallen and since that day, the night reigns in our spirits, a night streaked with the bloodshot lightning of the dead for four years. At that moment began the great insomnia of the world."[36] Dawn would break with the advent of the socialist millennium.

Such emotional outbursts were rare, but they are a reminder that Blum's fastidious intellect was fired by molten passion. His socialism was no mere abstract doctrine but the political expression of a burning moral imperative. He wrote:

Socialism is born of the concern for human equality because the society in which we live is founded on privilege. It is born of the pity and anger that is aroused in every honest heart by the intolerable spectacle of poverty, unemployment, cold, hunger . . . it is born of the contrast, scandalous and heart-rending, between the luxury of some and the privation of others, between crushing toil and insolent idleness. It is not, as has been so many times charged, the product of envy, which is the lowest of human motives, but of justice and compassion, which are the noblest.[37]

Indissolubly wedded to this philosophy, Blum had no hesitation in splitting from the Bolsheviks, who were, he observed, elevating terror into a system of government.

Nevertheless, in the spirit of Jaurès, he deplored sectarianism, that endemic disease of the Left. He remained conciliatory despite vilification from Thorez which was comparable to that of Maurras. Even while building up the Socialist Party during the 1920s (at the expense of the Communists) Blum hankered for proletarian solidarity and political synthesis. He also remained committed to the overthrow of the bourgeois state, though, a gentle Jacobin, he wanted "peaceful and fraternal" revolution.[38] Presciently forecasting a crisis of over-production in the United States in October 1929, Blum optimistically anticipated the collapse of capitalism. He reckoned that the Depression, when it came, had a greater social impact than either the French Revolution or the First World War. Although accepting the Marxist view that fascism was the last stage of capitalism, Blum, as a man of reason, could hardly conceive that Hitler would come to power. When he did, Blum had every patriotic and political motive for supporting the Popular Front.

At dawn on Saturday 7 March 1936 the Führer himself contributed to its future electoral success through "Operation Schooling." Choosing his moment with diabolical cleverness and using as his excuse the Sarraut government's ratification of the Franco-Soviet Pact, he sent a token force of 22,000 troops into the Rhineland. As they marched over the 50-kilometre-wide strip of territory bordering the Rhine, which had been demilitarised not only by the imposed peace of Versailles but by the negotiated treaty of Locarno, the inhabitants of the cities of Essen, Düsseldorf, Frankfurt, Mainz and Freiburg were at first stupefied and then jubilant. The citizens of Cologne watched with amazement as aircraft of the Luftwaffe circled round the spires of their cathedral and they cheered convulsively as infantry of the Sixth Army Corps crossed the Hohenzollern Bridge and goose-stepped into the Domplatz, where General von Kluge took the salute. Elsewhere crowds broke through police cordons, laughing girls showered soldiers with flowers, church bells pealed, flags flew and bands blared. Calculation of the financial benefit which the new garrisons would bring to the Ruhr's distressed areas enhanced patriotic euphoria. Even so, many of the Rhineland's 15 million people expected the French to retaliate and in Berlin Defence Minister Blomberg was ashen-faced with anxiety. Meanwhile Hitler, having torn up one international agreement, characteristically offered another—a 25-year non-aggression pact with France. He told an exultant Reichstag: "I look upon this day as marking the close of the struggle for German equality [of] status and . . . the path is now clear for Germany's return to European collective cooperation." That evening the Führer watched a torchlight parade of 15,000 brown-clad Storm-troopers from his Chancellery balcony. One of their songs included the refrain: "For today we own Germany and tomorrow the entire world."[39]

This was exactly what the French feared and Sarraut broadcast a belligerent riposte. If acts like Hitler's were permitted, he said, there could be no peace in Europe; France would neither negotiate under menace nor "let Strasbourg once again come under the fire of German guns."[40] A few others took this line. Pugnacious politicians—Reynaud, Paul-Boncour and Georges Mandel among them—maintained that this was the moment to stop Hitler; and in *The Gathering Storm* Churchill was to advance his classic argument that action now would have made the Second World War unnecessary. With hindsight and in theory one may judge that the anti-appeasers were right for, as Bismarck had warned, he who seeks to buy the friendship of his enemy with concessions will never be rich enough. At the time, however, concession was almost inevitable. Germany's occupation of the Rhineland was "one of the most heavily telegraphed moves in Europe since 1918,"[41] yet French governments had made no plans to react and Sarraut's ministers were surprised by the speed and boldness of Hitler's action. General Gamelin, whose mentality, like his army, was organised for defence, did not possess a single unit ready for combat. Nothing could be done without full mobilisation, he said, a slow, costly and dangerous move which he deprecated. Most of Sarraut's colleagues were equally passive, and when the War Minister voiced their views Flandin (now at the Quai d'Orsay, where he was sometimes lachrymose and always less combative than his officials) concluded: "Well, there we are; I see there is nothing to be done."[42]

France did receive offers of support from Czechoslovakia and, more equivocally, from other members of the eastern entente such as Poland. But its vital British ally, resentful about French softness towards Italy over Ethiopia, could not (as Baldwin told Flandin) "accept the risk of war."[43] However, what ultimately paralysed France—its eventual appeal to the

League amounted to immobility—was the state of public opinion. Here, as in Britain, the vast bulk of the populace revolted at the prospect of another Armageddon when they were already enduring the rigours of the Depression. This was the most frequent comment heard on the streets of the capital and seen in newspapers that Parisians rushed out to buy. "Above all, no war," trumpeted *L'Action française* and youths scattered leaflets with the same message from the balcony of the Comédie Française.[44] At the other end of the political spectrum the Communist *L'Humanité* called only for "sanctions"[45] while the Socialist *Le Populaire* refused to admit that a "diplomatic conflict," in which Germany's stand was not unreasonable, could be a casus belli.[46] Right and Left had their own motives for wanting to avoid war. Maurras insisted, "We must not march against Hitler with the Soviets."[47] Though by no means a complete pacifist, Blum believed that the best defence against fascism was to repudiate the creed of militarism. He advocated disarmament, the alleviation of economic ills, occupation of the moral high ground.

In retrospect this seems a hopelessly idealistic response to the Nazi menace, but at the time it won Gallic hearts and minds. The anti-fascism of peace crusaders was more attractive than the defeatism of nationalist appeasers, especially those who preferred Hitler to Blum. Some Frenchmen feared that (as right-wing manifestos maintained) behind the Popular Front lurked the shadow of Moscow. More believed that the left-wing alliance could create a new earth, if not a new heaven. As Blum said in the only election speech he was well enough to make, which was broadcast from the balcony of the Gothic town hall in his Narbonne constituency: "I am not describing a Utopia, a visionary paradise. I am describing a society all of whose elements exist, ready to be fused into life by your will."[48] At the polls the Popular Front won a decisive victory—376 seats against 222. The Communists did so well at the expense of the Radicals that Blum, being leader of what was now the largest party, was bound to become the next Prime Minister. Sitting in a restaurant when he heard the news, he was so surprised that he poured salt over his strawberries. "Millions of Frenchmen felt as though they were emerging from a tunnel"[49] and Blum himself glowed with happiness at the prospect of power. But with characteristic candour he expressed doubts about his capacity to exercise it. Nervous members of the bourgeoisie had no doubt that the leader of France's first Socialist government would overthrow the State—despite Blum's expressed intention of acting within his mandate and the Communists' refusal to serve in his administration (which they nevertheless supported). In May 1936, during the month-long interval before he was constitutionally permitted to take office, there was a further flight of capital. People talked of barricades and tumbrils. As though the word were father to the deed, France became engulfed by the largest wave of strikes in the history of the Third Republic.

THESE were partly a result of reflex action by Communists and trade-unionists who had long been trying to mobilise workers and now felt that they might succeed. Partly, though, the strikes were a spontaneous rebellion by workers against the harsh rule of bosses and the inhuman despotism of machines, an attempt to realise their new political power on the shop floor. They were a contagious protest, carried out in a "climate of effervescence,"[50] against low pay and poor conditions. They were a revolt against the Depression.

Beginning with the occupation of aviation factories as far apart as Le Havre and Toulouse, the strikes spread like the revolutionary Great Fear. Soon infected were the important engineering plants of the Paris region: the Nieuport works at Issy-les-Moulineaux; the Lavalette automobile accessories concern at St. Ouen; the Hotchkiss armaments complex at Levallois. On 28 May the epidemic reached Renault's factory at Billancourt. This was the buckle on the Parisian Red belt. It was also the largest industrial concentration in France, containing the most modern assembly line in Europe. A jumble of barracks-like buildings, Billancourt produced not only cars but vans, lorries, tractors, tanks, fire engines, aircraft motors and so on. Communists in the artillery workshop began the strike, "sitting in" the works (then quite a novel tactic) to stop Renault importing black-leg labour. Within two hours all 30,000 workers had downed tools. Though afraid that they would be evicted and sacked, the strikers were ecstatic about their success. Suddenly the 7-ton steam-hammers had ceased their infernal cannonade. The 800-ton Deering presses for cutting out chassis, mudguards and bonnets were silent. The gantries stopped, the hydraulic cranes lay idle, the iron foundries came to rest, the Bessemer converters cooled. The smoke from furnace chimneys evaporated, the air cleared and the sky brightened. In workshops making cylinders, crank-shafts, axles and gearboxes, the murderous rhythms of metal gave way to the exhilarating strains of dance music played on mouth organs, accordions, radios and gramophones. "The public, the bosses, Léon Blum himself, and all who are strangers to this life of slavery are incapable of understanding what was decisive in this affair," wrote one striker. "Independent of all other considerations, this sit-in is in itself a joy, a pure joy."[51]

What the workers of Billancourt chiefly rejoiced about was the overthrow, however temporary, of the old order. They were now "the lords and masters of Renault's." So they looked the foremen in the eye, defied the smoking ban, indulged in wild horseplay and Grand Guignol. That afternoon thousands processed to the vast new plant on the Ile Seguin in the Seine—it was nicknamed "Devil's Island." They crossed the iron bridge to board this great industrial battleship, waving red flags and shouting "Down with the Boss."[52] Later they burned Louis Renault in effigy and threw the charred corpse into the river. Their animus was understandable, for Renault had done much to earn his punning title "Le Saigneur [i.e. lord and blood-sucker] de Billancourt."[53] As one of his employees remarked, "The Old Devil knows how to make his slaves sweat blood . . . he's like a Pharaoh!"[54]

Actually Renault had more in common with Henry Ford: indeed, when they first met the two motor-car moguls had such a strong rapport that, though neither spoke the other's language, they were said to have communicated happily without an interpreter. Like Ford, Renault was an untaught mechanical genius with powerful authoritarian leanings. He started by tinkering in the shed of his family's property at Billancourt, in what was then a leafy suburb of Paris, and became the first Frenchman to mass-produce automobiles. During the Great War Renault built tanks and his tracked lorries made a vital contribution to the defence of Verdun. He expanded his works, buying up adjoining land and sometimes forcing out neighbours reluctant to sell by testing his vehicles outside their houses all night long. Renault brought this kind of finesse to all his activities. Shy and saturnine, with coarse, dexterous hands and sharp, mesmeric eyes, he could think of nothing to say to women except to ask them to sleep with him. When one of his office-boys answered back, Renault chased him round the factory and, failing to catch him, fired all the office-boys at Billancourt. Though as boorish and grasping as a Balzacian peasant, Renault had a bourgeois fear of the masses. He regarded them as primitive, dangerous and physically loathsome. But he also considered them responsive to forceful leadership. The fascist writer Pierre Drieu la Rochelle, who had an affair with Renault's ambitious wife, compared him to the frog in the fable who tried to inflate himself into a bull. And Renault certainly tried to turn his concern into a model police state. Employees were subjected to secret surveillance and martinettish control. Those giving a hint of political involvement were sacked at once and placed on a blacklist. Such was the "climate of suspicion" at Billancourt that workers were alienated from one another, not even daring to compare pay-slips—documents of Byzantine complexity. Unlike Ford, Renault offered little in the way of welfare and every year, during the fallow autumn season, he laid off thousands of his human robots. During the Depression wage cuts accompanied further lay-offs, while Renault imported cheap Arab labour and employed more women. In the words of a worker who moved from Billancourt to Javel, where the yoke of amiable, improvident André Citroën was somewhat easier: "I found I had left an Empire for a Republic."[55]

Yet for all their ceremonial *lèse-majesté*, the Billancourt strikers did not want to topple the Emperor from his throne. As *L'Humanité* said, they were simply "tired of low wages, work speed-ups, fines and military discipline."[56] They demanded more money, better conditions, a 40-hour week, paid holidays and union recognition. They had, without doubt, precipitated a situation that was dangerously volatile. But they were not, despite the fears of the middle class and the hopes of Leon Trotsky, a revolutionary crowd. Rather they were truants from travail. They sang the "Internationale" but with equal fervour they sang the popular song of the moment, "Madame la Marquise." They gave the clenched-fist salute but protected Renault's property, though some strikers did sleep in his new touring cars in their dirty blue overalls while a few others got drunk and were sick over the seats. The strikers shouted Bolshevik slogans but their watchword was "Calm," chalked on every available surface. Pickets wore hammer-and-sickle badges or displayed the triple-arrowed escutcheon of socialism. But workers spent most of their time talking, drinking, reading the papers, playing cards on upturned packing cases, dancing among piles of scrap iron to an impromptu orchestra of cornet, flute, violin and concertina, and foraging for bread and cigarettes—local shops had run out of both. The workers' organisation was chaotic and, when Renault made a few concessions, they were willing to go home for the long Whitsun weekend. Most of the 100,000 strikers in and around Paris followed suit and the contagion seemed to have run its course.

However, on Tuesday 2 June it broke out again with renewed strength. Not only Renault but the whole of France's engineering industry ground to a halt. Other trades joined in and Blum took office on the Thursday in an atmosphere of mounting crisis. He demanded calm and his Minister of the Interior Roger Salengro declared that, "The Popular Front stands for order."[57] But by 6 June a million workers were on strike, a figure which doubled over the next few days. France was crippled. Almost every industry was affected throughout the Hexagon and beyond. Farms were occupied as far afield as north Africa. Dockers struck in Marseilles and street cleaners stopped work in Le Havre. At Bouchain bargemen blocked the canal and in Valenciennes miners slept on the railway tracks to prevent the movement of coal. In Paris, which was bedecked with red flags and tricolors, waiters refused to serve in restaurants and guests at the Hotel Majestic had to make their own beds. The lorry drivers of Les Halles ceased to operate, food piled up at railway stations and housewives began to hoard—prices rose and soon shops would sell only two pounds of potatoes to each customer. Petrol was unobtainable and so were most newspapers. The sweated assistants at big stores such as the Galeries Lafayette, Au Printemps and Bon Marché took possession of the premises, men and women sleeping on different floors "for reasons of decency."[58] The drivers of Black Marias withdrew their labour, as did film-makers and music hall artistes. After attempting to run the Delespaul Havez chocolate factory near Lille themselves, workers resolved to "make a free distribution [of their spoiling goods] to the town's poor."[59] Despite such law-breaking the police did not make their habitual parades of force and the Croix de Feu was quiet. Essential services were maintained and everyone remained surprisingly calm. But the holiday spirit was gradually being overtaken by a mood of irritation.

At Billancourt mock funerals were held of workers who stayed at home. A show trial was staged of de la Rocque, who was represented by a chained figure locked in a cage resting on two broomsticks and begging for mercy. He was condemned to death and his dummy, wearing swastika and Croix de Feu armbands, was hanged and burned. During the second phase of the strike an oligarchy of activists emerged who controlled it much more strictly. Indeed, they established a system of rules and punishments which some thought on a par with those of Louis Renault himself. They also banned wine and women. But they did encourage song, and anything else that would keep the strikers happy—dances, cinema shows, boxing matches, boule competitions, games of football. They also distributed free newspapers to complement their propaganda pageants. And when a general settlement was finally reached they organised a piece of peripatetic theatre which demonstrated how far political consciousness had grown among the workers.

Marshalled according to their workshops and replete with bands and banners, 20,000 Renault workers marched through the streets and squares of the Boulogne district in an enormous victory parade led by left-wing politicians. They were accompanied by floats representing different aspirations of the Popular Front. Reconciliation was symbolised by a lorry-load of musicians alternately playing the "Marseillaise" and the "Internationale." Unity was embodied in icons of Blum, Herriot and Alfred Costes, the local Communist deputy who had formerly been a machinist at Renault. Proletarian power was personified by a tableau vivant of workers wearing Phrygian caps. Peace was typified by a trident-bearing angel vanquishing war in the shape of a gladiator. Meanwhile, throughout Paris similar processions celebrated what Blum's paper *Le Populaire* described as not so much a victory as "a triumph!"[60]

It was enshrined in the Matignon Agreement, so called after the Prime Minister's official residence. (In fact Blum used the Hôtel Matignon only as an office, meeting colleagues in the Cabinet Room which was decorated with tapestries depicting the adventures of Don Quixote.) Inspired by terror of revolution, bosses and bourgeoisie put up little resistance to the proletariat's radical demands. So workers won a fortnight's holiday with pay, a 40-hour week, collective contracts and wage rises of roughly 12 per cent. In quick succession the government passed scores of further laws, some equally far-reaching. It suppressed the fascist leagues, nationalised the Bank of France and large parts of the arms industry, fixed wheat prices, began a substantial programme of public works, raised the school-leaving age to 14. Altogether it shifted power significantly towards the working class. This was the French New Deal. Blum's opponents scorned it as "Rooseveltism for Lilliputians."[61] But the French Premier, having no mandate for revolution, was happy to alleviate the effects of the Depression even if he could only do so in small ways. He admired Roosevelt and sought to emulate him. As the American Ambassador, William Bullitt, told FDR (in a characteristically ingratiating letter) after the President's 1936 election victory, Blum

> entered the front door, flung his broad-brimmed black hat to the butler, his coat to the footmen, leaped the three steps to the point where I was standing, seized me and kissed me violently! I staggered slightly but having been kissed by Stalin, I am now immune to any form of osculation, and I listened without batting an eye to as genuine an outpouring of enthusiasm as I have ever heard . . . Blum himself said to me that he felt his position had been greatly strengthened because he is attempting in his way to do what you have done in America.[62]

In providing a favourable climate for the massive growth of union membership and the practice of free collective bargaining, Blum unquestionably resembled Roosevelt. Yet, ironically, the measures for which the Popular Front is best remembered—the encouragement of recreation— bore certain similarities to fascist initiatives. Blum appointed Léo Lagrange Under-Secretary for Sport and Leisure (he was derided as the "Minister for Idleness")[63] who organised everything from people's aviation clubs to cheap railway fares. At a time when Hitler was attempting to turn the Berlin Olympics into a "symbol of the conquest of the world by National Socialist doctrine,"[64] Lagrange built swimming-pools and athletics stadiums as monuments to the vitality of the French race. The cult of fitness flourished. Camping and youth hostelling boomed. Tourists formed a market for new products such as Orangina, Ambre Solaire and Lacoste shirts. Bicycling was such a national passion that competitors in the gruelling Tour de France had long taken drugs to improve their performance— early tests were primitive and one cyclist whose urine sample proved negative was "warned that he was pregnant."[65] But with the birth of "le week-end" millions more French people pedalled their way to pleasure. For the first time better-off wage-earners could also take longer holidays and explore remoter regions of their own country. Sometimes it proved a shock: Renault workers found a Brittany that seemed to be in "the Middle Ages."[66] Often it was a delight: 60 per cent of the tens of thousands who visited the Riviera had never seen the sea. Well might Blum feel gratified by the sight of processions of

> jalopies, motor-bikes and tandems ridden by working-class couples wearing matching pullovers . . . All this made me feel that, in spite of everything, I had brought a ray of sunshine into dark, difficult lives . . . not only made family life easier but opened up a vision of the future and created hope.[67]

Hope was soon disappointed, for the social gains were blotted out by the economic losses. Blum had thought that by increasing the buying power of the masses he would stimulate industrial growth. Instead production fell because workers put in fewer hours and employers put in less cash, having too little confidence to invest in the future. Moreover prices rose by as much as a fifth during the summer of 1936, threatening the franc and eroding the benefits of Matignon. This in turn led to a belated and ineffectual devaluation (by about 30 per cent) in September, and to a swift decline in the currency's value thereafter. It also caused increasingly violent industrial unrest, not just because workers were trying to ensure that their wages kept up with inflation but also because revanchist managers sought to claw back the concessions which had been extorted from them. So, until a greater conflict supervened, there was constant guerrilla warfare on the French industrial front, culminating in occasional pitched battles.

Louis Renault complained that, after the events of June 1936, his works became the object of massive attack from extremists. "Continual stoppages, repeated acts of indiscipline, a systematic slow-down in production," he said, "rendered the atmosphere of our factory more and more poisonous."[68] Having tasted freedom, the denizens of Billancourt were unwilling to accept renewed servitude, even if on easier terms. One replied to a foreman's reprimand that "he had had enough, that it had to blow up, and that the next time workers would not hang foremen and bosses in effigy but for real."[69] It was a token that, in the years before the Second World War, France would continue to be a prey to bitterness and tumult.

MEANWHILE, another Popular Front was facing a challenge more violent than anything seen at the time in France. In mid-July 1936 a military insurrection—a *pronunciamiento*—was launched against the Republican government of Spain. Recently elected in conditions of turmoil, it too had aimed at "moderate" reform,[70] arousing visionary expectations among its adherents and corresponding fears of Red revolution among its adversaries. Weak in armaments but strong in mass support, it was soon engaged in a ferocious civil war against General Francisco Franco's Nationalist coalition. So opened a still more tragic play within the European play. Many people regarded it as a microcosm of the world-wide struggle against fascism. But for the French it was a seismic extension of the great rift which threatened to split the Hexagon in half. It was a fight in which Spanish blood was being shed for French ideals. It was another stage in the conflict which was kindling during the Concorde riots and perhaps due to culminate in a global conflagration. As the Communist writer André Chamson put it: "The Spanish War was a shock even more profound than that of February 6th. We saw there the symbol of liberty in peril and the prefiguration of our future."[71]

The burning question thus became: would the French Popular Front help its Spanish counterpart? When the leader of the Madrid government, José Giral, appealed for arms, Blum's first instinct was to agree. He was supported outside the government by the Communists and within the administration by left-wing colleagues such as Léo Lagrange and Pierre Cot, the Aviation Minister. However, opposing the move were not only the predictable friends of Franco in France but pacifists, moderates, Catholics, ex-Premiers Herriot and Chautemps, and members of a bourgeoisie petrified by the spectre of Communism. The novelist François Mauriac voiced their views: "If it were found that our rulers are actively collaborating in the Iberian massacre, we would know that France is governed not by statesmen but by gang bosses acting on the orders of what must be called the International of Hatred."[72] This message was discreetly but influentially echoed by an "extremely worried" British government.[73] It had a "strong pro-rebel feeling"[74] and shrank from what promised to be a dress rehearsal for a second world war—perhaps even its opening night. Blum too feared that aiding Spain might precipitate a general conflict, one in which Britain could remain neutral and "half of France would not follow me."[75] There was also, Blum said subsequently, an associated danger:

"In France we too were on the verge of experiencing a military coup d'état."[76]

Blum was too cautious to risk more French civil strife. He was too scrupulous to force his convictions on a divided nation. He was too civilised to imitate fascist governments, desiring instead to set the world an example of "conciliatory politics."[77] As André Malraux later observed, "Blum valued conciliation to the same extent as General de Gaulle valued inflexibility."[78] So the Premier changed tack and, in agreement with other countries, adopted the policy of "non-intervention"—a term which, as Talleyrand had said, roughly corresponded in meaning to "intervention." Blum's "non-intervention"—he denied Madrid more than a clandestine trickle of French munitions—actually helped Franco, who was in receipt of substantial supplies from Mussolini and Hitler. This in itself was an unsafe course, as Blum knew: the menace of fascist encirclement was worse than the threat of Bismarck's hostile Prussian-Iberian alliance—the Iron Chancellor had proposed to apply the Spanish mustard plaster to the back of France's neck. So Spain became his "torture."[79] It lacerated his soul. When he died, Blum said, Spain would be written on his heart as Calais had been written on the heart of Mary Tudor.

The Premier made much of his anguish and his idealism, which were, no doubt, quite genuine. Indeed, it was the essence of Blum's tragedy that his qualities rather than his defects led him to abandon Spain. Yet he was not a complete stranger to political chicanery. He extolled press freedom but closed down a Trotskyist journal and passed a gagging law on newspapers when their attacks on his government became too fierce. He held enlightened views about the equality of the sexes but included three women in his cabinet chiefly to avoid embracing female suffrage, which would have increased the conservative vote. Though a socialist and a Jew, Blum welcomed Schacht to Paris on the grounds that nothing could be gained by treating ideological barriers as insurmountable. Where Spain was concerned, the principled Blum capitulated to circumstances. Other considerations apart, the lingering Depression, which thwarted nearly all the ameliorative efforts of the Popular Front, made it impossible for France to compete successfully against Germany and Italy in supplying arms to Spain. It was therefore better, as Eden said, to have a dam that leaked than no dam at all. So Blum persevered with the charade of non-intervention even though it became plain almost immediately after Mussolini and Hitler had signed the agreement in August 1936 that they had no intention of abiding by its provisions, which were neither enforceable nor legally binding.

Understandable and perhaps even inevitable though it was, Blum's wary, legalistic policy towards Spain proved disastrous for France. It allowed Germany and Italy to seize the initiative: to exploit Spanish mineral wealth for the purposes of rearmament; to use the peninsula as a military testing-ground and a political distraction; to seal the Rome-Berlin Axis; to demonstrate the invincibility of fascism. Meanwhile democratic France (like Britain) looked feeble as well as hypocritical. Belgium no longer trusted its neighbour: seeking safety in neutrality, King Leopold III withdrew from the Franco-Belgian Pact, leaving an unfortified frontier north of the Maginot Line. The Pyrenees would mark another hostile border. Soviet confidence in France as an ally against Germany was further shaken—a feeling powerfully reciprocated in Paris because of Stalin's purges. Clinging to Britain, a demoralised France lost the power to act alone. By failing to stand beside its Spanish alter ego the Popular Front discredited itself. Blum's government prepared France for future capitulations.

Echoing Haile Selassie, the famous Communist firebrand Dolores Ibarruri—La Pasionaria—emphasised this point on her visit to Paris early in September 1936. She made no impression on Blum himself, who sorrowfully wiped his eyes on a silk handkerchief, filling her "with moral and physical revulsion."[80] But she electrified a vast rally in support of the Spanish government at the huge bicycling stadium in the 15th arrondissement, the Vélodrome d'Hiver. She also belied her reputation as a maenadic mob-orator—in a classic atrocity story *L'Action française* had just accused her of biting a monk to death in the streets of Madrid. Her dress black, her greying hair tied in a bun, her strong face radiant with emotion, the Basque Joan of Arc spoke in Spanish but held her listeners spellbound with "the most beautiful voice ever heard on any French platform." Mellow as a viola, it performed every modulation from scorn to pathos, from anguish to anger. La Pasionaria's message was simple and vatic. Her courageous compatriots needed guns and aeroplanes from France, for they were engaged in a universal struggle against fascism. "It is Spain to-day, but it may be your turn tomorrow."[81] In that very stadium, after the great round-up of June 1942, Jews were held before being sent to German concentration camps.

Nevertheless this 30,000-strong meeting was, like so much during the years of the Popular Front, politics as spectacle. With its red and gold Spanish flags, its streamers, slogans, icons and music, the demonstration bore certain resemblances to rallies in Nuremberg, Rome and Moscow. French choreographers knew how to dramatise their propaganda with processions and incantations. They employed imaginative special effects such as sky-writing and releasing thousands of pigeons. Their *son et lumière* performances were particularly impressive—the "sudden darkening" of venues such as the Vélodrome d'Hiver, the floodlighting of immense portraits of Socialist saints like Jaurès, "the singing of the Internationale, *sotto voce,* in the darkness by all those thousands of men, exploding as the light returned." Indeed the Popular Front was influenced by a student of totalitarian techniques of mass brainwashing named Sergei Chakhotin. He believed that the democracies too should engage in the "psychical rape" of crowds, but that it should be "scientifically planned" along Pavlovian lines for the purpose of "saving . . . humanity."[82] The fact was, however, that where Hitler and Mussolini starred in a brutal theatre of power the Popular Front staged tinsel fêtes of fraternity. These were in some ways a form of escapism, a cathartic flight from the hardships and hazards of the time. But by the summer of 1936, with the outbreak of the Spanish Civil War following so fast on the occupation of the Rhineland, it was becoming harder to avoid reality.

Spain fatally divided the Popular Front, compelling its members to take sides over the issue of non-intervention, just as it impelled democrats everywhere to take sides in the greater conflict between fascism and Communism. Neutrality remained possible. So did lukewarmness. The workers of Billancourt, for example, were hampered in helping "the heroic people of Spain" by their wish to preserve the Popular Front in France.[83] And Winston Churchill's son Randolph was not far wrong in asserting that the British public regarded the Spanish Civil War as "just a lot of bloody dagoes killing each other."[84] But for many Spain seemed to insist on the existential duty to choose, to decide whom to back in what the trade union leader Léon Jouhaux called this "struggle of the light against the night."[85] Of course, in an era when systematic obfuscation contrived false dawns, blinding mirages and crepuscular delusions, light and darkness could be confused. They often were; but the Iberian issue seemed clear. For both Right and Left the Spanish Civil War was a "holy war,"[86] a "crusade,"[87] "the last great cause,"[88] "the struggle for the soul of Europe."[89] Spain reinforced the powerful Manichean tendencies of the age, the belief that the world was the scene of a cosmic duel between good and evil. Even sceptics could convince themselves for a time that the lesser of two evils was wholly good. So commitment was commonplace, particularly as André Malraux's prophecy was in the process of coming true. "Fascism has spread its great black wings over Europe," he had said. "Soon there will be action, blood for blood."[90]

In the summer of 1936 Malraux himself experienced action and bloodshed. Probably the first French writer to enter the cold, sunlit arena of Spain, he anticipated hundreds of intellectuals and thousands of workers, an international brigade who "presented their lives"[91] in what they believed to be a just cause. Despite an adventurous career Malraux was by no means altogether the stuff of which heroes are made. Bibliophile, arachnophobe, pornographer, mythomaniac, this dandy from Montmartre claimed to have been a Kuomintang commissar in Canton when he had really gone to Indo-China in search of loot and narrowly missed a term in gaol. Always exuding a whiff of charlatanism, he seemed not to take himself seriously—except as a great novelist (he had lobbied ruthlessly to ensure that *La Condition humaine* won the Goncourt Prize in 1933). Some of his habits were odd: he not only chain-smoked but ate a kilogram of sugar lumps a day. Like Malraux's character, his appearance was (to use a slang term he favoured) *farfelu*, bizarre. He had a long, lank forelock, a pointed chin and huge eyes whose pupils were like dark yolks set high in pools of white. His gaunt, pallid countenance was disfigured by tics. His conversation was punctuated by "awe-inspiring nervous sniffs" which sounded to Arthur Koestler like "the cry of a wounded jungle beast" and were "followed by a slap of his palm against his nose."[92] Yet Malraux's "fearless, dangerous talent" was, as Léon Daudet said, "at once sombre and luminous like some chiaroscuro painting."[93] He was not only a writer of genius but a determined fellow-traveller. To defeat fascism he was prepared to sacrifice a measure of intellectual integrity. He hailed Russia as a land of freedom, for example, even though the Moscow edition of *La Condition humaine* had been altered without his permission to express Soviet views of the Chinese revolution. Furthermore, this self-intoxicated opportunist was willing to sacrifice his life to create a "legend"[94] like that of T. E. Lawrence, who haunted his imagination. Only in the sky, Malraux obviously concluded, could he play such a decisive role.

Taking advantage of the indecision of the French Popular Front in July and early August 1936, Malraux recruited pilots (nearly all mercenaries) and acquired a job lot of aircraft, mostly Dewoitine fighters and Potez 540 bombers. Other flying "coffins"[95] he claimed to have bought at a flea market, including Douglases, Blochs, Bréguets and the Emperor Haile Selassie's personal aeroplane. With the secret connivance of Blum and Cot, Malraux spirited this aerial armada out of France just before the non-intervention embargo came into force. Standing with his "legs spread, hands in his pockets, a cigarette in his mouth," as the planes took off from Montaudran airport near Toulouse, he looked to one observer "like a music-hall owner during a dress rehearsal."[96]

Once across the Pyrenees himself, "Coronel" Malraux commanded the España Squadron which was initially based at Barajas airport outside Madrid. Much has been made of the "inestimable services"[97] rendered by Malraux and his flying foreign legion to the cause of the Republic at a time when its resistance was still disorganised. But the truth is lost in a cumulus of myth louring over the high sierras. Malraux himself was no pilot—he apparently flew as a gunner-bombardier.[98] His mercenary fliers were, in the opinion of an American airman, "a bunch of racketeers." His machines, some "so slow it was a crime,"[99] were no match for Fiats, Savoias or Junkers. "It was never a question of engaging in combat with fascist fighters," writes a recent scholar, "but of returning to the aerodrome in one piece."[100] Early missions mainly involved reconnaissance and attacking enemy factories, sometimes by throwing bombs out of the plane windows or dropping them by hand through latrine vents. Nevertheless, Malraux's courage and example, together with his squadron's challenge to fascist mastery of the air, did much for Republican morale. And in mid-August 1936 at the village of Medellin (birthplace of Cortés, conqueror of Mexico) Malraux's planes damaged a motorised column which Franco was thrusting towards Madrid.

The novelist gave a graphic account of the raid in *L'Espoir*. He described how six rickety planes, the Douglases armed with 1913 machine-guns, flew through the heat haze which quivered across the harvest-coloured earth of Estremadura. They passed over the time-scarred city of Badajoz with its Alcázar and deserted bull-ring. They followed the road to Medellin, "a ribbon of incandescent light" against the blinding glare. There they rained destruction on the advancing convoy, the Moors, specks of khaki dotted with white turbans, fleeing like panicked ants. Finally they attacked its main body in the narrow streets of the village.

> The falling bombs flickered across a belt of sunlight, vanished, and sped on with the free movement of torpedoes. The square began to fill with smoke, and bursts of sudden flame exploding everywhere like mines. Upon the highest flame, in a swirl of dense brown smoke, a plume of white shot up; then, suddenly, above it, a tiny black lorry turned a fantastic somersault and fell back into the murk below.[101]

Perhaps Malraux exaggerated the destructive effect of the air raid, just as his own role in Republican resistance was exaggerated. But such accounts rang true to a generation which feared bombers as much as their children would fear nuclear missiles. The Spanish Civil War brought home to contemporaries not only the horror but the imminence of a European— perhaps even a global—civil war. To the French in particular, so long preoccupied with their domestic crisis, it was a terrible adumbration of the catastrophe to come.

PART THREE

CANYON

XV

THE COMING OF THE SPANISH
CIVIL WAR

IT is ironic that Spain, a baffling *terra incognita*, should have become the screen on to which outsiders projected their own concerns with such luminous clarity. The more fractured and opaque that rough Iberian square, the more those abroad made it the focus of their certainties. The Spanish Civil War appeared to alien eyes as a clash of international creeds. It seemed to crystallise the universal opposition between bosses and workers, between Church and State, between obscurantism and enlightenment. In the words of Jason Gurney, a Briton who came to fight for the Republic,

> Everybody saw Spain as the epitome of the particular conflict with which they were concerned. It was for this reason that the writers of the Western world became so emotionally involved in the Spanish conflict. For myself, and a great number of people like me, it became the great symbol of the struggle between Democracy and Fascism everywhere.[1]

Spain did indeed become an ideological battleground whose armies were loud in their determination to crush Communism or to "smash Fascism."[2] The American Alvah Bessie even asserted that his comrades in the International Brigades were "among the first soldiers in the history of the world who really knew what they were fighting for."[3]

However, they thought they knew almost everything because they actually knew almost nothing about Spain. Propagandists grossly simplified and distorted the issues. The "art of lying," as one authority has said, "attained new levels of perfection during the Spanish Civil War."[4] Foreigners saw what they wanted to see in this bloody combat. They accepted it as a dramatic struggle between good and evil just as they accepted the touristic view that Spain was a land of contrasts. *"Sol o sombra,"* said Premier Manuel Azaña, confirming the cliché with a metaphor drawn from the bull-ring, whose seats are so named depending on whether or not they are protected from the glare. "Spain is like that . . . it is always sun or shade."[5]

Amid confusion which hung over the Spanish arena like dust on a hot afternoon, strangers missed the nuances of this duel to the death.

Spain was not so much a land of contrasts as "a bundle of small bodies tied together by a rope of sand."[6] It was "a geographical expression,"[7] a cultural medley, a linguistic discord reverberating through giant cordilleras. It was a confederacy of cantons linked by tenuous communications—few roads were metalled and there were three different railway gauges. Detached from Africa yet isolated from Europe, Spain's 24 million people owed little allegiance to Madrid. They identified with their *patria chica,* or "regional homeland." Their loyalties were to remote Galicia, a granite mosaic of tiny farmsteads; or to the rugged Basque provinces, Catholic, semi-industrialised and militant for autonomy; or to mountainous Navarre, with its equally quixotic devotion to Church and King; or to golden Catalonia, with its flourishing vineyards, its thriving textile trade and its anarchist, separatist traditions; or to warm Valencia, whose fertile *huerta* was the rice bowl and the orange grove of Spain; or to austere Castile, its bare *meseta* alternately parched and frozen; or to voluptuous Andalusia, supposedly created by God as a refuge if He ever got bored with heaven, but actually a kind of hell for the destitute quasi-serfs on its vast feudal estates.

Here, as in neighbouring Estremadura and other impoverished parts of Spain, "the autochthonous life of the villages,"[8] with their local customs and costumes, superstitions and vendettas, had hardly been affected by the modern world. Men used Stone Age harrows, sickles which had not changed since the Bronze Age, threshing-boards like those described in the Old Testament, ploughs such as were depicted on ancient Greek vases. Peasants might wear black corduroy suits but they had an essentially medieval mentality: some feared witchcraft, others thought that Protestants had tails. Many peasants belonged neither to the nation nor to a party: they "belonged to the land."[9] They belonged to tribal villages, which they would often guard during the Civil War while refusing to send men to the front. They belonged to sleepy *pueblos* whose sordid, zigzag streets were flanked by grey adobe houses, most of them flea-ridden hovels where the floors were beaten earth, the windows were black holes and the rooms reeked of smoke and dung.

Fierce "village patriotism"[10] might have produced unity even in diversity. But, riven by regionalism, Spain was also fragmented by factionalism. The deepest fissure was between rich and poor: over half of Spain went to bed hungry each night. Wages were so low in Galicia that handmade lace could compete with factory products. But the worst-off were in the south, where labourers were known as "machines of blood."[11] They earned as little as 2 pesetas (1 shilling or 24 US cents) a day and spent about a third of the year in enforced idleness. Thus they ate, as they lived, less well than their masters' donkeys. At Castilblanco desperate men were arrested for gathering acorns, a crop consecrated to pigs. Near Ciudad Real famished peasants fed on grass. Although ill-educated and often illiterate—the governing classes did not want "men who think, but oxen who work"[12]— Spain's dispossessed inevitably contrasted their lot with that of the 10,000 families which owned half the country's cultivable land. As a result simmering agrarian troubles constantly threatened to boil over and social antagonism was more acute than anywhere else in Europe. One peasant recorded:

> We hated the bourgeoisie, they treated us like animals. When we looked at them we thought we were looking at the devil himself. And they thought the same of us. There was a hatred between us—a hatred so great that it couldn't have been greater.[13]

Aristocrats hated too. One would blame the Civil War on "modern drainage: prior to this, the riff-raff had been killed by various useful diseases; now they survived and, of course, were above themselves . . . When the war is over we should destroy the sewers."[14]

In the land which (according to Pliny) had invented wars in order to fight them and which gave the term *guerrilla* to the world, in the land of the Conquistadores and the *furia española,* in the land of Torquemada and Goya, primitive peasants were incipient brigands if not outright revolutionaries. They were kept in check by a moribund government, a bloated bureaucracy and rapacious political bosses called *caciques,* whose instrument of repression was the Guardia Civil. This was a notoriously brutal police force which had been founded by the nineteenth-century "strong man" General Narváez who, when invited on his deathbed to forgive his enemies, replied that he had none because he had killed them all. The Civil Guard was a virtual army of occupation. Its men wore green uniforms and tricorn hats like enamelled coffins. They had shiny black boots and (according to the poet García Lorca) "patent leather souls."[15] Almost as blatantly the Church aided the State, though, since nothing was simple in Spain, some priests identified with their flocks and their regions. The ecclesiastical hierarchy, however, in a country barely touched by the Enlightenment, let alone by the Reformation, retained an *auto-da-fé* mentality. It used the confessional for surveillance, the pulpit for propaganda and the catechism to damn liberals to hell. Long opposed to "the disastrous mania for thinking,"[16] the clergy sometimes stopped the teaching of reading in schools to prevent children from being corrupted by Marxist literature. Preaching the merits of poverty while laying up treasure on earth, the Church implicitly endorsed the proverb that "Money is a good Catholic." So this rich, hypocritical organisation was loathed in Spain with a ferocity which foreigners found incomprehensible. What had been a consolidating force during the long re-conquest of the Iberian peninsula from the Moors was now more than a source of social dissension; it was an incitement to violence.

The most vigorous protest against the authority of the Church—against all authority, indeed—was anarchism. This was not just a revolutionary movement, it was a rival creed. Since its fortuitous introduction to Spain at the behest of Mikhail Bakunin in 1868, anarchism had spread through the country like pentecostal fire, establishing itself particularly strongly in Catalonia and Andalusia. Anarchists believed that "Money and power are the diabolical philtres that turn a man into a wolf." Anarchists wanted to liberate human beings not only from the baneful sway of the capitalist State but from their own base nature. They aimed to establish a brother-hood of workers on the ruins of civil society. Anarchists were not afraid of ruins according to one of their leaders, Buenaventura Durruti, a swarthy metal worker from León who during one spell of exile had found employ-ment with Renault. "We are going to inherit the earth," he said. "We carry a new world, here, in our hearts."[17] To achieve the day of secular salvation, anarchists preached a new puritanism. They frowned on drinking, smok-ing and bull-fighting; they praised sexual abstinence and condemned prostitution; they proselytised tirelessly for self-improvement. They also espoused terrorism. Echoing Diderot, Bakunin had forecast that the mil-lennium would arrive only when the last king had been strangled with the entrails of the last priest. Catching the mood of chiliastic exaltation, his followers burned convents and churches, which they anathematised as dens of "incense and darkness."[18] They mounted savage strikes, robbed banks and threw bombs. They assassinated politicians, insisting on the righteousness of murder without hate. It is true that moderate anarchism was by no means a contradiction in terms and it was increasingly strong among trade-unionists in Barcelona. But for so-called "uncontrollables" violence was the legitimate tactic of free men: "Nothing great has ever been achieved without violence . . . the sins of the old corrupt system can only be washed away in blood."[19]

Such extremism appealed to many of the other sects struggling over the carcass of Spain. But with their powerful support and their unruly tactics the anarchists, above all, made political moderation impossible. Conserva-tive governments could only achieve stability when they were led by an "iron surgeon"[20] such as General Primo de Rivera, the erratic 1920s dictator whom King Alfonso XIII had boastfully called "my Mussolini"—the King's subjects jested that he was Primo de Rivera but "*secundo de* Mussolini." Radical governments could only survive by making local concessions (such as granting self-rule to Catalonia) which sapped both their own strength and the integrity of the nation. Thus after the peaceful establishment of the Republic in 1931, Spain lurched from Left to Right, falling apart in the process.

The global economic crisis made matters worse. It depressed iron and steel production, reduced the export of olive oil and citrus fruits, and increased unemployment, especially in the Basque provinces. But being protected by its "relative backwardness and isolation,"[21] Spain was less seriously damaged than other major countries. It was tormented by political afflictions which were worse than economic woes. Whichever pretender to the throne they supported, monarchists could not accept the new dispensation. Communists, of whatever persuasion, were just as determined to set up a dictatorship of the proletariat. Different varieties of nationalists, conservatives, clericals, traditionalists, centrists, liberal democrats, separatists, radicals, left republicans, socialists and syndicalists were equally intransigent. If these irreconcilables were doomed at last to come to blows, it was the anarchists, living up to their name with a vengeance, who were to ensure that the Spanish Civil War was alloyed with revolution. They also helped to ensure that the revolution would not succeed. For, to quote Malraux's expression, it proved impossible "to *organize* the Apocalypse."[22]

No one tried harder to sustain the State against extremist assaults during the early 1930s than Manuel Azaña. Indeed, he came to seem the embodiment of the Republic. With his humane instincts, his lucid mind and his cultivated tastes, Azaña was in some ways the Spanish equivalent of Léon Blum. Born in 1880 in Alcalá de Henares near Madrid—the birthplace of Cervantes, whose house was in sight of his own—Azaña seemed made for literature. Shy, taciturn, precocious, he made books his closest companions, taking no interest in his father's soap factory or in the society of the charming old cathedral town with its evening promenades and its storks nesting on the roofs. Although he qualified as a lawyer, Azaña preferred to become a government official in Madrid with leisure to write. He quickly achieved eminence as a man of letters, though he did not win a popular audience—the philosopher Unamuno said that Azaña was "capable of starting a revolution" in order to get his books read.[23]

Actually Azaña was keener on abstract citizens than flesh-and-blood revolutionaries. But he was passionately committed to freedom, which might not make men happy, he was fond of saying, but at least made them men. As a boy, Azaña later recalled, he had played with a silver buckle and a majestically-plumed helmet belonging to his grandfather, himself a fighter for freedom, which he had cherished "like a personal religion." These military relics had transmitted

> across the dark gulf of the past century when all Spain was aflame with the struggle for liberty, a sense of that epic quality—indescribable and, in the soul of a child, ineradicable—which for me, since my earliest days, has been the splendid essence of Spanish liberalism.[24]

So Azaña plotted to rid Spain of the yoke of Church and King, spending months in hiding from the police before Alfonso was forced into an exile made sweeter by the huge sums of money he had smuggled abroad. Azaña devoted this period of enforced leisure to fiction and when the Republic was proclaimed, in April 1931, he remarked, "Another month and I would have finished the novel!"

Instead he became Minister of War and then Prime Minister (1931–33), making a reputation with his tongue that he could not gain with his pen. Azaña's speeches were masterpieces of eloquence, overwhelming in their power of thought and their clarity of expression. Appealing to reason, he was anything but a demagogue. Yet, as he hoped, his dazzling phrases pierced the hearts of hearers like "darts of fire." Fellow parliamentarians were so transfixed that they compared him to Mussolini. The magic of his utterance even seemed to transform Azaña's physical appearance—from frog to prince. His opponents frequently likened him to a frog, for Azaña was short, balding, glaucous and as corpulent as perpetual sweet-eating could make him. With his thick lips, bespectacled eyes and pendulous jowls, Azaña had, said the writer-diplomat Salvador de Madariaga, "the face of a man with few friends."[25]

His bilious pallor was accentuated by the artificial light of the Cortes, the Spanish parliament, a beautiful amphitheatre whose doors were guarded by bronze lions cast from ancient cannons, whose ceiling was supported by Corinthian columns and decorated with historical paintings and whose walls were adorned with marble memorials to former political leaders, many of them victims of violence. Here Azaña occupied the ministerial blue bench. Cool, aloof and enigmatic in repose, the ash on his cigarette growing so long that it fell on to the grey-blue British wool suitings that he favoured to cover his paunch, the Premier achieved a majestic metamorphosis once he rose to his feet. As the American Ambassador to Madrid, Claude Bowers, recorded: "His genius revealed itself when, in speaking, his face lit up amazingly. His eyes were keen, expressive, changing with the mood of the moment. His manner was serene."[26] Seeing himself as both teacher and ruler, Azaña was prone to long-windedness as well

John Heartfield's 1936 photomontage,
Fascist Memorials of Honour: Memorial of the Duce in Abyssinia

A prisoner inside Dachau, Hitler's first concentration camp

The public face of the SS, 1933: its leader, Heinrich Himmler, is third from the right, front row

A gateway into the Gulag on the anniversary of the October Revolution

Stalin's pillory: painted wooden images of unsatisfactory government employees—shirkers, drinkers and other such "criminals"—set up in Moscow's Park of Rest and Culture

Nippon's descent into the "dark valley": Japanese troops invade Manchuria, 1931

Hirohito, worshipped as the 124th Emperor of Japan, reigned from 1926 to 1989

Mao Tse-tung mobilises the Chinese masses, c. 1935

Civilians flee during a Japanese air raid on Canton, June 1938

Politicians, including Daladier (*left*), Herriot (*third from right*)
and Blum (*second from right*), at the Tomb of the Unknown
Soldier in Paris, Armistice Day 1936

A cross-section of the Maginot Line

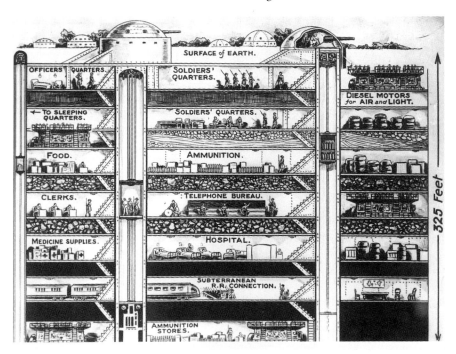

"Today Spain, tomorrow the world":
an anti-fascist poster issued by the united parties of the Spanish Left

General Francisco
Franco Bahamonde,
Caudillo of Spain

The Wehrmacht
parades at Hitler's tenth
Nuremberg Rally,
12 September 1938

as egocentricity, and his didactic style, so effective in the Cortes, was less well suited to popular audiences. But much could be forgiven a statesman whose mind was as sharp as a Toledo blade and whose purpose was to educate Spain in the principles of liberal democracy.

Unfortunately Spain could not learn his lessons during the 1930s. The Left derided liberals such as Azaña for planning "a brilliant future in the past" while the Right damned them for creating an "anti-Spain" in the image of Antichrist.[27] Moreover, Azaña, graceful in word, proved clumsy in deed; he was a polemical bull-fighter but a political bulldozer. In his efforts to introduce a welfare state, including a minimum wage, sickness benefits and paid holidays, Azaña did not really tackle the intractable problem of peasant poverty. True, some land redistribution did take place; but Azaña was so concerned about the nation's "finances" that he put balancing Spain's budget before trying to achieve proper agrarian reform.[28] However, he did establish a secular state. He broke the Church's hold on education, legalised civil marriage, expropriated Catholic property, suppressed the Jesuits and even appeared to tolerate the burning of ecclesiastical buildings. "All the convents in Spain," he memorably remarked, "are not worth a single Republican life."[29] Azaña gave Catalonia autonomy. He imposed modest tax increases on the rich, who invariably behaved as though their incomes were exempt from this indignity. Like other liberal leaders, Azaña made no bones about continuing to censor the press in the interests of what he took to be public safety. He exiled his enemies to North Africa and founded a force of blue-uniformed Assault Guards. This did not, however, put a stop to extremist efforts to throttle the young Republic. The anarchists were responsible for constant disturbances, sporadic strikes, often brutally suppressed, and occasional insurrections. Equally menacing was the right-wing coup of 1932 led by the fire-eating General José Sanjurjo, whose nickname was "Lion of the Rif"[30] and whose watchword was *"Viva España Indivisible!"*[31]

To unify Spain by force was to provoke civil war and to promote military dictatorship. But these consequences were obscured, as was the rebellious temper of the army, by the abject failure of Sanjurjo's *pronunciamiento*. Thereafter Azaña himself, who had witnessed Sanjurjadist skirmishers in action from the windows of the Ministry of War, underestimated the military threat. Yet, glorying in his ability to "pulverise"[32] the army with hard-hitting reforms, he had made bitter enemies within its ranks. Azaña had certainly done what was needful. In 1931 Spain's forces were corrupt, anachronistic and top-heavy. Although half the national budget was devoted to the armed services, they possessed almost no modern equipment. They had no tanks and some of their cavalry regiments had no horses. Their artillery was so obsolete that they had been out-gunned by the Moroccans. Most of their rifles were museum pieces and all their ammunition would have been exhausted by a battle lasting more than 24 hours. With no fighters and only one bomber (its largest bomb weighed 11 pounds), their air force consisted of flimsy reconnaissance planes. Spain boasted 800 generals and an officer corps the same size as that of the German army in 1914. Azaña had pensioned off two-thirds of its members on full pay, creating a formidable dissident cadre in the process. He had made the army more democratic, begun to provide it with new arms, and reorganised it in other ways. Not least, he closed the Saragossa Military Academy, the Spanish Sandhurst or West Point, whose director was Francisco Franco Bahamonde. Although he was the ablest general in the army, Franco also found himself reduced in rank as a result of Azaña's reforms.

Franco was a dangerous and a devious foe. He was ruthless and self-righteous, cold-blooded and courageous, ambitious and patriotic. Like Azaña, he longed for the regeneration of Spain, though their views on how this could be achieved had nothing in common. Franco's creed, though sometimes expressed in the vocabulary of fascism, was the old-fashioned nationalism of duty, honour, country. It seemed all the more passionate because he came from Galicia, a kind of Iberian Celtic fringe where bag-pipes and reels took the place of flamenco and fandango. Indeed, Franco's origins were as remote from Castile as Hitler's were from Prussia. Born in 1892 at the port of El Ferrol, the son of a rakish civil servant whom he detested and a devout mother whom he adored, Franco would have entered the navy but for its virtual annihilation during the Spanish-American War. Instead, aged 15, he enrolled in the Military Academy at Toledo. Here the "Little Matchstick," as he had been nicknamed, was the smallest of the cadets. He was a frail figure with a high-pitched voice, pro-tuberant ears and a long, Semitic face which seemed to confirm rumours about Jewish forebears. When seniors tried to bully him, though, he responded so fiercely that he soon earned their respect. Solitary and stu-dious, though also rather slow, he lived for his profession. And as a subal-tern he showed himself ready to die for it. Posted to Morocco, where a colonial conflict had simmered for years, he distinguished himself by his superhuman bravery.

Other soldiers treated Spain's turbulent Arab protectorate as "a brothel and an immense tavern."[33] To the puritanical, humourless Franco it was simply a battlefield. Like young Winston Churchill fighting against the Pathans, he paraded up and down the lines on a white horse, attracting and ignoring bullets. When one knocked the cork from his canteen he called across to the Moroccans, "Better shot next time."[34] Franco became the ace of the Spanish Foreign Legion, whose men were (in his words) "shipwrecked from life"[35] and whose motto (coined by General Millán Astray) was "Long live Death." Franco matched the cruelties of the Moroccan tribesmen, encouraging pillage and once commending a bugler for having killed and cut off the ears of an unarmed prisoner. For their part, the Moroccans thought that he was blessed with divine protection. However, in 1916 he earned the more substantial benefit of royal favour after being seriously wounded—he survived only by threatening to shoot the doctor who thought him too far gone to be worth evacuating to hospital. Decorated and promoted, Franco became a Gentleman of the Bedchamber. Alfonso XIII "sponsored" his marriage, which was twice postponed to accommodate his military duties.[36] The King addressed him with the familiar "tú" and sent him a medal blessed by the Virgin of Pilar. Yet when the Republic was proclaimed, no one seemed to swear it fealty with greater sincerity than the King's favourite general—the youngest European general, indeed, since Napoleon. The new regime was doubtless anathema to Franco. But he refused to commit himself to his friend Sanjurjo's tragi-comic coup. "Franco," wrote the royalist airman Juan Antonio Ansaldo, "is a man who declares himself, and then retracts; draws near, and then steps back, vanishes or slides away; always vague, never clear and categorical."[37] He was like the proverbial Galician peasant, of whom it is said that if you meet him on the stairs you can never tell whether he is going up or down.

Franco's reward for equivocation was command of the Balearics. Azaña's reward for contention was defeat in the elections of November 1933. By antagonising extremists he had alienated moderates. So centre-right parties emerged victorious. But not even the strongest of them, the Catholic alliance formed by an able young lawyer called José María Gil Robles, who had met Hitler and employed Nazi campaign techniques such as dropping leaflets from aircraft, could form a government alone. What followed, therefore, was the *"Bienio Negro"*—the two black years. During this time weak coalitions, dominated by the foxy, philandering Radical Republican Alejandro Lerroux, attempted to impose order on Spain. Their attempt was doomed. Conflict grew more acute as the government reversed most of Azaña's measures. Reactionary triumphalism provoked revolutionary terrorism—strikes, riots, sabotage, murder. Spaniards donned their martial liveries: the Carlists of Navarre, more royalist than the King, their red berets and yellow tassels; Catalan militiamen, rising to another challenge from Madrid, their green shirts; Falangists, members of the party recently founded by the dictator's handsome son José Antonio Primo de Rivera in emulation of Mussolini's Fascists, their blue blouses. They unfurled banners rich in symbolism: the anarchist flag, its colours adopted by the Falangists, was "Red for the struggle and black because human thought is dark."[38] They put on their badges: the Carlists, for example, festooning themselves with rosary beads, crucifixes and other religious talismans. They mouthed their slogans, none more potent than the cry *"UHP,"* or "Proletarian Brothers Unite," adopted by the coal miners of Asturias.

This region, indeed, witnessed the Spanish proletariat's first attempt to mount a full-scale revolution. It was prompted by Francisco Largo Caballero who, in his bowler hat, well-filled black suit and lace-up boots, looked like the stolid, pipe-smoking bricklayer and trade union leader he had been. However, he was misled by a thoroughly inappropriate title which the Communists, now eager to ally with the Socialists, bestowed on him—the "Spanish Lenin."[39] As such he threatened to fight if Gil Robles's supporters entered the cabinet. This they did in 1934, prompting fears that the Spanish Republic was about to go the way of Weimar. But the left-wing uprising which followed was quickly crushed everywhere except in Asturias. Here, though pay was relatively good, conditions underground were worse even than those in Russian mines. Socialists, anarchists, Communists and other working-class parties sank their differences to create a force of some 30,000 men. Although they could not overcome the Oviedo garrison they conquered much of the region, making up for their dearth of artillery with explosive charges accurately hurled by *dinamiteros* skilled at the game of pelota. In the course of this fighting the Church suffered and atrocities took place, much inflated by government propaganda. As Azaña had warned Largo Caballero, the revolt invited military repression.

Franco was put in command and he brought over units from the Army of Africa. After pitiless fighting it defeated the miners in the mountain fastness against which the Moorish wave had once broken and from where the Christian re-conquest had begun 12 centuries before. As if in revenge, Moroccan troops were given leave to rape, loot, mutilate and murder. Here was a foretaste of the "colonial" methods which Franco would later employ all over Spain. His most notorious henchman at this time was Major Lisardo Doval of the Civil Guard who was "determined to exterminate the seeds of revolution even in the bellies of the mothers."[40] He subjected his victims to such euphemistically-named tortures as the "tube of laughter" (a gauntlet of jeering, beating guards), the "concert hall" (a variety performance evoking "shrieks of torment") and the "aeroplane" (which jerked prisoners off the ground by their wrists tied behind their backs).[41] Franco tried to conceal these crimes by imposing an "iron censorship"[42] while the right-wing press created a smokescreen of atrocity stories about crucified priests and violated nuns. But as a woman who helped to expose the truth observed: "What is happening in Spain is like the delayed explosion of the dark medieval spirit."[43] Arguably the left-wing parties had sparked off this explosion for they initiated what was, in effect, a "dress rehearsal" for the Civil War.[44] They were, at any rate, morally ill-equipped to denounce military rebellion against democracy in 1936. On the other hand Franco, who was honoured by the Right with command of the Army of Africa while being dubbed by the Left "Butcher of Asturias," bore responsibility for retribution which cost 2,000 lives. Having sown dragons' teeth, he reaped a people's army.

Initially, though, what the Asturian conflict produced was the Popular Front. Reacting not only against the violence but against the corruption and ineptitude of the government, left-wing parties united to form the Spanish equivalent of Blum's coalition in France. It was, however, much less coherent. Along with 30,000 other political prisoners, most of its leaders had been gaoled after the Asturian uprising. Huddled in a heavy overcoat, thick muffler and blue beret against the icy blasts that swept down from the Guadarramas, Largo Caballero—the Spanish Lenin—rekindled his revolutionary ardour inside Madrid's Model Prison: for the first time he read the works of the real Lenin. Azaña, on the other hand, detained on board a prison ship at Barcelona, became demoralised and disillusioned. He could joke that he was proposing to charge his many visitors five pesetas a ticket. But he confided to his intimates that "The Republic is finished."[45]

His pessimism seemed justified at a great rally which he addressed, after his release, on a chilly, overcast Sunday in October 1935. Denied the use of Madrid's bull-ring, at least 200,000 people gathered on waste ground known as the Campo de Comillas in the working-class suburb of Carabanchel on the south bank of the Manzanares River. Despite Civil Guard hostility they had come by train, lorry, cart, bus, or burro and on foot—a few had tramped all the way from Asturias. Azaña's baroque periods, his disquisition on the budget and his appeal for tolerance, were uninspiring when they were not inaudible. His peroration was more effective: Spain, like all Europe, was "a battlefield" between democracy with its admitted errors and dictatorship with its manifest horrors—fanaticism, violence and war.[46] But when the crowd, roused at last to vociferous enthusiasm, gave the clenched-fist salute, Azaña was too proud and too fastidious to return it. A bourgeois liberal, he was incapable of riding the storm of a proletarian revolution.

However, it was as a broad-based coalition that the Popular Front succeeded at the general election of February 1936. Every influence had been used to defeat it, including a wild propaganda campaign. The Bishop of Barcelona declared that "A vote for the conservative candidate is a vote for Christ."[47] Gil Robles plastered Madrid with posters, one of which announced that there had been "no tuberculosis under the monarchy."[48] In this "battle of billboards" the Left published pictures of a top-hatted tycoon pushing the weeping mother of Liberty off a cliff. It also issued placards announcing that "Rightism is Fascism—Fascism is War."[49] Thanks to the vagaries of the Republic's voting system the Popular Front, which won a small majority in the polling-booth, won a large majority in the Cortes. Out of a total of over 470 seats, held by more than a dozen parties, the Communists had 14 and the Falangists had none—arithmetical proof that Spain was then anything but a reflection of the wider struggle between Bolshevism and fascism. All the same, everything pointed to civil war. The prophecies of the philosopher Ortega y Gasset seemed to be coming true: the triumph of "hyperdemocracy" was at hand in which "the mass acts directly, outside the law, imposing its aspirations and desires by means of material pressure."[50] Even the Surrealists were realistic about the impending conflict. Salvador Dali painted a premonition of it, as did Joán Miró, whose *Man and Woman in Front of a Pile of Excrement* is a phantasmagoria of burning landscapes under the pall of night.

As Azaña resumed the premiership, on 19 February 1936, the country was racked by further internal convulsions. Matters were made worse by inflation and by under- or unemployment which affected almost a fifth of the workforce. Spain had no unemployment relief and, as in Weimar Germany, the jobless swelled the ranks of the political activists and fatally undermined the stability of the regime. There were parades, strikes, brawls, shootings, lynchings, church burnings, peasant occupations of farms, attempts by commercial interests to subvert the Popular Front and rumours of conspiracies, coups and revolutions. When further pleas for moderation and reconciliation proved ineffective, Azaña hit back at the government's most provocative opponent. He arrested José Antonio Primo de Rivera and dissolved the Falange. But he failed to suppress it. Moreover, his steps to neutralise the army, among them the transfer of Franco to the Canary Islands, were equally unsuccessful.

Azaña was, in fact, helpless against those intent on using republican liberty to destroy the Republic. Perhaps the resources of Spanish democracy were inadequate to resist a dictatorship of some kind. But in the last resort Azaña, who had aged visibly, lacked the strength and the courage even to use them. Thus in May 1936 he was content to be elevated to the presidency. This largely honorific position gave him a commanding view of, but a spectator's role in, the unfolding Spanish tragedy. It began, he observed, with "radiant optimism," as the minds of nearly all his country-men were fired with messianic aspirations. One side was intent on saving Christian civilisation while the other proclaimed the birth of a new civili-sation: "Terrible hyperboles that easily inflame what is visionary in the Spanish soul."[51]

Azaña's friend and successor as Premier, the well-meaning Santiago Casares Quiroga, offered no comparable inspiration. A Galician sparrow whose shrill outbursts hardly concealed a basic frailty, he was buffeted from Left and Right. Largo Caballero, who had refused to join the govern-ment, was "the chief exponent . . . of the revolutionary idea."[52] Although opposed by moderate socialists under the dynamic, diabetic Indalecio Pri-eto, he terrified the bourgeoisie by saying that he wanted a Republic with-out class war, "but for this it is necessary that one class disappears."[53] Rivalling even the anarchists, socialist gunmen were so active that some kind of working-class insurrection did seem to be the main danger facing the Republic. On the other hand, Falangists raced through slums in auto-mobiles spraying the inhabitants with bullets. Monarchists were muster-ing. And quasi-fascist politicians such as José Calvo Sotelo publicly called for the army to rescue the Fatherland from Bolshevism.

Ever since the Popular Front's victory a military plot had, indeed, been brewing. Its director was General Emilio Mola, who, like his co-conspirator Sanjurjo, was later killed in an air crash. This would leave the stage clear for Franco, but for the time being he remained coyly uncom-mitted. Sanjurjo complained that Franco would "always be in the shad-ows, because he is crafty."[54] Mola went so far as to call Franco "the biggest old hen"[55] of all the generals and they themselves nicknamed him "Miss Canary Islands 1936." With his feminine voice, his clammy handshake, his pot belly and his double chin, Franco did not seem an incipient dictator. But there was an adamantine will behind his quiet manner and his eyes were chips of ice. As late as June, when his warning to Casares Quiroga about the perils of "collective indiscipline"[56] was ignored, Franco still hesi-tated. In the same month Gil Robles gave the Cortes a memorable (and doubtless unreliable) inventory of the violence that had taken place under the Popular Front: 269 political murders, 1,287 people wounded, 113 major strikes, 160 churches gutted, 10 newspaper offices destroyed, and so on. "Spain is in anarchy," he pronounced. "And we are today present at the funeral service of democracy."[57]

Calvo Sotelo followed with a bitter diatribe against the government, threatening it with a military revolt. In the uproar that followed, the pale-faced, black-garbed figure of La Pasionaria allegedly rose and, pointing her finger at him, intoned: "That was your last speech."[58] If the story is true, and she always denied it, this was a vatic utterance. On 12 July, in revenge for a Falangist murder, Assault Guards took Calvo from his house and shot him dead, dumping his body at Madrid's East Cemetery. Here was spine-chilling proof that the government could no longer govern. It prompted Franco to throw in his lot with the conspirators and it enabled them to present their sedition as patriotism. From his headquarters in Pamplona the cunning, bespectacled Mola signalled the start of the uprising with a coded broadcast message: "All over Spain the sky is cloudless."[59] It was vital, he believed, to hold the country back from "the very brink of the abyss."[60]

NEEDLESS to say, the rebellion plunged Spain into the abyss. What the generals hoped would be an old-fashioned *pronunciamiento,* leading to the speedy establishment of authoritarian rule according to precedents established by Narváez, Primo de Rivera and other "strong men," provoked widespread resistance, social revolution and civil war. Each side adopted the European terminology of the day. Nationalists (as the rebels quickly came to call themselves) used the rhetoric of fascism, not least to secure aid from Mussolini and Hitler. Republicans spoke the language of democracy, presenting themselves as the defenders of an ideal with international appeal. Most foreigners accepted these representations at face value. On the first anniversary of the rebellion's outbreak Salvador de Madariaga noted:

> By a tragic coincidence this war, essentially Spanish, has "caught on" abroad. Lured by somewhat shallow parallelisms, men, institutions and even Governments outside Spain have been adding fuel to the fire which is consuming our unhappy country. Spain is thus suffering vicariously the latent civil war which Europe is—so far—keeping in check.[61]

Thus illusion made reality more terrible. And reality in July 1936 was not just a State dividing against itself but a nation disintegrating along so many fault lines that father was often ranged against son, and brother did take up arms against brother.

In some places the issue was never in doubt. Burgos, the city of El Cid, declared for the rebels without a struggle. As one aristocrat boasted, "The very stones are nationalist here."[62] In monarchist Pamplona the uprising was greeted with spontaneous scenes of enthusiasm. Zamora, Palencia, Salamanca, Avila, Segovia, Huesca, Teruel and Cáceres were won by the Nationalists with little or no bloodshed. Spanish Morocco also quickly rallied to Franco. He flew to Tetuán from the Canaries in a chartered British Dragon Rapide biplane, paid for by the tobacco tycoon Juan March, and took command of the tough, professional Army of Africa which was to play such a crucial role in his victory. Elsewhere violence, trickery, accident and audacity achieved vital gains for his cause. Unarmed workers were unable to resist police, Falangists and troops in El Ferrol, Corunna, Vigo, Saragossa, Valladolid, Cadiz and Granada. In León the civil governor pretended to side with the government until a column of armed miners had set off for Madrid. A similar ruse secured Oviedo.

General Queipo de Llano, a flamboyant fire-eater who had once ordered the entire Spanish army to grow moustaches within 24 hours, captured Seville with a tiny force. This he paraded round and round the city to give the impression of strength, some of its men staining their faces with walnut juice to convince workers that the Moors had arrived. Once in control Queipo proved to be, in the American Ambassador's view, "the greatest radio warrior of all time," master of a medium with "illimitable possibilities" for "confusing the public mind."[63] The General reinforced real terror, applied even where there had been no resistance, with surreal threats uttered in a voice which seemed to have been marinaded in Manzanilla. He proposed to "peel" the bulky Prieto "like a potato."[64] Village Republicans, he vowed, would be ruthlessly hunted down: "If they hide beneath the earth I shall dig them out; even if they're already dead, I shall kill them again."[65] Queipo would achieve agrarian reform in Estremadura, Nationalists quipped, by giving the peasants land—six feet of it.

As it happened, the working class took advantage of military hesitations and gave the Republic control of more than half the land area of Spain. The Basques' passion for independence overcame their Catholic and conservative predilections and the provinces of Vizcaya and Guipúzcoa remained true to the government. The entire Mediterranean coast from Port Bou to beyond Malaga was saved from the rebels, often after bitter local fighting. Many local authorities had little appetite for revolt and in Barcelona the loyalty of the Civil Guard may well have been decisive. Often, too, the navy assisted, for most sailors (like most airmen) maintained their allegiance, though on many ships the ratings had to overpower their officers. In much of south-eastern Spain the rebellion was crushed, though pockets of resistance remained, notably in Toledo.

In Madrid the revolt precipitated a ministerial crisis and a popular convulsion. Since at least 1934 the capital had been "living in the shadow of revolution"[66] and, with this shadow frightening him more than the threat of military rebellion, Azaña fleetingly appointed a government to negotiate with Mola. But, to his despair, "everybody wanted to kill."[67] The generals rejected all overtures and metropolitan workers were in no mood to compromise. Increasingly angry demonstrations choked the streets. Trade-unionists took over police duties. Socialists, some brandishing pistols or ancient carbines, careered round the Puerta del Sol in placarded taxis. Anarchists in red sashes and Phrygian caps gave the clenched-fist salute as they drove requisitioned Cadillacs up and down the Gran Via. Loudspeakers blared La Pasionaria's echo of Pétain's Verdun slogan: *"No pasarán!"* Crowds converged on the Ministry of War shouting, "Traitors! Cowards!"[68]

Beating a swift retreat, Azaña commissioned his friend Professor José Giral to lead a new Popular Front administration. And it, in the sneering words of a German diplomat, "armed the mob."[69] In the warm dawn of Sunday 19 July truck-loads of rifles were distributed to trade union members, many of whom had no idea how to use them and clicked their bolts excitedly like castanets. The trouble was that only 5,000 of the rifles had bolts. The rest were stored in the rebel-held Montaña Barracks. From the cobblestone Plaza de España, where the lance of the bronze statue of Don Quixote seemed to point the way, workers and Assault Guards bloodily stormed this hill-top fortress and slaughtered most of its defenders. Sporadic resistance was quelled elsewhere. Some districts of the city became little battlefields, criss-crossed with sandbags and barricades and dotted with dead men and horses. In others *madrileños* went about their normal lives. They sat in the Calle de Alcalá drinking villainous brandy and eating fried sardines, which those who could afford it liked to smother in chocolate sauce. As the acrid smoke from burning churches mingled with the atmosphere of tobacco and garlic, they watched the rickety yellow trams clang past and engaged in chaff which, one foreigner remarked, "would have made an English horse blush."[70] But normality could not last. Power was now in the hands of the people, many of whom put on the uniform of revolution. This was the workman's blue overall, done up with a novelty zip and known as the *mono*. Columns of militia, sustained only by zeal, streamed forth to meet the foe. In the city, decorated with huge posters of Lenin and Largo Caballero, revolutionaries began what the British chargé d'affaires called a "reign of terror."[71] All Azaña's gloomiest forebodings were realised. Haunting the National Palace like the ghost of sovereignty, he was appalled by the indiscriminate executions, many of which took place in the bosky Casa de Campo just across the river, almost within sight of his bedroom window. But his plea that they should stop was ignored.

In Barcelona, where the fighting had been even more bloody, social revolution followed Republican victory with still greater vengeance. Workers mounted a spontaneous assault on the bourgeoisie and the Church. There was no looting—anarchists scorned luxuries—though pawnshops had to give up their pledges. But at night, reported the American Consul, the city centre "means a reign of silence and fear and a few furtive shadows along walls." Thousands of killings took place. They began as a purge against subversives and as a prelude to expropriation. They finished as the frenzy of visionaries and criminals. The latter, freed from gaols, were often employed to take members of rival factions "for a ride" and their "executions and cruelties" continued for months.[72] About 700 clergy were murdered and there was an orgy of iconoclasm. The sacred images of the rich were smashed, some of the most "valuable" turning out to be fakes made of paste and papier mâché.[73] Almost every religious building in Barcelona was put to the torch. On the night of 19 July 1936 the city was honeycombed with fire and, as a witness wrote, church walls rose up "translucent and gold with flames, each tiny pinnacle and turret bright against the sky."[74] There were further atrocities: priests' ears were cut off and passed round like those of bulls; nuns' corpses were exhumed and exhibited (even to children) in a variety of disgusting poses and states of decomposition. Only a Church which had epitomised fierce obscurantism since the days of the Inquisition could have provoked such pathological anticlericalism. Little of it was accompanied by "demoniac excitement"; it was mostly just an "administrative business."

Nevertheless, there was in Barcelona an "indescribable atmosphere of political enthusiasm."[75] The city, coincidentally host to the Workers' Olympiad, rival to the official games being held in Berlin, was placarded with lurid posters. It was draped with red and black flags and daubed with the initials of working-class organisations: CNT-FAI (anarchist), UGT (Socialist), PSUC (Communist), POUM (Marxist). This alphabet soup was also splashed over commandeered private vehicles. Many of the trams, taxis and horse-cabs were painted red and black. But the bourgeois traffic lights, done away with to the peril of pedestrians, were blank. Overnight Barcelona became proletarian. Middle-class people, when they emerged from hiding, disguised themselves in shabby clothes and frayed *alpargatas* (rope-soled shoes). Denizens of slums such as the sordid, evil-smelling Fifth District took possession of the Ramblas, Barcelona's Park Lane. It was a curious architectural mélange with

> houses looking like wedding-cakes, houses with domes and cupolas and mounted by eagles, houses in the "style moderne" of 1900, with metal ivy railings, and shell-shaped balconies, and "stalactite" porticos, and tiled fronts, dotted with little blue flowers.[76]

Formerly the preserve of smart men in felt hats and fashionable women in black mantillas, the broad, leafy avenue, its central precinct gay with blooms, umbrellas and open-air markets, was now the haunt of the bare-headed, tie-less, shirt-sleeved multitude. Many carried rifles. Loudspeakers blared revolutionary songs into the small hours, sometimes varying them with the current hit "The Music Goes Round and Round," but mostly playing and re-playing "To the Barricades!" and "Sons of the People."

"People too full of humanity," as the novelist Ramón Sender said, dreamed of "freedom, of the good, of justice."[77] Waiters refused tips, though, unlike some villages, Barcelona did not abolish the symbol of exploitation itself—money. Beggars vanished. Prostitutes were frowned on, though women generally gained in terms of respect and equality. They even enjoyed a degree of sexual liberation—as one Catalan remarked, "Revolution is a great aphrodisiac." Illiterate militiamen could be seen laboriously spelling out ballads about proletarian brotherhood or trying to make sense of anarchist manifestos with titles such as "The Organisation of Indiscipline." Large buildings, pockmarked by bullets and shells, were requisitioned in the name of the common weal. The Liceo became the Catalan People's Theatre. The Ritz first did duty as an Emergency Blood Hospital and then served as a public canteen, shedding the light of its chandeliers on persons who would not previously have been permitted to darken its doors. Over the entrance trade-unionists placed a huge red sign saying "HOTEL GASTRONOMIC No. 1."[78] All enterprises, ranging from mines, farms and factories to cafés, cinemas and barbers' shops, were taken over by the workers. For a short time even the brothels were collectivised—under the auspices of the caterers' union. So were the bootblacks, noted George Orwell, who vividly conveyed the furious idealism which pervaded the Catalan capital:

> Shop-walkers looked you in the eye and treated you as an equal. Servile and even ceremonial forms of speech had temporarily disappeared. Nobody said *"Señor"* or *"Don"* or even *"Usted";* everyone called everyone else "Comrade" and "Thou," and said *"Salud!"* instead of *"Buenos días."* . . . All this was queer and moving. There was much in it that I did not understand, in some ways I did not even like it, but I recognized it immediately as a state of affairs worth fighting for.[79]

Many Spaniards agreed. As the Republic's social experiment took its protean forms, as workers' committees proliferated and local authorities competed, militias massed for battle. Regarding their officers as equals, getting the same pay, eating the same food, wearing the same uniforms, these rag-tag volunteers had little in common with standard soldiers. They had no proper supplies: at noon on 22 July 1936 the first column set off from Barcelona down the Paseo de Gracia amid scenes of feverish jubilation; at 2:00 P.M. a messenger arrived back to say that they had forgotten to take any food and lorries had to be filled with whatever local grocery stores could provide. The militias sported a bizarre assortment of weapons: some carried arquebuses and pikes; villagers near Toledo equipped themselves with a collection of armour worthy of Don Quixote, swords, lances, breastplates, bucklers. They were untrained, prone to deserting their posts to pick grapes or go home for weekends. Worst of all, these ill-led units were almost as hostile to one another as to the forces of Franco, almost as intent on destroying capitalism as on killing fascists. Foreigners were appalled by them. The poet John Cornford said that they "showed not the slightest sign of military discipline."[80] George Orwell averred that the position held by his *centuria* might have been stormed by "twenty Girl Guides armed with battledores."[81]

The achievements of the militias in the first three months of the Civil War certainly confirmed the German Ambassador's assessment that their military value was "nil."[82] Exultant columns stormed into Aragon but failed to advance far or fast. Durruti, for example, "the avenging angel of the poor,"[83] wreaked more havoc on his own side than on the enemy and stalled in front of Saragossa. The Madrid contingents only just managed to halt Mola's advance through the Guadarramas, even though the Nationalists were crippled by a lack of ammunition. After a ferocious struggle, Irún and San Sebastian fell to the Nationalists, cutting the Basque country off from France. Franco's Army of Africa proved impossible to stop once German Junkers had ferried it across the Straits of Gibraltar—the first great "airlift" in history was given the Wagnerian codename "Magic Fire." Advancing in fleets of multicoloured coaches, their roofs stacked with provisions and loot, their radiators decked with mascots ranging from the Virgin Mary to Mickey Mouse, these hardened troops constantly outflanked the raw Republicans, who had no capacity to manoeuvre and stuck to the roads.

Having vanquished towns and villages, the Nationalists "pacified" them by means of systematic terror. Civilian spies known as "Green-sleeves" ferreted out government supporters and "Black Squads" of killers dispatched them mercilessly.[84] Among their victims in Granada was García Lorca, one of whose executioners apparently said: "I fired two bullets into his arse for being a queer."[85] Everywhere the rebels took control they dispensed murder. The French novelist Georges Bernanos was horrified by the atrocities which he witnessed in Majorca, where officials registered those shot as having died from "congestion of the brain."[86] After the costly capture of Badajoz, where foreign legionaries sang their battle song "Betrothed to Death," over 1,500 people (many identified as Republicans by rifle bruises on their shoulders) were herded into the bull-ring. Here, providing a spectacle to local gentry, they were shot in batches. Their blood stained the white walls, drenched the grey sand and mixed its odour with the scent of jasmine. Then the insurgents advanced through Estremadura towards Madrid. But Franco, ever sensitive to the importance of "spiritual factors,"[87] by which he meant propaganda and morale, turned aside from the capital to raise the siege of Toledo's Alcázar—one of the most famous episodes in the Civil War.

The Alcázar was not a fortress despite its name—a corruption of the Latin *castra,* or "military camp," prefixed by the Arabic definite article. Nevertheless the drab, granite bulk of the Military Academy, standing with its four square towers like the tip of Toledo's spearhead and almost moated by the Tagus River, dominated the ancient city. Here an obscure, grey-bearded colonel, José Moscardó, whose main interest was football, collected a scratch force of 1,100 soldiers, Civil Guards and Falangists, and raised the red and gold standard of Spain. Unable to dislodge them, Republican militias took their revenge on local priests, none of whom had joined Moscardó. Other "fascists," defined by their possession of servants, were also executed. Moscardó's son Luis was captured and made to tell his father that he would be shot if the Alcázar did not surrender. Their final dialogue, perhaps apocryphal, echoed round the world: " 'If it is true,' replied Moscardó, 'commend your soul to God, shout *"Viva España!"* and die like a hero. Good-bye, my son, a kiss.' 'Good-bye, Father, a very big kiss.' "[88]

Moving though this may be, it should not obscure the fact that Moscardó himself killed about 100 left-wing hostages inside the Alcázar. Still, there is no denying the courage of its 70-day resistance. Shells breached the thick bastions. High explosive smashed the double-headed eagles, emblems of Charles V, whose palace it had once been and whose courtyard statue (the Emperor was symbolically portrayed trampling a Moor) was also damaged. Huge mines, the detonation of which could be heard more than 40 miles away in Madrid, reduced much of the Alcázar's fabric to rubble. The attackers tried to set fire to it with burning petrol. Planes bombed it, though they did as much damage to the yellow ochre walls and vermilion roofs of the surrounding houses, and to the nearby Plaza de Zocodover, where heretics, entering through the Gate of Blood, had once been burned. All day (except during siestas) the turrets were peppered with rifle fire—tourists from the capital liked to come down and take pot-shots. At night the fusillade continued, assisted by powerful arc-lamps from a Madrid film studio which bathed the ruined Alcázar, "extraordinarily squat against the dark immensity of the sky," in a "vivid, theatrical effulgence."[89]

Meanwhile the defenders had to exist on a diet of mule stew, husked grain and stagnant water. Even more taxing for some, they had nothing to smoke except rose petals and the leaves of elm, acacia, mulberry and eucalyptus—the last made them sick, yet they were still willing to climb trees in view of enemy snipers to pick them. (Later, Republicans threw their enemies packets of cigarette papers over-printed with propagandist slogans.) Putrescent corpses that could not be buried added danger as well as squalor to the siege. Disease was rife, especially among the 550 women and children huddled in the Alcázar's foetid catacombs. Some of the women were so distressed by their filthy state that they refused to be seen in daylight; they manufactured face powder from plaster scraped off the cellar walls. Medical supplies were limited and doctors amputated limbs with a meat saw. The defenders' boots and uniforms fell to pieces and some arrayed themselves in the panoply of Napoleonic hussars filched from the Academy Museum. Yet Moscardó's men resisted all assaults until, on 27 September 1936, the relief column finally appeared. Emerging from their devastated ramparts, the survivors had "that ghastly pale-green colour, that gaunt expression and that far-away mysterious look in the eye" of figures painted by El Greco.[90]

In the ensuing reprisals the gutters of Toledo literally ran with Republican blood. But Franco, increasingly convinced that he had been chosen by God as saviour of Spain, was heartened. Now acclaimed as Generalissimo and soon hailed as Caudillo, or Leader, he believed that this symbolic victory had won him the war. In fact, it probably lost him the capital. For resistance stiffened as his forces closed on Madrid, driving before them a pathetic flock of refugees—mostly weather-beaten peasants in smocks and straw hats leading carts piled high with household goods; some even herding sheep, cattle, pigs and goats through main streets which had banned mule and donkey traffic since 1930. Placards warned that Franco would shoot half the city, not an absurd estimate in view of Queipo de Llano's assertion that the generals had agreed to the death of "three or four millions"—a tenth of whom would be *madrileños*—to achieve their "final triumph."[91] Other slogans announced that Madrid would be "the tomb of Fascism" and "the Verdun of Democracy." Wits quipped, "Why not somewhere else?"[92] But most citizens responded to the challenge with perfervid idealism. The German writer Gustav Regler noticed "a spirit of intoxication in the people, an infectious eagerness for sacrifice, a hot-blooded unreason and fanatical belief in freedom."[93]

Largo Caballero's new government of Republican solidarity, which replaced Giral's weak administration, did much to foster, but little to tap, this spirit. Azaña, the liberal figurehead, was increasingly disillusioned and discredited, especially when he retreated to Barcelona on pretence of visiting the front line. Largo himself, "with the smooth face of a monk and the glinting grey eyes of a power-hungry tycoon,"[94] was out of his depth as a war leader. He intimidated his military underlings, one of whom said that his "eyes, like those of Philip II, make your blood run cold." But he constantly revealed his "incapacity."[95] And the more catholic his coalition grew—it first included keen Communists, then unwilling anarchists—the less unified it became. Thus the Prime Minister would not permit Socialist workers to help build fortifications outside Madrid for fear that they would defect to the anarchists. Worse still, he discouraged the digging of trenches because it was unworthy for Spaniards to fight in such a way.

Towards the end of October 1936 he announced over the radio that there would be a counter-attack against the advancing enemy. Sure enough, Moorish cavalry was routed by the first Russian tanks, bought with enough gold from the Republic's vaults to pave Red Square; gold which, Stalin gloated, the Spaniards would never see again any more than they would see their own ears. But the Nationalists pressed on and even total mobilisation could not prevent them, by 6 November, from hammering at the gates of Madrid. The Prime Minister then left sealed orders for two generals (placing them in the wrong envelopes) and secretly departed for Valencia. He was accompanied by his cabinet and by many officials, who took with them vital information about, for example, the sites of ammunition dumps in the capital. Charged with its defence, General José Miaja sat at Largo's desk in the Ministry of War. Portly, rubicund, bespectacled, he seemed an improbable saviour. He pressed bells: nobody came. He telephoned subordinates: few answered and some who did simply laughed. According to Ernest Hemingway, this "brave-and-as-dumb-as-a-bull" defender of Madrid even had to inspect his defensive lines by bicycle because all the official cars had gone.[96] However, the efficient Communist Fifth Regiment (which had reintroduced regular practices such as ranks, salutes and insignia) rallied to his call. Miaja gathered his commanders together, told them that the government had gone, and announced, "I want those who stay with me to know how to die."[97]

That, at least, is the heroic myth. What remains unclear is the extent to which Miaja, no revolutionary himself, was a Communist puppet. For as Russian arms appeared and foreign volunteers gathered to serve in the Comintern-organised International Brigades, the poisonous tendrils of Stalinism started to smother Republican Spain. Soviet officers, NKVD agents and political commissars began to assume control. Thus Moscow paranoia compounded Madrid spy mania. This itself was exacerbated by Mola's boast that he had a "fifth column" of secret supporters in the capital. The most terrible incident in the resulting purge was the massacre of over 1,000 Nationalist detainees in the Model Prison, who were taken off in red double-decker buses and shot just outside the city. The atrocity caused Azaña to remark that he did "not want to preside over a Republic of assassins."[98] However, Communist ruthlessness seemed, especially to the hundreds of thousands now joining the party, less dangerous than anarchist fecklessness. (Characteristically the anarchists thought Madrid was better off without a government but tried to force ministers to return to the capital.)

The Communists certainly proved their worth in the defence of Madrid. They mounted a massive propaganda campaign whose message was, in the headline of their newspaper *Mundo Obrero,* "All Out to the Barricades: The Enemy is Across the River."[99] The first Russian planes dropped leaflets urging Madrid to emulate Petrograd. This plea was repeated by orators, posters, radio and films. Cinemas showed Soviet classics such as *Chapaev* and *The Battleship Potemkin*—Franco, himself an *aficionado* of the screen, would acknowledge the important morale-boosting role these films played by regularly shelling the Gran Via as crowds emerged from the final evening performance. Madrid was galvanised. Granite blocks were torn up from the streets and used to build barricades in the grey slums of Carabanchel. Trenches were dug among the rolling woods of the Casa de Campo. Volunteers streamed to the city's defence, often in hastily formed companies of barbers, bakers and candlestick-makers. Some took a five-centimo tram ride to the front and for the first time male tram conductors were replaced by women. Indeed, women served everywhere, even picking up the rifles of fallen militiamen and filling gaps in the line. Behind it they prepared boiling oil to pour on the Moors and hundreds marched down the Gran Via on the afternoon of 7 November with huge streamers which proclaimed: "Defending Madrid, we fight for the honour of our mothers and the lives of our sons."[100] Despite such demonstrations it was widely reported abroad that Madrid had fallen. Radio Lisbon broadcast a circumstantial account of Franco's entry into the city on a white charger and in the Ministry of War General Miaja received telegrams of congratulation addressed to the Generalissimo. In the event, assisted by the fortuitous discovery of the Nationalist plan of attack, the resolute Republicans decisively parried what was supposed to be the final thrust into the heart of the city. The battle, which culminated with fierce hand-to-hand fighting in the Casa de Campo, proved that the Army of Africa was not invincible. It charged the Republic with new optimism.

This glowed more brightly as, simultaneously, the first contingent of the

International Brigades arrived in Madrid. A people in arms joyfully welcomed what seemed like a real army. Indeed, the battalions marching down the Gran Via in their khaki corduroy uniforms and brown glengarry caps were taken for Russians. They were kitted out with tin helmets and rifles that were not blunderbusses. Their officers had swords and revolvers. They appeared well drilled and disciplined. All this was something of an illusion, born of comparison with Republican militias (which, much to anarchist disgust, the government was now trying to turn into a regular force). The fact was that the first international units were called to Madrid before their "training was over, and without proper equipment."[101] But this did not stop Spaniards from weaving instant legends around the foreign volunteers, who were "transfigured into demi-gods."[102]

No doubt their courage merited such éclat for they were at once thrown into the line, where they acquitted themselves heroically. On 9 November they mounted a costly but successful counter-attack in the Casa de Campo, leaving piles of enemy dead under the ilex trees. This stiffened Republican resistance in Carabanchel, where the Moors proved less adept at house-to-house fighting. But the green-uniformed anarchists of Durruti (himself shortly to be killed, probably by accident) were a disappointment. After they took over the Casa de Campo section of the line, the Nationalists lunged across the river (more a rivulet) and into the University City. Just when it looked as though they would penetrate to the Plaza de España a pistol-packing Miaja rallied his forces: "Cowards! Cowards! Die in your trenches. Die with your General Miaja!"[103]

The battle now raged round the half-built fortress of learning. The Internationals recaptured the gutted red-brick Hall of Philosophy, barricading themselves behind tomes of German metaphysics and Indian transcendentalism which proved, one ironically remarked, "quite bulletproof."[104] Some even perused the thick volumes, none of which propagated a theology to compare with that of militants such as John Cornford, who remarked that the single thing in the universe which gave him most satisfaction was "the existence of the Communist International."[105] In other faculty buildings Republican forces fought for floors and even rooms, sniping round doors and sending hand grenades up in lifts. Death arrived haphazardly and there were hairbreadth escapes. In the uncompleted Clinical Hospital 50 Moors died from eating experimental rabbits, hens and sheep injected with germs. A shell splinter circumcised one foreign volunteer as "neatly as a practised rabbi."[106] By the end of November 1936 the two sides had fought themselves to a standstill. They dug in, put out barbed wire and prepared for a war of attrition.

Meanwhile Franco sought to break the spirit of Madrid with air raids heavier than anything hitherto seen. The city had virtually no defences against this form of attack. In lieu of searchlights, cinema projectors were mounted beside rooftop machine-guns. A partial blackout had been improvised: the street lamps were painted an eerie indigo and militiamen shot at windows where candles flickered. However the Junkers and Savoias provided by the Führer and the Duce had no difficulty in finding the capital and the bombing reached a climax during the third week of November. Madrid became what one American correspondent called "a nightmare of slaughter and living horror. A seething hell which makes Dante's masterpiece a tame thing by comparison."[107] During the day the capital was obscured by clouds of smoke and dust; at night it was lit up by incendiaries and fires. Bengal flares turned darkness into noon and transformed streets around the Gran Via into "rivers of green flame."[108] "Treading blood and breathing sparks,"[109] people took refuge in the metro or sheltered in dank cellars. They lived the life of troglodytes.

Journalists had a grandstand view of the holocaust from Madrid's only skyscraper, the white, steel-and-concrete Telefónica opposite the Gran Via Hotel. Arturo Barea, who worked there as a censor and produced (paradoxically) one of the most revealing accounts of the war, said that looking down on the city from the parapeted roof of this 13-storey building was like gazing into an old well inhabited by slimy beasts. Occasionally the veil of darkness was rent.

> Bundles of light swept through the street alongside the screeching sirens mounted on motor-cycles, and the drone of bombers invaded the sky. The nightly slaughter began. The building quivered in its roots, the windows rattled, the electric lamps waxed and waned. And then everything was choked in a pandemonium of hisses and explosions, of red, green, and blue glares, of twisting, gigantic shadows cast by crashing walls and disembowelled houses, of madly tolling fire bells, of whistles, of shouts, of cries.

Yet the vision of those watching the blitz from the telephone exchange was more than usually partial.

They could see the battlefield laid out before them with theatrical clarity: the grey stores, apartment blocks and cinemas flanking the arterial canyons around the Gran Via; the white cube of the Fine Arts Club and the green trapezium of Retiro Park; the red and yellow tiles of the tenements around the Toledo Bridge; the silver arc of the Manzanares; the swart necklace of shacks that ringed the city; the dark woods and umber fields beyond; and in the distance the blue-black ramparts and glowing crests of the snow-capped Guadarramas. They could see the fighting: the rivets on the Savoias' metal skins; the pilots' faces as they dropped bombs resembling steel eggs; the toy soldiers engaging in their homicidal manoeuvres; the ululating shells which thrashed the treetops of the Casa de Campo and burst "like puffs from a cigarette."[110] But as the battle froze into winter stalemate the Telefónica became something of an ivory tower, even a castle in Spain. That monument to American capitalism, which still held about 20 American Telephone and Telegraph Company staff (who were rumoured to be preparing a lavish welcome for Franco), at first seemed not only bomb-proof but immune to attack. It fostered an illusion of security along with an equally misleading view that Madrid was an "earthquaked city."[111]

In fact, *madrileños* became inured to the bombardment and quickly nerved themselves for the rigours of the ensuing siege. Although civilians were deliberately strafed, food queues formed early. In the cratered, glass-strewn Puerta del Sol bootblacks, newsboys and vendors of lottery tickets continued to ply their trades. Shops boarded up their windows and adapted to new circumstances—one formerly dealing in holy images sold kneeling shepherds painted to look like militiamen taking aim. Tram lines and overhead cables were quickly repaired and the service was maintained. In the Gran Via, christened the "Avenue of Death," bars and cinemas kept up a ghostly existence before the curfew. Platinum blondes ran out of per-oxide but appeared as "zebra-haired odalisques."[112] Soap, too, was scarce but women managed to wash clothes and those near the front line hung them out to dry on the barbed wire. Couples made love behind the barri-cades. Children played with red-hot shrapnel among the shell-holes.

Many people, it is true, crowded into the wealthy Salamanca district, where the presence of foreign embassies (themselves sheltering thousands of Nationalists) ensured safety for the refugee camps which sprang up in their midst. Many more thanked their stars when bad weather prevented raids. The fact is, though, that casualties were few and damage was lim-ited, particularly when judged by later standards. The bombing looked worse than it was, especially when seen from above by journalists whose apocalyptic descriptions were freely transmitted and eagerly perused. Far from demoralising the inhabitants, as Franco had hoped, the air raids steeled resistance and intensified "the bitterness of the struggle."[113] The Generalissimo would have to find other ways to win, and more help from abroad. It would have to be more practical help, perhaps, than could be bestowed by the mummified hand of St. Teresa of Avila, which had just been presented to him by Carmelite nuns. (He was to keep it close to him until the day of his death.)

One of the Republicans' most striking posters pictured a lighthouse sit-uated in the centre of a red Iberian peninsula with its beams pouring out over Europe; its caption read, "Spain will be a light to the world."[114] Madrid's own lighthouse was the Telefónica, that lofty sentinel which at once guarded the capital and transmitted news from its front. By the end of 1936 the building was shell-scarred and brick-patched, for the Nationalists had taken exception to its use as an artillery observation post. But from their lines across the Casa de Campo it was still "clearly outlined," a British journalist later remembered, like St. Paul's Cathedral towering over blitzed London.[115] Everything, including the lifts, functioned. Telephone lines remained open though the operators sometimes had to retreat to the cellars. And this "proud New York baroque tower" had become, according to the American writer John Dos Passos, not so much a "symbol of the colonizing power of the dollar" but a symbol, in the minds of *madrileños*, of "the defence of the city."[116]

As a beacon of communication it was, however, an equivocal symbol, especially to those who knew its workings. For it was the headquarters of a "combination of censorship and propaganda" which one correspondent described as "flawless."[117] Incoming messages as well as outgoing dispatches were censored, so that foreign journalists were cut off from their newspapers. Elaborate efforts were made to play down the revolutionary aspects of Republican life, to conceal the vicious in-fighting between factions and to portray the conflict as a struggle between fascism and democracy. The nuances of the war were lost in transmission and its quintessentially Spanish character was obscured. To add to the confusion, truth was often mixed with falsehood and foresight with fantasy. The most insistent warning broadcast from Republican Spain was that "the armies marching on Madrid, Barcelona and Valencia are also marching against London, Paris and Washington."[118]

XVI

FRANCO'S VICTORY

THE governments in London, Paris and Washington saw the defence of Madrid in a very different light, and they were determined not to become embroiled in war on account of Spain. Their cautious, calculating attitude towards the Iberian struggle contrasts strikingly with the bold idealism of those whose spirits, as Louis MacNeice wrote, found "their frontier on the Spanish front."[1] The democracies did not accept Radio Madrid's claim that the Spanish capital was "the universal frontier that separates liberty and slavery."[2] Instead they reckoned that the opposing forces stood for different forms of tyranny. Of course Baldwin's followers tended to be Francisco Franco–phile—much was made in Britain of the General's "praiseworthy golf handicap"[3]—whereas Blum's supported the Spanish Popular Front. Most British Conservatives, although less extreme than the French Right, regarded the civil war as a matter of "Rebel versus Rabble."[4] But both governments, who wanted to protect their large Spanish commercial interests, feared that a Republican victory would turn Spain Red. As anxious to contain Communism as to contain war, they embraced neutrality.

Roosevelt, who seemed to think that Franco was fighting Bolsheviks in order to establish a "liberal"[5] regime and who sought to win the Catholic vote at home, took the same line. More, he pandered to American isolationists by refusing to join the non-intervention pact. He even, in due course, refused to admit Basque refugee children, who were exceptionally well treated in Russia. Hoping to prevent the conflict from spreading and conscious that two-thirds of Americans were indifferent to Spain, Roosevelt simply imposed an embargo on arms sales, first moral, later legal. Franco said that FDR had behaved as a "true gentleman."[6] For, like the non-intervention accord itself, the embargo applied only to munitions. It did not stop the Nationalists obtaining raw materials and manufactured goods (such as Ford trucks) from the USA. In particular Shell-Standard provided nearly all their oil on credit, contributing to Franco's "ultimate victory."[7]

Needless to say, non-intervention failed to prevent the Republic from falling under the sway of the Communists. Rather it assisted the process. This was because the Soviet Union was the only power prepared to sell it the military aid which Germany and Italy were bestowing on Franco. There was a pleasing symbolism about the non-intervention flag, to be flown by all ships in the international force supervising the operation (or, rather, non-operation) of the scheme: two black balls on a white background.

Appropriately, too, the non-intervention committee, representing 27 nations, met in London where it was sustained above all by the British, masters of the art of hypocrisy. While Hitler, Mussolini and Stalin intervened ever more blatantly, slippery diplomats papered over the international cracks. As Winston Churchill concluded, they were engaged in "an elaborate system of official humbug."[8] Yet, like most other people in Britain and elsewhere, Churchill initially supported non-intervention. It seemed a useful myth. It concealed the clandestine support Britain was giving the Nationalists: in Gibraltar, for example, the Royal Navy provided supplies and other assistance while the Gordon Highlanders nearly drowned one of Franco's airmen in whisky when "toasting a quick victory."[9] Under the chairmanship of a patrician nincompoop named Lord Plymouth, the non-intervention committee preserved Britain's façade of impartiality. Like the equally ineffectual League of Nations, it let members blow off verbal steam. Permitting European poisons to drain away through the Spanish ulcer, it helped to prevent the spread of what Anthony Eden called "the War of the Spanish Obsession." On the other hand, in an age of obfuscation the futility of the non-intervention policy could hardly have been more apparent. There was no proper system of enforcement or verification. So arms (those from Germany packed in crates marked "Christmas Decorations") and men reached Spain almost unhindered. Yet the fact that they had done so was invariably said to be "unsubstantiated."[10] Turning a blind eye to breaches of the pact did not save Britain's face. It advertised democratic timidity. Like France, Britain undermined collective security, which alienated the Soviet Union and strengthened Italy's ties with Germany.

Scornfully interpreting conciliation as decadence, Mussolini became yet more convinced that his future lay with Hitler. Mussolini's Spanish policy was, as always, egotistical and off the cuff. In the words of a leading Italian diplomat, the Duce lacks the patience which mediocre men have to go deeply into problems and the spirit of continuous application of men who lack imagination. Anything that is not spontaneous intuition fails to attract and seduce him. In this way he creates round himself a dangerous atmosphere of messianic expectation . . . which he enjoys as a sign of blind faith in him.[11]

At the same time Mussolini did have identifiable purposes in Spain, where he had long been attempting to stir up trouble. He was moved by strategic considerations, aiming not so much to turn the Mediterranean into an Italian lake as to secure access to the Atlantic. He had ideological motives, wanting to ruin the French Popular Front, check international Communism and demonstrate fascist solidarity. Above all, he yearned to build on his Ethiopian triumph, to enhance his prestige and augment his glory. Hence the dispatch to Spain of a total of 72,000 involuntary "volunteers." They were accompanied by some 660 aeroplanes (plus pilots), 150 tanks, 800 big guns and masses of other *matériel*. This powerful force was charged with winning speedy and spectacular Italian victories.

It failed. Admittedly, Mussolini's troops did start by capturing Malaga. But in March 1937 they took part in a third attempt to encircle Madrid, two previous attacks having miscarried (at Boadilla and in the Jarama valley) thanks in part to the International Brigades. Now 35,000 Italian soldiers, supported by Moroccans and Spaniards (one division led by Moscardó), launched a confident offensive from the north towards Guadalajara. Among the units ranged against them was the Garibaldi Battalion of the XIIth International Brigade. It consisted mostly of Italian anti-Fascists bent on continuing the struggle against Mussolini vicariously. They followed in the footsteps of Carlo Rosselli, socialist founder of the "Justice and Liberty" movement, who was soon to be murdered in France (with his brother Nello) at the Duce's behest. Likening the era of Franco's uprising to "the darkest stages of the Risorgimento when practically nobody dared hope," Rosselli had proclaimed that the Italian volunteers would achieve redemption abroad and at home: "TODAY IN SPAIN, TOMORROW IN ITALY."[12] Fired by this aspiration, the Garibaldi Battalion gave a good account of itself in the defence of Guadalajara. It extinguished the ardour of the Duce's Black Flame division, killing some and capturing others. It induced still others to desert by amplified appeals to proletarian solidarity— Luigi Longo and Pietro Nenni, future political leaders in Italy, were responsible for this propaganda.

During the battle mist, sleet and snow further hampered Mussolini's men, many of whom were equipped for Ethiopia (which they had expected to be their destination). They lost command of the air. Their trucks got stuck in the thick clay of the *meseta*. Their light tanks proved no match for the Russian T-26s, let alone the monster TB-5s. Their commander, trying to direct operations with the aid of a Michelin road map, was badly outmanoeuvred. As H. R. Knickerbocker put it in a contemptuous (and censored) dispatch: "The Italians fled, lock, stock and barrel-organ."[13] The final result was not quite "a second Caporetto,"[14] as enemies of the mortified Mussolini claimed. Nevertheless it was "Fascism's first defeat"[15]—all the more reason for Mussolini to declare it "a real victory."[16] Guadalajara also provided conclusive proof that elements of Italy's regular army were fighting in Spain. *New York Times* reporter Herbert Matthews could now give the lie to those on his newspaper who had refused to accept that fact. He had talked to prisoners and read their documents. He had even smoked their blue-packaged Macedonia cigarettes—a vast improvement on Spain's "anti-tanks," so called because of the lung-piercing power of their black tobacco. As if to acknowledge that the subterfuge was no longer possible, Mussolini's Ambassador in London, Dino Grandi, proclaimed defiantly that no Italian volunteers would leave Spain until the Civil War was won. In spite of this apparently fatal stroke, however, non-intervention survived. The British government kept it in being, preferring a farce to a tragedy.

Angered by Mussolini's arrogance, Franco probably got a sour satisfaction out of Italian humiliation at Guadalajara. Certainly the Caudillo's priorities were different from the Duce's. As Franco explained to the Italian Chief of Staff,

> In a civil war, systematic occupation of territory, accompanied by the necessary purges, is preferable to a rapid defeat of the enemy armies, which in the end leaves the country still infested with enemies.[17]

However much they may have infuriated Mussolini, these Fabian tactics suited Franco's other main ally, Adolf Hitler, to perfection. The Führer was, as he said more than once, interested in the "continuation of the war."[18] It helped him to create the Anti-Comintern Pact and the Rome–Berlin Axis in October 1936, persuading Japan that he was an active foe of Communism and attracting Italy into his sphere of influence. It also had the effect of weakening Mussolini's Roman empire and distracting his attention from Hitler's ambitions in Austria and Czechoslovakia. Towards the end of the Civil War the Führer actually admitted that he would like the most industrialised part of Spain to remain in Communist hands: "A red Catalonia would be like a thick, fat bone before the Italian dog kennel, and Mussolini could stand around gnawing at it, while he does not trouble himself worrying about other things in Europe."[19]

Uneasily aware that he was the victim of this strategy, the Duce railed against the restraints of the "brutal friendship" and cursed Hitler for hiding his moves behind the Spanish smokescreen. But after Guadalajara he could not afford to lose face by quitting the peninsula. Meanwhile Hitler's intervention demoralised the French Popular Front. It exposed the irresolution and weakness of Britain. It kept Soviet Russia isolated: indeed, frustrated in his attempts to build a bloc against Germany, Stalin began to consider other policies. The German economy, particularly the rearmament programme, benefited from the import of Spanish minerals on favourable terms. Finally Spain became, as the German tank commander Wilhelm von Thoma memorably remarked, "a European Aldershot."[20] It provided Hitler with a training- and testing-ground for the weapons and tactics which he could (or would) employ in the Second World War. Most important from this point of view was a detachment of the Luftwaffe, whose firepower was greater than that of the combined air forces of the First World War. It consisted of 150 aircraft and 5,600 men (reinforced and replaced from time to time) and was known as the Condor Legion.

Commanded by General Hugo Sperrle, who in both character and appearance strangely resembled Hermann Göring, the Legion had as its Chief of Staff and driving force Colonel Wolfram von Richthofen. He was a cousin of the famous "Red Baron," "air ace" and pioneer of formation flying, with whom he had served successfully during the Great War. The Colonel was also a prototypical Prussian officer. He had gimlet blue eyes, cropped blond hair, chiselled Aryan features and a ramrod Junker bearing. But he was a technocrat as well as an aristocrat. He loved engineering and he worshipped efficiency. He treated his brown-uniformed men (who wore Spanish insignia of stars and bars) like cogs in a military machine. Austere, impatient and demanding, von Richthofen was a strict disciplinarian. He detested small talk, confining conversation to professional matters. Driving his fliers hard, he drove himself harder, in more senses than one: he handled his 3.7-litre Mercedes like a Messerschmitt. He was a flute-playing fitness fanatic who did physical jerks every morning, yet he had only one lung and smoked 40 cigarettes a day.

The Colonel also permitted his juniors certain indulgences. One squadron was allowed to decorate its aircraft with pictures of Mickey Mouse, a friendlier icon than the Legion's own, which was a swooping condor with a bomb in its talons. Moreover, a special brothel was established for legionaries in a luxury villa outside Vitoria, staffed by 20 medically-inspected girls who entertained officers in blue bedrooms and other ranks in green cubicles. To the amusement of Spaniards, the Germans made love as they made war. They marched to the brothel in formation, lined up in single file and advanced on the "stentorian command of a sergeant-major"[21]—paying 100 pesetas for 15 minutes. It is clear, however, that in von Richthofen's eyes recreation was simply a reward for ruthlessness.

In the campaign launched against the Cantabrian provinces in the spring of 1937, when it became apparent that Madrid could not be taken, the German Colonel was openly contemptuous of the Spanish high command. He accused Mola to his face of "want of energy."[22] He insisted that attacks from the air should be quickly followed up by ground assaults. The bombing of Durango von Richthofen considered a success, though not one of the 258 people killed was a soldier. Afterwards he did remind "all concerned" to aim at military targets; but they should do so "without regard for the civilian population."[23] It was his "golden rule" that if aircraft could not reach their targets they should drop their bombs on enemy territory, irrespective of whether they might hit population centres.[24] The Colonel was a student of General Douhet, who had painted a "dark and bloody picture" of future warfare. In particular he had maintained that the "merciless pounding" of cities by unstoppable aerial armadas carrying "inhuman weapons" would ensure swift capitulation.[25] Von Richthofen himself believed in stimulating "fear . . . because it affects morale. Morale is more important in winning battles than weapons. Continuously repeated, concentrated air attacks, have the most effect on the morale of the enemy."

On the sunlit evening of 25 April 1937, von Richthofen attended an operational conference in Burgos, driving the 75 miles from Vitoria in as many minutes. In the three-storey town hall senior officers, presided over by Colonel Juan Vigón, Mola's capable Chief of Staff, sat on carved, high-backed chairs around a long, polished oak table which glowed under the light of heavy chandeliers. Their purpose was to decide on the best method of exploiting the setbacks of the Republic's disorganised northern forces, which were being squeezed into a diminishing pocket of resistance. The Basques, geographically and culturally remote from Madrid, were ill-armed and more divided in their allegiance than any other part of Iberia. Catholic and conservative, they clung to the Republic because it promised autonomy and democracy. Accordingly bourgeois Basques in blue berets fought beside Asturian miners in red-and-black forage caps. The white, green and scarlet standard of free "Euzkadi" flew alongside the red flag of Santander socialism. Confusion was worse confounded in that each Basque province had its own frontiers and its own currency, while each valley (almost) had its own loyalties and its own dialect: according to a Spanish proverb, Satan himself was baffled by the language, leaving after seven years of being "unable either to understand or to make himself understood."[26] A common defence was virtually impossible. Furthermore the war at sea had swung against the Republic, preventing the import of munitions and food. The non-intervention agreement aggravated the effects of the Nationalists' naval blockade: France refused even to export medical cotton wool in case it was used for filling shells. In murky Bilbao, the Basques' industrial capital, the shops were empty. The staple diet was chickpeas and a black bread which was said to cause abortions in women and insanity in men—some preferred to eat cats and dogs. From the front line demoralised defenders, outgunned by Mola's forces, were falling back towards the Basques' spiritual capital, Guernica. At the Burgos conference von Richthofen declared: "The Reds have broken . . . Nothing is unreasonable that can further destroy enemy morale, and quickly. It is already crumbling because of the air attack."[27]

Early cloud and haze soon cleared the next day and, after a final consultation with Vigón, von Richthofen ordered the attack on Guernica. Over 40 aircraft, German planes marked with the St. Andrew's cross, were armed. Most were tri-motor, corrugated-metal Junkers 52s, known as "trams" because they seemed to clang through the air. A few were new Heinkel 111s, camouflaged in light brown and pale grey but distinguished by their white wing tips. To provide fighter cover and to strafe, there were tortoise-like Heinkel 51 biplanes with open cockpits, all wires and struts. These were supported by Italian Fiats and (perhaps) by fast Messerschmitt BF 109 fighters, more than a match for any Republican machines.[28] Stukas, von Richthofen's most accurate bombers, were not used, which belied his later claim that the Rentería Bridge was the Legion's prime target. So did the Legion's bomb load, which consisted of incendiaries and shrapnel as well as high explosive. So did the tactics employed: waves of aircraft flew abreast to carry out the first European exercise in "carpet-bombing."[29] It was also the first attempt to obliterate an entire town from the air. Von Richthofen, though he spoke fluent Spanish, may well not have appreciated that Guernica was the national shrine of the Basques. He may not have known that their parliament had met in front of its sacred, black-trunked oak. He may not have been aware that in its church of Santa María Spanish sovereigns had sworn to preserve their immemorial liberties—whereupon bonfires were lit on the highest surrounding peaks, Gorkea, Oitz, Sollube, Ganekogortu and Kolitza. So von Richthofen was perhaps innocent of trying to "wound the Basques in their very soul." But even if his intention was only to disrupt the enemy's retreat and to keep him on the run, he must have realised that massive civilian casualties were inevitable. The evidence suggests that, acting in concert with the Spanish high command—Mola himself had threatened to "raze all Vizcaya to the ground"[30]—von Richthofen was guilty of carrying out an unprecedented "experiment in terror."[31]

Guernica was certainly a tempting target for saturation bombing. Situated in a valley patchworked with farms and pine copses at the head of the Mundaca estuary, it was crowded with old wooden buildings. The working-class district was "compact as peat,"[32] a labyrinth of narrow streets flanked by small shops, ancient dwellings and dingy taverns. As well as three convents, two churches and one monastery, Guernica had combustible factories producing sweets and small arms. It possessed no air defences and only a few ill-prepared shelters. On the sunny afternoon of Monday 26 April the town's 7,000-strong population was swollen by country folk coming to market and to watch pelota. Farmers wearing smocks drove livestock into town or arrived aboard solid-wheeled wooden ox-carts. Some were deterred by the flash and thud of shell-fire in the distance. Others worried about the presence of refugees and stragglers from the front. But Guernica was surely a safe haven, a sanctuary. As it happened, the local garrison commander was intent on turning the town into a fortress, another Alcázar. But few realised this, certainly not von Richthofen, who seems to have been unaware that there were any troops at all in Guernica.

At about 4:30 P.M. look-outs on the roof of the Carmelite convent rang their warning bell. It was at once echoed by a peal from Santa María church. A single Heinkel III appeared. It was flown by Major Rudolf von Moreau, the pilot who had dropped supplies inside Toledo's Alcázar. He crossed the town once, as its inhabitants ran for cover in cellars and bunkers. Then, encountering no flak, von Moreau flew back, straight and level at 4,000 feet, and dropped 6 bombs around the railway station near the town centre. The 1.5 tons of high explosive caused havoc among passengers waiting for the Bilbao train, gashed open the front of the Hotel Julián and left the station plaza strewn with smashed bodies and smoking debris. As a cloud of dust mushroomed skywards, witnesses heard the "wild shrieking of terrified people."[33]

A quarter of an hour later, just as rescue workers were beginning to drag survivors from the wreckage, the Condor Legion struck in force. The first flight, zooming in much lower than von Moreau, again hammered at Guernica's heart. Their bombs tore buildings to pieces. They flattened the fire station, killing the dray horses and the stable-boy. They hit the sweet factory, igniting cauldrons of liquid sugar and incinerating a young woman worker. They devastated the market-place, setting alight the canvas stalls, splintering the plane trees, spilling lumps of flesh and gobs of blood over the cobbles. They splashed burning thermite on to a couple of bullocks, who broke from their pen, stampeded through the square and fell into a large crater.

Every 15 minutes the raiders returned. They pulverised the town, creating a miniature fire-storm in its ruins. They destroyed three-quarters of the buildings, including the church of San Juan, the old men's home, the "El Liceo" cinema, the Bank of Vizcaya, the sports club and the pelota stadium. But they missed the bridge and the arms factory. Also unscathed were the old stone parliament surrounded by its curved iron railings and Santa María church, where the priest extinguished an incendiary bomb with communion wine—some of his congregation thought they had witnessed a miracle. Whether the inhabitants prayed or screamed, fled or cowered, they were pursued by flights of fighters which, "like flashing dancing waves on shingle,"[34] machine-gunned them from as low as 200 feet. These mechanical harpies also attacked surrounding farmsteads, which burned "like little candles in the hills."[35] From the hills, said one witness, it was like "having a preview of the end of the world."[36]

Dusk ended the three-hour massacre. But Guernica continued to blaze, unexploded incendiaries occasionally flaring into life. Driving across the mountains from Bilbao with other journalists that night, clever little George Steer and big brash Noel Monks, who had both reported the Ethiopian conflict, saw from a distance of ten miles the town's crimson death throes reflected on the clouds. The sky "seemed to move and carry trembling veins of blood." Over the last incline Steer perceived through the smoke a vision of hell: at "every window piercing eyes of fire"; where every roof had stood "wild trailing locks" of flame; the streets "a carpet of live coals."[37] Kept from the centre by the conflagration, he picked up dud fire-bombs, glittering aluminium tubes branded with the German imperial eagle. Like the other correspondents, Steer watched weeping soldiers retrieving charred bodies from gutted buildings. He viewed the beginnings of an exodus: the dazed inhabitants, unable to find their way around their own town because familiar landmarks had disappeared, sought refuge behind the "Ring of Iron," Bilbao's Maginot Line. Steer also questioned eyewitnesses, pieced together the sequence of events and estimated that the dead were numbered in hundreds.

On 28 April *The Times* and the *New York Times* published his story, which was all the more shocking for being written so dispassionately. The facts were confirmed by other accounts, many printed in equally conservative journals. Moreover, *The Times* stood by Steer's story, though it later disparaged him, just as it had earlier censored some of his reports from the

Basque country.[38] (Less than a month after the martyrdom of Guernica the editor, Geoffrey Dawson, responded to a temporary Nazi ban on his paper by saying that he had not attempted "to rub it in or harp upon it" and made his notorious confession that "I do my utmost, night after night, to keep out of the paper anything that might hurt [German] susceptibilities." It is plain, despite special pleading by *The Times's* official history, that he omitted news as well as opinion.)[39] Anyway, the news from Guernica burned itself into the contemporary psyche. It provoked global outrage. As the *New York Times* wrote, "This climax of cruelty horrifies the world more than any other barbarity of a barbarous war."[40] The world's emotions were, of course, epitomised by Picasso's passionate masterpiece. It was painted in violently contrasting black, white and grey newspaper tones which suggested (as Stephen Spender said) "the despair of light and darkness in air raids: despair of the darkness because it is too complete and you are lost; despair of the light because it is too complete and you are revealed to the enemy raiders."[41]

In Britain and the United States especially, the tide of public opinion now turned against Franco. His only recourse was to muddy the waters, for he could not admit that the Spanish Civil War was anything less than a crusade—the Caudillo was depicted flanking Jesus Christ in photomontages distributed to Nationalist troops. So the myth was born that the retreating Republicans had themselves burned Guernica, as they had burned Irún, as part of a scorched earth policy and for propaganda purposes. To murder innocents and then accuse their fellows of the crime struck Fr. Alberto de Onaindía, who had personally experienced von Richthofen's "trial in totalitarian warfare," as "almost worse than the burning of the town" itself. But everyone from Queipo de Llano to Joachim von Ribbentrop, from Catholic cardinals in Rome to Conservative MPs in London, put the blame on "Asturian dynamiters."[42] Franco endorsed the story. He even established a "Commission" of investigation which tried to discredit Steer, condemned the "apocalyptic extravagance" of Republican propaganda and came to its pre-determined conclusion.[43] Von Richthofen, having claimed in a secret dispatch to Berlin that "the concentrated attack" had been "the greatest success,"[44] now charged "Reds" with torching the town after "tossing gasoline cans into the ground floors."

Despite the irrefutable evidence, that legend lingers on today.[45] Its long life is only partly attributable to the size of the lie. Democratic governments, fearful of being forced by their own people to face up to the dictators, engaged in an unspoken conspiracy to obscure the truth. American Secretary of State Cordell Hull disingenuously informed congressmen that there was "no evidence" of Germany's being involved in Spain. The Quai d'Orsay exerted financial and other pressure on the Havas agency to distort news about Guernica, though *Le Canard Enchâiné* mocked the self-immolation story by suggesting that Joan of Arc had lit her own funeral pyre. The British Foreign Office received a full account of the air raid from its Consul in Bilbao, who visited the scene within 24 hours, and confirmation from its Ambassador that the Germans had "bombed Guernica to smithereens." Yet in the House of Commons Anthony Eden, the Foreign Secretary, claimed to have had no "considered reports"[46] on the episode. He even told the imperial conference of May 1937 that Germany was cooperating "loyally, efficiently and zealously" in non-intervention.[47] Actually the committee was scared even to mention the name Guernica in case von Ribbentrop walked out. Bowing to German pressure, it finally agreed to a craven resolution condemning the destruction of open towns whether by aerial bombardment or by fire.

Hitler had no doubt that aerial blitzkrieg, the technique which von Richthofen went on to refine in Poland and Russia, won the Civil War for Franco. "People speak of an intervention from Heaven," he later remarked, but it was the intervention of "von Richthofen and the bombs his squadrons rained from the heavens that decided the issue."[48] Actually here was another myth rising from the ruins of Guernica—that air power was invincible. Images of unprecedented destruction obscured the fact that Guernica, like Ethiopia, had been defenceless. Pundits, echoing Douhet, harped on the irresistible power of a "flying fortress" of bombers.[49] Propaganda and fiction fed "popular fears."[50] The British in particular became obsessed by the Luftwaffe's potential to deliver a "knockout blow."[51] But the Germans also learned the wrong lesson from Guernica, only discovering the vulnerability of massed formations of bombers on daylight raids during the Battle of Britain. Aviation alone, for all the horrors it engendered, was not omnipotent. Certainly the Basques were demoralised by the cataclysmic superiority of their foes in the air. They fell back on Bilbao, where the "Ring of Iron" quickly dissolved, and then on Santander. But the Nationalists, who clinched their decisive victory in Asturias by October 1937, crushing the last resistance on the Cantabrian coast and winning the war in the north, triumphed because they were also stronger at sea and on the ground.

MEANWHILE, Catalonia, which should have been the powerhouse of the Republic, was defeating itself. Where Franco fused the disparate elements in the Nationalist coalition, forcing Carlists to don the blue shirt of the Falange and Falangists to adopt the Carlist red beret, the Republican factions remained at daggers drawn. The anarchists and their allies, notably the POUM (Marxist Workers' Party), wanted to continue the social revolution because fascism could only be defeated by smashing capitalism. The Communists, uneasily supported by Socialists, wanted to win the war, which could only be done by a centralised State and a unified army. They had the better case for, as Prince Kropotkin had said, revolutionary government is a "white blackbird."[52] Workers' control gave power to "uncontrollables."[53] Thanks largely to the anarchists, Catalonia was in a state of "complete dissolution," wailed Azaña. "There, nothing remains: government, parties, authorities, public services, law and order; nothing exists."[54] But the alternative to "chaos," as the American Consul in Barcelona pointed out, was "tyranny."[55] It was the extension of Communist dictatorship to Spain.

Stalin had become involved in the Civil War reluctantly, as part of his policy of trying to preserve collective security. Spain was "a pawn in his power game."[56] His aim was to prevent France from being encircled by fascist powers at a time when Russia herself was in danger of encirclement by the anti-Comintern forces of Germany and Japan. Perhaps he had other motives. But his methods were certainly familiar. He exerted brutal pressure on the government of Largo Caballero, who was so infuriated by the demands of the Russian Ambassador that he once threatened to throw him out of the window. Communist propaganda was as unscrupulous as it was preposterous. One celebrated communiqué announced that "the advance continued without the loss of any territory";[57] and after the battle of Jarama, it was said, "the dead were recovered with their arms stiff in the revolutionary salute."[58]

Stalin heightened the atmosphere of secrecy and treachery by reinforcing the Republican air force with what a Dutch pilot called the "flesh-clad robots of the U.S.S.R."[59] Breakfasting on eggs, ham and chopped liver and enjoying at Gaylord's Hotel in Madrid other luxuries unobtainable in the Soviet Union, the Russians were kept in sterile isolation. It was as if they might be infected with alien heresy—though Stalin still executed many of them on their return. He preferred, in fact, to employ foreign Communists as senior functionaries. And he chose men like Palmiro Togliatti, whose secretary said that he would sleep with her just as coldly as he would shoot her; Vladimir Copic, who caused a massacre in the Abraham Lincoln Brigade at Jarama by assuring them that Spanish troops were advancing in their support when the Americans could see that they were not; André Marty, "crazy as a bedbug,"[60] in Ernest Hemingway's apt phrase, and homicidal to boot. Slavishly obedient to their master, these apparatchiks did their best to build Stalinism in another country.

Marty, for example, who had led a mutiny in the French Black Sea fleet when it was ordered to support the Russian Whites in 1919, created a microcosm of the Soviet State at Albacete, the International Brigades' base. He organised spies and commissars—known variously as "Red Chaplains"[61] and "comic-stars."[62] Then, with the help of sinister functionaries such as Walter Ulbricht, nicknamed "Comrade Cell,"[63] he instituted witch-hunts and purges. Many volunteers committed "suicide à la Beckmann,"[64] a euphemism for being tortured to death like the German Brigade captain of that name. Marty confessed to having executed 500 men, 5 per cent of the International Brigades' entire fatalities. This gross character, with his thick eyebrows and grey moustache, his liquid eyes and pendulous jowls, had contracted in virulent form what Gustav Regler called "Russian syphilis"[65]—Stalin's pathological fear of Trotskyite subversion. In May 1937 that disease became epidemic, spreading from its birthplace to distant Catalonia.

There tension between the competing parties had taken the form of increasingly hysterical denunciations of the "Trotskyist-fascist" POUM[66] and growing street violence in Barcelona. George Orwell, just back from fighting with the POUM militia in Aragon, was struck by the stench of hatred. He also noticed that, like the flaming revolutionary slogans on public buildings, the signs of working-class dominance had faded. Hats and ties had returned while blue overalls and red bandannas were disappearing. Communist officers sported "elegant khaki uniform" plus pistols. (These were almost unobtainable at the front, where Orwell, a picturesque figure wearing a coffee-coloured balaclava, long khaki scarf, yellow pigskin jerkin, corduroy riding breeches, khaki puttees and size 12 boots "clogged in mud," had been armed with a 50-year-old German rifle.)[67] Fashionable restaurants in the Ramblas were full while bread queues lengthened in the slums—tins of food were opened in the shops to prevent hoarding. The police were aggressive. Beggars and prostitutes were back in business. Egalitarian forms of speech were on the wane. The few smoked smuggled Lucky Strikes while the many could afford only cigarettes filled with "sliced liquorice root."[68] Those in the anarchist camp were embittered by the revival of bourgeois privilege. But Communists were bent on sacrificing revolution on the altar of discipline—even though, as a high official admitted, Catalonia was now "not at war."[69] On 3 May, Assault Guards tried to take over the telephone exchange from the anarchists, who not only tapped Communist calls but sometimes interrupted the conversations of leaders like Azaña to give gratuitous advice. Shooting broke out and the conflict spread. Soon revolutionaries, whether anarchist or Marxist, were tearing up the square cobblestones of the city to make barricades. It was "a civil war within the civil war."[70]

Other towns in Catalonia also became involved but the bloodiest clashes took place in Barcelona. Buildings were besieged and stormed. Machine-gun and sniper fire raked the streets. Grenades were hurled at passing cars. There were ambushes, skirmishes, murders. The fighting kept most people indoors, including Azaña, who was concerned about his personal safety. ("That cowardly fairy is behaving like an hysterical whore," fulminated Prieto.)[71] Business ground to a halt. Food, apart from oranges, ran short. Rubbish piled up in the gutters and corpses lay where they fell in the squares. The situation was confused by tortuous political manoeuvres and moving appeals for working-class unity. Proletarian brothers fraternised. Police occupying the ground floor of the telephone exchange (which continued to function) sent up sandwiches to the anarchists above. Assault Guards in the luxurious Café Moka, at the end of the Ramblas, gave beer to POUM militiamen in the nearby Hotel Falcón. But it was not until the arrival of 4,000 armed men from Valencia that peace was fully restored, on 8 May 1937.

The Communists claimed that they had ended a conflict caused by bad leadership as well as by Trotskyite subversion. They then engineered the downfall of Largo Caballero. He was replaced as Premier by the Finance Minister, Juan Negrín. Professor of Physiology at Madrid University, Negrín was a high-living, clear-thinking, tough-talking socialist. But the Communists believed him to be more biddable than Largo and he was certainly willing to lose the revolution in order to win the war. The first fruit of this new determination was the outlawing of the POUM. The "Trotskyist organisation"[72] which Trotsky himself had condemned for its "betrayal of the proletariat,"[73] was pictured as a figure whose slipping hammer-and-sickle mask revealed a fiendish swastika-scarred face. Its leader, Andrés Nin, was imprisoned, tortured and killed. And in the ensuing purge many of his followers suffered the same fate.

George Orwell, back in Barcelona after having been shot in the neck, had to become a fugitive and he escaped from Spain thanks only to the inefficiency of the police. Orwell's account of his adventures, *Homage to Catalonia,* is one of the seminal books of the age. A vivid personal narrative, it also scythes down the rich "crop of lies" propagated by the war.[74] This exposé was the prime concern of the tall, pencil-moustached old Etonian with self-consciously proletarian habits—even Spaniards were appalled by the strength of the black shag tobacco he rolled in his cigarettes. Orwell was shocked not so much by the rise of left-wing totalitarianism as by its power to obscure the truth. "History stopped in 1936,"[75] he once remarked, meaning that propaganda had taken its place. No one, though, had a sharper eye for what actually happened than George Orwell.

Born (in 1903) Eric Blair, he was the son of a shabby-genteel colonial official whose income mainly went on "keeping up appearances."[76] He was thus "lower-upper-middle-class"[77] and, suffering "snobbish agonies" at fee-paying schools where most boys were better-off, he conspired to hide his humiliating poverty.[78] School also gave him an early experience of authoritarianism, though he would never have claimed, like W. H. Auden, that "at school I lived in a Fascist state."[79] As a young policeman in Burma Orwell "saw the dirty work of the empire at close quarters"[80] and decided that the concealed object of that empire was theft. He railed in secret against the "slimy" humbug of "the white man's burden" and the suffocating constraints of the "pukkah sahib's code."[81] To expiate his guilt and to find material for the books he returned home to write, he became tramp, dish-washer, hop-picker, book-seller and school teacher. He did not espouse Bohemian chic. Indeed he branded as cranks the modish contemporary army of simple-lifers, food faddists, spook-hunters, sexual nonconformists and community hikers. Above all, he despised hedonism. He seemed to take a masochistic pleasure in good old-fashioned discomfort and inconvenience, which became more pronounced with age. Late in life he advised V. S. Pritchett to keep goats, saying that they would be certain to cause him a lot of trouble and to lose him a lot of money and getting "quite carried away as he expounded on the 'alluring disadvantages' of the scheme."[82] During the 1930s Orwell developed a distinctive vision. He fashioned a translucent style, which also reflected his "crystal spirit."[83] He found a voice that was radical, incisive and painfully honest. Unlike many bourgeois writers on the Left, he did not regard "intellectual self-castration" as "a small price to pay for achieving some likeness to Comrade Ivan Ivanovich."[84] Like Thomas Mann, he rejected the notion that useful lies, those that served the anti-fascist cause, were better than harmful truths.

So Orwell's account of the Spanish heresy hunt provided a startling insight into the nature of Stalinism. It showed that Communists did not scruple to use the methods of fascists and that both sides were the enemies of common decency. However, the Left could not bear too much reality, though its blithe certainties were to be shaken by Orwell just as those of the Ancien Régime had been shaken by Voltaire. *Homage to Catalonia* was rejected unread by Orwell's fellow-travelling publisher, Victor Gollancz.

And Kingsley Martin, editor of the socialist *New Statesman,* refused to print his articles on Spain. Nevertheless Orwell had uncovered the essential features of a new "kind of hate-world, slogan-world" which had struggled into life during the 1930s. It was a world of cant phrases, clockwork responses, coloured shirts, rubber truncheons, barbed wire, food queues, secret police, processions, rallies, posters, and "loudspeakers telling you what to think."[85] It was a world evoked for the ages in *Animal Farm* and *1984.* Yet, ironically, Orwell was no mere observer of that world. He belonged to it. In *Homage to Catalonia* he did not simply paint too rosy a picture of the Spanish militias. He later admitted to writing more "sympathetically" about the POUM than he actually felt.[86] For all his intellectual integrity, Orwell was at times prepared to commit the sin of Squealer (the propagandist pig) and Big Brother. He altered the past to suit the needs of the present. During the war, when the Soviet Union became Britain's ally, he found himself describing Stalin, in a BBC broadcast, as "wise" and "large-minded."[87]

However, to quote Ilya Ehrenburg's misquotation of Lope de Vega, "Blood shouts the truth in soundless books."[88] If the meaning of Stalinism remained obscure to the outside world, Spaniards on the Republican side soon began to grasp its sanguinary character. During the summer of 1937 the terror spread to include anarchists and Catalan separatists. Communists began to crush the collectives. Commissars imposed more draconian discipline on the International Brigades, where the military salute replaced the clenched-fist gesture. The Republican secret police adopted all the methods of their mentors in the NKVD, spying, blackmailing, kidnapping and murdering their victims. Some they confined to lunatic asylums. They also established private gaols with torture chambers—one, designed to disorientate prisoners, consisted of a spherical black room with a solitary electric light at the top. Even a Communist commander like the bearded El Campesino was horrified by these excesses. Yet he had been, in his own words, "brought up in a school of terrorism," was "guilty of ugly things myself " and, as a Spaniard, regarded life as tragic and death in war as a fitting end for man.[89] His disillusionment was commonplace. The "spontaneous revolutionary ardour"[90] of the first months of the Civil War had vanished. The International Brigaders talked less of a crusade, more of a struggle. In Madrid spirits sank as supplies dwindled: there was little to consume except a liquor laced with vanilla extract which tasted like varnish remover and "Dr. Negrín's victory pills"—lentils.[91] Barcelona too was haunted by the spectre of defeat.

. . .

THIS the Communist leadership tried to exorcise with further offensives. In July they mounted a huge assault 35 miles west of Madrid. It was directed towards Brunete, a tiny village with a muddy pond and white adobe houses in the midst of the harsh Castilian plain, bleached and baked rock-hard by the sun. In heat that turned tanks into pressure cookers and bathed the horizon in a shimmering haze, parched men advanced across stubbly fields with little cover except rough scrub and occasional ravines. They were held up by pockets of ferocious resistance. Finally Nationalist reinforcements, artillery and aircraft drove them back, littering the landscape with blackened, bloated corpses. The International Brigades suffered heavy casualties. Among them were Oliver Law, who was fighting for "national independence" for the "Negro people"[92] in Spain and was the first black American ever to command a company of whites; Jackie Shirai, probably the only native-born Japanese to take part in the conflict; and George Nathan, the immaculate British officer who had climbed out of "the pit of worklessness" to remake himself in Spain[93] and had gone into battle carrying a gold-tipped swagger-stick. The consequent desertions and minor mutinies better reflected the result of the battle than Communist claims of victory.

During August the Republic applied new pressure on the Aragon front. Some of the fiercest fighting took place in the little town of Belchite, where observers saw "a picture of the horrors of war which no Hollywood film could ever give."[94] Republicans built parapets of rotting bodies stacked eight high and fought in gas masks because they could not bear the stench. So great was the danger of epidemics that they finally turned the site into a vast crematorium. They soaked the corpses in petrol and burned them. As the American volunteers departed they saw in the smoky light of the funeral pyre an advertisement for ZETSO— EXTERMINATOR.[95] What this was they never discovered. But it seemed symbolic, for they left behind a town so devastated that when Ernest Hemingway visited it the following month he could not tell where the streets had been. Scattered with mule carcasses, scorched timbers, cooking pots, lithographs and sewing machines covered in flies, Belchite suggested a Surrealist collage.

Franco slowly tightened his stranglehold on the Republic. In the summer of 1937 he persuaded Mussolini to reinforce the Nationalists' naval blockade by means of piracy. In London the Admiralty, which had broken the Italians' naval code (thanks to their amiable habit of enciphering leading articles from *Il Popolo d'Italia*), knew perfectly well that the Duce was sinking British merchant ships, as well as those of France, Russia and other countries. But, fearful that the Royal Navy was over-stretched, it sustained the pusillanimous fiction that "unknown" submarines were responsible. Nobody was fooled. Mussolini was hailed as "the Unknown Statesman" and Parisians took to calling the Boulevard des Italiens the "Boulevard des Inconnus."[96] For once France acted decisively and organised an international conference. It met at Nyon in Switzerland in September 1937 and promptly resolved that the British and French fleets would retaliate. This strong line, it has been said, "could have marked the beginning of the end of appeasement."[97] For, as Admiralty cryptographers discovered, Italian submarines were ordered to withdraw before the conference even met. And although Mussolini boasted to Hitler that the submarine sinkings would continue, they ceased (though shipping still suffered from sporadic air attacks). However Neville Chamberlain, who had succeeded Baldwin as Prime Minister in May 1937, considered such a stand "dangerous."[98] He also showed at Nyon that he was committed to conciliating fascism while keeping Communism at arm's length. Italy, but not the Soviet Union, was given an area of sea to patrol. No wonder Ciano gloated in his diary, "From suspected pirates to policemen of the Mediterranean—and the Russians, whose ships we are sinking, excluded!"[99]

The Republic's response to being starved of arms was, once again, to attack. Prompted by the needs of propaganda as much as strategy (and aided by French willingness to let in a trickle of supplies), this was a measure of desperation. In December 1937 the Republicans directed an offensive against Teruel. Where Brunete had been a kind of Omdurman, the grim walled capital of lower Aragon was another Valley Forge. Temperatures fell to 0 degrees Fahrenheit, winds "shrieking down from the north"[100] gusted to 50 miles an hour, and thick flurries of snow reduced visibility to a few yards. Engines seized up and not even blow torches could move them. Thousands of troops suffered frostbite and some had limbs amputated without anaesthetics. Others, having tried to warm themselves with *aguardiente,* died of exposure in their sleep. Even the lice froze—which gave them mighty appetites when the thaw came. Taking advantage of the weather, Republican forces enveloped the town, a jumble of crags and cavities like a mouthful of bad teeth. They then proceeded to crush resistance, as Ernest Hemingway and other reporters observed:

> In the afterglow of the setting sun, with all around the town the flashing of guns, yellower than trolley sparks but as sudden, we saw these kids [dynamiters] deploy a hundred yards from us, and, covered by a curtain of machine-gun and automatic rifle fire, slip quietly up the last slope to

the town's edge. They hesitated a moment behind a wall, then came the red and black flash and roar of their bombs, and over the wall and into the town they went.[101]

Miraculously the medieval Mudéjar towers survived the onslaught, but much of Teruel was wrecked. The bitter struggle for possession of the ruins provided Hemingway with a display of the "most godwonderful housetohouse fighting"[102] [sic] he had ever seen.

This comment was typical of the macho exhibitionism which Hemingway brought to life in general and to Spain in particular. Like Roy Campbell, the South African poet who supported Franco, Hemingway made a fetish of virility and felt compelled to exaggerate his own. Seriously wounded on the Italian front while working for the Red Cross in 1918, he gave the impression that he had been engaged in combat. So mad about bloodsports that he thought nothing of machine-gunning sharks from his boat or shooting coyotes from a low-flying Piper Cub, Hemingway embellished his own exploits shamelessly. Nothing appealed to him more than the bloody theatre of the bull-ring and during the 1920s he saw literally hundreds of taurine deaths in the afternoon. No Scott Fitzgerald, he drank as though to prove his masculinity. Already Hemingway's tall, well-balanced frame and handsome, wide-mouthed face were ravaged by whisky, absinthe and tequila—which did not improve his behaviour. At his worst he was a parody of the leather-jacketed, corduroy-trousered tough guys in his stories, a swaggering, bullying poseur trying desperately to live up to his legend.

Yet Hemingway was charming, generous and brave as well as jealous, petulant and quarrelsome. He showed off to the men of the International Brigades, but he welcomed them to his first-floor room in Madrid's Hotel Florida. With "splurging magnificence"[103] he handed out whisky and ham from his store in the tall, mirrored armoire. He let them take hot baths, allowed them to sprawl in his cretonne-covered armchairs and listen to the victrola, even supplied them with girls. The obverse of Hemingway's callow sentimentalism was the fierce realism his fiction displayed. He beat out a staccato, quasi-vernacular style, using his Corona typewriter (as he once said) like a mitrailleuse. He provided a fresh vision of the inter-war years, with their sombre intimations of impotence and death. As Rupert Brooke had done a generation earlier, he indelibly stamped his mark on his age. Moreover, Hemingway's affection for Spain was genuine. He cherished memories of "the loops of twisted garlics; earthen pots; saddle bags carried across the shoulder; wine skins; the pitchforks made of natural wood."[104] He supported the Republicans because theirs was the cause of the downtrodden majority. He shunned the abused word "crusade." But, like Robert Jordan in *For Whom the Bell Tolls*, he experienced during the Civil War

> a feeling of consecration to a duty toward all of the oppressed of the world that would be as difficult and embarrassing to speak about as religious experience and yet it was authentic as the feeling you had when you heard Bach, or stood in Chartres Cathedral or the Cathedral at León and saw the light coming through the great windows.[105]

Notwithstanding its false heroics, facile melodrama and male chauvinism, Hemingway's novel is one of the most powerful evocations of the war. It faced the fact that atrocities had occurred on both sides. While asserting that Communist control had provided the only hope of victory, the book fulfilled its promise to dissipate the fog of lies resulting from that control. Hemingway etched an acid portrait of André Marty and was less than flattering about La Pasionaria—who "always made me vomit always."[106] In short, Hemingway compensated in his art for the propaganda to which he devoted much of his life during the war. Accepting the temporary "necessity for all the deception"[107] in the interests of defeating Franco, Hemingway ignored its corrupting effects while hostilities lasted. He tacitly endorsed Communist terror. He told American audiences that writers had a special stake in fighting fascism because it was the only form of government that prevented them from telling the truth—as though Stalin were wedded to the First Amendment. Above all, in his newspaper dispatches Hemingway distorted the facts. He inflated Republican victories and Nationalist defeats. He also indulged in personal "military Munchausenism."[108] Often, for example, Hemingway implied that he was on his own in exposed positions when he was with other journalists in relative safety. At Teruel he depicted himself in a particularly noble light, showing a young soldier how to knock the jammed bolt of his rifle free with a rock, instructing welcoming civilians to stay indoors, receiving the surrender of the city.

Actually it did not surrender until 8 January 1938, by which time Hemingway was en route to New York. Nationalist relief columns, pouring towards what Franco called the "witches' cauldron"[109] of Teruel, had been impeded by more blizzards. But when the sky cleared they began to besiege the besiegers. Franco launched a massive assault which extended northwards along the Aragon front. Here artillery, aircraft and even cavalry were used to crushing effect. On 17 January, as dusk blanketed the stone-cold sierras, the heavens themselves seemed to shine forth the death of the Republic. An ambulance driver recorded:

the night sky suddenly lit with a vast sheet of cherry-coloured, mauve-red fire . . . Faint bars of white striation moved through it. The whole thing was too big to have been started by man, at even his pulp-magazine worst. Troops moving down the mountain are terrified. Morale, uncracked by, my God, how many weeks of broiling in the icy Teruel furnace, is gone.[110]

A hush fell over ten miles of battlefield as men gazed awestruck at this explosion of light. It seemed as though a giant fist had punched a hole in the firmament and was beckoning with opalescent fingers. Was it flame-throwers, liquid fire, some kind of mirage, the reflection of a burning town, a death ray? It was, in fact, the aurora borealis, hardly ever seen so far south. Within a few minutes it faded away and the guns resumed their own pyrotechnic display, to murderous effect.

Teruel fell and the Republicans were driven back with huge losses. Refugees thronged towards Barcelona, where they suffered in the heaviest air raids of the war. Mussolini was "delighted that the Italians should be horrifying the world by their aggressiveness for a change, instead of charming it by their skill at playing the guitar."[111] But although Franco seems to have agreed to the bombing he was also reported as saying that it strengthened Republican morale, a "blunder" for which the Duce was to blame.[112] The Caudillo drove swiftly towards the sea, cutting the Republic in half and isolating Catalonia from Valencia and Madrid. Meanwhile Negrín tried to strengthen his government. In particular he got rid of the socialist Prieto, who was both defeatist and hostile to the Communists— he gibed that Stalin feared the discovery of what all the world knew, namely that Russia was selling them arms. Negrín put out peace feelers at home, which Franco spurned. Doing his utmost to show that the Republic was a bourgeois democracy, he looked for salvation abroad, which was not forthcoming thanks to Chamberlain's *rapprochement* with Mussolini. At the same time Negrín stiffened the Republic's resistance. The Prime Minister was often dismissed as an impossible voluptuary, with an appetite for women to match Mussolini's and a taste for food to rival Herriot's— some evenings he would eat one dinner at home, another at a restaurant, and a third at a nightclub. Yet he never succumbed to outside control (though he shut his eyes to Communist crime in return for Communist help) and he became the incarnation of resistance to fascism. When the Nationalists pushed towards Valencia in July 1938 Negrín inspired a counter-move across the River Ebro from beleaguered Catalonia. It was, *mutatis mutandis,* the Republic's Ardennes counter-offensive.

It was also the boldest and bloodiest operation of the war. On a moon-

less night 80,000 men massed on the muddy banks of a 20-mile bend in
the tawny, fast-flowing river. Among them were all five International
Brigades, some of whom sang softly in the darkness revolutionary songs in
many languages—"El Himno de Riego," "La Bandiera Rossa" and the
Internationale. After crossing by boat or pontoon bridge, or even swimming, they advanced on a broad front towards the little town of Gandesa.
The Nationalists were taken completely by surprise, but they resisted
stubbornly and contained the attack before it had gone ten miles. Then
commenced a furious slogging match in which artillery and aircraft
wrought havoc on the exposed Republicans. Perhaps the worst carnage
occurred in a *barranca* (ravine) just outside Gandesa which the Internationals christened "Death Valley." One wrote in his diary:

> The place stank with the smell of dead and decomposing bodies . . .
> Shells screamed directly overhead as we lay against the rock wall of a ter-
> race; some dropped ten, twenty metres away. Hugged wall. As dark
> came, enemy began to use tracer bullets in rifles and machine-guns, and
> shelled the hillside methodically, the shells tracing a horseshoe against
> the sides of the bottle-neck-shaped gully. Bullets were always in the air;
> the reddish and pink tracer bullets seemed to move slowly and weirdly.
> Sounds of men screaming *"Socorro, socorro!"* (Help, help!) and groaning
> *"Madre mia,"* kept up all night.

Standing wheel to wheel, Nationalist guns laid down the mightiest barrage since the First World War. Republican troops hung twigs and bags of
camphor around their necks, respectively to bite on during the cannonade
and to counter the stench of death. The Republic poured in its last
reserves but flesh stood no chance against this weight of metal. Glorying
in their air supremacy, Nationalist fighters pointed bombers to their targets by sky-writing huge arrows of white vapour in the vault of Prussian
blue. Negrín could only retaliate diplomatically. On 21 September 1938 he
announced the withdrawal of his foreign volunteers in the hope of winning international support and obliging Franco to reciprocate. Unfortunately this gesture coincided with the Munich crisis. So, while the world
watched the dismemberment of Czechoslovakia, the Republic continued
to bleed to death on the Ebro.

The disbanding of the International Brigades marked the Republic's
failure (despite all its propagandist efforts) to transform the Spanish Civil
War into a global crusade against fascism, a crusade in which it would
have stood a winning chance. Negrín could only live in hope, but it was
now apparent that the democracies would pursue appeasement even at the
cost of terminal humiliation. It was also apparent that the early euphoria
of the foreign volunteers was wellnigh extinguished. Attempts were made

to re-kindle it at moving farewell parades in Barcelona, now so battered that it looked like "the skeleton of a Hollywood make-believe town thrown on the scrap heap."[113] The survivors of Madrid, Jarama, Guadalajara, Brunete, Belchite, Teruel, the Ebro and other battles marched past to tumultuous cheers. Squadrons of planes thundered overhead, dipping their wings in a final salute. Under impassive portraits of Stalin, spectators wept. Hundreds of girls in native costume rushed forward, kissing the departing heroes and "pressing huge bouquets of flowers into their arms."[114] La Pasionaria made an emotional speech:

> You can go proudly. You are history. You are legend. You are the heroic example of democracy's solidarity and universality. We shall not forget you, and, when the olive tree of peace puts forth its leaves again, mingled with the laurels of the Spanish republic's victory—come back![115]

Few could revive the first fine, careless rapture that had brought them to Spain. Mostly working-class Communists, they had come to strike a blow against capitalist Depression as well as fascist dictatorship. Like Frenchmen (who formed the largest contingent), Americans had intended to forge their own "Popular Front on the Spanish battlefield."[116] Anti-Nazis like Hans Biemler, who had strangled an SS guard in Dachau and escaped wearing his uniform, had hoped to "get back to Germany through Madrid." "Many were Jews," as Gustav Regler said, and their bullets in the darkness had been "aimed at Hitler."[117] Similarly, Italians had fought Mussolini by proxy. Eager to create socialism at home, Britons like Fred Copeman, sometime Invergordon mutineer and hunger marcher, had been unable to "ignore the plight of Spain."[118] Of course some had had more personal reasons for crossing the Pyrenees. There were adventurers, homosexuals and sufferers from ennui, such as the Belgian Nick Gillain. There were vagrants, drunkards, neurotics and criminals. But in an arena which for a time was the focus of the world, most volunteers had deliberately acted as the conscience of their age. Now many were disillusioned. They had quailed before the homicidal despotism of André Marty. They had witnessed ruthlessness compounded by cynicism, incompetence and hypocrisy. They had heard so much mendacious propaganda that they hardly knew what to believe. As Jason Gurney bitterly concluded, "We deceived ourselves and were deceived by others."[119]

On the other hand, some of the survivors found that their ideals had been tempered in the Spanish furnace. A number, particularly those who could not risk returning home, took Spanish citizenship to continue the defence of the Republic. More pledged themselves to fight on elsewhere, "merely changing the fronts and the weapons."[120] Men such as these had never seen the civil strife in Spain as a "domestic conflict" and they regarded the Second World War, when it came, as just the next round in "the struggle between the forces of Fascism and democracy."[121] It was, of course, precisely foreign inability to perceive the Spanish Civil War in Spanish terms that helped to make it part of the wider conflict. Intervention, and non-intervention, turned the Iberian peninsula into a battleground of outside interests and alien creeds.

So Franco's victory, achieved by 1 April 1939 after the conquest of Catalonia and the collapse of Madrid, was a victory for Hitler. Mussolini shared in it to a lesser extent—Spain had cost Italy far more than Ethiopia. But Pope Pius XII, in a jubilant message to Franco, thanked the Lord for "Spain's desired Catholic victory."[122] The losers were Stalin, who moved from appeasement towards a fatal alliance with Hitler, and the democracies. They had let slip their chance to form a united front with Russia against Germany. They had demonstrated the impotence of international arbitration and led Hitler to believe that he could go on freely expanding in Europe. Thanks to them the fascist grip had strengthened on the Mediterranean and Madrid had come close to the Rome–Berlin Axis. Franco was much more committed to the dictators than his subsequent neutrality and propaganda suggested. On his eight-foot-long desk in the high-ceilinged Bishop's Palace at Salamanca, which was guarded by Moorish lancers in turbans and white capes, the Caudillo had framed photographs of the Führer and the Duce. In January 1939 Franco told von Richthofen that he would not think of turning to Britain and France because they "had antiquated political and economic convictions and were declining powers whose methods were not suited to a rising Spain."[123] Far from rising, Spain was (in the words of the exiled Azaña) "behind bars."[124] Franco proved a merciless gaoler, every inch a "murderous little Christian gentleman."[125] However, although he liked to boast that he had eliminated the Enlightenment, his intentions were obscure. That he would concentrate on domestic repression rather than foreign aggression could not be known in 1939. But by then Azaña's prophecy did seem to be coming true: he had forecast that if the Republic were defeated Britain and France "would have lost the first campaign of the future war."[126]

In retrospect, then, the civil conflict in Spain can be seen as the hinge between global slump and global war. For the Depression not only fostered extremism, it also undermined liberalism. It sapped the will of Britain, France and (to a lesser extent) the United States to resist fascist aggression. As a recent historian has written, acute economic competition drove the three democracies "into a Hobbesian condition of each against all."[127] The events in Spain, it is true, did begin to concentrate moderate minds. Faced with atrocities like Badajoz or Guernica, even pacifists began to consider the advantages of rearmament. But the British, in particular, were slow to read the writing on the wall. "The fact is," said fellow-travelling writer T. C. Worsley, "we are absurdly cushioned from the realities in comfortable, safe, blind old England."[128] There was much to be said, as Arthur Koestler decided, for a country run by Blimps rather than Commissars, a country

> suspicious of all causes, contemptuous of systems, bored by ideologies, sceptical about Utopias, rejecting all blueprints, enamoured of its leisurely muddle, incurious about the future, devoted to its past.[129]

Yet such happy pragmatism could easily be confused with complacent laziness. Certainly George Orwell thought so. Returning home from Catalonia to the green and pleasant land of his childhood, he found it almost impossible to believe in foreign emergencies. Posters told of cricket matches and royal events. Men in bowler hats wandered among the pigeons in Trafalgar Square. Red buses and blue policemen patrolled the streets. Everyone was "sleeping the deep, deep sleep of England, from which I sometimes fear that we shall never wake till we are jerked out of it by the roar of bombs."[130]

PART FOUR

DEEPENING GLOOM

XVII

BRITAIN'S ROYAL STATE

SIREN voices did try to alert John Bull during the mid-1930s, none louder than that of Winston Churchill; he warned Britons, "Do not close your eyes to the fact that we are entering a corridor of deepening and darkening danger."[1] At first he made little impression. Weapons were plainly lacking to ensure the safety of the British Isles, let alone the British empire. But the National Government was still traumatised by the Depression. It was reluctant to jeopardise the frail economic recovery by spending more money on arms. Neville Chamberlain, who succeeded Snowden as Chancellor of the Exchequer, was haunted by the prospect of "another crisis like that of 1931."[2] He therefore preferred to "take risks with defence rather than finance."[3] Once Lord Mayor of Birmingham, Chamberlain was more than usually afflicted by political tunnel vision, doubtless the result of looking at world affairs (as Churchill said) "through the wrong end of the municipal drain-pipe."[4] He could not see that the two policies he espoused, rigid frugality at home and supple diplomacy abroad, were incompatible. By starving the military of cash Chamberlain ensured that British plenipotentiaries would always negotiate from a position of weakness. Covenants without swords are but words. Thus the nation began to slide towards a new kind of appeasement, from dignified conciliation to humiliating concession. What had long been an attempt to preserve the status quo became an endeavour to achieve what the Conservative minister Oliver Stanley called "peace with as little dishonour as possible."[5] This perilous progress was largely obscured by a combination of official secrecy and regal flummery. Recalling Théophile Gautier's maxim that one can pass through one's own age without seeing it, the top Foreign Office mandarin Sir Robert Vansittart commented: "that was particularly true of the thirties."[6]

Vansittart, handsome, clever and rich, was another member of the British élite who tried to raise the alarm about a renascent Germany. His estimates of the speed with which the Luftwaffe was growing were much more accurate than the smug forecasts of the Air Ministry. Stanley Baldwin did not know what to believe, lamenting that as far as British Intelligence was concerned Germany was "a dark Continent."[7] Nevertheless, in November 1934 he accused Churchill of exaggerating the danger and assured the House of Commons that Britain still had an ample margin of safety. Baldwin promised to maintain "parity" with the Luftwaffe. However, not even Britain could insulate itself from the awful sense which pervaded Europe, according to Aldous Huxley, "of invisible vermin of hate, anger crawling about looking for blood to suck."[8] The cabinet decided both to increase the RAF budget (at the expense of the other services) and to seek a general arms agreement with Germany. France was uneasy. But Baldwin reckoned that he won Laval's assent to the overture by feeding him on "salmon trout, mixed grill, very mixed, Kentucky ham which tasted like crystallised nectar, plum pudding and brandy sauce."[9]

Hitler was not thus to be seduced. When, in March 1935, a government White Paper cautiously declared that the security of Britain demanded further rearmament the Führer renounced Versailles. He openly acknowledged the existence of the Luftwaffe and introduced conscription. The British Ambassador in Berlin warned that "The rapidly-growing monster of German militarism will not be placated by mere cooings, but will only be restrained from recourse to its *ultima ratio* by the knowledge that the Powers who desire peace are also strong enough to enforce it." But other voices insisted that Hitler "did not want war" and that he would be satisfied once he had gained equality of armaments.[10] So British politicians had evidence of Hitler's intentions but did not know how to interpret it. They saw what they faced but they could only grope towards an understanding. Confused and confounded, the government took contradictory measures.

At Stresa in April, where a "gaga"[11] Ramsay MacDonald relied on Vansittart for everything (including collar studs) and the interpreter had to make up a speech from the prime-ministerial ramblings, Britain tried to form a united front with France and Italy. But MacDonald's successor at 10 Downing Street torpedoed this initiative by concluding a unilateral pact with Hitler. Confessing that he had completely underestimated Germany's strength in the air, and authorising a further modest expansion of the RAF, Stanley Baldwin placed a theoretical limit on Germany's sea power. He signed the Anglo-German naval agreement. Challenged in Far Eastern waters by the waxing power of Japan, Britannia aimed to rule the waves by a negotiated settlement. Diplomats such as Vansittart even hoped that Hitler's undertaking to restrict the production of warships might be extended to other weapons of war. But the main result was that Britain's Stresa partners were alienated, France looking for an alliance with

Russia, Italy looking for a conquest in Ethiopia. Yet though the naval agreement violated the Treaty of Versailles and damaged the principle of collective security, it assuaged public fears in Britain. For the prospect of another war with Germany seemed to have faded.

This was the horror which haunted the sceptred isle during the 1930s and few people could bring themselves to acknowledge, with Churchill, that there were worse things than war. King George himself so dreaded war that he once threatened to join a mob shouting for peace in Trafalgar Square. "I fear War more than Fascism," confessed Vera Brittain, author of that poignant memorial to the lost generation, *Testament of Youth* (1933).[12] To avoid another Armageddon she campaigned against rearmament. Most progressives agreed, including the historian A. J. P. Taylor, who was anything but "blind to the reality of Nazi Germany."[13] They believed that investing in weapons was not only wasteful but dangerous, since an arms race would inevitably culminate in an armed struggle. This was why the Labour party considered that "the worst defence that any country can have is a large army."[14] But at a time when the government was holding aerial manoeuvres and rehearsing blackout and gas mask drill (which seemed only exercises in propaganda since the bomber always got through), idealists like Vera Brittain espoused not just peace but pacifism.

Actually the so-called Peace Ballot, a poll of over 11 million British people conducted by the League of Nations Union which reported in the early summer of 1935, was not a vote for pacifism. It was a vote for international disarmament and collective security. Over half those asked seemed prepared to resist aggression. But at least 100,000 Britons supported that charismatic asthmatic, the Rev. Dick Sheppard, in his absolute renunciation of war. Their high-minded revulsion against this criminal, obsolete folly was perhaps best summed up in Canon Charles Raven's cry: "It is utterly inconceivable that Christ could be the pilot of a bombing aeroplane."[15] Popping this bubble, a critic pointed out that it was equally impossible to imagine Christ driving a car along the Kingston bypass or going to a Walt Disney film. However, pacifism was a faith, one of many clamouring for adherents during the 1930s. So it was largely impervious to reason, though in due course the implacable malignity of Nazism did change minds, including those of Bertrand Russell and Aldous Huxley. Pacifism was a broad church and its apologists were very various. They ranged from principled proponents of non-violence in the spirit of Tolstoy and Gandhi to neurotic cranks living on carrot-juice and lentils. Some even believed in stopping war by force.

As this fecund diversity illustrates, the familiar stereotypes of the 1930s are always misleading. Labels like "the Auden generation"[16] are particularly inadequate. Some young poets, Laurie Lee for example, had never heard of Auden. The writer Rayner Heppenstall could declare that, "Auden, Spender and Day Lewis did not, from any point at which I found myself, in the least appear to dominate the age."[17] Plays such as *The Dog Beneath the Skin* were eclipsed by patriotic effusions such as *Cavalcade* (of whose author, Noël Coward, Auden remarked: "Is it like this/In Death's other kingdom?").[18] *New Verse* was as much a minority interest as *New Writing* at a time when even the successful Left Book Club could not compete with Boots Circulating Library. John Betjeman's happy conceit about "Love in a Valley" amid the "cushioned rhododendrons"[19] of suburban Surrey reflected the English temper better than Auden's anguished vision: "That valley is fatal where furnaces burn."[20]

Britain pullulated with conflicting creeds. The evangelist Frank Buchman preached Moral Rearmament. Major Douglas and his green-shirted supporters espoused Social Credit, the last word in something-for-nothing economics. Functionalism, especially in architecture, was all the rage: Evelyn Waugh complained that "the post-war Corbusier plague" had left Britain scarred with "villas like sewage farms, mansions like half-submerged Channel steamers, offices like vast beehives and cucumber frames."[21] Freudianism was in fashion. Surrealism had its moment of glory when Salvador Dali gave a London lecture, on "Authentic Paranoiac Phantoms," wearing a diving suit (to show that he was plumbing the depths of the human mind) and nearly suffocated. Dali, clutching two borzois and a billiard cue while talking through his helmet, represented artistic anarchy; but even Britons committed to sterner imperatives were reluctant to conform. Wyndham Lewis rejected fascism when it became, as a mass movement, too democratic for his taste. Searching for the light, Hewlett Johnson, the "Red" Dean of Canterbury, found that atheistic Marxism was "profoundly Christian."[22] Giving another account of what it meant to be a Christian, Bishop Headlam of Gloucester said that church-persecuting Nazism "represented a strong spiritual influence."[23] Conservative MP Harold Macmillan denounced "the Casino Capitalism" of his own party and was in turn denounced, by his old nanny, as "a dangerous Pink."[24] Aneurin Bevan was called a "Bollinger Bolshevik,"[25] while bourgeois Communists were described (by Beatrice Webb) as "mild mannered desperadoes." Rose Macaulay stigmatised British intellectuals, with some reason, as "the not-so-very-intelligentsia."[26]

Amid all these contradictions only loyalty to royalty seemed to unite the nation. During the Silver Jubilee of May 1935 no more than two houses in England, it is said, flew the red, white and green banner of Chartist republicanism. When the Mayor of Bermondsey refused to meet the King, on the grounds that the cost of the ceremony would deprive 30 poor crippled children of a week's holiday by the seaside, an angry crowd burned him in effigy outside his own town hall, to the strains of the National Anthem. The first silver, and the last imperial, jubilee was a conscious effort to rally the whole nation behind its most revered talisman, the Sovereign. Baldwin, ever conscious that civilisation rested on gossamer set over "deeps of chaos and anarchy," was especially keen to parade the Crown as the "great symbol of our race and of our unity."[27] Under its magic influence, the cabinet hoped, internal divisions would vanish. Devotion to a dynasty would translate into allegiance to the State, perhaps even into votes for the National Government. It spared neither pains nor cash (spending 250,000 pounds on illuminations alone) to organise a public affirmation which would put Nuremberg into the shade. Of course George V's jubilee was a brilliant display of pomp, not a barbaric extravaganza. It was designed to foster social cohesion, not to exalt dictatorship. But it also aimed to satisfy irrational appetites which even socialists shared: Harold Nicolson once recorded that Herbert Morrison "spoke of the King as Goebbels might have spoken about Hitler."[28] As Britain's constitutional authority Walter Bagehot taught, the masses deferred to "the 'theatrical show' of society . . . a certain charmed spectacle which imposes on the many and guides their fancies as it will."[29]

So on 6 May 1935 King George V and Queen Mary celebrated the twenty-fifth anniversary of his reign by driving from Buckingham Palace to St. Paul's Cathedral in an open carriage pulled by six grey horses. Balding and bearded, he was dressed in the scarlet uniform of a field marshal, with a plumed hat, glittering decorations and the green ribbon of the Thistle across his chest. Stiff but voluptuous, she wore a hydrangea-pink embroidered lace gown set off by the blue sash of the Garter, a silver wrap collared with a huge white fox fur and a gleaming toque embellished with a pale pink feather. Arrayed with equal splendour were the dignitaries, including foreign royalties and six Commonwealth prime ministers. They were conveyed in the 300 carriages and cars which made up the royal procession, escorted by Life Guards, Horse Guards, Dragoons, Lancers and Hussars. Other troops, 14,000 of them, lined the grey streets, which had blossomed in the fine weather with a colourful profusion of banners, streamers, bunting, garlands and red, white and blue rosettes. The Mall was especially picturesque: festoons of blue and gold flowers hung from tall white poles surmounted with crowns and lions, and linked with chains of fairy lights.

As the cavalcade jingled past, church bells pealed and bands along the route blared at their appointed times. In response to bowing and waving from the royal carriage, the vast crowds cheered themselves into a "delirium of joy." So compacted was this human maelstrom that many fainted and one man was crushed to death. But nothing affected the stately progress of a "pageant unsurpassed in the history of the empire."[30] Greeted by a fanfare of trumpets, the royal pair stepped on to the red carpet leading to the national shrine. As they entered spears of sunshine pierced the gloom of the nave. Enthroned at last in gilded crimson armchairs beneath Wren's baroque dome, the King and Queen became the central figures in a scene from a medieval tapestry. There were heralds in gorgeous tabards of scarlet and gold, white-gauntleted Gentlemen at Arms grasping tasselled pikes, high officers of army and State in ceremonial uniforms, a gleaming motley of bronze medals, silver swords and gold braid. Even more exotic were the spangled satraps of empire, Nepalese potentates in pearled skull-caps adorned with the yellow plumage of birds of paradise, Indian maharajas whose turbans flaunted emeralds and rubies that might have glowed at the courts of Akbar and Aurangzeb. Surrounded by religious images, notably Holman Hunt's *The Light of the World,* and by monuments to secular glory (including memorials to Nelson, Wellington, Gordon and Kitchener) the gold-coped Archbishop of Canterbury, Cosmo Gordon Lang, bestowed a divine blessing on earthly majesty. From the marble pulpit he declared that George V embodied the national "spirit of unity" and had "come to be not only the King but the Father of his People."[31] Lang's words were relayed through hundreds of loudspeakers to the London multitude. But evidently George himself was less affected by the endorsement than by the unpunctuality of the Established Church. Complaining that 26 ancient prebendaries had held up the returning procession, he told the Dean: "I didn't know there were so many damn parsons in England."[32]

Nothing else marred the Mardi Gras spirit. The police promptly suppressed a few Communist attempts to "challenge"[33] the Union Jack with the Red Flag. And the vast majority of the King's subjects enjoyed themselves. London looked like "Epsom Downs on Derby Day,"[34] complete with musicians, fortune-tellers, "stop-me-and-buy-one" ice-cream vendors and hawkers selling paper hats and patriotic favours. People broke into spontaneous song, the favourites being "Tipperary" and "Rule Britannia." Dancers performed in fancy dress. Confetti was thrown from West End hotels. Street parties filled the East End, where banners proclaimed that Cockneys were "Lousy but Loyal."[35] Matching celebrations took place all over the country. Indeed, the whole empire was *en fête:* from Ottawa to Sydney, from Gibraltar to Delhi, from Jerusalem to Christchurch, from Cape Town to Hong Kong. Some manifestations of Jubilee spirit were curious: ultra-loyalists in England painted their fingernails red, white and blue; to honour the imperial patriarch a jungle tribe in India swore to "forsake wife-beating" for six months.[36]

In the evening London was illuminated as never before, with two hundred million candle-power of electricity. Every important building was floodlit. Coloured lights were used on a large scale for the first time. Horse Guards Parade was bathed in a dim blue hue. Westminster Abbey became "a poem in old ivory."[37] St. James's Park, scented with red may and white hawthorn, yellow tulips and purple irises, was "turned into a fairyland."[38] Buckingham Palace was "a stately miracle in white."[39] Members of the royal family were dazzled as they repeatedly emerged on to the balcony to greet the ecstatic throng. It responded by singing "God Save the King" and "For He's a Jolly Good Fellow." From the palace George electrically ignited a huge bonfire in Hyde Park, which was watched by 250,000 people. This in turn was the signal for 200 other fires (the highest on the summit of Ben Nevis) to be lit throughout the kingdom, binding it together in a web of light. Ramsay MacDonald, himself glowing with emotion, flew over the capital. He witnessed, according to one reporter, the "nation spelling out its joy in letters of flame." It was the "most awe-inspiring spectacle man has ever presented to the heavens."[40]

As if anxious to prove that the Jubilee was no mere silver lining to the economic cloud, but signalled its passing, the festivities continued for weeks. At the same time, ironically, violent fluctuations in the silver bullion market indicated the persistence of the Depression. And Britain was caught in the grip of the iciest spring weather for a century. The King gallantly soldiered on, taking part in countless further ceremonies. Under the massive oaken hammerbeams of Westminster Hall, where William Rufus had feasted and Charles I had stood trial, he received a loyal address from parliament. At Olympia he viewed the Royal Tournament, which included a historical pageant entitled "The Spirit of Cooperation." He attended a Jubilee Concert at the Albert Hall featuring 2,000 performers gathered from choirs all over the country. He watched an RAF fly-past at Mildenhall and inspected the Royal Navy at Spithead. He participated in wreath-layings, parades, presentations, banquets and Jubilee Balls.

All this was good for business, which cashed in on patriotism, and it did wonders for national morale. But it also encouraged Britons to mistake shadow for substance. Hypnotised by sumptuous ritual, they failed to appreciate their country's relative decline in power and wealth. Of course they could not be expected to perceive the King as he really was: a respectable father figurehead who mercilessly bullied his family; a hard worker who protested if affairs of State interrupted important events on the social calendar, such as the Newmarket races; a frugal traditionalist who squeezed secret tax concessions from a deferential Treasury; a conscientious squire with anti-Semitic prejudices and a penchant for prostitutes. Fascinated by the apparition of majesty, they did not see in the archaic *tableau vivant* a revelation of Britain's obsolescent state.

THE 160 ships that steamed past the sailor King at Spithead (many of them brought back from the Mediterranean despite the impending confrontation with Italy over Ethiopia) were mostly of Great War vintage. Few had been modernised and the fleet now had only a dozen battleships—compared to 61 in 1918. Moreover, such was Britain's industrial stagnation that capital ships commissioned after 1935 did not come into service before the Second World War and the Admiralty had to purchase armour-plate abroad—some from the Ruhr. Similarly the aircraft which saluted George V were old-fashioned biplanes of wood and canvas. Competition with the Luftwaffe was hampered by the backwardness of aircraft production and the lack of a trained workforce. And despite Britain's victory in the Schneider Trophy, its designers resisted innovation: in the early 1930s they regarded monoplanes as "un-English."[41] Equally outmoded was the army, with its nostalgic, even "mystical,"[42] devotion to the horse. Needless to say, this was duplicated by ground forces all over the world. It was not even absurd, in view of their heavy reliance on animal-drawn transport. But the British took "Hippophil conservatism"[43] to extremes. As a subaltern Field Marshal Montgomery had to pass an army examination in which the first question was, "How many times in each 24 hours are the bowels of a mule moved?"[44] During the 1930s cavalrymen conducted a long rearguard action against "those petrol things,"[45] tanks. They were assisted by politicians such as Duff Cooper, Minister of War in 1935, who said that there would always be a role in modern warfare for the well-bred horse. Infuriated by this Blimpishness, a progressive colonel called Dorman-Smith emerged from the War Office every evening and engaged in a little charade. He formally bowed to the nearest Whitehall lamp-post. In due course he hoped to see Duff Cooper hanged from it for neglecting to prepare the army for the coming war. Later Dorman-Smith, who was a friend of Hemingway, circulated a design for a new tank with a special attachment for releasing horse manure.

Throughout the summer and autumn of 1935 the issue of rearmament rumbled across Britain like distant thunder. It was made more ominous by Mussolini's growing threat to Ethiopia. This roused the spirit, if it did not concentrate the mind, of His Majesty's Loyal Opposition. At its annual conference Labour resolved to endorse whatever measures the League of

Nations took to resist Italian aggression. The party therefore rejected the Christian pacifism of its leader, George Lansbury. Side-whiskered, ruddy-complexioned, blue-serge-suited, Lansbury was revered as the conscience of English socialism. But his notion of a diplomatic initiative was to propose going to pray for peace with Hitler. Having been reviled by Ernest Bevin for hawking his conscience around the country, Lansbury resigned. His successor was Clement Attlee, a laconic middle-class social worker compounded in equal parts of mousiness and steeliness. Attlee endeavoured to keep his party together by vigorously supporting collective security while adamantly opposing rearmament.

Baldwin could thus claim, during the November general election, that Labour wanted Britain to act as policeman of the world while refusing to provide either helmet or truncheon. It was a convincing charge and it helped to conceal Conservative hesitations over the country's defences. Baldwin could not afford to alienate the anti-militarist vote, so he promised Britain safety but without "great armaments" or "huge forces."[46] These pledges were ambiguous, though not as dishonest as Churchill later claimed. But Baldwin brazened out his equivocations with a massive show of candour. Wrapping himself in the Union Jack and basking in the reflected glory of the Jubilee, he played the role of British bulldog. This impression was confirmed in cinema newsreels, which must have seriously damaged Labour's standing with the electorate. The film companies pretended to be neutral, but they projected an unflattering image of Attlee. He had to speak perching on a chair, fumbling with his notes on his knee and showing his hairless pate to the camera. By contrast, Baldwin appeared on a specially built set backed by leather-bound books and Greek columns. He read his speech fluently and sonorously from a roller on the desk in front of him. The Prime Minister was all the more persuasive because he had been secretly shown a copy of Attlee's script. When Baldwin concluded, "I think you can trust me," the Gaumont newsreel flashed up on the screen, to the sound of cheering, the legend "AND YOU DO!"[47]

They did. The National Government, now little more than a front for the Conservative party, convincingly won the last British general election before 1945. It secured 432 seats, as against 154 for the Labour party, which itself staged something of a recovery from the low ebb of 1931. With the campaign behind him Baldwin's Foreign Secretary, Sir Samuel Hoare, could concentrate on the Ethiopian problem. Hoare had gained immense prestige from his September speech at Geneva. Banging the table for emphasis, he had pledged his country's "unwavering fidelity"[48] to the League of Nations and its principle of international resistance to unprovoked aggression. In practice Hoare hid behind the League, restricting Britain's commitments to those feebly promulgated in Geneva and privately making emollient overtures to Rome. Nothing occurred to stop Mussolini's invasion of Ethiopia in October. The League, hampered by Laval's refusal to offend the Duce, imposed mild economic sanctions. Hoare, who confessed to being "a very dull speaker,"[49] was at first loath to disappoint the expectations raised by the most successful oration of his life. Having pronounced so boldly, he was unable to see how Britain could avoid imposing an "oil embargo."[50] But, thin-lipped and bad-tempered, he eventually moved towards conciliation. The Foreign Secretary was about to embark on one of the most inglorious episodes in British diplomatic history.

There was a tragic inevitability about his fate. Hoare was a pocket Machiavelli who felt out of place in the ample seat of Lord Palmerston. Hoare had professed reluctance to move from his previous quarters: as Secretary of State for India his snug billet had been an oak-panelled room with nabob furniture and Persian miniatures looted from the Red Fort in Delhi. Yet he only had to walk down the mosaic corridors of power in the Italianate *palazzo* which housed both offices (not to mention many others, linked by pneumatic tubes for conveying messages). Doubtless the building as a whole expressed a self-confidence he did not share. The entire edifice was, in fact, a resounding affirmation of British might. It was a classical structure, designed at Palmerston's insistence by that champion of neo-Gothic, Sir George Gilbert Scott—vestiges of his original, rejected plan can be seen embodied in St. Pancras Station. The Foreign Office was approached through an imposing courtyard. It was entered up a grand staircase which was crowned with a gilded dome—the sun at its centre surrounded by signs of the Zodiac—and flanked by alabaster statues of former foreign ministers. The walls were embellished with allegorical frescoes in yellow ochre, Venetian red and cobalt blue depicting the "expansion and triumph of the British Empire,"[51] one of which appears to be a rape scene. Inside were vast staterooms such as the barrel-vaulted, Corinthian-capitalled Locarno Suite and the glass-roofed, granite-columned Durbar Court. Before Hoare's office three gold-braided flunkeys guarded their master's privacy in a cavernous antechamber containing colossal oil-paintings of Hanoverian sovereigns. The Foreign Secretary's room itself was a study in diplomatic dominance. Forty-two feet long and half as high, the heat from its coal fire barely reaching the scattered easy chairs let alone the gold-starred, green-grey walls, it had accommodated Lord Salisbury in splendid isolation. From its five panelled windows (curtained in heavy brown satin) which overlooked Horse

Guards Parade and St. James's Park, Sir Edward Grey had seen the lamps going out all over Europe. Behind its massive desk Lord Curzon had sat, writing so fluently that he never needed to pause for thought. Under its painted, chandeliered ceiling Austen Chamberlain had conversed with Stresemann and Briand in a new language—European. Now the Lilliputian Hoare took control of the Brobdingnagian "national palace."[52] Here was his chance to deploy a talent for intrigue developed over 25 years in public life.

He had exercised it most recently and successfully by moving India a few hesitant steps towards self-government. Nor was it a disadvantage to have thus incurred the wrath of Winston Churchill, whose views on the subcontinent where he had served as a subaltern were antediluvian compared to those of Hoare. Opposing appeasement, the great political freebooter was serving his term in the wilderness, and his hatred for the prim, dapper little high churchman burned no less fiercely for that. During one of their disputes Churchill expostulated: "I will break this bloody rat Hoare's neck."[53] Perhaps Churchill would have liked to strangle him with their old school tie, for Hoare too had been at Harrow. Indeed, Hoare later prevented its grounds from being occupied by an unsightly barrage balloon hangar, loyalty to the Alma Mater apparently overriding concern for national air defence. Of course Churchill was the antithesis of Hoare, a ducal bird of paradise to the Foreign Secretary's common or garden baronet (sprung from Quaker banking stock). True, after an outstanding Oxford career, Hoare had married into the purple, though it was apparently a union of convenience. But he remained a political Mr. Slope. As a young MP he was "pale, ascetic and fragile-looking . . . with a simpering voice that suggests a newly ordained and nervous curate." After his Commons speeches there were calls of "the collection will now be taken" and "Amen."[54]

Hoare had served with military intelligence during the First World War, sending his masters much misinformation from Russia. His report of Rasputin's murder, however, was so early and so accurate that the tsarist authorities suspected him of complicity in it. Afterwards Hoare rose through the Tory ranks by devious and diligent means. He became a client of Lord Beaverbrook, who first puffed him as a future premier in the *Daily Express* (the political kiss of death) and later secretly paid him large sums of money in return for information. Pompous, petty and nakedly ambitious, the vulpine Hoare was little liked by his colleagues. Indeed, they were apt to sneer, particularly when he invited them to a Park Lane club where, dressed in black tights, he demonstrated his skill as an ice skater. The vain Foreign Secretary had no understanding of intimacy. He was a cold fish. He was also a calculating one. But by his own confession the ailing, arthritic Hoare now lacked judgement, being literally and figuratively unbalanced by fainting fits.

Hoare judged that oil sanctions and the measure which could have decisively stopped Italy's rape of Ethiopia—denying it the use of the Suez Canal—were too risky. Baldwin's injunction to avoid war at all costs rang in his ears. He accepted Vansittart's view that Italy must be bought off so that Britain could concentrate on the greater menace of Germany. Although Hoare described the service chiefs as "the worst pacifists and defeatists in the country,"[55] he was alarmed by their warnings of British military deficiency. He was intimidated by fascist propaganda, some of it passed on by the British Ambassador in Rome, who insisted that Mussolini "will act like a mad dog."[56] Hoare shrank from conflict. Was he right?

Certainly Britain was anxious for peace. According to General Pownall at the War Office, its people were morally and psychologically unprepared to fight for "'poor little Ethiopia.' Black races to an Englishman are always niggers and we don't see why we should be plunged into war on their account."[57] Less offensively, *The Times* agreed: "The fantastic notion of a European war, as an alternative preferable to an Abyssinian war, has never for a moment entered the head of any sober Englishman."[58] There is no doubt that, despite having denuded its Far Eastern forces, Britain remained terribly vulnerable closer to home. The Mediterranean fleet had only a few minutes' supply of anti-aircraft ammunition. According to an Italian analysis, it "could not defend Egypt or the Suez Canal," let alone fight for the Covenant.[59] Britain's fourth arm of defence, the economy, was as feeble as its other three. There were, says a recent authority, "overwhelmingly plausible strategic and economic reasons" for avoiding war with Italy.[60]

On the other hand, it can be persuasively argued that this was the most promising moment before 1938 to have confronted fascism with force. Hoare could have administered a serious check to Mussolini, whose position would have been damaged by a tame response and perhaps destroyed by a "mad-dog act." Such a course would have enhanced Britain's prestige, with incalculable consequences. Nor was it impractical. Even that arch-appeaser, the Christian Scientist Marquis of Lothian, urged the Foreign Secretary to emulate Palmerston:

> If Mussolini defies the League and defies us, and gets away with it, while we find excuses for doing nothing, because the League will not agree to effective sanctions, we shall have had the worst humiliation since Yorktown.[61]

Hoare himself well knew that the League would follow a British lead: he had told the King from Geneva that "the head of almost every delegation wished to see me to take my orders."[62] For all Laval's zigzagging, French support was inevitable in the event of war: Hoare had Herriot's personal assurance that "As between Italy and England, France must always choose England."[63]

Despite the acknowledged inadequacies of the fleet, attacks of gloom and a general reluctance to jeopardise Britain's global defences, the heads of Britain's armed services had no doubt that they could defeat Mussolini. Admiral Chatfield spoke for them all when he said, "The bumptiousness of Italy is so great that it may be worth fighting her now to re-assert our dominance over an inferior race."[64] The confidence, if not the arrogance, of the Admiralty was surely justified, not least because the sailors on the spot were dying to have a crack at the Italians. Of course there were miscalculations: the massing of ships at Aden gave the Germans "a cryptanalyst's feast" and enabled them to crack British naval codes.[65] But the Royal Navy's superiority over Mussolini's fleet was to be amply demonstrated during the Second World War. Even in 1935 Italy, which imported 80 per cent of its raw materials, could have been cut off from its forces in Ethiopia and bottled up in the Mediterranean. Anthony Eden later concluded that Hoare missed a great opportunity in not calling Mussolini's bluff in 1935. His sometime secretary Oliver Harvey agreed: by taking a firm stand against Italy, Britain could have isolated Germany, impressed Japan, freed the Mediterranean and prevented Spain from becoming "an international complication."[66] The distinguished military historian Sir Basil Liddell Hart declared: "Never again would there be so good a chance to check an aggressor so early, and the failure to do so in this case was the most fateful turning point in the period between the wars."[67]

This is speculation enhanced by hindsight. Britain's tragedy was that it had been so weakened and so demoralised by the Depression that most of its leaders could see no alternative to appeasement. Even Churchill, who wanted to keep his powder dry for Hitler, was occasionally afflicted by the malaise. In any case he regarded Ethiopia as unfit to be an "equal member of a league of civilised nations."[68] Nevertheless he was "deeply incensed"[69] by Mussolini's aggression. In pugnacious moods he was eager for "strong action" which would, he believed, force Mussolini to "climb down."[70] Yet the people were also angry. And this was one occasion when the government might have done well to heed its democratic masters. In their view Mussolini was committing daylight robbery abroad, whereas Hitler, when he later reoccupied the Rhineland, was only moving into his own backyard. Despite General Pownall's doubts, the level of popular indignation suggests that in 1935 a majority of Britons would have backed a moral stand. This is further indicated by the Peace Ballot, which Beaverbrook called the "Blood Ballot" because it could be used to sanction war on behalf of collective security.[71] That poll certainly suggests the spuriousness of government claims that it invariably had to reflect public opinion. So, in a different way, does the remark of Rex Leeper, the head of the Foreign Office Press Department. When Hoare opted to appease Mussolini, Leeper said: "It would take three weeks to prepare the public mind for a negotiated settlement instead of sanctions."[72]

Leeper, who aimed to transform newspaperdom into "a gramophone repeating the F.O. dope,"[73] proved a poor prophet. On 7 December 1935, looking "blue and mottled from fatigue and stress,"[74] Hoare set off for a holiday in Switzerland. He paused in Paris just long enough to agree with Laval that the Lion of Judah's share of Ethiopia should be given to Mussolini. The plan, devised by Vansittart and Grandi (the Italian Ambassador in London), initially proved acceptable to the British cabinet. But the howl of outrage which greeted the leaked news of it quickly drove Baldwin into retreat. Most newspapers were hostile. *The Times* was particularly scathing about the link between Haile Selassie's diminished realm and the sea. To protect the interests of the French railway line from Djibouti, this "strip of scrub" would be denied a railway and "restricted to the sort of traffic which has entered Ethiopia from the days of King Solomon, a corridor for camels."[75] Hard-headed City men described the plan as "the most miserable document that has ever disgraced the signature of a British statesman."[76] Liberal Tories condemned it as a wicked betrayal, reactionaries as a cowardly "scuttle," and all longed for a face-saving "get-out."[77] Hoare had suffered another blackout while skating and had broken his nose—Churchill, still in homicidal mood, wished it had been his neck. Now the Foreign Secretary returned home to become the government's scapegoat. Mustering as much dignity as any politician with a plastered nose can, he spoke from the corner of the third bench below the House of Commons gangway, the traditional refuge of ministers forced to resign. He defended himself effectively. But at last, wishing his successor more luck than he had enjoyed, Hoare's voice cracked. He burst into tears and crept out of the Chamber a "broken man."[78] Having at first urged acceptance of the Hoare-Laval plan, King George, with his fondness for rough humour, regaled his discredited minister with one of the current club jokes: "No more coals to Newcastle, no more Hoares to Paris."[79] He was disappointed that Sir Samuel (who was perhaps lucky to avoid regal ribbing about "hoar-frost in Switzerland")[80] did not laugh.

. . .

THE chain-smoking King enjoyed few further moments of levity. His health deteriorated and he worried about the succession. He deplored his eldest son's infatuation with Mrs. Ernest Simpson and actually forecast that Edward would ruin himself within 12 months of inheriting the throne. By the beginning of 1936 the King was obviously failing. He cannot have been cheered by news of Rudyard Kipling's death—supposedly the trumpeter of empire went first to herald its Sovereign into eternity. On 20 January George, wearing a flowered dressing gown, held a final Privy Council meeting in his bedroom at Sandringham. He could barely sign his name and soon lapsed into a coma. His doctor, Lord Dawson of Penn, issued that celebrated announcement: "The King's life is moving peacefully towards its close."[81] Dawson himself fulfilled this prophecy with a remarkable act of euthanasia, only recently revealed. He injected a lethal mixture of morphine and cocaine into the King's jugular vein. This was done, with the royal family's approval, to ease the King's suffering and to ensure that his death was reported with suitable dignity in the morning papers, notably *The Times,* rather than in "the less appropriate evening journals."[82]

In her diary Queen Mary wrote, "the sunset of his death tinged the whole world's sky."[83] But the fading of royal glory, like the lowering of house lights, had to be stage-managed. Even in death—particularly in death—veneration for the monarchy had to be kept alive. The King's body was embalmed to guard against its exploding during the funeral procession as the Duke of Teck's had done. George V's exit was a bizarre culmination of a long, intensive propaganda campaign which aimed, as Leonard Woolf wrote, "to establish in the people a superstitious 'loyalty' towards the royal family."[84] According to an American resident in London, the "royal publicity machine," which outdid "that of any film star," was responsible for the central paradox of English life. This was the coexistence of an "advanced political democracy" with a "retrogressive social aristocracy." The British themselves had no difficulty in accepting the paradox, observed the American. They were shocked by the deification of Stalin and Hitler but they failed to see that their own adulation of royalty surpassed that "inspired by any Dictator in Europe."[85]

Doubtless this was an exaggeration. But now a people which had rejoiced at the Jubilee was encouraged to indulge in a communal catharsis. The nation donned black. The air waves resounded to a perpetual threnody. The BBC devoted so much time to prayers, hymns, incantations, tolling bells and solemn music that some wondered whether king-worship had taken over from faith in God. (At his first State banquet the future Lord Longford absent-mindedly genuflected to the King.) Equally mournful were the press and the cinema. They provoked a frenzy of grief, as if trying to convince their audiences that the King's death was "the greatest event in human history since the Crucifixion."[86] The arrival of his body in London aroused something close to mass hysteria—a foretaste of the emotions generated, six decades later, by the passing of Diana, Princess of Wales. Slowly and sadly, in cold pale sunshine, the funeral cortège made its way from King's Cross Station to Westminster Hall. The coffin, shrouded in the royal standard and surmounted by the Imperial State Crown, a gold circle encrusted with gems such as the fiery white Cullinan diamond and the massive blood-red ruby given to the Black Prince and worn by King Henry on St. Crispin's Day, travelled on a gun carriage. As it entered New Palace Yard, the apex of the diadem, a Maltese Cross containing St. Edward's huge sapphire, the oldest crown jewel of all, jolted loose and flashed to the ground. A Grenadier sergeant major retrieved it and King Edward VIII, following the bier, exclaimed: "Christ! What will happen next?"[87]

Some of his subjects regarded this mishap as a terrible omen. But most were overwhelmed by poignant emotions engendered during George V's lying-in-state. Conservative MP and diarist "Chips" Channon, who watched the coffin being placed on its purple catafalque, was "left with the feeling that nothing matters . . . almost an eve-of-war reaction."[88] Over the next four days almost a million people queued for hours in hushed awe to pay their last respects to the King. Late one evening his four sons came down to the dimly-lit hall and took over the duties of the long-booted, plume-helmeted Household troops keeping silent vigil at each corner of the catafalque. It was another "excellent piece of public relations," according to Edward VIII's official biographer, though in order not to cheapen the gesture news of it was not given out in advance. The new Sovereign had another reason for being discreet: "King Carol of Rumania might have come and insisted on standing on top of the coffin."[89]

Almost everything else in Edward VIII's short reign was a blaze of indiscretion. This chiefly arose from his dangerous liaison with Wallis Warfield Simpson. She seemed to have bewitched him. She had, declared Mrs. Baldwin, "stolen the fairy Prince."[90] A Baltimore girl who was said to have spent her youth in "much seduced circumstances,"[91] Wallis had, according to malign gossip, learned the arts of love in Chinese brothels. But the secret of her success with Edward was probably not Eastern sexual techniques but Western ruthlessness. Certainly she looked more determined than beautiful, having obstinately straight hair, hard sapphire eyes and a firmly pointed chin. With her svelte figure and lustrous complexion, she seemed "chic rather than feminine, half artifice, half steel."[92] Often she would spend a whole day on her make-up, burnishing an appearance which combined animal allure and *soignée* sophistication. Loving jewellery, bibelots and *objets d'art* with a passion worthy of Queen Mary (who rightly saw her as an adventuress), Wallis herself was a sparkling social ornament. She was brittle and witty, punctuating tart, staccato sentences with salvoes of silver laughter. She was vital, clever, modern, flirtatious . . . and voracious.

Unlike her deferential English rivals, she had no hesitation in meeting Prince Charming's quasi-masochistic needs. Perhaps because he had been bullied and spoiled throughout his early years, Edward yearned for a regime of strictness tempered with tenderness. Soon after their affair began in 1934 Wallis was ordering him to fetch her cigarettes while forbidding him to smoke. She criticised his clothes and got him to paint her toenails. He loved her "madly tenderly adoringly" and, it is clear, sexually—despite giving George V his word of honour that she was not his mistress. Wallis responded firmly, coolly, even contemptuously. She told him that he had not grown up where love was concerned and she occasionally reduced him to tears. His billets-doux were often puerile, sometimes infantile and always full of self-abasement. Complaining that Mussolini seemed to have planned the Ethiopian crisis just to ruin his holiday, he wrote to her: "Your blue-eyed charmer is the most disappointed small boy you can imagine."[93] Now King Edward flouted convention by insisting that Mrs. Simpson be invited to royal occasions, neglected his duties to visit her, smuggled Paris fashions into the country for her, showed her the confidential government papers (which he dismissed as bunk) in his red boxes. His Private Secretary was aghast at such irresponsibility: "Before her the affairs of state sank into insignificance . . . every decision, big or small, was subordinated to her will."[94]

At first this was little more than a political inconvenience. The government suspected that Mrs. Simpson was an informer of the German Ambassador Ribbentrop, though it found evidence only that she was an agent of the American press magnate William Randolph Hearst—to whom Edward later wrote in "ardent admiration."[95] Many in official circles believed that the King himself was "pro-Nazi."[96] Ribbentrop himself thought that he was "a kind of English National Socialist."[97] Certainly the King threw his weight against intervention when Hitler reoccupied the Rhineland in March 1936. But Britain's failure to resist was already a foregone conclusion. The opinion of Sovereign and subjects coincided. This was not the case over the exiled Haile Selassie, who was now in Britain. To receive him at Buckingham Palace would be a popular gesture, urged Anthony Eden, Hoare's successor at the Foreign Office. The King replied that it would not be popular with the Italians. Mildly anti-Semitic, Edward had stronger prejudices against other races: when the Theosophist Annie Besant disclosed that the King was the reincarnation of the Emperor Akbar, he was "not over-pleased at the idea of having been a 'black man.'"[98] But despite signs that Edward was veering towards dictatorship, despite his threat to crush the BBC, despite the excited speculations of diplomats, the King was a political pawn. He might keep Baldwin waiting for 80 minutes, but he had no real power. Fancying himself as "Edward the Innovator," he later confessed that the only two changes he had made were inaugurating the King's Flight of aircraft and permitting the Yeomen of the Guard to shave off their spade beards. The King had no serious world-view. Like Lady Astor, he changed his mind as often as he changed his clothes. He re-set his watch, it was said, by every clock he passed. He flirted with fascism because it was fashionable. For its part, the government censored what went into his red boxes and kept him under the surveillance of the security services.

They discovered that where possible the King continued to behave as though he were Prince of Wales—the slight, baby-faced, buttercup-blond playboy of the Western world. His ornamental functions apart, Edward had spent his whole life in the hectic pursuit of pleasure. His private universe was a kind of X-certificate version of P. G. Wodehouse's Drones Club. Or *Vile Bodies* in a Cartier setting. It was filled with wine, women, song and sport. It consisted of smart nightspots, louche weekends, high jinks, horseplay, jazz and jigsaw puzzles. It was embellished with gold lighters and jewelled cigarette cases, Art Deco cuff-links and Fabergé boxes. Edward sympathised with the poor but associated with the rich. Amusing plutocrats eminent in society were his delight, such as Emerald Cunard and Chips Channon. Emerald, who hailed from San Francisco, had married a shipping heir and used his money to subsidise her lover, Sir Thomas Beecham. Chips, who came from Chicago, had married a brewing heiress and used her money to buy his way into bed with the likes of Terence Rattigan. Emerald addressed Edward as "Majesty Divine"[99] and hoped to become Mistress of Robes to Queen Wallis. Chips sometimes instructed his butler to lace the cocktails with benzedrine and aspired to be the Court Pepys.

The Channons' palatial mansion, 5 Belgrave Square, might have been designed specifically to entertain the King and Mrs. Simpson. Its *pièce de résistance,* approached through a dark antechamber guarded by two torch-bearing figures—one Chinese and the other Nubian—clad in magnificent gold liveries, was the "Amalienburg" dining-room. Decorated by Stéphene Boudin with gilt nymphs, dolphins, scallop shells and exotic birds, it shimmered like a blue and silver sea. The table top was made of squares of mirror which reflected thickets of Meissen and Dresden figures. Ocean-green silk curtains surged up to the coved ceiling. Soft candle-light from the huge crystal chandelier glinted in ornate golden looking-glasses. They in turn multiplied the host of blooms and the "brilliantly burnished silver decoration"[100]—argent chairs, albedo sideboard, pearl-grey carpet and nests of gorgeous bric-à-brac. It was a rococo dream. As the guests processed in to dinner, men wearing evening dress and (at the King's insistence) decorations, women accoutred in long gowns, diamond tiaras and ropes of gems, even Edward gasped. Formality and frivolity combined at the sumptuous meals (caviare in blinis, sole Muscat, Boeuf Provençal), which were followed by films or dancing. The King told his hostess that he "approved of splendour."[101]

Mrs. Simpson described herself as "Wallis in Wonderland." She basked in the caresses of those eager to ingratiate themselves with the King. Lady Colefax (so socially predatory that her Chelsea mansion was dubbed "Lions' Corner House")[102] expressed "delighted admiration for not only your immense wisdom & lovely common (so miscalled!) sense, but also for your unfailing touch of being exactly right in all judgements."[103] Less sycophantic members of high society made jokes about the royal paramour: "Honi soit qui Wally pense."[104] Among the informed élite hostility grew after her notorious summer holiday with the King on board the luxury yacht *Nahlin*. The couple were pictured together in poses of startling informality. Of course, there was nothing to compare with the royal exhibitions of the late twentieth century. But it was scandalous enough that a king of England should appear wearing nothing but shorts and gold crucifixes while evidently alert to the sound of his mistress's voice.

The British newspapers either did not print such photographs or airbrushed Mrs. Simpson into Trotsky-like oblivion. Foreign journals reported the romance with relish. The Madrid correspondent of *Paris-Soir* complained that his paper found the "massacre of a hundred Spanish children" less interesting than a sigh from Mrs. Simpson.[105] However, alien newspapers were banned from Britain or mutilated on arrival. For months the sovereign people were kept in the dark. The government was not responsible for a conspiracy of silence. Lord Beaverbrook arranged an informal "gentleman's agreement" among newspaper editors, who knew their place in a deferential society. Foreign correspondents in London, especially Americans, were amazed by Fleet Street's "habit of suppressing or 'playing down' unpalatable news," regarding it as "another sign of the deterioration of British democracy."[106] But this was to misunderstand the situation. The fact was that an authoritarian ruling class and an Olympian Civil Service had always seen universal suffrage as a threat to their monopoly. Mistrusting the populace, especially during times of social tension, they never accepted democracy—in the sense of accepting that only an informed electorate can properly exercise its vote. The gentlemen-in-waiting of the press (including the editor of the *Daily Worker*) would no more talk about royal peccadilloes in front of the masses than patricians would discuss family failings in front of the servants. In public journalists might expatiate grandly on the duty of disclosure incumbent on the Fourth Estate. In private they followed Lord Northcliffe, founder of the popular press, who had solicited hints from Buckingham Palace "as to what or what not to publish."[107] Unhappily *suppressio veri* in the interests of the monarchy seemed to legitimise *suggestio falsi* on behalf of the government. It helped to justify the newspapers' deceit about appeasement and the imminence of war. Hiding the truth about Mrs. Simpson contributed to what one historian has called the "moral paralysis" afflicting so much of the press during the Depression decade.[108]

Towards the end of 1936 "the King's matter" also induced a kind of political paralysis. It was exacerbated by the ever-increasing lethargy of Baldwin. Husbanding his failing energies for what he apparently regarded as the major problem of the day, the Prime Minister begged Anthony Eden not to trouble him "too much with foreign affairs just now."[109] Churchill himself was distracted by the issue, which obsessed the British Establishment to the point of "mania."[110] The couple fed the mania by behaving more and more recklessly. The King caused particular offence by refusing to open new hospital buildings at Aberdeen; he preferred to meet Mrs. Simpson, who was coming to stay at Balmoral. Nevertheless, it was extraordinary that at a time of mounting international tension the vital interests of the country and the empire should have taken second place in the minds of British leaders to an essentially trivial concern.

After all, the King could still perform his duties with panache. He cut a splendid figure at the State Opening of parliament, though he was almost overcome by the smell of mothballs from the peers' robes. He inspired sailors while inspecting the fleet with Sir Samuel Hoare, now restored to office as First Lord of the Admiralty in reward for his having remained eloquently dumb. On a notably successful tour of distressed areas in South Wales the King brought a ray of hope to dismal pit villages. But after Mrs. Simpson secured her divorce from the complaisant Ernest, rumours abounded in the smart world and abroad that Edward intended to marry her. They provoked horror. Somehow the British aristocracy (though not the bourgeoisie) was more offended by her being an American than by her being a divorcée. Noting occasional insinuations in the newspapers, an alarmed Chips Channon remarked that "the monarchy has lost caste enormously." Oddly, he blamed not the *mésalliance* itself but poor public relations. The King was "at his worst with Fleet Street, off-hand, angry and ungracious; he never treats them in the right way, or realizes that his popularity depends on them."[111] When the King heard that the press could not be kept quiet for much longer, he told Baldwin that if the government opposed his marrying Mrs. Simpson he would abdicate.

As the Prime Minister considered options and took soundings, the floodgates burst. Apparently keen to encourage more royal church-going, the Bishop of Bradford declared that the King showed few signs of being aware that he needed God's grace. The press then broke the news to a startled nation. It wrote respectfully, though Edward, accustomed to servility, felt that he was being treated like a common felon. Around him began to form a curious cavalier party which included disaffected elements ranging from Communist to Fascist. Beaverbrook was a leading light, apparently wanting to use the crisis to "bugger Baldwin."[112] Winston Churchill had much the same ambition. But all his chivalric instincts were aroused by the royal plight—his wife Clementine called him the last believer in the divine right of kings. Churchill advised Edward to play for time. He should barricade himself in Windsor Castle, summon the Beefeaters and defy Baldwin. But Baldwin had correctly gauged the disapproving temper of country and empire. Moreover, Edward knew his constitutional limitations and determined to go. He negotiated a generous financial settlement by the simple expedient of lying about his private wealth and pleading poverty, thus "conforming to established royal strategy."[113]

Then, on 10 December 1936, he quit the throne. The Duke of Windsor, to give him his new title, famously broadcast to his former subjects that he could not discharge his duties without the help of the woman he loved. Archbishop Lang, also famously, replied that Edward had sought his private pleasure in an "alien" social circle and "In darkness he left these shores." The Archbishop was duly reviled for kicking his man while he was down: "Old Lang swine, how full of Cantuar."[114] However, the most important victim of the abdication was Winston Churchill. He had alienated MPs by going "on the rampage" in the Smoking Room and declaring that he would not permit the King to be "strangled in the dark."[115] Appealing for delay in the Commons, he had been brutally howled down and had left the Chamber muttering that he was finished. Charges that he had genius without judgement revived and his campaign of resistance to the dictators was correspondingly discredited. Even friends turned against him. Churchill's star would rise again; but now he had to endure a dark night of the soul.

The abdication crisis also cast a shadow over the palace. Or rather, to change the metaphor, it let daylight in upon royal magic. It exposed the mystery of monarchy, which Bagehot had considered its life, to the common gaze. The new King, George VI, feared that the "whole fabric" of the institution might "crumble under the shock and strain of it all."[116] True, only five MPs supported a republican motion in the Commons. But one Tory reckoned that as many as a hundred might have done so on a free vote. Moreover, there were worrying signs of public disaffection. Edward had been the most popular figure in the country, if not the world. George had none of his transcendent glamour and savoir-faire. He was nervous, shy, dull, irascible and afflicted by a crippling stammer. Indeed, so ill-equipped was he to occupy the throne that some consideration was allegedly given to passing him over in favour of one of his younger brothers. Rumours abounded, too, that he was incapable of fulfilling his functions as Sovereign. It was therefore vital to cancel "the painful impression caused by an adored monarch who in a moment had thrown on to the scrap heap all the millions of mugs and plaques adorned with his face" and to build up "popular affection" for his replacement.[117]

This was speedily done. Newspapers vied with one another in stressing the new King's hitherto well-hidden talents. They praised his devotion to duty, simple tastes, concern for his subjects. They lauded his soundness as a family man, noted the comforting similarities he bore to his father and even professed to see the first sproutings of a nautical beard on his chin. There was no hint in George of his brother's addiction to "exotic" pleasures, now disparaged with extreme unction by *The Times*.[118] The King's "lack of more superficial, spectacular gifts," intoned the *Spectator,* "merely serves to emphasise the qualities, valuable and firm-based, that are part of his essential make-up."[119] Chips Channon thought that the press campaign would make the new regime popular and he was right. George VI became a living illustration of Bernard Shaw's maxim that kings are not born but made by universal hallucination.

Ironically his coronation, a gigantic cyclorama of majesty, was the subject of Mass Observation. This pseudo-science was a detailed attempt to examine society by, and on behalf of, its own members. It was founded by cannibal anthropologist Tom Harrisson and poet Charles Madge, whose first project was an immense survey of "the immediate human world" on 12 May 1937, the day when George was crowned. What emerged from the (inevitably subjective) observations of their volunteer reporters was that many people were sceptical about "the patriotic jingo of flag-wagging." But many more were entertained by the carnival atmosphere. They were thrilled by the glittering spectacle. They were moved, often to tears, by the broadcast ceremony. They recognised that the coronation was "colourful make-believe,"[120] but they were seduced by it all the same.

Certainly no effort was spared to make this a golden occasion. The Silver Jubilee decorations and illuminations were eclipsed. Everything was branded with patriotic motifs, from dinner services to linoleum, from coal scuttles to red, white and blue girls' "undies." *The Times* ululated: "Coronation Day breaks upon the world like some sublime chord that is the climax of a long crescendo . . . The Crown is the necessary centre, not of political life only, but of all life."[121] Eight grey horses pulled the gold coach, sprung with leather straps on the backs of four massive tritons (the rear pair carrying imperial fasces), through euphoric crowds. At Westminster Abbey the solemn ritual was enacted: the anointing with holy oil, the oath-swearing, the investing with regalia, the crowning. Chips Channon thought that the high points of the ceremony were the kneeling bishops drawn up like a flight of geese, a shaft of sunlight catching the King's gold tunic as he sat on the throne, the peeresses putting on their coronets, a thousand white-gloved arms sparkling with jewels. When a Socialist MP complained of having to sit behind the peers, Channon retorted: "It's their show, after all. You are lucky to be here at all."[122]

This was fair comment. Despite the self-congratulatory talk of a "truly democratic"[123] monarchy, the coronation was a feudal affair confined almost exclusively to a social élite. The people were only allowed a glimpse of the proceedings. Live television coverage, which could not be censored, was prohibited. Newsreels were admitted but (as the *Daily Mirror* reported without irony) the Archbishop of Canterbury, "ever vigilant of public interest and good taste, will carefully scan the films" and, with the help of the Duke of Norfolk, cut out "anything which may be considered unsuitable for the public at large to see."[124] What Chips Channon saw was that the aristocracy continued to rule the country. If this was a romantic illusion it contained, as a recent authority has said, a "germ of truth."[125] The masses were consumers, powerful yet manipulable. They were like the shoppers in Oxford Street, mesmerised by Selfridge's window display entitled "The Empire's Homage to the Throne"—it was afterwards bought to embellish the palace of an Indian prince. Ordinary Britons did not see the parade of magnificence as an insult to their lowly lot. Indeed, threadbare hunger marchers applauded the caparisoned cavalcade and the meaner the streets, the brighter their decorations. All the same, the contrast between the classes was palpable. It was physical as well as sartorial. Caught among a royalist, mainly lower-middle-class crowd in Trafalgar Square, George Orwell was struck by their "puny limbs, sickly faces" and bad teeth (often no teeth at all).[126] Other witnesses, from Mass Observation to the social anthropologist Bronislaw Malinowski, concluded that the loyalty was sincere and that it generated increased confidence in the "security" of the British empire.[127] Few but Communists and foreigners regarded the coronation as "imperialist propaganda"[128] or "a sort of whistling in the dark."[129]

Their views may have been sour but they were not unsound. The last imperial coronation disguised the fundamental weakness of the empire and diverted popular attention from the real dangers it faced. As Winston Churchill wrote, "Foreign affairs and the state of our defences lost all claim upon the public mood."[130] And in this mood the public could not conceive that the bright panoply of pomp was a hollow shell. The empire made Britain great. Without it, as its statesmen and service chiefs privately reiterated, the mother country would be an insignificant island anchored forlornly off the coast of Europe. Yet the Cabinet Secretary himself, Maurice Hankey, acknowledged that Britain had nothing more than "a façade of Imperial Defence."[131] What he meant was that the country was hopelessly over-stretched. Britain's resources did not match its reponsibilities and it had few means of protecting the vast bulk of its colonies and dominions which lay east of Suez. Their most likely attacker and, in the government's opinion, an even more immediate threat to peace than Germany, was Japan. Indeed, it was against Japan, not Italy, that skimpy defences had been put in place at Suez. But the menace was economic as well as military: Japan had obviously embarked on a national drive "to capture the markets of Asia and beyond."[132]

The British could not decide how seriously to take the danger or how best to counter it. Instinctively they reached for Gilbertian and Kiplingesque stereotypes, often contradictory ones. The Mikado's realm brooked no compare and his subjects were quaint and queer. They were also "bad little men who know too much,"[133] creators of a counterfeit civilisation. The British Naval Attaché in Tokyo took a different line: the Japanese had "peculiarly slow brains"[134] as a result of the intellectual effort they devoted to learning a script that made hieroglyphics seem child's play. On the other hand, Japan had taken enormous strides—though this suggested that it, too, was grossly over-stretched. The War Office seemed to believe both that the Emperor had a powerful modern war machine and that his soldiers were "coolies in uniform."[135] British diplomats warned that the Japanese also had a "mad-dog temper."[136] Vansittart assessed the situation more clearly and coolly. Early in the decade he pronounced:

We are incapable of checking Japan in any way if she really means business and has sized us up, as she clearly has done . . . By ourselves [i.e.
without US help] we must eventually swallow any & every humiliation
in the Far East.[137]

Uncle Sam would neither prop up John Bull nor tolerate a *rapprochement*
between London and Tokyo. In fact, America determined Britain's policy
in the Far East just as Britain determined France's in Europe. Consequently the Foreign Office dithered, now trying to conciliate Japan,
now issuing stiff protests. It attempted to "hunt with the hare—develop
China—and ride with the hounds—co-operate with Japan."[138] Britain put
on shows of strength: during the Ethiopian crisis one old cruiser and four
destroyers had to career around trying to convince Nippon that they were
the China Station fleet. Confused about their own policy, the British were
mystified about the policy of the Japanese. How was it made and where
would it end? The Land of the Rising Sun was as opaque as the dark side
of the moon. Or, in the preferred British terminology: "It was always difficult to know what was going on inside the anthill."[139]

XVIII

THE RISE OF JAPANESE MILITARISM

AT any rate Japan resembled the ant rather than the proverbially idle grasshopper and it was plainly building a garrison state. Despite hardship, the proportion of Japan's budget spent on arms rose from below a third to nearly a half during the three years following its withdrawal from the League of Nations in February 1933. Under the double goad of economic depression and diplomatic isolation, the Japanese fortified themselves against the world and threatened the peace of Asia. Their industry was formidable. As one journalist remarked, Japan was a "sweated nation."[1] Not a shard of metal was wasted, visitors observed, which might augment Nippon's clanking panoply. Instead of tin signs there were wooden ideographs. Hedges did for iron railings and pegs for nails. Bamboo poles took the place of wire clothes lines, a feature which foreigners were apt to notice since country women often remained naked to the waist while hanging out the washing. Japan also bought scrap in bulk, not least broken-up American warships which were transported for recycling straight to the Imperial Navy's dockyards in Osaka. But such preparations seemed only prudent in a world where other nations were erecting tariff barriers and signs saying "Strangers not Admitted."[2]

In these circumstances Japan's army leaders not only continued to exploit Manchukuo, they also concluded that no market or source of raw materials was secure unless they controlled it. Without colonies the Fatherland was unsafe. Itagaki wrote: "No fundamental solution can be found within the boundaries of naturally poor Japan that will ensure a livelihood for the people at large."[3] So Japanese imperialists, like their British predecessors, justified expansion on grounds of self-defence. At a time of such fierce economic competition, it was a matter of life or death. Britain, as the nation with the greatest interest in preserving the global status quo, now found this attitude difficult to comprehend. But no one could mistake the growing Japanese resentment about international inequities. It was best summed up by the diplomat Amo Eiji, who was shocked, at a Thames-side restaurant in the late 1930s, when a leisured lady spent on her lapdog what it would have cost to feed several poor but hard-working Japanese labourers. Was not this vignette enough, he asked the British Ambassador bitterly, "to suggest a fundamental problem among nations?"[4]

The problem was not just to do with disparities of wealth, though most Japanese could not afford budgerigars, let alone pet poodles—they contented themselves with large green singing crickets in wicker cages. The problem was the gulf between hard actuality and manifest destiny. Nationalist pretensions had always been overweening and, as pressure mounted for Nippon to take its proper place in the world, they became menacing. Extreme patriots appealed for Asian *Lebensraum* and preached the gospel of the sword. Vowing that Japan would not concede an inch gained in Manchuria even "should the country be burnt to the ground," Foreign Minister Uchida advocated "scorched-earth diplomacy."[5] None spoke in 1933 with more messianic fervour than the War Minister, General Araki:

> Needless to say, the Imperial Army's spirit lies in exalting the Imperial Way and spreading the National Virtue. Every single bullet must be charged with the Imperial Way and the end of every bayonet must have the National Virtue burnt into it. If there are any who oppose the Imperial Way or the National Virtue, we shall give them an injection with this bullet and this bayonet.[6]

Japan did not seek merely to lead the Great Asia Association, founded in March 1933 to save the Orient from Soviet Communists as well as Western imperialists; it aspired to what one historian has called "colonial totalitarianism."[7] As the decade progressed there was less talk of *wangtao*, the "principle of benevolent rule," and more of *koninka*, "imperialisation." In other words, the empire was being incorporated into a Greater Japan. But even this was not enough: the Son of Heaven should command universal vassalage. Soon, in time-honoured fashion, nationalism was masquerading as cartography. Just as the seventeenth-century English lawyer John Selden had demonstrated the twin proposition that the sea could be owned and that Charles I owned it, so the Professor of Geography at Kyoto Imperial University now claimed that all the oceans of the world should be named the Great Sea of Japan. Just as the eighteenth-century Emperor of Cathay, Qianlong, had rejected European maps because "China should be in the centre of the world,"[8] so Japanese now consigned the West to its periphery.

Such notions were strengthened by the lonely struggle in Manchuria. No people were more racially pure than the Japanese, they claimed, and adversity encouraged a corresponding ideological uniformity. War stifled unorthodoxy. Isolation was an antidote to disintegrating individualism, of the kind epitomised by George Bernard Shaw. Arriving in Tokyo soon after Matsuoka had walked out of Geneva, the playwright dramatised himself as a "mental earthquake."⁹ Actually he was more of a gadfly: he proposed that the Japanese should turn their guns on their slums (as a preliminary to building new houses); and he asked, "Why don't you worship your descendants?"¹⁰ But Shaw was pertinent as well as impertinent. He told his hosts that they were stirring up Chinese nationalism which *bushido* could not quell. And he said that Japan's poverty would (and should) dispose it to embrace Communism. Official persons he met such as Araki and Prime Minister Saito (an "amiable old nincompoop" with whom he exchanged pleasantries on the subject of senescence) agreed that this was a possibility. But they regarded it not as an economic problem but as a "thought problem."¹¹ Correct indoctrination would provide the solution.

So the police stepped up their campaign against "dangerous thoughts." They mounted a vast surveillance operation, aiming to "hear what has no sound and see what has no shape."¹² Over the next three years they arrested 60,000 "thought criminals." They also detained more than a million other suspects under different pretexts—offences could include anything from practical jokes to tattooing one's body. They virtually destroyed the Communist Party. By methods including brainwashing, physical torture and imprisonment, they "cured" or "converted" many offenders.¹³ These terms are not altogether misleading, for the emphasis was on enlightenment rather than coercion. Moreover, reformed Communists were liable to come out with exclamations like this: "What supreme bliss it is to be born a Japanese with the privilege of sacrificing oneself for the sake of . . . the Emperor."¹⁴ Hirohito's police state (though the Emperor himself never sought to create such a thing) resembled Bismarck's rather than Hitler's. But it indulged in characteristic fascist follies. Censors spent ages counting the petals on chrysanthemums in films, cutting out those containing between 12 and 20 in case they were confused with the 16-petalled imperial crest. Campaigners for linguistic purity tried to outlaw the universally used "mama" and "papa." The song "Lean on Your Shovel" was banned.¹⁵

In mid-1933, after a truce had been agreed with the Chinese in Manchukuo, Japan was swept by a genuinely popular song: "Tokyo Ondo." It was sung by the geisha Katsutaro and could be heard everywhere. It floated from wooden houses, new apartment blocks and stages set up on street corners for the annual *O-Bon* Festival, the joyous reunion of the living with the spirits of the dead. To its strains people in bright summer kimonos bought ice and water melons from stalls which sold charcoal and roasted hot potatoes during the winter months. Under lanterns black with insects they lit up Golden Bats: each ten-sen, green and gold packet of ten cigarettes was provided with a little holder so that every flake of tobacco, a government monopoly, could be smoked. As the music went round and round, householders chattered and danced away the tropical nights. But the authorities were determined to promote the "Japanese spirit" in everything from school text-books to popular culture. So gradually the cheerful melody of "Tokyo Ondo" was drowned by the earnest "Song of Young Japan."

> Brave warriors united in justice,
> In spirit a match for a million—
> Ready like the myriad cherry blossoms to scatter
> In the spring sky of the Showa Restoration.[16]

This seemed to imply the restoration of direct rule by Hirohito, a realisation of the power nominally restored to the Meiji Emperor in 1868, but it was really a euphemism for a khaki shogunate. And in July 1933 another military coup was nipped in the bud. Self-proclaimed *Shinpeitei,* or "soldiers of the gods," plotted to strike during the day on which Hirohito visited the Military Academy, the Japanese version of St. Cyr. These callow jingoists were members of secret societies like the Black Dragon and they were financed, ironically, by a dealer who hoped to make a killing on the stock exchange. They proposed to "massacre the cabinet" and to exterminate other politicians as well as capitalists and financiers. The army would then, they hoped, declare martial law and bring about a "second restoration."[17] Probably senior military and even royal figures were implicated. But they distanced themselves from the conspiracy when police arrested the ring-leaders, whose arsenal amounted to little more than a few swords and hundreds of samurai headbands.

Further threats of terrorism followed, all designed to smash the compromise which Prince Saionji had manufactured after Inukai's murder. Saito's cabinet of national unity, in which both party politicians and army officers served, satisfied nobody. It was riven by internal strife, complicated by factionalism in the armed forces. It was further injured by the trial of Inukai's assassins, whose burning sincerity was contrasted with government corruption. One defendant aroused particular sympathy by declaring:

Producing rice for the nation, the farmers were unable to obtain food for themselves. Eighty per cent of the soldiers are farmers. The politicians and financiers have strayed from the spirit of patriotic brotherhood which is the fundamental characteristic of the nation. I felt the need of awakening them and we acted with that motive.[18]

Still more ominously, it was also said during the trial that "The present Imperial Household is similar to the House of Romanoff when it disintegrated. Only there is no Rasputin in Japan."[19] Yet there were forces just as sinister. Super-patriots questioned the patriotism of Araki himself. The General became "quite run down" because young subalterns would jump over his fence and wake him up in the middle of the night with the question: "What happened to the promises you made before you assumed your post as Minister?"[20]

The atmosphere of crisis was heightened by fears that an overtly "Fascist regime,"[21] perhaps led by Baron Hiranuma, might succeed Saito. In fact Saito, the bulky, snowy-haired, garrulous Premier, consolidated his government in the autumn of 1933 by making Hirota Koki, a suave professional diplomat, Foreign Minister. This was a shrewd move as Hirota had forged strong links with the ultra-nationalist organisations such as *Genyosha* (the Dark Ocean society) yet also had good claims to be an internationalist. He was a disciple of the high priest of political terrorism, Toyama Mitsuru, yet made himself agreeable to that ineffable specimen of diplomatic orthodoxy, Sir Robert Craigie. His position was so ambiguous that even his own countrymen did not know where he stood. One described him as a person who "hides innate prudence and studied discretion beneath a cloak of Oriental nonchalance and retains his own way of thinking, though mingling constantly with those tainted with occidentalism."[22] Foreigners were even more confused about this "subtle equilibrist in careerism."[23] The German Ambassador, for example, could not understand how Hirota's passionate nationalism was to be reconciled with his "kind, moderate and almost slow behaviour."[24] Even today it is unclear whether Hirota was a misunderstood liberal who tried obliquely to control the excesses of the military or a cunning chauvinist who deserved his final punishment—he was the only Japanese civilian hanged as a war criminal.

Born in 1878, the son of a Fukuoka stonemason, Hirota soon changed his given name to Koki, which means "firm of purpose." But later, when asked (as public men often were) for a sample of his handwriting, he would invariably pen four Chinese characters meaning "adapt to whatever comes." Climbing the diplomatic ladder, after graduation from Tokyo Imperial University, Hirota was famously impassive. Whatever the crisis, during the time he served in Britain and the United States, he wore an ivory mask. Bitterly disappointed at being sent as Ambassador to Holland in 1927, he composed a haiku:

> A windmill
> Taking a nap
> Until the next breeze blows.[25]

The occasional tapping of his long-stemmed, small-bowled pipe on a desk was the only sign of anger the silent, delicate, toothbrush-moustached Hirota ever gave. At home he was more forthcoming. Devoted to books, baths and puns, he amused his children with his early-morning judo exercises. He also took them hunting for truffles among the pine roots near his seaside retreat north of Tokyo. Here, as in all country districts, the early morning cockcrow, *kokka-koh-koh,* seemed to proclaim that, "Filial piety is the root of national prosperity."[26] Hirota's family clearly took the maxim to heart.

All shared his extraordinary spirit of self-sacrifice, the Japanese spirit of living as though already dead. When he felt unable to desert his post in Holland to see his ailing mother, she starved herself to death; and his eldest son committed suicide after failing his exams. Stoicism in Japan was often the "façade of a tumultuous soul."[27] Perhaps this was true of Hirota for, apart from drinking rather heavily, he showed no emotion about these tragedies. In office he remained inscrutable, avoiding all forms of ostentation. Hirota was just a man in mufti, albeit discreetly well tailored. He disliked wearing *haikara* (high collar), white tie and tails, which made him feel like a street musician. He loathed the Prussian-style Court dress of gold-embroidered jacket, white sash and braided trousers which, he said, made him look like a hotel commissionaire. His policies were also bafflingly disguised. He paid lip-service to liberalism, insisting that he was working for a gradual increase in international trust. He even faced down General Araki, whose emergency plans for conflict with Russia had provoked opposition in the army. But while Hirota advocated global peace he had also supported the Manchurian war. For a time the Foreign Minister's sphinx-like manner helped to sustain this contradiction. His tragedy, and Japan's, was that he could not resolve it.

Hirota's ambivalence, while by no means unusual, was one more obstacle in the way of understanding Nippon. Japanese statements about foreign policy were increasingly "couched in enigmatic terms."[28] As the army's grip on the body politic tightened, military sedition became "a topic like a lady's lost virtue; there were hints and innuendos, but no one . . . [would] speak plainly."[29] The Emperor himself grew ever more worried about his country's "dual—civilian and military—foreign policy."[30] Both Chinese and

Americans complained that Japan spoke with many voices. When Chiang Kai-shek wondered which top Japanese to negotiate with, an aide said that he could not go far wrong if he chose a colonel, a major or a captain. Henry Stimson maintained that Japan was not a normal country because control was exercised from below. The American Ambassador in Tokyo, Joseph Grew, wrily remarked that visiting tourists knew as much about the place as he did.

Grew approved of Hirota and appreciated his conciliatory endeavours. It was, after all, Hirota's opposition to "spasmodic military hysteria" that helped to force the resignation of Araki in January 1934. His successor at the War Ministry, General Hayashi Senjuro, was every inch a soldier—from khaki cap to gold spurs. The son of a former *daimyo* (feudal baron), he had the reputation of being the "Japanese version of an English gentleman." There were rumours, it is true, that the thickly-moustached General associated with political racketeers. Moreover, he stated in a pamphlet worthy of Mussolini that, "Battle is the father of creativity and the mother of culture."[31] Nevertheless he was a tough, taciturn, decisive character, bent on restoring discipline. He seemed a guarantee that there would be "no more hysterico-politics from the lower senior ranks."[32] Then, in the spring of 1934, the Foreign Ministry official Amo Eiji made an embarrassing *démarche*. He issued a declaration saying that the Western powers should be prohibited from playing any significant role in China. He seemed to be slamming the Open Door. But there was much confusion about the pronouncement and the American State Department, which could not even get an official translation, was left "groping about in something of a fog."[33] In private Hirota professed to be surprised and offended by Amo's initiative. Yet he himself had said much the same thing in more diplomatic language. And he did not repudiate in public what came to be seen as an Asian Monroe Doctrine.

The Amo Declaration marked another significant stage in the army's forward march. True, the removal of the anti-Communist Araki had helped to dissipate what Litvinov called "the darkest thunder-cloud on the international political horizon."[34] Now, however, the Supreme Command talked not of bullets but of steel mills, not of preparing for immediate conflict but of mobilising the whole nation for total war. This suggested that the hard heads of Hayashi's "Control" faction were even more dangerous than the hotheads of Araki's "Imperial Way." Hayashi's supporters, men such as General Nagata Tetsuzan, chief of the Military Affairs Bureau at the War Ministry, demanded not just blood but ever-increasing amounts of treasure.

It seemed possible to foot their bill because the country had risen above the Depression. In 1934 the government actually declared that it was over for Japan. Production was rising at more than ten per cent a year. Between 1930 and 1936 exports doubled, despite international trade restrictions aimed at everything from textiles to bicycles, tinned tuna to electric light-bulbs. The chemicals industry boomed. During the 1930s the metals and machinery workforce rose from 250,000 to 1.7 million. Japan now made more rayon than America and had "dethroned" Lancashire in the field of cotton fabrics, producing well over a third of the world's supply before the end of the decade. By then, too, its economy was stronger than Italy's and it had overtaken France in manufacturing capacity. At last Nippon could be "properly classified an 'industrial society.'"[35]

But military maturity was still lacking. Indeed, Japan's unique economic success encouraged primitives in the army to become greedier, not wiser. Having installed Pu Yi as Emperor (his reign was named *Kangte,* "Tranquillity and Peace") in one of many endeavours to "disguise" Manchukuo as "an independent nation,"[36] the soldiers now wrested formal control over it from the Tokyo government. There were more plots and rumours of plots. Matsuoka attacked the degenerate, Westernised party system. In the summer of 1934 financial scandals finally brought down Saito's ministry. But although Saionji managed to secure the appointment of another government of national unity, led by poor, honest Admiral Okada Keisuke, Hirota and Hayashi remained in place. And the Supreme Command became still more domineering.

The Soviet Ambassador, who recognised the trend of events, likened Japan to the cat in the Russian fable. A cook caught it eating meat and gave it a stern lecture: the cat listened but continued to eat meat. In November 1934 Lieutenant-Colonel Matsumoto told the Ex-Soldiers Association in Kobe that Japan could and should defeat the decadent United States, which stood in the way of its becoming "just ruler of the world." Matsumoto and his ilk were "perfectly capable," Joseph Grew concluded, "of committing what might well amount to national hara-kiri in a mistaken conception of patriotism."[37] But the process seemed unstoppable. In the same month students in the Military Academy and others, whom Saionji called the army's "habitual criminals,"[38] attempted another coup, which was quickly stifled. At the beginning of 1935, when the soldiers made a boundary dispute in Jehol the excuse for further aggression, an embarrassed Hirota had to ask in cabinet what they were doing and whether he could be kept informed. Yet he also announced publicly that there would be no war while he was in office. And he elevated his envoy in China to ambassadorial status. But military zealots, encouraged by feuding politicians, again undermined his efforts. In June 1935 the army lunged into the provinces of Hopei and Chahar. Premier Okada wryly admitted that he could do nothing. Finance Minister Takahashi complained that he was losing control of his budget. Foreign Minister Hirota was torn between holding Chiang Kai-shek's hand and slapping his face. In fact, the government was virtually paralysed. Despite his aversion to "ultra-nationalistic actions and movements,"[39] the Emperor himself could not assist.

HIROHITO found shades of the prison-house closing upon him as the decade progressed. At its beginning he was merely a captive of convention. He was occasionally paraded as a pageant, usually immured as a fetish. Before his people the Emperor manifested himself in all the trappings of divine kingship. He could not smile or wave lest it should impair his dignity, though he was obliged to appear in ill-cut clothes because tailors had to guess his measurements, not being permitted to touch him. When he was on tour spectators were not allowed within 100 metres of his maroon Rolls-Royce. His situation was epitomised by the weird communion he held with his subjects while on fleet manoeuvres in Kinko Bay during the autumn of 1931. After dusk, while his ship's company were having their evening meal, the Emperor was observed on the aft deck standing alone, stiffly at attention, saluting towards the land. It was five or six miles away and totally obscured by the murk. But a telescope revealed two rows of flickering lights, evidently lanterns waved by fishermen and bonfires blazing on hill-tops. A chamberlain wrote:

> At such a distance the people on the coast could not possibly have seen the ship, so they must simply have timed this demonstration of their loyalty and affection according to the predicted hour of the ship's passage. The emperor's response to this must have been intuitive, for unless he was aided by some temporary change or quirk in atmospheric conditions, it is unlikely that he could see the lights with the naked eye. It was quite a moving sight . . . the emperor saluting people he could not see, and the people hailing the emperor they could not see.

At first the ship's Captain could not think how to acknowledge their greeting. Then he slapped his knee and exclaimed, "The searchlights! We'll turn on the searchlights, and they will know we are here."[40] As their beams burst through the gloom and played over the undulating shores of the Satsuma and Osumi peninsulas, the vessel became a seaborne temple of light. The eyes of crew and courtiers blurred with tears as they witnessed the imperial aureole and thought of the joy it would inspire. Yet it is clear that, in their perceptions of each other, the living god and the anonymous masses remained in the dark.

For the most part Hirohito was quite invisible, shut up in the Imperial Palace. It was guarded by an azure moat, massive grey walls of unmortared stone, heavy iron-studded gates and the Towers of Tenshu, with their protecting "arms from Heaven."[41] No sightseers were admitted and from the outside nothing could be discerned of the Palace, a maze of pavilions built on the site of the ancient Tokugawa castle, except porcelain tiled roofs shaped like Mongolian tents. Twice a year, at cherry blossom time in the spring and when the autumn chrysthanthemums were in bloom, the Emperor gave garden parties. Privileged visitors, the men in top hats and frock coats, the women in European dress or gorgeous silk kimonos, saw a 300-year-old horticultural masterpiece. It contained ancient plum trees and gnarled pines, lotus pools and bronze fountains, waterfowl and butterflies, vines and water lilies, willow-pattern bridges and lacquered pergolas, purling brooks and rockeries banked with cryptomeria. It was another Eden, a place of sublime confinement.

The first telephone was admitted to the Palace only in 1928, the first journalist in 1933. He was Ward Price, star reporter of the London *Daily Mail* and a celebrated lickspittle of totalitarian regimes. He owed his entrée to having given Japan "very favourable publicity"[42] in the past, and he would soon trumpet the army's "most categorical assurance" that it had no aggressive intentions towards China.[43] Now Price afforded his readers an awestruck glimpse of the Japanese holy of holies. Footmen in cocked hats and heavily gold-laced liveries ushered him into the single-storeyed, wood-carved, temple-like Palace. A master of ceremonies conducted him through richly carpeted apartments decorated with gilded screens and hung with tapestries of medieval battle scenes. After an anxious rehearsal—the frock-coated visitor had to make three bows at intervals of two yards—he had his private audience in the Phoenix Room. It was empty apart from the Chair of State, panelled in gold with dragon designs and flanked with two large, flower-filled *cloisonné* vases. Standing throughout, the bespectacled Emperor declared that he wanted good relations with Britain and (despite having left the League) "peace in the Far East."[44] But, like General Hayashi, who was in attendance, Hirohito was dressed in khaki uniform, complete with red facings, peaked cap, gold badges of rank and sword.

As these accoutrements suggest, the peace-loving Emperor was ever more in thrall to the army. Since 1931, heeding Saionji's counsel, he had said as little as possible when meeting the Supreme Command in order not to sully himself with controversy. He had reluctantly submitted to the appointment of Honjo Shigeru, conqueror of Manchuria, as his military aide-de-camp. The General, while always being profoundly humbled or "deeply moved by His Majesty's sentiments," did not hesitate to counter them with martial opinions. He favoured higher military expenditure. He charged that the Court was responsible for "the weak-kneed foreign policy." He also assured Hirohito that the army was not "acting contrary to the theory of imperial sovereignty" when it disagreed with him "on specific issues."[45] Paradoxically, the more the soldiers exalted the Emperor as a god, the more they reduced him to the status of a puppet. This was because they could pull the strings in a theocracy, whereas if the Emperor were a constitutional monarch Japan would be a parliamentary democracy with the army remaining subject to civilian control.

Hence the explosive debate, which rocked Japan to its volcanic foundations in 1935, over whether the Emperor was a mere "organ" of government. This view had been put forwards by a dull legal scholar named Minobe Tatsukichi, who now became the victim of a heresy hunt comparable to that involving Salman Rushdie in a later age. The irony is that Minobe, who supported the authoritarian Meiji constitution, would elsewhere have been deemed a conservative. However, he did defend civil rights such as freedom of speech and he attacked the army for making war "the basis of our national policy."[46] The soldiers and their factious political supporters retaliated with an "epoch-making" assault on liberalism.[47] Minobe, as Saionji said, became "the scapegoat."[48] Few had read his works and fewer understood the intricacies of the academic argument. But the campaign ripped across the country like an earthquake. Minobe was invited to kill himself. He was denounced in the Diet. Reservists at Tokyo's Military Club ceremonially burned his books. The government (somewhat ambiguously) condemned his theory. In order to avoid prosecution Minobe withdrew into private life. His books were banned. Later he was wounded in an assassination attempt. It was no wonder that, at the height of the furore, the fiery visionary Ishiwara could declare: "I am going to be the leader of a dictatorship in Japan a few months from now."[49]

The Emperor fought back. In the spirit of Minobe, he advised and encouraged the government. He warned Prime Minister Okada to "guard against being led by the nose by the military forces stationed overseas."[50] He also helped to remove a "gangrenous sore"[51] from the body politic— General Mazaki Jinzaburo. One of the most rabid members of the Imperial Way faction, Mazaki had evidently been behind the Military Academy plot in 1934 and he was now ousted from his post as Inspector-General of Military Education. This threw the army into renewed turmoil and provoked the assassination of one of Mazaki's chief opponents. On 12 August 1935 a fanatical former fencing instructor named Lieutenant-Colonel Aizawa Saburo burst into General Nagata's office at the War Ministry, slashed him across the face with his sword and, after a struggle, stabbed him to death. Aizawa was astonishingly insouciant about the whole matter. He was concerned about his cut finger and lost cap, sorrowful only that he had not dispatched Nagata with a single stroke, and convinced that he could now proceed to his new post in Taiwan. In fact Aizawa was arrested before he left the building, only to find himself approached by a major-general who shook his hand and thanked him. Taking responsibility for the Nagata incident, War Minister Hayashi resigned. His successor, General Kawashima Yoshiyuki, was told that the "Emperor personally wishes to supervise all diplomatic and military affairs."[52] Kawashima said that he did "everything without talking" and "staked everything on stricter control of the army."[53]

This was yet another false dawn. Like the pearly mist which so often veiled the morning face of Tokyo, aggression was in the air. The city was tense with anxiety and rife with rumours of further terrorism. Court officials were given police guards. Saionji believed that the country was taking the path of German or Russian dictatorship. When in mid-January 1936 Japan finally walked out of renewed London negotiations to limit naval rearmament, after once more being denied parity, Takahashi feared that political and military extremists would unite to bring about fascism. When Foreign Minister Hirota complained that the soldiers had sabotaged his pacific overtures towards Chiang Kai-shek, Premier Okada smilingly retorted that it was better for them to be spending most of their budget in north China than distributing it to "*ronin* [desperadoes] and rightists" at home. The Supreme Command itself could not rein in "the runaway army."[54]

Signs that its *enragés* would precipitate some new putsch were legion. In what Saionji called his "humble shack," actually an elegant, two-storeyed villa whose many windows looked over the sea at Okitsu, the Prince heard that young officers of the 1st Division were "trying to stir up something prior to their departure for Manchukuo."[55] The military police discovered the plot and kept its leaders under surveillance—but only during the day. The ring-leaders even held a dress rehearsal, making a mock attack on the Metropolitan Police Station in Tokyo: screaming soldiers with fixed bayonets charged up the front steps and into the building. Hints of the conspiracy reached the royal family. Hirohito's brother, Prince Chichibu, was rumoured to be encouraging the young officers: he had given one of them a set of his underwear. It was clear, in fact, that some new libation of blood was about to be offered on the altar of the Showa Restoration. But the Japanese convention of tacit understanding operated to a bewildering degree. The coup was common knowledge in government circles and even received a measure of official collusion. It was foreshadowed but unmentioned.

Agitated by the Minobe debate and stimulated by the trial of Aizawa, which took place at the beginning of 1936, the plotters, a score of modern samurai none higher in rank than captain, had steeled themselves to act. They held the leadership in common, but they were not an entirely homogeneous group. Many streams, some flowing from Nazi and revolutionary sources, fed their murderous idealism. But its essential well-springs were nationalistic. The plotters were in revolt against the degenerate alien creeds of liberalism, capitalism, fascism, socialism and Communism. They modelled themselves on the 47 *ronin* in the classic morality tale, whose vengeful self-sacrifice for the sake of personal obligation answered the deepest yearnings of the Japanese soul. In fact the current which swept these young soldiers to destruction was that of native religious fundamentalism. No one has analysed this better than the writer Mishima Yukio, who shared their utopian ambition to purge Japan of foreign defilement and their "supreme resolution to die a fanatic's death."[56] In his novel *Runaway Horses* he paints a vivid picture of their sympathy with the suffering poor during the Depression, their indignation at the irresponsibility of the moneyed class whose interests were served by effete bureaucrats, corrupt politicians and evil courtiers, their impatience with the self-seeking cliquishness of the military high command, and their search for imperial salvation. Mishima's hero declares:

I had faith that the dark clouds would one day be blown away and that a bright and clear future lay ahead for Japan . . . Th[e] sun is the true image of His Sacred Majesty. If people could only bathe themselves in its rays, they would shout with joy. The desolate plain would then become fertile at once . . . But the low-lying cloud of darkness covers the land and shuts off the light of the sun. Heaven and earth are cruelly kept apart . . . To join heaven and earth, some decisive deed of purity is necessary. To accomplish so resolute an action, you have to stake your life, giving no thought to personal gain or loss. You have to turn into a dragon and stir up a whirlwind, tear the dark, brooding clouds asunder and soar up into the azure-blue sky.

In other words: the more hopeless the cause, the nobler were the motives of those prepared to die for it.

Like Mishima's fictional terrorist, the young officers thought not in terms of killing people but only of "destroying the deadly spirit that was poisoning Japan."[57] They had little or no political programme, believing that everything would automatically come right once the light of the imperial countenance shone directly upon the nation. Inspired to glory, some went out for a drink on the eve of the uprising and told an astonished waitress: "Tomorrow we are going to die."[58] At the same time Joseph Grew was entertaining senior Japanese officials, including ex-Premier Saito and Grand Chamberlain Suzuki Kantaro, at the American embassy. They watched, with every sign of enjoyment, a trite Hollywood musical called *Naughty Marietta* starring Nelson Eddy and Jeanette MacDonald—one of its songs was "Ah, Sweet Mystery of Life." Snow was falling thickly as they drove home, blanketing the city in a sinister silence. In his Palace the Emperor, tired from his afternoon skiing in the Fukiage Gardens, slept peacefully.

At two o'clock the next morning, 26 February 1936, bugles sounded reveille within earshot of the Palace. Fourteen hundred troops of the 1st and Guards Divisions donned heavy greatcoats and packs, drew live ammunition and mustered in their barracks. Many of them expected another night exercise. But, obedient to a fault, they carried out their ferocious orders to the letter. Separate squads set out to assassinate seven prime targets. One burst into the house of the white-bearded, 82-year-old Finance Minister Takahashi, Japan's answer to Maynard Keynes. They shot and slashed him to death in his bed, shouting "Traitor!" and "Heavenly Punishment!" As they left a lieutenant said to Takahashi's terrified servants, "Excuse me for the annoyance I have caused."[59] Another group of rebels forced their way into the residence of the former Premier, Saito, whom they found in his night kimono and gunned down, wounding his wife in the process. Then some of them went on to kill Watanabe Jotaro, Inspector-General of Military Education.

However, four of their intended victims escaped. Prince Saionji, whom the nationalist writer Kita Ikki regarded as the last of the "plump worms oozing from the corpse" of the Meiji Restoration,[60] took refuge with the police. At the Itoya Inn in the hot-springs resort of Yagawara, 60 miles from Tokyo, policemen detailed to protect Count Makino fired on his attackers, who set the building alight and machine-gunned anyone who fled from the flames. It seemed as though the former Lord Privy Seal must succumb to this slaughter, but in the confusion his 20-year-old granddaughter led him to safety. In his Tokyo residence Grand Chamberlain Suzuki fell to the floor under a hail of bullets. As the soldiers moved in to give him the *coup de grâce* Suzuki's wife, kneeling in a pool of his blood, begged to be allowed to administer it herself. The captain in charge agreed, saluted the supposedly dying man and said to her: "I am particularly sorry about this but our views differ from His Excellency's, so it had to come to this."[61] Suzuki survived to become a future premier. The man occupying that post at the time, Okada Keisuke, saved his life but fatally lost face. By mistake troops killed his brother-in-law, who resembled him, and Okada hid first in a shed and later in a laundry closet. Everyone assumed that the Prime Minister was dead. But he eventually appeared, wearing a shabby kimono and three days' growth of beard. And although the undignified details of his escape were hushed up, everyone was embarrassed by his post-insurrection resurrection.

Meanwhile the mutineers had occupied much of central Tokyo, including the War Ministry, the Metropolitan Police Station, various government offices, important official residences and the unfinished Diet building, a great white edifice with massive columns and ziggurat tower. The troops put out barbed wire, invaded several newspaper plants to issue propaganda and displayed flags bearing the Meiji legend: "Revere the Emperor, destroy the traitors."[62] There was virtually no opposition: fishmongers going to market before dawn saw soldiers leading away policemen. But the rebels failed in their attempt to secure the Imperial Palace and with it the person of the Emperor—as vital a capture for them as Montezuma had been for the *Conquistadores*. In the darkness some Guards did manage to bluff their way into the compound. But their purpose was discovered and the Palace Guards ordered them out at gunpoint. So they never had a chance to fortify themselves at the main Sakashita Gate and flash the torchlight signal to their shivering confederates on the roof of the police station. Mishima later claimed that if the ruthless Kita Ikki, whose eclectic radicalism inspired so many of the rebels, had acted with them, they would not have made this mistake. But it was a mistake which, according to Mishima, typified "the fragile and ethereal beauty of the righteous army which forbore the slaughter of even one woman or child. And because of this very 'blunder,' the affair will forever leave . . . the imprint of its spiritual values on the pages of history."[63]

The Emperor was appalled by such perversions of the samurai spirit and opposed the rebels vigorously. In fact he showed more resolution than at any other time in his career—until he took it upon himself to announce Japan's surrender in August 1945. "So they have done it," he exclaimed, when woken with news of the revolt early on the Wednesday morning of 26 February. His immediate instinct was to take personal responsibility: "It's all due to a failing in me."[64] But he soon changed his mind and determined not to tolerate further appeasement of the army. He placed the blame squarely on the mutineers and angrily insisted that they should be crushed. His advisers were more circumspect. Among others, Honjo, whose son-in-law was implicated in the conspiracy, objected to Hirohito's use of the term "rebels." To avoid provoking them further Honjo himself employed euphemisms such as "activist troops."[65] War Minister Kawashima tamely transmitted their singularly imprecise demands to the Emperor and ignored Hirohito's order to quell them—though he was deeply humbled by it. Passing through the rebel lines, Kawashima returned to the War Ministry, where he negotiated with some of the young officers in the audience hall.

The confrontation was confused. Mazaki, whom the rebels counted on to lead a reformed government, revealed his sinister "double personality":[66] at first he offered to help them, later he threatened to shoot them. Ishiwara, previously sympathetic to the rebels even though he had once featured on their death list, now declared that since rearmament amounted to a Showa Restoration, whereby the Emperor was exercising direct rule through the army, no "incident" was necessary. Asked what he would do, the prime mover of the Manchurian Incident snapped: "Persuade them to withdraw. And if they don't listen, raise the colours and wipe them out." "Why, you bastard!" cried a 2nd lieutenant, approaching Ishiwara with drawn sword as the hall resounded to shouts of "Cut him down."[67] Bloodshed was only just averted and Ishiwara left calmly. Yet later he himself burst into the cabinet room, sword in hand, demanding to present the "views of the army." Recovering from their alarm, ministers told him that the War Ministry would do that, and Ishiwara sulkily withdrew.

Like the city under snow, the Imperial Palace was shrouded in uncertainty. There, without Hirohito's sanction, General Araki held a meeting of the Supreme Military Council which approved first the motives and then the actions of the plotters. Later Araki claimed that this was an attempt to take official control of the uprising. But to connive with the rebels was not to conquer them. This emerged starkly on 27 February, when martial law was declared and the mutineers themselves were charged with its enforcement. They were even supplied with provisions by loyal troops, who could be distinguished only by their white armbands. Apart from a short, neutral radio announcement of the "incident" and army bulletins saying that various ministers "had died immediately" after visits from activist soldiers,[68] there was a complete news blackout. Kita Ikki, a gaunt figure in a Chinese robe, assured the rebels that they had massive popular support and some of them began to celebrate victory, singing and dancing with their shoes off at the Koraku and Tameike tea-houses. In fact the public were curious but indifferent and the jubilant young officers did little to promote their cause.

Meanwhile the Emperor was becoming ever more furious. "To kill the venerable subjects whom I have trusted most," he told Honjo, "is like gently strangling me with floss-silk."[69] Hirohito threatened to lead the Imperial Guard into battle himself and kept insisting that the mutiny must be suppressed. Informed of his opinions for the first time by Araki, the rebels dismissed them as ambiguous, the emanations of evil counsellors. The Emperor was reluctant to issue a direct command in case it was disobeyed. However, the armed services and the Court closed ranks behind him. Loyal reinforcements, backed by the Navy, gradually tightened their noose round the heart of the city. The rebels then sent a message to the Palace saying that they would surrender and commit suicide if the Emperor gave the order. Honjo tearfully requested him to do so but he would not honour them with even that dubious recognition. They had been responsible for "terrible atrocities," the Emperor said. "Do such actions conform to the ideals of *bushido*? I find it difficult to understand what the army is saying."[70]

Angered by imperial intransigence, the rebels prepared to fight. Tokyo, which had preserved a façade of normality, with workers scurrying about their tasks in the glare of the Ginza neon, now took on an air of ominous calm. In the distance the Hakone Mountains shone with crystal clarity but nearer at hand Mount Fuji loured over the city like a grey giant. Trains, buses and trams ceased to run, though the occasional military truck tore through the streets. Civilians were evacuated from the danger zone. Children were kept indoors and schools closed. Postmen, pedlars, news vendors and grocers' boys vanished. Telephone and cable links with the outside world were cut. The business district was deserted and an "unnatural silence brooded over the usually active area."[71] Rebel banners, made of tablecloths filched from the Peers' Club, flew from the Sanno Hotel and the Prime Minister's residence. In surrounding lanes loyal detachments, supported by tanks and artillery, prepared for action. To give their guns a clear field of fire they cut down the palmettos in Hibiya Park.

But during the morning of 29 February the rebels were subjected to a fierce attack of propaganda. Radio messages urged capitulation. Suspended from a balloon above the Imperial Aeronautical Association building, a long ideograph streamer bade soldiers to obey the imperial command and exhorted: "Your fathers, mothers, brothers and sisters are all weeping because you will become traitors."[72] Bombers dropped leaflets saying that, "His Majesty orders you to return to your barracks."[73] Those who complied were promised pardon; the rest would be shot. By noon the resistance, like the snow, had melted. Several young officers committed suicide. Most planned to continue the struggle, like Aizawa, in the courtroom. They would be disappointed. The trials were held secretly in the summer of 1936 and 13 executions followed almost at once. Kita Ikki and three others were shot later, under cover of a wider war. As they faced the firing squad, one proposed that they should shout a banzai for the Emperor. Unorthodox to the last, Kita replied: "I'd rather not."[74]

FROM the young soldiers' point of view the uprising had been a failure—"A dragon's head with the tail of a snake."[75] But for their pragmatic seniors it was a triumph. After Okada's tearful resignation, Saionji was forced to choose Hirota as Prime Minister and to watch while the army virtually monopolised power. Hirota himself summed up his situation graphically:

> The military are like an untamed horse left to run wild. If you try head-on to stop it, you'll get kicked to death. The only hope is to jump on from the side and try to get it under control while still allowing it to have its head to a certain extent.[76]

The lowly Premier had no chance of bridling the well-born new War Minister, Terauchi Hisaichi. Indeed the tall, stately General excluded important liberals from the cabinet. He told Hirota that the disgraceful February rebellion was a "turning-point" and that the army now proposed a "complete reform of the administration."[77] It established a stranglehold on the government by reviving the convention that its existence depended on the inclusion of serving senior officers. Terauchi also attacked democracy itself, suggesting that the money for the Diet building would have been better spent on two new divisions. He did not succeed with his plan to replace the parliamentary system with a "military despotism." But society was subjected to even stricter discipline. More telephones were tapped; more letters were opened; new laws were passed to control "writings of a disquieting nature."[78] Censors even took their craft to its ultimate absurdity by refusing to reveal what it was they had censored. A week after the February rebellion journalists were instructed not to print news about a rumour that soldiers "in Kagoshima prefecture 'did something.' "[79]

The Emperor himself was intimidated. In the excitement of the uprising he had called for a thorough purge of the army. He was glad when Terauchi conducted one, though the War Minister suppressed an imperial censure on the forces of Nippon, putting it in his desk drawer where his successor found it gathering dust. On reflection, however, Hirohito held that he had overstepped the bounds of his constitutional authority in February. Courtiers and diplomats had thought his "wonderful" conduct "a small ray of hope in an otherwise depressing and thunder-laden outlook."[80] But now he made greater efforts to conciliate the military. He avoided confrontations with his new aide-de-camp, a more assertive and mendacious character than Honjo, who had resigned because of his suspected complicity in the rebellion. The Emperor clung to the status quo, telling a surprised Hirota to protect the position of the nobility. Masking his diminished role, he accepted an inflated title: Emperor of Greater Japan. He hid more timidly behind punctilio and protocol. Silence became his stronghold. He avoided direct statements in favour of elliptical questions and oblique gestures. Privately he could still be outspoken and during a two-hour audience he shouted at the quasi-fascist Baron Hiranuma. Newly appointed as President of the Privy Council (in the teeth of liberal opposition), Hiranuma emerged looking seared, "like a man who had been in a steam bath."[81] Furthermore, Hirohito consistently tried to halt "the snowballing impetus towards war."[82] But in general he abided more than ever by the shadowy conventions of "oracular sovereignty."[83]

While driving inexorably towards aggression, the army also gave conflicting signals. This was because military infighting grew so intense that Terauchi, like his predecessors, could not maintain discipline over the army. Nor could Ishiwara, despite his firebrand reputation. He now wanted a period of peace to prepare for the "decisive battle" against Russia.[84] But when he tried to restrain the Kwantung Army a colonel riposted, amid mocking laughter: "We are only putting into practice in Inner Mongolia what we learned from you."[85] Defiantly they made another stab across the borders of Manchukuo. Ishiwara roared, "The next time I visit the Kwantung Army I'm going to piss on the floor of the commander's office."[86] Meanwhile Hirota expected to be killed by one lot of partisans or another. And the Foreign Ministry was virtually powerless. Military factions inspired diplomatic initiatives such as the Anti-Comintern Pact with Germany, which was negotiated by Japan's perfervidly pro-Nazi Ambassador, General Oshima Hiroshi, and signed in November 1936. When a committee of the House of Peers quizzed one senior staff officer about the direction the Supreme Command proposed to take, he kicked aside his chair and refused to disclose anything they could not find in the newspapers. But, as the arms budget rocketed, war seemed inevitable.

The obvious target was China, whose mineral and other resources looked ripe for exploitation. As General Isogai Rensuke had told the British emissary Sir Frederick Leith-Ross, Japan was a young man "deeply in love with Miss China." She was a "beautiful girl" and, although she kept giving the "glad-eye to Britain and America," Japan was determined to marry her. Leith-Ross retorted that it looked as though Japan "wanted to rape Miss China," which the amused General did not deny.[87] In the early summer of 1937 Tokyo buzzed with rumours that the "young officers overseas might start something before the August promotions and transfers."[88] By now Prince Konoe Fumimaro was Prime Minister (Hirota and his two short-lived successors having succumbed to military intrigues) and Saionji hoped that his immense social prestige might inhibit the army. But although Konoe was a strong nationalist, his government was weak. He could not even discover which military cabal was in the ascendant. So, on 7 July 1937, Japan was flung into a catastrophic war with China. As Ishiwara correctly forecast, China would become to Hirohito "what Spain was to Napoleon, an endless bog."[89]

Yet even today it is unclear why the initial skirmish occurred: details of its origins are "lost in the darkness which enveloped this fracas."[90] Possibly the Chinese themselves were responsible. Despite bitter internal strife a mood of national unity was forming in the country. Urged on by Stalin, Mao Tse-tung's Communists were ready for an alliance of Chinese forces to fight against Japan. Nationalist supremo Chiang Kai-shek was himself under pressure to lead the coalition, though he regarded the Japanese as a boil on the skin of China whereas the Communists were a disease of the vital organs. But whether the first shots were fired by the Chinese eager to provoke a conflict with the Japanese, or whether they were simply an accident, the whole episode seemed to most people at the time "alarmingly akin" to the Manchurian Incident of 1931.[91] They could only read the present in the light of the past. They were not privy to the bewilderingly divided counsels of the Japanese: counsels reflected in Tokyo's War Guidance Section, which veered from demanding peace to declaring war and back again within a couple of months; counsels which forced Hirota (once again Foreign Minister) to negotiate with the army *through* the navy; counsels which caused the decision to mobilise to be reached and cancelled four times in as many weeks. So most contemporaries blamed Japan for the "China Incident"—war was not officially declared. They discerned in it a pattern of aggression which, however confusing, was unmistakable. There is much to be said for their view.

On the night of 7 July 1937 a full moon shone over Peking. It illuminated the mossy, seventeen-metre-thick walls, the sixteen iron-embossed gates, the yellow grid of streets and the purple nucleus of the Forbidden City. On the Hill of Ten Thousand Years it silvered the onion-shaped Dagoba shrine. It danced on Pei Hai Lake, whose waters glimmered with the lanterns of pleasure barges and the lights of the Temple of Eternal Peace. A few miles south-west lay the Marco Polo Bridge, named after the famous visitor to Kublai Khan's court who had admired its graceful arches and its grey pillars, which were adorned with a pride of marble lions. Here from time immemorial caravans of Bactrian camels from central Asia had crossed the Hun River, making their final halt at the fortress town of Wanping before plodding on to the capital. It was here that the Emperor Qianlong had raised a stele fifteen feet high to honour the beauty of the setting moon as seen at dawn from the magnificent stone bridge. And here, on that serene summer night in 1937, units of Peking's 4,000-strong Japanese garrison on manoeuvres—part of the force detailed to secure the still-contested province of Hopei—were attacked by unknown assailants under cover of darkness. They returned fire. Soon the grey-clad Chinese soldiers in Wanping found themselves besieged. Despite fitful attempts to limit the strife, it spread like bubonic plague until it threatened to infect the entire world. Yet it remained a hidden contagion. As *Time* magazine noted in June 1941, "World War II's biggest front, its oldest battle, its largest protagonist, are unknown."[92] Few war correspondents witnessed the fighting. The unimaginable vastness of China fostered Kafkaesque confusion. And Japanese propaganda stood truth on its head. Satirising this trait, a graffito duly appeared on the wall of the Marco Polo Bridge: "Birthplace of Peace in East Asia."[93]

The conflict swiftly flowed over the plains of north China. There were brief hopes that Peking would become another Madrid. But at the end of July long lines of Chinese infantry, some swathed in blood-stained bandages, others wild-eyed with fear, all filthy, forlorn and exhausted, straggled out of the city. Accompanying them along shuttered Front Gate Avenue was a motley baggage train of iron-wheeled carts and ancient guns drawn by shaggy Mongolian ponies. As dusk fell soldiers cursed and whips cracked, bringing "momentary life to the almost ghostly passage of defeated men." Two days later the victorious Japanese forces rode under the tiered pagoda-like roofs of the city's main gate, which had swung open unprotestingly on its stone rollers, and paraded down the tree-lined Avenue of Everlasting Peace. First came the drab-coloured tanks, armoured cars and artillery, ploughing up the warm asphalt, then cavalry units on rangy Australian Walers, then troops in American-built trucks, and finally an Asahi beer wagon. The invaders hoisted rising-sun flags on the walls and shouted banzais. But they committed no outrages: instead a Japanese plane dropped coloured leaflets proclaiming, "Peace and Harmony between the Peoples of East Asia."[94] Elsewhere the Japanese were shocked by the pugnacious spirit of their despised enemies. Admittedly Chiang Kai-shek could only organise an uneasy coalition of warlords—but they were sometimes prepared to fight to the last coolie. As an American observer noted, "The current expression to cover all [China's] ills is *pu i-ting* ('not certain or not definite'), and it sure as hell hits the mark."[95]

Nevertheless the Japanese were enraged by any resistance. They determined to "punish the barbaric Chinese."⁹⁶

Atrocities occurred on both sides and few prisoners were taken. When a Russian adviser to the Chinese asked to interrogate two newly captured Japanese soldiers he was told, "They died a little en route."⁹⁷ However, the Japanese mounted a sustained campaign of terror against the civilian population. They pillaged farms and scorched the Chinese earth. They surrounded villages, put them to the torch and shot the inhabitants as they fled. They razed towns, destroyed hospitals and schools, murdered, looted and raped on an inconceivable scale. When the war spread south, they deluged Shanghai with a "tempest of steel."⁹⁸A Japanese, surveying the pulverised ruins, could only exclaim: "Just like our earthquake."⁹⁹ The devastation was made worse, after the fall of the Chinese city, by the systematic removal of metal for scrap. Machinery was wrenched from factories and houses were gutted of lead pipes, brass fittings, copper hinges, iron nails. When buildings collapsed the Japanese set the debris alight. The suburb of Chapei was almost obliterated by its own funeral pyre, while "bursts of flame splashed a reddish glare on the thick haze of billowing ashes."¹⁰⁰ Four square miles, containing the homes of a million people, were consumed by "one of the great conflagrations in the history of the world."¹⁰¹ The Japanese caused lesser holocausts in other cities of the populous Yangtse basin, leaving "corpses as thick as flies on fly-paper."¹⁰² But nothing compared in horror to what was aptly christened "the rape of Nanking."

Once the metropolis of the Ming dynasty, this was now Chiang Kai-shek's capital. So it offered General Matsui Iwane, who was much tougher than his wizened, palsied appearance suggested, an alluring opportunity "to dazzle China even more greatly with Japan's military glory." He proclaimed that "the devil-defying sharp bayonets" of his army would be "unsheathed so as to develop their divine influence" over the Nanking government and to chastise "the outrageous Chinese."¹⁰³ By the second week of December 1937 most officials, including the Generalissimo and Madame Chiang Kai-shek, had left Nanking. Using planes, tanks and artillery, the Japanese drove the defending forces over the stubbly rice marshes and grassy dykes, thrusting them behind the vast, crumbling, crenellated fortifications of the city. Guided by two sausage-shaped observation balloons, they bombarded Nanking from distant Purple Mountain, where gleamed the blue-roofed, white marble mausoleum of Sun Yat-sen, father of the Chinese Republic. The attackers blasted their way through the Kungwha Gate and scaled the medieval bulwarks. Panic-stricken Chinese troops, deserted by their officers, tried to escape by lowering themselves down the 70-foot-high walls on straw ropes or cats' cradles of belts and puttees. Large numbers fell to their deaths. But below, the junks and sampans, already under fire, could not contain the frenzied mob who swarmed aboard. Many capsized and sank. Survivors were bombed and strafed. Once again, as in the Taiping Rebellion, the muddy Yangtse foamed with blood.

Thousands of Chinese soldiers left inside the city, encouraged by the score of heroic foreigners who stayed behind to supervise the Safety Zone, put their faith in leaflets dropped by Japanese aircraft promising to protect good citizens. They shed their uniforms—one reporter observed "the wholesale undressing of an army that was almost comic"[104]—and tried to blend in with the population. It was hopeless. Once in occupation, the Japanese automatically executed men with calloused hands or knapsack marks on their shoulders. But they did not restrict their atrocities to suspected combatants. They embarked on a saturnalia of destruction such as had not been seen since the sack of Magdeburg during the Thirty Years War. They murdered, tortured, raped, robbed, pillaged and burned. Groups of prisoners were mown down by machine-guns, torn apart by savage dogs, doused in kerosene and set on fire, buried alive. Many were used for bayonet practice: as one company commander later explained, this form of execution provided "a finishing touch to training for the men and a trial of courage for the officer. After that a man could do anything easily."[105] Perhaps 50,000–60,000 died, though controversy still rages over the figures.[106] One witness counted 500 civilian corpses in a single street. Another saw a mound of bodies six feet high at the Hsiakwan Gate. A Japanese newspaperman noted, "I've seen piled-up bodies in the Great Quake in Tokyo, but nothing can be compared to this."[107]

The horrors seemed casual but they were also calculated, as though cold-blooded conquerors wanted to brand their mark on the hide of China in letters of fire. One man was found with his "head burned cinder black—eyes and ears gone, nose partly, a ghastly sight."[108] At least 20,000 women were raped, many in broad daylight. At night gangs of soldiers, frequently drunk, roamed the streets, breaking into houses, dragging out females of all ages, raping them as often as 40 times in a session and infecting many with venereal diseases. Those who resisted, and many who did not, were killed. Others became "comfort women" in the military brothels which the Japanese army soon set up in response to the outcry about rape, thus systematising their sexual abuse of conquered peoples. Babies were bayoneted. Everything of value was stripped from the city and about half of it was reduced to charred rubble. The inhabitants were left destitute and starving. But pariah dogs flourished and black crows, always a sinister feature of the Nanking sky, grew fat on human flesh—for several weeks Japanese soldiers insisted on leaving the bodies of their victims in the streets, asserting that "Chinese don't need to be buried."[109]

At serious risk to their own lives the Westerners in the Safety Zone—businessmen, missionaries, doctors—tried to stem the tide of violence. One heroic German, John Rabe, prevented many barbarities by brandishing his swastika emblem at Japanese troops. They took more notice of that than of their own embassy staff, who were horrified by the pogrom, which lasted for eight weeks, gradually diminishing in intensity. Diplomats, whose own cables were censored by the army, urged the foreigners to publicise the facts, which might force Tokyo to impose order. But army spokesmen blandly denied that anything untoward had occurred, on the grounds that it would have been contrary to the Meiji rescript on military discipline. To sustain the lie, Chinese crowds were made to celebrate and wave rising-sun flags for the benefit of newsreel cameras. Tourists were conducted around parts of Nanking which had been specially cleared of corpses. Japanese papers painted an idyllic picture of the city, saying that it had suffered at the hands of *Chinese* looters but that peace had been swiftly restored under the beneficent influence of imperial soldiers. However, the culprits themselves inadvertently provided evidence of their own bestiality in photographs which they sent to be developed in Shanghai. Overwhelming independent testimony confirmed the story these pictures told, giving the world a hideous adumbration of future war crimes.

The crimes of Nanking doubtless stemmed from the conviction that heaven-born Japanese were licensed to exterminate *Untermenschen*. This was a holy war officially blessed by the Emperor (despite his private reservations); he sometimes rewarded his troops with cigarettes bearing his emblem which they smoked reverently, preserving the divine ash. This was also total war in which victory was the only duty and terror was a means to that end. Brutalised by their own superiors, the soldiers of the sun could hardly be expected to have mercy on their enemies. And they were indoctrinated with the idea that in China "every mountain and stream, every tree and blade of grass was the enemy."[110] Apparently the army felt no shame; but Prince Kanin, the Chief of Staff, did issue a "VERY SECRET" order calling for more discipline because regrettable practices damaged Japan's reputation.[111] Ironically the two senior figures who were most outraged were both executed, after the Second World War, for their part in the rape of Nanking. They were General Matsui, who gave his subordinates a "scathing reprimand,"[112] and Foreign Minister Hirota, who was "violently angry" when he heard of the atrocities.[113] Having pursued risky peace negotiations with China, which the army monitored and sabotaged,

Hirota again courted assassination. He apologised profusely for attacks on British and other vessels guarding the Yangtse. Among them was the American gunboat *Panay*, which was sunk during the storming of Nanking. But although a few officers were cashiered or transferred, among them Hashimoto Kingoro, founder of the Cherry Blossom Society, who had deliberately fired on survivors, no one at the top accepted guilt for the general carnage, least of all the Prime Minister.

Tall, elegant and imperturbable, with delicate hands and sparkling eyes, Prince Konoe seemed a statesman of immense distinction. His record was almost as impressive as his looks, breeding and intelligence. He had made out a persuasive case against the Versailles settlement, which kept his country in thrall to the West. He had championed a New Deal for Japan, coining the term "welfare state" and advocating economic recovery through imperial expansion. Konoe had also rallied the nation behind the war effort. He had inaugurated the National Spiritual Mobilisation Campaign at Tokyo's Hibiya Hall, which was decorated with slogans like "Loyalty and Patriotism" and "Work for the Sake of the Country."[114] Konoe was obviously steering the nation to victory and its war spirit was stirred to a new pitch by the fall of Nanking. People unfurled flags, drank sake and shouted banzais all over Tokyo. At night thousands marched from the Marunouchi business district to the gates of the Imperial Palace, where the reflections of their lanterns flickered on the Stygian waters of the moat. Yet for all the zeal Konoe inspired, he himself was a fundamentally frivolous character.

The Prince played at politics. Charming, cynical and witty, he preferred gossamer arguments to solid conclusions. So indiscreet was he that Hirota would discuss nothing confidential in cabinet in case it reached the ears of the Russian Ambassador. Konoe was notorious for retiring to bed with some ailment, perhaps indigestion, when faced with intractable problems. He appointed ministers casually, often ineptly, and, as the Emperor said, handled them "as though they [were] someone else's responsibility." Konoe even dared to relax with the Son of Heaven, golfing and gossiping, rambling on aimlessly about matters of State, cracking jokes that were sometimes misunderstood and lounging with long legs crossed in a way that perturbed the starched court chamberlains. The Prime Minister frequently offered to resign and told the Emperor: "It is an extremely difficult thing for a dreamy person like myself, who is popular yet has no power, to take charge of affairs indefinitely."[115]

Like all Japanese premiers, Konoe was only a first among equals. But his powerlessness largely resulted, of course, from the irresistible rise of the army. It first arrested his peace envoys to Chiang Kai-shek and intercepted his coded telegrams. Later it demanded increased budgets but refused to discuss strategy. Just before the fall of Nanking, Konoe was "very much surprised" when the Emperor revealed the "plan of military operations until next March" since the Prime Minister "had never heard of it from the supreme command headquarters."[116] Like Hirota, Konoe tried to retain his influence with the army by giving way to it. Saionji called him a puppet and Konoe himself lamented that he was a robot. But he had little choice and, in any case, the militarists represented his id. Hence his uncompromising declaration, made on 16 January 1938, that he would no longer deal with Chiang Kai-shek. This, perhaps more than anything else, ensured that the "China Incident" would become a prolonged war. Characteristically, Konoe later acknowledged that his declaration had been "an utter blunder"[117] and he went on conducting negotiations with the Chinese Nationalists in secret.

The die had been cast, however. Japan was sucked into the Continental morass just as Ishiwara had forecast. Ishiwara himself was removed from his post for insisting that Chiang Kai-shek would resist as long as he held an acre of territory. China was not like Abyssinia, Ishiwara declared; rather it resembled an earthworm which, if cut in two, would "still keep wriggling."[118] Or, to change the metaphor, China was a vast blanket in which the invaders could hold only the seams—roads, railways, rivers, canals. Nippon might win every victory but was doomed to lose the war. Furthermore the aggression against China was provoking hostility elsewhere, which would ultimately be fatal to Japan. Roosevelt fancied himself a Sinophile and liked to dwell on his family's long connection with China, traces of which littered his house at Hyde Park—the large blue-and-white porcelain pot in the library, the bronze bell used as a dinner gong, the prized Peking and Hong Kong stamps in the President's collection. But FDR was in any case more perturbed by Japanese expansion than by German. He accepted the euphemism "China Incident" since he was thus able to export arms to Chiang Kai-shek, the Neutrality Act banning their sale only to nations at war. He also demanded, in his famous "quarantine" speech of 5 October 1937, that the forces of "international anarchy" should be ostracised like the carriers of infectious disease.[119] This alarmed isolationists in the United States and Roosevelt, only willing to lead when Americans were willing to follow, temporised. He even responded softly when the *Panay* was sunk. Neville Chamberlain's sour opinion—that nothing could be expected from the American government except words—was confirmed. But the British Prime Minister was actually relieved. He considered that sanctions would incense Japan and that appeasement was a panacea which would also work in the Orient.

Appeasement had also been Russia's policy before Japan became embroiled in China. Scores of skirmishes had taken place each year on the Soviet Union's frontier with Manchukuo. Running for 3,000 miles across forests, mountains and deserts, it bristled with pillboxes, barbed wire and observation posts. The last major clash had occurred on the Amur River just a few days before the fatal sparks flew at the Marco Polo Bridge. Then Moscow had retreated ignominiously, convincing Tokyo that Stalin's purges were incapacitating Russia. But once its enemy's back was turned the Bear unsheathed its claws. Stalin quickly concluded an agreement with Chiang Kai-shek and sent him military aid, delighted that the Chinese were doing his fighting in the Far East as the Spanish were in Europe. The Japanese fumed and chafed, particularly since many of the soldiers regarded Communist Russia as more of a menace than Nationalist China. To modern samurai consumed by an unbearable sense of hardship and injustice, acquiring one enemy was no reason for losing another. Nobody expressed the chauvinists' creed more ardently than Matsuoka Yusoke, who had led Japan from the League of Nations and was soon to take an even more prominent role in his country's destiny. With the stern fatalism so typical of his compatriots on their long march through the dark valley, Matsuoka proclaimed that the Anti-Comintern Pact was now the guiding star of Nippon. Imperial Japan would go forward with Nazi Germany, he declared, "even if it means committing 'double suicide.'" [120]

XIX

THE SOVIET PURGES

As Japan thrust deep into China it seemed that the Soviet Union was also bent on suicide. Stalin had not been satisfied with exterminating the kulaks and devastating the countryside. He was now mangling the Communist party, shattering his own instrument of repression, the NKVD, and decapitating the Red Army. The entire nation was sucked into this vortex of terror. What strangely interested the Supreme Command in Tokyo was that during these monstrous purges many Russians it had never heard of (and who themselves had scarcely heard of Nippon) confessed to being Japanese spies. Here was proof pathological that the USSR was in no state to impede the soldiers of the sun. About Stalin's motives the Japanese were as much in the dark as his victims. Those newly arrested in Russia repeated *"Za chto?"*—"What for?"—so often that fellow prisoners described the expression as "Record No. 1" and told them to switch it off. For some condemned to death the words *"Za chto?"* were their last, scrawled on the walls of their cells in blood.

The question echoes down the ages and even now there is no clear answer. But, having sown famine, Stalin evidently decided that he must reap a harvest of his enemies. Certainly he studied, and was impressed by, the Führer's method of cutting such a crop. At a Politburo meeting after the Night of the Long Knives he exclaimed: "Good chap, that Hitler! He showed how to deal with political opponents!"[1] Soon Stalin found the excuse he needed to imitate Hitler, except that his pogrom destroyed millions and took a thousand nights to reach its ghastly climax. As the writer Eugenia Ginzburg famously said, the year 1937 began on 1 December 1934—the date on which Sergei Kirov, head of the Communist Party in Leningrad, was assassinated.

Whether Stalin was responsible for his death, creating a dramatic incident which he could exploit as Hitler had exploited the Reichstag fire, remains a mystery. According to a recent investigation, the evidence against him consists of "unverified facts, rumours and conjectures."[2] Still, it would unquestionably have convicted Stalin in one of his own courts, where "the accused has to prove that he is innocent."[3] Guilty of countless murders where the motive was obscure, Stalin could hardly have convinced a people's judge that he was blameless in a case where he had so much to gain. For the shot that dispatched Kirov eliminated not one enemy but all. It enabled Stalin to set the seal on the most homicidal tyranny the world had ever seen. Much about Kirov's killing, moreover, suggests that the Kremlin was indeed involved.

His assassin, a disgruntled Party member called Leonid Nikolaev, had previously been detained in suspicious circumstances, only to be released by the NKVD. Yet he gained entry to the Smolny, headquarters of the Leningrad party, a honey-coloured classical building with columns, pediment and portico which stood in its own park overlooking the Neva. Kirov, for all his open, smiling looks, had many foes, not only inside the Party: he had declared "war" on the kulaks and employed many of them to build the useless White Sea–Baltic Canal, which cost up to 200,000 lives. The Smolny, once a school for aristocratic girls and later Lenin's sanctum, was carefully protected. Nevertheless on that dark, wintry afternoon the guards were inexplicably negligent. So, according to the familiar story, Kirov met his end. Dressed in a khaki cap and light overcoat, his boots echoing on the parquet, he walked alone towards his spartan third-floor office, its huge desk cluttered with models of machinery. Unhindered, Nikolaev stepped out of the lavatory where he had been hiding and shot him in the back of his beefy neck with a Nagan revolver.

On hearing the news, Stalin set off for Leningrad accompanied by half the Politburo. He also issued a decree lifting legal restraints on the speedy prosecution and execution of terrorists. From the first, therefore, he treated Kirov's death as the tip of a conspiratorial iceberg. But, taking personal charge of the investigation, he ensured that almost all the evidence was eradicated. Nearly everyone involved was shot, imprisoned, killed in convenient accidents or otherwise removed from the scene. Leningrad itself quaked under Stalin's wrath. According to Solzhenitsyn, a quarter of the population was arrested. Almost certainly the figure ran into tens of thousands, including every person bearing the common surname "Nikolaev." Indeed, so many inhabitants joined the "Kirov torrent" to Siberia that it seemed as if the curse of Peter the Great's estranged wife—that the city would be empty—were about to be realised. Leningrad's housing problem was said to have been cured at a stroke.

Back in Moscow, Stalin denounced White counter-revolutionaries, Trotskyists, wreckers, class enemies, terrorists, spies and saboteurs. But while anyone could be caught in this net, Stalin particularly directed the purge against the old guard of the Communist Party. Perhaps he saw himself as a renascent Ivan the Terrible, whose mistake had been, Stalin considered, to succumb to qualms of conscience and kill too few nobles. Certainly he determined to destroy the boyars of Bolshevism: they were, he said, "a millstone round the neck of the revolution."[4] As former acolytes of Lenin, Lev Kamenev and Grigori Zinoviev seemed still to be the greatest menace. Kamenev, a solid, dignified figure with a goatee beard and a pince-nez, was one of the Party's ablest theoreticians. Zinoviev, energetic, mercurial and vain of his vulpine profile, was (despite his squeaky voice) an outstanding orator. In fact both men were ciphers. Kamenev was damned by his association with Trotsky—they were brothers-in-law. Zinoviev had been corrupted by power—he seduced women with the help of meals cooked by the late Tsar's chef. Once wont to sneer at Stalin's clumsy formulations of Marxism, Kamenev and Zinoviev had long since abased themselves before him. But they were arrested, together with a number of associates. While the NKVD were searching his apartment Zinoviev (who for years had been so cowed that he would not reveal his state of health to foreign journalists without consulting the Kremlin) scrawled a frantic note to Stalin. He was guilty of "nothing, nothing, nothing," he insisted, "I swear to you by all that may only be sacred for a Bolshevik, I swear to you by the memory of Lenin."[5] But the NKVD, staffed by men who boasted that they could have got Marx to confess to being an agent of Bismarck, soon extorted pleas of guilty. Kamenev and Zinoviev were convicted of moral responsibility for Kirov's death.

Following their imprisonment, in January 1935, a "quiet" purge continued for 18 months. The Politburo demanded "genuine Bolshevik vigilance."[6] Hundreds of thousands of members were expelled from the Party. Many others were "unmasked," detained, gaoled and sent to concentration camps. There "class enemies" were held collectively responsible for Kirov's murder, even though they had been behind barbed wire at the time, and punished with additional hard labour.[7] In April 1935 a new law decreed that children aged 12 and above were subject to the full penal code, including execution—an instrument of immense power in the hands of Lubyanka torturers, who used it against even younger children. The NKVD was strengthened, until its administration cost two-thirds as much as that of all other government departments put together, and it managed that huge segment of the Soviet Union's economy (a quarter, according to one estimate)[8] which was accounted for by slave labour. Nevertheless, in comparison to the butchery which followed, this was, as Anna Akhmatova said, a "vegetarian" terror.[9]

Moreover, Stalin disguised it by continuing the thaw begun at the 17th

Party Congress in 1934. While flaying the Party, he caressed the people. Bread rationing was abolished. More meat was on sale. So was *The Book of Healthy and Tasty Food* which Anastas Mikoyan, who was in charge of supplies, introduced with Stalin's words: "Life has become better, life has become merrier."[10] That personification of merriment, Mickey Mouse, appeared on Soviet cinema screens. Stalin revived tsarist rewards and disciplines. In the army, the NKVD, the administration and elsewhere he established a whole hierarchy of ranks and orders. School uniforms returned to favour. Lipstick, nail varnish, plucked eyebrows, jewellery, silk stockings and evening gowns suddenly ceased to be decadent. The same went for smart suits, stiff collars and creased trousers. The Cossack corps, formerly the White spearhead against Reds, was revived. Old forms were given new life. Russia was once again the "Motherland." Christmas trees came back into fashion. Diplomats took lessons in etiquette. Marshal Voroshilov insisted that his senior officers learn ballroom dancing.

More leisure became available, albeit in regimented form. A new kind of festival was staged at Moscow's Gorky Park: the greenery was filled with large model frogs, butterflies, grasshoppers and birds; the Pioneer Lake was transformed into a "'fairy-tale sea' with huge representations of the legendary 'golden fish,' the sturgeon, the pike, the whale";[11] and all the entertainments, from carnival parades and Ferris wheel rides to concerts and circus performances, were illuminated by fireworks and searchlights. The secret policemen also had a ball. It was a masquerade, held at the NKVD's luxurious club, and it rivalled anything seen in Montmartre or on the Kurfürstendamm. Men wore dinner jackets or dress uniforms—Henrikh Yagoda designed a new uniform complete with white gold-braided tunic, light-blue trousers, shoes of patent leather (which had to be imported) and a gilt dirk as sported by tsarist naval officers. Women appeared in long gowns or decorated costumes borrowed from the wardrobe of the Moscow Grand Opera. Tables were laden with champagne and caviare. A jazz band played. And from the ceiling a large revolving ball made of tiny mirror prisms "strewed upon the whole place a veritable snowfall of little gleaming lights."[12] Yagoda, head of the NKVD, made a habit of raping his secretaries. But the Communist Party now extolled family values: divorce, contraception and abortion became correspondingly harder to obtain.

Amid tight security precautions Stalin himself appeared more often in public. He was photographed with children, airmen and Stakhanovites. When Stalin inspected locks on the new Moscow–Volga canal, which (thanks to slave labour) improved the water supply of the city as well as turning it into a major inland port, he was recognised by passengers on an excursion boat named *In Memory of Kirov.* As the deck band struck up the Internationale, they waved handkerchiefs, clapped and cried: "Thank you, Comrade Stalin, for the happy life." Stalin also went to see the capital's new underground railway, riding, if *Pravda* is to be believed, in "a car with passengers—workers of Moscow."[13]

The metro was a Soviet showpiece, a symbol of what could be achieved by Communist planning. It was also the most dramatic element in a Moscow that was undergoing metamorphosis at an ever-increasing pace. Demolition vied with construction as the city was remodelled along the grandiose lines envisioned by the Kremlin hierarchs. Bulldozed or blown up, buildings "disappeared like theatre sets."[14] The maze of narrow alleys and wooden slums gave way to paved roads and radial boulevards, spacious parks and fountain-filled squares, granite embankments and soaring bridges. Churches were torn down and factories or underground railway stations were built on their ruins. The Russian Cinema was erected where once the Holy Week Monastery had stood. Ancient monuments such as the Iversk Gates and the Sukharev Tower disappeared, while the Dynamo Stadium and the *Pravda* office became new landmarks. In front of the Kremlin the old city market, full of taverns, warehouses, hovels and stalls selling vegetables, fish and game, was razed to make room for edifices such as the Moscow Hotel and the Council for Labour and Defence Building. Red Square was made more accessible, not so much for the benefit of secular traffic as for parades sacred and military. To revere Lenin and salute Stalin, processions from the six districts of Moscow could now all pour into the square at the same time.

Gorky Street was widened. New department stores were built. So many automobile works, iron foundries, rayon plants and other industrial enterprises were established that by the end of the decade Moscow alone manufactured 40 per cent more than the whole of Russia had done in 1913. It even boasted a scent factory, whose most exotic perfume was christened "Breath of Stalin." Schools, hospitals, nurseries, theatres and libraries proliferated. But dramatic façades still hid shabby courtyards. Incipient public affluence was marred by inveterate private squalor. All accommodation was bursting at the seams and, as even the Communist apologist Lion Feuchtwanger acknowledged, "everyone is huddled together like so many sheep in a pen."[15] Despite the careful stipulations of the so-called Stalin Plan, moreover, "Socialist reconstruction"[16] seemed chaotic. One visitor wrote:

Moscow as a whole appeared to be dreadfully incomplete and very noisy. The streets had been excavated; there were long, muddy trenches floored with dirty planks; heaps of soil lay everywhere. The whole city was in a mess, and heavily loaded lorries were busy shifting the accumulated debris. Everywhere one saw long fences around the Metro stations that were under construction; everywhere [wooden] scaffolding shrouded half-built skyscrapers and houses. In every quarter of the city the earth shook with the ringing of hammers, the banging, bumping and screech-ing of single-bucket excavators, concrete mixers and machines that turned out mortar. Thousands of men worked day and night with almost fanatical diligence. Packed trams rumbled along the streets. There were only a few cars to be seen, of all makes and vintages. The streets were full of one-horse carriages, their boxes occupied by surly drivers. In the cen-tre of the city there were some large, very up-to-date trolley buses.[17]

These were soon to supersede trams, but Stalin refused to allow double-deckers because he feared that they would overturn.

However, he and Moscow's Party chief, Lazar Kaganovich, did sanction the proposed change from the French and German method of digging underground railway lines—shallow open trenches along main roads—to the deep tunnelling system used in England. The resulting catacombs would provide Muscovites with air raid shelters, and bombs were dropped on the sites to test the depth at which they would be invulnerable. In case of attack Lenin's mummified body would be safely stored at a special sta-tion near Red Square. Stalin would get a subterranean bolt-hole from the Kremlin, via a purpose-built branch line to Kuntsevo. Furthermore, when Kaganovich's lieutenant, young Nikita Khrushchev, became convinced that escalators (which he had never previously heard of) were better than lifts, this suggestion was also accepted.

Burrowing through Moscow's marshy soil was exceptionally hazardous. Subsidences were so massive that nearby buildings were imperilled and new techniques had to be adopted to stabilise the ground: the earth around shafts was first frozen solid and then the concrete was heated to make it set. Human sinews had to make up for lack of machinery: pick-axes, shovels and wheelbarrows were the main tools employed. The 70,000 workers, many of them women, who excavated the dark tunnels of the metro suffered unimaginable privations. Some were sucked into quicksands or drowned in underground streams. Others got "the bends" from pressurised caissons or were buried alive when roofs collapsed. Some contracted diseases from toiling for months up to their knees in water. Others collapsed from inadequate food and brutal treatment. The most ruthless methods were used to keep the project going without a pause. Vil-lages around the capital were demolished to provide bricks. Citizens were punished for refusing to do "voluntary" work. No expense was spared. Visiting Berlin incognito, Kaganovich discovered that its subway entrances were mere holes in the ground and proclaimed: "we are going to have beautiful pavilions."[18]

So they did, with spacious staircases, wide platforms, lofty roofs and rich materials such as onyx and malachite. Marble mosaics and porphyry facings, bronze panels and stained glass, brass fittings and crystal chandeliers, multi-coloured faience tiles and gold-studded stucco were freely used to make each station an individual work of art. The station at Dzerzhinsky Square was resplendent with rare Caucasian granite. That at Arbat Square featured a massive ceiling portrait of Stalin sculpted in semi-precious stones. Stalin's own favourite was apparently Mayakovskaya station on Gorky Street, embellished with stainless steel, flecked grey marble and 36 oval cupolas, a model of which won the grand prize at the World's Fair in New York. Everywhere the illumination (which extended through the tunnels) was indirect, often being filtered through tinted glass. No smoking was permitted and no advertisements marred these glittering crypts. But each station, Kaganovich declared, was "a palace shining with . . . the light of advancing, all-victorious socialism."[19] And each "miracle of engineering" won converts to Communism.[20] Although there were queues for tickets and the crowded blue trains did not run on time, *muzhiks* wagged their heads at the subterranean splendour and remarked that "in truth our government is doing fabulous things."[21] Spanish miners who came to excavate the subway after the Asturias uprising were equally captivated. Even El Campesino, who was later sent to dig the underground as a punishment for his alienation from Stalinism, hailed it as a "masterpiece of construction."[22] Visitors from Rose Kennedy to H. G. Wells, who had no conception of the human cost, shared his opinion.

It was an achievement which helped to answer the question of whether Soviet Communism was, as Sidney and Beatrice Webb suggested, *A New Civilisation?* Perhaps their massive tome (which famously dropped the question mark from its title in the second edition) was as much a product of senility as gullibility. The Webbs seemed incapable of critical analysis, making up their minds before they embarked and ignoring admonitions from their nephew-in-law Malcolm Muggeridge. Excuses can be made for them. Their three-week tour, which resembled a royal progress, was certainly stage-managed with care. Less credulous investigators than the Webbs were taken in by intimations of Utopia, especially those enshrined in the new Soviet constitution—a travesty of the socialist Magna Carta it purported to be. Gorky himself was hoodwinked with the help of a copy of *Pravda* specially printed for him. Towards the end of 1935, moreover, the followers of that superhumanly energetic coal miner Alexei Stakhanov were breaking so many production records that Russia seemed a wonder of the world. Even Pasternak paid tribute to the men of the Kremlin, though in daringly ironical fashion. Addressing a writers' congress at Minsk in February 1936, he called for the exercise of genius, against which there could be no law; for if "there were such a decree, then some of our leaders would have to impose a prohibition on themselves."[23] While not quite hailing Party bosses as geniuses, the Webbs did think they resembled Wells's "Samurai," who had a vocation for leadership. The old Fabians also likened Stalin and his acolytes to the enlightened specialists whom Auguste Comte had called the "Priests of Humanity."[24] Such views, not surprisingly, outraged the exiled Trotsky. To prescribe Stalinism for the Bear but only Fabianism for the Lion was crazy, he thought; England was "the last ward of the European madhouse."[25]

ACTUALLY the Soviet Union was succumbing to lunacy. In the summer of 1936 it became a vast glass darkly reflecting the homicidal mania of its leader. This national psychosis is often called the Great Purge and it began with the first of the three major show trials, whose star defendants were Kamenev and Zinoviev. Recalled from prison to Moscow, these old Bolsheviks were accused of having planned a Trotskyite version of the coup which Franco had just mounted in Spain. In hoarse Georgian accents Stalin himself urged the NKVD to "Give them the works until they come crawling to you on their bellies with confessions in their teeth."[26] Kamenev and Zinoviev did manage to secure a final meeting with Stalin in the Kremlin, where they extracted a promise that their lives would be spared if they cooperated at the trial.

This took place in the October Hall, the upstairs ballroom of what had once been the Nobles' Club and was now the Trade Union Building. Where tsarist aristocrats had once waltzed, Communist revolutionaries now danced with death. In the musicians' gallery Stalin orchestrated the proceedings from behind an opaque screen, occasionally signifying his presence with puffs of smoke from his Dunhill pipe. Across pale blue walls supported by white Corinthian columns, and embellished with a stucco frieze of dancing girls, hung a huge slogan which read: "Workers of Moscow! To the mad dogs—a dog's death."[27] But the 350-strong audience, sitting on cushioned benches under crystal chandeliers, were not workers. They were junior members of the NKVD under orders to create a distur-bance if any of the accused strayed from their meticulously rehearsed scripts. Behind a low brown balustrade, guarded at each corner by ram-rod-stiff, scarlet-and-blue-capped soldiers with fixed bayonets, sat the 16 defendants. According to some observers, they looked haggard and spent, with dark rings under their eyes and putty-coloured skin that hung in folds. But others thought that they were "in good health and even in good spirits."[28] Zinoviev, it is true, had bloodshot eyes. He seemed "cowed"[29] and everything about him drooped except his shock of dark hair. But his state was attributable to asthma (made worse, as it happened, by his having been incarcerated in a stifling cell). Zinoviev quickly removed his collar and tie; sometimes he even smiled.

Opposite the dock was a desk occupied by the State Prosecutor, Andrei Vyshinsky. He was a slight figure with sparse red hair and a florid countenance, a trim moustache over thin lips, and grey eyes magnified behind steel-rimmed spectacles. In his stiff collar and smart suit Vyshinsky looked like a stockbroker. But he behaved like the Grand Inquisitor. Behind the scenes he urged that the harshest torments should be unleashed against the prisoners. On stage he took full advantage of their resulting docility. Jutting out his lantern jaw and sometimes foaming at the mouth, he hurled bizarre abuse at the accused. They were "liars and buffoons, despicable pygmies, pug dogs and puppies."[30] No documentary evidence was presented but no substantive defence was offered. On the basis of their confessions, said Vyshinsky, these rabid curs deserved to be shot. What baffled foreign reporters was that the curs themselves agreed. They did not fight for their lives but admitted to fantastic crimes, supplying a wealth of detail that seemed authentic. Although cursing Trotsky and blessing Stalin, they did not "testify like men coerced." Maybe each prisoner was, as the Russian proverb had it, lying like an eyewitness. Surely there was more to their extraordinary performance than appeared. But as the accused men made their final speeches, some denouncing their co-defendants, others sobbing "like camp-meeting converts," *New York Times* journalist Harold Denny concluded with a classic inversion of the truth: "There is free speech in the shadow of the executioner."[31]

The three uniformed judges, seated at a raised table covered with a green baize cloth at the end of the lofty room, also acted as jury. Their guilty verdict was inevitable—one of them, I. T. Nikitchenko, declared prior to the Nuremberg war crimes tribunal on which he served that judicial impartiality would "lead to unnecessary delays."[32] (When instructed by Moscow to oppose lenient sentences passed by his Western colleagues, Nikitchenko had to consult the rest of the panel over how to give a dissenting opinion.) Even judges like him, however, seemed impressed by the dignified way in which the white-haired Kamenev heard his doom pronounced. Zinoviev, by contrast, looked crushed. Apparently he continued to protest his innocence and to beg for mercy in the few hours remaining before he was shot in the cellars of the Lubyanka. Afterwards, in the

Kremlin, a witness gave an imitation of Zinoviev's frantic last moments which reduced Stalin to tears of helpless laughter.

The Russian people, though, were transfixed by the grisly drama enacted in the October Hall. In the thrall of propaganda, they increasingly took shadows for substance. Hermetically sealed inside their own national theatre of the absurd, they confused illusion with reality. They were, for the most part, convinced by the new "Method" of acting exhibited at the trial: where Stanislavski had brought out his players' latent powers of self-expression by precept and practice, Stalin did so by torture and intimidation. Russians suspended disbelief, moreover, because they saw in the October Hall not only a mystery play but a transparent fable designed to convey the truth that enemies of the people would be executed. It was hard, even for Stalin, to distinguish between people and enemies of the people. "That is why it was necessary," wrote Fitzroy Maclean (who attended a later show trial), "for there to be so sharp a contrast between good and evil, between darkness and light, for the characters to be portrayed in such crude colours, to correspond accurately to the conventional figures of Communist Heaven and Hell."[33]

The defendants had indicated other candidates for perdition. They thus prepared the way for a second Stalinist pogrom more widespread, though somewhat less bloody, than that accompanying the collectivisation of agriculture. In factories and institutions all over the country mass meetings clamoured for action against spies, saboteurs, traitors and terrorists who had yet to be unmasked. Newspapers magnified the cry, demanding an investigation into the treachery of those senior Communists who had been implicated, notably Tomsky, Radek, Piatakov, Rykov and Bukharin. Stalin tried to lull Mikhail Tomsky into a false sense of security, calling at his dacha with a bottle of wine. But Stalin had violated the unwritten compact, dating back to Lenin's time, whereby Russian revolutionaries would not spill one another's blood—outsiders remained fair game—in some Bolshevik Thermidor. After a blazing row, Tomsky drove his visitor from the house with a volley of screamed obscenities. Stalin left, still clutching the bottle of wine, and shortly afterwards Tomsky committed suicide. The State Publishing House, which he had run, was at once exposed as a "nest of Trotskyists."[34]

After ordering the death of 5,000 Party members already under arrest, Stalin craftily distanced himself from the growing witch-hunt. In September 1936 he dismissed Yagoda as head of the NKVD and appointed in his place Nikolai Yezhov. It was a measure of the ghetto-like isolation in which diplomats lived, shunned like typhus carriers by Soviet citizens and cut off from most Russian reality, that so shrewd an observer as the British Ambassador, Lord Chilston, interpreted this appointment as an attempt to curb the power of the secret police. Quite the opposite was true. But Yezhov did not quite warrant the position he was to occupy in popular demonology. This tiny man, with his shrill voice, bandy legs and rotten teeth, has usually been portrayed as terror incarnate. He was "a pigmy with the face of a murderer,"[35] a bisexual "dwarf-monster" who massacred the innocents.[36] Certainly Yezhov was a vicious little sadist whose crimes were legion; but like everyone else in the USSR he was the victim of Stalin's insensate lust to kill. He played midget Faust to the Kremlin Mephistopheles. Yezhov was so frightened of Stalin that his fine features were convulsed by nervous tics, the upper lip twitching, the left eyelid fluttering. Unable to sleep, often reeking of vodka, he hid himself in a Lubyanka labyrinth patrolled by armed guards. He was, nevertheless, seen as the "Iron Commissar."[37] *Yozh* means hedgehog in Russian—a spiky cartoon character of that name briefly eclipsed Mickey Mouse, who was deemed to represent the meek proletariat under the heel of capitalism—and Yezhov's victims were known as his prickles. The next two years became the *Yezhovshchina,* the Yezhov era. Even sophisticated journalists like Ehrenburg believed, so he said, that Yezhov was responsible for the reign of terror. And many people on both sides of the barbed wire exclaimed despairingly with Pasternak: "If only someone would tell Stalin about it."[38]

In fact Stalin was making repression a way of life. He was also softening up his next major victims. "The greatest delight," he had once said, "is to mark one's enemy, prepare everything, avenge oneself thoroughly, and then go to sleep."[39] By January 1937 everything was ready for the October Hall's second judicial masque. Seventeen men stood trial, the most famous being Yuri Piatakov, who had helped to revolutionise industry, and Karl Radek, Stalin's most brilliant sycophant. Like many of their kind, both had blood on their hands. Both, moreover, had called for the deaths of Kamenev and Zinoviev, Piatakov even volunteering to act as executioner. Now they had been through the NKVD mincing machine. Piatakov, a quixotic figure with greying hair and rufous goatee, looked like a living corpse. Radek, slim, bespectacled, brown-suited, his skull-like visage fringed with chestnut whiskers, had survived better by turning his confession into a valedictory *jeu d'esprit.* He sipped lemon tea and had the gall to assert that "It was not I who was tormented, but I who tormented the examining officials." All, though, admitted to charges which seemed stranger than fiction. They confessed to treason, espionage, terrorism, wrecking on a grand scale and "counter-revolution of the most vile, loath-some, fascist type." These crimes emanated, of course, from "the suffocat-ing underworld of Trotskyism."[40]

As in the previous trial, some testimony was demonstrably false. The alleged Oslo conference between Piatakov and Trotsky could not have taken place because Norwegian records, refuting the prosecution's case, proved that no plane had landed. Such flaws added to foreigners' bewil-derment. Simone de Beauvoir dismissed as "the merest imbecility" *Le Matin*'s claim that the confessions had been extracted by means of an American "truth drug" but added helplessly, "What explanation could one offer in its stead?"[41] Keynes professed himself "absolutely baffled for the correct explanation. In a way, the speeches of the prisoners made me feel they somehow *believe* their confessions to be true."[42] Others were scepti-cal. Lord Chilston reported to the Foreign Office that the indictment as a whole was "utterly unworthy of belief." Like most diplomats and most reporters, he believed that false confessions had been extorted by "unavowable methods."[43] And he was glad that the trials helped to dis-credit the Soviet government abroad. Some were ribald about the hypoc-risy. Céline, who visited Moscow in 1936, thought it worse than the terror itself. He said that the Soviets had had the effrontery to dress up a turd and "pass it off as a caramel."[44]

However, those predisposed to favour the regime, such as the American Ambassador Joseph E. Davies, were credulous to a fault. Davies accepted the guilt of the accused and said that Vyshinsky conducted the trial "in a manner that won my respect and admiration as a lawyer."[45] It was to the uncomprehending Davies, apparently, that the journalist Alfred Cholerton made his classic comment on the 1937 show trial: "I believe everything but the facts."[46] But cynicism was powerless against the true fellow-travelling faith. The German writer Lion Feuchtwanger did not agree with friends who were disillusioned by the "tragi-comical, barbaric, incredible" proceedings at the October Hall. As he observed the trial his "doubts melted away" and he wrote:

> Read any book or any speech of Stalin's, look at any portrait of him, think of any measure which he has taken . . . It at once becomes as clear as daylight that this modest, impersonal man cannot possibly have com-mitted the colossal indiscretion of producing, with the assistance of countless performers, as coarse a comedy, merely for the purpose of hold-ing a sort of festival of revenge, with Bengal lights to celebrate the humiliation of his opponents.[47]

Most of those opponents were shot, though Radek postponed his death for a time by implicating Nikolai Bukharin, philosopher-editor of *Izvestia*, and Marshal Mikhail Tukhachevsky, moderniser of the Red Army. The importance of this trial, though, was that it removed the last restraints on a universal heresy hunt. All over the country mass meetings and demonstrations, in which even school children participated, demanded death for counter-revolutionary bandits. In Red Square, in a temperature of –27 degrees centigrade, Nikita Khrushchev whipped a crowd of 200,000 people into a frenzy of hatred for fascist-inspired Trotskyite agents and hailed Stalin as "the beacon of all progressive humanity."[48] Stalin himself overcame the last vestiges of resistance inside the Party, assisted by the suicide of the forthright Politburo member Sergo Ordzhonikidze. This was successfully disguised as a heart attack at a time when, it was said, Russians no longer believed there was such a thing as natural death. Addressing the Central Committee in March 1937, Stalin projected his own paranoia on to the vast Soviet screen. The dark side of their industrial success, he declared, was that Communists had become blind to the ever-increasing dangers of capitalist and Trotskyist subversion. Their agents had infiltrated "nearly all our organisations," often in the guise of loyal Party members and hard workers.[49] They must be arraigned without mercy and crushed like vipers. So the purge entered its most manic phase, sweeping the country like a Siberian blizzard and blasting the lives of millions.

MEETINGS were held at which anybody suspected of deviating from orthodoxy by a hair's breadth was denounced. "Everyone was a traitor," wrote an NKVD officer, "until he proved the contrary by exposing someone else as a traitor."[50] People were generally accused of being spies or saboteurs, often both. They were involved, as one young Communist zealot declared, in the "poisoning of workers, terror, wrecking of factories, arson, and diversion . . . on the instructions of the German and Japanese intelligence service."[51] Charges ranged from the sublime to the ridiculous: one woman was indicted both for plotting to kill Stalin and for surreptitiously inserting swastikas into the pattern of tea-cups she designed. At a Party meeting in the Ukraine a woman tried to incriminate the deputy chief of the Regional Health Department: "I don't know that man over there, but I can tell from the look in his eyes that he's an enemy of the people." The official probably saved his life, Khrushchev records, by refusing to defend himself and responding quickly: " 'I don't know this woman who's just denounced me, but I can tell from the look in her eyes that she's a prostitute'—only he used a more expressive word."[52]

Both Pasternak and the Georgian novelist Grigol Robakidze, who defected to Germany, suggested that Stalin had been inspired by Dostoevsky's *The Devils,* in which the nihilist Shigalyov visualised a despotism based on unlimited surveillance and unbridled denunciation.[53] And one of Stalin's last victims said that the dictator had realised the nightmare world of conspiracy, suspicion and calumny which Swift satirised in Gulliver's voyage to Laputa. Stakhanovite spy-catching was as illogical as the scatological investigations which the Dean proposed—discovering which hand suspects used to wipe "their posteriors,"[54] examining ordure to find out who was an assassin and who "thought only of raising an insurrection and burning the metropolis."[55]

Witches' sabbaths were followed by mass arrests. Whole cadres were seized. Newspapers printed long lists of the condemned, though they included only a "very small proportion of the total number of 'disappearances.'"[56] Most at risk were senior officials in local government, industry and the professions—about whom their juniors and non-Party members experienced considerable *Schadenfreude.* Leningrad, special focus for Stalin's hatred, was worst affected. "Black Ravens" (as Black Marias were called) worked overtime, trundling through the sub-arctic summer nights and taking away virtually all political and economic leaders—"beheading the community."[57] Elsewhere, as new appointees to top positions were mown down in their turn, the casualty rate rose above 100 per cent. Technical experts of all sorts were favoured targets.

Railwaymen, who had an *esprit de corps* going back to tsarist times, were assailed with particular ferocity when Kaganovich warned that every branch line had its wreckers. They were a convenient scapegoat for railway accidents which happened, on average, once every five minutes. So many station masters, signalmen, guards and other railway workers were detained that special prisons had to be set up for them, with the overflow being locked for months in cattle trucks shunted into lonely sidings. When Communications Commissar I. V. Kovalev arrived to take up his new post at Minsk in 1937, he found nothing but empty offices. His predecessors and their deputies had all been arrested.

I looked for anyone, but there was only a strange and terrible silence. It was as if a tornado had passed through. I was amazed that the trains were still running and wondered if anyone was controlling this enormous operation. I went to the apartment of an acquaintance who worked in the railway administration. To my surprise I found him at home with his wife, who was in tears. "Why aren't you at work?" I asked before even greeting him. "I'm waiting. They said they'd come for me today. See, I've got some clean shirts packed. Nasedkin of the NKVD is purging every second man. He's probably paralysing the railway." Having got the picture and recovered my composure, I phoned Stalin in Moscow—after all, if the railway didn't work as it was supposed to, I'd be the next on the list. Poskrebyshev [Stalin's bald, round-headed factotum] answered. I told him of the situation. Somehow the rampage was rapidly brought to a halt. Anyway, there was no one left to put in gaol.[58]

Smaller élites suffered similar ravages as Stalin, who had long been suspected of planning the "total extermination of the educated class in Russia,"[59] laid waste the "empire of knowledge."[60] The Union of Writers lost a quarter of its members. Historians vanished at such a rate that one old Bolshevik feared Stalin would be able to establish the "phantasmagoria of these trials" in the minds of future generations as "official truth."[61] Architects reluctant to realise Stalin's monumental aspirations, notably the modernist Mikhail Okhitovich, were consigned to a "pantheon of devils."[62] The lives of poets, artists and musicians were also squandered. Khrennikov, head of the Composers' Union, was so scared of Stalin that in his presence he messed his pants, a common occurrence according to Shostakovich. Dramatists and performers bit the dust. Stalin heard that spies and terrorists had tried to take over the Red Banner song and dance ensemble, which was apparently riddled with anti-Soviet elements. Most of its members were arrested.

Journalists became such transient figures that at *Izvestia* they ceased to put name-plates outside their doors. The propagandist (though sometimes indiscreet) *Journal de Moscou* replaced the name of the editor on its masthead with the day of the week, prompting Foreign Minister Litvinov to inquire whether it was now being edited by "Tuesday." Pressmen, Isaac Babel remarked, sat on the edge of their chairs. The axe even fell on Mikhail Koltsov, hitherto a trusted agent of the Kremlin. He had served heroically enough in Spain to earn Hemingway's admiration and had once remarked that if Stalin said he (Koltsov) was a traitor, he would believe it and declare himself guilty. Now, shortly before his doom, the buck-toothed newspaperman stumped agitatedly around his *Pravda* office: "I feel I'm going crazy," he exclaimed, "I should be able to explain the meaning of what is happening, the reasons for so many exposés and arrests. But in fact I, like any terrified philistine, know nothing, understand nothing. I am bewildered, in the dark."[63]

Scientists were persecuted, for only Stalin's experiments were deemed innocent in the vast laboratory of the Soviet Union. Surgeons were sent to Siberia in such numbers, it was said, that patients requiring difficult operations should go not to Moscow but to Magadan. Bacteriological research virtually came to a halt because the NKVD thought those engaged in it were "always working out new ways of poisoning the population or the troops,"[64] or the livestock. Between 1931 and 1938 all 13 secretaries of the Kiev Academy of Science were arrested. So were biologists who fell foul of Trofim Lysenko, the charlatan plant breeder (backed by Stalin) who blighted the entire study of genetics. Equally vicious, though less notorious, was the destruction of Soviet astronomy. Some of its practitioners proved guilty of wrecking on the stellar front—they took a non-Marxist line on sunspots. But generally their fault was in themselves, not in their stars. They had nurtured cosmopolitan connections, a tradition of "international cooperation,"[65] a spirit of "world-camaraderie."

All this, which obviously involved spying, had become apparent in June 1936, when they played host to many foreign colleagues who had come to observe a total eclipse of the sun. The British expedition had been notably well treated and near Omsk, where weather conditions were perfect, it had witnessed an unforgettable spectacle. Direct sunlight vanished and darkness covered the earth. The temperature dropped. Mercury, Mars and Venus became visible. As the sun ringed the black orb of the moon, "the corona shone in all its glory."[66] The heavens, like Russia itself, might have been mourning the departure of Gorky, who had just died. Or they might have been foreshadowing the catastrophe about to overwhelm Russia's 100-strong corps of astronomers. Within a year 30 of them were detained or dead. The rest were discredited and terrified. When the director of the Moscow Planetarium, now an NKVD man, sent minions to find an astronomer to settle a midnight dispute between Molotov and Kaganovich about whether Orion or Cassiopeia was shining over Stalin's dacha, the first one they called on had a heart attack in the doorway and the second committed suicide by jumping out of a window. Their subject fell under a penumbra of official suspicion which lasted for decades.

Anyone else with foreign contacts, however tenuous, faced repression: returning emigrés, diplomats and secret agents, athletes who had competed abroad, volunteers for Spain, Seventh-Day Adventists and other religious sectarians, philologists, philatelists and Esperantists (though the young Stalin had himself studied that aspirant universal language in prison). Communists from Germany, Italy, Poland, Finland, Hungary, Bulgaria and elsewhere who had sought sanctuary or work in the Soviet Union were more viciously persecuted there than at home. Minor ethnic groups were scythed down—Chinese, Persians, Jews, Letts, Estonians, Karelians, Armenians and many others. The terror overflowed the Soviet borders, not just in the murder of Spanish dissidents and assorted defectors elsewhere but in the vast secret purge conducted by Stalin's Mongolian satrap, Marshal Choibalsan, which left only five people "in the entire country with more than high-school education."[67]

Also counting as alien, the non-Russian Soviet Republics were marked for torment. Ten out of the eleven lost their presidents inside six months, along with most other senior apparatchiks. The leadership of the Ukraine, despite its unflinching efforts to kill kulaks and spread famine, was "liquidated" together with anyone who could be branded a nationalist—there were 150,000 arrests in this Republic alone during 1937. Stalin's homeland was not spared. Indeed, the NKVD over-fulfilled their quota in Georgia. Stalin's mother was said to have fainted when a contingent of them arrived at her house; but they were only there to guard her and she died a natural death in 1938, still regretting that her son had not become a priest. A more objective assessment of Stalin's vocation came from the Georgian old Bolshevik Budu Mdivani, who had known him for 30 years: he joked that the dictator's mother was being guarded to ensure that she did not give birth to another Stalin. Mdivani apparently told his interrogators: "Stalin won't rest until he has butchered all of us, beginning with the unweaned baby and ending with the blind great-grandmother!"[68]

The secret police were all too aware of Stalin's catholic taste in homicide. Yezhov soon announced that he would "get rid of all the scum which the revolution and the Civil War had sent sloshing into the organs of state security . . . sweep out all that grime with an iron broom."[69] Over 3,000 NKVD officers were shot in 1937, though the pay of those who remained was quadrupled and they were given extravagant privileges, each rank smoking a different brand of cigarette. The staff of Lefortovo, an old tsarist prison now said to be the most dreaded destination in Moscow, was wiped out in its entirety four times. Similarly, after the judicial murder of Marshal Tukhachevsky (whose confession is still extant, marked with brown spots of blood shed by this immensely strong man), the Red Army was purged. How many victims Stalin claimed remains the subject of dispute, with estimates ranging from 10 to 50 per cent of the officer corps. Evidently the purge destroyed "three or four times"[70] as many top commanders as the 600 who fell in the Second World War. And it seems that a total of about 40,000 officers were executed, imprisoned or discharged (though many were later reinstated) during the *Yezhovshchina*. The other services hardly fared better and for a time military science suffered accordingly—the *arme blanche* and airborne cavalry, in the shape of Douhet's massed bombers, were favoured above tanks and fighters.

In numerical terms, however, none of this compared with Stalin's assault on Soviet society in general. According to some estimates as many as ten ordinary citizens were purged during the late 1930s for every one Party member. Sometimes, to meet the quota of arrests assigned to them, the secret police simply counterfeited their victims' confessions and shot them out of hand. Their actions were both arbitrary and haphazard. Anything could activate their inquisition—a joke, a misprint, a breach of the rules at work, the breakdown of a machine, a chance remark, a complaint about queueing, admiring Tukhachevsky's handsome looks, accidental damage to a portrait of Stalin. Logic was outraged as well as justice: the essence of the terror was its cruel "irrationality."[71] Children were gaoled as terrorists, hermits as conspirators, blind men as spies. Solzhenitsyn records the case of a deaf and dumb carpenter who was convicted of counter-revolutionary agitation because he hung his cap and jacket on a bust of Lenin. Pyotr Yakir, adolescent son of a purged general (who had tried to save his family by blessing Stalin with his last breath, which provoked curses in the Kremlin), was charged with "having organised a band of Anarchist cavalry."[72] Accusing a sleek couturière of armed insurrection, the NKVD man himself laughed at the absurdity of the indictment—but she was still imprisoned for eight years.

Any connection with someone stigmatised as an enemy of the people could be fatal. Relations were guilty by blood. (But, said an NKVD officer, loved wives got eight years, unloved five.) Friends and colleagues were tainted. Neighbours were vulnerable. A black joke circulating round Moscow as Franco's forces advanced in Spain summed up the situation: "They've taken Teruel." "You don't say so. And his wife as well?" "No, no. Teruel's a town." "Good heavens! They've started arresting whole towns?"[73] Complicity was catching, like the Black Death. After the execution of State Prosecutor Nikolai Krylenko, a celebrated climber who had named many peaks in the Pamirs after prominent Communists (Stalin got the highest), hundreds of other mountaineers were martyred. Altogether a chain of guilt by association was forged long enough to shackle the entire people.

There is some evidence that the process got out of control. In the hot summer of 1937, for example, *Pravda* itself complained of "excesses."[74] Economic growth fell from 12 to 2 per cent as industrial leaders were winnowed and workers were "terrorised."[75] Living standards declined, even for the privileged: one NKVD agent had never seen an orange until he was sent to Copenhagen, whereupon he bought a squeezer and drank a quart of orange juice each morning. The Great Purge disrupted every walk of life. Street names kept changing. State bankers disappeared so rapidly that rouble notes finally had to appear without an official signature. Libraries were in turmoil as they responded to the demands of a capricious censorship: Balzac's novels went in and out of favour; what should be done with Kamenev's edition of Lenin's writings? Textbooks were in a permanent state of revision, so that school children often had to do without them altogether. The gaols bulged and in many cells there was standing room only. Sixty-six women were crammed into the narrow, high-windowed tower chamber in Moscow's Butyrka Prison which had once contained only Pugachev, leader of the peasants' revolt against Catherine the Great. Monasteries and bath-houses were converted to hold prisoners and in Siberia they were immured in huge pits, dug and roofed over for the purpose.

Terrified of finding themselves incarcerated, NKVD officers dared not lessen the momentum of detentions. They drew up more dossiers, increased the pace of arrests and speeded up the process of interrogation. Stalin authorised physical brutality as a standard practice in August 1937. So instead of relying on the "conveyor"—torture by fatigue took a long time and often exhausted the interrogators—they beat out confessions with rubber truncheons or metal rods. Often they would smash their prisoners in the face, knocking out a few teeth, at the start of questioning, in an effort to demoralise them. Then barbaric forms of cruelty were often employed. Torturers broke bones, gouged out eyes, kicked testicles, crushed fingers, made captives drink spittle and eat excrement. Dungeons rang with the shrieks of victims and the curses of inquisitors. Listening to this hellish cacophony was more than many inmates could bear. Famished, they stuffed their ears with pellets of bread.

Some who experienced such horrors felt that they were living in a hideous dream. It was as though they were entombed alive, a Dostoyevskyan sensation enhanced when they were shut, *en route* to interrogation, in one of the coffin-like cupboards which lined the carbolic-clean corridors of the main Moscow gaols. This was done to prevent one prisoner seeing another; the newcomer's approach was signalled by guards snapping their fingers in Lefortovo and tapping a key on a belt buckle in Butyrka and the Lubyanka. The illusion of premature burial was made more vivid by the "special prison light"—the "dull-red incandescence" of an ever-burning bulb at night, the "perpetual twilight"[76] of a masked window by day. On the wall of a condemned cell in Lefortovo someone scratched Mandelstam's line: "Am I real and will death truly come?"[77]

In their limbo, blue-grey phantoms waited to be cast into outer darkness. Once the NKVD had decided a sentence—anything between 5 and 25 years' "loss of freedom," or death—pronouncing it became a 3-minute formality. Few were found innocent. No precise figures exist, but it seems that the *Yezhovshchina* devoured up to 4 million people, possibly more. Some 750,000 of these were shot, though the NKVD did experiment with other means of dispatching their victims, including the gas chamber. The crematorium in the cellars of the Lubyanka worked at full blast, its chimney depositing a fine ash on the barbed-wire-enclosed roof where prisoners exercised. Those who escaped a bullet in the back of the neck, which might be fired by any member of the NKVD—there were no special executioners—embarked for labour camps.

THIS vast penal colony, initiated as early as 1918, spread like a cancer across the face of the Soviet Union. It consisted of thousands of concentration camps, a scatter of land-girt Devil's Islands which Solzhenitsyn aptly named the "Gulag Archipelago"—GULAG was the acronym for Chief Administration of Corrective Labour Camps. They ranged from the Solovetski Monastery northwest of Archangel, where Ivan the Terrible had isolated his enemies in caves known as "stone sacks," to Magadan, capital of the "Land of White Death" in the Soviet Far East.[78] They included a large number of enterprises with demands for labour that had become insatiable by 1937 (when the supply of kulaks was exhausted). Among them were coal mining (at Vorkuta), lumbering (Kargopol), canal-building (Belomor), railway work (Pechora), canned meat (Krasnodar) and agriculture (Karaganda). These are names which ought to be etched on the memory along with Dachau and Buchenwald, even Belsen and Auschwitz; for what all these places had in common was a policy of treating inmates as subhuman. Stalin was personally responsible for initiating this regime in the Soviet Union: in 1937 he called for prisons to be prisons and not rest homes. When a brave geologist protested at one camp that "These people might die," an official smilingly replied: "What people? These are enemies of the people."[79]

They were, in general, less well looked after than animals. But when, for that reason, one bold prisoner asked to be re-classified as a horse, he was sent to one of "Stalin's villas"—a punishment cell. Starved, clad in verminous tatters, housed in freezing wooden barracks, consigned to back-breaking toil, bitten by swarms of gnats, midges, horseflies and mosquitoes, a prey to scurvy, pellagra, tuberculosis, malaria, typhus, frostbite and gangrene, bullied by guards and savaged by their Alsatian dogs, exposed to the brutish violence of common criminals (*urkas*) sharing their captivity, healthy men and women became skeletal wrecks within thirty days of entering this slave empire. One prisoner described a work brigade as it trudged before dawn from the searchlight-bright camp "zone" to the snowy wilderness. It consisted of "dirty scrofulous shadows wrapped in torn rags held together with string, gripping their empty mess-cans and swooning from cold, hunger and exhaustion."[80]

Of all the camps probably those in the Kolyma network east of Siberia, still the coldest inhabited region on earth, were the *ultima Thule* of cruelty. Kolyma was an Arctic wilderness of mountain, marsh and virgin forest. Its economic purpose was to extract gold from ice. Those sent to its mines were quite simply worked to death. It is true that the regime became relatively tolerable for a time, after prisoners had endured the initial agony of chiselling the port of Nagayevo from the barren cliffs which command the Sea of Okhotsk and building the nearby town of Magadan on permafrost swampland more porous than that of St. Petersburg. Kolyma's first NKVD chief, E. P. Berzin, reckoned that he could only squeeze "golden sweat" from men with flesh on their bones.[81] So the prisoners, though not regarded as "quite human," were valued. They were treated rather like black American slaves "during the period described in *Uncle Tom's Cabin*."[82] However, in 1937 Stalin had Berzin shot. Kolyma then became, so to speak, the Arctic circle of Dante's inferno.

The first ordeal which those destined for it had to endure was the railway journey across the boundless grey steppe of Soviet Russia. Exiles were packed into windowless cattle cars—over 100 Communists occupied space formerly allotted to 48 tsarists or 12 horses. These trucks bore the legend "Special Equipment" and elaborate efforts were made to hide their contents from the civilian population. When trains halted, even in the middle of nowhere, absolute silence was enjoined on pain of death. To stop notes being thrown from trucks the guards confiscated every scrap of paper, in lieu of which intellectuals would sometimes recite Russian classics by heart. During the odyssey, which took many weeks, prisoners were starved of food and, more unbearably, of water. Sometimes they froze, sometimes they suffocated. Always "politicals" were liable to be robbed and killed with impunity by the *urkas,* tattooed demons who seemed to have been vomited up from the underworld. By the time they staggered into the vast transit camps outside Vladivostok (where Mandelstam died, a deliverance at least from Kolyma) the health of many prisoners was broken. They were filthy, unrecognisable: Eugenia Ginzburg only realised that she was looking at herself in a mirror because she now resembled her mother. Attempts were made to de-louse them. Men and women were shaved of all their bodily hair by (male) barbers. But their shrivelled flesh was subjected to a new assault—by voracious bugs marching in formation like soldier ants. Another scourge was night blindness, caused by vitamin deficiency. It particularly afflicted the intelligentsia, who were singled out for physical punishment. Many with the clearest vision of what was happening to the Soviet Union had to grope their way through the darkness, fluttering their hands in front of them like the antennae of some creature of the deep.

Winter lasted eight months in Kolyma but, once the sea had melted, new arrivals were quickly mustered for embarkation. One described the process:

> When we came out on to the immense field outside the camp I witnessed a spectacle that would have done justice to a Cecil B. De Mille production. As far as the eye could see there were columns of prisoners marching in one direction or another like armies on a battlefield. A huge detachment of security officers, soldiers, and signal corpsmen with field telephones and motor-cycles kept in touch with headquarters, arranging the smooth flow of these human rivers.[83]

Directed by whistles and flags, women, cripples, old men, teenagers and others manoeuvred in military formation. The operation took hours and the shorn convicts were herded aboard rusty prison ships for a voyage which bore comparison with the "middle passage." They were battened down so tightly in foetid holds that they could hardly breathe. Scenes now took place which might have inspired Hieronymous Bosch. At best the *urkas* would terrorise the "politicals," committing multiple rape (putting out the eyes of anyone who resisted) and murder. At worst there would be a major disaster: in 1934, for example, when the S.S. *Dzhurma* got stuck in the pack ice, not a prisoner survived and some of the crew went mad. Men and women who spent a week or more in one of these ocean-going dungeons, awash with human detritus, received a fitting introduction to Stalin's island of the damned.

Kolyma was, of course, on the continent. But those marooned there always thought of it as a place apart, another world. It was remote and primeval, and its rocky shore loomed out of a leaden sea. The land itself had a wild beauty: in spring blue mountains were bright with green larch and pink-purple fire-weed. On the road to Magadan, though, wooden watchtowers reminded new exiles that only the silvery gulls wheeling overhead were free. The "city of gold" itself was a squalid frontier town built on the bones of prisoners. It consisted of little brick, more timber and much mud. But Magadan, where the temperature never sank below -50 degrees centigrade, was civilisation compared to barbed-wire stockades in the depths of the taiga, where a man's hot soup might turn to ice before he had time to drink it. It was appropriate, for instance, that Elgen, the second largest camp, meant "dead" in the local (Yakut) language. Here prisoners were made to feel at home by a large green-painted wooden arch bearing the legend in huge red letters: "Long live the great Stalin."[84] But almost everything else was so unfamiliar as to seem extraterrestrial. The "white nights" were not platinum like those of Leningrad: instead the icy "flush in which normal outlines were held in quivering suspense" conveyed "a feeling of something deeply hostile to man." The camps were populated by zombies, their emaciated bodies supporting huge heads, brick-red from frostbite, with bloodshot eyes starting from purple sockets. The prisoners looked "Martian."[85]

They were victims of what was deliberately intended as a killing regime. Yezhov set out "to purge the already purged."[86] In Kolyma and elsewhere prisoners were deprived of fur coats and felt boots. Instead they were given grey wadded jackets and trousers, which soon fell to pieces, and canvas shoes. So camp doctors, often convicts themselves who showed what humanity they could, were forever amputating corpse-white, frostbitten toes. Punishments grew more harsh: one was tying a naked man outside to be eaten alive by mosquitoes which, prisoners joked, the NKVD had gathered from all corners of the earth for their delectation. Rations were reduced while work quotas increased. At Kolyma the rule was: "No gold, no bread."[87] But those who dug the mines, which needed no pit props because the earth was frozen solid, were caught in a lethal trap. If they fulfilled their quotas, they worked themselves to death; if not, they starved or were shot as saboteurs. Those in the last stages of malnutrition were known as "goners." They haunted the "zone" like wraiths, scavenging for fish heads and cabbage leaves on kitchen refuse tips, eating bark and moss. Death was their inevitable release: there were no old people in Kolyma.

Nor was there anything to make life worth living. Little joy came from the pathetic prisoners' band. Drunken orgies fuelled by eau-de-Cologne, antifreeze or floor polish often numbed the senses for good. There were fleeting, often brutal, sexual contacts and young *urkas* engaged in masturbation races, but most libidos were exhausted. Inmates got little satisfaction from their active form of passive smoking—inhaling the breath of those who possessed tobacco. Escape was a fantasy. Some reckoned that the bliss of a few days in hospital was worth the price of self-mutilation, even though it was a capital offence. Yet suicide was rare. It was certainly nothing to challenge the administration's monopoly on murder. As production fell, executions increased. The gravedigger at one small camp complained that his job was no longer a sinecure: he had buried 3 men in 1936, 4 in 1937, but in 1938 he filled more than 10 pits, each holding over 30 corpses. Throughout the vast Kolyma complex in that year 40,000 prisoners were executed and many more expired from hunger and exhaustion. The climate took its own fatal toll, not least the blizzards which raged with unparalleled fury, freezing bone-marrow and reducing visibility to nil. Caught in the so-called "Valley of Death" near Shaivinsk Camp during one such storm, a party of several thousand prisoners and guards lost its way and perished to a man.[88] Only the few lucky enough to find some kind of light, inside job emerged from the icy holocaust of Kolyma. According to some estimates this complex, throughout its Stalinist years, may have claimed more lives than Auschwitz. And as surely as the survivors of Auschwitz bore their tattooed numbers, those of Kolyma carried the scars of trophic ulcers, stigmata of starvation.

YET, just as some inmates of German concentration camps could hardly believe in the horrors they were experiencing, Stalin's victims often found it difficult to credit the evidence of their senses. They were innocent so there must be some mistake, for which neither Stalin nor the Party could be held responsible. Or perhaps they really were guilty: Communists, like Christians, carried about with them (as one purged historian wrote) a "sense of sin, a vague and indefinable feeling of having transgressed, combined with an ineradicable expectation of inevitable punishment."[89] In some obscure fashion, then, many thought the NKVD right. This was certainly the view of free workers in Magadan, as Eugenia Ginzburg recorded:

> Their naive trust in official propaganda was so strong that they simply refused to believe what their own eyes told them about the realities of Kolyma. Anything that appeared in a newspaper carried more conviction with them than what they saw in the street.[90]

To add to the obfuscation, even ideologues who recognised the character of Stalin's despotism did not necessarily want to reveal it to the Party faithful outside Russia. "If you deprive them of their illusions," said Roberta Gropper, formerly a Communist member of the Reichstag who was imprisoned in Butyrka before being handed over to Hitler, "you rob them of their last hope."[91]

Beyond the barbed wire there was a widespread disposition to accept that the "corrective labour camp" lived up to its name—instead of being, as one Kolyma prisoner said, "an incubator for all the vilest human instincts."[92] Molotov trumpeted the official line, which the Depression made less implausible. Conditions in the Gulag, he said, were better than the "real slavery that exists in capitalist society."[93] This became a Communist chorus. Widely disseminated inside the Soviet Union and published abroad was a fairy-tale account of how criminals, some with "flowers in their buttonholes" and assisted by only 37 OGPU officers, had been "reforged" through work on the White Sea–Baltic Canal.[94] (This achievement was celebrated with the issue of a brand of cigarettes called Belomor, though the chain-smoking Nadezhda Mandelstam called the tobacco "shit from burial mounds.")[95] The theme of salvation through labour also found expression in Nikolai Pogodin's play *The Aristocrats,* warmly applauded in 1935 at Moscow's Realist Theatre.

Western fellow-travellers, some of whom were taken in by "Intourist" prisons, echoed Soviet propaganda. None was more fatuous than Shaw, who said that in England the convict entered gaol an ordinary man and left a criminal, whereas in Russia the opposite was the case—"but for the difficulty of inducing him to come out at all."[96] Such remarks muddied the waters. So did the capitalist efforts to boycott goods produced by slave labour. They made the humanitarian outcry against conditions in the camps, ample evidence of which filtered out, seem part of a plot to do down Communism. Foreigners could therefore profess honest bewilderment about what went on in the Gulag, just as they could regard the purge trials as (in Thomas Mann's phrase) "ugly riddles."[97]

Still puzzling today is the question of how much Russians knew and understood about the Great Purge itself. Many seemed quite sincere in taking official pronouncements at face value. During his free-booting trips through the Soviet Union in 1937 Fitzroy Maclean discovered an "absolute lack of independent thought" and a general propensity to parrot the views of *Pravda* and *Izvestia*.[98] Of course, in the presence of aliens, as another visiting Briton found, the average Russian became "a gramophone record of Stalin."[99] Nevertheless, there is copious evidence to support the view that the nation had been brainwashed. Stalin received millions of letters from petitioners, who must have hoped that he would right their wrongs—in fact most of these missives were bundled up unopened and burned. Confident of their innocence, some Communists, even when arrested, were not terrified by the terror. The leader cult continued to work its malign magic. Many people, including the mature and the well educated, felt not just genuine pride in the regime but a real love for its presiding genius. The clever children's writer Kornei Chukovsky described in his diary Stalin's appearance at the Komsomol Congress in December 1936:

> Something extraordinary had happened to the audience! I looked round . . . every face was full of love and tenderness, inspired . . . For all of us, to see him, simply to see him made us happy . . . We reacted to every movement with reverence; I had never supposed myself capable of such feelings . . . Pasternak kept whispering rapturous words in my ear. Pasternak and I went home together, both revelling in our own happiness.[100]

Such veneration was commonplace. Even after his father's judicial murder Anton Antonov-Ovseyenko held Stalin's name "sacred."[101]

That their idol should be engaged in a Machiavellian betrayal of the revolution seemed less likely than that the charges against his enemies were true. The very fact that these charges were so incredible, it was said, made them easier to believe. After all, the world's "most accomplished mystery writers could hardly have invented such a case."[102] (George Orwell punctured this paradox with his comic skit about a monstrous Churchillite conspiracy to overthrow the British empire by means which ranged from blowing up the House of Lords to spreading "foot and mouth disease in the Royal racing-stables.")[103] But even informed members of the Soviet élite swallowed similar stories about Trotskyites, not least because "the unpredictable, incomprehensible and treacherous daily reality of the Soviet system fed perceptions of omnipresent conspiracy."[104] General Gorbatov, one of the few to return from Kolyma, accepted Tukhachevsky's guilt. Stalin proved once more the efficacy of the big lie.

On the other hand, all Russians knew that they were living through an appalling cataclysm. Moreover, recent research into secret police files reveals that dissonant views could often be heard in jokes, verse, rumours, letters and conversation. "This 'shadow culture' ensured that official propaganda was never able to secure a total monopoly on popular opinion."[105] Despite indoctrination and secrecy, many grasped the import of the show trials. Victor Kravchenko, who later defected to the West, said that no one he met in Moscow attached the slightest value to the confessions of defendants. They were simply "puppets in a political morality play not in the least related to truth."[106] Another contemporary was still more scathing: "Even the simplest fool knew that all those thousands were not 'traitors,' 'enemies of the people,' or 'spies.'"[107] Shostakovich obviously put Russians who claimed to be unaware of what was happening on a par with Germans pleading ignorance of the death camps: "Of course they understood."[108] Eugenia Ginzburg exposed the reality with Humean logic which shocked some of her fellow prisoners: "But if everybody is supposed to have betrayed one man, isn't it easier to think he has betrayed them?"[109] Few had the courage to express such blatant scepticism behind bars (jailbirds were often stool pigeons or, as prisoners said, "broody hens") let alone inside the greater panopticon of the Soviet Union itself.

According to one (probably exaggerated) estimate, every fifth citizen was an NKVD nark. Russians joked about the man looking at himself in the mirror who says, "One of us must be an informer."[110] So although there was (according to a leading authority) "mass discontent with Soviet rule,"[III] people kept their own counsel. "Today a man only talks freely with his wife," Babel memorably remarked, "at night, with the blankets pulled over his head."[112] Yet, according to another of Stalin's victims, by the time of the Piatakov trial, "we were all thinking the same thing"—namely that the charges were "rubbish."[113] The gulf between what could be voiced and what could be thought was deep but it was also murky. For what Stalin's subjects said with their lips tended to corrupt their minds. They took refuge from the yawning gap between private and public opinion in the licensed schizophrenia which Orwell called "doublethink." As a student of this "dual consciousness" has written:

> At public meetings, and even in private conversations, citizens were obliged to repeat in ritual fashion grotesque falsehoods about themselves, the world, and the Soviet Union, and at the same time to keep silent about things they knew very well, not only because they were terrorized but because the incessant repetition of falsehoods which they knew to be such made them accomplices in the campaign of lies inculcated by the party and state.[114]

Universal mendacity was inevitable. It was a time, as Solzhenitsyn noted, when the "permanent lie becomes the only safe form of existence."[115]

Yet even Russians who tried to think straight, to make sense to themselves of the Great Purge, were bemused. It is, indeed, still unclear whether Stalin was a dictator committed to a revolution that devoured its children—a Communist Kronos—or a tyrant hell-bent on eradicating his enemies—the figure memorably foreshadowed by the nineteenth-century Russian writer Alexander Herzen, Genghis Khan with a telegraph. It has been argued recently that "the key to understanding" Stalin (and Hitler) is to recognise that he was entirely serious about his historic role and devoted his life to what he saw as a "higher cause."[116] Certainly, in private letters to Molotov, Stalin gave every sign of believing that the Soviet Union was menaced by counter-revolutionary enemies within. On the other hand, he had all the hallmarks of a malevolent despot. There is a chilling cynicism about the aphorisms attributed to Stalin: "Death solves all problems. No man, no problem!"[117] "One death is a tragedy, a million just statistics."[118] He seemed about as much hampered by ideological considerations as Al Capone. Throughout the 1930s Stalin kept the door open for an agreement with Hitler. Nothing now seems more preposterous than Ambassador Davies's assertion that the purpose of the "terrific" purge was to keep in power a government "sincerely desirous of elevating the condition of the common man."[119] More plausible is Boris Pasternak's suggestion that the *Yezhovshchina* was prompted by the failure of collectivisation.

This could not be admitted and "every means of intimidation had to be used to make people forget how to think and judge for themselves, to force them to see what wasn't there, and to maintain the contrary of what their eyes told them."[120] Stalin acquired absolute power to make facts as plastic as Salvador Dali's clocks. He was the Surrealist of *Realpolitik*.

Delving deeper into Stalin's mentality is even more problematic, for retrospective psychoanalysis is little more than guesswork. Khrushchev's verdict, which echoed that of Bukharin and was subsequently echoed by Molotov, is convincing: Stalin had a "sickly suspicious" mind.[121] Plainly a man who said that he trusted nobody, not even himself, exhibited signs of paranoia. Pathologists may refine that diagnosis. Historians are more likely to conclude that Stalin's motives lie hidden in the black hole where madness and evil meet.

Madness and evil were palpable towards the end of 1937. They were rampant in Red Square during the all-day parade marking the twentieth birthday of the revolution, when Stalin was guarded so neurotically that NKVD officers marched past with empty holsters and loudspeakers provided the cheering. Equally sinister and spurious was the subsequent celebration of "the glorious anniversary of the CHEKA–OGPU–NKVD, the unsheathed sword of the working class."[122] As lights blazed in the Lubyanka and snow melted in the warm weather, Muscovites looked forward to a "black Christmas."[123] And as the Great Purge approached its climax Russia trembled. Dread was written on the faces of passers-by, in their shifty glances, forced smiles and crumpled expressions. People froze when the telephone rang, kept a bag permanently packed, slept in their clothes. Fears slid everywhere like shadows, wrote the poet Yevgeny Yevtushenko, but all too visible were those with "death sentences shining inside them like white crosses on the doors of Huguenots."[124] The cities and the élite were most afraid, for they were Stalin's main target. The bonds of humanity were destroyed. The assault on the past was a mind-numbing portent of the future. Men and women became as though they had never been. After unspeakable tortures V. E. Meyerhold, the immensely popular theatre director, was turned into an "unperson." At the other end of the scale, Yagoda, previously ubiquitous, vanished: he was erased from books and photographs; he was replaced by a lifebelt in D. M. Nalbandyan's famous painting of Stalin inspecting the White Sea–Baltic Canal; and his colossal rock statue at the entrance to that canal was dynamited into oblivion.

Outsiders could hardly grasp the scope of the terror, the scale of the horror. Pasternak's cousin Olga Freidenberg cast a retrospective ray of light into the Soviet heart of darkness.

No one who has not lived in the Stalin era can appreciate the horror of our uncertain position. A person's life was poisoned secretly, invisibly, as witches and sorcerers were hounded in the Dark Ages. Something mysterious was accumulating under the earth and coming to the boil. A person felt at the mercy of an inescapable force aimed at him and certain to crush him.[125]

Some did attempt to escape, hiding in the woods or getting arrested for a minor criminal offence. Some sought to obliterate all traces of heresy from their homes, thus threatening to choke the Moscow sewage system: a prohibition was issued against putting books down the lavatory. Some took refuge in silence, isolation, insanity or suicide. Children as young as ten, many abandoned when their parents were imprisoned, killed themselves. But there was no real resistance to repression, as would have occurred if a tithe of Stalin's charges had been true. Russians were slaughtered because they were, in more senses than one, innocent. They were also passive, petrified by "unheard-of terror"[126] like Jews during the Holocaust. Stalin shuffled his subjects "like a pack of cards."[127] Huge queues were "formed by people awaiting execution."[128] The Kremlin's master did not need to cut off heads, observed Mandelstam: "they fly off by themselves like dandelions."[129] Stalin's homicidal mania inspired a shell-shocked fatalism, if not a giddy complicity, in his victims. No one evoked their state, as they listened for the black whisper of doom, more movingly than Anna Akhmatova. In her "Requiem" for another lost generation she wrote:

> Madness has already covered
> Half my soul with its wing,
> And gives to drink of a fiery wine
> And beckons into the dark valley.[130]

XX

AMERICA IN ISOLATION

OPAQUE as it was, the Stalinist horror haunted the world during the latter part of the 1930s, a time when the problems of the Depression were eclipsed by the dangers of war. In the course of the 1936 American election campaign, for example, the President was severely embarrassed by an endorsement he received from a Comintern newspaper. It revived charges that the New Deal was stars-and-stripes Bolshevism, that Roosevelt himself was a Yankee Stalin and that the FBI was an "American OGPU."[1] In his opening speech the President issued a forceful refutation. The "malicious" opponents trying to paint him Red resembled those who had accused Washington of wanting to make himself king and Jefferson of planning to set up a guillotine, who had damned Lincoln as a "Roman Emperor" and Woodrow Wilson as "a self-constituted Messiah." Not content with denouncing the "menace" of Communism, Roosevelt said, he had immunised the United States against it; for his home-grown plan to eradicate the Depression safeguarded constitutional liberties.[2]

This was a strong case. But, as it happened, Roosevelt was already contemplating a radical change which did smack of authoritarianism. He proposed to make the Supreme Court—seen as the major threat to the New Deal—more amenable to the White House. Observers noted that on the drenching day of FDR's second inauguration Chief Justice Charles Evans Hughes, a white-bearded figure who looked like Cecil B. De Mille's idea of Jehovah, "spoke slowly and with especial emphasis" when he came to that part of the oath requiring the President to uphold the constitution.[3] It was thus vital for Roosevelt to distance himself from Communism and from any other form of dictatorship. Even if he had been prepared to flout the hardening views of the isolationists, he was bound to reject the invitation issued by Litvinov to support the Soviet policy of collective security. For the purge trials convinced most Americans that there was nothing to choose between the hammer and sickle and the swastika. Communism was simply Red fascism.

Yet most Party members and many fellow-travellers in the United States kept their faith in Stalin. They saw him as both a surgeon cutting gangrened flesh from the Soviet body politic and a sorcerer presiding over a magic country of the mind. Such writers as Lillian Hellman, Dashiell Hammett, Irwin Shaw, Dorothy Parker and Upton Sinclair took the purge trials at face value. So did many other progressives, countering the conclusions of philosopher John Dewey, whose commission convicted Stalin of monstrous perfidy. Others on the American Left were so perplexed by the Great Purge that they suspended judgement until the facts could be known. Trying to get at the truth now, they declared, was as futile as asking, "Who won the San Francisco earthquakes?"[4] More surprisingly, many liberals who believed that the trials were a wicked sham remained sympathetic to the Communist cause. Despite everything, they felt, Russia was the greatest bulwark against fascism. Stalin sustained the loyalists in Spain, cockpit of the Popular Front. The Kremlin stood for the proletariat at a time when American trade-unionists were engaged in life-or-death struggles and it was still tempting to measure civil rights in purely economic terms. As the author Alfred Kazin said, "It did not matter how deceitful and murderous Stalin was showing himself to be in the purges; the Soviet Union, a 'workers' state' stained only with the unaccountable sins of its leadership, still represented the irreversible movement of human progress."[5] Malcolm Cowley, literary editor of the *New Republic,* found a memorable image to sum up the creed of fellow-travellers of all intellectual persuasions. The mist of ages had blown away to reveal that

> chasms lay on all sides of us, and that beyond them were mountains rising into the golden sunlight. We could not reach the mountains alone, but perhaps we could merge ourselves in the working class and thereby help to build a bridge for ourselves and for humanity.[6]

Most Americans, however, were alienated from the Soviet Union and the Communist Party as a result of the purges. Some of the fiercest opposition came from disillusioned champions of the October Revolution whose grail had been shattered by Stalin's apostasy. None was more vocal than Max Eastman, once editor of *The Masses.* He was horrified by the witch-hunt. He was sickened by the fact that "supposedly intelligent people" should believe that all old Bolsheviks had been "treacherous and contemptible fiends, except only one, and that one, by a sublimely improbable accident, the very man who had managed to concentrate power into his hands."[7] With the confidence of one who had at last seen the light, Eastman anatomised the delusions of those who still bowed the knee to the Kremlin Baal.

When historians look back, I believe the fading of religious faith in this era will seem the chief explanatory factor of its madness. Men haven't got used yet to the emptiness of the sky, and so they worship gods of clay again—what crude and bloody ones!—and believe in myths and promises of heaven on earth. Soviet Russia was far enough away, and sufficiently insulated by the language barrier, to function wonderfully in the place of Kingdom Come. All you had to do was dismiss all the plain facts as atrocity stories—they are horrible enough to sound like it—and believe the whole state-owned propaganda, and you could be as tranquil amid the falling ruins of civilisation as an infant in the arms of Jesus.[8]

Those who had never succumbed to Bolshevik blandishments merely had their worst fears confirmed by the purges. Communism was just another chapter in the dark annals of tyranny. Stalin and Hitler were Tweedledum and Tweedledee. Even if those purged were guilty, their behaviour was a crushing indictment of the system. It spawned crime like a Surinam toad. Yet conservatives themselves found the picture clouded. Influenced by its reporter Walter Duranty, who pronounced the trials authentic, the *New York Times* was slow to move from agnosticism about "what goes on behind the Soviet veil."[9] Respected figures like Newton D. Baker and Mauritz Hallgren agreed with John Gunther that no "fair-minded person can read the verbatim report of the second trial and still believe the confessions could have been fabricated."[10] As ever during the 1930s, dogma was rampant while certainty was elusive.

American confusion about Russia, so pregnant with future consequences, was nowhere better reflected than in the conflict between Roosevelt's new Ambassador, Joseph E. Davies, and the career officials at the Moscow embassy. Davies has invariably been portrayed as the naïve amateur who allowed himself to be bamboozled by the men of the Kremlin. So he was, but that is not the whole story. A Midwesterner of Welsh Nonconformist stock, Davies was born in 1876 and brought up on the maxims of Horatio Alger. Although he had backed Woodrow Wilson and made friends with Franklin Roosevelt, his political career had not been a success. But he had made a small fortune as a lawyer—he numbered Henry Ford and the Dominican dictator Trujillo among his clients—and in 1935 he married a large fortune. His new (and second) wife was Marjorie Post, the General Foods heiress. Nicknamed the "Lady Bountiful of Hell's Kitchen"[11] for her work in the New York slums during the depths of the Depression, she was also described as "the most stunning woman outside *Harper's Bazaar*." She had favoured a secret wedding, costing a mere 100,000 dollars—it was embellished with 5,000 specially dyed chrysanthemums to match the 300-pound blush-pink cake. Davies's own gift to his wife was the cachet of their Moscow appointment. After extravagant farewell parties they set out accompanied by a retinue of servants, 50 pieces of hand luggage and 30 cabin trunks. They took masses of crystal glass, silverware and domestic appliances, truck-loads of Birdseye frozen food (including oysters) and 2,000 quarts of ice-cream. They installed new plumbing at the embassy, Spasso House, and when their imported refrigerators blew all the fuses they brought in a transformer from Helsinki. Altogether the couple seemed less suited to be envoys to Stalin's Kremlin than to Louis XIV's Versailles. Even the French Ambassador was "dazzled" by the lavish soirées of the "Frigidaire Queen."[12]

Davies, a silver-haired Babbitt with a penchant for flattering the press, paid much more attention to the likes of Walter Duranty than to his own staff. Dedicated experts such as Loy Henderson, George Kennan and Charles Bohlen actually considered resigning *en masse* in protest at Davies's appointment. They were incensed when, discovering that his office was bugged, the Ambassador simply said that the Russians would hear only of American friendship. The professional diplomats resented the fact that Davies spent most of his time going on jaunts and collecting *objets d'art*. Many of these were the confiscated property of purge victims. But the Soviet authorities, who always preferred to deal with frank capitalists rather than idealistic fellow-travellers, were extremely generous. Molotov's wife, who was particularly fascinated with Marjorie's flamboyant opulence, typified by lipstick-red gowns and strings of diamonds, invited her to choose what treasures she fancied in the Kremlin store-rooms. She was allowed to purchase gold and silver chalices of Peter the Great's time and other such antiques, paying for them by weight alone—Catherine the Great's salt-cellar was so heavy that, later, Andrei Gromyko's wife thought it was fixed to the Davies' dining-table. The Ambassador waxed lyrical about Moscow's "beautiful prison of luxury" with its cornucopia of armorial weapons, decorated bibles, Court plate, royal coaches, embroidered altar cloths and jewelled images.[13] He and his wife bought so much in the way of paintings, icons, china, imperial porcelain, Fabergé trinkets and gem-encrusted cigarette cases that Stalin lowered the diplomats' exchange rate from 45 to 7 roubles to the dollar, causing "economic hardships" at every embassy in Moscow.[14] Still more infuriating to officials like Kennan, they had to translate for Davies in the October Hall; they found that he disagreed with their sceptical view of the purge trials; and at lunch-time they were obliged to fetch his sandwiches.

Of course, Davies was wrong about the trials. But his advisers were less right than they liked to think. While dismissing charges of a top-level conspiracy, Kennan believed that some of Piatakov's co-defendants were guilty of espionage and that others were "active in the maintenance of the skeleton of a Trotskiist organisation." Kennan concluded that no Westerner could plumb the Soviet depths.

> The Russian mind, as Dostoevski has shown, knows no moderation; and it sometimes carries both truth and falsehood to such infinite extremes that they eventually meet in space like parallel lines, and it is no longer possible to distinguish between them.[15]

This view was understandable. Yet Kennan and his disenchanted colleagues boldly concluded that the purges had cut at the root of Soviet power.

Davies, who travelled himself and relied on his Russophile Military Attaché Colonel Faymonville, was nearer the mark when he told Roosevelt that the Bear was "fat" enough to "waddle through" the crisis.[16] Not only did Davies testify to the vast strength of Russian resources, he correctly judged that here was an intensely nationalistic state—whereas Kennan believed that the Soviet Union was primarily committed to world revolution. Compared to the sophisticated Kennan, of course, Davies was generally crass and credulous. He considered Stalin kindly and trustworthy, a friend to children and dogs. Yet he also forecast that in due course the democracies would be glad of help from Russia despite its "terrible tyranny over the human spirit and human life."[17] Moreover, albeit for "the wrong reasons,"[18] Davies was right about Soviet might. Almost alone of presidential advisers he maintained that Russia could withstand the German onslaught in 1941. When the United States entered the war Davies urged that American aid should be sent to the USSR. His recommendation, added to the still more influential urging of Harry Hopkins, carried greater weight with Roosevelt than the cautious counsels of the State Department.

Also of considerable assistance to the Soviet Union, and fortuitously coinciding with the attack on Pearl Harbor, was the publication of Davies's ingratiating account of his diplomatic stewardship, *Mission to Moscow*. Kennan and his friends dubbed it *Submission to Moscow*.[19] Apparently encouraged by the President—"Jack this picture *must* be made"[20]—Warner Brothers produced a cinematic version of the book in 1943. It was a grotesque distortion of history: the main purge trials, for example, were conflated into a single one designed to show that the defendants were guilty of a Trotskyite conspiracy supported by the Axis warmongers. When screened in Russia, the movie gave Shostakovich his one good laugh of the war. Even the Soviet propaganda machine, he thought, would not have had the gall to produce such a travesty of the truth. In the United

States the film provoked a "roar of protest"[21] from liberals and it convinced conservatives that Hollywood was the focus of a Communist conspiracy. But what worried the protesters most about *Mission to Moscow* was not its falsehood but its verisimilitude. For all its blatant staginess, the picture contained much newsreel footage which gave it an air of documentary authenticity. And for all the portentous absurdity of statesmen twirling globes as they pondered about world war and peace, the atmosphere was one of dour introspection similar to that of *film noir*. When it came to dressing up fantasy as fact no organisation could compete with Hollywood. For motion pictures, ubiquitous expression of American culture, were the most powerful mythopoeic medium of the age.

HOLLYWOOD dazzled cinema audiences all round the globe. Luminous, numinous images projected on to a screen through veils of cigarette smoke invaded the public mind like a phantom army. As the French novelist Céline wrote, "Dreams waft upwards in the darkness to join the mirages of silver light."[22] The coming of sound, one of the swiftest technological revolutions in history, had transformed film. As well as being a popular entertainment, it was now a profoundly resonant experience. It was more akin to the brave new world of Aldous Huxley's "feelies" than to the flickering enchantment of the magic lantern show. Like an opiate, it created irresistible illusions. Synchronous music and speech added new dimensions to plot and character. Film stars became at once human and superhuman, figures whom the watching millions could identify with and worship. In fact the picture palace was something between a brothel and a church. Inside fantasies could be hired for a short time and faith might be sealed for life. Customers could be seduced by synthetic romance and won by sublime love. They could dream individual dreams in the dark and see communal visions of light. Above all, immersed in Hollywood's radiant hallucination, they could escape from the grim reality of the times.

The irony was that Hollywood itself could not escape the Depression. During the 1920s, when 100 million Americans went to the movies each week, the film industry had seemed another Klondike. Its controllers invested lavishly in motion pictures and in new cinemas to show them. These edifices were as garish as Hollywood itself. Their architecture aped Chinese pagodas, Egyptian temples, Italian gardens, Persian mosques. They were embellished with golden dragons, marble colonnades, silver fountains, bronze domes. Along a thousand main streets neon signs proclaimed Paramount or Fox. Along New York's "Great White Way," as the popular song had it, a million hearts beat quicker in the flicker of a million lights. None burned more brightly than those of the Roxy, whose pyrotechnics could have illuminated a city of 250,000 people. The Roxy's façade, decorated with forests of gold leaf, was reminiscent of the cathedral at Valladolid. Its twisted columns were modelled on Bernini's baldachino in St. Peter's, Rome. Its baroque rotunda, which contained the largest oval carpet on earth and was lit by a 2.5-ton crystal chandelier, was "one of the most overwhelming public rooms in the world this side of Napoleon's tomb."[23] The red plush seats in the air-conditioned auditorium accommodated some 6,000 patrons, many attracted by the cinema's glamorous live dance troupe, the Rockettes. The stage was so huge that, comedians said, no one should be caught on it without food and water.

This so-called "Cathedral of the Motion Picture" and its subsidiary basilicas, most of them staffed with attendants dressed like the Household Cavalry of Ruritania, were re-equipped to take sound at the end of the 1920s. Despite the stock market collapse the rage for talkies was such that it looked as if the expenditure—around 20,000 dollars a cinema—would reap handsome dividends. Double features began in 1931, giving audiences extra value for money. The Roxy attracted patrons by supplying free tobacco. New refreshment counters were installed: popcorn was popular and yielded over 100 per cent profit. Films promoted consumer goods, at a price. By such means Hollywood hoped to beat the big bad wolf of Depression. Walt Disney's animated film *Three Little Pigs* (1933), with its desperately cheerful theme song "Who's Afraid of the Big Bad Wolf?," was the movie-makers' paean of hope. The eldest pig, who resembled Herbert Hoover but possessed Franklin Roosevelt's jauntiness, provided a model of successful self-reliance. It turned out, however, that the movie moguls had built their heavily-mortgaged houses of straw.

During the first years of the Depression attendances plummeted to 60 million a week. Box-office receipts fell accordingly, reaching their nadir in 1933. By then nearly a third of all American cinemas had doused their lights and closed their doors for good. The large companies suffered staggering losses. Some, like Paramount and RKO, went bankrupt. Others, like Warner Brothers, sold assets to pay their debts. Nearly all changed hands. Yet, like the Seventh Cavalry in countless westerns, bankers and financiers rode to the rescue. They wanted to save their own investments and they recognised the potential of a near-monopolistic industry that dominated the world: 80 per cent of films shown in Britain were American and even in Japan the figure was around 35 per cent. But the price of salvation was, on the whole, stultifying blandness.

In a frantic effort to drum up trade during the early 1930s producers had offered the public a more red-blooded diet. Mervyn Le Roy reflected the current mood of despair in his sombre tragedy *I Am a Fugitive from a Chain Gang* (1932). Violent gangster movies challenged some of the smug assumptions of the day: going to school, remarks Tommy Powers (James Cagney) in *The Public Enemy* (1931), means "learning to be poor." Comedians could be more subversive still. The Marx Brothers, whose early films were triumphs of comic anarchy, seemed bent on knocking down society and dancing on its ruins. W. C. Fields was sometimes equally outrageous. So was Mae West, who spiced her films with provocative sexuality. *She Done Him Wrong* (1933), which fizzed with saucy scenes and risqué dialogue, was an especially flagrant assault on Mrs. Grundy.

In 1934 the puritans, who were mostly Catholics, retaliated. They formed the "Legion of Decency," which was headed by Al Smith and blessed by Pius XI, who pronounced that the spiritual and mental faculties of audiences sitting in "darkened theatres" were "for the most part dormant."[24] The Legion accused the film industry of manufacturing salaciousness and instituted boycotts of its products. Decent Legionaries marched behind banners proclaiming "An Admission to an Indecent Movie is a Ticket to Hell."[25] Hollywood thereupon experienced one of its periodic fits of morality. The film producers submitted slavishly to the restrictive code of their chosen censor, Will Hays. He not only excised words like "God," "damn," "lousy," "floozy," "virtuous" and "sex," he also banned whole areas of experience—miscegenation, drugs, abortion, incest. Censorship produced its inevitable crop of absurdities. While MGM gave actresses who needed them false breasts complete with nipples, the Hays Office ordered Disney to take the udders off his cartoon cows.

Money being the motive power of the so-called "dream factory," it was still prepared to turn out anything that seemed likely to pay. Producers would sometimes risk challenging or even shocking audiences. Films such as Fritz Lang's *Fury* (1936) tackled gritty social issues—in this case lynching—to spine-chilling effect. In *Modern Times* (1936) the gigantic industrial machinery which threatened to crush Charlie Chaplin became a chilling metaphor for the dehumanisation of American society. Despite its assembly-line studio system, Hollywood would even fabricate a masterpiece pillorying in the process the boss of one of the country's most powerful vested interests. Orson Welles's *Citizen Kane,* based on the life of William Randolph Hearst, employed a host of novel techniques such as mixed sound effects, flashbacks and compelling contrasts. Thanks to new incandescent lighting and high-speed panchromatic film, Welles could juxtapose theatrical glare with deep pools of shadow. He thus created a study in black and white which brilliantly reflected the enigmatic character of the press magnate and of the pre-war era.

During the worst years of the Depression, however, Hollywood dealt less in pungent archetypes, more in saccharine stereotypes. Gone were Little Caesars and Blonde Venuses; in their place reigned G Men and Snow Whites. Actresses like Mae West, Jean Harlow and Marlene Dietrich were drained of their erotic charge, bleached of their humanity as if "by the insipid Hollywood sun."[26] Mickey Mouse was anthropomorphised from zany, skinny rodent into trusty, cuddly doll. Hollywood took refuge in banal sentimentality, trite formulae and anaemic artifice. It even pandered to foreign prejudices, getting Fascist approval for a film of *The Eternal City* and rejecting Herman Mankiewicz's scenario about Hitler entitled "The Mad Dog of Europe." Hollywood also collaborated with the grotesquely restrictive British censors: on the eve of the Second World War their chief declared that "We may take pride in observing that there is not a single film showing in London today which deals with any of the burning issues of the day."[27]

For home consumption Hollywood's plots ceased to be dangerous explorations of subliminal desires. They became instead nostalgic evocations of small-town virtues, treacly affirmations of New Deal values. This was fair enough in the sense that most movie-goers had no wish to be purged with pity and terror. They wanted release from care and pain, "fairyland" pictures which would "supply the lacks in their existence."[28] They craved short cuts to Nirvana. Still, it suited the government that too much reality did not appear on the screen. President Roosevelt was doubtless familiar with the lines of New Yorkers who gathered as early as 8:00 A.M. under the lights of Broadway, Times Square and 42nd Street to take refuge in theatres showing three features. Certainly he prescribed the celluloid anodyne. "During the Depression," he said, "when the spirit of the people is lower than at any other time, it is a splendid thing that for just fifteen cents an American can go to a movie and . . . forget his troubles."[29]

So Hollywood manufactured optimistic myths to cheer a depressed civilisation. The movie magnates dispensed tinsel and glitter, as befitting their flashy emblems—Columbia's torch of liberty, the star-circled mountain peak of Paramount, the questing searchlights of Twentieth Century Fox. Hollywood sold a "gaudier version of religion," said writer Ben Hecht, in the shape of "Mother Goose platitudes and primitive valentines."[30] It transported audiences to Shangri-La and the Land of Oz. Often, they found, the balsa-wood Wild West was more substantial than the asphalt jungle outside the doors of the picture palace. The gimcrack underworld became more solid than the world of flesh and blood. Once enter "the dark of the theatre," said director Josef Von Sternberg, and "the thin line dividing what is real and what is imagined is severed."[31] Fact blurred into fantasy like images dissolving on the screen. Authentic grief and joy carried less conviction than the glycerine tears and the orthodontic smiles of film stars. True lovers paled beside Clark Gable and Greta Garbo. Genuine thugs had less charisma than Edward G. Robinson and George Raft. Even monsters like Boris Karloff and Shirley Temple did not seem incredible. Everyday life was eclipsed by the glamour and melodrama of films such as *Gone with the Wind.* The cinema provided a surrogate existence for many people. They spoke like Humphrey Bogart. They vamped like Marlene Dietrich. They postured like Errol Flynn. Life imitated Hollywood.

Nowhere was this more true than in Hollywood itself. Los Angeles' most celebrated suburb occupied a gigantic proscenium between sepia mountains and technicolor coast. Nature herself sometimes provided authentic dramas—flood, drought, fire and earthquake. But in all other respects the place, which housed only some of the film companies, seemed artificial. The sunshine appeared to have been switched on by Warner Brothers, thought J. B. Priestley. The gardens (with their scentless flowers) and the orchards (with their tasteless fruits) looked like the work of Metro-Goldwyn-Mayer. The streets resembled a vast junkyard of studio sets, all "slapdash cheap picturesqueness."[32] Oil derricks punctuated the skyline like exclamation marks, while the foreground was a jumble of white apartment buildings, stucco bungalows, flimsy stores, hamburger stalls, petrol pumps, blinking signs and lurid hoardings advertising such enticing amenities as "Los Angeles' fastest growing cemetery."[33] Freak buildings turned up like the lost properties of some bizarre spectacular. Restaurants were constructed to resemble ice-cream cones, brown bowler hats, monstrous women. And film stars throwing parties in them accomplished further metamorphoses, transforming them into cardboard ships or papier mâché cathedrals. Beyond the fringe of Hollywood, in gilded enclaves like Pasadena, Beverly Hills, Bel-Air, Santa Monica and Malibu, architectural mimesis ran riot. Houses were not houses but Art Deco *palazzos,* Mexican haciendas, Gothic castles, Tudor manors, French châteaux, Swiss chalets, Japanese temples, Tuscan villas, Samoan huts or any combination of such styles. Greta Garbo lived in a green-shuttered Algerian monastery. Charlie Chaplin inhabited a red-brick colonial mansion. Marion Davies's beach house was a "white-pillared manse, huge as a railway terminal."[34] Everything was sham and fantasy. No wonder that film director James Whale exclaimed, "All the world's made of plaster of Paris!"[35]

It was a pardonable exaggeration. From the vast studio hangars came a cascade of scenery as substantial as a Dadaist delirium. Here, in painted canvas and plywood, mocked-up lath and plaster, was a cyclorama featuring the entire history and mythology of mankind. No one conjured up the chaos of conflicting images more vividly than Nathanael West. Stumbling past flapping marble porticoes and cellophane waterfalls, his hero (in *The Day of the Locust*) encounters

> the skeleton of a Zeppelin, a bamboo stockade, an adobe fort, the wooden horse of Troy, a flight of baroque palace stairs that started in a bed of weeds and ended against the branches of an oak, part of Four-teenth Street elevated station, a Dutch windmill, the bones of a dinosaur, the upper half of the *Merrimack,* a corner of a Mayan temple.[36]

Like these evanescent tableaux, the costume drama overflowed from the studio lots. Sunset Boulevard and its surroundings witnessed a perpetual masquerade, a strutting procession of mimic men and women dressed for their parts. Females wore mink coats over purple lounging pyjamas. Males sported green trousers, orange sneakers, pastel handkerchiefs. Stars con-cealed themselves behind dark glasses with large white rims, "a triumph of conspicuous anonymity."[37] Extras competed in exhibitionism. Hollywood attracted a huge company of supporting players—small-town beauty queens and vaudeville midgets, cabaret dancers and circus strong men, burlesque comedians and opera soubrettes. Following like prospectors in a gold rush came barkers, mountebanks, swamis, "healers," beauticians, morticians. Of all the make-belief merchants none were more extraordi-nary than the so-called "cinemoguls" or "cellulords."

Almost without exception these men—they were all men, many of them Jewish—had risen from humble beginnings. Sam Goldwyn had been a glove salesman, Louis B. Mayer a rag-picker, Harry Cohn a furrier, Eddie Mannix a bouncer in an amusement park. The Warner brothers were butcher's sons. The Schenks had owned a drugstore. Marcus Loew and Adolph Zukor had run penny arcades. Most had come to Hollywood via the slums of show business: flea circuses, theatrical agencies, nick-elodeons, vaudeville. Once established as the rulers of movie-land they became, as often as not, a prey to fantasy, vanity and megalomania. They confused cinema with *vérité:* Walt Disney reckoned that the centaur sequence in his cartoon film *Fantasia* would be the making of Beethoven. Monarchs of the "marzipan kingdom" moved in "an aura of greatness," said Ben Hecht, "and reports of their genius would have embarrassed Michelangelo."[38] Like royalty, Sam Goldwyn never carried money. The film producers became pocket dictators. Louis B. Mayer of MGM declared that directors should learn to crawl before they could walk. Harry Cohn of Columbia bugged and purged his employees, exploited his starlets sexually and modelled his office on that of Mussolini. "I don't have ulcers," he said, "I *give* them."[39]

Cohn also vouchsafed an explanation of what the film industry was all about: "It's cunt and horses."[40] This was not so much a definition as a characteristically crude declaration of philistinism. And it would have amply confirmed the low esteem in which the movie tycoons were held. Writers, who ranked in the studio hierarchy above hairdressers but below heads of publicity, particularly despised them. They were always (in an expression attributed to Sam Goldwyn) "biting the hand that lays the golden egg."[41] Thus Dorothy Parker complained that she was working for cretins. S. J. Perelman described them as hoodlums of great wealth. Ben Hecht called them trash-pedlars who had lamed the American mind. Josef Von Sternberg, who wielded pen as well as lens, said that his bosses knew what they wanted but didn't know how to spell it. Another writer, who wished to get out of his contract with Columbia, offered to act as Harry Cohn's interpreter on a trip to England. But it was Sam Goldwyn who attracted the most joyous ribaldry. Bald, jug-eared and hook-nosed, he was the prototype of the language-garbling, cigar-chewing Hollywood Napoleon. His verbal solecisms—"Include me out," "In two words, im possible"—were notorious and (mostly) apocryphal. His greed was legendary. Goldwyn "beat at your mind like a man in front of a slot machine," said Hecht, "shaking it for a jackpot."[42] His taste was execrable. Like Walt Disney, he tended to equate art with obscenity.

Yet writers, who invariably have the last word in the struggle between culture and commerce, gave a false impression of film producers. They inflated the already bizarre follies and foibles of the caliphs of California, caricaturing them as ignorant clowns, lunatic charlatans, sacred monsters. Part of the writers' animus stemmed from the fear that their literary talents were atrophying in Hollywood, which they variously compared to Devil's Island and the Sargasso Sea. More galling still, they were shackled to Goldwyn and his ilk with golden chains. As one memorably expostulated, "They ruin your stories. They massacre your ideas. They prostitute your art. They trample on your pride. And what do you get for it? A fortune."[43]

Fortunes were made because the film tsars were skilful salesmen. They had a shrewd grasp of public taste, which they did not intend to go bust by overestimating. There was a method in their seeming madness: they made money even more prodigiously than they wasted it. P. G. Wodehouse, who admitted that he had been paid huge sums for doing practically nothing in Hollywood, nevertheless recorded: "Studio life is all perfectly normal, not a bit crazy."[44] He claimed, regretfully but erroneously, that it would not afford him a single comic story. "Sam Goldwyn," said another author, "goes up the hill and teaches the foxes to be smart."[45] Goldwyn and his kind were particularly smart when it came to defending their fiefdom against the only man of letters who ever seriously threatened it. This was Upton Sinclair, who sought election as Governor of California in 1934 on the Democratic ticket and a utopian socialist platform. "What does Sinclair know about anything?" growled Louis B. Mayer. "He's just a writer."[46]

Sinclair knew a good deal and he was not impressed by the New Deal. An old-time muckraker, he had become famous by denouncing many American evils, from the meat-packing industry to the child labour laws. Now he began the EPIC crusade to "End Poverty in California." Normally Sinclair could be dismissed as a crank. He preached more "isms" than Horace Greeley: feminism, spiritualism, food faddism, prohibitionism, Fourierism. He attempted to uplift humanity, as H. L. Mencken gleefully noted, through sex hygiene, Esperanto, telepathy, twilight sleep, chiropractic, war gardens, *vers libre* and paper-bag cookery. Though not a Communist, Sinclair was an ascetic defender of Soviet Russia. Nevertheless, at a time when one in seven inhabitants of California was on relief, Sinclair's radical nostrums seemed so attractive that people paid to attend his political meetings. What he proposed, in brief, was to tax according to means and to set up cooperatives producing for use rather than profit. He even had ideas about generating jobs in the film industry: "Why should not the State of California rent one of the idle studios and let the unemployed actors make a few pictures of their own?" Louis B. Mayer was appalled and he led his fellow magnates in a bitter assault on the muckraker. It demonstrated that Hollywood was not simply in the business of conjuring up a candyfloss world. When provoked, it could create vicious as well as vapid distortions of reality.

Sinclair asked for trouble, not least by likening movie bosses to Jewish traders of yore who had sold Christian girls into concubinage. But he was taken aback by the dirty tricks that followed. A slight, professorial figure with pince-nez, pursed lips and an expression of quizzical geniality, Sinclair expected others to share his fundamental benevolence. Instead he found himself pilloried as "Utopian Sincliar," a "red devil," the fourth Horseman of the Apocalypse riding his hobby in an attempt to catch up with Mussolini, Hitler and Stalin.[47] MGM freely issued California cinemas with bogus newsreels in which respectable Americans pledged their support to the Republican candidate, Frank Merriam, while shabby aliens said they would vote for Sinclair because, "His system worked vell in Russia, vy can't it vork here?"[48] The most notorious of these frauds showed a train-borne invasion of hoboes, drawn to the Golden State by Sinclair's promise of jobs. Fake still photographs had long been used to discredit political figures: the Los Angeles *Times,* for example, had depicted labour leader Samuel Gompers trampling on the Stars and Stripes. But this was the first time the movies had made such propaganda. Their controllers, who threatened to move their business to Florida if Sinclair won, did not defeat him alone. Other great vested interests contributed, including the first advertising agency to become involved in a political campaign. Sinclair warned his followers not to be surprised if they heard that he was calling for "the overthrow of our Government, or the abolition of the Christian religion, or the nationalisation of our virgins, or the cutting up of babies for soup-meat."[49] However, the masters of make-belief had proved that their dark art could change reality as well as mould fantasy. Hollywood was a lie factory as well as a dream factory.

For the most part, however, Hollywood avoided overt political propaganda. Certainly there, as elsewhere, reactionaries vied with Reds, who were said to be a compound of "high ideals and low IQs."[50] But the "isms" chiefly on display in the film colony were not fascism and Communism; they were narcissism and solipsism (to say nothing of plagiarism). And if Hollywood liked to contemplate its own navel, or admire its own face in the glass, other Americans did not look far beyond their own noses during the Depression. Their vision was impaired by the economic blizzard. After a second election victory the President himself was unsighted and lost his political way. He became fixated on the prospect of the collapse of the New Deal as a result of a conspiracy in the Supreme Court.

THAT a cabal of nine old men, most of them conservative, should strike down reforming laws at a time when (as Roosevelt said in his second inaugural address, on 20 January 1937) one third of the nation was "ill-housed, ill-clad, ill-nourished," was widely regarded as an insult to democracy. There was much to be said for this view, though even the "four horsemen of reaction" on the bench were remarkably liberal on matters of civil rights.[51] During Roosevelt's first term Chief Justice Charles Evans Hughes and his hardline brethren invalidated more legislation in a shorter time than had ever been done before. Furthermore they had done so on flawed and inconsistent grounds, here ruling that the federal government had no right to regulate agricultural production, there deciding that state governments could not fix minimum wages. Al Smith could well crow, after the nullification of the AAA early in 1936, that the Supreme Court was throwing out the New Deal "alphabet three letters at a time."[52]

It was easy to perceive the spectre of judicial dictatorship behind the white marble façade of the new Supreme Court building. This palace of justice, just across the plaza from the Capitol, was part of the Depression building boom designed to invest official Washington with neo-classical dignity. Opened in 1935, it was a grandiose monument to the majesty of the law. It had twin rows of Corinthian columns, bronze doors featuring Homeric scenes, and "fine big windows to throw the New Deal out of." [53] Above was a pediment whose frieze contained nine figures, some allegorical, others real. In the centre was Liberty enthroned, holding the scales of justice and guarded by Order (a Roman soldier with *fasces*) and Authority (a medieval knight with sword). Immediately to the right was the figure of Chief Justice Hughes himself, supposedly sculpted without his knowledge. He did know enough, however, to insist that the motto which gleamed from the east portico should read "JUSTICE THE GUARDIAN OF LIBERTY."

No doubt Hughes saw himself as the embodiment of this ideal as he presided over the Court's deliberations in its magnificent 24-columned chamber, which was walled with ivory-veined Spanish marble and draped with red velvet hangings. He liked to quote William Pitt's maxim— "Where law ends, tyranny begins"—and to add that their business was to see that where "law begins, tyranny ends." [54] Hughes was meticulous and peremptory in his dealings: he was said to have cut off a voluble counsel in the middle of the word "if." Eyes flashing and beard bristling, the dark-robed Chief Justice laid down the law as if it were holy writ. Certainly the sloppy formulae and coercive implications of the New Deal were anathema to him. He condemned its more vulnerable provisions with all the force and ingenuity at his command. Cloaked in high-minded phrases though the Supreme Court's opposition was, it came close to being an abuse of judicial power. Many thought that the Court was acting unconstitutionally in the name of the constitution. Professor Felix Frankfurter denounced its "long course of misbehaviour" and recommended that "the fear of God should be instilled" into the justices. [55]

This was a notion that had appealed to Teddy Roosevelt and his cousin adopted it eagerly. But FDR was too eager. His general rule was to gauge public opinion first and to act afterwards. Clare Boothe Luce plausibly charged that Roosevelt's characteristic gesture, matching Hitler's Nazi salute and Churchill's "V" sign, was to hold his wetted finger up to the wind. However, Roosevelt had just won a larger majority of votes than any previous president. He became the victim of hubris—and nemesis. In putting forward his plan, on 5 February 1937, to increase the membership of the Supreme Court and to "pack" it with up to six of his own appointees, Roosevelt made the greatest political mistake of his life.

He offended friends as well as enemies by springing the scheme on them without warning. He initially justified it by impugning the competence of the aged judges. This argument offended the octogenarian (but liberal) Justice Louis Brandeis, who helped to demolish it by showing that he and his colleagues were abreast of their work. Then the President frankly accused the Supreme Court of sabotaging the New Deal. With Machiavellian guile, Hughes riposted by persuading the flexible Republican Justice Owen Roberts to make a tactical switch. Together, in the spring of 1937, they sustained measures such as Senator Wagner's National Labour Relations Bill—the trade unions' Magna Carta. Hughes also reversed the Court's previous decision against a minimum wage law. Wits repeated, "A switch in time saves nine."[56] Certainly Hughes took the wind out of Roosevelt's sails. So long as it appeared impartial, Americans revered the Supreme Court. They believed in the separation of executive, legislature and judiciary, whereas Roosevelt now seemed bent on achieving a monopoly of power. Isolationist Democrats such as Senator Burton K. Wheeler of Montana saw fearful portents abroad: "It is an easy step from the control of a subservient Congress and the control of the Supreme Court to a modern democracy of a Hitler or a Mussolini."[57]

Obstinate and petulant, the President persevered. But he was thwarted by fate. In the blazing heat of a Washington summer, Joe Robinson, the formidable Senate majority leader to whom Roosevelt had promised the first available seat on the Supreme Court, went home to his dismal apartment in the Methodist Building, across the park from the Capitol, and suffered a fatal heart attack. All Robinson's horse-trading came to naught and the "packing" bill was buried with him. But in their turn the Supreme Court judges, who were mortal as well as malleable, also began to vanish. So Roosevelt was able to pack the Court without risking disaster. He claimed that he had lost the battle but won the war. In fact he had suffered a major reverse. The President had alienated much middle-class opinion and divided his own party. He had fostered an abiding distrust of his policies. And he had suggested that the main threat facing the United States was from the rise of totalitarianism at home rather than abroad.

Other events in 1937 focussed the attention of Americans on their own affairs. Labour was entering a new phase of militancy. Encouraged by the powerful miners' leader John L. Lewis, it came off victorious in a series of bitter and often violent industrial disputes. Lewis ran his own union as though he were a Tammany boss. But he inspired unskilled workers everywhere with his vision of how unionism could transform their lot: it would be like the breaking of dawn after a "dark night."[58] With apostolic fervour Lewis proselytised for the Committee (later Congress) of Industrial Organisation, gaining some three million members in a year. He also ensured that the novel technique of the sit-down strike (as employed in France and elsewhere) proved effective against foes like General Motors.

The world's largest manufacturing company opposed independent trade-unionists with what its workers saw as an "industrial Cheka." Lewis retaliated with ferocity, finesse and tub-thumping oratory that swooped from the sublime to the ridiculous. Ogre-faced, beetle-browed, lion-maned, he hectored allies and enemies alike. The Governor of Michigan, Frank Murphy (formerly Mayor of Detroit), received his heaviest broadside. Murphy came under pressure from the courts to remove the strikers from General Motors' property by force. The Governor was, in fact, an ambitious liberal who, to paraphrase one of his critics, invariably tempered justice with Murphy. Sustained by Roosevelt, he had no intention of spilling car workers' blood. Nevertheless, as Lewis embellished the story in after years, the union leader crushed the Governor by threatening to resist any attempted eviction order in person:

> I shall then walk up to the largest window in the plant, open it, divest myself of my outer raiment, remove my shirt, and bare my bosom. Then when you order your troops to fire, mine will be the first breast that those bullets will strike![59]

Deprived of official support, General Motors settled on reasonable terms.

During 1937 nearly five million workers, some of them women, went on strike and those who occupied their workplaces were particularly successful. Lewis trumpeted, "No tin-hat brigade of goose-stepping vigilantes or Bible-babbling mob of blackguarding corporation scoundrels will prevent the onward march of labor."[60] The giant United States Steel, which produced almost as much steel as Germany, actually granted union recognition without a struggle. Lesser steel companies refused to compromise and bloody conflicts ensued, the worst being the "Memorial Day Massacre" during which the Chicago police killed ten strikers. Conservatives warned that the masses, led by Lewis, were "invading the domain of sovereignty."[61] That invasion sowed trepidation in the hearts of America's middle class. Later in the year, according to Harold Ickes, it became a "psychosis of fear"[62] as America was struck by the so-called "Roosevelt recession."

The recession was partly caused by the higher wages which stronger unions had gained for their members, and the corresponding reduction in profits and investment. But the main reason for rising unemployment, falling farm prices and manufacturing production, and the collapsing stock market (which dropped faster in 1937 than in 1929), was Roosevelt's return to orthodox economics. Urged on by his dour Treasury Secretary Henry Morgenthau Jnr., the President resumed his quest for that ever-receding grail, the balanced budget. He cut federal expenditure by over two billion dollars. This measure may have been financially prudent but it incurred a frightful cost in terms of human misery. About 2.5 million people lost their jobs. Destitution and malnutrition increased. Bread lines lengthened and more children scavenged in refuse bins. Cities such as Cleveland, Chicago and St. Louis found it impossible to relieve distress. Harry Hopkins reported that in 17 southern states people were starving. By the end of 1937 it looked as though 1933 had returned. The New Deal seemed finished.

Roosevelt himself was demoralised by the extent of the tragedy. He was, to be sure, still idolised by the "forgotten man" and the "invisible man" (to employ Ralph Ellison's term for the unseen black American), who gave FDR's picture the "place of honour" in their houses.[63] But better-off citizens were now vilifying the President in scabrous, even pathological, terms. They whispered that he was a syphilitic who deserved to be assassinated. The New Deal was stigmatised as the "Jew Deal." Roosevelt saw himself as the victim of an "unconscious conspiracy" by moneyed interests.[64] He was apprehensive, tetchy, irresolute, a "cornered lion" who "did not know where to put his strength to bring about recovery." He tried to talk the country out of Depression, as Hoover had done, and then waxed furious when members of his cabinet also uttered "Hooverisms." At last, in April 1938, Roosevelt responded to the logic of Keynes and the entreaties of Hopkins. He decided once again to spend his way out of trouble, requesting three billion dollars for relief and public works. This halted the decline though it was not enough to end the Depression. But it scared Morgenthau—Henry the Morgue—"to death."[65]

Roosevelt, by contrast, began to regain self-confidence even though his domestic woes continued throughout 1938. In the spring Congress rejected the President's attempt to reorganise government agencies. This was little more than an administrative reform designed to increase efficiency. But having sown the suspicion that he was an incipient dictator with his Court-packing plan, Roosevelt now reaped a harvest of distrust. No fewer than 108 Democrats helped to vote down the reorganisation scheme in the House of Representatives. Some convinced themselves, in the spirit of Sinclair Lewis's ironically entitled novel *It Can't Happen Here*, that America could be reorganised into fascism. Others feared that the President, having shown himself sympathetic to rampant trade unionism, would pack the administration with blue-collared radicals and Sovietise the United States. A symptom of these anxieties was the setting up, in May 1938, of the House Un-American Activities Committee, whose oafish Texan chairman, Martin Dies, found Communism in every organisation from the Roman Catholic Church to the Boy Scout movement. Hollywood was particularly tainted, and suspicion even fell on Shirley Temple. Roosevelt ridiculed Red scare-mongering. Yet he himself had already authorised Hoover's FBI to keep both Communists and fascists in the United States under surveillance, a move charmingly endorsed by Cordell Hull: "Go ahead and investigate the hell out of those cocksuckers."[66]

Now, stung by the unprecedented defection of so many congressional supporters, Roosevelt attempted to "purge" reactionary Democrats at the 1938 elections. He seemed to be deliberately driving a wedge between conservative Southerners and Tammanyites on the one hand and, on the other, progressive elements in the party whose candidates he openly supported. His intrusion into local politics was much resented and largely abortive. Paradoxically, however, this increased the chances that Roosevelt would be elected for a third term. The more divided the Democrats became, the more it appeared that only Roosevelt could unite them. Similarly he seemed to be the only pilot who could weather the rising international storm.

DISILLUSIONED voters, it is true, suspected Roosevelt of looking for opportunities abroad to disguise his domestic failures. As the prominent Unitarian minister John Haynes Holmes asked, "Is it not inevitable that the President, in good old dictatorial fashion, will take us into war to cover up the mess at home?"[67] Unquestionably Roosevelt saw the political advantages of persuading Americans that "dangers within are less to be feared than dangers without."[68] He also appreciated the advantages of rearmament: the demand for munitions boosted business confidence, though the Depression had had such a traumatic effect that as late as 1941 many industries were reluctant to accept large military orders which required the construction of new plants. But the Depression was a cause of war since war was a way out of the Depression. Also, economic rivalry sharpened national pugnacity. As totalitarian aggression threatened to engulf both Europe and Asia, Roosevelt's emphasis on the external menace seemed reasonable. Its first manifestation was, of course, the "quarantine" speech in October 1937.

Roosevelt had discussed what he would say with his cautious Secretary of State, Cordell Hull. But the President took a somewhat bolder line than that advised by the lisping, high-voiced Tennesseean who, with his black suit and neck-tie and his white hair and eyebrows, looked like the Victorian free-trader he was. Nor did Roosevelt allow himself to be deterred by a huge notice on a warehouse opposite the Chicago platform on which he spoke. In letters ten feet high it said simply "UNDOMINATED"[69] and it had been painted on the orders of Colonel McCormick, the rabidly isolationist publisher of the Chicago *Tribune*. Said to have the finest mind of the thirteenth century, McCormick had been at Groton school with Roosevelt but he now denounced the President as a "panty-waist Hitler."[70] Roosevelt did not mention the Führer or the Duce in his speech. Indeed, they affected to believe that he was referring to Japan or Russia. But the President did say that "the present reign of terror and international lawlessness" had "reached a stage where the very foundations of civilisation were seriously threatened." He also declared that "peace-loving nations must make a concerted effort in opposition."[71]

However, his emphasis was on peace rather than collective security. For this reason most Americans at first took a favourable view of the speech. Isolationists reacted strongly, condemning it as sabre-rattling. The day after the speech William Randolph Hearst wrote, "I think we are on our way to war"; and, although Roosevelt personally reassured him, the newspaper magnate launched a hysterical press campaign against the warmonger in the White House.[72] Hearst and McCormick were on the Right of the loose alliance of isolationists which stretched across the entire political spectrum to pacifists such as Oswald Garrison Villard and socialists such as Norman Thomas on the Left. Their views were various. But they were at one in their refusal to permit what historian Charles Beard called "the killing of American boys in a struggle over the bean crop in Manchuria." Even more dangerous, isolationists considered, were plots to embroil the United States in the conflicts of Europe. Its chancelleries, according to Senator Homer Bone, were full of "megalomaniacs, egomaniacs, and psychopaths, who are literally preparing to dip their hands in blood."[73]

At all costs, isolationists believed, the New World should steer clear of the Old, with its monsters and demons, war-makers and war debtors, totalitarians and imperialists. As early as 1934 the President had warned that America must either prepare to meet the challenge of the rearming dictators or face "another period of long night—such as the Dark Ages."[74] Thus the isolationists had some justification for seeing him as an instinctive internationalist. He did not believe that the American continent could be an island, cutting itself off from the troubles of the rest of the planet. He agreed with Cordell Hull, who thought the isolationists were like "the somnambulist who walks within an inch of a thousand-foot precipice without batting an eye."[75] He was so perturbed by the "hair-trigger times"[76] that he occasionally toyed with hair-trigger expedients. General Hugh Johnson warned that during the New Deal Roosevelt had "shot craps with destiny" to the tune of several billion dollars a year but that this was as nothing to the great gamble of war.[77]

Yet the "quarantine" speech, which sounded like a clarion call to resist Nazi aggression or to impose sanctions on warring Japan, turned out to be little more than the first of a series of "verbal gestures" by which the President essayed to talk his way out of conflict.[78] This was because Roosevelt found he had only meagre support. So, when questioned about the import of his words, he was studiously vague. He gave soft answers and avoided hard actions. He refused to be provoked by the sinking of the *Panay* in December 1937, tamely accepting Japanese apologies and indemnities. Roosevelt was constrained even more by congressional opinion than by public opinion. Not a single senator, it was said, would have supported armed retaliation against Nippon. Moreover, early in 1938 Representative Louis Ludlow's move to restrict the President's war-making power was only just defeated in the House. Even had Roosevelt wanted to treat the *Panay* incident as a *casus belli* (as Henry Morgenthau urged) America's military weakness would have inhibited him. Its powerful navy was essentially an instrument of defence, and in any case the joint Far Eastern fleet manoeuvres which he suggested in order to deter the Japanese were rejected by the British. Furthermore the navy was no compensation for a small, obsolescent air force and an army—really a mounted border constabulary, still equipped with 1903 Springfield rifles—which ranked seventeenth in the world.

Thus Roosevelt sought safety in detachment. He disguised the policy with high-minded appeals for international concord, which annoyed the hard-headed British leader. Roosevelt himself was always irritated by Chamberlain, who had been in the habit of pompously referring to himself as the Chancellor of the Exchequer. Now, as Prime Minister, Chamberlain rebuffed Roosevelt's various charm offensives and peace initiatives with barely concealed contempt. And the President, who was nearly "as myopic in his judgement of European, indeed of world, politics as Stalin," suspected that the devious Premier was engaged in a conspiracy to divide up Europe with the dictators.[79] Nevertheless he unwillingly followed Chamberlain's lead, approving the goals of appeasement "while avoiding any public identification and expressing private doubts about the morality and practicality of Britain's concessions."[80] Like the Prime Minister, the President was indignant but passive when Germany occupied Austria in March 1938. The following month, when Chamberlain sought to detach

Mussolini from Hitler by recognising Italy's conquest of Ethiopia, Roosevelt reluctantly commended the accord. Despite liberal pressure to lift the arms embargo on Spain, Roosevelt (with an eye on the Catholic vote at home) continued to support Britain's policy of non-intervention. The President also proposed an international conference to solve the German Jewish refugee problem, which was held at Evian-les-Bains in July 1938. The American government's real purpose, as a State Department official wrote, lay in "forestalling attempts to have the immigration laws liberalized." This was duly achieved by all the 32 nations represented. Wringing their hands but closing their doors against more refugees, their delegates took part in a hypocritical charade which the Nazi leadership interpreted as a back-handed endorsement of its anti-Semitic policies. Roosevelt, who had made Jews a feature of America's governmental landscape, bore a full measure of responsibility for what has been called the "Jewish Munich."[81]

As the Nazis prepared to assault Czechoslovakia the President remained silent. Privately he inveighed against international desperadoes but he felt that America could do nothing except wait for Europe to blow itself up and then help to pick up the pieces. He also told the cabinet that England and France would betray Czechoslovakia and then "wash the blood from their Judas Iscariot hands."[82] Yet he informed the British Ambassador that he would be the first to cheer if pressure on Czechoslovakia from the European democracies bore fruit. He sent Chamberlain his famous cable—"Good man"—when the Prime Minister embarked on his final, doomed attempt to wrest peace with honour from Hitler. The President rejoiced at the outcome and tried to "share in the credit."[83] Even when doubts set in he declared himself "not one bit upset over the final result of Munich" since it opened up a better world prospect.[84]

All over the world, of course, jubilation was quickly overtaken by shame. Roosevelt soon distanced himself from the Munich settlement and he raised another 300 million dollars for rearmament. The President was horrified by *Kristallnacht,* the mass attack on German Jews in November 1938, and recalled his new Ambassador to Berlin, Hugh Wilson. Like his British counterpart, Sir Nevile Henderson, Wilson was a champion of appeasement. He admired aspects of Nazism, such as the "Strength through Joy" movement. He denounced America's "Jewish controlled press" for its "hymn of hatred" against Germany.[85] He favoured Munich, arguing that it was unrealistic for the democracies to defend Czechoslovakia's borders and making the point by flying to Prague in a Messerschmitt borrowed from the Luftwaffe. Yet Roosevelt only envisaged Wilson's withdrawal as a temporary measure and would have sent him back in March 1939 had not Hitler chosen that month to complete his occupation of Czechoslovakia.

That April, following the British and French example, the United States recognised Franco's regime in Spain. Roosevelt also issued a further peace appeal. In it he reviewed the Asian as well as the European situation, deploring Japan's slamming of the Chinese Open Door, which had brought only mild American retaliation in the shape of a loan to Chiang Kai-shek. And the President offered to arrange a disarmament conference if only aggressor nations would renounce the use of force. Roosevelt's overture was largely directed at his domestic constituency but he cannot have anticipated Hitler's brutal retort. The Führer dismissed the President as a "contemptible creature" and asked why, if he believed that all problems could be solved at the conference table, the United States had not joined the League of Nations. Hitler also stressed that he was merely righting wrongs in Europe, an argument craftily calculated to win the hearts of American isolationists.

One of their leaders, Senator Hiram Johnson of California, gloated that Hitler had won the argument. The President's aim, in the Senator's view, was "to knock down two dictators in Europe so that one may be firmly implanted in America."[86] Johnson also said that Jews and Britons wanted to fight to the last American and he helped to stop Roosevelt from revising the Neutrality Acts. The President was thus prevented from giving significant aid to the democracies in the event of war. In the summer of 1939 he also found himself unable to persuade William Borah, the so-called "Lion of Idaho" but in fact another senatorial ostrich, that war was imminent. At a conference in the White House Borah rejected all such warnings. He said that he had not only got better information than the State Department but that he had paid for it. What this meant, it transpired, was that he subscribed to *The Week,* a London scandal sheet edited by Claud Cockburn, who often breached Britain's wall of official secrecy but who freely admitted (in his later autobiography) to inventing stories which mirrored his Communist convictions. Even more remarkable than Borah's simple faith in *The Week* was the fact that the President, too, relied heavily on this titillating but tainted source.

What went on inside Roosevelt's head kept even his intimates guessing. Strangers could not penetrate his baffling façade of affability at all. When Charles Lindbergh met the President in 1939 he felt as though he were "talking to a person who was wearing a mask."[87] Nevertheless Lindbergh and his fellow isolationists were convinced of Roosevelt's belligerence. They had some evidence: responding to public opinion, the President was openly hostile to Japan and applied trade sanctions in July 1939. However, he kept the fleet firmly in San Diego for fear of provoking military reprisals. Furthermore Roosevelt also reflected the views of those 94 per cent of his compatriots who, in September 1939, wished to avoid becoming involved in a European war. Believing as he did that the presidency was a place of moral leadership, he could certainly have given "a strong presidential lead [in opposing totalitarianism] between 1937 and 1939."[88] Instead, despite his personal convictions, he was willing to face humiliation in order to keep America out of the front line. After *Kristallnacht* the feisty little Mayor of New York, Fiorello La Guardia, appointed a 12-man police detail to protect the German consulate: it consisted entirely of Jews and was led by Captain Max Finkelstein. By contrast the President cut all references to proper names, including Germany, Hitler and Goebbels, from a radio address given by his blunt Secretary of the Interior on the subject of Nazi persecution of the Jews: Roosevelt did not want Harold Ickes to say anything to "arouse Germany."

In fact, Ickes was quite outspoken enough to enrage the Nazis and to embarrass the State Department, whose "tender consideration of the dictatorships" he deplored.[89] He further annoyed Cordell Hull (as well as irritating the President and most of the cabinet) by his stubborn refusal, despite many months of pressure, to permit the sale of helium to Germany. America alone produced significant quantities of this buoyant, non-combustible gas, which Germany needed to keep its Zeppelin air fleet in commercial service. Hydrogen, traditionally used in airships, had proved lethal as a lifting agent. Alone it could not be ignited: dirigibles struck by lightning had crackled with tongues of St. Elmo's fire (sparks even spurting from crewmen's fingertips) and yet they had survived. But hydrogen leaking into oxygen made an explosive mixture and during the 1920s and early '30s American, British, French and Italian airships had suffered a series of catastrophes, many of them bursting into flames like incendiary bombs. The German *Graf Zeppelin,* however, had broken records crossing the Atlantic in 1928, had gone on to circumnavigate the world in 1929 and had travelled to the Arctic in 1931—voyages partially financed, for their news value, by William Randolph Hearst. Thereafter it engaged in a profitable transatlantic service, covering a million miles without accident and establishing itself as the leviathan of the skies.

Vaster than any battleship but lighter than air, the *Graf Zeppelin* was 775 feet long and 100 feet wide and supported a gondola which was fitted out like a luxury liner. It had lounges, observation decks, a smart restaurant, cabins complete with showers, even a sealed smoking-room. It flew with uncanny smoothness and silence. Wine glasses did not have to be secured on tables and passengers could hear sounds from the ground, as often as not cheering from people (and not only Germans) afflicted with "Zeppelinomania." The dirigible did not resemble a bird but, in the words of its creator, Hugo Eckener, "a fabulous silvery fish, floating quietly in the ocean of the air . . . [which] when it appeared far away, lighted by the sun, seemed to be coming from another world and to be returning there like a dream."[90] Inside the balloon's glossy skin—in the belly of the whale—the Zeppelin was equally fantastic. On an early flight Arthur Koestler ventured into its interior. Crossing the high central catwalk, he found himself in a space more cavernous than a cathedral "filled with darkness, the smell of bitter almonds, and a dull, subdued sound as if invisible bats were lazily flapping their wings." The noise came from the fluttering of gas bags, which hung upright in rows like enormous pears amid "a labyrinth of girders, rafters, lattices, trusses and buttresses, a jungle of steel and aluminium."[91] The smell was caused by the presence of hydrocyanic gas. It was a trace of the fatal weakness in the behemoth's bladder. It was the whiff of impending holocaust.

However, the addition to Germany's airship fleet which was launched in 1936, the *Hindenburg,* showed no sign of weakness. It seemed, indeed, to confirm that airships were as powerful as they looked—an aerial force of the future. The *Hindenburg* was the largest flying machine ever built. It outdid all previous Zeppelins in speed and sophistication. Although never admired by Hitler (who preferred Junkers and Messerschmitts), it became an emblem of Nazism. It dropped millions of propaganda leaflets from the air, played "Deutschland Über Alles" from its powerful loudspeakers, flaunted huge swastikas on its tail fins. During ten successful transatlantic journeys this great argosy of the heavens established its ascendancy even in New York. Suspended over the streets at night it seemed like a magic apparition, its shiny, cigar-shaped hull reflecting the glare of searchlights and its "contours exaggerated by the contrast of light and darkness."[92]

Even on its final voyage, in May 1937, everything appeared auspicious. When the 36 passengers and 61 crew members set off from Frankfurt the band played "Ein Feste Burg." They got a wonderfully clear view of Cologne Cathedral. The *Hindenburg* glided serenely through Atlantic storms and, flying low over icebergs off Newfoundland, it became wreathed in rainbows. Ships saluted it in Boston harbour and drivers stopped their cars to gaze and wave and honk their horns. On the Empire State Building, tallest of what looked from the air like nails embedded in the sidewalks of New York, people could be seen taking photographs of the airship. Although delayed by thunderstorms, the *Hindenburg* seemed set to make a perfect landfall at Lakehurst, New Jersey. But as the mooring lines were dropped from 120 feet there was a muffled bang from the vicinity of the top fin. Through the dusk and drizzle spectators on the ground saw a dull glow which almost immediately turned into a fireball visible ten miles away. In the famous words of radio reporter Herbert Morrison:

> It is bursting into flames. This is terrible! This is one of the worst catas-trophes in the world! The flames are 500 feet into the sky. It is a terrific crash, ladies and gentlemen. It is in smoke and flames now. Oh the humanity! Those passengers! I can't talk, ladies and gentlemen. Honest, it is a mass of smoking wreckage.[93]

For those on board the *Hindenburg* "it was like a scene from a medieval picture of hell."[94] Yet nearly two-thirds of them survived, for the flames spiralled upwards, over the gondola and through the colossal carapace, bursting from the nose of the ship like a giant blow-torch. In just 32 sec-onds the *Hindenburg* became a scorched and twisted skeleton on the soft earth. Today it seems impossibly remote, the relic of a primitive monster too cumbersome to escape extinction. At the time it seemed as if all that was needed to revive the cause of the airship was copious transfusions of helium.

Although many people, including Hitler, suspected that the *Hinden-burg* was the victim of sabotage, a more likely explanation for the fire was that a ruptured gas bag had been ignited as a result of the electrical storm. Hugo Eckener was determined that its new sister ship, named the *Graf Zeppelin II,* should not suffer the same fate. Tall, white-whiskered, bow-tied, grey-suited, invariably smoking a pungent black Brazilian cheroot, Eckener was hailed as the "Columbus of the Air"[95] and he testified impres-sively before the Senate Military Affairs Committee. Congress was per-suaded that Germany would employ airships only for peaceful purposes and it authorised the sale of helium to Germany. But in 1938 Ickes inter-vened, arguing that the US Navy itself regarded airships as weapons of war. His stand provoked such a heated debate that, he quipped, "In future we'd better spell helium with two *l*'s!"[96] Eckener himself, a "fine, hearty, jolly, old man"[97] whom Ickes admired for his open dislike of the Nazis, argued his case with the Secretary of the Interior. But when Ickes insisted that helium could help to sustain the German war machine Eckener retorted angrily: "Yes, if we were German idiots, we could also try fighting with medieval swords instead of machine-guns, but you wouldn't expect us to be such fools."[98]

Eckener was right. In 1940 Germany broke up its airships and melted down the metal for use in fighter aircraft. The United States did the same: as a British expert observed, "Aeroplanes breed like rabbits, airships like elephants."[99] On the other hand, Ickes was not wholly wrong. Although bound up in the New Deal and loth to spend money on arms when Americans were starving, the Secretary of the Interior recognised that Hitler was aggression personified. He perceived that sooner or later America would have to abandon isolationism, face reality and fight for its life. Ickes spearheaded the attack on Nazism. He branded fascist countries outposts of the Ku Klux Klan, "Nations in Nightshirts."[100] Knowing much less about war than the President, the Secretary of the Interior divined that Nazi Germany would use any weapons that came to hand, even obsolete ones. So it proved in the summer of 1939, when the *Graf Zeppelin II* was turned into a spy ship. It was filled with electronic equipment and flown high over the North Sea to analyse British radar transmissions. Held up by hydrogen, the dirigible was an explosion waiting to happen. It could well have ended its days a charred ruin like the *Hindenburg,* another "mournful symbol" of what Hugo Eckener "expected to be the final outcome for Germany."[101]

XXI

THE FÜHRER'S PATH TO WAR

NINE months before its fiery demise, the *Hindenburg* took part in the most spectacular propaganda exercise ever staged by the Nazis. This was the Berlin Olympic Games, held during the first half of August 1936. On the rainy opening day the airship was cheered to an echo as it cruised over the city and the nearby athletics stadium trailing a giant Olympic banner. Its five linked rings, the multicoloured insignia of international unity, contrasted starkly with the black swastikas, emblems of aggressive nationalism, emblazoned on the airship's tail fins. Yet this juxtaposition, multiplied a million-fold in the forest of flags on the ground, reflected the paradoxical nature of the eleventh Olympiad. It also suggested, to those with eyes to see, the barefaced duplicity of Nazism.

The Games, though revived in 1896 by Baron Pierre de Coubertin to propagate the Prussian style of physical education and the English tradition of schoolboy sports, had long been consecrated to ideals of global harmony. It was for this reason that Hitler had previously denounced them as "an invention of Jews and Freemasons."[1] Once in power, though, the Führer saw the Olympics as "a splendid chance of enhancing our prestige abroad."[2] Mounted with appropriate pageantry, they could be a brilliant advertisement for the Nazi State and the Nordic race. At least part of this plan was thwarted by the prowess of a young black American athlete, Jesse Owens, who for a while stole the spotlight. "The bright glow of romance," said his home-town newspaper, "hovers over such a feat."[3] However, the Olympiad did realise much of the Führer's fell purpose. According to the French Ambassador to Berlin, André François-Poncet, it was "a great moment, a climax of sorts, if not the apotheosis of Hitler and his Third Reich."[4]

Certainly preparations for the event were made on a "Wagnerian scale."[5] The Führer personally authorised the construction of a new stadium, at the Grunewald race-course, to hold more than 100,000 people. At his insistence glass and concrete were shunned in favour of Franconian limestone, Saxon porphyry, Württemberg travertine, basalt from the Eifel, dolomite from Anröchte, granite and marble from Silesia—Hitler's concentration camps were often strategically situated near quarries. The complex surrounding this vast crucible was equally extravagant: the spacious assembly area known as the May Field; the swimming-pool flanked by steeply rising stands; the fine gymnastic amphitheatre; the slender 243-foot tower for the 16-ton Olympic bell inscribed with Schiller's line, "I summon the youth of the world." Monuments to international sport, the Olympic edifices were also a potent and uncompromising expression of Nazism. The same was true of the Olympic village at Döberitz. A signal improvement on the accommodation pioneered for the Los Angeles Games of 1932, it included 160 tile-roofed bungalows nestling amid woods and lakes in a landscape specially sprayed to get rid of the mosquitoes. Here the male athletes were both housed and pampered. Their hosts catered for national tastes in sleeping as well as eating, providing mattresses for Americans, duvets for Swiss, tatami mats for Japanese. But, built by army engineers, the village had a double purpose: after the Games it became an infantry training centre.

Berlin itself, as the American novelist Thomas Wolfe observed, was "transformed into a kind of annex" to the Olympic stadium.[6] Prior to this metamorphosis the capital had been drab and pinched, full of dilapidated buildings, run-down enterprises and dingy shops besieged by food queues. It was so depressed that even New York seemed buoyant by comparison, as a Berliner enthralled by Times Square observed:

> The dazzling display of flickering advertisements, figures and names, flashing and disappearing in uninterrupted glitter, was bewildering— like a mirage, a fairy-tale of plenty. Poor old Europe—fortunate America! The difference between the Old and the New World seems symbolised in this mélange of colour and light.[7]

Now Berlin sought to outshine New York. It was cleaned, primped, painted, polished and swathed in miles of banners and bunting. The cosmetic process began along the main routes into the city. Houses facing the railway tracks had uniform window decorations and each mainline station was festooned with 700 square yards of swastika flags and 500 square yards of Olympic flags, as well as 4,200 metres of oakleaf garlands and 50 gigantic wreaths. The streets and squares of Berlin, sprouting green, loudspeakered flagpoles at regular intervals, were tricked out in similar fashion. None was more magnificent than the so-called Via Triumphalis, which led from the Lustgarten through Unter den Linden, beneath the Brandenburg Gate (itself bristling with flags and garlands), along the broad avenues of the Tiergarten to the Olympic stadium. For the benefit of visitors the capital was filled with uniformed interpreters. The legion of prostitutes, which had dwindled since the dissolute days of Weimar, was reinforced by recruits summoned from the provinces. But the city was purged of pickpockets and petty criminals. To disprove tales of Nazi censorship, alien journals and books once consigned to the flames reappeared in shop windows, while Julius Streicher's poisonous newspaper *Der Stürmer* was nowhere to be seen.

Furthermore the President of the International Olympic Committee, Comte Henri de Baillet-Latour, persuaded an angry and reluctant Hitler to take down anti-Semitic signs. Foreigners had been shocked by photographs of the entrance to the Winter Olympics at Garmisch-Partenkirchen which bore a prominent notice, "Jews Forbidden Entry."[8] Abroad consciences were pricked. There was some hostility to British participation in the Games; many feared it would be used to persuade the German people that Hitler's anti-Semitism was "condoned by the world" and "as a chance of Nazi glorification."[9] The *Daily Herald* made play with a book written by the Nazis' chief athletics coach, Kurt Muench, who acknowledged that "non-political, so-called 'neutral' sportsmen are unthinkable in Hitler's state" and described Jews as a "devilish power in the life of the people."[10] But generally opposition was muted in Britain. The Labour MP Philip Noel-Baker was persuaded by his fellow ex-Olympic athlete Harold Abrahams, himself a Jew, to drop his attack on the Berlin Games in *The Times* (though he did protest in the *Manchester Guardian*) because opinion in Britain was "more pro-Nazi than it has been at any time."[11] In the United States, however, there was an outspoken campaign to prevent American athletes from competing "under the Swastika." Its supporters pointed out that German Jews, banned from public swimming-pools and sports centres, could neither train nor compete on equal terms. "Despoiled of goodwill, sportsmanship and fair-play, the Games can have no meaning except as a prestige-building enterprise for the Nazi regime."[12]

In order to undermine American attempts to boycott the Olympics, the Nazis made small concessions. For example, a few token Jews, including the foil champion Helene Mayer, who looked every inch an Aryan, were selected to represent Germany. The "chosen handful," as the *Manchester Guardian* put it, were "paraded before foreign eyes, food for the credulous."[13] Yet such gestures were effective. So was Goebbels' charge that transatlantic protests about Nazi anti-Semitism were consummate hypocrisy. Athletic apartheid was as prevalent thoughout the United States as other forms of racism—though, according to a smug piece of special pleading in the *New York Times,* few literate Americans "made a philosophy of the thing." Instead they practised racial discrimination in "the good, old thick-headed, prejudiced, irrational human fashion."[14] It was doubtless in this fashion that Avery Brundage, President of the American Olympic Association, allowed himself to be convinced that it was not the Nazis but proponents of the boycott who were trying "to use the Games as a political weapon." He concluded, indeed, that the boycott was part of a vicious Jewish-Communist conspiracy and that the Games must go on (as the parrot phrase had it), to ensure that politics were kept out of sport. Brundage was accused of being "a Jew hater and Jew baiter."[15] Without question he was hopelessly bamboozled by the Nazis. Yet, as the British Ambassador Sir Eric Phipps noted, they would never be able to succeed in their aim of deceiving *everybody all the time.* "[16] Although, like other Germans, SA men were under orders to behave politely to all guests irrespective of their race, even Hitler could not stop them from getting drunk in the streets of his Potemkin city. There they bawled: "When the Olympics are past, the Jews will be gassed."[17]

Such proleptic horrors were eclipsed by the glittering rituals, many of them invented or elaborated by the Nazis, which led up to the Olympic Games. The most sensational was the torch run. This was a relay of 3,075 athletes, each carrying the "sacred fire"[18] one kilometre towards Berlin from the starting-point at Olympia in the Peloponnese. Here Nordic immigrants, Nazis maintained, had founded the ancient Greek games. Here, on 20 July 1936, the flame was kindled from the sun's rays by a posse of modern Greek virgins—who were perhaps as synthetic as the ceremony itself. Visiting dignitaries listened to a long message, delivered by a Greek orator, from Baron de Coubertin. He was happily able to discern the outlines of a new Europe emerging from "thick morning mist" and recommended for its guidance "an eternal Hellenism that has not ceased to light the way of centuries."[19]

Among the onlookers was Leni Riefenstahl, who was making a Nazi-sponsored film of the Olympiad. She found the torch-lighting rite dull and the torch-bearer inauthentic—instead of gym shorts, she insisted, he should have worn "a classical loincloth."[20] So she created her own reality, projecting it on to the world in her superb but sinister documentary *Olympia* (1938). Riefenstahl staged key episodes such as the flame-kindling ceremony—accompanied in the film by music which conjures up "the magic fire lit by Loge at Wotan's command in *Die Walküre*"[21]—specially for the camera. It dwelt lovingly on the straining sinews of the torch-bearers, particularly those of the young athlete Anatol Dobriansky, who looked so like a Greek god that Riefenstahl, herself "as pretty as a swastika,"[22] virtually kidnapped him for a brief affair. The lens also focussed on a hauntingly romantic odyssey, set against an eerie backdrop of moonlit sea, dusky mountains and Delphic remains, in which lone runners loped towards the German capital, each clutching his portion of the eternal flame. Actually, the runners were almost always accompanied. And, once, one of the steel magnesium flares (made, ironically, by Krupps) went out, so that the next torch had to be lit with a match. This disaster was concealed. The advancing flame, its progress punctuated by solemn ceremonies and pro-Nazi demonstrations (notably in Vienna), and monitored by stirring radio broadcasts, captured the world's imagination. It seemed like the coming of the Grail.

The excitement was further whipped up in Berlin itself by a hectic succession of displays, parades, salutes, fanfares, flag-raisings, wreath-layings and the like, each performance accompanied by interminable renderings of the Horst Wessel song and "Deutschland Über Alles." At 1:00 P.M. on 1 August a gathering of 28,000 "Aryan" youths greeted the Olympian flame at the Lustgarten. They were drawn up in fanatically precise ranks and harangued by Goebbels—"Holy flame, burn, burn, and never go out!"[23] During the afternoon the flame followed in the wake of Hitler's cavalcade, a phalanx of black Mercedes-Benzes which drove along the Via Triumphalis, flanked by frenzied crowds and ramrod-stiff troops, to the Grunewald stadium. As the Führer made his entrance it exploded with *"Heil"*'s, bellowed from more than 100,000 throats. Attired in his brown uniform, Hitler cut a more virile, modern figure than members of the Olympic committee, who were spatted, top-hatted, frock-coated and gold-chained. He presided with simple dignity over more pageantry, notably the march-past of the competitors.

They were a kaleidoscope of colour: Greeks leading in their blue and white national costume; Egyptians in red fezzes; Danes and Poles wearing scarlet blazers; Indians in silver-grey coats and turbans; Germans at the rear, all immaculate in white. Each of the 153 teams acknowledged Hitler in its own way. The Americans clapped their straw hats over their hearts and turned their eyes right but (by tradition) refused to dip their flag. The goose-stepping Bulgarians gave the Nazi salute. The French essayed the Olympic salute, which resembled it, and were applauded for their apparent obeisance to the Führer. The British did not give the Nazi salute, earning themselves a rebuke from the historian Arthur Bryant: they should have "gone a little out of their way to make this friendly gesture to their hosts."[24] (Chamberlain's government evidently agreed, since it seems to have "played a leading role in forcing the English [football] team to give the Nazi salute in the Berlin stadium in 1938.")[25] After official speechifying, Hitler declared the Games open. Flags flew, guns thundered, thousands of released pigeons fluttered into the sky, and Richard Strauss conducted the Olympic Hymn which he had composed specially for the occasion. As its echoes died away a slim, blond, white-clad athlete appeared carrying the Olympic fire. He ran along the red cinder track and up the grey steps to a marble daïs holding an enormous brazier. Then, after a dramatic pause, he lit the flame. It was, the German News Service remarked, 22 years to the day since the "torch of war"—the war to end war—had blazed into light. The present "peaceful combat," Germany hoped, would help to achieve "universal understanding among the world's peoples."[26] A symbol of that hope was the presentation to Hitler by the aged Greek peasant Spiridon Loues, who had won the 1896 marathon, of an olive branch from the sacred grove in Olympia. The Führer, preparing to depart amid further flourishes and pyrotechnics, seemed much moved by the gift.

He was also thrilled, once the Games began, by the German victories, beaming and slapping his thigh each time a medal was won. To secure these results the athletes had been meticulously prepared, though without regard to the Olympic code of amateurism. The Reich had financed the training of many competitors, such as the women's figure-skating champion who had been coached for over a year at the ballet school of the Munich opera. The German equestrian team had practised for 18 months on a full-scale replica of the exceptionally difficult Olympic cross-country course—and duly took the gold medal. But no State subsidy could create an innate talent like that of "the hero of these Games,"[27] Jesse Owens. He sprinted with the fluid grace of a panther, gliding over the ground as though he were dancing across hot coals. He was "as beautiful as an animated statue of bronze."[28] His seemingly effortless triumph in the 100 metres immediately established him as one of the "immortals of athletics."[29] Better still, three more gold medals did not alter the smiling modesty of his demeanour—he had trained under Jim Crow and learned humility from Booker T. Washington. Seeking to capitalise on his popularity, Reemtsma, Germany's largest tobacco firm, used pictures of Owens to advertise its cigarettes. But, though he was worshipped by the crowd, Owens was reportedly snubbed by the Führer. In fact, having congratulated the first winning German athletes, Hitler was asked not to show such favouritism. Thereafter he congratulated no one in public. However, when Baldur von Schirach, Reich Youth Leader, suggested that Hitler might strengthen the mood of internationalism by having his picture taken with Owens, the enraged Führer apparently responded: "Do you really think that I will allow myself to be photographed shaking hands with a negro?"[30]

Owens was a particular affront since his superlative athleticism made nonsense of Nazi theories of Nordic supremacy—though even American coaches were apt to explain that black runners excelled because they were "closer to the primitive."[31] But the agonies and ecstasies caused by non-Aryan victories in general showed that the Olympiad was not so much a global festival of sport as a contest between rival nations. George Orwell thought it inevitable that events like the Berlin Games would lead to "orgies of hatred."[32] Yet the Nazi regime deliberately made matters worse, stirring up chauvinistic passions until the Olympic stadium seethed, and sometimes erupted, like a volcano. The German spectators had much to acclaim since their team won far more medals—33 gold, 26 silver and 30 bronze—than that of any other country. The Nazis took the credit. With shining eyes Goebbels declared that, "The national spirit created by this régime was responsible for the German victories."[33] His opinion was widely held and so was its corollary, that athletic failure was a mark of national decline. Commenting on Britain's pitiful performance (4 gold medals, 7 silver and 3 bronze), *The Times* worried about the decadence of the imperial race. The head of the Foreign Office, Sir Robert Vansittart, reckoned that it was "going to make us look like a C³ nation."[34]

Vansittart was in Berlin on a diplomatic "busman's holiday" and, like other distinguished visitors, he was subjected to a barrage of hospitality designed to reinforce the message of the Games. The Nazi leaders vied with one another to mount the most dazzling entertainments. Ribbentrop gave his guests a feast of roast ox and vintage champagne. Göring, who had recently told the German people that the shortage of fats was a blessing because they were inclined to eat too much, was more extravagant still. In the grounds of his palatial new Air Ministry in the Leipziger Platz he built a fantastic mixture of funfair and fairy-tale village (complete with outdoor cafés groaning with food) which was suddenly illuminated by rooftop searchlights. Goebbels invited 2,000 guests to his "Sommerfest," held on the idyllic Peacock Island, in the Wannsee, which was linked to the mainland by a specially built pontoon bridge. The ancient trees were transformed into huge chandeliers, with lights in the shape of butterflies, and the firework display sounded like an artillery bombardment. "For half an hour the German Himmel blazed with coloured light," Chips Channon recorded, "and the noise was deafening. When at last the fireworks were over, the skies were still light for some time before the darkness dared to steal back and defy Goebbels." Nothing like these revels had been seen since the days of Nero, remarked Channon, though, on second thought, he decided that they resembled "the fêtes of Claudius, but with the cruelty left out."[35]

Many other visitors, taken in by the ostentation or by the camouflage associated with the Olympics, were inclined to admire Hitler's Germany. As William Shirer recorded, some Americans disbelieved the hostile accounts of foreign correspondents like himself, preferring to accept the evidence of their own senses. They were "favourably impressed by the Nazi 'set-up.'"[36] Britons returning home after the Games wrote to the newspapers praising the "community spirit" fostered by "that remarkable man of vision who directs the destinies of Germany."[37] The French press, too, acknowledged that the organisation of the Games was proof of German efficiency, prosperity, discipline and strength. Doubtless these characteristics were intimidating but they did not necessarily presage war. Indeed, at the Games Hitler not only made a successful bid for international respectability, he plausibly presented himself to the world as a man of peace. But by no means everyone was fooled by the "Olympic truce."[38] Thomas Wolfe said that the Berlin Games symbolised the new collective might of a people "desperately ill with some dread malady of the soul."[39] Sir Eric Phipps was confirmed in his opinion that there was "no such thing as sport for sport's sake in Germany. There is only sport for the sake of war."[40]

War was certainly on Hitler's mind as the Olympiad drew to a close. The final ceremonies, it is true, foreshadowed a time of peace which he thought would last for at least four years, when Japan would act as host to the Games. His view was echoed at the valedictory climax in Berlin. In the darkness the Olympic flame guttered out and dead silence reigned around the stadium, broken by a deep spectral voice, as though God were addressing the multitude over the loudspeakers: "I summon the youth of the world to Tokyo." But after the Olympics had been held in Japan, Hitler told Speer, "for all time to come, they will take place in Germany."[41] In 1937 the Führer laid the foundation stone at the Nuremberg site of this perpetual home for the Games, work on which was still continuing as late as 1944. Like other architecture with which Hitler was associated, it was designed on a scale appropriate to "the ruler of the whole world."[42] As a preliminary to global conquest, the Führer retired to his eyrie at Berchtesgaden immediately after the Games and formulated a plan to speed up the evolution of a self-sufficient and rearmed Reich. Within four years, he said, "the German economy must be fit for war."[43]

To this end the Führer put Hermann Göring in charge of a new Four Year Plan, Germany's equivalent to the Soviet drive for military and industrial might. Göring's task was to secure the Nazi grip on the economy, to reduce Germany's dependence on imports by creating home-produced substitutes and to rearm for all-out conflict. Schacht, who had done so much to combat the Depression, was outraged by the appointment. He said that Göring understood nothing whatever about economics—whereas, he supposedly informed Papen, Hitler's grasp of the subject was at least "that of a sixth-form schoolboy."[44] Others, then and later, have been equally inclined to dismiss Göring as a bad joke, a homicidal buffoon whose contribution to the development of the Third Reich need not be taken too seriously. Historians have often drawn him larger than life-size, a figure of monstrous geniality and baroque tastes, "a manicured mountain of perfumed flab."[45] According to a recent account, Göring was a flamboyant mixture of Nero and Al Capone, with the emphasis on fiddling and tax-fiddling.

Göring's antics as the Reich Master of the Hunt and of Forests seemed especially to be the stuff of black comedy. He imported unusual creatures, conserving elk and cherishing bison who, though generally sullen towards visitors, gave "the impression that they knew Göring personally."[46] While people were being sent to concentration camps, Göring issued stringent regulations to prevent the suffering of animals. He appeared in a variety of bizarre hunting costumes, complete with hunting horn, hunting knife and Scandinavian spear, when showing off the delights of Schorfheide. This was the region of forests, lakes and moors north-east of Berlin in which Göring chose to create Carinhall, a combination of hunting lodge and mausoleum for his first wife. At the very time when Göring was exhorting his countrymen to tighten their belts, it was enlarged on a pharaonic scale and furnished with Babylonian opulence—he later contemplated moving the palace of Minos from Crete to Carinhall. Visitors, seeing him in this setting, understandably waxed satirical. Sir Eric Phipps, who reckoned that Göring would probably reach the apogee of his career upon the scaffold, portrayed him as a kind of murderous Michelin man bouncing around in a Gothic horror show.

It must be said that Hitler's most powerful lieutenant lent himself to this kind of caricature. He embroidered the feats which had admittedly won him the *Pour le Mérite* and command of the Richthofen Squadron during the First World War. Having been shot in the groin at the time of the Beer Hall Putsch, he succumbed to morphine addiction during the treatment that followed. He had spells in a Swedish lunatic asylum, where he developed paranoid fears about the Jews: in one hallucination he screamed that Abraham was "driving a red-hot nail into his back."[47] Once the Nazis gained power, Göring embarked on a course which would make him the greatest plunderer of Europe since Napoleon. He acquired money, land, furniture, precious stones, works of art and other treasures in astonishing abundance. Göring soothed himself by running cascades of gems through his podgy fingers—his hands, noted America's Under Secretary of State Sumner Welles, "were shaped like the digging paws of a badger."[48] Peroxided, powdered and rouged, he dressed up (or, rather, was dressed by his valet) in comic opera uniforms, green silk pantaloons, violet kimonos and purple togas, holding the ensemble together with jewelled brooches, gold sashes and gem-encrusted belts. Göring was a tailor's dream, not least because, alternately gorging on sausages, pastries and whipped cream, and dieting to reduce his sweating 20-stone bulk, he required his clothes to be constantly altered. Moreover, new orders and medals, for which he frankly lusted, were always being added to the constellation of stars and spangles which adorned his person—Ribbentrop called him "that Christmas tree."[49]

As this suggests, Göring appeared to wear his heart upon his sleeve, or on his chest. His peacock vanity was so artlessly displayed that he seemed sincere. His Falstaffian bonhomie was paraded with such gusto that he gave the impression of being an honest rogue. Some visitors to Berlin even took him at his own valuation—as Hitler's paladin. Lady Londonderry told him that he was "a Siegfried of modern times."[50] Other Britons, notably Phipps's successor as ambassador, Sir Nevile Henderson, found Göring in certain respects "sympathetic" and "attractive."[51] Clearly he was more amenable than the Führer himself. As another British diplomat remarked, "Göring was preferable because, unlike Hitler, he ate, drank, and slept with women just like a normal human being."[52] At the time the *Manchester Guardian* described him as "moderate and responsible."[53] Even historians have pronounced Göring "by far the most reasonable of the Nazi leaders."[54]

In fact his air of affable moderation, tempered by the occasional rough sally, was a pose. Göring's role was to present himself as the acceptable face of Nazism. But he was a romantic nationalist who had sold his soul to the Führer and he could barely mask the dark side of a nature that was cunning, cruel and corrupt. Hitler's interpreter, Paul Schmidt, who often translated for Göring, noted the diplomatic adroitness concealed behind his elephantine manoeuvres. Göring handled delicate situations "with a finesse which the German people would not have believed possible in this swashbuckling heavy-weight."[55] Göring was a ruthless anti-Semite, though he sometimes tried to disguise the fact or to make light of it: he once suggested that Jews should share enclosures at Schorfheide with animals that were "damnably like [them]—the elk too has a hooked nose."[56]

When he became Reichsmarschall the truth about him was engraved in stone over the porch at Carinhall—his coat of arms featured "a mailed fist grasping a bludgeon."[57] Hitler admired Göring's brutal energy and said that after talking to him he felt he had taken a bath in steel. The Führer indulged Göring's "Renaissance"[58] vices, especially ambition, cynicism and greed. He turned a blind eye to Göring's crimes, notably theft, blackmail and extortion. He loaded him with honours and offices. By 1936 Göring was, among other things, President of the Reichstag, Prime Minister of Prussia, commander of the Luftwaffe, boss of a huge clandestine telephone-tapping agency (known as his "Research Office") and overlord of the German economy. Far from being a reasonable or moderate figure, let alone an independent one, Göring was Belial to Hitler's Lucifer.

As such Göring had no scruples about ensuring that the German people gave up butter for guns. Nor did he hesitate to promote autarky, the ultimate form of protectionism. For a nation still in the shadow of the Depression, the policy seemed reasonable since it held out the promise that Germany could stand on its own feet. However, it was designed not just to defend against economic blockade but to prepare for war, which, by sharpening Germany's hunger for raw materials, it made more likely. Schacht opposed autarky as a form of self-strangulation. But Hitler supported Göring. The latter was willing to make any sacrifice to forge a *Wehrwirtschaft*, a war economy, so that Germany could "gain a *Weltreich*,"[59] a world empire. Relying on its own resources, Germany became more than ever a realm of the *ersatz*. From Ruhr coal came synthetic oil, petrol, rubber, ammonia, soap, even (it was claimed)[60] butter. Leather was made from fish skin. Clothes were fabricated from wood pulp. Even when it was cheaper to import, say, high-grade iron ore from Sweden, inferior German minerals were preferred, which involved the construction of new smelting plants. Schacht despaired about "the dissolution of all economic order and the introduction of jungle morality."[61] Economic autarky, he declared, led to "mental autarky,"[62] a narrowing of minds and an increasing estrangement between the great powers. Schacht exchanged angry words on the subject with both Hitler and Göring. The latter once banged his fists on the table and roared: "I tell you, if the Führer wishes it, then two times two is five."[63] After a long struggle Schacht, who resembled "the kingpin in a skittles game,"[64] was knocked aside. He resigned his economic portfolio in 1937. Later Göring telephoned him triumphantly from the office which he (Schacht) continued for a time to occupy as President of the Reichsbank: "Herr Schacht, I am now sitting in your chair."[65]

As self-styled "master of the German money,"[66] Göring was less competent but more powerful than Schacht. By his own admission Göring could not understand graphs or statistics, and he refused to read documents longer than four type-written pages. He delegated much but intrigued against able subordinates such as Erhard Milch, who rebuilt the Luftwaffe, for fear that they might challenge his supremacy. He was more interested in appearance than reality and sometimes valued quantity above quality. "The Führer," said Göring, "does not ask me how big my bombers are, but how many there are."[67] The Four Year Plan was ill-conceived and provided no well-regulated system of State direction. Instead rival agencies competed for priority and private companies scrambled for raw materials. German industrial growth was slow and there were few incentives to efficiency: taxes were high, wages were kept low, consumer goods were scarce, trade stagnated and by 1938 living standards had hardly risen above the level reached ten years earlier. To augment its might Germany sacrificed not only liberty, as Winston Churchill said, but also prosperity.

However, Göring was able to command the economy because Hitler had provided jobs; and workers, in short supply by 1937, were inspired as much by gratitude as by pride in a revived Fatherland or by fear of the concentration camp. So the government directed labour and investment, controlled prices and inflation, interfered in banking and manufacturing, increased public expenditure on construction and heavy industry, encouraged private saving, and even used workers' unemployment insurance contributions to finance rearmament. Göring extended State control into almost every sphere of life and by 1938 he was spending well over half the government's budget, mostly on weapons of war. In the same year he beat off a military challenge to his authority by helping to ensure Nazi control of the army high command, getting himself made Field Marshal in the process. Before the Four Year Plan was over the Hermann Göring Reichswerke, the nucleus of Germany's rearmament programme, had become the largest industrial organisation in Europe. Like Hitler, Göring believed that "only a nation that stakes everything on its armaments will be able to continue its existence."[68] He ordered the Reich authorities to "direct all energies to a lengthy war."[69]

Göring's achievement in sustaining the myth of his own moderation, despite everything, owed much to the Olympic pause, the 18 months or so after the Games during which the Nazis consolidated their position. During this time, in fact, he was talking of "vassalising"[70] central Europe while Hitler was secretly drawing up war plans directed towards securing German living-space from the supposedly subhuman Slavs. Hitler's plans, adumbrated in *Mein Kampf,* were best expressed in the so-called Hossbach Memorandum of November 1937 which, if less than a blueprint, was much more than a daydream. Nevertheless, the Führer promised that there would be no further surprises like the occupation of the Rhineland. He also drew closer to Mussolini through their joint support for Franco, thus weakening Italy's resolve and ability to resist a German fusion with Austria. *Anschluss* had always been Hitler's aim. The demand for a union of all Germans was the first article in the Nazi programme of 1920 and in *Mein Kampf* Hitler said that it was the supreme task of his life. Thwarted at first, he was always on the look-out for fresh opportunities and complained at the Berghof that he had to view his native land "through field glasses."[71] Because Vienna talked of independence, he declared, six million Germans ran the risk of being "turned into Swiss."[72] For the time being, though, Hitler waited.

However, he did not trouble to conceal his Austrian ambitions from visiting Britons, who failed to discourage him. The aged Lloyd George, who was impressed by the hard work which he saw being done in Dachau and returned his daughter's satirical Nazi salute with a serious one because Hitler "really is a great man,"[73] told parliament that Britain would never go to war again for an Austrian quarrel. Lord Halifax, who came ostensibly to see Göring's International Hunting Exhibition but actually to appease Hitler on behalf of Neville Chamberlain, conceded in November 1937 that the position of Austria (and of the Sudetenland and Danzig) might have to change. Subjected to the Führer's rant on this subject, Halifax preferred the more diplomatic Göring. He was a gangsterish schoolboy whose "composite personality," Halifax famously and fatuously wrote, included "film star, great landowner interested in his estate, Prime Minister, party-manager, head gamekeeper at Chatsworth."[74] The Austrian Chancellor himself, Kurt von Schuschnigg, concluded that Göring was a pacific influence and "would not be persuaded into some violent adventure against Austria."[75] Yet Schuschnigg's own Foreign Minister, who also attended Göring's Hunting Exhibition, noticed a map there on which no border line was marked between Germany and Austria. Göring commented, with a wolfish grin: "Good huntsmen know no frontiers."[76]

Many Austrians dismissed fears based on such remarks as Nazi phantoms. But Göring was at least as rabid as Hitler on the subject of the *Anschluss* and he took a major part in achieving it. Göring thought nothing of threatening that if the government in Vienna did not toe the Nazi line "we would march in, and that would mean the end of Austria."[77] He even tried to bully Mussolini, declaring that Italy should relinquish its role as protector of Austria for the sake of the alliance with Greater Germany. Nazi support for the Duce in the Mediterranean, Göring suggested, depended on his keeping his "hands off Austria."[78] Actually Mussolini had already decided that his Abyssinian adventure precluded Italy from being, as he put it, fossilised on the Brenner. So by the end of 1937 Austria was ripe for the plucking.

THIS had always seemed to be the destiny of the rump of the Habsburg empire, an artificial creation of the Versailles settlement which suffered from a profound "malaise of national spirit."[79] The post-war truncation wrecked everything from the Civil Service to the financial system, from the railway network to the car industry. Vienna, once the imperial capital, became a massive hydrocephalic head perched on a puny body. Moreover it was a Red head, whereas the body was black—clerical and reactionary. During the 1920s Vienna became a model of progressive endeavour, its "pores seeping with socialist spirit, with proletarian will—a red city through and through, not only at skin level and in its administration . . . but in its life, its blood and its nerves."[80] Vienna's health, housing, educational and welfare programmes were notably advanced for their time. Huge working-class apartment blocks such as Karl-Marx-Hof, over a kilometre long, ringed the baroque old city. They were socialism in bricks and mortar. And they seemed poised to overwhelm the bourgeoisie, especially when the Depression subjected Austria to terrible new hardships. The failure of the Rothschild Creditanstalt Bank exacerbated an already poisonous anti-Semitism. Unemployment affected about a third of the workforce, many of whom scavenged for food and became a prey to political extremism. In 1934 authoritarian measures provoked a short but bloody civil war in which Vienna's "residential citadels"[81] became ferro-concrete fortresses which were shelled by government troops. Democracy was crushed, trade unions were outlawed and the Fatherland Front secured power. This was a "clerico-Fascist" party, whose symbol was the Greek "crutch" cross. Here was an aspirant theocracy, which sought to intervene in almost every aspect of life—chemists selling contraceptives could not advertise "Olla's Rubbers," only "Olla's Rubber-sponges."[82] But the Front, for all its waving of red-white-red flags, was unable to give Austria a true sense of national identity.

It was outflanked from the Right by the Austrian Nazi party. Although suppressed after their attempted putsch, in which the charismatic little peasant leader Engelbert Dollfuss was murdered, the Austrian Nazis (faction-ridden though they were) drew strength from the north. Hitler articulated the anti-Semitic prejudices of his compatriots. Göring would have found many Viennese to agree that theirs was no German city because it had been wholly judaised—it must be purged, he said, and "the

Jew must go."[83] Nazis expressed the pan-German sentiments of many Austrians more powerfully than the Fatherland Front. Schuschnigg himself, who succeeded Dollfuss, believed in a Greater Germany, though he rejected Prussian hegemony and toyed with mystical notions of restoring the Holy Roman Empire. However, in return for a guarantee of independence, Schuschnigg did sign a "gentlemen's agreement" with Hitler in the Olympic summer of 1936 to the effect that Austria "recognised herself to be a German state."[84] It was a fatal mistake, tantamount (as one German diplomat put it) to "committing suicide through fear of death."[85] Schuschnigg had sold the pass of Austrian sovereignty and he proved unable to resist further Nazi pressure. He was, indeed, that paradoxical creature—a diffident dictator. Decorated for his war service, the Jesuit-educated Tyrolean was unquestionably courageous. But he was also meek, austere, cerebral, devout and, above all, reserved. No one quite plumbed the depths of this fair-haired, chain-smoking lawyer with horn-rimmed glasses which concealed eyes of unfathomable blue. "You can't get near to the Austrian Chancellor," remarked a contemporary; "he is always behind his spectacles."[86] But by 1938 Hitler saw that he was strong enough to coerce Schuschnigg. In February the Führer issued an invitation to Berchtesgaden which the Austrian Chancellor, anxious to stop Nazi demonstrations in Vienna, could not refuse. Intending to intimidate, Hitler ensured that two of his most brutal-looking generals, Sperrle and von Reichenau, were in attendance, together with the new Chief of Armed Forces High Command, Wilhelm Keitel. Schuschnigg, he said, "must be made to tremble."[87]

Almost as soon as Schuschnigg arrived, Hitler, wearing black trousers and a brown Stormtrooper's tunic complete with swastika armband, launched into a furious tirade:

> The whole history of Austria is just one uninterrupted act of high treason . . . I am going to solve the so-called Austrian problem one way or another . . . Perhaps you will wake up one morning in Vienna to find us there—just like a spring storm . . . such an action would mean blood . . . Don't think for a moment anybody is going to thwart my decisions . . . I give you once more, and for the last time, the opportunity to come to terms . . . Think it over, Herr Schuschnigg, think it over well. I can only wait until this afternoon.[88]

Hardly able to interrupt and forbidden to smoke in the Führer's presence, Schuschnigg was shattered by the experience. The virtual ultimatum with which he was presented after a frugal lunch shocked him still more. It stipulated that two Austrian crypto-Nazis, Arthur Seyss-Inquart and Edmund Glaise-Horstenau, should be appointed respectively as Ministers of the Interior and of Defence. Nazis imprisoned in Austria were to be released and the ban on their political activities was to be lifted. Military and economic "coordination"[89] was to take place between the two states. It was thus inevitable, Hitler reckoned, that they would soon be coordinated into a single nation. Schuschnigg hoped against hope that he could prevent outright invasion, though that seemed imminent when Hitler made a great show of calling General Keitel into the room. So, bullied, humbled and expecting to be arrested on the spot, Schuschnigg signed the document. As the dazed Austrian Chancellor drove back towards Salzburg through the grey fog of a winter's night, Papen, who had accompanied him throughout, memorably remarked that, whatever his behaviour on this occasion, at other times "the Führer can be absolutely charming."[90]

Schuschnigg had wondered, when he set out on the fatal journey to Berchtesgaden, whether a Viennese psychiatrist should go in his place. Afterwards Schuschnigg felt as though he had met a "madman who thinks he is a God." Hitler seemed like "someone from another world"[91] and the pious Tyrolean had no idea how to respond to him. His tactic was to play for time by behaving as though the Berchtesgaden protocol was a final settlement. But the Führer made no secret of the fact that it was the last stage on the road to *Anschluss.* In a speech to the Reichstag he denounced as race traitors those of German blood who did not favour unity under the Reich, provoking a thunderous response across the border. In Graz, Linz and Vienna demonstrations occurred during which, Hitler's admirer Unity Mitford reported to Winston Churchill, "one could not move in the streets for people shouting, *'Heil Hitler!' 'Anschluss!'* & waving swastika flags."[92] At night in the mountains Nazis set fire to brushwood piled into the shape of swastikas, blazing their message clear across the valleys. In desperation Schuschnigg announced that a plebiscite would be held on 13 March 1938. Austrians were invited to vote for him and for: "a free and a German Austria, an independent and a social Austria, a Christian and a united Austria; for peace and employment and for the equality of all who stand for their people and their nation."[93] This composite formula, which was bound to be endorsed, prompted a flurry of Austrian patriotism. Socialists and Communists, liberals and clericals marched together in the sunshine along the Kärntnerstrasse and the Graben, shouting *"Heil Österreich!"* and "Red-White-Red unto Death!" Loudspeakers broadcast Austrian military marches. Aeroplanes dropped thousands of leaflets calling for a *"Ja"* vote. The breeze "caught them up and held them quivering against the railings of the Hofburg and the bare branches of the trees around the Ringstrasse, until the city seemed to have been visited by some strange white blossoming."[94]

Taken by surprise, Hitler reacted with fury. He mobilised his forces and disseminated lies about Bolsheviks raising the hammer and sickle in Austria. Unable to get help from abroad and unwilling to spill German blood, Schuschnigg moved from appeasement to capitulation. He agreed to Hitler's demand, conveyed by Göring through Seyss-Inquart, that the plebiscite should be abandoned. Göring now revealed what Genghis Khan could have done with a telephone. In a series of urgent trunk calls he relayed the Führer's orders to Seyss-Inquart. Schuschnigg and his cabinet were forced to resign. Stormtroopers in Nazi uniform were authorised to act as police. Göring nominated ministers in the new government headed by Seyss-Inquart. Acting on Göring's long-distance instruction, he requested Germany to send troops to re-establish law and order in Austria. In fact, the only threat of violence came from the Nazis, who were determined to punish those who, like the defiant President Miklas, did not actively promote the impending *Anschluss*. In the Ballhausplatz, outside the yellow walls of the Chancellery, a Nazi mob howled for blood. Inside sinister men with close-cropped hair and sabre-scars on their cheeks strutted about and slammed doors: the Gestapo had arrived. Schuschnigg prepared to leave his office, the office from which Metternich had once dominated Europe. The high, square room with its red and gold brocade hangings was overlooked by a large portrait of the Empress Maria Theresa. On another wall, more ominously, the death mask of Schuschnigg's murdered predecessor Dollfuss "glowed in the dusk."[95]

Schuschnigg refused to flee from Vienna and for the next seven years he remained a prisoner of the Nazis. So did his country; but most Austrians rejoiced in their captivity. The Wehrmacht, which marched in without firing a shot, was welcomed with unfeigned enthusiasm. It was greeted by so many new brown uniforms and swastika flags that factories ran out of cloth and towns succumbed to "decorative monotony."[96] Church bells pealed and loyal addresses were read in front of cheering crowds. Men saluted and bellowed *"Sieg Heil."* Women wept for joy and uttered thanksgivings. Girls garlanded steel-helmeted troops as though they were an army of liberation. When the Führer arrived, on the afternoon of 12 March 1938, people even knelt in the tracks of his big black Mercedes to collect the dust its wheels had touched. Hitler was so moved by the manifestations in his home town of Linz that, over a dinner of pea soup and rice at the Hotel Weinzinger, he abandoned the temporary expedient of making Austria a satellite state and decided to restore fully his "homeland to the German Reich."[97] In Vienna the former down-and-out was received with "an ecstasy of emotional fervour."[98] "The whole city behaved like an aroused woman, vibrating, writhing, moaning and sighing lustfully for orgasm," wrote one witness, George Clare, who stated that this was no purple passage but an "exact description."[99] The climax came on 13 March in the Heldenplatz, where 200,000 people took part in an orgy of adoration as Hitler spoke from the balcony of the semicircular Hofburg. Austria's new mission, he said, was to be the youngest bastion of the German nation. It was a mission which the vast majority embraced, including Cardinal Innitzer. He hailed Hitler, flew Nazi banners from St. Stephen's Cathedral and urged Catholics to "do their duty to the German Fatherland."[100] Innitzer subsequently recanted, but by then 99.73 per cent of the electorate had voted for the *Anschluss* which he had sanctified. Austria had become Ostmark, a province of greater Germany, and postcards were on sale in Vienna showing "a swastika sun rising over the Stephanskirche."[101]

Why the Austrian mood swung so sharply towards Hitler has never been quite clear, even to Viennese analysts of the national psyche. It seemed inconceivable that such a hideous change could suddenly overtake a people famed for their golden-hearted *Gemütlichkeit* and blithe *Schlamperei,* for their addiction to light waltzes and sentimental operettas, for their indulgence in café conversation accompanied by pâtisseries, croissants, strudels, pancakes so thin that a newspaper could be read through them, and a hundred varieties of coffee, best served with whipped cream. Doubtless Austria's surrender to the Führer can partly be explained as a release from pent-up tension, an emotional catharsis. Partly it was due to Nazi propaganda, which played so effectively on the susceptibilities of the mutilated state. More important, in a country still reeling from the Depression, were hopes of economic improvement and full employment. These not only were realised but were reflected in a 300 per cent rise in Vienna's birth rate, formerly one of the lowest in the world. But on a more sinister level the *Anschluss* was welcomed because it liberated monsters from the Austrian id.

Many Austrians, who (as the writer Alfred Polgar sardonically observed) made bad Nazis but good anti-Semites, burned to unleash their hostility on the country's 400,000 Jews. There was a massive attack, the ferocity of which embarrassed even the Gestapo. As the German playwright Carl Zuckmayer wrote,

> The city was transformed into a nightmare painting by Hieronymus Bosch . . . [the] air filled with an incessant, savage, hysterical screeching from male and female throats . . . [in an] uprising of envy, of malevolence, of bitterness, of blind vicious lust for revenge.[102]

Mobs shouted "Destruction to the Jews."[103] Thugs daubed anti-Semitic signs on walls and smashed Jewish windows. Looting was rampant: when

Stormtroopers took 6,000 Austrian schillings from Sigmund Freud's apartment he remarked wryly, "Never have *I* been paid so much for a single visit."[104] Repulsive scenes occurred in which Jews were forced to eat grass in the Prater park or to scrub pavements and public lavatories while crowds jeered that Hitler had at last found work for parasites. Aptly enough, Jews had nicknamed the moustached Führer "Pemsel"—"brush" for cleaning lavatories.

However, the cataclysm of arrests, beatings and murders did have one great incidental benefit for Austria's Jews. They were not lulled into a sense of false security like the Jews of Germany, where anti-Semitism was less acute and the persecution mounted more gradually. Instead, they sought to flee. One British diplomat recorded that his consulate was "stormed by hundreds of terrified hysterical Jews begging for a visa to go anywhere out of Austria."[105] He called the police. Other diplomats were equally unhelpful, reflecting the reluctance of their countries to admit Austrian Jews— Switzerland even insisted that their passports should be stamped with a large red "J." When Hitler mentioned his plan to solve Europe's "Jewish problem by way of emigration to the colonies" the Polish Ambassador promised the Führer that, if it was successful, "we will erect him a beautiful monument in Warsaw."[106] Neither scheme was realised and everywhere doors slammed against Jewish refugees. Austrian passport offices bore signs saying, "All frontiers are closed to the Jews."[107] Yet most of them managed to escape, though some only travelled as far as France, Czechoslovakia or Italy, where they were later caught by the Nazis. Driven to despair, thousands took a more direct way out, a route endorsed by Göring, who publicly said that he "could not put a policeman behind every Jew to prevent suicides."[108] This hardly squared with his promise to Sir Nevile Henderson that Austrian Jews would be treated with "tolerance and leniency."[109] Nevertheless, Viennese newspapers and radio insisted that foreign reports of "de-Jewing" were an "orgy of lies."[110]

Absurd though official denials were, outsiders were bound to acknowledge that Austria had submitted voluntarily to Germany. Opponents of Hitler might harp on "the rape of Austria," and in due course the myth that Austria was the first victim of Nazi aggression became enshrined in the heart of the nation. It even helped to ensure Austria's post-war independence from the Soviet Union. However, as Ward Price remarked (with characteristic crudity) after accompanying German troops to Vienna, "If this was rape never have I seen a more willing victim."[111] Price ignored the fact that many Austrians, and not only Jews, were horrified by the invasion. But other observers, like the Chicago *News* cartoonist who showed Austria being crucified on a *Hakenkreuz,* the crooked cross of the Nazis, ignored the fact that even more Austrians saw Hitler as a saviour. Their euphoria convinced foreigners that, far from seeking to resist the *Anschluss,* they should consider it a family matter. It had been settled brutally and Hitler's methods were widely condemned. But the union seemed natural, inevitable. Even Mussolini, whose position was most damaged and whose inaction drew effusive thanks from Hitler, acknowledged that one "ambiguity had been removed from the map of Europe."[112] The reaction in London was similar. It was summed up in a letter from Sir Alexander Cadogan, who had replaced Vansittart as head of the Foreign Office, to Sir Nevile Henderson: "Thank goodness Austria is out of the way."[113] The way, indeed, seemed to have been cleared for a peaceful settlement with Hitler. Siren calls (uttered by Litvinov, among others) for a grand alliance to resist the Reich by force were ignored. So were pleas such as that of the former British ambassador in Vienna, Sir Michael Palairet. He believed that the *Anschluss* should have been opposed because it involved the swallowing of "peaceful, tolerant, cultured and predominantly Christian" Austria by a Germany which was none of these things. He also warned that Hitler's Reich "will not stop short at the absorption of Austria."[114]

CZECHOSLOVAKIA would obviously be Hitler's next target. He had actually intended to strike there first and only seized Austria when the chance presented itself. The *Anschluss,* it has been rightly said, exemplified Hitler's "extraordinary combination of consistency in aim, calculation, and patience in preparation with opportunism, impulse and improvisation in execution."[115] Now he was ideally situated to embark on his long-planned quest for *Lebensraum* in the east. Czechoslovakia, surrounded by German territory on three sides, was like a bone in the jaws of the Nazi mastiff. Yet Hitler claimed that it was a spearhead in the side of the Fatherland. More plausibly, he asserted that the three million so-called Sudeten Germans living within Czechoslovakia should be reunited with the Reich. Their return accorded with the very principle of national self-determination underlying the Versailles settlement which had created Czechoslovakia. Amid the ruins of the Austro-Hungarian empire, it is true, that principle had been virtually impossible to apply. So the state consisting of Bohemia, Moravia, parts of Silesia, Slovakia and Ruthenia (sub-Carpathian Ukraine) was an ethnic and linguistic jigsaw puzzle. Although a successful democracy with a strong industrial base, it was an all-round invitation to irredentism. The Nazis in particular damned Czechoslovakia as degenerate and redundant. Göring, licking his lips over its economic resources even while digesting those of Austria, denounced the Czechs as a "vile race of dwarfs without any culture."[116] Their country was "the vermiform appendix of Europe! We shall have to operate."[117]

"Operation Green" was the codename given to Hitler's plan to destroy Czechoslovakia. It provided for a lightning strike against strong frontier defences followed by an immediate conquest of the whole country. The excuse for aggression was to be found in the plight of the Sudeten Germans, who did have genuine grievances. Hitler ordered their leader, a handsome gymnastics teacher called Konrad Henlein, to step up his agitation: violent incidents were duly magnified in the German press, which sometimes took "names at random from the telephone book to publicise them as martyrs to Czech brutality."[118] Henlein was told to demand so much from the Prague government that he could never "be satisfied."[119] Hitler envisaged that a brief, local conflict would be sparked off by some manufactured incident, such as the murder of the German Ambassador. However transparent the pretext, he was convinced that the democracies would only posture and admonish. They would not intervene and, without them, nor would Russia. France, though bound by treaty to help its eastern ally, would be discouraged from doing anything effective by Hitler's new West Wall. Actually this bastion was a mere shadow of the Maginot Line, but the Führer correctly calculated its deterrent effect. So defeatist was the French high command that in the event of a general war it proposed to attack a softer, remoter and wholly irrelevant target—Italian forces in Libya. The British, Hitler thought, were still less ready and willing to defend Czechoslovakia. And, indeed, the chiefs of staff reported to the cabinet: "we can do nothing to prevent the dog getting the bone, and we have no means of making him give it up" except through a long, hazardous conflict.[120] This, Hitler sensed, the governments in London and Paris (and probably Moscow too) wished at all costs to avoid. His confidence was sustained during the summer of 1938 when Britain and France sought a full settlement with Germany by extorting concessions from Czechoslovakia.

Its President, Dr. Edvard Benes, intellectually dynamic though prevented by a squeaky voice from being personally charismatic, could only plead, delay and yield. He sought help where he could, even supping with Stalin, whom he characterised as "gracious, thoughtful and accommodating."[121] Hitler, though, succeeded better by stimulating the appetites of Czechoslovakia's immediate neighbours, egging on the greedy Poles and telling the nervous Hungarians that "those who wished to share in the meal would have to help with the cooking."[122] When negotiating with Henlein, Benes procrastinated as much as he dared, earning himself an impatient rebuke from Lord Runciman, the British mediator, but gaining time to fortify Czechoslovakia's exposed Austrian flank. He thus added to the screen of pillboxes, tank traps and barbed wire, modelled on the Maginot Line, against which the Führer himself feared that German forces might bleed to death in a terrible "repetition of Verdun." Nevertheless Hitler was determined to crush the Czechoslovaks. "Long live war," he exclaimed to Henlein on 1 September 1938, "even if it lasts two to eight years."[123]

Within a few days, though, Benes accepted all Henlein's demands, despite the fact that this gave the Sudeten Germans virtual autonomy within Czechoslovakia. Its President made the sacrifice in response to overwhelming pressure from the Western democracies, whose leaders clung to their belief that by appeasing Hitler they could avoid war. Not to be deprived of this consummation, the Führer became more bellicose. He abused Benes and insisted on the right to full Sudeten self-determination. He fomented disorder inside Czechoslovakia, giving Henlein an excuse to break off negotiations with the President. Germany was poised to strike. Then, prompted by the French, who were torn between dishonouring their treaty obligations and engaging in a war they feared to lose, the British Prime Minister intervened. The world gasped as the 69-year-old Neville Chamberlain made his famous flight to Berchtesgaden. But the Czechoslovak Ambassador in London, Jan Masaryk, took a shrewder, sourer view: "I am very much afraid that the senile ambition of Chamberlain to be the peacemaker of Europe will drive him to success at any price, and that will be possible only at our expense."[124]

Hitler proceeded to dupe Chamberlain. He flattered the Prime Minister's vanity, letting it be known that he considered him "a man."[125] The Führer persuaded Chamberlain of his good faith. Above all, at Berchtesgaden he convinced his guest that he was willing to precipitate a world war over the Sudetenland but that the cession of ethnic German areas to the Reich would bring a general peace. So Chamberlain flew back to England, where he persuaded his cabinet colleagues and the French leaders that Czechoslovakia's German fringe must be trimmed. Benes was bullied into accepting what he rightly considered a bad bargain: an international guarantee of the new frontiers to compensate for the loss of vital territory. On 22 September Chamberlain returned to Germany, this time to the spa town of Bad Godesberg on the Rhine, where he expected to clinch agreement with Hitler. But, still intent on launching Operation Green, Hitler now demanded more. Czech outrages against the Sudeten Germans had increased, he said, and his forces would have to occupy their land by the end of the month. Moreover, the Poles and the Hungarians must be satisfied. Back home once more, Chamberlain faced stiffening resistance in the cabinet and in the country to what the *Daily Telegraph* called "an abject and humiliating capitulation."[126]

As both Britain and France steeled themselves to fight, Chamberlain made two final appeals for peace. The first was to Hitler, who remained intransigent and several times shouted at the British envoy, Sir Horace Wilson: "I will smash-sh-sh the Czechs."[127] The second was to Mussolini, who grabbed the chance to avoid a conflict for which Italy was unprepared. He added his voice to those of Göring and Goebbels, who argued that a deal could be made which would give Hitler everything he wanted except the blitzkrieg against Czechoslovakia. But what may have swayed the Führer more was the lack of war spirit apparent in the glum crowds at a Berlin military parade on 27 September. He exclaimed, "I can't lead a war with such a people"—to which Goebbels replied that all they needed was more "enlightenment."[128] In lieu of that a four-power conference, from which the Czechs (and the Soviets) were excluded, was convened at Munich. Chamberlain and Daladier accepted Nazi proposals which Mussolini put forward as his own. They barely modified Hitler's Godesberg demands. Czechoslovakia was to surrender not only the Sudetenland but important centres of communication, major industrial areas and its vital fortifications (the experimental bombardment of which would convince the Wehrmacht that it was "perfectly possible"[129] to break through the Maginot Line). Benes could not resist the dismemberment of his country, though he lamented Czechoslovakia's base betrayal by the democracies and forecast that it would produce its own punishment. Returning home from Munich after what Winston Churchill called this "total and unmitigated defeat,"[130] Chamberlain and Daladier were greeted as conquering heroes. For having acted as dishonest broker, Mussolini plausibly posed as the arbiter of Europe. Hitler, though still angry at having been denied the conflict he craved, had become the master of the entire Danube basin.

Perhaps the Führer was prompted to reflect on Bismarck's maxim that he who holds Bohemia holds the continent. At any rate, the day after the Munich agreement was signed Hitler made it clear to subordinates that he intended to engorge the rump of Czechoslovakia as soon as he got the chance. To this end the Führer mercilessly harried the Czech *Untermenschen,* as he called them. He took as much territory as he could, and fostered Slovak separatism as well as Polish and (later) Hungarian rapaciousness. Appeasement whetted Hitler's appetite for aggression and he ordered Göring to organise a "gigantic armaments programme which would make insignificant all previous achievements." Among other things the Luftwaffe would become five times larger, ready, as Göring put it, to "burst upon the foe like a chorus of revenge."[131] All this would be done by driving the Jews out of the economy altogether and severely squeezing the rest of the population. Hitler was unperturbed by the consequences of devoting almost 80 per cent of public expenditure, by 1939, to preparing for war. "If we win," he said, "the billions we have spent will weigh nothing in the scales."[132] Of more concern to him was the pacific bent of the German people, who had shouted *"Heil Chamberlain"* with embarrassing enthusiasm. In November Hitler secretly addressed senior newspaper editors:

> It has now become necessary to psychologically change the German people's course in a gradual way and slowly make it realise that there are things that must, if they cannot be carried through by peaceful means, be carried through by methods of force and violence.[133]

Propaganda would imbue the *Volk* with properly Teutonic ferocity.

So would the example of the SA, who conducted a pogrom against the Jews on the night of 9–10 November 1938. It was a reprisal for the assassination of an official at the German embassy in Paris by a young Jewish refugee named Herschel Grynszpan, who was maddened by the news of his family's sufferings at the hands of the Nazis. The Stormtroopers' vengeance, Goebbels claimed, was spontaneous. In fact it was calculated and encouraged from the top—Hitler said that the SA "should be allowed to have a fling."[134] The Gestapo in Berlin organised the terror, sending out directives to the provinces. Starting under cover of darkness, Stormtroopers (soon joined by freelance hooligans) went on the rampage all over Germany. They burned synagogues, smashed houses, looted shops and attacked Jews. Irrespective of age and sex, the victims were beaten up and subjected to disgusting indignities. At Leipzig, for example, Jews were thrown into a stream in the Zoological Park and spectators were ordered to "spit at them, defile them with mud and jeer at their plight."[135] Nearly 100 Jews were killed and over 20,000 were sent to concentration camps, from which many never returned. The destruction gave one Jewish girl, brought up as a godless Communist, a new vision: "What reverberated through my ten-year-old atheist mind was: 'This is what Hell is like, this must be Hell.' "[136]

To add insult to injury, the Jewish community was literally made to pay for *Kristallnacht,* so called on account of the avalanche of broken glass littering the streets. A collective fine of a billion marks was imposed, amounting to about 20 per cent of the wealth of the 300,000 Jews left in Germany. Goebbels considered this "a nice bloodletting."[137] Göring was less satisfied. He thought it would teach the Jews a lesson: "The pigs won't commit another murder."[138] But, he told Heydrich, "I wish you had killed two hundred instead of destroying such valuables."[139] Göring then proceeded with further spoliation, "aryanising" surviving Jewish businesses. Jews who remained in Germany faced mounting persecution. Addressing the Reichstag in January 1939, Hitler foreshadowed "the obliteration of the Jewish race in Europe."[140]

Nothing shocked world opinion more than the dawning appreciation that Hitler's anti-Semitism was not rhetoric but reality. Many Germans, too, were horrified by *Kristallnacht* and its aftermath. Yet, in spite of barbaric actions to match savage words, most citizens of the Reich continued to revere the Führer precisely because they could still regard him as a dictator of peace. Unlike Mussolini, Hitler did not glorify war for its own sake. More to the point, he had miraculously succeeded in overturning the Versailles settlement without bloodshed. Even generals and diplomats plotting against Hitler, whose disastrous course they could foresee more clearly than did the public at large, were disconcerted by his triumph at Munich. The wind was further taken out of their sails in March 1939 by his peaceful "liquidation" (as the Nazis liked to call it) of the Czechoslovakian rump, despite the promised Anglo-French guarantee of its borders. Now the separatist Slovaks acted as the Third Reich's Fifth Column. They were prodded into declaring independence, which gave Hitler the excuse to bully Benes' successor, the aged and ailing Emil Hacha, into submission.

The Führer's harangue seemed to turn Hacha to stone—only his frightened eyes revealed that he was alive—but his ordeal in Berlin reached its climax when Göring threatened that the Luftwaffe would blast half Prague into ruins within two hours. The Czech President collapsed and had to be revived with injections administered by the Führer's personal physician. Hacha capitulated, ordering his troops not to fire on the Wehrmacht. Proclaiming that he was the greatest German in history, a euphoric Hitler invited his secretaries to kiss him—which they did, on both cheeks. He then followed his forces to Prague, driving into the sullen city at dusk during a snowstorm. At the Hradcany Palace, ancient Gothic seat of the kings of Bohemia, he ate a cold supper and went so far as to drink a "tiny glass" of Pilsener beer.[141] Hitler pronounced Bohemia and Moravia to be German protectorates; Slovakia soon suffered a similar fate, while Ruthenia was thrown to the Hungarians. Without delay Göring began to exploit the economic resources of the captive provinces, which reinvigorated the flagging Four Year Plan. An especially potent asset was the giant Skoda munitions plant at Pilsen: this recent loss to the French Schneider Creusot concern became an immediate gain to the Hermann Göring Reichswerke.

The rape of Czechoslovakia was quite different from the rape of Austria. That, Litvinov had said, was the most serious event to have occurred since the First World War. The new violation—of non-German territory containing aliens whom the Führer had specifically said he did not want in the Reich—presaged the Second World War. It provided hard evidence of Hitler's insatiable lust for conquest, thus, as Ciano observed, "profoundly agitating public opinion throughout the world."[142] It confirmed beyond a shadow of doubt that he was as untrustworthy as he was predatory. The British were particularly outraged. This was because, as the German Ambassador explained (in a priceless diplomatic formulation), they had interpreted the Führer's statement that the Sudetenland was his last territorial claim in Europe "in too drastic and unpolitical a manner."[143] In other words, they had believed it. The revelation of Hitler's mendacity so appalled Chamberlain that he announced Britain's determination to oppose any attempt at global domination. A few days later Hitler took back the Baltic port of Memel from Lithuania and warnings reached London that he would shortly seize Danzig. So, at the end of March, Chamberlain told a cheering House of Commons that Britain and France would support Poland in resisting a German attack. Yet, contrary to appearances, this declaration did not mark the end of appeasement: it was an attempt to give the policy teeth. Britain still tried to conciliate Germany, the Bank of England handing over six million pounds' worth of Czech gold, *The Times* softening the commitment to Poland. But Chamberlain was trying to draw a line in the sand. The aim was "to contain and deter Hitler rather than to defeat him."[144]

However, Chamberlain had conceded so much for the sake of peace that no mere declaration of intent could persuade Hitler that he was suddenly ready to wage war. Ironically, it was now the Führer who became the victim of illusions about the Prime Minister, instead of vice versa. He was convinced that in the last resort Chamberlain, and with him Daladier, would leave the Poles in the lurch. Hitler had seen the democratic "worms" at Munich, he said, and he could not believe that they would turn. Indeed, his main fear was that "some *Schweinehund*"—despite the new animal imagery, he obviously had Chamberlain in mind—"will make a proposal for mediation."[145] As usual, Ribbentrop confirmed his leader's view of the situation, threatening personally to shoot any of his officials who presumed to prophesy war in the west. But although Hitler thought Chamberlain was bluffing, he also considered his Polish guarantee to be part of a plot to encircle Germany. When news of it reached him at the Reich Chancellery the Führer flew into one of his famous frenzies. The veins on his forehead throbbed, his eyes glared malevolently, he tore across the room and beat his fists on the marble table, shouting: "I will brew him a devil's drink."[146]

The concoction contained three main ingredients. First Hitler ordered that Operation White, the attack on Poland, should be ready by 1 September 1939. Other enemies, such as Britain and France, could be dealt with later: Poland's unbearable obstinacy over Danzig must be punished at once. Secondly, when Mussolini, humiliated by being kept in the dark over Czechoslovakia, sought to restore Italian prestige by invading Albania, Hitler supported him with enthusiasm. Six weeks later, on 22 May 1939, the Axis powers forged the Pact of Steel, a military alliance which was supposed to secure Germany's southern flank. Finally Hitler ensured that he would not have to fight a war on two fronts by coming to terms with Stalin. He thus outmanoeuvred the Western democracies, who were making their own overtures to the Soviet Union. But whereas they hesitated to ally with the Bolshevik Bear, Hitler had no scruples about doing an ideological volte-face in the interests of *Realpolitik*. It could easily be reversed. The Führer confessed privately that he was "in no wise altering his fundamental anti-bolshevist policies; one had to use Beelzebub to drive out Satan."[147] Assisted by the dialectic, Stalin was equally cynical about abandoning principle in order to avoid his own war on two fronts, against Germany and Japan. Like Hitler, he had no faith in the will of Britain or France to fight for Poland; indeed, he suspected them of trying to engineer a titanic struggle between Nazism and Communism. Furthermore, he looked forward to territorial gains from a new partition of Poland and to economic advantages from trade with Germany. So, on 23 August Ribbentrop arrived in Moscow with full powers to clinch a deal. In two meetings the Nazi and Soviet negotiators resolved all outstanding issues and agreed on spheres of influence from the Baltic to the Black Sea. Then they signed the "Non-Aggression" Pact, which made aggression against Poland inevitable.

Hitler's motives for embarking on this colossal gamble are anything but clear. Part of the explanation is that he *was* a gambler, eager to live dangerously and prepared to risk everything on his hunch that the war against Poland could be contained. As Hitler told Göring, who preferred to play safe, he had only ever wanted to break the bank. But at a more visceral level Hitler felt that the Reich must start its "racial fight" against miser nations which hoarded "oilfields, rubber, treasures of the earth."[148] It was a fight for the resources that would equip Hitler's military machine to crush lesser breeds and thus to win living space for the German people. It was also a viciously circular struggle, war achieving conquest and conquest fuelling war, which could only end in world domination. This was a long-term goal but it was real enough for all that. During the summer of 1939, standing before a model of the great meeting hall planned for Berlin, Hitler pointed to the swastika in the claws of the German eagle at the apex of the vast dome. "This is to be altered," he told Speer. "Instead of the swastika, have the eagle perched on top of the globe."[149]

The first stage of this process had to be initiated at once, Hitler thought, because Germany held the political and economic whiphand, a situation that might not last long. Moreover he himself, embodying more authority than any leader in the nation's history, might be assassinated. The fate of the Reich depended on his iron will. With megalomaniac clairvoyance Hitler saw that the moment of destiny had arrived. His vision was never sharper than when he ascended to the rarefied atmosphere of the Berghof.

> In the broad horizons of the land around Berchtesgaden and Salzburg, cut off from the everyday world, my creative genius produces ideas which shake the world. In those moments I feel no longer part of mortality, my ideas go beyond mortal frontiers and are transformed into deeds of great dimensions.[150]

It was at times such as these, said François-Poncet, that Hitler became incapable of reason. Instead, like some demiurge in the grip of madness, he dreamed of overthrowing nations and continents, of re-writing geography and history. Occasionally nature itself seemed to endorse the Führer's sanguinary intuitions. On the evening of 24 August 1939 he and his entourage witnessed from the terrace of the Berghof a particularly brilliant display of the Northern Lights. The sky shimmered with rainbow hues and across the darkened valley the legend-haunted Untersberg shone with a livid glow. Their faces and hands, Speer recorded, were bathed in red light. The spectacle induced a pensive mood. Hitler turned abruptly to one of his adjutants and said, "Looks like a great deal of blood. This time we won't bring it off without violence."[151]

XXII

THE FASCIST AXIS

BLOOD was on the minds of both the Duce and the Pope as Italy veered unsteadily into the orbit of Germany during the pre-war years. Mussolini ensured that his Ethiopian promised land ran with blood rather than milk and honey. Mass murder would quell the rebellious natives, he told Graziani, and anyone remotely suspected of resistance must be "shot without delay."[1] But he also thought that blood-letting invigorated the mother country and he regretted that fewer than 2,000 Italians had been killed in the Ethiopian campaign. More were destined to die in Spain and their example would, Mussolini hoped, toughen Italy in the increasingly violent struggle for existence. So would persecuting Jews, whom he vilified, along with "niggers," as a disintegrating force in civilisation. "Jews even refuse to breed because it costs pain," he averred. "They don't realise that pain is the only creative factor in the life of a nation."[2] Hardly consistent with this idea was his conclusion, as he drew closer to Hitler, that Jews should not be permitted to defile the purity of Italian blood by intermarriage. The ban brought him into fresh conflict with Pius XI, who had long opposed "Nazi doctrines of 'blood and race.'" Catholicism was incompatible with the worship of that new trinity—*Volk, Reich* and *Führer.* It was Hitler's Germany as well as Stalin's Russia that the Pontiff had in mind when he addressed his cardinals at Christmas 1935: the horizon was obscured by clouds, he said, "dark, threatening, already tinged with blood."[3]

By then the Pope was bitterly disappointed over the Concordat which he had signed with Hitler two years previously. It had been negotiated in haste: the Nazi threat to suppress Catholic schools and youth movements had roused Vatican fears of another Bismarckian *Kulturkampf.* In return for State acceptance of the Church's educational and cultural role (as well as other tenuous benefits such as a secret compact against Bolshevism), Hitler received real political advantages. He eliminated the Catholic Centre party, consolidated the Nazi dictatorship and gained international respectability. In fact, as *Le Temps* commented at the time, the Concordat was a triumph for the National Socialist government: "Catholicism in Germany has lost everything but its life."⁴ Some thought it had lost its soul. Like Italian churchmen after 1929, German clerics began to laud nationalist dictatorship. Bishops talked of creating a "synthesis between Teutonism and Christianity," of forging a link between the swastika and the cross. Priests gave Nazi salutes and employed Hitlerian terminology: "Jesus is our Führer." As late as 1937 the entire German episcopate endorsed Archbishop Gröber's view that the Concordat was "proof that two powers, totalitarian in their character, can find agreement, if their domains are separate."⁵ From the first, though, cynicism reigned in the Vatican, where the Concordat was regarded as the least of various evils. It would certainly be violated, said the Pope's ascetic Secretary of State (and successor), Eugenio Cardinal Pacelli. But, he observed with a smile, the Nazis would probably not violate all its articles "at the same time."⁶

Actually, they initiated a comprehensive persecution of the Church almost at once. They imprisoned priests, subverted monastic orders, attacked confessional schools, undermined Church organisations, suppressed religious journals, brutalised pilgrims to Rome, victimised Catholics of Jewish descent. Mussolini thought this uncompromising policy ill-advised since, as he told the German Ambassador, it was easy to win over the Church: he himself had given tax concessions and "other small favours to the higher clergy . . . so that they even declared the war in Abyssinia a holy war."⁷ But Hitler had both ideological and political motives for this campaign: the system of organised mendacity presided over by "the senile officiant" in St. Peter's chair "must be smashed" and the State "must remain absolute master."⁸ Nazi propaganda played its familiar part and the Pope himself came under fire. Himmler's repellent journal *Das Schwarze Korps* pictured him in front of a huge sack of gold with the caption, "A safe stronghold our God is still." Pius felt "particularly wounded" by the repeated lie that he was of Jewish origin.⁹ He raged at Hitler's Ambassador to the Vatican, "We never expected to be treated so by Germany."¹⁰ He also fulminated at the "Germanophile" Pacelli, who favoured conciliation and discouraged him from "protesting openly" about breaches in the Concordat.¹¹ While Nazi and Fascist forces alone seemed capable of holding back the Red tide in Spain, the Pope heeded such counsel. He was particularly influenced by the General of the Jesuits, who was "so obsessed by the Bolshevik danger that he regarded Mussolini in the light of a Saviour."¹²

However, by 1937 the European situation was changing. Stalin's purges had discredited Soviet Communism. In Spain Franco seemed poised to defeat the forces of Republican godlessness. The French Popular Front had abstained from revolution. In Germany, however, the Nazis were not only attacking the Church directly but attempting to replace it with an idolatrous cult. They promoted their racialist religion, one Vatican official said, with "a frenzy of primeval barbarism." Plagued by cardiac and respiratory problems, the embattled old Pope seemed incapable of resistance. Small, frail, his skin as transparent as parchment, he appeared to be "bowed down under the sins and follies of the world."[13] But if the Pope's heart was failing, his mind remained vigorous and his will stubborn. He husbanded his strength, eating little meat but much cooked fruit, drinking some red wine and taking regular exercise in his beautiful gardens. Even in decrepitude he retained his autocratic manner. "Everyone is terrified of him in the Vatican," recorded the Italian Foreign Minister. Illustrious cardinals, whom he treated "with arrogance," trembled at his approach. Pacelli had to take dictation from the Pontiff as though he were a "little secretary."[14] Certainly the sibylline cardinal was in no position to prevent the Pope from publicly denouncing the Nazi assault on Christendom. So, in March 1937, the famous encyclical *Mit brennender Sorge* (With burning anguish) was written, secretly distributed and read from pulpits all over Germany. It condemned violations of the Concordat, accused the Nazis of waging a war of annihilation against the Church and excoriated their "mad attempt to imprison within the frontiers of one people, within the pedigree of a single race, God, creator of the world."[15]

This was the noblest official utterance to emerge from the Vatican during the pontificate of Pius XI. It identified the evil at the heart of Nazism and implicitly acknowledged the failure of the Concordat policy. No tribute was more flattering to *Mit brennender Sorge* than that of the Nazis themselves. They suppressed all mention of it, confiscated every copy they could find, shut down print shops and stepped up the persecution of the clergy. Their fury was also expressed in vindictive pin-pricks: towns and villages with religious names, such as Gottesberg and Heiligenstadt, were made to change them. Pius XI himself was vilified in revolting ways and when he died Goebbels told his minions in the Propaganda Ministry to spit (metaphorically) on the coffin. Hitler was particularly incensed because the papal condemnation was expressed forthrightly and not in the oracular language usually favoured by the Holy See. This was strange since Cardinal Pacelli apparently had a hand in drafting the encyclical and, as he showed on becoming Pope Pius XII in 1939, there was no more accomplished master of the art of circumspection. Throughout the entire course of the war he never directly referred to the fate of the Jews, the greatest sin of omission ever perpetrated by a successor of St. Peter. Even when Jews were being rounded up for transportation to Auschwitz beneath his own windows in 1943, Pius XII contented himself with a Delphic declaration to the effect that all men, of whatever race or creed, benefited from his solicitude. The German envoy von Weizsäcker was pleased that the statement was couched in "the Vatican's distinctive style" since "only a small number of people will recognise in it a special allusion to the Jewish question."[16] People had certainly recognised the intention of *Mit brennender Sorge*.

Yet for all its plain speaking, the encyclical did not mention anti-Semitism as such. It concentrated on wrongs done to the Church and affronts against religion. It did not condemn Nazism in so many words. In fact, as one historian has concluded, the Roman Catholic Church's opposition to Hitler was "carefully circumscribed; it was rooted in a concern for her institutional interests rather than in a belief in freedom and justice for all."[17] Unquestionably Pius XI felt personal sympathy for the Jews. He told a group of Belgian pilgrims that Christians could not "take part in anti-Semitism" because "in Christ we are all Abraham's descendants . . . Spiritually we are all Jews." But this unique statement was hardly publicised at all, perhaps because of the Church's traditional antipathy to "the race of murderers of the Lord," perhaps because of its more recent phobia about the "Bolshevik-Jewish conspiracy." The Vatican drew a careful distinction between Christian and Nazi anti-Semitism, putting Alfred Rosenberg's embodiment of the latter, *The Myth of the 20th Century* (1934), on the Index. But it did not proscribe *Mein Kampf.* It did not condemn *Kristallnacht.* During 1938 the Jesuit journal *Civiltà Cattolica* published articles in which "hatred towards the Jews was no less vehement than that of the secular anti-Semitic Fascists."[18] For unknown reasons Pius XI did not even publish the encyclical denouncing Nazi racial policies, *Humani Generis Unitas,* which he secretly commissioned not long before his death. Perhaps this was just as well. The draft warned against the "spiritual contagion" to which Christian souls were exposed by contact with Jews and declared that the "unjust and pitiless . . . campaign against the Jews has at least this advantage, if one can put it so . . . that it recalls the true nature, the authentic basis of the social separation of the Jews from the rest of humanity."[19]

If the Pope had pronounced an unequivocal anathema against anti-Semitism, he might have checked Mussolini. After all, the Duce's proposal to build a mosque in Rome in order to substantiate his claim to be "Protector of Islam" was scotched by a protest from the horrified Pontiff. Yet on this more important issue Mussolini was left free to follow his own impulses. More, he was encouraged. In his endeavours to make Italians act as members of an imperial race after the Ethiopian victory, he could largely count on the Church's support. Cardinal Schuster of Milan, for instance, hailed Mussolini as "the new Constantine." Schuster, indeed, was so keen on "playing the super-Fascist" that, as Roberto Farinacci wryly remarked, "we sometimes thought he was presenting himself as a candidate for the Secretaryship of the Party."[20] But it was easy for proselytising clerics to believe that Mussolini was doing God's work in Ethiopia. This was particularly so in 1937 when he outlawed *"madamismo,"* cohabitation (though not sexual congress) between white men and native women. Ecclesiastics endorsed the Duce's insistence that Italians in Ethiopia should maintain their "racial dignity."[21] From this it was but a step to advocating racial supremacy at home, especially since Mussolini blamed world Jewry, typified by Léon Blum, for backing sanctions against Italy. The writing was on the wall for racial tolerance in Italy, for what Nazi propagandists sneeringly called "Kosher Fascism."[22]

On the subject of anti-Semitism, as on everything else, Mussolini was as capricious as quicksilver. In earlier days he had often decried it, notably in its Hitlerian form, as barbarous, cruel and absurd. In conversation with Emil Ludwig he had denied the existence of a biologically pure race and ridiculed its mongrel champions. He told the Jewish leader Nahum Goldmann that the Führer was a fanatical rascal while he himself, the Duce, was a Zionist. He publicly announced (with characteristic coarseness) that Italy had no Jewish problem:

> The Jews have been in Rome since the time of the kings; doubtless it was they who supplied the clothes after the rape of the Sabine women; there were fifty thousand at the time of Augustus and they asked to weep over the corpse of Julius Caesar. They will remain undisturbed.[23]

There were still only about 50,000 Jews in Italy, mostly affluent and assimilated bourgeois. Many spoke no Yiddish, which, as Primo Levi recorded, often proved fatal when they were unable to communicate with other inmates in Nazi concentration camps. Many were Fascists who, in the words of a Turin rabbi, admired "the noble figure of Il Duce, powerful, gifted with amazing, I would almost say divine, qualities."[24] Other Italian Jews simply accepted Fascism as part of the air they breathed. As one wrote, "I lived in the belly of the monster, totally unaware of its existence."[25] But the Fascist monster was always uncomfortably aware of harbouring potential adherents to alien creeds—Zionism, Bolshevism, even liberal democracy. As Italian nationalism grew more furious under the spur of war—actual in Ethiopia and Spain, potential in Europe as a whole—Jews could be represented as the fifth column of internationalism.

· · ·

THE roots of Fascist anti-Semitism did not run deep and its evil flowers were only to blossom after a generous application of Nazi manure. Meanwhile its growth was just one expression among many of Mussolini's endeavour, in the wake of the Ethiopian struggle, to revitalise his regime. Racism was a kind of social autarky, to match the new drive for economic self-sufficiency, which would prepare the nation for total war. Sanctions had not only aggravated the Duce's belligerence but intensified his siege mentality. Now he stockpiled commodities and controlled their supply. He tried to develop synthetic substitutes for imports such as petrol and rubber, an endeavour for which extravagant claims were made—artificial wool was said to have been produced from milk and textiles were manufactured from a variety of sources, "including genets [civet-cats]."[26] Italian coal was preferred to British though it cost more, and iron was regarded as a "precious metal."[27] The modern Italian film industry was born of State subsidies, in order to reduce dependence on America. Mussolini increased government controls over banking, industry and trade. In October 1936 he devalued the lira by 41 per cent, which boosted exports. But inflation rose even faster and, despite price restraints and wage increases, living standards fell. Mussolini was unperturbed. He continued to spend twice as much of the national income (11.8 per cent) as Britain on armaments and when his Minister of Exchange and Currency warned of imminent bankruptcy he declared that economics had never "halted the march of history."[28]

At any rate tighter discipline (mitigated by advances in health insurance and the introduction of paid holidays) would inure Italians to tighter belts. So schools and youth organisations were regimented more strictly. "Mass leisure"[29] was more sternly ordered, especially on "Fascist Saturday," when Starace tried (often in vain) to make Italian males parade. In 1938 the employment of women, who amounted to a quarter of Italy's workforce, was curtailed by law. Domestic dictatorship, Fascists maintained, should also be revived, as advocated in Fernando Loffredo's notorious treatise *Politics and the Family* (1938): "Women must return under the absolute subjection of men—father or husband; subjection and therefore spiritual, cultural and economic inferiority."[30] The regime's propaganda grew more strident, especially over the air waves. As more people acquired wireless sets this "magical instrument with its irresistible fascination became the official voice of the State, amplifying the sonority of the Duce's voice, extending his charismatic relationship with the public."[31] No broadcasts were more shrill than those directed at increasing Italy's birth rate. Mussolini denounced bourgeois egoists who kept dogs and cats but did not breed children. Male deserters from the battle of life would be punished by shame—those of Turin, who failed to live up to the name of the city of the bull, were particularly culpable. So were women who wore small-breasted, narrow-waisted Parisian fashions, which militated against procreation (though Mussolini also banned Gino Boccasile's provocative tabloid *Grandi firme* with its big-bosomed, long-legged cover girl, who seemed "as dominant and emancipated as a man").[32] Fecundity and virility, not sexuality, were the characteristics of an imperial race. In the Duce's words, "nations with empty cradles could not conquer an empire"[33]—or defend it.

Yet Mussolini simultaneously stated that colonies strengthened the mother country by draining off her surplus population. Landless peasants and unemployed workers should be encouraged to cultivate foreign soil for the benefit of the homeland. According to the familiar argument, these "Legionaries of Labour"[34] would produce raw materials, provide markets for manufactured goods and garrison strategic outposts of greater Italy. This imperial vision was a mirage. Yet it was sustained even where it was most obviously illusory, in Libya. Seized with barbaric cruelty and held with brute force, Italy's so-called "fourth shore" was supposedly transformed into a model colony after 1934 by Air Marshal Italo Balbo. Although the "conquering eagle of transoceanic flights" (as one admirer hailed him) hated being "caged among the palm groves of Tripoli,"[35] he had certainly made the best of his exile. In pith helmet, dark glasses and khaki tunic, the goateed Governor-General had sweated to turn Libya into a personal advertisement and a "Fascist triumph."[36] He had modernised Tripoli, demolishing Arab slums, laying out wide boulevards and spacious gardens, constructing new offices, hotels, shopping arcades. He had made strenuous efforts to bring fertility to a wilderness of scrub, stone and sand. He had attracted tourists by staging air rallies and Grand Prix automobile races. Moreover he had built the "Balbia," a strategic road which ran 1,822 kilometres along the north African coast from the frontier of Tunisia to the border of Egypt. It was a heroic feat of engineering carried out in temperatures reaching 49 degrees centigrade in the shade (when there was any) by a 13,000-strong army of (mostly) Libyans, dark men "looking like white shadows in the blinding blaze of the sun."[37] In March 1937 Mussolini himself came to inaugurate this extravagant project, the last link in a highway connecting the Atlantic to the Nile.

It was a typical piece of Fascist theatre, made more exotic by the *Arabian Nights* setting. Balbo spared no expense. He re-painted and renovated whole areas of Tripoli, draping all the public buildings in flags and illuminating them brilliantly at night. He erected triumphal arches and gigantic slogans. He arranged motorcades and cavalry parades. He staged a Lucullan feast in the desert and a performance of *Oedipus Rex* in the restored Roman amphitheatre of Sabratha. To acclaim the Duce he mustered multitudes, including nomads who took months to ride their camels from remote oases in the parched hinterland. Mussolini himself rode into Tripoli on horseback, accompanied by an enormous retinue and preceded by two Libyans carrying large papier-mâché *fasces*. His visit, he declared, was

> the consecration of the achievement of Fascist Italy in North Africa . . . the glorification and the apotheosis of imperial triumph attained in far distant East Africa . . . [in the face of the] most ignoble and absurd coalition in history.[38]

The climax of the melodrama was Mussolini's acceptance of the Sword of Islam, which he brandished from the saddle with the Arab cry of *"Uled !,"* as a symbol of his promise to protect Moslems—a symbol which might have been more convincing had it not turned out that the sword was made in Florence. The last great scene, one "to make Mr. Cecil B. De Mille green with envy"[39] according to a foreign reporter, was the Duce's reception at the massive brown castle-palace formerly occupied by the Turkish governor and now Balbo's headquarters. Its white cupolas blazed with light and fountains reflected the multicoloured illuminations. A rich incense rose from thickly planted flower-beds. The guard of Zaptiehs, with drawn blades and long scarlet and argent burnous, stood like statues in archways and along paths. Through the throng of dress-uniformed, bemedalled men and women wearing sky blue and silver cloaks moved Mussolini, a tall plume waving in his hat, his huge jaw tilted at a suitably imperial angle.

The "demographic colonisation" of Libya, as Fascists christened mass migrations which were said to have "no parallel in history," also relied on showmanship. Balbo, the impresario of convoys of Italian "Soldiers of the Soil"[40] to his African satrapy, employed all the arts he had learned when conducting squadrons of aeroplanes on transatlantic flights. In 1938 he recruited an "army of rural infantry"[41] from the mother country. They were carefully selected: loyal Fascist families, literate, sturdy, philoprogenitive, mainly from the north. In October they began their momentous journey, converging on Genoa in 17 special trains. As instructed, they wore their best clothes, the women dressed in white blouses, many of the men clad in grey-green or black uniforms, sporting medals and cards coloured to indicate their precise destination. Most of the peasants smoked rank pipes or asphyxiating Tuscan cigars. Some had never seen the sea. In the pouring rain Balbo improvised a motorised cavalcade to the docks, leading it through welcoming crowds in a blue sports car. He supervised every detail of the embarkation. Then his luxurious flagship, the *Vulcania,* led the fleet from port amid a cacophony of bands and sirens. Six more vessels joined the original nine in the bay of Naples where a firework display lit up Vesuvius. As they departed hundreds of rockets released tiny white parachutes trailing green, white and red streamers. Off the coast of Gaeta Mussolini inspected the flotilla from the bridge of the cruiser *Trieste,* which was accompanied by four destroyers, all cleaving the calm water at 16 knots. The colonists' steamers listed to starboard as they crowded along the rails, saluting and crying: *"Duce! Duce! Duce!"*

At Tripoli Balbo's 20,000 found everything meticulously prepared to receive them, including a tented camp on the shore for their first night. Disembarking in two hours with military precision, they assembled in the Piazza del Castello which was overlooked by a monstrous silhouette of the Duce's head encased in a steel helmet. Balbo, in a peaked cap, bade them welcome and unveiled a bronze equestrian statue of Mussolini holding the Sword of Islam. Then, after exhortations and prayers, the colonists dispersed to enjoy their allowance of free food, drink, cigarettes and entertainment. The next day they set off in columns of trucks for their new habitations, which were clustered across the tawny steppes of Tripolitania and Cyrenaica. The villages contained stores, post offices, medical centres, political offices, schools and churches of great size and peculiar ugliness, one resembling a power station, another a railway terminus, another a grain elevator. Surrounding them stood the uniform white concrete farmsteads that had been built, furnished, provisioned with firewood and food and given access to artesian water in anticipation of the colonists' arrival. The holdings had been planted and provided with livestock so that the settlers could get off to a good start. Many of the farmhouses were equipped with electric light and water closets—a novelty to most peasants. It all testified to the truth of the slogan which had greeted them in Tripoli: "Mussolini redeems the earth and establishes cities."[42]

This was the message that was assiduously promulgated to the world's press, many of whose representatives accompanied Balbo on his epic voyage. The propaganda even helped to attract more settlers—Balbo led another contingent of 10,000 in 1939. Yet on almost every count this imperial enterprise was a sham. Worthwhile crops could hardly be squeezed out of the barren and thirsty soil of Libya: one journalist saw fields of grain reaching a height of only nine inches, "a pathetic little fur upon the sand," while peasants went "down on their knees, picking it, even imploring it to grow."[43] The colony therefore cost far more than it could ever return, draining the mother country of human and financial resources which would have been better invested in depressed areas closer to Rome. Reflecting on the fact that Italy spent ten times as much running its colonies as the value of their imports, the Minister of Foreign Trade told Mussolini that the empire was devouring the homeland. And far from strengthening Italy strategically, Libya added to its defence burdens. When war broke out Balbo described his military position as hopeless, caught between the British in Egypt and the French in Tunisia "like a slice of ham in a sandwich."[44] Italy's navy could hardly keep open communications with Libya and soon two-thirds of the Duce's merchant marine was at the bottom of the sea which he had aspired to turn into "mare nostrum."

Not content with that Latin ambition, Mussolini had grandiose notions of conferring on all the people of his empire the right to say: "Civis Romanus sum." Accordingly, in January 1939, he announced that the four coastal provinces of Libya were now part of metropolitan Italy and that their 700,000 inhabitants could become Italian citizens. But this too was fake. The Duce had recently given racial prejudice the force of law at home and even he could not simultaneously eradicate it abroad—though token changes were made, such as the removal of the different-coloured lights which distinguished white from native brothels. In the last resort, moreover, nothing could disguise the fact that Libya was held by force of arms: so little were native troops, Spahis, trusted that they had to hand in their rifles at night. Thus Arabs, many of whom had been displaced by Italians on the best land, remained second-class citizens, ripe for revolt when the opportunity presented itself. Meanwhile Balbo, who in general hated the German alliance, did his best to protect Libya's 20,000 Jews. He even invited a few of them to dinner when Göring visited Tripoli—the corpulent Field Marshal feigned illness to avoid their company.

Balbo's recalcitrance infuriated Mussolini less than the flair for publicity which had originally caused his banishment to Africa. The trumpetings which attended his first mass migration were anything but music to the Duce's ears for they threatened to drown paeans in his own praise. Mussolini was especially sensitive to outside opinion and scrutinised the foreign press minutely, seeing in the most superficial article, as one of his ministers wrote, "double-crosses, intrigues, 'coldnesses,' at every moment."[45] Thus he soon ordered his own press and radio to keep quiet about Balbo's colonists and in Italy nothing more was heard of them, "for all the world as though they had been swallowed up by the Syrtes."[46] Furthermore Balbo was personally ostracised, like other prominent Fascists whom Mussolini regarded as rivals. In the words of the Air Marshal himself, "As soon as he sees too much light shining on us, he turns off the switch."[47]

JEALOUSY, suspicion and mistrust accounted for the frequent and notorious changes of the ministerial guard under Fascism. Success was punished and corruption was rewarded—Mussolini joked that he could not sack *gerarchi* (Fascist functionaries) who had made their fortunes because they would make way for those with their fortunes still to make. In fact he promoted pliable mediocrities who represented no threat, and servile lackeys who owed everything to him and competed against one another. During the later 1930s this had the paradoxical effect of permitting him to devolve power without losing authority. He was then much preoccupied with his ambitious young mistress Claretta Petacci, who spent a good deal of her time lying on a couch in a garish dressing gown in the star-spangled Zodiac Room at the top of the Palazzo Venezia. There she drank tea and played solitaire while waiting for her fickle, passionate and sometimes violent lover, for whom she was, as she assured him, "crazy with desire."[48]

Also during these years the Duce suffered from periodic and painful bouts of ill health, which some, including Balbo, attributed to syphilis rather than to gastritis. Without doubt he was visibly ageing: fat and bald, he presented "the visage of a dissolute Roman emperor of the decadence."[49] So he was content to leave routine matters in the hands of obsequious clients like Dino Alfieri (Minister of Press and Propaganda), Fernuccio Lantini (Minister of Corporations) and the ineffable Party Secretary, Achille Starace. Giuseppe Bottai, who had been a sincere admirer of the Duce and became Education Minister in 1936, was a cut above the rest and now held a correspondingly low opinion of Mussolini, describing him as an autodidact who was a bad teacher and a worse student. The most disastrous of the latter-day promotions, however, was that of the Duce's son-in-law, Galeazzo Ciano, appointed Foreign Minister in June 1936 at the age of 33. This was blatant nepotism made more outrageous by Ciano's obvious fecklessness. A Roman riddle asked whether this playboy could do anything well: the answer was that he made an excellent cuckold, though, on second thought, even for that Ciano needed the help of his wife. Americans joked that the son-in-law also rises.

Ciano's Fascist credentials, at least, were impeccable. His father was a naval hero, Count Constanzo Ciano, who had so flourished under Fascism that he became Mussolini's designated successor. Evidently recognising his son's susceptibility to the pleasures of the flesh, the Count had early tried to instil a measure of nautical discipline, dressing him in a sailor suit until he was fifteen to stop him from accompanying his friends to the brothel. The measure proved ineffectual and the young Ciano became a compulsive libertine, later instructing diplomats to act as pimps for him during trips abroad and lusting in Berlin for that notorious "temple of sexual gratification,"[50] the Salon Kitty. He pursued the opposite sex in the spirit of Mussolini, whose lieutenants transformed his maxim "many enemies much honour" to "many women much honour."[51] In that sense, as his biographer drily remarks, Ciano was the most honoured Fascist of his era. Certainly a woman helped to win him swift advancement. After a whirlwind courtship he married Mussolini's favourite daughter, Edda, in 1930. Ingratiating as well as handsome, Ciano was given a series of plum jobs, which did not stop further philandering. In her autobiography Edda—herself addicted to dry martinis, poker games, fast cars and Roman gallants—wrily recorded Joseph Kennedy's reaction to her husband:

> I have never met such a pompous and vain imbecile. He spent most of his time talking about women and spoke seriously to no one, for fear of losing sight of the two or three girls he was running after.[52]

Ill-camouflaged infidelities proved no bar to Ciano's progress and he further improved his prospects by commanding the *Disperata* Squadron in Ethiopia. He even won a silver medal for valour, though wits said that he should be awarded a gold medal for his bravery in accepting the silver one. As master of the Chigi Palace he aroused yet more envy. Italians, convinced that his sole claim to distinction was to have wedded Mussolini's daughter, nicknamed him "Ducellino."

Like Chips Channon, Ciano possessed *par excellence* the qualities of a good diarist; and his diaries, which he kept in a massive safe in the Chigi Palace's Hall of Victories (once Mussolini's office), do indeed give a vivid, if sometimes imaginative, account of the decline and fall of the Fascist empire. Their author was frivolous, egotistical, exhibitionistic and indiscreet. These characteristics were precisely those which should have disqualified him from the task of diplomacy. Admittedly he was also observant, cynical, witty and astute. He bubbled with cocktail-party banter and exuded dance-floor charm. His manner was usually as smooth as his well-pomaded hair and the more he disliked the foreigners with whom he had to deal, the more oleaginous he became. With such a capacity for insincerity he might not have disgraced a lowly post (such as he had earlier occupied) in the Shanghai legation. Yet as Foreign Minister Ciano was a wholly irresponsible figure. He was idle and, as his mother-in-law herself said, addicted to "luxury, social fads and high living." Foreign affairs took second place in his life to love affairs. Rather than meeting his ambassadors or reading their dispatches, he preferred to lounge on the beach at Ostia ogling his entourage of film starlets or to disport himself at the Acquasanta Golf Club in the company of his "harem."[53]

At his grand house in the Via Angelo Secchi, sumptuously furnished and embellished with a fine collection of Chinese porcelain, he liked to entertain with champagne supplied by Ribbentrop—which Ciano loudly disparaged. Better still, he enjoyed swapping scandal and conducting intrigues at the exquisite soirées held by Isabella Colonna, an opulent Levantine who combined the roles of Princess, procuress and mistress. So intimate was she with Ciano that Italy's Foreign Ministry was said to be located not in the Palazzo Chigi but several hundred yards away in the Palazzo Colonna. Even when Ciano did attend diplomatic receptions, pleasure came before business. The American Ambassador, William Phillips, recorded that he had to invite the "youthful favourites"[54] of both Galeazzo and Edda Ciano, whose louche behaviour shocked older guests. Ciano himself pinched bottoms with abandon and "blithely scratched himself in places where Ribbentrop would have endured an infestation of fleas without moving a muscle."[55] Phillips concluded soberly that Ciano was "less a Foreign Minister than a young man with a roving eye."[56]

In a vain attempt to acquire more *gravitas* Ciano modelled himself on Mussolini. Initially, at least, the Foreign Minister idolised his father-in-law. His journal is full of genuflections to the sacred person of the Duce, hosannas to his heroism, oblations for his invariable rightness—so much so that it seems almost to have been composed for Mussolini's eyes, just as it was written in an imitation of his script. Ciano aped his master's mannerisms. He perfected the peacock strut and the basilisk glare. He combined the granite-jawed stance and the mailed-fist gestures. He moved his sensuous lips in an exaggerated fashion and spoke in staccato sentences. His language became cutting and dismissive—he declared that Dino Grandi, Italy's Ambassador in London, had "the brains of a mosquito."[57] This might all be dismissed as play-acting, but Ciano possessed a genuine streak of ruthlessness. He thought nothing of plotting the murder of opponents of Fascism, such as the Rosselli brothers, assassinated in 1937, or King Zog of Albania, who saved his skin by fleeing his country in 1939. Ciano also introduced a "Fascist tone" into the business of foreign affairs. Rather than engaging in the effete manoeuvres of old-fashioned diplomacy, he reached brutal decisions and made uncompromising pronouncements. Ciano entrusted Blackshirt gangsters such as Farinacci with important missions instead of career diplomats, whom he despised as much as did Mussolini and Hitler. In the Chigi Palace these dignified functionaries became so insubstantial that they were known as "shadows."[58] Ciano worked instead through his "cabinet" of Fascists, reducing "the traditional apparatus to an empty shell."[59]

Between 1936 and 1939, therefore, Ciano had a malign effect on the foreign policy of his country. He adopted Mussolini's rhetoric, proclaiming that the conquest of Ethiopia had made Italy a great and, at last, a satisfied power. Yet he did nothing to abate the Duce's continuing adventurism. Ciano, who spoke good English, did make sporadic attempts to restore the traditional alliance with Britain. This resulted in a fatuously named "Gentlemen's Agreement" (January 1937), designed to heal the Ethiopian wounds, and an Anglo-Italian accord (April 1938), a nervous response to the *Anschluss*. Both proved abortive: Spain drove a wedge between Fascism and democracy, which Germany hammered home. Moreover, in Ciano's opinion, Britain's gestures of appeasement only demonstrated its feebleness. For at the very time Italian troops in Spain were flagrantly breaching the non-intervention agreement, Italian submarines were committing acts of piracy in the Mediterranean, and Italian radio was broadcasting that "the future is Fascist." (The propaganda issuing from Bari, a hapless British diplomat complained, was entirely mendacious, quite unlike that of London, which presented British news and views "objectively and factually, though favourably by a process of selection and omission.")[60] So Ciano did not quarrel with Mussolini's characteristic pronouncement that the English kept their brains in "the seats of their trousers"[61] and that young, virile nations such as Italy and Germany would soon have to assert themselves against the stupid, decadent democracies by means of war.

According to Dino Alfieri, Ciano could have exerted a "beneficent influence" on Mussolini. He was clear-sighted and well informed enough to have warned his father-in-law not only of the failings of Fascism but also, in 1939, of the dangers of Nazism.[62] In fact, Ciano was too weak to do much more than act as Mussolini's echo. He did, indeed, puff himself up like a bullfrog in the press. Newspaper editors like Giovanni Ansaldo were left in no doubt as to how his speeches were to be treated, as this extract from a telephone call intercepted by Mussolini piquantly reveals.

> *Ciano:* Ansaldo!
> *Ansaldo:* Commander, Excellency!
> *Ciano:* Remember in particular not to omit any of the parentheses in the text of the speech.
> *Ansaldo:* To what do you refer, Excellency?
> *Ciano:* To the applause, the cheering of the eager crowd. Do I make myself clear?

Ansaldo: I won't fail, Excellency!

Ciano: Especially at the end. The final applause! Make sure that I really had a lot. Emphasise it with bold type! Don't skimp on the bold type![63]

Ciano thus became enough of a presence to help isolate his father-in-law. Many thought that he obscured the Duce's vision and cut him off from reality. As one observer remarked, Ciano was "another diaphragm between Mussolini and the world."[64]

Using the word in another sense during his speech in Milan's Piazza del Duomo on 1 November 1936, Mussolini declared that the new line agreed between Rome and Berlin was "not a diaphragm but an axis."[65] Around it, he said, all peaceful states could revolve. Actually the Axis was formed with aggressive intent. It was a compact of convenience aimed at the democracies, especially Britain. Mussolini had long shared Göring's view that the League of Nations "represented for England a sort of invisible alliance against Italy and Germany."[66] So even while he and Ciano made overtures to London after the Ethiopian war, the Duce privately inveighed against the nation of shopkeepers and threatened to "bomb the English to bits." As for the French, they were "sick, senile." They had "raised the art of cooking to a principle" and had become victims of the "culture of the stomach."[67] Yet their Popular Front government was hostile to Italy. Thus on becoming Foreign Minister Ciano had held his first official meeting with the German Ambassador, whom he had assured of Italy's "friendly inclinations."[68] Then, in the autumn of 1936, he had visited Germany, where he relished a welcome which was always enthusiastic and sometimes "quite delirious." He lapped up the Führer's flattering assertion that the Duce was the world's leading statesman and agreed with him over the dangers of Bolshevism and British encirclement. The result was the totalitarian Axis, as Mussolini announced. However, Italy and Germany had by no means reached, as Ciano claimed, a "perfect accord."[69] In fact their relationship bobbed up and down convulsively. As a punster in Ciano's ministry remarked (playing on the Italian word *asse,* which also means board), "Give me an axis and I will make you a see-saw."[70]

The political attraction between Fascist Italy and Nazi Germany was counterbalanced by a personal repulsion. The leading figures in the two regimes had real affinities but little affection. The Führer generally admired Mussolini but he was happy, for the amusement of his entourage, to mimic the Duce's more grotesque oratorical posturings. He also remarked that in an uncertain world the only thing that could be relied on was the unreliability of Mussolini and the Italians. The Duce was progressively hypnotised by Hitler. But he often denounced the Führer's boring monologues, his treacherous behaviour and his insane capacity to "set the world ablaze."[71] Mussolini thought Ribbentrop a loathsome idiot, while the Führer described Ciano as "that disgusting boy."[72] Himmler was likened by his Italian counterpart to a laughing hyena in the zoo. And almost everyone in Rome shared the Duce's view that Göring was "a ridiculous figure."[73] Like many of his countrymen, Göring himself despised the entire Italian race, a lazy, sensual, frivolous people who were "lower than Slavs."[74] After the war Göring said that Germany might have won if only the Italians "had been our enemies instead of our allies."[75] He was unwittingly echoing Field Marshal Blomberg, who came to the conclusion, after inspecting Mussolini's armed forces in 1937, that victory in the next war would go to whichever country did not have Italy on its side.

Prussian arrogance exacerbated ill feeling over meatier issues. While sanctions were in force Germany took advantage of Italy's economic weakness, exploiting its dependence on coal imports and making inroads into its Balkan and Danubian markets. The Fascist government feared that Hitler had designs on the South Tyrol, despite his assurances to the contrary and the care he took not to offend Italian sensitivities. Hitler even insisted that towns in school atlases should appear with their German names in brackets after their Italian ones—Bolzano (Bozen), Merano (Meran) and so on. Quite unmistakable, however, was the Führer's intention to achieve the *Anschluss* and as early as 1936 Mussolini dropped hints that he would not stand in the way, though he wanted Austria to keep a semblance of independence. His tacit abandonment of the role of protector of Austria was an admission of weakness. So, indeed, was his continued flirtation with Britain, itself a matter of some embarrassment. As Ciano wrote, if, in the event of the *Anschluss,* Greater Germany should

> press on our frontiers with the weight of its whole seventy million, then it would become increasingly difficult for us to reach an agreement or even talk with the English, since it would be impossible to prevent the entire world interpreting our policy of *rapprochement* with London as a journey to Canossa under German pressure.[76]

Above all, Mussolini worshipped strength. His velleities about Germany dissolved before the one great fact of Nazi might. He had no doubt that the Third Reich represented a "revolution of the old Germanic tribes of the primeval forest against the Latin civilisation of Rome."[77] But, like decadent emperors of old, he reckoned that his best chance of survival lay not in beating the barbarians but in joining them.

That conclusion was reinforced by his momentous visit to Germany in September 1937, when Hitler put on a display of power not seen by an

Italian ruler since the invasion of the Huns and the Goths. *En route* the Duce's armoured train was guarded by soldiers with fixed bayonets, one to every telephone pole. In Munich SS men stood shoulder to shoulder facing huge crowds which gave Mussolini a tumultuous welcome. Although he was only there for nine hours the city had never been more "elaborately adorned," the *pièce de résistance* being a huge triumphal arch in front of the Karlsplatz, draped with Fascist black, wreathed with laurel and crowned with a massive golden "M." Mussolini witnessed a mock tank battle at Mecklenburg, where the sky was darkened by the aircraft of the Luftwaffe. He visited the Krupp munitions plant at Essen, where he saw the drilling of naval guns and the hammering of red-hot blocks of iron weighing 300 tons, ready to be forged into armour-plate. There were lighter moments: Leni Riefenstahl mustered "some of Germany's prettiest girls"[78] to have tea with the Duce and the Führer; Göring showed Mussolini his toy trains; and, in a bizarre tableau representing the amity between their countries, maidens sporting plaits and peasant costumes held hands with youths wearing togas.

The spectacle presented by Berlin was on the largest scale, eclipsing that of the Olympics and "exceeding in magnificence and grandiosity anything previously attempted."[79] The city was a sea of flags, the buildings were almost submerged by bunting and "prosaic streets [were] made over into a composite fairyland." The illuminations, now a standard feature of Nazi pageants, gave the equivalent of two million candle-power, the only black hole being the Soviet embassy. Unter den Linden, where four rows of 33-foot pylons topped with gilded eagles were lit from below by searchlights, was transformed into a gigantic pillared hall "whose roof is the sky." In a carefully rehearsed manoeuvre (lampooned by Charlie Chaplin in *The Great Dictator*) the trains carrying Hitler and Mussolini travelled side by side towards the specially constructed station outside the city, the Führer's advancing rapidly at the last moment so that he could greet the Duce on the platform. Then there were parades, processions, inspections, ceremonies. Mussolini, in his fez with its red cordon of honour, his blue-grey Fascist uniform and azure sash, apparently made a good impression. At any rate the million-strong multitude, enjoying a paid holiday, were in good voice, many having been given cheering lessons at their factories. Mussolini, looking bronzed and bouncy, acknowledged the applause with radiant smiles. He saluted snappily and walked so briskly that the Führer, taller by several inches and plainly-uniformed in brown, had to hurry to keep up with him.

The climax of the visit took place at the May Field, adjoining the Olympic stadium. Despite meticulous arrangements, Hitler himself checking details, the evening turned into something of a fiasco. The tired crowd, dazzled by the lights and recalling the blackout practice recently carried out as an air raid precaution, chanted at Göring: "Hermann, make it dark."[80] Hitler's speech coincided with a torrential downpour. Mussolini, bellowing into the microphone in a strong Italian accent, was virtually incomprehensible to all but radio listeners. After a military tattoo in the Olympic arena, which echoed to the sound of dozens of massed bands, the drenched spectators were caught in a crush as they hurried to leave. They joked among themselves: "Tomorrow we shall, of course, read in the papers that the organisation was quite perfect."[81] Nothing, though, could dampen Mussolini's spirits. He was thrilled by his reception and impressed to the core of his being by the invincibility of Nazism. Psychologically he was now wedded to Hitler's Germany, which did not stop him from periodically contemplating divorce. However, the totalitarian states had not concluded a more formal alliance and no one knew the precise political significance of their demonstration of friendship. Outsiders wondered whether the visit was anything more than a piece of showmanship conjured up by "two of the world's master magicians in mass control."[82] Journalists puzzled still more about the import of one item in the cornucopia of gifts which Mussolini took back to Rome. The curator of the Berlin zoo had presented him with three crates of geese.

Perhaps they were a reminder of the geese that had saved the Capitol in ancient Rome. Or maybe they were an intimation of the *passo Romano,* the Latin goose-step which Mussolini introduced early the following year. This was disliked by the military and derided by the people, who suggested that since Germany had given Italy the *passo Romano* Italy would give Germany the *passo Brennero.* King Victor Emmanuel also objected to the alien form of marching; but, Mussolini sneered, that was because the half-pint Sovereign could not do it without making himself look ridiculous. In any case, the Duce insisted, the parade step was not an import from Prussia: "The goose was a Roman bird."[83] However, it was obvious that Mussolini was copying the Nazis and hoping, by means of a mobile show of aggression, to instil their martial spirit into his own forces. For the same reason he introduced a greeting "Salute the Duce," which was the Fascist equivalent of the Nazis' *"Heil Hitler."*

More important, the Duce proceeded to pit himself sharply against the democracies. His contempt for them had recently increased: they had modified the tough stand which they had initially taken at Nyon against the "unknown" submarines sinking neutral ships supplying the Spanish Republicans and invited Italy to help patrol the Mediterranean. So on 6 November 1937 Mussolini signed the Anti-Comintern Pact with Germany and Japan. In theory this was directed against international Bolshevism but, as Ciano wrote, it was "in fact unmistakably anti-British." It was also anti-Semitic. Ciano thought, for example, that the Japanese, adopted as honorary Aryans now that Italy had perforce turned against its former friends the Chinese, regarded as their "greatest obstacle the Jewish-British plutocracy which wants to arrest the march of young peoples."[84] That march, Mussolini believed, was unstoppable. Although the Pact was little more than an expression of ideological solidarity, he boasted that Italy was now "at the centre of the most formidable politico-military combination that has ever existed."[85] In December he felt strong enough to leave the "tottering temple"[86] of the League of Nations. But his true strength could be gauged from his confession to Ribbentrop that he was tired of mounting guard over Vienna. By February 1938 the Duce was saying that he positively favoured "the nazification of Austria."[87] He vacillated characteristically when the *Anschluss* occurred: Hitler's fervent thanks emphasised how much Germany had gained and Italy had lost. But the Duce himself seemed at a loss, and seeds of doubt about his infallibility began to germinate in the mind of Ciano. The Foreign Minister himself regretted the speed with which the Austrian cockerel had found its way into the German pot.

HITLER aimed to reconcile Italy during his official visit in May 1938, an uphill task since popular attitudes towards the Third Reich ranged from "weary cynicism"[88] to harsh antagonism. Mussolini's extravagant preparations to greet the Führer prompted wry jokes: workmen repairing hundreds of miles of roads were said to be digging trenches against the German invasion; or perhaps they were looking for the Axis. Nothing daunted, the Duce aimed to stage an exhibition of Fascist pomp to eclipse his own welcome by the Nazis and to outshine the triumphs of the Caesars. He did not merely redecorate the Eternal City, he presented Hitler with "the resurrected Rome of Augustus." Thus the Führer drove under the radiant Arch of Constantine, laid a wreath at the pristine Pantheon and witnessed the Colosseum ablaze with crimson fire—magnesium flares lit up the whole arena and "each archway in the three-storied circle framed a dark vision of a soldier in a steel helmet with fixed bayonet standing out against the red glow."[89] Dazzled by Italy's classical heritage, Hitler was also exposed to its current might. Knowing that Germany could not match the Italian navy, the Duce displayed 190 beflagged warships in the sunny Bay of Naples. Destroyers, with pom-poms blazing, burst through smoke-screens laid by seaplanes. Eighty-five submarines dived and surfaced in perfect formation, firing their deck guns to deafening effect. Zig-zagging torpedo boats performed a mock attack on the battleship *Cavour*, from which Hitler and Mussolini watched the manoeuvres. When darkness fell the fleet's searchlights helped to turn night into day and, competing with the livid corona of Vesuvius, a giant sky-sign proclaimed HEIL HITLER.

This sound-and-light show signified little in terms of power. Mussolini threatened to use his armada to break out of the Mediterranean prison guarded by Gibraltar and Suez; yet its fast, lightly armoured, short-range vessels were not designed for oceans but for the inland sea. Even there they were handicapped by lack of training, radar and aircraft carriers—Mussolini famously maintained that Italy itself was an unsinkable aircraft carrier. So perhaps he was more impressed than Hitler by the naval review. The other armed services on parade were still less imposing, though the Führer was said to have formed an "over-favourable impression"[90] of them. Italy's aircraft were too slow, its tanks were too light and its artillery was obsolete—most of it was horse-drawn and some cannon dated from the time of Garibaldi. Some of the armoured cars driving past carried wooden guns and many soldiers bore rifles designed in 1891. The Duce's "genius for bluff"[91] included a preternatural capacity for self-deception, nowhere more marked than in his estimation of Italy's military strength. But Hitler must have observed the hollowness of his legions. There was such a palpable gap between reality and Mussolini's rhodomontade about having eight million bayonets, and aeroplanes "so numerous that they could blot out the sun."[92] That gap, indeed, was emphasised by the presence of so many ceremonial troops, cuirassiers in plumed silver helmets and gold-decorated breastplates, colonial cavalry in scarlet cloaks and white burnouses. Hitler was impatient with the trappings of anachronism. Nothing irked him more in Italy—not even the discovery that the apparent cheering of the Florentines was actually a recording played over loudspeakers—than being caught up in regal flummery.

King Victor Emmanuel, as head of state, was his official host. So the Führer drove into Rome with him, perched on what he described as "a badly slung carnival carriage"[93] and attended by scarlet-liveried footmen; while the Duce rode alone in a motor car, the proper vehicle for a modern dictator. Hitler occupied Crown Prince Umberto's private apartments in the Quirinal Palace, once the popes' summer residence but now, according to its peevish guest, a dirty old museum smelling of the catacombs. He disliked his host, that "acid and untrustworthy little man,"[94] and was overheard urging Mussolini to abolish the monarchy, to lance the royal abscess on the Fascist body politic. Goebbels, observing the throne in the Quirinal Palace, was equally free with his advice: "Keep that gold and velvet object. But put the Duce on it. That chap [indicating the King] is too small."[95] Victor Emmanuel got his own back on the Nazis by spreading rumours that their leader was a drug-taking degenerate—Mussolini himself believed that Hitler rouged his cheeks to hide their pallor. Bound by protocol, the Führer underwent a number of indignities, not least appearing after a performance of *Aïda* dressed in a top hat and tails; ludicrous pictures taken of him, looking "like a cross between a head waiter and a chimney sweep,"[96] were suppressed. He could only relax and enjoy his visit away from the stifling formality of the Court—with Mussolini himself. But even then everything did not go according to plan: on one occasion a band struck up the wedding march from *Lohengrin* and amused spectators asked one another whether the Duce and the Führer were exchanging rings.

The alliance sought by Hitler, for whom the Axis represented mere courtship, was a military one. Although he did not let Mussolini into his plans, it was clear that his ambitions now centred on Czechoslovakia. He needed to secure his southern flank without committing himself to realising Mussolini's Mediterranean dreams. Thus Hitler declared his "unalterable will" that the Alpine frontier would remain "for ever inviolable"[97]—which did not stop Mussolini reinforcing the Brenner Pass. Nor would the Duce, at the very time when Chamberlain was praising his "good faith"[98] and expressing confidence in their Easter accord, agree to a formal treaty with Germany. This provoked a "violent discussion between von Ribbentrop and Ciano in grotesque contrast with what was being offered to the public in the grandiose official demonstrations." But such demonstrations tend to build up their own, often barely perceptible, momentum.

Italians were moved by the "lyrical impetus"[99] of Hitler's pledge to keep the Alps between them. Mussolini sensed that the juggernaut of totalitarianism was gaining pace and raised the tempo. He put his civilian officials into uniform. He replaced the Fascist Militia's fez with a Germanic helmet, complete with eagle. He tried to make Italians use *voi* (you) instead of the alien and effeminate *lei*. He abused the democracies more freely, ordering a "wave of Gallophobia in order to liberate Italians from their last remaining slavery: servility towards Paris."[100] He attacked the Pope, who, ignored by Hitler, had shut up the Vatican, moved to his summer residence at Castelgandolfo and deplored the appearance in Rome of a "cross that is not the cross of Christ."[101] Mussolini also took a stronger line against the Jews, many of whom had been arrested or banished from cities which the Führer visited. In July 1938 the Ministry of Popular Culture issued a piece of spurious scholarship setting out the Fascist attitude to race in the form of an anti-Semitic decalogue, mockingly dubbed the "Ten Commandments of the Axis."[102] Both the King and the Pope expressed dismay that Italy should be imitating Germany in this matter. Mussolini responded furiously: those who said that the Fascist government copied anyone were half-wits and it was difficult to know whether they deserved pity or contempt. But in reply to a private enquiry from the Vatican the Duce denied that he had been referring to the Pontiff.

During the summer and autumn of 1938 Mussolini introduced a series of anti-Semitic decrees. Jewish teachers and pupils (and books) were excluded from Italian schools. The rights of foreign Jews to live in Italy were restricted and citizenship granted to those who had settled after 1918 was revoked. Mixed marriages were forbidden. Jews were purged from organisations such as the armed services. They were not permitted to own land or run businesses employing more than 100 people. Behind the scenes Mussolini sometimes worked himself up into a frenzy about Jews, saying that he wholeheartedly approved of *Kristallnacht* and was pleased to have infected Italians with the germ of anti-Semitism. He also smiled on Farinacci, who was quite happy "to exterminate all Jews"[103] but who, like other prominent Fascists, enriched himself by "aryanising" those who could purchase exemption from the legislation. It was, in fact, "almost universally unpopular in Italy, even among most Fascists." There was a revulsion against Nazi Germany, as the source of anti-Semitic poison. One member of a Turin crowd answered Mussolini's assertion that "the peddling of lies" was one of the ills of the world by saying that Italy too suffered from the disease. There were cries of "*Abbasso* Hitler!"[104]

Mussolini's measures also attracted widespread foreign condemnation, especially in the United States, and Ciano had to insist that there was no "persecution" of Jews, only "discrimination" against them. Irritated by the sophistry, Sumner Welles threatened retaliation against Italians in America, which made the Italian Ambassador turn "a brilliant purple in the face."[105] However, the American government was more concerned with protecting its own Jewish citizens in Italy than with attacking the principle of anti-Semitism (just as the Holy See mainly complained that the ban on mixed marriages breached the Lateran Concordat). Roosevelt even took a favourable interest in Mussolini's scheme to found a "Jewish concentration colony"[106] in Ethiopia, only to be embarrassed when the Duce decided not to give "a square centimetre" of Africa to the Jews and proposed instead that they should go to America. Mussolini professed to be indifferent to opposition at home and abroad. In fact, towards the end of 1938, he planned to give the screw of his racial legislation "an even sharper turn."[107] As the global scene darkened he felt ever more impelled to ally with the strong against the weak, with Germany (and Japan) against the democracies. Soon he was being hailed as "Gauleiter of Italy."[108]

The gibe was justified, even though Mussolini seemed to have emerged triumphantly from the Munich settlement. In fact he acted throughout as Hitler's lieutenant. Despite being uncommitted by a military pact and unprepared for the speed of Hitler's move against Czechoslovakia, the Duce gave his full support to Germany. Although he was unhappy that the Führer had stolen another march on him, Mussolini had been influenced not only by the iron resolution of the Nazis but by the flabbiness of the pot-bellied democracies. Swallowing bitter pills was what they were made for, he said. Britain, in particular, lost face through its willingness to sacrifice the Sudetenland on the altar of European peace. It was clear, Ciano wrote, that the "English will do everything to avert a conflict, which they fear more than any other country in the world."[109] When Chamberlain asked Mussolini to intercede with Hitler, the Duce reckoned that the British must be suffering from some sort of menopausal disorder. The Prime Minister's flight to Germany was a further sign of weakness. Mussolini exclaimed:

> As soon as Hitler sees that old man, he will know that he has won the battle. Chamberlain is not aware that to present himself to Hitler in the uniform of a bourgeois pacifist and British parliamentarian is the equivalent of giving a wild beast a taste of blood.[110]

Mussolini himself appeared a confident figure at Munich. Laced into his uniform, speaking all the requisite languages, and combining parliamentary cut with dictatorial thrust, he even seemed to dominate the proceedings.

These were held in the spacious red-columned salon on the first floor of the new Führerhaus, a classical edifice on the Königsplatz, whose cream and pink marble Doric façade was interrupted by a huge bronze eagle with wings outstretched. The leaders sat around a massive fireplace in armchairs, which was not conducive to business. Nor was the lack of a chairman and a set agenda; so progress was slow. Chamberlain yawned incessantly; Daladier fortified himself with Pernod; Hitler scowled and fidgeted. Mussolini alone appeared at ease, though not at rest. According to François-Poncet, his mobile features reflected each eddy in the flow of argument. He smiled or pouted; his brows rose in surprise or knotted with menace; his eyes registered curiosity or amusement, or they darted fire. Dismally monoglot, Hitler not only followed these fugitive expressions closely, he even imitated them. Yet in reality the Führer was the puppet-master animating the Duce, whose peace proposals, like his race laws, emanated from Germany. This did not stop him from being saluted, on his return to Italy, as the "Saviour of Europe." He was also called the "Saviour of Peace,"[111] not a title relished by one who maintained that war is to man what maternity is to woman. Welcomed in Rome with a triumphal arch covered in laurel branches, Mussolini shouted angrily: "Who dreamt up this carnival?"[112]

The Caesar of the Fascist carnival, ever more bellicose and erratic, was increasingly out of step with his own people. Sensing this, he issued mordant denunciations of the bourgeois spirit, which was the antithesis of Fascism. However, as the British Ambassador contemptuously remarked, alluding to Mussolini's famous dictum that it was better to live for a day as a lion than for a century as a sheep, the Italians were "becoming tired of perpetual roaring and would prefer to graze in peace."[113] Chauvinistic appeals made little impression on them, though Ciano did stir up excitement in parliament by talking about the "natural aspirations of the Italian people."[114] Thereupon the deputies, in an apparently impromptu but actually well-orchestrated demonstration, rose to their feet baying for Tunis, Djibouti, Corsica and Nice. They seemed to have forgotten, France's new Ambassador, François-Poncet, drily remarked, that the road to these desirable destinations "would be over the bodies of 45 million Frenchmen."[115] Daladier was equally forthright, but not all his compatriots took the matter that seriously: some besieged the Italian embassy in Paris demanding "Venice for our honeymoon couples."[116] Mussolini vainly tried to stir up more Gallophobia, most delicately expressed in his anonymous article entitled "France is a Spittoon."

In fact, inside Italy popular feeling was more hostile to the Fascist regime than at any time since the murder of Matteotti, almost 15 years previously. This could be inferred from the enthusiasm with which Romans greeted Chamberlain and Halifax in January 1939. Mussolini privately damned his visitors as possessing nothing of the stuff of splendid adventurers such as Sir Francis Drake, who had won the empire which they would lose. But the crowds, for once not marshalled by the authorities but massing spontaneously, cheered the British Prime Minister so loudly that conversation inside the Palazzo Venezia became difficult and they were silenced by the touch of a bell on the Duce's desk. Characteristically, Mussolini was still arranging a *rapprochement* with Britain, which had recognised the conquest of Ethiopia in return for the removal of 10,000 Italian troops from Spain, at a time when he had just decided to conclude a military alliance with Germany and Japan in order to re-draw the map of the world. Diplomatic schizophrenia matched personal megalomania, best enunciated in the Duce's telephoned instruction to a bemused surveyor:

"The course of the Tiber winds too much—prepare a plan to straighten it."[117] But the zigzag course of foreign policy was apparently a matter of Fascist pride. Ciano boasted to the German Ambassador, "The Italian programme is to have no programme."[118]

Actually the Italian programme was to respond to German *faits accomplis.* Mussolini was more shocked by Hitler's invasion of Czechoslovakia than he had been by the *Anschluss.* As usual the Führer, mistrustful of the Court camarilla in the Quirinal Palace, gave the Duce no warning. Instead Mussolini received, to his chagrin, a mollifying message when it was too late to object. The very stones of Rome would rise up against a German alliance after this, he said, and briefly considered siding with the hated French. However, in his bosom, admiration for Hitler's brutal coup struggled with apprehension. The Führer was establishing a hegemony of Europe and he must be conciliated. This was also, incidentally, the view of the new Pope, Pius XII, who refused to join the democracies in protesting against the occupation of Prague. Most Italians, however, resented the current subservience to Hitler, jesting that, "Things were much better under Mussolini."[119] In the Chamber of Fasces and Corporations, recently appointed to replace the elected Chamber of Deputies, Italo Balbo, defying the order not to wear royal decorations, accused the Duce of licking the Germans' boots. Determined to assert the continuing virility of Fascism and to present Hitler with a *fait accompli* of his own in a region where he feared German incursions, Mussolini approved a scheme long hatched by Ciano. On 7 April 1939—Good Friday—Italy invaded Albania.

It was a move calculated to make headlines rather than to make real gains for Italy. Albania was so poor that, according to a wartime British officer, people would murder you for the lice in your shirt. The country was already an Italian protectorate—annexing it, Mussolini's critics said, was like raping your wife. King Zog, actually a tribal chieftain who had climbed over many corpses to mount a throne of his own creation, was a Fascist in all but name. Concealed by propaganda worthy of Baron Munchausen, the invasion itself was conducted with astounding incompetence. Radio communication was so ineffective that a senior officer had to fly back and forth to Albania to report on the situation. As Ciano's Chief of Staff, Filippo Anfuso, memorably remarked, "If only the Albanians had possessed a well-armed fire brigade, they could have driven us back into the Adriatic."[120] Zog, whom Italians called the "White Negus,"[121] escaped with buckets full of rubies and emeralds as well as a substantial part of the country's gold reserves. Ciano himself might have succeeded to his crown. But in the event King Victor Emmanuel received it from four burly, surly Albanians in dress suits, whose progress in open State carriages conducted by bewigged coachmen and attended by liveried flunkeys was watched by the Roman crowd in absolute silence. The spiritless little Sovereign believed in accepting crowns, even crowns of Ethiopia and Albania. But while loyal Fascists enthused about the acquisition of an Italian "fifth shore,"[122] Victor Emmanuel reckoned that Mussolini had merely grabbed a few rocks.

Albania was in one sense a victim of the democracies' appeasement policy; and so, in due course, was Italy. The protests of the Western powers against this fresh act of Fascist aggression were muted for fear of driving Mussolini more surely into the arms of Hitler. The attitude of leaders such as Chamberlain was indeed hardening: he privately condemned the Balkan "smash and grab raid," which Mussolini had carried out with "complete cynicism."[123] But the tone of the democracies remained soft and their very moderation provoked the Duce's extremism—he dismissed Roosevelt's plea for a ten-year truce as the product of spreading paralysis. Hitler, by contrast, congratulated him on a Fascist triumph and on the consequent strengthening of the Axis. He drew the Duce inexorably into his thrall, daring him to be bold. Observing the process, Bernardo Attolico, the Italian Ambassador in Berlin, described Mussolini's attitude towards the Reich as "that of a person who, when asked to jump into the street from the ground floor, insists on jumping from the roof."[124] So, in May 1939, the Duce plunged into what he wanted to call the "Pact of Blood," though it was finally dubbed the "Pact of Steel." The name mattered less than the content, which Ribbentrop drew up and which Ciano, in a singular act of Fascist dynamism, accepted without proper scrutiny. He thus committed Italy to come to Germany's aid in the event of war. He failed to stipulate that Italy should be consulted about such a conflict and simply took Hitler's word for it that he would keep the peace for at least three years. Ciano already knew that Poland was Hitler's next target and that plans were being made to ensure that Soviet Russia did not interfere. Yet throughout the early summer of 1939, preoccupied with parties, flirtations and trips to Capri, he maintained that there was no danger of an immediate conflict. Ciano dismissed Attolico's admonitions to the contrary as the vapourings of a neurotic who was frightened of his own shadow.

By early August, however, as Nazi antagonism towards Poland sharpened, Ciano grew alarmed. He arranged to meet Ribbentrop at the luxurious lakeside Schloss Fuschl, near Salzburg, which the German Foreign Minister had confiscated from an Austrian Jew murdered by the Gestapo. Talking in English, Ciano asked: "Do you want Danzig?" "More than that," Ribbentrop replied. "We want war!"[125] Shocked and disillusioned,

Ciano tried for ten hours to convince Ribbentrop that an attack on Poland would lead to a general conflict. His arguments made no impression and at Berchtesgaden, over the next two days, Hitler proved yet more implacable. The Führer worked himself into a rage over Polish brutalities—castrations, killings, rapes—inflicted on German minorities. As Ciano sardonically observed, he seemed to believe his own atrocity stories. In fact there was ample reason to disbelieve everything Hitler said, especially after his volte-face over Bolshevism. Mussolini endorsed the Nazi-Soviet agreement even though it cleared the decks for war. Ciano and other senior Fascists urged him to remain neutral, to break the Pact of Steel. The Duce swung to and fro like a weathercock in a storm. He yearned to march with Hitler. He lusted for triumphs and spoils. He ached to turn his warlike rhetoric into reality. But, as Dino Grandi wrote, his Nietzschean warmongering had always been a game, "a bluff, a fraud."[126]

Mussolini wanted war as St. Augustine had wanted chastity—not yet. He knew that Italians were unwilling to fight beside Germans and that the nation was unprepared for a major conflict. His troops were short of basic necessities, such as uniforms. His ships lacked fuel and nobody seemed to know how many aeroplanes he had—Ciano suggested that someone should be sent round the airfields to count them. Italy was desperately short of raw materials and, running such a large trade deficit that it resorted to selling munitions to the democracies, its capacity for imports was only "about one-half of what it had been in 1913."[127] So the Duce told the Führer that he could not fight unless Germany supplied Italy with millions of tons of coal, oil, steel, arms and other *matériel*. The demand could not be met and Mussolini therefore espoused "non-belligerence"—a less shameful term, in his view, than neutrality. This was a wise course for, when Hitler's victories did finally tempt him to fight, Italian forces made little progress during the "hundred hours' war" against France. But in September 1939 Mussolini was mortified by his inglorious stance. Europe was going up in flames, he remarked to Ciano, and after 18 years of bellicose propaganda the Duce of Italy had become the champion of peace. The dogs of war were unleashed but the Fascist lion lay down like a lamb. At a time when there was "Darkness Over the Earth"—to quote the title of Pius XII's first encyclical, issued shortly after Hitler invaded Poland—Mussolini stayed safely at home.

XXIII

FRANCE'S LEAN YEARS

WAR and peace were the inescapable themes of the time and they were
strikingly rehearsed during the International Exposition held in Paris in
1937, to which Italy made a flamboyant contribution. The Exposition
was nominally devoted to the display of arts and sciences. Among its 240
pavilions, which spread along the banks of the Seine and clustered
between the Trocadéro and the Champ de Mars, were cultural and industrial exhibits providing, it was claimed, "an inventory of the civilisation of
today and tomorrow."[1] The Palace of Discovery, situated in the Grand
Palais, contained a machine which generated the largest electrical spark in
the world. The nearby Palace of Cold was crowned by a tower of snow, 40
metres high, which never melted. French commercial enterprises appeared
in every shape and size: there was a Palace of Aviation which had an aero-
dynamic profile and a Pavilion of Tobacco reminiscent of a box of cigars.
Each undertaking had its showcase, from television to toy trains, from
ceramics to linoleum, from brown biscuits to bananas, from *haute couture*
to sewage disposal. Furthermore, 42 nations exhibited their own claims to
fame. In the glassy Italian pavilion, for instance, the delights of Tuscany
and Umbria were extolled, as were the achievements of national figures
from Romulus to Balbo, whose epic flight across the Atlantic was celebrated by a great bronze Winged Victory. However, patriotic show often
turned into political propaganda. Also exalted was Mussolini's Roman
empire, with huge photographs illustrating the conquest of Abyssinia,
while an enormous equestrian statue symbolised the "genius of Fascism."[2]

The French hoped that an assembly of nations would promote international amity and the organisers of the Exposition asserted that its dominant purpose was enshrined in the Pavilion of Peace. There, among other
things, a speaking clock announced that four soldiers had been killed and
nine mutilated for every minute of the First World War. However, Léon
Blum himself regarded the Exposition as a battleground where "democracy would deal fascism in all its forms its death-blow."[3] And if the Italians

responded pugnaciously enough, others beat more loudly still on the jingoistic drum. The German and Soviet pavilions, which glowered at each other on either side of the Right Bank end of the widened Pont d'Iéna, were uncompromising monuments to might. Both were built in the familiar style of neo-classical brutalism. The Nazis, though, won the contest for architectural virility. This was not only because of their seven-metre statues of "aggressively nude Teutons"[4] (before whose prodigious loins amused spectators would photograph one another) but because the German eagle clutching the swastika overshadowed the hammer and sickle opposite. The juxtaposition gave rise to conflicting myths: an inhabitant of affluent Passy "distinctly saw" the eagle flying off with the Soviet emblems in its talons; but a resident of "Red" Bobigny, "better informed about the tricks of aerial perspective," plainly witnessed "the sickle cutting off the eagle's wings."

It was understandable that spectators should conjure up fantasies before these "two formidable works of public intimidation."[5] At a time when the USSR was racked by Stalin's purges the extravagant Soviet pavilion gave a particularly strong stimulus to the imagination. Thus Parisians nicknamed the statues holding the hammer and sickle, two giant proletarians fashioned in stainless steel whose clothing streamed in the breeze, "Hurrying to the Lubyanka." Yet genuine revelations were also to be found in the Soviet pavilion. With walls made of marble quarried in Turkistan and motifs picked out in gold and precious stones, it smacked more of capitalist luxury than Communist austerity and visitors discerned monumental hypocrisy in this temple to the Workers' State. Moreover, something of the essence of Stalin's Russia was captured by a fresco in the Great Hall portraying the old Bolshevik leaders. As they disappeared into the maw of the NKVD, frantic last-minute efforts were made to disguise the purges "by adding, for instance, a beard to Marshal Tukhachevsky's face, side-burns to Radek, hair to Zinoviev."[6]

The Exposition could be seen as a paradigm of the contemporary condition in other respects. The American pavilion recalled the skyline of New York and featured national achievements from TVA dams to Hollywood villas. The Tokyo-educated, Paris-based architect of Nippon's pavilion eschewed a pagoda but created a bonsai garden, helping his native country to present "a new civilisation which is essentially Japanese."[7] The Pontifical pavilion offered spiritual sustenance at regular celebrations of the Mass but its campanile, crowned with a copper Madonna, was dwarfed by the symbols of secularism. Austria erected a "Grand Hotel of Vienna" at which waiters in national costume served Viennese coffee with whipped cream and strudels. British hospitality was dispensed at a tavern bearing the archaic sign, "Buttery." Ironically, genteel leisure was depicted as the main preoccupation in what had once been the workshop of the world. Life there now seemed to revolve around a permanent country-house weekend. Britain represented itself as largely pastoral and "entirely upper-class," displaying "an elegant pattern of golf balls, a frieze of tennis rackets, polo sets, riding equipment, natty dinner jackets," plus coronation robes and a cardboard cut-out of Neville Chamberlain fishing in long rubber boots.[8] Here was a "vision of regression"[9] that had nothing in common with Mussolini's projection of himself as a Roman Emperor. There was much recrimination about the humiliating contrast between the colossal endeavours of the totalitarian states and the derisory effort made by the motherland of the world's greatest empire. British critics likened their pavilion to "a sweet stall" and "a suburban cinema."[10] Even Republican Spain, embroiled in civil war, put on a more ambitious exhibition. Indeed, the Spanish pavilion stole the show with Picasso's apocalyptic memorial to Guernica, a latter-day Massacre of the Innocents explosively irradiated by that emblem of modernity, an electric light-bulb. French artistic efforts were also impressive, notably Raoul Dufy's immense mural on the history of electricity in the Palace of Light.

At a time when much of rural France was still not electrified and those houses that were seldom used more than 40-watt bulbs, the Exposition was a glorification of the entire spectrum of light. Among the most brilliant events were 18 Fêtes de la Lumière. They presented a "new art form"[11] (to reach maturity with the scintillating "mechanical 'ballet'"[12] in the Lagoon of Nations at New York's World's Fair in 1939) featuring light, music, fireworks and fountains. In the Seine a great machine pumped up thousands of jets of water in hundreds of different shapes—bouquets, birds, fans, rockets, rivulets—which were illuminated by powerful, multi-coloured lights. The dazzling aqueous theatre was embellished with clouds of silvery smoke rising like wraiths from the river in the path of the light which was projected from moored rafts as well as from the banks. There huge crowds watched "an unforgettable spectacle of radiant phantasmagoria." Since these symphonies of light and water had to compete with many other kinds of illumination, the organisers of the Exposition took special care to avoid "luminescent anarchy." They achieved a "marvellous fusion of effects . . . through contrasts between lights and shadows as well as by nuances of colour."

Their *pièce de résistance* was the Eiffel Tower, a "cathedral of light"[13] which eclipsed even the floodlit pavilions of Berlin and Moscow. Over 700 thousand-watt searchlights shone on it from all angles. Its iron filigree was threaded with ten kilometres of fluorescent tubing. A huge flaring fan opened and closed towards the new Chaillot Palace, while towards the Ecole Militaire gleamed the red, blue and white colours of France. Firework displays immersed the whole structure in flame. After viewing one from his balcony in Passy, the novelist Julien Green wrote: "It was an extraordinarily beautiful sight. The whole sky was set in a blaze, and the conflagration was suddenly transformed into a shower of emeralds and diamonds. It gave an impression of a bomb exploding in an immense jeweller's shop."[14] Equally entranced, E. M. Forster saw the high-voltage Tower as a scientific swan, an inspired giraffe, a crimson plesiosaurus; but he sensed in the "music and light, lusic and might" surrounding it a portent of war. To others the Eiffel Tower seemed like "a gigantic phantom rising to vanish into the celestial regions,"[15] a pillar of fire in the gloom.

Despite national rivalries, the Exposition was itself a beacon in a drab decade. It was an attempt not only to foster global harmony but also to revive industry and to boost morale at home. In these last respects it even gained a measure of success. It cheered visitors, who travelled between the pavilions in electric buggies, sat in the pavement cafés or picnicked under the flowering chestnut trees. It provided a host of entertainments, with performers ranging from Fred Astaire and Ginger Rogers to La Scala Opera Company. It also promoted Paris as the capital of fashion at a time when French *haute couture* was in disarray and more than 10,000 of its workers were unemployed. The Palace of Elegance, situated on the Quai d'Orsay and veneered with light-blue imitation faience, provided fashion designers with an international stage on which to parade their wares.

Elsa Schiaparelli, in particular, took full advantage of it. An Italian aristocrat and an anti-Fascist autocrat, who had contrived an evening ensemble based on an Ethiopian warrior's tunic with trousers of imperial purple to honour Haile Selassie, she was by 1935 the "undisputed queen of Paris fashion."[16] She had won the position, toppling Coco Chanel from her throne, largely by dint of audacity. Reacting against the subdued pastels, beiges and navies formerly thought sophisticated, Schiaparelli produced clothes in Fauvist hues: canary yellow, Mars orange and shocking pink (her trademark). Other schools of artists—Futurists, Dadaists and Surrealists—also contributed to her more avant-garde outfits. Thus she fabricated hats shaped like television sets, vegetable baskets, shoes. She created *trompe-l'oeil* skeleton sweaters and fingernail gloves. She sold buttons that looked like lollipops, necklaces apparently threaded with aspirins, a handbag resembling a telephone, a white satin evening gown decorated with a huge Daliesque lobster. No garment-maker better appreciated the publicity value of being different: at the Exposition Schiaparelli caused a sensation by burying a naked plaster mannequin in flowers and stringing up a washing-line on which she hung "all the clothes of a smart woman, even to panties, stockings and shoes."[17] Gendarmes had to hold back the crowds.

However, Schiaparelli owed her own vogue to practicality as well as to eccentricity. She used natural fabrics which moved with the body, as well as cheap synthetics such as rayon. Like Chanel, she appealed to the young with functional sports garb, well-cut suits and neat little black dresses. But whereas Chanel had made proletarian styles elegant, producing *apache* sweaters for the *beau monde* and dungarees *à la mode,* Schiaparelli, as Jean Cocteau wrote, invented "for all women what was once the privilege of few—to be individual."[18] She also made them less androgynous, accentuating soft curves and fluid lines at a time when, thanks to diet and exercise, better-off women were more willowy than ever before. She narrowed waists and emphasised busts, moving away from the tubular shape of the 1920s and in 1935 pioneering padded brassières. She also broadened shoulders, perhaps adumbrating the epaulettes of war, perhaps echoing the Balinese *bapangs* (projecting collars) seen at France's Colonial Exhibition of 1931. Certainly Schiaparelli ransacked the globe for inspiration, finding it in Indian turbans, Cossack jackets, Mexican boleros, Tuareg pantaloons, Italian masks. Chic versions of such exotica were displayed at her boutique, the first of its kind, at 21 Place Vendôme. There, in what was said to be the most famous window in the world, customers discovered an Aladdin's cave of sartorial fantasy. It doubtless represented an "escape from reality"[19] at a time of Depression. Maybe, too, it was a protest against the uniform garb and the uniform mentality of totalitarianism. But it also reflected other influences, especially, in 1937, that of the International Exposition. Its glitter provoked an explosion of spangles and sequins. Its extravagance prompted the use of brighter colours, richer fabrics, more exuberant embroideries and more opulent styles—puffed and frilled tulle capes, for example. Schiaparelli called her mid-season collection "Paris, 1937"[20] and won plaudits at home and abroad for her new, tall, svelte evening silhouette.

The scene behind the high fashions and the bright lights was much less *comme il faut.* Blum had hoped that the Exposition would be "a triumph for the working class, the Popular Front and liberty."[21] Instead it ultimately attracted far fewer visitors (only 31 million) than previous national exhibitions and lost money (220 million francs). Even as it was being erected the Exposition became a focus for the industrial strife which had plagued France since the advent of the Popular Front. Convinced that they were being exploited and worried about unemployment once the work was done, the 20,000 builders spun out their tasks, restricted overtime and periodically went on strike. They ignored inducements from employers, appeals by Blum and the coaxing of their own trade union leaders. Labour relations on the site deteriorated, outbreaks of violence occurred and some men carried arms to work. Others spat at sightseers and shouted "parasite."[22] The official opening had to be postponed. Even when it did take place, on 25 May 1937, most pavilions were unfinished, though, Parisians joked, "The Eiffel Tower is ready."[23] So, embarrassingly enough, were the edifices constructed by the totalitarian powers, Germany, Italy and the Soviet Union. To avoid the potholes and rubble President Lebrun conducted his inaugural tour of the Exposition from the Seine. Elaborate efforts were made to hide the incompleteness, including the copious use of plasterboard and whitewash. But nothing could prevent visitors from seeing that America's skyscraper was only one storey high. No cosmetic could disguise the fact that much work remained to be done on France's Pavilion of Labour. Blum now set himself to deal with the crisis of which this was such a poignant symbol. He thus precipitated his own downfall and the withering away of the Popular Front.

IT had already been grievously weakened. Many of its keenest supporters were disillusioned by devaluation and non-intervention in Spain. Right-wing newspapers hounded ministers so ferociously that one of them, Roger Salengro, falsely accused of having deserted during the First World War, committed suicide. Far from achieving industrial peace through concessions such as the 40-hour week, embodied in the Matignon Agreement, Blum's ministry had to face many damaging disputes. These fostered hopes and fears of social revolution, which in turn undermined national solidarity against external foes. Communists looked to Moscow while, according to one foreign observer, "some of the most prominent industrialists would rather see the establishment of fascism in France with the armed support of Hitler and Mussolini than submit to the dictation of labour."[24] Inflation rose and productivity fell, notably in France's shrunken munitions industry, which proved unable to meet the government's new orders. The *"real tragedy of the Front Populaire,"*[25] insisted the British journalist Alexander Werth, was that it had to sacrifice expenditure on social improvements to the increasingly urgent needs of rearmament. Thus in February 1937 Blum announced a "pause"—really a suspension of the Matignon Agreement in an attempt to balance the budget. He also tried to curb strikes. But the financial crisis grew more acute and, faced by a flight from the franc, Blum complained that he was a victim of the "wall of money."[26] French capital, he plausibly asserted, had itself gone on strike against the Popular Front. Then, on 16 March, the Prime Minister became personally involved in an incident which proved a turning-point in his government's fortunes. A violent confrontation took place between left-wing demonstrators and police at Clichy, a working-class district described by Céline as Paris's doormat, on which everyone wiped their feet. Six people were killed and hundreds injured. Blum visited the scene, hot-foot from the Opéra and wearing full evening dress. He was promptly implicated in the carnage by a vicious cartoon captioned: "Who said this man has no French blood?"[27]

If the Clichy clash raised the spectre of the Concorde riot, the resulting six-hour general strike conjured up the prospect of another Commune. Foreign reports even claimed that civil war was imminent and that Daladier, the War Minister, was concentrating an army at the gates of Vincennes. In parliament Blum mocked these scare stories. Less easy to dismiss was the sinister assertion of a right-wing deputy that Nazi Germany would not tolerate a Communist country on its border. A more immediate danger, by June 1937, was a renewed fall in industrial production and a further run on the franc. France was said to be unique in passing from one depression to another without an intervening period of prosperity. To stop the rot Blum asked for plenary powers. His aim was to restore confidence, as Poincaré had done through massive devaluation in 1926. But, in an age of dictators, the Radicals in the Chamber were suspicious of an economic autocracy. Vehement for moderation, they were fearful of truly radical measures such as exchange controls and tax reforms. Consequently they refused to support Blum. So did the Senate, where the Prime Minister was blamed for having persuaded French workmen that "freshly roasted larks"[28] would fall into their mouths. The tide of public opinion had plainly now turned against the Popular Front. On June 20, therefore, Blum resigned. He was worn out by his ordeal and disappointed that the bright promise of the previous year had not been fulfilled. Yet he hoped that the Popular Front could be kept in being under new management.

The new manager was Camille Chautemps, who had survived the disgrace of being Prime Minister during the Stavisky scandal and had wriggled back into power as a leading Radical. In fact, Herriot described him as an eel, though according to the American Ambassador, William Bullitt, Chautemps was generally "considered a jellyfish with lots of common sense."[29] Certainly he was smooth, slippery and prone to drift. But, lacking drive and conviction himself, Chautemps was adept at reconciling colleagues of different views. He kept the Popular Front flag flying but supported, for example, the conservative (and ultrasinuous) Georges Bonnet

as his Finance Minister. Gliding towards the wall of money, Chautemps
was able to obtain the powers denied to Blum. But, though his government raised taxes, cut social spending and eroded the 40-hour week, it had
no more success in mending the French economy. The franc was allowed
to float—and it sank. Industry stagnated. Strikes spread, involving metallurgical workers at Lille, power operatives at Lyon, employees in the Peu-
geot motor works at Souchaux, seamen at Le Havre, hotel and café staff in
the capital. Recalcitrance was so rife at Billancourt that Renault foremen
actually struck against "union tyranny."[30] Sit-ins occurred in a number of
other factories around Paris and transport workers withdrew their labour
in sympathy—in December 1937 army lorries had to deliver food to Les
Halles. Despite the simultaneous threat of right-wing violence, realised in
sporadic bombings carried out by members of a secret society known
as the Cagoulards, Chautemps did throw a few sops to the Left. French
railways were nationalised, for example. But the three classes of travel
remained. This was one indication among many that Chautemps would
never implement the egalitarian programme of the Popular Front, which
as a result finally broke up at the beginning of 1938. Chautemps' conduct of foreign policy was, if possible, even more supine than his domestic
leadership. He lived up to his reputation for solving problems by dodg-
ing them and, significantly, resigned on 10 March 1938—the eve of the
Anschluss.

The Quai d'Orsay had long accepted that, as its top official Alexis Léger
said, Hitler's "share of the swag resulting from the Rome–Berlin axis, viz.,
in the first instance the swallowing of Austria, will come to him without
the use of force."[31] But, fatalistic in anticipation, France was paralysed by
the event. Daladier later claimed that, as War Minister, he had proposed
mobilisation but that other members of the cabinet "felt they were merely
shadows, carrying on 'les affaires courantes,' so the fresh crime of the Nazi
gangsters went unpunished."[32] Chautemps and his fellow shadows blamed
French stasis on British refusal to help. Yet no special pleading could disguise the fact that France was neither ready nor willing to intervene under
any circumstances. The best that could be done was to form a government
of public safety and national unity. Blum tried. He even put forward a
quasi-Keynesian proposal to stimulate the economy by means of massive
deficit spending on arms. It was ironic, as no one appreciated better than
Blum himself, that an apostle of peace should be imitating the plans of
Göring and Stalin. But, he insisted,

We shall proceed in such a way that around the manufacture of armaments there will be an economy which will be the basis for a more abun-

dant production in all domains, so that in the very midst of this painful task, undertaken and carried out in common, the work of social solidarity and human fraternity shall be continued and amplified.[33]

The tragedy was that Blum's loftier ideals were inappropriate to the age of the *Anschluss*.

This explains why his new ministry lasted less than a month: it seemed more of an attempt to revive the irrelevant Popular Front than to create the vital Union Nationale. Other factors also frustrated Blum. The press exacerbated fears that he would impose confiscatory taxation. Further strikes occurred, notably in defence industries. There was an upsurge of anti-Semitism, mainly directed at Jewish refugees from Austria. In *Je Suis Partout* Lucien Rebattet, who had witnessed the Nazi pogrom that "smashed the ghetto" in Vienna, praised it as "a splendid example of distributive justice."[34] In the Chamber deputies shouted "Down with Jews" and "Jews to the scaffold."[35] The British government, whose influence on French affairs waxed with the German menace, barely concealed its hostility to Blum. This was not a matter of racial prejudice, though Léger had once felt it necessary to hold Blum in conversation beside a statue of Disraeli at 10 Downing Street so that their Tory hosts could see that he too, although a Jew, was "a gentleman and an statesman."[36] No, what mainly concerned Neville Chamberlain was Blum's socialism, his suspected intrigues with the Labour Party in Britain and his open sympathy for the Communist Party in Spain and Russia—which might lead to war with Germany. So Britain's National Government rejoiced when Blum's ministry gave way to what seemed to be a French national government, led by the supposed strong man Edouard Daladier, in April 1938. And behind the scenes the new British Ambassador in Paris, Sir Eric Phipps, helped to jockey Georges Bonnet into the Quai d'Orsay. The new French Foreign Minister was, in Winston Churchill's phrase, "the quintessence of defeatism."[37]

In fact, as a recent historian has written, Bonnet "is one reason why appeasement has become a dirty word."[38] If Chautemps resembled an eel, Bonnet put contemporaries in mind of a snake—specifically a sidewinder. To quote one of Bonnet's few friends: "When he walks, he does not go straight but moves sideways in such a manner that all one sees of him is a long powerful nose that seems to scent every danger and every prey."[39] When danger did threaten, Bonnet would, according to his more robust colleague Georges Mandel, "hide under any flat stone to avoid it." This was not quite fair. Bonnet did possess courage, even if it was primarily the courage of his own lack of conviction. Lord Halifax found him "not so black (or so yellow) as he is painted."[40] Furthermore Bonnet was clever, sophisticated, energetic and charming. In many respects he was an asset to the government. The son of an affluent Dordogne magistrate, he had good connections, a wealth of political experience and an attractive wife called Odette whose high ambitions matched his own. Inevitably she was nicknamed "Soutien-Georges"—a well-worn play on the French word for brassière, which had earlier been applied to King George V's ample-busted Queen Mary.

Bonnet needed all the support he could muster for he exuded dishonesty. His blue eyes were hooded, shifty and veiled in mist, as if to conceal thoughts he dare not avow. Bald-pated and spindle-shanked, he was supposed to be "congenitally uncandid."[41] He lied, it was said, like a tooth-puller. General Gamelin thought Bonnet wholly untruthful and described him as a "vile ferment"[42] at the heart of government. Daladier himself acknowledged that he could "not have full confidence"[43] in Bonnet, who tampered with diplomatic documents at the time and tried to distort the historical record subsequently. Bonnet used his inside knowledge as Foreign Minister, notably at the time of Munich, to speculate on the Bourse. Still more reptilian were his attempts to insinuate himself into the good graces of Nazis. Bonnet once told the German Ambassador that it was fortunate so many Communists had been killed in Spain since the Parisian Red Belt was now more thinly populated. On another occasion he assured him, quite erroneously, that French cabinet ministers were all sincere admirers of the Führer. Plainly Bonnet regarded dishonour as a small price to pay for peace. Daladier was, or appeared to be, more scrupulous and determined. But nothing better revealed his essential feebleness than his refusal to dismiss Bonnet, even when he knew that the Foreign Minister was betraying his trust. The Premier was understandably mocked for being a "reed posing as a lance." In the end, chiefly because of his equivocations over Bonnet and the policy he represented, Daladier was a broken reed.

Yet although resolute for irresolution, Daladier did possess a kind of dogged integrity. Unlike Bonnet, Chautemps and their kind, he was unsullied by financial scandal—though Parisians joked that his plump mistress, the heiress to a tinned-sardine fortune who had married the impoverished Marquis de Crussol, was a "sardine who thinks she's a sole."[44] Daladier was a patriot who made serious efforts to augment the power of France. On becoming Premier he retained the War Ministry and stayed at the Rue Saint-Dominique instead of moving to the Hôtel Matignon. Despite a gruff exterior—furrowed brow, pursed lips, rumpled suit—and a cold tone said to resemble the mistral of his native valley, he made a good impression in both offices. One witness, Jean Daridan, wrote:

> Of medium height but massive presence, with eyes very blue and pene-trating, sparse hair, thick nose and quizzical mouth, Daladier breathed courage—the effect, incidentally, of a certain detachment, as if he viewed problems from afar. He was able to laugh at himself but, applied to oth-ers, his irony could be corrosive. With a benevolent manner free of all pomposity, he excelled at drawing out his colleagues and communicating his trust in them. His knowledge was vast, his intelligence lively, and I have never seen anyone grasp an issue so quickly or master a brief with such ease.[45]

Daladier also established a rapport with the electorate, keeping uncannily in tune with public opinion. Abroad he slapped Mussolini down but bent over backwards to conciliate Hitler. At home he imposed greater discipline and espoused sound money, devaluing the currency again in May 1938. He reversed the costly reforms of the Popular Front in order to strengthen the "fourth arm of defence"[46]—the economy. He stepped up rearmament and where possible ruled by decree. Sometimes, as the hostile journalist "Perti-nax" observed, Daladier was a dictator in spite of himself.

Daladier's grim authoritarianism went some way to conceal his own weakness and that of France. Of course he could not dispel prevalent fears. Frenchmen reminded one another obsessively that theirs was a land of 40 million peasants whose chief enemy was an industrial nation twice its size. In the summer of 1938 war seemed inevitable, defeat likely and, to those of military age, death or injury certain. Henri de Montherlant advised a young friend not to worry about his future since "in a year you'll be killed in the war." The friend replied, "That's what my mother tells me."[47] A character in Sartre's novel *The Reprieve* buys a photograph of a shattered face—noseless, with a bandage over one eye—because, he says, "I want to know what I shall look like next year."[48] Alarm was not confined to the public. General Vuillemin, head of the air force, embarrassed Daladier by coming close to panic. Duped by the Luftwaffe, which fitted planes with new registration numbers and switched them from one base to another during manoeuvres at which he was a guest, Vuillemin forecast that, in the event of war, the French air force would be annihilated in a few days.

By contrast Maurice Gamelin, Chief of Staff of National Defence, remained "astonishingly calm and confident."[49] He would talk of the French army slicing through Germany like a knife through butter. And until the spring of 1939 he was insouciant about the dangers of blitzkrieg. Gamelin had learned imperturbability from "Papa" Joffre during the First World War and, like him, refused to be disturbed between the hours of

8:00 P.M. and 8:00 A.M. But his composure smacked of complacency. Even if he fostered the illusion of France's military might only in order to maintain prestige or to confuse foes, the results were sometimes unfortunate. Believing that the French could defend both themselves and their allies, the British were encouraged to neglect their own army. Frenchmen too were deceived. Léon Noël, Ambassador to Poland, complained that he and other senior officials had been kept in the dark about the "terrifying unpreparedness" of France's army: "Under the pretext of propaganda aimed at foreigners, we ourselves were misled about the real state of our armaments."[50]

Disillusionment set in with such a vengeance after the defeat of 1940 that people exaggerated the nation's decadence between the wars. France was said to have been the sick man of Europe. The French, led and misled by cowardly poltroons, had been corrupted by "ignorance and error."[51] In recent years the fashion has changed, notably (and ironically) among Anglo-Saxon historians, who have sought to play down the French malaise and to rehabilitate figures such as Gamelin. Their efforts are unconvincing. It is true that Gamelin was neither a ninny, as Sartre reckoned, nor, as General Beaufre asserted, a noodle. He was an intellectual soldier with sensitive political antennae and a shrewd conception of modern warfare. But he lacked martial spirit. He was better at talking about war than preparing for it—or waging it. And even in discussion he was equivocal, keen to tease out academic subtleties, anxious to avoid commitment, only willing to profess "half certainties,"[52] reluctant to look his interlocutors in the eye. In counsel he was cautious, enigmatic, inconsistent and somnolent: subordinates called him "Gagamelin." He frequently overestimated German strength, thus undermining Daladier's tenuous fortitude and bolstering Bonnet's inveterate pusillanimity. In 1938, for example, Gamelin declared that Germany's West Wall was a formidable barrier when he knew that its concrete was not dry. His judgement about more distant armed forces was equally at fault: he considered Poland, and bizarrely, Romania more powerful than the Soviet Union. Suave and studious, a son of the church and a disciple of Bergson, Gamelin might have made a Jesuit or a philosopher. As France's Commander-in-Chief between 1935 and 1940, he was little short of a disaster.

The task of preparing to fight Germany was anything but straightforward. Its chief difficulty was that past and present Depression cast a longer shadow than future war. Daladier, earlier responsible for drastic reductions in military spending, was now loth to increase it too fast for fear that a temporary boom should result in a subsequent slump. Even so the defence budget, fixed at 14 billion francs in 1936, had doubled by 1938.

But France's industrial capacity was now so restricted that money could not be turned into munitions overnight. A B-1 heavy tank, for example, took two years to build—in three separate factories. Indeed, some machine tools were so old that workers constructed tanks with little more than hammers and files. Efficient production depended on large orders, which were not forthcoming. The removal of munitions plants from the vulnerable Paris region, notably Pierre Cot's transfer of the entire aviation industry to Toulouse, Bordeaux and Marseilles, further disrupted rearmament. There were shortages of skilled workers, especially in engineering and metallurgy. Still, France made such strides that by 1939 it was outproducing Germany in both tanks and fighter aircraft. Furthermore France's military equipment was in certain respects superior to that of the Third Reich. Gamelin not only had more tanks, some with thicker armour and heavier guns, he also had more artillery than Germany. True, only 44 of his 200 artillery regiments were motorised. But the Wehrmacht itself was more of a "military anachronism" than a "mechanised juggernaut":[53] when Hitler invaded Russia in 1941 he fielded 3,350 tanks and 650,000 horses, over four times as many as had Napoleon in 1812.

However, arms mattered less than men—and ideas. Gamelin and his generals had learned little and forgotten nothing since Verdun. They did not even appreciate the value of the infiltration tactics which had enabled the Germans to make such dramatic advances in 1918, well before the blitzkrieg was envisioned. It was not so much in war *matériel* that France was old-fashioned—though Vuillemin said that the obsolescence of the air force scared him out of his wits—it was in military doctrine.

Gamelin considered aviation an adjunct to the army and even a progressive such as Charles de Gaulle had little notion of employing aircraft in combined operations with tanks. The French army relied on firepower rather than mobility, understandable perhaps since its infantry, burdened with heavier equipment, was slower in 1939 than it had been in 1914. Gamelin allowed himself to be distracted by Italy and developed no plans to attack Germany. Any offensive, he said, would result in "a modernised form of the battle of the Somme."[54] As this suggests, Gamelin was as defence-minded as Daladier who, as War Minister, declared that "the first and last word in military art is to build a trench and hold it."[55] Yet the Maginot Line was palpably incomplete. Like its leaders, the French army was cautious, bureaucratic, fossilised by tradition. Few of its officers envisaged the tank as much more than a lumbering gun platform designed to support ground troops—not one of the copies of General Guderian's *Achtung! Panzer!,* a German textbook of tank warfare which was translated and distributed to garrisons all over France, had its pages cut. In fact the

Nazi propaganda booklets, sold on the streets in support of the
Winter Aid campaign (*reproduced actual size*)

The Physical Culture Parade in Red Square, Moscow, 1936

Modern Times, 1936: Charlie Chaplin becomes a cog in the industrial machine

Nazi propaganda:
the idealised Aryan,
featured on a poster

Nazi propaganda:
the demonised Jew,
pictured on a beermat

Ethiopians learn to salute the Duce

Emperor Haile Selassie of Ethiopia leads his troops against the Italians

Edward VIII leaves Windsor Castle after his abdication broadcast,
10 December 1936

George VI and other members of Britain's royal family, wearing their
coronation robes, try to revive the mystique of monarchy

Winston Churchill visits his Epping constituency during the general election of 1935

Partially obscured by spray from illuminated fountains in the River Seine,
the Nazi tower confronts the Soviet pavilion

Neville Chamberlain brings home the good news from Munich

Molotov signs the Nazi–Soviet Pact, 23 August 1939, watched by
Ribbentrop (*centre*) and Stalin

Icon of the leader who claimed to embody his nation

military leadership was reluctant to fit tanks with radios because it wanted to limit their capacity for manoeuvring *en masse*. Moreover the abstemious Gamelin neglected to equip his own Vincennes headquarters with radio or telegraph, relying instead on telephone and messenger. Still, he was less obscurantist than Pétain, who thought that France was defeated in 1940 because electronic communications had taken the place of carrier pigeons.

I F the French high command worried about their own ground forces they despised those of their closest ally. Britain had a mere "parade-ground army,"[56] weaker even than the Red Army, itself little more than an internal constabulary with a gutted officer corps. Gamelin tried to persuade the British to strengthen their forces and to forge armoured divisions. But the Treasury kept tight hold on the purse-strings at a time of Depression and, as Gamelin discovered, his own country had no monopoly on military conservatism—British regiments which received self-propelled guns, for example, slowed down their rate of fire by retaining elaborate procedures to control non-existent horses. Nevertheless, the British alliance was a matter of life and death for France.

Only with the help of John Bull—his powerful navy, his burgeoning modern air force and his immense imperial resources—could Marianne survive a prolonged Teutonic assault. As Daladier himself acknowledged: "Everything depends on the English; we must follow them."[57] Bonnet was more slavish still, saying that he would accept English guidance "with my eyes closed."[58] Daladier wondered aloud why Great Britain went to the expense of maintaining an embassy in Paris when it had one which cost nothing—at the Quai d'Orsay. That France did retain some diplomatic initiative is indicated by the countercharge, noted by Sir Nevile Henderson, that with Phipps at its head the British embassy was only a branch of the French Foreign Ministry. However, few doubted that Paris was dancing to London's tune. Fewer denied that the English alliance was as necessary as that between the horseman and the horse (though Paul-Boncour echoed Talleyrand's warning that "we must try not to be the horse").[59] So, to promote the entente, King George VI and Queen Elizabeth made a state visit to France in July 1938. It was a spectacular democratic display designed to outshine the barbaric pageantry of the Axis.

Behind the scenes the democratic machinery proved cumbersome, clogged by protocol and bureaucracy. There were difficulties over what official gifts would be appropriate for the royal couple: the King wanted an inscribed gold cigarette case to add to his collection but he had to make do with an engraved glass table-service. The French tried to pack his programme with formal engagements and he rejected several which would have imposed "extra fatigue." He also refused to broadcast his speech from the Elysée Palace: his Private Secretary feared that the "additional nervous strain"[60] might adversely affect the stammering Sovereign's delivery. However, the King did submit to the request that he should wear uniform, despite the discomfort, at the British embassy dinner. The British also agreed to satisfy the insatiable French appetite for honours and decorations, though courtiers worried about the cheapening effect, and Buckingham Palace ran out of insignia. The royal visitors also proved indulgent about an entertainment arranged for them by the playwright Sacha Guitry in which the French composer Lully was credited with writing the tune of "God Save the King." Despite the contretemps, both sides were determined to make the visit a model of harmony, not only to raise their own people's morale but to impress "the dictator states."[61] Nothing better symbolised Gallic eagerness to please than the curtsy with which Madame Lebrun greeted her regal guests. Since she was the wife of the French head of state there was much controversy about its propriety, to say nothing of its elegance. One critic described the curtsy as a *"génuflexion catastrophique."*[62]

The Republic as a whole paid extravagant obeisance to royalty—even the Communist press bade them welcome. Paris smothered itself in flags and bunting. The Eiffel Tower flew a Union Jack 1,500 square yards in size and the Boulevard des Capucines was a tunnel of red, white and blue. A chiropodist's shop displayed corns and bunions against a background of the British banner. The Exposition had been cleared away and unsightly scenes were hidden by hoardings proclaiming "God Save the King." The words of the anthem, spelled out phonetically, were distributed to the crowds, themselves swollen by provincials in their rustic garb and city folk who had postponed their holidays for the occasion. *"Vive le Roi,"* they roared as the King (dressed in admiral's uniform) and the Queen (in a pale cream costume trimmed with silver fox fur) made their ceremonial entry into the capital. They drove in open cars with the Lebruns, and a shaft of sunshine, which had pierced the grey clouds as their train drew into the Bois de Boulogne station, followed them all the way to the Place de la Concorde "while everywhere else was in shadow."[63] Despite this celestial spotlight, though, the spectators did not see much of the visitors. The French government, terrified of another royal assassination, surrounded the King and Queen with a phalanx of Republican Guards and packed the streets with gendarmes. "What has my brother ever done against France," quipped the Duke of Windsor, "that he needs such elaborate police protection?"[64] More ominously, Diana Cooper had noticed that the soldiers posted every hundred yards along the railway line to guard the royal train stood "in blood-red pools of poppies and seem[ed] to be advertising a second world war."[65]

The functions which followed had been arranged largely to remind the French and British people of their common sacrifice during the First World War. Thus George VI broke precedent by not going to the races. Instead, as he arrived at the port of Boulogne, a statue of Britannia was unveiled to commemorate the disembarkation of the first British troops in 1914. The King visited the Military Hospital in Paris. He laid a wreath at the tomb of the Unknown Soldier. He watched a march-past of 50,000 troops at Versailles and attended a State banquet in the Hall of Mirrors, the first time it had been used for such an event since Clemenceau presided over the signing of the Peace Treaty. The 260 guests, served by waiters wearing powdered wigs, scarlet and blue liveries, knee breeches, white silk stockings and rubber-soled shoes, were offered a menu fit for a king. It included caviare flown in from Moscow, iced melon and Amontillado, salmon trout with crayfish, young lamb chops, quail stuffed with foie gras, breast of Rouen duck with peas and salad, creamed chicken with asparagus, Perigord truffles, iced mousse and peaches. This was accompanied by 13 wines of surpassing rarity and excellence, some the same age as the royal guests. Justice could not be done to this feast in less than three hours but, to the chagrin of the ten chefs who had created it, only 45 minutes were allocated to its consumption—which must have tested King George's fragile digestive system however sparingly he ate. Still, it was no small matter that a gastronomic seal had been set on the democratic concord.

Furthermore the King completed his engagements with a poignant reminder of the imperial contribution to the British war effort. At Villers-Bretonneux he unveiled a memorial to Australians killed on the Western Front and recalled events which had bound France to Greater Britain "with ties that the passing years can never weaken."[66] It was significant, however, that although the words expressed solidarity, the symbolism implied appeasement—of which the King was privately an ardent supporter. Cemeteries like the one at Villers-Bretonneux evoked a war so terrible that it should have ended war. Monuments to the glorious dead put up all over France during the epidemic of inter-war "statue-mania"[67] were not just recollections of heroism but adumbrations of danger to be avoided at all costs. Their iconography was mainly secular: few crosses to indicate the afterlife of individual soldiers; many obelisks, triumphal arches, Gallic cocks and allegorical figures to denote the survival of the nation. The highest form of patriotism often seemed to be the promotion of peace: the socialist administration of Lille changed the wording on the great memorial in the city centre from *"Morts pour la France"* to *"Morts pour la Paix."*[68] As Diana Cooper discovered, the French saw the royal visit as "a safeguard against the dreaded war."[69] Their enthusiasm was correspondingly effusive. According to Phipps, "No celebration since the Armistice has aroused such united and deep feeling."[70] American observers were particularly impressed by the fact that the European democracies were such "good box office." In the words of the *New York Times,* "Messrs Hitler and Mussolini surely missed a bet if they didn't have costumers, stage designers and production directors on hand to make notes." Berlin and Rome could not have put on a better show, "and neither could Hollywood."[71]

KING George and Queen Elizabeth went home warmed by what they considered an essentially *"personal"* triumph.[72] Their glow would have been extinguished had they heard Daladier's subsequent animadversions to William Bullitt—who promptly passed them on to Roosevelt. The King was "a moron," the French Premier declared, and his wife was "an excessively ambitious woman who would be ready to sacrifice every other country in the world in order that she might remain Queen Elizabeth of England."[73] Actually this outburst was part of a prolonged diatribe against perfidious Albion. It was inspired by resentment at being kept "in the dark"[74] (as France was well into 1939) about British diplomatic and military intentions, by fears of betrayal and by anger about what seemed to be blackmail. During the State Visit Lord Halifax had insisted that Britain would withdraw support from the Franco-Czechoslovak alliance unless Paris increased pressure on Prague to make concessions over the Sudetenland. Despite his vexation, though, the French Premier was not wholly averse to the policy of appeasement. He sounded bellicose and insisted that France's commitment to Czechoslovakia was "sacred and immutable";[75] but privately he confessed to seeking some honourable way to escape it. Bonnet himself hardly tried to conceal "a terror of war so deep . . . [that he was] prepared to accept any solution, however unjust or fraught with future disaster, so long as it did not impair Franco-German relations."[76] It was not only another huge blood-letting that he feared but the destruction of the social order and "the disappearance of the privileged classes."[77] He himself fully expected to be thrown into the Seine.

So, with British connivance, Bonnet sapped Daladier's crumbling will to resist. He got ammunition from Phipps "to fire off at any possible war-mongers"[78] in the cabinet, such as Georges Mandel. He intrigued with corrupt and defeatist ministers such as Anatole de Monzie and Charles Pomaret. He informed Benes that France would not fight for the Sudetenland, a *démarche* not hidden from Hitler. He suppressed Litvinov's offer to hold staff talks, thus keeping France's most powerful confederate at arm's length. How the Soviet Union would have supported France in the event of war over Czechoslovakia remains unclear. But, as de Gaulle observed, whatever horror his compatriots felt towards the Communist regime, to combat Hitler they had to ally with the Russians: it was like "Francis I making common cause with the Muslims against Charles V."[79] Bonnet naturally preferred an American alliance, but when he tried to imply that it was evolving, during a speech at the opening of an American war memorial at La Pointe de Grave on 4 September 1938, Roosevelt flatly denied any involvement in a "Franco-British front."[80]

If the President thus gave encouragement to the Führer, Bonnet continued to undermine Daladier's self-confidence. On 8 September the Premier was still threatening that the French would march to a man. A week later, as Chamberlain made his first peace-seeking flight to Germany, Daladier was close to capitulation. On 18 September he submitted to British and Bonnétiste pressure to agree to the cession of Sudeten territories with a German majority. Yet he knew that this would deliver up the frontier fortifications on which Czechoslovak security rested in return for an Anglo-French guarantee that could hardly be worth more than the treaty on which France was reneguing. Put to the test, Daladier characteristically took the line of least resistance and shuffled off responsibility on to others. Worse still, he helped Bonnet to weaken the moral fibre of the French people themselves. He did nothing to rally popular support for Czechoslovakia. Indeed, far from invoking the heroic spirit of Verdun, like the right-wing deputy Henri de Kérillis, or proclaiming, like de Gaulle, that "no sword struck heavier blows than our sword,"[81] the government did its best to "anaesthetise opinion."[82] Here was the climax of an era aptly described as one of "make-belief and spiritual betrayal."[83]

From mid-September public meetings concerned with international affairs were banned. The radio was controlled more tightly. Its bosses even cut the final sentence from one of Chamberlain's speeches because it was thought too "pessimistic."[84] The press was strongly called to heel. When, after Hitler increased his demands at Godesberg, the Foreign Office in London stated that Britain would join France in resisting a German attack on Czechoslovakia, the Quai d'Orsay dismissed the communiqué as "false news" and compliant papers said that anyone who attached credence to it was a warmonger. Police also tore down Flandin's poster asserting that the public had been deceived into accepting war as inevitable. In fact, there was little to counteract the predominant mood of defeatism, now fostered mainly by those on the Right—they were more vehement than left-wing pacifists whose convictions began to fracture under the pressure of events. So as Frenchmen were called up, during Daladier's fit of recalcitrance over the Godesberg timetable by which Hitler would occupy the Sudetenland, the French mind was mobilised against war.

Right-wing propaganda was intense and Parisian walls were papered with placards. The message was simple. France should not be sacrificed for Czechoslovakia, itself less a nation than a *macédoine.* To fight Germany was to commit mass suicide, since the Luftwaffe would flatten French cities in a fortnight—the capital's fire chief reckoned that 50 incendiary bombs would set all Paris ablaze. This time civilians would suffer with soldiers, whose fate would be that of the defenders of Verdun. Sartre was typical in anticipating that the new land battles would echo the old. War would be a thunderbolt to

> shatter this smooth-faced world, plough the countryside into a quagmire, dig shell-holes in the fields, and fashion these flat monotonous lands into the likeness of a storm-tossed sea—war, the hecatomb of righteous men, the massacre of the innocents.[85]

Overwhelmed by the prospect of another Armageddon, some felt that, "It is better to live as a German than to die as a Frenchman."[86]

The public, like the Premier himself, was subject to abrupt mood swings as France writhed on the horns of its cruel dilemma—dishonour or war. Two intellectuals classically expressed the agonising ambivalence of the time: Sartre said that the democracies could not go on appeasing Hitler for ever, yet felt that the prospect of imminent conflict was too dreadful to contemplate; Blum, anticipating an unworthy peace, found himself "divided between cowardly relief and shame."[87] By contrast, the men who were mobilising quickly became fatalistic about resuming the death grapple with Germany. Reservists, some still clad in workmen's blue cotton jackets and trousers, wore an air of grim resignation as they gathered at railway stations and set off to defend France at one remove. The atmosphere was very different from that of 1914. No one cried of *"à Berlin"* or sang the Marseillaise, though some Communists did bawl the Internationale—a raucous counter to "international fascism,"[88] of which Hitler was the incarnation.

However, in the few days before Munich the prevailing climate was one of panic. It was encouraged by the obvious ineptitude of the air raid precautions: the comical failure of the blackout practice; the patent shortage of gas masks and shelters; the wan piles of sand in the streets for use against fires, which became playgounds for children and lavatories for cats. Equally inadequate were the evacuation measures—except in the case of government ministries. Politicians seemed especially prone to "blue funk."[89] The Aviation Minister, certain that "the destruction of Paris would pass all imagination," sent his family to Brittany and advised others to do the same.[90] These others had to fend for themselves. So from Lille to Strasbourg there was a "stampede of the well-to-do."[91] Cars packed with people and possessions jammed the roads leading south and west. Huge crowds besieged the railway stations and people fought for seats on trains. Six hundred thousand Parisians fled in a week. The capital felt empty, though queues still formed outside savings banks. The shops were deserted, apart from those selling trunks. The Louvre closed and its works of art were packed into crates. Factories were camouflaged, trenches were dug in parks, street lamps dimmed to a glimmer. Doctors profited by issuing medical certificates granting exemption from military service. A brisk trade arose in houses for sale or rent in areas remote from invasion routes. Country cousins became popular. By 29 September 1938, in fact, France was consumed by a war scare reminiscent of the Great Fear of 1789. In Paris, Strasbourg, Dijon and elsewhere mobs attacked Jews and looted their shops, shouting: "Down with the Jewish war."[92] The spirit of Bonnet stalked the land. "Let us not be heroic," he urged; "We are not up to it."[93]

At Munich Daladier was hungry for conciliation. As usual, he looked combative and made a continuing show of resistance. But he was a willing victim of the British "plot," as Lord Halifax's private secretary put it, "to frighten the French into ratting and then get out on their shoulders."[94] Daladier revealed his true colours by remarking that the *bellicistes* in his own cabinet wanted to push France into an "absurd and above all impossible war,"[95] a war that might cost the lives of three million Frenchmen. Harrowed by his country's weakness, especially in the air, he agreed to the carve-up of Czechoslovakia. But his scowling countenance and hunched posture betrayed his anger. Daladier recognised that Munich was a crushing humiliation for France, but he did not expect it to be hailed with "frenetic joy."[96] By treating the story of Daladier's return to France as the climax of his post-war novel *The Reprieve*, Sartre made it famous: expecting to be booed (if not mobbed) by the crowd at Le Bourget airport but finding himself cheered, the dumbfounded Premier turned to Léger as they disembarked from the plane and said through gritted teeth, "The cunts!" Ironically, Sartre's lover Simone de Beauvoir participated in the general euphoria. She was "delighted" with Munich and "felt not the faintest pang of conscience" about the betrayal of Czechoslovakia: "Anything, even the cruellest injustice, was better than war."[97]

Most newspapers were inclined to forget Czechoslovakia in their paeans of exultation over "Peace! Peace! Peace! That is the word, this morning, joyously written in every eye and heard on every lip. The world breathes again. We can all live."[98] Daladier was adulated for saving husbands from butchery, wives from widowhood, children from orphanages. As he and Bonnet were driven in an open Hotchkiss from the airport to the Rue Saint-Dominique, their progress took on the character of a victory parade. The crowds surged forward, wreathed the car with flowers, tried to kiss the Premier. As one witness observed, the welcome overflowed into alien forms:

> The crowd waved flags like the Japanese, clapped as though they were in a theatre, unconsciously stretched out their hands in the fascist manner; and now from the tall buildings they were pouring out the waste-paper baskets and flooding down the leaves of calendars as if they were in the United States.

On the Concorde Bridge a blind old soldier waved his white stick and shouted, "Long live peace!"[99]

With characteristic cynicism Jean Cocteau took up the cry: "Long live the shameful peace!"[100] Certainly many were ashamed by what had happened. The sight of Daladier's triumphant return made Michel Clemenceau, the Tiger's cub, weep. The following day the political theorist Raymond Aron spent the first half-hour of his lecture at l'Ecole de Saint-Cloud commenting on Blum's "cowardly relief" and denouncing the "merchants of sleep" who had lulled Frenchmen into thinking that the price of valour would not be high.[101] Even more scathing about the national torpor, Georges Bernanos thought that France had been raped by hooligans while she slept. Rape might be followed by murder: the Czechoslovak Foreign Minister, like Haile Selassie and La Pasionaria before him, prophesied that the fate of his country today would be visited on others tomorrow. André Tardieu agreed, saying that the German triumph was just one more stage in resurrecting the Europe of 1914. De Kérillis declared that Daladier had achieved a diplomatic Sedan, a view shared by Laval. None excoriated the "surrender" more pungently than de Gaulle, whose imagery perhaps reflected the fact that France's last public guillotining had taken place the previous summer—at Versailles, in front of a huge and appreciative crowd. By conjuring with the hideous spectre of war, he said, the corrupt press had terrified the nation into sacrificing its honour. But Munich would bring only "a brief respite, like old Madame du Barry with her head on the block begging: 'Just a few more seconds, Mr. Executioner!'"[102]

Despite Daladier's rapturous reception, it seems that France as a whole was divided and confused by Munich. According to a primitive opinion poll, 37 per cent of Frenchmen (women were not asked) disapproved of the agreement, whereas 57 per cent approved. Writers argued amongst themselves: Gide thought Munich a triumph of "reason (if not justice and right) . . . over force";[103] Bernanos heard in the "ignoble rejoicing . . . the Te Deum of cowards."[104] Newspapers of the same stamp disagreed over the issue: some left-wing journals were elated, some were hostile and some were uncertain, while *Vendredi* was "so radically split . . . that it abandoned politics altogether, changed its name to *Reflets,* and restricted itself to purely cultural matters."[105] It was not surprising, therefore, that the Prime Minister was once again at odds with himself. In parliament, where only the Communists (and two others) opposed him, Daladier defended Munich as an honourable settlement which preserved Czechoslovakia and promised peace in Europe. But to the American Ambassador (who gave him a bouquet on his return from Munich) Daladier acknowledged it as an immense defeat and said that unless France recovered its national spirit "a fatal situation will arise within a year."[106]

CENTRAL to that renaissance was economic revival, without which massive rearmament could not be achieved. About this there was a large measure of agreement, though many on the Left remained committed to the social gains of the Popular Front. The Premier was adamant, though, that sacrifices would now have to be made. In its own modest way France was obliged to imitate the Soviet Union and starve itself great. As Daladier told an American financier, "You can have guns, butter or leisure. If you go for guns you must reduce your butter ration and lose some of your leisure."[107] To put France on a war footing Daladier appointed the ablest member of the cabinet, Paul Reynaud, Finance Minister and gave him plenary powers. Reynaud did not mince his words about the dangers of the existing situation. In a broadcast made on 12 November 1938 he told his countrymen, "We are going blindfold towards an abyss."

Reynaud now issued a series of decree laws so draconian that they shocked the cabinet itself. He raised taxes and increased arms spending from 29 billion francs to 93 billion. He cut price controls and reduced the public works programme. To improve output he also ended the so-called "week of two Sundays."[108] The Saturday holiday had taken on a "sacred character"[109] and its abolition precipitated further clashes with organised labour. Another sit-in took place at Billancourt, where Louis Renault was one of many bosses seeking revenge on employees for the concessions extorted in 1936. The government was determined to crush any threat to defence industries and thousands of police were sent to evict the strikers. They encountered barricades of oil drums and scrap iron as well as a hail of missiles—ball-bearings, pistons, crankshafts, carburettors. The gendarmes used a lorry as a battering-ram and hurled tear gas bombs, then a novelty. After a long struggle the defeated workers, over 2,000 of whom were later dismissed, had to march out of the factory "making the fascist salute to cries of, 'Long live the police.'"[110] This was the penultimate act of the pre-war drama at Billancourt; the last was the resignation of 2,000 Renault workers from the Communist Party in the week after the signing of the Nazi–Soviet Pact.

As employers everywhere regained the whip-hand, hopes kindled by the Popular Front were extinguished. Workers suffered a momentous defeat when a general strike, called for 30 November, proved a damp squib. It proved too that the Popular Front was not only dead but buried. Still, if social relations were embittered and many on the Left were politically alienated, the economy did begin to revive under Reynaud's spur. Confidence and capital returned. Trade improved and inflation ceased. By the summer of 1939 unemployment had fallen by 10 per cent and industrial production had risen by 20 per cent. Yet output had still not returned to the level of 1929 and France had by no means developed a full-blown war economy. Renault himself was more concerned to increase the manufacture of cars than tanks: when the conflict came only 18 per cent of his production consisted of war *matériel*.

The government's growing authoritarianism at home signalled an erosion, but not a termination, of the policy of appeasement abroad. Bonnet, mortified that Chamberlain had extracted his famous piece of paper from Hitler (in which the Führer, apparently endorsing the common desire for peace, had agreed to consult over the removal of future sources of difference), sought a similar guarantee for France. Having ensured that news of *Kristallnacht* was played down in the French press, he welcomed Ribbentrop to Paris on 6 December 1938. The Nazi Foreign Minister, lavishly entertained at the Quai d'Orsay (which only a few months before had been sumptuously redecorated for King George), proved expansive. Doubtless he relished the fact that, at the express request of the German Ambassador and probably with the approval of Daladier, Bonnet had not invited Jewish ministers such as Jean Zay and Georges Mandel. But Ribbentrop also appreciated the gushing obsequiousness of his Gallic counterpart, especially his indiscreet revelation of France's "indifference with regard to the East"[111]—which evidently gave Germany a free hand in Poland.

Bonnet also seemed willing to exchange French colonies for European peace. Indeed he agreed with pacifists who could not believe that any parliament would be criminal enough to unleash a war which would wreck Europe for the sake of "a few hundred scroungers on acres of sand infested with crocodiles."[112] But Georges Mandel, Minister for the Colonies, possessed something of the spirit of his mentor Clemenceau. The saturnine Mandel, described as "the Mephistopheles of the French Chamber,"[113] was determined not to lose a single acre of imperial sand. When Daladier suggested, as a concession to Mussolini, making Djibouti a free port, Mandel replied: "We'll give the Italians a pier and that's all."[114] The Premier's backbone was duly stiffened, though he remained apt to wobble on the international stage. But he drew strength from the public, which was becoming ever more hostile to Hitler—and to Chamberlain. Frenchmen now called the English architect of appeasement *"Monsieur J'aime Berlin"* and Paris shops could not sell the "lucky umbrellas" which had been so popular immediately after Munich.

The French public also appeared indifferent to the fact that Daladier had virtually dispensed with parliament. They did not seem to care that, in his drive to strengthen the country and to stop democracy from being "a regime of contradictions,"[115] he had learned other practices from the dictators. None was nastier than his appeal to xenophobia, a prejudice which became more virulent as Jewish and other refugees fled to France. It must be said that France was more generous in providing asylum than any other European country, or than the United States. The wretched of the earth had traditionally found sanctuary in Marianne's bosom and after 1918 immigrants had been regarded as a demographic asset. But with the onset of the Depression foreigners were seen as competitors for jobs and scapegoats for all the troubles of the Hexagon. They were damned as *métègues* (dagos). They became targets of violence. As early as 1933 Daladier considered them a "Trojan horse of spies and subversives,"[116] a view echoed by Communists intent on concealing the naked racism of their cry, *"La France aux Français."*

Of course, like everyone else, Daladier was worried about the nation's "lean years." Despite the acquisition of Alsace-Lorraine and the alien influx, France's population was barely one per cent larger before the Second World War than it had been before the First. The Prime Minister even went so far as to consult Bullitt over how to increase the birth rate—the Ambassador's solution, facetiously confided to Roosevelt, was "to have Joe Kennedy transferred to Paris."[117] Yet some of Daladier's earliest and fiercest decree laws were directed towards the control, internment and expulsion of foreigners. Matters became worse at the beginning of 1939 when Franco finally crushed Catalonia and almost 500,000 refugees made their tragic exodus from Spain.

These scarecrow beings limping through the cold Pyrenean passes were the jetsam of defeat. They were the wreckage of the Republic, "the weary crowd of peasants and workpeople, the escaping officials, the hungry women, the lost and orphaned children, and the broken fragments of a valiant army." Some were more broken than others. A few, terrorised by the strafing of their ragged columns, gave way to panic. More were emaciated, sick, wounded. Once, a file of blind soldiers was to be seen, with bandages over their eyes, "holding each other's hands and groping along the road."[118] But most troops reached the border with heads high and rifles shouldered. Remnants of the International Brigades even marched into Le Perthus "with flags flying, songs on their lips and fists raised in the Popular Front salute."[119] What shocked all the fugitives, however, was their brutal reception. The French, after some hesitation about whether to close the frontier altogether, treated them not as exiles but as criminals. The refugees were surrounded by Gardes Mobiles who interrogated them, confiscated their weapons, searched their pathetic bundles of possessions and on occasion made them throw away handfuls of earth which they had snatched up from their native villages. Women and children were separated from males of fighting age, who were herded off to improvised concentration camps. Watching the humiliation of men of "courage high as mountains, and of faith deep as an abyss," Gustav Regler discerned a still deeper abyss. "The dirty road on which the disarmed men stood was not merely the frontier between two countries, it was an abyss between two worlds."[120]

The sympathy and understanding which might have bridged this gulf were notable by their absence. The Spaniards anticipated fraternal aid and comfort from a republic which still paid lip-service to the ideals of the Popular Front. The French feared that the invaders would be at best a drain on their meagre resources and at worst a source of Communist (or anarchist) contagion. Prejudice was rampant, especially in the right-wing press, which complained that France was being "blackmailed with pity." *Le Petit Bleu* ranted in the manner of Céline:

After the Italian anti-Fascists and the German refugees, and the undesirables of the whole world; after the procession of beggars and international crooks and professional unemployed and murderers; here are our next visitors, the Spanish "republicans," among them the most dangerous revolutionary agitators, dripping with blood, and running away from the punishment they deserve for their "political" crimes.[121]

Reflecting something of this spirit and eager to encourage their unwelcome guests to return home, the French authorities confined them behind barbed wire on open beaches guarded by Senegalese troops who, one prisoner reported, "kick us about and use their rifle butts on us."[122] Men slept on the bare ground and survived on 1,600 calories a day. There were no latrines. Disease was rife but the few doctors had scant resources and the death-toll was high. Friends of the victims accused the French authorities of "clear and definite murder."[123] The cellist Pablo Casals, who visited the seaside camps, likened them to Dante's Inferno.

Worse still were the "punishment" camps for political extremists suspected (not always mistakenly) of being hell-bent on murder and insurrection. At Le Vernet, for example, hard labour, torture, and semi-starvation soon turned inmates into "grey-faced, hollow-eyed, apathetic wrecks."[124] In terms of food, accommodation and hygiene Le Vernet was regarded, by those who had sampled both, as being worse than Dachau. Enough became known about conditions in the French camps and about the fate of the Spanish women and children, whose squalid dwellings aroused "horror"[125] among witnesses, to provoke an international outcry. The portly little Minister of the Interior, Albert Sarraut, toured Mediterranean camps and pronounced that everything was in perfect order, though he did not see much since he was averse to getting sand in his shoes. Protests continued and soon shelter and sanitation were provided, while food and medical services improved. France received much blame from the outside world, but little assistance. The *New York Times* instructed its reporter Herbert Matthews not to file "any sentimental stuff"[126] about the refugee camps.

Equally unsentimental, Daladier recognised Franco's government at the end of February 1939. Fearful of having a third fascist enemy on his borders, the French Premier returned Spain's gold and art treasures. He also sent an Ambassador, Marshal Pétain, calculated to please the Caudillo. Daladier was less accommodating towards the British, who now worried that a demoralised, pacifist France might refuse to fight against Germany. Chamberlain offered military help in case of attack and kept urging Daladier to propitiate Mussolini. He refused, a policy which politicians at the time and historians subsequently condemned as "short-sighted."[127] Yet the Duce would surely have interpreted any concession as confirmation of Gallic-cum-democratic decadence, which could only have strengthened his adhesion to the Axis. Moreover, Daladier had good reason to believe that Fascist rapacity was insatiable, having secretly heard that Mussolini looked on Munich as "a beginning, not an end."[128] Through good intelligence, too, the French Prime Minister was less surprised than the Duce when Hitler entered Prague in March 1939. Britain now took a stronger line in eastern Europe, as France had long advocated. Its guarantee of Czechoslovakia having proved worthless, it now guaranteed Poland and (with France) Romania and Greece. However, urgent French efforts to secure a military alliance between the democracies and the Soviet Union foundered on British hesitation and mutual mistrust. Most Frenchmen were now inclined to resist further Nazi aggression and Gamelin said that his forces were ready for war; but many inside and outside the government still espoused appeasement. "Why die for Danzig?" reiterated *L'Oeuvre,* most famously on 10 July. Daladier himself veered from the firmness of Reynaud to the elasticity of Bonnet, "following the ebb and flow"[129] of current opinion.

During the summer of 1939 the mood in France swung between hectic gaiety and oppressive gloom. Prosperity was returning; the stock market crept higher; farmers harvested bumper crops; Schiaparelli's salon had never been more crowded; Parisian fêtes were unusually extravagant; dancing was all the rage. Indeed, the favourite film of the moment was *Toute la Ville danse.* The most splendid ball of the season took place on a warm July night at the Polish embassy. Ministers and diplomats sipped champagne while an orchestra played and beautiful women in frothy gowns waltzed with military officers. "In the gardens white marble sphinxes gleamed beneath the stars . . . and pots of red fire threw on the scene the glow of a conflagration." The Polish Ambassador, Julius Lukasziewicz, believed that Bonnet was "definitely seeking some legally valid escape" from French obligations, news of which accounted for increased "blustering" in Berlin.[130] The shadows quivered. All thought war imminent and some were reminded of the ball "given by Wellington on the eve of Waterloo."[131] Watching a mazurka, Reynaud remarked: "It is scarcely enough to say that they are dancing on a volcano. For what is an eruption of Vesuvius compared to the cataclysm which is forming under our feet?"[132]

No brief revival of confidence, it seemed, could eradicate the pervasive fear that Marianne was caught up in a dance of death. Jean Renoir marvellously evoked her whirling doom in his film *La Règle du Jeu.* Opening in July 1939 but banned as too demoralising by September, it portrayed a corrupt and disintegrating society held together only by deception. "We live at a time when everyone lies," says one of the characters, "drug ads, governments, radio, movies, newspapers."[133] The French people were not only confused by institutional mendacity. They were demoralised by the Depression, lacerated by social strife and haunted by the prospect of a war in which the whole country, besieged behind the Maginot Line, would become a monstrous Verdun filled, Laval forecast, with "millions of corpses."[134] Yet, as the decade advanced, more and more Frenchmen bitterly concluded that the alternative to war was slavery, that their choice lay *"between Verdun and Dachau."*[135] Hence the incessant panics, the visions of catastrophe and the "nightmare of fear"[136] (Julien Green's phrase) which afflicted France throughout the 1930s.

Disquiet aggravated disunity as Hitler set his sights on Poland. Bonnet sought to squirm out of French obligations. Daladier wavered and procrastinated, his outbursts of anger being invariably followed, as "Pertinax" remarked, by gestures of impotence. Even when he did declare war the Prime Minister tried to keep the door open to peace. Many of his compatriots shared his ambivalence. On the one hand, they knew that unless France fought Germany it was finished as a great power. They resembled the departing soldiers whose excellent morale was, a journalist noted, "curiously mental":[137] the *poilus* were not moved by patriotic fervour but by the grim conviction that a dirty job had to be done at once. On the other hand, a significant section of French society shared Daladier's mental reservations and such people grew increasingly anxious that the war should remain as phoney as possible. They hoped that there would be little fighting and tried to believe that France was safe behind the Maginot Line, which would, some said, become the largest tourist attraction in Europe after the war. But as propagandists and censors went about their business and the newspapers appeared with large blank spaces, no one knew what was happening. Albert Camus wrote in his journal, "Never has the individual been more alone in the face of the lie-making machine."[138] An air of gloomy unreality permeated the capital. With its street lights painted dark blue, Paris resembled a ghost city. Car headlamps were also coloured blue and looked like large aquamarines bowling down asphalt canyons. Squares and alleys were full of shadows. The prostitutes carried gas masks, as did the tin-helmeted policemen, slung from their shoulders in dung-coloured satchels. "Everything, underlying everything," wrote Simone de Beauvoir, "a feeling of unfathomable horror."[139]

XXIV

CHURCHILL, CHAMBERLAIN
AND APPEASEMENT

As the British and French governments each tried to shift the responsibility for their foreign policies on to the other during the pre-war years, one Englishman strove to stiffen the resistance of both. Winston Churchill was an ardent francophile. He idolised Napoleon as (in Michelet's view) only the uneducated could and possessed an almost mystical faith in French military prowess. A British intelligence officer's prediction that German forces would overrun France in less than a month "nearly made him froth with rage . . . 'The unshakeable glory of France' was an obsession."[1] Witnessing a display of that glory at celebrations marking the 150th anniversary of the fall of the Bastille, Churchill intoned fervently: "Thank God for the French Army."[2] He paid other visits to Paris during the late 1930s in an attempt to inspire friends—Mandel, Reynaud and even Flandin among them—with his own faith and fortitude. His efforts were ultimately frustrated in the case of Reynaud, Churchill claimed, by the Frenchman's mistress Madame de Portes, "who—ah—possessed facilities which were not in my capacity to offer."[3]

To the authorities on both sides of the Channel Churchill's pugnacious endeavours were a source of alarm, tinged with amusement. Churchill's French was a particular cause of mirth: he was proud of his command of the language but he spoke so volubly, in a John Bull accent with grammar and vocabulary to match, that only Frenchmen with a colloquial knowledge of English could understand him. Reporting to the Foreign Secretary about one foray during which Churchill urged the formation of "a solid Anglo-French block against Germany," Sir Eric Phipps wrote that his French was

> most strange and at times quite incomprehensible. For instance to Blum and Boncour the other night he shouted out a literal translation of "We must make good," by "Nous devons faire bonne (not even bon)." This

clearly stumped Boncour, who may even have attributed some improper meaning to it. You will get a most eloquent first-hand account of this hectic and electric week-end from its brilliant animator.

As the Ambassador's last sentence suggests, Churchill remained a compelling figure, for all his comic quirks, and a statesman of the front rank even though he had been for so long confined to the back-benches. Phipps spared no pains to discredit him with the French, assuring Herriot and others that Churchill only spoke for a very small section of the British public and that his utterances should be taken with "liberal sprinklings of salt."[4]

It was not surprising that Churchill should have provoked mistrust. For although he was brave, eloquent, witty, industrious, dogged, versatile and supremely talented, with most great offices of state under his belt and many gorgeous feathers in his cap, Churchill had given more hostages to fortune than any other politician of his day. Britain's leading parliamentarian had changed parties twice and policies so often that, Lord Beaverbrook declared, he had held every view on every question. Said to be a warlord at sea during Armageddon, Churchill had sired the Dardanelles disaster. He had treated strikers as the enemy within and earned a reputation as warmonger towards foreign foes. He had returned the pound to the gold standard at too high a rate. He had attacked progress towards Indian independence, branding himself as a blimpish reactionary. In a mood of cavalier romanticism during the abdication crisis he had championed Edward VIII. In short, Churchill seemed to be brilliant but unsound. It was an opinion to which most leading figures of the day subscribed. According to Asquith, Churchill thought with his mouth and had "genius without judgement."[5] He possessed a powerful brain, noted Lloyd George, but it was prevented from running true by "a tragic flaw in the metal."[6] Baldwin repeated (and modified) a story told by an early biographer that at Churchill's birth the good fairies came trooping in with their gifts—imagination, daring, energy, guts—and then a bad fairy arrived to deny him wisdom. It became a commonplace to depict Churchill as a buccaneer: picturesque certainly, but rash, ambitious, dangerous and volatile. R. A. Butler, Under-Secretary of State at the Foreign Office before the war, considered him "the greatest adventurer of modern political history."

Butler also cast aspersions on Churchill's origins, calling him a "half-breed American."[7] This was a typical instance of the character assassination by association to which he was subjected. Undoubtedly, though, Churchill's stock was lowered as much by his raffish relations as by his disreputable friends. They all seemed to identify him as "a particularly way-ward, rootless and anachronistic product of a decaying and increasingly discredited aristocratic order."[8] Churchill's mother was not only the daughter of a notorious Wall Street speculator, she also acquired a train of unsuitable husbands and lovers. His father, the erratic and syphilitic Lord Randolph, was a striking example of ducal degeneracy. For "all his remark-able cleverness" Lord Randolph was, in the estimation of the fifteenth earl of Derby, "thoroughly untrustworthy: scarcely a gentleman, and probably more or less mad."[9] Winston's staunch belief in Churchills against the world seemed less like family loyalty than tribal chauvinism when other members of his clan were considered: vapid dilettantes such as Moreton Frewen, known as "Mortal Ruin"; blue-blooded boors such as "Sunny," ninth Duke of Marlborough, whose wife Gladys said that he was ruled by "black, vicious personal pride like a disease";[10] the unwelcome and non-paying Guests; and, the greatest trial of all, Churchill's spoiled son Ran-dolph, who jovially acknowledged that he was not fit to be allowed out in private.

Churchill's friends were cast in the same mould, with the partial excep-tion of the vegetarian, non-smoking, teetotalitarian Professor Frederick Lindemann. (Even he was a social carnivore—he once took counsel's opinion about what place he was entitled to occupy at high table in his Oxford college, Christ Church.) They were high-living and often hard-drinking freebooters who dwelt on the outer edge of respectability. F. E. Smith, Lord Birkenhead, was considered to be a "fluent and plausible bounder"[11] early in his career, while later, to his fury, he was represented as a "crapulous and corpulent buffoon."[12] Lord Beaverbrook was aptly nick-named "Been-a-crook"[13] and seemed to be "a kind of Dracula, Svengali, Iago and Mephistopheles rolled into one."[14] Brendan Bracken, the red-haired financial and political chancer who was (wrongly) rumoured to be Churchill's illegitimate son, appeared to be a charlatan incarnate. "Every-thing about you is phoney," said a journalist; "Even your hair, which looks like a wig, isn't."[15] With friends and relations like these, Churchill under-standably offended the bourgeoisie, though he did not let that worry him. He used "middle-class" as a term of abuse, shared his father's disdain for suburban "lords of pineries and vineries" and despised "adjectival grocers"[16]—what he would have made of an adjectival grocer's daughter can only be imagined.

Churchill's extravagant style of life was also an affront to more modest folk, especially during the Depression: adopting F. E. Smith's maxim, he professed to be easily satisfied with the very best. He behaved like a nabob, crowned with flamboyant hats out of doors and robed in garish dressing-gowns at home. With the body of an unrepentant sybarite and "the face of a self-indulgent cherub,"[17] he exuded an aura of cigar smoke, eau-de-Cologne and good liquor. (His wine merchant's bills, which were large and paid slowly, as he had a lordly way with tradesmen, included many half bottles of champagne—not for sharing. But he was no alcoholic for, as C. P. Snow said, no alcoholic could drink that much.) Churchill's appetite for food was gargantuan: he liked roast beef as well as white wine for breakfast, with other meals on an equally carnivorous scale. He made no secret of his patrician taste for gambling, polo and hunting (foxes not women). Servants were part of the tenure of his existence, running his life on oiled wheels. His country house, Chartwell Manor, near Westerham in Kent, was organised like a miniature Blenheim Palace.

Churchill adored Chartwell and spent huge sums on renovating and improving it, with mixed results. The dining-room, for example, scene of oratorical as well as gastronomic feasts, had to accommodate great girders which made it much too low for its length. It was like eating in a basement—except for the wonderful views over Churchill's happy valley. This he cherished. He planted and dug, laid out a tennis court and excavated a swimming-pool which was heated so that it steamed. He built enormous walls, laying bricks with more energy than skill and often dictating letters as he went. He created lakes, dams, waterfalls, fish-ponds, treating his black swans, golden orfe and other creatures with anthropomorphic indulgence. He farmed in a lavish but inexpert fashion, telling Lloyd George that he was determined to make agriculture pay, "whatever it costs!"[18]

Churchill often guyed himself thus, giving involuntary colour to hostile interpretations of his character and conduct. Equally provocative in deed, he was himself largely responsible for the fact that pre-war contemporaries saw him in caricature terms—as a fabulous soldier of fortune forever plotting some fantastic coup. That view of Churchill was almost entirely effaced by his great achievements during the Second World War and by his subsequent account of them. Since Churchill hung on to his prime-ministerial papers, this account was authoritatively documented as well as unashamedly partisan. History would be his judge, he liked to jest, and he would write the history. So for a generation Churchill remained a gleaming titan marching triumphantly to broad sunlit uplands through the pages of his own works—and those of his many admirers. His was the spirit that inspired the nation in its finest hour. His was the voice that gave the lion's roar. He was the colossus who won victory over the forces of darkness. A. J. P. Taylor famously summed up that verdict in his volume of the *Oxford History of England:* Churchill was "the saviour of his country."[19]

Recently, however, this idyllic picture has once more been modified. Historians, chipping away at the gloss and supplying *lacunae* in the monumental official biography (or rather chronicle), have rediscovered the "rogue elephant"[20] in Churchill. They have restored the pre-war perspective, portraying him as a wild, egotistical and often malign force, more of a danger to friends than to enemies. Scholarly reappraisals like those of Robert Rhodes James and John Charmley have undoubtedly damaged Churchill's reputation. He can no longer be viewed through rose-tinted, or even Violet-Bonham-Carter-tinted, spectacles. No more can he be seen as—in a world of worms—the perennial glow-worm. This is all to the good: a Churchillian legend is no more desirable than a Napoleonic legend. Historians should be euhemerists: their task is to expose the reality within the myth, to reveal the flesh and blood behind the godhead. Faced with hagiography, particularly Establishment hagiography, they might well adopt Victor Hugo's motto: "Je suis *contre.*"[21] On the other hand, much of the recent assault on Churchill smacks less of wholesome revision than of downright iconoclasm, image-smashing for its own sake or in the interest of a hidden political agenda. For example, neo-conservative critics of Churchill such as Maurice Cowling conjure with the notion that the empire might somehow have been preserved, and the nation saved from socialism, if only Britain had let the Nazis fight it out with the Communists and had held aloof from, or negotiated its way out of, Churchill's "war of moral indignation." This phrase is a perverse, not to say impudent, description of what might fairly be called, at least on the part of the democracies, a just war.

Churchill's critics are on surer ground when they point out that he was inconsistent and opportunistic towards the dictators during the 1930s. He more or less condoned the Japanese invasion of Manchuria. For a long time he admired Mussolini and supported Franco. Even his opinion of Hitler was seriously flawed. He was willing to believe that such a "great man" might resurrect German honour without recourse to arms. As late as 6 November 1938, three days before *Kristallnacht,* Churchill repeated his hope that, if Britain were ever defeated in war, "we should find a Hitler to lead us back to our rightful position among the nations."[22] Such views, though, can best be considered as aberrations fed by ambition. Churchill's warnings about the Nazi menace were long and loud, early and prescient. Only a few weeks after the Führer came to power he alerted the House of Commons to "the tumultuous insurgence of ferocity and war spirit"[23] in

Germany. He denounced Nazi anti-Semitism and declared that Hitler's barbarous tyranny was inculcating a blood lust not seen since pagan times. Churchill collected and disseminated information about German rearmament and prophesied that it would lead, via lesser acts of aggression, to war. Only through a massive revival of martial strength and political will, he insisted, could Britain deter and resist the Third Reich. Churchill was not infallible about facts, still less about forecasts: shortly before the Second World War he ordered a waterproof suit to wear in the trenches. Yet as a voice crying in the wilderness about the Nazi peril he was without peer. A recent authority rightly concludes:

> Churchill's exaggerations were more accurate than Chamberlain's realism . . . His judgement of Hitler and his intentions was always sounder than that of the dozens of European statesmen who made the pilgrimage to Berlin and Berchtesgaden.[24]

Churchill's tragedy, and Britain's, was that during the late 1930s he found himself cast in the role of Cassandra.

Churchill's detractors, none of whom was more determined to keep him in the wilderness than Neville Chamberlain, would have been given pause for thought had they seen him reading and dictating with inexhaustible fecundity in his Chartwell bedroom. Surprisingly small and austere, with photographs of Lord Randolph and a wide bedside bookshelf crudely installed by the estate carpenter for his papers, it was not the boudoir of a hedonist but the billet of a campaigner. It plainly contradicted Chamberlain's view of Churchill as a gaudy magnifico, improvising policies (some good, more bad) between drinks and sustaining them with nothing more than facile rhetoric. In fact Churchill did his homework quite as meticulously as Chamberlain himself, devoting particular attention to his parliamentary "impromptus." Still, there is no denying that the two men were opposites without mutual attraction. Chamberlain, who succeeded Baldwin as Prime Minister in May 1937, might admire Churchill's wit and brilliance, his courage and vitality, but he had always felt that there was an unbridgeable "gulf between him and me."[25] In his opinion Churchill was unstable and amoral. Taking issue with him was "like arguing with a brass band."[26] He must at all costs be kept out of the cabinet, which he would dominate and even silence. When the War Minister, Leslie Hore-Belisha, urged Churchill's inclusion, Chamberlain replied: "I won't have anyone who will rock the boat."[27] For his part, Churchill professed respect for the tough imperial pioneer who had struggled unsuccessfully for seven years to grow sisal on his father's estate in the Bahamas. But he was essentially out of sympathy with Chamberlain, regarding him as narrow-minded, cold-hearted and dusty-souled. Theirs was the perennial opposition of the Puritan and the Cavalier. It was the opposition, too, "between Birmingham Town Hall and Blenheim Palace."[28]

CHAMBERLAIN was often disparaged for being unable to see beyond the confines of local government and petty commerce. Lloyd George maintained that he would have made a good Lord Mayor of Birmingham in a lean year and that he had "a retail mind in a wholesale business."[29] Experienced diplomats such as Sir Alexander Cadogan said that Chamberlain equated the conduct of foreign affairs with the handling of trade disputes. With a prissy manner, a reedy voice and a smug expression habitually imprinted on his corvine features, Chamberlain seemed every inch the political haberdasher. His conventional clothes added to the impression: the old-fashioned starched wing-collars; the black jacket and striped trousers; the inevitable umbrella, sceptre of the bourgeoisie since the time of Louis-Philippe—almost the only time Chamberlain showed anger was when his umbrella got broken. Although he was quite a cultured man, his amusements were on a similarly modest scale: he liked Christmas cracker jokes and games of musical chairs—at Cliveden, the Astors' country house, he was allowed to win because it meant so much to him. Chamberlain's international outlook was equally naïve: America was "a nation of cads";[30] Russia was "semi-Asiatic"; and the French could not "keep a secret for more than half an hour, nor a government for more than nine months."[31] Obviously Neville was a mere shadow of Joseph Chamberlain, lacking his father's Olympian manner, global vision and volcanic eloquence. Indeed, like his siblings, Neville was "dwarfed and scorched by the towering inferno of his father's personality."[32] He once said that reading about his father reminded him of studying the planets: his "own significance diminished with every step."[33]

Determined to prove himself, though, Chamberlain grew in self-confidence, even arrogance, with every step he took up the political ladder. Having entered parliament in 1918, aged almost 50, he made his name as a reforming Minister of Health during the late 1920s and as a masterful Chancellor of the Exchequer from 1931 to 1937. Stiff, reserved, penny-pinching and self-righteous, he was not a popular figure. Even his half-brother Austen remarked on his killing coldness. But such was his dedication to business, so logical were his policies and so lucid his speeches that he dominated the National Government. Once in 10 Downing Street, Chamberlain became a democratic despot. He was as masterful as Sir Robert Walpole, a portrait of whom (by Vanloo) hung over the marble fireplace behind his leather-upholstered chair in the long, Corinthian-columned cabinet room.

Furthermore Chamberlain drew around himself an inner circle of subservient mediocrities, most of them knights remote from the practice of chivalry. Sir John Simon, a serpentine lawyer described as a snake in snake's clothing, was singularly lacking in resolution at the Treasury: he had sat on the fence so long, Lloyd George famously remarked, that the iron had entered into his soul. Sir Samuel Hoare, now at the Home Office, had learned no lessons from the dictators: he was later said to have "passed from experience to experience, like Boccaccio's virgin, without discernible effect upon his condition."[34] Sir Thomas Inskip, Minister for Coordination of Defence, had little ability, less power and no perceptiveness: "He could look with frank and fearless gaze at any prospect, however appalling—and fail to see it."[35] Other acolytes, such as Sir Horace Wilson, with his "temporising, 'play for safety,' formula-evolving mind,"[36] and Sir Kingsley Wood, who on the outbreak of war opposed the bombing of munition works in Germany because they were private property, were equally unable or unwilling to stand up to Chamberlain.

Compliance seemed to validate his growing assumption of infallibility, which was expressed with the jauntiness of a schoolboy and the primness of an old maid. Flattery fed Chamberlain's vanity for, as one official noted, "he likes to be set on a pedestal and adored, with suitable humility, by unquestioning admirers." There was "no surer way of gratifying him than to make some allusion to the exceptional importance of his position."[37] By the same token, criticism, mockery and disrespect infuriated him. Chamberlain became increasingly intolerant of disagreement, equating loyalty to himself with patriotism. He squashed or squared the press with unprecedented vigour, using lobby journalists to manipulate public opinion while contemptuously accusing the occasional dissenter of being duped by "Jewish-Communist propaganda."[38] Chamberlain deployed his own secret propaganda organ, the supposedly independent journal *Truth,* to discredit opponents. He tapped their telephones. He harried ministers and extended his control to every aspect of government. He crushed parliamentary debate, treating the Labour opposition with open contempt and imposing a ruthless discipline on his own rank and file. One Tory MP said that "they had now a Führer in the Conservative Party."[39] Anthony Eden, the Foreign Secretary, believed that Chamberlain "*au fond* had a certain sympathy for dictators, whose efficiency appealed to him."[40] Ironically, the champion of appeasement in Europe was not a weak Prime Minister but an exceptionally strong one. The would-be conciliator of the continent was a domestic autocrat.

His foreign policy was eminently defensible, so much so that, despite its arrant failure, its defence has become almost a new orthodoxy among historians. Chamberlain started from the unimpeachable premise that war is the abomination of desolation. The noblest ambition an English statesman could have, he thought, was to make "gentle the life of the world." Determined, like nearly all his countrymen, that there should be "no more Passchendaeles," Chamberlain thought that peace could be purchased by righting the injustices of the Versailles settlement. But it would be fatal to negotiate from a position of weakness: the corollary of his search for *détente* was rearmament. Force was the only language dictators understood and diplomacy without guns could not protect Britain's overstretched empire from a hostile coalition of Germany, Italy and Japan. On the other hand, Chamberlain, like Daladier, regarded prosperity as the fourth arm of defence. "If we were to follow Winston's advice and sacrifice our commerce to the manufacture of arms," he wrote, "we should inflict a certain injury on our trade from which it would take generations to recover." Chamberlain was as much haunted by the Depression as by Armageddon. His nightmare was that a feverish munitions boom would be followed by a disastrous slump and political defeat, with an incompetent Labour party having "to handle a crisis as severe as that of 1931."[41]

Unsighted by the economic blizzard, Chamberlain failed to perceive the full danger of Nazi aggression. He could hardly believe that either Hitler or Mussolini, despite their wild rantings and bellicose posturings, wanted "to go to war."[42] Rather than risk the catastrophic loss of blood and treasure, they would surely be amenable to a deal. It was just a matter of making friendly overtures, seeking acceptable terms and catching the dictators in the right mood, when they would give anything they were asked for. Creating his own image of the dictators, Chamberlain pronounced about their opaque designs with astonishing assurance—and inaccuracy. Hoping to use former German colonies as bargaining chips in a European settlement, for example, he never appreciated how little importance Hitler attached to them. Austen Chamberlain had memorably chaffed Neville with knowing nothing about foreign affairs and his deficiency was made worse by the patent inadequacies of official information gatherers. The Secret Intelligence Service, for instance, was so underfunded that its head, "Quex" Sinclair, had "to appeal to relatives for money and was still unable at the time of Munich to afford wireless sets for his agents."[43] Yet, working in the dark, Chamberlain was obstinately convinced that he knew how to reach an understanding with the Führer and the Duce. Such was his confidence that he culpably neglected potential allies. Unlike Churchill, he did not strain every nerve to woo the United States away from isolationism, though he took care not to alienate America by making major concessions to Japan. He kept France at arm's length until 1939. Worst of all, succumbing to prejudice as much as ignorance, he failed to clinch an agreement with the Soviet Union.

Chamberlain also misjudged the issue of rearmament, making "a conscious choice to take risks with defence rather than with finances."[44] Perhaps he was right not to embark on an all-out arms race in 1937, which could have saddled the services with obsolete equipment and might have damaged the country's economy in peace and war. But even Lord Halifax reckoned that the Treasury worried too much about Britain's capacity to buy abroad, since aid from America, which was bound to defend democracy at least by proxy, would be forthcoming in time of war—as it was, in the shape of Lend-Lease. In any case, Chamberlain could have done more to provide the sinews of war without jeopardising exports and foreign exchange reserves. He could have eradicated manufacturing bottlenecks, trained and mobilised manpower, given industry longer-term munitions contracts, alerted the public and achieved, as Hore-Belisha wanted, "a greater intensification of our efforts."[45] General Pownall also advocated "maximum" effort, damning Chamberlain's pernicious idea of preparing for a "half-hearted" war when "we shall again be *fighting for our lives*." British survival in 1940 owed less to Chamberlain than to the recession of 1938, which released skilled labour, machine tools and raw materials for arms production. But by then the government's emphasis had changed from deterrence to self-defence. This was reasonable in the case of the air force and even the navy; but the army remained hopelessly ill-prepared. The skinflint Treasury initially restricted its strategic role—"The tail wagging the dog,"[46] growled Pownall—and ultimately contributed to the débâcle of 1940. Even during the last months of peace the increase in rearmament was "more apparent than real."[47] Soldiers understandably gibed that the real concern of Whitehall's financial mandarins "was not to fight a war, but to be able to pay an indemnity after losing it."[48]

Chamberlain's rearmament programme sent out to the dictators a feeble message about British strength; his appeasement policy sent out a powerful message of weakness. Together these signals invited the aggression they were designed to prevent. Certainly they afforded minimal encouragement to German opponents of Hitler, particularly the military plotters who might have toppled him in 1938. Anthony Eden gave a more robust impression. He was young, glamorous and energetic. He had a fine war record and his speeches, though banal in style, were idealistic in content. As the champion of the League of Nations and the foe of Mussolini, Eden had won golden opinions at home. The Nazis actually described him as "a notorious firebrand."[49] This was an absurd characterisation. As Lord Beaverbrook said, Eden was a rebel in velvet gloves. His outlook was as conventional as his handsome appearance, smart suits and patrician drawl. Eden agreed with Chamberlain's foreign policy, declaring that his constant purpose was "the appeasement of Europe."[50] But he was less consistent and more temperamental than the Prime Minister. Eden was the son of a half-mad baronet and an exceedingly beautiful woman, and he was said to be a bit of both. Certainly he was volatile and highly strung, prone to rows and rages. With all his grace and charm, he was also a prima donna, "terribly vain and egocentric."[51] Chamberlain ruffled Eden's feathers by his impatience to come to terms with the dictators. The Foreign Secretary preferred to face down the detested Mussolini in the Mediterranean and to keep Hitler guessing through diplomatic procrastination in Europe. However, when Lord Halifax was invited to meet the Führer in November 1937, under the guise of attending the International Hunting Exhibition, Eden at first agreed to the visit. Soon, though, probably piqued by the growing significance attached to this mission, he changed his mind. Still suffering from a bout of influenza, Eden protested to Chamberlain, who concluded their acrimonious interview by telling him to go home and take an aspirin.

Edward Wood, third Viscount Halifax, was admired during the 1930s as an impeccable gentleman-amateur of politics. Tall and aloof, he seemed to be above the fray and indifferent to worldly ambition. He was a sincere high churchman much given to private devotions and to family prayers. Although born without a left hand, he became a dedicated Master of Foxhounds and seldom allowed the business of government to stop him hunting on Saturdays. Like Arthur Balfour, whose aristocratic detachment he shared, Halifax seemed to acquire the glittering prizes of life without effort and without emotion. He was not even moved when, as Viceroy of India, Hindu terrorists bombed his train: he went on reading a work of divinity, explaining later that he was "inured to that kind of thing by the Cona Coffee machine which was always blowing up."[52] Having tried to conciliate India, Halifax endorsed appeasement in Europe. As the conscience of the Tory party, he invested the policy with moral weight. Such were his principles that he refused Göring's invitation to shoot Pomeranian foxes "on the false plea of a strained shoulder."[53] Chamberlain felt that Halifax was the ideal person to negotiate with the Nazis. Some historians have agreed. Maurice Cowling describes Halifax as "the embodiment of Conservative wisdom."[54] John Charmley avers that behind his "languid exterior there was Yorkshire granite."[55]

Actually Halifax had no idea of how to cope with the Third Reich—

he was like a eunuch in a brothel. Caught in a Tractarian time warp, the lofty Englishman was remote even from his own compatriots. He regarded remarriage after divorce as tantamount to bigamy. He treated senior Civil Servants as flunkeys, instructing them, for example, to make his appointments with the barber. While President of the Board of Education in 1935, he had favoured a new church school for the villagers of Hickleton, his family seat in Yorkshire, "to train them up for servants and butlers."[56] His insouciant ignorance of foreign affairs amazed Chaim Weizmann: if he knew as little about other areas as he did about the Middle East, the Zionist leader exclaimed, "God help this poor country."[57] As Beaverbrook said, Halifax had led a sheltered life, cosseted, flattered and never obliged to face harsh realities. He was "an earnest and an honest fellow—not quite stupid, but inexperienced in worldly affairs."[58] Halifax was a feudal anachronism. He lacked the imagination, even the will, to comprehend Hitler's Germany.

He raised his black bowler in response to Nazi salutes. He liked Goebbels and, of course, Göring, a "picturesque and arresting figure" with his green leather jerkin, red-sheathed dagger and chamois-tufted hat. Halifax was impressed by the Hunting Exhibition (which included stuffed heads of animals shot by King George and Queen Elizabeth) and he was "interested to see the very curt and peremptory way in which our 'bodyguard' of sport officials of all sorts cleared our way" through the crowds. The whole enterprise was "a monument to showmanship, enthusiasm and thoroughness . . . a wonderful effort, down to a gramophone reproducing the roar of a stag in the Imitation Forest." On arrival at Berchtesgaden Halifax mistook the Führer for a footman, and was only prevented from handing him his hat and coat by a frantic whisper from the German Foreign Minister. At their meeting Halifax quickly sold the pass by volunteering that Britain would accept changes in the positions of Austria, Czechoslovakia and Danzig provided that they were carried out peacefully. When Hitler told him that the film *Lives of a Bengal Lancer* was used to instruct the SS in how to deal with inferior races and went on to state that the way to control India was to shoot Gandhi first and then Congress supporters in dozens or hundreds as necessary, Halifax seemed to regard him not as an evil tyrant but as an outlandish vulgarian. It was almost as if contact with the Führer had blunted his famous moral sense, though it was, to be sure, scarcely acute about racial matters in the first place. As Viceroy of India he had been tickled by the "delicious" suggestion that Afghans lived in trees.[59]

Yet although, as Halifax plaintively reiterated, they spoke different languages, he did discern something of Hitler's attitude towards himself and his government. Halifax wrote in his diary:

He gave the impression of feeling that, whilst he had attained power only after a hard struggle with present day realities, the British Government was still living comfortably in a world of its own making, a make-believe land of strange, if respectable, illusions. It had lost touch with realities and clung to shibboleths—"collective security," "general settlement," "disarmament," "non-aggression pacts"—which offered no practical prospect of a solution of Europe's difficulties.

Correct though these perceptions were, they seemed to make no impression on Halifax's mental retina. He went away with his illusions intact, still mouthing the shibboleths of conciliation. He believed that Hitler sincerely wanted peace, which should be obtained through "a frank examination of what every nation may be able to put into the pot for general appeasement."[60] Halifax even likened Hitler to that other inspirational leader, Mahatma Gandhi. Perhaps he saw the Führer as a fakir in jackboots.

Responding to complaints about British newspapers from both Hitler and Goebbels, Halifax put a measure of censorship in the appeasement pot. He had actually agreed with the Führer about "the dangerous influence of the press," telling him that criticisms of Germany doubtless stemmed from lack of information in Britain. Naturally Halifax was anxious to escape the charge that the government was controlling the media. So he avoided anything in the nature of a "formal arrangement," preferring a "personal and confidential understanding [with newspapermen] . . . to guide them along the lines desired."[61] These lines had been set out for him by Britain's dapper, snobbish Ambassador in Germany, Sir Nevile Henderson, who deeply sympathised with the Nazis' "great social experiment."[62] He explained to Halifax that:

HMG cannot go so far as to wash their hands of Austrians and Sudetendeutschen; that would look too cynical and immoral. Ultimately, however . . . we shall have to fall back on the line of self-determination under suitable guarantees that it is freely exercised.[63]

Duly influenced by Halifax, *The Times* printed an editorial to the same purpose, which gave pleasure in Berlin and pain in Prague. Halifax would later declare that "no attempt had been made by instruction, request or suggestion to prevent newspapers from expressing their considered views."[64] But at the time he broadened the scope of his efforts, trying to suppress unfavourable portrayals of the Nazis by cartoonists such as Low and Dyson. The latter, for example, drew a character representing "The Peace of Mind of Europe" handing over a little black girl to a slavering Nazi with the words, "Take my child, but spare, oh spare me!"[65]

As a comment on Chamberlain's plans for colonies like Tanganyika this was strikingly apt; but Halifax complained that it was "unjustly cruel"[66] to the Nazis. The owner of the *Daily Herald,* Lord Southwood, who knew nothing about newspapers except how to print them, meekly followed his direction. So did other proprietors and their underlings. As the "silent censorship" grew tighter one diplomatic correspondent remarked on "the 'twilight' creeping over foreign policy."[67] This is not to say that free expression was stifled in Britain, though the intelligentsia derived wry amusement from the revelation that one of the country's poison gases had the initials "BBC." Churchill contrasted Britain's happy fate with the terrible condition of countries "where everything is cooked and doctored and pervaded, by rule and decision, and you can only tell by getting hold of foreign newspapers what is happening in the great world outside."[68] British newspapers were often admirably well informed and outspoken, none more so than the *Yorkshire Post.* Heterodoxy flourished. The *New Statesman* was a cult. Claud Cockburn's scurrilous journal *The Week* in some respects anticipated *Private Eye.* The Left Book Club attracted 60,000 members and its founder, Victor Gollancz, aspired to create "the most powerful body of educated public opinion that any country has ever had."

Yet the mainstream press ignored bodies like the Left Book Club, conducting, the Club claimed, "an open conspiracy of silence to blot out whatever conflicted with the political aims of the Government."[69] Moreover, the Club itself imposed a "voluntary censorship" on members, as Evelyn Waugh pointed out, providing only material which confirmed "their existing opinions."[70] They would, said Cyril Connolly, choke on its "brimstone aridities."[71] Certainly the Club's Communist propaganda muddied the wells of knowledge. The BBC did nothing to clear them. The Corporation remained Mr. Chamberlain's poodle; and his opinion, expressed by his Private Secretary in April 1939, was that, "It is definitely undesirable that, at times like the present, issues of foreign policy should be discussed in a controversial spirit on the air."[72] Such was the "conspiracy of silence"[73] in which it engaged during the Munich crisis that, at the government's request, even talks about world affairs on *Children's Hour* were cancelled. Plainly there was no commitment in Britain to informing the electorate, let alone to acknowledging the sovereignty of the people. R. A. Butler summed up the opinion of the political élite in what today would be regarded as a breathtaking inversion of the truth: "Good government flourishes in the dark."[74]

Fed on pap, most Britons behaved in a callow fashion and did not challenge the prevailing code of secrecy. They accepted their humble place in the social order and hardly impugned the right of those at the top to direct opinion or to oversee the fate of the nation. No one, for example, questioned the appointment of Major Harding de Fonblanque Cox as an official film censor even though he was 81 and suffered from a form of *lethargica* which caused him to fall asleep when he read anything. On the contrary, the *Sunday Express* reported quite seriously that Major Cox, author of such works as *Chasing and Racing, Fugleman the Foxhound, Dogs, Dogs and I,* and *Dogs of Today,* would "not countenance vulgarity. No, my boy, let us show clean films in the old country. I shall judge film stories as I would horse flesh or a dog. I shall look for clean lines."[75] The leaders of the old country belonged to an exclusive club. Its membership was generally ordained by birth, though many qualified to join were kept out by the convention that government was an esoteric matter, only susceptible to the understanding of mature men. Ladies might wear fashionable swastika charms but they should be swathed in clouds of unknowing. Débutantes were taught that it wasn't done to talk politics or, indeed, to say anything interesting at all. Meanwhile, outside the magic circle ordinary folk simply got on with their lives. As Louis MacNeice wrote in his *Autumn Journal,* they worked, took holidays, did the football pools, gossiped, cuddled, smoked and drank. Blinkered by habit, "Most are accepters, born and bred to harness/And take things as they come."

A minority, MacNeice continued, refused the bridle and espoused one of the fierce creeds of the day. Those cleaving to the Left wanted to abolish the

> System that gives a few at fancy prices
> Their fancy lives
> While ninety-nine in the hundred who never attend the banquet
> Must wash the grease of ages off the knives.[76]

Those on the Right supported Yeats's view that equality was "muck in the yard": "Historic nations grow/From above to below."[77] But in both camps faith imposed its own tunnel vision. As late as November 1936 the Labour MP Sir Stafford Cripps declared that although defeat by Germany would be "a disaster" for capitalists it would be no "bad thing for the British working classes."[78] A couple of years later Harold Nicolson encountered three young peers in his club who stated that "they would prefer to see Hitler in London than a Socialist administration."[79] That even parliamentarians should have invoked the Führer was not only a measure of public ignorance but a monument to the immaturity of British democracy.

HITLER would have taken further comfort from events in Britain at the beginning of 1938. In January Sir Robert Vansittart was removed as senior mandarin at the Foreign Office and given a high-sounding but powerless advisory role. Vansittart was the Beau Brummell of bureaucracy, elegant, flamboyant and provocative. He outshone Eden sartorially, eclipsing his double-breasted waistcoats. He also patronised the Foreign Secretary, who connived at his spurious promotion with the Prime Minister. (Chamberlain was himself so distrustful of Vansittart that for a time he kept him under surveillance by MI5.) Vansittart also irritated colleagues with elaborate aphorisms which never quite came off: "To tell the truth about Germany in Britain was to put the cat among the stool-pigeons."[80] Still, he was probably the staunchest and best-informed foe of the Nazis in Whitehall. By contrast his replacement, Sir Alexander Cadogan, was (in the words of Hugh Dalton) "a tame and colourless civil servant with less character and less persistence in arguing with politicians when he thought they were wrong."[81] Before the *Anschluss* Cadogan wrote in his diary, "I almost wish Germany would swallow Austria and get it over."[82]

Cadogan was an unsatisfactory lieutenant for someone as prone to vacillation as Eden. The Foreign Secretary veered between complaining about defeatists in the cabinet and endorsing the same defeatists' defence policy. He thanked Chamberlain for taking such a close interest in foreign affairs but flew into a rage when the Prime Minister rejected Roosevelt's peace initiative. The President's proposal for a conference to tackle the economic causes of the political turmoil was just the kind of woolly, high-minded enterprise to annoy Chamberlain, who feared that it would upset his plans to negotiate directly with the dictators. However, it attracted Eden, who valued American cooperation and supported the cause of international morality with every cliché at his command—quite an arsenal. As Richard Crossman later wrote, Eden was "that peculiarly British type, the idealist without convictions."[83] He eventually resigned from the government on 20 February 1938, not because he opposed the principle of appeasement— he thought the policy could work where Germany was concerned—but because he objected to the speed with which Chamberlain was trying to implement it *vis-à-vis* Italy. The Prime Minister was prepared to lose his Foreign Secretary because, he wrongly believed, a quick settlement with Mussolini might forestall the *Anschluss*. He was encouraged to think so by his sister-in-law Ivy, who wore a Fascist badge and acted as a private intermediary with Mussolini—a role which, Halifax later said, reflected "well-intentioned stupidity" on the part of the Prime Minister.[84] The Italian Ambassador, Dino Grandi, also hinted that this was the last chance for an agreement. He himself witnessed confrontations between Eden and Chamberlain, who took the Italian line, at which they behaved "like two cocks in true fighting posture."[85] Grandi so despised Eden that he refused to meet him at the Foreign Office on the grounds that he was play-ing golf.

By replacing Eden with the more amenable Halifax, Chamberlain ful-filled his ambition to be his own Foreign Secretary. Eden made little political capital out of his resignation, which, though regarded abroad as a victory for totalitarianism, was played down by the media at home. Afterwards he kept his distance from Churchill, who said that he "repre-sented a spirit of resistance to the Dictator Powers."[86] Eden also acted towards Chamberlain in a "most careful and circumspect" manner, as though smoothing his path back to office.[87] So the British government's campaign to come to terms with the dictators was barely interrupted by the *Anschluss*. Of this Halifax remarked, anxiously pacing the Foreign Office: "Horrible! Horrible! I never thought they would do it!"[88] But Britain merely sent a protest, which Hitler treated with contempt. And neither Chamberlain nor Halifax concluded that the Führer was possessed by a Napoleonic lust for conquest. Churchill disagreed and advocated the formation of a grand alliance to resist it. Chamberlain rejected this as impractical. To indicate that Britain would not be bullied he did accelerate rearmament. But he failed to ensure that it would be, as he promised, the nation's top priority. Continually hampered by financial constraints, Hore-Belisha found that "Hitler is my best ally; when he rattles his chains the Treasury give a little more."[89]

At the same time Chamberlain did everything possible to mollify Hitler, even giving the chairman of Lewis's department stores a "high-powered rocket"[90] for boycotting German goods after the *Anschluss*. The Prime Minister also repeated his determination to rely on diplomacy rather than force. He would not commit Britain to support Czechoslovakia, or France if it went to Benes's aid. According to an early opinion poll a surprising 33 per cent of Britons opposed Chamberlain on this issue. But 43 per cent supported him and the rest did not know. Jan Masaryk, Prague's Ambas-sador in London, said that he spent most of his official life "explaining that Czechoslovakia is a country and not a contagious disease."[91] Churchill insisted that for Britain the unfamiliar jumble of letters forming the word Czechoslovakia spelled "nothing less than self-preservation."[92] He sounded the alarm with a great outburst of oratory, soon "getting the ear of the nation."[93] On 24 March 1938 he declared that "this famous island [was] descending incontinently, fecklessly, the stairway which leads to a dark gulf."[94]

This was a fair assessment. Britain's foreign policy was not only damned by its short-sightedness but doomed by its internal contradictions. On the one hand Chamberlain tried to persuade Hitler not to take the Sudetenland by force, which could provoke war with France and Britain. On the other hand the Prime Minister put such pressure on Czechoslovakia to make concessions that the Führer was bound to conclude that the Western powers would not fight. As one senior diplomat wrote, "the ambivalence of our policy . . . was not long concealed."[95] Official British warnings to Germany were weak and vague. Unofficial indications made it clear that Chamberlain regarded Czechoslovakia as an opportunity to achieve a European settlement rather than a bulwark of democracy to be defended. In Berlin Sir Nevile Henderson so truckled to the Nazis, who were, he thought, anathema only to Jews, Communists and ideologues, that Halifax had to admonish him not to suggest that Britain would abandon the Czechs under all circumstances. But in the summer of 1938 Halifax himself apparently told Hitler's special envoy, Fritz Wiedemann, that before his death he would like to see "the Führer entering London at the side of the English King amid the acclamation of the English people."[96]

No such ingratiating messages came from Prague. In order to influence the "pig-headed" Benes and his "miserable little nation"[97] (Henderson's words), the British government appointed a supposedly independent mediator to investigate Sudeten claims. He was Lord Runciman, a stiff-collared, morning-coated elder statesman who, as Lloyd George remarked, "would make the temperature drop, even at a distance."[98] Arbitrating, as Runciman said, on the brink of Niagara, he discovered that Benes was conciliatory while Henlein was intransigent. But his report did not show this. Although it claimed to reflect the principle of Sudeten self-determination, it was an exercise in appeasement dictated from Downing Street. *The Times*'s suggestion on 7 September that Prague should cede its "fringe of alien populations" to Germany (which not even Hitler himself had yet demanded) may also have been inspired by Halifax. He repudiated it publicly. In private he was unperturbed by the indiscretion, though he did seem increasingly bemused—"not a noble stag at bay," as Noel Annan phrased it, "but a bewildered, timorous rabbit."[99] The Foreign Secretary felt that he was "groping like a blind man trying to find his way across a bog, with everybody shouting from the banks different information as to where the next quagmire is!"[100]

Like others on the road to Munich, Halifax did show occasional "flashes of spirit";[101] but they were quickly smothered. When the government received secret information about Hitler's timetable of aggression against Czechoslovakia from an anti-Nazi in the German embassy, the Foreign Secretary told Henderson to deliver a stern warning that Britain could not stand aside from the general conflict which would inevitably follow. However, he then accepted Henderson's hysterical plea (scrawled on blank pages torn from a book of detective stories because the Ambassador had forgotten to take writing paper to Nuremberg) that this message would drive the Führer "right off the deep end."[102] Instead Henderson wanted the British press to present Hitler as "the apostle of peace."[103] Chamberlain agreed that the German leader should not be upset and went so far as to praise Hitler's self-restraint. The Prime Minister's private scheme, code-named "Plan Z," was to settle German grievances at a personal meeting with the Führer. The plan was so unconventional and daring, Chamberlain boasted, that it almost took Halifax's breath away. But on 14 September the cabinet approved it. As Hore-Belisha said, the proposal to fly to Berchtesgaden was "an adventurous one which would appeal to the imagination of the whole world."[104] No one was more anxious for peace than the War Minister, warned by the Chiefs of Staff that Germany would overrun Czechoslovakia in a week and that British intervention would be like "a man attacking a tiger before he has loaded his gun."[105] Yet, like Duff Cooper and others, he feared that Chamberlain was embarking on "something which might involve us in dishonour."[106] Vansittart was more hostile still, comparing the Prime Minister's odyssey to Henry IV's humiliating pilgrimage to Canossa.

Most people, though, acclaimed Chamberlain's dramatic gesture. Aged 69, this latter-day paladin of peace was embarking on his maiden journey by aeroplane to save the world from the horrors of a new Armageddon. Never had the Prime Minister seemed more resolute. During the seven-hour flight through storm-filled skies he remained "aloof, reserved, imperturbable, unshakably self-reliant."[107] British newspapers vied with each other to express their readers' feelings of relief and gratitude. On 16 September, while Chamberlain was at Berchtesgaden with Hitler, *The Times* replaced its leading article with a poem by John Masefield, the Poet Laureate, which stated that the Prime Minister was "divinely led." The object of this adulation clearly began to believe in his myth as well as his mission. He also felt unable to disappoint the hopes his peace-making foray had raised. So, in return for the assurance that Hitler would not resort to arms at once and that he had no further territorial demands, Chamberlain agreed in principle to the cession of areas of the Sudetenland where Germans were in a majority—he did not even insist on a plebiscite.

The Prime Minister knew that the Führer was untrustworthy and believed that he was half mad. Yet he vainly assumed that Hitler would keep his word because he had given it to him. So Chamberlain got agreement from his own cabinet: Halifax thought that the transfer of territory could easily be achieved since "a few British regimental bands marching up and down the Sudeten areas would suffice to keep the peace."[108] The red-faced Daladier reluctantly fell into line: with him, Chamberlain observed waspishly, "the darkest hour was always before lunch."[109] Benes was bullied into submission with the assistance of Lord Runciman, who was brought in (as Halifax's secretary noted) to do the government's "dirty work."[110] Reading the diplomatic documents much later, Lord Cranborne, who had served Eden in the Foreign Office and resigned with him, said that Britain's readiness to "batter the Czechs and to do anything however contemptible to avoid war makes me blush."[111]

On 22 September Chamberlain once again set off from Heston airport, where scattered booing from the crowd indicated that public opinion was hardening against his policy—a poll showed that 22 per cent supported it while 40 per cent were opposed. At Godesberg he was ferried across the river from the Petersberg Hotel to the Dreesen, where Hitler was surrounded by so many senior Nazis that the main hall resembled the "domestic establishment of some great barbarian chieftain of Germanic heroic legend."[112] Reporting that he had gained acceptance for the Berchtesgaden terms, Chamberlain leaned back with a satisfied expression on his face, the German interpreter recalled, "as much as to say 'haven't I worked splendidly during these five days'!"[113] He was correspondingly shocked by Hitler's new demands that Poland and Hungary should participate in dismembering Czechoslovakia, which must let German forces into the Sudetenland by the end of the month. Yet when he got home again Chamberlain argued "quite calmly for complete surrender."[114] The Prime Minister told cabinet colleagues that he had established an influence over the Führer, who respected him, and that Hitler would keep his word and conduct an orderly occupation. This was better than a general war, which Britain was unprepared to fight, and it should be the prelude to a general peace.

By now, though, the reaction against appeasement was gaining strength and comedians concluded that things had gone from bad to Bad Godesberg. Protest meetings were held throughout the country and demonstrators in Whitehall chanted, "Stand by the Czechs; Chamberlain must go."[115] The press generally condemned the Godesberg demands, which represented "not the basis of negotiation for a peaceful settlement but a dictation to an enemy beaten in the field."[116] Even *The Times* said that every Briton would favour resistance if Hitler planned "the violent annexation . . . of the Sudeten territory, at least so long as the way of peaceful transfer is open."[117] The "Old Lady of Printing House Square" made so bold as to question whether the Nazis were "seeking to murder a nation because it is in the way."[118] The Labour party also took a tough stand, though it usually talked loudly while refusing to carry a big stick—a position as intellectually bankrupt as Chamberlain's was morally bankrupt. Dire warnings came from senior Conservatives such as Churchill, Eden and Leo Amery. The last wondered if "our empty sacks can muster up sufficient courage to stand on end and say 'NO.'"[119] The Foreign Office was in revolt and Cadogan, who now preferred defeat to dishonour, helped to change Halifax's mind. Cabinet ministers also stood up to Chamberlain. Extolling the Premier's flight to Berchtesgaden as "an inspiration of genius," Hore-Belisha said that in the Godesberg deal "we are appearing as the allies of Germany."[120] He, Duff Cooper and other ministers wanted the fleet to be mobilised and a declaration made that Britain would fight beside France if Hitler invaded the Sudetenland. Chamberlain unwillingly followed this course. But his illusions about building an Anglo-German *rapprochement* on the ruins of Czechoslovakia apparently remained intact.

So for a few days Britain reluctantly but doggedly prepared for war. Families queued for gas masks. The unemployed helped to dig trenches in public parks. City children were evacuated to the countryside. Efforts began to safeguard works of art and plans were made to kill poisonous reptiles in zoos. Fifty million ration cards were prepared and the authorities warned against hoarding. But the perils of "night starvation" had been all too widely advertised and there was a run on tinned food, as well as on vacuum flasks, candles, torches and oil lamps. Air raid precautions were tested. Churchill's growls grew louder and became more expressive of the national mood. He asserted that if Hitler violated Czechoslovakia a roar of fury would arise from the free peoples of the world proclaiming "nothing less than a crusade against the aggressor."[121]

Equally tenacious, but by now close to a nervous breakdown, Chamberlain continued his crusade for peace. He sent Sir Horace Wilson on his hopeless mission to plead with Hitler. He approved a speedy timetable for Czech withdrawal from the Sudetenland—a compromise between the Berchtesgaden and the Godesberg terms—which Halifax insisted that Benes "must adopt."[122] The continual late-night meetings, the Foreign Secretary complained, spoiled his eye for the high birds; but by now the Prime Minister himself, who liked to boast that he was tough and wiry, confessed to "wobbling all over the place."[123] Certainly he sounded at the end of his tether in the famous broadcast he made on the evening of 27 September:

> How horrible, fantastic, incredible it is that we should be digging trenches and trying on gas masks here because of a quarrel in a far away country between people of whom we know nothing.[124]

After the cabinet had refused to accept the capitulation recommended by Wilson, Chamberlain issued a final appeal to Hitler, saying that he could get all he wanted without war and without delay. Chamberlain also asked Mussolini to intercede. The Führer's invitation to the four-power conference at Munich arrived at such a dramatic moment, just as the Prime Minister seemed to be telling the Commons that conflict was inevitable, that there were suspicions that it had been stage-managed. Certainly it was greeted with "heartfelt acclamations" and Churchill himself congratulated the Prime Minister on his luck. Scrambling back from the edge of the abyss, Chamberlain had accomplished a theatrical transformation "in which the shadow of death seemed turned into morning."[125]

On his return from Munich Chamberlain was greeted as though he were a victorious general. When he flourished the accord which Hitler had signed and proclaimed that it represented "peace with honour" and "peace for our time,"[126] the crowds roared until they were hoarse. Lord Halifax (who did not suspect that Hitler had dismissed the piece of paper as having "no significance whatsoever")[127] cheered until his tonsils showed. The journalist Godfrey Winn saw "no sacrilege, no bathos"[128] in praising God and Chamberlain in the same breath, and the Archbishop of Canterbury called for a day of national thanksgiving. The King stood with Chamberlain on the balcony of Buckingham Palace. As the wave of euphoria swept the country (and Downing Street was deluged with letters, flowers, fishing-rods and umbrellas), regal endorsement of the Prime Minister's triumph seemed only natural—*The Times* offered its exclusive picture of the balcony scene as a Christmas card. But appearing with Chamberlain in this public fashion was, as Lord Altrincham later said, "the biggest constitutional blunder that has ever been made by any sovereign this century."[129] The Crown had associated itself with a policy which caused the resignation of one cabinet minister, Duff Cooper, and provoked significant opposition in parliament. Britain had, as Churchill famously said, sustained a total defeat. The "German dictator, instead of snatching his victuals from the table, had been content to have them served to him course by course."[130] Czechoslovakia, Churchill concluded, would not satisfy his appetite.

WITH surprising speed a reaction set in against Munich. Feelings of joy at Britain's deliverance from war were overtaken by feelings of shame at the betrayal of Czechoslovakia. Many who had saved their skin would no longer, in the words of Louis MacNeice, damn their conscience. What had seemed a brave bid for peace in September appeared, as autumn progressed, to be a fatal act of cowardice in the face of alien might. Brendan Bracken's joke gained currency: "One Funk in the German cabinet, and twenty-two in the British."[131] More vulgarly, Claud Cockburn said that Chamberlain had "turned all four cheeks" to Hitler.[132] By 320 votes to 266 the Oxford Union carried a motion deploring "the Government's policy of peace with honour."[133] On Bonfire Night Harold Macmillan burned a guy dressed in a black Homburg and a frock coat, equipped with a neatly rolled umbrella. The government did badly in by-elections, and china ornaments celebrating Chamberlain the peace-maker remained unsold in shops.

The Foreign Office feared that Munich had been a "débâcle."[134] Furthermore Britain might have to wriggle out of the guarantee given to the rump of Czechoslovakia, a guarantee which Duff Cooper compared to insuring a man's life after dealing him a mortal blow. Con O'Neill, 3rd Secretary at the Berlin embassy, delivered an even more cutting indictment of British foreign policy when resigning from the diplomatic service in protest against Munich. He wrote, soon after *Kristallnacht:* "Such ruthlessness is the essential method of Nazi policy, which they not only prefer, having a consistent and indeed respectable philosophy of the use of terror in a world of rabbits, but also *cannot avoid.*" The Third Reich thus represented "a direct threat" to Britain, O'Neill continued, which in any case had "no right" to be indifferent to the sufferings of Jews and others who offended the Nazis.[135] Yet *Kristallnacht* was a mere crystallisation of Nazi horrors which were known to Chamberlain, as *Time & Tide* later reminded him, "when by his signature on the Munich Agreement he extended the area of Nazi sadism to the Czechs."[136]

Irrespective of the moral rights and wrongs of Munich, its defenders have always argued that it was inescapable. Domestic and imperial reluctance to oppose the principle of national self-determination, however brutally expressed, together with the military feebleness of the democracies allegedly made Chamberlain's bid for peace at the expense of Czechoslovakia a "tragic necessity."[137] In fact Chamberlain only invoked the popular will, anyway subject to official manipulation, when it corresponded to his own views. The same was true of opinion among Commonwealth leaders, who relied on London for information and were not told that Hitler's aggression in Europe represented a direct threat to the British empire. Of course, as the Chiefs of Staff vehemently insisted, Britain was quite unprepared for war (though senior soldiers such as Hastings Ismay reckoned that Germany could have been defeated in 1938). But in general the military and intelligence services failed to appreciate the weakness of the Third Reich.

The Luftwaffe and the German navy could have done little damage to Britain in 1938, while Hitler's own high command forecast catastrophe if the Wehrmacht had to fight on two fronts. The Chief of Staff, General Beck, resigned over the issue and his successor, General Halder, maintained that if only Chamberlain had stood firm a military conspiracy, finalised "to the last gaiter button,"[138] would have toppled Hitler. Whatever the truth of that, the Western democracies, supported by 35 well-equipped Czecho-slovak divisions (to leave the Red Army out of the equation), were in a better position to take on Germany in 1938 than was the case a year later. During that year their position deteriorated. This was partly because Chamberlain, convinced that Munich was the foundation for a lasting settlement and committed to conciliation despite every setback, did not go all out for rearmament. There was some acceleration and the country's defences were signally improved by the spread of radar coverage, which augmented Chamberlain's confidence both in appeasing and (ultimately) in opposing Hitler. But in 1938 the British did not match the "effort of blood" made by the Germans and demanded by the French. Indeed, on returning from France in November Chamberlain remarked that the British army was so small that it was hardly worth worrying about whether it was ready or not.

At the very time when Chamberlain was resisting arms expenditure at home he was unprofitably increasing imports from Italy and surreptitiously giving more foreign credits to Germany in an effort to promote appeasement by economic means. The Prime Minister assumed that the dictators shared his own opinion about the dangers of a further slump and about the current failings of autarky. Hitler could be civilised, he thought, by being drawn into closer trading relations with the British empire. However, as Professor Paul Kennedy has said, this was "a remarkably myopic view" considering that, for example, the British Commercial Attaché in Berlin repeatedly warned that Germany only wanted "continuing access to sterling so as to stockpile tropical raw materials for a future war."[139] Hitler regarded Chamberlain's economic overtures—his "silver bullets"—as another sign of weakness. Mussolini took the same view of the Prime Minister's visit to Italy in January 1939. Chamberlain hardly cut a heroic figure on that occasion. At first he refused to have an audience with the Pope for fear of offending the Duce. He gave the French grounds for thinking that he would betray their interests at a "second, Mediterranean, Munich." And his ineffectual, last-minute attempt at inducing Mussolini to tell Hitler that under certain circumstances the democracies would fight "did no more than convey an impression of timidity."[140]

Yet Chamberlain took heart at the slightest encouragement—the cheering of the crowds, the lavishness of the accommodation, even the fact that the Duce honoured his guests by making one of his rare appearances in evening dress. The Prime Minister dismissed Fascist demonstrations against the French as he did Nazi attacks on the Jews: they were foolish impediments to the peace process. He did worry, during the winter of 1938–9, about French disaffection and rumours of imminent German aggression; and "on these waves of fear," in the view of the War Office, "we get propelled a little further each time, sinking into lazy hollows in between."[141] In the troughs Chamberlain was buoyed up by his own self-esteem: things must be going well because he was in charge. Despite hostile auguries, he could not resist saying periodically that Europe was entering a period of tranquillity, that Hitler had missed the bus, that Britain was getting on top of the dictators, that the danger of war receded every day. Churchill made hay with his forecasts and predicted that Chamberlain would repeat them. The Prime Minister ran true to form. On 9 March 1939, in an unattributable briefing not cleared with the Foreign Office, he told lobby correspondents that the European situation looked promising. The next day, when the newspapers were full of this glowing prospect, Sir Samuel Hoare compounded the gaffe with a speech looking forward to a new "golden age."[142] Five days later, at just about the time Henderson was penning another dispatch stating that Hitler prided himself on being a man of his word, German troops occupied Prague.

Chamberlain's first response was disappointment tempered by a determination not to be deflected from his quest for peace. He was also relieved that, since Czechoslovakia had ceased to exist, the British guarantee, initially said to be a moral obligation and subsequently described as transitory, was null and void. Prague was lost but Britain's face was saved. Chamberlain promised to shun further continental commitments, though he would take the "bold step" of consulting actual and potential allies to resist further aggression. Halifax rejected the view that this was "not a very heroic decision."[143] But ever since Munich the Foreign Secretary had been drifting apart from the Prime Minister. Now he feared that Poland and Romania would succumb to Hitler, making it impossible for Britain to contain Germany and destroying the balance of power in Europe. He was also influenced by public indignation and parliamentary clamour over the triumph of evil. Fleet Street was generally outraged by Hitler's naked aggression and flagrant duplicity, disillusioned with appeasement and keen to resist a "stark tyranny unknown since Napoleon's time but darker than his."[144] In the Foreign Office Vansittart stated flatly that the Nazis were "criminals whose hands are still dripping with blood and who have just slapped our embarrassed faces before the world."[145] Something had to be done, as Chamberlain himself soon recognised. Halifax plumped for another guarantee—this time for Poland—even though he could get little in exchange from Colonel Josef Beck, Warsaw's Foreign Minister, a sly debauchee whose face was said to resemble that of "a ravisher of little girls."[146]

Britain nevertheless went ahead unilaterally and unconditionally. The decision to support Poland was not a calculated initiative so much as an expression of outraged *amour propre*. It was formulated in an atmosphere of "panic, humiliation and moral hysteria."[147] Here was no diplomatic revolution, in which Chamberlain, as one historian put it, beat "his furled umbrella into a flaming sword."[148] Rather it was a confused attempt to reach the goal of appeasement by other means. Chamberlain hoped to deter Hitler by the threat of a war on two fronts and to mollify him by the prospect of some territorial negotiation—as *The Times* pointed out on April Fool's Day, he had guaranteed only Poland's independence, not its frontiers. But by extending Britain's own frontier from the Rhine to the Vistula (as Daladier said), Chamberlain miscalculated. Britain was now liable to be sucked willy-nilly into a European conflict. Worse still, London was holding aloof from Moscow—partly to allay fear in Warsaw, partly to avoid anger in Berlin. Churchill said that Chamberlain had stopped in No Man's Land, under fire from both trench lines. Lloyd George urged the government to clinch an alliance with the only power which could master Germany. As he spoke, Harold Nicolson recorded, "the round, brown head of Maisky, the Soviet Ambassador, [could] be observed grinning like a little gnome above the clock" in the Commons gallery.[149]

Chamberlain retained his instinct to return soft answers to the Axis powers, despite growing provocation. On 5 April 1939 General Lord Gort, the Chief of the Imperial General Staff, dismissed reports that Mussolini was about to invade Albania as "bilge."

> It would take weeks of preparation and we would be bound to know of it. Besides, Mussolini had given the assurance that there was no intention on the part of Italy to interfere with Albania's integrity.[150]

The attack, launched two days later, was thus a shock to the British government. But Chamberlain, who wished that the Duce had made the invasion "look like an agreed arrangement,"[151] at first tried to play down its importance. Soon, though, he was overtaken by a sense of personal betrayal: "Mussolini has behaved to me like a sneak and a cad."[152] The Prime Minister therefore agreed to add Greece and (at French insistence) Romania to the list of guaranteed countries, prompting the popular jest: "A guarantee a day keeps Hitler away."[153]

Conscription would have been a stronger deterrent, but when Hore-

Belisha urged its introduction Chamberlain upbraided him angrily for having "a bee in [his] bonnet."[154] However, even *The Times* was changing its tune on this subject. As the journalist Colin Coote told the War Minister, "The Squeaker (formerly the Thunderer) won't go further than daily hints; but would lead a chorus of praise if conscription were adopted."[155] Within four days of his altercation with Hore-Belisha, Chamberlain approved compulsory military service—a decision furiously opposed by the Labour party. He also established a Ministry of Supply. But he refused to appoint Churchill to run it, despite the fact that 56 per cent of the population wanted him in the cabinet (only 26 per cent were opposed) and that most Britons thought that his "influence far transcends that of either of the official oppositions."[156] Nor was he influenced by extraordinary full-page press advertisements, apparently paid for by ex-servicemen, featuring pictures of the Cenotaph, notional appeals from the Unknown Soldier for volunteers to serve their country and Churchillian rallying calls, one of which cited Gibbon's denunciation of a ruler for betraying "a pusillanimous aversion to war."[157] Chamberlain continued with his attempts to conciliate Hitler: offering more Danegeld, courting Stalin with obvious reluctance, hinting that concessions might be forthcoming over Danzig. As Hore-Belisha privately complained, Chamberlain, Wilson, Simon, Butler, Henderson and their peace-at-any-price supporters "still hope to buy their way back to normality. That is an illusion, because the price of 'normality' in this sense is nothing less than the British empire."[158]

Chamberlain still did not think hostilities with Germany inevitable, particularly since Britain was rearming so much faster than before. "Hitler has concluded that we mean business," he wrote on 23 July 1939, "and that the time is not ripe for a major war."[159] In fact, probably nothing but Churchill's entry into the government would have convinced Hitler that Britain meant business, particularly as the Führer continued to receive hints about the possibility of a Polish Munich. Horace Wilson talked to an unofficial German negotiator about a pact that "would enable Britain to rid herself of her commitments *vis-à-vis* Poland."[160] Halifax refused to go to Moscow and Britain was represented by a low-ranking, slow-moving delegation. Even if its members had been fully empowered they could not have spoken for the Poles, who feared (as Colonel Beck put it) that the Russians endangered their souls whereas the Germans endangered only their lives. Stalin had no difficulty in choosing between the languid democracies and a dictator who wooed him so urgently and proffered such a handsome dowry.

The Nazi-Soviet Pact had been in the cards for some time, perhaps since Molotov had replaced the Jewish Litvinov as Soviet foreign minister. But it came as a shock to Britons, who regarded it as a prelude to war. The

Labour party was as much shocked by the cynicism of Stalin as the Tory party was shocked by the opportunism of Hitler. Most shocked of all were British Communists and fellow-travellers, who had expected to be ranged against fascism in "the coming struggle for power." John Strachey himself, the author of the book of that title, at first argued that the Pact was a necessary stage on the dialectical road to socialism, taking refuge in the Marxist heart of Hegel's labyrinth. Then he began travelling away from his fellows, selling 1,000 pounds' worth of Russian Five Year Plan bonds and investing the money in General Motors. The appeasers did not give up their own struggle so easily. Henderson told Hitler that Chamberlain had proved his friendship by keeping Churchill out of the cabinet. Even after he had almost come to blows with Ribbentrop and shouted at Hitler, the British Ambassador still considered that German proposals over Danzig were "not on the whole too unreasonable."[161] The Director General of the BBC suggested that "it would be a good idea to relay to Germany 'the famous song of the nightingale' in Bagley Woods as a token of Britain's peace-loving intentions."[162]

To the end, and afterwards, Chamberlain and Halifax hankered for a peaceful compromise. They used strange intermediaries and even stranger analogies—the Foreign Secretary somehow expected to hunt down Hitler through negotiation and professed to see the Führer as a "beaten fox."[163] They implored Mussolini to restrain Hitler. They begged Roosevelt to urge Beck to be more flexible (while themselves cold-shouldering Japan, which was disenchanted with pro-Soviet Nazism, in order to placate the United States). They pressed Beck to delay mobilisation so as not to provoke Hitler, thus impairing Polish defence when war came. The Führer was encouraged to believe that he could localise the war against Poland, despite a formal alliance between London and Warsaw backed up by stern warnings from Whitehall about the consequences of aggression. The warnings reflected a stiffening of resistance during the last days of peace. Chamberlain's cabinet feared that, with arms production at full blast, Britain's economic position (and thus its capacity to wage a long war) could only worsen. Diplomats were increasingly ashamed of Henderson's antics. Clifford Norton, in the British embassy in Warsaw, wrote to William Strang in the Foreign Office:

> The historian of the future may well ask what right Henderson had to falsify the British spirit and attempt to drag our name in the mud again! God knows that if Poland fights it will be hell for her and all of us. But there is a worse hell for cowards and traitors than for those who go down because they kept their word.[164]

A new spirit was also detectable throughout Britain, where trenches were being dug, barrage balloons inflated, babies fitted with gas masks. In Harold Nicolson's words, gloom had "changed into determination, the gloom of anticipation melting into the gaiety of courage."[165]

Chamberlain did at least take a united nation into the war, a nation inspired, once the dithering had stopped, by a clear sense of purpose. As Ismay wrote, the three years prior to the outbreak of hostilities were more difficult and anxious than the three disastrous years that followed. This was because, once the war began, "we lived in a world of reality. There were concrete problems to deal with. But in the years before, we lived in a world of imagination . . . trying to pierce the veil of the future."[166] No one pierced that veil more incisively than Winston Churchill, whom Chamberlain was obliged to take into the cabinet as First Lord of the Admiralty on the outbreak of war.

In charge of the navy, he made grievous errors and enjoyed his usual pleasures without seriously damaging his reputation as a war leader. As a *Times* journalist wrote in his diary, Churchill was

> stoking himself unduly with champagne, liqueurs etc. Dines out & dines well almost every night. Sleeps after luncheon, then to the House of Commons, then a good & long dinner, & doesn't resume work at the Admiralty till after 10 pm, & goes on till 1 or 2 a.m. He has got into the habit of calling conferences of subordinates after 1 a.m., which naturally upsets some of the Admirals, who are men of sound habits. So there is a general atmosphere of strain at the Admiralty, which is all wrong. Yet Winston is such a popular hero & so much *the* war-leader that he cannot be dropped.[167]

Less than a week after this was written he became Prime Minister. Churchill was the right choice because he possessed pre-eminently the courage and the will to win. These qualities were epitomised in a letter which he had recently sent to his chief rival for the premiership, Lord Halifax, who would acknowledge in his subsequent autobiography that his own cardinal fault was taking the line of least resistance. That, declared Churchill,

> leads to perdition. Considering the discomfort and sacrifice imposed upon the nation, public men charged with the conduct of war sh'd live in continual stress of soul. Faithful discharge of duty is no excuse for Ministers: we have to contrive & compel victory.[168]

It was a noble exhortation. Churchill was, in his unique fashion, the embodiment of the British samurai spirit.

XXV

NIPPON IN CHINA

ALMOST as self-indulgent as Winston Churchill, Prince Konoe fostered a fierce chauvinism in Japan as the conflict with China continued. His government regimented the nation in an increasingly dictatorial manner; in fact, Japanese took to using the word "totalitarianism" during the later 1930s, though the system was said to be incompatible with the Imperial Way. Patriotic slogans proliferated: "National Unity"; "Untiring Perseverance";[1] "One Hundred Million with One Spirit."[2] Individuals were urged to make sacrifices for the greater good: "Away with frivolous entertainment"; "One soup and one side dish (per meal)."[3] Posters, films, broadcasts, lectures and meetings repeated the message, creating a mood of harsh austerity throughout Nippon. By the winter of 1937–8, when school children doffed their warm coats in sympathy for the fighting troops, life at home seemed to be "an extension of the battle line." "Never before," declared a Tokyo journal, "have the sentiment and mode of life of the Japanese people witnessed such a great change during so brief a period."[4] To support the soldiers of the sun abroad no domestic self-denial seemed too extravagant. The Prime Minister himself was subject to right-wing criticism for eating unnecessary lunches. But when death threats followed, Konoe remained languidly indifferent.

The pressure to pinch and scrape left its mark on the entire population. They were pressed to renounce costly ornaments, seasonal gifts and new clothes. Women wearing bright kimonos, cosmetics and permanent waves were publicly rebuked. Later kimonos were compulsorily abbreviated to save material; and some were dyed khaki, while others bore patriotic motifs—arrows, fans, bells. Frills and pleats were removed from Western dresses, though women who really wanted to identify with the military adoped *mompei,* drab peasant pantaloons. Men wore single-breasted jackets, shirts with attached collars and shortened tails, and trousers without turn-ups. Brass buttons and hair-pins were banished. Iron was as scarce as gold and children were no longer given metal toys. To save timber, matches were shaved by 0.029 of an inch. To save leather, handbags were made of bamboo, willow or cellophane. Shoes were fashioned from shark or whale skin, and there was a campaign in favour of cloth slippers *(zori)* and wooden clogs *(geta)*. Chemists from the Ministry of Agriculture experimented with tanning rat skins. Designs were even advanced for a national uniform costing 30 yen (less than £2), to be worn by officials and, if times got harder, by everyone.

Economies, enforced by the police, took many forms. Dance halls and mah-jongg clubs were shut down. Shops, restaurants, theatres, cinemas, brothels and other places of entertainment had to close early. Rubber balls, including golf balls, were banned. As well as the "control of pleasure," the authorities insisted on the "utilisation of waste"⁵—old newspapers, broken pens, beer bottle tops. The government sponsored a huge programme of substitution: raffia for rubber bands; soya bean stalks for wood pulp; plastic, porcelain and glass for metal; rayon for cotton and wool. Many goods were rationed—including petrol, which resulted in the spread of asphyxiating charcoal-fuelled cars, lorries and buses. Japanese fishing-boats reverted to sails. Imports were restricted and over 300 foreign commodities disappeared from the shelves of department stores, including soaps, perfumes, cosmetics, tooth powder, cameras, stationery and clothing. The Ginza was darkened, the "prohibition against neon signs" being officially described as "an enlightened act."⁶ The Tokyo Olympic Games, scheduled for 1940, were abandoned because the metal for the stands could be used to build a destroyer. For similar reasons Mitsubishi stopped work on its huge new building in the Marunouchi business district. Even the Emperor was subject to the spartan imperatives of the day. He had to give up foreign wine and cigarettes (for others—he himself did not smoke). When the government's drive to wring gold from its citizens began, he was obliged to swap his gold spectacles for cheap metal ones and change his gilded crests to silver. Until Saionji intervened, Hirohito was actually prevented from convalescing after an illness in his modest, grey-boarded, seaside house at Hayama. He also had to seek military approval before doing anything as effete as collecting marine specimens, a task which involved courtiers in full morning dress wading into the water, bowing and beaching the imperial boat.

Like Stalin's Russia, Konoe's Japan seemed bent on starving itself great. Movements were launched to eliminate company banquets and to cut down the amount of food served in private houses. This was small enough in all conscience: the breakfast and dinner of a typical university professor might consist of nothing more than rice and pickled radish, while lunch would be something like fish soup and boiled cabbage. People were encouraged to eat half-hulled rice, partly because it was more nutritious but mainly because the polished article was over-dressed and gave the "impression of a degenerate western dish."[7] Patriots, incidentally, served their children rice with a pickled plum in the centre to replicate the national flag. Through its National Mobilisation Act (passed in March 1938) the government not only took control of capital and industry, wages and labour, training and research; it also mobilised goods and materials. It aimed to reduce daily necessities "to the minimum required for sustenance."[8] So, at a time when eggs, butter, milk and cheese were almost unobtainable at home, they were exported to obtain foreign exchange. In due course other Japanese foods were sold in Peking when they could hardly be found in Tokyo—milled flour, canned crab, fish, fruit, jam. Writing during the Second World War, a diarist named Kiyoshi Tomizuka recalled an English story about a poor knight who went hungry to buy a splendid suit of armour, only to be killed because he was too weak to fight in it: "This is just what happened to Japan."[9]

The tightening of the national belt concentrated the nationalist mind. Japan had always been strictly disciplined but now intellectual uniformity was deemed a matter of survival. Teachers were told to instruct their pupils in "Japanese science" based on "the Imperial Way."[10] This apparently excluded evolution, since the Japanese claimed divine descent: the police reacted furiously when an animal welfare society, anxious to protect a colony of monkeys in Hakone Pass, erected a sign saying, "Be kind to our ancestors." School sports became more martial. General Araki, now Minister of Education, tried to weed out "spiritual borrowings" from outsiders and to harmonise Japanese sport to the "way of the warrior," *bushido.* This meant more emphasis on marching, judo and kendo, though baseball, duly purged of alien terminology, remained acceptable. However, declared Araki, "Bats, balls and gloves must be handled with loving care, such as a samurai would expend on his sword . . . All games must be played with the solemnity of two swordsmen battling for their lives."[11] Nothing, children were taught, was more glorious than to die the death of a warrior.

To assist with their spiritual mobilisation Araki banished books by writers such as Mill, Hardy, Gissing, Shaw, Russell and Aldous Huxley. Subsequently a production of *Hamlet* was forbidden in case it should provoke dangerous thoughts about royalty. "Thoughts are contraband,"[12] wrote a foreign journalist, and the police were especially keen to stop them from being smuggled into universities. They arrested, intimidated and vetted lecturers. To induce students to sympathise with suffering soldiers, they prohibited café proprietors in university districts from employing nubile waitresses. They even uncovered heresy at Kyoto's Doshisha ("all with one thought") University—long-haired students, mistakes in reciting imperial poems, Christian principles—and rooted it out. As the British Ambassador recorded, higher education was "being gradually confined within the mental strait-jacket."[13]

So was society at large, thanks to General Araki's indoctrination and the moral purification drive of Admiral Suetsugu, the Home Minister. Everything about the war was obscured, including the fact that it was a war. If pressed, officials might concede that it was a "*special* undeclared war";[14] but they continued to call it the "China Incident," even when mocked by a German diplomat who remarked that between 1914 and 1918 he had taken part in the "World Incident."[15] Censorship was tightened up, though it never became as all-embracing as that of Nazi Germany or Soviet Russia. "There is just enough freedom of the press left in Japan," wrote the journalist W. H. Chamberlin, "to permit an occasional editor to say there is none." But the sole news agency, Domei, was completely under the government's thumb. Propaganda was ubiquitous. News reports were often fabricated and newspapers printed nothing but optimistic accounts of the war. Journalists were wary about even hinting at setbacks. The *Japan Advertiser* got into serious trouble for revealing that Chinese living along the Canton–Hankow railway were selling for scrap at 20 cents per pound the fragments of bombs which cost Japan 35 dollars each. Hundreds of journals were suppressed for lesser crimes.

Those that remained wreathed even innocuous items in a fog of circumlocution. When 50,000 people massed in the Tokyo terminus plaza to welcome the 1st Division home from China, newspapers reported that they had gathered at "a certain station" to greet troops returning "from an undisclosed place."[16] Other media of communication were equally unilluminating. Newsreel theatres had multiplied at the beginning of the war but they showed nothing except the official version of events. Films such as *La Grande Illusion* were banned. The wireless was painfully discreet. Police also made efforts to stifle the "bamboo wireless," the gossip mill by which, so the cliché ran, news travels fast in the East. They forbade the families of soldiers who were killed from revealing the fact even to friends—most of the severely wounded men were kept abroad. Short-wave radio sets—capable of receiving overseas broadcasts—were confiscated even from foreign residents; long-wave sets—ministerial megaphones— were given away in poorer rural districts. Post, telephone and telegraph all came under government control. The occult itself was gagged: fortune-tellers were instructed to predict only good luck.

As the war dragged on into 1938 many Japanese seemed reluctant to be spiritually mobilised and General Itagaki complained that people were not sufficiently tense. The root of the trouble was that the propaganda was increasingly at odds with reality. As a visiting journalist noted, it is hard "to keep up a mass-deception over a term of years."[17] The public had been led to expect a short war: the Chinese barbarians would quickly succumb to "a more civilised nation and a more virile race."[18] General Sugiyama had even told the Emperor that the China Incident would be all over in a month. Yet although the forces of Nippon advanced faster than those of Genghis Khan and won battle after battle, so much so that nothing remained to be done apparently except to mop up irregular elements of the shattered Chinese armies, there was no end in sight. In the spring of 1938 Suetsugu came close to admitting as much, even acknowledging that the term "Incident" was a misnomer. But he did so in characteristically contradictory fashion. China's policy of "long-term warfare" was "out of the question" for Japan, he said. However, the

> present "incident" is, of course, a large-scale war, and to deal a crushing blow to the enemy is by no means an easy task. Long-term warfare may, therefore, in certain circumstances be unavoidable.[19]

Yet by now Japan's economy was faltering from shortages of labour and raw materials. Wages were rising, especially for munitions workers, who were said to be paid more than cabinet ministers. But inflation followed suit and taxes rocketed, from (on average) 19 yen per head in 1936 to 31 yen per head in 1938. Consumption fell at home and Japan seemed bent on destroying its markets on the mainland. One Japanese diplomat observed that in its economic policy towards China, Nippon resembled an octopus eating its own tentacles.

As working hours increased and working conditions deteriorated (rest periods and meal breaks vanished), the people, like their Emperor, appeared haggard and emaciated. The Japanese government, like others at the time, took some welfare measures, notably in the field of health care and insurance. But its main endeavour was to intensify the propaganda barrage. This was a disastrous course, heightening expectations of a swift peace yet fostering a pathological jingoism which made it impossible to achieve. As Konoe realised very soon after declaring that he would have no dealings with Chiang Kai-shek, only by conciliation and compromise could Japan extricate itself from the Chinese morass. No such settlement could be reached because the Japanese people had been persuaded that the reward for their sacrifices would be an overwhelming victory. Other contradictions followed, compounded by differences inside the Japanese military and political leadership. Hirota tried yet again to come to terms with the Generalissimo behind the scenes, while telling the press that Chiang would "be decapitated by the Japanese Army if captured."[20] Konoe secretly negotiated with Chiang while he publicly reaffirmed that Japan was bent on destroying him and "eradicating this disease of the Far East."[21]

Such language reinforced a national intransigence which disturbed outsiders. W. H. Chamberlin admired the Japanese for their stoicism, frugality, tenacity and capacity for disciplined common effort, but he was struck by their "insular one-sidedness of outlook." The "average Japanese can only recognise two viewpoints," he asserted, "the Japanese viewpoint and the wrong viewpoint."[22] The veteran American Ambassador Joseph Grew summed up the Japanese attitude towards China thus: "How can you expect us to compromise when you refuse to accept our views?"[23] Tunnel vision augmented xenophobia and vice versa. One expression of both was the adoption of anti-Semitic measures despite the virtual absence of Jews in Japan. Another was the virulent spy mania. Visitors to Japan were subjected to such intense surveillance that the tourist industry suffered. The situation was even worse in occupied territories such as Formosa, where female missionaries were particularly suspect and foreigners were harassed by no fewer than five separate agencies: the foreign section of the provincial police, the secret police, the water police, the military police and counterespionage associations. Linguistic cleansing continued apace. On signs and hoardings Japanese characters replaced Roman type. Words derived from English were deemed enemy aliens: for example, the Japanese *hakama* supplanted the Westernised *sukato* (skirt). Similarly, Golden Bats changed their name to *Kinski*. These were valued all the more because of the dearth of foreign cigarettes; for the Japanese were not merely, like other people, addicted to nicotine, they had imported the word *tabako* as early as the seventeenth century and they regarded smoking as "one of the most magical and fantastic of all the arts."[24]

It was on Britain, chiefly, that Nippon beat out its frustrations over China. America was loathed because of its informal economic sanctions against Japan, and Russia was feared for seeking to spread the Communist contagion, but provoking these giants was fraught with peril. Britain was an easier target and was, moreover, the flagrant embodiment of a world order in which the "have" powers continued to lord it over the "have-nots." Embroiled in Europe, John Bull had dazzling possessions in Asia: colonies, such as Malaya, rich in natural resources; a necklace of strategic and commercial strongholds, including Singapore and Hong Kong; more than half of all the foreign investments in China, worth 250 million pounds; shipping so extensive that Nippon itself could charter nearly half a million tons for war work in 1938. Japanese resentment was palpable and understandable: Britain was trying to support China and check Japan in order "to maintain her monopolistic rights and interests which have been secured by lawless means over a long period of years."[25] Privately British diplomats agreed with this assessment. One wrote, "We acquired our dominant position in China as a result of our wars with that country in the nineteenth century and we can now only keep it by the same or similar methods."[26]

However, Britain was now incapable of defending its Far Eastern prizes by force. The British empire relied on prestige. But that in itself, with its overtones of racial arrogance, was calculated to incense the Japanese. Ambassador Grew liked to tell of an Englishwoman landing in Japan who grandly remarked to her host: "Ah, so this is Kobe. Tell me, who is our Governor-General here?"[27] The prime cause of the "blaze of hatred for Great Britain" which flared up after the China Incident was the "British habit of regarding Japan as a second-class nation comparable to China."[28] Efforts were made to improve relations on both sides but the auguries always seemed bad. Just as the new British Ambassador, Sir Robert Craigie, was proposing his first toast to Anglo-Japanese friendship in September 1937, a typhoon blew open the embassy windows with a crash. Soon afterwards Prince Chichibu made a goodwill flight to London in an aircraft named "Divine Wind," *Kamikaze*.

Japanese hostility to Britain was particularly fierce towards the end of 1937. In November a crowd invaded the compound of the British embassy waving placards with slogans such as "Great Britain, Hands off China" and "Japan Must Fight Britain to Death." An "Opposition to Britain" League was formed and its message was amplified at mass meetings across the country. The British government, which invariably underestimated the Japanese, pooh-poohed such manifestations. One Foreign Office diplomat observed loftily that "the Japanese are somewhat hysterical people (it is the Malay strain in them) and they are prone to these unreasoned hatreds."[29] Nevertheless Craigie generally favoured "cooperation" with Nippon, cherishing the illusion that he could thus "bring about a redirection of Japanese policy."[30] His optimism was encouraged by the appointment of General Ugaki in place of Hirota as Foreign Minister in the spring of 1938. The two men discussed an accommodation between their countries. Ugaki produced a gnomic formula. Where China was concerned he favoured "sleeping in the same bed but dreaming different dreams," while in the case of Britain he advocated "sleeping in different beds but dreaming the same dream."[31]

What that meant, it seemed, was that Japan should take over Britain's imperial role in the Far East. The aspiration was more bluntly expressed by Rear Admiral Inagaki, Chief of the Naval Air Force's General Affairs Bureau, who told the German Naval Attaché at a summer geisha party: "China was only a means to an end, only a step on the way to a final reckoning with *England*."[32] Dimly perceiving this, Halifax chided Craigie for being insufficiently firm. The British government, believing that Japan was too deeply engaged in China to take on another major adversary, was anxious to form a common front with the United States in Asia. Thus Halifax supported a plan to prop up China's currency with a 20-million-pound loan. As he declared, with his usual blend of holiness and foxiness:

> China is fighting the battle of all law-abiding states and she is incidentally fighting our own battle in the Far East, for if Japan wins our interests there are certainly doomed to extinction . . . Every consideration, therefore, of honour and self-interest impels us towards doing what we can to keep China alive.

However, when Chamberlain proved unwilling to offend the Axis as a whole, Halifax characteristically capitulated. He advised against the loan because of "the risk of an adverse reaction in Japan."[33]

THE Japanese were not mollified since by this stage Britain was the prime scapegoat for their failure to subjugate China. This failure was harder to bear because, under the hammer of Thor, China was evidently being forged into a united nation. To be sure, the country was so vast, amorphous and diverse that it was less a state than a geographical expression. Bounded by steppe, mountain, desert, forest and ocean, it stretched from the harsh brown plains of the arid north to the lush green uplands of the subtropical south, from the Himalayan peaks of Tsinghai to the Yangtse basin in Kiangsu. The threads holding this immense territory together were sparse. By 1938 China had only 70,000 miles of high road and 10,000 miles of railway track. Language was an equally inadequate means of communication: the province of Fukien alone was said to have 108 dialects. Foreigners were often assumed to be speaking a regional patois and vain attempts were made to talk to them by spelling out words in Chinese characters. Differences of race, religion and even diet (rice versus noodles) further divided the inhabitants. In any case, they were for the most part virtually embedded in their native earth. Ninety per cent of the 500 million souls were peasants: at the mercy of flood, famine, drought and disease; subject to warlords, landlords, money-lenders and tax-collectors. The Chinese peasant was so poor, a British ambassador noted, that whereas his equal in the Dutch East Indies could always get a banana, he would "often be heartily thankful if he could get a share in an old banana skin."[34] Yet the Communist Chairman, Mao Tse-tung, discerned in the ground-down peasant an incipient revolutionary and the Kuomintang Generalissimo, Chiang Kai-shek, perceived him as an instinctive national-ist. Neither was wrong. Under the agonising imperative of the Japanese invasion, the Chinese masses were mobilised as a political force as never before.

No leader had done more to unite the nation than Chiang Kai-shek. The son of a village merchant, he was born in 1887 near the port of Ningpo and he always spoke (in his high-pitched voice) with the sibilant accents of Chekiang province. His mother brought him up strictly, accord-ing to Confucian precepts, and the discipline seemed to be imprinted on his face. It was a mask so expressionless that it often caused comment among Westerners schooled on tales of Oriental inscrutability. The visit-ing British writers Auden and Isherwood, for example, thought Chiang "almost a sinister presence; he has the fragile impassivity of a spectre."[35] Yet behind that frozen countenance wild passions raged. Sometimes they erupted into violence. When provoked he would shout, curse, weep, bang the table, throw things, complain of torments like those "Buddha suffered in hell."[36] He might threaten to commit suicide and his face would change colour, first to "pale green," then to "terrible white." Often his tantrums culminated in the order of a thrashing or a beheading. But they were soon over, like his periodic "gusts of passion,"[37] one of which caused him to try to rape the 13-year-old girl who later became his second wife. Chiang's strongest driving force was a brave, stubborn, cunning and utterly ruthless ambition. To achieve power he made every sacrifice, employed every expe-dient and tapped every well-spring.

After cutting off his pigtail in defiance of Manchu custom, Chiang scraped and struggled to get the best possible military education—in Japan. In 1911 he returned to fight in the revolution which would, Sun Yat-sen hoped, plant in China the three principles of nationalism, socialism and democracy. Chiang also acquired a less wholesome patron in Tu Yueh-sheng, boss of the notorious Green Gang and head of Shanghai's criminal underworld. There the young officer engaged in activities which appar-ently ranged from "intense dissipation"[38] (one reward for which was gon-orrhoea) to extortion, robbery and murder. In 1923 Chiang visited Russia and with Soviet help he was appointed commandant of Whampoa Mili-tary Academy in Canton, China's Sandhurst or West Point. On Sun Yat-sen's death in 1925 Chiang was expected to emerge as the pre-eminent military leader, a Chinese Trotsky. But two years later, having identified

Bolshevism as "Red imperialism,"[39] he purged the Kuomintang's Communist allies. He also tried to establish his legitimacy as head of the Nationalist party by marrying Mei-ling Soong, the beautiful, American-educated
sister of Sun Yat-sen's widow. Although he wrote her love letters and called
her "Darling" (one of his few English words) it is clear that this marriage,
his third, was a dynastic one. It was, like his subsequent conversion to
Christianity, a "calculated political move."[40] Not only did it make him
Sun's heir and gain him Croesus-rich brothers-in-law (T. V. Soong and
H. H. Kung), it helped to win him friends in the West at the very time he
needed them. Within a year Chiang had marched north, captured Peking[41]
and become, in the eyes of the world, the leader of a unified China.

This was a gigantic illusion. As the American journalist Edgar Snow
wrote, Chiang was nothing more than "the apex of a loose pyramid of
sand."[42] He was a national warlord who had failed to conquer his regional
compeers and had to rely on a quasi-feudal fealty, which was often with-
held. From his capital, Nanking, he exercised direct control over only five of
the lower Yangtse provinces. Elsewhere his rule was constantly challenged
in local revolts amounting at times to civil war. In the long run, of course,
Chiang's most dangerous enemies within were the Communists. Outlawing these "bandits" and putting a huge price on the heads of their leaders,
he attempted to crush them in a series of bitter campaigns. He failed,
though Mao Tse-tung's forces were eventually driven into the remote
fastness of north Shensi. Nor was Chiang successful in dealing with the
external threats to his regime: the alien wedge of Western powers in their
privileged concessions, the louring Russian menace and the aggression of
Japan. In his house were many mansions and to remain even nominal
landlord he had to engage in a perpetual struggle.

Chiang drew strength from various sources, foreign and domestic.
He learned from Hitler, whom he admired, when trying to weld the
faction-ridden Kuomintang into a party which would command allegiance
throughout the country. His aim, he told the Blue Shirts, an élite band
formed in 1932 on the model of Nazi Stormtroopers, was "to spread our
revolutionary spirit to the masses of the entire nation." German military
advisers also helped to modernise Chiang's army, which was taught the
goose-step. His security chief, Tai-Li, turned the euphemistically named
Central Investigation and Statistics Bureau into such a Gestapo that he
was known as "China's Himmler."[43] Yet Chiang often spoke the language
of Western democracy, especially when Mei-ling was acting as his interpreter. And he did more than simply pay lip-service to capitalist ideals:
he achieved much in the way of promoting education, improving communications, developing industry and stabilising the currency. After initial

doubts, the publications of Henry Luce in the United States hailed Chiang as a "sagacious" leader and they "clearly preferred Mei-ling to her American counterpart, Eleanor Roosevelt."[44]

Chiang's "New Life Movement," launched in 1934 in an attempt to revitalise China spiritually, was a more eclectic affair. With its prohibitions against spitting, smoking, drinking, over-eating, foot-shuffling, using lipstick, burning joss-sticks and letting off firecrackers; with its processions bearing multicoloured dragons and shining pagodas from which fluttered slogans urging people to kill flies and rats, to avoid gambling and women; with its Boy Scout spies to discover miscreants and its squads of bully boys to beat them up, the Movement seemed a cross between Fascism and Evangelicalism. Yet with its emphasis on the ancient virtues of courtesy, righteousness, integrity and a sense of shame, the New Life Movement drew on the tradition of Confucius. Many Westerners disliked its combination of intolerance and hypocrisy, Madame Chiang Kai-shek coming in for harsh criticism on both scores. She was so fond of sermonising that, not content with subjecting Chinese pilots to a course of moral uplift, she "laid down some golden rules for air tactics."[45] Yet in defiance of the precepts of the new purity campaign, she smoked mentholated English cigarettes, painted her face, imported Paris lingerie, slept between silken sheets and used the most delicious perfume that Auden and Isherwood had ever smelled. According to her socialist sister Ching-ling (Sun Yat-sen's widow), she spent 4 million Chinese dollars a year on toilet articles, including medicinally-impregnated lavatory paper at 20 dollars a sheet. Still, Chiang made up for his wife's extravagance by his monastic austerity. Frugal, taciturn, teetotal and non-smoking, he wore an unadorned tunic and seemed a fine advertisement for the New Life Movement. It impressed many Chinese.

It also helped to cloak the fact that Chiang's regime was fundamentally reactionary and corrupt. Behind Chiang stood the gangster, Tu Yueh-sheng, his Green Eminence. With a long egg-shaped head, close-cropped hair, bat ears, dead eyes, cruel lips, large yellow decayed teeth, and the sickly complexion of an addict, the blue-gowned Tu seemed like a caricature of the fictional Fu Manchu. In fact, he was nastier than he looked. It was with his help that the Generalissimo attempted to monopolise the nation's drug traffic, now more profitable than ever since Chinese opium was increasingly being used to produce morphine and heroin. This was "an act of stupendous government criminalisation." It was, as Sun Yat-sen had said, "tantamount to selling out the country."[46] But it was also an important revenue-yielding enterprise (a standard one, secretly employed by Mao at Yenan, for example) which did much to sustain Chiang's regime. And it was disguised with consummate cynicism. Drug shops carried out their business, supervised by the police, under the name of de-toxification clinics. The Opium Suppression Bureau, far from eradicating the trade in narcotics, actually managed it. One of the Bureau's members was Tu himself, described in the British-edited Chinese *Who's Who* of 1933 as a "well-known public welfare worker."

Whatever his associations, Chiang was widely regarded as the strong man of weak China. The British considered him powerful and dynamic. The Japanese recognised that he was chiefly responsible for the national revival; as a Foreign Ministry spokesman in Tokyo later said, "His figure shines brighter than anyone else in the Kuomintang and the government."[47] Stalin thought he had much more to gain from Chiang Kai-shek than from Mao Tse-tung. This was a reasonable assumption since until 1937 Chiang seemed to be succeeding in his campaign to appease the Japanese in order to destroy the Reds. With a ferocity all his own, he had followed the traditional Chinese policy of tackling domestic rebels before foreign aggressors. "Rather slay a thousand innocent men," he insisted, "than let one Communist escape."[48] By 1934 the Nationalists had almost exterminated the Communists, who set off on the epic retreat to north China which is known as the Long March. It became, in the theology of Chinese Marxists, an exodus like that of the Children of Israel. The chosen cadres also had their own Moses, in the person of Mao Tse-tung.

These are not original analogies, for the odyssey has attained the status of a national myth, with Mao himself as its hero. The Long March has been represented as the migration of the Red Nation, carrying with it, like the Ark of the Covenant, the pure faith that would revolutionise China. Mao himself was not just the leader but the saviour. He emerged from the ordeal as a superhuman figure charged with "elemental vitality."[49] Foreigners were particularly apt to hail him as a "monumental genius."[50] To one Western devotee, who met him soon after the Long March, the character of this tall peasant-philosopher, with his long hair and his effeminate hands, was plainly written on his face. She discerned wisdom in his "high, square forehead"; "patience and untold suffering in [his] sparse, painfully knitted brows"; shrewdness and irony in his "large black eyes"; "determination, in his high cheekbones"; "sensuality in his full lips"; sensitiveness to beauty in his "nervous, finely shaped ears"; kindness in the "soft curve of his chin"; "sense of humour in the corners of his eyes and of his mouth."[51]

Such romance hid a reality that was hardly less fantastic. The Long March was not an inspired national migration but an improvised military evacuation. Threatened with encirclement by the forces of Chiang Kai-shek, some 86,000 men, mostly young soldiers so countrified that they had never seen a locomotive or an electric light, abandoned their Kiangsi soviet south of the Yangtse River in search of a safe haven. The Red Army stole away at night, in accordance with principles of deception recommended by ancient Chinese war manuals, shedding its skin like a golden cicada and moving "intangibly as a ghost in the starlight."[52] But it also deceived those left behind—old, young, sick, female—who received no mercy from the Kuomintang. The Red Army was equally ruthless with the men in its own ranks. Moreover, although imbued with revolutionary idealism, some of them even with virginal innocence, they were not above rape, robbery, kidnapping, extortion and murder, their usual victims being landlords, not peasants. Nevertheless the army's positive achievements were worthy of celebration in song and story.

Particular events stand out: the running fights, swift manoeuvres and guerrilla stratagems by which Chiang Kai-shek was eluded and deluded; the clashes with remote hill tribes such as the Miao and Yi (the latter liked to strip stragglers of all their possessions, including clothes, and leave them to starve or freeze); the climbing of the Great Snowy Mountains, where troops were "told to talk in whispers because there was so little oxygen";[53] the still more hazardous voyage through the marshy, unmapped grasslands on the empty plateau between the watersheds of the Yellow and Yangtse rivers. But no episode was more famous than the storming of the iron-chain suspension bridge over the Tatu River, a swirling torrent that flowed through jagged narrows with the speed of a galloping horse, at Luting. To capture it ahead of Kuomintang reinforcements, Mao sent shock troops racing up the gorge. They wound in "dragon lines" along steep cliffs, and at night their split-bamboo torches sent "arrows of light glinting down the dark face of the imprisoning river."[54] They arrived before the Nationalists. Assault teams, armed with sub-machine-guns, Mauser pistols and hand grenades, swung themselves across the hundred-yard-long bridge link by link, since the wooden flooring had been removed on their side. On the far side it remained intact and the Kuomintang guard, which had been shooting wildly, poured kerosene on the planks and set them alight. The attackers charged through the flames and secured the bridgehead. But even this crucial victory is overshadowed by the oft-repeated statistics of the Long March: in a year Mao's force travelled 6,000 miles, crossed 18 mountain ranges and 24 rivers, captured 62 towns and broke through the armies of 10 warlords. Only a few thousand survivors (including a handful of women) reached Shensi province, walled and moated by nature, where Mao set up his headquarters in the tiny, ancient city of Yenan, "South of the Clouds."

Living in a candle-lit cave in a bleak, loamy valley so narrow that the sun penetrated only for a few hours each day, eating cabbage and millet, reading and writing copiously, cultivating tobacco in his little garden, Mao rapidly became acknowledged as the warrior-sage of the Chinese revolution. Yet he had begun the Long March in a litter and had not taken command for three months. Despite his growing reputation as a military genius his tactics had sometimes led to bloody reverses in the field and his strategy so reduced the strength of his own contingent that he barely survived the struggle for power inside the Red Army. That he prevailed was a tribute to the peasant stubbornness which ran through his character like "a steel rod."[55] Beaten as a boy by his father, who had raised himself from poverty by hoarding grain to keep up the price, Mao had revolted against the bucolic life. In 1911, aged 18, he had left his Hunan village to study at Changsha, where, he later joked, he invaded the provincial library "like an ox let loose in a vegetable garden."[56] Although he acquired a veneer of education, wrote poetry and became a Marxist, Mao never strayed far from his earthy roots.

He valued manual labour over intellectual endeavour. He admired primitive rebels, distressed farmers who became the outlaw heroes of Chinese novels, the "bandits of despair."[57] He reviled foreign devils and denounced Chinese subservience to them: "If one of our foreign masters farts, it's a lovely perfume." Chewing red peppers and chain-smoking Pirate cigarettes, he remained dirty, dishevelled and uncouth—happy to search his trousers for lice in front of visiting journalists such as Edgar Snow. Privately he sinned against the canons of sexual puritanism which (after earlier espousing free love) he publicly prescribed. Employing brutal means and enduring cruel setbacks, he had struggled for years to exploit the revolutionary potential of the armed *rural* working class. This he came to appreciate better than anyone, visualising hundreds of millions of peasants rising "like a tornado or tempest—a force so extraordinarily swift and violent that no power, however great, will be able to suppress it."[58] But at Yenan he grew fat, literally and metaphorically. Bloated on adulation, he was a peasant emperor in the making. Puffed up by vanity, he was a proleptic dictator of the proletariat.

Paradoxically, Mao's most down-to-earth qualities—his simplicity, self-deprecating humour, rustic common sense—assisted in his deification. His very weaknesses were a source of strength. Mao's chronic constipation became a cause for concern throughout the Red Army: at Yenan a cheer would go up as news spread that "the Chairman's bowels have moved."[59] Mao was a poor orator who "spoke as if his mouth were full of hot congee";[60] but this endeared him to the huge audiences at his open-air meetings outside Yenan, where listeners at the front relayed his words to those at the back amid murmurs of approval. His awesome popularity, though, rested on his transcendent abilities and achievements. Despite the set-backs Mao had proved his mastery of guerrilla warfare during the Long March, escaping entrapment with bewildering feints and dazzling forced marches, living off the land yet making friends with most of its inhabitants, transforming the whole campaign into a prelude to revolution. At Yenan Mao deployed his formidable organisational skills to build the élite which would mobilise the masses. To turn China Red required certain key measures: creating a model soviet (many peasants thought this was a person), free from exploitation, beggary, unemployment, prostitution, infanticide, child slavery, opium-smoking, foot-binding; seeking Moscow's blessing, not least by setting up a secret police (given the innocuous title, "Social Affairs Department") modelled on the OGPU; simultaneously endorsing democracy and human rights in order to conciliate the West; above all, forming a popular front with Chiang Kai-shek to "drive out the invading dwarfs" of Nippon.[61] Currency notes printed in Shensi bore such slogans as "Stop Civil War!" and "Unite to Resist Japan!"[62] Before he would seek allies against the Japanese, though, Chiang himself was bent on wiping out every Communist soldier in China.

However, the case that Chinese should not fight Chinese but combine against Japan won increasing support. None championed it more ardently than the warlord Chang Hsueh-liang, known as the Young Marshal, whose father (the Old Marshal) had been assassinated by the Kwantung Army in 1928. Failing to persuade Chiang Kai-shek, he sought to coerce him. When the Generalissimo visited Sian in December 1936, the Young Marshal staged a mutiny. Chiang was staying just outside the ancient city, in the temple-hotel at the hot springs resort of Lintung. He rose early to meditate cross-legged in his night-shirt before an open window. Shots rang out as the Young Marshal's troops overwhelmed his bodyguard. Leaving behind his slippers and false teeth (which he only wore at night, his wife would complain, when visiting a concubine), Chiang climbed out of the window, scaled a wall and dropped 30 feet, injuring his back in the fall. He limped up a bare, snowy hillside in the grey dawn, seeking refuge and praying for help. It came, he later told a journalist, in the shape of "two white hares. I knew, instinctively, that God had sent them as a sign and that they would lead me to safety."[63] Chiang followed them and found a small cleft in the rocks where he hid. But the soldiers soon found him. Chiang expected the worst and pleaded for a quick death. Instead he was carried down the hill on an officer's back and imprisoned in the Palace of Glorious Purity, built for Tang emperors within the walls of Sian. There he was visited by the Young Marshal, who bowed low and apologised for the inconvenience.

News of the kidnapping astonished the world. Confusion reigned, compounded by strict censorship and unbridled propaganda. London (agog with the abdication crisis) was predictably baffled by the "Chinese Puzzle."[64] Tokyo blamed a Comintern plot. Moscow asserted that Chiang was the victim of a Japanese coup, a claim so absurd that Chinese papers would not print it for fear of ridicule. Apparently Mao's first instinct was to urge the trial and punishment of the Generalissimo, who "owes us a blood debt high as a mountain."[65] But, pressed by the Kremlin, the Chinese Communist Party soon determined to use him to promote the struggle for national salvation, which would become, Mao hoped, the crucible of social revolution. Having caged Chiang, the Young Marshal's supporters were fearful of "setting the tiger free back to the mountains."[66] But Mao's urbane lieutenant Chou En-lai argued convincingly that Chiang was indispensable. As the Generalissimo himself told the Young Marshal, *"I am the government."*[67] Tortuous negotiations took place to secure his release, which was bought at the price of ending the civil war and concentrating on the foreign aggressors. Chiang showed his gratitude by locking up the Young Marshal for life. But he did not renegue on his main pledge. Paradoxically, the "Sian Incident," as it was called, made Chiang "the popular symbol of what he had opposed for years: a genuine united front against Japan."[68] As leader of the Chinese, he had to follow them.

So when conflict with Japan exploded at the Marco Polo Bridge, the warlords rallied to the central government—for the first time in the history of republican China. They were, to be sure, reluctant and unreliable allies. Furthermore, Chiang and Mao continued to regard each other as rivals: their forces, which were never integrated, clashed as early as 1938. Still, the Generalissimo did not go quite so far as his former henchman Wang Ching-wei, later the puppet ruler of Japanese-occupied China, who maintained that cooperation with the Communists was "tantamount to drinking poison in the hope of quenching one's thirst."[69] As the Japanese attacked, Chiang encouraged the Chinese Red Army to engage in guerrilla warfare. It was often effective against an enemy which in many districts controlled only the territory within a rifle-shot of the highway. But the Red Army was ill-equipped: Russian arms went to Nationalists, not Communists, who complained, "Weapons for the bourgeoisie, but books for the proletariat."[70] Moreover, the success of Mao's forces was inflated by propaganda not just from Yenan but from Tokyo, which magnified the

Red Menace in order to present the Japanese invasion as "a defence action against Communists."[71] At the War Exhibition in Ueno Park, for example, a large mural showed red war-planes rising from Moscow, changing colour in mid-flight, and landing at Wuhan in the blue-and-white livery of the Kuomintang. Contrary to the myth that was soon established, Mao husbanded his army as "the germ plasm of the Chinese revolution."[72] Chiang, on the other hand, flung his best troops into the fray, hoping to show Japan that the cost of fighting to the finish would be too high.

Once or twice they scored a victory, notably at Taierhchuang in March 1938, which was hailed as another Guadalajara. Sixteen thousand Japanese soldiers were surrounded and killed, many in vicious hand-to-hand fighting. But for the most part Chiang's armies were hopelessly outclassed in leadership, training, tactics and equipment. A Russian adviser was appalled to see Chinese units being ferried across the Yellow River on ox-hide rafts as old as the Great Wall. An American military observer described Chiang's grey-clad troops, who sometimes satisfied their craving for salt with the gunpowder in bullets removed from their cases, as a "goddam medieval mob."[73] They resisted in order to stop the Chinese becoming "the coolies of Japan";[74] but when routed they merged into the countryside to become peasants again. From north and east the "blood-spot flag" steadily advanced towards the nation's industrial heartland, the triple city of Wuhan, known as China's "three furnaces." Chiang was trading too much space for too little time. Yet retreat was the only way to stave off defeat. Not only did Japan's murderous firepower prove irresistible on land but Nippon controlled the waters and the skies. Chinese courage and patriotism were not enough. Nor was Chinese propaganda. At an official briefing in Hankow on 9 March 1938 journalists learned that "Of seven planes brought down by Chinese forces, fifteen were destroyed by infantry."[75]

As the fortresses guarding Wuhan fell one by one amid slaughter and rapine, the Japanese sensed victory. The capture of the urban complex on the Yangtse, often regarded as the Chicago of China, would, the Chief of Staff of the Japanese Operations Section declared, "deal the Chinese a truly decisive blow."[76] To ward it off Chiang employed his most potent weapon, deliberately precipitating a "disaster of fantastic size for military ends."[77] The vast, turbid Yellow River drained the land of 100 million people and regularly flooded to such catastrophic effect that it was known as "China's Sorrow." For centuries the inundations had grown worse because, instead of dredging its heavily silted bed, the Chinese had built up its banks. Thus the river did not flow through a sunken channel so much as along a colossal aqueduct, some 25 feet higher than the land on either side of it and well above the roof-tops of riparian cities such as Kaifeng. It was less a moat than a wall of water. To block the approach to Wuhan, Chiang unleashed this "malignant muddy dragon." In June 1938 his engineers dynamited the earthern dykes east of Chengchow. After the explosion (which Chiang later tried to blame on the Japanese) the river seemed to hesitate for a moment. It

> pounded, swirled and bubbled . . . with a sound very much like a loud, sardonic, hissing laugh; then, finally, with a terrible roar, it turned, and, with a sudden burst of power, ripped through the breach.[78]

The tawny deluge poured across the plain, engulfing 11 large towns and 4,000 villages. It killed livestock, destroyed crops and devastated much of the farmland in the provinces of Honan, Anwei and Kiangsu. Millions of Chinese were left homeless and untold numbers died. But many Japanese also perished. Their tanks and artillery stuck in the mire, their vessels grounded on the empty lower reaches of the river, and they were forced to withdraw. Having first scorched the earth, Chiang had now drowned it.

Both sides re-grouped. Chiang put pressure on Stalin, with whom he had signed a non-aggression treaty in 1937, to provide more aid, especially in the shape of aircraft and pilots. The aviators were the avatars of Bolshevism. They were adept, intrepid and unsmiling automata—like those in Spain, where some of them, indeed, had served. They lived apart and demanded borscht, black bread, potatoes and sweet tea, receiving instead (at best) shark's fin soup, steamed bread, rice and jasmine-flavoured tea, and at worst "fried bamboo grasses, assorted leaves, something like little worms and beetles."[79] Russia more than made up for the loss of German military assistance, which Hitler finally withdrew in the interests of the Anti-Comintern Pact. (Mussolini also supported both sides, though his flying instructors in China made aerial surveys of strategic districts and sold them to the Japanese, while members of the Fascist friendship mission to Tokyo despised their hosts and said that "cooperation" between their two countries would result in nothing more than "the exchange of opera singers.")[80] By the autumn of 1938, however, the Japanese noose again tightened around the shabby tenements and dingy smoke-stacks of Wuhan. Despite widespread sickness and oppressive heat, the forces of Nippon advanced remorselessly by road, rail and river, using poison gas as they came.

Wuhan was proclaimed another Madrid, or "the Chinese Verdun."[81] But Chiang's defence was as insubstantial as his rhetoric, "a sort of dream world of correct words and resounding phrases."[82] Ill-trained Chinese fliers in obsolete machines proved easy meat during dog-fights. Air raids grew more frequent, unimpeded by the few searchlights and the noisy anti-aircraft fire. In one attack many of Chiang's fully-loaded bombers were destroyed on the ground, along with his largest ammunition dump. An eyewitness described

> millions of white and green and red tracer bullets exploding in bunches, unfolding like magnificent, prehistoric flowers; clusters of shells bursting into fluffy smoke like the ripe heads of cotton plants. Hundreds of high-powered bombs tearing erratic holes into this luminous floral design . . . Volleys of flares, hurled into space, and floating slowly back to earth like pleiades of baby moons, illuminating the pandemonium below with their dazzling cold white light.[83]

Foreigners found the last days of Wuhan exhilarating. Among them a fevered, artificial gaiety reigned: cafés and cabarets were full, and champagne flowed at all-night parties and farewell dinners.

The Chinese were also "immensely stirred, fiercely alive and intense." But they were in more immediate peril and many of the city's inhabitants joined the tide of dispossessed humanity, amounting to tens of millions, which swept across the continent. They left from the westernised bund under the yellow glare of kerosene lamps in sooty steamers, flimsy sampans and ramshackle junks. They went by rail, filling the dark-blue coaches of the Shanghai Express and packing less salubrious rolling-stock until it overflowed: passengers perched on roofs and steps, clung to doors and windows, until the trains resembled "half-dead centipedes crawling with ants."[84] They travelled by road, on foot or in rickshaws, on donkeys or Mongol ponies, aboard bullock-carts or cars, in battered buses or wheezing lorries. A banker's wife, anxious about her household goods, even managed to commandeer one of the scarce ambulances—whose red crosses were expunged from their roofs because they proved such an irresistible target to Japanese airmen that Chinese wounded otherwise refused to ride in them.

Meanwhile myriad coolies transported over 100,000 tons of machinery to Chungking, the first large city above the Yangtse gorges, at the hub of distant Szechuan. They manhandled the huge turbines, arsenals, factories and mills which formed the core of a new industrial base. It would be operated by many thousands of skilled and semi-skilled workers, who also joined in the flight. They were accompanied, in a mass migration almost as remarkable as the Long March, by doctors with the contents of hospitals, government clerks with official records, professors with university libraries, craftsmen with the tools of their trade, farmers with their flocks and herds, to say nothing of an army of camp-followers including prostitutes. That autumn, as the persimmons grew red, as the pink and brown kaoliang ripened, as the green shoots of winter wheat sprouted and the air filled with millet chaff from peasant flails, refugees were the main harvest of China's ochre land.

When the Japanese entered Wuhan, on 25 October 1938, they found a ruined shell. Admittedly, some of the destruction which Chiang ordered had not taken place, since dynamite was removed and fuses cut by those from the foreign concessions, including British bluejackets, anxious to protect property. But much plant was blown up or set on fire and everything possible was taken away by the Chinese, from pontoons on the river to manhole covers in the streets. Still, the Japanese (who committed no outrages) rejoiced in their victory. In Tokyo huge flag and lantern parades were held and on 3 November, the anniversary of the Meiji emperor's birthday, Prince Konoe proclaimed a "New Order in East Asia." Chinese youths spelled out the message in gigantic human ideographs at celebratory athletics meetings which they were forced to attend in Peking. Such displays have plausibly been described as "an Oriental version of the Nazis' Nuremberg spectacle."[85]

Konoe's declaration amounted to a peace offer. It proposed an Asian confederation, which Japan would protect and develop, against Western and Soviet imperialism. This was an ideal genuinely embraced by some nationalists, notably intellectuals in the Prime Minister's brains' trust, the Showa Research Association *(Kenkyukai)*. But "co-prosperity" was essentially a euphemism for exploitation. And "cooperation" was a disguise for the hegemony which Konoe now seemed in a position to secure. Nippon occupied the eastern half of China, the ancient heartland of Cathay. It was in possession of all the major cities and ports—Canton had fallen without a struggle earlier in October as Japanese forces, encouraged by Chamberlain's having "sold out Czechoslovakia"[86] and convinced that Britain would "put up with any indignity rather than fight,"[87] ignored neighbouring Hong Kong. Nippon controlled nearly all China's industry, railways, motorised vehicles, electrical generating power and invested capital. Furthermore, Chiang's regime was virtually cut off from outside assistance, except for a narrow-gauge railway to Indo-China, a bad motor road to Burma and a caravan route to Sinkiang. True, the Japanese blockade proved surprisingly porous: postal services continued throughout the war, as did smuggling, known to Nippon as "special trade." But with a million troops in the field, the Japanese were convinced that the war was over. They expected Chiang to come to terms at once.

However, he knew that to come to *their* terms, which in any case the army kept stiffening, would be to lose his job, his country and probably his life. He also knew that backwardness as well as size gave China an immense resilience. The loss of cities meant little to a nation of peasants. Inflation could be discounted too: "China has no finances," boasted one Kuomintang official, "that is our strength."[88] Sir Robert Craigie put the point more soberly when he noted that China did not collapse because "her economic structure is inorganic and without nerve centres."[89] So, like Napoleon in Moscow, General Hata waited in vain at Wuhan for a national surrender. When it did not materialise he could do little more than guard his extended lines of communication, govern and exploit the subjugated territories through puppet regimes, engage in limited "rice-bowl campaigns" to supply his own troops, while trying to wear out the resistance and destroy the morale of his foes. After the fall of Wuhan, said one Japanese colonel, "We bogged down, deeper and ever deeper, in that endless morass of attrition."[90]

Chiang not only destroyed bridges, railways and ferries in his wake, he retreated to the greatest natural stronghold in China. Ringed by high mountains, Szechuan was a populous province full of broad terraced valleys lush with wheat, sugar, beans, oranges, peaches, poppies, and orchids sporting translucent petals and perfumed like citrus fruits. The walled city of Chungking, standing high on a spur of rock at the confluence of the Yangtse and Chialing rivers, was the region's barbican. Tier upon tier of dilapidated buildings clung to the cliff which rose from the water's edge, forming a colossal grey rampart. Even the tough, turbaned coolies who carried cargoes up the steep, twisting, sewage-strewn alleys to the central coign found the going hard. So far was Chungking from modern civilisation that rickshaws were novelties while buses, piped water, telephones and electricity were marvels; but the city seemed protected by its feudal remoteness. It was also hidden by the prevalent mists and fogs, which made Chungking seem "an insubstantial thing, floating in haze, a mirage . . . a shadow city."[91] The refugees, who doubled Chungking's poor and largely illiterate population in a matter of months and hated the humid, malarial summers as much as the damp, rheumatic winters, felt safe in streets to which they lent a cosmopolitan air, with smells of grilled Peking duck, sounds of staccato Cantonese and business signs from Shanghai, Nanking and Hankow.

Yet this sense of security was an illusion, for Chungking was peculiarly vulnerable from the air, even on moonless nights. It was silhouetted between the two stretches of water which reflected any vagrant gleams of light, "making it a near perfect target." Early in May 1939 there was a lunar eclipse, when the Chinese traditionally beat gongs to scare off the giant dog of heaven who tries to devour the moon. The Japanese bombers, which arrived almost simultaneously, were less easy to deter, despite the stutter of machine-gun fire and the cough of anti-aircraft guns. Their first raid caused considerable damage but their second, a day later, created a fire-storm. The planes arrived at dusk, flying so high that they seemed "like gnats floating in the dark." Then the bombs fell and a thunder of explosions rolled across the city, which "boiled in a sudden upheaval of flying wreckage."[92] A vast pall of dust billowed over the shambles and smoke rose from a multitude of individual blazes. They coalesced into a roaring sea of flame which threatened to engulf the entire promontory. It was, a distant eyewitness wrote,

> a scene of appalling beauty. Fire streamed up in long pennons and banners, bending a little in the slight draft of night breeze. Flames whipped from their roots, soaring into the whirling columns of smoke like flapping wings.[93]

As troops with masked faces fought the conflagration and dug desperately in the smouldering ruins, streams of terrified survivors fled to the river or to the hills under the milky glow of a nearly full, white moon.

The raid, which occurred when the streets were crowded with people returning home after work, caused 7,000 deaths and many more injuries. In the opinion of one contemporary, it "shocked a world horror-hardened by Guernica and Barcelona."[94] Yet when the initial panic subsided, the inhabitants of Chungking returned to resurrect the city. Normal services were quickly restored. Blue-clad labourers and khaki-uniformed soldiers cleared debris, filled in craters, salvaged anything of value and buried corpses. Bamboo scaffolding sprang up as though growing from the ashes. Soon new buildings of purple sandstone and grey shale were being raised on the remains of rat-infested shacks and lice-ridden hovels. Fire lines were left between them and other air raid precautions were introduced. The Chinese devised a long-range warning system, dug cave shelters and improved the blackout by turning off the main switch at the city's generating plant and allowing the police to shoot at lighted candles and cigarettes. The Japanese bombers often returned; but they could not destroy Chungking, let alone China, in fabric or in spirit. Signs in the city's shops announced: "Business as usual"; "The more we are bombed, the more we are strong to endure"; and (a play on the word *tan*, which means eggs or bombs) "Fresh eggs, direct from Tokyo."[95]

THUS the war became a bloody stalemate. Many senior Japanese soldiers and politicians wanted peace but they were still reluctant to lose face, sacrifice security or give up the spoils of war. By so doing they not only risked the wrath of a disillusioned people but assassination by fanatical ultra-nationalists, who were again plotting and threatening. It was therefore impossible to generate a consensus for peace-making such as had developed spontaneously, through the growth of patriotic feeling, for making war. The army was, as always, riven by internal faction. It remained at odds with the navy, whose officers sought to check the soldiers through the characteristic expedient of agreeing with them. Konoe's cabinet, said one of its members, resembled a conclave of Chinese warlords: "all of them have different opinions and have someone backing them."[96] Konoe himself was still popular. "Why, nobody is opposed to him," an admirer remarked without irony, "not even the people."[97] Yet he was, if anything, more indecisive than ever. His friend Kido said that he possessed neither principles nor opinions, only eccentric tastes. Konoe himself admitted that he lacked the courage to face political problems. Certainly he allowed power to slip still further into the hands of the military. In December 1938 he made another pugnacious peace proposal, offering China friendship at the point of a bayonet, which Chiang predictably refused. The following month, "utterly disheartened and despondent," he gave up the premiership and became Lord Privy Seal. In the upbeat estimation of *Contemporary Japan,* the "wayward Prince was passive in doing constructive things, but positive in the manner of his resignation."[98]

Konoe swapped places with Baron Hiranuma, a stately, cadaverous lawyer who had founded one of the ultra-nationalist societies, *Kokuhonsha,* and had long been characterised abroad as Japan's "Fascist leader."[99] To liberals at home, Hiranuma was anathema. Saionji regarded him as the prototypical champion of the empty, drum-beating, sloganising movement to turn Japan into a one-party state. The Emperor himself, in his Delphic way, wondered whether Hiranuma was not "egotistical."[100] But even the new Prime Minister's supporters were repelled by his forbidding manner. He was notoriously cold and unsociable, fond of reciting Noh dramas and Chinese poems, playing *go* and practising archery. When a group of citizens honoured him by meeting his train en route to a function, he "never uttered a word" to them throughout the remainder of the journey, fully earning his sobriquet "the Silent."[101] Hiranuma did now pay lip-service to constitutional democracy, for which he was branded by former friends a worn-out "old tiger."[102] But his increased drive for national unity seemed to be a shift in the direction of totalitarianism. So it was, though in a peculiarly Japanese fashion. Hiranuma, like Konoe before him, kept having to defer to the army in order to maintain his own leadership and, more important, to preserve the Imperial Way. He yielded to the sword in order to defend the throne, even though he offended its occupant in the process. As Hiranuma told Konoe, "I might do something entirely opposed to the will of the Emperor, but I cannot help that. I shall be fully responsible for my action."[103]

Under Hiranuma, therefore, Japanese militarism became still more unbridled. He himself maintained a fierce hostility towards the Chinese, saying that as for those who continued to oppose Japan "we have no alternative than to exterminate them."[104] For the rest there would be the bliss of friendly cooperation, though even this was expressed in sinister, even bizarre, terms. China and Japan were as close as lips and teeth, it was often said. To effect sincere "Asiatic co-ordination," the Director of the Japanese Foreign Office's Information Bureau, Kawai Tatsui, told a gathering of Chinese in Shanghai, the two nations "must be naked in their minds." He thereupon took off his clothes and danced in the nude before his hosts, who "heartily applauded." As a result, according to Craigie's sardonic account of the episode, "Mr. Kawai's popularity with the Chinese has been greatly enhanced."[105] Less endearing was Hiranuma's policy of tightening up Nippon's economic monopoly over the conquered territories, which inevitably aggravated Japan's relations with China's other major trading partners. Both the United States and Britain protested frequently about the obstruction of their commerce as well as the habitual indignities and occasional violence which Japan inflicted on their nationals. For instance, Westerners arriving at Kobe were now made to provide both a urine and a stool sample; and John Masters, then a regular soldier, was further surprised when the Japanese customs stamped all the cigarettes in his case individually. However, Washington and (to a lesser extent) London were reluctant to act or react in concert for fear of provoking Tokyo. Thus the loans which both Western governments now gave to stabilise Chiang Kai-shek's rapidly inflating currency were not coordinated. The democracies reckoned that helping China was less risky than retaliating against Japan.

Intent on wrecking the finances of Nationalist China, Hiranuma bitterly resented the intervention. So did his countrymen and once again superior, old-fashioned, cowardly, domineering Britain became Japan's chief whipping-boy. By the spring of 1939, Prince Saionji learned, "anti-British fever [was] thoroughly spreading in all directions."[106] One ultra-nationalist told Craigie that Japan would not shirk from conflict with Britain even if "it meant that every Japanese subject was to fall fighting by the Emperor's side."[107] Thus Nippon sought closer relations with Britain's European enemies, Germany and Italy. Just how close they should be was the subject of a long and involved struggle between Japan's leaders. Most army men, including Itagaki (now War Minister), wanted an aggressive alliance with Italy and Germany. They were supported by Hiranuma himself (after initial opposition) and other cabinet ministers, as well as by the Japanese ambassadors in Berlin and Rome. These envoys, in the opinion of the snowy-haired Arita Hachiro, who had succeeded Ugaki as Foreign Minister the previous year, were so spellbound by their hosts that they were indistinguishable from them. With the backing of the navy, the older *zaibatsu,* and liberals such as Saionji, Arita managed to postpone a full-blooded coalition with Hitler and Mussolini until the Anti-Comintern Pact was invalidated by the Nazi-Soviet agreement. The Foreign Minister, who was threatened with assassination, also received help from the Emperor. Hirohito expressed disquiet about the extension of Japan's commitments, which left the War Minister "greatly awed." But it also provoked talk of setting up a military shogunate. The Emperor signally failed to restrain the "shameful"[108] anti-British demonstrations in Tokyo, which were led by the military police and financed by the army. In China, meanwhile, the Japanese further harassed British subjects and increased restrictions on British enclaves. They surrounded the concession at Tientsin, for example, with both barbed wire and an electric fence.

This large trading city, situated 80 miles south-east of Peking, became the focus of the most dangerous crisis to occur between Japan and Britain during the inter-war years. What angered the Japanese most about the British concession at Tientsin was that it kept Chiang's currency in circulation and harboured Chinese terrorists. Matters came to a head in April 1939 when a Chinese collaborator was shot, four men were arrested and, despite alleged confessions, the British refused to hand them all over to the Japanese authorities. General Homma thereupon instituted a rigorous blockade of the concession, his sentries strip-searching Britons of both sexes at bayonet point. This provoked a furious outcry around the world as the yellow press waxed lurid about the Yellow Peril. The Japanese declared that the blockade would remain in force until Britain had agreed to a series of humiliating conditions, notably the withdrawal of support for China. Lord Halifax, who had responded uncertainly to the crisis, now maintained that Britain could not "capitulate" over Tientsin because of "general reactions here and in the United States."[109] However, appeasement in Europe had not equipped Britain for resistance in Asia. So Chamberlain overruled him.

Craigie was told to negotiate a compromise. His July conversations with Arita took place in an atmosphere charged with tension. One huge rally passed a resolution saying that:

> We, the seven million citizens of Tokyo, embodying the rising aspirations of Asian peoples, have determined upon a thorough bombing of Britain, the enemy of justice and humanity.[110]

But, through tact and tenacity, Craigie managed to get both the blockade and most of the Japanese conditions lifted. He did have to acknowledge, though, that Nippon's forces in China needed to take steps to meet their "special requirements," which Britain would do nothing to prejudice.[111] With his usual optimism Craigie thought the accord would give "strong impetus" to the "movement for rapprochement" with Britain which leaders like Hiranuma favoured. Less sanguine observers, such as the British Ambassador in China, the pipe-loving Sir Archibald Clark Kerr, dismissed this hope, tartly observing that Japanese politicians were always bounced by militarists "bent on conquest" and the "expulsion of foreigners."[112] The Chinese themselves regarded the Tientsin settlement as a Far Eastern Munich. Americans were so disturbed by it that (without consulting Britain) Roosevelt announced the termination of the 1911 commercial treaty with Japan. One Whitehall mandarin subsequently said that the weakness displayed by Britain over Tientsin "may perhaps have contributed to the Russian decision to make an agreement with the Germans rather than ourselves."[113]

As it happened, just when Britain was back-pedalling over Tientsin, the USSR was attacking Japanese forces at Nomonhan, on the frontier between its Outer Mongolian satellite and Manchukuo. This was the bloodiest of the many border clashes which took place between the two great Far Eastern powers during the 1930s and nothing better illustrated the atavistic aggressiveness of the soldiers of the sun. At a time when they threatened to come to blows with the British empire and were engaged in a conflict with China that had already cost them 50,000 lives, Japanese nationalists initiated actions likely to provoke war with the Soviet Union. Of course, the likes of Hiranuma and Itagaki had long advocated this conflict. Most Japanese, moreover, believed that sooner or later they would have to face a showdown with Russia. But it took General Tojo Hideki to express his country's antagonism towards the Bear in its crudest form.

Admittedly, Tojo, born into a military family in 1884, was anything but sophisticated. He was frighteningly ignorant of the outside world: after the war Tojo revealed that, although he had heard of Munich, he did not know what had happened there. His dislike of foreigners extended to all manifestations of alien culture, from jazz to Charlie Chaplin. Ishiwara dismissed Tojo as "uneducated" at best and at worst "mentally defective."[114] His more considered verdict was that Tojo had the pettifogging mentality of a sergeant-major. Yet not for nothing was the heavily moustached general known as "the Razor." Despite his balding head, his bespectacled countenance, his scrawny, diminutive physique and his crumpled, ill-fitting uniform, Tojo impressed even the supercilious *New Yorker:* he came "about as close as a Japanese can to looking important."[115] Westerners were often repelled by Tojo's gruff, brusque manner but they felt that his "quick movements and erect carriage denote energy and determination."[116]

Certainly he was exceptionally self-disciplined and hard-working. Tojo often said that he was on duty 24 hours a day—sustained by sweet rice cakes and cigarettes. Smoking, 60 a day, was his only pleasure. His only duty lay in being "completely subservient"[117] to the Emperor, whom he approached with an exaggerated obeisance that was much appreciated at the Palace. Later, as Premier, Tojo claimed to be a mere reflection of his sovereign's glory: "Were it not for this light I should be no better than a pebble by the roadside."[118] But Tojo's brand of imperial fundamentalism was essentially a doctrine of belligerence. It amounted, as stated in his war crimes trial, to "ultra-nationalism, blind devotion to authority, belief in Japan's ambition of being dominant in Asia, belief in Japan's superiority and divine mission, and belief in the necessity of military aggression."[119] As Deputy War Minister in Konoe's government Tojo had summoned a group of leading industrialists and, barking at them "as if he were laying down the law to a company of new recruits,"[120] stated that the army would ensure that they no longer put profit before the national interest. This lay in preparing the country to face not only the hostility of Britain and America, but to fight wars simultaneously against both China and Russia.

Tojo was well aware that Soviet forces in the Far East had been immensely strengthened by the summer of 1939 and that they had fought the Japanese to a standstill during the previous major border conflict, at Changkufeng. But this in itself spurred on the fire-eaters of the Kwantung Army to ignore the restraining hand of Tokyo and teach Moscow a lesson. They were, in any case, convinced that the Red Army had been incapacitated by the purges and would be no match for troops inspired by devotion to the Emperor. As the "Nomonhan Incident" developed from a frontier skirmish into a small war, the Japanese infantry did, indeed, fight with fanatical courage. They stopped Soviet tanks with Molotov cocktails. They made bayonet charges over open ground against murderous firepower. Under cover of darkness they became homicidal shadows, faithful to their training motto, "The night is worth a million reinforcements." They took part in so-called "special attacks"—suicide missions—acting as "human bullets" and mocking their foes for having a "despicable urge to live."[121] They themselves preferred death to surrender. However, as General

Georgi Zhukov threw in more armoured and mechanised forces, the Japanese found themselves having to execute a "lateral advance,"[122] otherwise known as a retreat. Both in the air and on the ground they were outnumbered, out-manoeuvred and comprehensively out-gunned. Soviet batteries often fired more shells in a minute than Japanese artillery could afford to use in a week.

Through good intelligence, much of it supplied by the well-placed Soviet spy in Tokyo, Richard Sorge, Stalin was confident that Hiranuma's government would not let the Nomonhan Incident turn into an all-out war with Russia. He was correct, despite the perennial insubordination of the Kwantung Army. Its ardour was cooled by Zhukov's crushing victory and some officers began to look for softer targets. However, what really destroyed the rationale of the fight against Russia was the Nazi-Soviet pact, news of which hit drought-stricken Japan like an earthquake on 23 August 1939. That their prospective European ally could be guilty of such "treachery"[123] shocked nationalists such as Konoe. It caused the army grave loss of face, though this was a matter, Hiranuma concluded, on which it would be wise to remain silent. With the government in total disarray, he himself resigned.

The aged Prince Saionji, who regarded the German betrayal as the "biggest failure" in Japanese foreign policy "since the beginning of our history," hoped that a new ministry would bring about a diplomatic revolution in favour of Britain and the United States. But the Emperor was unable to find a political leader who could break free of army thraldom. In fact no one was qualified to form a cabinet, Saionji remarked, "unless he has tasted the bitter suffering of drinking three 'to' [about 12 gallons] of vinegar through the nose."[124] With the red wens on his face, the new Prime Minister, retired General Abe Nobuyuki, looked as though he had done just that. But he was quite incapable of controlling the soldiers, whose aggression did not abate. It did, however, change direction—southwards, where the imperialist powers, now beleaguered by war in Europe, offered easier opportunities than did Russia. As Stalin told Ribbentrop in September, when crowing over the fact that the Japanese were suing for peace after having sustained 20,000 casualties at Nomonhan: "They have understood my language."[125]

XXVI

THE MAKING OF THE
NAZI-SOVIET PACT

SOVIET citizens also understood Stalin's language, despite his Caucasian heavy breathing, but his purpose remained obscure. He talked in deceptively simple terms and his actions spoke louder than words. But it was not clear, as the Great Purge continued with unabated fury into 1938, what Stalin intended or where he was bound. On the one hand, a malevolent despotism appeared to have become entrenched. Terror was now a matter of routine. When people were arrested a standard procedure was followed: their children were packed off to institutions, their furniture was left in place for new occupants and their jobs were filled by eager young Bolsheviks. Furthermore, the Motherland was as regularly invoked as the Comintern was ignored, and the phobia about foreigners had become so universal that diplomats from abroad were shunned even by prostitutes. So it seemed possible that Stalin was engaged in a cruel but rational process of recreating the Party in his own image and preparing the nation for war. On the other hand, there were further signs that the locomotive of history was running away with its driver. The terror had apparently taken on a life of its own. NKVD men became something of "a power unto themselves."[1] They chose victims who had not been tipped the black spot by the Kremlin, adding another element of chance to the national game of murder in the dark. To the British Ambassador, at least, it seemed quite as plausible that Stalin was a "homicidal maniac" whose mania was being exploited by a "band of bloodthirsty police spies" as that he was a "cold and calculating tyrant" systematically killing off his opponents.[2]

However, as the liquidation of top managers took its toll on the economy and the armed forces suffered a further assault, few doubted that Russia's capacity to resist alien aggression was being seriously impaired. So on 24 January 1938 Stalin touched the brakes and changed direction, just as he had done by writing his article "Dizzy with Success," condemning the excesses of collectivisation in 1930. Now he launched a campaign against false informers, those who had denounced others in order to save their own skins. He turned his withering gaze on the secret police, who had reckoned that their "personal salvation lay in swimming" with the tide of terror.[3] The purgers themselves should be purged, though no one knew who would accomplish this or how far they would go. The purge was "rather like the plague," a contemporary scientist observed, "and you could never tell who would catch it next."[4] Often Russians did not even know who *had* caught it. One of the few indications that prominent figures had become infected was the removal of their photographs from Moscow's Children's Park of Rest and Culture.

In certain cases, of course, public enemies were pilloried in public. Those being prepared to appear in Stalin's last great show trial, which took place in March 1938, were subjected to the most lurid abuse. In particular the Soviet press demanded that Nikolai Bukharin, the star defendant, should be indicted for conspiring with the Trotskyite traitors already found guilty, those "liquidated double-dealers, murderers, spies, and rabid enemies of the working class." Stalin was especially anxious to get rid of Bukharin, who had been Lenin's favourite Bolshevik and remained the most attractive embodiment of the Party's early idealism. This is not to say that Bukharin was a Communist Candide. During the Russian revolution he had cited Saint-Just to the effect that those who cannot rule with law must rule with iron. And he had produced vicious apologias for Red violence against the Whites: "Humpbacks are only cured by death."[5] During the decade after the revolution Bukharin did much to promote the rise of the Stalinist State. He proposed to mould intellectuals as in a factory. Seeking to ingratiate himself with his leader, he conducted heresy hunts against the opponents of Stalin—for whom Nietzsche might have coined his aphorism that gratitude is hatred wearing a mask. Bukharin supported the Cheka, an organisation he honoured to his dying day. Professor Ivan Pavlov opposed Bukharin's election to the Academy of Sciences because he was "up to his knees in blood."

However, Bukharin duly came to see Stalin as Genghis Khan and to espouse "proletarian humanism."[6] He resisted the growing power of the OGPU, which had lost, he thought, its pristine ideological purity. He defended the rights of nationalities and condemned the coercion of peasants. He objected to the kind of cultural conformity which required poetry to be rhymed slogans. To the fury of Stalin, who was implacable about the acceptance and implementation of the "general line," Bukharin conjured with Marx's slogan "Doubt everything." In 1929 he was expelled from the Politburo as a "right deviationist." In fact, Bukharin was not really a politician at all. He was, as Trotsky suggested, a perpetual student of politics. Stalin put it more harshly: Bukharin was "a typical representative of the spineless, effete *intelligent* in politics."[7] He chased ideas with the same youthful ardour as he chased butterflies. Bukharin lacked the strength of Lenin and the unscrupulousness of Stalin. He was a creature of emotion, highly strung, easily moved to love, laughter or tears, prone to nervous collapse. But he possessed (after Lunacharsky) the subtlest, best-informed and most versatile mind in the Communist Party. So, once he had confessed his sins and asked for absolution, he won renewed approval. This was dangerous, since Stalin was always inclined to ask who had organised applause. According to one account, Bukharin's speech at the 1934 Writers' Congress in Moscow was greeted with such a huge ovation that, on returning to his seat, he whispered to friends: "What have you done? You have signed my death warrant."[8]

Bukharin was undoubtedly too captivating for his own good. Born in 1888, the son of a minor clerk and school teacher, he was not only a philosopher of revolution but a paragon of charm. His conversation was seductive: witty, ironical, sometimes malicious, occasionally savage, always full of zest. He never put on airs or stood on his dignity: as editor of *Izvestia* (1934–6) he allowed his staff, during countryside walks, to throw him into the air and catch him again; and to amuse his beautiful third wife, Anna Larina, he walked on his hands in Montmartre. She was also impressed by the fact that he could spit like a *muzhik* and whistle like a *bezprizornik*. Bukharin remained the Bohemian of Bolshevism, given to salty language, living in unpretentious simplicity, dressing in peaked cap, baggy leather jacket and high boots. In appearance he rather resembled Lenin, having a small stocky frame, a thin red goatee, a domed forehead and eyes alight with intelligence. Like Lenin, he was incessantly active, painting, hunting, swimming, mountaineering, reading with voracious speed. He also wrote quickly, seldom crossing out and producing work which ranged from *The ABC of Communism* to abstruse essays on the theory of dialectical materialism. He championed the kind of science that worked for society, influencing British scientists such as Julian Huxley and J. D. Bernal, Professor of Physics at Cambridge University, who pronounced that "science is communism."[9]

Bukharin also studied natural history. He loved not only lepidoptera but animals of all sorts and, to the delight of Stalin's daughter, Svetlana, who adored him, he collected a menagerie. It included hedgehogs, grass-snakes, marmosets, a bear cub, a crippled hawk and a tame fox which long outlived its owner and years later was still "racing round the Kremlin."[10] Bukharin's popularity was obviously seen as a threat by Stalin himself. Partly as a matter of self-protection and partly in the interests of Party unity, the rebel attempted to mollify the dictator during the early 1930s.

He extolled Stalin's brilliance and lauded his policies in grovelling terms. But Bukharin could not resist using veiled expressions, commonly known as "Aesopian language," to hint that there was really nothing to choose between Stalin and Hitler, with whom he believed war to be inevitable. (Squeezed between Germany and Japan, Russia's millions might have to find a place for themselves, he prophesied darkly, in one of the furnaces at Magnitogorsk.) Bukharin also discovered in von Ranke's account of the Borgia pontiffs, with their Inquisition, their Jesuit cadres and their "wild mass extermination of heretics," a means to suggest the true nature of Stalinism: "Among the popes there were not only simple criminals, there were true masters of dirty, bloody enterprises, virtuosos of murder."[11]

By 1936 Bukharin was sure that he would be one of the Red Pope's next victims. In the spring of that year, on a visit to France, he privately depicted Stalin as a vengeful, malicious demon who could not bear the existence of anyone who was his superior in any way. Stalin even seemed jealous of the Bukharinite-Leninist high brow, ordering the photographic re-touchers in Soviet press offices to increase the size of his own forehead by one or two centimetres. "And now he's going to kill me," Bukharin told André Malraux.[12] Yet the Russian, loathing the émigré life, would not go into voluntary exile. He returned home, determined to drain his bitter cup to the dregs. Once again he was struck by the similarities between Stalinism and Nazism. Both systems dehumanised their own people by suppressing intellectual liberty through force and fraud. In the last article he wrote for *Izvestia,* on 6 July 1936, Bukharin made the identification as explicit as he dared. At a time when every utterance was combed for hidden meanings, it was tantamount to a manifesto: "A complicated network of decorative deceit in words and action is a highly essential characteristic of Fascist regimes of all stamps and hues."

Thereafter a pall of official hostility descended over Bukharin. He was not detained but for months he lived as a virtual recluse in the Kremlin, spending much of his time, ironically, in Stalin's old bedroom—they had earlier swapped apartments. From this limbo he sent desperate appeals to members of the Politburo. One expressed joy that "the dogs" Zinoviev and Kamenev had been shot, for the latter's accusations against Bukharin were so "monstrously base" that he (Bukharin) had lost all sense of reality: "Is it a dream, a mirage, a madhouse, a hallucination?"[13] In another he implored Stalin to investigate the charges that were poisoning his life: "Interrogate me! Turn me inside out!"[14] His pleas were in vain. Listening to the Spassky Tower bell counting down the hours to his doom, Bukharin contemplated suicide; but he lacked the courage to pull the trigger of the gold-plated revolver given to him by Voroshilov. However, still asserting his innocence, he went on hunger strike. Hauled before the Central Committee, Bukharin apologised for his protest but declared that he would not tell lies about himself as Kamenev and Zinoviev had done. Molotov shouted: "If you don't confess, that will prove you're a fascist hireling. Their press is saying that our trials are provocations. We'll arrest you and you'll confess."[15] Knowing that the axe was about to fall, Bukharin wrote a letter to future Communist leaders and consigned it to the memory of his young wife. In it Bukharin swore that he was a good Bolshevik transformed into a villain by the OGPU's wonder-working organs in order to satisfy the "sick, suspicious mind of Stalin." He wrote: "I feel my own impotence before a devilish machine which, by using in all probability medieval methods, has come to possess gigantic power, enough to fabricate organised slander."[16]

Finally, in February 1937, Bukharin was arrested. So the secret police had more than a year to work on him before the show trial. Little is known of what he endured in the Lubyanka. Ignorance has encouraged speculation, classically formulated by Arthur Koestler in *Darkness at Noon* (1940). That novel, whose hero, Rubashov, owes much to Bukharin, carries powerful imaginative conviction. Indeed the "grandeur"[17] of its central argument, whereby Rubashov is induced to confess falsely to counter-revolutionary crimes in order to do a last service to the Party which (for all its faults) is conducting "the most promising social experiment in history,"[18] converted a number of young French intellectuals to Communism. As it happens, Koestler did get uncannily close to the justification, which has recently come to light, that Bukharin sent Stalin from prison. Proclaiming himself innocent of the crimes to which he had confessed under interrogation, Bukharin said that he would submit to the Party because he had concluded that there was some "great and bold political idea behind the general purge" which overshadowed all else. "It would be petty of me to put the fortunes of my own person on the same level as those tasks of world-historical importance, which rest above all on your shoulders."[19] Bukharin developed this theme during his famous final speech from the dock. In a passage from which Koestler quotes, Bukharin said that he had given in to the prison investigators after having completely reevaluated his past.

> For when you ask yourself: "If you must die, what are you dying for?"—
> an absolutely black vacuity suddenly rises before you with startling vivid
> ness. There was nothing to die for, if one wanted to die unrepented. And,
> on the contrary, everything positive that glistens in the Soviet Union

acquires new dimensions in a man's mind. This in the end disarmed me
completely and led me to bend my knees before the Party and the country . . . For in reality the whole country stands behind Stalin; he is the
hope of the world.

Sophisticated though this thesis is, however, it reflects only part of the
truth.

As Koestler himself shows, the secret police had blunter instruments
at their disposal than moral persuasion. These were certainly permitted
and perhaps employed in Bukharin's case. According to one account, he
held out for three months before being locked in a "special cell"[20] which
invariably produced confessions. Furthermore, he tortured himself. Unlike
the cold, calculating Rubashov, Bukharin was an ideologue of flesh and
blood. As emerges from his frantic, adoring and self-abasing prison letters
to Stalin, Bukharin was a constant "prey to torments." He was terrified
that his wife and son would be killed. He dreaded the prospect of a bullet
and begged to be dispatched by poison or morphine. He was so lacerated
by fear that he succumbed to bouts of "hallucinatory delirium."[21] Bukharin's capitulation was thus more a matter of psychological collapse than
intellectual surrender. He hinted at this during his trial. Bukharin scorned
the notion that the interrogators of the Lubyanka employed drugs or hyp-
notism to create a slave spirit. Instead, he suggested, they disintegrated
their victims from within, inducing a "semi-paralysis of the will" and a
"peculiar duality of mind."[22]

Bukharin displayed that condition to a bewildering degree during the
ten days of what Trotsky called Moscow's ultimate "judicial phantasmagoria."[23] He was arraigned in the October Hall with 20 other defendants,
including prominent old Bolsheviks such as Krestinsky, Rykov, Rosengoltz and Yagoda. The last of these, having masterminded similar cha-
rades, looked the most crushed: once so lithe and arrogant in his OGPU
uniform, he now huddled in a dark suit, his shoulders stooped, his hair
noticeably greyer, his face a portrait of despair. The beaky, bespectacled
Krestinsky stunned the court on the first day by withdrawing his plea of
guilty: but he recanted the next morning, reportedly after spending the
night in a cell heated to a temperature of 120 degrees Fahrenheit by four
great arc-lamps while being forced to drink glasses of salty water and to
look at pictures of worse tortures. However, Bukharin stole the show with
a performance designed to preserve his integrity without destroying his
family. Despite the agony he had endured before and after his arrest, he
walked this tightrope with dazzling panache.

Bukharin's technique was to admit, with every sign of sincerity and penitence, responsibility for counter-revolutionary transgression in general but to deny particular instances. Thus he pleaded guilty to terrorism but not guilty to terrorist acts, such as the assassination of Kirov and the attempted murder of Lenin. He also deftly discredited the case for the prosecution, insinuating its absurdity and undermining evidence resting solely on confession, which he described as a medieval principle of jurisprudence. Moreover, his confessed "insurrectionary orientation" seemed to be little more than opposition to Stalin's personal rule, while his conspiratorial programme involved "a lapse into bourgeois-democratic freedom." Again and again the flustered Vyshinsky tried to brand Bukharin a criminal rather than a heretic but failed to pin him down. Asked to be specific about his crimes, Bukharin replied wryly that it was hard for him to select from so many. Quizzed about a certain conversation, which Vyshinsky called "this" conversation, Bukharin answered that Hegel considered "this" to be "the most difficult word."[24] Told that he was a criminal, not a philosopher, Bukharin settled whimsically for being a criminal philosopher. Such sallies provoked laughter even among the picked audience and Vyshinsky sweated inside his blue double-breasted suit. In lieu of argument (not to mention proof) he increased the volume of abuse: "this was the first instance in history of a spy and a murderer using philosophy, like powdered glass, to hurl it into his victim's eyes before dashing his brains out with a footpad's bludgeon [i.e., his general confession]."[25] Bukharin was visibly contemptuous of the State Prosecutor, exposing Vyshinsky's elementary logical mistake of assuming what he was trying to prove. After scribbling away on the bulky indictment in blue pencil, Bukharin made a challenging final speech. It was "a brilliant composition, delivered in a matter-of-fact manner," reported the *New York Times,* and containing "no trace of bombast, truculence or cheap oratory."

Of course, no forensic skill could have altered the verdict. For weeks resolutions had been pouring into Moscow from committees and organisations throughout the country (often couched in the same language) calling for the death of the accused. The entire Soviet press had condemned them as "highway robbers," "despicable reptiles," "bloody hounds of fascism"[26] and, in what *The Times* called a "grimly proleptic phrase," "Trotskyist carrion."[27] Hearing that they had variously spied for foreign governments, tried to poison Yezhov, slaughtered Soviet stallions, filled the workers' butter with glass and nails, the courtroom audience broke into "murmurs of rage, horror and disgust." In that "strange, tense atmosphere" even sceptics such as Fitzroy Maclean (who once, unforgettably, noticed Stalin silhouetted by an ill-directed arc-lamp inside his screened private box) found themselves "unconsciously yielding to the power of suggestion."[28] So the defendants had no hope, which did not stop them writing final petitions for mercy. Bukharin alone looked "manly, proud and almost defiant"[29] to the end. The others, only three of whom escaped an immediate death sentence, seemed utterly demoralised. Yagoda made a pathetic plea to be allowed to do hard labour on one of his own canals. Rykov, a tall figure with bleary eyes and straggling beard, giggled incoherently and wept. Rosengoltz attempted to ingratiate himself with the court (and to save his children) by averring that Bolshevism had created in Russia for the first time "a full-blooded life, scintillating with joy and colour." He even recited the hit song from the film *Circus:*

> Native land of mine, so beautiful . . .
> There is no other land the whole world over,
> Where man walks the earth so proud and free.[30]

Circus "presented to the world the benign face of the idealistic socialist state."[31] That the film's hymn to the Motherland should have been quoted at the climax of the purge trials was a final irony in one of the most macabre episodes in the annals of totalitarianism.

ACCORDING to a recent authority, the last show trial sent out a "signal that the worst of the Terror was over."[32] Actually it seems to have sent out quite the opposite signal. The last show trial was another allegory of death. It sharply dramatised the continuing liquidation of Stalin's enemies. In particular the destruction of Bukharin, despite his ingenious apologetics and appealing high-mindedness, indicated that the mills of Yezhov would grind on, and grind exceeding small. To be sure, the NKVD now concentrated on exposing secret enemies within the Party, those who, as Vyshinsky said in his summing-up, had "spent the whole of their lives behind masks."[33] Moreover, some of those earlier arrested and imprisoned were rehabilitated. Nevertheless the Great Purge showed few signs of moderating by the summer of 1938. Indeed, the climate of fear grew more oppressive and suspicion filled the air like fog.

Rather than risk revealing their thoughts people increasingly talked in Party jargon, in the stock phrases imprinted on the minds of the newly literate—almost everyone in the rising generation. Or they took refuge in silence. Not all spontaneity was stifled and jokes, many of Jewish origin, could still be heard in whispers. One concerned an old man called Rabinovich who holds a placard thanking Comrade Stalin for his happy childhood: when the police protest that Stalin had not even been born when Rabinovich was a child he replies, "That's exactly what I want to thank him for."[34] Still, it was in 1938 that Mandelstam devised a gesture for the suppression of jokes—moving the lips silently and slicing the hand across the throat. Soon he himself was crushed by the juggernaut, which seems to have killed about as many people in 1938 as it had in 1937. Towards the end it claimed especially such victims as Komsomol leaders, provincial apparatchiks, members of factory committees, religious devotees, NKVD men and officers in the army of the Far East. In the first eight months of the year 35 per cent of Moscow's Party officials were dismissed. Of 175 commissars in the People's Republics, 150 lost their lives. At least 44 per cent of all senior diplomats were purged. On 12 December 1938 Stalin approved the shooting of 3,167 people. As one Muscovite who survived the camps wrote: this "accursed Tamerlaine smashed and trampled everything. He took the future away from citizens who were not yet born."[35]

What really signified the end of the Great Purge was not the last show trial but the dismissal of Yezhov as People's Commissar for Internal Affairs, head of the NKVD. This may seem a paradoxical claim since his removal was announced on 8 December 1938, four days before Stalin issued his mass death warrant, and his replacement was Lavrenti Beria, a sadist even more malign than Yezhov himself. However, it is clear that the monstrous witch-hunt was running out of steam towards the end of the year, if only for want of victims. In November the Central Committee adopted the highly critical report of an investigatory commission into the purges, and condemned the NKVD for "gross violations of legal norms."[36] Yezhov became the chief scapegoat. Long hated and feared, he had once been likened to the

> wicked urchins of the courts in Rastereyeva Street, whose favourite occupation was to tie a piece of paper dipped in paraffin to a cat's tail, set fire to it, and then watch with delight how the terrified animal would tear down the street, trying desperately but in vain to escape the approaching flames.[37]

Now the persecutor became the prey. Yezhov languished for a few weeks as Commissar for Water Transport, drinking vodka, saying nothing at meetings and making little paper aeroplanes, which he sent flying and retrieved even if he had to crawl under a chair to do so. Just before the 18th Party Congress in March 1939 Stalin asked him ominously if he was fit to be a member of the Central Committee. Yezhov turned pale and stammered that "he loved Stalin more than his own life"[38] and did not know that he had done anything wrong. Stalin replied that top NKVD officials had plotted to assassinate him when Yezhov had been their boss. A few days later Yezhov was arrested. He seemed relieved, handing over his gun and saying: "How long I have been waiting for this!"[39] In 1940 he was executed.

Beria's first act—the replacement of most of the NKVD officials who had worked for Yezhov with seasoned thugs of his own, many of them Georgians—scarcely encouraged Russians to hope for a relaxation of the terror. Nor did Beria's record inspire optimism. Born in 1899, he had risen to become chief of the Georgian secret police as early as 1926, by dint of intrigue and by spilling blood like water. His opponents in the Caucasus complained of "unprecedented horrors and terror carried out by the Cheka in its torture chambers."[40] Beria's appearance belied his nature. Although he liked to wear a military jacket and riding breeches tucked into boots, he looked flaccid. His eyes bulged behind pince-nez, his lips curled girlishly, his hands were limp and damp, his physique was flabby and his skin was sallow. But in reality Beria was violent, cruel, adamantine.

He was a serial rapist, using his bodyguard to kidnap young women from the streets of Moscow and bring them to his house. He liked to toy with his political victims, dangling them over the abyss. Most he cut off in their prime but some were saved for future games of cat-and-mouse. Thus while Bukharin's second wife, an invalid, was brutally treated and executed, Anna Larina merely suffered a long term of imprisonment, her baby being sent to an orphanage. Beria obviously relished the interview with Larina, offering her grapes and threats. Having discovered from an informer that she had written a poem about an evil black raven which gorged on corpses and spread fear, slavery, oppression and shame throughout Russia, he enquired sardonically whom it was meant to represent, but did not press for an answer. Eventually he delivered the *coup de grâce:* "If you want to live, shut up about Bukharin. If you don't shut up, here's what you'll get [he aimed his right forefinger at his temple]."[41] She agreed to shut up, concluding his sport. As well as playing with prisoners, Beria also enjoyed torturing and shooting them with his own hand. Stalin promoted him because he recognised a kindred spirit. "The two were lone wolves," noted an acute observer. "And their alliance was lupine."[42]

What that alliance achieved in 1939 was a gradual alleviation of Russia's long agony. Beria continued to stress that enemies of the people must be unmasked but he declared that not all Soviet ills could be blamed on them. NKVD men, whose pay he doubled, went on with their barbarous tasks; but the number of arrests dwindled and torture was employed more selectively. Beria, who was as astute as he was callous, put terror on a businesslike basis. Appeals against the more bizarre convictions now sometimes succeeded. The regime in the camps became less severe. More prisoners were released and reinstated. Incarcerated after translating Dante's *Inferno,*

Mikhail Lozinsky was freed on Stalin's orders to complete the work with *Purgatorio* and *Paradiso*. (Stalin enjoyed such ironies: during the war, when he needed the Church's support, he encouraged it to start a paper staffed by former employees of the journal *Atheist*.) In 1939 the Soviet press printed fewer denunciations of spies and wreckers. The 18th Party Congress congratulated itself on the defeat of the enemy within and the victimisation of major officials virtually ceased, though many diplomats were removed and Vyshinsky fell under a cloud. Stalin, who admitted that mistakes had been made, seemed to think that he could now maintain total control of the Soviet Union with only token bloodletting. Under these circumstances socialist discipline occasionally lapsed. Facing a factory committee (including an NKVD officer) which was trying to make "voluntary" labour compulsory, a young female worker turned round, bent down, lifted up her skirt and declared: "Comrade Stalin and you all can kiss me wherever it is most convenient to you." She strode out, leaving her audience stunned and numb with fear. Finally a voice broke the silence: "Did you notice, she didn't have pants on?"[43] Laughter eased the tension and no further action was taken.

Onlookers outside the USSR understandably tried to gauge the effect of the Great Purge on Soviet foreign relations. Their bewilderment grew accordingly, for the internal convulsion seemed calculated to add to Russia's discredit abroad. Both the *Völkischer Beobachter* and the *New York Times* argued that the Soviet regime stood condemned by the purges and the show trials whatever the truth about them: if the victims were guilty, Bolshevik ranks had been filled from the start with saboteurs, traitors, assassins and "scum";[44] if they were innocent, the USSR was governed by a homicidal dictator and "we are back in the torture chambers of the Aztecs and the Druids."[45] More inexplicable than these crimes, in alien eyes, was the blunder of crippling the Soviet Union when the external threat had never been greater. Mussolini wondered, during the arraignment of Bukharin, if Stalin had secretly become a fascist, since he was "doing a notable service to fascism by mowing down in large armfuls his enemies."[46] The Polish Chief of Staff General Stachiewicz detected a "cracking of the whole Soviet structure."[47] For such a rupture, some contemporaries and historians concluded, there could be only one explanation. This was that the nationalist leadership felt bound to destroy every shred of left-wing opposition in order to bring about a diplomatic revolution—nothing less than the alignment of Communism with Nazism. According to this theory, Stalin, fearful about Russian vulnerability, had been covertly aiming for an alliance with Germany ever since the rise of Hitler. The massacre of the old Bolsheviks "performed a specific role in asserting the pro-Nazi orientation of Soviet foreign policy."[48] George Kennan stated the case with his usual clarity: the Russian "purges made some sense" only in the context of the search for an accommodation with the Third Reich, "though even then only to a very abnormal mind."[49]

This is an enticing notion and it is sustained by clear evidence that Stalin, who seems to have admired Hitler's ruthlessness, always kept open the option of improving relations with Germany while never losing his suspicion of the imperialist powers, whose weak leaders he despised. Certainly he did not allow ideological considerations to get in the way of political advantage and he saw merit in restoring the kind of economic and military cooperation which had benefited both Russia and Germany between 1921 and 1933. Moreover, as Nazi strength waxed, Stalin seemed ever more intent on seeking a rapprochement with the Third Reich. In the view of one well-placed German diplomat, he was "upset" by the *Anschluss* but took it as proof that the democracies "were not sufficiently determined to be good partners." After the rape of Czechoslovakia there was "near unanimity among the Western embassies in Moscow that Stalin had a higher regard for the Germans" than for the British and the French.[50] This opinion has been echoed by students of the period, who have tended to interpret the Nazi–Soviet Pact as the product of a long germination process. As newly released documents show, however, this is misleading: Stalin only threw in his lot with Hitler at the last moment. Indeed, before the spring of 1939 he was preoccupied by domestic affairs, directing only that the construction of a common front against aggressive fascism would best serve the USSR but leaving the details to his Foreign Commissar, Maxim Litvinov. Far from carrying out the purges to assist his foreign designs, Stalin sacrificed Russia's bargaining position abroad to the overwhelming imperatives of his domestic holocaust.

This was literally the case, in that so many Soviet diplomats were shot or imprisoned that it became almost impossible for the rest to function. Their job involved contact with foreigners, yet they knew that this could prove fatal. Loy Henderson, of the American embassy in Moscow, said that "officials of the People's Commissariat of Foreign Affairs are so patently in abject terror that one must pity them."[51] A tense Litvinov, surrounded by a few paralysed old stagers and many inexperienced new recruits, whispered to the French Ambassador: "How can I conduct foreign policy with the Lubyanka across the way?"[52] Stalin made Litvinov's task harder still by undermining the policy of collective security: his brutal violation of the liberal values which the democracies professed made them reluctant to cooperate with the Soviet Union. The British government in particular regarded the "semi-Asiatic savages" in the Kremlin as natural foes rather than potential friends. The decapitation of the Red Army—nearly all the commanders trained in Germany disappeared during the purge, hardly an indication that Stalin was courting Hitler—served to confirm that view. The British had never been impressed by Russia's military strength and they concluded that the purged Red Army had little offensive (but much defensive) capacity. The Soviet Union would be a weak, unreliable and undesirable ally. As an enemy, it was unlikely to become efficient enough to be dangerous. In any case, a serious conflict might provoke economic breakdown and another revolution. As the British Ambassador noted, every move of Soviet policy clearly reflected "intense anxiety to avoid war."[53]

So Stalin's aggressive domestic policy militated against his defensive foreign policy. The purges alienated the democratic allies he wanted as a bastion against German expansion. A few days after the *Anschluss,* which coincided with the grisly conclusion of the last show trial, Moscow drew attention to the menace now confronting Czechoslovakia and expressed Soviet readiness to join in collective actions to counter it. But, like other such initiatives, this one fell on stony ground. London deemed it "inappropriate." Paris failed to respond at all, which typified, said Litvinov, Gallic "indecision, inertia and credulity in the face of events creating a threat to peace and a direct danger to France."[54] The French high command would not even listen to its own Military Attaché in Moscow, who reported in April 1938 that the Red Army, now nearly two million strong, was recovering from the purges and had developed a formidable *"potentiel de guerre."*[55]

Certainly its fighting spirit, if not its skill, was demonstrated in a major clash with Japan at Changkufeng during the summer. And its strength was augmented between 1937 and 1939 by a programme which "doubled or trebled" the production rate of tanks, aircraft, artillery and other *matériel.*[56] But the French did not wish to know this, any more than they wished to believe Litvinov's repeated assurances that the Soviet Union would honour its treaty obligations to Czechoslovakia provided that France did likewise. To quote the title of a devastating indictment of Stalin's duplicity by the exiled former Communist Ante Ciliga which was published in 1938, how could anyone credit anything concocted *Au Pays du Grand Mensonge*? For their part the British entirely distrusted Litvinov, supposing that Russia, which lacked a common border with Czechoslovakia, also lacked the will and the power to make war against Germany. Alternatively, Stalin might help Czechoslovakia as he had helped Spain, spreading the bacillus of Bolshevism and trying to drag in the democracies to fight fascism. Chamberlain therefore sought a peaceful compromise, sending Lord Runciman to mediate over the Sudetenland. However, as the Soviet Ambassador in London, Ivan Maisky, soon discovered, Runciman was inexperienced, "deaf, ponderous, and even somewhat ignorant of where Czechoslovakia was."[57] He was dispatched only to lend a measure of dignity to that country's dismemberment.

Litvinov also thought that Czechoslovakia would be betrayed. But he strained every nerve in his energetic body to prevent it. Sophisticated though unrefined, Litvinov was sometimes disparaged by foreign members of the diplomatic corps. One German called him a "typical clever little dealer from a Jewish suburban store." There was a strain of anti-Semitism, too, in British animadversions—to the effect that Litvinov was not only a coarse, shameless, sarcastic bully but a "corpulent paterfamilias" married to an "English Jewess."[58] But though he was said to have no friends, only colleagues who disliked him, no one could deny Litvinov's prodigious intelligence. It was combined with immense industry, unusual candour, biting (and sometimes obscene) wit and "strong character."[59] Fortitude, especially, was what Litvinov tried to instil into the French. They were privately informed that the Soviet Union had deployed 30 infantry divisions on its border, all prepared for combat. Litvinov publicly announced that "a possible bloc of peace-loving states" would be stronger than any hostile force, an advantage that would be lost if they pursued a "policy of non-resistance to evil and bartering with the aggressors."[60] At the same time Litvinov attempted to woo Chamberlain away from appeasement, proposing a British-French-Soviet conference and informing Halifax via Churchill that the USSR was prepared to tackle Germany. But Halifax, like the Prime Minister, preferred to deal with the Third Reich rather than the Soviet Union, which he considered "the anti-Christ."[61]

Only the Czechoslovaks, it seemed, believed that Russia would intervene if they were abandoned by the democracies. When the Soviet Ambassador, Sergei Alexandrovsky, drove through Prague on 21 September, patriotic demonstrators around the Hradcany Palace at first shouted abuse at his smart Packard, one man putting his head through the window and calling him a "pot-bellied bourgeois." Then they realised who he was and their tumultuous cries sounded "like an impassioned appeal to fight fascist Germany." The Czech mood, Alexandrovsky reported complacently, was one of "all but zoological Russophilia." So the crowd pulled back behind a cordon of red-faced, sweating policemen and the Ambassador proceeded through the Hradcany gates. He found the stylish halls of Maria Theresa given over to war preparations. Desks and cots littered the floors; army officers hurried to and fro; workmen glued paper on to windows. The corridors were lit by dim, blue-coloured bulbs and on a table in Benes's office overlooking the Vltava River sat a gas mask. The President appeared confident to the point of arrogance, referring to Gamelin as his subordinate and expecting aid from Britain as well as France and the Soviet Union. The last Alexandrovsky now confirmed. Benes repeated that he would "rather 'fall under Stalin' and lose his little green-grocery than fall under Hitler and become a shareholder of a cartel selling oxhides to Germany."[62]

The prospect of help from the democracies receded during the next few days, but Benes preserved a brave front, at least for the benefit of Alexandrovsky. The Ambassador rightly suspected that the President was trying to inveigle the Soviet Union into the conflict on its own. Despite claims to the contrary, it now seems plain that "there was no unilateral offer of Soviet aid."[63] Stalin had no wish to do battle with Germany alone. On the other hand, he did as much as he could to reveal his country's "readiness to fight"[64] alongside Britain and France. He mobilised massive forces, secured a passage across Romania and sent war-planes to Czechoslovakia. He warned Poland (in vain) not to become Germany's jackal and, when conflict seemed imminent, ordered Soviet diplomats in Berlin to burn their codes. Litvinov may have been wrong in thinking that the Führer would have backed down over Czechoslovakia if faced by the real prospect of a war on two fronts. But he was surely right in advocating collective security. For even if the democracies could not have averted a war in September 1938 they were far better placed to fight, with Czechoslovak and Soviet participation, than was the case a year later.

The Munich agreement shocked Stalin. He had been excluded from the conference—Lord Halifax claimed that there was no time to issue an invitation to Moscow—and he now feared that the USSR would become the next item on Hitler's menu. The Czechoslovak sop, Stalin said, had done nothing but "whet the aggressor's appetite."[65] Moreover, the famous declaration of 30 September, in which Chamberlain and Hitler expressed the desire of their two peoples never to go to war with each other again, sounded ominously like a non-aggression pact directed against Russia. *Mein Kampf* was closely studied in the Kremlin, where the Führer's expressed ambitions to carve *Lebensraum* out of Soviet territory were taken with the utmost seriousness. In return for peace in the west, Britain appeared to be giving Germany a free hand in the east. Maisky's indignation over Munich was understandable: "The League of Nations and collective security are dead. International relations are entering an era of the most violent savagery and brute force." Yet however much the Soviets mistrusted the democracies, their sole counter to anti-Comintern aggression was collective security. Litvinov tried to breathe new life into it. He had no doubt that Britain and France preferred to strike a deal with Germany. But they would keep the Soviet Union in the complex game of bluff and manoeuvre which all the powers were playing in order to improve their own chances with Hitler, who might anyway raise the stakes too high. As Litvinov prophetically wrote in October 1938, it was not to the advantage of Chamberlain and Daladier-Bonnet "to make a clean break with us right now, or they would lose their trump card when negotiating with Berlin. They will turn to us only if no agreement can be wangled with Berlin and if the latter puts forward demands even they would find unacceptable."[66]

Between the capitulation at Munich and the seizure of Prague, it seemed that the democracies were evolving a *modus vivendi* with the Axis powers, mainly through appeasement. They allowed the Führer every latitude in his brutal occupation of the Sudetenland. They appeared willing to give ground in some sort of colonial settlement. In the Kremlin's view they made more noise than Hitler himself about his designs on the Ukraine, with the aim of poisoning relations between the Third Reich and the Soviet Union. It was no wonder, therefore, that in his speech to the 18th Party Congress on 10 March 1939 Stalin flayed Britain and France. Desperate to hold on to their empires, they would stop at nothing to "rake the fire with somebody else's hands"[67]—in other words to get the USSR to fight Germany on their behalf. Some observers, alert to suggestions from various quarters of an imminent diplomatic revolution, took this famous statement as a hint that Stalin was seeking a rapprochement with Hitler. But though that was not ruled out in the Kremlin, Stalin's speech was also scathing about the fascist "incendiaries of war" who tried to express their military alliances in terms of harmless geometrical "axes" and "triangles."[68] Stalin's opinion of the aggressor states was vindicated five days later, when Hitler entered the Hradcany Palace. Stalin's opinion of the democracies was vindicated soon afterwards when they rebuffed Soviet moves to form a common front and proposed to guarantee Poland's security unconditionally, an offer which Colonel Beck memorably "accepted between two flicks of ash from my cigarette."[69]

Stalin could not believe that Chamberlain really expected to deter Hitler by means of this guarantee. To be sure, he had been told that the British Prime Minister had claimed the Führer and his generals would never "risk war if they knew that they would have to fight on two fronts."[70] But, according to Maisky's report, Lloyd George (who had been the recipient of Chamberlain's remark) laughed the Premier to scorn on learning that the second front would be Poland. As Lloyd George had said, that country was hopelessly weak compared to the vital element in a serious second front—the Soviet Union. Stalin, like Hitler, concluded that Chamberlain was bluffing over Poland. The British had obviously given Beck his guarantee to mollify anti-Nazi opinion at home and to camouflage their continuing policy of turning Hitler's aggression towards the steppes. This was by no means a paranoid suspicion. Reading between the lines of Chamberlain's comments, one senior British diplomat concluded that "the real motive for the Cabinet's attitude is the desire to secure Russian help and at the same time to leave our hands free to enable Germany to expand eastward at Russian expense."[71]

However, Chamberlain could not ignore the public clamour for a grand alliance. As for Stalin, he still had no realistic alternative. His dismissal of Litvinov, on 3 May 1939, might have been a signal that he was open to offers from Germany, and Hitler certainly took it as such. But Litvinov's successor, the Soviet Premier Vyacheslav Molotov, did not slam the door on the democracies. Naturally Molotov obeyed Stalin's ukase, "Purge the ministry of Jews."[72] He initiated a "new wave of reprisals and arrests"[73] against the staff of the People's Commissariat of Foreign Affairs, replacing them with officials who were deemed well qualified because they spoke only Russian and had never had any contact with foreigners. But the Jewish champion of collective security was allowed to retire to a dacha in the woods outside Moscow where he played bridge, learned to type and read poetry and novels. Fearing a night-time visit from the NKVD, Litvinov kept a pistol beside his bed. But though Beria personally tortured one foreign ministry official into confessing that his former boss was the head of a counter-revolutionary terrorist group spying for Germany, Litvinov never had to choose between the Lubyanka and suicide.

WHERE Litvinov was suave and cosmopolitan, Molotov was crude and elemental—he prided himself on his native hardness, taking his Bolshevik alias from the word "hammer." His real name was Skriabin; he was distantly related to the composer and he had even supported himself as a young revolutionary by playing the mandolin. But Molotov, born in 1890, had no cultural interests, no creative instincts, no finer feelings, no original thoughts. The son of a clerk, he himself became the chief clerk of Communism. Lenin, who criticised Molotov for fostering mindless bureaucracy but was impressed by his capacity to sit at a desk, apparently dubbed him "Stone-bottom." Stalin, in whose shadow Molotov always walked, valued his unflagging industry, his machine-like memory and his cold-blooded willingness to sign death warrants. His loyalty, too, was shatter-proof. It survived Stalin's mockery of his teetotal, vegetarian fads, several threats that he would be purged and the post-war imprisonment of

his wife. Outside observers were mainly struck by Molotov's robotic qualities: the stiff movements of his short arms and stumpy legs; the automa-
ton-like responses voiced in jerky, stuttered syllables; the flat, granite face
scarcely softened by glittering pince-nez and bristling moustache; the
fleeting "smile of Siberian winter."[74] Dull and impassive in his shabby grey
suit, Molotov personified the anonymous Soviet apparatchik. But, contrary to a recent verdict,[75] he was by no means a boneheaded nonentity.

Foreign diplomats, who noticed that he alone in the Kremlin "would
talk to his chief as one comrade to another,"[76] found him incisive, efficient
and formidable. They were regularly made to perch on low chairs in front
of Molotov's elevated desk. When in June 1939 British and French envoys
went to his office (a door of which always remained ajar so that, they surmised, Stalin could eavesdrop on the proceedings), Molotov subjected
them to a tirade. He castigated their governments for rejecting the renewed Soviet offer of a treaty guaranteeing the integrity of the small eastern European states from Finland to Turkey. Instead the distrustful
democracies had put forward counter-proposals limiting their own obligations (notably in the Baltic) while trying to commit Russia to defend
Poland and Romania. His pasty face reddening and his ice-blue eyes
flashing, Molotov declared angrily that if they believed the Soviet Union
would accept these proposals "then you must think we are nitwits and
nincompoops."[77]

If the British Prime Minister heard of this warning, he did not heed it.
As tension mounted over Danzig and his government came under increasing pressure to secure a coalition with Russia, Chamberlain continued to
treat with Stalin in order to settle with Hitler. But British prevarications
merely confirmed Soviet suspicions. On 29 June 1939 *Pravda* accused the
democracies of deliberately "dragging out the negotiations" in Moscow so
as to reach agreement with Berlin. Chamberlain's diplomatic smokescreen
was all too transparent, never more so than when, at the end of July, he
reluctantly consented to the dispatch of a military mission to Russia. No
embassy has been more palpably doomed from the start. Its leader was not
only obscure, but also rejoiced in a farcical name—Admiral Sir Reginald
Aylmer Ranfurly Plunkett-Ernle-Erle-Drax. He was also encumbered with
a decoration, the Order of the Bath, which the Russians (who apparently
translated it as "washtub") found hilarious. A tall, high-coloured, bushy-
eyebrowed aristocrat, the Admiral was considered bold by the navy. But
as a French member of the mission later wrote, Drax was slow of speech
and "not very quick in the uptake."[78] While the French delegates, led by
General Doumenc, were told to bring back an agreement at all costs, Drax
was instructed to proceed with caution, to volunteer no military informa-

tion, to bear in mind the possibility of Soviet-German collusion and to spin out the talks for as long as possible. The principle of procrastination was also applied to the mission's means of transport. An aeroplane was ruled out and Halifax said that a warship "would have the effect of attaching too much importance to the mission." General Ismay suggested facetiously, "They might bicycle." Drax himself mentioned that "there is also the route via Vladivostok."[79]

In the event they took a slow steamer, the *City of Exeter,* an imperial relic with an Indian crew. During the five-day voyage the large Anglo-French contingent ate curries served by turbanned waiters, took part in a deck tennis competition (which Drax won) and discussed their instructions in the children's playroom. By the time the ship docked at Leningrad, under a bright, opaline, midnight sky, they had reached no very definite conclusions. The Russians greeted the delegation with scant ceremony, as befitted its lowly status. After sightseeing in Leningrad, Drax and his colleagues took the Red Arrow express to Moscow, where their host was Marshal Voroshilov. A semi-literate ex-metalworker who believed that horses should not be replaced by machines and that the Red Army should not be equipped with automatic weapons for fear it should run out of bullets, he proved more than a match for Drax. The opening session of the negotiations took place on 12 August in the banqueting hall of the Spiridonovka Palace, once owned by the Tsars and later occupied by General Frunze (the founder of the Red Army), and the Admiral found the atmosphere literally overpowering. He was already "uncomfortably hot" in his "blue uniform frock-coat."[80] Then Voroshilov "lit up a strong, black *papirosa* cigarette, and most of the delegates immediately followed suit."[81] The white marble, mock-Gothic hall, dominated by a monumental fireplace, a portrait of Stalin and an oak ceiling copied from that in London's Westminster Hall, filled with smoke. Drax, who suffered from a weak throat, began to cough and his voice became a croak.

He almost choked when Voroshilov, brandishing his own authority to sign a military agreement, asked to see the credentials of the Anglo-French delegation. General Doumenc produced a letter from Daladier which passed muster. But Drax, feeling "a trifle non-plussed,"[82] had nothing to show and Voroshilov, himself no more than a "paper plenipotentiary,"[83] scored a cheap initial triumph. Worse followed. The Marshal, ever more dictatorial, posed a series of awkward questions. What forces could the democracies put into the field? What plans had they to combat the Axis? What part should Russia play if Germany invaded Poland? The democratic allies, referred to scathingly by the Soviets as "the yielding (or surrendering) powers,"[84] were first evasive and then mendacious about their military preparations (though even when multiplied threefold the number of British divisions seemed to Voroshilov inconceivably small). But what Drax could not hide was the fact that the Poles, fearful of another partition, refused to admit the Red Army even if its purpose was to repel the Wehrmacht. By 17 August, as the French vainly tried to change minds in Warsaw, the talks had stalled.

Drax had time for more sightseeing. He inspected the Kremlin Museum. He witnessed an air display outside Moscow, where Stalin appeared with a red-haired woman in a green-windowed car. Drax visited the People's Park of Rest and Culture, which surprised him by charging an entry fee; once in the park he found that culture amplified by loudspeakers made rest impossible. He descended into Lenin's chilly mausoleum. "The cold is necessary to preserve the great man from decay," Drax recorded, "but he already looks in his glass coffin so pallid and waxen that one feels that his mortal remains are not long for this world." Chivvied by sentries, the Admiral emerged into the daylight "feeling that the tomb of Lenin is no pleasant addition to the attractions of the City."[85] Finally a bombshell struck: Ribbentrop's advent was announced. But before he arrived the Anglo-French negotiations had foundered, ostensibly on the rock of Polish intransigence. The true reason for their collapse, however, was that Chamberlain did not really want an alliance with Stalin. Nor, indeed, did Drax, who left for home on 25 August. His relief at escaping from constant Soviet surveillance was so heartfelt that, on arriving at the first railway station in Finland, he alighted from the train and "executed a little dance on the platform."[86]

The Western allies thus sacrificed their last chance of finding "the only alternative to a war waged on German terms."[87] Chamberlain, his vision clouded by the dark deeds of the Kremlin, lost sight of his own country's national interest. This was to erect a firm barrier around the most dangerous potential aggressor, as the Chiefs of Staff and 84 per cent of the British people wanted. If approached with determination, the USSR would have completed the encirclement of Germany. As late as 1 September 1939 Stalin, fearful of betrayal by Hitler, tried to revive negotiations with Chamberlain and Daladier. Six days afterwards he privately remarked: "We would have preferred an agreement with the so-called democratic countries . . . but Britain and France wanted to use us as hired men and not even pay us anything for it."[88] Stalin had suspected that Britain would renegue on its commitment to Poland, leaving the Soviet Union to face Germany alone. In the Far East, too, the Bear was fighting the battles of the Lion. Nothing demonstrated Anglo-French pusillanimity more plainly, in the Kremlin's view, than the low rank of the delegates sent to

Moscow. Chamberlain and Daladier went to Munich, Molotov growled to Ribbentrop, "but who do we get here? Admiral Nobody and General Inconnu!"[89]

Molotov sat "stiff and dumb" with democratic negotiators whereas, responding to the suit being urgently pressed by Hitler at the beginning of August, he was "communicative and amiable" towards German diplomats.[90] Aiming to prevent the formation of a hostile coalition that would force him either to fight on two fronts or, more probably, to call off the attack on Poland and hold a face-saving "Party rally of peace,"[91] the Führer conducted his wooing with a passion of which Chamberlain could hardly conceive. Fervent messages flew from Berlin to Moscow, culminating in an authoritative declaration that the ideological barriers between Nazism and Communism could be broken down and that no issue between the Baltic and the Black Sea stood in the way of the "restoration of friendly cooperation" between them. Convinced by the middle of the month that the Anglo-French negotiations were going nowhere, Molotov told the German Ambassador that this "pregnantly and clearly expressed" overture had made a "decisive" impression on him.[92] It had, of course, made a decisive impression on Stalin. He wished to proceed step by suspicious step; but Hitler was marching to the beat of a different drum.

The Führer needed to secure Russian neutrality well before the autumn rains turned the Polish flatlands into a morass that would bog down his blitzkrieg. So he at once accepted the terms of a non-aggression treaty proposed by Molotov, and Ribbentrop pressed for an immediate meeting at which all could be settled and signed. Now it was Molotov's turn to procrastinate. He did so, the Germans reckoned, for "political reasons," hoping to squeeze advantage from Hitler's impatience and offering "transparent pretexts"[93] for the delay. Hitler fretted and fumed until aides feared for his health. Then he cut the Gordian knot by writing direct to Stalin, asking that Ribbentrop should be received no later than 23 August. Stalin agreed. So, in the early afternoon of that day the German Foreign Minister and his party, so large that two Focke-Wulf Condor aircraft were required to carry them, landed at Moscow airport. There, beside hammer and sickle banners, flew Nazi swastikas (some back to front and none visible outside the airport) borrowed from a Soviet film studio. A band, hastily rehearsed, played "Deutschland Über Alles." NKVD officers shook hands with their opposite numbers in the Gestapo. Ribbentrop, dressed in a long leather coat, a black jacket and striped trousers, inspected the German embassy staff who were lined up in military style to meet him. He then drove in Stalin's personal limousine along boulevards lined at ten-yard intervals by policemen wearing white summer jackets. In the city the

old Austrian embassy had been hastily prepared for him. At 3:00 P.M.
Ribbentrop entered the Kremlin. He was accompanied by the popular
and handsome German Ambassador, Count von der Schulenburg, who
gasped when he found himself in the presence of Stalin as well as Molotov.
Throughout his four years in Moscow the Count had never met the Red
Tsar.

Stalin, having first engaged in the standard charade of inviting Molotov
to act as the Russian spokesman, conducted business with his usual accuracy and authority. A form of words was hammered out with remarkable
speed. Stalin likened political communiqués to the shields of the Romans
and his drafting corrections were later commended by Hitler himself.
Stalin deleted Ribbentrop's imaginative eulogy to Soviet-German friendship because it would insult public opinion conditioned to emnity, since
for years "we have been pouring buckets of shit over each other's heads."[94]
The non-aggression agreement, to come into immediate effect, was secured,
each state promising not to assist the other's enemies in time of war. But a
secret protocol, designating separate spheres of influence, required an
adjournment while Ribbentrop solicited a final concession, over Latvia,
from Hitler. Within three hours this was granted and the Kremlin meeting resumed. When Ribbentrop announced that the Soviet Union had got
its way in the Baltic, Stalin seemed to quiver with joy, as though experiencing a political orgasm.

After the drafting came the drinking. Toasts were repeatedly proposed,
to the Führer, to Stalin, to Ribbentrop, to the new era in Russo-German
relations. As other members of the Politburo and the German delegation
arrived to celebrate, the talk grew more expansive. Stalin said that if weak
England dominated the world it was only because stupid nations allowed
themselves to be bluffed: "It was ridiculous, for example, that a few
hundred Englishmen should dominate India."[95] Ribbentrop declared that
the Anti-Comintern Pact was directed against the Western democracies,
not the Soviet Union. Stalin spoke respectfully of the French army but
Ribbentrop harped on France's numerical inferiority and stated that the
West Wall was five times as strong as the Maginot Line. The signing of the
freshly typed pact was recorded for posterity. A Russian photographer set
up an "enormous prehistoric camera" on an "antediluvian tripod"[96] and
exploded a black powder flare which rattled windows and filled Molotov's
brown office with dense smoke.

Heinrich Hoffmann, Hitler's personal photographer, employed his lens
more discreetly. He also kept his eyes open: Hitler had instructed him to
observe minute personal details, of interest to the Führer alone. Hoffmann noted that Stalin's handshake was firm and his lynx-like eyes radi-

ated power. Moreover, his ear lobes were "separate and Aryan" and not, as Hitler had wondered, "ingrown and Jewish."[97] During the vodka toasts Stalin drank only from his personal flask, which apparently contained water. But later, according to Hoffmann, he got "well and truly lit up" on Crimean champagne—Goebbels would joke that at last Hoffmann had found someone to drink with him. Stalin remained sober enough, though, to admonish one of the photographers not to print snapshots of them drinking on this solemn occasion. Later, for similar reasons, Hitler considered Hoffmann's photographs unpublishable. Stalin was always pictured with a cigarette—he favoured Herzegovina Flor, though he sometimes broke out the tobacco for use in his pipe. Smoking at such a historic moment, said Hitler, "smacks of levity." The photographs were published, but only after Hoffmann had "duly expunged" the cigarettes.[98]

Such were the delicate sensibilities of the dictators on the brink of "the abyss"[99] into which, as Schulenburg observed, Europe would now surely plunge. Even totalitarian states could not wholly ignore public opinion. Stalin made further efforts to justify the monstrous volte-face to bemused Russians who for some hours replaced the traditional greeting "How d'you do?" *("Zdravstvuite?")* with "What does it mean?"[100] They were literally as well as figuratively in the dark, since the Nazi-Soviet Pact coincided with the longest blackout practice so far held: it was enforced by cutting off electric power at source (which also silenced radio sets) and was intended to prepare the civilian population for German aggression. Now, however, booths were set up in Gorky Park where speakers explained the new foreign policy, though in truth this attraction was eclipsed by the All-Union Agricultural Exhibition which featured everything from colossal statues of workers (brought back from the Paris Exposition) to prize live-stock (including a cow fitted with false teeth). Press, radio, cinema and theatre were mobilised to propagate the pro-German line. On 1 September *Pravda* carried Molotov's denunciation of short-sighted people "carried away by simplified anti-Fascist agitation." To ask how Communists could agree with Nazis was to ignore essentials, he declared, since the Pact was between states, not systems. Stalin himself devised two simple diagrams to instruct the army in the diplomatic revolution. The first showed a triangle with "London" at the apex and "Berlin" and "Moscow" at either end of the base: it was captioned "What did Chamberlain want?" The second showed a triangle with "Moscow" on top and "Berlin" and "London" at the bottom corners: it was captioned "What did Comrade Stalin do?"[101] What Stalin had done was to keep the Soviet Union above the impending battle.

This policy seems to have been as popular outside the Kremlin as within it. According to one well-informed foreign correspondent, most Russians suspected that Chamberlain was trying to trick them into fighting Hitler on Britain's behalf and they probably congratulated themselves on "having 'out-Muniched' the Prime Minister."[102] Stalin had donned the mantle of appeasement and, at a time when the Nomonhan Incident was reaching its bloody climax, ensured that Russia would not be assailed on two fronts. The Molotov-Ribbentrop accord not only undermined the Anti-Comintern Pact; it was, *Pravda* asserted, an "act of peace."[103] But it also gave the Soviet Union a breathing space in which to prepare for war. During that time Russian industry, assisted by trade with Germany, could forge new weapons for reconstructed Red forces. Furthermore, there were spoils to be won in eastern Europe and the Baltic, notably through another partition of Poland and the acquisition of countries—Lithuania, Estonia, Latvia—within Russia's new sphere of influence. The Communist tide might sweep even further westwards if the Axis powers and the democracies battered themselves to a standstill. Compared to imperial dreams which were more extravagant than those of the tsars, the Führer's immediate ambitions seemed modest. It was no wonder that Stalin gloated to Khrushchev: "I know what Hitler's up to. He thinks he has outsmarted me, but actually it is I who have outsmarted him."

Of course, Hitler had outsmarted Stalin. By a sublime irony the embodiment of morbid mistrust continued to put his trust in the Führer, despite mounting, damning evidence that he would betray it, until Zhukov woke him in the early hours of 22 June 1941 with the news that German aircraft were bombing Russian cities. Or, to be more precise, Stalin distrusted Hitler less than he distrusted the democratic leaders who were, he was sure, trying to create a rift between Moscow and Berlin, something he tried to prevent by means of appeasement more abject than anything countenanced by Chamberlain. In the long run, at all events, the Nazi-Soviet Pact proved a disaster of staggering proportions for the USSR. It struck at the root of the Communist faith, exposing its moral hollowness to all but the most blinkered devotees. New Bolshevik had often seemed to be old tsarist writ large; but now, it plainly appeared, Stalinism was akin to Hitlerism. Stalin's cynical act of *Realpolitik* wrecked collective security. It gave the green light to Operation White, Hitler's murderous assault on the so-called "Bastard of Versailles," Poland. This was justified by a fabricated attack on the German radio station at Gleiwitz, evidenced by murdered concentration camp inmates dressed in Polish uniforms—a deception that deceived no one. And it was initiated by the 11-inch guns of the aged battleship *Schleswig-Holstein,* ostensibly paying a "courtesy visit" to Danzig to honour the German dead of the First

World War. These Krupp monsters opened fire, in a distant echo of the first salvo in the battle of Verdun, at the fortification commanding the inner harbour at 4:45 A.M. on 1 September 1939.

At the beginning of the Second World War Stalin's benevolent neutrality, sustained by illusions as chimerical as any in that age of shadows masquerading as substance, enabled Hitler to crush all but one of his enemies piecemeal. Then, having triumphed in the west, the Führer was free to turn eastwards and conquer the living-space he had always craved. "Russia," he reportedly said, "will be our India!"[104] But, taking advantage of the secret protocol in the Pact, Russia itself had moved west. On Stalin's orders Soviet forces left their strong border bastion, the Stalin Line, and established feeble new defences within sight of the Wehrmacht. These were quickly smashed and overrun when Hitler launched the most terrible campaign, Operation Barbarossa, in the most destructive war in history. During its bloody course the Soviet Union, much more than its allies, bore the brunt of Nazi fury, endured inconceivable sufferings and turned the tide of the conflict.

PART FIVE

CHASM

CONCLUSION

ONE by one, between September 1939 and December 1941, the great powers slid into the fiery chasm of conflict. There was a terrifying inevitability about the descent, yet almost everyone was unprepared for it. No war in history has been more widely telegraphed, yet it still came as a shock. Ordinary people, with memories of Verdun, the Somme and Passchendaele, regarded it as unavoidable but inconceivable. They feared the worst but hoped for the best. Even after the signing of the Nazi-Soviet Pact many expected Hitler to back down. Finding it hard to face the prospect of another bloodbath, they engaged in endless "wishful thinking."[1] So did their leaders. Well into the summer of 1939 Chamberlain still thought that he could appease Hitler. Even later Bonnet, if not Daladier, reckoned that he could contrive a Polish Munich. On the eve of war, 31 August, the Führer himself professed to "hear the wings of the angel of peace."[2] If he supposed that at the last minute the democracies would betray Poland, which would then fall to him without a struggle, Hitler miscalculated. Mussolini also miscalculated, hoping to enjoy the fruits of Hitler's swift victory in France through a largely rhetorical contribution to the fight. But no one miscalculated more grievously than Stalin, who in 1941 refused to credit overwhelming intelligence, including that provided by his own spy Richard Sorge and by Ambassador Schulenburg, to the effect that Germany would attack Russia. On the other side of the world, Washington was ludicrously unready to be a wartime capital: a public road crossed the runway of the city's only airport, Hoover Field, and pilots had to land and take off during breaks in the traffic. Although deciphered signals showed that hostilities in the Pacific were impending on the morning Pearl Harbor was bombed, Roosevelt had no thought of "an attack on any American possession."[3]

Of course, it is easy to forget that the past was once the future and to expose failures in foresight with the benefit of hindsight. Today almost invariably misreads tomorrow, sometimes grossly. In 1919, for example, the journalist Philip Gibbs concluded the first edition of his admired book *Realities of War* with a prophecy that ruined Europe was about to be engulfed by chaos. Introducing a revised edition in August 1929, he declared that the "crash which I anticipated has not come," thanks to "renewed prosperity."[4] However, when it did come, bringing the Slump in its train, statesmen and citizens found it still harder to pierce the veil of the future or even to see what was happening at the present. The Depression cast a pall over the world. It was the worst peacetime crisis to afflict humanity since the Black Death. More, it was the economic equivalent of Armageddon. During the 1930s, therefore, the globe was enveloped by something like the fog of war. It was a time of systematic obfuscation, darkness at noon. Governments fought to maintain control by manipulating minds and mobilising opinion. They did so in a fashion "unprecedented in history," employing new means of mass communication and even drawing on the advertising techniques which had lifted the cigarette from "its status of lowly 'coffin nail' to that of a national necessity." Instead of protecting truth with a bodyguard of lies, they threatened to liquidate it. They confused friends as well as foes, distorting reality or attempting to change its nature, fostering "the illusion that we live entirely in a world of propaganda myths."[5] But the Depression not only occluded the contemporary vision of war, it also made war more likely.

The old liberal world order, which had been severely damaged by the First World War and was further undermined by the Communist revolution in Russia, finally collapsed during the 1930s. The Depression wrecked the Weimar Republic and brought Hitler to power in Germany. It smashed the fragile internationalist, parliamentary consensus in Japan, opening the door to the militarists. It prompted Mussolini to seek domestic dividends by means of foreign adventures. It completed the isolation of the Soviet Union, which claimed to be immune to the crisis but starved its citizens in order to arm socialism for the apparently inevitable clash with fascism— the last stage of doomed, desperate capitalism. The mutual hostility of the rival totalitarian systems, each bidding to transcend and fulfil the historical process, each polarising opinion accordingly, did much to form the character of the age. Before 1939 their antagonism was most memorably expressed in the Spanish Civil War. This was a national struggle that seemed to be a prelude to a world war; C. Day Lewis and many others viewed it "quite simply as a battle between light and darkness."[6]

The Depression also sapped the strength and self-confidence of the democracies. Britain experienced a naval mutiny, fascist demonstrations and hunger marches. France was lacerated by the worst civil strife since the Commune. To avert what appeared to be incipient revolution, Roosevelt embarked on the most far-reaching federal programme in American peacetime history. Other nations responded to the catastrophe, which hit the poorest countries hardest, in different ways. But all the major currencies eventually went off the gold standard, dethroning the "old idol of liberal economics."[7] And to balance their budgets governments abandoned laissez-faire in favour of protectionism. The tariff barrier became the economic analogue of the Maginot Line. Bitter commercial contention, with rival devaluations, replaced the ideal of international cooperation. In fact, trade ceased to be a matter of mutual advantage and turned into a system of "beggar-thy-neighbour."[8] Economic nationalism easily developed into political aggression.

The process was exacerbated by palpable inequalities in the world order. Imperial powers such as Britain and France were seen to benefit from having exclusive sources of raw materials and captive markets for their manufactured goods. This encouraged "have-not" states to create "co-prosperity spheres" of their own, in defiance of the feeble League of Nations. Japan annexed Manchuria and tried to conquer China, challenging Britain's position in the Far East. Italy seized Ethiopia and flexed its muscles in the Mediterranean, which, when Franco subjugated Spain, seemed in danger of becoming a fascist lake. Germany occupied fringe territories, tearing up the Treaty of Locarno as well as the Peace of Versailles and upsetting the balance of power in Europe. In fact, the formation of an embattled Axis hostile both to the democracies and to international Communism posed a clear threat to *global* equilibrium. America further destabilised the situation by refusing to pull its weight internationally: Roosevelt could do little, particularly as he needed the support of isolationists to implement the New Deal. Meanwhile the Depression had so demoralised the leaders of Britain and France that they were reluctant to imperil recovery by spending too heavily on munitions. They thus found themselves adopting increasingly humiliating postures of appeasement, particularly after missing a crucial chance to check Mussolini over Ethiopia. In stark contrast, Hitler helped to revive the German economy by making rearmament his priority. The logical conclusion of Nazi autarky was war.

Cordell Hull may well have been right that trade wars are the germs of shooting wars. The Depression undoubtedly sharpened national animosities. To a large extent the mass political movements of the 1930s were a crystallisation of multitudinous personal resentments over hardship. The great causes of the day were forged from countless individual ideals, hammered out on the anvil of the Depression. War was a continuation of cutthroat competition by other means. However, it was not pre-determined by the economic crisis—though today tends to assume that yesterday had to become what it was. Clearly the prime mover of the Second World War wanted it for his own fell purposes—revenge, *Lebensraum,* genocide, global domination. The Führer was interested in blood rather than money: he disdained Chamberlain's "silver bullets" except in so far as they enabled him to buy lead bullets. For Hitler the Depression was a burning grievance to exploit and a golden opportunity to show that rubber truncheons can reduce unemployment and concentration camps can prevent inflation. His methods did have some effect and he claimed to have revived Germany by a supreme effort of will. The claim was greatly exaggerated but widely credited. Like the first hundred days of the New Deal, which made Roosevelt President for life, Hitler's supposed conquest of the Depression so augmented his prestige that he became virtually unassailable at home. Certainly it helped to nourish the Führer's illusions about his own infallibility, as did that triumph of *Realpolitik,* the Nazi-Soviet Pact.

During the precipitous descent into war and for several years thereafter the Führer retained his illusions. But he was not alone, for in the Avernal gloom misapprehensions gathered like wraiths. Britain fought, at least in part, to preserve an empire that was already doomed. No one in France anticipated that the nation whose spirit of resistance was symbolised by Verdun and embodied in the Maginot Line could be reduced to vassalage in six weeks. When Operation Barbarossa was launched few expected the Soviet Union to survive for much longer—Hitler gave Stalin four months. Japan made war in order to create a self-sufficient empire; but it was, in more than one sense of the word, indefensible. Americans had no idea what it would take to quell Nippon, or that Nazi Germany would fight to such a finish, or that the necessary but tragic investment in mass destruction would finally dispel the Depression. The war, which produced the lineaments of a new world order, plumbed new depths of human torment. Not until 8 May 1945 could Churchill congratulate Stalin, the Red Army and the Russian people on emerging from the shadow of death into "the sunshine of a victorious peace." Here at last was an end, he said, to "the sacrifices and sufferings of the Dark Valley through which we have marched together."[9]

Notes

Unless otherwise stated, the place of publication for the following books is London.

CHAPTER I

1. A. Horne, *The Price of Glory* (1962), 70.
2. G. Blond, *Verdun* (1965), 38.
3. J. Romains, *Verdun* (St. Albans, 1973), 244.
4. J. M. Winter, *The Experience of World War I* (1988), 141.
5. Patrick Shaw Stewart's phrase is quoted in J. MacKenzie, *The Children of the Souls: A Tragedy of the First World War* (1986), 192.
6. H. Desagneaux, *A French Soldier's War Diary 1914–1918* (Elmfield, 1975), 17.
7. H. Barbusse, *Under Fire* (1917), 214–15.
8. D. Englander, "The French Soldier, 1914–18," *French History* I (Mar., 1987), 52.
9. D. Lottman, *Pétain: Hero or Traitor* (1985), 57.
10. Horne, *Price of Glory*, 133.
11. Barbusse, *Under Fire*, 257.
12. A. Horne, *To Lose a Battle: France 1940* (1969), 29.
13. P. Fussell, *The Great War and Modern Memory* (Oxford, 1979 edn.), 321.
14. A. Prost, "Verdun" in P. Nora (ed.), *Les Lieux de Mémoire* II: *La Nation* (Paris, 1986), 129.
15. J. Winter, *Sites of Memory, Sites of Mourning* (Cambridge, 1995), 95.
16. Blond, *Verdun*, 249.
17. C. Dyer, *Population and Society in Twentieth Century France* (1978), 78.
18. F. Caron, *An Economic History of Modern France* (1979), 180.
19. E. Spears, *Assignment to Catastrophe* I (1954), 206.
20. Quoted by B. Hüppauf, "The Birth of Fascist Man from the Spirit of the Front: From Langemarck to Verdun" in J. Milfull (ed.), *The Attractions of Fascism* (New York, 1990), 67.
21. J. Toland, *Adolf Hitler* (1976), 62–3.
22. A. Hitler, *Mein Kampf* (1969 edn.), 185–7.
23. B. Pasternak, *Doctor Zhivago* (1958 edn.), 396.
24. Russia was still using the Julian calendar, which lagged 13 days behind the Gregorian. As far as the West was concerned the revolutions took place in March and November. During the war St. Petersburg, afterwards Leningrad, was renamed Petrograd.
25. M. Ignatieff, *The Russian Album* (Harmondsworth, 1988), 111.

26.   W. B. Lincoln, *The Romanovs* (1981), 718.

27.   G. F. Kennan, *Soviet–American Relations, 1917–1920: Russia Leaves the War* (1956), 15.

28.   N. Stone, *The Eastern Front* (1985 edn.), 283.

29.   A. de Jonge, *Stalin and the Shaping of the Soviet Union* (1986), 35.

30.   E. E. Smith, *The Young Stalin* (1968), 329.

31.   See A. J. P. Taylor's introduction to J. Reed, *Ten Days That Shook the World* (Harmondsworth, 1977), xvii.

32.   R. M. Slusser, *Stalin in October* (Baltimore, Md., 1987), 255.

33.   R. H. McNeal, *Stalin* (1988), 34.

34.   N. N. Sukhanov, *The Russian Revolution 1917* (Oxford, 1955), 273.

35.   D. Shub, *Lenin* (Harmondsworth, 1977), 216–17.

36.   O. Figes, *A People's Tragedy* (1997 edn.), 495.

37.   Sukhanov, *Russian Revolution,* 640.

38.   Reed, *Ten Days,* 129.

39.   Shub, *Lenin,* 360.

40.   A. Solzhenitsyn, *The Gulag Archipelago 1918–1956* (1986 edn.), 21.

41.   G. Leggett, *The Cheka: Lenin's Political Police* (Oxford, 1981), 359–60.

42.   S. White, *Britain and the Bolshevik Revolution* (1979), 13.

43.   C. Andrew, "The British Secret Service and Anglo-Soviet Relations in the 1920s," *Historical Journal* 20, 3 (1977), 684.

44.   E. H. Carr, *The Bolshevik Revolution 1917–1923* III (1953), 190.

45.   P. Brendon, *Winston Churchill* (1984), 91–2.

46.   Kennan, *Soviet–American Relations,* 272.

47.   R. H. Mitchell, *Thought Control in Prewar Japan* (Ithaca, N.Y., 1976), 94, 185 and *passim.*

48.   *The Memoirs of Herbert Hoover* I (1952), 433.

49.   L. Ardzooni (ed.), *Thorstein Veblen: Essays* (New York, 1934), 37.

50.   H. Nicolson, *Peacemaking 1919* (1944 edn.), 32.

51.   T. A. Bailey, *Woodrow Wilson and the Lost Peace* (Chicago, 1963 edn.), 111.

52.   J. M. Keynes, *The Economic Consequences of the Peace* (1924 edn.), 38. Keynes's remark about Wilson's short legs was probably an imitation of Lytton Strachey's similar observation on Dr. Arnold in *Eminent Victorians.*

53.   Lord Riddell, *Intimate Diary of the Peace Conference and After 1918–1923* (1933), 78.

54.   *Ibid.* 51 and 57.

55.   W. K. Hancock, *Smuts: The Sanguine Years 1870–1919* (Cambridge, 1962), 523.

56.   P. Mantoux, *The Deliberations of the Council of Four* I, edited by A. S. Link (Princeton, N.J., 1992), 64.

57.   D. R. Watson, *Georges Clemenceau* (1974), 327.

58.   B. H. Liddell Hart, *Foch: Man of Orleans* II (1937 edn.), 431.

59.   Nicolson, *Peacemaking,* 333.

60.   Keynes, *Economic Consequences,* 37.

61.   Brendon, *Churchill,* 87.

62.   D. Lloyd George, *The Truth About the Peace Treaties* I (1938), 405.

63.   A. J. P. Taylor (ed.), *Lloyd George: A Diary by Frances Stevenson* (1971), 183.

64.   G. Dallas, *At the Heart of the Tiger* (1993), 567.

65. *Memoirs of Hoover* I, 437.

66. C[hurchill] A[rchives] C[entre], HDLM, Box 11, file 6, Headlam-Morley's interview with Balfour 6 July 1920.

67. A. Tardieu, *The Truth about the Treaty* (1921), 102.

68. E. Holt, *The Tiger* (1976), 235.

69. Lloyd George, *Peace Treaties* I, 406.

70. Riddell, *Intimate Diary*, 78.

71. H. Elcock, *Portrait of a Decision* (1972), 247.

72. M. Fitzherbert, *The Man who was Greenmantle: A Biography of Aubrey Herbert* (1983), 219.

73. R. J. Schmidt, "Hoover's Reflections on the Versailles Treaty" in L. E. Gelfand (ed.), *Herbert Hoover: The Great War and its Aftermath 1914–23* (Iowa City, 1979), 66.

74. P. Rowland, *Lloyd George* (1975), 495.

75. H. Hagenlücke, "Germany and the Armistice" in H. Cecil and P. H. Liddle (eds.), *At the Eleventh Hour* (Barnsley, 1998), 46.

76. *Hitler's Table-Talk*, introduced by H. R. Trevor-Roper (Oxford, 1988 edn.), 224.

77. A. J. P. Taylor, *The First World War* (1963), 207.

78. R. Rhodes James (ed.), *Memoirs of a Conservative: J. C. C. Davidson's Memoirs and Papers 1910–1937* (1969), 92–3.

79. Nicolson, *Peacemaking*, 368.

80. J. Headlam-Morley, *A Memoir of the Paris Peace Conference 1919* (1972), 179.

81. I[mperial] W[ar] M[useum],[Harada-]Saionji [Diary], AL 5118/1, "Naval Disarmament Treaty Supplement," 82.

82. L. Connors, *The Emperor's Adviser: Saionji Kinmochi and Pre-War Japanese Politics* (1987), 3.

83. Yoshitake Oka, *Konoe Fumimaro* (Tokyo, 1983), 28.

84. J. Winter and B. Baggett, *The Great War and the Shaping of the 20th Century* (1996), 351.

85. A. Salter, *Recovery: The Second Effort* (New York, 1932), 28.

86. M. A. Ledeen, *The First Duce* (Baltimore, Md., 1987), 14.

87. A. Bonadeo, *D'Annunzio and the Great War* (1995), 127.

CHAPTER II

1. I. Kirkpatrick, *Mussolini: Study of a Demagogue* (1964), 64.

2. M. G. Sarfatti, *The Life of Benito Mussolini* (1925), 210.

3. *Popolo d'Italia*, 2 July 1921,

4. G. Giudice, *Pirandello* (1975), 152.

5. F. Chabod, *A History of Italian Fascism* (1961), 47.

6. R. J. Young, "Reason and Madness: France, the Axis Powers and the Politics of Economic Disorder, 1938–39," *Canadian Journal of History* XX (Apr. 1985), 69.

7. *Times,* 14 Aug. 1922.

8. *N[ew] Y[ork] T[imes]*, 26 Oct. 1922.

9. R. Mussolini, *My Life with Mussolini* (1959), 45.

10. A. Lyttelton, *The Seizure of Power* (1987 edn.), 95.

11. T. H. Koon, *Believe Obey Fight* (Chapel Hill, N.C., 1985), 7–9.

12. P. Morelli, *Mussolini: An Intimate Life* (1957), 93.

13. *NYT,* 31 Oct. 1922.

14. *Hitler's Table-Talk,* 10.

15. *NYT,* 31 Oct. 1922.

16. C. Hibbert, *Benito Mussolini* (1962), 37.

17. W. S. Churchill, *Thoughts and Adventures* (1974 edn.), 186 and 191–2.

18. *Times,* 31 Oct. 1922.

19. C. Sheridan, *In Many Places* (1945), 211–12.

20. Hibbert, *Mussolini,* 37.

21. D. Mack Smith, *Mussolini* (1981), 82.

22. M. G. Sarfatti, *Dux* (Verona, 1932), 314.

23. K. G. W. Lüdecke, *I Knew Hitler* (1938), 72.

24. Lyttelton, *Seizure of Power,* 19. Mussolini borrowed Corradini's phrase.

25. M. Gallo, *Mussolini's Italy* (1974), 223.

26. E. Eyck, *A History of the Weimar Republic* I (Cambridge, Mass., 1962), 229.

27. K. Heiden, *Der Fuehrer: Hitler's Rise to Power* (1967), 106 and 112.

28. F. K. Ringer, *The German Inflation of 1923* (New York, 1969), 91.

29. D. H. Aldcroft, *From Versailles to Wall Street 1919–1929* (Harmondsworth, 1987), 136.

30. N. Ferguson, *The Pity of War* (1998), 417.

31. Viscount d'Abernon, *An Ambassador of Peace* II (1929), 95 and 123.

32. A. Fergusson, *When Money Dies: The Nightmare of the Weimar Collapse* (1975), 177.

33. M. J. Bonn, *Wandering Scholar* (1949), 286.

34. S. Zweig, *The Invisible Collection* (New York, 1926), *passim.*

35. A. E. Simpson, *Hjalmar Schacht in Perspective* (The Hague, 1969), 12.

36. Ringer, *German Inflation,* 125.

37. E. D. McDonald (ed.), *Phoenix: The Posthumous Papers of D. H. Lawrence* (1967 edn.), 108–9.

38. A. de Jonge, *The Weimar Chronicle: Prelude to Hitler* (1978), 134.

39. C. Bresciani-Turroni, *The Economics of Inflation* (1937), 288.

40. W. Carr, *Hitler: A Study in Personality and Politics* (1978), 5.

41. W. Shirer, *The Rise and Fall of the Third Reich* (1964 edn.), 87.

42. N. H. Baynes (ed.), *The Speeches of Adolf Hitler, 1922–39* I (New York, 1969), 44.

43. E. Canetti, *Crowds and Power* (1962), 186–8.

44. E. Hanfstaengl, *Hitler: The Missing Years* (1957), 33 and 22.

45. Carr, *Hitler,* 19.

46. Hanfstaengl, *Hitler,* 83.

47. Hitler, *Mein Kampf,* 98.

48. Hanfstaengl, *Hitler,* 69.

49. Toland, *Hitler,* 132.

50. H. Barbusse, *Stalin* (1935), 274.

51. I. Kershaw, *Hitler 1889–1936: Hubris* (1998), 192.

52. A. Bullock, *Hitler: A Study in Tyranny* (1965 edn.), 106.

53. H. J. Gordon, *Hitler and the Beer Hall Putsch* (Princeton, N.J., 1972), 288 and 351.

54. d'Abernon, *Ambassador,* 270.

55. J. C. Fest, *Hitler* (1973), 190.

56. Toland, *Hitler,* 191.

57. Fergusson, *Money Dies,* 214.

58. *NYT,* 9 Sept. 1923.

59. O. M. Poole, *The Death of Yokohama* (1968), 31.

60. W. Weston, *A Wayfarer in Unfamiliar Japan* (1925), 192.

61. P. Verney, *The Earthquake Handbook* (1979), 131.

62. *NYT,* 9 Sept. 1923.

63. *Times,* 8 Sept. 1923.

64. *NYT,* 6 Sept. 1923.

65. *NYT,* 9 Sept. 1923.

66. R. Storry, *The Double Patriots* (1973 edn.), 34.

67. *NYT,* 9 Sept. 1923.

68. *NYT,* 12 Sept. 1923.

69. F. S. G. Piggott, *Broken Thread* (Aldershot, 1950), 178.

70. *NYT,* 6 Sept. 1923.

71. Lord Northcliffe, *My Journey Round the World* (1923), 108.

72. S. L. Gulick, *Toward Understanding Japan* (New York, 1935), 118.

73. W. H. Chamberlin, *Japan over Asia* (1938), 20.

74. IWM, Saionji (May, 1939), 2541.

75. Storry, *Double Patriots,* 28.

76. R. J. C. Butow, *Tojo and the Coming of War* (Princeton, 1961), 79.

77. *Contemporary Japan* (June 1935), 103.

78. Chamberlin, *Japan over Asia,* 27.

79. U. Close, *Challenge: Behind the Face of Japan* (1935), 106.

80. L. Mosley, *Hirohito: Emperor of Japan* (1966), 18.

81. B. H. Chamberlain, *Things Japanese* (1939 edn.), 87.

82. D. Cannadine, "The Context, Performance and Meaning of Ritual: The British Monarchy and the 'Invention of Tradition,' c. 1820–1977" in E. Hobsbawm and T. Ranger (eds.), *The Invention of Tradition* (1983), 120 and *passim.*

83. Mikiso Hane, *Emperor Hirohito and his Chief Aide-de-Camp: The Honjo Diary, 1933–36* (Tokyo, 1982), 58.

84. IWM, Saionji (Nov. 1937), 1930.

85. IWM, Saionji, "The Assassination of Chang Tso-lin," 11.

86. *NYT,* 11 Nov. 1928.

87. *Japan Today and Tomorrow* (1928), 17.

88. B. W. Fleisher (ed.), *The Japan Advertiser Enthronement Edition* (Tokyo, 1928), 28.

89. S. Bradford, *George VI* (1989), 210.

90. *Japan Advertiser,* 27 Sept. 1929.

91. E. Seidensticker, *Tokyo Rising* (1990), 26.

92. *Japan Today and Tomorrow* (1929–30), 81.

93. O. D. Tolischus, *Tokyo Record* (1943), 12.

94. *Japan Today and Tomorrow* (1929–30), 56.

95. P. G. O'Neill (ed.), *Tradition and Modern Japan* (Tenterden, Kent, 1981), 106.

96. *Japan Today and Tomorrow* (1929–30), 149.

97.   P. Duus (ed.), *The Cambridge History of Japan* VI: *The Twentieth Century* (Cambridge, 1988), 762.
98.   Duus (ed.), *Cambridge History of Japan* VI, 592–3.
99.   *Japan Advertiser,* 17 Dec. 1927.
100. W. M. Fletcher, *The Search for a New Order: Intellectuals and Fascism in Prewar Japan* (Chapel Hill, N.C., 1982), 3.

CHAPTER III

1.   *Contemporary Japan* (1933), 455.
2.   IWM, Saionji (June 1936), 1529.
3.   N. and J. MacKenzie (eds.), *The Diary of Beatrice Webb* (1985), 198.
4.   White, *Britain and Bolshevik Revolution,* 40.
5.   J. Mahon, *Harry Pollitt* (1976), 127.
6.   G. Blaxland, *A Life for Unity* (1964), 198.
7.   R. McKibbin, *Classes and Cultures: England 1918–1951* (Oxford, 1998), 148.
8.   N. and J. MacKenzie (eds.), *Diary of Webb,* 254.
9.   W. McElwee, *Britain's Locust Years 1918–1940* (1962), 115.
10.   P. Brendon, *Our Own Dear Queen* (1986), 107.
11.   C. Andrew, *Secret Service* (1985), 234.
12.   T. Jones, *Whitehall Diary* I (1969), 101.
13.   G. Orwell, *The Road to Wigan Pier* (Harmondsworth, 1962), 19.
14.   G. A. W. Tomlinson, *Coal-Miner* (1940), 17 and 97.
15.   M. Morris, *The General Strike* (1976), 108.
16.   J. Skelley (ed.), *The General Strike* (1976), 363.
17.   J. Symons, *The General Strike* (1957), 29.
18.   *Manchester Guardian,* 4 May 1926.
19.   R. Page Arnot, *The General Strike* (1926), 176.
20.   *Manchester Guardian,* 4 May 1926.
21.   W. H. Crook, *The General Strike* (Chapel Hill, N.C., 1931), 414.
22.   *British Gazette,* 5 May 1926.
23.   A. Williams-Ellis, *All Stracheys are Cousins* (1983), 106.
24.   D. Cooper, *Old Men Forget* (1953), 150.
25.   K. Martin, *The British Public and the General Strike* (1926), 29.
26.   A. J. P. Taylor, *English History, 1914–1945* (1967 edn.), 246.
27.   C[ambridge] U[niversity] L[ibrary], B[aldwin] P[apers], 22, f. 73.
28.   Jones, *Whitehall Diary* II, 23.
29.   K. Middlemas and J. Barnes, *Baldwin* (1969), 300.
30.   CUL, Add. 7938, G. M. Young to A. W. Baldwin, 25 Oct. 1949.
31.   *British Gazette,* 5 May 1926.
32.   *Times,* 10 May 1926.
33.   CUL, BP, 23, f. 10.
34.   CUL, Add. 7938, J. C. C. Davidson to A. W. Baldwin, 29 Oct. 1952.
35.   Middlemas and Barnes, *Baldwin,* 28.
36.   Lord Home, *The Way the Wind Blows* (1976), 48.
37.   Jones, *Whitehall Diary* II, 63 and 19.

38. R. Blythe, *The Age of Illusion* (Harmondsworth, 1964), 181.
39. P. Ryan, "The Poor Law in 1926" in Morris, *General Strike*, 376–7.
40. Brendon, *Churchill*, 105.
41. E. S. Turner, *Dear Old Blighty* (1980), 186–9.
42. Rhodes James (ed.), *Memoirs of Conservative*, 246–8.
43. R. Page Arnot, *The Miners: Years of Struggle* (1953), 435.
44. P. Johnson (ed.), *Twentieth-Century Britain* (1994), 267.
45. Blythe, *Age of Illusion*, 48.
46. CUL, BP, 18, f. 5, Reith to Davidson, 6 May 1926.
47. J. Curran and J. Seaton, *Power without Responsibility* (1981), 152.
48. J. R. Clynes, *Memoirs 1924–1937* (1937), 82.
49. K. Rose, *King George V* (1983), 343.
50. CUL, BP, 18, f. 5, Birkenhead to Baldwin, 23 Sept. 1926.
51. J. Campbell, *F. E. Smith First Earl of Birkenhead* (1983), 775.
52. A. Bullock, *The Life and Times of Ernest Bevin* I, (1960) 337.
53. P. Williamson, "The Doctrinal Politics of Stanley Baldwin" in M. Bentley (ed.), *Public and Private Doctrine* (Cambridge, 1993), 182.
54. S. Ball, *Baldwin and the Conservative Party* (1988), 14.
55. Clynes, *Memoirs*, 92.
56. C. Forman, *Industrial Town: Self Portrait of St. Helens in the 1920s* (Newton Abbot, 1978), 234.
57. CUL, BP, 18, f. 54, Churchill to Baldwin, 10 Sept. 1926.
58. CUL, BP, 15, f. 139, Evan Williams to Baldwin, 10 Nov. 1926.
59. G. Woodcock, "My Worst Journey" in K. Fraser (ed.), *Worst Journeys* (1991), 13.
60. D. F. Calhoun, *The United Front: The TUC and the Russians* (Cambridge, 1972), 233.
61. C. Brooks, *Devil's Decade* (1948), 13.
62. G. White and J. Maze, *Harold Ickes of the New Deal* (Cambridge, Mass., 1985), 89.
63. M. Sullivan, *Our Times V, The Twenties* (1935), 444.
64. J. Braeman, R. H. Bremner and D. Brody (eds.), *Change and Continuity in Twentieth-Century America: The 1920's* (Columbus, Ohio, 1968), 412–13.
65. G. Thomas and M. Morgan-Witts, *The Day the Bubble Burst* (1979), 21.
66. P. Collier and D. Horowitz, *The Fords* (1988), 101.
67. See J. Weightman, "The Solar Revolution," *Encounter* (Dec. 1970).
68. M. Etherington Smith and J. Pilcher, *The "It" Girls* (1988 edn.), 241.
69. H. L. Mencken, *Treatise on the Gods* (New York, 1930), 296.
70. J. Dos Passos, *U.S.A.* (Harmondsworth, 1960), 776.
71. *The Autobiography of Calvin Coolidge* (1929), 29.
72. I. Stone, "Calvin Coolidge: A Study in Inertia," in I. Leighton (ed.), *The Aspirin Age 1919–1941* (1950), 136.
73. W. Allen White, *Puritan in Babylon* (Gloucester, Mass., 1973 edn.), 294.
74. R. Lewitt, *George W. Norris: The Persistence of a Progressive 1913–1933* (Chicago, Ill., 1971), 308.
75. Walter Lippmann's phrase is quoted by F. Freidel, *America in the Twentieth Century* (1966 edn.), 248.
76. *Memoirs of Hoover* II (1952), 157.

77. G. H. Nash, *The Life of Herbert Hoover: The Engineer 1874–1914* (1984), 569.
78. D. Burner, *Herbert Hoover: A Public Life* (New York, 1979), 167.
79. G. H. Nash, *The Life of Herbert Hoover: The Humanitarian 1914–1917* (1988), 370.
80. G. H. Nash, "The Social Philosophy of Herbert Hoover" in L. Nash (ed.), *Understanding Herbert Hoover: Ten Perspectives* (Stanford, Cal., 1987), 35.
81. *Memoirs of Hoover* II, 142.
82. W. Irwin, *Herbert Hoover* (1929), 301.
83. J. Tebbel and S. M. Watts, *The Press and the Presidency: From George Washington to Ronald Reagan* (New York, 1985), 418.
84. Burner, *Hoover*, 167.
85. M. and H. Josephson, *Al Smith: Hero of the Cities* (1969), 40 and 162.
86. R. O'Connor, *The First Hurrah: A Biography of Al Smith* (New York, 1970), 115.
87. M. and H. Josephson, *Smith*, 381.
88. Burner, *Hoover*, 204.
89. Baltimore *Sun*, 23 July 1928.
90. Kansas City *Star*, 7 Nov. 1928.
91. *Memoirs of Hoover* II, 184.
92. F. D. Mitchell and R. O. Davies, *America's Recent Past* (1969), 201.
93. Nash, *Hoover: The Humanitarian*, 367.
94. R. S. McElvaine, *The Great Depression: America 1929–1941* (1984), 52.
95. *Memoirs of Hoover* II, 222.
96. See A. M. Schlesinger Jr., *The Cycles of American History* (1987), 381 and *passim*.
97. *Memoirs of Hoover* III (1953), 354 and 357.
98. Burner, *Hoover*, 246.
99. Thomas and Morgan-Witts, *Day the Bubble Burst*, 64.
100. B[ancroft] L[ibrary], Berkeley, Hearst Papers, Brisbane to Hearst, 5 Feb. and 23 June 1927.
101. W. Z. Ripley, *Main Street and Wall Street* (New York, 1927), 352.
102. R. Sobel, *The Great Bull Market: Wall Street in the 1920s* (New York, 1968), 95.
103. R. Sobel, *Panic on Wall Street* (New York, 1972 edn.), 371.
104. Thomas and Morgan-Witts, *Day the Bubble Burst*, 226 and 178–9.
105. Sobel, *Panic on Wall Street*, 366.
106. J. K. Galbraith, *The Great Crash 1929* (Harmondsworth, 1961), 95.
107. Thomas and Morgan-Witts, *Day the Bubble Burst*, 260, 331 and 351.
108. *NYT,* 25 and 29 Oct. 1929.
109. *NYT,* 25 Oct. 1929.
110. Galbraith, *Crash*, 135.
111. *NYT,* 31 Oct. 1929.
112. A. Sinclair, *Corsair: The Life of J. P. Morgan* (1981), 231.
113. Quoted by K. S. Davis, *FDR: The New York Years 1928–1933* (New York, 1985 edn.), 148.
114. G. Rees, *The Great Slump: Capitalism in Crisis 1929–33* (1970), 60.
115. E. Wilson, *The Shores of Light: A Literary Chronicle of the Twenties and Thirties* (1952), 496.
116. R. Sobel, *The Big Board: A History of the New York Stock Market* (New York, 1968), 283.

CHAPTER IV

1. *NYT,* 22 Oct. 1929.
2. New York *Daily News,* 30 Oct. 1929.
3. H. L. Stimson and McGeorge Bundy, *On Active Service in Peace and War* (1948), 52.
4. J. Rublowsky, *After the Crash: America in the Great Depression* (1970), 85.
5. McElvaine, *Great Depression,* 30.
6. B. Mitchell, *Depression Decade: From New Era to New Deal* (New York, 1947), 31.
7. G. Martin, *Madam Secretary: Frances Perkins* (Boston, 1976), 146.
8. F. Perkins, *The Roosevelt I Knew* (New York, 1946), 94.
9. J. N. Leonard, *Three Years Down* (New York, 1939), 121.
10. S. Terkel, *Hard Times* (1970), 61 and 71.
11. A. Rogers and F. L. Allen, *I Remember Distinctly* (1947), 126.
12. M. L. Fausold, *The Presidency of Herbert C. Hoover* (Lawrence, Kans., 1985), 111.
13. Burner, *Hoover,* 264 and 257.
14. L. R. Parks, *My Thirty Years Backstairs at the White House* (New York, 1961), 229.
15. E. E. Robinson, and V. D. Bornet, *Herbert Hoover* (Stanford, Cal., 1975), 169.
16. *Nation* 132 (14 Jan. 1931), 44.
17. A. M. Schlesinger, *The Age of Roosevelt* I (1957), 250 and 251.
18. Tebbel and Watts, *Press and Presidency,* 424.
19. Fausold, *Hoover,* 141.
20. Burner, *Hoover,* 261.
21. *NYT,* 2 May 1931.
22. E. Wilson, *The American Jitters: The Year of the Slump* (1932), 133–4.
23. G. Perrett, *America in the Twenties: A History* (New York, 1982), 422.
24. W. A. Swanberg, *Norman Thomas: The Last Idealist* (New York, 1976), 125.
25. *NYT,* 16 June 1931.
26. S. Rosenman, *Working with Roosevelt* (1952), 58.
27. Davis, *FDR,* 242.
28. [S. Rosenman (ed.),] *[The] P[ublic] P[apers and Addresses of Franklin D.] R[oosevelt]* I (New York, 1938–), 471.
29. A. J. Toynbee (ed.), *Survey of International Affairs 1931* (1932), 60 and 58.
30. Stimson and Bundy, *Active Service,* 57.
31. Toynbee (ed.), *International Affairs 1931,* 60.
32. R. S. McElvaine (ed.), *Down and Out in the Great Depression: Letters from the "Forgotten Man"* (Chapel Hill, N.C., 1983), 20 and 46.
33. *PPR* I, 624–5.
34. McElvaine (ed.), *Down and Out,* 18.
35. See *NYT* and *New York Herald Tribune,* 17 Mar. 1932.
36. D. A. Shannon (ed.), *The Great Depression* (Englewood Cliffs, N.J., 1960), 29.
37. A. Gottfried, *Boss Cermak of Chicago: A Study of Political Leadership* (Seattle, Wash., 1962), 249.
38. C. Phillips, *From the Crash to the Blitz* (1969), 62.
39. C. H. Trout, *Boston, the Great Depression and the New Deal* (New York, 1977), 92.
40. M. N. McGeary, *Gifford Pinchot: Forester-Politician* (Princeton, N.J., 1960), 372.
41. *Nation* 134 (8 June 1932), 651.
42. Terkel, *Hard Times,* 123.

43. *NYT,* 16 June 1931.
44. J. K. Ohl, *Hugh S. Johnson and the New Deal* (De Kalb, Ill., 1985), 82.
45. J. Gerassi, *The Premature Antifascists* (New York, 1986), 46.
46. Wilson, *American Jitters,* 297.
47. *NYT,* 14 June 1931.
48. *Nation* 132 (28 Jan. 1931), 81.
49. *NYT,* 5 Dec. 1931.
50. *NYT,* 23 Nov. 1930.
51. W. A. Swanberg, *Luce and His Empire* (1972), 81.
52. M. H. Vorse, "Rebellion in the Cornbelt: American Farmers Beat Their Plow-shares into Swords," *Harper's* CLXVI (Dec. 1932), 3.
53. D. J. Lisio, *The President and Protest: Hoover, Conspiracy and the Bonus Riot* (Columbia, Miss., 1974), 80.
54. C. M. Green, *Washington* (Princeton, N.J., 1963), 371.
55. F. Daniels, *The Bonus March* (Westport, Conn., 1971), 167.
56. J. F. Vivian and J. H. Vivian, "The Bonus March of 1932: The Role of General Van Horn Moseley," *Wisconsin Magazine of History* (Autumn 1967), 34.
57. Daniels, *Bonus March,* 174.
58. *Nation* 135 (10 Aug. 1932), 116 and (17 Aug. 1932), 138.
59. *NYT,* 6 Nov. 1932.
60. M. Freedman (ed.), *Roosevelt and Frankfurter: Their Correspondence, 1928–1945* (Boston, 1967), 78. This story expresses the truth but it cannot be precisely correct because Roosevelt was at Albany on 28–9 July.
61. *Nation* 134 (15 June 1932), 670 and 135 (3 Aug. 1932), 96.
62. Burner, *Hoover,* 315.
63. W. Johnson (ed.), *Selected Letters of William Allen White 1899–1943* (New York, 1947), 309–10.
64. *Nation* 134 (1 June 1932), 616.
65. *New York Herald Tribune,* 8 Jan. 1932.
66. F. Freidel, *Franklin D. Roosevelt: The Triumph* (Boston, 1956), 299.
67. Schlesinger, *Age of Roosevelt* I, 467.
68. T. Morgan, *FDR: A Biography* (1985), 108.
69. *New York Herald Tribune,* 11 Feb. 1932.
70. Morgan, *FDR,* 271–2.
71. A. B. Rollins Jr., *Roosevelt and Howe* (New York, 1962), 376.
72. E. K. Lindley, *Franklin D. Roosevelt: A Career in Progressive Democracy* (Indianapolis, 1931), 21.
73. R. Moley, *After Seven Years* (New York, 1939), 11.
74. *PPR* I, 646.
75. Morgan, *FDR,* 352.
76. B. N. Timmons, *Garner of Texas* (New York, 1948), 168.
77. Burner, *Hoover,* 315.
78. Moley, *After Seven Years,* 45.
79. Burner, *Hoover,* 316.
80. H. Feis, *1933: Characters in Crisis* (New York, 1966), 13.
81. Boston *Globe,* 17 Oct. 1932.
82. P. Brendon, *Ike: His Life and Times* (New York, 1986), 63.

83. *New York Herald Tribune,* 25 Sept. 1931.

84. R. Steel, *Walter Lippmann and the American Century* (1980), 300.

85. *NYT,* 5 Mar. 1933.

86. F. Freidel, *Franklin D. Roosevelt: Launching the New Deal* (Boston, 1973), 205.

87. R. S. and H. M. Lynd, *Middletown in Transition* (1937), 20.

88. *NYT,* 4 and 5 Mar. 1933.

89. Morgan, *FDR,* 376.

CHAPTER V

1.   F. Kafka, *America* (Harmondsworth, 1967), 13.

2.   B. Brecht, *Gedichte* II (Frankfurt, 1960), 158.

3.   W. Laqueur, *Weimar: A Cultural History 1918–1933* (1974), 148.

4.   F. Ewen, *Bertolt Brecht* (1970), 196.

5.   H. Rauschning, *Hitler Speaks* (1939), 76.

6.   Fest, *Hitler,* 98.

7.   C. Reiss, *Joseph Goebbels* (1949), 87.

8.   C. Isherwood, *Down There on a Visit* (1962 edn.), 26.

9.   H. L. Poor, *Kurt Tucholsky and the Ordeal of Germany 1914–1935* (New York, 1968), 153.

10. J. Heygate, *Those Germans* (1940), 60.

11. A similar joke was made about the wooden lions outside Lord Beaverbrook's London residence, Stornoway House.

12. H. R. Knickerbocker, *Germany—Fascist or Soviet?* (1932), 5.

13. E. Fröhlich (ed.), *Die Tagebücher von Joseph Goebbels* I (Munich, 1987), 196–7.

14. This was a smart suburb of Berlin where Goebbels lived with his wife.

15. Hanfstaengl, *Hitler,* 191.

16. Lüdecke, *Hitler,* 383.

17. A. Speer, *Inside the Third Reich* (1970), 17.

18. J. Goebbels, *Der Kampf um Berlin* (Munich, 1941), 86.

19. *Der Angriff,* 5 Oct. 1930.

20. Fröhlich (ed.), *Tagebücher von Goebbels* I, 185.

21. Reiss, *Goebbels,* 52.

22. R. Taylor, "Goebbels and the Function of Propaganda" in D. Welch (ed.), *Nazi Propaganda* (1983), 38.

23. A. Werth, *France in Ferment* (1934), 46.

24. Hitler, *Mein Kampf,* 439.

25. E. K. Bramsted, *Goebbels and National Socialist Propaganda* (1965), 20.

26. d'Abernon, *Ambassador* II, 52.

27. W. H. Nelson, *The Berliners* (1969), 112.

28. R. Manvell and H. Fraenkel, *Doctor Goebbels* (1960), 86. Goebbels not only anticipated Roosevelt's "arsenal of democracy" phrase, he has some claim to have coined Churchill's expression "the iron curtain."

29. V. Reimann, *The Man who Created Hitler: Joseph Goebbels* (1976), 110.

30. A. Nicholls and E. Matthias (eds.), *German Democracy and the Triumph of Hitler* (1971), 20.

31. Reimann, *Goebbels,* 106.
32. J. W. Wheeler-Bennett, *Hindenburg: The Wooden Titan* (1967 edn.), 333.
33. *NYT,* 7 June 1931.
34. Hitler, *Mein Kampf,* 307 and 301.
35. Fest, *Hitler,* 266. Hitler made so many prophecies about the time of his assumption of power that some of them were bound to be right.
36. H. A. Turner Jr. (ed.), *Hitler—Memoirs of a Confidant* (Yale, 1985), 111.
37. *The Ribbentrop Memoirs* (1954), 32.
38. I. Kershaw, *The "Hitler Myth": Image and Reality in the Third Reich* (Oxford, 1989), 30.
39. *Memoirs of Ernst von Weizsäcker* (1951), 94.
40. E. Larsen, *Weimar Eyewitness* (1976), 146–7.
41. S. Delmer, *Trail Sinister* (1961), 102.
42. Kershaw, *Hitler 1889–1936,* 336.
43. Wheeler-Bennett, *Hindenburg,* 342.
44. S. Spender, *World within World* (1953), 110–11.
45. [E. L. Woodward and R. Butler (eds.),] *D[ocuments on] B[ritish] F[oreign] P[olicy 1919–1939],* 2nd series, I (1946–), 478–9.
46. A. Dorpalen, *Hindenburg and the Weimar Republic* (Princeton, N.J., 1964), 204.
47. F. Stern, *Dreams and Delusions* (New York, 1987), 121–2.
48. de Jonge, *Weimar Chronicle,* 216.
49. E. M. Remarque, *All Quiet on the Western Front* (1929), 309–10.
50. M. Broszat, *Hitler and the Collapse of Weimar Germany* (New York, 1987), 33.
51. *Times,* 8 Dec. 1930.
52. *DBFP,* 2nd series, II, 225.
53. Reiss, *Goebbels,* 94.
54. Toland, *Hitler,* 256.
55. Dorpalen, *Hindenburg,* 234.
56. C. Isherwood, *The Berlin Stories* (New York, 1954), 86.
57. T. Sender, *The Autobiography of a German Rebel* (1940), 273.
58. J. Goebbels, *My Part in Germany's Fight* (1935), 45.
59. *NYT,* 5 Mar. 1932.
60. J. Goebbels, *Wetterleuchten: Aufsätze aus der Kampfzeit* (Munich, 1939), 270.
61. Manvell and Fraenkel, *Goebbels,* 100.
62. Delmer, *Trail Sinister,* 149–50.
63. Fest, *Hitler,* 328.
64. O. Friedrich, *Before the Deluge* (New York, 1972), 363.
65. F. François-Poncet, *The Fateful Years* (1949), 23.
66. K. Heiden, *A History of National Socialism* (1971 edn.), 182.
67. *The Diaries of Harry Kessler* (1971), 419.
68. H. W. Blood-Ryan, *Franz von Papen* (1940), 139.
69. *Diaries of Kessler,* 423.
70. Lüdecke, *Hitler,* 341.
71. J. Simon, *Retrospect* (1952), 188.
72. Rauschning, *Hitler Speaks,* 172.
73. *NYT,* 7 June 1931.
74. H. James, *The German Slump* (Oxford, 1986), 8.

75. Goebbels, *Germany's Fight*, 134.
76. Turner (ed.), *Hitler*, 182.
77. Wheeler-Bennett, *Hindenburg*, 410.
78. Goebbels, *Germany's Fight*, 181 and 183.
79. Lüdecke, *Hitler*, 413.
80. Goebbels, *Germany's Fight*, 207.
81. *Ibid.* 236–7.
82. D. Reed, *Insanity Fair* (1938), 127.
83. Wheeler-Bennett, *Hindenburg*, 435.
84. Dorpalen, *Hindenburg*, 447.
85. *NYT*, 11 Oct. 1931.
86. Stern, *Dreams and Delusions*, 120.
87. Rauschning, *Hitler Speaks*, 15.

CHAPTER VI

1. J. Gunther, *Inside Europe* (1936), 204.
2. M. Muggeridge (ed.), *Ciano's Diary 1939–1943* (1947), 321.
3. M. Gallo, *Mussolini's Italy* (1974), 176.
4. R. Gildea, *Barricades and Borders* (Oxford, 1987), 256.
5. H. Rhodes, *The Vatican in the Age of the Dictators 1922–1945* (1973), 20.
6. A. Randall, *Vatican Assignment* (1956), 58.
7. Rhodes, *Vatican*, 19.
8. J. Gaillard, "The Attractions of Fascism for the Church of Rome" in Milfull (ed.), *Attractions of Fascism*, 208.
9. I. Kirkpatrick, *The Inner Circle* (1959), 47.
10. D. A. Binchy, *Church and State in Fascist Italy* (Oxford, 1970 edn.), 186.
11. Binchy, *Church and State*, 105.
12. A. C. Jemolo, *Church and State in Italy 1850–1950* (Oxford, 1960), 212.
13. Rhodes, *Vatican*, 45.
14. Randall, *Vatican Assignment*, 62.
15. Binchy, *Church and State*, 188–9.
16. *NYT*, 13 Feb. 1929.
17. *Times*, 13 Feb. 1929.
18. *L'Osservatore Romano*, 13 Feb. 1929.
19. Jemolo, *Church and State*, 213.
20. *L'Ere Nouvelle*, 14 Feb. 1929.
21. J. Pollard, *The Vatican and Italian Fascism, 1929–1932* (Cambridge, 1985), 50.
22. *Italy Today* (Feb. 1931), 13.
23. Jemolo, *Church and State*, 233.
24. *Italy Today* (Aug. 1929), 10–12.
25. Pollard, *Vatican and Fascism*, 60.
26. E. Delzell (ed.), *The Papacy and Totalitarianism between the Two World Wars* (California, 1974), 29.
27. G. Seldes, *The Vatican Yesterday—Today—Tomorrow* (1934), 369.
28. *Italy Today* (Sept.–Oct. 1932), 25.

29. V. Zamagni, *The Economic History of Italy 1860–1990* (Oxford, 1993), 252.

30. *Italy Today* (Jan. 1929), 7.

31. *O[pera] O[mnia di Benito] M[ussolini]* XXIV (Florence, 1958), 311.

32. G. Seldes, *Sawdust Caesar* (1936), 285–6.

33. C. P. Kindleberger, *The World in Depression 1929–1930* (Harmondsworth, 1987), 135.

34. S. B. Clough, *The Economic History of Modern Italy* (New York, 1964), 247.

35. H. Finer, *Mussolini's Italy* (1935), 183.

36. New York *Evening Post*, 20 Aug. 1930.

37. C. R. Coote, *Italian Town and Country Life* (1925), 53.

38. *OOM* XXII (1957), 47–8.

39. R. C. Fried, *Planning the Eternal City* (1973), 39.

40. S. Kostof, "The Emperor and the Duce: The Planning of Piazzale Augusto Imperatore in Rome" in H. A. Millon and L. Nochlin (eds.), *Art and Architecture in the Service of Politics* (1978), 309, 295 and 322.

41. Gallo, *Mussolini's Italy*, 236.

42. C. Levi, *Christ Stopped at Eboli* (Harmondsworth, 1982), 123, 65 and 137.

43. L. Paserini, *Fascism in Popular Memory* (Cambridge, 1987), 32.

44. Paserini, *Fascism*, 45.

45. I. Silone, *Fontamara* (1965 edn.), 13.

46. Levi, *Christ*, 34.

47. Finer, *Mussolini's Italy*, 305 and 302.

48. *DBFP*, 2nd series, I, 383.

49. Seldes, *Sawdust Caesar*, 318.

50. New York *World*, 29 July 1929.

51. J. P. Diggins, *Mussolini and Fascism: The View from America* (Princeton, N.J., 1972), 54.

52. K. D. Bracher, *The German Dictatorship* (1970), 256.

53. R. T. Clough, *Looking Back at Futurism* (New York, 1942), 37.

54. *Independent*, 11 Apr. 1990.

55. L. Chamberlain (ed.), *Marinetti: The Futurist Cookbook* (1989), 41, 55, 21, 37, 144, 61 and 67.

56. E. Gentile, *The Sacralization of Politics in Fascist Italy* (1996), 112–15.

57. Finer, *Mussolini's Italy*, 397

58. C. G. Segrè, *Italo Balbo* (Berkeley, Cal., 1987), 97.

59. G. Pini and D. Susmel, *Mussolini—L'Uomo e L'Opera* I (Florence, 1953), 359.

60. Clough, *Futurism*, 150.

61. Finer, *Mussolini's Italy*, 140.

62. R. De Felice, *Mussolini il duce* I: *Gli anni del consenso, 1929–1936* (Turin, 1974), *passim*.

63. S. Trambaiolo, "The Child and the She-Wolf: Memories of a Fascist Childhood" in Milfull (ed.), *Attractions of Fascism*, 12.

64. *Italy Today* (Nov.–Dec. 1932), 3–4.

65. L. de Bosis, "The Story of my Death" in F. Keene (ed.), *Neither Liberty nor Bread* (New York, 1940), 97.

66. I. Origo, *A Need to Testify* (1984), 70.

67. *Times*, 4 Oct. 1931.

68. I. Balbo, *La Centuria Alata* (Milan, 1934), 284.

69. *NYT,* 16 July 1931.

70. E. R. Tannenbaum, *Fascism in Italy* (1973), 264.

71. Finer, *Mussolini's Italy,* 305.

72. Kirkpatrick, *Mussolini,* 256.

73. Pollard, *Vatican and Fascism,* 167.

74. Kirkpatrick, *Mussolini,* 271.

75. Finer, *Mussolini's Italy,* 405.

76. C. Falconi, *The Popes of the Twentieth Century* (1967), 202.

77. E. Ludwig, *Talks with Mussolini* (1932), 173.

78. P. C. Kent, *The Pope and the Duce* (1981), 193–5.

79. Kirkpatrick, *Mussolini,* 275.

80. M. Muggeridge (ed.), *Ciano's Diary 1937–8* (1952), 115.

CHAPTER VII

1. T. Zeldin, *France 1848–1945: Ambition and Love* (Oxford, 1979), 304.

2. Werth, *France in Ferment,* 40.

3. Kirkpatrick, *Mussolini,* 164–5.

4. D. Hart-Davis (ed.), *In Royal Service: The Letters and Journals of Sir Alan Lascelles 1920–1936* II (1989), 54.

5. C. M. Andrew and A. S. Kanya-Forster, *France Overseas* (1981), 249.

6. R. Binion, *Defeated Leaders* (New York, 1960), 293, 198 and 239.

7. T. Zeldin, *France 1848–1945: Anxiety and Hypocrisy* (Oxford, 1981), 301.

8. B. Oudin, *Aristide Briand: La Paix: une idée neuve en Europe* (Paris, 1987), 526.

9. D. W. Brogan, *The Development of Modern France* (1967 edn.), 655.

10. Oudin, *Briand,* 528.

11. G. Clemenceau, *Lettres à une Amie* edited by P. Brive (Paris, 1970), 640.

12. *NYT,* 24 Nov. 1929.

13. L. Daudet, *Clemenceau* (1940), 296.

14. *NYT,* 25 Nov. 1929. The *New York Times* was one of many journals which repeated the myth that Clemenceau was buried in a perpendicular position.

15. Dallas, *Tiger,* xi.

16. Binion, *Defeated Leaders,* 295.

17. A. Sauvy, *Histoire Economique de la France entre les deux Guerres* I (Paris, 1965), 115.

18. W. Wiser, *The Crazy Years: Paris in the Twenties* (1983), 229–30.

19. J. Flanner, *Paris was Yesterday 1925–1939* (1973), 67–9.

20. P. Reynaud, *In the Thick of the Fight* (1955), 8.

21. A. Sauvy, "The Economic Crisis in France," *Journal of Contemporary History* IV, No. 4 (1969), 21.

22. G. Orwell, *Down and Out in Paris and London* (Harmondsworth, 1964), 80.

23. I. Ehrenburg, *The Life of the Automobile* (New York, 1976 edn.), 33.

24. Binion, *Defeated Leaders,* 307.

25. J. Paul-Boncour, *Entre Deux Guerres* II (Paris, 1945), 213.

26. R. Cobb, *Promenades* (Oxford, 1980), 49.

27.　Binion, *Defeated Leaders*, 306.

28.　*NYT*, 11 Feb. 1934.

29.　T. Zeldin, *France 1848–1945: Politics and Anger* (Oxford, 1984 edn.), 214.

30.　*NYT*, 18 Mar. 1934.

31.　J. M. Wallace-Hadrill and J. McManners, *France: Government and Society* (1970), 227.

32.　E. Talbott (ed.), *France since 1930* (New York, 1972), 43.

33.　Binion, *Defeated Leaders*, 295.

34.　S. Hoffmann *et al.*, *France: Change and Tradition* (1963), 3.

35.　Werth, *France in Ferment*, 127.

36.　E. Paul, *Narrow Street* (1942), 157.

37.　D. H. Pinkney, *Napoleon III and the Rebuilding of Paris* (Princeton, N.J., 1958), 79.

38.　E. Zola, *Le Ventre de Paris*, edited by M. Baroli (Paris, 1969), 426.

39.　N. Evenson, *Paris: A Century of Change, 1878–1978* (1979), 301.

40.　H. Lüthy, *The State of France* (1955), 22.

41.　See M. Crozier, *La Société bloquée* (Paris, 1970), *passim*.

42.　G. Wormser, *Clemenceau vu de près* (Paris, 1979), 261.

43.　Oudin, *Briand*, 23, 49 and 15.

44.　G. Suarez, *Briand* VI (Paris, 1938–52), 308.

45.　Oudin, *Briand*, 528.

46.　*L'Action française*, 8 Mar. 1932.

47.　Binion, *Defeated Leaders*, 299.

48.　V. Rowe, *The Great Wall of France: The Triumph of the Maginot Line* (1959), 39.

49.　R. J. Young, *In Command in France* (1978), 60.

50.　A. Kemp, *The Maginot Line: Myth and Reality* (1981), 17.

51.　E. Eis, *The Forts of Folly* (1959), 226.

52.　Rowe, *Great Wall of France*, 16.

53.　C. Serre (ed.), *Evénements Survenues en France de 1933 à 1945* I (Paris, 1947), 233.

54.　P. C. F. Bankwitz, *Maxime Weygand and Civil-Military Relations in Modern France* (Cambridge, Mass., 1967), 54.

55.　A. Huxley, *An Encyclopaedia of Pacifism* (New York, 1972 edn.), 34.

56.　A. Read and D. Fisher, *The Deadly Embrace* (1988), 158.

57.　Kemp, *Maginot Line*, 15.

58.　"Pertinax," *The Gravediggers of France* (New York, 1944), 19.

59.　*Journal officiel de . . . Débats Parlementaires* (15 Mar. 1935), 1045.

60.　J. M. Hughes, *To the Maginot Line* (Cambridge, Mass., 1971), 203.

61.　Dyer, *Population and Society in France*, 95.

62.　R. Griffiths, *Marshal Pétain* (1970), 132.

63.　N. Greene, *From Versailles to Vichy: The Third French Republic, 1919–1940* (Arlington, Ill., 1970), 60.

64.　F. Kupferman, *Laval* (Paris, 1987), 20.

65.　G. Warner, *Pierre Laval and the Eclipse of France* (1968), 3.

66.　Kupferman, *Laval*, 23, 85 and 78.

67.　François-Poncet, *Fateful Years*, 11.

68.　Warner, *Pierre Laval*, 23.

69. H. Stuart Hughes, *The Obstructive Path: French Social Thought in the Years of Desperation 1930–1960* (New York, 1963), 103.

70. P. Bernard and H. Dubief, *The Decline of the Third Republic 1914–1938* (Cambridge, 1985), 195.

71. J.-B. Duroselle, *La Décadence 1932–1939* (Paris, 1979), 56.

72. P. J. Larmour, *The French Radical Party in the 1930's* (Stanford, Cal., 1964), 7.

73. J. Jackson, *The Politics of Depression in France 1932–1936* (Cambridge, 1985), 47.

74. Larmour, *French Radical Party*, 74 and 71.

75. S. Jessner, *Edouard Herriot: Patriarch of the Republic* (New York, 1974), 2.

76. A. Adamthwaite, *France and the Coming of the Second World War 1936–1939* (1977), 98.

77. L. Levy, *The Truth About France* (Harmondsworth, 1941), 141.

78. M. Sachs, *Day of Wrath* (1953), 184.

79. G. Wright, *Rural Revolution in France: The Peasantry in the Twentieth Century* (Stanford, Cal., 1964), 14.

80. Serre (ed.), *Evénements* I, 237.

81. Z. Sternhall, *Right nor Left: Fascist Ideology in France* (Stanford, Cal., 1986), 266.

82. W. H. Schneider, *Quality and Quantity: The Quest for Biological Regeneration in Twentieth-Century France* (Cambridge, 1990), 186.

83. Werth, *France in Ferment*, 15.

84. E. Weber, *Action Française: Royalism and Reaction in Twentieth-Century France* (Stanford, Cal., 1962), 315.

85. H. Tint, *The Decline of French Patriotism 1870–1940* (1964), 196.

86. Werth, *France in Ferment*, 83, 80 and 95.

87. Weber, *Action Française,* 324.

88. Werth, *France in Ferment*, 110. The paper doubtless owed this phrase to Prosper Mérimée, who had complained, when editing Napoleon's correspondence, that the early letters to Josephine consisted of nothing but "kisses, in places the names of which are not found in the Dictionary of the French Academy." [T. Aronson, *Napoleon & Josephine* (1990), 78.]

89. *NYT,* 11 Mar. 1934.

90. M. Beloff, "The Sixth of February" in J. Joll (ed.), *The Decline of the Third Republic* (1959), 35.

91. *NYT,* 7 Feb. 1934.

92. *Times,* 8 Feb. 1934.

93. E. Herriot, *Jadis* II (Paris, 1952), 376–7.

94. *Le Matin,* 7 Feb. 1934.

95. *NYT,* 10 Feb. 1934.

96. A. Tardieu, *France in Danger!* (1935), 151.

97. N. Rostow, *Anglo-French Relations, 1934–36* (1984), 247.

CHAPTER VIII

1. R. Graves, *Goodbye to All That* (Harmondsworth, 1957), 240.

2. D. Hart-Davis, *Hitler's Olympics* (1988 edn.), 97.

3. A. Boyle, *Montagu Norman* (1967), 188.

4. D. Marquand, *Ramsay MacDonald* (1977), 514.
5. J. C. Cairns, "A Nation of Shopkeepers in Search of a Suitable France 1919–40," *American Historical Review* 79 (1974), 727.
6. J. L. Garvin, quoted by D. Carlton, *MacDonald versus Henderson: The Foreign Policy of the Second Labour Government* (1970), 29.
7. Marquand, *MacDonald,* 514.
8. R. Skidelsky, *Politicians and the Slump* (1967), 63.
9. Marquand, *MacDonald,* 127, 281 and 69.
10. M. MacDonald, *Titans & Others* (1972), 12.
11. R. A. Jones, *Arthur Ponsonby: The Politics of Life* (1989), 97.
12. M. A. Hamilton, *J. Ramsay MacDonald* (1929), 160.
13. M. A. Hamilton, *Remembering My Good Friends* (1944), 120.
14. *Daily News,* 25 June 1929.
15. Hamilton, *Remembering,* 125.
16. M. Muggeridge, *Chronicles of Wasted Time* I: *The Green Stick* (1972), 49.
17. P. Snowden, *Autobiography* II (1934), 876.
18. Marquand, *MacDonald,* 498.
19. Jones, *Ponsonby,* 155.
20. N. MacKenzie (ed.), *The Letters of Sidney and Beatrice Webb* III: *Pilgrimage 1912–1947* (Cambridge, 1978), 239.
21. *Annual Register* (1929), 55.
22. Marquand, *MacDonald,* 527 and 543.
23. Campbell, *Smith,* 258.
24. O. Mosley, *My Life* (1968), 231.
25. S. Bradford, *George VI* (1989), 93.
26. R. Skidelsky, *Oswald Mosley* (1975), 180.
27. K. Young (ed.), *The Diaries of Sir Robert Bruce Lockhart* I: *1915–1938* (1973), 99.
28. C. L. Mowat, *Britain Between the Wars 1918–1940* (1968 edn.), 358.
29. Skidelsky, *Politicians and Slump,* 94.
30. Hamilton, *Remembering,* 110–11.
31. R. Graves and A. Hodge, *The Long Weekend* (1965 edn.) 242.
32. B. Pimlott (ed.), *The Political Diary of Hugh Dalton 1918–40, 1945–60* (1986), 63.
33. C. Cross, *Philip Snowden* (1966), 251.
34. Jones, *Whitehall Diary* I, 253.
35. J. Barnes and D. Nicholson (eds.), *The Empire at Bay: The Leo Amery Diaries 1929–1945* (1988), 68.
36. *Parliamentary Debates, House of Commons,* 239, Col. 1355.
37. O. Mosley, *The Greater Britain* (1934), 59–60.
38. Pimlott (ed.), *Diary of Dalton,* 130.
39. Skidelsky, *Mosley,* 216.
40. P. Clarke, *The Keynesian Revolution in the Making 1924–1936* (Oxford, 1988), 314. The debate about the validity of Keynesian analysis continues and it is by no means clear how much impact public works could have had on what Keynes himself acknowledged to be the intractable problem of unemployment. The case that there were no "easy and workable solutions" is ably made by R. McKibbin, "The Economic Policy of the Second Labour Government 1929–1931," *Past & Present* 68 (Aug. 1975), 102 and *passim.*

41. A. Morgan, *J. Ramsay MacDonald* (Manchester, 1987), 163.

42. N. and J. MacKenzie (eds.), *Diary of Beatrice Webb*, 232.

43. A. J. P. Taylor, *My Darling Pussy: The Letters of Lloyd George and Frances Stevenson 1913–41* (1975), 141–2.

44. Skidelsky, *Politicians and Slump*, 297.

45. S. Roskill, *Hankey Man of Secrets* II: *1919–1931* (1972), 544.

46. N. Branson and M. Heinemann, *Britain in the Nineteen Thirties* (1973), 31.

47. Marquand, *MacDonald*, 605.

48. Taylor, *English History*, 290.

49. Cross, *Snowden*, 292.

50. Jones, *Ponsonby*, 187.

51. Marquand, *MacDonald*, 635.

52. J. Pope-Hennessy, *Queen Mary* (1959), 565.

53. P. Brendon and P. Whitehead, *The Windsors* (1994), 30–1.

54. M. Crawford, *The Little Princesses* (1950), 94.

55. M. Bloch, *The Reign and Abdication of Edward VIII* (1990), 19.

56. N. and J. MacKenzie (eds.), *Diary of Beatrice Webb*, 228.

57. R. Gray, *The King's Wife: Five Queen Consorts* (1990), 333.

58. D. Duff, *Queen Mary* (1985), 181.

59. Viscount Templewood, *Nine Troubled Years* (1954), 59.

60. Rose, *George V,* 92.

61. J. A. Thompson and A. Mejia Jr., *The Modern British Monarchy* (New York, 1971), 45.

62. Rose, *George V,* 375.

63. H. J. Laski, *Parliamentary Government in England* (1938), 396 and 388.

64. R. Rhodes James, *A Spirit Undaunted* (1998), 86.

65. Snowden, *Autobiography* II, 957.

66. L. Wincott, *Invergordon Mutineer* (1974), 65.

67. S. Roskill, *Naval Policy Between the Wars* II: *The Period of Reluctant Rearmament 1930–1939* (1976), 34.

68. A. Carew, "The Invergordon Mutiny, 1931: Long-Term Causes, Organisation and Leadership," *International Review of Social History* 24 (1979), 166.

69. A. Ereira, *The Invergordon Mutiny* (1981), 11 and 6.

70. D. Divine, *Mutiny at Invergordon* (1970), 159.

71. *NYT,* 18 Sept. 1931.

72. *Times,* 18 Sept. 1931.

73. R. Vansittart, *The Mist Procession* (1958), 425.

74. *NYT,* 19 Sept. 1931.

75. E. O'Halpin, *Head of the Civil Service: A Study of Sir Warren Fisher* (1989), 189–90.

76. T. Jones, *A Diary with Letters 1931–1950* (1954), 33.

77. H. Dalton, *Call Back Yesterday* (1953), 294–5.

78. Middlemas and Barnes, *Baldwin,* 664.

79. Cross, *Snowden,* 319.

80. Branson and Heinemann, *Nineteen Thirties,* 55.

81. Mowat, *Britain Between the Wars,* 432.

82. J. Schumpeter, *Business Cycles* (New York, 1939), 917.

83. S. N. Broadberry, *The Productivity Race* (Cambridge, 1997), 211.
84. T. Willis, *Whatever Happened to Tom Mix?* (1970), 109 and 112.
85. Blythe, *Age of Illusion,* 186.
86. E. Wilkinson, *The Town that was Murdered: The Life Story of Jarrow* (1939), 191.
87. J. B. Priestley, *English Journey* (1934), 319 and 411.
88. J. Hanley, *Grey Children* (1937), vii.
89. W. Greenwood, *Love on the Dole* (1933), 227.
90. Hanley, *Grey Children,* 171.
91. W. Hannington, *The Lean Years* (1940), 54.
92. *Times,* 13 Feb. 1936.
93. R. M. Titmuss, *Poverty and Population* (1938), 308.
94. Lord Boyd Orr, *As I Recall* (1966), 117.
95. C. Booth, *Life and Labour of the People in London,* 2nd series I (1902), 172.
96. H. Massingham, *I Took off my Tie* (1936), 2–3.
97. Jones, *Diary with Letters,* 100.
98. CUL, BP, 9, f. 272.
99. W. Manchester, *The Caged Lion: Winston Spencer Churchill 1932–1940* (1988), 42.
100. N. and J. MacKenzie (eds.), *Diary of Beatrice Webb,* 279.
101. *Criterion* XI (1932), 467.
102. M. Stannard, *Evelyn Waugh* I (1986), 348.
103. H. G. Wells, *Experiment in Autobiography* II (1934), 750 and 781.
104. J. Strachey, *The Coming Struggle for Power* (1932), 245.
105. Skidelsky, *Mosley,* 284.
106. Brendon, *Churchill,* 124.
107. N. Mosley, *Rules of the Game* (1982), 159.
108. Mosley, *Life,* 168.
109. Mosley, *Rules of the Game,* 201 and 96.
110. J. Lees-Milne, *Another Self* (1970), 97.
111. Wells, *Autobiography* II, 782.
112. *Evening Standard,* 17 Apr. 1933.
113. Skidelsky, *Mosley,* 254.
114. Pimlott (ed.), *Diary of Dalton,* 193.
115. J. Charnley, *Blackshirts and Roses* (1990), 49.
116. P[ublic] R[ecord] O[ffice], M[osley] P[apers], HO 144/20140/166 and 169.
117. Wells, *Autobiography* II, 782.
118. *Times,* 23 Apr. 1934.
119. *Daily Mail,* 23 Apr. 1934.
120. PRO, MP, HO 144/20140/28, 59 and 116.
121. Mosley, *Rules of the Game,* 231.
122. *NYT,* 12 June 1934.
123. PRO, MP, HO 144/20140/28 and 276.
124. Citrine's protest to the Home Secretary in PRO, MP, HO 144/20141/58.
125. *News Chronicle,* 12 June 1934.
126. *Daily Telegraph,* 8 June 1934.
127. H. Daley, *This Small Cloud* (1986), 139.
128. PRO, MP, HO 144/20141/10.
129. C. Cross, *The Fascists in Britain* (1961), 123.

130. R. Thurlow, *Fascism in Britain: A History 1918–1985* (1987), 107.

131. *Fascist Week,* 9 Mar. 1934, 4 and 11 May 1934.

CHAPTER IX

1. G. M. Wilson, *Radical Nationalist in Japan: Kita Ikki 1887–1937* (Cambridge, Mass., 1969), 171.

2. H. Cortazzi and G. Webb (eds.), *Kipling's Japan* (1988), 70.

3. Chamberlin, *Japan over Asia,* 292.

4. *NYT,* 7 June 1931.

5. W. J. Macpherson, *The Economic Development of Japan c.1868–1941* (Basingstoke, 1987), 45.

6. W. H. Chamberlin, "Kansai: Land of Shrines and Smokestacks," *Contemporary Japan* (Sept. 1936), 181.

7. *Contemporary Japan* (Dec. 1932), 477–8.

8. IWM, Saionji, "Naval Disarmament Treaty Supplement," 105.

9. F. Utley, *Japan's Feet of Clay* (1936), 146.

10. Fukutake Tadashi, *Rural Society in Japan* (Tokyo, 1978), 5.

11. *North-China Herald,* 19 Jan. 1932.

12. E. B. Schumpeter (ed.), *The Industrialization of Japan and Manchukuo, 1930–1940* (New York, 1940), 145.

13. C. Browne, *Tojo: The Last Banzai* (1967), 37.

14. T. R. H. Havens, *Farm and Nation in Modern Japan* (Princeton, N.J., 1974), 114.

15. R. Hofstadter, *The American Political Tradition* (1971 edn.), 302.

16. Mishima Yukio, *Runaway Horses* (1973), 220.

17. Duus (ed.), *Cambridge History of Japan* VI, 628.

18. *Contemporary Japan* (Dec. 1932), 534.

19. S. S. Large, *Organized Workers and Socialist Politics in Interwar Japan* (Cambridge, 1981), 137.

20. *NYT,* 27 Aug. 1931.

21. W. W. Lockwood, *The Economic Development of Japan* (Princeton, N.J., 1954), 63.

22. J. W. Morley (ed.), *Japan Erupts: The London Naval Conference and the Manchurian Incident, 1928–1932* (New York, 1984), 29.

23. Senate Committee on Foreign Relations, *Hearings on Treaty on Limitation of Naval Armaments,* 26.

24. M. Montgomery, *Imperialist Japan* (1987), 294.

25. Morley (ed.), *Japan Erupts,* 83.

26. IWM, Saionji, "Naval Disarmament Treaty Supplement," 55.

27. IWM, Japanese War Trials, Box 144, Defence Document # 2502, 4.

28. IWM, Saionji, "Naval Disarmament Treaty Supplement," 249.

29. *NYT,* 27 Aug. 1931.

30. A. Wray and H. Conroy (eds.), *Japan Examined* (Honolulu, 1983), 311. For a discussion of the inadequacy of the term "fascism" to describe Japanese extremist movements, see P. Duus and D. I. Okimoto, "Fascism and the History of Pre-War Japan: The Failure of a Concept," *Journal of Asian Studies* 21 (1979), 72 and *passim.*

31. Sadako N. Ogata, *Defiance in Manchuria: The Making of Japanese Foreign Policy, 1931–1932* (Berkeley, 1964), 30.
32. IWM, Saionji, 104.
33. Ogata, *Defiance in Manchuria*, 30.
34. IWM, Japanese War Trials, Box 143, CC-8.
35. Maruyama Masao, *Thought and Behaviour in Modern Japanese Politics* (Oxford, 1969), 168.
36. D. Bergamini, *Japan's Imperial Conspiracy* (1971), 381.
37. M. R. Peattie, *Ishiwara Kanji and Japan's Confrontation with the West* (Princeton, N.J., 1975), 36.
38. *NYT,* 27 Sept. 1931.
39. Duus (ed.), *Cambridge History of Japan* VI, 292.
40. IWM, Japanese War Trials, Box 144, Defence Document # 2502, 4.
41. Wilson, *Kita Ikki,* 83.
42. Morley (ed.), *Japan Erupts,* 139–40.
43. Peattie, *Ishiwara,* 95.
44. Mikiso Hane, *Honjo Diary,* 8.
45. IWM, Saionji, 55.
46. Morley (ed.), *Japan Erupts,* 181 and 197.
47. IWM, Saionji, Pt. I, 40 and 42, and Pt. II, 75.
48. Storry, *Double Patriots,* 83.
49. IWM, Saionji, Pt. II, 66.
50. P. Fleming, *One's Company* (1934), 84.
51. *NYT,* 20 Dec. 1931.
52. IWM, Saionji, Pt. II, 76.
53. R. Craigie, *Behind the Japanese Mask* (1946), 27.
54. Murakami Hyoe, *Japan: The Years of Trial, 1919–52* (Tokyo, 1982), 31.
55. J. B. Crowley, *Japan's Quest for Autonomy* (Princeton, N.J., 1966), 115.
56. IWM, Saionji, Pt. II, 127.
57. Peattie, *Ishiwara,* 129.
58. IWM, Saionji, Pt. II, 176.
59. Ogata, *Defiance in Manchuria,* 100.
60. C. Thorne, *The Limits of Foreign Policy: The West, the League and the Far Eastern Crisis 1931–1933* (1972), 138.
61. F[oreign] R[elations of the] U[nited] S[tates]: Japan 1931–1941 I (Washington, 1943), 89.
62. *NYT,* 16 May 1932.
63. IWM, Saionji, Pt. II, 245.
64. Fukuda Ippei, "Korekujo Takahashi—Japan's Sage of Finance," *Contemporary Japan* (Mar. 1933), 617.
65. Nakamura Takafusa, *Economic Growth in Prewar Japan* (New Haven, Conn., 1971), 233.
66. Lockwood, *Economic Development of Japan,* 140.
67. *Contemporary Japan* (June 1934), 73.
68. IWM, Saionji, Pt. II, 485.
69. *Contemporary Japan* (Sept. 1935), 270.

70. D. K. Nanto and Takagi Shinji, "Korekiyo Takahashi and Japan's Recovery from the Great Depression," *American Economic Review* 75 (May 1985), 373.

71. Close, *Face of Japan*, 203.

72. *Contemporary Japan* (June 1934), 66.

73. IWM, Saionji, Pt. II, 137 and 789.

74. B. Shillony, *Revolt in Japan* (Princeton, N.J., 1973), 31.

75. Fukuda Ippei, "Araki—The Man of the Crisis," *Contemporary Japan* (Dec. 1932), 390.

76. J. B. Crowley, "Japanese Army Factionalism in the Early 1930's," *Journal of Asian Studies* 21 (1962), 315.

77. A. D. Coox, *Nomonhan* I (Stanford, Cal., 1985), 60.

78. IWM, Saionji, Pt. II, 1533.

79. K. Singer, *Mirror, Sword and Jewel* (1973), 35.

80. E. Snow, *Far Eastern Front* (1934), 81.

81. *The Diary of Marquis Kido, 1931–1945* (Frederick, Md., 1984), 26.

82. M. B. Miller, *Shanghai on the Métro* (1994), 250.

83. H. Sergeant, *Shanghai* (1991), 146.

84. *North-China Herald*, 20 Oct. 1931 and 19 Jan 1932.

85. IWM, Saionji, Pt. II, 232.

86. *North-China Herald*, 2 Feb. 1932.

87. Snow, *Far Eastern Front*, 206.

88. Thorne, *Limits of Foreign Policy*, 233 and 262.

89. *FRUS I*, 199.

90. Snow, *Far Eastern Front*, 223.

91. IWM, Japanese War Trials, Box 142, HH-20.

92. E. Behr, *The Last Emperor* (1989), 204.

93. Snow, *Far Eastern Front*, 229.

94. Thorne, *Limits of Foreign Policy*, 204.

95. Snow, *Far Eastern Front*, 234.

96. Mosley, *Hirohito*, 111.

97. P. Williams and D. Wallace, *Unit 731* (1989), 32.

98. A. Vespa, *Secret Agent of Japan* (1938), 29 and 53.

99. R. Benedict, *The Chrysanthemum and the Sword* (1967 edn.), 151 and 224.

100. Snow, *Far Eastern Front*, 236.

101. IWM, Saionji, Pt. II, 469, 258–9 and 277.

102. J. W. Dower, *Empire and Aftermath: Yoshida Shigeru and the Japanese Experience, 1878–1954* (Cambridge, Mass., 1979), 100.

103. F. C. Jones, *Manchuria Since 1931* (1949), 22.

104. M. D. Kennedy, "The Reactionary Movement of 1932," *Contemporary Japan* (Mar. 1933), 625.

105. IWM, Saionji, Pt. II, 261.

106. *NYT,* 16 May 1932.

107. H. Byas, *Government by Assassination* (1943), 25.

108. Murakami, *Japan: Years of Trial*, 47.

109. IWM, Japanese War Trials, Box 144, Defence Document # 2502, 36.

110. *Contemporary Japan* (Dec. 1932), 389.

111. Murakami, *Japan: Years of Trial,* 48.
112. *Contemporary Japan* (June 1934), 16.
113. *Contemporary Japan* (Sept. 1933), 254.
114. Craigie, *Japanese Mask,* 30.
115. J. C. Grew, *Ten Years in Japan* (1944), 44.
116. IWM, Saionji, Pt. II, 503 and 495.
117. *Japan Weekly Chronicle,* 16 Mar. 1933.
118. IWM, Saionji, Pt. II, 520.
119. *NYT,* 19 Feb. 1933.
120. IWM, Japanese War Trials, Box 144, Defence Document # 2502, 24.
121. W. Fleisher, *Volcanic Isle* (1942), 40.
122. Dower, *Yoshida,* 103.
123. A. J. Toynbee (ed.), *Survey of International Affairs 1933* (1934), 496.
124. G. Slocombe, *A Mirror to Geneva* (1937), 291.
125. B. Nichols, *Cry Havoc* (1933), 126.
126. Thorne, *Limits of Foreign Policy,* 361.
127. I. Nish, "An Aspect of Tradition and Modernity: Matsuoka and Japanese Diplomacy at Geneva, 1932–33" in P. G. O'Neill (ed.), *Tradition and Modern Japan* (Tenterden, Kent, 1981), 122
128. N. Hillson, *Geneva Scene* (1936), 47.
129. *Times,* 25 Feb. 1933.
130. *League of Nations Official Journal Special Supplement* 112 (Geneva, 1933), 17.
131. *NYT,* 25 Feb. 1933.
132. I. Nish, *Japan's Struggle with Internationalism: Japan, China and the League of Nations 1931–3* (1993), 216.
133. Hillson, *Geneva Scene,* 69.
134. G. Scott, *The Rise and Fall of the League of Nations* (1973), 240.
135. Thorne, *Limits of Foreign Policy,* 336.
136. IWM, Saionji, Pt. II, 707.
137. Wilson, *Kita Ikki,* 81.
138. IWM, Saionji, Pt. II, 547.
139. Peattie, *Ishiwara,* 192.

CHAPTER X

1. A. Amba, *I Was Stalin's Bodyguard* (1952), 69.
2. D. Volkogonov, *Stalin: Triumph and Tragedy* (1991), 198 and 281.
3. J. Fishman and J. B. Hutton, *The Private Life of Josif Stalin* (1962), 72.
4. De Jonge, *Stalin,* 243.
5. E. Lyons, *Assignment in Utopia* (1938), 98.
6. Muggeridge, *Green Stick,* 218.
7. P. Scheffer, "Stalin's Power," *Foreign Affairs* (July 1930), 559.
8. Amba, *Stalin's Bodyguard,* 84.
9. P. Levi, *Boris Pasternak* (1990), 165.
10. O. Mandelstam, *Selected Poems,* translated by C. Brown and W. S. Merwin (Harmondsworth, 1977), 98.

11. D. Rayfield, "Stalin, Beria and the Poets"—inaugural professorial lecture at Queen Mary College, London, 1992.

12. *NYT,* 18 Jan. 1931.

13. Wells, *Autobiography* II, 806.

14. Lyons, *Utopia,* 390.

15. De Jonge, *Stalin,* 324.

16. Amba, *Stalin's Bodyguard,* 152.

17. N. Mandelstam, *Hope Abandoned* (1974), 205–6.

18. J. E. Bowlt, "Russian Sculpture and Lenin's Plan of Monumental Propaganda" in Millon and Nochlin (eds.), *Art and Architecture,* 185.

19. N. Tumarkin, *Lenin Lives!* (1983), 205.

20. I. Zbarsky and S. Hutchinson, *Lenin's Embalmers* (1997), 78.

21. E. E. Cummings, *Eimi* (1933), 243–4. E. Wilson, *Travels in Two Democracies* (New York, 1936), 322.

22. F. Maclean, *Eastern Approaches* (1974 edn.), 28.

23. R. C. Tucker, "The Rise of Stalin's Personality Cult," *American Historical Review* 84 (1979), 349.

24. *NYT,* 22 Dec. 1929.

25. R. W. Davies, *The Industrialisation of Soviet Russia* 3: *The Soviet Economy in Turmoil, 1929–1930* (1989), 139.

26. S. F. Cohen, *Rethinking the Soviet Experience* (New York, 1985), 101.

27. *NYT,* 14 June 1931.

28. *NYT,* 13 Oct. 1929.

29. N. Mandelstam, *Hope Against Hope* (1975 edn.), 243.

30. M. Lewin, *Russian Peasants and Power* (1968), 476.

31. G. G. Grigorenko, *Memoirs* (1983), 36.

32. B. Souvarine, *Stalin* (1939), 424.

33. Lewin, *Russian Peasants,* 477.

34. S. G. Wheatcroft, "More light on the scale of repression and excess mortality in the Soviet Union in the 1930s" in J. Arch Getty and R. T. Manning (eds.), *Stalinist Terror: New Perspectives* (Cambridge, 1993), 277. The historical debate about the number of Stalin's victims has been revived by evidence emerging piecemeal from Russian archives in the wake of *glasnost.* Many scholars now tend to accept lower estimates than those of, say, Robert Conquest. But the debate continues and the true figures will never be known. See E. Bacon, *The Gulag at War* (1994), 6–22 and *passim.*

35. Solzhenitsyn, *Gulag Archipelago,* 26.

36. V. Serge, *Memoirs of a Revolutionary* (1963), 247.

37. Solzhenitsyn, *Gulag Archipelago,* 197.

38. M. Hindus, *Red Bread* (1931), 101.

39. I. Deutscher, *Stalin* (1968 edn.), 325.

40. M. Fainsod, *Smolensk Under Soviet Rule* (1959), 248.

41. Figes, *Tragedy,* 521.

42. L. Kopelev, *The Education of a True Believer* (1981), 235.

43. Figes, *Tragedy,* 641.

44. Fainsod, *Smolensk,* 241.

45. A. Sisman, *A. J. P. Taylor: A Biography* (1993), 102. See also P. Hollander, *Political Pilgrims* (Oxford, 1981), 161 and *passim*.

46. E. Lyons, *Modern Moscow* (1935), 100.

47. E. H. Carr, *A History of Soviet Russia: Socialism in One Country* I (1958), 122.

48. Lewin, *Russian Peasants*, 29.

49. D. Rayfield (ed.), *The Confessions of Victor X* (Dover, N.H., 1984), 64.

50. Fainsod, *Smolensk*, 213.

51. R. W. Davies, *The Industrialisation of Soviet Russia* I: *The Socialist Offensive* (1980), 220 and 228.

52. T. J. Colton, *Moscow: Governing the Socialist Metropolis* (1995), 262.

53. Volkogonov, *Stalin*, 234.

54. Lyons, *Moscow*, 233.

55. B. Pasternak, *People and Propositions,* edited by C. Barnes (Edinburgh, 1990), 73.

56. L. T. Lih, O. V. Naumov and O. V. Khlevniuk (eds.), *Stalin's Letters to Molotov 1925–1936* (1995), 162.

57. Deutscher, *Stalin,* 123.

58. W. A. Rukeyser, *Working for the Soviets* (1932), 98.

59. L. Fischer, *The Life and Death of Stalin* (New York, 1952), 136.

60. There were almost two roubles to the dollar at the official exchange rate, but in terms of purchasing power in the open market the rouble was worth about two cents.

61. N. Shimotomai, *Moscow Under Stalinist Rule, 1931–34* (1991), 169.

62. E. K. Poretsky, *Our Own People* (1969), 102.

63. M. Heller and A. Nekrich, *Utopia and Power* (1986), 226.

64. R. O. G. Urch, *The Rabbit King of Russia* (1939), 120 and 195.

65. Lyons, *Utopia*, 413.

66. Swanberg, *Luce,* 100.

67. S. F. Starr, "Visionary Town Planning during the Cultural Revolution" in S. Fitzpatrick (ed.), *Cultural Revolution in Russia 1928–1931* (1978), 218.

68. V. Kravchenko, *I Chose Freedom* (1947), 31.

69. Lyons, *Moscow,* 262.

70. *DBFP*, 2nd series, VII, 168.

71. E. H. Carr, *The Twilight of the Comintern, 1930–1935* (1982), 18.

72. J. Degras (ed.), *Soviet Documents on Foreign Policy* II (Oxford, 1952), 465.

73. J. Haslam, *Soviet Foreign Policy, 1930–33: The Impact of the Depression* (1983), 2.

74. Davies, *Soviet Economy in Turmoil,* 471.

75. Lih *et al.* (eds.), *Stalin's Letters,* 200.

76. *DBFP,* 2nd series, VII, 186.

77. Davies, *Soviet Economy in Turmoil,* 96.

78. *DBFP,* 2nd series, VII, 136–7.

79. S. N. Harper, *The Russia I Believe in* (Chicago, 1945), 185.

80. M. Lewin, *The Making of the Soviet System* (1985), 248.

81. I. Ehrenburg, *Men, Years—Life III Truce: 1921–33* (1963), 222.

82. Rukeyser, *Working for Soviets,* 200.

83. Lewin, *Making of Soviet System,* 252.

84. T. Scott, *Behind the Urals* (1942), 9

85. A. C. Sutton, *Western Technology and Soviet Economic Development 1930 to 1945* (Stanford, Cal., 1971), 62–3.

86. Scott, *Behind the Urals,* 46.

87. Sutton, *Western Technology,* 76.

88. S. Kotkin, *Magnetic Mountain: Stalinism as Civilization* (Berkeley, Cal., 1995), 86.

89. H. Kuromiya, *Stalin's Industrial Revolution* (Cambridge, 1988), 315.

90. P. Short, *Mao* (1999), 505.

91. Grigorenko, *Memoirs,* 42.

92. Lyons, *Moscow,* 194.

93. R. Conquest, *The Harvest of Sorrow* (1986), 3.

94. S. O. Pidhainy (ed.), *The Black Deeds of the Kremlin* I (Toronto, 1953), 294.

95. D. G. Dalrymple, "The Soviet Famine of 1932–1934," *Soviet Studies* 15 (1964), 262.

96. R. Crossman (ed.), *The God that Failed* (1950), 68.

97. A. Orlov, *The Secret History of Stalin's Crimes* (1954), 53.

98. Pidhainy (ed.), *Black Deeds of Kremlin,* 281.

99. H. Kostiuk, *Stalinist Rule in the Ukraine* (1960), 15.

100. Pidhainy (ed.), *Black Deeds of Kremlin,* 235.

101. Orlov, *Secret History,* 318.

102. R. Medvedev, *Let History Judge* (1972 edn.), 94.

103. E. Ammende, *Human Life in Russia* (1936), 60.

104. Kravchenko, *Freedom,* 129.

105. H. H. Fisher, *The Famine in Soviet Russia 1919–1923* (New York, 1927), 62.

106. Conquest, *Harvest of Sorrow,* 151.

107. Lyons, *Moscow,* 269.

108. S. Zweig, *The World of Yesterday* (1943), 255.

109. A. Koestler, *Arrow in the Blue* (1969 edn.), 327.

110. Deutscher, *Stalin,* 341.

111. Heller and Nekrich, *Utopia and Power,* 230.

112. H. R. Mussey, "Russia's New Religion," *Nation* 134 (4 May 1932), 512.

113. Muggeridge, *Green Stick,* 210.

114. A. Koestler, *The Invisible Writing* (1969), 62, 65 and 188.

115. CAC, STRN 4/5, Sir Reader Bullard to W. Strang, 3 Oct. 1932.

116. Muggeridge, *Green Stick,* 243–4.

117. Ammende, *Life in Russia,* 218.

118. H. Thompson, *Tintin: Hergé and his Creation* (1991), 32.

119. Muggeridge, *Green Stick,* 223.

120. *NYT,* 31 Mar. 1933.

121. F. E. Beal, *Word From Nowhere* (1938), 131 and 253. Beal's vehemence doubtless owed something to American clemency.

122. Pasternak, *Zhivago,* 495.

123. Quoted from the *New Statesman* by A. Monkhouse, *Moscow, 1911–1933* (1933), 344.

124. K. Bourne and D. C. Watt (eds.),] B[ritish] D[ocuments on] F[oreign] A[ffairs Part] II, Series A, 14 (USA, 1986–), 133.

125. L. Kolakowski, *Main Currents of Marxism* III: *The Breakdown* (Oxford, 1977), 477.
126. Medvedev, *Let History Judge,* 226.
127. M. G. Smith, *Language and Power in the Creation of the USSR, 1917–1953* (New York, 1998), 146.
128. W. H. Chamberlin, *Russia's Iron Age* (1935), 296.
129. G. Orwell, *Inside the Whale* (Harmondsworth, 1966), 164.
130. B. I. Nicolaevsky, *Power and the Soviet Elite* (1966), 29.
131. A. Ulam, *Stalin: The Man and His Era* (1974 edn.), 374.
132. Amba, *Stalin's Bodyguard,* 216.
133. D. Rayfield, "Stalin the Poet" in *P & N Review* 41 (1984), 45.
134. Volkogonov, *Stalin,* 129.
135. A. Kemp-Welch, *Stalin and the Literary Intelligentsia, 1928–39* (1991), 131.
136. M. Eastman, *Artists in Uniform* (1934), 6.
137. E. Pasternak, *Boris Pasternak: The Tragic Years 1930–1960* (1990), 5.
138. J. Berger, *Shipwreck of a Generation* (1971), 44.
139. A. Gide, *Back from the USSR* (1937), 78.
140. Chamberlin, *Iron Age,* 108.
141. Ammende, *Human Life in Russia,* 216.
142. S. F. Cohen, *Bukharin and the Bolshevik Revolution* (1974), 345.
143. R. Conquest, *Stalin and the Kirov Murder* (1989), 27.
144. A. Antonov-Ovseyenko, *The Time of Stalin* (New York, 1981), 86.
145. D. Shostakovich, *Testimony* (1979), 276.
146. A. Barmine, *One Who Survived* (1945), 247–8.

CHAPTER XI

1. P. G. Filene, *Americans and the Soviet Experiment, 1917–1933* (Cambridge, Mass., 1967), 259.
2. T. A. Bailey, *America Faces Russia* (Ithaca, N.Y., 1950), 264–5.
3. Wilson, *Shores of Light,* 531.
4. R. Long, *An Editor Looks at Russia* (New York, 1931), ix.
5. R. Tugwell, "The Principle of Planning and the Institution of Laissez-Faire," *American Economic Review* 22, Supplement (Mar. 1932), 75 and 92.
6. R. G. Tugwell, *The Brain Trust* (New York, 1968), 139.
7. W. E. Leuchtenburg, *The New Deal* (New York, 1968), 25.
8. Martin, *Perkins,* 23 and 34.
9. R. W. Steele, *Propaganda in an Open Society: The Roosevelt Administration and the Media* (Westport, Conn., 1985), 22.
10. *PPR* II, 65.
11. D. MacArthur, *Reminiscences* (New York, 1964), 101.
12. M. and H. Josephson, *Smith,* 444.
13. S. D. Cashman, *America in the Twenties and Thirties* (New York, 1989), 160.
14. Morgan, *FDR,* 382.
15. P. Bonnifield, *The Dust Bowl* (Albuquerque, N.M., 1979), 70.
16. Feis, *1933,* 105.

17. E. L. and F. H. Schapsmeier, *Henry A. Wallace of Iowa* I (Ames, Iowa, 1968), 188–9.

18. J. B. Martin, *Adlai Stevenson of Illinois* (New York, 1976), 104.

19. E. L. and F. H. Schapsmeier, *Wallace*, 177.

20. R. E. Sherwood, *Roosevelt and Hopkins* (New York, 1950), 2 and 33.

21. S. F. Charles, *Minister of Relief: Harry Hopkins and the Depression* (Westport, Conn., 1963), 24.

22. J. F. Carter, *The New Dealers* (New York, 1934), 191.

23. D. W. Brogan, *Roosevelt and the New Deal* (1952), 167.

24. E. F. Goldman, *Rendezvous with Destiny* (New York, 1952), 263.

25. R. Talbert, *FDR's Utopian: Arthur Morgan of the TVA* (Jackson, Miss., 1987), 74.

26. P. J. Hubbard, *Origins of the TVA* (Nashville, Tenn., 1961), 77.

27. P. Cutler, *The Public Landscape of the New Deal* (New Haven, Conn., 1985), 133.

28. *NYT,* 25 June 1933.

29. *PPR* II, 123.

30. J. Mitchell, "Utopia—Tennessee Valley Style," *New Republic* (18 Oct. 1933), 272.

31. Talbert, *Morgan,* 114.

32. T. K. McCraw, *Morgan vs. Lilienthal: The Feud within the TVA* (Chicago, Ill., 1970), 33–4.

33. J. Huxley, *TVA: Adventure in Planning* (1943), 76.

34. M. J. McDonald and J. Muldowny, *TVA and the Dispossessed* (Knoxville, Tenn., 1982), 224.

35. McCraw, *Morgan vs. Lilienthal,* 36.

36. R. Biles, *Memphis in the Great Depression* (Knoxville, Tenn., 1986), 80.

37. J. F. Bauman and T. H. Coode (eds.), *In the Eye of the Great Depression* (De Kalb, Ill., 1988), 173.

38. D. R. Richberg, *The Rainbow* (New York, 1936), 288.

39. Schlesinger, *Age of Roosevelt* II, 100.

40. Ohl, *Johnson and New Deal,* 14 and 101–2.

41. F. Perkins, *The Roosevelt I Knew* (1948), 162.

42. *The Secret Diary of Harold Ickes* I (1955), 52.

43. Perkins, *Roosevelt,* 164.

44. Ohl, *Johnson and New Deal,* 146.

45. H. S. Johnson, *The Blue Eagle from Egg to Earth* (New York, 1935), 206.

46. S. Fine, *The Automobile Under the Blue Eagle* (Ann Arbor, Mich., 1963), 78 and 37.

47. Ohl, *Johnson and New Deal,* 218 and 149.

48. *NYT,* 20 Aug. 1933.

49. Ohl, *Johnson and New Deal,* 140.

50. R. Moley, *The First New Deal* (New York, 1966), 354.

51. *NYT,* 11 Aug. 1933.

52. T. E. Vadney, *The Wayward Liberal: The Political Biography of Donald Richberg* (Lexington, Ky., 1970), 3 and 143.

53. Schlesinger, *Age of Roosevelt* II, 157.

54. *NYT,* 20 July 1933.

55. Brogan, *Roosevelt and New Deal,* 48.

56. P. Brendon, *The Life and Death of the Press Barons* (1982), 146.

57. G. White and J. Maze, *Harold Ickes of the New Deal* (Cambridge, Mass., 1985), 4 and 137.

58. CUL, Cordell Hull MS 3591, Reel 9, C. P. McKinney to Hull, 1 Mar. 1933.

59. Phillips, *Crash to the Blitz,* 108.

60. *NYT,* 18 June 1933.

61. Schlesinger, *Age of Roosevelt* II, 121.

62. Wells, *Autobiography* II, 793–4.

63. J. Alsop, *"I've Seen the Best of It"* (New York, 1992), 136.

64. J. P. Lash, *Eleanor and Franklin* (New York, 1971), 424.

65. J. B. White, *Upstairs at the White House* (1974), 15.

66. CUL, Cordell Hull MS 3592, Reel 10, J. H. Paul to Hull, 23 Oct. 1933.

67. *Secret Diary of Ickes* I, 104.

68. J. A. Garraty, "The New Deal, National Socialism and the Great Depression," *American Historical Review* 78 (1973), 911.

69. M. Heald and L. S. Kaplin, *Culture and Diplomacy* (Westport, Conn., 1977), 183.

70. *NYT,* 25 Nov. 1933.

71. B. Sternsher, *Rexford Tugwell and the New Deal* (New Brunswick, N.J., 1964), 348 and 366.

72. R. G. Powers, *Secrecy and Power: The Life of J. Edgar Hoover* (1987), 185.

73. *NYT,* 21 May 1933.

74. Mosley, *Greater Britain,* 1.

75. Wells, *Autobiography* II, 796.

76. Schlesinger, *Age of Roosevelt* III, 526.

77. Perkins, *Roosevelt I Knew,* 267.

78. M. R. Beschloss, *Kennedy and Roosevelt* (New York, 1984), 85.

79. Bauman and Coode, *Great Depression,* 83 and 101.

80. W. J. Cash, *The Mind of the South* (1971 edn.), 362.

81. Washington *Evening Star,* 15 Apr. 1935.

82. C. A. Henderson, "Letters from the Dust Bowl," *Atlantic Monthly* 157 (May 1936), 551.

83. Bonnifield, *Dust Bowl,* 2.

84. D. Worster, *Dust Bowl* (Oxford, 1979), 17.

85. J. Steinbeck, *The Grapes of Wrath* (Harmondsworth, 1963), 214 and 211.

86. W. J. Stein, *California and the Dust Bowl Migration* (Westport, Conn., 1973), 48.

87. Worster, *Dust Bowl,* 99.

88. CUL, Cordell Hull MS 3591, Reel 9, Hull to W. Phillips, 11 July 1933.

89. W. E. Leuchtenburg, *Franklin D. Roosevelt and the New Deal* (New York, 1963), 201.

90. A. Allfrey, *Man of Arms: The Life and Legend of Sir Basil Zaharoff* (1989), xvii.

91. R. Dallek, *Franklin D. Roosevelt and American Foreign Policy 1932–1945* (New York, 1979), 95.

92. Cashman, *America in Twenties and Thirties,* 200.

93. N. Halasz, *Roosevelt through Foreign Eyes* (New York, 1961), 78.

94. Schlesinger, *Age of Roosevelt* III, 657.

CHAPTER XII

1. G. Weinberg, "Hitler's Image of the United States," *American Historical Review* 69, No. 4 (1964), 1010. For a discussion of Hitler's ultimate objectives see I. Kershaw, *The Nazi Dictatorship* (1993 edn.), 125 ff.
2. James, *German Slump*, 381.
3. D. Irving, *Göring* (1989), 114.
4. H. Mommsen, *The Rise and Fall of Weimar Democracy* (1996), 535.
5. D. Reed, *The Burning of the Reichstag* (1934), 17.
6. F. Tobias, *The Reichstag Fire* (1962), 74.
7. F. von Papen, *Memoirs* (1953), 268.
8. Delmer, *Trail Sinister*, 188–9.
9. R. Diels, *Lucifer ante Portas* (Stuttgart, 1950), 194.
10. H. Mommsen, "The Reichstag Fire and Its Political Consequences" in H. Holborn (ed.), *Republic to Reich: The Making of the Nazi Revolution* (New York, 1972), 173.
11. Quoted in *NYT,* 2 Mar. 1933.
12. Reed, *Burning of Reichstag,* 18.
13. C. Isherwood, *Mr. Norris Changes Trains* (1987 edn.), 223.
14. G. J. Giles, *Students and National Socialism in Germany* (Princeton, N.J., 1985), 131.
15. *NYT,* 6 and 11 May 1933.
16. R. Grunberger, *A Social History of the Third Reich* (1971), 307.
17. *NYT,* 10 May 1933.
18. N. Hamilton, *The Brothers Mann* (1978), 271.
19. F. V. Grunfeld, *The Hitler File* (1974), 172.
20. Friedrich, *Before the Deluge,* 385. Freud joked that the Nazis had advanced from medieval times, when the authors would have been burned.
21. Baynes (ed.), *Speeches of Hitler* I, 568.
22. W. Laqueur, *Russia and Germany* (1965), 169.
23. Rauschning, *Hitler Speaks,* 134.
24. Giles, *Students and National Socialism,* 254.
25. Bracher, *German Dictatorship,* 267, 261 and 268.
26. *Spectator,* 18 Dec. 1936.
27. Hitler, *Mein Kampf,* 507.
28. J. C. Fest, *The Face of the Third Reich* (1970), 188.
29. J. Noakes and G. Pridham (eds.), *Documents on Nazism, 1919–1945* (1974), 347.
30. A. Richie, *Faust's Metropolis* (1998), 311.
31. O. Kokoschka (ed.), *Oskar Kokoschka Letters 1905–1976* (1992), 155.
32. Grunberger, *Social History of Third Reich,* 416.
33. Rauschning, *Hitler Speaks,* 95.
34. K. Usborne, *"Elizabeth"* (1986), 39.
35. W. Maser, *Hitler* (1973), 67. The Congress Hall in the Palace of the Soviets was designed to contain 21,000 seats and the whole edifice was to be topped by a statue of Lenin so vast that "one could play badminton in its boots." (V. Cunningham, *British Writers of the Thirties* [Oxford, 1988], 179.)
36. O. Dietrich, *The Hitler I Knew* (1957), 146.
37. Carr, *Hitler,* 51.

38. Speer, *Inside Third Reich,* 46 and 53.

39. Rauschning, *Hitler Speaks,* 268.

40. Fest, *Hitler,* 541.

41. Hans Mommsen's controversial phrase is quoted by R. J. Evans, *Rethinking German History* (1987), 68.

42. T. W. Mason, "The Primacy of Politics—Politics and Economics in National Socialist Germany" in S. J. Woolf (ed.), *The Nature of Fascism* (1968), 173.

43. Brendon, *Churchill,* 148.

44. *Ribbentrop Memoirs,* 29 and 31.

45. Fest, *Face of Third Reich,* 75.

46. N. Mühlen, *Schacht: Hitler's Magician* (New York, 1939), iv.

47. H. Schacht, *My First Seventy-Six Years* (1955), 310.

48. François-Poncet, *Fateful Years,* 221.

49. *NYT,* 26 May 1937.

50. A. M. Cienciala, *Poland and the Western Powers, 1938–1939* (1968), 16.

51. Simpson, *Schacht,* 86.

52. W. Carr, *Arms, Autarky and Aggression* (1972), 39.

53. CAC, LKEN 1/20, 12 Sept. 1936.

54. R. Klein, *Cigarettes are Sublime* (1995 edn.), 12.

55. Grunberger, *Social History of Third Reich,* 332.

56. W. Deist *et al.*, *Germany and the Second World War* I (Oxford, 1990), 132.

57. M. Gallo, *The Night of Long Knives* (1973), 77.

58. Rauschning, *Hitler Speaks,* 155. Convincing though he seems, Rauschning is increasingly regarded as an unreliable source.

59. Lüdecke, *I Knew Hitler,* 597 and 649.

60. R. Macgregor-Hastie, *The Day of the Lion* (1965), 210.

61. H. Baur, *Hitler's Pilot* (1958), 60.

62. *D[ocuments on] G[erman] F[oreign] P[olicy 1918–1945]*, Series C, IV (1962), 109.

63. Gallo, *Night of Long Knives,* 106.

64. Baur, *Hitler's Pilot,* 64.

65. H. Höhne, *The Order of the Death's Head* (1969), 113.

66. Dietrich, *Hitler I Knew,* 29

67. H. G. Gisevius, *To the Bitter End* (1948), 159 and 167.

68. D. Irving, *Goebbels* (1996), 190.

69. Baynes, *Speeches of Hitler* I, 322.

70. Höhne, *Order of Death's Head,* 133.

71. R. J. Evans, *Rituals of Retribution* (Oxford, 1996), 649.

72. H. L. Leonhardt, *Nazi Conquest of Danzig* (Chicago, Ill., 1942), 103.

73. Kershaw, *Hitler Myth,* 86.

74. A. J. Toynbee (ed.), *Survey of International Affairs 1934* (1935), 325.

75. Prince Starhemberg, *Between Hitler and Mussolini* (1942), 170.

76. J. W. Wheeler-Bennett, *The Nemesis of Power* (1964), 325.

77. Fest, *Hitler,* 470. This telegram sounds suspiciously like an invention by Hitler. Cf. G. Reitlinger, *The SS: Alibi for a Nation* (1956), 69.

78. H. Krausnick *et al.* (eds.), *Anatomy of the SS State* (1968), 130.

79. R. Coe, *The Vision of Jean Genet* (1968), 115 and 132.

80. P. Loewenberg, "The Unsuccessful Adolescence of Heinrich Himmler," *American Historical Review* 76 (1971), 614.

81. *Hitler's Table-Talk*, 167.

82. *I[nternational] M[ilitary] T[rials] N[urnberg: Nazi Conspiracy and Aggression]* II (Washington, 1946), 187 and 201.

83. E. Kogon, *The Theory and Practice of Hell* (1950), 35.

84. Reitlinger, *The SS*, 464.

85. *NYT*, 27 July 1933.

86. T. Hoess, *Commandant of Auschwitz* (1959), 80 and 236.

87. *IMTN* I (Washington, 1946), 961.

88. P. Wallner, *By Order of the Gestapo* (1941), 91.

89. G. R. Key (ed.), *Dachau* (1939), 43 and 136.

90. P. Berben, *Dachau* (1975), 29 and 108.

91. Krausnick *et al.* (eds.), *Anatomy of SS State*, 435–6.

92. Key (ed.), *Dachau*, 33.

93. *NYT*, 5 and 23 Apr. and 26 July 1933.

94. A. Gill, *The Journey Back from Hell* (1988), 248.

95. *NYT*, 10 Oct. 1933 and 20 Sept. 1936.

96. O. Woods and J. Bishop, *The Story of The Times* (1983), 295.

97. Key (ed.), *Dachau*, 41.

98. Rauschning, *Hitler Speaks*, 275.

99. Evans, *Rituals*, 679.

100. D. J. Diephouse, "The Triumph of Hitler's Will" in J. Held (ed.), *The Cult of Power* (New York, 1983), 51.

101. W. L. Shirer, *Berlin Diary* (1970 edn.), 22–3.

102. S. Roberts, *The House that Hitler Built* (1937), 140.

103. H. T. Burden, *The Nuremberg Party Rallies: 1923–39* (1967), 81.

104. Speer, *Inside Third Reich*, 59.

105. Burden, *Nuremberg Rallies*, 86.

106. D. Welch, *Propaganda and the German Cinema* (Oxford, 1983), 147.

107. Diephouse in Held (ed.), *Cult of Power*, 61.

108. CAC, LKEN 1/20, 20 May 1936.

109. T. Abel, *Why Hitler Came to Power* (New York, 1938), 244.

110. Noakes and Pridham (eds.), *Documents on Nazism*, 463.

111. *Sunday Express*, 17 Nov. 1935.

112. Turner, *Hitler*, 196.

113. D. C. Watt, "The Anglo-German Naval Agreement: An Interim Judgement," *Journal of Modern History* 28 (1956), 174.

114. Brendon, *Churchill*, 92.

115. Muggeridge (ed.), *Ciano's Diary 1937–1938*, 8.

116. *DGFP*, Series C, IV, 688 and F. D. Laurens, *France and the Ethiopian Crisis, 1935–1936* (The Hague, 1967), 23–30.

117. E. Cerruti, *Ambassador's Wife* (1952), 150 and 124.

118. E. Wiskemann, *The Rome–Berlin Axis* (1966 edn.), 67.

CHAPTER XIII

1. G. W. Baer, *The Coming of the Italian-Ethiopian War* (Cambridge, Mass., 1967), 4.
2. E. M. Robertson, *Mussolini as Empire-Builder* (1977), 7.
3. D. Mack Smith, *Mussolini's Roman Empire,* 68.
4. A. Del Boca, *The Ethiopian War 1935–1941* (Chicago, 1969), 7.
5. The name Abyssinia stems from an Arab word implying mixture of races. The name Ethiopia, "Land of the Dark-faced men," was adopted by the Emperor Menelik to give cohesion to his state.
6. E. Santarelli, "The Economic and Political Background of Fascist Imperialism" in R. Sarti (ed.), *The Ax Within: Italian Fascism in Action* (New York, 1974), 166.
7. Baer, *Italian-Ethiopian War,* 30.
8. L. Farago, *Abyssinia on the Eve* (1935), 153.
9. Del Boca, *Ethiopian War,* 5.
10. Baer, *Italian-Ethiopian War,* 29.
11. J. H. Spencer, *Ethiopia at Bay* (Algonac, Mich., 1984), 23.
12. G. Steer, *Caesar in Abyssinia* (1936), 202.
13. T. M. Coffey, *Lion by the Tail* (1974), 13.
14. Brendon, *Queen,* 112.
15. H. G. Marcus, *Haile Selassie I: The Formative Years 1892–1936* (Berkeley, Cal., 1987), 64.
16. E. Waugh, *When the Going Was Good* (Harmondsworth, 1959), 87.
17. W. Thesiger, *A Life of My Choice* (1988 edn.), 43.
18. K. Nelson and A. Sillivan (eds.), *John Melly of Ethiopia* (1937), 114.
19. *Spectator,* 19 July 1935.
20. Spencer, *Ethiopia at Bay,* 64.
21. H. de Monfreid, *Vers Les Terres Hostiles de l'Ethiopie* (Paris, n.d.), 229–30.
22. Asfa Yilma, *Haile Selassie Emperor of Ethiopia* (1936), 234.
23. Farago, *Abyssinia on the Eve,* 106.
24. N. Cunard (ed.), *Negro* (1970 edn.), 387 and 283.
25. *The Autobiography of Emperor Haile Selassie I: My Life and Ethiopian Progress 1892–1937* (Oxford, 1976), 208.
26. E. Virgin, *The Abyssinia I Knew* (1936), 83.
27. G. Rochat, *Militari e Politici Nella Preparazione della Campagna D'Etiopia* (Milan, 1971), 377.
28. Earl of Avon, *The Eden Memoirs: Facing the Dictators* (1962), 193. Other foreign ministers of the 1930s were equally ill-informed: Lord Halifax could not distinguish Somalia from the Sudan.
29. P. Reynaud, *La France a sauvé L'Europe* I (Paris, 1947), 157.
30. E. de Bono, *Anno XIII: The Conquest of an Empire* (1937), 118.
31. *DBFP,* 2nd series, XIV, 149.
32. Muggeridge (ed.), *Ciano's Diary 1937–1938,* 206.
33. L. S. Amery, *My Political Life* III (1955), 166.
34. *DBFP,* 2nd series, XIV, 280–1.
35. Robertson, *Mussolini as Empire-Builder,* 160.
36. Avon, *Facing the Dictators,* 225.

37. V. Mussolini, *Vita con mio padre* (Rome, 1957), 62.
38. Slocombe, *Mirror to Geneva,* 308.
39. G. Salvemini, *Prelude to World War II* (1953), 237.
40. *Times,* 1 Aug. 1935.
41. J. Pearson, *Citadel of the Heart* (1991), 243.
42. W. Churchill, *The Second World War I: The Gathering Storm* (1948), 129.
43. R. A. C. Parker, "Great Britain, France and the Ethiopian Crisis 1935–1936," *English Historical Review* 89 (1974), 310.
44. G. Stolper, "European Kaleidoscope," *Foreign Affairs* 14 (Jan. 1936), 216.
45. *NYT,* 3 Oct. 1935.
46. A. Mockler, *Haile Selassie's War* (Oxford, 1984), 54.
47. L. Farago (ed.), *Abyssinian Stop Press* (1936), 109.
48. De Bono, *Anno XIII,* 281.
49. Coffey, *Lion by the Tail,* 164.
50. *Manchester Guardian,* 13 Nov. 1935.
51. Baer, *Italian-Ethiopian War,* 263.
52. *DBFP,* 2nd series, XV, 330.
53. A. J. Toynbee (ed.), *Survey of International Affairs 1935* II (1936), 284.
54. *DBFP,* 2nd series, XV, 448.
55. *OOM,* XXVII, 203.
56. *Times,* 19 Dec. 1935.
57. F. Charles-Roux, *Huit ans au Vatican* (Paris, 1947), 135.
58. Del Boca, *Ethiopian War,* 75.
59. D. Omissi, *Air Power and Colonial Control* (Manchester, 1990), 160 ff. Winston Churchill, for one, was "strongly in favour of using poisonous GAS, against uncivilised tribes." (*Times,* 29 Nov. 1998.)
60. J. W. S. Macfie, *An Ethiopian Diary* (1936), 77.
61. Coffey, *Lion by the Tail,* 263.
62. A. Cooper (ed.), *Mr. Wu and Mrs. Stitch: The Letters of Evelyn Waugh to Diana Cooper* (1991), 53.
63. E. M. Spiers, *Chemical Warfare* (1986), 95.
64. Steer, *Caesar in Abyssinia,* 283.
65. Coffey, *Lion by the Tail,* 275, 288 and 234.
66. Del Boca, *Ethiopian War,* 62 and 172.
67. P. Badoglio, *The War in Abyssinia* (1937), 66.
68. E. W. Polson Newman, *Italy's Conquest of Abyssinia* (1937), 145.
69. Steer, *Caesar in Abyssinia,* 325.
70. R. Higham, *Air Power* (1972), 81.
71. L. Mosley, *Haile Selassie: The Conquering Lion* (1964), 216.
72. Toynbee, *Survey of International Affairs 1935* II, 356.
73. R. Katz, *The Fall of the House of Savoy* (1972), 294.
74. *Il Giornale d'Italia,* 13 May 1936. Cf. Binchy, *Church and State,* 648–51.
75. *OOM,* XXVII, 394.
76. L. Barzini, *The Italians* (1964), 146.
77. A. Brissaud, *Mussolini* I (1983), 406.
78. Millon and Nochlin (eds.), *Art and Architecture,* 303.

79. De Felice, *Mussolini il Duce* I, 597.
80. See *Times Literary Supplement,* 31 Oct. 1975, for Denis Mack Smith's devastating criticism of this verdict.
81. R. and E. Packard, *Balcony Empire* (1943), 17.
82. Coffey, *Lion by the Tail,* 340.
83. *NYT,* 2 and 1 July 1936.
84. Del Boca, *Ethiopian War,* 158–9.
85. Starhemberg, *Hitler and Mussolini,* 218.
86. *NYT,* 2 July 1936.
87. Mosley, *Haile Selassie,* 241.

CHAPTER XIV
1. A. Werth, *The Destiny of France* (1937), 59 and 62.
2. H. R. Lottman, *The Left Bank* (1982), 78.
3. *L'Humanité,* 6 Apr. 1934.
4. J. Santore, "The Comintern's United Front Initiative of May 1934: French or Soviet Inspiration?," *Canadian Journal of History* XVI, 3 (Dec. 1981), 411.
5. Roskill, *Hankey* II, 137.
6. Santore, in *Canadian Journal of History* (Dec. 1981), 413.
7. J. Haslam, "The Comintern and the Origins of the Popular Front 1934–1935," *Historical Journal* 22, 3 (1979), 689.
8. K. Ross, *Fast Cars, Clean Bodies* (Cambridge, Mass., 1995), 16. The phrase was Emile Pouget's.
9. Sternhall, *Right nor Left,* 267.
10. G. Navel, *Man at Work* (1949), 96.
11. J. Jackson, *The Popular Front in France Defending Democracy, 1934–38* (Cambridge, 1988), 98.
12. Werth, *France in Ferment,* 263.
13. R. Girault, "The Impact of the Economic Situation on the Foreign Policy of France, 1936–9" in W. J. Mommsen and L. Kettenacker (eds.), *The Fascist Challenge and the Policy of Appeasement* (1983), 209 and 223.
14. Jackson, *Politics of Depression,* 100 and 105.
15. Reynaud, *Thick of the Fight,* 22.
16. J. Lacouture, *De Gaulle* I (1990), 139.
17. Jackson, *Politics of Depression,* 180.
18. *L'Oeuvre,* 12 July 1935.
19. M. Bloch, *Strange Defeat* (Oxford, 1949), 167.
20. Jackson, *Popular Front,* 47 and 73.
21. *Le Populaire,* 8 Oct. 1935, from *L'Oeuvre de Léon Blum (1934–1937)* (Paris, 1964), 126.
22. Werth, *Destiny of France,* 202.
23. Warner, *Pierre Laval,* 127.
24. *Le Populaire,* 26 Feb. 1935.
25. P. N. Furbank, *E. M. Forster: A Life* II (1978), 193.
26. D. R. Brower, *The New Jacobins* (Ithaca, N.Y., 1968), 27.

27. *NYT,* 14 Feb. 1936.
28. M. Chavardès, *Eté 36: la Victoire du Front Populaire* (Paris, 1966), 16–17.
29. J. Lacouture, *Léon Blum* (New York, 1982), 79 and 201.
30. J. Colton, *Léon Blum: Humanist in Politics* (1974 edn.), 59.
31. Jackson, *Popular Front,* 251.
32. Weber, *Action française,* 374.
33. J. Joll, *Intellectuals in Politics* (1960), 5.
34. Colton, *Blum,* 8.
35. G. Fraser and T. Natanson, *Léon Blum* (1937), 150.
36. L. E. Dalby, *Léon Blum* (New York, 1963), 241. Actually Jaurès was solidly petty bourgeois. See H. Goldberg, *The Life of Jean Jaurès* (Madison, Wis., 1962), 181 and *passim.*
37. Colton, *Blum,* 68.
38. W. Logue, *Léon Blum: The Formative Years 1872–1914* (De Kalb, Ill., 1973), 118.
39. *NYT,* 8 Mar 1936.
40. M. Baumont, "The Rhineland Crisis: 7 March 1936" in N. Waites (ed.), *Troubled Neighbours: Franco-British Relations in the Twentieth Century* (1971), 163.
41. J. T. Emmerson, *The Rhineland Crisis* (1977), 105.
42. Reynaud, *Thick of the Fight,* 129.
43. P. Flandin, *Politique française 1919–1940* (Paris, 1947), 208.
44. W. F. Knapp, "The Rhineland Crisis of March 1936" in Joll (ed.), *Decline of Third Republic,* 69.
45. *L'Humanité,* 11 Mar. 1936.
46. *Le Populaire,* 7 Mar. 1936.
47. *L'Action française,* 9 Mar. 1936.
48. *L'Oeuvre de Blum (1934–1937),* 243.
49. A. Thirion, *Revolutionaries Without Revolution* (1976 edn.), 373.
50. B. Badie, "Les Grèves du Front populaire aux usines Renault" in *Le Mouvement Social* 81 (Oct.–Dec. 1972), 81.
51. S. Weil, *La Condition ouvrière* (Paris, 1951), 169.
52. Werth, *Destiny of France,* 296–7.
53. A. Rhodes, *Louis Renault* (1969), 73.
54. Saint Loup, *Renault* (1957), 209.
55. Rhodes, *Renault,* 114.
56. *L'Humanité,* 29 May 1936.
57. *Le Populaire,* 4 June 1938.
58. *NYT,* 6 June 1936.
59. J. Danos and M. Gibelin, *June '36* (1986), 117.
60. *Le Populaire,* 8 June 1936.
61. Werth, *Destiny of France,* 331.
62. O. H. Bullitt (ed.), *For the President: Personal and Secret: Correspondence Between Franklin D. Roosevelt and William C. Bullitt* (1973), 178.
63. Bernard and Dubief, *Decline of Third Republic,* 312.
64. Hart-Davis, *Hitler's Olympics,* 83.
65. R. Holt, *Sport and Society in Modern France* (1981), 98. The sportsmen of other nations also used dubious substances to stimulate their performance. In 1939, for example, both teams in Britain's F.A. Cup Final received weekly injections of

gland extract from bulls, rabbits and other animals, as pioneered by the Australian A. Menzies Sharpe, who had "introduced gland therapy into football." (*Evening Standard,* 20 Apr. 1939.)

66.   Jackson, *Popular Front,* 137.
67.   G. Lefranc, *Histoire du front populaire* (Paris, 1974), 339.
68.   P. Fridenson, *Histoire des Usines Renault* (Paris, 1972), 266–7.
69.   M. Seidman, "The Birth of the Weekend and the Revolts Against Work: The Workers of the Paris Region during the Popular Front (1936–1938)," *French Historical Studies* XII, 2 (1981), 259.
70.   G. Brenan, *The Spanish Labyrinth* (Cambridge, 1976 edn.), 301.
71.   D. Caute, *Communism and the French Intellectuals* (1964), 117.
72.   *Le Figaro,* 25 July 1936.
73.   *FRUS* II (1936), 448.
74.   G. Warner, "France and Non-Intervention in Spain, July–August 1936," *International Affairs* 38, No. 2 (Apr. 1962), 205.
75.   C. Sforza, *Contemporary Italy* (1946), 294.
76.   P. Broué and E. Temime, *The Revolution and the Civil War in Spain* (1970), 329.
77.   J. Bowyer Bell, "French Reaction to the Spanish Civil War, July–September, 1936" in L. P. Parker and W. C. Askew (eds.), *Power, Public Opinion and Diplomacy* (Durham, N.C., 1959), 294.
78.   A. Malraux, *Antimemoires* (1968), 94.
79.   Lacouture, *Blum,* 353.
80.   D. Ibarruri, *They Shall Not Pass* (1966), 129.
81.   Werth, *Destiny of France,* 383–4.
82.   S. Chakhotin, *The Rape of the Masses: The Psychology of Totalitarian Propaganda* (1940), 241, 273 and 278.
83.   S. Schweitzer, "Les Ouvriers des Usines Renault de Billancourt et la guerre civile espagnole," *Le Mouvement Social* 103 (Apr.–June 1978), 115.
84.   A. Lunn, *Spanish Rehearsal* (1937), 43.
85.   A. J. Toynbee (ed.), *Survey of International Affairs 1937* II (1938), 142.
86.   See, e.g., Jacques Maritain, "The Idea of Holy War" in J. O'Brien (ed.), *From the N.R.F.* (New York, 1959).
87.   Cf. E. O'Duffy, *Crusade in Spain* (1938) and J. Gurney, *Crusade in Spain* (1974).
88.   S. Weintraub, *The Last Great Cause: The Intellectuals and the Spanish Civil War* (1968)—the title comes from Jimmy Porter's phrase in John Osborne's play *Look Back in Anger.*
89.   Stephen Spender in Crossman (ed.), *God that Failed,* 244.
90.   J. Lacouture, *André Malraux* (1975), 167.
91.   W. H. Auden, "Spain" in R. Skelton (ed.), *Poetry of the Thirties* (Penguin, 1964), 135.
92.   Koestler, *Invisible Writing,* 302.
93.   Lacouture, *Malraux,* 141.
94.   Spender, *World within World,* 206
95.   L. Fischer, *Men and Politics* (New York, 1941), 354.
96.   W. G. Langlois, "Before L'Espoir: Malraux's Pilots for Republican Spain" in B. Thompson and C. A. Viggiani (eds.), *Witnessing André Malraux* (Middletown, Conn., 1984), 111.

97. P. Nenni, *La Guerre d'Espagne* (Paris, 1959), 163.

98. In an article entitled "This is War" (*Collier's*, 29 May 1937), however, Malraux seems to represent himself as piloting a plane.

99. E. Finick, "I Fly For Spain" in *Harper's Magazine* 176 (Jan. 1938), 141 and 139.

100. R. S. Thornberry, *André Malraux et L'Espagne* (Geneva, 1977), 42.

101. A. Malraux, *Days of Hope* (Penguin, 1970), 94–9.

CHAPTER XV

1. Gurney, *Crusade*, 18.

2. E. Romilly, *Boadilla* (1971 edn.), 50

3. V. Brome, *The International Brigades* (1965), 34.

4. D. W. Pike, *Conjecture, Propaganda, and Deceit and the Spanish Civil War* (Stanford, Cal., 1968), 205.

5. L. A. Fernsworth, *Spain's Struggle for Freedom* (Boston, Mass., 1957), 176.

6. R. Ford, *A Hand-Book for Travellers in Spain* (1966 edn.), 7.

7. R. Carr, *The Spanish Tragedy* (1977), 7.

8. G. Brenan, *South from Granada* (1957), 45.

9. R. Fraser, *Blood of Spain: The Experience of the Civil War, 1936–1939* (1979), 84.

10. J. A. Pitt-Rivers, *The People of the Sierra* (1971 edn.), 202.

11. A. Beevor, *The Spanish Civil War* (1982), 31.

12. Brenan, *Spanish Labyrinth*, 56.

13. Fraser, *Blood of Spain*, 96.

14. P. Preston, *Franco* (1993), 191.

15. F. García Lorca, *Obras Completas* IV (Buenos Aires, 1945 edn.), 51.

16. E. A. Peers, *The Spanish Tragedy 1930–1937* (1937), 6.

17. A. Paz, *Durruti: The People Armed* (Montreal, 1976), 229.

18. B. Bolloten, *The Spanish Civil War* (1991), 66 and 51.

19. Carr, *Spanish Tragedy*, 13.

20. A. Hopkins, *Spanish Journey: A Portrait of Spain* (1992), 285.

21. J. Harrison, *The Spanish Economy in the Twentieth Century* (1985), 103.

22. Malraux, *Days of Hope*, 113.

23. S. de Madariaga, *Spain* (1942), 297.

24. M. Azaña, *Obras Completas* II (Monterey, Mexico, 1966), 692.

25. F. Sedwick, *The Tragedy of Manuel Azaña* (Columbus, Ohio, 1963), 76, 152 and vii.

26. C. G. Bowers, *My Mission to Spain* (1954), 10.

27. G. Jackson, *The Spanish Republic and the Civil War 1931–1939* (Princeton, N.J., 1965), 480.

28. E. E. Malefakis, *Agrarian Reform and Peasant Revolution in Spain* (New Haven, Conn., 1970), 253.

29. M. Maura, *Así cayó Alfonso XIII* (Mexico, 1962), 251.

30. Among other holders of this promiscuously bestowed nickname was the Rif leader, Abd el Krim.

31. Beevor, *Spanish Civil War*, 30.

32. S. G. Payne, *Politics and the Military in Modern Spain* (Stanford, Cal., 1967), 275.

33. A. Barea, *The Track* (1943), 29.
34. J. W. D. Trythall, *Franco* (1970), 32.
35. F. Franco, *Diario de una bandera* (Madrid, 1922), 19.
36. B. Crozier, *Franco* (1967), 73.
37. Payne, *Politics and Military in Spain*, 290.
38. I. Ehrenburg, *Eve of War 1933–1941* (1963), 111.
39. F. Borkenau, *The Spanish Cockpit* (1986 edn.), 54.
40. Beevor, *Spanish Civil War*, 37.
41. L. Manning, *What I Saw in Spain* (1935), 126–33.
42. H. Buckley, *Life and Death of the Spanish Republic* (1940), 153.
43. Manning, *Saw in Spain*, 136.
44. F. Jellinek, *The Spanish Civil War* (1938), 163.
45. Sedwick, *Azaña*, 140.
46. Azaña, *Obras Completas* II, 291.
47. J. Alvarez del Vayo, *Freedom's Battle* (1940), 13.
48. Bowers, *Mission to Spain*, 182.
49. Fernsworth, *Spain's Struggle*, 180.
50. J. Ortega y Gasset, *The Revolt of the Masses* (1932 edn.), 18.
51. Bolloten, *Spanish Civil War*, 56.
52. *DGFP*, Series C, V, 310.
53. R. Carr, *Spain 1809–1939* (Oxford, 1966), 642.
54. Preston, *Franco*, 134.
55. Hills, *Franco*, 223.
56. Crozier, *Franco*, 517.
57. Fraser, *Blood of Spain*, 90.
58. R. Low, *La Pasionaria: The Spanish Firebrand* (1992), 58.
59. I. Maisky, *Spanish Notebooks* (1966), 40.
60. R. A. H. Robinson, *The Origins of Franco's Spain* (Newton Abbot, 1970), 291.
61. *Times,* 19 July 1937.
62. M. Junod, *Warrior Without Weapons* (1951), 98.
63. Bowers, *Mission to Spain*, 334–5.
64. G. Brenan, *Personal Record 1920–1972* (1974), 297.
65. Fraser, *Blood of Spain*, 128.
66. S. Juliá, "Economic crisis, social conflict and the Popular Front: Madrid 1931–6" in P. Preston (ed.), *Revolution and War in Spain 1931–1939* (1984), 148.
67. Fernsworth, *Spain's Struggle*, 237.
68. Beevor, *Spanish Civil War*, 56.
69. *DGFP*, Series D, III, 23.
70. Buckley, *Spanish Republic*, 78.
71. *DBFP*, 2nd series, XVII, 107.
72. J. W. Cortada (ed.), *A City in War* (Wilmington, Del., 1985), 5 and 50.
73. Jellinek, *Spanish Civil War*, 323.
74. M. Laird, "A Diary of Revolution," *Atlantic Monthly* (Nov. 1936), 520.
75. Borkenau, *Spanish Cockpit*, 73.
76. V. Cunningham (ed.), *Spanish Front: Writers on the Civil War* (Oxford, 1986), 92.
77. R. Sender, *Seven Red Sundays* (1936), 15.
78. J. Langdon-Davies, *Behind the Spanish Barricades* (1937), 141 and 136.

79.   G. Orwell, *Homage to Catalonia* (Harmondsworth, 1966), 8–9.
80.   P. Stansky and W. Abrahams, *Journey to the Frontier* (1966), 327.
81.   Orwell, *Homage to Catalonia*, 28.
82.   *DGFP,* Series D, III, 94.
83.   Borkenau, *Spanish Cockpit*, 195.
84.   I. Gibson, *The Death of Lorca* (1973), 71–2.
85.   Carr, *Spanish Tragedy,* 123.
86.   G. Bernanos, *A Diary of My Times* (1938), 104.
87.   Crozier, *Franco,* 207.
88.   C. D. Eby, *The Siege of the Alcázar* (1965), 72. Moscardó's son was shot a month later in reprisal for an air raid.
89.   Malraux, *Days of Hope,* 174.
90.   H. G. Cardozo, *The March of a Nation* (1937), 129.
91.   Jellinek, *Spanish Civil War*, 286. In more unbuttoned mood Queipo asserted that "more than half of the population must be wiped out." See J. Martín Blázquez, *I Helped to Build an Army* (1939), 355.
92.   R. Colodny, *The Struggle for Madrid* (New York, 1958), 162 and 43.
93.   G. Regler, *The Owl of Minerva* (1959), 273.
94.   Delmer, *Trail Sinister,* 263.
95.   Blázquez, *Helped Build an Army,* 129 and 202.
96.   E. Hemingway, *For Whom the Bell Tolls* (1976 edn.), 208 and 212.
97.   Colodny, *Struggle for Madrid,* 45.
98.   Bolloten, *Spanish Civil War,* 165.
99.   *Mundo Obrero,* 7 Nov. 1936.
100. Colodny, *Struggle for Madrid,* 54.
101. P. Sloan (ed.), *John Cornford: A Memoir* (1938), 236.
102. J. Last, *The Spanish Tragedy* (1939), 120.
103. Colodny, *Struggle for Madrid,* 65.
104. J. Sommerfield, *Volunteer in Spain* (1937), 150.
105. Sloan (ed.), *Cornford,* 122.
106. K. Scott Watson, *Single to Spain* (1937), 171.
107. H. E. Knoblaugh, *Correspondent in Spain* (1937), 102.
108. F. C. Haighen, *Nothing but Danger* (1948), 147.
109. L. Delaprée, *Mort en Espagne* (Paris, 1937), 187.
110. A. Barea, *The Clash* (1946), 179 and 191.
111. *Nation,* 12 Dec. 1936.
112. Delmer, *Trail Sinister,* 299.
113. G. Cox, *Defence of Madrid* (1937), 132.
114. H. Thomas, *The Spanish Civil War* (1990 edn.), 310.
115. N. Monks, *Eyewitness* (1955), 72.
116. J. Dos Passos, *Journeys Between Wars* (1938), 366.
117. Knoblaugh, *Correspondent in Spain,* 131.
118. Colodny, *Struggle for Madrid,* 145.

CHAPTER XVI

1. L. MacNeice, *Autumn Journal* (1939), 29.
2. Thomas, *Spanish Civil War*, 481.
3. K. Martin, *Editor* (1968), 212.
4. D. Little, *Malevolent Neutrality* (Ithaca, N.Y., 1985), 241. The expression was that of Sir Henry Chilton, non-resident Ambassador in Spain, who also said that Franco was defending the interests of "our class."
5. Azaña, *Obras Completas* IV, 630.
6. Thomas, *Spanish Civil War*, 576.
7. R. Whealey, "How Franco Financed his War—Reconsidered," *Journal of Contemporary History* XII (Jan. 1977), 147.
8. W. S. Churchill, *Step by Step* (1939), 332.
9. J. Larios, *Combat over Spain* (n.d., 1968?), 93.
10. J. Edwards, *The British Government and the Spanish Civil War, 1936–1939* (1979), 47.
11. J. F. Coverdale, *Italian Intervention in the Spanish Civil War* (Princeton, N.J., 1975), 18.
12. C. F. Delzell, *Mussolini's Enemies* (Princeton, N.J., 1961), 156.
13. Monks, *Eyewitness*, 71.
14. *NYT*, 24 Mar. 1937.
15. To quote the subtitle of O. Conforti's *Guadalajara* (Milan, 1967).
16. *Il Popolo d'Italia*, 17 June 1937.
17. J. F. Coverdale, "The Battle of Guadalajara, 8–22 March 1937," *Journal of Contemporary History* IX (Jan. 1974), 70.
18. G. L. Weinberg, *The Foreign Policy of Hitler's Germany* (1970), 298–9.
19. R. H. Whealey, *Hitler and Spain* (Lexington, Ken., 1989), 60.
20. B. H. Liddell Hart, *The Other Side of the Hill* (1973 edn.), 122.
21. Larios, *Combat over Spain*, 89.
22. R. L. Proctor, *Hitler's Luftwaffe in the Spanish Civil War* (Westport, Conn., 1983), 122.
23. G. Thomas and M. Morgan-Witts, *The Day Guernica Died* (1975), 63.
24. P. Wyden, *The Passionate War: The Narrative History of the Spanish Civil War, 1936–1939* (New York, 1983), 352.
25. G. Douhet, *The Command of the Air* (London, 1943), 156 and 52.
26. G. Borrow, *The Bible in Spain* (1959 edn.), 373.
27. Thomas and Morgan-Witts, *Day Guernica Died*, 146 and 120–1.
28. G. Howson, *Aircraft of the Spanish Civil War 1936–1939* (1990), 136 and 233.
29. A. Galland, *The First and the Last* (1970 edn.), 30. Galland uses the term but claims that the first instance of "co-ordinated mass bombing" took place at Oviedo.
30. H. R. Southworth, *Guernica! Guernica! A Study of Journalism, Diplomacy, Propaganda and History* (1977), xiii and 189. In a telegraph message to Cordell Hull the American Ambassador Claude Bowers said the destruction of Guernica was "in line with Mola's threat to exterminate every town in province unless Bilbao surrenders." (*FRUS* I [1937], 290.)
31. Jackson, *Spanish Republic and Civil War*, 381.
32. G. L. Steer, *The Tree of Gernika* (1938), 240.

33. Thomas and Morgan-Witts, *Day Guernica Died,* 227.

34. Steer, *Tree of Gernika,* 238.

35. *Times,* 28 Apr. 1937.

36. Thomas and Morgan-Witts, *Day Guernica Died,* 275.

37. Steer, *Tree of Gernika,* 241–4.

38. Beevor, *Spanish Civil War,* 176.

39. I. McDonald, *The History of the Times* V: *Struggles in War and Peace 1939–1966* (1984), 465–6. Cf. Vansittart, *Mist Procession,* 507. Also Pimlott (ed.), *Diary of Dalton,* 227.

40. *NYT,* 1 May 1937.

41. *New Statesman,* 15 Oct. 1938.

42. Southworth, *Guernica!,* 139–40, 35.

43. *Guernica: The Official Report of the Commission appointed by the Spanish Nationalist Government* (1938), 14.

44. Thomas and Morgan-Witts, *Day Guernica Died,* 282.

45. Irving, *Göring* (1989), 174–5.

46. Southworth, *Guernica!,* 187, 231 and 228.

47. L. R. Pratt, *East of Malta, West of Suez: Britain's Mediterranean Crisis, 1936–1939* (Cambridge, 1975), 72.

48. *Hitler's Table-Talk,* 569.

49. L. E. O. Charlton, *The Menace of the Clouds* (1937), 47.

50. R. Overy, *The Air War 1939–1945* (New York, 1981), 206.

51. U. Bialer, *The Shadow of the Bomber: The Fear of Air Attack and British Politics 1932–1939* (1980), 151.

52. R. N. Baldwin (ed.), *Kropotkin's Revolutionary Pamphlets* (New York, 1927), 238. Noam Chomsky's case for the anarchists, put forward in *American Power and the New Mandarins* (1969), is unconvincing.

53. Bolloten, *Spanish Civil War,* 426.

54. J. Haslam, *The Soviet Union and the Struggle for Collective Security in Europe 1933–39* (1984), 133.

55. *FRUS* I (1937), 286.

56. W. G. Krivitsky, *I Was Stalin's Agent* (1939), 110.

57. Brome, *International Brigades,* 166.

58. R. A. Rosenstone, *Crusade of the Left* (New York, 1969), 92.

59. O. de Wet, *Cardboard Crucifix* (1938), 56.

60. Hemingway, *Bell Tolls,* 366.

61. Broué and Temime, *Civil War in Spain,* 223.

62. A. H. Landis, *The Abraham Lincoln Brigade* (New York, 1967), 30.

63. C. Stern, *Ulbricht: A Political Biography* (1965), 31.

64. R. D. Richardson, *Comintern Army* (Lexington, Ken., 1982), 162.

65. Regler, *Owl of Minerva,* 293.

66. Bolloten, *Spanish Civil War,* 429.

67. B. Crick, *George Orwell: A Life* (1980), 215–16.

68. Orwell, *Homage to Catalonia,* 107–11.

69. Borkenau, *Spanish Cockpit,* 176.

70. V. H. Drath, *Willy Brandt: Prisoner of His Past* (Radnor, Penn., 1975), 221.

71. Bolloten, *Spanish Civil War,* 450.

72. *Daily Worker,* 11 May 1937.
73. L. Trotsky, *The Spanish Revolution (1931–39)* (New York, 1973), 209.
74. S. Orwell and I. Angus (eds.), *The Collected Essays, Journalism and Letters of George Orwell* I (Harmondsworth, 1971 edn.), 301.
75. Orwell, *Homage to Catalonia,* 233–5.
76. Orwell, *Wigan Pier,* 108.
77. M. Gross (ed.), *The World of George Orwell* (1971), 77.
78. G. Orwell, *Keep the Aspidistra Flying* (Harmondsworth, 1973), 46.
79. H. Carpenter, *W. H. Auden* (1981), 26.
80. Orwell, *Wigan Pier,* 127.
81. G. Orwell, *Burmese Days* (Harmondsworth, 1972), 37 and 66.
82. R. Rees, *George Orwell: Fugitive from the Camp of Victory* (1961), 150.
83. To employ Orwell's own phrase, which George Woodcock used as the title for his *Study of George Orwell* (1966).
84. Crossman (ed.), *God that Failed,* 58.
85. G. Orwell, *Coming up for Air* (Harmondsworth, 1963), 149 and 158.
86. Orwell and Angus, *Collected Orwell* I, 345 and 404.
87. M. Shelden, *Orwell: The Authorised Biography* (1991), 377.
88. Ehrenburg, *Eve of War,* 179. He was apparently quoting from *Arte nuevo de hacer comedias* (1609) in which Lope says that "the truth is wont to call out from mute books." I am grateful to Dr. Melveena McKendrick for finding this reference.
89. El Campesino, *Listen Comrades* (1952), 19.
90. E. H. Carr, *The Comintern and the Spanish Civil War* (1984), 45.
91. P. Preston, *The Spanish Civil War 1936–39* (1986), 118.
92. *The Book of the XV Brigade* (Newcastle, 1975), 156.
93. T. Wintringham, *English Captain* (1939), 66.
94. Landis, *Abraham Lincoln Brigade,* 298.
95. C. Eby, *Between the Bullet and the Lie: American Volunteers in the Spanish Civil War* (New York, 1969), 165.
96. D. Carlton, *Anthony Eden* (1981 edn.), 109.
97. D. A. Puzzo, *Spain and the Great Powers 1936–1941* (New York, 1962), 199.
98. P. Gretton, "The Nyon Conference—the naval aspect," *English Historical Review* 90 (Jan. 1975), 110.
99. Muggeridge (ed.), *Ciano's Diary 1937–1938,* 15.
100. *NYT,* 20 Dec. 1937.
101. W. White (ed.), *By-Line: Ernest Hemingway* (1970), 266–7.
102. C. Baker (ed.), *Ernest Hemingway Selected Letters 1917–1961* (1981), 462.
103. J. Herbst, "The Starched Blue Sky of Spain," *The Noble Savage* I (1960), 93.
104. C. Baker, *Ernest Hemingway: A Life Story* (1969), 275
105. Hemingway, *Bell Tolls,* 210.
106. Baker, *Hemingway,* 415.
107. Hemingway, *Bell Tolls,* 206.
108. K. S. Lynn, *Hemingway* (1987), 446.
109. *DGFP,* Series D, III, 576.
110. Landis, *Abraham Lincoln Brigade,* 374–5.
111. Muggeridge (ed.), *Ciano's Diary 1937–1938,* 92.
112. *DGFP,* Series D, III, 626.

113. *NYT,* 20 Jan. 1938.
114. E. Rolfe, *The Lincoln Battalion* (New York, 1939), 305.
115. Thomas, *Spanish Civil War,* 853.
116. Rosenstone, *Crusade of the Left,* 88.
117. Regler, *Owl of Minerva,* 285 and 284.
118. F. Copeman, *Reason in Revolt* (1948), 78.
119. Gurney, *Crusade,* 188.
120. B. Alexander, *British Volunteers for Liberty: Spain 1936–1939* (1982), 245.
121. W. Gregory, *The Shallow Grave* (1986), 178.
122. Fernsworth, *Spain's Struggle,* 236.
123. *DGFP,* Series D, III, 819.
124. Ehrenburg, *Eve of War,* 209.
125. Weintraub, *Last Great Cause,* 150. The expression was H. G. Wells's.
126. Sedwick, *Azaña,* 196.
127. R. Boyce and E. M. Robertson (eds.), *Paths to War: New Essays in the Origins of the Second World War* (1989), 57.
128. T. C. Worsley, *The Fellow Travellers* (1971), 108.
129. Koestler, *Invisible Writing,* 517.
130. Orwell, *Homage to Catalonia,* 221.

CHAPTER XVII

1. M. Gilbert, *Winston S. Churchill* V (1976), 652.
2. F. M. Miller, "The Unemployment Policy of the National Government, 1931–1936," *Historical Journal* 19, 2 (1976), 456.
3. R. P. Shay, *British Rearmament in the Thirties: Politics and Profits* (Princeton, N.J., 1977), 286.
4. A. L. Rowse, *All Souls and Appeasement* (1961), 103.
5. Pimlott (ed.), *Diary of Dalton,* 198.
6. Vansittart, *Mist Procession,* 533.
7. W. K. Wark, *The Ultimate Enemy: British Intelligence and Nazi Germany, 1933–1939* (1985), 42.
8. G. Woodcock, *Dawn and the Darkest Hour* (1972), 193.
9. Jones, *Diary with Letters,* 153.
10. C. Barnett, *The Collapse of British Power* (1984 edn.), 388–9 and 400.
11. N. Rose, *Vansittart: Study of a Diplomat* (1978), 161.
12. V. Brittain, *Diary of the Thirties 1932–1939: Chronicle of Friendship* (1986), 256.
13. A. J. P. Taylor, *A Personal History* (1984 edn.), 162.
14. Clement Attlee in *Daily Herald,* 4 Apr. 1935.
15. M. Ceadel, *Pacifism in Britain 1914–1945: The Defining of a Faith* (Oxford, 1980), 205.
16. The title of Samuel Hynes's excellent study (1978).
17. N. Wood, *Communism and the British Intellectuals* (1959), 72.
18. Carpenter, *Auden,* 165.
19. J. Betjeman, *Collected Poems* (1988 edn.), 23.
20. *Selected Poetry of W. H. Auden* (New York, 1958), 17.

21.   *Country Life,* 26 Feb. 1938, Supplement XII.

22.   H. Johnson, *Searching for the Light* (1968), 154.

23.   M. Gilbert and R. Gott, *The Appeasers* (1967 edn.), 65.

24.   A. Horne, *Macmillan 1894–1956* I (1988), 105 and 109.

25.   J. Charmley, *Churchill: The End of Glory* (1993), 502.

26.   Wood, *Communism and Intellectuals,* 75 and 71.

27.   *Daily Telegraph,* 4 May 1935.

28.   J. A. Thompson, "Labour and the Modern British Monarchy," *South Atlantic Quarterly* 70 (1971), 347.

29.   Brendon, *Queen,* 226.

30.   *NYT,* 7 May 1935.

31.   *Illustrated London News,* 11 May 1935.

32.   Rose, *George V,* 395.

33.   *Daily Worker,* 1 and 2 May 1935.

34.   *Daily Herald,* 6 May 1935.

35.   Graves and Hodge, *Long Weekend,* 312.

36.   *Daily Telegraph,* 4 May 1935.

37.   *NYT,* 6 May 1935.

38.   *Daily Mail,* 30 April 1935.

39.   *NYT,* 6 May 1935.

40.   *Daily Mail,* 7 May 1935.

41.   E. Garnsey, "An Early Academic Enterprise: A Study in Technology Transfer," *Management Studies* (Research Paper 7/92), 2.

42.   B. Bond, *British Military Policy between the Two World Wars* (Oxford, 1980), 130.

43.   L. Graecan, *Chink* (1989), 125. See also 116 and 143.

44.   *The Memoirs of Field-Marshal the Viscount Montgomery of Alamein, K. G.* (1958), 28.

45.   *The Memoirs of Captain Liddell Hart* I (1965), 241.

46.   Middlemas and Barnes, *Baldwin,* 864–5.

47.   N. Pronay and D. W. Spring (eds.), *Propaganda, Politics and Film 1918–1945* (1982), 136.

48.   *Times,* 12 Sept. 1935.

49.   J. A. Cross, *Sir Samuel Hoare* (1977), 112.

50.   Roskill, *Hankey* III (1974), 186–7.

51.   S. Goetze, *Mural Decorations at the Foreign Office* (1936), 5.

52.   I. Toplis, *The Foreign Office: An Architectural History* (1987), 164.

53.   Brendon, *Churchill,* 127.

54.   Cross, *Hoare,* 35.

55.   CUL, Templewood MSS VIII:3, Hoare to Eden, 17 Sept. 1935.

56.   CUL, Templewood MSS VIII:3, Drummond to Hoare, 27 Aug. 1935.

57.   B. Bond (ed.), *Chief of Staff: The Diaries of Lieutenant-General Sir Henry Pownall* I (1972), 79.

58.   *Times,* 23 Sept. 1935.

59.   R. Quartararo, "Imperial Defence in the Mediterranean on the Eve of the Ethiopian Crisis (July–October 1935)," *Historical Journal* 20, 1 (1977), 220.

60.   P. Kennedy, *The Rise and Fall of the Great Powers* (1989 edn.), 435.

61.   CUL, Templewood MSS VIII:3, Lothian to Hoare, 18 Oct. 1935.

62.   CUL, Templewood MSS VIII:4, Hoare to Wigram, 14 Sept. 1935.

63. CUL, Templewood MSS VIII:3, A. Chamberlain to Hoare, 1 Dec. 1935.

64. A. J. Marder, *From Dardanelles to Oran* (1974), 83.

65. E. D. MacLachlan, *Room 39* (1968), 77.

66. J. Harvey (ed.), *The Diplomatic Diaries of Oliver Harvey 1937–1940* (1970), 299.

67. *Memoirs of Liddell Hart* I, 290.

68. K. Feiling, *A Life of Neville Chamberlain* (1970), 264.

69. CUL, Templewood MSS VIII:1.

70. Young (ed.), *Diaries of Lockhart*, 330.

71. A. J. P. Taylor, *Beaverbrook* (1972), 354.

72. D. Waley, *British Public Opinion and the Abyssinian War 1935–6* (1975), 13.

73. R. Cockett, *Twilight of Truth* (1989), 19.

74. Middlemas and Barnes, *Baldwin*, 881.

75. *Times*, 16 Dec. 1935.

76. Parker, *English Historical Review* 89 (1974), 322–3.

77. CUL, Templewood MSS VIII:1, C. M. Patrick to Hoare, 12 Dec. 1935.

78. H. Nicolson, *Diaries and Letters: 1930–1939* (1966) 233.

79. Eden, *Facing the Dictators*, 317. *Pace* Kenneth Rose (*George V*, 400), there is no reason to doubt Eden's account.

80. Young (ed.), *Diaries of Lockhart*, 330.

81. Rose, *George V*, 402.

82. F. Watson, "The Death of George V," *History Today* (Dec. 1986), 28.

83. Duff, *Queen Mary*, 201.

84. L. Woolf, *Quack, Quack!* (1935), 33.

85. "An American Resident," *The Twilight of the British Monarchy* (1937), 22 and 14.

86. P. Gibbs, *Ordeal in England* (1938), 12.

87. F. Donaldson, *Edward VIII* (1974), 181.

88. R. Rhodes James (ed.), *Chips: The Diaries of Sir Henry Channon* (1967), 55.

89. P. Ziegler, *King Edward VIII* (1990), 246.

90. M. Bloch, *The Reign and Abdication of Edward VIII* (1990), 31.

91. Manchester, *Caged Lion*, 225.

92. Brendon, *Queen*, 123.

93. M. Bloch (ed.), *Wallis and Edward* (1986), 196, 118 and 134.

94. M. Thornton, *Royal Feud* (1985), 89.

95. BL, Hearst Papers, Duke of Windsor to Hearst, 9 May 1947.

96. M. Gilbert, *Finest Hour* (1983), 700.

97. Ziegler, *Edward VIII*, 260.

98. P. Ziegler (ed.), *The Diaries of Lord Louis Mountbatten 1920–1922* (1987), 239.

99. O. Sitwell, *Rat Week* (1986), 61.

100. *Country Life* (26 Feb. 1938), 224.

101. Rhodes James (ed.), *Chips*, 83.

102. B. Masters, *Great Hostesses* (1982), 153.

103. Brendon, *Queen*, 188–9.

104. A. de Courcy, *Circe: The Life of Edith, Marchioness of Londonderry* (1992), 264.

105. R. Payne, *The Civil War in Spain 1936–1939* (1963), 153.

106. *We saw it happen* by Thirteen Correspondents of "The New York Times" (1939), 171.

107. P. Brendon, "Amendment Envy," *Columbia Journalism Review* (Nov.–Dec. 1991), 68.

108. S. Koss, *The Rise and Fall of the Political Press in Britain* II (1984), 543.

109. Eden, *Facing the Dictators*, 410.

110. R. Buckle (ed.), *Self Portrait with Friends: The Selected Diaries of Cecil Beaton 1926–1974* (1979), 47.

111. Rhodes James (ed.), *Chips*, 77.

112. *Sunday Times*, 24 Apr. 1966.

113. P. Hall, *Royal Fortune* (1992), 78.

114. J. G. Lockhart, *Cosmo Gordon Lang* (1949), 405.

115. Barnes and Nicholson (eds.), *Amery Diary*, 431.

116. J. W. Wheeler-Bennett, *King George VI* (1958), 283.

117. W. Gerhardie, *God's Fifth Column* (1981), 310.

118. *Times*, 14 Dec. 1936.

119. *Spectator*, 11 Dec. 1936.

120. H. Jennings and C. Madge (eds.), *May the Twelfth 1937* (1987 edn.), 416, 272 and 305.

121. *Times*, 12 May 1937.

122. Rhodes James (ed.), *Chips*, 126–7.

123. *Times*, 12 May 1937.

124. *Daily Mirror*, 6 Mar. 1937.

125. D. Cannadine, *The Decline and Fall of the British Aristocracy* (1990), 206 and 210.

126. Orwell, *Wigan Pier*, 87–8.

127. P. Ziegler, *Crown and People* (1978), 46.

128. *Daily Worker*, 12 May 1937.

129. "American Resident," *Twilight of Monarchy*, 42.

130. Churchill, *Second World War* I, 171.

131. P. Haggie, *Britannia at Bay* (Oxford, 1981), 59.

132. B. A. Lee, *Britain and the Sino-Japanese War, 1937–1939* (Stanford, Cal., 1973), 7.

133. R. Kipling, *From Sea to Sea and other Sketches: Letters of Travel* (1900), 435.

134. Roskill, *Naval Policy* II, 188.

135. M. and S. Harries, *Soldiers of the Sun* (1991), 93.

136. F. S. Northedge, *The Troubled Giant* (1966), 468.

137. I. Nish (ed.), *Anglo-Japanese Alienation 1919–1952* (Cambridge, 1982), 39–40.

138. *DBFP*, 2nd series 1933–36, XX, 668.

139. Haggie, *Britannia*, 51–2.

CHAPTER XVIII

1. Chamberlin, in *Contemporary Japan* (Sept. 1936), 183.

2. Tota Ishimaru, *Japan Must Fight Britain* (1936), 275.

3. J. Toland, *The Rising Sun* (1970), 7.

4. Nish (ed.), *Anglo-Japanese Alienation*, 95.

5. C. Gluck and S. R. Graubard (eds.), *Showa: The Japan of Hirohito* (1992), 162.

6. Maruyama Masao, *Thought and Behaviour*, 94.

7. G. Henderson, *Korea: Politics of the Vortex* (Cambridge, Mass., 1966), 103 and *passim*.

8. A. Peyrefitte, *The Collision of Two Civilisations* (1993), 145.

9. H. V. Redman, "Shaw in and on Japan," *Contemporary Japan* (June 1933), 120.

10. M. Holroyd, *Bernard Shaw* III: *The Lure of Fantasy* (1991), 300–1.

11. *Contemporary Japan* (June 1933), 121.

12. E. K. Tipton, *The Japanese Police State* (1990), 89.

13. Mitchell, *Thought Control,* 101–3, 185.

14. Tsurumi Kazuko, *Social Change and the Individual: Japan Before and After Defeat in World War II* (Princeton, N.J., 1970), 51.

15. J. Patric, *Why Japan Was Strong* (1944), 142.

16. Shiroyama Saburo, *War Criminal: The Life and Death of Hirota Koki* (Tokyo, 1977), 97.

17. *NYT,* 12 and 15 July 1933.

18. Byas, *Government by Assassination,* 70–1.

19. IWM, Saionji (3 Aug. 1933), 655.

20. IWM, Saionji (Sept. 1933), 686.

21. *Contemporary Japan* (Dec. 1933), 537.

22. *Contemporary Japan* (Mar. 1934), 624.

23. J. Gunther, *Inside Asia* (1939), 91.

24. H. von Dirksen, *Moscow, Tokyo, London* (1951), 154.

25. Shiroyama, *Hirota,* 5, 167 and 49.

26. *Daily Mail,* 8 Mar. 1933.

27. W. Price, *Key to Japan* (1946), 16.

28. J. W. Morley (ed.), *Dilemmas of Growth in Prewar Japan* (Princeton, N.J., 1971), 86.

29. Byas, *Government by Assassination,* 79.

30. Mikiso Hane, *Honjo Diary,* 147.

31. G. J. Kasza, *The State and the Mass Media in Japan, 1918–1945* (Berkeley, Cal., 1988), 125.

32. *Contemporary Japan* (June 1934), 66–71.

33. D. Borg and Okamoto Shumpei, *Pearl Harbor as History* (1973), 110. The British Foreign Office knew from decrypts of Japanese diplomatic traffic that Amo's declaration was official policy. See A. Best, *Britain, Japan and Pearl Harbor* (1995), 9.

34. *Contemporary Japan* (Dec. 1933), 742.

35. H. Patrick (ed.), *Japanese Industrialization and its Social Consequences* (1976), 97 and 65.

36. IWM, Saionji (Sept. 1934), 993.

37. Grew, *Ten Years,* 132 and 136.

38. IWM, Saionji (Nov. 1934), 1074.

39. IWM, Saionji (June 1935), 1253.

40. Osanaga Kanroji, *Hirohito* (Los Angeles, 1975), 120.

41. *Daily Mail,* 8 Mar. 1933.

42. IWM, Saionji (15 May 1933), 607.

43. *Daily Mail,* 14 May 1933.

44. *Daily Mail,* 8 Mar. 1933.
45. Mikiso Hane, *Honjo Diary,* 106, 144–5 and 140.
46. F. O. Miller, *Minobe Tatsukichi* (Berkeley, Cal., 1965), 182.
47. Borg and Shumpei, *Pearl Harbor,* 501.
48. IWM, Saionji (Feb. 1935), 1166.
49. IWM, Saionji (1 June 1935), 1236.
50. Mikiso Hane, *Honjo Diary,* 149.
51. IWM, Saionji (July 1935), 1276.
52. IWM, Saionji (Aug. 1935), 1305.
53. *Japan Today and Tomorrow* (1935–6), 112.
54. IWM, Saionji (Sept. 1935), 1305.
55. IWM, Saionji (31 Jan. 1936), 1410.
56. Mishima Yukio, *Hagakune* (Harmondsworth, 1979), 16.
57. Mishima, *Runaway Horses,* 393–4.
58. Shillony, *Revolt in Japan,* 133.
59. Toland, *Rising Sun,* 17.
60. G. M. Wilson, "Kita Ikki's Theory of Revolution," *Journal of Asian Studies* XXVI, No. 1 (Nov. 1966), 95.
61. E. Behr, *Hirohito: Behind the Myth* (1989), 163.
62. Shillony, *Revolt in Japan,* 143.
63. Noguchi Takehiko, "Mishima Yukio and Kita Ikki: The Aesthetics and Politics of Ultranationalism in Japan," *Journal of Japanese Studies* 10, No. 2 (Summer, 1982), 452.
64. Osanaga, *Hirohito,* 126.
65. Mikiso Hane, *Honjo Diary,* 215.
66. IWM, Saionji (Feb. 1936), 1417.
67. Murakami, *Japan: Years of Trial,* 57–8.
68. A. Morgan Young, *Imperial Japan* (1938), 281.
69. S. S. Large, *Emperor Hirohito and Showa Japan* (1992), 69.
70. Mikiso Hane, *Honjo Diary,* 172.
71. *NYT,* 1 Mar. 1936.
72. R. Storry, "Fascism in Japan: The Army Mutiny of February 1936," *History Today* (Nov. 1956), 726.
73. *NYT,* 1 Mar. 1936.
74. Marukami, *Japan: Years of Trial,* 61.
75. Shillony, *Revolt in Japan,* 209.
76. Shiroyama, *Hirota,* 149.
77. *Contemporary Japan* (June 1936), 136.
78. Baba Tsunego, "Hirota's 'Renovation' Plans," *Contemporary Japan* (Sept. 1936), 173.
79. Fleisher, *Volcanic Isle,* 206.
80. *DBFP,* 2nd series, XX, 788.
81. Irie Sukemusa, "My 50 Years with the Emperor," *Japan Quarterly* XXX, No. 1 (Jan.–Mar. 1983), 40.
82. C. Sheldon, "Japanese Aggression and the Emperor, 1931–1941, from Contemporary Diaries," *Modern Asian Studies* 10 (Feb. 1976), 2.
83. D. A. Titus, *Palace and Politics in Prewar Japan* (New York, 1974), 40.

84. Irye Akira (ed.), *The Chinese and the Japanese* (Princeton, N.J., 1980), 233.

85. Marukami, *Japan: Years of Trial,* 62.

86. Peattie, *Ishiwara,* 278.

87. F. Leith-Ross, *Money Talks* (1968), 215.

88. IWM, Saionji (June 1937), 1816.

89. M. A. Barnhart, *Japan Prepares for Total War* (Cornell, 1987), 89.

90. J. B. Crowley, "A Reconsideration of the Marco Polo Bridge Incident," *Journal of Asian Studies* 22, 2 (May 1963), 281.

91. *NYT,* 8 July 1937.

92. *Time,* 16 June 1941.

93. Grew, *Ten Years,* 224.

94. J. Bertram, *North China Front* (1939), 83.

95. F. Dorn, *The Sino-Japanese War, 1937–41* (New York, 1974), 45 and 56.

96. J. W. Morley (ed.), *The China Quagmire: Japan's Expansion on the Asian Continent 1933–1941* (New York, 1983), 235.

97. A. Y. Kalyagin, *Along Alien Roads* (New York, 1983), 122.

98. R. Farmer, *Shanghai Harvest* (1945), 85.

99. H. J. Timperley, *What War Means: The Japanese Terror in China* (1938), 149.

100. Dorn, *Sino-Japanese War,* 85.

101. J. G. Andersson, *China Fights for the World* (1939), 172.

102. *North-China Daily News,* 24 Sept. 1937.

103. IWM, Japanese War Trials, Box 143, MM-4.

104. *NYT,* 18 Dec. 1937.

105. M. Gilbert, *A History of the Twentieth Century* II (1998), 163.

106. Hata Ikuhiko subjected the inflated claims of Iris Chang and others to incisive analysis in "Nanking: Setting the Record Straight," *Japan Echo* 25, No. 4 (Aug. 1998).

107. I. Chang, *The Rape of Nanking* (New York, 1997), 48.

108. Timperley, *Japanese Terror,* 41.

109. E. Wickert (ed.), *The Good German of Nanking: The Diaries of John Rabe* (1999), 115.

110. Shiroyama, *Hirota,* 194.

111. M. and S. Harries, *Soldiers of Sun,* 408.

112. J. Goette, *Japan Fights for Asia* (1945), 52.

113. Shiroyama, *Hirota,* 194.

114. T. R. H. Havens, *Valley of Darkness* (New York, 1978), 13.

115. IWM, Saionji (Mar. 1938), 2050 and 2067.

116. *Diary of Kido,* 181.

117. J. H. Boyle, *China and Japan at War 1937–1945* (Stanford, Cal., 1972), 82.

118. Peattie, *Ishiwara,* 307.

119. B. W. Tuchman, *Sand Against the Wind: Stilwell and the American Experience in China, 1911–45* (1970), 174–6.

120. J. W. Morley (ed.), *Deterrent Diplomacy: Japan, Germany and the U.S.S.R., 1935–1940* (New York, 1976), 214–15.

CHAPTER XIX

1.   C. Andrew and O. Gordievsky, *KGB: The Inside Story* (1990), 187.
2.   Getty and Manning (eds.), *Stalinist Terror,* 47. More recent research still, by Yuri Zhukov, tends to confirm this view. See *Guardian,* 23 May 1998.
3.   A. Kuusinen, *Before and After Stalin* (1974), 133–4.
4.   R. C. Tucker, *Stalin in Power: The Revolution from Above 1928–1941* (1990), 265.
5.   W. Laqueur, *Stalin: The Glasnost Revelations* (1990), 206.
6.   J. Haslam, "Political Opposition to Stalin and the Origins of the Terror in Russia, 1932–1936," *Historical Journal* 29, 2 (1986), 409.
7.   D. J. Dallin and B. I. Nicolaevsky, *Forced Labour in Russia* (1947), 255.
8.   N. Tolstoy, *Stalin's Secret War* (1981), 11.
9.   Mandelstam, *Hope,* 99.
10. R. Medvedev, *All Stalin's Men* (Oxford, 1983), 35.
11. R. Sartoris, "Stalinism and Carnival: The Aesthetics of Political Holidays" in H. Günther (ed.), *The Culture of the Stalin Period* (1990), 66.
12. Orlov, *Secret History,* 147.
13. Tucker, *Stalin in Power,* 330.
14. V. Paperny, "Moscow in the 1930s and the Emergence of a New City" in Günther (ed.), *Culture of Stalin Period,* 231.
15. L. Feuchtwanger, *Moscow 1937* (1937), 32.
16. M. F. Parkins, *City Planning in Soviet Russia* (Chicago, 1953), 36.
17. Quoted from Oskar Maria Graf by R. Medvedev, *Khrushchev* (1982), 17.
18. Medvedev, *Stalin's Men,* 124.
19. Colton, *Moscow,* 327.
20. Thomas, *Spanish Civil War,* 124.
21. J. von Herwarth, *Against Two Evils* (1981), 41.
22. El Campesino, *Listen Comrades,* 72.
23. Pasternak, *People and Propositions,* 243.
24. Mackenzie (ed.), *Letters of Webb* III, 405 and viii.
25. *Trotsky's Diary in Exile* (1935), 84.
26. Orlov, *Secret History,* 129.
27. A. Vaksberg, *The Prosecutor and the Prey: Vyshinsky and the 1930s' Moscow Show Trials* (1990), 81.
28. D. N. Pritt, *The Autobiography of D. N. Pritt* I (1965), 110.
29. *BDFA,* II, Series A, 13, 312.
30. Vaksberg, *Prosecutor,* 82.
31. *NYT,* 21 and 23 Aug. 1936.
32. R. E. Conot, *Justice at Nuremberg* (1983), 19.
33. Maclean, *Eastern Approaches,* 118.
34. *NYT,* 27 Aug. 1936.
35. M. Litvinov, *Notes for a Journal* (1955), 212. Litvinov's journal was a forgery, but it was plausible enough to deceive E. H. Carr. See J. Haslam, *The Vices of Integrity* (1999), 174.
36. E. Ginzburg, *Into the Whirlwind* (1967), 193.
37. F. Beck and W. Godin, *Russian Purge and the Extraction of Confession* (1951), 31.
38. Ehrenburg, *Eve of War,* 197.
39. *Trotsky's Diary,* 66.

40. W. P. Coates (ed.), *The Moscow Trial* (1937), 222 and 212–13.

41. S. de Beauvoir, *The Prime of Life* (1962), 230.

42. Martin, *Editor*, 230.

43. *BDFA*, II, Series A, 14, 23 and 31.

44. L.-F. Céline, *Mea Culpa* (1937), 34.

45. J. E. Davies, *Mission to Moscow* (1942), 54.

46. C. E. Bohlen, *Witness to History 1929–1969* (1973), 52.

47. Feuchtwanger, *Moscow*, 161–2. Apparently Feuchtwanger did have private doubts, but suppressed them.

48. D. J. Dallin, *From Purge to Coexistence* (Chicago, Ill., 1964), 116.

49. Coates (ed.), *Moscow Trial*, 249.

50. Krivitsky, *Stalin's Agent*, 171.

51. Fainsod, *Smolensk*, 423.

52. S. Talbott (ed.), *Khrushchev Remembers* I (1971), 114.

53. B. Pasternak, *An Essay in Autobiography* (1959), 92, and G. Robakidze, *Die gemordete Seele* (Berlin, 1933), *passim*.

54. Y. Rapoport, *The Doctors' Plot* (1991), 148.

55. *The Works of Jonathan Swift*, edited by D. L. Purves (Edinburgh, 1889), 178.

56. *BDFA*, II, Series A, 14, 226.

57. A. Bullock, *Hitler and Stalin: Parallel Lives* (1991), 727.

58. Volkogonov, *Stalin*, 306.

59. T. Tchernavin, *Escape from the Soviets* (1933), 88.

60. To quote the title of A. Vucinich's book (Berkeley, Cal., 1984).

61. Kravchenko, *Freedom*, 283.

62. H. D. Hudson Jr., "Terror in Soviet Architecture: The Murder of Mikhail Okhitovich," *Slavic Review* 51, No. 3 (Fall 1992), 461.

63. Medvedev, *Let History Judge*, 402.

64. A. Weissberg, *Conspiracy of Silence* (1952), 306.

65. R. A. McCutcheon, "The 1936–1937 Purge of Soviet Astronomers," *Slavic Review* 50, No. 1 (Spring 1991), 117.

66. S. I. Luck, *Observation in Russia* (1938), 226 and 221.

67. J. Becker, *The Lost Country: Mongolia Revealed* (1992), 94.

68. Conquest, *Great Terror*, 340.

69. B. Starkov, "Narkom Ezhov" in Getty and Manning (eds.), *Stalinist Terror*, 30.

70. B. Bonwetsch, "The Purge of the Military and the Red Army's Operational Capability during the 'Great Patriotic War'" in B. Wegner (ed.), *From Peace to War* (1997), 396.

71. A. Sakharov, *Memoirs* (1990), 32.

72. P. Yakir, *A Childhood in Prison* (1972), 34.

73. M. Buber, *Under Two Dictators* (1949), 9.

74. J. Arch Getty, *Origins of the Great Purges* (Cambridge, 1985), 179.

75. B. G. Katz, "Purges and Production: Soviet Economic Growth 1928–1940," *Journal of Economic History* 3 (Sept. 1975), 585.

76. Ginzburg, *Into the Whirlwind*, 45 and 147.

77. Mandelstam, *Hope*, 458.

78. Dallin and Nicolaevsky, *Forced Labour*, 169 and 121.

79. R. Conquest, *Kolyma: The Arctic Death Camps* (1978), 78.

80. G. Herling, *A World Apart* (1951), 91.

81. Dallin and Nicolaevsky, *Forced Labour*, 153.

82. V. Petrov, *It Happens in Russia* (1951), 161.

83. Conquest, *Kolyma*, 23.

84. E. Lipper, *Eleven Years in Soviet Prison Camps* (1951), 125.

85. E. Ginzburg, *Within the Whirlwind* (1981), 9 and 117.

86. V. Kravchenko, *I Chose Justice* (1951), 239.

87. V. Conolly, *Beyond the Urals* (1967), 313.

88. Dallin and Nicolaevsky, *Forced Labour*, 73.

89. Beck and Godin, *Russian Purge*, 156.

90. Ginzburg, *Within the Whirlwind*, 216.

91. Buber, *Two Dictators*, 156.

92. Lipper, *Eleven Years*, 150.

93. Dallin and Nicolaevsky, *Forced Labour*, 223.

94. A. Williams-Ellis (ed.), *The White Sea Canal* (1935), 11 and 7.

95. C. R. Proffer, *The Widows of Russia* (Ann Arbor, Mich., 1987), 15.

96. D. Caute, *The Fellow Travellers* (1973), 100.

97. T. Mann, *Tagebücher 1935–1936* (Frankfurt, 1978), 358.

98. *BDFA*, II, Series A, 14, 274 and 132.

99. W. Citrine, *I Search for Truth in Russia* (1936), 256.

100. E. Radzinsky, *Stalin* (1996), 363.

101. R. W. Thurston, "Fear and Belief in the USSR's 'Great Terror': Response to Arrest, 1935–1939," *Slavic Review* 45, No. 2 (1986), 227.

102. Coates, *Moscow Trial*, 8.

103. Orwell and Angus (eds.), *Collected Orwell* I, 368–9.

104. G. T. Rittersporn, "The Omnipresent Conspiracy: On Soviet Imagery of Politics and Social Relations in the 1930s" in Getty and Manning (eds.), *Stalinist Terror*, 115.

105. S. Davies, "Stalin, Propaganda and Soviet Society during the Great Terror," *The Historian* 56 (Winter 1997), 29.

106. Kravchenko, *Freedom*, 282.

107. Thurston, in *Slavic Review* 45, 223.

108. Shostakovich, *Testimony*, 135.

109. Ginzburg, *Into the Whirlwind*, 119.

110. De Jonge, *Stalin*, 276.

111. Fainsod, *Smolensk*, 449.

112. Conquest, *Great Terror*, 383.

113. Weissberg, *Conspiracy*, 54–7.

114. Kolakowski, *Marxism* III, 96.

115. Solzhenitsyn, *Gulag*, 325.

116. Bullock, *Hitler and Stalin*, 400.

117. A. Rybakov, *Children of the Arbat* (1988), 559.

118. De Jonge, *Stalin*, 341.

119. Davies, *Mission*, 152.

120. Pasternak, *Zhivago*, 495.

121. Talbott (ed.), *Khrushchev Remembers*, 585.

122. *Moscow News*, 29 Dec. 1937.

123. Poretsky, *Own People,* 171.
124. A. Platonov, *The Fierce and Beautiful World* (1970), 8.
125. E. Mossman (ed.), *The Correspondence of Boris Pasternak and Olga Freidenberg 1910–1954* (1982), 163.
126. M. Gilbert, *The Holocaust* (1986), 368.
127. Pasternak, *Pasternak: Tragic Years,* 107.
128. V. Grossman, *Life and Fate* (1985), 214.
129. Mandelstam, *Hope,* 357.
130. S. N. Driver, *Anna Akhmatova* (New York, 1972), 132.

CHAPTER XX

1. C. Gentry, *J. Edgar Hoover: The Man and The Secrets* (New York, 1991), 214.
2. *PPR* V, 383–4.
3. Ickes, *Secret Diary* II (1955), 52.
4. F. A. Warren, *Liberals and Communism* (Bloomington, Ind., 1966), 175.
5. A. Kazin, *Starting out in the Thirties* (1966), 86.
6. M. Cowley, *The Dream of the Golden Mountains: Remembering the 1930s* (New York, 1980), 118.
7. M. Eastman, *Love and Revolution: My Journey through the Epoch* (New York, 1964), 624.
8. B. L. Grayson (ed.), *The American Image of Russia 1917–1977* (New York, 1978), 143.
9. *NYT,* 26 Aug. 1936.
10. Gunther, *Inside Europe* (1937 edn.), 497.
11. K. D. Eagles, *Ambassador Joseph E. Davies and American–Soviet Relations 1937–1941* (1985), 87.
12. R. Coulondre, *De Staline à Hitler* (Paris, 1950), 113.
13. Davies, *Mission,* 67.
14. R. C. Williams, *Russian Art and American Money 1900–1940* (Cambridge, Mass., 1980), 231 and 253.
15. *FRUS: The Soviet Union 1933–1939,* 365 and 369.
16. Eagles, *Davies,* 164.
17. G. L. Weinberg, *The Foreign Policy of Hitler's Germany: Starting World War II 1937–1939* (Chicago, Ill., 1980), 354.
18. R. H. Ullman, "The Davies Mission and United States–Soviet Relations, 1937–1941," *World Politics* 9 (1956–7), 239.
19. R. Nisbet, *Roosevelt and Stalin: The Failed Courtship* (1989), 16.
20. O. Friedrich, *City of Nets* (1987), 154.
21. D. Culbert, "Our Awkward Ally: Mission to Moscow (1943)" in J. E. O'Connor and M. A. Jackson (eds.), *American History/American Film* (New York, 1979), 134.
22. L.-F. Céline, *Journey to the End of the Night* (1934), 214.
23. B. M. Hall, *The Best Remaining Seats* (New York, 1961), 123.
24. C. Carlen, *The Papal Encyclicals 1903–1939* (Raleigh, 1990), 520.
25. E. Rosow, *Born to Lose: The Gangster Movie in America* (New York, 1978), 176.

26. Wilson, *Shores of Light,* 665.

27. *Spectator,* 29 June 1991.

28. R. S. and H. M. Lynd, *Middletown,* 261.

29. R. Pickard, *The Hollywood Studios* (1978), 439.

30. B. Hecht, *A Child of the Century* (New York, 1954), 469.

31. J. Von Sternberg, *Fun in a Chinese Laundry* (1966), 68.

32. J. B. Priestley, *Midnight on the Desert* (1937), 174 and 198.

33. I. S. Cobb, *Exit Laughing* (New York, 1941), 473.

34. J. Tebbel, *The Life and Good Times of William Randolph Hearst* (1953), 40.

35. J. R. Taylor, *Strangers in Paradise* (1983), 107.

36. *The Complete Works of Nathanael West* (1957), 352.

37. L. C. Rosten, *Hollywood: The Movie Colony* (New York, 1970 edn.), 46.

38. Hecht, *Child of Century,* 476 and 471.

39. B. Thomas, *King Cohn* (1967), 137.

40. Pickard, *Hollywood Studios,* 282.

41. A. Marx, *Goldwyn: The Man behind the Myth* (1976), 225.

42. Hecht, *Child of Century,* 482.

43. Rosten, *Hollywood,* 310.

44. F. Donaldson (ed.), *Yours Plum: The Letters of P. G. Wodehouse* (1990), 126.

45. Marx, *Goldwyn,* 77.

46. Taylor, *Strangers in Paradise,* 112.

47. U. Sinclair, *How I Got Licked and Why* (1935), 151 and *passim.*

48. *NYT,* 4 Nov. 1934.

49. L. Harris, *Upton Sinclair: American Rebel* (New York, 1975), 308.

50. E. Lyons, *Red Decade* (1941), 284.

51. R. Maidment, "The New Deal Court Revisited" in S. W. Baskerville and R. Willett (eds.), *Nothing Else to Fear* (Manchester, 1985), 38.

52. Cashman, *America in Twenties and Thirties,* 205.

53. *New Yorker,* 21 Sept. 1935. *The New Yorker* viewed the world as "a vast cocktail party" despite the Depression, and its political interests did not extend much further than complaining about the coloured lights on the Empire State Building— Al Smith obligingly had them changed to white. See B. Yagoda, *About Town:* The New Yorker *and the World it Made* (New York, 2000), 224 and *passim.*

54. M. Pusey, *Charles Evans Hughes* II (New York, 1963), 723.

55. N. L. Dawson, *Louis D. Brandeis, Felix Frankfurter and the New Deal* (Hamden, Conn., 1986), 143.

56. W. E. Leuchtenburg, "Franklin D. Roosevelt's Supreme Court 'Packing' Plan" in H. M. Hollingsworth and W. F. Holmes (eds.), *Essays on the New Deal* (Austin, Tex., 1969), 96.

57. A. A. Ekirch, *Ideologies and Utopias* (Chicago, 1969), 199.

58. M. Dubofsky and W. Van Tine, *John L. Lewis* (New York, 1976), 219.

59. I. Bernstein, *Turbulent Years* (Boston, 1970), 516 and 548.

60. M. E. Parrish, *Anxious Decades* (New York, 1992), 357.

61. *American Mercury* (June 1937), 138.

62. Ickes, *Secret Diary* II, 241.

63. I. Bernstein, *A Caring Society* (Boston, 1985), 307.

64. Ickes, *Secret Diary* II, 241.

65. J. M. Blum (ed.), *The Morgenthau Diaries* I (Boston, Mass., 1959), 394 and 420.
66. Gentry, *Hoover,* 207.
67. Ekirch, *Ideologies and Utopias,* 226.
68. W. S. Cole, *Roosevelt and the Isolationists 1932–45* (Lincoln, Neb., 1983), 296.
69. D. Brinkley, *Washington Goes to War* (1989), 16.
70. J. E. Edwards, *The Foreign Policy of Colonel McCormick's Tribune, 1929–41* (Reno, Nev., 1971), 117.
71. R. Dallek, *Franklin D. Roosevelt and American Foreign Policy, 1932–1945* (New York, 1979), 148.
72. BL, Hearst Papers, Hearst to J. F. Neylan, 6 Oct. 1938 and E. D. Coblentz to Hearst, 22 Oct. 1938.
73. M. Jonas, *Isolationism in America 1935–1941* (Ithaca, N.Y., 1966), 72 and 105.
74. A. Nevins, *The New Deal and World Affairs* (Yale, Conn., 1950), 81.
75. C. Hull, *The Memoirs of Cordell Hull* I (New York, 1948), 667.
76. E. B. Nixon (ed.), *Franklin D. Roosevelt and Foreign Affairs January 1933–January 1937* II (Cambridge, Mass., 1969), 437.
77. Jonas, *Isolationism in America,* 121.
78. M. Leigh, *Mobilizing Consent* (Westport, Conn., 1976), 34.
79. D. C. Watt, *How War Came* (1989), 125.
80. D. Reynolds, *The Creation of the Anglo-American Alliance 1937–41* (1981), 32.
81. L. Baker, *Days of Sorrow and Pain: Leo Baeck and the Berlin Jews* (New York, 1978), 226–7.
82. Ickes, *Secret Diary* II, 468.
83. F. W. Marks, "Six Between Roosevelt and Hitler: America's Role in the Appeasement of Nazi Germany," *Historical Journal* 28, 4 (1985), 975.
84. A. A. Offner, *American Appeasement* (Cambridge, Mass., 1969), 268.
85. J. H. Stiller, *George S. Messersmith* (Chapel Hill, N.C., 1987), 128.
86. Dallek, *Roosevelt and Foreign Policy,* 187.
87. Cole, *Roosevelt and Isolationists,* 289.
88. Leigh, *Mobilizing Consent,* 48.
89. Ickes, *Secret Diary* II, 545 and 677.
90. L. Payne, *Lighter than Air* (1977), 178.
91. Koestler, *Arrow in Blue,* 381–4.
92. J. G. Vaeth, *Graf Zeppelin* (New York, 1958), 182.
93. Payne, *Lighter than Air,* 231.
94. M. G. Mather, "I Was on the Hindenburg," *Harper's Magazine* (Nov. 1937), 593.
95. L. Lochner, *What About Germany?* (1943), 41.
96. Vaeth, *Zeppelin,* 213.
97. CAC, LKEN 1/19, 27 Feb. 1936.
98. H. Eckener, *My Zeppelins* (1957), 180.
99. D. H. Robinson and C. L. Keller, *"Up Ship!"* (Annapolis, Md., 1982), 229.
100. Ickes, *Secret Diary* II, 173.
101. Eckener, *Zeppelins,* 170.

CHAPTER XXI

1. Hart-Davis, *Hitler's Olympics,* 49.
2. *Hitler's Table-Talk,* 426.
3. Quoted by W. J. Baker, *Jesse Owens* (1986), 4.
4. François-Poncet, *Fateful Years,* 203.
5. B. F. Gordon, *Olympic Architecture* (New York, 1983), 37.
6. T. Wolfe, *You Can't Go Home Again* (Harmondsworth, 1968 edn.), 572.
7. B. Fromm, *Blood and Banquets: A Berlin Social Diary* (New York, 1990 edn.), 198–9.
8. *Manchester Guardian,* 6 Dec. 1935.
9. CAC, NBKR, 6/54/1, Will ? to P. Noel-Baker, 26 Nov. 1935.
10. *Daily Herald,* 31 Dec. 1935.
11. CAC, NBKR, 6/54/1, P. Noel-Baker to W. P. Crozier, 4 Dec. 1935.
12. CAC, NBKR, 6/54/1, Manifesto of the Organization of American Good-Will Olympic Association, 13 Dec. 1935.
13. *Manchester Guardian,* 7 Dec. 1935.
14. *NYT,* 14 July 1936.
15. A. Guttmann, *The Games Must Go On: Avery Brundage and the Olympic Movement* (New York, 1984), 71 and 73.
16. Hart-Davis, *Hitler's Olympics,* 38.
17. R. G. Reuth, *Goebbels* (1993 edn.), 214.
18. *NYT,* 3 Aug. 1936.
19. R. D. Mandell, *The Nazi Olympics* (1972), 130.
20. C. C. Graham, *Leni Riefenstahl and Olympia* (New York, 1986), 61.
21. P. Conrad, *Modern Times, Modern Places* (1999), 497.
22. *Daily Mirror,* 9 Nov. 1938. The phrase was Walter Winchell's.
23. Hart-Davis, *Hitler's Olympics,* 167.
24. A. Roberts, *Eminent Churchillians* (1994), 296.
25. S. G. Jones, *Workers at Play* (1986), 184.
26. *NYT,* 1 Aug. 1936.
27. *Spectator,* 7 Mar. 1936.
28. Guttmann, *Brundage,* 79.
29. *Times,* 4 Aug. 1936.
30. Hart-Davis, *Hitler's Olympics,* 195.
31. Baker, *Owens,* 45.
32. Orwell and Angus (eds.), *Collected Orwell* IV, 62.
33. *BDFA,* II, Series F, 47 (1994), 242.
34. *DGFP,* 2nd series, XVII, 769.
35. Rhodes James (ed.), *Chips,* 112 and 111.
36. Shirer, *Berlin Diary,* 59.
37. *Times,* 27 Aug. 1938.
38. *DGFP,* 2nd series, XVII, 758.
39. Wolfe, *Home Again,* 576.
40. CAC, PHPP 10/2, Phipps's "Berlin Diaries" (10 Dec. 1936), 170.
41. G. Sereny, *Albert Speer: His Battle with Truth* (1995), 154.
42. J. Thies, "Hitler's European Building Programme," *Journal of Contemporary History* XIII (1978), 424.

43. K. P. Fischer, *Nazi Germany* (1995), 377.
44. Papen, *Memoirs*, 388.
45. Irving, *Göring*, 161.
46. P. Schmidt, *Hitler's Interpreter* (1951), 54.
47. Irving, *Göring*, 88.
48. S. Welles, *The Time for Decision* (1944), 92.
49. R. J. Overy, *Goering, The 'Iron Man'* (1984), 73.
50. de Courcy, *Circe*, 271–2.
51. N. Henderson, *Failure of a Mission* (1940), 80.
52. Quoted by G. MacDonagh, *A Good German: Adam von Trott zu Solz* (1990), 101.
53. *Manchester Guardian*, 24 Jan. 1938.
54. L. Mosley, *The Reich Marshal* (1974), 216.
55. Schmidt, *Interpreter*, 30.
56. J. and A. Tusa, *The Nuremberg Trial* (1983), 282.
57. R. Manvell and H. Fraenkel, *Hermann Göring* (1962), 102.
58. *Hitler's Table-Talk*, 206.
59. CAC, Christie Papers 1/5/57–8, Memorandum of a conversation with Göring, 28 July 1937.
60. Lochner, *Germany*, 33.
61. Simpson, *Schacht*, 142.
62. H. Schacht, "Germany's Colonial Demands," *Foreign Affairs* 15 (Jan. 1937), 230.
63. Simpson, *Schacht*, 146.
64. Cerruti, *Ambassador's Wife*, 188.
65. Manvell and Fraenkel, *Göring*, 151.
66. Simpson, *Schacht*, 141.
67. D. Irving, *The Rise and Fall of the Luftwaffe: The Life of Erhard Milch* (1973), 54.
68. Overy, *Goering*, 78.
69. R. J. Overy, "Hitler's War and the German Economy: A Reinterpretation," *Economic History Review* 35 (May 1982), 279.
70. CAC, Christie Papers, 1/5/57–8, 28 July 1937.
71. J. Gehl, *Austria, Germany, and the Anschluss 1931–1938* (1963), 135.
72. K. von Schuschnigg, *The Brutal Takeover* (1969), 90.
73. Schmidt, *Interpreter*, 59.
74. CAC, HLFX, 410.3.2.
75. Schuschnigg, *Takeover*, 170.
76. Manvell and Fraenkel, *Göring*, 156.
77. *DGFP*, Series D, I, 381.
78. *Ibid.* 376.
79. R. Luza, *Austro-German Relations in the Anschluss Era* (Princeton, N.J., 1975), 8.
80. J. Lewis, *Fascism and the Working Class in Austria 1918–1934* (Oxford, 1991), 78, quoting a Social-Democrat newspaper of 1931.
81. E. Lichtenburger, *Vienna: Bridge Between Cultures* (1993), 94.
82. G. E. Gedye, *Fallen Bastions* (1939), 152.
83. Schuschnigg, *Takeover*, 65.
84. G. Brook-Shepherd, *Anschluss: The Rape of Austria* (1963), xxi.
85. *DGFP*, Series C, VI, 1088.
86. Starhemberg, *Between Hitler and Mussolini*, 174.

87. Gehl, *Anschluss,* 169.

88. K. von Schuschnigg, *Austrian Requiem* (1947), 20–5.

89. *BDFA,* II, Series F, 14, 279.

90. Schuschnigg, *Requiem,* 279.

91. Brook-Shepherd, *Anschluss,* 80 and 65.

92. CAC, CHAR 2/328/75, Unity Mitford to Winston Churchill, 5 March 1938.

93. Schuschnigg, *Takeover,* 255.

94. Gedye, *Bastions,* 288.

95. Schuschnigg, *Requiem,* 50. Schuschnigg's description of scar-faced Gestapo men only held true for a tiny minority of senior officers. The Gestapo was primarily recruited from career policemen, very few of whom had been to university where they would have got sabre scars. See G. C. Browder, *Hitler's Enforcers: Gestapo and the SS Security Forces in the Nazi Revolution* (Oxford, 1997), Appendix.

96. *BDFA,* II, Series F, 14, 322.

97. E. B. Bukey, *Hitler's Hometown* (Bloomington, Ind., 1986), 168.

98. R. H. Bruce Lockhart, *Guns or Butter* (1938), 253.

99. G. Clare, *Last Waltz in Vienna* (1982 edn.), 195.

100. R. Schwarz, "Bürckel and Innitzer" in F. Parkinson (ed.), *Conquering the Past: Austrian Nazism Yesterday and Today* (Detroit, Mich., 1989), 138.

101. Gedye, *Bastions,* 268.

102. P. Gay, *Freud: A Life for Our Time* (1988), 619.

103. G. E. Berkley, *Vienna and its Jews* (Cambridge, Mass., 1988), 253.

104. S. Gardner and G. Stevens, *Red Vienna and the Golden Age of Psychology, 1918–1938* (New York, 1992), 124.

105. *BDFA,* II, Series F, 14, 360.

106. J. Lipski, *Diplomat in Berlin 1933–1939* (New York, 1968), 411.

107. *Daily Telegraph,* 16 Mar. 1938.

108. *Times,* 19 July 1938.

109. *BDFA,* II, Series F, 14, 340.

110. *Ibid.* 359–60.

111. Lockhart, *Guns,* 246.

112. Brook-Shepherd, *Anschluss,* 209.

113. D. Dilks (ed.), *The Diaries of Sir Alexander Cadogan OM 1938–1945* (1971), 70.

114. *BDFA,* II, Series F, 14, 290–1.

115. A. Bullock, "Hitler and the Origins of the Second World War," *Proceedings of the British Academy* 53 (1967), 271.

116. Toland, *Hitler,* 472.

117. François-Poncet, *Fateful Years,* 257.

118. R. Kee, *Munich* (1988), 144.

119. Noakes and Pridham, *Documents on Nazism,* 539.

120. R. A. C. Parker, *Chamberlain and Appeasement* (1993), 137.

121. I. Lukes, *Czechoslovakia between Stalin and Hitler* (Oxford, 1996), 56.

122. Weinberg, *Foreign Policy of Germany 1937–1939,* 409.

123. T. Taylor, *Munich: The Price of Peace* (1979), 722 and 721.

124. V. S. Mamatey and R. Luza, *A History of the Czechoslovak Republic 1918–1948* (Princeton, N.J., 1973), 247.

125. Cooper, *Old Men Forget,* 229.

126. *Daily Telegraph,* 26 Sept. 1938.

127. Henderson, *Mission,* 160.

128. Gisevius, *Bitter End,* 325.

129. M. Toscano, *The Origins of the Pact of Steel* (Baltimore, Md., 1967), 81.

130. Brendon, *Churchill,* 132.

131. *IMTN* II, 425.

132. Fest, *Third Reich,* 47.

133. Fest, *Hitler,* 536–7.

134. L. S. Dawidowicz, *The War Against the Jews 1933–45* (1975), 101.

135. M. Gilbert, *The Holocaust* (1986), 70.

136. S. Rodgers, *Red Saint, Pink Daughter* (1996), 161.

137. Reuth, *Goebbels,* 241.

138. *IMTN* I, 981.

139. Conot, *Nuremberg,* 342.

140. *IMTN* I, 984.

141. *The Memoirs of Field-Marshal Keitel* (1965), 81.

142. *DGFP,* Series D, VI, 15.

143. *DGFP,* Series D, VI, 38.

144. D. C. Watt, "Misinformation, Misconception, Mistrust: Episodes in British Policy and the Approach to War, 1938–1939" in M. Bentley and J. Stevenson (eds.), *High and Low Politics in Modern Britain* (Oxford, 1983), 244.

145. *IMTN* III (1946), 585.

146. M. Bloch, *Ribbentrop* (1992), 220.

147. *The Von Hassell Diaries* (1948), 66.

148. *IMTN* III, 574.

149. Sereny, *Speer,* 186. For further evidence of Hitler's "globalist" intentions see M. Michaelis, "World Power Status or World Dominion," *Historical Journal* 15 (1972), 331–60.

150. Carr, *Hitler,* 51.

151. Speer, *Inside Third Reich,* 162.

CHAPTER XXII

1. G. Rochat, "L'Attento a Graziani e la repressione italiana nel 1936–37," *Italia Contemporanea* 118 (1975), 21.

2. Muggeridge (ed.), *Ciano's Diary 1937–1938,* 9.

3. T. E. Hachey (ed.), *Anglo-Vatican Relations, 1914–1939* (Boston, Mass., 1972), 277 and 341.

4. *Le Temps,* 5 July 1933.

5. G. Lewy, *The Catholic Church and Nazi Germany* (1964), 165, 160 and 93.

6. *DBFP,* 2nd series, V, 525.

7. *DGFP,* Series D, I, 967.

8. *Hitler's Table-Talk,* 143.

9. Rhodes, *Vatican,* 198 and 200.

10. G. O. Kent, "Pope Pius XII and Germany: Some Aspects of German–Vatican Relations 1933–1943," *American Historical Journal* 70 (Oct. 1964), 62.

11. O. Friedländer, *Pius XII and the Third Reich* (1966), 4.

12. Hachey (ed.), *Anglo-Vatican Relations*, 360.

13. *Ibid.* 379 and 370.

14. Muggeridge (ed.), *Ciano's Diary 1937–1938*, 147.

15. *Acta Apostolicae Sedis* 29 (Rome, 1937), 149.

16. Delzell (ed.), *Papacy and Totalitarianism*, 72.

17. Lewy, *Church and Nazi Germany*, 326.

18. D. Carpi, "The Catholic Church and Italian Jewry Under the Fascists (To the Death of Pius XI)," *Yad Vashem Studies* IV (1975), 48, 46 and 56.

19. G. Passalecq and B. Suchecky, *The Hidden Encyclical of Pius XI* (1997), 252 and 247.

20. Binchy, *Church and State*, 673–4.

21. Sarti (ed.), *Ax Within*, 192.

22. M. Michaelis, *Mussolini and the Jews* (Oxford, 1978), 95.

23. *OOM* XXIV, 82.

24. A. Stille, *Benevolence and Betrayal: Five Italian Jewish Families under Fascism* (1992), 53.

25. D. V. Segre, *Memoirs of a Fortunate Jew* (1987), 49.

26. Keene (ed.), *Neither Liberty Nor Bread*, 219.

27. *BDFA*, II, Series F, 13, 7.

28. M. Knox, *Mussolini Unleashed 1939–1941* (Cambridge, 1982), 12.

29. V. de Grazia, *The Culture of Consent* (Cambridge, 1981), 185.

30. Quoted by A. de Grand, "Women under Italian Fascism," *Historical Journal* 19, 4 (1976), 965.

31. Quoted by D. Thompson, *State Control in Fascist Italy* (Manchester, 1991), 124.

32. V. de Grazia, *How Fascism Ruled Women* (Berkeley, Cal., 1992), 214.

33. *BDFA*, II, Series F, 12, 72.

34. M. Moore, *Fourth Shore* (1940), 18.

35. Segrè, *Balbo*, 293.

36. G. L. Steer, *A Date in the Desert* (1939), 132.

37. Segrè, *Balbo*, 297.

38. *BDFA*, II, Series F, 13, 25.

39. E. D. O'Brien, "With the Duce in Libya," *English Review* 64 (May 1937), 553.

40. Moore, *Fourth Shore*, 13 and 18.

41. Segrè, *Balbo*, 313.

42. Moore, *Fourth Shore*, 117.

43. Steer, *Date*, 162.

44. Segrè, *Balbo*, 378.

45. D. C. Watt, "The Rome–Berlin Axis, 1936–1940: Myth and Reality," *Review of Politics* XXII (1960), 523.

46. D. Alfieri, *Dictators Face to Face* (1954), 53.

47. F. W. Deakin, *The Brutal Friendship* (Harmondsworth, 1962), 63.

48. A. Collier, *Duce!* (1971), 376.

49. Kirkpatrick, *Mussolini*, 333.

50. E. Dollmann, *The Interpreter* (1967), 159.

51. G. B. Guerri, *Galeazzo Ciano* (Milan, 1979), 69.

52. E. Ciano, *My Truth* (1975), 86.

53. Dollmann, *Interpreter,* 220 and 160.
54. W. Phillips, *Ventures in Diplomacy* (1955), 116.
55. Dollmann, *Interpreter,* 154.
56. Phillips, *Ventures,* 92.
57. G. A. Craig and F. Gilbert, *Diplomats 1919–39* (Princeton, N.J., 1953), 515.
58. P. V. Cannistraro, *Historical Dictionary of Fascist Italy* (Westport, Conn., 1982), 228.
59. Craig and Gilbert, *Diplomats,* 517.
60. *BDFA,* II, Series F, 13, 70 and 69.
61. Muggeridge (ed.), *Ciano's Diary 1937–1938,* 13.
62. Alfieri, *Dictators,* 197.
63. Guerri, *Ciano,* 388.
64. *BDFA,* II, Series F, 12, 60.
65. Wiskemann, *Axis,* 86.
66. M. Muggeridge (ed.), *Ciano's Diplomatic Papers* (1948), 87.
67. *DGFP,* Series C, V, 1002 and 1000.
68. *DGFP,* Series C, V, 637.
69. *DGFP,* Series C, VI, 32.
70. Wiskemann, *Axis,* 102.
71. Starhemberg, *Hitler and Mussolini,* 170.
72. Mack Smith, *Roman Empire,* 140.
73. Starhemberg, *Hitler and Mussolini,* 238.
74. R. Overy, *The Road to War* (1989), 170.
75. Library of Congress, Spaatz Papers, Box 134. Göring's view was also shared by Georges Mandel, who forecast victory against Hitler in six months, or in three months if Italy fought on the side of Germany.
76. Muggeridge (ed.), *Ciano's Papers,* 162.
77. Starhemberg, *Hitler and Mussolini,* 170.
78. *NYT,* 25 and 26 Sep. 1937.
79. *BDFA,* II, Series F, 13, 63.
80. *NYT,* 30, 27 and 29 Sep. 1937.
81. *BDFA,* II, Series F, 13, 64.
82. *NYT,* 26 Sep. 1937.
83. Mack Smith, *Mussolini,* 217.
84. Muggeridge (ed.), *Ciano's Diary 1937–1938,* 27 and 47.
85. Knox, *Mussolini Unleashed,* 35.
86. Muggeridge (ed.), *Ciano's Papers,* 152.
87. Muggeridge (ed.), *Ciano's Diary 1937–1938,* 73.
88. Binchy, *Church and State,* 660.
89. *NYT,* 2 and 4 May 1938.
90. Weizsäcker, *Memoirs,* 129.
91. J. Whittam, "The Italian General Staff and the Coming of the Second World War" in A. Preston (ed.), *General Staffs and Diplomacy Before the Second World War* (1978), 93.
92. Clough, *Economic History of Italy,* 262.
93. *Hitler's Table-Talk,* 268.
94. D. Mack Smith, *Italy and its Monarchy* (1989), 295.

95. Muggeridge (ed.), *Ciano's Diary 1937–1938*, 114.
96. R. Spitzy, *How We Squandered the Reich* (1997), 209.
97. Baynes (ed.), *Speeches of Hitler* II (1969), 1462.
98. *NYT,* 3 May 1938.
99. Toscano, *Pact of Steel,* 19 and 23.
100. Muggeridge (ed.), *Ciano's Diary 1937–1938*, 124.
101. *NYT,* 7 May 1938.
102. Binchy, *Church and State,* 614.
103. H. Fornari, *Mussolini's Gadfly: Roberto Farinacci* (Nashville, Tenn., 1971), 185.
104. *DBFP,* 3rd series, III (1950), 497 and 350.
105. *FRUS 1938,* II (1955), 591 and 596.
106. Michaelis, *Mussolini and Jews,* 195.
107. *DGFP,* 3rd series, IV, 547.
108. Muggeridge (ed.), *Ciano's Diary 1939–1943,* 56.
109. Muggeridge (ed.), *Ciano's Diary 1937–1938,* 148.
110. Kirkpatrick, *Mussolini,* 348.
111. *DBFP,* 3rd series, III, 349.
112. Gallo, *Mussolini's Italy,* 290.
113. *DBFP,* 3rd series, III, 500.
114. Muggeridge (ed.), *Ciano's Papers,* 251.
115. *DGFP,* Series D, IV, 533.
116. Mack Smith, *Roman Empire,* 136.
117. Collier, *Duce,* 150.
118. *DGFP,* Series D, IV, 533.
119. *Hassell Diaries,* 44.
120. B. J. Fischer, *King Zog and the Struggle for Stability in Albania* (New York, 1984), 279.
121. *BDFA,* II, Series F, 15, 26.
122. S. Pollo and A. Puto, *The History of Albania* (1981), 225.
123. Watt, *How War Came,* 214.
124. Toscano, *Pact of Steel,* 283.
125. Ciano, *Truth,* 161.
126. De Felice, *Mussolini il Duce* II: *Lo Stato totalitario 1936–1940* (1981), 653.
127. Zamagni, *Economic History of Italy,* 271.

CHAPTER XXIII

1. *NYT,* 18 Apr. 1937.
2. P. Dupays, *Voyages Autour du Monde* (Paris, 1938), 102.
3. *BDFA,* II, Series F, 23, 20.
4. A. Werth, *The Twilight of France* (1942), 139.
5. Dupays, *Voyages,* 226.
6. O. Bernier, *Fireworks at Dusk: Paris in the Thirties* (Boston, Mass., 1993), 260. Ironically the organiser of the Soviet pavilion was recalled to Russia in 1937 and arrested on charges of "spying for France." (*Memoirs of Ivanov-Razumnick* translated by P. Squire [1965], 307.)

7. Dupays, *Voyages,* 109.
8. Martin, *Editor,* 209.
9. P. Greenhalgh, *Ephemeral Vistas* (1988), 133.
10. Dupays, *Voyages,* 88.
11. *NYT,* 8 Aug. 1937.
12. *Illustrated London News,* 29 Apr. 1939.
13. P. Dupays, *L'Exposition Internationale de 1937* (Paris, 1938), 156, 230 and 201–3.
14. J. Green, *Personal Record 1928–1939* (n.d., 1940), 287.
15. E. M. Forster, *Two Cheers for Democracy* (Harmondsworth, 1965 edn.), 16. Dupays, *L'Exposition,* 203.
16. P. White, *Elsa Schiaparelli: Empress of Paris Fashion* (1986), 172.
17. E. Schiaparelli, *Shocking Life* (1954), 79.
18. White, *Schiaparelli,* 176.
19. V. Steele, *Paris Fashion* (Oxford, 1988), 250.
20. *NYT,* 30 Apr. 1937.
21. Seidman, in *French Historical Studies* (1981), 266.
22. Adamthwaite, *France and Second World War,* 58.
23. D. and M. Johnson, *The Age of Illusion* (1987), 111.
24. *BDFA,* II, Series F, 23, 16.
25. A. Werth, *France and Munich* (1939), 104.
26. Duroselle, *Décadence,* 309.
27. Lacouture, *Blum,* 375.
28. CAC, PHPP 1/19, Phipps to Eden (quoting Joseph Caillaux), 9 Nov. 1937.
29. Bullitt (ed.), *For the President,* 173.
30. A. Prost, "Le Climat Social" in R. Rémond and J. Bourdin (eds.), *Edouard Daladier, Chef du Gouvernement* (Paris, 1977), 102.
31. CAC, PHPP 1/19, Phipps to Eden, 30 Sept. 1937.
32. CAC, PHPP 1/20, Phipps to Halifax, 28 Mar. 1938.
33. Colton, *Blum,* 303.
34. P. Lazareff, *Deadline: The Behind-the-Scenes Story of the Last Decade in France* (New York, 1942), 203.
35. *BDFA,* II, Series F, 23, 154.
36. Craig and Gilbert, *Diplomats,* 391.
37. Churchill, *Second World War* I, 236.
38. R. J. Young, *France and the Origins of the Second World War* (1996), 30.
39. *Times,* 19 June 1973.
40. Adamthwaite, *France and Second World War,* 103.
41. A. and V. M. Toynbee (eds.), *Survey of International Affairs 1939–1946: The Initial Triumph of the Axis* (1958), 170.
42. M. Gamelin, *Servir* II (Paris, 1946), 333.
43. W. Jedrzejewicz (ed.), *Diplomat in Paris 1936–1939* (New York, 1970), 263.
44. V. Cronin, *Paris: City of Light, 1919–1939* (1994), 291.
45. E. de Réau, *Edouard Daladier 1884–1970* (Paris, 1993), 61.
46. M. S. Alexander, *The Republic in Danger* (Cambridge, 1992), 144.
47. E. Weber, *The Hollow Years: France in the 1930s* (1995), 244.
48. J.-P. Sartre, *The Reprieve* (Harmondsworth, 1963), 58.
49. *BDFA,* II, Series F, 23, 180.

50. Duroselle, *Décadence,* 280.
51. Bloch, *Strange Defeat,* 168.
52. Y. Lacaze, *France and Munich* (Boulder, Col., 1995), 330.
53. To quote the title of R. L. Dinardo's book (1991).
54. Gamelin, *Servir* II, 345.
55. "Pertinax," *Gravediggers,* 89.
56. Alexander, *Republic in Danger,* 45.
57. Rémond and Bourdin, *Daladier,* 228.
58. Jedrzejewicz, *Diplomat in Paris,* 72.
59. H. Noguères, *Munich* (1965), 22.
60. CAC, PHPP 4/3, Hardinge to Phipps, 2 June 1938.
61. CAC, PHPP 4/1, Phipps to George VI, 1 Feb. 1938.
62. Werth, *France and Munich,* 205.
63. *NYT,* 20 July 1938.
64. *NYT,* 17 July 1938.
65. D. Cooper, *The Light of Common Day* (1959), 221.
66. *NYT,* 23 July 1938.
67. D. G. Troyansky, "Monumental Politics: National History and Local Memory in French *Monuments au Morts* in the Department of the Aisne since 1870," *French Historical Studies* XV (Spring 1987), 122. See also A. Gregory, *The Silence of Memory* (Oxford, 1994), 158–9 and *passim.*
68. P. M. H. Bell, *The Origins of the Second World War in Europe* (1997 edn.), 99.
69. Cooper, *Light,* 223.
70. BDFA, II, Series F, 23, 170.
71. *NYT,* 22 July 1938.
72. Bradford, *George VI,* 273.
73. Bullitt (ed.), *For the President,* 210.
74. J. E. Dreifort, "The French Role in the Least Unpleasant Solution" in M. Latynski (ed.), *Reappraising the Munich Pact* (Washington, D.C., 1992), 39.
75. G. Fergusson, "Munich: The French and British Roles," *International Affairs* 44 (Oct. 1968), 654.
76. S. Butterworth, "Daladier and the Munich Crisis: a Reappraisal," *Journal of Contemporary History* 9 (July 1974), 207.
77. Lacaze, *Munich,* 321.
78. CAC, PHPP 1/20, Phipps to Halifax, 14 Sep. 1938.
79. C. de Gaulle, *Lettres Notes et Carnets 1919–Juin 1940* (Paris, 1980), 442.
80. Noguères, *Munich,* 99.
81. de Gaulle, *Lettres,* 475.
82. A. Adamthwaite, "France and the Coming of War" in Mommsen and Kettenacker, *Fascist Challenge,* 254.
83. Lacaze, *Munich,* 361. The remark was Bernard de Montferrand's.
84. Rémond and Bourdin, *Daladier,* 259.
85. Sartre, *Reprieve,* 42.
86. Noguères, *Munich,* 206. The remark was made by the Secretary-General of the teachers' union.
87. *Le Populaire,* 20 Sep. 1938.
88. *L'Humanité,* 20 Sep. 1938.

89. Werth, *France and Munich*, 302.
90. Bullitt (ed.), *For the President*, 297.
91. *BDFA*, II, Series F, 23, 182.
92. J. M. Sherwood, *Georges Mandel and the Third Republic* (Stanford, Cal., 1970), 213.
93. Bernier, *Fireworks*, 289.
94. Cooper, *Old Men Forget*, 240.
95. Lacaze, *Munich*, 176.
96. G. Bonnet, *De Washington au Quai d'Orsay* (Geneva, 1946), 294.
97. De Beauvoir, *Prime of Life*, 267.
98. *Paris-Soir*, 1 Oct. 1938.
99. Noguères, *Munich*, 305–6.
100. Cronin, *Paris*, 295.
101. R. Aron, *Mémoire* (Paris, 1983), 147.
102. Quoted by A. Adamthwaite, *Grandeur and Misery: France's Bid for Power in Europe 1914–1940* (1995), 201.
103. *The Journals of André Gide* III: *1929–1939* (1949), 405.
104. S. Albouy, *Bernanos et la politique* (Toulouse, 1980), 183.
105. De Beauvoir, *Prime of Life*, 268.
106. Bullitt (ed.), *For the President*, 287.
107. Réau, *Daladier*, 299.
108. T. Kemp, *The French Economy 1913–39* (1972), 156.
109. Rémond and Bourdin, *Daladier*, 93.
110. Jackson, *Popular Front*, 111–112.
111. J.-P. Azena, *From Munich to the Liberation, 1938–1944* (Cambridge, 1984), 18.
112. Duroselle, *Décadence*, 238.
113. *BDFA*, II, Series F, 23, 202.
114. Sherwood, *Mandel*, 216.
115. Werth, *France and Munich*, 433.
116. T. Maga, "Closing the Doors: The French Government and Refugee Policy, 1933–1939," *French Historical Studies* XII (Spring 1982), 429.
117. Bullitt (ed.), *For the President*, 350.
118. L. Stein, *Beyond Death and Exile* (1979), 22.
119. H. L. Matthews, *Half of Spain Died* (New York, 1973), 217.
120. Regler, *Owl of Minerva*, 323.
121. Quoted by Werth, *France and Munich*, 427.
122. *Nation* (6 May 1939), 542.
123. I. de Palencia, *Smouldering Freedom* (1946), 67.
124. A. Koestler, *Scum of the Earth* (1955), 97.
125. L. Guilloux, "The Betrayal of the Refugees," *New Republic* 98 (22 Feb. 1939), 68.
126. Regler, *Owl of Minerva*, 321. Conservative newspapers in Britain censored the story for the sake of good relations with France.
127. W. I. Shorrock, *From Ally to Enemy* (Kent, Ohio, 1988), 271.
128. *Documents Diplomatiques Français 1932–1939* 2e serie, XIII (Paris, 1979), 824.
129. J. Moch, *Une Si Longue Vie* (Paris, 1976), 153.
130. Lazareff, *Deadline*, 220.
131. A. Maurois, *Why France Fell* (1940), 24–5.

132. W. L. Shirer, *The Collapse of the Third Republic* (Richmond Hill, Canada, 1971 edn.), 416.

133. C. W. Brooks, "Jean Renoir's *The Rules of the Game*," *French Historical Studies* VII (Fall 1971), 273.

134. Warner, *Laval*, 147.

135. Horne, *Price of Glory*, xvi.

136. Weber, *Hollow Years*, 243.

137. Flanner, *Paris*, 222.

138. H. R. Lottman, *Albert Camus* (1979), 209.

139. Beauvoir, *Prime of Life*, 303.

CHAPTER XXIV

1. R. W. Thompson, *Churchill and Morton* (1978), 72.

2. Maurois, *Why France Fell*, 33.

3. J. McMillan, *The Way It Happened 1935–1950* (1980), 106.

4. CAC, PHPP 1/20, ff 14, 15 and 22, Phipps to Halifax, 28 Mar. 1938.

5. P. Stansky (ed.), *Churchill: A Profile* (1973), 52.

6. R. Rhodes James, *Churchill: A Study in Failure 1900–1939* (1970), 90.

7. J. Colville, *The Fringes of Power* (1985), 122.

8. D. Cannadine, *Aspects of Aristocracy* (1994), 132.

9. R. E. Foster, *Lord Randolph Churchill* (Oxford, 1981), 177.

10. H. Vickers, *Gladys* (1979), 227.

11. Brendon, *Churchill*, 112.

12. J. Campbell, *F. E. Smith* (1983), 821.

13. A. Chisholm and M. Davie, *Lord Beaverbrook* (New York, 1993), 163.

14. M. Foot, *Debts of Honour* (1980), 79.

15. C. Lysaght, *Brendan Bracken* (1979), 196.

16. Brendon, *Churchill*, 12.

17. *Life*, 9 Jan. 1939.

18. Lord Beaverbrook, *The Decline and Fall of Lloyd George* (1966), 306.

19. Taylor, *English History*, 4.

20. Charmley, *Churchill*, 441.

21. A. J. P. Taylor, *From Napoleon to the Second International: Essays on Nineteenth-Century Europe* (1993), 374.

22. *Times*, 7 Nov. 1938.

23. Gilbert, *Churchill* V, 457.

24. G. Craig, "Churchill and Germany" in R. Blake and R. Louis (eds.), *Churchill* (Oxford, 1994 edn.), 36.

25. D. Dilks, *Neville Chamberlain* I (Cambridge, 1984), 441.

26. N. Rose, *Churchill: An Unruly Life* (1994), 181.

27. R. J. Minney, *The Private Papers of Hore-Belisha* (1960), 130.

28. P. Addison, *Churchill on the Home Front 1900–1955* (1992), 278.

29. Jones, *Diary with Letters*, 422.

30. K. Middlemas, *Diplomacy of Illusion* (1972), 54.

31. Feiling, *Chamberlain*, 323.

32. D. Cannadine, *The Pleasures of the Past* (1989), 311.
33. Dilks, *Chamberlain* I, 32.
34. "Cato," *Guilty Men* (1940), 41.
35. A. Salter, *Memoirs of a Public Servant* (1961), 256.
36. W. J. Brown, *So Far . . .* (1943), 222.
37. Colville, *Fringes of Power,* 79.
38. Cockett, *Twilight,* 8.
39. Pimlott (ed.), *Diary of Dalton,* 225.
40. Harvey (ed.), *Diaries of Oliver Harvey,* 48.
41. Feiling, *Chamberlain,* 321, 317, 314 and 292.
42. Middlemas, *Illusion,* 116.
43. Andrew, *Secret Service,* 408.
44. R. P. Shay, *British Rearmament in the Thirties* (Princeton, N.J., 1977), 286.
45. CAC, HOBE 1/5/12, 14 Mar. 1938.
46. Bond (ed.), *Chief of Staff,* 99 and 129.
47. S. Newton, *Profits of Peace* (Oxford, 1996), 111.
48. J. P. D. Dunbabin, "British Rearmament in the 1930s," *Historical Journal* 18, 3 (1975), 598.
49. Spitzy, *Reich,* 184.
50. Carlton, *Eden,* 82.
51. E. Shuckburgh, *Descent to Suez* (1986), 131.
52. A. Roberts, *'The Holy Fox': A Biography of Lord Halifax* (1991), 31.
53. CAC, HLFX, Halifax to Sir Eric Mieville, 29 Oct. 1939.
54. M. Cowling, *The Impact of Hitler* (Cambridge, 1975), 9.
55. J. Charmley, *Chamberlain and the Lost Peace* (1989), 18.
56. Lord Birkenhead, *Halifax* (1965), 326.
57. W. P. Crozier, *Off the Record* (1973), 71.
58. Taylor, *Beaverbrook,* 270.
59. Birkenhead, *Halifax,* 248.
60. CAC, HLFX, 410.3.2.
61. *Ibid.*
62. Henderson, *Mission,* 23.
63. CAC, HLFX, 410.3.2, Henderson to Halifax, 23 Nov. 1937.
64. Cockett, *Twilight,* 65.
65. *Daily Herald,* 1 Dec. 1937.
66. CAC, HLFX, 410.3.2.
67. Cockett, *Twilight,* 53.
68. *Times,* 23 Nov. 1938.
69. J. Lewis, *The Left Book Club: An Historical Record* (1970), 43 and 102.
70. C. Sykes, *Evelyn Waugh* (1975), 184.
71. "Palinurus," *The Unquiet Grave* (1946 edn.), 24.
72. A. Adamthwaite, "The British Government and the Media, 1937–1938," *Journal of Contemporary History* 18 (1983), 291.
73. P. Scannell and D. Cardiff, *A Social History of Broadcasting* (Oxford, 1991), 88.
74. Brendon and Whitehead, *Windsors,* 76.
75. J. Richards, *The Age of the Dream Palace* (1984), 102.
76. MacNeice, *Autumn Journal,* 17

77.   R. Ellmann, *Yeats: The Man and the Masks* (1949), 281.
78.   *Times,* 15 Nov. 1936.
79.   Nicolson, *Diaries 1930–1939,* 342
80.   Rowse, *All Souls,* 77.
81.   Pimlott (ed.), *Diary of Dalton,* 231.
82.   Dilks (ed.), *Cadogan,* 47.
83.   V. Rothwell, *Anthony Eden: A Political Biography 1931–57* (Manchester, 1992), 250.
84.   CAC, STRN 4/1, Halifax to Strang, 7 Jan. 1957.
85.   Carlton, *Eden,* 127–8.
86.   *Times,* 25 Feb. 1938.
87.   R. A. Butler, *The Art of Memory* (1982), 51.
88.   Northedge, *Troubled Giant,* 491.
89.   CAC, HOBE 1/5/42, 9 Feb. 1939.
90.   *The Memoirs of the Earl of Woolton* (1959), 132.
91.   R. Bruce Lockhart, *Jan Masaryk* (1956 edn.), 18.
92.   *Daily Telegraph,* 15 Sept. 1938.
93.   *Liverpool Weekly Post,* 11 May 1938.
94.   Gilbert, *Churchill* V, 927.
95.   Lord Strang, *Home and Abroad* (1956), 134.
96.   N. Ferguson (ed.), *Virtual History* (1997), 282.
97.   *DBFP,* 3rd series, II, 11 and 21.
98.   Noguères, *Munich,* 77.
99.   N. Annan, *Our Age* (1995 edn.), 267.
100.   *DBFP,* 3rd series, II, 256.
101.   H. Aulach, "Britain and the Sudeten Issue, 1938: The Evolution of a Policy," *Journal of Contemporary History* 18 (1983), 251.
102.   Henderson, *Mission,* 147.
103.   *DBFP,* 3rd series, II, 257.
104.   CAC, HOBE 1/5/22.
105.   Minney, *Hore-Belisha,* 146.
106.   CAC, HOBE 1/5/23.
107.   Strang, *Home and Abroad,* 137.
108.   Harvey (ed.), *Diaries of Oliver Harvey,* 187–8.
109.   Middlemas, *Illusion,* 351.
110.   Harvey (ed.), *Diaries of Oliver Harvey,* 187.
111.   U. Bialer, "Telling the Truth to the People: Britain's Decision to Publish the Diplomatic Papers of the Inter-War Period," *Historical Journal* 26, 2 (1983), 357.
112.   Strang, *Home and Abroad,* 140.
113.   Schmidt, *Interpreter,* 96.
114.   Dilks (ed.), *Cadogan,* 107.
115.   *Daily Telegraph,* 23 Sept. 1938.
116.   *Daily Telegraph,* 26 Sept. 1938.
117.   *Times,* 26 Sept. 1938.
118.   *Times,* 27 Sept. 1938.
119.   Barnes and Nicholson (eds.), *Amery Diary,* 485.
120.   CAC, HOBE 1/5/38.

121. *Daily Telegraph,* 15 Sept. 1938.
122. *DBFP,* 3rd series, II, 571.
123. Taylor, *Munich,* 884.
124. *Times,* 28 Sept. 1938.
125. *Daily Telegraph,* 29 Sept. 1938.
126. Feiling, *Chamberlain,* 381.
127. Spitzy, *Reich,* 254.
128. M. Muggeridge, *The Thirties* (1967 edn.), 325.
129. Brendon and Whitehead, *Windsors,* 106.
130. *Times,* 6 Oct. 1938.
131. Young (ed.), *Diaries of Lockhart,* 406.
132. Graves and Hodge, *Long Weekend,* 440.
133. R. Eatwell, "Munich, Public Opinion and Popular Front," *Journal of Contemporary History* 6, 4 (1971), 126.
134. D. Lammers, "From Whitehall after Munich: The Foreign Office and the Future Course of British Policy," *Historical Journal* 16, 4 (1973), 832.
135. CAC, STRN 4/2, O'Neill to Strang, 29 Nov. 1938.
136. *Time & Tide,* 4 Nov. 1939.
137. Strang, *Home and Abroad,* 153.
138. R. J. O'Neill, *The German Army and the Nazi Party 1933–39* (1968 edn.), 231.
139. P. Kennedy, *The Realities Behind Diplomacy* (1981 edn.), 303. It must be said, though, that some officials, including the government's chief economic adviser, Sir Frederick Leith-Ross, considered the "silver bullets" a sound investment.
140. P. Stafford, "The Chamberlain-Halifax Visit to Rome: a reappraisal," *English Historical Journal* 98 (Jan. 1983), 79 and 89.
141. Dunbabin, in *Historical Journal* (1975), 603.
142. Templewood, *Troubled Years,* 328.
143. Charmley, *Chamberlain,* 170.
144. *Observer,* 26 Mar. 1939.
145. S. Newman, *March 1939: The British Guarantee to Poland* (Oxford, 1976), 136–7.
146. Muggeridge (ed.), *Ciano's Diary 1937–1938,* 85.
147. Newman, *March 1939,* 136.
148. J. W. Wheeler-Bennett, *Munich: Prologue to Tragedy* (1948), 376.
149. Newman, *March 1939,* 207.
150. CAC, HOBE, 1/5/58.
151. Charmley, *Chamberlain,* 178.
152. Andrew, *Secret Service,* 420.
153. Mowat, *Britain Between the Wars,* 640.
154. CAC, HOBE, 1/5/72.
155. CAC, HOBE, 1/5/77, 23 Apr. 1939.
156. *Spectator,* 2 June 1939.
157. *Evening Standard,* 11 May and 26 Apr. 1939.
158. CAC, HOBE, 1/5/80.
159. Boyce and Robertson (eds.), *Paths to War,* 254.
160. A. J. P. Taylor, *The Origins of the Second World War* (1971 edn.), 245.
161. Henderson, *Mission,* 273.
162. A. Adamthwaite, *The Making of the Second World War* (1977), 92.

163. Roberts, *Holy Fox*, 171.
164. CAC, STRN 4/3, 30 Aug. 1939.
165. S. Howarth, *August '39* (1989), 190.
166. *The Memoirs of General Lord Ismay* (1960), 84.
167. CAC, LKEN 1/23, Leo Kennedy's diary, 4 May 1940.
168. Gilbert, *Finest Hour*, 190.

CHAPTER XXV

1. Havens, *Valley*, 13.
2. Kasza, *State and Mass Media*, 177.
3. Oka Yoshitake, *Konoe*, 73.
4. *Japan Today & Tomorrow* (1940), 87.
5. *Ibid.*
6. Havens, *Valley*, 17.
7. *BDFA*, II, Series E, 17, 224.
8. H. Abend, *Chaos in Asia* (1940), 43.
9. S. Okita, *Japan's Challenging Years* (Sydney, Aus., 1983), 26.
10. Havens, *Valley*, 30.
11. *BDFA*, II, Series E, 17, 162–3.
12. E. O. Hauser, "Japan's Die-Easy Liberals," *Asia* (Jan. 1939), 36.
13. *BDFA*, II, Series E, 17, 67.
14. F. Oliver, *Special Undeclared War* (1939), 18.
15. A. Young, *China and the Helping Hand* (Cambridge, Mass., 1963), 107.
16. S. Lillico, "Knowing Not What They Do," *Asia* (Jan. 1939), 24.
17. J. Bertram, *North China Front* (1939), 494.
18. *Contemporary Japan* (Mar. 1939), 149.
19. *BDFA*, II, Series E, 17, 72.
20. *North-China Herald*, 9 Mar. 1938.
21. *BDFA*, II, Series E, 17, 72.
22. W. H. Chamberlin, "Looking Back at Japan," *Asia* (July 1939), 378.
23. Mosley, *Hirohito*, 169.
24. *Contemporary Japan* (Apr. 1939), 229–30.
25. *BDFA*, II, Series E, 16, 246.
26. Lee, *Britain and Sino-Japanese War*, 142.
27. Grew, *Ten Years*, 189.
28. *BDFA*, II, Series E, 16, 318–19.
29. Lee, *Britain and Sino-Japanese War*, 60.
30. Sato Kyozo, *Japan and Britain at the Crossroads 1939–1941* (Tokyo, 1986), 207.
31. Morley (ed.), *China Quagmire*, 329.
32. J. W. M. Chapman (ed.), *The Price of Admiralty* I (Brighton, n.d., c. 1981), xxiv.
33. *DBFP*, 2nd series, XXI, 749 and 820.
34. CAC, KNAT 1/11/118, Sir H. Knatchbull-Hugessen's diary, 16 Nov. 1937.
35. W. H. Auden and C. Isherwood, *Journey to a War* (1973 edn.), 58.
36. P. P. Y. Loh, "The Politics of Chiang Kai-shek," *Journal of Asian Studies* 25 (1966), 436.

37. Ch'en Chieh-ju, *Chiang Kai-shek's Secret Past* (Boulder, Col., 1993), 227 and 40.

38. S. Segrave, *The Soong Dynasty* (1985), 158.

39. K. Furuya, *Chiang Kai-shek: His Life and Times* (New York, 1981), 196.

40. B. Crozier, *The Man Who Lost China* (1976), 115.

41. It was subsequently called Peiping, but for ease of identification the name Peking is used here throughout.

42. E. Snow, "China's Fighting Generalissimo," *Foreign Affairs* XVI (July 1938), 616.

43. Crozier, *Man Who Lost China*, 165 and 10.

44. R. E. Herzstein, *Henry R. Luce* (New York, 1994), 101.

45. R. Sues, *Shark's Fins and Millet* (Boston, Mass., 1944), 166.

46. F. Wakeman, *Policing Shanghai* (1995), 259 and 275.

47. Boyle, *China and Japan*, 278 and 152.

48. H. Suyin, *Eldest Son* (1994), 85.

49. E. Snow, *Red Star Over China* (1968 edn.), 90.

50. K. E. Shewmaker, *Americans and Communists 1927–1945* (Ithaca, N.Y., 1971), 188.

51. Sues, *Shark's Fins*, 283–4.

52. G. Benton, *Mountain Fires* (Berkeley, Cal., 1992), 19.

53. H. Salisbury, *The Long March* (1985), 234.

54. Snow, *Red Star*, 197.

55. A. Smedley, *Battle Hymn of China* (1944), 122.

56. T. Terrill, *Mao* (New York, 1980), 27.

57. Coox, *Nomonhan* I, 66.

58. S. Schram, *Mao Tse-tung* (1967), 64 and 85.

59. Salisbury, *Long March*, 121.

60. J. R. and S. R. MacKinnon, *Agnes Smedley* (1988), 193.

61. H. Forman, *Horizon Hunter* (1942), 162.

62. Snow, *Red Star*, 229.

63. H. Abend, *My Years in China 1926–1941* (1944), 233.

64. J. M. Bertram, *Crisis in China* (1937), ix.

65. Suyin, *Eldest Son*, 151.

66. Tien-Wei Wu, "New Materials on the Xi'an Incident," *Modern China* 10 (Jan. 1984), 116.

67. Bertram, *Crisis*, 146.

68. H. L. Boorman (ed.), *Biographical Dictionary of Republican China* (New York, 1967), 329.

69. Boyle, *China and Japan*, 189.

70. J. Haslam, *The Soviet Union and the Threat from the East, 1933–41* (Pittsburgh, Pa., 1992), 105.

71. H. Conroy, "Japan's War in China: Historical Parallel to Vietnam?," *Pacific Affairs* 43 (1970), 61.

72. J. C. Hsiung and S. I. Levine, *China's Bitter Victory* (New York, 1993), 82.

73. Dorn, *Sino-Japanese War*, 7.

74. Abend, *Chaos*, 149.

75. Auden and Isherwood, *Journey*, 226 and 44.

76. A. D. Coox, "Effects of Attrition on National War Effort: The Japanese Army Experience in China, 1937–1938," *Military Affairs* 32 (1968), 57.

77. *North-China Herald*, 6 July 1938.

78. J. Belden, *Still Time to Die* (1945), 113 and 164.
79. Kalyagin, *Alien Roads,* 12.
80. *BDFA,* II, Series F, 14, 30.
81. Kalyagin, *Alien Roads,* 129.
82. Dorn, *Sino-Japanese War,* 185.
83. Sues, *Shark's Fins,* 298.
84. H. Suyin, *Destination Chungking* (1969 edn.), 58 and 84.
85. Boyle, *China and Japan,* 339.
86. IWM, Saionji, 2329.
87. Haggie, *Britannia,* 128.
88. Auden and Isherwood, *Journey,* 135.
89. *BDFA,* II, Series E, 17, 298.
90. *Military Affairs* (1968), 61.
91. Suyin, *Chungking,* 143.
92. R. B. Ekvale, "The Bombing of Chungking," *Asia* (Aug. 1939), 471–2.
93. Suyin, *Chungking,* 197.
94. *Asia* (Aug. 1939), 472.
95. Suyin, *Chungking,* 207.
96. IWM, Saionji, 2364.
97. *Asia* (Jan. 1939), 36.
98. *Contemporary Japan* (Mar. 1939), 33–4.
99. *NYT,* 22 May 1932.
100. IWM, Saionji, 2349.
101. *Contemporary Japan* (Mar. 1939), 57.
102. G. M. Berger, *Parties out of Power in Japan 1931–1941* (Princeton, N.J., 1977), 206.
103. Storry, *Double Patriots,* 248.
104. Abend, *Chaos,* 203
105. *BDFA,* II, Series E, 18, 159.
106. IWM, Saionji, 2470.
107. *BDFA,* II, Series E, 17, 244.
108. IWM, Saionji, 2495 and 2602.
109. *BDFA,* II, Series E, 18, 180.
110. Nish (ed.), *Anglo-Japanese Alienation,* 88.
111. F. C. Jones, *Shanghai and Tientsin* (Oxford, 1940), 176.
112. *BDFA,* II, Series E, 18, 200 and 202.
113. Lee, *Britain and Sino-Japanese War,* 202.
114. Coox, *Nomonhan* I, 101.
115. Butow, *Tojo,* 3 and 435.
116. Craigie, *Mask,* 127.
117. Irokawa Daitichi, *The Age of Hirohito* (1995), 82.
118. Maruyama Masao, *Thought and Behaviour,* 17.
119. IWM, Japanese War Trials, Box 149, XX–24.
120. Browne, *Tojo,* 74.
121. Coox, *Nomonhan* II, 1064, 1083 and 1089.
122. Watt, *How War Came,* 342.
123. *Diary of Kido,* 222.

124. IWM, Saionji, 2619 and 2628.

125. C. Boyd, *The Extraordinary Envoy* (Washington, D.C., 1980), 150. Stalin claimed 20,000 dead; the correct figure was nearly 20,000 dead *and* wounded.

CHAPTER XXVI

1.   R. W. Thurston, *Life and Terror in Stalin's Russia, 1934–1941* (1996), 112.

2.   *BDFA,* II, Series A, 14, 327.

3.   Z. K. Brzezinski, *The Permanent Purge* (Cambridge, Mass., 1956), 118.

4.   D. Holloway, *Stalin and the Bomb* (1994), 27.

5.   Cohen, *Bukharin,* 368 and 99.

6.   Nicolaevsky, *Soviet Elite,* 14 and 17.

7.   Lih *et al.* (eds.), *Stalin's Letters,* 155 and 168.

8.   Berger, *Shipwreck,* 107.

9.   Wood, *Communism and British Intellectuals,* 133.

10. S. Alliluyeva, *Letters to a Friend* (1967), 37.

11. T. Bergmann, G. Schaefer and M. Selden (eds.), *Bukharin in Retrospect* (New York, 1994), xvii.

12. Cohen, *Bukharin,* 365.

13. Volkogonov, *Stalin* 295–6.

14. Radzinsky, *Stalin,* 362.

15. Medvedev, *Let History Judge,* 174.

16. R. Medvedev, *Nikolai Bukharin: the last years* (New York, 1980), 136.

17. K. A. Jelenski, "The Literature of Disenchantment," *Survey* 41 (Apr. 1962), 115.

18. A. Koestler, *Darkness at Noon* (Harmondsworth, 1987), 131.

19. Radzinsky, *Stalin,* 378.

20. A. Larina, *This I Cannot Forget* (1993), 238.

21. Radzinsky, *Stalin,* 378 and 376.

22. R. C. Tucker and S. F. Cohen (eds.), *The Great Purge Trial* (New York, 1965), 666–7 and 665.

23. *NYT,* 8 Mar. 1938.

24. N. Leites and E. Bernaut, *Ritual of Liquidation* (Glencoe, Ill., 1954), 166.

25. Tucker and Cohen (eds.), *Great Purge Trial,* 331, 340 and 517.

26. *NYT,* 13 and 7 Mar. 1938.

27. *Times,* 2 Mar. 1938.

28. Maclean, *Eastern Approaches,* 95 and 93.

29. *NYT,* 13 Mar. 1938.

30. Tucker and Cohen (eds.), *Great Purge Trial,* 655.

31. R. Stites, *Russian Popular Culture: Entertainment and Society since 1900* (Cambridge, 1992), 90.

32. Thurston, *Life and Terror,* 114.

33. Tucker and Cohen (eds.), *Great Purge Trial,* xv.

34. D. Volkogonov, *The Rise and Fall of the Soviet Empire* (1998), 90.

35. Volkogonov, *Stalin,* 339.

36. A. Knight, *Beria* (Princeton, N.J., 1993), 89.

37. Nicolaevsky, *Soviet Elite,* 48.

38. Conquest, *Stalin,* 208.
39. R. Medvedev, *On Stalin and Stalinism* (Oxford, 1979), III.
40. Knight, *Beria,* 22.
41. Larina, *Forget,* 203.
42. Knight, *Beria,* 96.
43. Thurston, *Life and Terror,* 196.
44. Tucker, *Stalin in Power,* 412.
45. *NYT,* 13 Mar. 1938.
46. Tucker, *Stalin in Power,* 503.
47. *BDFA,* II, Series A, 14, 369.
48. J. Hochman, *The Soviet Union and the Failure of Collective Security, 1934–1938* (Ithaca, N.Y., 1984), 123.
49. G. F. Kennan, *Russia and the West under Lenin and Stalin* (1961), 316. Kennan's argument was anticipated in G. Hilger and A. G. Meyer, *The Incompatible Allies* (New York, 1953), 293.
50. Herwarth, *Evils,* 115 and 162.
51. T. J. Uldricks, "The Impact of the Great Purges on the People's Commissariat of Foreign Affairs," *Slavic Review* 36 (June 1977), 192.
52. M. J. Carley, "End of the 'Low, Dishonest Decade': Failure of the Anglo-Franco-Soviet Alliance in 1939," *Europe–Asia Studies* 45, 2 (1993), 315.
53. *BDFA,* II, Series A, 14, 403 and 347.
54. G. Roberts, *The Unholy Alliance* (1989), 86.
55. Carley, in *Europe–Asia Studies* 45, 310.
56. M. Harrison, *Soviet Planning in Peace and War, 1938–1945* (Cambridge, 1985), 8.
57. I. Maisky, *Who Helped Hitler?* (1964), 78.
58. *BDFA,* II, Series A, 14, 359.
59. A. Roshchin, "People's Commissariat for Foreign Affairs before World War II," *International Affairs* (May 1988), 109.
60. J. Haslam, "The Soviet Union and the Czechoslovakian Crisis of 1938," *Journal of Contemporary History* 14 (July 1979), 452.
61. Carley, in *Europe–Asia Studies* 45, 321.
62. "Munich: Witness's Account," *International Affairs* (Dec. 1988), 128–31.
63. B. Cohen, "Moscow at Munich: Did the Soviet Union Offer Unilateral Aid to Czechoslovakia?," *New European Quarterly* 12, 3 (Fall 1978), 344.
64. G. Jukes, "The Red Army and the Munich Crisis," *Journal of Contemporary History* 26 (1991), 197. Opinions about this still differ. R. C. Raack (*Stalin's Drive to the West, 1938–1945* [Stanford, Cal., 1995], 19) thinks it "unlikely that Stalin really wanted to help the Czechs at all."
65. *1939: Lessons of History* (Moscow, 1989), 193.
66. Roberts, *Unholy Alliance,* 109 and 113.
67. G. Roberts, *The Soviet Union and the Origins of the Second World War* (Basingstoke, 1995), 65.
68. *FRUS: Soviet Union 1933–39,* 741 and 739.
69. Read and Fisher, *Deadly Embrace,* 68.
70. S. Aster, "Ivan Maisky and Parliamentary Anti-appeasement, 1938–39" in A. J. P. Taylor (ed.), *Lloyd George: Twelve Essays* (1971), 344.
71. Carley, in *Europe–Asia Studies* 45, 319.

72. A. Resis (ed.), *Molotov Remembers* (Chicago, Ill., 1993), 193.
73. Roshchin, in *International Affairs* (May 1988), 114.
74. Churchill, *Second World War* I, 288.
75. Watt, *How War Came,* 113.
76. Hilger and Meyer, *Incompatible Allies,* 301.
77. L. Mosley, *On Borrowed Time* (1969), 269.
78. A. Beaufre, *1940: The Fall of France* (1967), 97.
79. R. P. Ernle-Erle-Drax, "Mission to Moscow, August 1939," *Naval Review* XL (Aug. 1952), 251.
80. CAC, Drax 6/5, 10.
81. Read and Fisher, *Deadly Embrace,* 156.
82. CAC, Drax 6/5, 15.
83. J. Herman, "Soviet Peace Efforts on the Eve of World War Two: A Review of the Soviet Documents," *Journal of Contemporary History* 15 (1980), 597.
84. Drax, in *Naval Review* XL (Nov. 1952), 400.
85. CAC, Drax 6/5, 35.
86. Beaufre, *1940,* 142.
87. R. Craig Nation, *Black Earth, Red Star* (1992), 102.
88. A. Yakovlev, *The Events of 1939: Looking Back after Fifty Years* (Moscow, 1989), 8.
89. Read and Fisher, *Deadly Embrace,* 257.
90. *DGFP,* Series D, VI, 1075.
91. Deist, *Germany and Second World War,* 706.
92. *DGFP,* Series D, VII, 62 and 89.
93. *DGFP,* Series D, VII, 133.
94. Read and Fisher, *Deadly Embrace,* 252.
95. *DGFP,* Series D, VII, 227.
96. H. Hoffmann, *Hitler was my Friend* (1955), 109.
97. Bullock, *Stalin and Hitler,* 685.
98. Hoffmann, *Hitler,* 114.
99. Herwarth, *Evils,* 162.
100. *NYT,* 23 Aug. 1939.
101. Radzinsky, *Stalin,* 443.
102. *NYT,* 23 Aug. 1939.
103. *Pravda,* 24 Aug. 1939.
104. R. Overy, *Russia's War* (1997), 74 and 87.

CONCLUSION

1. T. Harrisson, *Living through the Blitz* (1976), 27.
2. P. Padfield, *Dönitz: The Last Führer* (1989), 187.
3. C. Andrew, *For the President's Eyes Only* (1995), 118.
4. P. Gibbs, *Realities of War* (1929), 9.
5. W. Albig, *Public Opinion* (New York, 1939), 284, 305–6 and 310.
6. *Authors Take Sides on the Spanish Civil War* (1937).
7. J. M. Roberts, *The Pelican History of the World* (1980), 848.
8. Kindleberger, *World in Depression,* 10.
9. CAC, CHAR 20/204B/119.

Select Bibliography

The notes indicate the literature on which this book is based and suggest lines of further reading and research. In view of their fullness, to say nothing of the comprehensiveness of academic bibliographies, it seems otiose to compile anything more than a brief selection of the most useful general books on the subject. They are in English (with a couple of exceptions) and the place of publication is London unless otherwise stated.

Adamthwaite, A. *The Making of the Second World War* (1977)

Andrew, C. *Secret Service* (1985)

Aster, S. *1939: The Making of the Second World War* (1973)

Baer, G. W. *The Coming of the Italian–Ethiopian War* (Cambridge, Mass., 1967)

Barnhart, M. A. *Japan Prepares for Total War* (Cornell, 1987)

Bell, P. M. H. *The Origins of the Second World War in Europe* (1997 edn.)

Bernard, P. and Dubief, H. *The Decline of the Third Republic 1914–1938* (Cambridge, 1985)

Bernier, O. *Fireworks at Dusk: Paris in the Thirties* (Boston, 1993)

Binchy, D. A. *Church and State in Fascist Italy* (Oxford, 1970 edn.)

Brenan, G. *The Spanish Labyrinth* (Cambridge, 1976 edn.)

Broszat, M. *Hitler and the Collapse of Weimar Germany* (New York, 1987)

Bullock, A. *Hitler: A Study in Tyranny* (1965 edn.)

Butow, R. J. C., *Tojo and the Coming of War* (Princeton, 1961)

Cannadine, D. *The Decline and Fall of the British Aristocracy* (1990)

Cashman, S. D. *America in the Twenties and Thirties* (New York, 1989)

Cole, W. S. *Roosevelt and the Isolationists 1932–45* (Lincoln, Neb., 1983)

Colton, J. *Léon Blum: Humanist in Politics* (1974 edn.)

Conquest, R. *The Great Terror* (1973 edn.)

Conrad, P. *Modern Times, Modern Places* (1999)

Cowling, M. *The Impact of Hitler* (Cambridge, 1975)

Crozier, B. *The Man Who Lost China* (1976)

Dallek, R. *Franklin D. Roosevelt and American Foreign Policy, 1932–1945* (New York, 1979)

Davies, R. W. (*et al.*, eds.), *The Economic Transformation of the Soviet Union, 1913–1945* (Cambridge, 1994)

de Grazia, V. *How Fascism Ruled Women* (Berkeley, 1992)

Deist, W. (*et al.*), *Germany and the Second World War* I (Oxford, 1990)

Delzell, C. F. *Mussolini's Enemies* (Princeton, 1961)

Duroselle, J.-B. *La Décadence 1932–1939* (Paris, 1979)

Duus, P. (ed.), *The Cambridge History of Japan* VII: *The Twentieth Century* (Cambridge, 1988)

Fraser, R. *Blood of Spain: The Experience of the Civil War, 1936–1939* (1979)

Freidel, F. *Franklin D. Roosevelt: a rendezvous with destiny* (Boston, 1990)

Galbraith, J. K. *The Great Crash 1929* (1961 edn.)

Gentile, E. *The Sacralization of Politics in Fascist Italy* (1996)

Gilbert, M. *Winston S. Churchill* V (1976)

Gluck C. and Graubard, S. R. (eds.), *Showa: The Japan of Hirohito* (1992)

Graves, R. and Hodge, A. *The Long Weekend* (1965 edn.)

Grunberger, R. *A Social History of the Third Reich* (1971)

Haslam, J. *Soviet Foreign Policy, 1930–33: The Impact of the Depression* (1983)

Haslam, J. *The Soviet Union and the Threat from the East, 1933–41* (Pittsburgh, 1992)

Ickes, H. *The Secret Diary of Harold Ickes* (2 vols., 1955)

Jackson, J. *The Politics of Depression in France 1932–1936* (Cambridge, 1985)

Jackson, J. *The Popular Front in France defending democracy, 1934–38* (Cambridge, 1988)

James, H. *The German Slump* (Oxford, 1986)

Kennedy, P. *The Rise and Fall of the Great Powers* (1989 edn.)

Kershaw, I. *Hitler 1889–1936: Hubris* (1998)

Kimball, W. *Forged in War: Churchill, Roosevelt and the Second World War* (1998)

Kindleberger, C. P. *The World in Depression 1929–1939* (Harmondsworth, 1987)

Knox, M. *Mussolini Unleashed 1939–1941* (Cambridge, 1982)

Kravchenko, V. *I Chose Freedom* (1947)

Large, S. S. *Emperor Hirohito and Showa Japan* (1992)

Lazareff, P. *Deadline: The Behind-the-Scenes Story of the Last Decade in France* (New York, 1942)

Leighton, I. (ed.), *The Aspirin Age 1919–1941* (1950)

Leuchtenburg, W. E. *Franklin D. Roosevelt and the New Deal* (New York, 1963)

Lyons, E. *Assignment in Utopia* (1938)

Mack Smith, D. *Mussolini* (1981)

Maruyama Masao, *Thought and Behaviour in Modern Japanese Politics* (Oxford, 1969)

Mazower, M. *Dark Continent: Europe's Twentieth Century* (1998)

McElvaine, R. S. *The Great Depression: America 1929–1941* (1984)

McKibbin, R. *Classes and Cultures: England 1918–1951* (Oxford, 1998)

Medvedev, R. *All Stalin's Men* (Oxford, 1983)

Medvedev, R. *Let History Judge* (1972 edn.)

Michaelis, M. *Mussolini and the Jews* (Oxford, 1978)

Mommsen, W. J. and Kettenacker, L. (eds.), *The Fascist Challenge and the Policy of Appeasement* (1983)

Morley, J. W. (ed.), *The China Quagmire: Japan's Expansion on the Asian Continent 1933–1941* (New York, 1983)

Mowat, C. L. *Britain Between the Wars 1918–1940* (1968 edn.)

Overy, R. *Goering, The 'Iron Man'* (1984)

Overy, R. *The Road to War* (1989)

Parker, R. A. C. *Chamberlain and Appeasement* (1993)

Peattie, M. R. *Ishiwara Kanji and Japan's Confrontation with the West* (Princeton, 1975)

Pollard, J. *The Vatican and Italian Fascism, 1929–1932* (Cambridge, 1985)

Preston, P. *Franco* (1993)

Pronay, N. and Spring, D. W. (eds.), *Propaganda, Politics and Film 1918–1945* (1982)

Reimann, V. *The Man who created Hitler: Joseph Goebbels* (1976)

Reynolds, D. *The Creation of the Anglo-American Alliance 1937–41* (1981)

Rhodes James, R. *Churchill: A Study in Failure 1900–1939* (1970)

Robertson, E. M. *Mussolini as Empire-Builder* (1977)

Rosten, L. C. *Hollywood: The Movie Colony* (New York, 1970 edn.)

Sarti, R. (ed.), *The Ax Within: Italian Fascism in Action* (New York, 1974)

Sauvy, A. *Histoire Economique de la France entre les deux Guerres* I (Paris, 1965)

Schlesinger, A. M. *The Age of Roosevelt* (3 vols., 1957–60)

Shirer, W. *The Rise and Fall of the Third Reich* (1964 edn.)

Short, P. *Mao* (1999)

Skidelsky, R. *Politicians and the Slump* (1967)

Snow, E. *Red Star Over China* (1968 edn.)

Southworth, H. R. *Guernica! Guernica! A Study of Journalism, Diplomacy, Propaganda and History* (1977)

Speer, A. *Inside the Third Reich* (1970)

Storry, R. *The Double Patriots* (1973 edn.)

Sues, R. *Shark's Fins and Millet* (Boston, Mass., 1944)

Taylor, A. J. P. *English History, 1914–1945* (1967 edn.)

Taylor, A. J. P. *The Origins of the Second World War* (1961)

Terkel, S. *Hard Times: An Oral History of the Great Depression* (New York, 1970)

Thomas, H. *Spanish Civil War* (1986 edn.)

Thurston, R. W. *Life and Terror in Stalin's Russia, 1934–1941* (1996)

Tucker, R. C. *Stalin in Power: The Revolution from above 1928–1941* (1990)

Vaksberg, A. *The Prosecutor and the Prey: Vyshinsky and the 1930s' Moscow Show Trials* (1990)

Volkogonov, D. *Stalin: Triumph and Tragedy* (1991)

Watt, D. C. *How War Came* (1989)

Weinberg, G. L. *The Foreign Policy of Hitler's Germany* (2 vols., 1970 and 1980)

Werth, A. *France in Ferment* (and 3 succeeding vols., 1934–1942)

Winter, J. and Baggett, B. *The Great War and the Shaping of the 20th Century* (1996)

Young, R. J. *France and the Origins of the Second World War* (1996)

INDEX

A Note About the Author

Dr. Piers Brendon is Keeper of the Churchill Archives and a Fellow of Churchill College, Cambridge. He is the author of twelve books, including biographies of Winston Churchill and Dwight D. Eisenhower. In addition to his work for the British and American press, he has contributed to numerous television documentary series.

A Note on the Type

This book was set in Adobe Garamond. Designed for the Adobe Corporation by Robert Slimbach, the fonts are based on types first cut by Claude Garamond (c. 1480–1561). Garamond was a pupil of Geoffroy Tory and is believed to have followed the Venetian models, although he introduced a number of important differences, and it is to him that we owe the letter we now know as "old style." He gave to his letters a certain elegance and feeling of movement that won their creator an immediate reputation and the patronage of Francis I of France.

Composed by Creative Graphics,
Allentown, Pennsylvania
Printed and bound by Berryville Graphics,
Berryville, Virginia
Designed by Anthea Lingeman